New Venture Experience

THIRD EDITION

Karl H. Vesper

VECTOR BOOKS

Seattle, Washington 98105

New Venture Experience
Third Edition

© Karl H. Vesper 2010

Published by Vector Books, 3721 47th Place N.E., Seattle, WA 98105-5224
Telephone (206) 522 5905

Cases in this book have been made possible by entrepreneurs, businesses, and other organizations which may wish to remain anonymous by having names, quantities, and other identifying details disguised. Basic relationships within the cases, however, are maintained. Cases have been prepared as a basis for class discussion rather than to illustrate either effective or ineffective handling of business situations.

ISBN 978-1-884021-32-9

To Joan

the only one of all

# Preface

This, the third edition of *New Venture Experience,* includes a completely rewritten text, different cases, a somewhat altered sequence of chapters, as well as significant additions to content and some innovations.

Like prior editions it includes a range of elements that can be chosen or not by the instructor for most emphasis, including:

1. **Text** with illustrative examples and footnotes to reference literature.
2. **Cases** at the back of the book matched to text information of the chapters, and there are two alternative cases for most chapters.
3. An **introductory list** in each chapter **of main topics** covered in the chapter.
4. **Opening questions** at the beginning of each chapter to trigger curiosity about issues in the chapter.
5. **Summary points** at the end of each chapter.
6. **Questions at the end** of each chapter (a) **for cases** related to the chapter, (b) for pursuing the option of developing a **venture plan**, and (c) for pursuing the option of writing a **venture history**.

Selecting among these elements leaves room for many alternative homework assignments and classroom activities.

Topic sequence

The sequence of topics, in ten parts through which are spread 23 chapters, follows the general logic of how a typical entrepreneur's thinking, to the extent that there is such, tends to go in pursuing a venture, as follows:

1. **Surveying** from a personal point of view preferences in type of venture/work and career activities;
2. **Searching** to find opportunities and for ideas about how best to exploit them;
3. **Screening** to assess whether a particular new product or service really can be made and sold, as well as whether the market size and potential return on investment justify following through to produce and deliver it;
4. **Planning** to map out what the strategy and design of the business should be and what specific steps, resources, and assistance will be needed to create and operate it;
5. **Financing** at some level to start moving the venture from concept toward reality as well as to live on until revenues generate sufficiently positive cash flow;
6. **Setting up** protections, paperwork, legal form, and facilities to begin enacting the venture;
7. **Teaming** more formally with both partners and outside helpers and stakeholders to create a combined capability for beginning the venture;
8. **Starting up** sales and operations to put the venture into motion;
9. **Finding and acquiring** an already ongoing business as an alternative path to start-up for entering independent business, and
10. **Managing downstream** from start-up the developmental trajectory and eventual disposition of the business, as well as the personal career that may flow from entrepreneurial endeavors.

Additions

Beyond this sequence of overall chapter topics, additions to this book since its earlier editions include:

1. **Expanded references** in the text to more recent literature of the field that has emerged since the earlier editions.
2. **Added examples** to illustrate more concepts.
3. **New conceptualizing and displaying tools** for designing, planning, and developing ventures.
4. **Extended topical coverage** to include strategic alliances, joint ventures, and franchising as both entry modes and strategies for growth. The first chapter newly includes a look at career options along the new venture life cycle. The Planning section newly includes a chapter on Business Design. The Financing section now separates debt from investor funding. And the concluding Downstream section is new with chapters on longer-run Trajectories of the venture as well as Eventualities for entrepreneurs.
5. The format has been changed to a **larger page size** to accommodate **more text and cases**, with a **soft-cover binding** for **lower weight and cost**.

Innovations

More exceptional changes that distinguish this edition from earlier editions and from other entrepreneurship texts are:

1. **Separate** chapters on discovery of **opportunity**, versus discovery of **ideas** for exploiting opportunity, as distinct from each other and from assessment of either.
2. Introduction of some elements of **new technology for discovering** venture ideas and thinking through ventures.
3. Introduction of a **"portfolio approach" option** for developing new venture designing, planning, and presentation skills and also for opening potential directions for practical research on entrepreneurship.

Important functions are offered by each of these three. The first, separating discussion of opportunity and ideas from each other and from evaluation of either, allows further and clearer treatment of how to search more powerfully for each. In other books definitions are sometimes absent, at other times vary, and sometimes switch position. Here *opportunity* is defined as a situation that someone can improve, and *idea* is defined as how the improvement can be rendered. Consequently, for a given opportunity many ideas may be solutions, some of which may even lead to other opportunities. A clearer map of this definition territory may be helpful to both individuals and teams in searching for competitive advantage.

Second, further help in the search task is new technology for finding venture ideas that has been developed by Jim Fiet at the University of Louisville. This and other systematic approaches for both opportunity discovery and idea discovery are also presented in Chapters 2A and 2B.

Another emergent technology to assist entrepreneurs comes from the work of Ron Mitchell at Texas Tech University, and concerns the deliberate identification and willful tuning of a personal "script" or individual modus operandi ("M.O.") for developing a venture or ventures. Introduction of this concept, coupled with a method of pursuing it and illustrative examples of prior students' efforts in doing so, appear as an important part of the first chapter on "surveying" or attempting to think ahead about personal entrepreneurial career options to gain perspective on topics of the chapters that follow.

This is analogous to the practice of athletes, who analyze their motions, identify patterns they follow, then experimentally and systematically reshape those patterns through practice to improve performance. In entrepreneurship the patterns are ways of thinking and acting in designing and implementing new ventures. Mitchell's research on hundreds of entrepreneurs indicates that they have repeating patterns of thinking and acting about it, and Mitchell's experimentation with classes has indicated that entrepreneurship students too can learn from study and experimentation with their "entrepreneurial M.O.'s." Exercises in the first chapter are illustrative.

A third novelty in this edition is the introduction of a "portfolio approach" for developing facility in venture discovery and development. It essentially invites students to keep considering the possibility of developing successive facets of a venture plan while feeling free to change the concept that the plan applies to, rather than staying with the original venture concept that may have become revealed as unpromising at some stage in the planning process. Rather than starting over from the beginning, the student changes to a different venture concept, but takes up planning for that concept at a later stage in the planning sequence. This could be analogous to an art student who might practice drawing hands alone at one point and flowers at another point without having those two different things being part of an overall integrated picture.

By "fine-slicing" facets of the venture creation process into sub-tasks that can be studied and practiced repeatedly, the student may gain more personal strength for accomplishing them better.

Such fine-slicing may also reveal opportunities for independent study projects or student theses. Investigation of and experimentation with fine slicing has yielded innumerable advances in other technologies ranging from car racing to industrial production and scientific advancement. Perhaps it will be found to have similar potential for developing and advancing a technology of new venture creation.

Acknowledgements

As with earlier editions of the book, I owe thanks to many who helped. Entrepreneurs, some of whose real names are used in the cases, gave both access to their ventures for case information and education from their experiences. Colleagues who helped with case development included Joe Crosswhite, Bill Gartner, and Nancy Tieken. Institutions that especially helped were Babson College, Baylor University, Harvard Business School, Syracuse University, and the University of Calgary.

Professors Alex DeNoble of San Diego State University, Jim Fiet of the University of Louisville, Don Kuratko of the University of Indiana, Tom Lee of the University of Washington, Ed McMullan of the University of Calgary, Mike Morris of Oklahoma State University, Ron Mitchell of Texas Tech University, and Don Sexton of Baylor University were very helpfully supportive, as was the late Peter Drucker of Claremont University.

I also greatly owe Jim Adams of Stanford University, who guided me to consider an academic career in the first place and helped me make a go of it. Arthur Lipper has long been a source of valuable insights and encouragement.

Dr. William Paulin helped in experimental use of some of the cases during our joint development of an "entrepreneurism" course series for the Jacobs School of Engineering at the University of California, San Diego, as did Jack Savidge, whose idea the course series was and who gave crucial guidance to the process.

Vital assistance in preparing the manuscript for publishing included copy editing by Sharon Hermann, layout and innumerable helpful corrections from Lesley Zanich, and cover help from Vimala Koushik and Lesley Zanich, as well as crucial tolerance and assistance in virtually every area from my wife, Joan.

Faculty members at other schools who used prior editions and/or parts of the book and/or also provided support and comments that gave the book opportunity to survive especially included, among many others: MacRae Banks, John Butler, Radha Chaganti, Gary Hansen, Gerald Hills, Charles Hofer, Paul Lapides, Brian McKenzie, Rebecca Reuber, Bud Saxberg, Harriet Stevenson, and David Wilemon.

Contents in Brief

Contents

CASES (In order of chapter assignment)

CASES (Alphabetically)

Part 1

SURVEYING

This, the first of ten parts in the book, consists of one chapter giving an overall look at what entrepreneurs do, what capabilities they draw upon, and what processes are involved in doing it.

The job of an entrepreneur is to offer something sufficiently better to the marketplace so that customers will support a new venture to deliver it. The venture may or may not be one of high-growth ambition, depending on its potential market and competition, what it will offer, what the founder(s) want it to become, what resources they can marshal, and how well they do their job.

Five key ingredients necessary for venture creation–personal contacts, the idea or concept for the business, technical capability, resources, and customer orders–are identified. An outline of topics for the written plan of a new business is briefly sketched, as are typical steps in venture start-up.

A prospective entrepreneur can make choices about what type of venture to attempt to initiate or join, and in what capacity. Each venture will create opportunity for potential roles that may include being the sole founder or, alternatively, one member of a team of founders. Beyond that are still other possible non-founder roles for participating in a venture through employment either within or outside of it. All roles related to the venture are likely to change over time, including adding new ones and phasing out others. By studying entrepreneurship an individual should be able to make better-informed choices about what roles to seek, and how to find and prepare for them.

Four types of knowledge necessary in founding new ventures are described, along with the observation that some are more crucial than others. All can be deliberately sought, but some depend on the type of venture and line of business to be pursued.

Contrasting modes of thinking involved in designing and managing the start-up process are also described, along with the suggestion that a balance among them is called for that depends both on the problems to be resolved and the people who are involved in thinking them through. Neglect of any mode, can cause problems. Focused emphasis on one versus another mode may enhance performance. Among those thinking modes a person can choose to follow whatever pattern of emphasis seems to come naturally, or alternatively to manage the emphasis with an aim of enhancing performance further than might happen naturally.

Individuals can not only choose to seek whatever information they prefer, but also to assess and manage the mental routines or "expert scripts" they follow in managing venture creation processes.

The conclusion of the first chapter presents an overview of chapters to follow.

CHAPTER 1 – Choices

Topics

1. Five key ingredients
2. Venture types
3. Role possibilities
4. Knowledge acquisition
5. Entrepreneurial thinking

Checkpoints

a. Define entrepreneur.
b. In what sequence should key ingredients for a venture be obtained?
c. How can ventures be classified for choosing a preferred type?
d. What is an entrepreneur's invisible organization?
e. What four types of knowledge apply to entrepreneurship?
f. What five thought modes apply to venturing?
g. What is the significance of an entrepreneur's *expert script*?

1. Five key ingredients

Anyone can choose to pursue entrepreneurship or self-employment, putting together a new job rather than accepting one under somebody else. Some definitions used here are

An **entrepreneur** is one who introduces **something better** to the world of commerce by taking *initiative* and *risk* that results in **business ownership** and management **for a profit**.

Entrepreneurship consists of leading in creation of a new business to produce and deliver that something better, in the view of customers, to the marketplace.

The something better, which is essential to the process, may be a new product or service, lower cost, more convenience, faster or more reliable delivery and follow-up, a more pleasant buying experience, or any combination of such elements. The "better" is important, and should be sought constantly in as many aspects of the venture as possible. The entrepreneur may or may not invent the something better personally. It could be the creation of another person that the entrepreneur makes available by leading in active management to deliver it.

The path to entrepreneurship, self-employment, owning and managing a business, may take many alternative routes.

A prospective business student has developed with some friends an innovative screen-saver software package. Sales have been rising, but to expand them further, more money and considerably more work time would be required. Should he drop it and go to school, postpone school and concentrate on the software, try to do both at the same time, or look for other possibilities?

— · —

Two women, one a lawyer and the other a beautician, have designed what they believe to be a better backpack for a mother to carry her baby. Both have some acquaintance with business, but neither has previously been involved in manufacturing and selling a product. How should they start?

— · —

An artist has developed an improved surface for drawing and painting on. He has found art supply stores interested in carrying it. But after producing some in his garage he has become frustrated with that activity and its interruption of his artwork. How best can he benefit from his invention, which is not patented?

No situation is "the typical" jumping-off place for becoming an entrepreneur. As these three examples illustrate, many starting points are possible. Examples throughout the book will illustrate much more variety. Exercises in the book will offer avenues for exploring personal venturing possibilities.

Five key ingredients

Five key ingredients are usually necessary and sufficient for starting a venture. They are personal contacts, a good idea, physical resources, technical know-how, and customer orders, as described more fully below. There is no "right sequence" for obtaining them, and in fact what the sequence is may depend on how the observer chooses to distinguish some of them. But sooner or later they all must be there to complete the start-up picture, as illustrated diagrammatically in Exhibit 1-1.

It is worth noting that four of them, the first two plus the last two, often tend to be linked to each other through prior experience, particularly from jobs, education (especially if it is technical), or hobbies. Most entrepreneurs work from what they learned through prior experience that is related to their venture.

For Microsoft, it appears that the founders followed this sequence:

Technical know-how In high school Paul Allen and Bill Gates chose the option of learning to work with computers. During summers they also learned something about how business works by operating a small computer service enterprise that measured traffic flow and that performed program

Five key ingredients in detail

Typically, the following five types of ingredients are requisite for venture creation.

1. ***Contacts*** Venturing is a human activity requiring at least two people, founder and customer, and generally many more, particularly to help a founder produce and deliver value to customers. Even though it is not possible to know in advance who will be most essential, some types of needed help can be anticipated and will be identified below. Gaining skill in identifying, meeting, evaluating, and cultivating personal relationships, plus building a good reputation, can make strategic networking to get needed help easier and more effective.

2. ***Good idea*** Not just any venture concept, but one that connects to a market that will pay enough for what the company produces to net an attractive return on investment will be needed, preferably early on, but probably after some development and evolution. Possibly the idea will come from a personal contact, as may other key ingredients.

3. ***Physical resources*** All enterprises require some physical resources, although some can get by with much less than others. Computers, peripherals, and desk space have gone a long way for some spectacular start-ups in recent years. Others need to lease or buy storefronts and furnishings, inventory, and processing equipment. Sometimes needed assets can be borrowed.

4. ***Technical know-how*** Somebody working for the company must have a task-relevant skill set for producing what the company delivers well enough for the venture to survive against competitors. Weak skills may be enough, at least temporarily, in situations where the (1) stronger ones are easy to learn, (2) there is a temporary shortage of supply, (3) the entrepreneur has some special connections who can help cut some slack, or (4) the entrepreneur has customers who don't much care about a particular purchase deal because to them it is very small. If the industry is new enough, competition may be absent. But it soon will escalate. The venture's initial technical know-how will likely continue over time as its core competence and other facets of the business, such as its customer list and brand, are developed based on this special know-how.

5. ***Customer orders*** Continuing orders from customers who pay their bills are required for the company to survive. The lead entrepreneur of the venture is usually the person who obtains the first order at least.

Exhibit 1-1 Five key ingredients

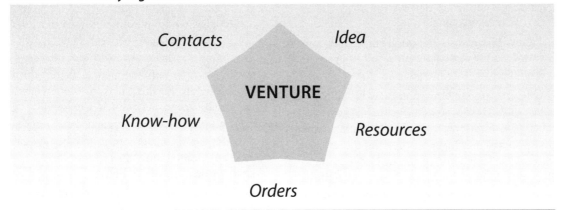

debugging. While Gates was still in college, Allen joined a computer company, Honeywell.

Idea It had occurred to them that there might someday become available such a thing as personal computers and that they might be able to do worthwhile things with them. When in 1975 Popular Electronics ran a cover story about the first microcomputer for consumers, the Altair kit offered by MITS Corporation in Albuquerque, they undertook to develop for it a software program.

Contact They called the founder of MITS, Ed Roberts, and told him they could provide a Basic program for his new computer. Then, while flying to his headquarters in Albuquerque, New Mexico, they wrote code for it. Amazingly, when they fed the brand new untested program they had just written into the machine via a punched paper tape reader, it worked on the first try.

Customer order Roberts made a deal with Gates and Allen to offer his prospective customers their software, which worked well, bundled with his hardware, which didn't.

Resources With that order came advertising and channels to the market. Financing needs beyond that were apparently minimal, just enough to live on and move forward. Eventually Gates and Allen decided to move back to their hometown, Seattle, and continue selling the product on their own. Roberts sued them for breaching what he thought had been a contract to continue working together. But he lost, and Microsoft was on its own.

A different sequence from that of Microsoft in acquiring the key ingredients can be seen in the experience of Jerry Kaplan, who invented the tablet computer in 1987 and founded a company called GO to make it.

Technical know-how Jerry Kaplan had completed a PhD in artificial intelligence at the University of Pennsylvania and joined Stanford's computer science department for "a dream job, with virtually no responsibilities other than to think about something interesting and write up my ideas once in a while."

Contacts Mitchell Kapor, founder of Lotus Computer, an early microcomputer software company dropped in on Kaplan, introduced himself and inquired what artificial intelligence might mean for personal computers. Kapor hired Kaplan as a consultant, and Kaplan began traveling to Boston once a month where he met other technical acquaintances of Kapor.

Idea On a flight in 1987 with Kapor, who was impatiently trying to organize notes he had scribbled at various times on scraps of paper and put them into a personal computer, Kaplan got the idea of making what would one day turn out to be a laptop, except that instead of a keyboard it would have a screen that responded to a pen. In the ensuing weeks, the two talked with potential confederates, all technical, but without solidifying a working relationship. Kapor suggested that Kaplan pursue the idea on his own.

Resources Kapor introduced Kaplan to John Doerr, a venture capitalist with a leading Silicon Valley firm, Kleiner, Perkins, Caulfield and Byers, who invited Kaplan to come chat about his idea. With no written business plan Kaplan described his idea to the group, using his leather folder to simulate a prototype. Several days later Doerr arranged to meet Kaplan for an hour when on flights in opposite directions their paths intersected for plane changes at the St. Louis airport. They reached agreement on a deal that would provide $1.5 million for a one–third stake of the start-up. Kaplan went to work recruiting technical people needed to develop the product and GO computer was underway.

Customer orders Although some sales revenues were eventually generated, they were nothing like expectations.

The time lapse in obtaining these key ingredients is fairly clear in some ventures but less so in others. Customer orders generally mark a clear time point, as may first occurrence of the venture idea and at least some of the needed resources. But acquisition of know-how can have roots at many points along the way, as can development of personal contacts vital to the venture.

Invisible organization

Personal contacts may lead the acquisition of any other key ingredients, a viable venture idea, know-how, resources, and sales orders. Leading or not, they will certainly be needed, and it makes sense for a venturer to begin listing them early for two reasons. One is to have a potentially helpful list available. The other is to build strength in understanding and selectively developing relationships with them. Which ones will become most helpful may not be foreseeable, but the more numerous they are, the better, if for no other reason than that through them can be found others as needed. Collectively they become an "invisible organization," as professor Ron Bassett has called it, a constituency built up over time that can be called into action quickly when the needs arise. This multiplies the strength of

the entrepreneur to make things happen faster and better.

Sociologists who have studied networks refer to "degrees of separation" between someone who wants to find another person with specified characteristics and the number of contacts they must work through to find that person. More degrees of separation mean more contact links must be gone through. It has been argued that by crossing six degrees of separation, it may be possible to find any desired individual in the world.

Distinctions are made between *close ties*, or acquaintances known well or for a long time, versus *distant ties*, which are newer and less well-known contacts. The former have the advantage of perhaps greater understanding and trust. But they also will tend to be contacts whose own acquaintances are more likely known in common with the entrepreneur's. Distant-tie contacts, who tend to be strangers, are more likely to have other acquaintances who are not in common with acquaintances the entrepreneur already has, and therefore may add a larger set of new contacts to the invisible organization.

Disciplined effort to enhance development of an invisible organization can include (1) making an address list of members and how they can help, (2) listing further capabilities desired and who might be added to provide them, (3) practicing ways to give help to people on the list, and (4) taking initiatives, including cold calling to recruit more members, particularly distant ties, and make them glad to belong.

2. Venture types

What the venture offers to whom, and how it either buys or produces what it offers, will largely determine not only how successful it is but also the kind of entity it becomes. Six contrasting types illustrate choices a would-be entrepreneur may be able to reach for.

Job-replacement or marginal ventures

Some people seek a business of their own because they have no job, cannot get one, or simply don't want to work for someone else, yet need to earn a living, however meager. For

most ventures that are easy to invent and attempt, such as restaurants, small retail stores, and services, the hours are long, wages low, and profits touch and go. Usually some investment has to be put at high risk to try such ventures, and many lose it. Competition is tough because existing operators have become highly skilled at the work and cut prices to survive. However, depending on individual tastes and circumstances, some job-replacement ventures also yield for their owners not only gratitude from their customers who receive desired services and goods, but also feelings of accomplishment, and the satisfaction of earning a respectable living, possibly with individual flair for their independent owner/operators.

Lifestyle ventures

Some entrepreneurs accept relatively low-paying ventures out of preference for particular kinds of work activities, hours, location, or companionship. Or they want to pursue ideas that regular jobs leave too little free time for. The appeal may be in art (professional photographers, landscapers, car builders), science (technical consultants, independent researchers), originality (engineers, inventors, craftspeople), or activities (outfitters, tour guides, independent instructors, some types of farmers). Whether or not it makes sense to complicate the task of competitive survival for lifestyle work is sometimes debated. But Mark Henricks, who studied entrepreneurs with such aspirations, found that some can, and do, happily succeed.[1]

High-pay, stably small ventures

High profits accrue to some small ventures that escape competition by focusing on markets that are high priced but either unnoticed by or too small to attract others, or that are protected by entry barriers such as personal favoritism, contacts, contracts, patents, proprietary assets, secrets, license protection, or special skills. Such ventures include highly skilled machine shops, independent health care professionals, real estate developers, some investment counselors, attorneys, and sports or theatrical agents.

High-profit growth ventures

Some types of competitive advantages coupled with large or rapidly expanding markets propel some ventures to become fast-growing gazelles, a term suggested by the CEO of Cognetics, Inc., David Birch. A top layer of this group is represented by Inc. magazine's list of 500 fastest-growing small companies. Interestingly the list's composition changes considerably over the years, both in terms of specific firms on it and in terms of the industries represented among the leaders. Growth causes include elements of science, art, timing, and luck. Electronics, computer, and software companies have been winners in recent decades. The fraction represented by manufacturing has gone down relative to that of services. Many gazelle founders first obtained high levels of education in science and engineering fields, but not all do.

> "I'm not sure if he graduated from high school, but he was brilliant," a colleague said of Malcolm McLean, a rural North Carolinian who sold a trucking business he had developed over 20 years to try shipping goods in containers. He began by fitting an old oil tanker with a reinforced steel deck with grooves to fasten the containers. This new approach eliminated having to unpack goods from rail cars or trucks, load them in slings, lower them into a ship's hold, and restack them, later to reverse the process at the other end, often accompanied by pilfering and other damage. It also reduced the labor and time, from one week with two shifts of 20 workers, to 10 hours with 20 crane operators, and ultimately formed part of the path to creation of "big box" stores like Wal-Mart. McLean sold his Sea-Land Corporation for $800 million.[2]

Later-takeoff ventures

Sometimes a venture can morph from one type to another. For instance, a prosaic grocery store or restaurant may, if it proves to have an extraordinarily strong format, be transformable into a larger chain that becomes a gazelle, as did such well-known firms as Starbucks, Wal-Mart, and many fast food enterprises like McDonald's. Or through acquisition an initial venture may be augmented to build a larger one or accumulate a diversified portfolio, as did Ling-Temco-Vought and Litton Industries, known in an earlier age as conglomerates. In the other direction, a business that grows large may spin off parts that are smaller but high performing, as happened when the Harley-Davidson Division of AMF Corporation was bought out by employees. Even a relatively prosaic small business can grow exceptionally among its peers.

Lifestyle ventures

High-pay, stably small ventures

High-profit growth ventures

Later-takeoff ventures

---

[1] Mark Henricks, *Not Just a Living* (Cambridge, MA: Perseus Books, 2002) pp. 199-200
[2] "A Gamble That Changed the World," *The Los Angeles Times*, April 24, 2006, p.C6

There were over 300 roofing companies in the Seattle Yellow Pages, and over 1,000 listed online for that area in 2006, many of them consisting of one or two people who hired additional workers by the job as needed. Many such companies do not last long because entry is easy and that line of work requires little capital. But one in Seattle, Jorve Roofing, begun 20 years earlier by a high school student, Ted Jorve, grew entirely from plowed-back profits to employ 175 roofers operating from 68 trucks. The "magic" appeared to include a combination of pricing high to pay for more careful work carrying a better guarantee, buying supplies by the truckload for lower cost, advertising to support high volume, providing more training, and careful management to retain workers with higher skills, plus constantly seeking out and applying what appeared to be generally known among managers as "best practices."

Further description of competitive advantages and how they work will be taken up later in connection with ways of seeking and screening new venture ideas.

3. Role possibilities

3. Role possibilities

Venture life cycle

As the long list of possible stakeholders may suggest, there can be many roles to choose from for participating in and learning about entrepreneurship, either as an insider or an outsider. Which person is the prime mover may change over time so that several different people may form, in effect, a sequence of lead entrepreneurs, as depicted along a hypothetical lifecycle curve of a start-up in Exhibit 1-2. An inventor may be followed by a company-starter who is then replaced by a company-runner, possibly with still others in between as helpers. Both full and fractional roles are possible, and a practical step may be to consider, "What kind of entrepreneur do I want to be, full or fractional, inside or outside the venture, and for what parts of the venture development path?"

Venture life cycle

Scientists discover new aspects of how things work. Their discoveries sometimes form the bases of new companies, in biotechnology, for instance, or semiconductors. Some go on to invent useful products and start companies based on their science, as did William Shockley, inventor of the transistor and founder of Shockley Transistor. Others, like Einstein, do not.

Inventors conceive new arrangements, either of physical elements including those of organizations, or of ways of doing things, sometimes patenting them, sometimes not. Some, like William Lear, inventor of a better car radio, the automatic aircraft landing system, and the Lear jet, go on to found one or several companies to exploit their inventions. Other inventors, like Robert Goddard, the "father of modern rocketry," do not. If complemented by assistance from someone with business inclination, training, and/or experience, however, and inventor may be more encouraged and enabled to accomplish start-up.

Starters like Sandra Kurtzig (ASK Computer, software) may not make scientific discoveries or noteworthy inventions, yet begin significant companies. Edison, although not a scientist, was certainly a prolific inventor and a starter, creating a company that eventually morphed into General Electric. Some starters, like Sam Walton but not Thomas Edison, go on to manage them to large size. Steve Wozniak did not, but his partner, Steve Jobs, did. Similarly, Bill Gates did, Paul Allen didn't. But both Bill Hewlett and Dave Packard did. Through teaming, a starter may be able to form an effective entrepreneurial partnership with an inventor, as noted above.

Serial starters begin one venture after another, sometimes in parallel, but don't stay with them as they mature into established businesses. The ventures of a given entrepreneur will likely range in level of success, quite possibly from high to failure. Milton Hershey failed with eight start-ups before succeeding with his candy company. Forrest Mars also failed several times before he hit on the Milky Way to build the company that gave us M&Ms. Steve Osher started a company that made an "electric lollipop," in which a battery-powered electric motor

Exhibit 1-2 Roles along a venture-growth curve

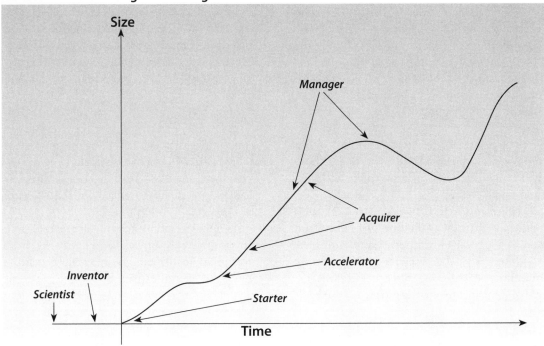

rotated the candy. He made enough money on it to go looking for other product possibilities, and upon walking through a pharmacy department noticed vibrational electric toothbrushes selling for around $100 each. He adapted his lollipop technology to make a much cheaper version of the toothbrush that rotated instead of vibrated. This product, too, succeeded and he sold it to Colgate. He used some of the proceeds to back a Broadway play, a kind of investment that usually loses. But his became a hit.

Runners carry start-ups further into more stable operation where things "get organized" and formal roles with greater organizational hierarchy develop in the company. The founding entrepreneur may not know how to, may not want to, or may not be allowed by investors to remain in charge at this stage. Founder CEOs in high technology firms, for instance, seldom last as long as three years, according to studies by Nesheim.[3] Runners who replace them may become long-term managers. As competitive arenas mature, typically margins narrow and

constant vigilance is needed to maintain quality, control costs, keep up morale, market against the competition, and ward off obsolescence. Managers must be good at keeping continual track of many complexities and activities of the business. Alfred P. Sloan built General Motors into the leading car company in the world, but he neither started it nor combined the companies that comprised it. Others did those things but failed at running it. Jack Welch became the most famous runner of his day at General Electric, but did not start it or any other company. However, Edwin Land, George Eastman, Henry Ford, and Howard Schultz all succeeded as both starters and runners.

Accelerators like Ted Turner take a company started by others, build upon it, and run it up a trajectory of high growth. Ray Kroc similarly made a multinational company and household word out of a hamburger store created by others. Some CEOs even move large companies from lower to higher trajectories as described by Jim Collins in *Good to Great*.[4] Interestingly,

[3] John L. Nesheim, *High Tech Startup* (Saratoga, CA: Electronic Trend Publications, 1992) p. 10.
[4] Jim Collins, *Good to Great* (New York: Harper Collins, 1991).

Collins found his accelerator-managers were not especially charismatic, but typically insiders who deeply understand the businesses they are in.

Acquirers at various points along the growth curve of a company, exemplified by Victor Kiam, who bought Remington Razor and turned it around, may enter independent business through purchasing a going concern that they then reshape and possibly sell off. Or they may take the buyout public, as did employees of Harley-Davidson and also those of the engine-rebuilding department of International Harvester.

Turnaround artists like Lee Iacocca, who took over Chrysler at the brink of failure and managed it back to prosperity, and later Carlos Ghosn who did likewise at Nissan[5], are sometimes regarded as entrepreneurial. Rather than starting new enterprises, they rebuilt existing ones.

Each of these roles calls for dealing with different types of problems, and quite possibly different personal style. Rarely is the same person a star at all of them. To what extent such alternative roles can be chosen as opposed to being imposed by talent and circumstance is not clear. It does appear, though, that in moving along the spectrum from scientist to manager, the need for dealing with people as opposed to things, and delegating rather than directing, increases.

Alongside the players of these roles are others who in part share them. Scientists have their colleagues, research assistants, and laboratory technicians. Inventors sometimes have shop workers who help in fabricating physical models of contrivances, and other specialists who help with non-technical aspects of developing the venture. Such collaborators may also contribute ideas that extend and improve the original concept.

It obviously may be possible to enter a venture in one role and then shift to another. For instance, a venture helper may succeed the entrepreneur as CEO while the former shifts to longer-range strategic thinking or returns to technical development. Particularly if a venture grows, there will be opportunities for role changes and career advancement regardless of the individual's entry point.

Changing roles by moving from one venture to another, as well as by moving from outside to inside employment in a venture or series of ventures is also possible. In some ways this may be analogous to changing jobs within one large employer. Because there may not be room to change bosses, co-workers, or functional specialties in a small organization, the best path for career advancement or variety may be to change organizations. In some ways this may seem less secure and comfortable than moving around in one big company. But in others it offers more security, because there are always many new start-ups with which to make application, whereas in one large organization there may be rigidity or even a process of decline that reduces the options to move around inside, while at the same time being buried out of contact with outside job possibilities.

4. Knowledge acquisition

General business knowledge

Traditionally entrepreneurs have learned how to start ventures through trial and error, rather than studying about the process. The aim of school is to shape learning more certainly and efficiently on a collapsed time scale with lower cost of error. To that end there is reason to organize knowledge about the subject more systematically.

Venturing knowledge can be divided into four types. The first here, general business knowledge, applies to business in general. The other three apply to entrepreneurship in particular.

General business knowledge

Traditional business school courses convey knowledge applicable to businesses in general,

---

[5] David Magee, *Turnaround* (New York: Harper Business, 2003).

whether start-ups or ongoing firms. Familiar categories of general business knowledge include marketing, finance, operations, human resources, business law, and accounting. Also included may be management of research and development, engineering, and other specialties that pursue product and service improvement.

Each of these subjects, although typically taught with an orientation toward established businesses, applies also to start-ups. An entrepreneur with knowledge of methods used in market research for established firms may be better equipped to check out the likelihood of customer acceptance for a new product or service to be offered by a venture. One with knowledge of accounting should be better able to prepare records and financial statements that a banker or investor will find reassuring in making a decision to advance money to the start-up, and so forth.

Problems in each of these business functional areas are bound to arise as a company gets started. The entrepreneur's responses will presumably be based on common sense, work experience, possibly formal study of business, and counsel from others. How effective the answers must be to make the venture succeed will depend upon how strong the venture's profit margin and strategic position are relative to competitors. A high margin enjoyed by a monopoly product or service, such as one protected by patents or licenses, can compensate for substantial mismanagement. Without such protection, however, managerial error can easily lead to failure. Moreover, even with such protection it is likely that the degree of success will be higher if the business side of the venture is more competently performed. Learning the facts and methods of business may help raise the level of competence with which the business side of the venture is performed.

This learning can be undertaken either before the venture is begun or after. Most entrepreneurs become involved in a start-up through some sequence of unanticipated events, find a need for certain know-how, sometimes through calamity, and then seek it, often through trial and more error than they would like.

The catch in this learn-only-when-needed approach is that (1) to a person without such knowledge the need for it may not be apparent, and (2) when the knowledge becomes acutely needed there may not be enough time available to seek it out. Countless other tasks and decisions may simultaneously be clamoring for attention. Developing the product or service, working out deals with customers and suppliers, arranging facilities and production, obtaining permissions from government agencies, setting up records for taxes, and many other chores also require acquisition of special knowledge. If at least some of the necessary knowledge can be acquired in advance, the bustle of start-up activities may go more smoothly.

General entrepreneurship knowledge

Some general business knowledge needs refinement for application to new ventures, as observed by David Birch, an MIT professor who started his own consulting company:

> I was starting in 1983, and I'd studied histories of 12 million companies. I knew it would take me 8 or 10 years to build the kind of business I wanted to build. I knew it wouldn't happen fast, that I wasn't going to get rich in a couple of years. I also knew that I wouldn't be able to grow in a straight line. I knew there'd be plateaus, dips, and bobs—that it would be erratic—and I was prepared for it. I knew I'd have to work 12 to 14 hours a day. I'd talked to a whole bunch of people and I knew what they went through.
>
> Profitability is not really a problem—cash is always the problem. They're very different. In my kind of company, profitability goes all over the place and is really quite manipulatable. If you want to grow, you expense every dollar you've got and keep it working in the company. Cash flow is a constant issue if you don't go for large outside financing, which we've chosen not to do. You've got a fixed payroll. Everything on the expense side is fixed, and everything on the revenue side is variable. Somebody gets sick and doesn't pay up on his receivable, or a salesperson gets lazy and doesn't sell for a couple months. All of a sudden your cash flow goes to hell. You find yourself constantly managing cash flow. It's a major issue.[6]

---

[6] "Coming of Age," *Inc.*, April 1989, p. 38.

Opportunity-specific knowledge

Venture-specific knowledge

That this type of entrepreneurship knowledge can be important seems evident in the findings of Stuart and Abetti[7], who reported from a study of 52 technical ventures that the number of previous ventures and the management roles played in them had by far the strongest relationship to performance of start-ups in their sample. They indicated that general management experience was not particularly important, which seems to suggest that knowledge about venturing is what counts. How important experience in the same line of business as the venture was could not be ascertained from the reported results, although many other studies have found a strong connection between line of business in the start-up and prior work in the same field.

Opportunity-specific knowledge

Of the different possibilities for classifying more industrially specific knowledge relevant to start-ups, two will be suggested here: opportunity-specific and venture-specific. Opportunity-specific knowledge is that possessed by a person who because of it recognizes the existence of a specific opportunity, but does not necessarily know how to take advantage of it. Inventors often consider themselves to be in this situation. Sometimes they are right.

> Chester Carlson was repeatedly rebuffed when he sought help to commercialize a process he had invented, which later became known as Xerography. As a patent attorney he became impatient with the available ways of making copies, carbon paper, photographic copying, and the like. They were too slow and cumbersome, and he came up with what could perhaps be a better copy technology. He thought he had hold of a great opportunity. But those he talked to, at firms like Eastman Kodak, General Electric, Polaroid, 3M, and other leading companies, did not. Sometimes inventors are wrong, thinking they have winning innovations when they really don't. But Carlson clearly was right. If anything, the opportunity was in his case vastly greater than he or anyone else anticipated. He had grasped the relevant opportunity-specific information and interpreted it effectively. The others he had talked to, until he approached the Battelle Institute, and through them a small company named Haloid, either didn't have it, couldn't grasp it, or couldn't interpret the information effectively.

Opportunity-specific knowledge is not limited to inventions or technological possibilities. It can also concern availability of resources or of possibilities for changing rules, such as zoning regulations, to make new businesses more possible. Perhaps most importantly, it may concern existence of potential customers for something the new venture can provide—who those prospective customers are, what they would like to have, and what they will regard as benefits of the new venture's product or service. Consequently, a good way to acquire opportunity-specific knowledge is to identify a possible market, then get acquainted with potential customers within it.

Venture-specific knowledge

Fourth is venture-specific knowledge, which roughly equates to the technical know-how for performing work the venture will be engaged in. It includes further information that those who have opportunity-specific knowledge require in order to capitalize on their ideas.

An example would be the possession of programming knowledge for developing a new Internet company. One person may have opportunity-specific knowledge and a conception of a site that could be profitable, but lack the programming knowledge required to set it up. A programmer may have that venture-specific knowledge even though not knowing of the opportunity.

Three ways to obtain venture-specific knowledge are (1) to take a job in such a business and learn it as an insider, (2) to undertake a start-up of the venture and learn what is required step by step, or (3) to develop a business plan for the venture through study and investigation. Each of these three approaches has its strengths and shortcomings.

How venture-relevant knowledge can be picked up over time can be seen in the experience reported by Anita Roddick, founder of The Body Shop. In 1991, when the firm had

---

[7] Robert W. Stuart and Pier A. Abetti, "Impact of Entrepreneurial and Management Eperience on Early Performance," *Journal of Business Venturing*, 5, no. 3, May 1990, p. 151.

grown to over 1,900 shops in 42 countries around the world, she commented on general knowledge about business.

> A great advantage I had when I started The Body Shop was that I had never been to business school. As I didn't know how things were supposed to be done, I didn't know the rules and I didn't know the risks. As far as I was concerned there were no rules, so I just went my own merry way working from gut instinct.[8]

Later in telling her story, however, she tells more about business experience she did get that might be regarded as part of her education. Her parents operated a café.

> My mother was the cook and my grandmother peeled potatoes in the garden out the back. As soon as we were old enough, all of us children were expected to help in the café after school and at weekends, taking orders, clearing tables, washing up, buttering endless slices of bread, operating the till. The work ethic, the idea of service, was second nature to us.

After a variety of teaching jobs and other adventures, including marriage and having children, she decided with her husband to try owning a bed and breakfast establishment, which they transformed partly into a hotel to cope with a shortage of customers in the off season. Next, they set up a restaurant, Paddington's, which they changed from upscale fare to burgers and fries when the former didn't sell. Modest success followed. Then, to escape the long business hours of the restaurant and get more home time, she decided to open a retail store.

> I already had an idea of what kind of shop I would like. It seemed ridiculous to me that you could go into a sweet shop and ask for an ounce of jelly babies, and you could go into the grocers' and ask for two ounces of cheese, but when you wanted to buy a body lotion you had to go into Boots and lay out five quid for a bloody great bottle of the stuff. Then, if you didn't like it, you were stuck with it.[9]

This situation where she believed improvement was called for was her opportunity-specific knowledge. With it she founded The Body Shop. She further commented on the education (venture-specific knowledge) that let her do so effectively.

> Sir Terence Conran, who also started out in business running a restaurant, says it is the best possible training ground for learning about service and for prospering in the retail trade.[10]

5. Entrepreneurial thinking

An entrepreneur's job, creating a new independent business, is arguably different from that of a manager, carrying forward the momentum of a firm already ongoing, and therefore calls for reconsideration of how thinking and acting about it should be done.

Five thought modes

An entrepreneur's decision process can be viewed as a pattern of emphasis among five different thought modes, each of which at certain times may be most important and all of which should work together. Five such modes, as summarized in Exhibit 1-3 and discussed further on the following page are:

(1) Absorptive,
(2) Analytic,
(3) Divergent,
(4) Projective, and
(5) Integrative.

In more detail these modes are as follows:

1. Absorptive mode

The absorptive mode of thought includes acquisition of the four types of knowledge described earlier for making decisions on a venture. To push the application and acquisition of knowledge beyond what comes naturally in considering a particular venture the following questions may be helpful.

a. What are the most important facts in this situation?

b. How certain are they?

Five thought modes

---

[8] Anita Roddick, *Body and Soul* (New York: Crown Publishers, 1991) p. 21.
[9] Roddick, *Body and Soul*, p. 68.
[10] Roddick, *Body and Soul*, p. 64.

Exhibit 1-3 Summary of thought modes

1. **Absorptive**
   What factual information and new knowledge is applicable or needed for proceeding and how does it apply?

2. **Analytic**
   What are issues, underlying causes, effects, options, pros and cons, and priorities? What does crunching the numbers reveal?

3. **Divergent**
   What possibilities lie off the beaten path? What are other alternatives?

4. **Projective**
   What happens next? What scenarios could ensue?

5. **Integrative**
   What is the big picture backed by details? What prescription should be followed and why?

c. What knowledge of skills and facts from school courses apply here?

d. What additional opportunity-specific or venture-specific facts would be most valuable, how could they be obtained, and would they be worth that cost?

e. What facts and/or lessons here might helpfully apply to other situations?

2. Analytic mode

The analytic mode is used for exploring and explaining how different aspects of the venture and its plan work. It can take several forms, including assessment of information, discovery of relationships between causes and effects, diagnosis of problems, quantification of important variables, prediction of the effects that changes in some variables will have on changes in others, and critical scrutiny of the logic in supposed relationships or arguments.

Some analytic questions to practice whenever opportunity permits for building venture analytic strength include the following:

a. Who will want the product or service of this venture?

b. How many will buy how much of it and how can that be brought about?

c. How big a profit margin will the venture enjoy?

d. How much time, money, and effort must be spent to try this venture?

e. What is the upside potential in terms of how much profit the venture could produce?

f. What is the downside risk in terms of how much money it could lose?

g. What are the likelihoods of upside potential or downside risk occurring?

Graphical depiction of quantities and relationships is a powerful tool for both analysis and communication. It is typically underutilized in venture plans. Graphs, histograms, and pie charts all can help in thinking through a venture and so should be used. Other graphical tools not limited to quantities, such as decision trees, flow charts, schematics, perspectives, machine drawings, freehand sketches, models, and photographs, also should be brought into the analysis wherever they can help clarify thinking. Simply writing out in words the logic of analysis and description can often be a powerful way to check for completeness and correctness.

3. Divergent mode

The analytic mode discussed above aims mainly at drawing correct conclusions from among choices already identified. The divergent mode, in contrast, seeks out additional possible choices. An early stage for applying it may be in searching out a venture idea or, perhaps earlier, more ways for looking for one. Most entrepreneurs turn out to have been lucky enough to have the venture idea come upon them without having to search for it. But leaving opportunity-discovery completely to chance probably reduces the odds of accomplishing successful entrepreneurship. Some questions that should trigger divergent thinking are the following:

a. What are other possible branches for a decision-tree of the situation in this case?

b. How could this be done better?

c. What other possibilities exist for solving problems?

d. What are the opportunity implications of possible future scenarios?

4. Projective mode

Projecting future business scenarios is crucial in entrepreneurship because its aim is to create businesses that do not yet exist. These scenarios can be grouped into two categories:

(1) speculative visions of the future, and

(2) prescriptions for what to do.

Speculative application of the projective mode explores such questions as:

a. If a particular set of actions is taken, what results will likely follow? And then what, and then what, etc.?

b. What should success look like and how can it be reached?

c. What might go wrong, what could be done if it did, and what action might forestall it?

Prescriptive application of the projective mode should work through details of implementing decisions. Relevant questions include:

a. What plan of action is recommended?

b. Who should do what, how, and when?

c. What should be the time line, milestones, Gantt chart and/or PERT chart picture?

d. What should the contingency plan(s) be?

e. What should be the costs and financial forecasts?

5. Integrative mode

Communicating the reasoning to others and implementing its conclusions is likely to work better if the reasoning is crystallized and presented in a way that is clear and coherent. Some further questions that may help in accomplishment of this goal include:

a. What is the logic behind this venture?

b. How have pros and cons of alternatives been weighed to reach conclusions?

c. Are priorities in the reasoning evident?

d. Is there a clear picture of where the action should lead?

e. Is there a phrase, slogan or tag line that captures the essence of what this venture aims for? (Such as Xerox's "office of the future" concept that led to invention of microcomputer icons and mice.)

f. Can the reason this venture may earn a profit against competitors for customers' money be quickly and easily discerned?

Three different alternative patterns for organizing the reasoning in presentation to others:

Diagnosis, identification of issues, alternatives for responding to the issues, pros and cons of the alternatives, and conclusions.

Future vision, rationale behind that picture, what it will take to get there, and recommendations for doing so.

Two or three **alternative scenarios** for development of the venture over time, comparison of those scenarios against criteria for success, choice of a particular scenario, and steps for implementing it.

In venture planning, how well these modes are applied and also how effectively the result is presented are both important. Vastly more important, however, is effective action, regardless of the plan.

Individual style

Emphasis among thought modes varies among people. One is an *idea person*, whose exhibition of divergent thinking generates many inventions. Like the numerous inventions of Thomas Edison, who seemed to be such a person, almost all the ideas may be worthless, but among them there may be some tremendously valuable gems.

Other individuals may be heavily analytic, a natural mode for laboratory work and much of engineering. Some may have encyclopedic memories crammed with great amounts of knowledge, a valuable strength among those who classify and study living organisms. Those with strength in projective thinking may be good at sketching out scenarios and hypothetical plans, while integrative thinkers are good at pulling it all together, communicating it to others, selling, and leading a project forward.

Arguably, individuals have default patterns of strength or emphasis among modes that serve well on some venturing tasks and less well on others. Ability to override a default pattern of emphasis and adopt a different one may help an individual become potentially more useful in more different venture situations. Therefore, it may be worth observing and reflecting on personal thinking patterns as part of preparation for venturing, either to choose better where to fit in, whom else to recruit as a complement in the effort, or what shift in personal-mode emphasis to introduce for thinking more effectively in new venture situations.

Expert scripts

Professionals and enthusiasts of many types can sometimes be seen to have a personal modus operandi, (M.O.) for pursuing goals. This refers to an individual style or pattern applied repeatedly in a particular area of expertise, whether as a manager, subordinate, or entrepreneur. An M.O. may be observable in a baseball pitcher, professional golfer, safecracker, fighter pilot, pool player, teacher, coach, orchestra conductor, or any number of other occupations. The same can be true of entrepreneurs who pursue one venture after another, sometimes referred to as *serial entrepreneurs*. Even if performing only one start-up, each individual may do it in a different way from how others would, and which could be construed as evidence of an individual M.O.

For a would-be entrepreneur, then, a reasonable objective to consider is how to develop an effective *entrepreneurial M.O.*, or style of thinking and acting to create ventures more likely to succeed.

For characterizing an M.O. in entrepreneurship, a useful concept from computer science may be that of *expert scripts*. These, according to the studies of Professor Ron Mitchell[11] at Texas Tech University, refer to patterns of logic developed through experience to handle similar logical problem situations. Some such routines in other fields include recipes, checklists, and formulas. Military people have standard operating procedures, production-shop operators have flow diagrams, pilots have checklists, judges have laws, players have rules, officials have regulations, and individuals have principles and ethics that are patterns of practices.

Expert thinking is obviously more complex than the simple characterization of a single checklist or routine only one layer deep. Beneath it lie myriad elaborations of details that a mind might consider. An expert chef goes by much more than a recipe written on paper. Sights, sounds, smells, tastes, feelings, and past experiences are doubtless part of the process. But similarities observable on the surface that are learnable, teachable, and can be critiqued and practiced to improve skills are present as well, complex as their underlying subroutines or subscripts may be.

Through asking hundreds of entrepreneurs how they think through problems such as opportunity assessment, forecasting, profitability analysis, and planning, Mitchell reported finding patterns, that indicated individual entrepreneurs develop expert scripts or routines for handling certain kinds of recurring venture decisions.

There are indications that refinement of ways to perform entrepreneurial functions is possible. For example, an unpublished study of bankers in various parts of the country by Howell and others back in the 1960s[12] found that some had refined their skills at working with ventures to a higher degree through

---

[11] Ron Mitchell, "Expert Scripts" in *Frontiers of Entrepreneurship Research, 1995*, eds. William D. Bygrave and others (Wellesley, MA: Babson College, 1995) p. 145.
[12] Henricks, *Not Just a Living*.

Mapping of expert scripts

Portfolio development

Topics ahead

practice. The study consisted of presenting to bankers a small number of high-technology venture-loan proposals and asking for their reactions. In regions where such ventures were rare, the bankers turned the proposals down, even though some of them were disguised proposals from companies that later prospered mightily, such as Hewlett-Packard. In Santa Clara, California, (Silicon Valley) where high-technology venturing was more common, bankers familiar with it would accept the proposals but impose stipulations, such as maintenance of certain ratios or hiring of certain kinds of expertise as tactics designed to raise odds of success and reduce financial risk. In short, it appears that they were applying venture-specialized expert-banking scripts, developed through experience, to help borrowers perform better.

More recently during the dot-com boom of the 1990s, so many start-up ventures were taken public that members of the underwriting community improved skills for expediting the intricacies of those processes, that is, improving their scripts. Much as it is regrettable that many people lost money from the frenzy of offerings and subsequent bust, the fact that this part of the venturing process could be refined is an encouraging sign that scripts for roles in venturing can be refined.

Mapping of expert scripts

Depiction of an entrepreneurial script can take any of many possible forms. It could be a list of related thoughts or actions, a sequence described in paragraphs, a flow diagram of mental events, or a sequence of circles with radiating spokes, some of which connect the circles in a sequence across the page.

A related concept is *mind mapping*, where combinations of radiating and connected spokes depict one thought leading to a variety of others in creative search for some desired idea to solve a problem. The purpose of a script depiction, which need not be graphical, is to describe pattern of thinking that repeats from one venture to another, rather than to generate and depict a burst of ideas for solving some task.

The point of identifying an individual's script is to improve how it works over time, possibly aided by comparing it with scripts of other people who have succeeded better in venturing. The starting point is to find a personally workable way of depicting the script so it describes the individual's thought process validly and then experiment in searching for improvements. Both of these tasks call for repetitive practice in depiction and analysis.

Portfolio development

One way to combine systematic learning with work toward a venture is to do a series of short projects that combine to form a new venture portfolio, analogous to the portfolio of an art or architecture student. Creating a portfolio allows concentrated practice on selected aspects of the venture creation process as a way of increasing skill in performing them. Musicians practice scales, and painters concentrate on perfecting elements of their work. Da Vinci practiced sketching hands, Goya refined a technique for painting eyes. Still earlier artists developed techniques for displaying perspective, all through repeated practice on selected parts of the picture. Students of surgery practice tying sutures, and engineering students practice designing machine components using CAD/CAM programs.

Topics ahead

The ensuing chapters follow a five-step scheme depicted in Exhibit 1-4: (1) This chapter covers choices of entrepreneurial job preference, personal capabilities, and style. Then come (2) searching for venture opportunities and ideas for how to exploit them, (3) screening those ideas for feasibility and attractiveness, (4) designing the venture itself and a plan for implementing it, all leading to (5) start-up steps for financing the venture and getting it going.

If this organization of chapters makes it seem that processes of discovering and implementing a venture idea are likely to be orderly and cleanly sequential, it will likely prove misleading. Venturing is an activity fraught with unpredictability and surprises—preferably on balance, happy ones.

Some readers may already have completed one or more of these steps and can therefore economize time and effort by skipping them to enter the sequence farther along. Or, if it is discovered at a later point the path is heading toward an unsatisfactory end, there may be advantage in going back to an earlier step to restart the sequence with the new knowledge in mind. The portfolio approach is designed to allow this.

Beyond start-up further relevant venture topics are alternatives for shortcuts through acquisition and for carrying the venture on through growth and eventual disposition, topics to be treated in chapters at the book's conclusion.

Exhibit 1-4 Start-up chapter topics sequence

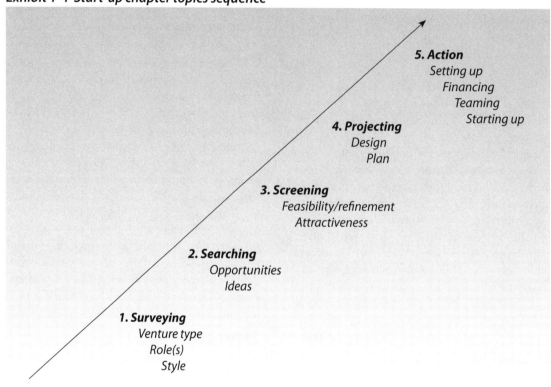

5. Action
  Setting up
  Financing
  Teaming
  Starting up

4. Projecting
  Design
  Plan

3. Screening
  Feasibility/refinement
  Attractiveness

2. Searching
  Opportunities
  Ideas

1. Surveying
  Venture type
  Role(s)
  Style

Exercises

Text discussion questions

1. Which of the four knowledge types is school best situated to impart and why?
2. Which of the four knowledge types would you consider most precious and what could you do about obtaining it?
3. If you wanted to influence the odds of your participating in start-up of a particular venture type, how could you do that?

Case questions (Cases appear in the back section of the book)

Case 1-1 Eric Chang
1. How were the "key ingredients" for Eric's venture obtained?
2. What "invisible organization building" is possible through this venture and how?
3. Explain how Eric's venture could become either of two different venture types.
4. What action steps should Eric take next and why?

Case 1-2 Kerry Tye
1. How, in rank order of importance, have Kerry's experiences equipped her, in terms of types of knowledge to contribute to the venture she is considering?
2. How do the key ingredients for Kerry's venture seem to have been obtained?
3. What roles have been required for creation of the venture she is considering, and how might the necessary roles change if it succeeds?
4. What personal agenda might she best adopt for contributing to the venture and to her fur ther career if she joins it?

Portfolio page possibilities (Some prior examples follow)
1. How would you rank the portfolio pages of some prior students that appear in at the end of this chapter, and why? What might be still better?
2. What criteria did you use for the above ranking?
3. On one side of one sheet of paper for each, prepare the following alternative pages you are as signed or wish to try. Indicate which one of them you are proudest of.
4. On at least one of your pages, list three new venture ideas you have thought of.

Page 1-1 Preferred venture type
1. What type of venture as listed in the chapter would you like to pursue, and why?
2. What roles over time in venturing do you imagine might suit your aspirations?

Page 1-2 Personal entrepreneurial script
Describe in some form (flow diagram, Mindmap, list, or other depiction) the script that your mind followed in generating and choosing one of your ideas to pursue.

Page 1-3 Knowhow acquisition
For one of the three ideas you have listed, briefly describe the know-how (1) you have and (2) would need to add for creating a venture to deliver it. (3) What would be your best way to acquire that know-how?

Page 1-4 Invisible organization directory
Spend at least 15 minutes listing names and potential business relevance of as many members of your invisible organization (contacts) as you can aside from family members, co-workers, and classmates to go with one of your ideas. Include at least one contact that you develop new for this assignment, and tell how and why you recruited that person.

Page 1-5 Marshalling key ingredients
Describe how you could best go about completing a set of key ingredients for one of your new business ideas.

Term Projects (individual or team)

Alternatives
1. Write the real start-up story of a local enterprise.
2. Write a complete venture plan or a feasibility analysis for a new start-up.
3. Start and operate a small enterprise during the term, keeping a log.
4. Pick a going enterprise and, with permission from the owner, prepare an agreement for purchasing it, including a reasonable price and terms.
5. Assist a local entrepreneur in starting or improving a business, and prepare a consulting report, including tasks accomplished and hours spent on them, such as a consultant might submit with a bill.

Here is some further description of what the first three of these alternatives might entail.

Venture history option

Develop a written history, based upon interviews with founders and initial backers, describing creation of a company begun five or less years ago. Prepare in advance for each interview session by making a list of questions to ask based upon both what you already know about entrepreneurship and upon what you are learning in your course. Then, if you wish, look at the list of suggested questions at the end of each chapter in this book for other ideas about what to ask. Select questions most likely to be significant and instructive. Interviews, preferably should be short and spaced over the term with time to think and write between them. It will likely help build confidence in the entrepreneur to take along each time a draft of what has been learned so far to let the person being interviewed see how your report is developing and possibly offer suggestions.

1. Some questions to start with include just what the company consists of, who owns it, what it delivers to customers and how, as well as where they hope it is headed.
2. Questions that apply to topics of this chapter include how the founder(s) came up with the five key ingredients, four types of knowledge and task relevant experience helpful for independent business entry.
3. Where do the founders think the company and they individually are headed, and to what extent do they believe they apply thinking styles (expert scripts) that distinguish them from other entrepreneurs?

Venture plan option

As a way of anticipating what should go into a venture plan, imagine yourself in the position of someone with savings who is being asked by an entrepreneur to invest in a start-up.

1. What information would you want to see in a plan to assess it for investment?
2. Where would you expect the entrepreneur might be able to obtain it?
3. Sketch a hindsight plan (what the start-up sequence must have been) for an existing business similar to one you might be interested in starting. Estimate, from interviews if possible, the role of venture-specific knowledge required and how it was obtained.
4. What events in the company's creation could most likely have been anticipated in planning, and how could that have mattered?

Prior student portfolio page example 1 of 1-1

1. Venture that I would like to pursue and why?

Venture: Lifestyle ventures

A lifestyle venture is one in which you leave your job because you prefer independence and like venture work better, or you might have an idea that prompts you to leave your job so that you have more time to follow that idea. I would like to pursue this type of venture for several reasons. First of all, I have a lot of hobbies and interests including cooking, scrapbooking, golf, etc. So I often think of ideas to help me improve my hobbies, whether it is a new tool or service. Also, a high degree of independence and being able to work on my own seems very appealing.

2. Roles over time in venturing

Being an insider in a venture gives you first hand experience to what it is like starting a business. At first, I would like to be more of a participant, part of the internal team, to gain knowledge on how things are done in a venture. Then, I would like to take one of my ideas and create a company from what I have learned from participating in that previous venture as well as all my other experience. It is important before starting something like this to gain as much knowledge as possible.

3. New product or service ideas

a. <u>Cell phone charger station in malls</u> — This machine would allow people who have forgotten to recharge their cell phones at home to do it while they are shopping. It would be a station with a computer screen where you would be able to choose your cell phone's brand and model. Then you would be able to place your phone inside a compartment with the specific charger needed that locks itself automatically after 5 seconds. It can only be opened with the credit card that was used to place it inside. It would do a full recharge in about 20 minutes for $2. You are able to shop while the phone recharges. If for some reason you forget your phone, no problem. When you placed your cell phone in this machine you entered your name and a home phone number along with a 5-letter password so the company will call you at the end of the day to say it is safe and it can be retrieved the next day. However, to make it easier on clients they are given a beeper to let them know when the twenty minutes are up and their phone can be picked up. Swipe your credit card and get your phone back fully recharged.

b. <u>Clue: University of Washington</u> — The game Clue for UW students (especially for new people so that they can get acquainted with the campus). However, this would be different from the original Clue, in the fact that it would not be a murder mystery but a game where someone has lost something. The game board itself would be an aerial map of the University and different professors would be the characters such as: a professor of economics, professor of dance, etc. Then the missing items could be things such as a skateboard, school books, a computer, etc.

c. <u>Scrapbooking Company - where we scrap for you</u> — A lot of times people don't scrapbook because they don't have time. However, they love the way it looks and wish they could have the same thing done for their pictures. Scrapbooking is the practice of combining photos, memorabilia and stories in a scrapbook style album. I would like to create a company where people would come into an office with their pictures and choose with a consultant which album and papers they would like to see used in their newly to be created album. They would leave their pictures at the office with a timeline of events and come back a week later for a consulting to see how they like the layout of the new album. The customer would come back one week later to pick up the final album.

*This page was replicated from a student paper and with permission.

Prior student portfolio page example 2 of 1-1

1. **What type of venture as listed in the chapter would you like to pursue and why?**

   I am most drawn to Job-Replacement and High-pay, Stably-Small ventures. My primary interest in entrepreneurship stems from a desire to be independent and to determine my own success, so these options naturally agree with me. Working for or managing a large corporation does not appeal to me; I would much rather be intimately involved with several aspects of a smaller business.

2. **What roles over time in venturing do you imagine might suit your aspirations?**

   Based on my aspirations, inventor, starter, runner, and manager roles are likely. The field and specific nature of the venture will of course determine whether the process begins at 'invention' or 'starting,' but the launching and continuation of a small business will certainly entail opportunities for me to assume the other roles. I am comfortable with the idea of all of them; my skills, experience, and my partners' abilities will ultimately determine which roles become my responsibilities.

3. **What are three new product or service ideas you can think of?**

   a) New wine bottle/cork design
      A wine "bag" with a one-way valve would allow wine to be poured without air coming into contact with the unused wine. This bag could be incorporated into a wine bottle (in order to maintain appearance, class, style, etc., which customers greatly prefer), with the valve acting to constantly equalize the pressure inside the bottle (surrounding the bag) with the ambient air pressure. This would maintain constant positive pressure on the liner bag, ensuring free-flowing wine without introducing oxygen.

   b) High-quality, customized online photo-printing
      Digital photos would be submitted electronically (online) for processing and printing. Pictures would be touched up and enhanced, and then high-quality prints would be made and shipped back to the customer. Higher quality and larger prints would be available as compared to in-store digital processing, and value is added through convenience, service, and quality. Intended more for high-end, large format printing than for normal snapshots.

   c) A steam closet for pressing clothes.
      A closet-like appliance in which washed and dried clothes would be hung, in order to steam the wrinkles out of them without manual labor (ironing, hand-steaming, etc). A water and electricity connection would be required, but otherwise the process would be entirely self-contained and automated.

Prior student portfolio page example 1 of 1-2

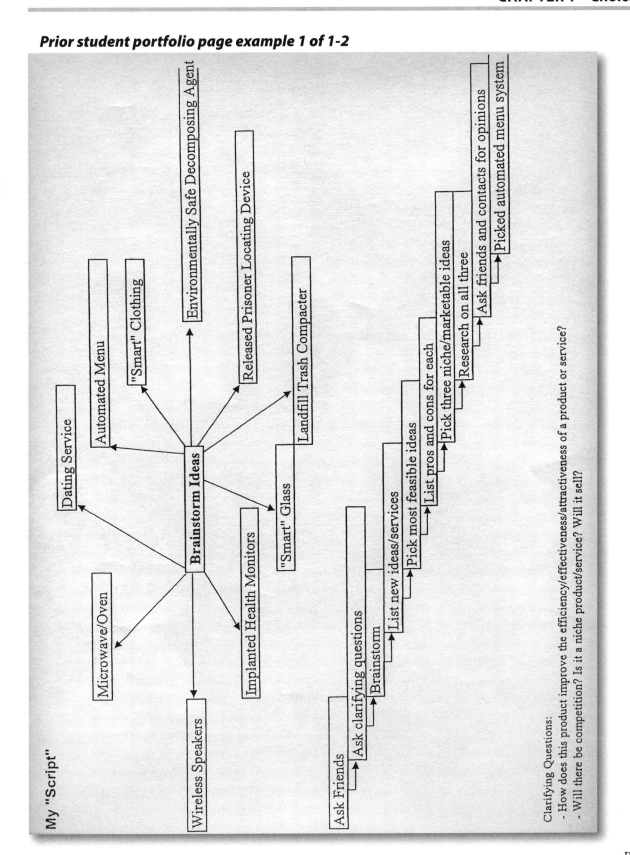

My "Script"

Brainstorm Ideas
- Dating Service
- Automated Menu
- "Smart" Clothing
- Environmentally Safe Decomposing Agent
- Released Prisoner Locating Device
- Landfill Trash Compacter
- "Smart" Glass
- Implanted Health Monitors
- Microwave/Oven
- Wireless Speakers

Ask Friends → Ask clarifying questions → Brainstorm → List new ideas/services → Pick most feasible ideas → List pros and cons for each → Pick three niche/marketable ideas → Research on all three → Ask friends and contacts for opinions → Picked automated menu system

Clarifying Questions:
- How does this product improve the efficiency/effectiveness/attractiveness of a product or service?
- Will there be competition? Is it a niche product/service? Will it sell?

Prior student portfolio page example 2 of 1-2

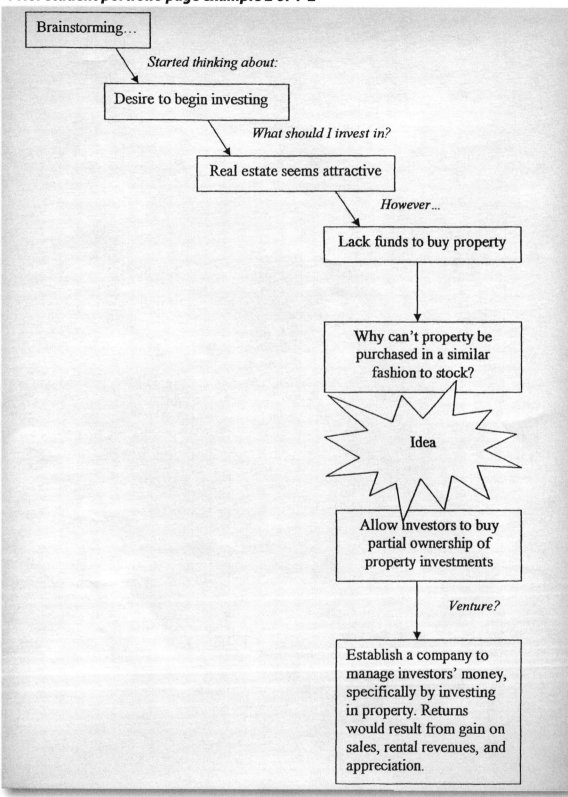

Brainstorming...

Started thinking about:

Desire to begin investing

What should I invest in?

Real estate seems attractive

However...

Lack funds to buy property

Why can't property be purchased in a similar fashion to stock?

Idea

Allow investors to buy partial ownership of property investments

Venture?

Establish a company to manage investors' money, specifically by investing in property. Returns would result from gain on sales, rental revenues, and appreciation.

Part 2

SEARCHING

This section presents two chapters on how ideas for "something better" to provide the basis for a new venture can be discovered. Both chapters conclude with systematic approaches for seeking viable venture possibilities.

Opportunity, which is centrally necessary to the entrepreneurship process, is the focus of the first chapter in this section. An entrepreneurial opportunity is defined as a situation where an entrepreneur can create an improvement and make it commercially available at a sufficient profit through forming a new business.

Awareness of the variety of forms opportunities take, which is to say types of opportunities, may help in identifying them sooner than competitors. Understanding of the causes that create opportunities may also help and are also classified in this chapter, as are different types of outcrops and clues that reveal opportunity existence.

Inevitably, some people are in better positions and are better equipped both to detect and to take advantage of a given opportunity than are others. Understanding this can help a would-be entrepreneur map a personal strategy either for pursuing an opportunity search that fits that person or for joining forces with other people to pursue it with winning combined capabilities. The chapter concludes with some systematic approaches for guiding opportunity search.

The second chapter in this section explores sources of product and service venture ideas, which are defined as conceptions for seizing and exploiting opportunities through entry into independent business. Thus, venture opportunities and venture ideas go together. Either can occur first. The venture idea discovery process sometimes arises from *capability push*, which builds from a question such as, "I wonder who might buy what can be developed from this capability?" At other times it arises from *market or customer pull*, which is triggered by such a thought as, "How could a new venture provide this product or service that people probably would like to have?" A list of such idea search questions is included in this second chapter. Also suggested are some criteria and further systematic approaches for searching that may be helpful for a person who wants to push the process of idea discovery, as opposed to simply waiting for it to happen spontaneously.

The idea to be chosen for implementation should be for something not only better, but sufficiently better to warrant the effort and other costs of venturing with it. That, in turn, depends upon such evaluation factors as product/service produceability, attractiveness relative to competition, market size, profitability, investment required and return on investment. Assessing prospective merit in such respects will be developed in two chapters on screening in the next part of the book that follow the two in this part on searching. This separate focusing of chapters on searching versus screening is for the sake of clarity and convenience. It should not obscure the fact that in practice searching and evaluating work together.

CHAPTER 2A – Opportunity

Topics

1. Opportunity and entrepreneurship
2. Two main opportunity types
3. Driving forces
4. Sequences
5. Discovery and searching

Checkpoints

a. Define opportunity.
b. Explain how opportunity and new ventures are related.
c. How are ideas different from opportunities and why does it matter?
d. How is opportunity created?
e. Explain the meaning and significance of dawn rate.
f. Illustrate perennial versus occasional opportunities.
g. Discuss overshoot and its consequences.
h. How is gap analysis supposed to work?
i. What are market holes?

Opportunities and ideas are both necessary in entrepreneurship. They are also two different things, and either may be discovered first. In this discussion, generally:

Opportunity is defined as a situation where one or more people can introduce an improvement.

Business opportunity is defined as a situation where the improvement can earn a profit.

Entrepreneurship opportunity is defined as a situation where the improvement can enable creation of an adequately profitable new business.

Ideas, in contrast to opportunities, are conceptions of ways to exploit opportunities, ways to render improvements, whether through businesses, entrepreneurship, or other avenues. For a given opportunity there may be multiple ideas about how to make the most of it. There may also be more than one opportunity that could be exploited through application of one idea. Discovery of either may lead to discovery of the other, or multiple others.

This chapter will concentrate on opportunities and how they can be sought. The companion, and in some ways overlapping, subject of ideas and seeking them will be left for the next chapter.

1. Opportunity and entrepreneurship

By defining *opportunity* as "a situation somebody can improve," and *entrepreneur* as "someone who introduces something better to the market through creation of a new firm," it follows that the existence of commercial opportunity is a necessary condition for entrepreneurship to happen.

Life, in hindsight, can be viewed as a series of opportunities, some taken and others missed.

Bill Gates and Paul Allen, thanks to their scholastic capabilities and their parents, had the opportunity to attend Lakeside, a high-quality private school in Seattle. Within the school were further opportunities they could accept or reject. One was made possible by the largesse of benefactors who had given the school a computer for students to learn on. Gates and Allen took this option, and from it learned computer programming.

Seizing this opportunity became part of a chain of events that eventually produced Microsoft. But this opportunity was one where the improvement possible was to learn more about using computers, not to start a company or earn a profit. It was a learning opportunity, but not a commercial one, although it eventually produced entrepreneurship, as did the following three situations where profitable business start-up occurred directly:

> A commercial malt-mixer salesman visited the hamburger stand of a customer who had been buying an unusually large number of the machines. He saw long lines of customers at the windows waiting to buy hamburgers.
>
> —•—
>
> A young man was troubled when he had to pay $40 in late fees when he returned a video he had rented from Blockbuster.
>
> —•—
>
> A saleswoman for the minicomputer division of a very large diversified company was asked by a prospective customer to provide software for inventory control. She replied that her employer did not offer that kind of software. The customer repeated his request.

Here can be seen the *outcrops* of three opportunity situations, evidence that circumstances were ripe for new venture development. The first prompted Ray Kroc's McDonald's; the second Reed Hastings' Netflix, which allows movie rental by Web with delivery by mail with no late fees; and the third, ASK, a minicomputer company whose name came from the initials of its founder, Sandra Kurtzig.

Tuning definitions

Opportunity is widespread because so many things can be improved, the nature of perfection being such that it is almost never attained. It may be impossible to improve works of Mozart or Shakespeare. But it is easy to envision what it might be like to have more available health care, simpler tax procedures, or less pollution. A particular chair could be lighter, the temperature

more comfortable, these shoes in better shape, work moving faster, paint fresher, gas mileage higher, service friendlier, and so forth.

Putting the word *business* in front of the word *opportunity* narrows its definition, because then improvement alone is not enough. Delivering the improvement must, in business, yield a profit. Further, to qualify it as *viable* for business, the profit must be justifiable in light of the time, resources, and risk level required to realize it. Fitting the definition to entrepreneurship in particular requires still further that the viable business opportunity be exploitable by entry into independent business ownership. Thus, the *definition of entrepreneurship opportunity becomes a situation where a better product or service can be introduced to the marketplace at a profit that warrants the requisite investment and risk.*

These qualifications help clarify challenges in the deliberate pursuit of entrepreneurial opportunity. If happenstance thrusts opportunity into view, the trick is to recognize it and act effectively. If outcropping evidence does not conveniently announce itself, then the trick is to search for clues, and the question becomes how to do that most effectively and efficiently.

Opportunity versus problem

The statement, "There are no problems, just opportunities," is arguable. A problem exists where something is wrong. But for an opportunity to exist there need be nothing wrong, just the possibility of something being made better. Still, choosing to view problems as opportunities may be useful by encouraging search for solutions that may pay off.

> Bill Lear encountered a problem when his plane would not start due to a low battery. He transformed this problem into an opportunity by searching for solutions, of which there could be many. The idea he liked best was to couple a small gasoline chainsaw motor with an aluminum-framed automobile alternator to produce a light-weight electric power generator from these already mass-produced, and therefore cheap, off-the-shelf parts.

Thus, a way to transform a problem into an opportunity is to seek ideas that solve the problem. To make the idea entrepreneurial, ways must also be found to fit it with a compelling value proposition and viable start-up business model.

Pursuing commercial viability may raise sub-problems, as it would in Lear's case above. Chainsaw motors are not designed for coupling with alternators. The two are designed to operate at different speeds, and the torque required to pull a saw chain may not match that needed to spin an alternator. Nor are the shafts or housings configured to match. But work on these mating problems might reveal more opportunities. What else could a chainsaw motor, geared down to lower shaft speed and higher torque, be useful for? Pocketbikes? Yes, they came later. But were they invented to solve a problem? Probably not. The opportunity they exploit seems to be one of just playing.

Opportunity versus idea

Idea, in contrast to *opportunity*, can be defined either as a way of solving a problem or of exploiting an opportunity. Any particular idea may or may not be useful, effective, or profitable, even though it may be aimed at a viable opportunity. An idea, like an opportunity, can be said to be viable for entrepreneurship if it is financially attractive (has business viability) and allows start-up as a major shareholder, not just a hireling. Plainly, it may, like an opportunity, be viable for an established business as well as for a start-up.

Why distinguish?

A value of distinguishing *idea* from *opportunity* is that for one opportunity, such as insufficient power in an aircraft battery, there may be more than one potentially worthwhile solution idea. For instance, shotgun shell charges, instead of chainsaw motors, can also be harnessed to crank over aircraft engines. Postponing the search for ideas may simplify the search for opportunities and allow more progress to be made on that, before shifting to a search for ideas to exploit the opportunities.

Starting with the latter, moreover, may make searching unduly random. It is too easy to generate ideas lacking valid purpose that way, which may produce confusing clutter. Often, ideas will occur automatically upon perception of opportunity. Or their discovery, which will be discussed in the next chapter, may reveal new opportunities.

Creation of opportunity

Opportunity is ubiquitous because there are always situations that people could improve, although requiring profitability reduces the array of possibilities. Anything that changes the status quo changes the opportunity array, eliminating some and creating others. For example, if in a river valley town there are some buildings needing paint, others with plumbing leaks, and still others with structural shortcomings, there are opportunities.

If governmental authorities decide to dam and flood the valley, those particular improvement opportunities will vanish. But then new housing may be needed for displaced occupants, creating a new array of opportunities.

A change of state or situation producing new opportunities may be caused by people, or by events. If by people, one or more of them may be entrepreneurs. Thus, opportunities can be created by, among others, entrepreneurs.

This fact could make discussion of whether or not entrepreneurs create their own opportunities a tautology. Being able to introduce change and thereby create opportunity implies that there was already an opportunity for that sequence. But that is not the point. Rather, it is to define any opportunity so that it includes room to consider alternative ideas as ways to exploit it.

Magnitude

Any potential improvement of a situation usually has one or more dimensions, such as how many people it helps, how many buy it, how much they value and are willing to pay for it, how long it lasts, and whether it needs replacement. Exploiting it can also have side effects that become part of its magnitude. Improvements in the form of innovations are sometimes characterized as *incremental* (small change) versus *radical* (major departure from how things were being done before). Radical changes may be *discontinuous* (sharp change on an otherwise fairly smooth rise in performance), *breakthrough* (change that had previously been impossible), or *disruptive* (seriously upsetting to an existing company's and/or industry's usual way of doing business).

Incremental innovations are more numerous and collectively can be extremely powerful. But it is hard for a given start-up venture to accomplish enough through incremental innovation to reach high success. Hence, venture investors typically seek the radical change ventures. They want opportunities that transform industries or, better yet, create new ones.

Entrepreneurs who discover such opportunities, however, need not be setting out with such ambitious goals. They may simply be responding to enthusiasms and opportunities that happen to deliver more than anticipated.

> Publication of *In Search of Excellence*, a best seller on how to run businesses effectively, succeeded far beyond the expectations of its authors, Tom Peters and Robert Waterman, who had left McKinsey & Company to start their own

consulting companies and hoped the book might help.

> — • —

> With only $500 Nolan Bushnell, a former Ampex engineer, started Atari, a company to make videogames. He was surprised when sales took off at $3 million the first year and a new industry resulted.[13]

> — • —

> Boolean algebra, the logic system on which digital computers are based, was invented by George Boole in the 19th century, long before anyone had such machines in mind. His goal for it was to prove logically the existence of God.

A mixed implication is that opportunities can be worth pursuing even when they do not seem great. But the fact that some are much greater than others warrants concern about which opportunity to pursue, how great it may be and how, if greatness is potentially there, to colonize it before others do, and survive when competition ensues.

2. Two main opportunity types

Perennials

Entrepreneurial opportunity rests on misalignment between supply and demand, and arises from the possibility of changing either or both. But there can be a lag between its existence and its exploitation. Such lag can create *perennial opportunities*, those that lie unexploited, awaiting action by either some existing enterprise or an entrepreneur. In contrast is a second type, *occasional opportunities* that arise newly, as opposed to lying in wait.

Perennials

There is always latent demand for **novel twists**, things simply not thought of yet that could be newly introduced almost any time. Games, toys, novelties, and fad items continually emerge as examples. Their discovery comes sometimes from companies and individuals who make a profession of discovering them and sometimes from amateurs just "playing around."

> Peter Adkinson, a Boeing employee, liked to play games. Partly as a hobby and partly as business effort he began producing and selling games at home. He was contacted by another man who

had invented a game and wanted financial support from Adkinson's "company" to develop it.

> Adkinson said he could not provide the support for that game, but if the man could devise a different game along certain lines Adkinson had in mind he would try producing it and, if it became successful, he would reconsider providing support for the man's game. The man devised a game along the lines Adkinson asked for, Adkinson began producing and selling it under the name "Magic," and within three years his company, Wizards of the Coast, had sales of over $150 million per year. Profits were not reported, the company being privately owned, but it seems clear that the margin on the game must be high, because it consists mainly of cards that are relatively expensive for consumers to buy but must be low cost to print.

High-margin perennial opportunity areas include health problems for which researchers find remedies (many of which subsequently show up on television commercials), technology-application potentials for new products such as the iPod, and desire for valuable rarities, as illustrated by the following history in

---

[13] John Kao, *Entrepreneurship, Creativity, and Organization: Text, Cases and Readings* (Englewood Cliffs: Prentice Hall, 1989) p. 44.

which can be seen a sequence of opportunities for different individuals, some of whom perceived and pursued them, and others of whom did not.

In 1867 15-year-old Erasmus Jacobs was sitting under a tree in the Transvaal when he saw "in the glare of the strong sun a glittering pebble" which he picked up, pocketed, and later gave to his youngest sister. A month later a neighbor, Schalk van Niekerk, saw the children playing a game with several stones, one of which was this pebble. He tried scratching a pane of glass with it. Seeing he admired it, the childrens' mother gave it to him.

Unsure whether the stone was really scratching glass or not, van Niekerk sold it for a few pounds to a trader, Jack O'Reilly, who shopped it around town without success until he came to the Acting Civil Commissioner, who sent it to an amateur mineralogist, W. Guybon Atherstone, who recognized and proclaimed it a diamond. Local newspapers took little notice, but the Local Colonial Secretary in Capetown to whom he mailed it in turn sent it to London where a prominent jewelry firm, Garrards, certified it as real, 21 ¼ carats, but passed it off as having been planted to swindle people into a land rush. Several months later a mineralogist sent by a London merchant reported back that any diamonds found in the vicinity had probably been carried there in the gizzards of wandering ostriches. He declared that the "geological character of the part of the country renders it impossible" that any diamonds could have been discovered there.

But a local shepherd, Swartbooi, had heard that Schalk van Niekirk was offering to buy "special stones" and stepped forward to sell one in exchange for 500 sheep, 10 oxen, and a horse. He got his price, and van Niekirk in turn accepted an offer of 11,200 pounds for it from a jeweler, Gustav Lilienjfeld, who put it on display as an 83½-carat diamond. Subsequently shipped to London, it was cut, polished, and sold for 30,000 pounds. As newspapers reported this and word spread throughout England, Europe, and America, a rush from around the world began, following closely on the heels of locals in South Africa. As in other areas of industrial opportunity, many new ventures sprang up, and with time most of them closed down, leaving a small number in prosperous long-term operation.[14]

Other potentially high-margin rarities include masterpieces, rights to exceptional talent, and bargains, such as under-priced real estate or antiques. Apparently advantage can be gained by developing appreciation for the value of high-value things.

Low-margin perennial opportunities are easier to find. Desire for lower prices generates sales for countless small businesses whose owners work harder, put in longer hours, or accept lower income to provide services. Small stores, barbershops, gardening services, and other such enterprises fill the Yellow Pages. Long hours and hard work in them tend to yield low pay, but a living. Occasionally, one of them will hit on a better idea that allows chain or franchise expansion to raise the payoff, but most do not.

Flexible labor, particularly at low wages, is also perennially in demand. Sometimes workers are able to *go solo* with their jobs to become contractors rather than employees for the companies they serve. The companies then need only employ their help when necessary, not permanently, while the former employees may then work for more than one company at a time to stay more fully occupied. Occasionally, a new start-up will result for a particular type of part-time worker. This new employer will take care of fringe benefits and payroll deductions so the other companies that buy their services can avoid that bother.

Especially intriguing among perennial opportunities are **currently overlooked improvement possibilities** such as products or services that could be introduced years earlier but aren't. Previous examples have included suitcases with wheels, surfboards with sails, and sushi restaurants with conveyor belts, all of which could have been done sooner. More examples of perennial opportunities will appear later in Exhibit 2a-2.

Occasionals

Occasional opportunities, the second main type, are created by one-time changes in circumstance of various types, such as governmental, technological, social, and economic.

---

14 Stefan Kanfer, *The Last Empire* (New York: Farrar Straus Giroux, 1993).

The circumstance changes, in turn, may result from a variety of events, such as demographic shifts, political elections, scientific discoveries, inventions, calamities, propaganda, advertising, and waves of sentiment. In the following case, opportunity was introduced by government action, but demand continued ever after.

Emperor Napoleon of France was frustrated by problems of feeding his army, with the result that in 1795 his government offered a prize of 12,000 francs to any patriot who could provide it with a method of providing wholesome food for its armies and navies at all times and in all circumstances. The country was fighting with the armed forces of Austria, England, Prussia, Sardinia, and Spain. Some Frenchmen were being killed in battle, but thousands were dying from the miseries of slow starvation and scurvy on inadequate diets of salt meat, smoked fish, and hard tack. They desperately needed fresher and more wholesome preserved food.

The result was a scramble by inventors seeking the prize, and one of them came up with a process for canning. Nicolas Appert, who had previous experience as chef, pickler, winemaker, brewer, distiller, confection maker, and government supplier of cooked provisions in large amounts, took up the challenge. Fourteen years later in 1809 he received the prize and promptly invested it to start a business applying his new technique. It consisted of sealing fresh or cooked meat, fish, eggs, and vegetables in air-tight bottles with corks tied down by wires which were then immersed in boiling water for varying periods determined through trial and error. It didn't always work and consequently led to problems at times, but it underwrote a business that his family carried on beyond him. His description of the process appeared in 1810 as *The Book for All Households*, or the *Art of Preserving Animal and Vegetable Substances for Many Years*. An American edition appeared in New York two years later. This was a half century before another Frenchman, Louis Pasteur, discovered not only that bacteria were a cause of disease and food spoilage, but also that they could be killed by sterilization, a process now known as pasteurization.[15]

Time window

There is a "window" time-wise for viewing and exploiting an occasional opportunity. Too soon means the market or antecedent technology is not ready. Too late means the market has dried up, the product or service has become obsolete, or competitors have already moved in too far, raising entry barriers and squeezing profits. Some opportunities stay available longer than others. Pet rocks went fast. Corn flakes have lasted long.

How time can change what kinds of opportunities are found can be surmised by looking at which types of firms grew fastest, as illustrated in Exhibit 2a-1 below, which contrasts leading businesses of the *Inc.* 500 in 1997 versus 2004.

Exhibit 2a-1 Inc 500 businesses of two contrasting years

1997	2004
1. Electric toothbrushes	1. Cell phone sales
2. Investment banking and IPOs	2. Web site software
3. Gas and electricity sales	3. Service call centers in India
4. Funding resources	4. Web link for ordering meals
5. Temporary employees	5. Large stock-block brokering
6. Computer products	6. Reengineering projects mgmt.
7. Residential property development	7. Environmental engineering mgmt.
8. Loan collections	8. Web site registrations
9. Management consulting	9. Medical image archiving
10. Digital photo image library	10. Life insurance buyback and resale

---

[15] Earl Chapin May, *The Canning Clan* (New York: Macmillan, 1937).

As more people come to accept the new order and find it familiar, a paradigm shift occurs through which things that seemed strange before now seem normal. The presence of cell phones, wireless networking, commonplace open heart surgery, and retracting automobile cup-holders were relatively unthinkable only a decade or two ago. But now they are ordinary, some individual having seen and acted on the opportunity first.

Exploitation lag

Some time lag is inevitable between existence versus exploitation of opportunity or going from recognition to action and effect. Of these, action is arguably the most vital. The sequence can vary, possibly beginning with action, such as buying something without the idea of a venture, receiving an offer for it from somebody else that makes obvious a profit possibility, and responding to produce a transaction that becomes the start of a business. Typically, action will follow recognition of opportunity, which in turn will follow some sort of business idea formulation, analysis, and decision to act.

Some ventures, such as production and sale of Trivial Pursuit, Pictionary, Magic, and virtually any other non-computer games, could have been done sooner, while others, such as Yahoo!, eBay, and Google had to wait until other elements were in place before they could be done.

Products that could have been done sooner and others that had to wait are listed in Exhibit 2a-2 below. A third column lists, with a

Exhibit 2a-2 Opportunity timing

	1 Had to wait	2 Could have been sooner	3 Still waiting. Never?
1	Lightweight surfboards	Happy massager	Tidal-electricity–generation
2	Digital watches	Hot-air corn popper	Fusion energy
3	Microcomputer software	Windsurfer	Fully functional electric cars
4	Microcomputer	Skateboards	Picture-phones
5	Space flight	Snowboards	Cures for the cold, cancer, AIDS
6	Internet communication	Fiberglas skis	Cheap solar cells
7	Cell phones	Turbojet	Space colonization
8	Pagers	Cargo containers	Control of aging
9	E-mail	Hub overnight air delivery	ESP, mental telepathy
10	Satellite TV	Discount brokerage	Disease elimination
11	iPod	Discount stores	Pills replace meals
12	DNA testing	Chunnel	Good petroleum substitute
13	Organ transplants	Antisubmarine countermeasures	Global warming remedy
14	Digital cameras	Knitting needles that glow in dark	Superconductivity uses
15	Laser printers	Internet?	Nuclear proliferation control
16	Bread machines	Web?	Universal clean air
17	Web marketing	Magic (Wizards game)	Crime elimination
18	Suburb shopping centers	Jet skis	Perfected genes
19	Flash memories	Bungee jumping	Space colonization
20	HDTV	Nail guns	Mental telepathy
21	Personal organizers	Current power mowers	Increased old-growth timber
22	Broadband	Wakeboards	Gravity regulation
23	Sex prediction	U.S. aseptic packaging	Star wars defense
24	Reliable jet engines	Short-stroke IC engines	True thinking machines
25	Aluminum cookware	Suitcases with wheels	Human cloning
26	Cigarette health warnings	Credit cards	Engineered humans
27	Privatized public services	Hula hoops	Economical massive desalination
28	Laboratory biological cloning	Trivial pursuit	Elimination of money
29	Cell phones	Pictionary	Replacement of universities
30	Transplanting hearts	Cylindrical "Frisbee"	Major ocean mining beyond oil

question mark, conceivable accomplishments that may or may not ever be achieved. Readers can no doubt quickly come up with additional items for each column. Thinking about the probable causes of such opportunities as these in conjunction with the reader's current situation and more recent events may stimulate imagination of further opportunities.

Antecedent capability

Some ventures cannot be done earlier because of missing technologies. A company that provides cell phone repair requires first the existence of cell phones, which in turn require development of the collection of technologies making up not only the phones but also the communication infrastructure needed for them to operate.

Other examples of changes that had to await technology development appear at the upper end of the first column in Exhibit 2a-2 below. Exceptions, however, include the last five items in that column as follows:

Aluminum cookware—public fear of poisoning delayed acceptance.

Shopping centers—required enough people with autos to be economical.

Health warnings on cigarettes—took massive amounts of proof of health damage.

Privatized public services—required experimentation and political pressure.

New drug availability—FDA approval requires much testing first.

The need to await antecedents for enacting a new device does not mean that a person cannot anticipate development of the opportunity for making it. Leonardo da Vinci anticipated inventions that came much later, including helicopters. The Dick Tracy comic strip conceptually predated cell phones with a wrist radio the size of a watch. One drawback it had compared to the present was a wire antenna that had to be worn up the arm. A shortcoming of both it and the modern cell phone might perhaps be anticipated by prediction of a future wrist video phone, whose screen will appear full-sized by projection on eyeglasses or the human retina.

Not only may the opportunity be imagined before the technology to implement it, but technical feasibility is often demonstrated long before application occurs. Picture phones, for instance, were demonstrated in the 1940s and are just spreading now via microcomputer attachments. The Internet itself was around for decades before it was made user-firendly and found wide use. Then it caused further cascades of venture opportunities that seem likely to continue indefinitely.

A way to seek advantage from the dependence of opportunity on precedent technology can be to ask (1) what future enabling may come from technology that is being developed now, or may be coming, and (2) what improvements may become possible if a particular technology were to be developed? Answers may provide clues to coming opportunities.

3. Driving forces

3. Driving forces

Business environment changes

Opportunities may last no longer than do the circumstances that create them and invite competition. The aim should be to stay a few steps ahead of competitors and on the move to new opportunities as driving forces behind existing ones play out. Such forces include the following.

Business environment changes

Less apparent to pedestrian consumers but very real in profit potential are opportunities that arise in commercial, as opposed to consumer, markets. To become aware of them may require informa-

tion searching efforts and commercial contact networks that the typical person does not have or, more importantly, does not reach for.

Economic dislocations

Commercial expansion or conversion, such as development of new industrial capacity or upgrading communications equipment, creates demand for new products and services that new firms may be better able to provide than old ones. Shifting production overseas opens a need for transaction and transportation services while at the same time making facilities and equipment available domestically for which new firms may generate uses.

Governmental actions

Waging wars (by whatever name) generates need for supplies of existing weapons and materiel as well as invention and development of new weapons. Regulation changes both produce opportunities for new companies to break into previously protected markets and for consulting services to help existing companies cope with the changes. Expanded labor rules, for instance, created opportunities for start-ups in temporary services to let existing companies avoid the new rules by hiring fewer people so they would not have so many permanent employees to care for.

Resistance reduction

A positive impulse to opportunity can be gained by reduction of resistance to it. Opportunity may be temporarily stymied by problems of bureaucracy, custom, corruption, communication, negotiation, reliability, and availability of money, even in localities rich with resources, such as parts of Africa, Latin America, and Asia.

Also necessary for entrepreneurship are trust, credibility, honesty, reliability, cooperativeness, willingness to let the other person realize a gain, understanding of high standards of performance, initiative, incentives, flexibility, and openness to change, as well as availability of resources. Many opportunities exploited in the U.S. that appeared in Exhibit 2a-2 could have been exploited elsewhere instead, if only the circumstances there were different in identifiable ways.

That gives reason for tuning in on change that may take place in situations where entrepreneurship is not occurring at present. A change in the governmental system of Mexico, the social attitudes toward venturing in Germany or Japan, or the political power of big conglomerates in Japan or Korea could herald cascades of new venture opportunities.

Development of local infrastructure can produce similar effects. The creators of Linux and Netscape, for instance, moved to Silicon Valley because of the type of venturing that was occurring there. Some software ventures have moved from Silicon Valley and other countries to Seattle because of the large number of programmers and programming industry there. Lifestyle can also be an attracting feature. Perhaps in time, coastal areas of developing countries will become magnets for new venture development when attractive real estate in the U.S. becomes sufficiently overcrowded and overpriced.

Laws may also preclude entry. The U.S. Postal Service monopoly on delivery to mailboxes is protected by law. Other monopolies can be unassailable because of requirements for licensing or obtaining contracts. However, monopolies based only on market or financial power can sometimes be exploited through licensing or selling out the better idea to them.

Enablers

As noted earlier, some innovations require precedent discoveries and technological advances for them to be possible.

Technical discoveries

Perhaps most widely evident in recent years have been opportunities arising from creation of chips that first made the microcomputer and then a wide range of other new products possible. Microcomputers themselves were followed by creation of software to go with them.

For three decades Moore's Law has held that the number of transistors on a chip of given size, roughly a gauge of chip performance, doubles every 18 months or so. Named after Gordon Moore, the chairman of Intel, the law has been the cornerstone of processes by which electronic goods have become more varied, cheaper, faster, and better—to the point that some gadgets, such as calculators and cell phones, cost a fraction of what they did when they first hit the market.[16]

Not all new technical capability improvements have been this widely obvious. For instance, small low-cost chainsaws gave artists another tool for carving works out of logs. Widespread air express delivery service empowered merchants to deliver

---

[16] Evan Ramstad, "The New Generation," *Wall Street Journal*, June 15, 1998, p. R4.

everything from flowers to junk auto parts faster to distant customers. Stereolithography[17] enabled expansion of prototype manufacturers and start-up of others. The spectrum of causes for such occasional opportunities has been developed in more detail elsewhere.[18]

Resource emergence

As education in technical subjects spreads worldwide, companies spring up to capitalize on the skills of less-expensive technicians from other countries. The Web becomes available and countless ventures arise to exploit it.

Impellers

Some aspects of industry structure, for example, whether it is oligopolistic, price-versus-service competitive, even innovative or not, do not much seem to influence the decisions of individual entrepreneurs. But other aspects do. Acquisition entrepreneurs, for instance, capitalize on advantages of consolidation where industries are fragmented, as happened with phone companies, auto companies, hospitals, and waste disposal firms.

Start-up entrepreneurs move according to what they see before them as possibilities to introduce something better. For them opportunity tends to correlate with market expansion and customers spending money differently. Defense spending goes up, and more entrepreneurs find ways to get part of it. The service sector expands, and entrepreneurs find more action in services.

Market emergence

The course of human and natural events is constantly changing circumstances and thereby creating new situations where things can be improved by new ventures, among other activities.

Supply-source withdrawal

An embargo clamped onto imports from Cuba in 1961 created opportunity for new sugar-growing companies in the U.S. Earlier, the oil cartel embargo caused gasoline prices to rise, which in turn enabled start-up of companies that converted cars and trucks to more economical operation on diesel fuel through replacement of gas engines with diesel engines. When the embargo ended, these converter companies went away.

When large aircraft purchasers shifted from propellers to jets, the propeller companies went out of production, which left the residual market of propeller users without supply. Consequently, smaller companies started offering a supply of used and refurbished propellers.

New demand

Because change is a constant, so is freshly emerging demand. Existing companies continually try to meet it but are not always suited to the new task, which leaves opportunity for new ventures. Introduction of microcomputers created demand for new designs of office furniture to accommodate them, as well as for accessories like mouse pads, which opened opportunities to meet the demand.

Population moves continually create need for new buildings, commercial as well as residential, and also for modification work on those in place. Development of new housing communities creates demand for new stores and services located more conveniently for them. Immigrants create demand for new types of foodstuffs and accommodation programs.

People's ages and lifestyles change, generating demand for different recreation equipment and services. Sports changes generate new product opportunities—from surfboards and snowboards, to skateboards and wakeboards, and to new safety gear and clothing to go with them.

Calamities such as earthquakes, hurricanes, pestilence, and war generate expanded demand for existing countermeasures as well as demand for research and its products to fight back with. At the same time, ever-present pressures to curb costs and improve results create demand for new methods and materials.

---

[17] Stereolithography: Ability to form solid objects from liquid plastic through hardening in 3D triggered by intersection of laser beams in the plastic.

[18] Vesper, *New Venture Mechanics* (Englewood Cliffs: Prentice Hall, 193) p. 4. Peter F. Drucker, *Innovation and Entrepreneurship* (New York: Harper Collins, 2000).

Profit chain evolution

As businesses and markets come and go, adapting to changes in population, transportation, and communication technologies, inevitably there arise reasons for channels of distribution to evolve as well. Both shortcuts and extensions of channels can represent opportunities for improving distribution.

Shortcuts

Buyers can sometimes be offered a novel choice through the elimination of some part of the value chain to give customers a lower price through buying directly from an earlier stage in the chain. Two examples:

> Amazon.com cut out the store, offering book shoppers more convenience through acceptance of orders on the Web and a slightly lower price in return for their giving up the opportunity to browse the shelves.
>
> — · —
>
> IKEA eliminated assembly steps in furniture making by redesigning it to allow assembly by the end user. This reduced costs in assembly, packing, shipping, and storage to give consumers a product that was cheaper and easier to carry home undamaged.

Sometimes a type of market that went away comes back, as illustrated by the evolution of the microcomputer industry in the time of Michael Dell.

> The first buyers of microcomputers had been mostly technical hobbyists who obtained them through mail order, and then assembled them and struggled to make them work. As the market expanded to include more people who wanted to use the computers without having to struggle with their technical failings, retail stores became a preferred purchase site because there, people could get help in selection, setup, and debugging. But the stores, many of them started by people lacking in technical or business experience, or both, had other failings. Their inventories were unreliable and their mark-ups were very high.
>
> As the stores struggled with these problems, microcomputer manufacturers were rapidly improving the design and reliability of their machines while at the same time lowering costs and prices, squeezing the margins of computer retail-

ers. More users were becoming microcomputer-savvy as they swapped assistance and benefited from books, articles, and classes providing education about the technology and equipment.

> More computer producers again began selling directly through the mail. From experience in upgrading his computers, and selling them to people he knew, Michel Dell took aim on high margins, observing that stores would charge $3,000 a microcomputer that could easily be built with $700 worth of parts. He recalled that, "I realized that if I could sell even more of them, I could actually compete with the computer stores—and not just on price but on quality. I could also earn a nice little profit and get all the things a high school kid would want.
>
> "But beyond that, I thought, 'Wow, there's *a lot* of opportunity here.'" When he drove off to enter the University of Texas, it was in a BMW bought with his high school earnings and carrying three PCs in the back seat.[19] Then microcomputer stores began phasing out, sometimes being replaced by sale of microcomputers in small departments of larger stores.

Thus here the opportunity for selling microcomputers began with mail order, then shifted to stores, only to have mail order sales rebound as the computers became more user-friendly and brand-name reliable.

Extensions

While some value chains are shortened, others are lengthened. For example, producers of commodities, such as plastics or metals, occasionally find demand for small orders of special variations in their products. Typically, they will charge extra for the trouble of producing, stocking, and delivering these low-demand goods. If later the demand goes up, these goods become highly profitable because of their high pricing to cover the special handling. Special distributors may then spring up to buy these goods in large quantities, for which they may be given volume discounts, because they relieve the commodity companies of the unaccustomed tasks of special handling.

Confluence

Although listed separately here, driving forces work together in confluence that is important to

---

[19] Michael Dell, *Direct from Dell* (NY: Harper Business, 1999) p. 9.

test for, lest one or more force of importance be overlooked. For instance, if incomes rise when a new technology emerges, the two may work together. Moreover, if it happens to enable products that fit a predominant age pattern, then that too may add strength to the net drive level. However, if at the same time capital happens to be short, that may impose a drag that in part nullifies the other forces and weakens the net driving force, and so forth.

4. Sequences

Chains

Trees

Cascades

Opportunities can multiply from a single source in the form of chains, trees, and cascades. Combinations of the three are most likely.

The introduction of preserving food in bottles introduced by Frenchman Nicolas Appert in 1809 was followed by a spreading series of developments in the United States as well.

In Boston, William Underwood started using Appert's methods to preserve cranberries, lobsters, salmon, and tomatoes. In New York, Thomas Kensett started using Appert's techniques in 1819 and went into partnership with his father-in-law, Ezra Daggett, filing for a patent on "an improvement in the art of preserving" that would use "vessels of tin" which was issued in 1825. They started canning in tin in 1839.

There followed a host of other innovations by other entrepreneurs; a steam cooker in 1843, a press of semi-automatically making can tops and bottoms in 1849, hermetic sealing in 1851, and the spread of canning to an ever-increasing variety of foods. With this variety came developments in ways of picking, sorting, and processing the foods as well, as new entrepreneurs initiated companies to make the materials, produce the machines, and set up processing lines over an ever-expanding geography.[20]

Chains

A company that starts with one toy or game is likely to see opportunities for additional toys or games. At the same time, some others who notice the success of the first game or toy will find that it triggers in them ideas for other similar products, possibly products that build upon the first one and that represent opportunities for them. Anticipating such effects, most companies and creative individuals consider it wise to protect such ideas through copyrighting, either by formal registration or by at least indicating the date and author's name in connection with publication. (The latter method offers somewhat less protection.)

Trees

The same ideas may sometimes be used to introduce lines of related products, such as when an author whose book catches on also licenses it for applications that branch into movies, action figures, and clothing.

Cascades

Rather than a chain of opportunity developing for just one company, a cascade of opportunities may develop that spills opportunities in many directions for one venture or many, as illustrated by the following two examples. The first starts with an event. The second starts with a venture.

Event: War

Impact For radar, better cathode ray tubes are developed.

Opportunity Those tubes can improve other applications.

Venture Tektronix starts by offering better oscilloscopes.

Impact Tektronix works on development of other display technologies.

Ventures Planar and other ventures spin off Tektronix to offer other display technologies.

Event: Apple starts

Impact Microcomputers become available for students, among others.

Opportunity With new software, spreadsheet calculation could be automated.

Venture Visicalc, followed by Lotus, begin by creating and offering that new software. Later comes Excel.

Impact The microcomputer market expands.

---

[20] May, *The Canning Clan.*

Opportunities—Other ventures start as suppliers of hardware, software, temp workers.

Multi-effect cascades

In more graphical form, such cascades can be seen in the "begat charts" that have been developed for several metropolitan areas, such as Austin, Minneapolis, and Silicon Valley. A chart for Silicon Valley beginning with Fairchild Semiconductor Corporation appears in Exhibit 2a-3 below. Although these examples pertain to electronic companies, others have occurred in different industries, such as airplanes, automobiles, shipping, steel, oil, construction, and services. When Sears, Roebuck and Company began and grew through introduction of mail order selling, numerous coattail opportunities arose for other ventures to spring up offering both new products and new sources of supply for Sears.

Overshoot and shakeout

The apparent vividness of hindsight on how successes were mined from cascades of opportunities can obscure the less-visible myriad failures that stemmed from the overshoot of too many aspirants joining the scrambles to capitalize on cascades once they became visible.

Multi-effect cascades

Overshoot and shakeout

Exhibit 2a-3 Fairchild Semiconductor begat chart

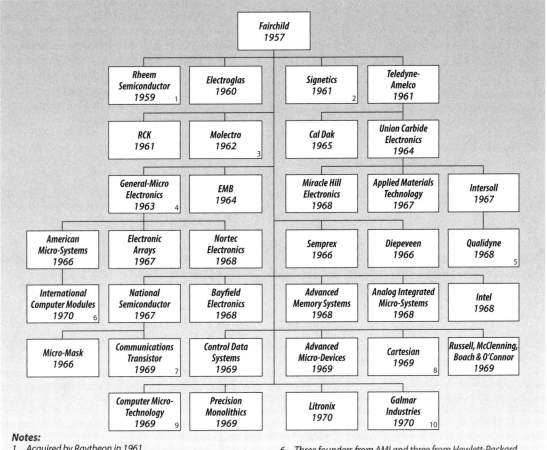

Notes:
1. Acquired by Raytheon in 1961.
2. Two founders were from Semiconductor Corp.
3. Assets of Molectro acquired in reorganization of National, which moved from Connecticut to California.
4. Acquired by Ford-Philco in 1966.
5. Other founders were from Circuit Engineering & Design, Fairchild, GE, and Union Carbide.
6. Three founders from AMI and three from Hewlett-Packard.
7. Two founders from Fairchild.
8. One founder from Philco-Ford Microelectronics.
9. Four founders from Fairchild and one from ITT Semiconductor.
10. Two founders from Fairchild, and one from Semimetals, Inc. and one from Peripheral Systems Corp.

Source: from Kirk P. Draheim "Factors Influencing the Formation of Technical Companies," in Cooper and Komives, 1972. With permission.

Too many miners joined the California gold rush of 1849, and most of them went broke, although some got rich. Others less visible in the cascade because they were not miners, but rather made their money by selling supplies to miners, prospered as well, Levi Strauss, the creator of Levi's jeans, being one of them.

Similar overshoot occurred in the Klondike gold rush and in other industries such as automobiles, airplanes,[21] and personal computers. Too many companies enter, costs drop as efficiencies are learned, but prices are cut faster, leading to shrinking margins. Some companies improve efficiencies fastest and survive, while others fall behind and are either squeezed out of business or absorbed by the survivors. Thus even though each of them looked to its founders like a very likely winner because the opportunity cascade was so massive, in fact they ended in obscurity. It may come quickly, as did the end of Bowmar, the company that introduced the first pocket calculator, only to be quickly eclipsed by Texas Instruments, Hewlett-Packard, and Casio. Or it may take decades, as was the fate of Digital Equipment Corporation, acquired by Compaq, which was ultimately acquired by Hewlett-Packard.

Misses versus hits

The hit of one person or company on an opportunity is usually in effect a miss by others who attempted to avail themselves of that opportunity. This may be due to differences in dawn rates (the rate at which existence of opportunities dawns on people, explained below), actions taken or not, or to other causes.

The microcomputer represented an opportunity that was missed by many companies who should have known better. Foremost among those missing it was IBM. Earlier, it had missed an opportunity to sell mainframe computers to the federal government because it insisted upon leasing rather than selling the machines, and upon providing the maintenance and software programming itself, rather than letting the customer do it. These were policies which had

won for the company previously, so it stuck to them and, this time, lost. A new mainframe competitor, Control Data, arose and took the government business IBM should have had.

Some years later an MIT computer expert proposed the idea of a smaller mainframe. IBM passed this idea by. Large mainframes were its business. Why undercut the existing successful product line with a smaller and cheaper model? Consequently, a new computer company was started in Cambridge, Massachusetts, Digital Equipment, which proceeded to become and remain dominant in the new industry of minicomputers.

Next, the microcomputer arose, not because IBM did not have one; it did. The big company had developed a prototype at its engineering facilities in Poughkeepsie, New York. But the product, apparently for lack of a strong champion or top management support, was shifted to a shelf in Boca Raton, Florida, and allowed to languish.

Only later, after introduction to the market by a small Albuquerque mail-order company, MITS, followed by a host of other start-ups, particularly Apple, Tandy Corporation, and Commodore, did IBM finally wake up to this opportunity and hastily enter the market.

To do so it acquired its operating system for the new machine through buying rights to one recently acquired by another small start-up, Microsoft. But IBM missed again, this time to get exclusive rights on that operating system, so that the big company in effect took the small end of that opportunity and gave the big end of the opportunity to Microsoft.

Obviously in hindsight, these are not the only companies who can justifiably conclude that they missed huge opportunities in microcomputers and should not have. So it is with a competitive economy in any number of areas: small cars, jet engines, Fiberglas skis, Gore-Tex, Formica, air express delivery and, of course, the Web. At an industry level, railroads missed the trucking and airline opportunities, while movie studios let television pass them by. At a national level, France, Mexico and Russia missed the opportunities they all had to hang on to what became parts of "Anglo" U.S. territory.

---

[21] Kenneth E. Knight and others, "Venture Survivability: An Analysis of the Automobile, Semiconductor, Vacuum Tube and Airline Industries," in *Frontiers of Entrepreneurship Research*, 1987, eds. Neil C. Churchill and others (Wellesley, MA: Babson Center for Entrepreneurial Studies, 1987) p. 138.

Two general types of misses are far misses and near misses. Far misses refer to opportunities that entrepreneurs should not regret missing, either because they could not have exploited them anyway or because they found better ones to exploit instead. Near misses are opportunities that in hindsight they did not have to miss and wish they had not. Most people have some of both.

Reasons why such misses occur can be grouped in three classes. First is failure to discover the opportunity at all. Second is to have discovered the opportunity but rejected it in error. Third is, after having seen the opportunity and selected it as worthwhile, to lose it through tardy or otherwise inadequate follow-through.

> Xerox consciously formed its Palo Alto Research Center (PARC), gave it a mission of inventing "the office of the future" and thoughtfully staffed it with leadership that was dedicated to computer distributed processing (i.e., separate smaller computers rather than a central mainframe) and talent with experience in disciplines compatible with that goal. The result included (1) invention of personal computers, (2) the mouse, (3) the graphical interface, (4) word processing software and (5) laser printers, all tremendous discoveries. Unfortunately for Xerox the additional steps of recognizing their potentials and then of introducing these products to the market in a way that capitalized on them through leadership in personal computers were not successful.
>
> This set of major misses was ironic in light of the fact that the Xerox process itself was an opportunity that had been presented by its inventor, Chester Carlson, to and rejected by, such distinguished giants as Eastman Kodak, Polaroid, 3M, General Electric, and others. Instead, a non-profit foundation, Battelle, and its small client company, Haloid, made off with the prize, later named Xerox.

5. Discovery and searching

The main reason for exploring different forms opportunity can take and patterns of its occurrence is to raise capability to seek it out at will.

A 1988 study by Koller[22] of 82 entrepreneurs randomly selected from the Yellow Pages found that most entrepreneurs:

Recognized, rather than sought out, business opportunities.

Learned of opportunities from someone else (business associates, relatives, and social contacts, in that order).

Found opportunities in fields where they had work experience. (Especially frequent was the response that they were attracted to the opportunity because it offered a chance to apply their prior training.)

Left open is the question of whether or not intentional efforts to seek out opportunities can improve discovery performance. Certainly they occur. But systematic studies of how well they work have yet to be reported.

As noted in the preceding chapter, opportunities tend to occur as a window in time whose shutter opens when the opportunity is available for seizure and closes when someone exploits it. In hindsight the opportunity can be seen to have had (1) a "total duration time." There can be (2) a "perception time lapse" or dawn time between when the window or shutter opens and when someone in a position to act upon it notices that it is open for exploitation. There can also be (3) a second or "response time" lapse between when someone notices that the opportunity shutter is open and when they act upon it, and (4) a third time lapse or "action duration time" between when the exploitation begins and when the opportunity has been exploited and becomes essentially closed.

Dawn rate

The rate at which existence of an opportunity dawns on someone can be complicated to describe. An individual's discovery of it may be slow or fast, as can expansion of awareness beyond one individual to others, whether through observation of the leader or through independent discovery. Moreover, a single opportunity

Dawn rate

---

[22] Roland H. Koller, "On the Source of Entrepreneurial Ideas," in *Frontiers of Entrepreneurship Research, 1988*, eds. Bruce A. Kirchhoff and others (Wellesley, MA: Babson Center for Entrepreneurial Studies, 1988) p. 194.

can be a composite of sub-problems and sub-opportunities, each having its own dawn rate.

IBM, having experienced a slow dawn rate in recognizing the potential of microcomputers, finally decided to create one, realized that it would need an operating system that would be expensive and, worse yet, very time consuming to develop and refine. Consequently, it went looking for an existing system and sent representatives to Microsoft to acquire the system it was using, which was called CP/M (control program/monitor).

Microsoft, apparently not seeing the great commercial opportunity that this inquiry might represent, informed IBM that they did not own the system and directed the IBM representatives instead to Gary Kildal, who had created and owned CP/M.

Kildal, not seeing the opportunity either, somewhat haughtily informed IBM that he would not be immediately available because he had other business to attend to and consequently directed its representatives to his wife. She in turn brought in CP/M's lawyer, and there followed an awkward chain of delays over several days, which eventually frustrated the IBM people so much that they gave up on CP/M and returned to Microsoft to ask whether there might be an alternative operating system somewhere else.

Meanwhile, the potential opportunity had dawned on Microsoft, which contacted Tim Paterson, who had developed an operating system similar to CP/M called DOS (disk operating system) and was willing to sell it. Apparently not seeing the magnitude of the opportunity at hand, Paterson sold it cheaply. Kildal got nothing.

IBM also did not see the vast profit potential of the operating system, only its own need for it. So it agreed to buy rights from Microsoft non-exclusively, which left Microsoft free to use or resell DOS to anyone else. As his lost potential dawned on Paterson, he decided to go after Microsoft, claiming on some basis they had shorted him. As a result, he got a bit more. Microsoft made multiple fortunes and its largest shareholder became the richest man in the world, financed mainly by the income from DOS.

Thus Microsoft at first missed the opportunity because their dawn rate was slower than the shutter. But window of opportunity opened again, and now they were ready. Then IBM missed, by not buying the property outright or else going to find another operating system that they could buy outright.

Outcrops and clues

Discovering opportunity is sometimes inextricably linked with having ideas about how to introduce something better. Hence, there will be some overlap between this chapter and the next about how entrepreneurs discover either ideas or opportunities. The term *outcrop*, sometimes used by geologists to describe clues indicating the presence of promising ore, will be used here to characterize clues to the presence of entrepreneurial opportunity. Some such outcrops, noted earlier,[23] include the following:

> Things have **changed**.
>
> Some market is **booming**.
>
> Something is **hard to get**.
>
> Available technology is **not being used**.
>
> **It's been a while** since quality/price improved.
>
> Margins seem to leave lots of **room for profits**.
>
> **Somebody else** is getting rich.
>
> Some resources are **sitting idle**.
>
> Someone has shown there is a better way but **not exploited it**.
>
> **Monopoly** is leading to complacency and poor performance.

Vantage points

The degree to which an opportunity is easy to glimpse can be a function of where it is relative to the vantage point, either mentally or physically, of any particular observer.

Opportunity clues, somewhat like radio signals, can be viewed in terms of a propagation radius, having greater strength closer to the opportunity source that diminishes outward from there. Most consumer industries broadcast their offerings and activities broadly to reach a widespread population. So do some commercial product industries, particularly when they are concerned about regulation, public relations, or their stock prices. But many care only about visibility in narrow markets, where they operate largely unknown to the public. How many people can name a manufacturer of

---

[23] Vesper, *New Venture Mechanics* (Englewood Cliffs: Prentice Hall, 1993) pp. 5-6.

O-rings, poison gas, crew-racing shells, screws, nails, or coffins? They are known almost exclusively to neighboring companies in their value chain, not to the public.

Hindsight effect

A striking characteristic of opportunities is that they can be so invisible in foresight but clear in hindsight. This may be because, like a nut and bolt going together, the possibility of fit is proven in the past but can't be proven in the future. Confirmation comes only after trying. Maybe this underscores a need to be ready to try things, and faster than others so they don't take the opportunity first.

In colonial days of the U.S. there were boundless resources available for the taking. What was the evidence of opportunity at the time? Imagine the unclaimed woods, unexplored minerals, unoccupied bays, and potential home sites? Who was in position to appreciate these, or to pursue exploitation of them, and how? There were resources available for the taking, but taking to where, by what means, and at what cost? Would the harvesting of furs, for example, warrant establishment of a logistical system to deliver them to wealthy Europeans?

With time, an increase in demand for whale oil to use in lamps signaled opportunity. Coincidentally, observation by sailors of numerous whales along the Atlantic coast was part of the same opportunity, a parallel outcropping of it. Many people certainly knew about the former, and the latter had been known for centuries. When a sloop from Nantucket blew off course into these offshore whales, it brought people who knew of the demand into contact with the supply, whereupon whaling at sea began. A cascade of further opportunities from this coincidence included development of new types of ships capable of processing whales at sea, as well as expeditions using them.

In hindsight, this opportunity is easy for anyone to see. But at that earlier time it took a storm impacting the right people at the right time to reveal the opportunity to some who would take action on it. That in turn led to other discoveries. Quite likely, many "wrong" people were exposed to these same clues, but missed them.

Visibility

Both perspective and illumination matter. Imagining opportunity as viewed through something like a camera lens raises the possibility of different viewing angles, some of which allow the opportunity to be glimpsed while others don't. Camera viewing allows focusing and zooming up close, which also can be important to understanding an opportunity.

Some opportunities seem to be brightly illuminated for a given person, while others may be more obscure for the same person. Presumably, the more vivid the illumination, the more visible the opportunity is to other potential exploiters as well.

Venture possibilities can come as surprises, first to those who carry them out and later, when they have become reality, to others. Michael Dell recalls plunging ahead with $1,000 in capital on the opportunity he saw in 1984.

> *I was pretty oblivious to the fact that the economy was in a state of turmoil when I started the company. That didn't really concern me too much. I mean, what I saw was the opportunity.... I wasn't particularly worried about whether I was going to make a lot of money. It just didn't really bother me very much.*

> *I think there are opportunities everywhere. The question is, which ones are the right ones, and which ones are the ones that will make a success? ... All markets will continue to be under pressure in terms of efficiency and pricing.*[24]

Proximity

For each opportunity some people are closer, or have a better vantage point for perception. It has been said that "no good oil deal makes it out of Texas," the presumption being that Texans will, being nearest to it, notice and pick it off first.

This is not to say that the person with highest proximity advantage to an opportunity will necessarily be the first notice or exploit it. Some individuals are more perceptive than others and so may operate with different perception ranges, and some have more resources or motivation.

Michael Dell was not in the computer business, but he was close to it from hanging around computer stores as a boy. One thing that caught

---

[24] *Inc*, March 2002, p. 71.

his attention was the large markup. "Let's say," he said, "that you buy a computer from a retail store, and you pay $4,000. The retailer sends $2,500 of that back to the manufacturer and keeps $1,500. The question I asked myself was: What was the retailer doing to earn his $1,500? Was he adding $1,500 of value to that machine for me, a knowledgeable computer buyer? The answer was no."

This inspired Dell to start selling computers. To make his product, he bought stripped-down IBMs and to them added options purchased from other suppliers. At first he sold through direct response advertisements, then through telemarketing, and finally through a sales force. In 1984 at age 19 he entered the industry. This was after competition had already squeezed many other entrants out. He not only survived as a newcomer entering late, but he built a company that by 1989 had sales of over a quarter billion dollars.[25]

Some miss opportunities that they arguably should not, given their proximity advantage. For them it might be better to collaborate in opportunity search with someone having more motivation or resources. At the same time, their oversight leaves opportunities available for discovery by others who search them out, even though they may start from less-helpful vantage points.

Searching by gap analysis

One methodical approach is first to pick an industry or market and then to look for what might be regarded by that market, or a segment of it, as a benefit worth paying to get. The technique for this process, formulated by White,[26] is called Gap Analysis. It involves ten steps for finding viable unserved market opportunities. Prior to White's ten steps is an implicit preliminary step, namely to choose an industry, such as, in an example he gives, the leisure industry.

White claims both entrepreneurs and established companies have found dozens of viable new product and service opportunities with this approach (although they are not listed in his book). He recommends group meetings for higher productivity. He also notes a reverse

White's ten steps

Briefly, here are the ensuing ten steps:

1. *List* criteria for search. These might include, for instance, market size, rate of return, capital intensity, mark-up level, degree of newness of the product or service and of the market, level of technology, outsourceability, and likely attractiveness to potential investors.

2. *Pick* an industry and segment its potential market population. Examples would be by age, income, or education. Pick one of these, such as adults between ages 35 and 45.

3. *Subdivide* for that segment in another way. For the above segment, a way to subdivide might be into workdays versus holidays, or vacation days. For instance, choose workdays of adults aged 35 to 45.

4. *Subdivide again*, for instance, into parts of the day.

5. *Eliminate*, with care lest something good be lost, sectors of the last subdivision that do not fit at all, but keep the rest in view.

6. *Brainstorm* to identify, for those remaining sectors, possible problems to which solutions might be sought. Some of the example problems White suggests for the end-of-workday sector include (1) when work ends, I am tired, (2) traffic is frustrating on the way home from work, and (3) my feet are tired and hot. His list includes 14 items beyond these three.

7. *Narrow* the above list to a smaller number (White picked four out of the 14 on his list) by eliminating those whose fit with the criteria of step one is weakest.

8. *List* the remaining problem aeas from step seven along one side of a worksheet and the criteria from step one across the top. Draw lines to make a matrix.

9. *List* possible solutions to each of the problem areas on the right side of the sheet. For traffic frustrations, White suggested intelligent street signs that would reroute traffic to reduce congestion. For tired and hot feet he suggested slippers containing vibrators.

10. *Assess* the solution ideas against each of the criteria listed across the page and further test them.

[25] Tom Richman, "The Entrepreneur of the Year," *Inc.*, January 1990, p. 43. Also, Joel Kotkin, "The Innovation Upstarts," *Inc.*, January 1989, p. 70.
[26] Richard M. White, *The Entrepreneur's Manual* (Radnor, PA: Chilton Publishing, 1971) p. 52.

Exhibit 2a-4 Product comparison grid on garden carts[27]

Garden carts

Carts Vermont Dumpfront Cart 26, $250.

Agri-Fab Poly Lawn Cart 45-02262, $100, A CR Best Buy.

Sierra Ranch Ultimate Dolly Cart DC103, $200.

Shop Smart You'll find smaller, $30 to $60 garden carts from Ames, Craftsman (Sears), Flowtron, and Rubbermaid at home centers. Larger or pricier carts from Agri-Fab, Carts Vermont, Gardener's Supply, Norway, Sierra Ranch, and Vermont Ware are sold at hardware stores, garden centers, and catalogs or online (see "Brands" on page 45). Consider your capacity needs. Look for large wheels. And think twice about buying all-plastic carts.

Overall Ratings By type, in performance order

Excellent ◉ Very good ◕ Good ○ Fair ◔ Poor ●

BRAND & MODEL	PRICE	CAPACITY (CU. FT.)	OVERALL SCORE (0-100 P F G VG E)	HANDLING	STRENGTH	LARGE WHEELS	PNEUMATIC TIRES	BALL BEARINGS	COMMENTS
LARGE CAPACITY *Mostly for large properties. These hold up to five 2-cu.-ft. bags of wood chips, or 400 lb., and require a roughly 33x40 -in. footprint stored on their nose.*									
Carts Vermont Dumpfront Cart 26	$250	13.6		◉	◉	✔	✔	✔	Especially easy to lift. Lengthy assembly.
Agri-Fab Farm/Yard Cart 45-01772	175	14		◉	◕	✔	✔	✔	Especially easy to lift. Lengthy assembly.
MEDIUM CAPACITY *Best for most buyers. These hold up to three 2-cu.-ft. bags of chips, or 300 lb., and require a roughly 26x31-in. footprint stored on their nose.*									
Gardener's Supply Medium Garden Cart 31-988	275	6		◉	◉	✔	✔	✔	Especially easy to lift and push. Wooden tray, padded handle. Lifetime warranty.
Norway Foldit Utility Cart	220	5.75 [1]		◉	○	✔	✔		All-metal; folds to 22x10 in. Especially easy to lift and push. Holds 330 lb., but wheels flexed under load. Padded handle.
Vermont Ware Town 'n Country Cart Model A Steel	250	5 [1]		◕	◉	✔	✔	✔	Especially easy to lift. Tipped forward under load. Metal tray, padded handle. Holds 350 lb.
E-Z Haul Garden Cart CT202	170	5.5		◕	◕		✔	✔	Especially easy to lift. Lifetime warranty.
Carts Vermont Home and Garden Cart 20	215	6.5		○	◉	✔		✔	Wooden tray. Lengthy assembly.
Agri-Fab Poly Lawn Cart 45-02262 **A CR Best Buy**	100	6		◕	○	✔		✔	Especially easy to lift. Gaps at wheels, but performance unaffected. Lengthy assembly.
Harbor Freight Tools Garden Cart 30422	75	6.5 [1]		○	◔	✔		✔	Damaged by 50-lb. sand bag and under maximum load. Wooden tray. Lengthy assembly. 30-day full warranty; 90 days on parts.
Craftsman (Sears) Yard Cart 87649	50	6.5		◔	◔				All-plastic. Hard to lift and push. Uncomfortable handle. Wheels flexed under load.
Flowtron Handy Hauler YC 500B	30	5		●	◔				All-plastic. Handle flexed and cracked under load. Hard to lift and push. Uncomfortable handle.
SMALL CAPACITY *For lighter-duty hauling. Most hold up to two 2-cu.-ft. bags of chips, or 175 to 250 lb., and require a roughly 22x23-in. footprint stored on their nose.*									
Sierra Ranch Ultimate Dolly Cart DC103	200	4 [1]		○	◉	✔	✔	✔	Pushing and lifting effort only average, despite features. Metal tray. Holds 175 lb. 1-year warranty on frame; 90 days on other parts.
Rubbermaid Roughneck 3706	50	4.75		◔	◔				All-plastic. Hard to push. Uncomfortable handle. Holds 200 lb. No warranty.
Ames Easy Roller Plus 2463875	40	4.5		◔	◔				All-plastic. Hard to push. Uncomfortable handle. Holds 250 lb. but wheels flexed under load. Lifetime warranty.

[1] *Estimate; capacity not stated by manufacturer.*

The tests behind the Ratings

Overall score reflects performance in our handling and sturdiness tests. **Capacity** denotes how many cubic feet a cart's tray can hold. Maximum weights are as stated by the manufacturer. **Handling** includes our judgments on stability and ease of pushing and lifting with 75 pounds of wood chips, based on outdoor tests over wood chips, leaves, and other varied terrain, and indoors over a wood-block obstacle course. **Strength** reflects the ability to carry maximum load and to withstand drop tests with 50-pound bags of sand. **Large wheels, pneumatic tires,** and **ball bearings** are features that ease pushing and rolling. **Price** is approximate retail. **Most carts have:** A warranty of 1 or 2 years. **Most large-capacity carts have:** Wooden trays. **Most medium- and small-capacity carts have:** A plastic or wooden tray with a metal frame and handle.

[27] "Garden Carts," *Consumer Reports*, May 2003, p. 43.

market-gap analysis is possible by seeking out, in already-served markets, suppliers that for one reason or another are not performing well, and creating a venture to outperform them.

Searching for market holes

A new offering can take the form of a different bargain not yet offered, a missing feature, or a combination of features. Such gaps within existing product lines can be viewed as *holes* in the market that some segment of it might like to have filled by a new product or service.

> Howard Head entered the snow ski market with metal-laminated skis selling for $135 a pair in contrast to the existing wooden skis that sold for $35 a pair. The difference in price proved to be justified by higher performance and longer life in the Head skis. But it left a price gap of $100. K2 filled that with skis made out of fiberglass, a material Head had considered but rejected. The K2 skis sold for $75 per pair, which attracted buyers to the gap. Before long, skiers found that K2 skis also performed better than Head's, which quickly became eclipsed in the market. Failing, the company was sold off for the value of its brand to a large firm, AMF.

A way to seek such holes can be to imitate, for some chosen market, the kinds of charts that display product comparisons in magazines such as *Consumer Reports* and those that concentrate on some kinds of products such as cameras, cars and microcomputers. These charts, **Product Comparison Grids**, typically list along one axis different features that have meaning for a particular product and along a second axis the brands offering that product, as shown in Exhibit 2a-4 below, which was printed from a *Consumer Reports* article about garden carts.

Searching by actions - Side street effect

Sometimes, successive revelations of a next problem, next possibility, or next opportunity demonstrate a kind of *side street effect*. That is to say that embarking on a venture is something like entering an avenue down whose side streets appear opportunities that cannot be foreseen. Initiative must first be taken and progress must be made before they can be seen. A similar effect has been described by Ronstadt in his discussion of a *corridor principle*.[28]

> When Norm Brodsky started a delivery service in New York City, he had great difficulty persuading anyone to use it. They already had such services, so why change? On a sales call he responded to rejection by asking if a potential customer had any problem at all with deliveries, and was told it was hard to link charges from delivery with the customer orders they applied to. This was an accounting, not delivery problem. But Brodsky went to work on it and ended up offering delivery service with a special twist that helped in accounting. This produced enough sales to put his company on the Inc. list of fastest-growing companies two years running.

An implication is that someone seeking opportunity might do well to take some initiative just to get into the flow of a chosen line of business, presumably one with favorable market trends, then look intentionally to see what new perspectives can be gained as a result and test their helpfulness in revealing unexploited opportunities.

Further ways of searching deliberately to discover potentially winning new possibilities will be described in the next chapter on ideas, which are here taken to mean ways of exploiting worthwhile opportunities.

Exercises

Text discussion questions

1. Discuss pros and cons of the proposition that entrepreneurs create their own opportunities.
2. How could a would-be entrepreneur go about looking for potential new venture opportunity outcrops and clues before looking for venture ideas?
3. Explain how considering opportunities in terms of chains, cascades, and trees could be potentially useful to a would-be entrepreneur.
4. What causes someone to miss an opportunity and what personal policies could they adopt to optimize the amount of missing they do?

---

[28] Robert Ronstadt, "The Corridor Principle," *Journal of Business Venturing*, Winter 1998, p. 31.

Case questions (Cases appear in the back section of the book)

Case 2A-1 Byron Osing

1. List the main opportunities Byron can be seen to have encountered. How would you characterize them as to their (1) main types, (2) outcrops, and (3) driving forces?
2. Whom else besides Byron would you suppose was likely in as good a position or better to detect and appreciate them?
3. What behaviors of Byron's seem to have caused him rather than someone else to win with them?
4. Describe the pros and cons of Byron moving ahead with Launchworks versus some other business activity you describe as an alternative.

Portfolio page possibilities (Some prior examples follow)

Each page, bearing the date and your name, should be one single-sided sheet, based upon this chapter, stating from your present impressions and information (quite possibly to change later) the following:

Page 2A-1 Opportunity identification

1. Identify an opportunity, noting its outcrops and clues.
2. Describe its driving forces and how they should play out.

Page 2A-2 Market hole chart

Develop a product comparison similar to Exhibit 2a-1 that reveals one or more market holes.

Page 2A-3 Future opportunity drivers

1. Identify a set of opportunity drivers and other forces at work or soon to arise.
2. List some opportunities those drivers should produce.
3. Predict when the forces would most likely play out and what impact that would have on the opportunity you identified.
4. Describe remedies to cope with that change if you seize the opportunity.

Page 2A-4 Gap analysis

1. Define a market sector and sketch, insofar as one page allows, a Gap Analysis to identify a potential new venture idea.
2. Note briefly the main events that occurred for you in each of the ten steps for finding this idea.
3. Comment on where this approach might be most versus least effective.

Term Projects (individual or team)

Venture history

1. What opportunity was the venture aimed at and to what extent was it the same as the one that the venture exploited?
2. What created the opportunity, how long had it awaited use, and what other opportunities were, in hindsight, passed over by the entrepreneur?
3. What outcrops and clues to the opportunity were present, which of them were perceived by the entrepreneur, and how?
4. To what extent did exploiting the opportunity create other opportunities?

Venture planning guide

1. Classify the topic areas in which you have been exploring for opportunity and the tactics you have used for looking. What other areas do they exclude and why?
2. To what extent have the above areas shifted as you have searched and why?
3. List information contacts (people as well as Web and literature) you have used for discovering and evaluating potential opportunity areas.

Prior student portfolio page example of 2A-1

1. Briefly describe the opportunity: Automated Touch Screens

Writing in terms of an opportunity in general, my opportunity would be based on the fact that I will be improving customer service and response time within the restaurant industry. With touch screens, customers won't have to wait for the waitress, and the restaurant employees will be able to focus more on their respective jobs. In the business opportunity sense, there must not only be improvement, but a monetary profit. In this case, I think that the time, resources, and risk level required to exploit it will justify profit made. The large profit margins will quickly take the company back to breakeven, where I can then begin to expand the product. Narrowing the definition even further, let's take a look at the entrepreneurship opportunity. I believe that this idea could definitely be used and expanded by one person. If I got the proper funding, I really think that I could launch this idea and create a new standard of restaurant dining experience.

2. Briefly note its type, dependencies, and apparent causes or driving forces.

- *Type:*

    Perennial opportunity — Ever-present possibilities — Small improvements This opportunity has always been available, but no one has really taken control and gone with it. People are continually eating out, and the automated menu service will definitely be able to increase the convenience and change in style for restaurant customers and owners.

- *Dependencies:*

    - Technology: seeing as this product is dependent on touch screen technology, it's a good thing that the technology is already available to make it all happen.
    - Situation: the success of this product and service is really dependent on people's willingness to change their customs of ordering and interacting with the waiters.
    - Resources: this venture is dependent on whether or not there will be available resources to actually cover materials, assembly, and shipping, along with other startup costs.
    - Time: the automated screens are definitely dependent on time. If too much time has passed between development and distribution, the touch screen might have already become obsolete, and restaurants will have found some other technology to replace it.
    - Industry Structure: ultimately, the restaurant business is dependent on whether or not people have money to spend. If there were large-scale depression, or a faltering economy, which does not provide enough for people to eat out, then our product would definitely be operating at a loss.

- *Driving Forces:*

    The largest driving force in this venture is the customer's need for faster and more efficient service. With lines in restaurants gradually increasing more and more of the population is working and can't afford to make healthy food at home, there becomes this need for express service at sit-in restaurants. If there's constant crowding at a favorite restaurant, the customer will definitely be discouraged and might even fail to return. This need for speed really pushes the idea of automation for part of the restaurant industry, yet still allowing for interaction and organization.

*This page was replicated from a student paper and with permission.

Prior student portfolio page example 1 of 2A-2

Sky Deli: *Market Hole*

	Convenience	Food Quality	Portability / Packaging	Price / Value	Customizability	Availability	Diet-Specific Options
Airline In-Flight Meals	Excellent	Average	N/A	Average	Average	Average	Average
Airport Cafés/Restaurants	Good	Good	Poor	Average	Average	Average	Average
Airport Fast Food Takeout	Good	Poor	Good	Average	Poor	Good	Poor
Food From Home	Average	Good	Average	Excellent	Excellent	Excellent	Excellent
Sky Deli	Excellent	Good	Excellent	Good	Excellent	Excellent	Excellent

Key: (w/ points allocated for scoring)

O	Poor	(1)
●	Average	(2)
◎	Good	(3)
✪	Excellent	(4)

Score Summary:

Airline In-Flight Meals	14
Airport Cafés / Restaurants	15
Airport Fast Food Takeout	14
Food From Home	23
Sky Deli	26

Prior student portfolio page example 2 of 2A-2

Market Hole Comparison						
	SolarWalk	Conven-tional Solar Array	Natural Gas	Nuclear Power	Hydro-Electric	Coal
Energy Efficiency						
Space Saving	☺☺☺ ☺☺	☺	☺☺☺	☺☺	☺	☺☺
Renew-ability Rating	☺☺☺ ☺☺	☺☺☺☺ ☺	☺	☺☺☺	☺☺☺	☺
Facility Cost	☺☺☺ ☺☺	☺☺	☺☺	☺	☺	☺
Maintenance Cost	☺☺☺ ☺☺	☺☺	☺☺☺	☺	☺	☺☺
Raw Material Cost	☺☺☺ ☺☺	☺☺☺☺ ☺	☺☺☺	☺☺☺	☺☺☺☺ ☺	☺
Initial Investment	☺☺☺ ☺	☺	☺☺☺	☺	☺	☺☺
TOTAL RATING=	29 ☺	16 ☺	15 ☺	11 ☺	12 ☺	9 ☺

KEY		
Excellent. Distinct advantage in this category.	☺☺☺ ☺☺	The SolarWalk system of solar energy harnessing has an advantage over the other 5 types of energy listed here, in these specific categories. Scoring 29 ☺'s, 13 more than the nearest competitor, its clear that the SolarWalk has the advantage. However, the energy efficiency percentage does not stand out as very impressive. I think that the real market hole that SolarWalk will be aiming for is energy within urban environments, and thus attributes such as "space saving" and "maintenence cost" could be viewed as more important and have greater weight in the rating process
Great. Many desired category elements.	☺☺☺ ☺	
Good. Average category performance.	☺☺☺	
Fair. Lacking major elements.	☺☺	
Poor. Much left to be desired.	☺	

CHAPTER 2B – Ideas

Topics

1. Where entrepreneurs find ideas
2. Two internal drivers of discovery
3. Choosing preferences
4. Focusing
5. Applying search tactics

Checkpoints

a. Explain why it can be useful to distinguish between opportunities and ideas.
b. What time intervals apply to ideas and how do they matter?
c. Where do venture ideas mainly tend to come from and why?
d. Explain what is meant in this chapter by drivers of venture-idea discovery.
e. Discuss the hierarchy of business idea types and why it matters.
f. Describe the nature and purpose of an idea scorecard.
g. Indicate steps a person could take to improve their performance in discovery of new venture ideas.
h. How can consideration of implicit search questions be helpful?

Opportunity, the subject of the preceding chapter, is about circumstance and the possibility of improving it. Ideas, the subject of this chapter, are about finding alternative ways to accomplish improvement.

Good ideas can come unsought, unanticipated, even somewhat by surprise. They arise from work, hobbies, acquaintances, and everyday observations as the result of unforeseen events. Trying to force discovery by *deliberately* searching for good, as opposed to any, ideas is hard. But if simply waiting and hoping for coincidence is not enough, there may be no other choice. This chapter will explore ways of searching.

1. Where entrepreneurs find ideas

Ideas are generally easy to find, but almost all of them are worthless, and good ones are very hard to find. For instance, many ideas for exploiting the opportunity to introduce microcomputers to the market were possible. But most fell short. Even venerable companies such as Texas Instruments, Digital Equipment, and NCR, as well as countless smaller firms, tried a range of ideas that failed for exploiting that opportunity.

Entrepreneurship researchers have come to see opportunity exploitation, although it may include a high point, as a process in which ideas unfold over time. Long and McMullan in 1984 devised and empirically tested a scheme for describing opportunity identification that included four stages.[29] *Pre-vision* consisted of a person's experiences and education leading up to the second, or *vision*, stage where the person recognized an opportunity, either by "feeling" it was there or through an "aha" epiphany. Third came *elaboration* of the opportunity concept in connection with a business idea. This third

---

[29] Wayne Long and Ed McMullan, "Mapping the New Venture Opportunity Identification Process," in *Frontiers of Entrepreneurship Research, 1984*, eds. John A. Hornaday and others (Wellesley, MA: Babson Center for Entrepreneurial Studies, 1984) p. 567.

Exhibit 2b-1 Where Inc. 500 founders got venture ideas

Source	Percent
Got idea while working in same industry	43%
Saw someone else try, figured I could do better	15
Saw unfilled niche in consumer marketplace	11
Did systematic search for business opportunities	7
Can't really explain it	5
Got idea from hobby or avocational interest	3
Other	16
Total	100%

Summarizing the results of this Inc. *study, its author, John Case, observed:*

"More common than out-of-the-blue inspirations were the explicable ones, the ideas that caught their creators by surprise, but in retrospect seem pretty logical…. The mythology of entrepreneurship celebrates such serendipity, propagating an image of the lone company-inventor suddenly flashing on the idea of a lifetime—and sometimes it happens that way."

stage appeared to last anywhere from moments up to seven years and involved reflection, information gathering, discussion, and actions leading to the fourth stage, *actual commitment* to start a particular business.

Gaglio and Taub clarified the sequence further, observing that, "In real life, the actual process is not so linear. Ideas can go through several iterations during development and ultimately bear little resemblance to the initial conception. Mistakes and failures can also prompt recognition of other opportunities, sometimes in apparently unrelated areas."[30]

Bhave[31] identified two developmental paths. In the first, which accounted for 41 percent of the start-ups he studied, the future entrepreneur encountered a need, worked at fulfilling it, and discovered along the way that a business could result. From this came a decision to start, after which idea refinement led to identification of business concepts and then development of a particular business concept. In the second, which accounted for the other 59 percent of the start-ups, a decision to start a business was made before scanning and filtration of potential opportunities began.

A 1989 survey of the *Inc.* 500 fastest-growing companies by the magazine asked the founders of those companies where they first got their venture ideas. Most (43 percent) said their ideas came from work. As can be seen in Exhibit 2b-1, the other categories of idea sources could overlap, either with this category (e.g., "saw an unfilled niche") or with others, such as hobbies, which was credited with only 3 percent of the ideas.[32]

Typically, though, the idea for a fast-growing business appears in much more pedestrian fashion. The structure of a marketplace shifts, maybe ever so slightly. A new niche opens up. And suddenly, people who may never have expected to become entrepreneurs are out on their own and amazed by their own success.

For Patrick Kelly, the founding CEO of PSS/World Medical, a major medical products wholesale distributor, the push for starting a company came partly from the fact that he had been fired as salesman for a similar company and failed to find satisfaction in two subsequent similar jobs, and partly from phone calls of a salesman like him at another company who kept proposing that they start a company together. Eventually, the two recruited a third salesman, took in as partner a neighbor who agreed to put up cash for a share of the business, and started the company. Over the next 15 years, it grew to a billion dollars in annual revenues.[33]

A very different sample from the *Inc.* 500 is that of the 1994 members of the National Fed-

---

[30] Connie Marie Gaglio and Richard P. Taub, "Entrepreneurs and Opportunity Recognition," in *Frontiers of Entrepreneurship Research, 1992*, eds. Bruce A. Kirchhoff and others (Wellesley, MA: Babson Center for Entrepreneurial Studies, 1992) p. 136.
[31] Mahesh P. Bhave, "A Process Model of Entrepreneurial Venture Creation," *Journal of Business Venturing*, May 1994, p. 223.
[32] John Case, "The Origins of Entrepreneurship," *Inc.*, June 1989, p. 54.
[33] Patrick Kelly, *Faster Company* (New York: Wiley, 1998).

eration of Independent Businesses, of whom Cooper et al. asked, "Where did you get the idea to go into this kind of business?" Again, the most frequent answer was "prior job," which accounted for 43 percent. Second most frequent, accounting for 18 percent, was a hobby or personal interest. Next came chance events (10 percent) and suggestions by others (8 percent). Interestingly enough, this was closely followed by "education/courses." Also interesting was the fact that those firms that did not survive the first year drew upon the same sources with about the same frequency, as seen in Exhibit 2b-2, which was derived from the study.[34]

Limitations of the statistics in studies to date include: (1) they don't say much about connections between idea sources and just how the ideas came about, and (2) how the generalities may apply in any individual case is not apparent. To learn more about these questions, a closer look at the following examples may help.

Prior job

Employment seems to be the main idea source in general.

> When Louis Krouse suggested to his employer, the NYNEX telephone company, that it consider the idea of arranging for its lower-income customers with no checking accounts to pay their bills someplace besides utility offices, which are scarce, and banks, which lose money on such transactions, NYNEX told him to investigate further. An experimental project in Albany worked, but NYNEX decided not to carry it further, and instead suggested that Krouse pursue it himself.

> Quitting his job, Krouse formed National Payments Network, Inc. (NPN) to collect for companies such as NYNEX for 50 cents per payment (less than banks charge). He then persuaded retail stores, such as 7-Eleven, for about 10 cents per payment to allow customers to pay through them. From the stores' standpoint this helps draw customers. In each store a point of sale terminal transmits payment to a central computer, which in turn arranges electronic funds transfer from the stores to the utilities. Founded in 1986, NPN was processing over $2 billion by 1988.[35]

Important to note in connection with getting ideas from a job are the employee's obligations (1) not to compete with an employer while employed, (2) not to take along or use proprietary information of the employer when leaving, and (3) not to violate any non-compete agreement after leaving that was signed as part of the employment. Each of these three injunctions is subject to interpretation that can be grounds for dispute and possibly lawsuit. Sometimes an employer will care, other times he or she may not. In this case the employer apparently gave permission for the entrepreneur to pursue the idea elsewhere.

Just what is proprietary information can sometimes be clear, as when an employer spells it out in writing as part of an employment agreement or when intellectual property is officially owned through a patent, trademark, or copyright. Actions taken by employers to assure secrecy about some aspects of their business can also make ownership clear. But other times the line can become fuzzy, as when an

Exhibit 2b-2 Where NFIB founders got venture ideas

Idea sources For percent of firms found to be	Discontinued	Sold	Surviving	Total sample
Prior job	42%	38%	43%	42%
Hobby/personal interest	18	16	18	18
Chance event	10	13	10	10
Someone suggested it	9	12	7	8
Education/courses	6	3	6	6
Family business	5	5	6	6
Activities of friends/relatives	6	6	5	5
Other	4	7	5	5
Total	100%	100%	100%	100%

[34] Arnold C. Cooper and others, *New Business in America* (Washington, D.C.: The NFIB Foundation, 1990).

[35] "The Emerging Entrepreneur," *Inc.*, January 1990, p. 59.

Recreation

Chance event

Personal contacts

employer charges that a former employee while employed recruited customers for a venture the employee later started, or that the employee before leaving recruited other employees to leave and join the new venture, possibly taking with them knowledge proprietary to the employer.

Even when there is a written agreement the lines can be fuzzy. Courts don't like the idea of someone being unable to pursue a livelihood. So if a non-compete agreement seems to the court too restrictive, they may not enforce it. The agreement must specify how long it will stay in effect, what activities it will apply to, and what geographical area it will cover. How restrictive any of these should be and remain enforceable can be contested in court.

Recreation

Ideas that come from recreational activities or other non-employment sources are generally safe from prior employer claims, but unfortunately also more rare.

> In 1989 Scott Griffiths formed a baseball team at his advertising agency, named it the Rhino Chasers, and had that name emblazoned on T-shirts and hats. He also made up labels with the name, and pasted them on bottles of beer for post-game parties. People began asking where they could obtain that brand of beer. Griffiths sought out a local micro-brewery to manufacture the product, and within a year was shipping 800 cases per month.[36]

Chance event

A business idea can crop up as a chance event for someone in quest of a job or business opportunity.

> Tom Stemberg had worked 12 years in the supermarket industry, starting as a management trainee with Star Market and rising to head of sales and merchandising. He then became division president of another supermarket chain, Edwards-Finast, where he developed a warehouse food business. But then he had a falling out with higher management and was fired.
>
> With a year's severance pay he was looking for a job and potential start-up ideas when he visit-

ed a discount warehouse in Langhorne, Pennsylvania, for an employment interview. In the store he noticed that the office supplies section was a shambles: empty boxes, torn packages, and goods spilled on the floor. He concluded that "this merchandise was moving very fast." Checking with industry analysts, he found that only 100 items in office supply sections accounted for up to 7 percent of the volume in such stores.

> He now envisaged a chain of discount stores selling just office supplies. Instead of buying from the half dozen major wholesalers who sold such supplies to retail stores, he would buy from manufacturers and sell direct, as did Toys"R"Us. Rather than continuing his job search, he next wrote a business plan, and took it to potential venture capital sources. The result was that "dozens of offers poured in." One venture capitalist commented that Stemberg "wasn't proposing just a chain of stores, but an entirely new retailing category. That really catches your attention. It slaps you in the face with the idea that this could be big." The deal chosen included $4 million in the first round and $31 million in three later rounds.
>
> The first Staples store opened on the outskirts of Boston in 1986. Not until 1989 did the company report a profit. But then it was $858,000 on $24.8 million in sales. In April of that year the company raised another $62 million through public offering.[37]

These three examples illustrate only part of the wide range of ways new venture opportunities and ideas are discovered. In each, the role of prior experience and unforeseen events can be seen. Also, in each case the opportunity was available for discovery by others. Only in the third example does it appear that the entrepreneur was actively searching. But even there the discovery came by surprise.

Personal contacts

It may not be surprising that other people are cited as an important source of new business ideas. For corporate ventures a study by Christensen and Peterson reported, "78.9 percent agreed wholly or partially that informal contacts were often the source of new opportunities, thus confirming the importance of social encounters.

---

[36] "Where Packaging Is Job One," *Inc.*, June 1990, p. 30.
[37] Stephen D. Solomon, "Born To Be Big," *Inc.*, June 1989, p. 94.
[38] Howard Aldrich and Catherine Zimmer, "Entrepreneurship Through Special Networks," in *The Art and Science of Entrepreneurship*, eds. Donald L. Sexton and Raymond W. Smilor (Boston: Ballinger, 1986).

It also supports Aldrich and Zimmer's (1988)[38] suggestion that social networks are an important source of new ideas as well as Koller's[39] (1988) observation that about half of his respondents had been suggested their ideas by someone else."[40] More surprising is the fact that the ways business ideas can be discovered through other people have not been extensively studied in order to learn how an entrepreneur might use that source most effectively.

2. Two internal drivers of discovery

The impulse toward a particular product or service idea for a new venture generally is triggered by one of two recognition drivers, either "capability push" or "customer pull." The trigger in this process can be either awareness (1) that capability is at hand or acquirable, or (2) that a market potential probably exists.

These concepts represent variations on earlier notions of technology push and market pull, but with some differences. Capability can be other than technological. Also, *customer* is more specific than market, although use of the term *market* can help make the point that usually it takes more than one customer to justify a venture. A nexus of capability and market, in other words potential supply and demand, is necessary, although not necessarily sufficient, for a venture to happen. Either can be first to trigger the idea.

Capability push

With capability push, the entrepreneur is impelled by the impression that he or she has, or can readily come by, the capacity to deliver something that somebody else might like to have. It may be a new product or service or something not new for which there will nevertheless be a demand that the entrepreneur can serve. The capability may be one of possessing something (oil on the homestead), being able to take control of some resources (oil on the next-door homestead for which an option may be obtainable), knowing how to do something (such as write computer code or bake a better pie), or being able to learn how to do such a thing. It may also be something bestowed, like the fortune Howard Hughes inherited from his father's oil tool

business and used to develop new ventures in aircraft, electronics, and movies.

Bill Lear built capability by reading up on radios as a youth and tinkering with improving the design of existing radios, partly as an escape from unpleasant family experiences. He devised a radio battery eliminator, then began producing and selling it on his own. He also took on contract troubleshooting and new product development for radio manufacturers. He designed a better coil for radios, and then built machines for coil making. Soon, he was building improved radios on contract for Zenith. His house became a radio factory.

For more space he moved the work to a warehouse, which was also headquarters for Galvin Manufacturing, later to become Motorola. Galvin hired him as chief engineer, but on a loose arrangement, which left him free to work for others as well. And in his basement, he started building radio sets as a product line of his own, and took on a partner to sell them.

A sometimes-effective way to develop capability for push, as well as to identify targets within an attractive market, is to begin by recruiting a team of appropriately expert individuals.

Norman Goldfarb, an electrical engineer whose technical experience had been limited to semiconductors, read about how Robert Swanson had telephoned Herbert Boyer, a world-renowned gene-splicing expert at Stanford University, and persuaded Boyer to join him in founding Genentech in 1976. By 1981 that venture had become the world's leading company in pharmaceutical biotechnology, and made its founders rich. Despite his lack of experience in the field, Goldfarb decided to try the same pattern in plant, as opposed to human, biotechnology. He telephoned a famous plant geneticist, Daniel Cohen, at the Uni-

Capability push

---

[39] Roland H. Koller, "On the Source of Entrepreneurial Ideas," in *Frontiers of Entrepreneurship Research, 1988*, eds. Bruce A. Kirchhoff and others (Wellesley, MA: Babson Center for Entrepreneurial Studies, 1988) p. 194.
[40] Peter Smed Christensen and Rein Peterson, "Opportunity Identification: Mapping the Sources of New Venture Ideas," in *Frontiers of Entrepreneurship Research, 1990*, eds. Neil C. Churchill and others (Wellesley, MA: Babson Center for Entrepreneurial Studies, 1990) p. 567.

versity of California at Davis, and persuaded him to collaborate in founding Calgene, a company that would specialize in the genetic engineering of plants to create better agricultural products. Goldfarb wrote a business plan, invested $500,000 from his family's trust, and recruited still other plant geneticists plus outside venture capital.

Some products created by the geneticists failed: corn plants modified to fix nitrogen did so, but failed to produce corn. But other products succeeded: a tomato containing a third less water consequently cost less to ship. Enough developments showed high promise to multiply the company's total equity investment of $9 million up to a cash-out for investors of $85 million in six years.[41]

Technology transfer

New technologies and products are always being generated by scientists and engineers employed by such organizations as research departments of corporations, technical departments of universities, and laboratories of the federal government. Much of this innovation output is put up for sale or license because producing the particular products that may be possible with it does not align with the mission or strategy of the organization that creates it. Consequently, licensing offices are set up in the organizations that seek to sell it to others, including entrepreneurs, who want to carry it forward to the marketplace.

A major impetus was given to such licensing activity in universities by Congressional passage in 1980 of the Bayh-Dole Act. This act authorizes universities, which develop technology under grants from federal agencies such as the Department of Defense, Department of Energy, and the Department of Health, Education, and Welfare, to retain rights to the technology which they can then grant licences on in return for royalties from others, including individual entrepreneurs and start-ups as well as established companies. Universities consequently set up technology transfer offices to seek patents on discoveries by faculty members and other researchers employed on the grants, and to seek ways of making money with them by selling them to entrepreneurs and established companies.

More recently, the emergence of entrepreneurship programs in business schools has led to internships and project courses in which entrepreneurship students develop business plans for exploitation of technologies identified by the university technology transfer offices.

However, there are challenges in seeking to transfer technology. A main one is that those who really understand the technology best generally remain employees of the organization that does not want to produce and sell the products that may come from it. So there is a danger that the technology-creating organization may lose key people as part of the transfer process.

In universities there may be arguments about whether a particular technology should be licensed to an existing company or to an entrepreneur, and whether a flat fee, a percentage royalty, or shares of stock should be sought as payment. Usually, universities have a policy of sharing rewards of the technology with the employees who create it. But just who deserves how much of the credit for its creation may also be a matter of legitimate dispute. Those hoping for rewards from exploitation of the technology, moreover, may prefer that it be pursued by experienced successful entrepreneurs who can give it full-time and appreciable investment of their own rather than by students who have less experience, more educational responsibilities, and no money.

Customer pull

With customer pull, entrepreneurs work back from an awareness that the market wants something, then marshal the capability to deliver it. Market-pull awareness, which is a form of opportunity-specific knowledge, may be revealed by an event such as a customer request for something that the prospective entrepreneur might be able to provide. Or it can be sought by will. In other words, belief that there will be customers may trigger a quest to acquire capability to serve them.

Simon Ramo and Dean Wooldridge worked as scientists for Hughes Aircraft on defense proj-

---

[41] Robert J. Kunze, *Nothing Ventured* (New York: Harper Business, 1990) p. 201.

ects. The Department of Defense, apparently becoming anxious that Hughes was receiving so much of the DOD's business, encouraged them to leave and set up their own company. They submitted resignation letters in July 1953, left the company on September 11, and established the Ramo-Wooldridge Corporation on September 16, which had a letter confirming a contract for strategic-missile development by September 18. The company went on to many other contracts, achieved listing on the New York Stock Exchange and, through merger with Thompson Products, eventually became TRW.[42]

General categories of potential customers obviously include consumers, businesses, governmental agencies, and non-profit organizations that can be further subdivided any number of ways. A starting point can also be the entrepreneurs themselves.

Egocentrism

The entrepreneur, by inventing what he or she wants, may automatically be aiming at a market of others with similar desires. The first Apple microcomputer was created because its inventors wanted it. A market followed. More recently, Linux came from a similar motivation.

Cooks create new foods, hobbyists create new toys, sports equipment, auto accessories, and games. Most don't become popular. But some do. It turns on how many other people see in the creation a benefit for themselves, and if so, how great. For some people this egocentric guidance mechanism works very well indeed, as illustrated by the following observation and recollections of innovators Ben Rosen, a venture capitalist who started Compaq Computer, and Steven Spielberg, the movie producer/director who commented:[43]

> I have no idea what other people want. I only know what I want. With Compaq, I just knew that I needed a portable to carry around.

> — • —

> All I know is about me. I know what I would love to see at that moment.

But with egocentrism there is also risk that the inventor is not representative of a broader market, as happens with artists who, by pleasing their own taste, find their work unappreciated and consequently unsalable. A visit to an inventors' show, which some cities periodically hold, will offer glimpses of unsuccessful inventions, often in the form of old prototypes that appear to have been displayed at the show year after year without consequence.

The alternative is to aim from the start at the desires of other people. These may be things they want now and realize it, things they want now but don't yet realize it, or things they will want in the future, whether they realize it or not.

Existing demand

Fred Smith, the father of the Fred Smith who would one day create Federal Express, made a fortune with a bus line. His father had been a successful riverboat captain. After successes as a truck salesman in the oil fields and in World War I an inspector in government truck procurement, he became sales manager for a truck company. One day in or around 1919, he told the owner of a company that provided taxi service across the state of Tennessee that a bus line would pay better. Then he kicked himself for giving the concept away, and told a car dealer who formerly employed him that "I've got a big idea." The dealer gave him a used truck and loaned him a thousand dollars to build his own bus body, which led to the start of the Smith Motor Coach Company, later to become Dixie Greyhound. A major step in his progress was to persuade the Tennessee legislature to pass a law in 1929 making intercity bus lines a public utility that could award exclusive routes. Later that year, Smith invested with a partner in a fast food chain, the Toddle House Restaurants. That same year he announced and then scrapped plans to buy two Ryan airplanes and start an airline between Memphis and Nashville. By 1930 his bus enterprise plus the developing chain of restaurants had become a $3 million concern.[44]

Future demand

Jack Simplot was an Idaho farm boy who would one day become a famous entrepreneur as the world's largest supplier of frozen potatoes for McDonald's. With winnings from that he became the principal backer of Micron Technology, a very successful microchip memory producer. Early on, his ability to anticipate fu-

---

[42] Simon Ramo, "Memoirs of an ICBM Pioneer," *Fortune*, April 25, 1988, p. 306.
[43] Jerry Useem, "The Start-up Factory," *Inc.* February 1997, p. 40.
[44] Vance Trimble, *Overnight Success* (New York: Crown Publishers, 1993) p. 103.

ture demand had shown up when he saw local farmers destroying hogs that, because of a glut on the market, were worth less than the cost of raising them. He gathered up young hogs that were consequently free for the taking, built pens, and fed them with local materials available free. Between sagebrush during the growing seasons and the meat of wild horses, which he shot, butchered, and fed to the hogs during winter, he had a supply of hogs by the following spring. Other farmers typically did not, and Simplot made what was for him a fortune selling to the pent up demand.[45]

Awareness of the demand does not necessarily lead to discovery of a solution for it.

Thomas Edison was enormously creative, but he did not invent the telephone. Instead, Alexander Graham Bell, who happened to be Edison's age, invented it. Bell was not deaf. His wife was.[46]

Implicit search questions

Some thinking patterns that could be adopted to seek venture ideas can be expressed in the form of implicit search questions. These may arise (1) through inquiry, (2) as a result of circumstances encountered, (3) through a process of evaluation, or (4) as a consequence of action decisions, as listed below.

Implicit search questions in detail

Inquiry

Venture ideas may be prompted by search questions that put the mind into a mode where it might be presumed to try different combinations and to seek answers that may turn out to be product and service ideas. This searching process may well operate subconsciously. Evidence that it happened appears when the mind pushes an idea forward to a conscious level. Search questions might include (with subquestions, in case the reader would like to tabulate a running tally to check or manage the search pattern over time):

1. What **a.** is bothering me, or **b.** might relieve a bother I have?
2. What else might I like to have?
3. What is **a.** a situation where something is missing, or **b.** what else might anyone else like to have?
4. How could this product or service be done differently than it is now?
5. What could I make or do with this **a.** resource or **b.** situation that I or others might want?
6. How could I follow the family tradition?
7. How could I do what I like doing?

Encounter

Idea prompting may occur from encounter with (1) someone else's idea, (2) a customer request, (3) some other person or information channel, or (4) some other event. Questions by which this process might produce a business idea include:

8. Somebody has asked me to provide them with something. **a.** Is it something I could provide?
9. Has this **a.** event, **b.** development, or **c.** circumstance changed, created an opportunity I could seize?
10. That seems to be done badly. **a.** Could there be a way to do it better, or **b.** could I do it better?
11. People went for something like (though not exactly the same as) this elsewhere. **a.** Could I play some role in providing it to a broader market?
12. This seems like a straightforward advance on what is working now. **a.** Could I play a role in providing it to a broader market?
13. I like this thing I encountered by accident. **a.** Could I play a role in providing it to a broader market?

---

[45] George Gilder, *The Spirit of Enterprise* (New York: Simon and Schuster, 1984).
[46] Peter C, Wensberg, *Land's Polaroid* (Boston: Houghton Mifflin, 1987) p. 23.

Implicit search questions (continued)

Evaluation

Evaluative reactions to a prompted idea might be:

14. Could I do this job I have on my own instead of as an employee?
15. I wonder if other people might like this idea. **a.** If I were they, would I like it?
16. I like the idea. I'll make one for me. If I like it, maybe others will too. **a.** I wonder if others might like this.
17. Somebody has asked me to provide them with something. **a.** If this person whom I have encountered wants it, might others too?
18. Should I take over this enterprise **a.** found through search, or **b.** as a result of encountering a seller's initiative?
19. Will doing this give me greater satisfaction than what I'm doing now?

Action decisions

Decisions to take action might take such forms as:

20. I think people will want this. **a.** So I'll offer it, **b.** and see if they go for it, or **c.** and I'm sure it will succeed.
21. I like this, so I suppose others will. I'll offer it.
22. This seems like a straightforward advance on what works now. So I will carry it out **a.** because I believe it will work, or **b.** to see how it will work.

3. Choosing preferences

For any given entrepreneur some types of ventures are preferable to others, as was discussed in the opening chapter. Reconsidering what those types are and what the relative preferences among them are may help hone the discovery process and make it more effective.

Line possibilities

Classification of ventures to shape idea preferences can be made according to such factors as capitalization, growth and profit potential, date of inception, convenience of location, or who plays what role in creating them.

The roughly 2,000 businesses started per day in the United States can be sorted by industry. The sample of 2,994 start-ups studied by Cooper et al.[47] was dominated greatly by retailing and services, as shown in Exhibit 2b-3. Within each of these categories, further breakdowns into virtually unlimited subdivisions can be made, as the Yellow Pages and *Thomas Register*, or any manufacturers' directories readily illustrate. Thinking about the variety possible may help trigger ideas.

Almost anyone can attempt start-up in lines of business where the largest numbers of people, over two thirds try it, namely retailing and services. But higher success rates, according to studies by Birch, are experienced in other lines such as manufacturing and professions.[48] Qualifications

Line possibilities

Exhibit 2b-3 Start-ups by line of industry[49]

Business	Percent
Retailing	46%
Services	19
Manufacturing	8
Construction	7
Professions	5
Finance	5
Wholesale	4
Other	6
Total	100%

[47] Cooper and others, *New Business,* p.15.
[48] David L. Birch, "The Truth About Startups," *Inc.*, January 1988, p. 14.
[49] Birch, "Truth."

Size of
Margin

Growth
Potential

Hierarchy of
attractiveness

for performing preferable types of start-ups can be acquired through prior job choices to gain appropriate experience, or through teaming up with people who already have it.

Size of margin

Patterns of attractiveness can be displayed in different ways, such as by profit margin versus line of business, which is illustrated in Exhibit 2b-4 below. Generally, the higher the margin, the better. Ability to estimate margin, and sensitivity to presence of high margin in either a venture encountered or a situation where it might be possible to undertake one, is a skill probably worthwhile for any would-be entrepreneur to pursue and practice as part of seeking venture ideas.

Only a minority of small ventures yields high earnings and attractive fringe benefits for owners. Most give low pay and not much security for long hours of work, topped by bookkeeping, tax preparation, and red-tape compliance that cut into evenings and weekends.

Ordinary ventures also typically do not give owners as much control over their lives as they expect. Cooper et al. found that whereas 78 percent of founders saw such control as an important motivation, 61 percent later were disappointed in the extent to which they attained it. At the same time, however, 82 percent of those whose businesses survived three years said they would form them again, even though 32 percent of them said they were disappointed in how well they had done.[50]

Growth potential

Potential for growth, as depicted in Exhibit 2b-5 is, like high margin, another indicator of attractiveness, but the two do not necessarily go together. A venture that can appeal to a bigger market will have more potential to grow than one confined to a smaller market. A surgeon's practice may be highly profitable, but not be able to grow large by industrial standards because it is a specialty confined to a particular individual whose work cannot be automated or parceled out to a hired workforce.

Most start-ups never grow large. Cooper et al. found that only 37 percent of start-ups added to initial employment in their first three years, and only 11 percent added four or more employees, while 11 percent, although they survived, actually shrank.[51] So staying small is generally to be expected. However, *Inc.* magazine found in a survey of its 500 fastest-growing small firms that although 175 (35 percent) had intended to grow only slowly, and 65 (13 percent) had not wanted to grow at all, their companies took off on high-growth trajectories.[52] Hence a reason for considering all types as starting points is that, as pointed out in the first chapter, a given venture can start as one type and transform into another.

Hierarchy of attractiveness

Generally, the most attractive type of venture, at least from an investment point of view, is one that combines both high profit and high growth potential. Also, although there can be exceptions, venture ideas tend to fit a hierarchy in terms of potential for margin, profit, and growth that follows the listing in Exhibit 2b-6, with protectable products at the top and ordinary, easy-to-copy services at the bottom.

First on this list, possession of patents, copyrights, and trademarks can give a venture the right to sue anyone who copies certain features of what the venture offers. One catch with patenting is that it may or may not be possible to claim important features as protectable, some-

Exhibit 2b-4 Margins versus type of for-instance business

	Service	**Product**
High margin	Licensed: physician	Patented: prescription drug
Low margin	Easy entry: house painting	Commodity: printing

[50] Cooper and others, *New Business*, pp.11-12.
[51] Cooper and others, *New Business*, p.1.
[52] Robert A. Mamis, "Growth Happens," *Inc.*, March 1997, p. 68.

Exhibit 2b-5 Many growth trajectories are possible

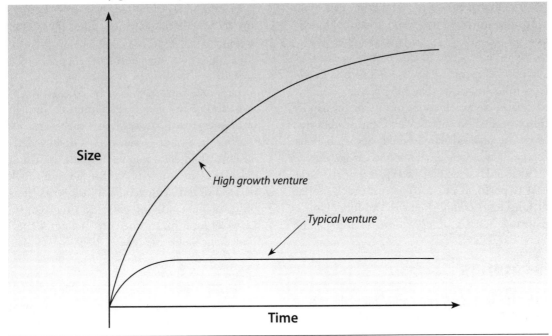

thing the government will decide. Another is that the suit filed against a copycat can cost a lot of money, and may or may not prevail in court. Secrecy about how the product is made is an alternative form of protection. Microsoft's operating system is a prime example of a product enjoying such protections.

At precaution to consider taking early in the process of looking for new ideas is to start writing down descriptions of them with dates in a notebook and having each entry witnessed and signed by another person to establish a record that may later be useful in seeking patent protection, if someone else seeks to patent the same idea and dispute arises over who first thought of it.

Second on the hierarchy are **scalable services**. These are services that can be sold on a wide geographic basis to spread thinly the fixed costs of

operating, such as advertising, training, research, development, and central management, and thereby gain high profits through economies of scale. Further benefits of scale include the ability to realize volume discounts from suppliers and to move down the learning curve faster. The coffee stores of Starbucks, chain merchandising of Wal-Mart, and fast food stores of major hamburger chains are examples of scalable services. As these businesses grow they also generally benefit from development of familiar brands, which of course they protect through trademarking.

Third on the list generally come **high-margin services**, many of which enjoy protection through governmentally sanctioned licensing, such as that which doctors, veterinarians, and banks possess. Sometimes the margins of services are protected simply through special expertise, such as how to

Exhibit 2b-6 Attractiveness hierarchy

Higher potential
1. Protectable product (patented, secret, and/or a strong trademarked brand)
2. Scalable service (maybe due to reputation, workforce, locations, or size)
3. High-margin service (may require license, rare skill, or reputation)
4. Ordinary product (may need investment or skills to produce)
5. Ordinary service (less skill or investment required)

Lower potential

put out oil-well fires with explosives, how to give legal testimony, or how to perform on stage.

Fourth are plain **products**, which, although **not protectable** by patents, copyrights, trademarks, or secrets, nevertheless require special skill and possibly expensive plant, equipment, or contacts to manufacture. Shipping pallets, wrought iron gates, extension cords, most types of handicrafts, printed brochures, clothing that does not have a recognized name brand, and numerous parts of houses would fall into this category.

Fifth and last are plain **services** that are fairly **easy to perform** and don't require much capital or long-term commitment to produce. House painting, restaurant operation, retailing, and

countless services advertised in the Yellow Pages are examples. Often for these services margins are low, hours are long, and failure rates are high. They are simply too easy to perform and attract too many competitors, who in turn push down margins and survival rates.

The above hierarchy has, of course, exceptions, and not all people share the aims of high profit and growth, as was noted earlier in connection with lifestyle ventures. Other general patterns of interest might segregate start-ups, and hence the kinds of venture ideas to look for, according to enjoyability of the work, flexibility of demands on personal time, convenience of location for the entrepreneur, or aesthetic appeal of some type.

4. Focusing

Target customer

For discovering good venture ideas there is as yet no dominant formula, although systematic approaches have been proposed, as will be described shortly. It has long been clear that trying to generate ideas will produce ideas but that most or all of them will be worthless. Entrepreneurs who have discovered good venture ideas through brainstorming or other such techniques are virtually impossible to find. But still, they do find ideas at least some of the time as part of wanting them. Moreover, there has been indication in studies of creativity that trying to get ideas yields more ideas and that trying to get better ideas yields fewer but better ideas. That is, setting criteria improves performance.

Target customer

Tying a product, service or venture idea to a potential customer will be needed, sooner or later, for it to work, and should therefore probably come into the search process early. It may take the form of either "what would this person like?" or "what person would like this?" That person, either way, should be demonstrably real, not just left as hypothetical, and beyond that person (who could be the entrepreneur to begin with), there need to be others whom that person typifies in the "right" way. That is, they must also predictably want the venture's product or service enough to buy it for a profitable price.

The target customer may be a person with unusual requirements, such as extra large shoes, or common requirements, such as protection from sunburn. In the following example it appears to have been anyone who wanted to get rid of whiskers.

King C. Gillette, a successful traveling hardware salesman and son of a patent agent, had already invented and patented a bushing and valve for water taps, as well as founded a company with his brother to make it, and seen the company fail. He had married the daughter of an inventor, William Painter, who invented the pop bottle cap and developed the still-successful Crown Cork and Seal company to produce it. Painter suggested that Gillette invent something with similar qualities, a disposable product people needed. Gillette asked, "But how many things are there like corks, pins, and needles?" Painter replied, "You don't know."

Gillette later confessed that Painter's suggestion became an obsession with him. Later he recalled that "one particular morning when I started to shave I found my razor dull, and it was not only dull but it was beyond the point of successful stropping and it needed honing, for which it must be taken to a barber or to a cutler. As I stood there with the razor in my hand, my eyes resting lightly as a bird settling down on its nest—the Gillette razor was born. I saw it all in a moment, and in that same moment many unvoiced questions were answered more with the rapidity of a dream than by the slow process of reasoning."

The same day, he said, he rushed to a hardware store, bought steel ribbon, bits of brass, files, and a small vise to build a prototype. In a letter to his wife, who was away visiting relatives, he wrote: "I have got it. Our fortune is made."[53]

Here it appears Gillette first decided on key characteristics of the product he wanted, something necessary and disposable. The idea trigger arose in the form of his own problem of needing razors re-sharpened. He was a target customer typical of millions. That intersection of recognition apparently yielded the product idea which became the basis for his company.

Attractive benefits

Market demand arises from what clusters of people with buying power exemplified by target customers perceive as benefits worth paying for, such as the following:

1. *New function* VisiCalc was the first microcomputer software program to liberate individuals from the laborious copying and writing required in preparing spread sheets. Because it ran only on the Apple II, it was highly influential in developing a market for that machine as well, and thereby contributed greatly to the survival of Apple amid the many microcomputers then on the market. It also illustrates the meaning of a new term, **killer-app**, a contraction of *killer application*, meaning a product that users feel they simply must have.

2. *Better performance* Lotus became a successful venture by introducing an improved spreadsheet program, 1-2-3, which was more functional and easier to use than VisiCalc. Consequently, the venture that introduced VisiCalc was eclipsed. The founder of Lotus, Mark Taber, got rich while Dan Bricklin did not. In a more prosaic industry, Buell got its start by modifying Harley-Davidson motorcycles to speed them up. Eventually, it was bought out to become a division of Harley-Davidson, with Mark Buell as its head.

3. *Fun* When Wizards of the Coast was trying to get started as a game company, it was the creation of the new card game Magic that brought success. Sales went from zero to over $150 million in about three years, and because the cost of creating cards is extremely low and they sell for a lot, the profits were tremendous. Other successful games introduced by start-ups have been Pictionary and Dungeons and Dragons, which was eventually bought out by Wizards.

4. *Variety* Tully's Coffee started by introducing essentially the same product with the same store atmosphere as Starbucks'. It even deliberately sought locations as close as possible to Starbucks'. The strategy was to capitalize on the availability of customers that Starbucks created and offer them an alternative, which inevitably some of them chose.

5. *Uniqueness* Some creations in glass are offered as individual works of art that have enabled their creator, Dale Chihully, to create a factory of artisans turning them out. Because each creation is different and there are many people who like them, these products command high prices.

6. *Health* Some biotechnology ventures, such as Genentech, raised large amounts of start-up capital and began as laboratories to develop proprietary medicines that, when successful, yielded enormous profits because of the value people placed upon the cures they offered.

7. *Convenience* Amazon.com was able to start, as have many dot-com ventures, by offering people greater ease of doing business, in this case buying books, through the Internet. The reason countless duplicative enterprises, such as filling stations, stores, restaurants, barber shops, and others to be found in the Yellow Pages, are able to start is they offer the same thing at what is for some customers a more convenient location.

8. *Efficiency* Electric toothbrushes introduced by Sonicare, a start-up, alledgedly clean faster and better with more healthful effect on gums.

9. *Reliability* Tandem's redundant computers compensated for weaknesses in reliability of computer technology when they were introduced and immediately made the start-up a huge success.

More customer benefits beyond these can easily be identified, such as the fulfillment of necessity offered by grocery stores, pharmacies, funeral parlors, and industrial suppliers; the ego satisfaction offered by custom autos, new clothing fashions, or sports; the safety offered by security companies; and the pleasure offered by new gourmet restaurants.

[53] Russell B. Adams, Jr., *King C. Gillette* (Boston: Little, Brown and Company, 1978) p. 21.

Features versus benefits

It is worth distinguishing between benefits of a product or service and the features that produce those benefits. Benefits are what it gives customers that they most care about. Features are what yield those benefits. Some features may be things customers don't like but will overlook because of the benefits they are after. Auto insurance provides features of protection from loss, which is why people buy it in spite of features they don't like, such as complex verbiage in the policies, necessity for spending time to work out coverage choices with an agent, and the price, whatever it is, that they must pay.

A more important reason for recognizing the difference between benefits and features is the trap that inventors and entrepreneurs sometimes fall into: designers can become infatuated with the features they may have worked hard to implement into a product or service, blinding them to the benefits the target market cares about, which are not necessarily the same at all.

Except at a bank or stock brokerage, a consumer generally invests to gain something other than a dollar advantage. A coat may be bought for warmth, feel, and appearance. These are benefits, not necessarily to be confused with features, such as type of fabric, stitching, and number of pockets. Features describe characteristics of the product; benefits describe what the product and its features do for the customer. Size is a feature. Fit is a benefit. Entrepreneurs often love to talk about the features they create and assume the benefits they think they are creating. But customers care about the benefits they get, and decide whether sales occur. For further examples:

> A manufacturer of hunting knives may see the sharp edge, its precision, and durability as centrally important. But the buyer may view the length of the blade, comfort of the handle, and decorativeness as the main reasons to buy.
>
> — · —
>
> A hairdresser may think store location and styling skill are what customers most value, whereas customers may care more about the social atmosphere and conversation during treatment.

Cost must also be considered from the customer's viewpoint, and dollar price may only be part of it. Additional non-dollar cost aspects in the customer's view may include inconvenience and time needed to buy. The purchase decision will probably be made based on the ratio of benefits to cost, which is sometimes referred to as the venture's **value proposition**.

A central part of the entrepreneur's job is to perceive, either from prior experience or from investigation, how decisions of a target customer, the type on which the venture will depend most for its sales, are going to be made about benefits versus features. One target customer may care more about different benefits and costs in a given product than another target customer does. One person may care most about whether the car is a coupe and what financing is available, while to another the brand, color, and price may matter more.

Whatever the deal, it must include not only a **compelling reason to buy** relative to alternative purchases, but as pointed out by Dr. Jeffrey Stamp of the University of North Dakota, also a **compelling reason to believe** what the venture presents as rationale to buy. Moreover, after sale, the product or service should satisfy the customer enough to produce repeat sales and/or word-of-mouth advertising by that customer that builds the entrepreneur's reputation, producing still further sales. Ideally, the sale should create a **compelling reason to buy again**. (Might for Starbucks part of the compelling reason to buy again be that not doing so may produce a headache?)

Specifications

How fully formed a venture idea is when it first occurs depends on a variety of factors, including experience with that line of work, degree of departure from the past that the idea represents, complexity of the technology involved, and the extent of available relevant information, ambition, and resources.

The idea for a product or service usually starts out vague relative to the way it must eventually be specified for delivery. Development of specifications may proceed through a series of fairly logical steps, eventually extended and refined by creative thinking techniques, with each step providing a basis for the next, as follows: (1) Needs or wants, (2) Benefits, (3) Features, (4) Performance specifications, and (5) Production specifications.

Performance specifications are what the customer can choose from in the way of results from the product or service. They may be divided into many different categories, depending on the product or service. In a restaurant they are what appears on the menu plus whatever else the customers care about in choos-

ing the place. For a flash memory they are the speed and capacity.

Production specifications are what the company gives its employees as guidelines for creating the product or service. Some may be simple, like how many of something to put in a bag and whether or not to write the price on it. Others may be complex, such as the precise temperature to which to heat the metal in making a spring, what to coat the hot metal with, and how fast to quench it so it will bend and spring back without breaking when deflected a certain distance.

5. Applying search tactics

Although would-be entrepreneurs usually don't discover ideas through use of systematic searching steps (except when pursuing acquisitions of ongoing firms), some deliberate tactics in searching can enhance performance.

Systematic search

Gap Analysis, a systematic approach described in the preceding chapter for seeking out opportunities, might coincidentally trigger product and service ideas as well.

Fiet systematic search methodology

More recently, Professor Jim Fiet at the University of Louisville, has developed and tested another systematic approach for discovering new venture ideas. It emphasizes both working from an individual's proven capabilities and the cultivation of information channels likely to feed information on a low-cost basis about possible product and service idea possibilities.[54]

He and his colleagues found that his method, in contrast to (1) just searching within the imagination based on present information, or (2) simply being alert for a "knock from opportunity," that might offer new information, substantially improved idea discovery in several contrasting groups of students who were tested

in controlled experiments reported by Nixon, et al.[55] On average the group using a constrained, systematic search method, achieved a 37.5 percent idea search success rate compared with an unconstrained group that succeeded 2.9 percent of the time. The article also presents detailed worksheets and specific steps that were used for applying the method.

His approach, which as used in the experiment noted above, involved a fairly complex set of steps over an entire one-term college course, centers on acquiring new information selectively as a key part of the process for searching systematically to identify new venture ideas. Underlying premises in this approach include:

Ideas come from information that an individual either already possesses or acquires additionally.

Seeking new information will help an idea search better than limiting the search to existing information.

Guidance for new information search should be based upon assessment of an individual's present proclivities and know-how as revealed by his or her experiences, accomplishments, and feelings of satisfaction about them. See Step 2 below for examples.

Systematic search

---

[54] James O. Fiet, *The Systematic Search for Entrepreneurial Discoveries* (Westport, CT: Quorum Books, 2002). Also James O. Fiet, *Perspectives on Entrepreneurship* (Cheltenham, UK: Edward Elgar, 2008).
[55] Robert D. Nixon et al, "Prior Knowledge and Entrepreneurial Discovery," *International Journal of Entrepreneurial Education*, 4: 2006, Senate Hall Academic Publishing, pp. 1-18.

Potential sources of new information are innumerable. See Step 3 below for examples. Tapping them systematically should work better than doing so randomly or impulsively.

A simplified alternative set of steps for applying Fiet's approach appears below.

One implication of Fiet's approach is that a person with more expertise from industrial or hobby experience would likely have acquired more potentially useful information sources, particularly personal contacts who might not only provide helpful information and ideas but also lead to still other contacts. A searcher with less practical experience might have to start more from scratch to build an effective working set of sources. The starting point would nevertheless still include reflection upon what seemed to be the searcher's previously demonstrated capabilities, strengths, and interests. A remedy for limited prior work or hobby experience could be to team up in searching with another person who already possesses more such search-relevant knowledge.

Although information sources that are less personal, such as periodicals, trade shows, the Web, and "just looking around" may be easier to tap and can yield helpful results too, greater help may come from cultivating new personal contacts who can provide fresher information, answer questions, and possibly add helpful advice. Moreover, in the future such contacts sometimes take initiative to pass along still more relevant information as they come across it.

> A California venture capitalist, when asked whether he had become better at making good investments through experience said "yes." When asked what he did differently as result of the experience that improved his performance he first looked puzzled and then said "not much." The key, he said, was not that he had changed, but that his contacts had become better at informing him about deals he should consider.

Six steps for applying Fiet's idea search approach

Briefly, here are the ensuing six steps:

1. *Recall and list* one or more prior productive accomplishments that you achieved either individually or through contribution to a team effort.
2. *Identify and list* personal capabilities that you drew upon most for making those contributions. These should not be virtues like honesty or industriousness, valuable as they may be, but rather productive capacities such as skills in problem solving, leadership, selling, organizing, conceptualizing, coordinating, inventing, finding suppliers, model building, code writing, or other technical or market savvy.
3. *Identify and list* information sources that you drew upon in producing the accomplishments listed in Step 1 above. These could be, most importantly, other personal industrial or technical contacts by name and address, but also publications, displays such as fairs and trade shows, Web sites, physical shopping sites, and even just walking around and dropping in on businesses.
4. *Start generating new* product and service ideas for venture creation that might likely link to or capitalize on the capabilities of Step 2 and/or information sources of Step 3 above. List these in a log with dates and a brief description of what might be important about each, such as whom it might serve, what benefits such recipients might gain, and how it might produce profits.
5. *Map out* a search plan of information sources that starts with those listed in Step 3 above and adds links to new ones to be tapped in some pattern along a future time line. Cluster these sources into half a dozen groupings or less that makes them easier to remember and develop strategies for tapping. In doing this, weigh the potential yield of information value of each cluster against the costs, particularly in time, required to tap it.
6. *Add to the idea log* begun in Step 4 above, a running performance assessment of information sources in the array of Step 5 and description of how the array is being modified in response to that assessment. Refine the clusters experimentally as most benefits the idea generation value versus costs of repeatedly tapping each over time.

How to show appreciation and reward personal information sources that help most, while spending less time on sources, whether personal or not, that help less, can be an art worth mastering through deliberate practice to improve discovery performance.

The potential power of searching through development of new personal contacts as well as using and refining existing ones is illustrated by experience of the following two entrepreneurs, each of whom developed his own method for doing so. Both happened to be engineers and sought to capitalize on their prior strengths.

Having obtained permission from his employer to do so, Ralph Astengo, a Seattle entrepreneur who sought the basis for a new venture, made it a practice to acquire at least one new contact every workday. He informed that person that he wanted to start a company and was looking for a way to do it. Within a year he had found a new partner and landed a contract for producing a boat-control mechanism. But that job was soon finished and the partnership ended. He restarted his search, and after making a series of new contacts learned about a medical invention, the rights to which were available through the University of Washington licensing office. This he followed up by recruiting help through still other contacts to start Advanced Technology Laboratories, a producer of Doppler blood flow meters, which was eventually acquired by a larger company, leaving him wealthy and looking for more ventures to start.

— • —

By visiting purchasing agents in established electronics companies and asking them what they were having trouble obtaining, a New England entrepreneur, Dick Brew, ran across a need for particular types of acoustic delay lines to use in electronic circuits. Based on this first-hand knowledge of an inadequately served market, he was able to recruit resources to start up his own firm and service it.

Using team help

Individuals produce creative ideas, but combining individuals into teams can further enhance idea discovery. How team thinking within a university helped pull together the design of Akamai, an Internet content distribution company, was reported by Teresa Esser

from interviews with Johnathan Seelig, one of its co-founders.

Before the company was incorporated, Seelig spent a great deal of time inside the office of an MIT professor of applied mathematics, Tom Leighton, hanging out with other like-minded folks and trying to figure out what the company was going to do. "We'd all show up with our backpacks from class, make a pot of coffee, and work through ideas about how this was going to develop as a business," Seelig remembers. "And then we'd go away and each person would try to pull together the pieces."[56]

High technology companies and companies that manufacture complex products use teams because they can work on many facets of the design job at once and also bring to bear different types of specialized knowledge needed to work out technical problems. Designing an airplane requires myriad types of specialized knowledge, including aerodynamic, structural, electrical, human factors, chemical, and thermodynamic. Designing a computer printer requires expertise in dynamic motion, color analysis, mechanical motion, electronic control, strength analysis, human factors, aesthetics, and so forth.

Jim Clark founded Silicon Graphics (SGI), a company that made workstations for manipulating 3-D graphics, but resigned after continual arguments with the CEO who had been recruited to run it. Emerging from $20 million to the good from SGI, Clark then set off to create another start-up. He did not know what its product would be, but experience had convinced him that capable people, not the product, should be sought out first. While vacating his office at SGI, he lamented to a friendly colleague that "I don't know how to start a company without engineers, but every good engineer I've ever known I've recruited here. And I can't take them with me."

The friend suggested contacting Marc Andreessen, who had recently moved to Silicon Valley from the University of Illinois, where he had worked on the program Mosaic to make Web browsing easier, but felt that his employer had been reaping all the benefits and not giving credit to the low-paid people who developed them. Around the end of January 1994, the two met over coffee and, Clark recalled, "decided that

56 Teresa Esser, *The Venture Café* (New York: Warner Books, 2002) p. 30.

Personal target practice

Scorecard

we'd begin to meet at my house with a kind of 'kitchen cabinet' I'd form to try to figure out what our new company would actually do." Marc's one condition was that its focus not be Mosaic.

For his part, Clark said, "Whereas Marc said he didn't want to have anything to do with Mosaic, I was more ambivalent. I simply didn't care one way or the other."

Clark also said that "Since I'd met Marc, the main objective had always been that we bring together the core group that had developed Mosaic. People who have worked well together in the past make all the difference in a start-up, where time can't be wasted getting people acquainted, integrating dissimilar personalities into a team."

At the same time, Clark felt he had momentum on potential projects that SGI had resisted. "It didn't make strategic sense," he said, "to start from scratch, trying to come up with something entirely novel."

A series of meetings at Clark's house followed, at which he and Andreessen were joined by other colleagues from SGI, one of whom he hired to become an "all-purpose assistant" to handle such things as schedules, phone calls, and food as the group sat around the table exploring ideas. Clark recalled that, "About all we assumed at that point was that whatever Company X did, it would involve the Internet in some way .... How could anyone make money on the Internet? I didn't have a specific answer to that yet, but I figured that with the Web- and Mosaic-enabled Internet already growing exponentially, you couldn't help but make money."

One carryover idea from SGI pursued was that of developing interactive TV. But when he flew to New York and checked with his contacts at Time Warner he concluded that they would not go for it. Andreessen proposed, in a twenty-page paper, the development of an on-line service for Nintendo for games over the Web. Clark put together a business plan to go with the technology plan. While waiting for a reply from Nintendo on the proposal, however, he worried that it was going to take months to get a decision from such a big company and at best would then bind the venture to only one customer who could kill it in a blink. Moreover, the Mosaic team back in Illinois would shortly graduate and disband to take other jobs.

He said to Andreessen, "You come up with something to do and I'll invest in it." Andreessen replied, "Well, we could always build a Mosaic killer ... build a browser that's better than Mosaic, put it out there, let it take over instead of Mosaic."

After brief further discussion, Clark said, "If you can hire the entire Mosaic team to do this, I'll invest in it. Screw the business plan and conventional investors."

Later he recalled, "Just like that, we knew what we had to do."[57]

Based upon the precedent of Mosaic they set about to develop the browser program and company, Netscape.

Personal target practice

Making discoveries requires somehow escaping the ruts of the present to reach new mental territory. To achieve uniqueness also requires escaping the ruts of others and searching new territory. A way to check for departure from ruts is to look for existing discovery patterns and then attempt to break into new ones.

Scorecard

A tool for displaying idea search patterns to identify which ones may be overlooked is the Idea Scorecard in Exhibit 2b-7 below. To apply it, first categorize the ideas thus far discovered according to where they fall on the Attractiveness Hierarchy of Exhibit 2b-6. Some types will be less represented than others. Trying to increase those numbers should challenge less familiar personal-searching modes and thereby perhaps strengthen them, while at the same time yielding ideas that are more exceptional and possibly also thereby more valuable.

Then categorize the ideas found by intended user (the one who first came to mind when the idea emerged), self, other consumers, businesses, and governmental and nonprofit customers. Then categorize them as to market pull versus capability push sources. Within market pull, consider and count whether the implicit purpose at discovery of the idea was to solve a present problem, to satisfy an apparent desire that is not necessarily a problem, to satisfy a desire that may or may not be there at present,

---

[57] Jim Clark, *Netscape Time* (New York: St. Martin's Press, 1999) p. 49.

or to satisfy a desire that will probably arise in the future.

Within capability push, consider whether the idea is one that derives from your own personal capability or from the personal capability of one or more other people with whom you might join forces.

After classifying in these ways and again counting how many of each type were found, display the count on the Idea Scorecard of Exhibit 2b-7. Some cells will doubtless have smaller numbers in them than others, which can again invite search for more of the rare types of ideas as suggested above for the hierarchy.

A question to consider then becomes, "Is my pattern typical of other people's patterns?" If it does seem to be typical, then an ensuing question is whether the typical pattern is more likely to yield valuable ideas or simply common ideas. If the ideas are common in some categories, then a better direction to look may be for ideas that fit the less-populated categories.

Beyond practice with this scorecard, it may be helpful to generate other scorecards, using different categories, such as were shown earlier in Exhibits 2b-1 through 2b-6, plus those in the sections on discovery search questions, and features markets like. Again, the aim would be to reach territory less populated, to prospect where other prospectors don't seem to be looking.

Exhibit 2b-7 Idea scorecard

Idea Triggered by	First User in Mind			
Market Pull	*For Self*	*For Other Consumers*	*For Businesses*	*For Gov't or Nonprofits*
Problem	1A	1B	1C	1D
Apparent Present Desire	2A	2B	2C	2D
Latent Present Desire	3A	3B	3C	3D
Anticipated Future Desire	4A	4B	4C	4D
Capability Push				
Own Capability	5A	5B	5C	5D
Others' Capability	6A	6B	6C	6D

(Service = S, High-Margin Service = HMS, Scalable Service = SS, Product = P, Protectable Product = PP)

Exercises

Text discussion questions

1. Describe how one or more venture ideas whose discovery is described in this chapter could have been discovered by someone other than the person who exploited it.
2. Describe how the venture ideas whose discovery is described in this chapter could have been discovered by a different path or idea triggering mechanism than the one by which it was actually found.
3. Are the implicit search questions listed in this chapter based more on capability push or on customer pull?
4. How might a group, as opposed to an individual, best attempt to apply principles of Fiet's approach to systematic search for discovering promising venture ideas?
5. What, in your judgment, is most likely to be the best way to search for a new venture idea and why?

Case questions

Case 2B-1 John Morse

1. How would you assess the sequence John followed in looking for a venture idea?
2. Where would the ideas he is finding most cluster on a "scorecard?" Is that good?
3. In what ways does the search approach John used align, or not, with that proposed by Jim Fiet as described in the chapter?
4. What should John do next?

Portfolio page possibilities (Some prior examples follow)

Each page, bearing the date and your name, should be one single-sided sheet, based upon this chapter, stating from your present impressions and information (quite possibly to change later) the following:

Page 2B-1 Scorecard

1. Briefly list the venture ideas you have generated so far this term.
2. Note for each the (1) hierarchy type, (2) sources, and (3) implicit search questions through which you discovered it.
3. Classify each with one of the cell numbers found in the Exhibit 2b-7 Scorecard of the text.
4. Deliberately seek ideas, note additional ideas for two different additional cells, and note for them also the characteristics referred to in item 2 above.

Page 2B-2 Target customer proposition

1. State the value proposition of what your venture will sell.
2. Describe the target customer for your value proposition and explain the rationale.

Page 2B-3 Benefits and features

State the value proposition of what your venture will sell.

Page 2B-4 Target performance specifications

1. List the performance specifications of what you intend your venture sell.
2. Explain the rationale behind those specifications and note the tradeoffs you considered in setting them.

Page 2B-5 Systematic search

Apply principles of the Fiet systematic search approach to your own venture idea search. Illustrate your steps and their results on not more than two page sides.

Term Projects

Venture history

1. How did the entrepreneur come upon the idea (versus opportunity) for the venture? What other ideas were rejected through what processes?
2. How could the main internal driver of the idea discovery be described?
3. What implicit search questions seemed most to be at work?
4. To what extent did the entrepreneur seem to use systematic search (whether implicitly or not) and to what extent did it happen to follow Fiet's rules?

Venture planning guide

1. If you have come up with ideas in connection with your product or service that you may want to patent, start a notebook describing them, date it, and have someone else whom you trust sign and date it as a witness. Repeat this as more ideas of potential value occur.
2. Brainstorm improvement possibilities for your main idea. Write out and save it for possible further use.

Prior student portfolio page example of 2B-1

Idea Source Scorecard

Idea Triggered By	First User in Mind			
Market Pull	For Self	For Other Consumers	For Businesses	For Gov't or Nonprofits
Problem				6p, 9p
Apparent Present Desire		2ss, 8pp		
Latent Present Desire		10pp		7pp
Anticipated Future Desire		3pp, 4pp	1pp, 5pp	

Capability Push				
Own Capacity				
Other's Capacity				

Hierarchy Type: Service = s   Scalable Service = ss   High Margin Service = hms
Product = p   Protectable Product = pp

Venture Ideas	**Sources**
1. Automated Menu	Got idea from friend
2. Dating Service	Saw someone else try, figured I could do it better
3. Microwave/Oven Appliance	Can't really explain it
4. "Smart" Clothing	Saw unfilled niche in consumer marketplace
5. "Smart" Glass	Got idea from prior job
6. Landfill Trash Compactor	Saw unfilled niche in consumer marketplace
7. Environmentally Safe Decomposing Agent	Saw unfilled niche in consumer marketplace
8. Wireless Speakers	Saw someone else try, figured I could do it better
9. Prisoner Locating Device	Read story about multiple offenders
10. Implanted Health Monitors	Read story about medical monitoring of ill

Implicit Search Questions

1. How can I make the ordering process faster?
2. How can I make the dating process better?
3. Can I combine these two appliances together?
4. Is it really possible for clothing to detect body temperature?
5. Can this color changing glass also be used for different purposes?
6. How can I reduce trash, save land space?
7. Is there a faster way to decompose trash?
8. How can I remove these wires?
9. How can we stop prisoners from repeated offenses?
10. Can we effectively monitor the ill in a constant manner?

*This page was replicated from a student paper and with permission.

Prior student portfolio page example of 2B-2

1. How would you describe a target customer for one of your product or service ideas?

Again, I will be using my automated menu service idea to answer this question. My target customer for my product would first lie in the restaurant industry. Although this product/service is first being directed towards restaurants, I'm sure there will be other interested industries once the product is transformed to fit other needs. For now, let's focus on the restaurant industry. To narrow the field, I will be focusing on middle to upper scale restaurants that can both afford this product. As an upper scale restaurant, new technological and innovative ways for customers to dine is seen as trendy, creating more demand for the automated menu. We will not be focusing on lower scale (fast food) restaurants, as those restaurants will simply don't need to rely touch screens to be efficient and speedy. After narrowing it down to middle and upper class restaurants, I can now divide those between the popular and regularly busy restaurants to the businesses with a random customer base. The service that this new product provides will work most effectively in a regularly busy environment, as the owners will be able to best utilize the speed of the automated menus. Lastly, the companies to target first should have a chain of restaurants, leading to a larger contract. If one piece of the chain likes the results that it is getting with the implementation of the new product, then the rest of the chain will soon follow as a new standard has been created. In the end, companies that can best use the automated menu system lean toward the Red Robin, Olive Garden, and Cheesecake Factory-esque restaurants.

2. What would be your value proposition to that customer?

The value proposition in this case is pretty simple. Let's take a look at benefit of the product and subsequent service in comparison to the cost of the product. Taking a look at the benefits, this system will definitely increase production, efficiency, and garner greater profits for the restaurant business. If you get more people in, you ultimately make more money. The touch screen system allows the customer to order own his own, and still gets that interaction with the waiter when they come and serve beverages, food, etc…This way; the wait time for food is drastically reduced. Along with a reduced wait time, the restaurant will be more organized. People will come in, the hostess will enter them onto a computer in the lobby, and they will automatically be put on a list. When customers are finished with their meal at the tables, they can press a "done" button that alerts the waitress. That button also sends a signal to the hostess that alerts them of a soon to be ready table. The network is also hooked up in the kitchen, where cooks can simply look off monitors for orders selected at the tables. What is this entire system going to cost? At $1000 per table, and a few thousand for the peripheral network linked to the hostess and kitchen, the restaurant will be saving thousands of dollars in the future. The organization and efficiency that the new system will provide will enable them to serve at least ten or more customers an hour. Taking food costs into consideration that equals $300 - $500 more per hour in pure profit. The restaurant can also reduce the number of waiters needed, as they won't have to be roaming to seat and serve customers. All you need is a couple beverage servers, a few meal servers, and a few busboys. It's as simple as that, and the end result is an irresistible value proposition.

Prior student portfolio page example 1 of 2B-3

3. What target specifications would you start with for that idea?

  The touch screen itself would be a 15 inch monitor, mounted on one side of the table. Coupled with paper menus, customers can sit down, read the menu, and go on to order their food without waiting for a server. The software package will display a button system that customers can simply touch and enter. Relayed to the hostess and the cooks through a LAN system network, the software will have a "sit down" stage, a button that is pushed after the customers have been seated, "order" stage, in which the customers have punched in their orders, and a "done" stage that signifies their completion of the meal. The print on the screen will be in 14 size Times Roman font so it can easily be read. The colors will be pale, but contrast enough to provide some kind of color scheme and still make it easy for the customer to read. The waiters can then come and pick up the payment, and quickly clean and prepare the table for the next party. The cost of purchasing the device and its software will come to approximately $1000, with concurrent training costs and future maintenance costs.

4. What basis did you use for those specifications?

  I asked a bunch of friends that have or are currently working as waiters and hostesses what they possibly wanted to see on an automated touch screen menu if it was available, and they gave me some specifications that I used to develop my target specifications. I took the specific specifications that they gave me, and first grouped them together according to what aspect of the product they were talking about. Second, I either took the best idea, or merged two good ideas together to form an even better one.

5. What sequence of steps might you follow to refine those specifications further?

  My first order of business would be to simply ask more questions. Asking experts in the restaurant business would definitely be useful in gathering even more suggestions for specific adjustments I can make to the product. I should also ask a larger contingency of people. Engineers, design artists, and other specialists would definitely be able to help improve my product.

Target Specification	Pre-Refining	Post-Refining
Price – Around $1000 to purchase	3	4
Cost to Use – Includes training, maintenance, etc...	4	5
Manufacturing/Production – Speed of production	2	4
Uniqueness – Is it different from anything we've seen?	3	4
Product Life – How long will it last?	3	3
User Benefits – How beneficial is it to the customer?	4	5
Value Added – How much value does it add?	4	5
Competitive Advantage – Does it give them an edge?	5	5
Patentability – Is it patentable?	2	2
Future Costs Saved – Will the business save money?	3	4
User Friendly – How easy is it to use?	4	5
Set-Up Ease – How easy is it to install?	3	4

Rank: 1 = low score 5 = high score

Price, cost to use, manufacturing/production, and set-up ease will definitely improve over time, as the company figures out ways to more effectively and efficiently assemble and improve the product. As more and more people use the touch screen system, we can leave room for a customer survey, allowing a vast amount of customer input into unique design creations as well as user benefits and user friendliness. As far as product life and patentability go, they don't really change due to the quickness of technology innovation and current availability of touch screens.

Prior student portfolio page example 2 of 2B-4

3-5. Specifications

Most of the following specifications come from a meeting with Paul, the director of operations for a small non-profit client of mine on Thursday, October 28th. I have set this client up with a Postnuke CMS, but they are interested in a CMS product that will do more for the organization and be easier to use.

I have split the specifications into two tables, the first containing those specs that are directly within the scope of this product, the second containing specs that may be beyond the scope of this product, but could be implemented in parts or in future modules.

To refine these specifications further, I would conduct more in-depth in-person interviews with potential clients and call/e-mail other potential clients in addition to current CMS users.

CMS Base Specifications

- Decentralized management
- Downloading data
  - PDF Format
  - Security: expiring links-by-email in lieu of attachments
  - VPN
- Interactive forms
  - Newsletter submission
  - Expense reports (to Access db)
  - Order management – POs, CC acceptance
  - Conference registrations
  - Surveys
- Intranet Content Capability
  - Policy Manual
  - HR forms
  - Training material
- Public info access
  - Public website
  - Sales literature

- Database management
  - Cross-sharing of data (e.g. address book, .vcf)
  - Presenting data graphically
  - Flowchart/diagram processes
- Uploading data
  - Simple for end-users
  - Photos/Graphics: simple resizing/editing
  - Audio/video capable
- Design Criteria
  - Security levels/Permissions
  - Cross-platform integration (e.g. PDAs, cell phones)
  - "Layered" Backup/Restore
  - Redundancy
  - Simplified admin. interface
  - Modular/compatible with 3rd party programs
  - Search capability (Google)

Potential Future Specifications

- Conferencing/Groupware
  - Forums (blogs)
  - Online meetings/Real-time chat
  - Messaging
  - Powerpoint capable
  - Audio/video conferencing

- Secure e-mail
  - SSL/PGP encryption
  - SPAM filter
  - Administrative functions built-in to webmail interface
  - Mailing list management
  - Multiple domains capable

Part 3

SCREENING

Discovering potential venture ideas is one thing. Deciding which of the myriad potential ideas is most worth pursuing, or pursuing at all instead of searching further, is another. Inevitably the two processes—searching for ideas, and screening to decide which to develop further—proceed together. The last section emphasized search; this treats assessment.

Two chapters comprise this section. Chapter 3A, on feasibility, concentrates on how likely the new product or service can be sold and delivered to customers. Whether it can be sold will probably have been partly established by the study of customers suggested in Chapter 2B. A step suggested by this section is to explore further with customers their actual willingness to buy based upon the evolving development and testing of the product or service. An early part of that process should be development in some form of a prototype. Testing it should establish that the product is legal, that it can physically be made, and that it can be properly produced and delivered in line with customers' expectation.

Selling and delivery will have to be done against the competition of established companies not only when the venture's product or service first appears but also after they react to its appearance. Consideration of this requires analysis and comparison not only of the venture's product or service against competitors, but also of the venture as a company pitted against the competitive advantage of other companies with which it will contend.

Chapter 3B, "Attractiveness," considers whether, assuming the venture is feasible, it will also be financially worthwhile. Whether it can earn a profit after entering competition is one issue. A second is whether that prospective profit looks large enough relative to what must be invested to start the venture. A third is whether the likelihood of success versus failure is high enough to go after that return on investment. In other words, will the upside potential profit justify the downside risk?

The main kinds of calculations required to explore these questions are breakeven analysis for rough estimation and pro forma financial statement projections if more detail seems called for. Key to both will be the basic numbers fed in as assumptions to the calculations. The hardest and most important to estimate of those numbers will be the projected sales figures.

Inevitably, judgments must be made both in guessing the input numbers to these computations and in deciding what to do about the output figures they produce. If the results are either extremely favorable or unfavorable, the action decision will probably be easy. But if the idea were very bad it would likely have been crossed off before the point of serious analysis. And the prospect of it being strikingly good is mitigated by the fact that competition, notwithstanding rare exceptions, tends to erode the upside prospects. Moreover, going ahead further w,ith the idea will likely reveal ways to improve on it further. But that will cost time and require risking money. So the action decision usually is not that easy but calls instead for thoughtful judgment beyond the analytic numbers.

CHAPTER 3A – Feasibility

Topics

1. Is the product/service workable?
2. How legal is it?
3. Is it a product or a business?
4. What is the verification path?

Checkpoints

a. Explain what is meant by feasibility analysis.
b. Describe the main purpose of a prototype.
c. Explain the different types of prototypes.
d. What different types of approval may be needed for a venture?
e. How is a business idea different from a product or service idea?
f. How is produceability different from salability?
g. What is a Competitor Companies Grid?
h. What is the purpose of a realness chart?
i. Why might side-street effect be important to a would-be entrepreneur?

The preceding chapter explored how potential new product and service ideas can be discovered. The next two will describe how to determine whether they are good enough to serve as the basis for starting a business. This chapter will concentrate on whether the product/service can work, be delivered, and be sold. A conceptual tool, the realness chart, will be introduced as a way of graphically tracking the degree to which the answers are affirmative. The next chapter on attractiveness will consider market size, profitability, and return on investment.

1. Is the product/service workable?

Creative design, as discussed in chapters leading up to this one, requires optimism that the something better, the new magic, can happen. Success too may call for optimism. But eventually it requires reality, and a worse mistake than failing is to fail more expensively than necessary. Hence, the new venture design process calls for checking reality along the way ahead of rises in time and money expenditures.

To economize time it can help in assessing the idea to attack first those issues most crucial to success. Some possibilities include those listed in Exhibit 3a-1 below. The first five of these concerns will be dealt with in this chapter and the rest in the next. A reader may

rightly decide that a different sequence from this will be most efficient for checkout of a particular venture idea. To economize time it may help in assessing the idea to attack first those issues most crucial to success. It may help to estimate priorities for treating these concerns, and reassess them as checkout of the venture idea progresses.

One good reason to try modeling the product or service during evaluation is that it may be cheaper and quicker than creating the real thing. It has been estimated that almost half of the resources used for conception, development, and launch of new products is spent on failures. Fewer than one out of five new product

Exhibit 3a-1 Some issues potentially crucial to success

Priority - Indicate ranking of the particular venture

1. ____ The product or service might be valuable but is not physically feasible and/or development would cost too much.
2. ____ Existence of forthcoming governmental regulations may render the venture either too cumbersome to pursue or illegal.
3. ____ Although legal, the venture would have dubious side effects, such as annoyances for neighbors, unsavory or unethical facets, or damage to "greenness."
4. ____ What the venture will produce may not gain some sort of independent certification needed to participate in its industry or market.
5. ____ It can be produced but people won't buy it.
6. ____ Some people will buy, but either there will not be enough of them, they would be too hard to find and sell to, or they won't pay enough to yield a profit.
7. ____ The venture would likely make some profit, but not enough to justify the investment required in time, money, or both.
8. ____ The return on investment would probably be attractive initially, but competitors in more advantageous positions would likely enter and shrink it prematurely.
9. ____ Such a venture could prosper adequately, but it doesn't fit this particular entrepreneur well enough.
10. ____ Although it may seem well fitted to the entrepreneur there are other alternatives that are still better.
11. ____ Going all the way to market is not feasible now, but that may change, so the project should be put on hold as a "real option" for reconsideration later.

projects that go into development in established companies ever become commercial successes. In some fields like biotechnology the fraction of successes is vastly less than this. Evaluation should seek to keep the cost of failures small.

Abstract modeling

The simplest test will likely be to ask for some opinions and/or experiment with pencil and paper. A sketch of the principal parts showing how they fit together and work may help. Architects use graphic software for laying out house designs, and rocket scientists use computer simulations, experiments, prototyping, and component testing long before trying the real thing.

Successively deeper penetrations in testing physical practicability can include the following:

1. **Imagine trying to implement** the idea, and guess what could interfere with making the product, having it work, or operating it at a competitively superior level of performance.
2. **Develop a written scenario** and sketches that show how the product or service will be produced and delivered with excellence, noting any legal, physical, or capability impediments for doing so.
3. **Solicit expert reviews** of whatever seem to be the most critical items in implementing the venture idea.
4. **Make a physical prototype** if the venture will make a new product, and use it to see what happens. If the venture will introduce a service, try performing it, and see how well that can be done.
5. **Develop and test a** series of progressively more realistic prototypes followed by pre-production and then production versions.
6. At each stage **try the conceptions out on others**, letting them see the drawings, prototypes, or other simulations as a basis for discussion. The objective of the discussion should be to look for problems, weaknesses, and ideas to render improvements, not to sell unless selling is truly the appropriate objective at that point.

Words and/or drawings

Sketches are an easy way to crosscheck imagination to evaluate the promise of alternative new designs to evaluate their feasibility. New restaurants, boats, toys, furniture, office layouts, and any products can be used to test reactions of potential customers. Written descriptions can also be used to present features such as service policies, steps for utilization, and the nature of sound, smell, ambience, and style. Such things obviously can apply not only to products but also services.

And, of course, entrepreneurs use sketches and written business plans, to present their ideas, not only to customers but also to funding sources. Sabeer Bhatia recalls presenting to venture capitalist Steve Jurvetson, the idea for Hotmail that he and his co-founder, Jack Smith, needed financing to implement:

> *Only in Silicon Valley could two twenty-seven-year-old guys get three hundred thousand dollars from men they had just met. Two twenty-seven-year-old guys who had no experience with consumer products, who had never started a company, who had never managed anybody, who had no experience even in software—Jack and I were hardware engineers. All we had was the idea. We didn't demo proof-of-concept software or a prototype, or even a graphic printed on a piece of paper. I just sketched on Steve Jurvetson's whiteboard.*[58]

Theory

Physical theory is sometimes helpful, particularly when designs may seem intuitively possible but in fact are not. Inventors are notorious for conjuring up perpetual motion machines, but there is no need to build them for testing because the laws of physics can prove they will not work. Such laws sometimes contradict intuition, as for instance in the nozzle of space rockets. Instead of converging to a narrow tip, like a nozzle on a garden hose whose purpose is to make the hose squirt harder, those on rockets flare outwards at the tip, also to make them in effect squirt harder. That is counterintuitive, but can be shown with pencil and paper using physics, to be the way nature works.

Physical theory is even more applied to tasks of getting dimensions right by other than expensive trial and error. How thick the beams in a bridge should be to give it strength enough plus a margin of error for any load it might reasonably encounter is computed by theory and physical data, not guessed at by construction engineers. How big the frontal area of a car radiator should be, how much oxygen and how much hydrogen to put in the tanks of a space rocket, how thick

a copper wire to use for a given load on a power line of given voltage, and what electrical components to combine in a chip are generally worked out with theory first, testing second, and experimental attempts third because that works fastest, cheapest, and most reliably.

Expert opinions

Most often, the entrepreneur possesses at least some of the expert industry-specific knowledge needed both to develop and to predict performance of the new venture's concept, including use of pencil-and-paper analysis. But in some cases he or she may not, and in others there may be call for crosschecking or treatment of some specialized aspect that the entrepreneur is not qualified to perform. Venture capitalists commonly use experts to perform confirmation of entrepreneurs' claims. If the issue is critical and the stakes are large, experts are even used to cross check opinions of other experts, as in the following example.

Jack Wireman had designed an electric motor for an airliner hydraulic pump that was required to run without servicing for 2,500 hours. When a unit failed due to a ruined ball bearing after only 750 hours, he was both surprised and alarmed. Without the pump the company that used the pumps in its airplanes was in trouble, and that meant so was Jack. The obvious remedy was to install a heavier bearing. So Jack pulled out the bearing catalog, chose one, had it installed in a motor, and put it on the test stand. To his surprise, this one failed after less than 500 hours and the test time had put deliveries seriously behind schedule.

In his anxiety, Jack called around, starting with the bearing manufacturers, and located two experts, one a ball bearing consultant and the other a professor of mechanical engineering at Caltech. Each expert reviewed the evidence and wrote a report with recommendations. The consultant said the failure was due to excessive load and advised using a still heavier bearing of the same type, but a custom design with closer tolerances that would be considerably more expensive than standard bearings. The professor said the cause was due to ball-skidding because of too light a load and advised using a lighter standard bearing with inner-race-centered balls rather than the present bearing that used outer-race centering.

Jack had only one test stand. The time, not to mention the cost, of building a second one, plus

---

[58] Po Bronson, *The Nudist on the Late Shift* (New York: Random House, 1999) p. 85.

Physical modeling

testing two motors in addition to the time and extra cost of introducing custom bearings, left him with a dilemma. What if doing all that also did not work? He chose a compromise. From the catalog of another bearing manufacturer he chose a heavier but standard bearing that had inner-race-centered balls. Testing on the stand proved it out. Installation in aircraft worked successfully. Jack wondered exactly why, but was glad.[59]

Physical modeling

Mention of prototypes in the preceding chapter centered on the objective of refining specifications for the product or service to enhance its competitiveness in the market place. However, having the specifications and being able to attain them are two different things. Hence, a second phase of prototyping may be needed to assess the feasibility of attaining required performance and being able to deliver it reliably to the marketplace at an acceptable price. If the idea seems novel enough to warrant pursuit of a patent, a parallel step is to begin a written and dated log of the development, as will be discussed in the chapter on Protecting Ideas.

Prototypes for testing and refining ideas can take a variety of forms, as described below.

Six forms of prototypes

Prototypes for testing feasibility and seeking improvements can take a variety of forms, as follows:

1. A **jury rig** is usually a combination of mechanical parts assembled to test principles of the way the mechanism will work. The jury rig of the first garden string trimmer consisted of an empty tin can, with pieces of plastic fish line poking out through small holes punctured around the side, with its bottom bolted to the shaft of a household vacuum cleaner motor. It did not work very well and quickly flew apart, but not before it proved capable of cutting grass that lawnmowers can't reach.

2. A **mockup** is usually a physical replica intended to show what the product would look like. New automobile designs are made out of wood, clay, and plastic combinations in the styling studios that design them. Later versions of these are good enough in appearance to be used for the photographs that appear in product brochures. Mockups of new airplanes are used for making sure that parts such as control cables, wires, and hydraulic machinery fit and allow motion and access as intended.

3. A **breadboard** usually refers to an electric or electronic circuit whose parts are fastened to a board with space between them to make it easier to connect and disconnect wires, or replace components experimentally. This allows testing of different parts and arrangements before committing to use them in a more compact final configuration.

4. An alpha **test model** or **working prototype** combines those features of the above types of prototypes in such a way that the model can be used to see whether all the intended functions operate properly. It may or may not quite look like the final version, but it should operate like one. Detroit automakers test new cars on tracks and highways in homely disguised forms called mules that allow road operation without revealing what the final new model styling will look like.

5. A **pre-production prototype** is intended to look and act like the final version. The difference is that it will have been made on a custom basis one at a time rather than on a production line. It is used for final testing and also for working out details of how best to manufacture the final parts in volume. Although almost identical to the final version sold to customers, largely because it was handmade, it may cost hundreds of times as much.

6. A **beta test version** usually refers to a customer-test model of a new computer or software product. It can also solidify the basis for gauging acceptance as well as for debugging and introducing refinements. Under special arrangements such as low- or no-cost and abundant technical support, the software or product is loaned to users who are selected to be like final customers so final debugging can be performed and operating manuals can be tested. If there is concern that the idea might be stolen, then those on whom it is tested should be selected with careful attention to both their reputations for integrity and the incentives they may be subject to. Additionally, they may be asked to sign a non-disclosure agreement in which they promise not to divulge the idea to others or take advantage of it themselves without approval. It may be appropriate to compensate such people for agreeing thus to bind themselves and for their efforts in improving the idea.

[59] Karl H. Vesper, *Engineers at Work* (Boston: Houghton-Mifflin Company, 1974).

Warren Avis recalled consequences of failing to test adequately a new manufacturing machine concept, which he backed in a 50/50 partnership.

> Soon after we'd signed the contract, my young partner insisted to my dismay that it wasn't necessary in this case to do the customary field testing.... With the fifty-fifty arrangement, I couldn't put my foot down.... So he forged ahead without testing the equipment thoroughly. He took it directly into various plants and had his people start assembling it. Before long the magnitude of the mistake began to surface.
>
> First of all, the technicians, who had handled the equipment only minimally in our warehouse, didn't have a clue about what they were doing in the assembly process. We asked them to take it apart and put it back together again at least ten times before shipping.
>
> "There's no way this machine is going to work!" they protested.
>
> A reverse prophesy, confirmed by a coup de grace: They hooked it up to the wrong kind of current and burned out all the motors.
>
> With some companies, this blunder might have presented some serious problems or setbacks that could still have been overcome. But for us, because of the high cost of the machinery (which ran into the tens of thousands of dollars), this mistake completely wrecked the company and its reputation.[60]

Construction

Physical models are also familiar simulations of the future. New major buildings are often laid out on a table in model form to attract investors, as are new condominium complexes to sell homebuyers.

The technology of prototype fabrication has advanced greatly in recent years thanks to computer simulation software. With CAD/CAM programs many features of new designs can be drawn, dimensionalized, and manipulated on screen, reducing the amount of physical cut-and-try needed in prototyping. The software can also help in preparation of drawings to make the parts and in directly machining parts with numerically controlled machine tools. Airplanes, autos, machined parts can be drawn, rotated, dimensionalized, and to some degree tested using CAD/CAM software as a cheap way of simulating reality. Some products can be simulated with CAD/CAM software and some cannot. New foods or perfumes would likely fall in the latter category.

In stereo lithography, a process categorized as fast prototyping, parts can be built up out of plastic that is hardened, deposited, or eaten away in three-dimensional space under computer control to produce parts directly without physical sawing, shearing, drilling, or other machining. Prototypes of new microcomputer mouse designs, for instance, have been made this way.

Professionals accustomed to helping with prototypes include job manufacturing shops, custom plastics molders, industrial designers, and testing laboratories. These can readily be located through the Yellow Pages and by asking around. To get the most help from them as economically as possible, it will probably be a good idea for the entrepreneur to attempt prototyping personally first, at least in the form of sketches, dimensions, target specifications, and, if possible, physical models. It will also be a good idea to obtain one or more price and delivery-time quotes and, if possible, to talk with other customers of the prototyping firms before choosing one.

Use

Physical working prototypes can be very powerful not only for determining that a concept is truly workable and for finding ways to improve upon it, but also checking potential user reactions, convincing potential backers to put up money and even for persuading customers to buy. In the following example a customer's enthusiasm for buying the prototype itself led to a premature sale.

> In 1968, a printing press mechanic who had recently arrived in Seattle, set up a repair shop. He also began development of a new four-color press that would produce greatly improved clarity but cost less than existing machines. He made two prototypes at a cost of $90,000 and began showing them to potential customers. One responded with a high-priced cash offer to buy the prototype itself. The mechanic, seeing how the cash could help him advance his ven-

---

[60] Warren Avis, *Takee a Chance to be First: The Secrets of Entrepreneurial Success* (New York: Macmillan, 1986) p. 187.

ture, agreed to sell it, provided he could set up and service it as well.

The machine was shipped to the customer in California and installed satisfactorily. But some operating problems developed soon after, and when the mechanic went to fix them he found himself blocked in California by a union contract provision allowing only their people to work on it. Union personnel hung a sign on the machine reading "Lost Horizon." Fearing that word of the machine's failure would spread and stymie future sales, the mechanic bought it back.

Even with the most sophisticated help, a venture can run into technical problems that just can't be solved within the bounds of rational investment. In the following example a whole squadron of start-ups ran aground on problems of physical infeasibility and sank.

Virtual I.O. was founded in 1993 "to do the next big thing in computing." It would produce a miniature computer with a "full-sized screen" by projecting the screen image onto a pair of wireless eyeglasses. The company recruited money and technical assistance and $30 million from a powerful industry cohort including TCI, Intel, Logitec, Bausch & Lomb, and Planar. Cooperative arrangements were worked out with electronic firms for help in developing a miniaturized screen, starting with the screen technology of video cameras.

The CEO Linda Rhode recalled, "we all knew it was risky, that it was hardware and therefore capital intensive, aiming at the leading edge for a home run or nothing. We aimed to create entry barriers in the form of intellectual property, strong financial backing, and equity partnerships with strong companies that could help with credibility and marketing as well as frightening off potential competitors."

From its powerful collaborators the company recruited an all-star board of directors from Fortune 500 consumer product companies. A "best of breed" product was created that earned virtually every major industrial design award. Sales in 1995 were $5 million with a loss, and in 1996 were $10 million with half as much loss. But performance was not yet good enough for customers, and now the camcorder companies were using larger viewfinder screens on their cameras, rather than further refining the smaller ones. Moreover, there was now a major new sink for venture capital investment in the rapidly rising popularity of the Internet. Virtual I.O. and its

other start-up competitors had all given up the chase by the end of 1997.

Field trials

Combinations of such approaches as these are usually more helpful than pursuing only one of them alone. But even that may not be enough. For some markets, in-depth understanding, coupled with quick response to change may be the only hope.

An emergency room physician and his wife developed a Macintosh-based system in 1989 for accumulating and processing data on medical operations. Successful installation in four west-coast hospitals encouraged them six years later to also develop the system for Windows. To attract venture capital, they engaged a professional manager, a seasoned CEO from a laboratory health care enterprise. Successful in raising $2 million, in September 1995 they began development of the new system. Notwithstanding a crash of the new system, which was now being modified to accommodate more tasks, coupled with sales delays, they further succeeded in obtaining a second round of $2 million in mid-1996.

By December 1996 the company had the new system working but was now experiencing sales delays. The way such equipment was bought had changed as insurance-claims processing had changed from single hospitals to multiple hospitals, which in turn had introduced new requirements for sharing information and consequent system-compatibility requirements. Adaptation to this and other preferences that potential customers requested in the product, such as "expansion from medical records and system tracking to capture everything that every insurance company wanted, and being user-friendly to everybody" had consumed valuable time and caused the venture to move the price up from $50,000 to $200,000, which in turn introduced different scrutiny and hesitation in the buying process. One major order was promised by a hospital by no later than February 1997, but as that date came and went without the order, management decided that heightened sales-force follow-through was needed.

By March 1997 company executives, short on cash, pleaded with their investors for one more round, urging that "we have $4 million worth of orders in the pipeline if we can just get one more shot for the sales organization to harvest and bring it home." One venture capitalist seemed favorably inclined, but the lead investor said no more money. In April, all employees were laid off.

As this example illustrates, a market can be a complex and fast-moving target, quick to change crucially and easy to misjudge by superficial assessment. For an entrepreneur who has limited resources and a new idea that is hard to evaluate based on the past, it can be especially helpful to seek advice from people who have had experience serving similar markets as well as from potential customers.

Gordon Bell, vice president of research at Digital Equipment Corporation when it was a top-performing star in the minicomputer industry, recalled a design review for a new computer under development.

> *I asked whether the design had been simulated or thoroughly reviewed. It hadn't, since the group was in such a hurry to meet the schedule that they wanted to skip the checking stage. On Saturday, I visited the project team to talk with its members and found that the management didn't understand the project and that four individuals each regarded himself as the project's sole architect and wanted the credit. The project had about four design styles, because it consisted of four large subsystems.*
>
> *By Thursday, no one wanted credit. Within six months the project was brought under control through many management changes and the introduction of a design process that required the use of design reviews and simulation to ensure the correctness of the design prior to building the hardware. The product ultimately shipped two years later than scheduled, whereas, left on its original course, it would probably never have shipped.[61]*

Quality

Testing of physical feasibility should not only show that the product or service can be produced, but also assure that it can be done well enough. According to a survey by *Inc.* magazine's 500 firms, 88 percent of founders attributed their success to exceptional execution of an ordinary idea, while only 12 percent said they succeeded because of an unusual or extraordinary idea.[62]

In their study of 2,994 firms, Cooper et al.[63] reported that odds of survival were on the average not higher among firms that *claimed* a reputation for quality as part of their strategy. However, firms that attributed more than 40 percent of their strategy to better service, and those that said 40 percent or more was focused on providing previously unavailable products or services, did have higher odds of survival. Emphasis on lower prices or on serving customer groups previously underserved was associated with higher failure rates.

What this suggests is that high quality, to the extent that it is perceived by customers as such, is typically a major key to raising odds of success. Hence, in evaluating plans for the venture, the entrepreneur should ask not just whether the product or service will be physically workable, but also how the presence of high quality in it can be made evident.

Kinds of excellence in performance that seem to distinguish winners in the *Inc.* 500 are illustrated by some examples such as the following.

> Tom Tjelmeland, who had worked on construction sites since age 14, entered a most prosaic line of work, the roof repair business, by concentrating on commercial customers and doing enough small things better than competitors so his firm would get the orders without need to give quotes. His tactics included clean white trucks and white uniformed workers in an industry notorious for the opposite. Use of computers gave him clearer awareness of costs in order to control them and facilitated reminders to customers about roof inspections. Careful sleuthing of competitors' performance in neighboring markets revealed which would be easiest to expand into. Questionnaire follow-ups of both jobs the company won and those it lost helped show why. Adding a 24-hour emergency service staffed by workers with cellular phones improved responsiveness. Numerous experiments with other ways of marketing and controlling helped identify which ones

---

[61] G. Gordon Bell with John E. McNamara, High-Tech Ventures (Reading, MA: Basic Books, 1991) p. 121.
[62] John Case, "The Origins of Entrepreneurship," Inc., June 1989, p. 54.
[63] Arnold C. Cooper and others, New Business in America (Washington, D.C.: The NFIB Foundation, 1990) p. 8.

worked best. All these activities helped set the company apart from competitors and propel it to *Inc.* 500 membership.[64]

In six years James Ake successfully expanded a six-employee shop that made bottle filling machines into a 100 employee company by emphasizing speed of delivery to customers. He achieved guaranteed delivery in 10 days by (1) devising control systems for ordering, manufacturing, shipping, and installing to cope with such difficulties as running with almost no backlog, (2) training, motivating, and compensating employees for flexibility and speed, and (3) managing inventory to allow fast production.[65] He also offered to subtract airfare for a visit to his plant if a customer bought. "If we can convince a customer to visit our place, we'll make the sale about 90 percent of the time.... When they see this company has meat on its bones and will be here to service the equipment, it means a lot."[66]

Part of what these examples illustrate is that the key to physical feasibility in some cases need not depend on technological breakthroughs or esoteric schooling. None of these apparently success-producing actions seems particularly exotic or difficult to accomplish compared to the start-up feats of some companies that clone genes or design microchip testers. Rather, it appears that these firms are winning by doing ordinary physical things extraordinarily well. In hindsight, the ability to perform them may seem straightforward common sense, something many entrepreneurs should be able to do. And yet the competitors of these firms apparently don't learn how to reach the same level of competence. Hence, a prospective founder should consider just how well his or her venture would be able to perform ordinary functions relative to its competitors.

2. How legal is it?

Government permissions

Sometimes it seems easy to tell that ideas won't sell. Examples might include such items, which actually were patented, as strap-on horns to make cows look like bulls for rodeos where suitable bulls were not available, a sleeping mask with ear plugs attached, a pillow shaped to accommodate women's hair curlers, a large plastic bag into which a person could be zipped up to the neck and washed by pumping in water, and a massage tool to be operated by the suction hose of a vacuum cleaner.

Those ideas may not have even seemed plausible at the time, but many other great failures did look good enough to draw large investments. They included "smell-o-vision," a movie that was shown with special vents under the seats so viewers could smell the cognac when a drink was poured on screen; the "Spruce Goose," the largest plane ever made at the time and held the size record for some years to come after it was actually flown in 1947, once only; and Zap Mail, a service introduced by the creator of Federal Express at great expense just before it was made irrelevant by cheap fax machines.

Government permissions

What markets would like to buy is one question. Permission to sell to them, however, can be another. For most products and services it can be taken for granted. But not for all.

Legality

It can, for instance, be legal to write books about how to make bombs, beer, or gold ingots, but not actually to make such products. Or, for another example, paralegal firms are banned in 11 states but not in California, where the practice was legalized by passage of a Senate bill.[67] Legal monopolies enforced by government at one level or another include license requirements that exclude competitors in such fields as medicine, barbering, law, taxi services, and broadcasting.

---

[64] Joshua Hyatt, "Out of the Ordinary," *Inc.*, December 1990, p. 110.
[65] John Case, "The Time Machine," *Inc.*, June 1990, p. 48.
[66] "On the Floor Sales," *Inc.*, August 1990, p. 108.
[67] Laurie Collister, "Legal Ease," *American Venture*, April-June 1999, p. 20.

Federal law prohibits competing with the U.S. Postal Service by delivering mail to home mailboxes.

Zoning laws prevent businesses in specified parts of town. However, some firms may have grandfather rights to operate such businesses in excluded zones because they got in before the zoning laws were passed. Occasionally, an entrepreneur will manage to get a zoning law changed to be able to set up, and will as a result get the jump on others who might like to do so.

New drugs cost so much to develop, test, and obtain approval from the FDA to sell, that new independent drug companies simply don't occur in the U.S.

In other lines of work there are controls over effluents, noise, and safety. Zoning sometimes restricts location of businesses.

Having noticed apparently attractive and functional prefabricated housing and office space in Europe, Warren Avis, the founder of Avis Rent-A-Car and an entrepreneur forthright enough to describe in his book failures as well as successes, recalled that he decided such housing should work marvelously in the United States and therefore set up a company to introduce it.

But, he recalled, *I had overlooked the fact that I would have to get building permits every time I wanted to put a structure up. You often have to wait ages to get those permits; and that sort of delay can play havoc with production schedules. We found that we had huge inventories building up which we couldn't sell because the go ahead hadn't come through from the government.*

Also, there was some community resistance. Neighbors were afraid that prefabricated housing would lower the quality of housing in the neighborhood. This required other government meetings, approvals, and permits.

Finally, there was a cultural problem. Americans, in general, don't like prefab housing. They prefer individual styling. Before long, it became apparent to me that the business simply wasn't going to work … so we quit and moved on to something else.[68]

But for the great majority of start-ups, such restrictions are not important. Often it is after the business has started that governmental burdens of reporting, taxation, inspections, and ordinances tend to become more serious. Part of the planning job should therefore be to explore and anticipate this.

There were no pre-made alcoholic "gelatin shots" in Ohio grocery stores when Brian Pearson's mother asked him and his friend, Nick Costanzo, to go pick some up there for his sister's 21st birthday party, apparently not realizing that grocery stores could not sell alcohol for consumption. Not finding it gave them the idea to make such a product, which they called "Zippers." Checking with the state Division of Liquor Control, Pearson was told that because it was a food product, no license was needed.

But when sales began the two men were told that they did need one, which they received after 13 months, in contrast to six to eight weeks normally required. The company began producing and expanding sales, before long to 26 states. But then Ohio rescinded the license. State agents raided and seized all the company equipment and records. Meanwhile, watchdog groups raised concerns that the product might be sold to teens, or tempt children because it looked like lunchbox gelatin. The company changed its packaging and pursued appeals with the state.

Six months after the raid, an Ohio grand jury decided not to indict the company. The company brought back laid-off employees, resumed production and marketing, introduced new flavors, and by 2003 was projecting sales of $8 million for 2004. Their conclusion was that it can be important to clarify carefully what laws may apply to a new product and, if necessary, hire specialized legal help to make sure any needed government permissions are in place before launch. [69]

Other permissions

Depending upon the entrepreneur's personal values and standards, some forms of business, although legal, may not measure up in terms of personal ethics or acceptable social impact. Examples include repairs that are over-priced, shoddy, or both, deceptive get-rich-quick schemes, cults, distasteful advertisements, and high-pressure selling of useless goods and services to poorly informed individuals.

Industry qualifications

For some new products and lines of work, formal performance standards must be met and certifications obtained if the new product or service

---

[68] Avis, *Take a Chance to be First*, p. 191.
[69] Jane Easter Bahls, "Neither Fish nor Fowl," *Entrepreneur Magazine*, February 2004, p. 68.

is truly to be viable in the marketplace. Airplanes need FAA certification, unless they are under certain dimensions. Appliances, unless they have Underwriters Laboratories approval, will be rejected by many retailers. Some sports products, unless certain associations approve them for tournament use, will not be bought by customers, as the following two examples illustrate.

In mid-1998 Black Rock Golf, a start-up maker of golf clubs, filed for Chapter 7 bankruptcy. Three years earlier it had begun by offering driver clubs that were 46 and 48 inches long, in contrast to the 43- to 45-inch length of clubs then in use. The inventors, golf pros Rocky Thompson and Jack Rule, found that the change gave them capability to hit the ball farther and concluded that they should produce it. Because such a length change would not be patentable they worried that the product would immediately be copied by other club manufacturers. To preclude that, they decided to move as fast as possible, not even stopping to ask for certification that the clubs conformed to standards of the U.S. Golf Association (USGA), as golf equipment manufacturers customarily did. Raising $1.2 million they commenced production and started selling directly through 800-number infomercials on the Golf Channel, thereby end-running the retail stores as well.

Sales quickly rose toward $5 million for the first year, and the founders took the company public in 1996 to raise another $5 million to finance production of a full line of clubs. Great promise was already showing early in the next year, when the USGA informed the company that markings on the clubs violated its rules. The company appealed the decision and had its Taiwan manufacturer re-label the incorrect clubs at a cost of $500,000. The appeal was successful within two months, but that turned out to be too late. Sales dropped, losses ensued, and the company went broke. Another manufacturer, Golfsmith International, acquired its assets out of bankruptcy for $483,000.[70]

In 1980 Laurence McKinney, based upon laboratory data from U.S. government studies of marijuana, designed a machine (The Maximizer) to cook the leaves through a heating cycle that would maximize potency. To implement his plan to sell the device through paraphernalia stores, he had packaging designed and started building up an inventory for sale. He also asked if he could apply for a patent on his process and was told by the U.S. Patent Office that he could. Before he could sell his product, however, state governments passed laws banning paraphernalia shops, leaving him with an apartment full of unsalable inventory.

There are several facets that may be worth remembering from these cases. One is that there can be opportunity to acquire bargains in bankruptcy cases. For a start-up, however, the moral may be to look during screening of a new business idea at the question of whether some sort of certification may be crucial to obtaining sales in the targeted market. Another is that that such certification, if obtainable, may be a degree of protection against entry by other competitors, especially if the protected company can reshape the certification requirements to fit more closely the specifications of its product or service. Yet another is that there may be opportunity to create a new certifying organization, either as a potentially profitable venture in itself or as an end run on existing certification obstacles. Finally, checking on certification rules may reveal the happy result that there is slack in the rules already that will allow entry by a product with new and different features, as happened in the following case.

Howard Head had revolutionized the snow ski industry by introducing laminated metal/plastic skis, which outperformed traditional wooden skis. Notwithstanding this advantage, his company, which had become beset by imitators and had also tried unsuccessfully to branch into clothing, got into serious trouble.

By selling out to AMF, Head had enough money to retire. Taking up tennis, he found it frustrating that he had to hit the ball in the relatively small "sweet spot" of the racket to get good performance. He experimented with alternative designs, such as putting weights on the rim to increase the polar moment of inertia around the racket's longitudinal axis. This, he found, helped make the sweet spot bigger, but unfortunately it also made the racket clumsier because of its greater weight. Another way of increasing the moment of inertia was to spread the racket wider and use lighter materials.

---

[70] "Shortcut Derails Maker of Long Golf Clubs," *Inc.*, August 1999, p. 25.

This, he found, solved both problems, and the Prince Racket was born. One more big break was needed, however. It had to be in conformance with tournament regulations. These, it turned out, had not ruled out such widening. Sales took off, and Head sold out for $65 million. Howard Head's comment: "I don't believe in marketing. I believe in making a better product. Then sales will take care of themselves."

3. Is it a product or a business?

"All right, it may be a feasible product or service, but is it a business?" is a question sometimes asked by venture capitalists when approached with requests for financing by enthusiastic inventors who think they may be bound for entrepreneurial glory.

Entry barriers

Every industry has barriers to new venture entry. Governmental barriers, which were mentioned earlier, exist in some industries. But in most the greatest barriers are other businesses competing for customers' money. Established firms want all the money they can get from customers, and they are set up and practiced at getting it by exploiting such advantages as the following:

- Prime location **leases**
- **Patents**
- Established **brands**
- Economies of **scale**
- Purchasing **clout**
- Working **relationships and special deals** with distribution channels
- Refined **habit patterns** of employees and customers
- **Experience** in competing
- **Proprietary** information possessed in both the minds of employees and the company files
- Ownership of other **property** such as tooling and equipment
- **Financial resources** not only for buying such advantages but also for staying power to weather mistakes and economic surprises, as well as to go after new opportunities.

It almost seems new ventures should not stand a chance of starting up, let alone surviving. But they do.

Contingency dependence

Sometimes the feasibility of a new venture under consideration is crucially dependent on the success of another new venture already underway that looks very promising. Perhaps it is expected that the new store should do well, because it has secured lease rights to a favorable location in a new shopping center under construction that is expected to flourish. But not all new shopping centers do flourish, so it may fail and take the new store with it.

Warren Avis learned of a grand new resort being built, in a foreign country by a millionaire, which would be one of the most elegant of its type in the world. That, Avis figured, would bode well for the real estate next door on which others could develop businesses to serve clientele attracted by the club, their friends, and so forth. Avis bought the land. The grand new club was completed with 200 rooms, and success seemed close.

But the millionaire bungled the resort development. The 200 rooms failed to achieve anything close to expected occupancy, the resort went broke, and Avis was stuck with an unproductive investment.

In hindsight, Avis, concluding that he had erred by letting his dreams get out of rationality and by going into unfamiliar businesses in a foreign country, resolved for the future to stay more with what he knew best how to do.[71]

Start-up advantages

Some reasons that the new venture may be able to generate its first sale and get started in spite of unfavorable entry barriers are listed in Exhibit 3a-2 below. It may be helpful to note for each and perhaps change over time as improvements are introduced, its target strength, if already attained with a rating from 0 to 3, or its shortfall with some negative number down to minus 3 if it is still to be worked on.

There are many in the business community who sympathize with start-ups. Just as experienced surfers will sometimes help a beginner

Entry barriers

Start-up advantages

[71] Avis, *Take a Chance to be First*, p. 193.

(so long as they are not competing for the same wave), entrepreneurs who have already succeeded are often willing to help another they see struggling to accomplish what they themselves did (so long as the start-up is not seen as a competitor). Some suppliers and professionals may help a venture in hopes it will become a customer.

Competitor Companies Grid

Use of comparison grids was suggested earlier for relative evaluation of competing product or service features. Here a further use of grids might helpfully compare the start-up as a company against other companies already established, rather than only comparing what it will sell against what they sell. Appropriate dimensions may include, among other things, the different types of entry barriers mentioned above. Four more general categories that can be used for comparison include:

Competitive edge of the company's product or service as discussed earlier.

Market strength Reputation, including that of the founders, contracts, contacts, selling skills, favorable visibility or press coverage, and possibly location can be crucial to sales volume. Also important is how promising the market demand versus how strong the competition seems likely to be.

Relative capability Special know-how for innovation, development, production, and delivery advantages, and allies may represent strength here.

Financial muscle How much money the venture has or can raise.

Historical evidence suggests that on average, market share is a powerful determinant of profitability, as is margin. Market share in turn seems to be driven by product or service quality and by value (roughly, performance divided by price) *as perceived by customers*. Dedication level and the willingness to work extra hours per dollar of income can also make an important difference.

Exhibit 3a-2 Status of start-up advantages

Status - Indicate the ranking from -3 to +3
1. ____ *The product or service is new, better, and available only from the venture, protected by a patent, secret, or production capability so far unmatched.*
2. ____ *There is a contract giving the venture privileged selling advantages (New York's taxi drivers buy exclusive operating-rights medallions).*
3. ____ *One or more of the founders has personal "in" with customers.*
4. ____ *One or more founders sells personally and is very persuasive.*
5. ____ *The venture owns or leases a better location.*
6. ____ *The venture offers a lower price, either because it can for some reason produce more cheaply, or because it is willing to sacrifice profit or high pay.*
7. ____ *The venture does a better job, possibly thanks to higher skills, or because in the excitement of start-up its employees work more conscientiously.*
8. ____ *The customer wants a second source of supply so as not to be at the mercy of a single supplier.*
9. ____ *Demand exceeds what other suppliers can deliver.*
10. ____ *The venture has a partner or ally who for some shared interest can and is willing to help.*
11. ____ *The venture owns an asset crucial to operating such a business, possibly special tooling, a mine site, a celebrity contract, or rights to a book or a performance.*
12. ____ *Competitors are unaware of or unconcerned about what they are losing to the start-up, due to preoccupation elsewhere, or to the stealth or speed of the start-up.*
13. ____ *The last item on this list may confer an advantage of surprise, with the start-up able to line up customers, saturate sales channels, or lock up key suppliers or assets before competitors can react*
14. ____ *Founders of the start-up may seek to start unobtrusively for the sake of such an advantage. Alternatively, they may choose to begin with a rush to scoop up customers, suppliers, and other collaborators as fast as possible and shut competitors out.*
15. ____ *Or it could be that even without these advantages the venture can prevail either because its something better is so powerful, or its competitors are too slack to respond effectively.*

Not to be overlooked is the possibility that competitors may retaliate when the venture, its concept, or its target market appear to have promise. In addition, an obvious possibility is that other companies or other start-ups may enter the market.

A layout for comparing these indicators of competitor advantages and potential threats is the Competitor Companies Grid displayed in Exhibit 3a-3 below. What items belong in such a competitor comparison grid must be deduced from consideration of the specific venture and relevant competitors as well as reflection on which elements are more versus less important.

After such factors have been assessed, likely moves or changes in competitors' and the venture's performances can be estimated, which should help provide a basis for assessing prospects of venture success still further into the future. Will competitors probably add offerings to match the venture? Should they cut price to match it? Should they be working on next generation designs now that will leapfrog what the venture introduces in the way of a product or service? What can or might they do about any legal protections the start-up might have such as contracts, leases, patents, trademarks, or copyrights? Might they sue the venture on such grounds? It's easier to get into a venture than it is to get out, particularly if the venture gets into trouble, and the time to anticipate troublesome eventualities is before taking the plunge.

Market entry prospects

Market entry is usually hard, but it happens all the time, sometimes with favorable results and other times not.

Failure

Much as one might wish otherwise, some product and service conceptions simply are too unlikely to work out and therefore should be scrapped. This is certainly true for established companies. Toy companies, for instance, are continually terminating design projects, as are high-technology giants, like Hewlett-Packard, whose employees sometimes hold wakes when their development efforts on new concepts are scrapped.

And, of course, new products that are followed through but still don't work out well enough in the marketplace are also junked, as illustrated by the following:

- Apple Computer introduced the **G4 Cube** computer in July 2000 and junked it in July 2001 when it proved too difficult to upgrade.
- IBM introduced its **ThinkPad TransNote**, a laptop with a touch pad and digital writing tablet in February 2001 and scrapped it in January 2002 when it did not sell because its sales price of $3,000 was too high.
- Motorola introduced a **PDA** that would clip to a cell phone in July 1999 and abandoned it in August 2000 when it was clear that the main effect of the device was to make a cell phone too cumbersome.[72]

Market entry prospects

Exhibit 3a-3 Competitor Companies Grid

	Venture	**Competitor 1**	**Competitor 2, etc**	**New Entrant 1**	**Entrant 2, etc**
Product/service edge					
Market strength or share					
Capability					
Financing					
Retaliation likelihood					

In hindsight, it would have been better to have foreseen these limitations and either modified the design specifications accordingly or scrapped the projects sooner so as to have avoided the development, tooling, and marketing expenses the projects entailed. Although they suffered expensive failures, at least the companies survived.

Survival

Thanks to flexibility in the economic system for trying to work things out in the face of failure, entrepreneurs many times manage through persistence to turn unworkable ideas around. Such was the approach that gave birth to Tupperware.

Earl Tupper, born in Berlin, New Hampshire in 1907, tried unsuccessfully to get permanent employment in the advertising industry. He worked as a tenant farmer and tended his parents' commercial greenhouses. He also operated a landscaping and tree surgery business of his own, which went bankrupt in 1936. He wrote about utopian dreams for a more ideal society, but also lived as a consumer of what were expensive luxuries for his time, such as fountain pens, a telephone, and new cars.

Meanwhile, seeking to enact his idealism, he invented and made prototypes of many inventions along the way, such as a knee-actuated harrow, a spray gun, a streamlined sled, and a top for auto rumble seats, but with little success. "I am too strapped for money, and have notebooks full of sketches and a house full of models and inventions," he wrote. Eventually, however, those models came to include his tremendously successful kitchen bowls and lids of polyethylene, which made Tupperware a household name and Tupper a fortune.[73]

Success

Even if redirection is not accomplished before the venture fails, however, there may still be the possibility of restarting to get the product specifications properly refined, as illustrated by the experience of another entrepreneur whose products have become household names.

Frank Mars, born in 1883, had polio as a child and remembered being carried to the kitchen so his mother could keep an eye on him while she made candy. Shortly after high school, having recovered, he started wholesaling candy, going from town to town making the rounds at dime stores. Shortly after his wife divorced him in 1910, he went bankrupt, as Milton Hershey had eight times before him in the candy business.

He and his second wife tried manufacturing candy in their Seattle home kitchen, and he went bankrupt again. Then trying yet again in Tacoma, he went bankrupt in 1914 at age 31. Moving in 1920 to the Minneapolis area, he and his wife tried yet again, first a butter cream bar, which did not catch on very well, and then in 1923 a nougat bar he named Milky Way, which was an immediate hit, taking his sales from $80,000 a year to ten times that much in its first year. In 1923 he made another hit with the Snickers bar, and another with Three Musketeers during the depression of 1932. (M&M's, in imitation of an English confection, were introduced in the 1940s by his son after Frank Mars' death.)[74]

The challenge looking forward is how to minimize the cost of failure, accomplish turnaround sooner rather than later, and make the most of the upside.

Although most new firms never grow large, some do, and some achieve very high profitability. The supreme example may be Microsoft, which in less than 20 years achieved a total valuation rivaling that of General Motors, made millionaires out of thousands of its employees and multibillionaires out of its two founders, Bill Gates and Paul Allen. In mid-1995 the *Seattle Times* reported that Gates had become the richest man in the world, with a net worth of $12.9 billion.[75] By 1999 that number had reached $80 billion and he was looking forward to giving it away to good causes.

High profits are possible when a venture enjoys a monopoly position in its product, service, location, talent, name brand, connections, or the like that makes it difficult for others to compete against it on price. The monopoly in Microsoft's case was its ownership of the DOS operating system used on roughly three-fourths

---

[72] "When Good Designs Go Bad," *Business 2.0 Magazine*, April 2002, p. 121.

[73] *Tupper Diary*, 18 June 1933, Archives Center of the National Museum of American History, Smithsonian Museum, Washington, DC. 470, Series 2.

[74] Jan Pottker, *Crisis in Candyland* (Bethesda, MD: National Press, 1995).

[75] *Seattle Times*, July 9, 1995, p. 1.

of all microcomputers. This ownership constituted a barrier to entry and price-cutting by any competitors. Other such barriers include patents, secrets, special know-how, licenses, special relationships with customers or suppliers, and special skills or talents.

If the new venture seems capable of mustering adequately strong advantages to enter the market, the next question becomes whether or not it can survive and become sufficiently profitable and otherwise rewarding enough to warrant the time, effort, and investment required to start it up. The next chapter will examine ways of exploring those questions further.

4. What is the verification path?

Realness Chart

The closer the product or service comes to actually being produced and sold, the higher the degree of proof that it is feasible. Those degrees can be laid out graphically on a Realness Chart, as shown in Exhibit 3a-4, whose horizontal axis displays the extent to which reality has been achieved in making the product or service and whose vertical axis shows degrees of closure in selling it.

The nature of the axis demarcations must depend on what the product is and would presumably vary from one product to another, although for just about any product the realness would be low at the verbal description stage and high at the ready-for-delivery stage of making it. Similarly, the degrees of realness in selling would range from speculating about sales at the low end of the scale to having a firm order at the high end, while in between the stages might differ from one product to another.

As with prototypes, an objective on either axis is to gain as much feasibility and potential performance information as possible at low cost. To do that, creative thinking will be called for in demarking the intervals on both axes. Then the task is to make investigations that move along those axes economically as far as makes sense, testing feasibility along the way. If the upper right hand corner can be reached, feasibility, though not necessarily profitability, will have been demonstrated.

Making it

Prototypes of various forms, as discussed earlier, allow the goal of making it to be approached gradually, in terms of both time and cost. But they can be powerful. Bell made the

following observations about their power at his employer, Digital Equipment Corporation.

Making it

> *An attractive, but superficial, mock-up of a product concept, or 'demo' may be built to sell investors and future employees. Although the product might be flawed in some way (e.g., a commodity, unbuildable, too expensive), the model can override rationality …. Being able to see or touch a product concept means an almost certain sale to product or company funders. At DEC, practically any physical model was a key to selling the development of a product.[76]*

Service compared to product

For both a service and a product, what stages in making it would fall along the scale from quickest, cheapest, and simplest at one end to achieving actual delivery to customers at the other would depend on the individual case. At the left end of the horizontal scale again would go just talk, maybe followed by graphics. But further along might come degrees of simulated experience for the customer. For a restaurant there might be mockups of menu and advertisements. For a business service there might be scenarios of where it fits, what it does, how a customer would be responded to, and possibly even fictional letters of appreciation from customers describing what things were done particularly well for them. A fictional video might display a scenario of the service being rendered, showing detailed views of some of the trickier or more sophisticated aspects of rendering the service that would distinguish it from competitors.

Not a sequence of actions for start-up

It is important not to confuse points on the realness chart scales with sequences of steps for

---

[76] G. Gordon Bell, *High-Tech Ventures* (Reading, MA: Addison Wesley, 1991) p. 189.

Exhibit 3a-4 Realness Chart

	Hand waving	Verbal description	Picture	Computer model	Physical mockup	Explicit specs	Working model	Test version	Production version
Purchase order in hand									**High Score**
Sell it ↑									
Formal in person interview(s)									
Phone interview(s)									
Mail or email correspondence									
Informal interviews									
Hopeful speculation	**Low Score**								

Make it →

start-up. It is possible that they could coincide, but steps on the chart should aim at accomplishing cheap and fast checkout rather than planning start-up procedures in detail. It is also possible that simply going ahead with start-up immediately could be quicker and more effective than performing extensive prior hypothetical check out analysis or planning, particularly if there is urgent need to get started fast to cope with competitors.

Selling it

For either a product or a service, the low end of realness on the vertical scale is probably hopeful speculation, and the high end is an order or more in hand. Having an order does not necessarily mean that there is the basis for starting a company or, if there is, that the company would succeed, or if it did that the success would return profits that justified the investment needed to achieve them. But, like a working prototype, it would be persuasive evidence that the idea of selling the new product or service was not just wishful thinking.

It might also give very helpful information about what would really be required to generate sales revenues. The experience of a marketing consultant in a situation where, although there was nothing wrong with the product or service, achieving the sale was impossible, illustrates how easy it is for sales expectations to be unfounded.

> Jack Savidge, as a route salesman for the meat packing company Armour, had been trying to edge out the competitor selling to Michael's Meat Market in Goshen, Indiana, but without success. Generally, what landed orders at other stores was a better price, but not so with Michael's. Finally, Jack became enabled to offer a price he was sure would be better than any other supplier serving Michael's.

> Jack gained a meeting with Michael, made his pitch with the new low price, and again was turned down. He recalled that finally he asked Michael why, because he was offering better price, quality, and service, he could get no order. Finally, Michael gave his answer. "Do you know Frank, the competitor's salesman? He's my brother-in-law."[77]

Here the top of the Realness Chart vertical scale was unreachable for a reason other than a failing of the product or service. The reason could not be seen until the selling attempt was made, illustrating how making the attempt can be important in making realistic assessment of feasibility.

Actions taken in order to move up the vertical scale on the Realness Chart should also provide progressively stronger evidence for substantiating ratings of the proposed product or service on the merit scales of Exhibit 3a-5.

These ratings should be used more as a guide for seeking further improvements than for evaluation. How could the product or service be altered to raise the score it deserves on each of them? Should any other dimensions be added to the left column? Should any items in any of the columns be altered to fit the venture better? After rating numbers are entered, what modifications in the venture's design might justify moving them higher?

Exhibit 3a-5 Rating need for the product or service

Dimension of need	Low rating of 1	Actual rating 1-5	High rating of 5
Need clarity	Fuzzy	_____	Clear
Need certainty	Hoped for	_____	Established
Need driver	Imagined	_____	Well validated
Benefit to customer	Low, nice to have (vitamin)	_____	High, must have (chocolate)
Customers	Unreachable, loyal to others	_____	Reachable, available, desirable
Utility	Customer unconvinced	_____	Customer sees it clearly
Life of need in marketplace	Short (<1 year) or unclear	_____	Long (>10 years)

[77] Jack Savidge, *Marketing Intelligence* (Homewood, IL: Irwin, 1992) p. 71.

Exercises

Text discussion questions

1. What is the practicality of trying to prototype services, as opposed to products?
2. How is an opponent-companies grid different from a competitive-products grid?
3. How might the categories on axes of a realness chart for a service differ from those of a product?
4. How might the steps on a realness chart be different from those for actual start-up?

Case questions

Case 3A-1 Michael Shane

1. What aspects of the marketplace appear to have given rise to the opportunity Michael is considering?
2. Invent a realness chart and verification path for pursuing the venture Michael Shane is considering.
3. Write out three questions Michael should ask in his market survey and indicate who should answer them.
4. What should Michael do next?

Case 3A-2 Laurence Osborne

1. Does the proposed venture in this case seem to be legal?
2. Is this proposed venture, as you see it, ethical? Why or why not?
3. What will determine whether this venture will succeed, and what can Laurence do about that?
4. List action steps Laurence should take next.

Portfolio page possibilities (Some prior examples follow)

Page 3A-1 Prototype

1. Describe some ways of prototyping your product or service and what potential weak spots they should test.
2. Either produce one, or tell in detail what would be required to do so.
3. Tell what it would be intended to test or demonstrate how it would work.

Page 3A-2 Target customer test

1. Try your product or service idea on a target customer.
2. Describe the customer.
3. Describe the test you made on that person, their reaction, and what it indicates.

Page 3A-3 Performance specifications

1. Describe performance specifications for your venture's product or service.
2. Indicate their relative importance and explain.
3. Indicate their relative difficulty for accomplishment and explain.

Page 3A-4 Realness Chart

Map a path of dates through cells on a realness chart for a venture idea, renaming steps on the vertical and horizontal axes as you think best suits that idea.

Page 3A-5 Competitor Companies Grid

1. Sketch a Competitor Companies Grid such as in Exhibit 3a-3 that might fit the introduction of one of your venture ideas.
2. Briefly describe how the competing would occur and change over time.

Term Projects

Venture history

1. What aspects of the venture concept were most worrisome in foresight and which were most troublesome in hindsight?
2. What, if anything, was done to check the idea out before spending cash on it?
3. Who, depicted on a comparison grid, were expected competitors and who turned out to be actual competitors when the venture got going?
4. To what extent were dimensions of need anticipated correctly?

Venture planning guide

1. Rate the need dimensions of your venture idea against the criteria of Exhibit 3a-5. Be prepared to say how you either did or would change the criteria list to fit your venture better and what happened when you tried to think of improvements to move the scores higher.
2. Devise a prototype of your product or service and try it on a target customer.
3. Apply whichever of the portfolio assignments above will in your judgment help your plan most.

Prior student portfolio page example of 3A-4

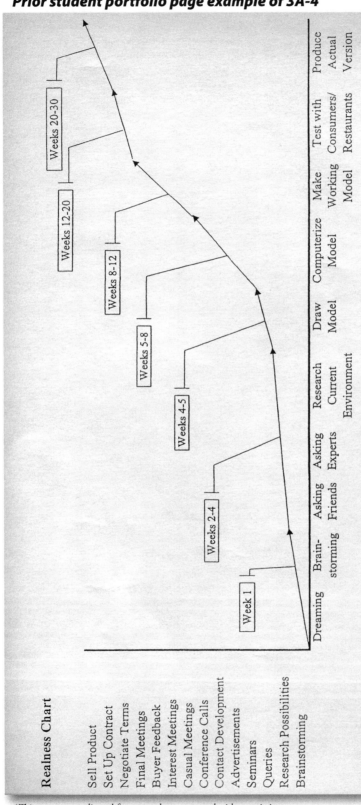

After talking with my cousin Felix, who has started his own IT consulting company, he was able to give me some insight on the business process and the steps it would take to complete the venture from beginning to end. Together, we were able to draw up a timeline, as he gave me approximations on the amounts of time I would have to put in to create the working product. Along with his testimonials, I was able to gather online some more approximations and stories as to entrepreneurs stabs at starting ventures relating to my industry. Coupled together, I was able to get a decent enough grasp on the topic to form my own realness chart

I purposely did not take into consideration the "angels" or venture capitalists recruiting process, because that would take up an entirely different realness chart. For VC's, you have to convince them that your product will become successful and create substantially high returns for them. You have to draw out forecasts and do extensive work to prove to them that you are worthy of their money. It's not that you don't have to do that for the restaurant owners as well, but there are some minute steps that are different, and would therefore be cause for a different realness chart (something I don't have room for).

Prior portfolio page example of 3A-5 student 1

Opponent Grid: 5 Year Prediction

	Restaurants (with Automated Menus)	Fast Food Restaurants	Restaurants (without Automated Menus)	Buffets	Copycat (Automated)
Product/Service Edge	Efficiency w/Restaurant Food	Fast Service/Cheap	Well Prepared Meals	Fast/Easy/Do-It-Yourself	Efficiency w/Restaurant Food
Market Strength/Share	Strong reputation/35%	Bad Reputation/20%	Medium-Strong Reputation/35%	Medium Reputation/2%	Medium Reputation/8%
Capability	Strong	Medium	Weak	Weak	Medium
Financing	Strong	Strong	Medium	Weak	Medium
Retaliation Likelihood	N/A	Strong	Strong	Weak	Strong
Overall Competitiveness	Strong	Medium-Strong	Medium	Weak	Medium-Strong

Restaurants w/ Automated Menus - My venture company will have a strong overall competitiveness because of its innovated design, and its ability to tie both efficient service and good food together. The touch screen menu provides that medium in between the two, and serves the purpose of propelling the restaurants that use my product heads and shoulders above the competition.

Fast Food Restaurants - Although the fast food industry doesn't make the best food, they do rake in the money. With profits in the billions of dollars, a retaliation is definitely likely to occur. I'm guessing they will strike back with their own attempts at an automated do-it-yourself menu. Lagging behind already, their best bet would be to work with me in developing something that would best suit their environment.

Restaurants w/out Automated Menus - As more and more people grow accustomed to the automated touch screen, they will start to create that standard of automation in restaurants. Although some people will most definitely still prefer the hands on technique that a waiter offers, I think we will gradually see the market share of the restaurants diminish over time. Those who haven't switched over either don't have the financial capabilities or refuse to switch over, and it's mostly likely that they will experience a fall in customers.

Buffets - Really don't play a major role, and therefore will not be affected by my product in too large of a manner.

Copycats - This is where I have to worry most, as companies and corporations will pounce on the opportunity to copy a successful product. To prevent this, I have to set up entry barriers; using patents, unique hardware, or other specifications that can't be duplicated. If the competition does come out with a product of their own, I have already refined my production process where I am low cost and efficient, resulting in a much higher profit margin and better product.

Prior portfolio page example of 3A-5 student 2

OPPONENT GRID taken from Figure 3b-4.			
	SolarWalk	Southwest Gas Corporation (SWGC)[11]	American Solar Electric (ASE)[12]
Product/Service edge	SolarWalk's not only supplies completely renewable energy at high efficiencies, but it also functions as pedestrian infrastructure.	SWGC provides consistent gas energy to heat homes, or create steam to produce electricity on the industrial level.	ASE does custom solar panel work for homes and businesses interested in cutting edge energy solutions. They are the biggest competition for SolarWalk.
Market strength or share	I project SolarWalk to break into the market in the southwestern U.S. and take 5% of that market immediately.	SWGC controls over 50% of the gas-energy market in the southwestern US, and is adding customers daily. This means cheap energy is in high demand.	ASE is a fairly small company, but managed to install over 900 killowatts of power since 2001. They are the main solar energy company in the SouthWestern US.
Capability	The dendritic web technology is already available, and costs are decreasing quickly. Therefore, capability is not an issue.	SWGC has rights to all natural gas facilities in Phoenix, and has a successful gas infrastructure.	ASE has the capability to produce a product similar to SolarWalk. They have the experience as well. However, they seem content to doing custom, low-end jobs.
Financing	SolarWalks initial financing will be through contracts from it's own customers after demonstrations are shown. Subsequent financing from investors.	SWGC is on the decline. A warm 2003 caused shares to decrease by 10%. Government regulations will cost the company $5 billion in the years to come.	ASE provides financial incentives to their customers to install grids, and offers government tax breaks to solar powered homes. They are financed soley by revenues.
Retaliation likelihood	It is likely that American Solar Electric will attempt to copy SolarWalk's designs, but we will already have many exclusive contracts signed with our customers.	The hotter the weather becomes, the better Solar Walk will do, and the worse SWGC will do. Therefore, SWGC may choose to go to solar energies in the future.	ASE could definitely compete directly with SolarWalk's product, and thus it will be necessary to stay ahead of them by enticing new customers and signing exclusive contracts.

[11] SouthWest Gas Corporation. *General Site*. <http://www.swgas.com/index.html> Oct 31, 2004.
[12] American Solar Electric. Services. <http://www.americanpv.com/projects.html> Oct. 31, 2004.

CHAPTER 3B – Attractiveness

Topics

1. How inviting is the industry?
2. How much can be sold?
3. How high will profits be?
4. How much cash will be needed?
5. Go further or not?

Checkpoints

a. Explain what characteristics affect industry attractiveness.
b. Discuss differences between survival and growth companies.
c. Explain what timing has to do with industry venturing attractiveness.
d. What different ways can sales of a new venture be forecast?
e. What are the main problems for an entrepreneur in forecasting for a venture?
f. What can be said about profits from a break-even analysis?
g. Explain the meaning of sensitivity analysis in a venture forecast.
h. How can the financial forecasts for a venture be crosschecked?
i. What explains the shape of a J-curve?

Financial attractiveness is a function of expected profits or net cash return, the likelihood of those profits occurring, and the amount that must be invested to achieve them. Expected profits are determined by prospective market size, competitive position, and costs. Competitive position is a function of how the product or service compares to competitors, as was discussed earlier in connection with product specifications, the makeup of the company, its game plan, how it compares to other companies or, more importantly, how it will compare to them in the future.

1. How inviting is the industry?

Choice of industrial sector and how that sector fares in general has implications for prospects of a business and consequently for its design. Hence, a significant strategic decision has already been made by the choice of product or service and what market segment it will serve.

Profitability

Some industries are more lucrative than others. For instance, as shown in Exhibit 3b-1, cosmetics have turned in high average profits and steel production low profits.

Overall, it appears that choice of industry has roughly a 20 percent impact on firm profitability.[78] But it is important to remember that those are averages. In the steel industry, for instance, Nucor as one company has grown and prospered mightily, despite the averages, while in pharmaceuticals many companies have failed, either because some of their drugs proved ineffective or because competitors came up with better ones. Similarly in airlines, Southwest has fared well when most of the industry did poorly, and then another new-

Profitability

---

[78] Richard Rumelt, "How Much Does Industry Matter?" *Strategic Management Journal* 1991; 12:167-185.
A.M. McGahan and M.E. Porter, "How Much Does Industry Matter, Really?" *Strategic Management Journal* 1997; 18:15-30.

Exhibit 3b-1 Relative profitability of business sectors

Above Average	Below Average
Cosmetics, toiletries (highest)	Automotive
Pharmaceuticals	Computer equipment
Soft drinks	Paper & forest products
Tobacco	Airlines
Food processing	Steel (lowest)

comer, Jet Blue, started up in a down market and prospered while other airlines declined. Plans to start Jet Blue were announced in February 1999, an order for its first 75 aircraft, costing $4 billion, was placed in April 1999, flights began in February 2000, and by December of that year revenues had reached $100 million.[79]

Statistical patterns are composed of many individual cases, some of which are typical and others not. Moving from industry patterns dominated financially by larger companies can be misleading about smaller companies, and both large and small can be misleading about start-ups, which within their own populations also may have majority patterns that fail to represent individual firms.

It is not clear to what extent overall industry profitability patterns are also true of start-ups in particular, or how they may vary with other parameters such as location. For instance, Kirchhoff et al. in 1993[80] reported from a study of 35,000 cohort ventures that choice of industry, through its effect on company growth rate, which correlates positively with survival, and choice of birth size both affect survival odds, whereas choice of region and emergence of other new firms in that region do not.

Survival

Failure rates for new ventures, as opposed to those of products as discussed in the preceding chapter, seem to average around 10 percent per year following inception—not as high as

has been commonly supposed. A popular estimate for a long time was that 80 percent of new firms fail in the first five years. More recent studies indicate that only around 50 percent do so. The study of 2,994 start-ups by Cooper et al. reported that 77 percent of new businesses formed in the U.S. during the mid-1980s survived three or more years, and another 4 percent were sold to new owners.

Odds of survival range among industries according to a number of studies performed over the years. An investigation by Birch[81] found that the most likely types of firms to survive were certain services. The top ten he reported in order of survival appear in Exhibit 3b-2.

Birch did not report the actual rates of survival, but the study of 2,994 start-ups by Cooper et al.[82] reported three-year survival rates of 73 percent in retail and 75 percent in non-professional services, compared to 85 percent in professional services, 83 percent in financial services, and 82 percent in manufacturing. A 1988 study of 3.6 million firms by Phillips and Kirchhoff, reported an overall survival percentage for start-ups of 40 percent for six years. The figures ranged from 35 percent for construction and 38 percent for retail firms, to 44 percent for wholesaling and 47 percent for manufacturing firms.[83]

Exhibit 3b-2 Top ten lines of business in order of survival

Veterinarians
Mortuaries
Dental offices
Savings banks (illustrating that times change)
Hotels and motels
Camps and trailer parks
Doctors' offices
Barbershops
Bowling and billiards
Cash grain crops

[79] Jet Blue Website, 2009.
[80] Bruce A. Kirchhoff and others, "Factors Affecting Firm Survival," in *Frontiers of Entrepreneurship Research*, eds. Neil C. Churchill and others (Wellesley, MA: Babson Center for Entrepreneurial Studies,1993) p. 319.
[81] David L. Birch, "The Truth About Startups," *Inc.*, January 1988, p. 14.
[82] Arnold C. Cooper and others, *New Business in America* (Washington, D.C.: The NFIB Foundation,1990).
[83] Bruce D. Phillips and Bruce A. Kirchhoff, "An Analysis of New Firm Survival and Growth," Babson Entrepreneurship Conference, Calgary, 1988. A more recent study by Kirchhoff cited in *The Christian Science Monitor* (May 7, 1993) states that no more than 18 percent of all start-ups fail in the first eight years, while 28 percent voluntarily terminate without losses to the creditors. The remaining 54 percent survive either with their original or new owners.

Exhibit 3b-3 Top ten types of firms in order of growth likelihood

Savings banks
Electrical parts manufacturing
Cardboard box manufacturing
Computer manufacturing
Paper products manufacturing
Plastic products manufacturing
Basic steel manufacturing
Pharmaceutical manufacturing
Commercial equipment manufacturing
Office fixture manufacturing

In fields such as high technology manufacturing, some researchers have found about 80 percent still in business after five years.[84] Moreover, even the 20 percent not found still in business may not necessarily have failed. They could have been sold, had their names changed, or simply have been closed down without failure by owners choosing to pursue other ventures.

Growth

Most likely to grow in findings of the Birch study was a different cluster of firms from those most likely to survive, with one exception, as can be seen in the Birch ranking of Exhibit 3b-3.

The main value of these statistical findings for a particular entrepreneur may simply be that industries vary in overall risk, profitability, and, consequently, attractiveness. Attractiveness often begins with margin and eventually settles out as profit and return on investment. If the industry has low survival rates, it will probably have low margins. So if the entrepreneur is entering with expectation of earning a high return, there is extra reason to consider with care just what it is that will permit that contrary outcome as well as how likely and for how long such a stunt can succeed.

Timing

Business trends often run in cycles both overall and within sectors, so that if a venture is to start up when its sector is doing badly, then the process of designing that venture should include consideration of the possibility that an upturn lies ahead, and plans should be made accordingly. Down cycles tend to squeeze companies out, so when the up cycle comes, there may be fewer competitors to deal with. In contrast, up cycles bring in more competitors, so just when prospects are looking good, times may be about to get harder.

A study by Sandberg found that industry life cycle was not a major factor in explaining venture outcomes.[85] Yet clearly, the oil embargo of 1974 took a toll on motor home sales, and hordes of filling stations went out of business, whether they were well run or not. The country simply did not need that many to pump the gas available. This event further caused Japanese and European automakers to look far-sighted, because their cars were smaller and used less fuel, while American automakers looked myopic because they concentrated on gas guzzlers (then in passenger cars and later in SUVs). Foreign car sales rose dramatically, and Detroit automakers scrambled to catch up. World War II gave a great boost to companies in aircraft production and other industries related to weapons manufacturing. In more recent years there was a burst of startups in e-commerce, telecommunications, and microcomputer software production. The first two of these over-expanded and collapsed, but the third did not. As noted earlier, the types of companies that head *Inc.* magazine's list of fastest-growing small firms shifts in pattern year by year.

Venture capitalists, particularly those who specialize in high technology, like to characterize venture ideas in terms of their power to create new industries or radically transform existing ones. Ideas that fall short of this can be good but not great, they say. Considering that possibility, the task of defining what competitive arena the venture will operate in becomes a more open question, and thoughtful imagination about possible scenarios becomes more useful than extrapolation of trends from past and present.

Growth

Timing

---

[84] Karl H. Vesper, *New Venture Strategies*, revised edition (Englewood Cliffs, N.J.: Prentice Hall, 1990) p. 32.
[85] W.R. Sandberg, "The Role of Strategy and Industry Structure," *New Venture Performance* (Lexington, MA: Lexington Books, 1986).

2. How much can be sold?

A comparison by Peters and Brush[86] of market-scanning activities used by 73 high- versus low-performing ventures in service versus 47 in manufacturing found appreciable contrasts:

- Higher performance firms did more market scanning than lower performers.
- Higher performance firms focused more on competitors, market share and strategy, whereas lower performers focused more on general trends.
- Higher performance firms made more use of networking, consultants, bussness contacts, and affiliates than did lower performers.
- Manufacturers tended to use more formal methods for market scanning and scan geographically more broadly than did service firms.

These findings are only tendencies on the average, and may or may not apply to any particular firm. Their greatest value may be in pointing up that there is a range of choices in regard to gathering market information, and no one set of choices is best for all.

Some entrepreneurs set aside the problem of forecasting and just start with customers already lined up for their products. Others just start selling and see what happens.

> Ken Draper, an employee at DHL in air freight shipping, reflected on the fact that large shippers received better prices than small ones and got the idea that banding together could give the small ones a better price break. In early 1987 he approached a shipping company with a proposal that he would organize a group of small shippers if the company would give a discount. The company agreed, provided he achieve sales of $10,000 per month within one year. He set a target of enrolling 12 small firms the first month but found he was able to get 85. The $10,000 per month quota was passed in the third month and sales by year-end were $250,000 per month. By 1999 his company, Unishippers, had expanded through franchis-

ing to serve 300,000 customers to become the largest transportation services reseller in the U.S.[87]

— • —

The risk of error during Dell's start-up seems to have been low, since he invested in no plant, working on microcomputer assembly and sales from his apartment. He did not have to design or manufacture parts, since he bought them off the shelf as needed, he paid little or nothing for labor, since he did assembly himself, and he sold only to individuals he knew would pay him.[88]

It is easy to be wrong in market foresight, and that can hurt if, in contrast to Dell's venture, the advance investment required is large. Even financially powerful companies can fail in trying to forecast sales with new products, as classic failures such as Ford's Edsel, which was researched but totally flopped, illustrate. When the product is truly new, even their massive resources for prediction can be helpless. Hewlett-Packard, for instance, undertook research to estimate the market for the pocket calculator and concluded that only a few thousand would ever be sold. Most people had too much trouble imagining what the product would be like before it existed, let alone how they would use it, or why they would want it. After all, there were adding machines, calculating machines, computers, slide rules, and besides, pencil and paper were available anywhere cheaply and didn't require batteries.

Anything that can be foreseen about customer reactions to a prospective venture's product or service can help in screening and refining the venture idea. Some of this foresight can be achieved by combining imagination with information a would-be entrepreneur already possesses, possibly to eliminate an idea or possibly to improve upon it. If the entrepreneur previously worked in the

---

[86] Michael P. Peters and Candida G. Brush, "Market Information Sources and Levels of Growth: A Comparison of New Service and Manufacturing Ventures," in *Frontiers of Entrepreneurship Research, 1993*, eds. Neil C. Churchill and others (Wellesley, MA: Babson Center for Entrepreneurial Studies, 1993) p. 150.

[87] Rhonda Greenwood, "Flying into New Territory," *American Venture*, April-June 1999, p. 14.

[88] Michael Dell, *Direct from Dell* (NY: Harper 1999).

industry and knows the customers personally, then information already known may confirm the venture idea and shape it to fit the market.

Unless there is prior confirmation of market potential such as might come from a hobby, experimentation with direct selling as part of checking feasibility, or prior employment in a related line of business, there will likely be a need to gather information about the hoped-for market, both to assess its potential and to design the venture to fit it. If the venture must recruit capital from outside sources, sales forecasting may be a requirement.

Difficulties of forecasting

Problems faced by entrepreneurs in attempting to forecast sales include the following:

■ The idea may be familiar to the entrepreneur because of dedication to it and immersion in it, but hard to explain to others because they lack such background.

■ Entrepreneurs have to be optimistic, and this can mislead them.

■ Some entrepreneurs may, because of prior accomplishments or exposure to customers, have credibility for investigating the market. But many lack this advantage for gaining access to decision makers, particularly in industrial markets.

■ Prospective customers may not want to be negative, may want to be encouraging, and may not want to offend the entrepreneur and so give misleadingly favorable responses to questions about the new product or service.

■ Entrepreneurs lack the money to hire professional help in market research, or may feel the money could be better spent on other necessary tasks of start-up.

■ Professional market researchers, accustomed to working for established companies, may fail to correct the calibration of their estimates when working with entrepreneurs who have less money, less brand reputation, and less experience to perform marketing follow through.

Nevertheless, some start-ups estimate markets well, even with little apparent forecasting effort. The venture capitalist who financed Hotmail as a start-up, Steve Jurvetson, remembers how founder Sabeer Bhatia presented his market prospects, as follows:

> Sabeer brought in these revenue estimates showing that he was going to grow the company faster than any in history. Sure, most entrepreneurs have that trait, but they are also concerned with looking like the fool. We dismissed Sabeer's projections outright, but he insisted, 'You don't believe we're going to do that?' He had hallucinogenic optimism. He had an unquenchable sense of destiny. But he was right. He grew the subscriber base faster than any company in the history of the world.[89]

In the majority of cases, however, sales estimates turn out to be overly optimistic, leading to suggestions that estimates should first be made and then be cut in half to add realism. Even if the levels come true, the time to reach them will probably be longer.

In the following case misestimation dealt with which customers would buy as well as at what price.

> Sequel, a company offering software for use in monitoring and managing the use of Intranet and Internet systems in large corporations, was initially aimed at serving a market consisting of many smaller companies. It would produce a shrink-wrapped CD selling for between $100 and $500 that smaller firms and branches of larger ones would install on their local computers. Conversations with potential customers revealed resistance to the price, making sales very hard.
>
> At the same time information from selling efforts and the business press, however, revealed that a better target would be larger *Fortune* 2000 companies. Installation would require a professional team over a week to 10 days. The selling price should be in the range of $75,000 to $100,000.
>
> Reorienting the start-up to provide this different product to a different market with different selling, servicing, and financing arrangements cost the start-up 85 percent of its $3.5 million seed capital plus an estimated 18 months delay, which it was lucky to survive.

---

[89] Po Bronson, *The Nudist on the Late Shift* (New York: Random House, 1999) p. 84.

This company managed to survive, despite the error in expected sales. Their hindsight conclusion was that further analysis of the market in advance would have greatly reduced the setback.

Broad market information

Expanding markets generally are preferable for start-ups because there is increasing sales potential to be shared. In times of flux, moreover, smaller firms that are less burdened with formalities, committees, rules, and conventions than older and larger firms can have a consequent advantage in flexibility. But expanding markets are also sought by many existing companies that want to grow and by companies in other industries that seek new territory for expansion by diversifying. Thus, industry growth is likely to attract competition. If that competition wants badly enough to gain market share that it will lose money to do so, it may make entry by others unattractive.

Support for the fast-growing-market theory of success abounded in recent years among start-ups in Internet, software, and telecommunications industries. Dot-com successes initially were numerous and in some cases so spectacular that they hid countless dot-com failures. The fact that failures among them were relatively low cost and the people who experienced them at first easily got other well-paid jobs or accomplished other successes, tended to obscure the failures in that particular line of venturing. Such low-penalty elements tend to be the exception rather than the rule among failures overall.

Over expansion of the market, however, has repeatedly been a killer for both start-ups and incumbents. Contracting markets can be even worse, if incumbents slash prices to hang onto dwindling numbers of customers. But exceptions, the specialty of entrepreneurs, also happen.

Pacific Propeller began selling airplane propellers when jets were replacing piston engines and the market for propellers was consequently collapsing. Because of that collapse the large propeller companies such as Hamilton Standard and Curtis Electric shut down. This left behind a market that was small for them but big for a small company, which entered it and prospered.

Still, there have to be enough potential sales to render start-up attractive, and it can be useful to ascertain just what the total market potential is. Even if competition for it is to be severe, a start-up may be able to find opportunity by joining forces with some other determined competitor and helping it win as part of a mutual benefit.

Whether a market in general is growing fast is usually not too hard to learn. It will likely be apparent in business magazines and common knowledge among people with jobs in it. Newspapers and other popular media will have reports about start-ups, hiring, new plant construction, and growth in stock prices of companies in the industry and others who supply them. Downturns, possibly temporary, will also be widely reported. Examples of broad trend characterizations can be seen in Gumpert's 1990 book, which includes business plans from several well-known ventures. Excerpts from two are as follows:

Ben & Jerry's – "The size of the total ice cream marketing in the United States is approximately 851 million gallons per year and is growing at the rate of 1-2 percent per year. The size of the ice cream market in New England is approximately 65 million gallons per year. The size of the super-premium segment of the national frozen desserts market grew from 11 percent in 1981 to 20 percent in 1982."

— · —

Pizza Hut – "In July 1973, the consumer price index for food away from home reached a level equal to food-at-home prices. With the exception of the March-May 1975 period, the index has reflected an advantage to eating away from home versus eating at home. This awareness has resulted in the fact that it is now stated that one in every three dollars spent on food is spent away from home, with the predictions that this figure will rise to one out of every two dollars."[90]

Five ways to gain such broad market information are listed on the following page.

---

[90] David Gumpert, *How To Really Create a Successful Business Plan* (Boston: Inc. Publishing, 1990) pp. 85-88.

Five sources of broad but relevant market information

1. ***Seeking out prior studies*** of the market or related markets by other companies, government agencies, or entrepreneurs. Asking a librarian and trying a Web search are good ways of seeking out data from prior studies and public sources. Some obvious sources are the Yellow Pages, the *Statistical Abstract of the United States*, publications and people of the U.S. Commerce Department, local newspapers whose advertising sales departments usually have helpful statistics and trade associations, of which there is at least one, and often several, for just about any line of business. These latter can be found through the *Encyclopedia of Trade Associations*.

2. ***Conducting surveys*** of population samples believed to typify customers. Mail questionnaires, advertisements incorporating feedback mechanisms such as mail-in responses, phone interviews and/or personal interviews may be used. Conducting surveys of potential customers may also give a basis for extrapolating to estimate total potential markets. For a start-up, however, these may or may not be practical. If the market is bounded, as in a given town, business area, or slice of the local population, the task may not be too hard. For geographically broader markets, seeking data online, or sending postal mail questionnaires to known groups or organizations may work.

3. ***Asking experts for opinions.*** Often, company founders are themselves experts in the markets they plan to enter and are therefore in a position to estimate both how much potential for sales is there and how severe competition for that market in the future is likely to be.

4. ***Speculating from demographic data on consumers.*** Information about age, income level, proximity to the company, and information about consumer interests can give clues about total market potential. Such data are readily available from secondary sources such as the federal *Statistical Abstract* or similar sources at state and local levels. Metropolitan newspapers, for instance, gather market data, which they are glad to share with the aim of gaining more classified, and other advertising customers.

5. ***Examining trade media to learn about industrial markets.*** Trade magazines, trade Web sites and trade associations can be helpful. Some industrial market companies are willing to share intelligence about markets they serve if helping the start-up could in turn help them as well.

Sharpening sales projections

Sales forecasting should aim to produce the top line for income statements showing volume by time period, such as monthly for a couple of years, then quarterly, then annually. To go from overall economic numbers about the market to specific estimates about how much a venture can sell, there are several approaches.

How many firm orders can be (and maybe have already been) obtained and from which specific prospective customers? A start on the answer to this question may have come from the feasibility analysis described in the preceding chapter. Part of that analysis was to seek sales orders as part of the realness test.

How many orders will the venture be able to fill? How many should it try to fill? Possibly capacity to deliver will be less than what could be sold, either because of a shortage of capital, or because building capacity will take time. Also, sales should be held down to what the venture is sure it can do a good job with.

What percent of the total market can the venture get? Venture capitalists deride such speculation as "if we can just capture 2 percent of this $100 million market we will have sales of $2 million," because the fact that 2 percent seems small does not mean it is obtainable; such faulty logic is known as the deadly 2 percent syndrome of thinking. The fact may be that any sales at all may be impossible to get. Still, the percentage approach may help add perspective. Possibly out of that large market there can be identified some small part held by competitors on which they are particularly vulnerable. It may be a small fraction that costs them most to serve, or that they for some reason care less about or are serving less well than

Sharpening sales projections

the rest. Identifying the weakest small fraction may at times be a realistic way to target and project sales for the new venture.

What sales trajectories have other companies entering this market followed? The venture may be modeled after one or some combination of those. Conjoint analysis is a mathematical method that correlates statistical factors with sales as a way of guessing by using historical data on similar businesses. For instance, in retailing, population within a specified radius, median income of the area, parking availability within a specified number of feet, competitors within a certain radius, rate of traffic flow, and extent of visibility are dimensions that may be used to make guesses about sales based upon sales of other stores. Deterrents to use of this method are that it is rather technical (worth learning to use it once?) and that figuring out which data to use and obtaining them may be expensive.

What do other people think the sales will be? Customers, suppliers, consultants, industry writers, and suppliers may all have worthwhile opinions.

What sales volume will make the venture an effective competitor? Too small, and the venture may be swamped by competitors. Too big, and it may be spread too thin to do the job well.

Segmentation studies

Two questions form the basis for estimating sales potential systematically beyond these methods. First, who is a typical target customer? Presumably, this question was explored when considering feasibility. Trying to make a pilot sale to be sure that at least somebody will buy what the venture has to offer should reveal good information about who that somebody can be, why they will buy, and how much they can be expected to buy. One or more of the founders in a prospective venture should be able to comment with first-hand knowledge on those questions.

Second, how many other potential customers like that one are there? What are the features common to them that distinguish them from other groups of customers somewhat similar

but not targeted by the company? What about the venture will enable it to sell to one segment if not the other? What might be required for expansion of sales to other segments later?

An experience illustrating quantification of a segment was described by Norm Brodsky:

> An entrepreneur had decided to create a new trade directory for sale to New York restaurateurs. It would provide information about such things as obtaining permits, kitchen supplies, and finding contractors. In addition to the sales price, it would derive revenues from companies that advertised in it. By the time he had sold 1,500 copies through personal calls, it was starting to become out of date. Worse, he had ordered a press run of 10,000 copies, which left 8,500 unsold, and now the printer was after him for payment that was more than he had collected. He had apparently not estimated what fraction of the total of 12,000 restaurants in the city would likely buy, particularly in view of the fact that the selling season was about four months. He had also apparently not noted that if he sold seven days per week for the four months he would have to make 100 sales contacts per day to talk to all those restaurants.[91]

David Gumpert[92] told of a market investigation that warded off trouble before it occurred in the case of a wholesaler of cut flowers who wanted to try selling directly to large-scale users such as restaurants, caterers, and funeral homes in the Boston area. This study took the following steps:

- Counting the number of such firms in the Yellow Pages.
- Learning the number of weddings and deaths per year from a state census office.
- Computing the number of caterings per wedding and deaths per funeral home to estimate the total cut flowers market potential.

The market potential in this case was judged sufficient to try as a next step calling on potential customers, presenting a value proposition, and seeking orders. As it turned out, those responses revealed enough barriers to discourage further pursuit of the idea. In hindsight perhaps, taking this last step might have eliminated need for the other

[91] Norm Brodsky, "No Accounting for Success," *Inc.*, June 1996, p. 25.
[92] Gumpert, *Successful Business Plan*, p. 81.

three. At the same time, perhaps the relatively small effort needed for the first three was needed to justify putting a serious effort on the sales attempts.

Ultimately, the sales forecast should include detailed lists of customers, market segments, geographic regions, and sales channels, and how much sales volume will flow to each. Future potential is what matters, but present patterns may be the best clue to that.

Writing this forecast out on a spreadsheet and estimating by month the actions that will be taken to produce those sales will set the stage for estimating an even more important quantity: profit.

One caution. John Osher, who had developed hundreds of consumer products and also started several successful companies, one of which he sold to Hasbro for $125 million, observed from his experience and that of other entrepreneurs that too often they compound the deadly 2 percent syndrome with still further over-optimism.

> They have already miscalculated the size of the market. Now they over-project their portion of it. They often say 'There are 200 million homes, and I need to sell (to) x number of them.' When you break it down, though, a much smaller number of those are really sales prospects. That makes it impossible to make their sales projections.[93]

3. How high will profits be?

Some entrepreneurs may be able to judge that their new venture will be profitable based on their work experience. But possibly the new venture will be significantly different. In that event further work on estimation may be prudent.

Five approaches for profit estimation are to:

1. **Ask** for opinions of knowledgeable people.

2. **Consider** performance of similar ventures.

3. **Examine** margin percentage.

4. **Analyze** breakeven.

5. **Work out** pro forma income statements based on a sales forecast.

The first three of these focus on computations. The last two use comparisons as ways of cross-checking for reasonableness and possible oversights of the computations. Beyond comparisons is the option of starting the venture up and seeing what profits come from it.

Short-cut profit estimations

Experienced opinions

Beyond possible prior experience of the entrepreneur, judgments of present or past managers of related businesses, bankers, suppliers, stock analysts, investors, and business brokers—people who have had first-hand experience with financial performance of such businesses—can be good bases for forecasting. People in sales of related products and services also develop a feel for where the money is, as well as which lines of work are prospering and which are not. The profitability information gleaned by reporters and other business writers generally shows up in print, often including reference to the people they talked to in obtaining it. Hence, contacting the sources they report can be a way to learn more details about profit prospects of potential ventures.

For ventures in some industries, special rules of thumb may apply. Insurance companies, for instance, are valued according to the policy amounts and premiums they have in force. Software companies are sometimes said to require sales on the order of $300,000 per employee to be financially attractive. But clearly it would depend on the kind of software, customers, competition, rate of obsolescence, possible tie-ins, and so forth.

Data on similar ventures

For some types of ventures, those where there are fairly clear historical precedents, a simple approach can be to make comparisons from published data of not only margins but other ratios as well. Examining financial informa-

Short-cut profit estimations

---

[93] Mark Henricks, "What Not to Do," *Entrepreneur*, February 2004, p. 86.

tion, such as might be found on the Web if the company is publicly traded (at smartmoney. com perhaps), examining case studies of real companies, visiting similar firms to see how they are doing, talking with employees, owners, and suppliers of them may give insights. Reading about comparable firms in business or trade magazines, or talking with other businesspeople may add insights about how highly they pay off, and how demanding they are in terms of skills, investment, and effort.

Two sources of published financial ratios are Dun and Bradstreet (*Industry Norms and Ratios*) and Robert Morris Associates (*Annual Statement Studies*). These are available in many public and university libraries.

In some cases stock market listings and financial reports of public companies can give guidance on typical financial relationships for an industry, although obviously they must be discounted to compare those companies with prospects of a start-up. If the payoffs of similar firms are high, then there is reason to hope that the venture's profitability will also be high.

Some trade associations also track financial ratios, so checking with them to see what is available and on what terms may be worthwhile. They can be found listed in the *Encyclopedia of Associations*, which is available in many libraries.

Margin assessment

One straightforward approach is to look at the margin percentage and see whether it seems high, then assume that profits will be correspondingly favorable.

> For Michael Dell, as noted earlier, healthy profit potential seemed obvious from the fact that he could easily put a computer together personally and sell it for over four times the cost of parts directly to customers with no advertising except word of mouth and no middlemen.[94]

For many businesses in manufacturing a 50 percent gross margin is healthy. If such a venture will manufacture something, one rough estimate could be that it should wholesale its product for at least twice the cost of labor plus

material. But entrepreneurs tend to thrive (or fail) by being exceptions.

Steve Jobs and Steve Wozniak sold their first computers to the Byte Shop for twice the cost of parts, not including labor.

If the venture makes a product and it is to be sold through an added retail layer, then probably the margin will have to be doubled again to provide for advertising, sales, and distribution. In a software venture, however, the margin should be vastly higher, because it costs almost nothing to produce the product once the code is written. There the problem is one of paying for the code and manual writing and then of getting sales, which may require advertising expenditures.

Margin rules of thumb are very rough, often don't fit a particular industry, and are typically on the low side anyway. If the venture is a store, for instance, the critical number is not margin percentage but rather margin in total dollars per month. The question is often how adequately that margin will cover rent, utilities, and staffing. If a larger investment is required, then profit and elapsed time are probably worth computing.

Profit computations

Using estimates of sales and costs to forecast profits through computation can be done in a variety of ways, ranging from simple to complex. The following example illustrates simple calculation.

> Richard Branson, who would later make more than one fortune as an entrepreneur and founded, among other enterprises, Branson Airlines, suffered from dyslexia and recalled that when he was young, it was "only when I was using real numbers that math made any sense to me." He recalled proposing to his father a venture to breed and sell small birds called budgerigars.
>
> "I worked out the prices, calculating how fast they could breed and how much their food cost, and persuaded my father to build a huge aviary." Writing from his boarding school to his father he asked, "Have you ordered any material we might want for our giant budgerigar cage? I thought our best bet to get the budgerigars at reduced rate would be from Julian Carlyon. I feel that if the shops sold them for 30 shillings, he would get say 17 shil-

---

[94] Dell, *Direct from Dell*.

lings and we could buy them off him for 18 or 19 shillings which would give him a profit and save us the odd 10 shillings per bird. How about it?"

His father complied, and the birds rapidly bred. But after selling to everyone locally, Branson found his aviary was still full. His mother wrote that rats had broken in and eaten them. But in fact she left the cage door open and they escaped. How much profit they actually yielded he did not report. [95]

What Branson did here was compute total margin, the difference between the cost of buying and feeding the birds and how much he could sell them for, and considered that total margin his profit. What he left out was any consideration of other costs a "real" business might have, such as rent and contingency expenses.

Breakeven

The next step beyond margin assessment can be to consider costs that are fixed as well as those that are variable and compute the volume of sales required to cover those fixed costs. If Branson, in the example above, paid rent on the space he used to house the birds, that cost would occur whether he sold any birds or not; rent would have been a fixed cost. Breakeven would have been defined as the amount he would have to sell, in number of birds or amount of money, to cover that fixed cost. Any further margin he earned through yet more sales would be profit, from which he could estimate the upside potential.

Thus breakeven estimation is done by adding up fixed costs of the venture, such as rent, wages, utilities, and advertising, and dividing by the number of cents per sales dollar left after paying variable costs on each unit sold. (Dividing fixed costs by the margin percentage expressed as a decimal fraction accomplishes the same thing.) If the sales level projected in the sales forecast is lower than the sales level needed to break even, then the venture is unlikely to succeed and it is time to move on to some other idea.

If the projected sales level is higher than that needed to break even, then the easy next step is to plug that sales level into the breakeven calculation (multiplying the sales figure by the margin fraction and subtracting fixed costs) to get an estimate of how high profits might be.

But it's easy to be too optimistic in such forecasts. For instance, the impact of competitor moves on sales is hard to foresee and so may be neglected, while at the same time some items of cost are almost certain to be missed, making profits look higher than they should.

David Birch, a former business school professor who started his own company, said he was surprised to learn in doing so that his "variable costs were fixed and fixed costs were variable." For instance, having very few employees, a major percentage drop in sales would be required to justify letting one go, thus his labor costs, normally considered variable in a breakeven analysis, were in fact fixed. And having a small office that was essentially all utilized meant that if sales rose and he had to hire another person, he would have to rent more space, thereby causing his rental expenses, normally considered fixed, to be variable.

Still, because it can be so quick and easy, estimating a linear breakeven can be worth doing to get a rough feel for financial promise of a venture.

Pro forma income statements

More complicated to prepare, but also more realistic and revealing about the relationship between sales and profits, is a pro forma income statement. To prepare it, sales and then cost figures are estimated one time period at a time, such as monthly or yearly. To get profits the costs are subtracted from sales for each of the periods. In these periods the "fixed" costs will not be fixed but will vary month by month, while the variable costs will not necessarily be a constant percentage of sales, but will vary with volume in ways that may reflect volume discounts and other economies of scale.

The approach involves listing all the items of a profit and loss statement, inserting the forecast of sales for each period, and then figuring the costs that will go with those periods. Generally, expenses are much easier to forecast ac-

Breakeven

Pro forma income statements

---

[95] Richard Branson, *Losing My Virginity* (New York: Random House, 1998) p. 30.

curately than sales, although there may be more details to check on. To save time it should help to put the most effort into only those items that represent the largest percentages of sales. For non-cash charges, such as depreciation, it may be practical simply to plan on a fast write-off, because the whole future of the venture is at this point problematic.

Owner compensation

Of personal interest to the founder in this forecast is the level of compensation it can provide him or her as well as what he or she must do to earn it. Will the return from a copy center, bicycle manufacturing, or software company be enough to live on?

Also relevant may be forms of compensation other than those purely financial. What will be learned from trying the venture? How much fun will it be? What are the odds that it might lead to other attractive opportunities? Starting a

venture is like entering an avenue down whose side streets lie contacts, adventures, and opportunities that cannot be discovered any other way than by proceeding. Just what constitutes success and how to gauge it is a question that each prospective founder must answer individually.

Sensitivity analysis

How important variables like income and compensation will vary with changes in key assumptions must also be considered, a process called "sensitivity analysis." With spreadsheet microcomputer programs it is relatively easy to vary the assumptions and see what happens to net cash flow and profits. In what month will the worst cash demand occur, and how much cash will be needed to get through it? How much worse will the need be if hoped-for events, such as collections from customers, are either below expectations or arrive later than anticipated? What is the downside worst case?

4. How much cash will be needed?

Short-cut estimations

Profits alone are not enough for assessing attractiveness. They must be related to the amounts put at risk to attain them. Theoretically, the correct approach for assessing financial attractiveness is to compute an expected return on investment and compare it to other alternative uses for the cash required.

Computing expected return and expected investment calls for making dollar projections of expenditures and revenues on a spreadsheet and then discounting them according to the probability of their coming true. In a more familiar business format, this involves making pro forma forecasts of an income statement, balance sheet, and cash flow statement and then guessing how likely they are to be right. The procedure for this is to work through the statements line by line making estimates of all the items—how much sales will be, when they will occur, when they will be collected, how much must be spent to achieve them, when the bills must be paid, and so forth.

Short-cut estimations

For quicker estimation of investment and return, as with profit forecasting, there are alterna-

tives such as opinions of relevantly experienced people and data from comparable companies.

Three-part simple estimation

Another simple-estimation approach for required investment is to add the sums guessed necessary for: (1) fixed assets, (2) working capital, and (3) losses during start-up.

Fixed assets Start-ups often find ways to minimize investment needed for setting up shop and obtaining equipment, either by outsourcing to suppliers, borrowing, or leasing. But still there may be some money needed to cover such things.

Working capital There will also be cash needs for (1) a bank account, (2) buying inventory, and (3) producing and delivery to customers. Suppliers and workers will want cash right away but customers may not pay for weeks or months.

Losses until profitability arrives Even after customers do pay, the company may lose money on sales for a while. Here the entrepreneur may simply have to guess a number. The longer the losses go on, the greater the investment. (At

Amazon.com losses went on for many years and even then profits were only very small, hardly enough to justify missing what the investment could have earned elsewhere.)

Adding these three main items, at least up to the time when profits are highly likely to occur, can give a first approximation of required start-up investment against which subsequent profits can be judged to guess return on investment (ROI).

Fuller projections

Beyond such simple estimation is the more comprehensive approach of working out full financial statement forecasts.

Pro forma balance sheets

Balance sheet forecasts, like income statement projections, must be done item by item across whatever time periods are chosen, presumably using a typical spreadsheet program.

Some balance sheet items, such as fixed assets and necessary cash balance, may be estimated as lump amounts. If the venture will have inventory, accounts payable and/or accounts receivable, those can be scaled in terms of "days on hand" or percentages of sales. For instance:

- If receivables will on average take one month to collect, then the balance sheet figure for that will be one month's sales. (Watch out for seasonality.)

- If creditors will require payment within one month on average, and if purchased materials amount to about one-third of the venture's selling price, then payables will be about one-third of one month's sales.

- If inventory will turn on average six times per year (in other words, two months' supply of it will be on hand), then the balance sheet figure will equal two months' cost of goods sold. If the company's gross margin is 50 percent, then the figure for inventory will be half of two months' sales revenue, which is one month's sales revenue.

From the pro forma income statement, as described earlier, should come information about sales level, which should guide balance sheet working capital numbers, and also give profits or losses that change retained earnings on the liability side of the sheet. Some figures that can

be hard to estimate include cost/volume shifts, seasonal sales variations, lags in collections, and both leads and lags in payments required. Figuring it can be work.

The "plug" figure to make assets and liabilities of the balance sheet equal each other in total is usually money from outside, either in the form of borrowing or through cash contributed by investors. Working the income and the balance sheet forecasts together may be needed for such smaller corrections as depreciation, tax payments, prepayments, interest payments, and deposits.

The plug is also used for comparing with profits to see what rate of return the venture should generate internally. Trading off debt versus equity can vary the proportion of the return that goes to owners versus lenders. But with that will go a tradeoff of risk at the same time. Higher debt means better return, but at higher risk to owners.

Cash flow forecast

Cash flow figures are usually most important of all, because without cash the business stops. Ultimately what determines financial return is how the cash that's been put in to the venture by its owners compares to the cash that went out to them. Along the way cash flow will determine whether the venture is solvent and able to continue. If the venture is simple enough, a budget using cash flows could be the first set of figures estimated to see whether the venture can be financed.

Regardless of whether cash flow estimation is the first forecasting step or the last one it will be crucially important, not just because it is the ultimate profit measure, but because it can warn in advance of cash shortfalls dooming the venture. Where net cash flow from operations is negative, the notion of *burn rate* is sometimes applied to describe how fast cash is running out or in effect how quickly the venture's cash supply is disappearing in dollars per day, week, month, or year.[96]

The cash flow forecast looks somewhat like an income statement, but with important differences. The top line is similar to sales, but shows only how much cash is collected from sales and when, which is usually later than when the sales occur.

---

[96] Michael Wolff, *Burn Rate* (New York: Simon and Schuster, 1998).

Expenses also may look similar to those of the income statement, but some may show up as paid for immediately, and for others, the payment may lag relative to where they would appear on income statement columns. Unlike an income statement, which does not tell about investments in equipment but only about what is depreciated on them, the cash flow statement shows how much cash is applied to them and when. Also unlike an income statement, it does show cash that is injected into the business from investors or lenders.

This forecast can be developed by following the seven cash flow forecasting steps listed below.

Cash flow forecasting steps

1. **Set up** a spreadsheet, skip a few lines and then list in a column at left the expenditures to be made in setting up the venture: investigation costs; lawyer fees; office supplies; fees for consultants, accountants, or other professionals; money spent on market investigation; sales estimation; design; prototypes; testing; equipment; tooling; producing and selling costs; and so forth.

2. **List** the sales forecast across the top by time period, monthly for at least the first year, later quarterly and perhaps annually.

3. Under the appropriate time points of this top line, **list** the dates when payment for those sales should show up as cash in the bank. For some ventures there may be advance payments on sales. For some the cash may come when the sales are made, as in a retail or service firm. For still others, such as product sales to industrial customers, the cash may not arrive for one or more months after deliveries are made.

4. Under this line **leave a blank** line for cash that will have to be pumped in by owners or lenders.

5. Below the blank line **list** under appropriate dates the payments that the venture will have to make as it gets under way for rent, purchases, wages, other expenses, and taxes. Some suppliers may let the venture wait a while—thirty, sixty, or perhaps ninety or more days—before they pay. But most will want payment either upon the venture's receipt of purchases or in some cases before it receives them. Landlords usually want advance rent payments, for instance.

6. **Subtract** the cash going out from the cash going in to obtain the net cash outflows and inflows.

7. **Add these flows cumulatively** over time and consider how much will have to be added at each time point to keep the company solvent. This shows how the company is faring financially over time. The monthly increments may not be exactly the same amounts as profit month by month, but over time their accumulation should approach accumulated profits. How does the accumulated amount of inflow minus outflow look as a reward for starting the business?

Most ventures lose money initially, and it is important to get a grip on how much that will be, lest the company run out of cash and have to fold before it can really get started. Also initially they usually have to make investments in things like rent prepayment, equipment purchases, set-up of facilities, and possibly development of products. In the case of this last item, biotechnology companies are an extreme example, many of them losing money for ten years or more before sales revenues allow either profitability or positive cash flow.

Graphically, this is illustrated by plotting either profits or cash flow from operations versus time, as shown in the "hockey stick" or "J-Curve" graph of Exhibit 3b-4.

This diagram illustrates that typically a venture loses money or burns cash initially while it attempts to gain sales and move toward positive cash inflow and profitability from operations. If things go well, sales build up, customers start paying their bills, and inflow moves upward, eventually becoming positive along with profits.

Exhibit 3b-4 The "J" or "Hockey Stick" curve

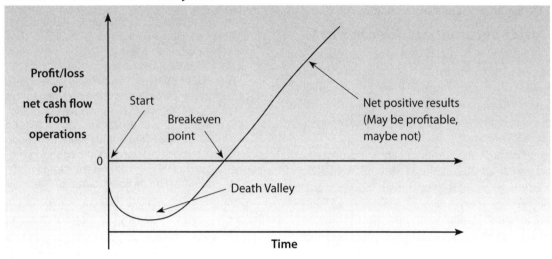

5. Go further or not?

Once complete, the cash flow and balance sheet exhibits will show investments required, while the income statements will show profit levels. The profits can then be divided by investments to compute return on investment (ROI). Venture capitalists typically require rates on the order of 30 percent per year and more. Other investors may accept less, but almost surely will want a return well above 10 percent to 15 percent for a start-up venture. This return, moreover, should be generated on a scale of invest-

ment that justifies the time and worry needed to work out and live with the venture deal.

A set of scales that might be used, depending on the hoped-for magnitude of the particular venture, for evaluating financial promise is shown in Exhibit 3b-5. As with previous similar scales, this one can be used first for rating what are deemed to be significant dimensions of financial promise for the venture, which may be different from those in the example above. Then the ratings can be written in. Then creative thought can

Exhibit 3b-5 Rating financial promise of the product or service

Dimension of merit	Best rating 5	Actual rating 1-5	Worst rating 1
Sales in 5 years	< $25M	_____	> $1 B
Sales growth	< 10% per year	_____	> 100% per year (for 5 years)
Gross margin	< 30%	_____	> 50%
Profit after tax	< 10%, fragile	_____	> 20%, robust
Asset intensity	Low sales/assets (<)	_____	High sales/assets (>)
Capital requirements	High, tough to fund	_____	Low, fundable
Time to Breakeven	< 1 year	_____	> 3 years
ROI	< 15%	_____	> 25%
Production costs	Lo margin, Hi fixed costs	_____	High margin, low fixed costs
Production assets	High asset requirements	_____	Low asset requirements

be applied to the question of what changes in the venture might warrant higher ratings.

Upside potential and downside risk

Alternative financial scenarios worth checking are both downside risk as well as upside potential of the venture. How much will be lost if the venture fails, how much will be recoverable and how hard will it be to recover any salvage value?

What happens if some of these numbers are off target can be explored through sensitivity analysis by preparing optimistic and pessimistic versions. Lowering sales estimates and raising expense estimates will push profit estimates down and the reverse will push them up in the forecast. Departure of reality from the forecast toward either lower sales or higher sales can cause the company to run out of cash. How fast and by how much should be tested with alternative assumptions.

Just going ahead

If the needed investment for start-up, which would include money and other resources that must be risked to make the venture go, as well as unpaid effort the founders put into it, is relatively small, the best test of attractiveness may be simply to go ahead, start the business, and if it fails write it off. Presumably, this would be done on as small a scale as practicable, figuring that if it shows promise more investment will be warranted, and if it does not the loss can be written off as education or entertainment.

The simplest case perhaps, is a service that risks only time in return for cash. Retailing can also be simple and low risk if the inventory is easy to liquidate at cost and only the rent (on a short-term lease with permission to sublet?) is at risk.

> Bill Lear, who would later develop the first car radio that could operate without separate batteries, the first automatic aircraft landing system, and the Lear Jet, was able to obtain his radio education without any cash outlay. Some of his learning came from the library and some from a stint in the Navy. Broke and out of work, he joined the Navy in 1920 to become a seaman radio technician.

> The next year he resigned and took other jobs, first as a Western Union operator and then in sales and repairs for a radio store, helping customers pick out sets or parts for building their own. He earned lodging by teaching his landlord's son about radios.

> Then Julius Buerkin, a wealthy customer, proposed they become partners in a new radio store in Quincy, Illinois, with Buerkin as president providing the money and Lear running it. Within two years Lear had sold out his share to Buerkin for $600, but not before he had begun to demonstrate technical originality in the design of circuits, antennas, and an early car radio.[97]

In this example there was not likely much need for tedious financial forecasting. Lear could quickly estimate from experience how much it would cost to stock the store. The rent was known and utilities probably low. There was no need for the store to finance receivables because customers would pay cash. And Buerkin, who was wealthy anyway, could doubtless provide whatever slack was needed to cover possible oversights. Attractiveness and financial confidence in the situation were likely generated by the fact that the radio industry was just entering explosive growth at the time. Radio manufacturers could not meet demand and in the stores people were waiting in line to buy sets and parts. There was no need for substantial capital investment. Lear's knowledge and ingenuity presumably provided competitive strength relative to similar stores.

But Lear's next venture provided support for the opposite case.

> Now 22 years old, Lear applied the stake provided from sales of his first venture to starting another one. This time he set up shop in his living room, repairing radios and designing new ones. Soon he moved to a rented basement shop downtown and carried on. But the venture failed. Why the expenses were too high relative to the sales is not clear, but he ran out of money within a few months, and also out of credit because he hadn't paid his bills. He and his wife packed up their Ford and left town, moving from Quincy to Chicago where he would soon undertake further ventures.

Whether financial forecasting would have saved the business can only be speculated. Lear

---

[97] Richard Rashke, *Stormy Genius* (Boston: Houghton Mifflin, 1985) p. 16.

continued throughout his life to soar and crash in a series of ventures.

Personal needs

Something all these forecasting approaches leave out is how much the founder and possibly others who might have quit their jobs to work in the start-up may have to spend personally to live on while starting the business. This too needs to be taken into consideration, although perhaps not by formal analysis, as part of assessing investment required by the business and whether the profit prospects are sufficient to justify it.

Finally, not only money is at risk. Family and business relationships, personal career, learning benefits, education from experience, new contacts, and glimpses of other opportunities can all be part of what comes with the venture and are probably worth considering by each entrepreneur on a personal basis.

Accept, refine, table, or reject?

How much analysis is enough? Successively deeper penetrations in deciding whether to improve further or drop the venture could include:

1. **Accept** this idea and move ahead to implement it.
2. **Keep checking** further aspects of this idea in successively greater depth to reach a verdict.
3. **Table** this idea for now and consider it a real option. Work on other ideas and maybe come back to this one later.
4. **Reject** this one and concentrate all processing capacity on either pursuing other ideas already found or seeking out still more ideas to check.

If the idea is to be rejected, then the sooner the better, so as to move on to minimize resource drain.

Exercises

Text discussion questions

1. If any financial forecast for a venture is likely bound to be wrong, why do it?
2. Explain which estimated, as opposed to calculated, number in a venture financial forecast will probably be hardest to estimate and why. Under what conditions would that one be easy, and then which would be hardest?
3. What are probable causes of the rankings in Exhibits 3b-1, -2, and -3 being the way they are and different from each other?
4. In what ways might an entrepreneur's expert script change through experience in forecasting for a series of ventures? (Base your answer on either what you see as your own script or that of some other individual whom you identify.)

Case questions

Case 3B-1 Luhrs and Williams

1. What industry are Janet and Renee entering and how attractive is it? Explain.
2. How profitable, in dollars, does their venture seem likely to become?
3. How could their financial forecasting methods be improved?
4. If assigned as part of a student team to help them, what would your work plan be?

Case 3B-2 Knight brothers (A)

1. Entrepreneurs must work in an unknown time frame, the future. This case presents, as a somewhat unknown time frame, the long past, making it a "back to the future" challenge.
2. Why might a venture like the Knight Brothers are considering work versus not work at its time and place?
3. What are potential weak spots in the venture and how might they be checked and/or fixed?
4. If the Knights wanted to refine their sales forecast, what steps could they take to do that?
5. List and describe actions the Knight brothers should take next and why.

Portfolio page possibilities

Page 3B-1 Breakeven
1. Work out as best you can an estimate of the breakeven point in sales dollars per month for one of your venture ideas, taking care to state your assumptions and how you came up with them as well as giving references to any outside data sources you may have used.
2. Include a statement of steps you might take in order to refine this estimate if you had time and resources to apply to that task.

Page 3B-2 Pro forma financials
1. Do the same as for portfolio page 3B-1 above, but for pro forma financial statements instead of breakeven.
2. Having done that, plot profit versus sales and net cash flow versus sales to identify the profit and cash flow breakeven sales levels respectively.
3. Footnote the data sources you used, particularly for estimating sales and gross margin, and especially identifying individuals, if any, who helped with estimating.

Page 3B-3 Upside potential
1. List an upper bound and a best guess total market for your product or service early on, making clear your reasoning and data sources used.
2. Estimate the upside profit and ROI based on the above.

Page 3B-4 Design improvement
Forecast the improvements that should be possible in terms of the performance specifications of your product or service. To the extent practical within the one-page limit, describe what it would take to make them happen.

Term Projects

Venture history
1. To what extent were sales breakeven and financial statements forecasted before starting and how was it done?
2. Were any alternate scenarios developed?
3. What were the greatest cash drain categories and how were they anticipated?
4. What, if any, unanticipated costs or savings arose?
5. How did the actual total profit and ROI compare to expectations and what produced the greatest gaps between expectations and reality?

Venture planning guide
1. Prepare pro forma financial forecasts for the first two years of your venture and compare them with the predicted performance of its three most threatening competitors.
2. Identify three start-ups comparable, on dimensions that you specify, to yours. Then indicate what performance yours should expect compared to theirs.
3. Prepare an estimate of the value that you have created thus far in working on your venture. For how much would you sell your rights to it? Who should most likely have any interest in buying and why?

Part 4

PROJECTING

The first chapter in this section will treat fuller design of the venture itself, as opposed to what it will offer customers, and the second will take up how to present that design effectively to different audiences in the form of a venture plan.

A venture can be designed much as can a product, a vacation, a military campaign, or any other human creation. Its design can be by default or deliberate choice and is usually some combination of both. Events in the commercial marketplace continually demonstrate that strategic design matters. Hence designing the venture, what all it will consist of, what it will offer, how it will compete and what it should accomplish for its various stakeholders is a part of venturing worth examination.

Whom to regard as the competition and how to deal with them initially and over time will influence the venture's design. Decisions about what variety to offer in the product or service, how to price it, and present it to the market will become part of the venture's strategy.

Careful venture design should help crystallize what the venture is to become and how, even though changes occur in the arena where it competes. What strengths to capitalize on and what weaknesses must be coped with will figure into this projection. One way of casting the projection is as a paragraph-style vision statement of the company as it should exist in the future.

Another is to characterize it in terms of a business model description that is elaborated from an initial conception of how the venture is supposed to make money through buying, producing, and selling into a series of choices about different facets of the business: its position in the value chain, its approach to customers, and its goals for satisfying stakeholders.

When the design is to be communicated to others, a written plan and oral delivery preparation may not only be in order, but may be absolutely necessary. Done well, a formally presented plan may help the venture recruit needed information, financing, and cooperation.

How to do this is a function of the nature of the venture, the make-up of the audience and what effect it is aimed to have upon the audience. Both written and oral presentations may be called for and worth the effort to perform well.

Although computer programs are available to help map out, write, and present the business plan, it is important that they not become a substitute for hard thinking about it. The plan is bound to be "wrong" no matter how it is done because it will inevitably be built upon incomplete information and before it can be implemented, the marketplace conditions on which it was predicated will have changed.

What will be of more value then will be reflexes developed by thinking the plan out, not by having a computer think it out. Having thought it out should have left the entrepreneur with memories of alternative paths of development that were considered but rejected and what combinations of impacts they might have had under different conditions. As the actual future introduces new and possibly surprising circumstances, some of that prior thinking and exploration should help produce better and faster rethinking of decisions to respond to the changed conditions.

CHAPTER 4A – Business Design

Topics

1. Competitive arena
2. Venture design elements
3. Initial strengths
4. Size implications
5. Longer run

Checkpoints

a. What makes up the competitive arena of a new venture?
b. Explain differences between business design and product or service design.
c. How may competition in the future differ from that at time of start-up?
d. What elements make up the competitive strategy of a venture?
e. What are the relative advantages of new versus established companies?
f. How is the strategy of a new venture to be described?
g. Define and explain the meaning and purpose of a business model.

How the design of a venture and the game plan or strategy by which it operates are developed is partly a matter of thinking and partly one of experimentation. These two activities must take place in that order, because thinking is required to determine what the experiments will be and to assess the significance of the errors or successes and decide what to do about them.

1. Competitive arena

Earlier discussion noted that odds of survival and growth vary with industry. Both customers and competitors change with time, and along with them both odds of success and a need to adapt for survival. Part of designing the venture should therefore be anticipation of how the market and competition may change. Four types of competition to consider, which may or may not have shown up on an Opponent Companies Grid thus far but should appear on one that is more future-oriented, are the following:

Existing look-alikes The venture may be motivated by other than having a new product or service, such as to expand supply of one that already exists. Or, its justification may be to offer better service or lower prices. But then existing businesses already offering that product or service may respond by lowering price, something to anticipate in design of the venture.

Copycats If the venture's product is new and begins to catch on, there will likely soon be imitators. Even though there may not be enough market to share, imitators unaware of that may enter and foolishly lose money, causing the new venture to lose as well. If it is first to market, the venture may thereby gain some advantages. But copycats have other advantages. They can wait to see whether the venture's approach will work. They can watch for weaknesses and avoid them. And copycatting will probably cost less, typically about one third.

Substitutes Something else is always there to attract a potential customer's money. Airplanes, buses, cars, and trains are very different but overlap in functions and hence can substitute for each other. Frozen dinners compete with fast foods and weldments compete with castings. The substitute for buying a new car may

Industry
development
patterns

Market
adoption
sequences

Future
scenarios

be to buy a used boat, or install a swimming pool. Hence, in considering what the competition for a new venture's product or service will be, some thought should be given to deflecting customer money from substitutes.

Leapfrogs The most worrisome competitive risk, however, may be that some other company or venture will jump ahead of the venture's product or service with one that is better.

The last of these particularly illustrates the need to think ahead strategically, which is of course what competitors will also be doing.

> One of the great success stories of Silicon Valley was Sun Microsystems, which in the mid-eighties upstaged microcomputer servers with much more powerful and higher-priced, although physically similar, servers called workstations. What let the company do so was that it developed its own more-powerful chips and software to go with them that would allow faster processing of more data.
>
> This was a strategic choice that paid off handsomely. But by then microcomputer chips advanced to where the workstations were matched in performance by conventional machines. Not only did this take away the ability of Sun to price its machines higher, it also left Sun matched by both conventional and cheaper software from Microsoft and free shareware from Linux. The value of Sun's shares dropped from $64.31 in September 2000 to $3.50 three years later.[98]

The issue is not whether Sun was right or wrong, but rather illustrates the fact that some decisions have consequences that can take time to play out and be difficult to rearrange along the way.

Industry development patterns

Customer populations take different forms. Government buying is fairly predictable in activities like road and dam building, but occurrence of a war or other disaster can cause rapid rise in buying followed later by precipitous drop. Fads similarly rise and fall rapidly. So a fad-bound venture must be ready to move in quickly and then get out before the market bubble either bursts from entry of too many competitors or simply evaporates.

Market adoption sequences

A pattern is discernable in high-technology product industries, such as pocket calculators, followed by microcomputers, followed by cell phones and hand-held computers, as well as the industries that support them, of adoption through a cascade of different user groups, beginning with "techies" and "show-offs," each of which for its own reasons will pay high to get the latest and greatest new technology. Following these groups come other sequentially later groups of adopters, the early majority, late majority, and the laggards, whose interests become progressively more utilitarian and cost-conscious until finally the products become low-margin commodities. Moreover, the shift from small to gigantic market can come quickly. Hence, it can be easy for a start-up pioneering the technology to be swept aside by later-entering companies better equipped to operate on larger scales.

Design of a venture to start with one of these groups as its customers for some new product and then to continue selling it to the later and much larger groups, calls for a major shift in both marketing method and operational scale, something that is very difficult if not impossible, according to Geoffrey Moore.[99] Therefore, early planning for the venture needs to anticipate this possibility, lest it be wiped out when a boom comes. The injunction from Moore is to focus first on one small market niche and then another, always becoming dominant niche by niche, and not allowing any other company to do the same within the sub-niches. Based upon study of the development of high technology cases, particularly in Silicon Valley, he says this can provide beachheads upon which to expand, possibly by forming alliances with larger companies.

Future scenarios

Some industries stay technologically fairly stable. Corn flakes, doorknockers, auto insurance sales, bus lines, auto repair shops, gardening, and housecleaning services don't change much over time. But other industries change

---

[98]Pui-Wing Tam, "Cloud over Sun Microsystems: Plummeting Computer Prices," *Wall Street Journal*, October 16, 2003, p. 1.
[99]Geoffrey A. Moore, *Crossing the Chasm* (New York: Harper Collins, 1991).

drastically. Sears' huge catalog operation was wiped out by the Internet, although Penney's was not. Microcomputers have become vastly faster and more powerful while at the same time dropping in price. TV cut in on movies. Color TV wiped out black and white TV. Videotapes cut in on TV. DVDs cut in on videotapes. Used CDs cut in on CDs.

Innovation S-curves

Technologies seem to follow what are called "S-curve" patterns of sales, where the initial sales growth rate of a new technology is slow as the market begins. That is followed by a steep rise to much greater volume as the market expands, after which the curve starts to level off toward its top. Meanwhile a second S-curve, that of a new competing technology has begun and grows, taking away sales from the old technology depicted on the first S-curve. Typically, incumbent companies of the old technology fight the new technology's encroachment. But eventually they lose. When transistors were introduced for electronic circuits by newcomers, companies that produced vacuum tubes, the older technology, improved their vacuum tubes by making them smaller, more reliable, and more energy-efficient. But before long the transistors, because they were still far better in all these respects, triumphed, and vacuum tube circuits disappeared.

This possible pattern of development too is something to be considered in planning for a new venture. Not that it can be a science. The problem in thinking about S-curves is that they become sharply definable only in hindsight. But new technologies eventually will come to eclipse whatever the venture begins with.

Part of the job of designing the business is to imagine and consider how new technologies may obsolete the present way of doing things. One way to do this is to read about technology in relevant magazines and Web sites. Another is to talk with experienced people in the industry as opportunity can be found, possibly at trade shows. A further step in planning can be to write one or more imagined scenarios of the industry's future, with the venture as a participant and other new ventures entering.

2. Venture design elements

Major elements to consider in refining design of the business include (1) the competitive arena in which the business will operate, (2) how that arena can be expected to change in the future, (3) the advantages and vulnerabilities that the venture will have, (4) what the purposes are that its founders, and after them its other stakeholders, want to serve, and consequently (5) what its mission should be, and (6) how it should be carried out as the venture develops into a business and matures.

But also, because nobody can fully foresee the future, designing the business must include willingness to make learn-as-you-go changes as experience reveals that some initial strategic suppositions happen to be wrong.

The initial ice cream venture strategy of Ben and Jerry's was to make ice cream and sell it in a scoop shop. They sought out a small town in New England where there was no other such shop and where there was a relatively young population they thought would buy. However, as Jerry recalled, "Ben and I had no long-term strategic plan for the business."

To reduce capital needs they sought out used equipment, occasionally making diversions to buy things that had nothing to do with the business whatever.

Just before they set up with their newly acquired equipment, another ice cream shop opened in the town they had picked. Consequently, they sought out another town and began again to set up.

Selling through their store turned out not to be profitable and they sought other customers. Soon they were both selling through the store and also carrying bulk ice cream to restaurants in the vicinity with a used truck they had bought. The company still lost money.

During trips to the restaurants they noticed mom 'n pop grocery stores along the way, from which they also began soliciting sales. This channel, it turned out, made the difference that let them become profitable. They thus advanced to larger volume, expanded territorial coverage, and applied in their advertising a theme of social responsibility, which caught on in a market for gourmet ice cream that turned out to be a popular trend of the times, a trend that other gourmet producers, such as Häagen-Dazs, also rode to success.

— • —

A novelty-product manufacturing start-up with three founders was tracked by Kao[100] as it grew to three additional full-time employees and four part-time staff selling to retailers. Kao's intention was to test the theory of renowned economist Joe S. Bain who had postulated that there were generally three types of entry barriers from incumbents: (1) economies of scale, (2) absolute cost advantages, and (3) product differentiation. Other possible barriers considered by Kao but found not to be a problem for this particular start-up were (4) governmental red tape, (5) shortage of equity capital, and (6) bank credit.

What did turn out to be significant barriers were

a. Access to department store and chain store buyers. These were found to have established buying relationships that made it hard for a new supplier to gain entry. They appeared disinterested in dealing particularly with a small start-up firm.

b. Suppliers not interested in providing small quantities of raw materials to the start-up. When they did so, typically they would charge more for the small quantities than they would have for large quantities.

Consequently, the start-up found itself obliged to adopt a set of policies arrived at through experimentation to get around these barriers. These included the following:

a. For product differentiation, what worked was to reach for high quality, incorporate some unique features of design, and stress that the product was domestically made.

b. For sales channels, in place of chain and department stores, a focus on small retail shops whose owners did the buying.

c. Sales representatives, it was found, could obtain helpful sales and product redesign information by asking certain questions of these buyers during sales calls.

d. Cost cutting was enhanced through imaginative searching that resulted, for instance, in using discarded cardboard boxes from stores to package shipments.

e. A continuing search process was adopted to find and change to the most economical suppliers.

f. One partner was assigned specific responsibility for quality control on every shipment.

g. All purchases of production machinery had to be approved by all partners.

These examples illustrate that each venture in its own way may have to shift and adapt as it works out a game plan and policies to succeed. These had to start with something, then search, rethink, and be flexible enough to make changes. Part of the value of thinking ahead can be to anticipate need for flexibility in order to make such changes.

Business models

At a general level, planning for a venture can be seen as moving from (1) discovery of an opportunity through (2) generation and refinement of ideas for exploiting it, (3) screening to assure that the ideas merit implementation, and (4) working out a business design for putting that implementation into effect. Along the way will be loops of evaluation where ideas are rejected and others take their place to move forward. Also along the way will be further elaboration of how the retained ideas will be enacted.

Simple model

The most simplistic business model is one that tries to explain, by describing what it will spend cash on and where revenue will come from, how the venture should make money. Emphasis is on economics of how the company is supposed to make profit.

Somewhat different is its *value proposition*, which tells how a customer wins. Both are different from the game plan or strategy of the company, which tells how the company will deploy and re-deploy its resources both in taking initiative and in responding to competition. It is also different from the company's future vision of itself and its activities, which is to say what assets and activities it will consist of and what they will look like, including what it hopes will be its image in the eyes of others.

---

[100]Raymond W.Y. Kao, "Entry Barriers and New Venture Strategies," *Journal of Small Business—Canada*, vol. 1, no. 2.

Exhibit 4a-1 Morris' business model's six core topics

1. *What does the venture offer to create value?*
2. *For whom is the value created?*
3. *What is the venture's main internal source of competitive advantage?*
4. *How does the venture differentiate itself from competitors?*
5. *How does the venture make money?*
6. *What ambitions of its managers and its investors does the venture aim to fulfill?*

Extended model

In between the most simplistic business model and a complex totality is the alternative of a model more elaborate than simply "how the business will make money." Six components, including that one, for a fuller model have been proposed by Michael Morris and are listed in Exhibit 4a-1.

A further elaborated worksheet for applying Morris' model appears as Appendix 4a-1. The application is relatively simple to perform and therefore limited, but not a bad place to start. Any model adopted at the start is bound to change as it comes into play amid the complex, not-fully anticipatable, and changing realities of the industrial marketplace, which also has its unpredictabilities but should be kept in mind and under observation from the start of serious planning.

Other facets to imagine in designing the business are its functional areas: marketing, engineering, finance, operations, accounting, and human resources. Each of these sub-areas can be considered at different levels of detail, ranging from overall to fine-grained, and each should be viewable as necessary for survival and prosperity of the business. In a sense the functional areas represent links of a chain, all of which must coordinate with the others. Designing them to operate as an interrelated whole can become complex as well as crucial, because failure of the wrong one at the wrong time can cause the business to miss major opportunities or possibly fail.

Business specifications

As with a product or service, design for a business may helpfully include specifications for how it should perform and what it should accomplish. Whether explicitly stated or not, it should be possible to read into the venture's development an implicit mission to which it is dedicated and how it should move forward on that mission. Some illustrations are as follows.

Mission statements

Company mission statements, which are often easy to find in their annual reports, can vary from a short paragraph to over a page. How they may vary in content and format is illustrated below by excerpts from the reports of Connor Peripherals versus Ben and Jerry's.

Connor Peripherals Connor's mission is to be the leading supplier of computer storage solutions by providing a comprehensive line of disk drives, tape drives, disk arrays, and data protection and storage management software for the entry, value, performance, and portable market segments.[101]

Ben and Jerry's Ben and Jerry's is dedicated to the creation and demonstration of a new corporate concept of linked prosperity. Our mission consists of three interrelated parts:

Product Mission: To make, distribute, and sell the finest quality all-natural ice cream …

Social Mission: To operate the company in a way that actively recognizes the central role that business plays in the structure of society by …

Economic Mission: To operate the company on a sound financial basis of …[102]

Each of these missions was further elaborated in the company's 1993 annual report.

Vision statements

Somewhat different from what the company aims to do is what future state or condition it aims to reach. Sometimes these two run together, as in the above statement from Connor Peripherals. Other times they may be distinct,

---

[101]Jeffrey Abrahams, *The Mission Statement Book* (Berkeley, CA: Ten Speed Press, 1995) p. 188.
[102]Abrahams, *Mission Statement*, p. 125.

as illustrated by the following two vision statement examples.

Continental Airlines To be recognized as the best airline in the industry by our customers, employees and shareholders.[103]

Microsoft A computer on every desk and in every home.[104]

Both mission and vision statements

Still other companies have at times chosen to make both mission and vision statements, as illustrated by the following.

Wendy's mission statement Deliver total quality.

Wendy's vision statement To be the customer's restaurant of choice and the employer of choice.[105]

Goals

A goal, like a mission statement, describes an accomplishment to be pursued, except that it is narrower. A mission statement or a vision statement may include any number of goals to be pursued, perhaps indefinitely; Ben and Jerry's mission includes several goals.

For the founders

Founders also have their goals in connection with the venture. Some may be coincident with business goals of the venture. Others may be personal to the founder, such as to pursue an idea, find adventure, make more money, or be more independent.

For other stakeholders

Each of the other stakeholders in the venture will also have goals, and part of the entrepreneur's job is to help in their accomplishment through effective management.

Consequent objectives

Objectives are similar to goals, except that they may be more specific and concretely attainable. A goal listed by Ben and Jerry's is to operate on a sound financial basis. An objective making this more concrete might be to maintain a two-to-one minimum ratio of current assets to current liabilities.

Milestones

Particularly in new ventures there are goals and objectives that advance dramatically with time. These advances represent milestones for gauging progress, and may be set either as calendar dates or as sequences. For managers, these show whether progress is happening as intended. Investors sometimes use them as decision points for either justifying or not the injection of more financial support.

Strategies, tactics, and policies

The moves a company makes, or the game plan it follows in pursuit of its goals and objectives, comprise its strategy. It can be flexible or rigid, thought-out or impulsive, effective or not. Thinking strategy out is likely to make it more effective.

Strategy can easily be seen in many companies. Harley-Davidson hangs on to nostalgia and tradition by retaining familiar features. It also keeps advancing technology and performance, albeit behind the Japanese cycle makers, who for their part started imitating the styling of Harley-Davidson when its strategy worked, not only in the United States but also in Japan. Wal-Mart builds big stores in relatively cheap locations and offers low prices through buying the biggest volumes. Starbucks emphasizes high-quality coffee, which is less simple than it might seem, plus familiar branding and, in most of its stores, a familiar ambience designed to be a third place to tarry in, along with work and home.

Also part of strategy are choices an enterprise makes on product line breadth, marketing mix, target market definition, degree of operational integration, motivation systems, and virtually all other conscious patterned decisions of the company.

Start-ups that get strategy wrong can hit major disappointments along the way, typically with less visibility because they have not yet reached a size where many notice them, although some have been fairly spectacular. *Inc.* magazine each year produces lists of hundreds

---

[103]Abrahams, *Mission Statement*, p. 191.
[104]Abrahams, *Mission Statement*, p. 396.
[105]Abrahams, *Mission Statement*, p. 590.

of top-performing new companies, but the lists change over time because some companies move up out of the start-up and small categories, while others, notwithstanding their early spectacular success, fail and drop out of the picture, as the following did.

Iron Computer—To remedy the destruction of microcomputers caused by operating in harsh environments such as hot restaurant kitchens and gritty machine shops, John Opincar, a software executive, designed a new airtight, temperature-controlled machine using mainly off-the-shelf components. With $50,000 from family and friends he formed a new company, Diehard, Inc., in 1993 to produce and sell it. Development was held up for nearly three months and valuable capital was consumed by legal action from Sears, Roebuck and Company in late 1994, claiming trademark infringement on its automobile battery. By mid-1995, with the new name Iron, the company had suspended operations to raise more capital and refine the product design. By early 1997, the plan was to raise cash for expanded product and at the same time generate publicity for the product through introduction of the first-ever fully registered stock offering on the Web. Costs of obtaining legal permission for the offering from the Securities and Exchange Commission, however, consumed more time and cash. When approval came for a 90-day offering period, the company started selling shares through its Web site. But instead of the $1.5 million to $9 million sought, the company was able to sell only $300,000 worth before time ran out. A subsequent attempt at a conventional public offering also failed, and in December 1998 the company entered Chapter 7 bankruptcy, owing approximately $250,000 to some 100 creditors. The few machines that had been sold at $4,000 each by the company apparently worked fine.[106] The last Yahoo entry for Iron Computer was May 1997.

Sometimes while some companies fail, others in the same industries and with similar products go on to success. Wrong choices in subsidiary elements making up the companies' strategies would seem most to deserve credit for the failures. Iron Computer management apparently tried to operate on a shoestring basis,

emphasizing the product rather than formalities like trademark research and advance planning. Such strategic choices sometimes work, but this time they simply did not.

Tactics

Whereas generally strategy is broad and longer run in perspective, tactics are thought of as being moves made by the enterprise to carry out strategy, that are smaller in scope and shorter in run. Coupon specials, bundling software with hardware, offering frequent flier miles or special customization, and outsourcing customer service to India are examples of tactics. Here are some others.

- Printer companies sell printers cheap to make money on cartridges and paper.
- Companies swap advertising tie-ins—moviemakers get free cars for showing them.
- Technology companies sometimes swap patent rights.
- Search engine companies sell position on the list of companies displayed.
- Money-back coupon offers let purchases be low-cost or free because many consumers don't return the coupons.
- Software companies sometimes give their programs free, and then sell upgrades.
- Most U.S. companies, at least in consumer products, offer money-back guarantees.

Policies

Rules for action to carry out strategy and tactics are policies. Thus a company will have policies for pricing, returns, quality control, employee vacations, advertising style, hiring criteria, direction of engineering efforts, and any number of other activities that are part of the cooperation needed to operate the organization effectively and efficiently over time.

Strategic bets

Although every venture is its own special case and entrepreneurs many times win by exceptions to the rules, there do seem to be some strategic choices that are generally better than others. More likely to win are strategies that (1) center on intelligence about individual customers, (2) capitalize

---

[106]Emily Barker, "Maker of Rugged PC's Crumbles in IPO Bid," *Inc.*, June 1999, p. 25.

on competence that favorably distinguishes the venture from its competitors, (3) focus sharply on a niche in the market, (4) aim for high share of the served market, (5) differentiate from competitors based on having higher quality rather than lower price, (6) invest in proprietary rights such as intellectual property, and (7) give the lead entrepreneur strong control and not many co-owners to deal with.

Less likely to win are strategies that (1) simply copy competitors, (2) go head to head against larger competitors, (3) try to follow one major breakthrough by pouring major resources into pursuit of another one, (4) try to integrate vertically, (5) try to advance on a broad frontier of market or technology, or (6) try to prevail through persistence on an idea that is not working.

SWOT check

A tool long and widely used for review of strategy is SWOT analysis, which stands for Strengths, Weaknesses, Opportunities, and Threats. The process involves thinking up lists of the most important aspects of each of these attributes, ranking and comparing them, then deciding how to make the most of those that are positive and minimize the detractions of those that are negative. A limitation of the approach is that it is too easy to generate the lists without thinking about them hard enough to gain true insights about how to render real improvement and avoid overlooking mistakes. A remedy can be to combine the SWOT check by thinking about strategy of the venture using other thinking tools, such as thought modes, failure mode analysis, creativity techniques, scenarios, and business models as well.

3. Initial strengths

In addition to help and encouragement from others such as suppliers, friends, family, and a network of entrepreneurs and stakeholders, strengths a start-up may have for breaking into its competitive arena should include:

- Something better to offer customers
- A contract with a customer
- Special "ins" with customers
- Advantageous location
- Licenses or working agreements
- Patents, trademarks, copyrights
- Lower price
- Harder-working participants
- A CEO who personally sells
- A better business model

Against some competitors the new venture may have the advantage of surprise, being able to line up customers, saturate sales channels, or lock up key suppliers or assets before those competitors can react. For that reason, the founders may seek to start unobtrusively. Others may choose to begin with a bang and garner customers, suppliers, and other collaborators as fast as possible to put competitors behind from the beginning.

To other competitors the venture may be essentially invisible until it becomes strong enough to impact them. Or it could be that even without these advantages the venture can prevail because its something better is so powerful, or its competitors are too slack to see it or to attack it even if they do see it.

Distinctive competence

What it is better at than other enterprises is sometimes referred to as a venture's distinctive competence. It may be special expertise of the founder or other key people connected to the venture, possibly in combination with other start-up strengths noted above. Identifying, utilizing, focusing on, preserving, and strengthening this should be of very high priority.

Sustainable competitive advantage

An elusive but desirable attribute to seek in designing a venture is some sort of sustainable competitive advantage. It may be competence or property, such as a patent or secret process. The problem is that such advantages tend to be frail when determined competitors attack them, by designing around patents, developing better processes of their own, or ganging up to marshal and apply greater resources. Paradoxically, the most enduring advantage may be something ephemeral, namely the customers' positive perception of the company's prior performance, reputation, or brand. Competitive advantage must be present to begin with and sustained by replacement if its initial basis runs out.

Pricing

Setting prices in a new venture poses questions, options, and dilemmas much the same as in established firms, except that the starting point is fresh. Some questions to consider are the following:

1. Are there competitive prices to be met?
2. What price will cover incremental costs?
3. How fast will a cream skimming (high initial) price attract competitors? Will a lower price dissuade them from trying to enter?
4. Will a lower price convey an image of cheapness and make it impossible to price higher?
5. How will customers feel later about what they paid?
6. What will the price/sales volume curve probably look like?

Although scientific methods can help explore some aspects of pricing, there is no science for determining prices themselves. Some ways to obtain information that may be helpful in an inevitably judgmental pricing process:

■ **Gather** information on competitors' prices and how they have changed relative to each other and over time.

■ **Compute** carefully what it will cost the venture to produce and sell what it produces.

■ **Ask** selected people in a focus group and/or survey what they think would be appropriate prices, how much they would pay, and what quality image different prices might convey.

■ **Ask** suppliers, agents, wholesalers, trade associations, and other members of the industry for their opinions on appropriate pricing.

■ **Plan** to experiment with different levels of price to determine what will work best, remembering that it will probably be easier to lower prices than to raise them, and that sooner or later competition will arise.

Price-cutting may only reduce margin, and possibly even imply lower quality without increasing sales, so unless there is some clear benefit for the company, the safest rule probably is don't cut price. Studies of the Strategic Planning Institute (PIMS) and others, suggest that the highest ROI correlates positively for market leaders with selling high-quality offerings and pricing them correspondingly high.[107]

But it is also possible to identify ventures where low price was a powerful advantage in getting started. One example is that of Michael Dell, whose core strategy was to eliminate the middleman and pass the savings along to customers by pricing lower. An earlier entrepreneur who used price-cutting as a key element was Henry Ford, who said:

> Our policy is to reduce the price, extend the operations, and improve the article. You will note that the reduction of price comes first. We have never considered any costs as fixed. Therefore, we first reduce the price to the point where we believe more sales will result. Then we go ahead and try to make the prices. We do not bother about costs. The new price forces the costs down. The more usual way is to take the costs and then determine the price; and although that method may be scientific in the narrow sense, it is not scientific in the broad sense…. Although one may calculate what cost is, and of course all our costs are carefully calculated, no one knows what a cost ought to be. One of the ways of discovering is to name a price so low as to force everybody in the place to highest efficiency. The low price makes everybody dig for profits.

This, said futurist George Gilder, "showed that high profits come from giving, through low prices and high wages, rather than from gouging for what the traffic will bear. This discovery is the moral core of capitalism."[108]

Discount shopping centers, including Wal-Mart, got their start by locating in lower rent areas, buying in larger volumes, eliminating frills, and passing along the savings of these moves to customers in the form of lower prices. By using low pricing, a venture may be able in effect to buy market share, which will increase its volume and from that reap savings from

---

[107]Robert D. Buzzell and Bradley T. Gale, *The PIMS Principles* (New York: The Free Press, 1987).
[108]George Gilder, *The Spirit of Enterprise* (New York: Simon and Schuster, 1984) p. 157.

economies of scale. It may even ward off some competitors who, seeing how low the prices are, decide that there is not enough profit margin to go after.

The venture has a choice. Pricing high may give the venture more needed revenue sooner and may enhance the image of what it offers as being higher quality. If it is able to charge a higher price, it will have more money to plow back into such things as quality improvement, advertising, and service in the short run. It may also be able to build through the higher revenues a stronger financial position so that when competitors attack, it can cut prices to fight back.

But with a lower price it may gain a bigger customer or user base and establish the venture more solidly in the marketplace. It may also reduce the attractiveness of the market to potential competitors, making their entry less likely.

Strategic pricing moves and countermoves are always easy to identify in a free market system. They particularly show up among commodity products, such as gasoline, airline tickets, steel, automobiles, and fast food. But they also show up in products that are not either identical or nearly so. Microcomputers, peripherals, and software compete on the basis of price versus performance where both are important. Upgraded new microcomputers come out at a higher price, which then drops, month by month, until the next upgrade when it goes back up again.

Profit chain focus

What the venture is very good at should determine where it could play a role in what can be regarded as a profit chain. Whatever gets delivered to the end customer can be viewed as the result of a chain of productive steps where each step adds some value (hence the term *value chain*, used in much strategic management literature). Products start with raw materials that may have begun with geological prospecting and then gone through various stages of refining and transporting, each of which was performed by a different enterprise. A venture may pick only one or several steps in this chain

of value adding as its segment of contribution, and that choice can be very important.

IKEA makes furniture but leaves out the assembly step to save money, which represents a saving to customers who are glad to do their own assembly, for example. Other companies sometimes change strategy by expanding back in the chain (backward integration), as did Henry Ford, when he bought rubber plantations to make his own tires, or forward (forward integration) as did Tektronix when it began selling its commercial electronic instruments to the public through its own catalog. Each industry has its possibilities for such expansion. Services can be sole site, chain, or franchise. Real estate development may include construction, architecture, retail sales, or renting. Distribution can include agency, freight forwarding, wholesaling, retailing, and service to any extent down the line. Virtual ventures, where there may be no plant or equipment other than a microcomputer and modem and everything else is outsourced, are an extreme form of selectivity in the profit chain.

Each part of the chain will offer its payoff potential, require its resources and skills, introduce its costs of negotiation, communication and coordination, bring on its competitors, and impose its risks. Limited resources generally push new venture founders toward choosing a narrow sector in the chain. But even companies with practically boundless resources may wisely choose to specialize. Microsoft, for example, subcontracts all of its manufacturing and even much of its software-writing with an aim of concentrating only on tasks it does best.

Producing in-house should allow better control of scheduling and quality. It can also build stronger capability inside the company faster, and it will probably be cheaper, because by using an outside producer, some of the profit earned by the product or service will have to be that of the supplier. But using an outside source may bring to bear greater production experience possessed by the source, reduce the amount of investment capital needed, and add flexibility, because contracts to the source can probably be cut back easier than the venture's own production establishment. This issue will be further considered in later chapters dealing with setting up shop and arranging for production.

Tradeoffs

Making tradeoff choices, such as whether to price high versus low and how much of the profit chain to occupy, will necessarily be part of designing the venture. Some other likely tradeoff areas include the following:

Speed versus refinement. How much to develop, test, and improve the product or service and its presentation must be weighed against potential penalties in both time and money. Whether to be sooner to market and scoop competitors, or to take longer and reduce the likelihood of poor performance or of being leapfrogged by competitors will have to be decided.

Sharing versus retaining ownership. Sometimes the only way to raise enough money or to recruit needed people may be to share ownership. Doing so may also help build a constituency and help the company grow faster. But it will leave the founders less to share later and may bring in more partners who prey on the venture for information and possibly try to interfere with management. The issue may boil down to determining how much to share and when.

Paying out or plowing back earnings. This can have major consequences for whether the venture grows and what it is like to manage. Partners, investors, and employees can all disagree about it; anticipating that possibility can have implications for how the venture

should be designed from the beginning as well as what potential participants are "promised" about its future.

Other tradeoffs

Limited size and limited resources may necessitate many other tradeoffs that it may help to consider during design of the venture, such as the following:

- Price versus:
  Quality
  Delivery speed
  Degree of customization
  Breadth of choice (line breadth)
  Support or warranty
- Channel choice—direct or other
- Brand development versus private labeling
- Alliance versus solo
- Commitment versus various risks
- Production cost versus flexibility
- Speed to market versus refinement
- Keeping versus sharing profits
- Anticipating the next generation versus waiting to be more sure
- How much geographical spread
- What kind of company—United, American, Southwest, Continental, or Northwest airlines management style
- Diversity versus concentration of strengths

Errors to avoid

Part of planning and of formulating the rules by which the venture will operate is to anticipate things that can go wrong and avoid them. A sampler of lessons from experience, reported by some entrepreneurs in their own words, follows as illustration.

Examples of errors to avoid

1. *Beware of bad ideas when you seem to be doing well. We tried a sort of fax machine for floppies that flopped. Do a survey beyond your family and friends. Ask people. It's not [about] how many good ideas you get in the shower.*
2. *Poor customer service.*
3. *We had no business plan, and it was a mistake. Planning would have helped us head off some problems and respond better to others.*
4. *We were too early, should have listed assumptions and planned contingencies.*
5. *We failed to ship when we said we would.*
6. *We became arrogant because of early success and that led us to put out products with bugs. We didn't know what we didn't know.*

Errors to avoid (continued)

7. *Failure to understand distribution channels tripped us up. Step One should be to learn who the target customer is and what channel reaches that customer.*

8. *Under-capitalization damaged us. Most software takes twice as long and costs twice as much as you think. If told it will take two engineers six months, assume it will take four a year. Competitors may have you outgunned. 'I thought I knew what cash flow meant until I didn't have any.'*

9. *Lack of awareness of competitors put us behind the curve. Aldus was apparently upstaged on its desktop publishing program before they knew it by Quark.*

10. *Shortage of the right talent, particularly in management, marketing and sales, let us fall behind. We were using the wrong strategy, which was to focus on a small niche, use low-cost guerrilla marketing, and make profits early. We should have moved to get big fast, blowing the doors off the market with heavy venture capital.*

11. *'Founderitis,' being afraid to share ownership, put us behind. It's not true that you can do everything. By not sharing you can wind up with 100 percent of nothing.*

12. *Constantly changing the business plan had us wandering all over and getting nowhere. Every month we based it on some new book or article.*

13. *We got bigger with an attitude of damn the costs and forget about controls. We did not measure sell-through across the retail counter and ended up thinking we were selling a lot more than we really were.*

14. *Be careful of contracts. I signed one with an infomercial company and they ended up taking my company away from me completely.*

15. *Design flaws killed us. You must have the specs up front or you get too many design changes. All software has bugs. Test, Test, and Test. And update. We put out a patch every month.*

16. *Don't miscast yourself. The CEO stopped personally selling and sales really dropped.*

17. *Have a war strategy. We were right, but they outspent us on litigation and we lost.*

18. *Don't venture indiscreetly. We tried branching into fitness equipment and it bombed.*

19. *Do forecast financials and analyze discrepancies. Otherwise you can run out of cash and die.*

20. *Do expect the boom cycle and the high margins to drop, because they will.*

21. *No guts, no glory. We passed up what turned out to be a really great opportunity because we were too conservative.*

22. *Do build a strong team and give it incentives to perform.*

23. *Do have an advisory board and heed its advice.*

24. *Check key links in your plan. We tooled up too late for the toy shows and missed the market.*

25. *Insurance can really be important. I know a harness maker who omitted it and was sued to death.*

26. *Avoid self-conflict—Computer leasing and computer consulting did not mix.*

It is not possible to know in advance which of these pitfalls or innumerable others will apply to any particular venture. The point in considering them is that part of designing the business should be to speculate about what might go wrong, try to build in safeguards, such as procedures to check for such things going wrong, and arrange for flexibility to make corrections that may be needed.

4. Size implications

Flexibility

As the venture starts to grow but is still small, some of the initial advantages discussed above should continue while others fade, preferably being replaced by new and better ones.

Flexibility

A great advantage of small firms is their ability to be flexible when they want to be. Big companies become efficient by developing and refining their systems, having their employees learn systems that work, and minimizing surprises. Through repetitive practice, they and their collaborators develop coordinated skills.

By the same token, however, they develop habits, and those are hard to change, which renders them less able to be flexible. Eventually, such inabilities to change may kill them off. Thus the *Fortune* 500 of half a century ago is a far different list from today's, many of its members having disappeared entirely, while others were swallowed up by other companies that rose during the period.

A small company can hold down fixed expenses by not investing in general purpose equipment or a permanent workforce to expand. Instead, it can outsource some items of output and hire temporary help for its workforce, all of which gives it flexibility to change with fewer complications than an established company. There are, in addition, some exemptions from federal regulations that apply to smaller firms, particularly in areas of hiring and firing, as well as sometimes in connection with zoning restrictions. Some local governments exempt firms of small size, either through applying special regulations, or by simply not enforcing other regulations that they would normally enforce against larger firms.

Perhaps the greatest flexibility advantages come simply from the organization structure in a small firm where there are no layers of decision-makers to be dealt with. The head person in the organization and the person at the bottom are personally acquainted and anyone can deal directly with either.

Growing other strengths

Progression from small to large introduces some disadvantages, the counterpoints to advantages of small just noted. But it also introduces advantages worth consideration in designing the business to make the most of them. Longer-run advantages to seek, depending on the particular venture, include:

> Expanding sales volume to achieve scale economies and experience build up that holds costs down. Some ways to gain such economies include:

> - Cultivating organizational learning with the aid of specialization. Total Quality Management systems (TQM) and Just In Time inventory control (JIT) are taught this way.
> - Automating to reduce labor costs, enhance consistency.

- Competitive bidding and stronger credit, to lower costs.
- Adding complementary lines to spread sales related overhead thinner.
- Providing cash, promotion, and other incentives to encourage a productive culture.
- Developing, possibly through investment in advertising, a brand name, reputation, connections, and buyer habits that build sales strength in the most appropriate market segments.
- Creating organizational, internal leadership, and cultural strengths that help employees do the work of the company with higher quality, more innovation, and lower cost.
- Developing and refining production and selling systems to both higher effectiveness and higher efficiency.
- Accumulating know-how and data from experience that helps decision-making.
- Building up financial and physical resources, as well as supplier relationships that give the company ability to marshal muscle fast to deal with emergence of new threats or new opportunities.
- Advancing technical development of the company's product or service so it does not fall behind but rather advances against the competition, coupled with protection of any intellectual property that is important to preserving such advances.

Although this list may not seem very long, it in fact covers an enormous number of smaller categories and angles, each peculiar to the circumstances of the individual business and the environment in which it operates, both of which are necessarily changing constantly.

Ways to accomplish this expansion will be further discussed in a later chapter. But some that can be noted briefly are:

- Expanding the market pie through product and service innovations, as well as advertising.
- Taking pie away from competitors through broader scope or better marketing.
- Vertically integrating (or other expansion in the value chain) to spread overhead thinner.

- Locking in users through families of compatible products.

- Creating add-ons, such as bundling, or complements such as accessories.

- Collaborating with allies in cooperative advertising or by cross-licensing technologies.

- Defending patents, trademarks, and copyrights, and protecting secrets as defenses against copycats.

Strategic evolution

Continuous improvement activities such as the above should reshape details, if not the major thrust, of strategy over time. Competitive pressures do the same. Kodak, when faced with the onslaught of digital technology, cut its dividend to invest in digital technology and product development.

The following contrasting examples may illustrate how strategy can reshape a venture and build strength over time.

For Nucor, the company most successful in exploiting the potentialities of mini-mill steel making, the winning strategy did not appear at the start. The company was begun in 1903 as an auto company, was nearly liquidated, then bought and sold, turned into a conglomerate in various lines of business, and by 1965 was nearly bankrupt. A new manager, Ken Iverson, was hired to run part of it that happened to make steel joists. He decided it would be cheaper to produce rather than buy steel for the joists, and so borrowed $6 million to build a mini-mill.

There followed a string of successes in which Nucor starred as a company that could both build and operate steel mini-mills with outstanding efficiency and profitability. Elements of strategy key to this accomplishment appear to have been the leadership of Iverson, who in 1986 was named "Best CEO in the Steel Industry" by *The Wall Street Journal*. His organizational policies, which included a very high degree of decentralization among the separate mills, a flat organizational structure with very few layers of management, and a powerful incentive compensation system that began low relative to industry norms and rose to high above them contingent upon performance for both workers and managers. Elements in the company's programs included profit sharing, discretionary bonuses, stock options, and schol-

arships for employees' children. Effort was also applied to minimizing status differences among employees. Investor Warren Buffett commented, "It is the classic example of an incentive program that works. If I were a blue-collar worker, I would like to work for Nucor."[109]

Clearly other key elements of strategy for the company included such things as how it organized employees, where it located plants, how it controlled costs, decisions it made about capacity, what other companies it collaborated with, and how it managed finances. These undoubtedly developed over time as the company grew subject to conscious decisions of an evolving management.[110]

In new industries, a tightening up of competitive standards is likely as the different competing companies become better at what they do and their customers become more sophisticated in choosing suppliers. Over time some ventures will be shaken out of the competition as they fall behind.

In 1980 as the microcomputer industry was taking off, scores of microcomputer manufacturers entered the business. Franklin and Fortune both stressed higher power, more memory, and sophisticated designs. Dot featured compactness, as would Osborne. Sinclair was cheapest, with a price of $99. Grid featured ruggedness. Texas Instruments had its own dedicated software and the muscle of a powerful parent. Coming along were microcomputers for Digital Equipment and Xerox, which had actually been the first with many features. None of these entrants survived in the business, though arguably any of them could have, given the right strategy. IBM had not yet introduced its PC.

Three companies seemed most likely to survive among the many entrants. Apple, which had not yet introduced the Macintosh (no graphical interface with icons was yet on the market, and would not be for several years), was working to build a base of users in the public schools, figuring that as children matured they, the market of the future, would be habituated to Apples. Commodore was betting on the international market as the big opportunity of the future, and had developed the largest user base overseas.

Radio Shack had the advantages of a well-known brand, large size, and, most importantly, its own retail outlets, where new users could buy with

[109] *Fortune*, December 19, 1988, p. 58.
[110] Pankaj Ghemawat and others, *Strategy and the Business Landscape* (Reading, MA: Addison-Wesley, 1999) pp. 10-11.

reliability this new, developing, and bug-riddled technology. The store could help them select, help finance the purchase, show them how to hook up and get started, and give them a place to come back to when things went wrong. The first microcomputer purchasers had been technical hobbyists who bought through the mail and then did their own debugging. But now the market was spreading to less technical people who had other uses for the product. They, so went the strategy, needed to buy through stores.

As it turned out, none of these strategies dominated. IBM won by the power of its brand name and reputation for reliability, but later lost ground as copycats undercut it by competing on low price. It also failed to capitalize on future potential by not obtaining exclusive rights to the DOS operating system it bought from Microsoft. As the technology became more reliable, the IBM name became less necessary and buyers started shifting back to buying through the mail, allowing the enormous success of Dell. Radio Shack computer stores phased out.

Still later, Apple started opening stores and expanding its product line to include iPods, iPhones, and later eBooks, which helped it expand its share of the microcomputer market, and the competitive game rolled on.

Threats with maturation

With growth, risks can occur in such areas as:

- Quality control
- Response to government actions including tax change
- Suppliers who are managing their own profit strategies and may hike prices when customers find supply short and become desperate to get some of it, while at other times providing great help when their production expertise, extension of needed credit, intelligence about the industry, or accelerated delivery may be vital
- Falling behind the curve on technology
- Growing "slack" by losing intensity and discipline

To deal with this, established companies work on many fronts. For example, they develop cost and financial accounting systems to warn of deteriorating conditions; they introduce programs that strive for greater efficiency, such as Just In Time (JIT) inventory control; they develop training and management systems that improve employee performance incrementally; and they adopt incentive systems to make high performance worthwhile for employees.

5. Longer run

In the broader picture, strategy is concerned with how pieces, aspects, resources, features, short- and long-term moves of the business fit together to make up the whole. Out of the combination come such characteristics as reputation, image, flexibility, synergy, atmosphere, responsiveness, culture, competitiveness, resilience, and eventually long-term return on investment.

A convenient example is the strategic makeup of Southwest Airlines.[111] As mentioned earlier, it began against strong resistance of existing airlines. Led by a maverick high-energy, legally trained CEO, it managed to become the top performer among all airlines on a consistent basis over a long time period. In hindsight, a pattern can be seen to its strategy that enables it to offer fast, frequent, and very low cost service to its customers relative to other airlines. The pattern is a combination of elements that includes highly motivated employees willing to be more

flexible among different tasks than employees of other lines typically are. This, in turn, can be attributed to such factors as how they are chosen, what leadership they have and the examples it sets, high pay, a high degree of informality and individuality that they can participate in, and their sharing in ownership of the line.

These and other elements of the combination that make up what can be regarded as the strategy of Southwest appear in Exhibit 4a-2 and are also illustrated in application of the Morris model of Appendix 4a-2.

Although such viewing of a company's strategy can appear to be clear and tidy in hindsight, in foresight or in operation it may not be so clear. Moreover, two different people may see the same strategy differently. One may even see it differently at different times. Regardless of the viewpoint, however, it is clear that the way elements of a com-

---

[111]Michael E. Porter, "What Is Strategy?" *Harvard Business Review*, November-December 1996.

Exhibit 4a-2 Strategic elements of Southwest Airlines

Strategic advantages	Causes	Behind causes
Low-priced tickets	Employees fast, flexible	High pay
Frequent departures	Limited agent usage	Employee stock ownership
Fast turnaround	Automatic ticket machines	Negotiated union flexibility
Cheerful service	Standardized fleet	Unusual CEO
Low costs	Limited amenities	Fuel contracts anticipated
	No baggage transfers	
	No other airline connections	
	Selected routes	
	Relatively cheap fuel	

pany's strategy fit and work together affects performance crucially.

Strengths relative to competitors must be found or created. Which parts or elements are most important to that relative strength depends on the nature of the venture and its particular opportunity. Identification of the venture's driving force, although not the same thing, may help clarify it.

In **retailing**, location tends to be a very important element of strategy. Merchandise selection, service, price, and promotion can also dominate.

In **high technology**, innovation, design talent, patent protection, and sometimes strategic alliances, particularly in biotech, are especially important.

In **banking**, having connections to money and an image of reliability, as well as capacity to handle details without error, are critical capabilities.

In **heavy manufacturing**, purchase and maintenance of equipment, choice of location and logistic methods, ability to deal with unions effectively, control of costs, management of quality, and adherence to delivery schedules all may be essential to survive.

A natural tendency for most companies is to follow the patterns prevalent in their industry. But a new venture has freedom to adopt a different pattern because it lacks established habits. It also has reason to look for a different pattern, because its competitors are probably already better at following their existing patterns than the new venture will be at imitating them.

Building image

The externally visible evidence of a company's strategy, which is to say of the pattern of action choices and priorities through which the company deals with challenges it faces, is sometimes relatively easy to see when the company is successful. The following are further examples:

- Brand power (McDonald's)
- Image of reliability (IBM, ATT)
- Low price direct selling (Dell, Wal-Mart)
- Innovation (Wizards of the Coast game company, Hewlett-Packard)
- Exceptional product performance (Head skis, Buell motorcycles)
- Style (Gargoyle sunglasses)
- Service (Amazon.Com, Snap-on tools)
- Alternative variation (Tully's Coffee across the street from Starbucks)
- Innovation capability (Hewlett-Packard, Apple)
- Financial power (Microsoft)
- Convenience (World Medical, HomeGrocer.com)
- Uniqueness (Chihuly handmade glass products, custom-built houses)
- Capability (new "killer-app" software)
- Efficiency for the user (electric toothbrushes)
- Health improvement (new medicines)
- Monopoly power (Windows, patented new drugs)
- Fun (Disney)
- Dominant shares of served markets (General Electric)
- Rapid product improvement (Integrated chip companies)

For the entrepreneur then, a key strategic question is, which of these types of strong points will the new venture seek to possess and capitalize on? In some cases clearly combinations of the above elements can apply, and typically the companies involved would like them to. These visible effects of strategy are only iceberg tips representing systems of facilities, people, organization, leadership, and activity that support them, sometimes well and other times not so well, at a less visible level.

Strategy evolution

The strategy that ends up deciding a company's longer-term fate may or may not be set mainly at the beginning. Typically, it will change form along the way. A study by Romanelli[112] reported that aggressive firms had higher growth rates in their start-up years, but a key was tailoring strategy to the conditions of the environment. New firms displayed strategic instability initially that took around two or three years to work out.

Two mechanisms for distilling some degree of focus out of what may be turning into a laundry list of hoped-for advantages on which the future of the venture may be staked are (1) a projected **opponent companies grid** for the venture similar to the one suggested for the near term in Chapter 3A, and/or (2) a brief **written scenario** of best estimates about how competitive events will unfold. Either of these is bound to be in error, the future being unknowable. The purpose at this point is not to spend great effort trying to guess that future. Thinking through the projection and displaying it in an easy-to-review form can be helpful in adding to the business plan for communicating it and demonstrating that the founder is thinking ahead in more explicit form than many do.

Strategy evolution

Exercises

Text discussion questions

1. How should an entrepreneur go about defining the industry in which his or her venture is to begin?
2. How should design of a venture be influenced by which features of the industry it will be in?
3. In what ways should the process of designing a venture be similar to or different from the process of designing a product or service?

Case questions

Case 4A-1 Mark Juarez

1. To what extent could Mark hope to create a business that would be consistent with his dreams, resources and business realties?
2. What would be the most salient points on a SWOT analysis for Mark's venture?
3. How would you describe a profit chain for Mark's venture and where it should try to fit?
4. List actions Mark should take at this point, in sequence.

Case 4A-2 Charles and Barbara Ewing

1. Prepare a quantitative one-page financial attractiveness estimate for the Ewings' venture.
2. Write out on one page a mission or vision statement for the Ewings' venture.
3. Write out a business model description for the Ewings' venture.
4. If a team of business school students wants to help them at this point, what should the Ewings ask the team to do, and what steps should the team take?

Portfolio page possibilities

Page 4A-1 Competitive arena

Describe the most consequential features of the competitive arena your venture will enter, noting both how those will likely change in the future and the external sources on which your depiction is based.

---

[112]Romanelli, Elaine, "Environments and Strategies of Organization Start-up Effects on Early Survival," *Administrative Science Quarterly*, 34(3) 1989, pp. 369-387.

Page 4A-2 Morris model

1. Write out a series of phrases that indicate what choices on the Morris Model depicted by Appendix 4a-1 that follows Chapter 10B of this book would best fit your venture, using one line per item. (For example "We create value primarily by offering services.")
2. Underneath this series of lines write a brief indication of choices you are most tentative about and how you might go about checking them out further.

Page 4A-3 SWOT

Present a SWOT analysis for some specified stage in development of your venture where you think it will be of most help.

Page 4A-4 Future opponent grid

1. Prepare a competitor grid for the company at two future points in time.
2. Include in each some indication of the four potential competition types.

Page 4A-5 Growth strategy

Describe a growth-generation strategy for your company.

Page 4A-6 Industry future scenario

Prepare a one-page forecast scenario in pictures and words describing developments in the industry of your venture.

Page 4A-7 Visions

1. Write a mission statement of what your company should accomplish.
2. Write a vision statement of how your company should accomplish that mission.
3. Write a picture of success describing what your company should look like at some defined point in the future.

Term Projects

Venture history

1. To what extent did the entrepreneur(s) develop on paper a design of the business?
2. What did the entrepreneur think the business model would be, what did it turn out to be, and what caused the difference?
3. How did actual strengths and weaknesses compare to expected ones, and what caused the differences?
4. What was the initial vision for the company's image in the public, how did it change, and why?

Venture planning guide

1. Rank the portfolio options above in terms of their potential value to your business plan and prepare those you ranked highest.
2. Prepare a commentary on the prospect of innovation S-curves as described in this chapter cropping up in your competitive arena and what that could mean for your venture.

CHAPTER 4B – Venture Plans

Topics
1. Purposes for planning
2. Alternative audiences
3. Matters of priority
4. Some elements to include
5. Presentation

Checkpoints
a. How can the time and expense of planning be justified?
b. Why do some entrepreneurs believe in formal planning and others do not?
c. For whom are business plans written and why does it matter?
d. Who should write the plan for a venture and why?
e. What are the most important aspects of venture business planning?
f. What should a venture plan include and what should it not?
g. How should a formal venture plan be organized?
h. What should be avoided in a business plan?
i. What is important to consider in presenting a plan orally?

This chapter will consider the reasons for planning before launching a business, audiences for whom plans may be useful, and how an entrepreneur can prepare and present plans to best effect.

1. Purposes for planning

Three broad purposes a venture plan may have are (1) to describe in concrete written detail how a venture can be started around a particular business idea, (2) to project likely financial and other requirements and returns for it, and (3) to communicate that scenario to other people. Typically, a business plan is a sales document for persuading people who can help that the venture is worth doing.

Feasibility study versus venture plan

Less biased than a venture plan is a feasibility study, the purpose of which is to investigate how well the venture can be done and how successful it likely will be. The purpose is not either to argue that the concept is a winner or that the venture should be carried out, and it need not go into detail about how, except for the most crucial actions. A feasibility analysis can sometimes usefully help as:

- An assessment of how possible it would be to implement a venture idea.
- An assessment of alternative ways of implementing a venture idea and finding the best.
- A test of the reasoning about design of a specific venture.
- A portrayal of a venture as a basis for seeking feedback to improve its design.
- A way to practice some aspects of the process of working up a venture plan.
- A sketch scenario against which founders can test their "fit."
- An exercise for learning about entrepreneurship.
- A device for obtaining counsel from others about venturing.
- A prelude to developing a fuller plan.

Feasibility study versus venture plan

Figuring out which purposes apply and why is important—it can be tricky to prepare a feasibility study that doesn't lapse into a venture plan whose purpose is to sell the venture idea rather than to evaluate it. The person preparing the study presumably picked the best venture idea he or she could. Hence, it should be loved. The study required work, which requires commitment. To what should this commitment be linked if not to an idea of great merit? Incentive for bias toward the idea is built in by effort on the analysis. Clarifying which of the above purposes apply and remembering them should help retain perspective.

Priority should be given to the most worrisome aspects of a prospective venture in developing a feasibility study, whereas a full venture plan calls for more complete coverage. For example, a plan should include biographies of the founders to let investors evaluate them. A feasibility study might not need to, unless there is a potential problem in recruiting some with particularly needed capabilities. A plan would more likely include description of how shareholders should hope to recover their investment. A feasibility study probably would not, unless that was known to be a critical issue for obtaining the investment. In fact, a feasibility study would less likely apply discussion to the issue of obtaining investment at all. It should, however, explore the level of return on investment to be expected.

If that return happens to be insufficient to justify the venture, it is no shortcoming of the feasibility study. The important thing is that the assessment of potential represented by the study point be realistic.

To that end it should be helpful to incorporate documentation that may have already been developed in applying previous chapters. Depiction of the market hole where the venture's product or service might fit should establish that there really is a place for it. Indication of whether capability push or market pull supports the impulse to fill that hole should, when combined with data from market study, confirm that the need for it has strength. Product

specifications, comparisons, and positioning diagrams should help clarify the market fit and relative competitive strengths of the offering. And a Competitor Companies Grid should show what the venture itself will have to contend with. Financial forecasts and analyses that were prepared in assessing attractiveness should give dimensions to the amount of profit and return rate to be expected. Description of the strategic design of the business, as discussed in the preceding chapter, 4a, should make clear what the venture aims to become and how, as a logical test of whether it really still seems to make sense.

Informal plans

Either a feasibility study or a business plan can be done as a short informal version with less detail. Most ventures, in fact, start without formal plans, and sometimes even major amounts of financial support are obtained that way.

> When Robert Noyce and Gordon Moore wanted to raise money for leaving Fairchild Semiconductor and starting Intel, the man they approached was Arthur Rock. Ten years earlier he had been the broker who had shopped their previous venture idea to 35 people, eventually landing Sherman Fairchild as a backer.
>
> Now for a business plan the two men had only a few notes on a couple of sheets of paper. Rock recalled: "Bob just called me on the phone. We'd been friends for a long time … Documents? There was practically nothing. Noyce's reputation was good enough. We put out a page and a half little circular, but I'd raised the money before people even saw it. If you tried to do it today, it would probably be a two-inch stack of paper. The lawyers wouldn't let you raise money without telling people what the risks are."[113]

Within a day in 1968, Noyce and Moore had start-up capital of $2.3 million for the initial financing of Intel based on a two-page plan.

Left out of this story, however, is how much Arthur Rock knew ahead of time about the industry, evolution of its technology, including how it had progressed at Fairchild where Noyce and Moore worked, what opportunity was being missed by Fairchild that could be exploited by these two employees, and how much invest-

---

[113] Tim Jackson, *Inside Intel* (NY: Penguin, 1997) pp.18, 22.

ment was typically required for this kind of work, judging from Fairchild and similar companies. From his experience as a venture capitalist who had bought into other high-technology companies, Rock knew what was needed to win, and he knew that Noyce and Moore, as insiders at Fairchild, were well-informed about it. Finally, Rock knew that technical talent, such as these two and not many others possessed, was the most powerful asset for succeeding. A lot could be read between the lines of the couple of sheets of paper that conveyed their plan, and Rock saw it. As the company grew, many plans in greater detail followed the first informal one.

Planning does not have to be done in written form to be useful. In their study of 2,994 new ventures, Cooper et al. found that 43 percent of the founders seriously contemplated business entry for a long time before taking action and 14 percent said they had thought someday they might do so. Undoubtedly some of these, particularly among the 43 percent, made formal plans. Another 13 percent said they entered business simply because it was the best alternative available, and 28 percent reported that the opportunity simply came along and they jumped into it.[114] It seems less likely that these last two groups formally planned. From this and much anecdotal evidence, it appears that most businesses start without formal planning and even more without *written* formal plans. Dave Thomas, the founder of Wendy's recalled:

> I always preach about having a plan, but ironically, I really didn't have a plan for Wendy's when I started out. What I had was a concept and plenty of operating experience, but there was no five-year plan with a restaurant-opening schedule or a financing program. There was nothing like that at all. For the sake of drama I wish I could tell you that it was more complicated than that, but it wasn't.[115]

Cooper et al. also point out that most firms start very small, 90 percent with fewer than 10 employees and over half with only one or two.[116]

This and other studies have also found that most firms stay small, under five employees. It might be supposed that these firms are therefore simple enough for owners to keep any planning in mind while at the same time keeping their enterprises flexible enough to respond to events quickly without much need for anticipation.

Of those ventures that do prepare formal plans many wait until after start-up, when cash from outsiders is needed to reach some next stage in progress of the venture.

Formal plans

A full venture plan will spell out in detail how the venture will be accomplished. It will assume feasibility is adequately established and fill in more about topics to be covered in the chapters running from here to the end of the book: recruiting help, raising money, setting up the business, starting it up, managing it downstream, and eventually exiting from it. Footnotes will give sources of data and appendices will include detailed financial statements, footnotes to go with them as well as other back-up data such as market research and resumes of key participants in the venture.

For most venture plans the question is not what can be done, as in a feasibility analysis. Rather it is to describe what should be done and how. It should describe a venture that is presumed, at least by the writer, to be both feasible and sufficiently attractive to be implemented. It should tell how feasibility and attractiveness have already been checked out and describe the strategy and future states that have been developed for the venture so that start-up, takeoff, and subsequent performance warrant the effort and investment required for implementation.

Plan writing can be the easiest part of developing a venture, and sometimes the least necessary. What makes a venture work is effective action by the founder(s) and others whose help is needed. If planning inspires that action, it is helpful. If planning does not lead to that action, the planning process may still have been educational. But that may be all.

---

[114] Arnold C. Cooper and others, *New Business in America* (Washington, D.C.: The NFIB Foundation, 1990) p. 18.
[115] R. David Thomas, *Dave's Way* (New York: Putnam's, 1991) p. 92.
[116] Cooper and others, *New Business*, p. 5.

Most venture plans are written to raise money from a bank or investors. But raising money is not the only justification for developing a plan. Some others include:

- To help in thinking through a start-up idea more thoroughly.
- To obtain credit from a supplier.
- To recruit needed partners.
- To recruit key employees.
- To convince a wanted customer that the venture will deliver.
- To provide guidelines to work from for founders and employees.
- To anticipate long lead times required for some action.
- To set up benchmarks for tracking performance.
- To use as a touchstone for guidance when events become hectic.

Although many entrepreneurs do not prepare extensive plans, others do, and some successful entrepreneurs believe strongly in serious formal planning. For instance, Steve Bostic, who built his start-up to top performer on the 1987 Inc. 500 list before selling it to Eastman Kodak for a reported $45 million, commented about his experience as follows:

> I'm saying it has to be planned. You have to take your vision, think it through, and turn it into a consistent strategy. And then you have to get it on paper. That's key. I maintain that if you can't put your vision on paper, you can never do it in the real world.[117]

When asked about the many companies that succeed without such planning, he continued:

> You're talking about companies that are one-man shows. Yes, if you're guiding the ship out front and pulling everybody else along, you don't need to write it down. But if you want to be able to walk out of the room and have life continue in an order-ly way, you'd better put your vision and your plan on paper.

In discussing partnerships through which software entrepreneurs get help from Microsoft in preparing their products, Mike Dusche, who received a couple hundred such requests per month, commented:

> To get my time or my developers' time, they really need to show us an articulate, crisp business plan about why we should be willing to invest our resources.[118]

There is empirical evidence that formal planning helps. Duchesneau and Gartner, for instance, found in contrasting a group of 13 more successful with 13 less successful fresh-juice distribution firms that the more successful firms on average spent more time (237 versus 85 hours) on planning. More recent analysis of a random sample of Swedish entrepreneurs by Delmar and Shane found that writing a business plan correlated with lower failure and higher new sales rates.[120]

Schwenk and Shrader identified 26 other studies on the helpfulness of planning, some of which showed a positive relationship while others did not. But from an analysis of all those studies combined, they concluded that the evidence "clearly demonstrates a planning/performance link across studies," and that "it strengthens the case for recommending the use of strategic planning in small firms." They also noted, "Since the effect sizes for most studies are small, however, it may be that the small improvement in performance is not worth the effort involved in strategic planning unless a firm is in a very competitive industry where small differences in performance may affect the firm's survival potential."[121]

---

[117] "Thriving on Order," *Inc.*, December 1989, p. 48.

[118] Christopher Caggiano, "Hotlinks," *Inc.*, October 1999, p. 75.

[119] Donald A. Duchesneau and William B. Gartner, "A Profile of Success and Failure in an Emerging Industry," *Journal of Business Venturing*, 5, no. 5, September 1990, p. 297.

[120] Frederic Delmar and Scott Shane, "Does Experience Matter? The Effect of Founding Team Experience on the Survival and Sales of Newly Founded Ventures," *StrategicOrganization*, Vol 4(3), pp. 215-47.

[121] Charles R. Schwenk and Charles B. Shrader, "Effects of Formal Strategic Planning in Financial Performance of Small Firms," *Entrepreneurship: Theory and Practice*, 17, no. 3, Spring 1993, p. 53.

2. Alternative audiences

All readers of business plans will care about central business issues such as viability, profit potential, downside risk, likely life cycle time, and potential areas for dispute and for improvement. But different types of readers will have different priorities among topics. Contrasting audiences include individual investors, venture capitalists, bankers, customers, and students.

What bankers look for

Most venture plans are written to raise money, and the source most common to businesses beyond founders' savings is bank borrowing. A banker's first concern has to be recovery of the loan. This is because banks are limited on the upside to a fixed interest rate, while on the downside they can lose everything. Moreover, most of the money banks lend is not their own, but rather that of depositors who expect to be able to withdraw it whenever they choose.

Consequently, questions a banker will have in reviewing a venture plan loan proposal include:

1. How reliable is this borrower? What has the person done before? What indication is there that he or she can be counted upon to repay?

2. What will be done with the money? To what extent will it be put into things that can be sold versus non-recoverable expenditures? How sure is it to generate profit?

3. What is the repayment schedule and reliability of repayment sources? Will the venture's customers be good credit risks?

4. What collateral will there be to ensure loan repayment? Will there be salable equipment or inventory, personal guarantee by a wealthy person, by the founder? How much equity capital coverage backs up the debt? Will the venture's debt/equity ratio be conservative for its type of business?

5. How gratifying will it be to handle this loan? Will it be hard or easy to set up? Will the venture's control system provide timely and accurate financial reports? Will the entrepreneur be easy to get information from and keep the bank up to date, especially if problems crop up?

Beyond these questions, the banker will be interested to know what the odds are that by lending to this particular enterprise, he or she will be gaining the loyalty of a customer with a future of growing prosperity and need to borrow more money.

What investors look for

Prospective investors accept more risk and care more about likelihood of profit growth than do bankers. The power and durability of the venture's competitive edge relative to those of future competitors is central to this. What the venture aims to become, and alternative future visions indicating the possibilities it has, will be particularly interesting parts of the plan. Investor questions will likely include:

1. How catchy (intriguing to read about) is the basic idea of this venture?

2. What benefit will the venture offer to customers and at what cost compared to other things they might buy instead?

3. What is the present stage of development and testing of the venture's product or service?

4. What levels of gross margin, net profit, and return on investment are projected for the venture, and what is the basis for believing they can come true?

5. What assurance is there that the venture's technology will not soon be bypassed or surpassed? What can be protected by patents?

6. What segments of which markets will the venture seek to dominate and how? How big can they be expected to become?

7. Who will make the sales and how? What evidence is there so far to assure they will happen?

8. How will production be done, and what will assure that it will hit cost and quality targets?

9. What competitors will the venture be up against, and what will be its relative strengths and weaknesses both initially and later?

10. Who will be on the board of directors?

Angel investors in particular

Individual investors who take risks on start-ups for reaching a next stage, often successful entrepreneurs themselves who like the idea of working with ventures of others both for satis-

What bankers look for

What investors look for

faction and profit, are sometimes called *angels*, an appellation that originated long ago referring to backers of Broadway plays. Questions they may add include:

1. How does the activity of this firm fit with my personal interests?
2. How much money will this endeavor need from me to reach a next stage, and what will protect my interest then?
3. What can I do to help raise the odds of winning besides through investing?
4. How will I get out?
5. Will I enjoy working personally with the founder(s)?

To maintain control of copies of the business plan left with investors for review, it is appropriate to limit the quantity of copies prepared and number them clearly. As will be further discussed in connection with raising capital, a legal risk of public offering can arise if too many copies, more than a dozen, or possibly two, are released.

What venture capitalists look for

Venture capitalists typically manage pools of other people's money to invest in ventures. They expect to take high risks for the sake of potential high returns, and they expect to spend time and money to make their investments work out. They want to make large multiples of their investments on large investments. Because the risks are high, most of their investments are disappointing. The few big winners among those investments must pay for the losers. Some questions of interest in addition to those of investors mentioned above are likely to include:

1. What new industry will this venture create?
2. What is the task-relevant experience of the founders, and what have they accomplished before?
3. Are the founders safe from litigation brought by present or former employers?
4. How well balanced is the management team?
5. What is the view of independent experts on the promise of the venture's new product or service?

6. What other venture capitalists have considered the plan, and how strong is their interest in investing?

Important to many venture capitalists is how well the technology or market of the venture aligns with what they consider to be their particular special areas of investment. Some work in communications, others software, or biotech, and so forth. How the plan is written cannot influence this fit, but at least it should be able to make it easy to assess.

The term *due diligence* that bankers use for assessing the credit worthiness of loan proposals is used also by venture capitalists in assessing ventures that seek money from them. The plan itself is only one piece of evidence among many, and usually serves them as a quick screening device to decide whether the venture is worth looking into.

Elevator pitch

Because their work obliges them to look through hundreds of serious, well-developed venture plans annually, venture capitalists value concise and direct expression that lets them get to the heart of a plan quickly. This need has given rise to the concept of an "elevator pitch," or quick statement describing the heart of how the venture should add something new, better, and highly profitable (assuming it can). The implication of the term is that if it takes longer than an elevator ride—and not one long enough to reach the highest skyscraper—to describe what a proposed venture will do to warrant venture capital investment, then the idea is not yet clear enough.

At the core of this pitch should be clear indication of what the venture will **enable customers to do**. At one end of the spectrum might be "to recover from AIDS." At the other might be such things as "conveniently enjoy a cup of coffee more," "have fun playing a new game with friends," or "make the paint job on my house look better." In between could be such things as "design my own Web page more easily," "get my products to customers faster," or "buy airline tickets cheaper." It is a cliché that people buy not products or services, but benefits. So

[90] David Gumpert, *How To Really Create a Successful Business Plan* (Boston: Inc. Publishing, 1990) pp. 85-88.

what is the benefit to be offered to customers by the new venture? How can that beat out competitors to create and capture a large and profitable market? And what will be needed by the venture to make it happen?

Other industrial audiences

Other possible industrial readers and their special concerns may include the following:

Customers Will the company be reliable as a supplier and as a source of follow-up service, warranty, and, if a product is involved, spare parts and repairs?

Suppliers How big a customer will the venture become, and how promptly will it pay its bills?

Employee recruits What kind of pay, advancement prospects, fringes, and work atmosphere will the venture offer?

Potential strategic partners How well will the venture's strategic interests align with ours, and what can it give us?

What to put in the plan for each of these audiences must be deduced from analyzing and understanding representative individuals in those audiences. Tuning the presentation to one may make it inefficient for review by other audiences. So focus deserves thought.

What instructors look for

School business plan assignments usually have learning as a primary purpose, which imposes different priorities. For instance, requirements that the venture show near-certain loan repayment and/or high profitability potential may no longer be realistic. Finding such deals is too much of a long shot for a school requirement. Also, expectation that such tasks as prototype construction or market research be done to a professionally adequate level in the limited time available for homework is an unlikely school requirement. Such time-consuming tasks can appropriately be cut short.

Instead, some things an instructor may take more interest in than a banker or investor would include:

- Evidence of good digging (e.g., pavement pounding). For many students, approaching strangers to obtain needed venture-specific information will be a new and therefore educational experience.

- Effective application of all thought modes described in Chapter 1. School can stretch the mind by pushing it to apply underused capacities.

- Good writing. Other things being equal, a better-written plan should be more successful in real life than a poorly written one. Usually in real ventures other things are not equal and the importance of those outweighs elegant writing. In school those other things cannot be required as important, but good writing can. If a plan is written by a team, then a particularly challenging part of the writing will be to coordinate sections well. Enough time should be reserved at term end for accomplishing that. Last minute combination of sections is not the way to win.

What competition judges look for

Many business schools conduct business plan contests at some level from campus to international. Judges in these contests include faculty members as well as venture capitalists, entrepreneurs, bankers, and other business professionals. Examples of the rating sheets used for judging plans at two universities, Texas and San Diego State, appear at the back of this book as Appendices 4b-1 and 4b-2. From these it may be seen that, in addition to contents of the written plan, two factors that count heavily are the quality of an oral presentation and the viability of the venture itself as estimated by the judges. Chances of winning may be enhanced by implementing a plan as far as possible before the contest, which is to say progressing as far as possible toward the upper right-hand corner of a Realness Chart described in Chapter 3A.

3. Matters of priority

Although venture plans can be fancy, there is no need for them to be. Some ventures have raised millions in start-up capital with very simple plans.

Sophisticated investors can look past flashiness to assess whether the founders and their venture have credibility, or at least they like to believe they

Other industrial audiences

What instructors look for

What competition judges look for

Developing the text

What to present first

Organization of the rest

can. If the venture is basically flawed, the remedy should be to redesign or abandon it, not waste effort on gimmicks to make it look good. Founders should also not assume that if they simply plan well enough, they can make any venture work. Validity, realism, truthfulness, and full disclosure of worrisome as well as encouraging factors are elements to reach for in creating a plan.

Developing the text

The purposes of the plan and nature of the venture should determine what it first describes. If the market is relatively apparent, as for something that will increase life or safety, then it may be best to start with description of the product or service, showing how the venture will be able to improve on what is now available in the marketplace. If the market is not so apparent, then the starting point may be to show readers what kind of need exists, how that was determined and what characteristics of it demonstrate that it can be profitable for the venture.

These are by no means the only two possibilities, as was suggested in the preceding chapter on screening. The objective is to start by letting readers know as directly as possible just what the venture will deliver, what the most outstanding virtue of the venture is and upon what basis that virtue rests. Maybe the basis is some unarguably unusual and powerful talent on the management team, unique property rights to an invention, or a location. It could also be a lucrative contract or access to endorsement by some party whose word is likely to be strongly influential with important customers.

A step for beginning to write a formal plan, unless another one occurs and looks better, is to brainstorm and write out answers to screening, designing, and portfolio page assignments given in earlier chapters. That will automatically provide some key sections.

An important thread for organizing action steps in the plan is a time line, Gantt or PERT chart of key events, milestones, and dates. Financial forecast development can build upon this time line.

Much of the plan's purpose will be to explain in more detail just what will cause the estimates for sales and expenses to come true. The writing process can in part work back from pro forma financial statements. They can help guide description of the product or service (categories of sales), who will buy how much of it (sales figures), what labor, materials and other expenditures will have to be in order to produce and deliver it (expenses), what physical items the company will need on hand to perform that work (assets), and where the financing (liabilities) will come from to obtain them.

What to present first

First in the presentation but last to be written should be an executive summary, summarizing the main points of the plan and dollar amounts.

Next should come a table of contents with page numbers for all main sections and for appendices.

Then should come an opening paragraph for the plan describing the rationale or logic by which the plan has been organized, and how its sequence of topics will flow.

Somewhere early in the plan should be a mission statement describing what the venture should productively accomplish and a vision statement of what the venture itself should become in the time interval that the plan covers.

Organization of the rest

In general, the organization of a venture plan should present more important aspects first and elaboration later, as a newspaper article does. If the reader needs explanation to understand an important point, then possibly the explanation should come first. But if only some readers, not all, will need the explanation, then it can be placed in an appendix, with reference in the text as to where it can be found.

The list of topics to be covered is fairly predictable, although there can be striking differences in sequences, as appropriate to the individual ventures. Collections of business plans have been published by the Gale Group. For example, Volume 6 in the series presents 24 actual business plans, mostly from service enterprises, plus two fictional examples.[122] In addition, it lists sources of help in business plan preparation. These should not be looked at as

---

[122] William H. Harmer and Terrence W. Peck, eds., *Business Plans Handbook* Vol. 6 (Farmington Hills, MI: The Gale Group, 1999).

models to imitate, but rather simply as a source of ideas for developing in its own way a plan that best fits the venture. A common characteristic of the plans is the absence of any graphics, so that adding them is a way for a new plan to set itself apart from the general pattern.

4. Some elements to include

The two main parts to the plan are the body and the appendices. The body should typically be no longer than about 10 to 20 pages. The purpose of appendices, which appear at the back, is to allow a reader to go through the plan without bogging down in all the details. The body might contain a summary of market research findings and simplified financial statements. But details, such as copies of questionnaires used in the market research, or more extended financial statements and footnotes explaining the figures, should be relegated to appendices. Within the body of the plan some of the main elements to include are as follows:

Business plan elements

A. Opening

1. **Tables of contents** vary in order of topics. A common feature they should share, however, is the listing of page numbers for both sections of the plan: the body and the appendices. A deficiency that makes some plans harder to read is that their tables of contents lack any page numbers, or list page numbers for the text only, not the appendices.

2. An **executive summary**, which follows the table of contents in a venture plan, should be an abbreviated version of the overall plan so a reader can catch the main features of a venture in one page, if possible. Making it brief, however, does not mean it should be vague. Wherever possible, specific facts and figures, such as the internal rate of return (IRR) should be given. Introducing specifics need not add much, if any, length. This page is extremely important in approaching any prospective professional backers who are accustomed to reading many plans. If it does not hold their attention, they will not read further and the rest of the plan will be wasted.

3. Following the executive summary, the plan should open with **a guiding paragraph** that briefly indicates (a) what the venture will sell, (b) what the principal competitive advantage of the venture is expected to be, (c) what the venture will need to be able to accomplish that, (d) what sequence of presentation the rest of the plan will follow and, (e) why that sequence. A vital function this paragraph should perform is to let the reader know the line of reasoning by which the remainder of the plan is organized and how it is laid out.

B. Description of product or service

Another task the front section of the plan must do, in both the introductory or executive summary and the plan's opening paragraph, is let the reader know just what the venture will offer to potential customers. Usually this can be done briefly at the outset and then be further elaborated in the body of the plan.

4. **Product (or service)** refers to what the company will sell. A section in the body of the plan should state clearly what the important features of the product or service are, what stage of development they are currently in, what will be needed to develop them further, and how the venture can be expected to do that as well as or better than anyone else. For readers who may be expert in the venture's technology, a few facts may suffice. For other readers, there may be need for an appendix that will enable them to educate themselves about it.

5. **Graphics** are worth reaching for. Even an amateur sketch, although perhaps not as elegant, can be a big help for readers of the plan. Pictures can truly be worth thousands of words and most business plans would be better if they used more graphics. Recruiting help by someone with art training may be worthwhile.

C. Market plan

The market arena and how it works encompasses the next five sections.

6. **Competitive analyses** should certainly have been part of the idea screening process, and it was suggested earlier that grids, matrices, and tables can be particularly helpful in that process. Examples of such tables appear regularly in prod-

uct-centered magazines such as *Consumer Reports, InfoWorld, Motor Trend, Motorcyclist* and microcomputer magazines. They can also be found online through search engines under "product comparisons."

7. **Market research methodology** can take many forms, including library search, questionnaires, interviews, test marketing, and focus groups. Market claims for a venture should, wherever possible, be based on factual information from such sources. In school it may be appropriate only to design and pilot test a market research investigation in a way much more limited than would be called for by the real thing. An appendix in the plan should show clearly how this study was performed, including sample questionnaires and protocols, if any were used.

8. **Market research data** should also be presented in an appendix. Excerpts in the appendix to this discussion illustrate use of both verbal description and tabular forms. The data need not be massive, particularly in a school study. Some data, however meager, are better than none, provided they are factual. The data should be accompanied by enough discussion to indicate clearly how they were analyzed.

9. **Market plan elements** may be simple or complex. Tabulating sales and where they will come from for a market plan can help the writer consider alternatives more thoroughly. Writing out tends to highlight any incompleteness. Noticing empty cells is a prompt to search for options that might fill them. If none are found, cells can still be left blank without diminishing value of the tabulation. The blanks can stimulate searching by readers, who also may be able to suggest more alternatives to formulate a better marketing strategy.

10. **Sales projections** will probably come directly from notes made during idea checkout. The text of the venture plan should contain at least a summary, perhaps in graphical form.

D. Operations plan

11. **Event schedules**, shown as lists, time lines, PERT and/or Gantt charts are useful tools for planning the sequence of important actions in getting a venture started and for communicating it to others. Simple versions in the text and backups as appendices with more detail may be helpful. Milestones should include in particular any key accomplishments upon which additional outside funding might be contingent.

12. **Organization charts**, both before and after the venture actually starts, should show clearly who will be the main leader and how other key members of the venture's workforce will be positioned in the power structure.[123] Somewhere in the plan there should also be indication of how ownership will be divided and a list of any key outside advisors. This should include, as soon as they have been chosen, names of any law and accounting firms that will be retained.

13. **Resumes** should be included as they do in the Prize-Winning Plan case herein. Of particular importance in them should be those aspects of prior experience that show relevance to the job tasks of this particular venture and evidence of accomplishment in prior challenging projects where something new had to be created under difficult circumstances.

E. Spending plan

14. **Applications of funds** will be a matter of considerable interest to whoever puts up money for a venture. Presumably some applications, such as advertising or administrative costs, will be unrecoverable in the event the venture terminates. Others, such as capital equipment, inventory, or development that results in patents, may continue to have value that will reduce potential losses.

15. **Cost breakdowns** must be made as part of forecasting both cash needs and profitability. The more that major elements of the costs can be subdivided and explained, or backed up with references, the more convincing the forecasts become. One option is to give limit effort on costs in the first draft of a plan but include a brief discussion of how the figures would be further refined if more time were available to work on them.

F. Pricing considerations

Price considerations should be given explicit attention from several perspectives in the venture plan.

16. **Pricing rationale** does not rest solely upon costs. But certainly the relationship between price and costs must be examined, including the way that costs are likely to vary with volume.

17. **Price/volume curves** can be important in formulating competitive strategy. Whichever company is able to move more quickly to lower costs, either by economies of scale or other ingenuity, can enjoy a pricing advantage. Competitors' prices, how they have changed in the past and what competitors might be able to do about them in the future should be explained.

---

[123] A two-stage organization chart example from a venture plan appears in Vesper, *New Venture Mechanics*, pp. 338-339.

G. Financial analysis

Financial analysis includes five different aspects. Each was called for in checking out the venture idea. All that should be required for the venture plan is to copy that analysis over with refinements of the calculations and explanations so that readers will understand how they were done. The text of the plan should include key summary elements of this analysis, with details relegated to backup appendices.

18. **Break-even analysis** can be made with either a numerical or graphical approach. The advantage of a numerical approach, dividing fixed costs by unit contribution or by gross margin percentage, is speed and simplicity. The advantage of a graphical approach, which can most accurately be done by using figures from a pro forma income projection, is that it can take into account non-linearity and should be more accurate. It may also be quicker and easier for a reader to absorb. Two different dimensions desirable for the horizontal axis are (a) sales volume and (b) target date.

19. **Pro forma financial projections** form a major structural element for most business plans. They set forth what the founders will have as goals in creating the new enterprise. The sensitivity of cash needs, profits, and return to influential assumptions should be explored by trying different numbers for such things as sales, expenses, and collection schedules. It can be helpful to include in the plan different forecasts, one optimistic, one pessimistic, and one most likely.

20. **Cash flow** projections. Notwithstanding the importance of pro forma financial statements for setting goals, cash flow is what the venture will most have to live by. The shortcut approach in creating cash flow projections is to add back non-cash charges to changes in the balance sheet. Much more useful, because non-cash charges don't actually tell where cash is coming from or going to, is to list all the actual cash inflows, outflows, and their sources by month.

21. **Footnotes to the forecasts** are vital for backing them up. Explaining sources of the numbers will enhance their credibility. Factual bases and important assumptions behind the numbers should be clearly stated and distinguished from each other. In an early draft plan, such as might be prepared as part of a one-term course in school, it may not be possible to have strong substantiation for the numbers. In that case, it is still important to say how they were arrived at, even though a fair amount of imagination may have been involved. Beyond that, it can help to describe what specific action might be taken if more time were available to work on increasing reliability of the numbers.

22. **Return on investment (ROI) analysis** can be added to save the reader time in computing it. The long run test of a venture may include many aspects, including survival and satisfaction of founders, employees, and customers. From a financial standpoint, the main test will probably be return on cash invested in the enterprise. An important aspect of this return will be the internal rate of return that the venture earns on assets entrusted to it. If this is strong, then the investors' return is likely to be strong also. How the figures are arrived at should be made clear in the plan.

23. **Risk factors** may or may not be listed in a section under that title. In principle, a business plan should be designed with maximum realism; in real life, risk is a part of the picture. In contrast to a legal brief or an advertisement, whose purpose is to bias a reader by loading all the arguments only on one side, a venture plan should be balanced, lest it make reader and writer antagonists rather than the collaborators they should be. Grouping risk factors into one section is sometimes an efficient way to introduce this balance. The facts on which those factors are based may speak adequately for themselves. Alternatively, risk factors may be pointed out at those points in the plan where important assumptions are made.

Help from other people

As a cross-check in evaluating the business plan, it can be helpful to have others read and comment. They may include friends or family members not necessarily familiar with business who can assess readability and perhaps also market feasibility, to the extent that they can empathize with the venture's potential users. For more solid business reactions, the opinions of people experienced in related lines of work may help. These might include prospective employees, suppliers, or sellers of what the company will offer. People affiliated with the Small Business Administration such as active and retired executives who volunteer their time may be good reviewers. Other successful entrepreneurs often like to help new start-ups and may be willing to look over their plans.

Surprisingly, perhaps, even future competitors may be willing to help, although obviously it can be risky to share an idea with them. How Hewlett-Packard reacted to what turned out to be a future competitor is illustrative:

Help from other people

William Hewlett temporarily left the company he had founded with David Packard to serve in the U.S. Army during World War II. There he met and was impressed by a young engineer, Howard Vollum, who had an idea for a new kind of oscilloscope. At Hewlett's suggestion, Vollum met with David Packard, who recalled:

During our conversation it became clear to both of us that rather than joining HP, Vollum really wanted to start his own company . . . and we helped him do just that. We lined him up with Norm Neely and many of our other sales representative firms across the United States. Thus was born Tektronix, the Oregon-based company that became the dominant oscilloscope supplier in the world.

As time went on it became quite clear that if we were going to offer a complete line of electronic measuring instruments, we needed to fill in the line with our own oscilloscope. So in 1956 we designed an oscilloscope, the model 150, which we hoped would provide a strong challenge to Tektronix.

Packard continued, pointing out that the model 150 was unreliable, and subsequent Hewlett-Packard challenges to Tektronix' dominance were unsuccessful for a number of years until his company developed a computer-managed system which eventually prevailed.[124]

Those most qualified to review plans in general may be venture capitalists, people who make a living at reviewing others' plans in a variety of businesses. *Inc.* magazine reached this conclusion after presenting each of 27 business plans to panels of experts, then tracking the ventures over time to see how they worked out. Of the 27, the number of ventures surviving two or three years later was 17.[125] *Inc.* ranked the experts it used in terms of quality of advice as proven by hindsight, as follows: (1) venture capitalists with positions in companies comparable to the start-ups they were evaluating; (2) operators of similar businesses; (3) direct competitors; (4) customers; and (5) observers, including academics and editors of trade journals. Venture capitalists were hands down best at foreseeing the ventures' futures, said the magazine, pointing out, however, that it was probably easier for the magazine to get counsel from them. It would be difficult for an entrepreneur in whose venture they were not actually investing to get venture capitalists to give much, if any, review effort.

According to the *Inc.* experts venture plans should anticipate a number of pitfalls, such as the following:

- Sales will grow more slowly than expected.
- Selling costs are vulnerable to underestimation on many items, from salespeople's salaries to conference attendance expenses.
- Most start-ups aim at markets that are too broad in terms of customers or geographic territories, or they introduce too many different products.
- People with experience crucial to the start-up are too often not given stock or other incentives to keep them dedicated to the venture.
- Operating costs and overhead easily rise, and too often are allowed to.
- Gaining a customer does not mean the customer will be loyal.

The *Inc.* editors also suggested some rules of their own from the way the ventures eventually turned out, including the following:

- *Nobody likes your product as much as you do.* The more successful entrepreneurs applied more effort to assessing the need for their products.
- *If you don't have experience, buy it.* Founders with prior experience in their industries did better than those without it.
- *Your competitors aren't dumb.* Studying how they operate and expecting them to respond to new entrants pays.
- *It isn't the sales. It's the sales cycle.* Founders tend to underestimate the capital needed, particularly for coping with the length of time it will take to gain market acceptance.
- *Don't underestimate how much time simply being the boss will eat up.* The only way to avoid being buried by the enormous amount of minutiae that will arise is through delegation. Each element by itself may be simple—government reporting, sick leave, holidays, little things that go wrong—but together they can become overwhelming without help.

Help from software

How about using a computer program? Ok, but there is risk it may not fit the venture well. Moreover, it cannot provide the substantiation that must lie behind the plan. Figuring out

---

[124] David Packard, *The HP Way* (New York: Harper Business, 1995) p. 78.
[125] Leslie Brokaw, "The Truth about Start-Ups," *Anatomy of a Startup* (Boston: *Inc.* Publishing, 1991) p. 364.

what that substantiation should be is part of the planning process and getting the substantiation is all that can give the plan strength. Also, planning is a thought process, and by letting a preformatted computer program determine its construction is to leave important parts of the thought process out. For some mechanical details, like running out the calculations on statements for instance, it may be helpful.

A number of microcomputer programs, such as Ronstadt's Financials, are available for help in planning. However, their output is limited by the quality of the planner's input. Their questions and prompts may indicate areas that need consideration. Financial forecasts can be generated either with a planning program or by using simple software. Either way, each major assumption used should be explicitly stated and keyed to the forecast with an appropriately positioned footnote, so that readers can judge the validity of the assumptions independently. Danger signals in the assumptions may include:

- Absence of footnotes to go with numbers that represent substantial fractions of total sales or total assets.
- Figures that, with no explanation, stay flat or escalate in regular steps over time.
- Amounts that seem unreasonable compared with industry averages such as those published by Robert Morris Associates or Dun and Bradstreet, those of comparable companies, or those to which the reader reacts based on prior experience.

Sometimes, of course, it is necessary in forecasting to pull numbers "out of the blue," even though they cannot be well supported. In such cases, the footnotes should admit that this has been done. Readers may then offer their own improved estimates.

Besides running the obvious computer cross-checks on spreadsheet totals and spell checking on textual sections, it may be helpful to apply a project management program, such as Microsoft's Project. Based on examination of 20 ventures, Dean[126] reported that project management techniques were useful in start-up planning for

- Examining the use of critical resources.
- Coordinating control of tasks in development of the venture.
- Reducing unnecessary duplication of work and increasing staff efficiency.
- Enhancing adaptation to a dynamic competitive environment.

Use of project management tools requires identification of tasks to be performed during the start-up, an estimated dollar cost for each, and beginning and completion dates. Entry of these into a project management software program will result in review displays such as Gantt and PERT charts, which are useful in uncovering potential omissions and conflicts in the plan. They are also helpful in showing the plan to others who, before undertaking the venture, can help with cross-checking and with implementation during start-up.

5. Presentation

Experts who have reviewed countless venture proposals point out that plans that are too sketchy or sloppy will discourage potential investors from struggling to discern what they mean, and also reflect adversely on the competence and craftsmanship of founders who submit them. Plans that are too long, elaborate, complex, or fancy may be rejected if they seem to reflect a misapplication of priority from substance to form. A balance between these extremes that is clean, clear, easy, and interesting to read should be sought. That still leaves room for creativity in written presentation, as experts Stanley Rich and David Gumpert have pointed out.

> Of all the hundreds of business plans that have been submitted to the MIT Enterprise Forum, one stands out as so exemplary in its format that it can serve as a model plan. This plan was like other plans in that it contained text on each right-hand sheet through the book; what distinguished it from other plans was that each

---

[126] Burton V. Dean, "The Project-Management Approach in the 'Systematic Management' of Innovative Start-up Firms," *Journal of Business Venturing*, 1 no. 2, Spring 1986, p. 149.

page was summarized on the left hand page. That is, each left-hand page—left blank in other plans—contained sets of bulleted highlight phrases, so that it was possible to read the summarized version of the entire business plan in somewhat under ten minutes!

Those of us who reviewed the plan… all felt that we had seen the ultimate in business plans. Each of us approached it the same way: We read the summary through, from cover to cover, to gain an overview of the company's objectives and approaches to achieving them. Once our appetites were sufficiently whetted, we then read the detailed document. This business plan truly turned into a book we couldn't put down until we had read through to the last page—in one sitting![127]

Mistakes to avoid

Things to avoid in plan writing, whether for school or for the real thing, include the following:

Length for its own sake It is easy to bulk up a plan with magazine articles about the industry and various kinds of literature or, even worse, with simple verbosity. No reader is likely to welcome that.

Adulation of the venture or its founders (e.g. "Our excellent product and highly talented management group…"). Such judgments as whether the founding team is competent and virtuous, whether the venture is highly likely to succeed and whether its product or service will be wonderful should be left to the reader.

Irrelevant information If there is a shortage of information on something important to the venture there may be a temptation to make up for it by including information on something else that happens to be conveniently available even though irrelevant. Such compensation does not help.

Duplication of reference materials readily **available elsewhere** It may be appropriate to excerpt sections selectively. However, references available in a library should simply be footnoted.

Directly imitating another plan or adopting a canned format Not letting the design of the plan follow from the logic of the individual venture introduces risks of mismatch in priorities, illogical reasoning, apparent imitation, and shallow thinking.

Reliance on the written document alone For a venture plan to be accepted, there will have to be personal meetings between the writer and the reviewer.

Tacking on elements such as financial forecasts, a mission statement, vision statement, story line, slogan, or elevator pitch without clear linkage to the reasoning that goes with them.

Finally, having someone other than the lead entrepreneur or member(s) of the founding team write the plan is usually a mistake. As with using a computerized routine for preparation, the problem is that the thinking will not be that of someone intimately familiar with what the venture is about and so will be wrong. By delegating the task of thinking the venture through, the founder(s) will be less well equipped to pursue it effectively.

Oral presentation

If the plan author(s) are called upon to present the venture plan orally, further steps are in order. Graphical displays can help both with clarity and as a pacing tool to stay within a time limit. Without being too complex to comprehend, they can still compress more information into less time.

Computer projection is fine, if the equipment can be depended upon and if the presenter is familiar with using it. For backup it will probably be wise to have available overhead transparencies and handouts as well, both as an aid for the audience to use in making notes and in case of computer or projector malfunction.

A further strength can be to have available alternative presentations of subsections with more details. These can be held in reserve and brought forth in response to listener questions or requests for more elaboration. Spare copies of the written plan on hand can serve a similar function.

But over-talking is also a risk. Keeping an eye on the audience and being ready to compress the presentation or skip ahead to a fresh point, even to stop earlier than planned if they look restless or their attention seems to be wandering, is also a desirable capability.

Physical demonstration of the product or service can be highly effective but also risky.

---

[127] Stanley R. Rich, and David E. Gumpert, *Business Plans That Win $$$* (New York: Harper & Row, 1985) p. 41.

Glitches can detract seriously. One alternative is a video display. Another is to set up physically but then shift to the video or handouts quickly if things start to go wrong.

Especially helpful should be multiple rehearsals ahead of time in front of one or more sympathetic but knowledgeable and critical audiences. If there is a time limit, then those rehearsals should be timed and practiced until they fit within the limit. The natural temptation will be to try packing too much into the available time and to do it by talking faster. But that will more likely lose listeners.

The following are some critical comments by a panel of experienced business people who were viewing oral presentations of half a dozen teams in an engineering entrepreneurship class at the University of California, San Diego. The comments have been regrouped but not restated.

Product

1. What is the value added (value proposition)? How is your technology actually better? How will it stay better?

2. Has your device been spec'd out?

3. What do you actually own? Who owns the patents and what do they cover? Could your technology be used in other industries? How fast will this become obsolete?

4. Did you check on packaging costs?

Strategy

1. How does your business model work? What is the revenue model? Did you consider just setting up as a technology licensing company?

2. I like the fact that you are scalable.

3. What does the competitive landscape look like? Tell us about competitors, their capabilities, and what they are up to. What is your sustainable advantage? What is going to separate you favorably from the competition? I liked that you covered competitors.

4. What are you seeking to become? Where will you be in five years—what is the scope of your business goals?

Marketing

1. What will be the experience of the user? What skills and time will be required of a user?

2. What will be your relationship with customers?

3. What is the cost/price relationship? What is the cost/price breakdown, and how much is left for investors?

Operations

1. What will your establishment physically consist of?

2. What makes you think your pilot run will be representative?

3. How will you manage security?

Financial

1. What is your proposition for investors? How do investors make out?

2. Let's see your financials. I see no explanation of money applications and milestones.

Presentation

1. You should walk us through the whole business plan in ten minutes. Have a dollar flow diagram early on that lays out the business model.

2. Big type on your slides—good. (different team) Your slides are hard to read. (different team) Your static display did not fit with points made.

It should help to listen carefully to such questions and comments from an audience, repeat them if necessary, and try to give listeners what they ask for. Replies should aim to add thought-out information about what is special in the venture.

The most reliable preparation for effective oral presentation will be to think through the venture and develop in-depth factual expertise about the technology, industry, key people, and what will be needed to have it work. With solid thinking about the venture as a foundation, even a less-than-elegant oral presentation can work, as illustrated by the following.

When Jerry Kaplan was setting out to develop a venture that would design and produce a "tablet" computer in 1987, he received, thanks to a prominent entrepreneur friend, an invitation to "drop by" and meet some partners in the well-known West Coast venture capital firm of Kleiner, Perkins, Caulfield and Byers. Thinking it was to be an informal get-acquainted meeting, rather than a formal presentation. "I was," he recalled, "unprepared." Wearing an informal sport jacket and shirt open at the collar, all he carried with him was a thin leather briefcase with a tablet of paper and pen inside. *No business plan, no*

35-millimeter slides, no charts, no financial projections, no prototypes.

Entering the conference room he found that another entrepreneur in suit and tie was wrapping up a presentation complete with a color graph on display and a prototype circuit on the table. As the man collected his belongings and left, a partner told him he would receive a response on his proposal in about a week. Then the audience faced Kaplan.

I was, Kaplan recalled, nearing a state of panic. I paused to size things up, knowing that the brief silence before diving in would create a momentary impression of authority. In reality, I was searching for a strategy.

I had a flash of déjà vu. I remembered facing this same kind of 'show me' crowd at my PhD dissertation defense. The key there was in recognizing that although the examination committee had the power, I had the knowledge.

Kaplan then described his concept for a tablet-type computer that would be controlled with a pen rather than keyboard, and he listed such applications as "to take notes; send and receive messages through cellular telephone links; look up addresses, phone numbers, price lists, and inventories; do spreadsheet calculations and fill out order forms." Then, after pledging his own commitment to the project, he described some of the technical difficulties that would have to be overcome. He recalled:

My audience seemed tense. I couldn't tell whether they were annoyed by my lack of preparation, or merely concentrating on what I was saying. Several people narrowed their eyes disapprovingly—or perhaps they were just deep in thought. I had been talking non-stop for about ten minutes, and I figured I'd better close.

Thinking I had already blown it, and therefore had little to lose, I decided to risk some theatrics. 'If I were carrying a portable PC right now, you would sure as hell know it. You probably didn't realize that I am holding a model of the future of computing right here in my hand.' I tossed my maroon leather case in the air. It sailed to the center of the table, where it landed with a loud clap. 'Gentlemen, here is a model of the next step in the computer revolution.'

For a moment, I thought this final act of drama might get me thrown out of the room. They were sitting in stunned silence, staring at my plain leather folder—which lay motionless on the table—as though it were suddenly going to come to life …

As Kaplan described it, the assembled partners then took over with discussion of technical challenges and possibilities. He got their full support, as will be discussed further in a later chapter on teaming.[128]

If the written and/or oral presentation succeeds, the real test to follow will consist of accomplishing its aims successfully. Implementing the venture will quickly give the entrepreneur(s) new information that makes the plan, part by part, obsolete even as its purpose is served and it becomes time to plan again.

Exercises

Text discussion questions

1. What are the arguments for and against formal venture plan preparation?
2. How can a computerized venture plan preparation program help and what are its limitations?
3. When should a venture plan be shown to whom and for what reasons?
4. Which elements of a business plan are most versus least important?
5. Which elements are most versus least difficult to prepare?
6. What part of a business plan should be written last and why?
7. What, in rank order, would you regard as the three most dangerous pitfalls of venture planning, and how might they best be dealt with?
8. What are the pros and cons of rehearsing oral presentation of a business plan?

Case questions

4B-1. Prize-Winning Plan

1. This plan is excellent, but no plan is perfect. Describe explicitly some ways it could be improved without changing how the venture itself would be done and without gathering any new information.

---

[128] Jerry Kaplan, *Startup* (New York: Penguin, 1994) p. 24.

2. In what specific ways should this plan be tailored to its expected audience?
3. On what aspects would this plan rate highest and which lowest on the contest rating sheets of Appendices 4b-1 and 4b-2?
4. If the team wants to follow the plan, what action assignments should it make for its members?

Portfolio page possibilities

Page 4B-1 Executive summary
Write an executive summary for one of your venture ideas.

Page 4B-2 Elevator pitch
1. Write out a two-minute elevator pitch for a new business idea of your own.
2. Explain how it is different from your executive summary and why.

Page 4B-3 Oral presentation
1. Prepare a set of slides that you summarize on one portfolio page.
2. Include some "back pocket" supplementary slides for response to expected questions.

Page 4B-4 Alternative plan outlines
List two different outlines for the plan of one venture. Explain the advantages and disadvantages of each.

Page 4B-5 Time line
Prepare a detailed time line of actions and events for the first year or two of your venture, explaining insofar as the page limit allows.

Page 4B-6 Gantt/PERT
Prepare a Gantt or PERT chart for the first year or two of your venture, elaborating insofar as the page limit allows.

Page 4B-7 Depiction
1. Prepare a picture showing one or more aspects of what your venture will offer.
2. Display on one page some other graphics such as charts or diagrams characterizing your venture.

Page 4B-8 Executive summary
Write a one-page executive summary for your business plan.

Page 4B-9 First paragraph
Write a first paragraph for your business plan that is appropriately different from the executive summary.

Term Projects

Venture history

1. What form did the entrepreneur's mental anticipation of future events in the venture take if not a written business plan?
2. To whom did the founder(s) find need to describe during start-up what the company would become, and what different ways was that done?
3. What feedback did the founders get ahead of time about how the venture would develop, whom did they get it from, and over what dates on the venture's timeline?
4. Did the founders become more convinced about the value of formal planning from doing the start-up, or less so?

Venture planning guide

1. Write the two most critical sections of a plan for your venture, explaining why they are such.
2. Prepare, and rate, alternative graphical aids for inclusion in your plan.
3. List features you could incorporate in your plan to make it unusually distinctive without compromising quality. Carry at least one out.
4. Perform an oral dress rehearsal of your plan, complete with visual aids. Time it with a stopwatch to be not less than 5 or more than 10 minutes. Role play a tough question and answer session.
5. Assess your plan using the rating sheets in Appendix 4b-1 and/or 4b-2.
6. Present your plan to a professional investor or banker and get feedback.

Part 5

FINANCING

This section presents three chapters on how ventures get financing: (1) inception or seed capital, (2) debt capital, the main sources for most ventures, and (3) outside capital, which is less commonly used and applies mainly to high-growth enterprises.

Initial seed capital, the subject of Chapter 5A, typically begins with the entrepreneur's personal savings, partly because that is simple and partly because other people's confidence for helping finance a venture is increased by the venture already having money in it and the entrepreneur having shown both an ability to pile up money and also enough confidence and commitment to the venture to commit savings to it.

It makes sense for a would-be entrepreneur to begin a personal savings campaign in order to have money to begin with when the venture opportunity comes into view. At that time it will also be wise to prepare estimates of how much will be needed both to live on and to start financing the venture. The amount needed may not be all that great, judging by the experience of prior success stories, including some that became very great. But the power of being able to get started on personal resources can be a great help in letting the entrepreneur concentrate on creating the business, as opposed to hunting capital. It will also allow retention of more ownership and control and put the entrepreneur in a better position to seek outside capital later on when the venture has become more a reality and less only a dream.

Borrowing, the subject of the Chapter 5B in this section, is usually where ventures get money next. Many entrepreneurs get it first from credit card borrowing, a source that is easy to draw upon, but that charges very high interest. Borrowing may also start with signing leases for equipment, which is in some important respects similar to borrowing where the equipment constitutes collateral. Or it may start with trade credit from suppliers if the venture looks to them fairly certain to pay its bills on time.

Typically after one or more of these potential debt sources has been tapped, a bank may loan the enterprise money. It will want to see that the venture seems to be taking off well, the entrepreneur has invested substantial personal capital in the business or can back the loan with personal collateral, or the business has customer orders that look certain to be paid. If the venture has been extending credit to customers and thereby gaining accounts receivable, the bank may loan against those. If it will not, they can probably be sold to a factoring company at a discount, which will in effect be high interest.

Chapter 5C in this financing section describes potential sources of equity financing for the business. They begin with private investors, or "angels." Usually millionaires, many of these people are themselves entrepreneurs who have become successful and would like to participate in other ventures by helping them get started by offering both money and advice.

Venture capital firms are easier to find but less likely to invest because their aim is to back only ventures with extremely high profit and growth potential. Their aim is to cash in when the venture is sold to another company or goes public. The latter is something the venture can attempt on its own. But it is a highly expensive process that must be justified by the promise of high returns on a large amount of money.

CHAPTER 5A – Inception Capital

Topics

1. Array of financing styles
2. Applications of first cash
3. Historical amounts needed
4. Sources of start-up cash
5. Terms

Checkpoints

a. Describe the array of individual funding styles.
b. Contrast cash needs of the entrepreneur versus the venture.
c. How can cash needs in a start-up be minimized?
d. What are the causes of shortfall in funding new ventures?
e. Describe the pitfalls that occur in forecasting start-up cash needs.
f. What seed financing patterns have been seen historically?
g. How do start-up cash needs vary by line of business?
h. What is the array of sources for obtaining first seed capital?
i. Explain the important criteria for choosing seed funding sources.

What are some differences in the ways start-ups get seed capital?

To an entrepreneur who wonders how to raise it, capital often appears to be the key to moving forward with a venture. In fact, the real key is evidence that the venture can justify capital with an appropriate positive cash flow. Capital represents social permission to use physical resources and efforts of others to produce something new. That financial permission may be inherited, gained in a speculation, or accumulated through work and savings. It can also be acquired as a loan or investment on the basis of a convincing track record, persuasive argument, business plan, or combinations of such factors.

This chapter will concentrate on starting with equity from working founders, leaving later chapters to describe use of debt, venture capital, and public offerings to raise cash.

1. Array of financing styles

The range of styles entrepreneurs use for financing ventures varies and any "typical" examples are bound to fall short of full representation. Here, however, are some types.

The **True Independent** starts and continues with savings. That way nobody else's permission is needed to apply resources for starting the business.

About half of the ventures in the Cooper, et al. study drew upon services of unpaid family members during start-up.[129] When they did, it was one member in half the cases, two in about a third, and three or more in the remainder. In about a third of the cases, the typical time given by those members was less than 10 hours per week and in another third it was 40 or more hours per week. Thus, family member "sweat equity" contributions are significant in many start-ups.

---

[129] Arnold C. Cooper and others, *New Business in America* (Washington, D.C.: The NFIB Foundation, 1990).

After working as manager of a record store, a young man decided he would rather work for himself by opening his own store. With a wife and two children to support, he did not make the decision quickly. He grew to dislike the job, and when he was told to shave, his discontent became severe. Conversations with some friends who operated their own record stores and told him how much money they made clinched the decision. "It made me mad," he said with a deleted adjective, "because I should have been doing this 15 years ago." He chose to specialize in what he knew from experience were harder to find kinds of music.

To finance the start-up he took advantage of a credit card advertisement that came in the mail and offered $15,000 in credit. Some of this he used to visit a distant record store that was having a sale at 50 percent off where he selectively bought inventory, initially storing it at home.

He found a store location near where he had worked before, figuring that old customers who knew him would more likely shop there. To get the site he even shaved, figuring it would help convince the landlord he was "a stand-up guy." He economized cash by enlisting a friend who knew carpentry, plus his father, to help with the cabinets and display furnishings. The only new thing he bought for the store was a cash register. Sales edged up within the first few months to $1,000 per day. With a markup of 50 percent on used records and CD's and 30 percent on new ones, he soon covered the rent and paid down his credit card debt, relieved to get rid of its high interest charges.

The **Partner** extends personal savings by joining forces with others to undertake the venture as a mutual effort. Family members of partners may also become involved, as with the True Independent. Examples of partnership beginnings include Apple, Intel, Microsoft, Hewlett-Packard, and Procter & Gamble. A common pattern is illustrated by the following venture.

In 1997 software developers at two different companies began having conversations about need for a program that would prevent reverse engineering of net-downloaded programs. The one whose employer most closely dealt in products of that type proposed that his employer develop it. The president declined, saying the market was too uncertain for such a gamble. Hence, the two began working on the program in their off hours.

When the program was ready in 1998, they began letting others know their plans, then with $40,000 between them from personal savings,

the two quit their jobs, formed the new company, and started recruiting customers. To save cash, nobody in the office received any salary until the fourth month and advertising was performed mainly via email. Within two months the company's cash flow, including founder salaries, had turned positive.

The **Enticing Deal Seller** hasn't adequate savings to start alone or as a family unit, possibly because of low wealth, or because the start-up requires large up-front investment. But the venture concept is so apparently attractive and/or the individual is so persuasive that other private investors put up the money. They may be family, friends, or individuals met through business contacts such as stockbrokers, other professionals, and other entrepreneurs. Their investment may be based on hardheaded business analysis, emotion, or both. An enticing deal, for instance, might be stock in the company, or a royalty in exchange for the personal guarantee of a loan at the bank. This could offer an infinite rate of return to the guarantor while restricting leverage of the borrower. However, the venture does not get to keep the money, and the guarantor could lose the amount of the loan.

An entrepreneur with a product claiming to be a "voice stress analyzer" needed money to have it produced and also pay to advertise it for sale by mail. His proposition to potential backers was that if they paid for the advertisements he would use all the cash that came in from sales first to pay them back, then to pay the producer. After that the initial backers would receive half again what they put up. Soon his advertisements appeared in airline magazines, generating orders and revenues that he distributed as promised.

The **Founding Team Creator** extends the partner concept to recruit complementary talents forming a balanced top management. The team may be dedicated to objectives other than ambitious profits, in which case the start-up financial resources will be limited to personal savings of the team members and those of their families and friends. Or the enterprise might be capital-intensive to set up a plant, employ the team, and generate capital gains. Historical examples of this approach include

Ford and DuPont corporations. One more recent is the following:

Taking up brewing as a hobby in 1991 led to the idea of starting a local brewery for a Florida resident who was educated as a mechanical engineer and worked for an auto manufacturer. He studied about brewing in his spare time, reading extensively, attending seminars, and even spending $1,500 to attend a Midwestern brewing school during vacation. By early 1993 he had completed a business plan for recruiting partners to produce keg beer for local accounts. It contained data about equipment and other costs as well as most appropriate cities for location, including several in the Rockies, Idaho, and North Carolina.

His personal savings let him commit $61, 000, but his forecasts called for $200,000 total. Figuring he could borrow $39,000 against purchase of brewing equipment left a need for $100,000 from partners.

He made a list of non-immediate family, friends, co-workers, and other acquaintances who might be able to invest, finally narrowing it to eight people. To these he made his pitch. Five invested, and three others who had learned of the venture second hand approached him to join. The effort he had applied to self-education and to development and careful refinement of a written business plan had, he concluded, paid off well.

Each of the investors' checks was deposited in an escrow account under a shareholder subscription agreement that guaranteed return of the money unless the total needed was received by a specified date. After several months the total was reached, and in 1994 the business began. Performance closely followed projections.

The **Venture Capital Sequence Follower** starts a company whose concept promises to justify high investment over a series of stages or financing rounds, which culminate in a liquidity event, permitting its investors to cash out, having taken high risk for high return. This event may be either a public stock offering or sellout to another company for cash or stock. The venture's potential for reaching this outcome is based upon such competitive advantages as exceptional talents on the team, powerful patent protection, or other major barriers to competitive entry, combined with a market of high profit and growth potential.

Voted a finalist for the "most promising new company" in 1999 by the Washington Software Alliance, "Avenue A" was seeded by personal savings of a lead entrepreneur plus three partners. The original intent of the company when it started in 1997 was to help Web site operators advertise more effectively. But after talking with companies that would buy the advertising, including some that used the Web for that purpose and others that did not, the founders decided that a better opportunity would be to help them by tracking and analyzing the click patterns they received, how many of those resulted in sales, and so forth. The first customers signed up in April 1998.

Following the personally financed seed money, the founders recruited some wealthy angel investors for a second round of cash injection. Then in 1999 came a third round, this time from venture capital firms to bring the total investment to $26 million. By 1999 the number of clients had risen to 50, and in February 2000, Avenue A commenced its fourth round, an Initial Public Offering (IPO) to sell stock to the public.

From contrasts among such individual styles and financing sequences, as well as other sources that will be noted in this chapter and others to follow, many patterns are possible. It therefore can behoove an entrepreneur to think flexibly and imaginatively in seeking resources for start-up. There will always be room for fresh approaches, as will be illustrated further. Choosing among them calls for awareness of what is to be gained or lost coupled with judgment about what can work for the type of venture and what matters most to the entrepreneur.

2. Applications of first cash

Start-up capital gives an entrepreneur permission to start a venture. Money from sales gives permission to continue it. The entrepreneur must add enough of the first to survive until the second arrives. Moreover, the first must have two parts. One is enough for the founder(s) to live on personally. The other is enough beyond that for the business to consume until it becomes sufficiently cash–flow–positive to support payroll for employees and the founders and meet commitments to backers.

Personal cash needs

Venture financing generally begins with the entrepreneur's own money from savings, wages, and possibly from family and friends. Often the longer that savings base can stretch, the stronger is the founder's bargaining position for continuing. It usually makes financial sense to adopt as soon as possible a personal lifestyle that builds savings. Tactics that can help include (1) avoiding debt on anything that does not increase in value faster than the rate of interest (i.e., pay credit cards before accruing interest charges if possible and don't borrow for consumer items like cars, clothing, or electronics), (2) living in low-cost accommodations such as with parents or roommates, (3) not buying expensive luxury items, (4) traveling only for essentials or business, (5) not loaning money except on a for-profit business basis, (6) driving a low-cost old car that has a cheap license and no collision insurance coverage, (7) avoiding expensive eating out or entertainment, and (8) possibly investing but (9) not gambling against professionals. Save with discipline.

Personal cash planning for start-up should anticipate not only usual expenses of food, clothing, and accommodations, but also emergencies that can and, for most people, do crop up by surprise. Inflation in living costs will inexorably occur, but increase of income to cope with it may not. Simply changing personal routines to work on the venture, such as by taking time off from a job or hiring others to perform home repairs rather than doing them personally, can increase living expenses during start-up.

Work time on the entrepreneur's regular job may have to be cut back or eliminated to pursue the venture. Promotions and raises may consequently stop, as may even the job when a present employer becomes aware that the entrepreneur has chosen another way to get ahead economically. Fringe benefits, medical coverage, vacation pay, and sick leave may end. And if the venture fails, these various former advantages may not return readily to a person who has demonstrated a preference for independence, let alone one with a recent failure.

Bill Lear made ends meet personally when beginning his long career as an entrepreneur by starting out as a consultant to radio manufacturers. He would, for pay, help them redesign their radios for higher performance. Through working on their problems he also developed some product ideas of his own that he could manufacture and, in some cases, patent personally. The consulting not only paid his living expenses, it also developed his contacts and identified customers for his own proprietary products, which in turn developed the basis for his own manufacturing enterprise.

Other ways to get by personally and build up a stake for venturing, aside from consulting, include working at a moonlight job to earn support income or, alternatively, working on the venture as a moonlight activity and/or having a spouse who earns income. The Cooper et al. study of 2,994 firms[130] found that 8 percent of the entrepreneurs held other full-time jobs during the first year of start-up, while 7 percent held part-time jobs and another 4 percent held irregular jobs. Thirty-five percent had a spouse who was employed full time outside the start-up, and another 11 percent had one employed outside part time.

Venture cash needs

Cash needs of the venture should be anticipated by generating financial forecasts, as was discussed earlier in projecting financial attractiveness. How those needs come into play can be seen in the following example of a start-up retail store to sell and install auto radios.

Total seed capital was $30,000, of which $5,000 was used to buy inventory, with suppliers agreeing to advance another $32,000 worth to be paid for within 30 days. The landlord was persuaded to wait 60 days for initial lease payments. Cash was then needed for the following items:

- City, county, state permits and licenses
- Building inspection costs
- Radio installation tools
- Insurance
- Leasehold improvements
- Office furniture
- Office supplies
- Salary for one employee

[130] Cooper and others, *New Business*, p. 16.

Other cash expenditures the company was able to defer, and fortunately the start-up process proceeded quickly, so that the founder was able to continue making ends meet until profits took hold.

Some further cash-consuming venture activities to consider appear in the next list below. It may help to rank order the items according to total first-year expenditure amount. Despite conscientious thinking to be complete, there will almost certainly be omissions. How will tax prepayments be handled? What if a supplier wants payment in advance, or a customer wants (or simply takes) extended credit? What if a supplier raises a price or tacks on some charge for service, COD, or late payment? Were all insurance coverages included? What if something breaks or is stolen? What will be done while waiting to replace it? What if there is a lawsuit over something? What if a personal emergency requiring cash arises for the entrepreneur at home? It is altogether too easy to see the need for start-up cash and at the same time to underestimate how great it will be.

- Travel expenses
- Correspondence
- Lawyer fees
- Prototype creation
- Logo design
- Advertisements
- Trade show booth
- Computers, software
- Phone, ISP
- Domain names
- Trademarks, patenting
- Tooling
- Travel
- Rental deposits
- Initial inventory
- Phone, fax, and mail
- Production equipment
- Accounting and tax help

Spreading these expenditures out month by month and adding them up will forecast the cash flowing out, which can be cumulated month by month to show a worst case of how much money must be raised in one way or another by the venture. This amount may come from investors, lenders, or customers. Assumptions about which of those people will provide how much cash to the company at what points in time must be made with care. What alternative actions can be taken if one or another of them either reneges, or simply delays payment?

Minimizing cash needs

Ways to reduce cash needed for business expenditures can also form a long list, including the following:

- Make do without (dining room table for desk?).
- Buy, don't make (use subcontractors).
- Make, don't buy (homemade production equipment?).
- Barter, don't pay cash (free samples for help, banner ads?).
- Buy used, not new (any auctions of other firms?).
- Do it yourself, don't hire (answer phones, sweep the floor, manage).
- Buy cheap (hire students, GIs off hours, homemakers).
- Lease, don't buy (copy machine, computer, space).
- Rent, don't employ (temporary help).
- Share, don't be isolated (office space, receptionist, shop, tools).

The catch with such need-minimizing approaches is that many extract tradeoffs in terms of quality, dependability, speed, or the entrepreneur's time. Sometimes less immediate cash outlay requires paying a higher total price, as in the case of leasing equipment. Thus, cash conservation may impose profit sacrifices, while raising cash may require sacrificing ownership, control, or both.

But compromise is not always costly. In 1990, the sales for the printing company Harvey Quadracci founded were $375 million; he recalled how in the early days of his company, he wooed customers through the impression that it was doing better than it was.

The client would come in and see rolls of paper stacked up but not know that in the middle they were hollow. Or we would have the press printing this one magazine, which had a run of maybe 15,000. The press would print 25,000 an hour. Here comes the client, and we'd start the press up and get him to move very quickly because the paper was going through. Then we'd get him out into the office, and suddenly the whole plant would shut down. "What was that?" he would say. "Oh, it must be everybody breaking for lunch." It's perception.[131]

Ken Hendricks, a roofing distributor with sales of $250 million in 1990, described how start-up economies continued even after his company had grown large.

> We still buy used, but nice, furniture. My desk came from somebody that had gone bankrupt. I've thought about the tears that had to fall on that desk, and it's something that reminds me every day that I'm not going to let this happen to me.[132]

Cash shortfall causes

The ultimate evidence of error in venturing is cash shortfall. How important cash solvency can be is illustrated by the following comment of Henry Quadracci, who was mentioned above.

> Nobody understands what cash flow is unless they've lived by it. The experience changes you permanently. I have a telephone in planes, trains, cars, and bedrooms because I have a phobia. I break out into a cold sweat if I'm away from a phone. It goes back to those days when I was always calling to ask, "Did the check come in the morning? OK, release those other checks."[133]

Ways that cash solvency can go wrong include the following:

- Not forecasting.
- Absence of good financial controls.
- Misapplying cash.
- Employing people who steal.
- Not correctly managing a bank balance.
- Waiting too long to seek capital.
- Asking for money without adequate preparation.
- Underestimating effort required to raise capital.
- Agreeing to a misunderstood deal.

- Pursuing capital sources that don't fit the venture.
- Getting too many shareholders too soon.
- Selling stock to an investor who has inadequate capability to help further.
- Selling equity when debt will do.
- Taking on too much debt.
- Paying too much for capital.
- Losing credibility by failing to meet commitments.
- Failing to back up records securely.

For each such cause of shortfall it is fairly easy to think of one or more preventative actions that could have headed off the problem.

Pitfalls in forecasting

Unless the entrepreneur has access to overwhelmingly sufficient cash relative to what the venture will need, an essential precaution will be to develop a cash flow forecast. Part of that precaution should be to consider ways the forecast can be wrong and by how much. How errors can enter in estimating cash needs include:

- Failing to list something for which cash will be needed.
- Underestimating how much something will cost.
- Falsely assuming suppliers will extend credit
- Underestimating how much inventory will accumulate
- Assuming customers will pay sooner than they will.
- Assuming nobody will make an error handling cash.
- Expecting loans will be processed quickly.
- Expecting investors will pay promptly.
- Not building margin for error into the forecasts.

As expressed by venture capitalist Ken Rich, "Happiness is a positive cash flow" in any new venture. Ultimately, profits must bring that about. Until then, however, most entrepreneurs must make it happen by a combination of frugality, foresight, and money raising.

---

[131] "Going for Broke," *Inc.*, September 1990, p. 36.
[132] "Going for Broke," p. 36.
[133] "Going for Broke," p. 35.

3. Historical amounts needed

Historical precedents usually help in forecasting. They show that cash needed for start-up can range widely from one venture to another, even in the same line of business. Amdahl Computer started with $17 million. But Apple Computer started with less than $1,000.

Probably fairly typical of small businesses in America are those in the 1990 study of National Federation of Independent Business (NFIB) firms by Cooper, et al, which are characterized in Exhibit 5a-1, showing that roughly a third were begun with seed capital of $10,000 or less.[134]

A contrast might be expected to appear among higher-growth companies than those of the NFIB, but it's hard to find. Among the *Inc.* 500 fastest-growing small firms in 1989, the fraction who had started with less than $10,000 was actually higher, 34 percent, as can be seen in Exhibit 5a-2 below.[135] Moreover in 1999, the figure was still higher, 37 percent,[136] and in 2003, notwithstanding inflation, the fraction

Exhibit 5a-1 Levels of start-up capital among NFIB firms

Start-up capital needed	Percent of firms
Less than $10,000	32%
$10,000–$50,000	41
$50,000–$100,000	15
$100,000–$250,000	8
$250,000 or more	4
Total	**100**

Exhibit 5a-2 Levels of start-up capital in Inc. 500 firms

Start-up capital needed	Percent of firms
Less than $10,000	34%
$10,000–$49,000	35
$50,000–$99,000	12
$100,000–$249,999	10
$250,000 or more	9
Total	**100**

that started with less than $10,000 had risen to 41 percent.[137]

The similarity of these patterns seems remarkable considering the difference in longer-term performance. The *Inc.* sample of the 500 firms out of all U.S. industries that have grown the most over the past five years is a very thin layer of top performers. These data seem to indicate that in terms of start-up capital most top performers begin with much the same level of resources as "typical" start-ups.

Notwithstanding exceptions, most companies, like most living creatures, begin small, even if later they become large. Some well-known companies and the amounts of money they were begun with include Singer Sewing Machines, $40; Avon, $500; Kodak, $3,000; Procter & Gamble, $7,192; Textron, $10,000; Ford, $28,000; and DuPont, $36,000.[138] Clearly, time worked in favor of these companies to compound the small start-up capital into greatness.

The effect of time on growth can be seen on the array of companies that became famous listed in Exhibit 5a-3 below. But the correlation is not fully direct. The set of companies in the table includes only ones that grew great, not others that stayed small or failed entirely. And among those that grew great there is also a range. Gillette multiplied its investment of $5,000 in 1903 by 150,000 times to a capitalization value ("cap value," or market value of all the stock shares outstanding, which equals the market value of one share multiplied by the number outstanding) of $7.4 billion from 1903 to 1991. Hewlett-Packard multiplied its investment of $538 in 1938 by 2.6 million times to a cap value of $13.1 billion in 1991.

Dependence on line of business

Important determinants of starting cash needed include the kind of business, how

---

134 Cooper and others, *New Business*, p. 28.
135 John Case, "The Origins of Entrepreneurship," *Inc.*, June 1989, p. 62.
136 George Gendron, "FYI," *Inc.*, August 1999, p. 11.
137 Case, "Origins," p. 58.
138 "Speaking Out," *Inc.*, October 1980, p. 20.

Exhibit 5a-3 Venture investment value increase[159]

Company	Began in year	With ($)	By 1991 worth ($)
Heinz	1875	1.00	10,000,000,000
Gillette	1903	5,000	7,400,000,000
United Parcel Service	1907	100	6,000,000,000
Walt Disney	1923	290	16,000,000,000

much of the profit chain it is to perform, and how fast its sales volume is to be expanded or ramped up.

Service businesses, small construction companies, firms selling software and Internet portals are often low in start-up cash requirements. To paint or clean houses, copy edit manuscripts, manage weddings or real estate properties, serve ice cream, coffee, or hot dogs from a cart, or offer management consulting can be done with little capital beyond personal needs. Correspondingly, there is little to protect such businesses from competitors, their profit levels tend to be low and failure rates high, and they almost never grow large. Hence, the risk of starting such businesses being a waste of time and money is high while upside potential is low.

Food and drink establishments typically require more capital than straight service start-ups, but they too tend to be low in profit and high in work hours and failure rate. Too many people start them, attracted perhaps by the familiarity of what they deal in. A serious restaurant can cost millions to set up. Even equipment for making bagels can cost over $100,000.

Biotechnology companies and banks generally require much more capital but differ from each other in time to break even, risk, and upside potential. The former can have very high potential, but carry high risk of failure, and take close to a decade to reach profitability, if ever. Banks also require major investment, and their risk is relatively low, but they require contacts with money and expert knowledge of the work.

Manufacturing companies usually require capital for buying equipment, setting it up and creating tooling to make products. Development of the products themselves can also require major capital for design, development, patenting, and selling. But if those hurdles can be surmounted, the result can be margins and profits which grow very healthy as sales volume grows, customer loyalty and brand image develop, work routines become refined, and products are improved with progressive engineering effort. Because of such business momentum and the capital investment in plant and equipment, manufacturing companies tend to be sought-after buyout targets, which makes them especially valuable to own. Foreign competition, however, has in recent years often eliminated U.S. plants and sometimes companies. Innovation, speed, uniqueness, and patents can still win.

Sales companies may require very little in the way of resources if, as manufacturers' representatives, they call on customers, discuss needs, display catalogs, and take orders for the one or several companies they may represent. But they are typically on 30-day-cancellable commission-only contracts, which makes them hard in work and high in risk. Wholesalers who maintain inventories may have substantial investments in warehousing and goods. Brokers may operate on either of these bases until customers go direct.

Government contract financing has enabled some start-ups to prosper with little initial capital, particularly if the contracts can be performed without much equipment. Rand Corporation, SAIC, and countless companies during wartime have managed to start based on government deals. However, such companies can find it hard to convert to production for civilian markets when the war exigencies go away.

---

[139] "Guess Who?" *Inc.*, September 1991.

4. Sources of start-up cash

As noted earlier, savings of the founder, possibly supplemented with a parallel job, provide the first cash for most ventures. Among *Inc.* 500 companies, for instance, the most important cash source for the entrepreneurs themselves and their families to live on during start-up was personal savings in 43 percent of the companies, support from spouse and other relatives in 12 percent, salary from another job in 17 percent, and salary from the start-up in only 20 percent of the cases.[140]

When respondents were asked which sources were most relied upon for capitalizing their enterprises, the fraction who nominated each category (some nominated more than one) was as shown in Exhibit 5a-4.

Interestingly absent from this list are other sources such as informal outside (angel) investors, venture capital investors, corporations, and public offerings. These sources too are sometimes used in start-ups, although more rarely. Another report on the *Inc.* 500 stated that for 56 percent the main source of seed money was personal savings, while 40 percent took out loans by mortgaging personal assets. Venture capital was used by fewer than 2 percent of the companies polled. (Among start-ups in general it has been estimated that fewer than one in 10,000 starts with venture capital.) Corporate loans in this later report showed a 41 percent response, compared to the earlier 33 percent above.[141]

The Cooper et al. study of 2,994 firms brought other sources into the picture, including outside individuals, venture capital firms, and suppliers, as can be seen in Exhibit 5a-5. This table may include overlap between "other individuals" and "former owners." From inclusion of the latter it appears that both start-ups and acquisitions were lumped together. This may also be true for the *Inc.* sample.

Something consistent through these lists is that personal resources and savings of the founders were the principal source of financing, followed by bank borrowing, which was probably based in whole or part upon the personal resources of the entrepreneurs, such as their homes and other personal assets such as securities.

Bootstrapping

Financing a venture by combining do-it-on-your-own practices for economizing needs with tactics for paying bills personally without having to raise cash from outside sources is sometimes referred to as *bootstrapping*. For many entrepreneurs it is a necessity because they don't have either contacts with "spare" money, enough credibility from past accomplishments, or enough time to seek out and recruit financial support.

Advantages of bootstrapping include that it removes formal money raising activities as distractions from the more important tasks of finding customers, selling, delivering, and col-

Bootstrapping

Exhibit 5a-4 Start-up capital sources of Inc. 500 firms[142]

Sources of capital used	Percent
Own resources	75%
Mortgage of own assets	35
Corporate loan from bank	33
Partner's assets	29
Personal loan from bank	23
Parents or other relative	20

Exhibit 5a-5 Fraction of NFIB firms using different capital sources[143]

Sources of capital used	Percent
Personal savings	74.6%
Banks	45.8
Friends/relatives	28.7
Other individuals	7.8
Suppliers/trade credit	6.3
Government guaranteed loans	3.2
Venture capital firms	1.3
Former owners (acquisitions)	8.9

[140] Case, *Origins*, p. 62.
[141] "The Year in Startups," *Inc.*, November 1989, p. 66.
[142] "The Year in Startups," p. 58.
[143] Cooper and others, *New Business*, p. 29.

lecting, activities which usually connect more directly to profits. That can get the company going faster by sidestepping capital hunting tasks that can take months or even years to work out. Bootstrapping automatically applies pressure to be frugal, which can save both money and such time as might be wasted on "shopping" to spend it. Some entrepreneurs have been notorious for wasting money that came into their ventures "too big too soon" by spending it on fancier than needed offices, furniture, and luxuries.

An entrepreneur operating without financial obligations to others is freer from constraints they might impose as part of any deal for financial support. There is less need to spend time asking for permission to spend, reporting about decisions made, or explaining actions taken, tasks that can interfere with speed and flexibility. Bootstrapping probably also enhances motivation to make decisions work, because there will be nobody else to blame them on.

Software start-up

Greg Gianforte knew something about how to write microcomputer software and about start-ups, having been part of starting one before and selling it off for enough money to retire at age 33 in the small college town of Bozeman, Montana. Deciding to try another start-up with minimal resources, he went looking for ideas on the Web in 1997. In this process it occurred to him that software to help companies respond to E-mail inquiries might be worth working on.

He wrote design specifications in the form of a data sheet for such a product. Then he cold-called customer-support managers, described his design, said he planned to release it in 90 days and asked if they would use it. Whenever they said no he asked why, then selectively added modifications he figured he could incorporate within the 90 days.

On schedule he released the new program, giving it away at first, working from his house with no employees, gathering feedback on how it worked and upgrading it. After three months he started charging at a price low enough to gain customers quickly. Four months yielded income of $20,000, but soon rose to $30,000 per month, at which time he started hiring people

to solicit sales by phone while his wife took care of accounting and operations. Rather than installing an elaborate phone system, he bought a separate 800 number line for each of his salespeople, which was much cheaper.

To accommodate customer requests for special modifications to the software, he hired a programmer and charged for that service, while also using ideas from it to upgrade his product. For more space the company moved to the back room of a real estate office, then to a former elementary school. Finally, in December 1999, less than two and a half years after beginning, Gianforte shifted from bootstrapping on minimal personal resources to raising $16 million from outside investors, moved to a new industrial building, and started recruiting experienced managers for his company, RightNow Technologies. By 2002 it employed 230 people on annual sales of $30 million.[144]

Entrepreneurs sometimes commandeer resources they don't have title to. In addition to borrowing, they may barter and even presume. Both receiving and giving favors is part of entrepreneurship. Author George Gilder has pointed out that the entrepreneur begins by a charitable act, putting forth effort and resources before getting anything back, in order to make a venture happen.[145] Other times entrepreneurs receive favors from sympathizers, including other entrepreneurs who wish them well, and community supporters who appreciate what ventures add to the store of available jobs, goods, and services. Effort, initiative, imagination, vision, and persuasion can be important forms of currency for obtaining use of other people's effort and resources.

Personal assets

Taking an inventory of personal assets that could be turned into cash may add some realism to the venture's funding picture. Steve Jobs and Steve Wozniak are said to have sold a Volkswagen van to raise money for starting Apple. Other assets of a would-be entrepreneur might include bank balances, stocks, bonds, mutual fund shares, life insurance cash value, and retirement plan balances that can be cashed in or borrowed against. If the

---

[144] Emily Barker, "Start with Nothing," *Inc.*, Feb. 2002.
[145] George Gilder, *The Spirit of Enterprise* (New York: Simon and Schuster, 1984).

entrepreneur owns real estate, a home-equity loan may be obtainable.

Any demonstrated ability to build wealth prior to attempting the venture can lift credibility in the eyes of others who may be asked to help. Not having been able to save money before will likely leave credibility correspondingly lower. Not having made an inventory of personal assets that could be applied to the venture would leave it lower still. Not being willing to apply those assets may leave it lowest of all and unable to pass what some investors have characterized as the "laugh test." ("You want me to put my savings at risk in this venture when you haven't committed your own to it? What a funny idea!")

Credit cards

A simple though painfully expensive way to extend personal assets, and one that may not be required to pass the laugh test because of the high interest charges it entails, is through borrowing against one, or even a collection, of credit cards. It was estimated in 1998 that one third of businesses employing fewer than 19 people used "plastic" as a funding source, twice the number that had done so five years earlier.[146] The following examples illustrate that sometimes it works.

> Dan Potter began his video store, Video Update, in St. Paul, Minnesota with his credit card. As he recalled, "We simply charged the purchase of 80 movies to our credit cards and lived in the basement of our store."[147]
>
> — • —
>
> Wilbert Murdock conceived of a computerized golf club and related software that would help in analyzing swing, stroke by stroke and also over time. While living with his mother in early 1998 he had his first prototypes tested. To reach this point he had invested all his personal cash, recruited $32,000 for 10 percent of the venture from some investors and borrowed $40,000 from his mother. Now credit card companies were hounding him for over $25,000 in charges he had rung up with them. He had stopped responding to their letters or phone calls. Instead, he was concentrating on living up

to such slogans as "succeed or die," and "failure is not an option," while hoping that his product would succeed and that some other established company, including the Taiwanese manufacturer that had agreed to produce his club, would not run off with his idea. The outcome of his venture was not reported.[148]

Care must be taken in using credit cards for business purposes so as not to mix business and personal expenses. Both business expenses and interest charged by the card company on those expenses are deductible for tax purposes. But personal expenses and any interest on those are not.

Customers

Some start-ups get financial advances from customers. Contractors, for instance, frequently receive advances and progress payments on construction projects. Both software and hardware makers in the microcomputer industry have been known to accept orders and advance payments for products to be made in the future. Three contrasting examples of capital coming from customers are the following:

> Pat Sayers founded Nursing Systems International with cash advances from hospitals more than a year before her product, a computerized expert reference system for nurses, existed. She had tried working as a consultant in selling a textbook and a slide series, from which she learned "how tough it really is to reach the market until people are out there saying, 'We want it.'" Consequently, when a hospital suggested she develop a system, she asked for payments up front, which she received. In return, she promised the contributors significant discounts on the product. The advances gave her credibility as well as cash that in turn helped her raise the remaining capital needed from other sources.[149]
>
> — • —
>
> Bob McCray raised half the $500,000 needed to start manufacturing electrical valve equipment from manufacturer's representatives who wanted to carry the product. Each representative was asked for a loan of $5,000 for every 1 percent of national market territory. In return, McCray promised to give the representative repayment on a short schedule, with interest at 1 percent over prime, plus exclusive territory rights and a

[146] Rodney Ho, "Banking on Plastic," *The Wall Street Journal*, March 9, 1998, p. 1.
[147] Jill Andresky Fraser, "Finance Twists," *Inc.*, April 1995, p. 115.
[148] Ho, "Banking on Plastic," p. 1.
[149] "The Year in Startups," p. 75.

discount of 50 percent off list in contrast to the customary 33 percent. McCray observed, "They look at us as more of a partner, which is good. We didn't want to be thought of as just another vendor. I certainly have no trouble getting them on the phone."[150]

— • —

RealCommunities, Inc., a 1998 Seattle start-up established to develop enterprise software to be released in mid-2000 for dot coms, began by establishing a relationship with a customer in which the customer agreed to prepay anticipated licensing fees for the product.

SBIR program

For research and development work in selected areas, agencies of the federal government will provide grants under its Small Business Innovation Research (SBIR) program.[151] By law, 10 federal agencies with research budgets must set aside 1.25 percent of the money in them for grants to companies with under 500 employees. Leads to the different federal agencies and information about the program can be obtained from the U.S. Small Business Administration.

Grants are given under two phases. The first phase provides up to $100,000 for the first six months for feasibility analysis of a proposed innovation of interest. The second phase, contingent on performance under the first, provides up to $750,000 additionally for up to two years.

By the end of the 1900s, over $1 billion per year was being disbursed by government agencies to small and start-up firms under this program. However, less than 15 percent of first-phase and 40 percent of second-phase proposals were being accepted as of 1989, and the trend was toward the number of proposals growing faster than the available funding. It also appeared that some enterprises were specializing in getting such grants as a way of operating their businesses on a continuing basis.

Friendly money

Family members, friends, and partners figure heavily in the initial financing of many ven-

tures, as could be seen in Exhibits 5a-4 and 5a-5, and are important alternatives to consider in bootstrapping, although, as will be discussed in a later chapter on teaming, there can be problems on that route.

Partner

Savings, then partners

Dave Thomas, the founder of Wendy's had worked for Kentucky Fried Chicken and taken part of his pay in the form of stock. Later, he got the idea of setting up a chain of stores to compete with McDonald's by offering a burger he thought people would prefer. He had the KFC stock, and with that he started his first store.

For his second store, he brought in partners who were going to work it, by selling them stock, which he loaned them the money to buy. Then they borrowed from a bank to buy equipment. He recalled, "When we went down to Bank One to borrow money for new equipment, eight of us—four co-owners and our wives—had to sign the notes individually."[152]

Family

Contract from father

George Getty was determined that his son, Jean Paul, would carry on the family oil business. Summers during college the young man worked in the oil fields between studies at the University of Southern California, then Berkeley, and finally Oxford. None of the schools inspired him to a very strong interest in scholarship. When he said he would rather become a diplomat than an oil-man, his father offered him a deal. George would pay his son $100 per month to scout low-cost oil leases. He would also pay drilling expenses, and on any wells that came in he would give the young man 30 percent of profits. Jean Paul accepted, and from there he went on to build his own multibillion-dollar oil empire.

Loan from father

Phil Knight wrote a business plan during his MBA program at Stanford on starting a company to distribute imported running shoes. He found a Japanese company to produce the shoes under a $25,000 contract. Having no investment money of his own, he turned to his

---

[150] "The Year in Startups," p. 71.
[151] Martha E. Mangelsdorf, " *Inc.*'s Guide to 'Smart' Money," *Inc.*, August 1989, p. 51. Also, a useful contact is the Small Business Administration's Office of Technology.
[152] R. David Thomas, *Dave's Way* (New York: Putnam's, 1991) p. 96.

father, who agreed to sign a blanket guarantee at the bank to back up the letter of credit needed to execute the contract. Then he got to work selling his Nikes.[153]

Backing from an in-law

Sam Walton had managed to accumulate about $5,000 by the time he had finished college, then worked as trainee at J.C. Penney and completed his World War II military service. He had also married a banker's daughter. His ambition was to own and operate his own retail store. Knowing this interest, a friend proposed that they team up to buy a St. Louis department store being offered for $40,000.

He approached his wife's father, who agreed to provide it. But Sam's wife didn't want to live in a big city like St. Louis. So he inquired with a franchiser, Butler Brothers, about whether they might have an available franchise for one of their Ben Franklin stores in a small town. The answer was yes, He bought the store for $25,000 plus $200 per month, or 5 percent of sales for rent. This cost turned out to be excessive and sales were slow, but Sam managed to boost them. He looked for a second store, with the help of his father in law, but the landlord there turned down his rent offer. That night Sam's father in law went to the landlord's house and talked her into accepting it. His retail store chain had begun.[154]

Friends

Loan from a friend

Since age 14 Freddie Laker had wanted to be involved with airplanes. During World War II he had learned to fly as a flight engineer with the Air Transport Auxiliary, which ferried new planes to the Royal Air Force. He also made friends in the aircraft industry. After the war he started selling spare aircraft parts he had obtained from various sources he knew out of the trunk of his car, handling the paperwork in his back seat. In 1947 he also helped his friend Bobby Sanderson sell some surplus bombers that Sanderson had become stuck with.

This favor was not forgotten. The next year, Laker, at age 26, was considering the attractiveness of twelve airliners being offered, together with spare parts to keep them running, by British Overseas Aircraft Corporation, BOAC. In a bar conversation he mentioned them to Bobby Sanderson, who asked Laker why he did not buy the planes himself. Laker said he would like to, but he had only 4,000 pounds and the price was 42,000. Sanderson pulled out his checkbook, wrote a check to Laker for 38,000 pounds and said, "Pay me back when you can."

From this major step up, Laker went on to make a large profit ferrying supplies with his airplanes during the Berlin airlift. Then he went on to offer charter flights and next he created his own airline, making a fortune by undercutting fares of the existing monopoly. Ultimately, he became very rich and was knighted by the Queen of England.[155]

These examples show there are many different ways of generating the first seed capital, and which of them will work best can depend upon the type of business as well as the circumstances of the entrepreneur and quite possibly the economic and technological times.

5. Terms

Sources, amounts, timing, and terms all are part of the venture resource acquisition process. Sometimes an entrepreneur must recruit several commitments simultaneously, a process known as "ham and egging," where the willingness of one to participate is dependent on assurance that another needed participant will also join the deal. Other times it may be necessary to demonstrate accomplishment at one stage in order to get participation at another stage.

The more successful a venture is at any stage, the easier time it will have getting capital for a later one. Suppliers, once they see that the venture can pay bills and is likely to continue, will begin to extend trade credit. Banks will usually loan something against accounts receivable. Potential investors will become easier to recruit, either as working partners or, if a way can be shown in which they are likely to recover their cash with a healthy profit, as silent partners.

---

[153] J.B. Strasser and Laurie Becklund, *Swoosh* (New York: Harcourt, 1991).
[154] Vance H. Trimble, *Sam Walton* (New York: Penguin, 1991).
[155] Roger Eglin and Berry Ritchie, *Fly Me, I'm Freddie* (New York: Rawson, Wade Publishers 1980).

What to seek

Financial and control aspirations of the founders can have major consequences for raising cash. One approach sometimes advocated is to "ask for more money than you need and take as much as you can get as soon as possible." A further argument is that by bringing in more money sooner, the venture may also gain stronger allegiance by more money providers who can help it in other ways, thus increasing the odds of success.

A contrasting view is that "it is best to hold off on raising outside capital as long as possible, because that way the company will be stronger when it seeks money and consequently less ownership will have to be shared to get it." In other words, the farther the company progresses, the less risky an investment it is, and hence the higher share price it can command. As to the prospect that with less money may come fewer or less intensely dedicated investors to help it, the contrasting view is that there will be fewer of them to require communicating with and distract the management from its main job of building the enterprise. Hence, the entrepreneur may have more flexibility, not only for operating the venture, but also for recruiting other investors later, who will not have to be concerned with so many existing owners if they should decide to join the effort.

More than just survival should be at stake. Prosperity should be the expectation, and the argument should really be about which course will maximize the stakeholders' satisfaction with that. Would the initial stakeholders be choosing between a bigger piece of a small pie versus a smaller piece of a bigger pie, and if so, which is preferable?

Keeping control

The "golden rule" (whoever provides the gold can make the rules) entitles those who put money into a venture to take some rights of control in return. This may take the form of written rules the company must follow, such as not to make any investments over a certain amount without permission, not to pay more than a certain amount to executives, to submit specified financial information on a certain timetable, to maintain certain balance sheet and income statement ratios, to appoint a certain number of directors, or to employ certain people in specified capacities.

It is natural for an entrepreneur not to want to share control. There is plenty to worry about in creating the venture without having to consider how investors feel about it. There is plenty for the entrepreneur to do without having to spend time interacting with investors. To the entrepreneur, sharing control can threaten distraction, interference, and wasted time.

It is also easy to see why an investor would want some control. Incentive to be careful with the money would be higher if it were the entrepreneur's own. To make up for this, the person with the purse attaches strings. It is possible to structure the arrangement such that the strings take hold only if the venture is falling too far short of its forecast.

Investors and lenders more experienced in dealing with ventures actually don't crave control. It can lead to interference that handicaps the venture and possibly destroys the enthusiasm and motivation of its creators. The founders, after all, are most expert about the venture. Lenders and investors don't know how to create it or run it well. Maybe they have some strings on the venture, but they should leave them loose as much as possible, stepping in only if the venture seems to be heading disastrously off track.

The entrepreneur should seek investors based upon their prior experience and reputations. In arranging a deal both sides should consider possible future problems, what will best motivate the founders and what sorts of deviations from course should trigger investor or lender action in the best interests of both their money and the enterprise.

Keeping ownership

Sharing ownership raises issues similar to those of control. Too much ownership sacrifice by entrepreneurs can reduce their incentives. Taking too little can limit investors to inadequate returns relative to their risk. In the end, division of ownership must be negotiated, and the investor usually has the upper hand. The entrepreneur may have some of the following choices:

- Taking a bigger piece of a small pie or a smaller piece of a bigger one.
- Keeping ownership by assuming the risk of borrowing, or giving up some ownership in return for someone else sharing the risk.
- Seeking more capital at early inception, even though that makes it more expensive. The alternative is to begin with less capital and wait until the venture grows to where it needs more. Seeking it then, however, may take time away from the many demanding tasks of building the venture, a sacrifice that may be serious or even fatal to the venture's continued development.

No standard formulas for choosing among such alternatives exist. They must be negotiated by each entrepreneur for each individual venture, with careful thought about alternative scenarios that can follow.

Bargaining

Founder(s) may have more or less choice about such matters, but very likely they can influence it. Starting with greater personal savings and having good relationships with more contacts who can help will give advantage, as will personal competence in activities most important to the venture. Being aware of the choices available, their implications and how to make persuasive arguments can help, as can having done homework on customers and financial forecasts. But being aware of tradeoffs between short and long run may be even more important. Putting over a win-lose deal too early can lead to sour relationships later that could even kill the company.

More variety in these choices and implications they carry will receive further attention in chapters to follow. But at an early stage one additional concept to keep in mind is the notion of capitalization value (cap value) of the venture, which was discussed above in connection with Exhibit 5a-3. As a total entity at different points in time, for how much should it be possible to sell the venture? How much did people pay per share of stock last time and how many shares are outstanding? Is it worth

half a million dollars or two million? Who in the company is doing most to make that value be there? Who can do how much to make it larger? Consequently, who should deserve how much of it?

This question just touches the surface, ignoring perhaps issues of risk—who has how much to lose? And ignoring perhaps fairness—who contributed how much or is working the hardest? But it is a starting point for thought about issues that can have major consequence for the venture.

Participation modes

Two main modes of financial participation are through debt and through equity ownership. Debt requires that the money be repaid, and it usually requires the borrower to pay interest. Equity constitutes a share of ownership and thus represents splitting the profits and the value of the business. It also usually carries with it a share of control proportionate to the share of ownership.

Each of these modes can be formulated to incorporate features of the other. Equity can be in the form of either common stock or preferred stock. Common stock represents directly proportionate shares of ownership, profit splitting, and liquidation rights. Preferred stock also conveys ownership, but each share may or may not convey as much of it as a common share does. Preferred can be voting or not, specify dividends, whether common shareholders get them or not, and give rights to assets upon liquidation whether there is anything left for common shareholders or not.

Either debt or preferred stock can also carry rights for conversion into common shares of stock. Debt can go in different directions among partners. One partner may loan money to the company or to another partner, who in turn may loan that money to the company or possibly use it to buy stock in the company. Variations on this theme with preferred shares are illustrated by the following example.

A surgeon who had lost a hand through excessive X-ray exposure complained about limitations of his artificial arm. The person to whom he complained, an investment counselor, undertook to design a better arm and made one for the surgeon. The surgeon was delighted with innovations in the new arm and proposed that they start a company to make them, he putting up the money and the counselor doing the work.

The counselor proposed a financing arrangement under which they would share the common stock equally, the surgeon would in addition receive preferred shares for his money, and the counselor would take no pay from the venture until the preferred shares had all been bought back from the surgeon at face value, the amount he had paid in.

Although preferred stock, rather than a loan agreement, was used in this case, the effect was much like a loan. The surgeon put up the money and it was repaid as if it had been debt. He got no interest, but the counselor also got no pay until the money was repaid. Had the preferred not all been redeemed, the surgeon could have foreclosed and taken over the business much as if the preferred had been debt. But the surgeon did get his money back, and then he got a further return on it when the counselor went on to buy out his common stock and ended up owning the business.

Sequence variety

As a prelude to the next two chapters which deal with sources of financing that usually come, if at all, only after the seed capital from sources just described, here are some indications of the variety of financing sequences that may develop.

Contracting

Personal savings are used for obtaining any needed bonding, as well as for small equipment and as down payments on bigger equipment for such work as home repair, maintenance, and construction.

Advances from the customer, if there is one, are used to pay for supplies and labor as the job advances.

Bank borrowing against real estate may be used by either the customer, if there is one, or the contractor, if there is no pre-sold customer, to help pay for the job. If costs overrun, there are several possibilities. The company may go broke or may be able to renegotiate with lenders and customers to see the job through.

Small manufacturing

Personal savings and possibly lease or time purchase are used for obtaining equipment. Any inventory and developmental expenses, as well as any costs of accounting and legal work to establish the company and apply for trademarks or patents are paid personally.

Partner money may be recruited to extend personal savings. The partner may be either a working partner or a silent partner.

Bank borrowing may be possible against personal assets initially and business assets later, after the business becomes established and has built up substantial net worth.

Trade credit should also become available after the company becomes solidly established.

Veterinary service

Personal savings of the founder are used (1) to live on, and (2) to provide initial working capital. A site is located based on demographics and where other clinics are not located and a lease is signed.

Bank borrowing is based on personal assets of the founder and possibly upon medical equipment in the office to do some advertising and commence operations.

Retailing

Personal savings of the founder are used (1) to live on, and (2) to provide initial capital in the business for initial equipment, rental and other deposits, opening inventory, and advertising. With that the company opens its doors and starts selling.

Partner money may be used to augment the main founder's stake, and this too will likely come from personal savings: those of the partner. The partner may be either a working partner or a silent partner who does not work in the business but invests for the sake of sharing the profits and possibly payment from sale of the business. Silent partners are sometimes referred to as *informal investors*.

Borrowing may be used if necessary to extend the personal savings investment, most likely after the company has gotten started. The loan may come from family and friends, or possibly from a bank against personal assets of the guarantee of a friend or family member. The founder probably also must guarantee repayment of any bank loan.

Trade credit will likely become available, but only after the business becomes financially secure. That, and further borrowing against accounts receivable can help with expansion. But they may not be enough. If the company's profits are not great enough relative to its needs to support its growth, or if something goes wrong, such as customers taking too long to pay what they owe the company, or inventory taking too long to move out, or expenses causing losses, the company may be hit with a cash shortage that can stymie its growth or even cause it to fail.

For a franchised dealer, say in cars or motorcycles, trade credit might apply from the start for "flooring" the merchandise.

Outside equity, through sale of interest to a few people on a private basis or to a larger number of people through a public offering, may be used to ward off a cash crunch. As the business takes hold and grows in sales, it needs more money for inventory and for providing credit to customers. This money may also be extendable through further borrowing against the assets it is used for.

Franchising the business may be another way of financing expansion. Under this method, the company basically rents its format to other people who in turn finance additional branches of the company and pay for use of the format through some sort of initial franchise fee plus an ongoing royalty to the company based on sales.

Software

Personal savings of the founder are used (1) to live on, and (2) to provide initial capital in the business for initial equipment, code-writing help, and advertising. Once the code and the manual are written and tested, the software is advertised and either sells or does not. If it sells, the company may go on upgrading and selling, using suppliers to produce the copies, or it may sell out to a larger software company.

Partner money may be used for helping to pay for the writing tasks. Bank borrowing based on personal assets of the founder and partner(s) may be used to extend the initial personal investments to a limited degree.

Outside capital may not be necessary, because suppliers provide the equipment, margins are so high, and the investment required for inventory is so small. Venture capital from professionals who specialize in software companies may be used if the company requires and can justify for major effort on writing and selling to capture market share faster than competitors do. Public sale of the company's stock, though perhaps not needed thanks to high margins, may be used to allow employees to sell their own stock, possibly after exercising options.

Biotechnology

Personal savings of the founding partners may be used for pulling together a team of talented scientists with an advisory board of other experts to back them up and to write a formal plan for the business.

Venture capital from professional venture capital firms and possibly established corporations is then sought to underwrite the research and development efforts required to create products for the company and get them appropriately approved by any federal agencies involved.

Public stock sales are used to augment the venture capital after the products are sufficiently well along to support wider interest in investing in the company. Expenses of the public offering are supported with advances from the venture capitalists, who may also take some money back out, with a good return for themselves, from the public offering.

Myriad other possibilities could be added to this brief list. Farms, freight forwarders, professional firms in law, accounting, medicine, dentistry, and all the other services listed in the Yellow Pages, manufacturers' directories, and Standard Industrial Classification lists are categories that could be subdivided further still in start-up financing variety. But at least these examples should show that there is no standard sequence and much room for creative design to fit the financing needs of each venture individually.

Exercises

Text discussion questions

1. Why do so many alternative funding mechanisms exist, rather than boiling down to one or a few over time as people learn what works best and concentrate on making companies go rather than spending precious time working out deals?
2. What would cause a person to choose one individual funding style versus another?
3. What is likely to be lost by skipping any steps in a typical high-tech venture capitalization cycle? What's to be gained?
4. What are the main pros and cons of three alternative funding sources for a new venture?

Case questions

5A-1 Ampersand (A)

1. Pick and explain from among the financing examples and sources described in the chapter, one or two that might be most similar to what Ampersand should use to raise cash.
2. What issues should be anticipated regarding ownership and control in Ampersand's early financing arrangements?
3. How should the issues be expected to change if the company takes hold and demonstrates it can win?
4. What are some things, for instance, that should be put in writing about both above types of issues, and who should sign it when?

5A-2 Knight brothers (B)

1. Describe two contrasting people who might reasonably consider putting money at risk on this proposed deal at the time of the Knight brothers (A) case.
2. What is your assessment of the Knight brothers' financing proposal from the viewpoint of each above potential investor? What changes would follow?
3. How might your answers to these questions be changed by today's hindsight?
4. Write out an elevator pitch for presenting the Knights' proposition for each of the two investors you chose for question 1 above.

Portfolio page possibilities

Each page, bearing the date and your name, should be one single-sided sheet, based upon this chapter, stating from your present impressions and information (quite possibly to change later) the following:

Page 5A-1 Cash budget

Prepare two cash budgets, for the first six months of a start-up venture and a second to cover your personal expenses for that period. Include footnotes explaining the assumptions you used.

Page 5A-2 Personal cash buildup

List a personal strategy and guidelines for accumulating cash to start a venture in five years. Include a forecast of the amounts you think you should be able to add by then to whatever it is you are starting with as a present personal net worth.

Page 5A-3 Friendly money sources

List your potential sources of money from friends and family for three time periods: (1) now, (2) at start-up, and (3) after break-even. Explain the extent to which you would use them and under what terms or conditions. Also tell how you would go about presenting your request to those from whom you would seek capital.

Term Projects

Venture history

1. What initial equity financing style did the founder(s) of the venture you are studying adopt?
2. By what processes were the inception cash needs of the venture determined and how far off target did they turn out to be?
3. Through what sequence of events, including dead ends, was the first significant equity capital picked and negotiated with what source(s)?

4. Had the founder(s) considered what other source(s) would have been tried next if the one used had not panned out, and if so what were they?

Venture planning guide

1. Assess the fit of the three most promising alternative sources of initial seed capital for your venture.
2. Formulate financing terms for your venture from the viewpoints of the above three.

CHAPTER 5B – Debt Funding

Topics

1. Early debt sources
2. Bank choices
3. Building credit
4. Non-bank debt sources
5. Beyond the loan

Checkpoints

a. Explain what may be wrong financing a start-up with debt.
b. What are the alternative early sources of debt for a venture?
c. Describe types of stakeholders that may advance debt financing.
d. How do bank and non-bank sources of debt differ in how they operate?
e. What differences between entrepreneurs and bankers matter and how?
f. How should an entrepreneur choose a bank?
g. Describe and explain seven C's of credit.

A main advantage of borrowing money, assets, and/or other people's efforts to create a business is that it helps allow retention of ownership. From the lender's viewpoint, however, such financing carries risk while limiting upside potential to the interest rate. Hence, borrowed money can be hard to get, particularly if the entrepreneur's own resources (needed for backing up the loan) or the entrepreneur's track record as assurance of capability to perform the venture, are limited. For most borrowing, the venture will have to show that it already possesses assets that can, if necessary, be sold to pay off the debts.

Advisability of venture debt

Nevertheless, on average more start-up capital for new ventures has come from debt (52.9 percent), as opposed to equity (46.7 percent), according to a study of 132 firms in Iowa by Carter and Van Auken,[156] who found also that most of the debt came from institutions, such as banks, not individuals (see Exhibit 5b-1). Of further interest was that a statistically signifi-

cant inverse correlation existed between owners' personal equity and first-year financial difficulties experienced by the firms. The reasons for this were not reported. Possibly, as the authors suggest, the entrepreneurs were deterred from investing heavily in riskier situations by having private information. Alternatively, greater equity investment may have reflected either that the firms were better financed and did not need more capital, or that their owners found it easier to raise more cash when needed because of the greater capital base.

Whether or not to try borrowing money for venture financing has both personal and business ramifications. Many people are in debt for much of their lives, buying a house, buying or leasing a late-model car, operating with charge accounts, and using credit cards are all ways of going in debt which many people live with. Some people don't mind that. Others do, and go out of their way to minimize or get rid of such debts entirely, either because they don't want to pay interest, or simply because they don't like the idea of owing money.

Advisability of venture debt

---

[156] Richard B. Carter and Howard E. Van Auken, "Personal Equity Investment and Small Business Financial Difficulties," *Entrepreneurship Theory and Practice*, 15, no. 2, Winter 1990, p. 51.

Exhibit 5b-1 Sources of capital as a percent of start-up total

Sources	Mean percent
Equity:	
Personal funds	35.6%
Partnerships	5.2
Stock to others	3.2
Other	2.7
Total	**46.7**
Debt:	
Institutional loans	43.8
Loans from individuals	5.3
Sale of bonds	1.1
Other	2.7
Total	**52.9**

Whatever the personal philosophy, borrowing for a venture raises some additional considerations. A major reason for not borrowing in a business can be to preserve its ability to borrow later if and when it really has to, for such reasons as the arrival of a big upturn in sales that may raise need for more working capital. Another is to avoid the risk of the business not being able to pay its bills if a downturn hits. Yet another is that the lender may impose requirements such as maintenance of certain financial performance ratios and provision of periodic reports. And, of course, with a loan there is usually interest to pay, generally higher with the higher risk of a young company. Finally, there is a risk for the company that the bank may choose to pull the loan, requiring repayment rather than making an extension that may be sorely needed if some adversity arises.

A reason for borrowing on behalf of the venture, personal biases notwithstanding, is that it may be the only way to continue or to expand the business without selling equity and thereby giving up ownership in the business, while at the same time acquiring co-owners to deal with. Besides, not all debt, supplier credit, or customer advances, for instance, require payment of interest. So people who avoid debt assiduously on a personal basis may very well use business debt all the time.

But the risks that go with debt are still there. Debt has to be paid, or else those to whom it is owed can take away assets of the business, and that can lead to total failure. Hence, it makes sense to be judicious about borrowing for a venture. Partly, the question is from where to borrow, and partly it is how much to borrow and on what terms. This chapter will explore a variety of choices on both these issues.

1. Early debt sources

Debt versus equity is not always a choice the entrepreneur has freedom to make. Early investors may decide to buy shares, loan the company or the founder money, or guarantee a loan in return for some incentive. Rarely will anyone except for close relatives loan venture money without solid business incentive.

From the viewpoint of a resource provider, lending normally buys a promise of definite repayment, with interest, and possibly coupled with the pledge of some specific assets as collateral, which presumably lowers the risk of losing. At the same time, of course, lending for only repayment and possibly interest has a limited upside for a lender. So a lender justifiably wants assurance that the venture will make good on the repayment promise. This can make borrowed money hard to get, particularly if the entrepreneur's own resources, as back-up for the loan, or track record, as an assurance of ability to perform the venture, are limited. A rational lender, which an individual may or may not be but another business likely will be, should consider the following in making a loan:

Liquidity How easy will it be to get the loan repaid?

Security What collateral and personal commitments are there to back up the loan so it can be repaid in case of default and how much cash could be recovered from it?

Cost How much time and trouble will it cost to handle the loan compared to the return it will yield in interest?

Profitability How much will the interest or other compensation from the loan be worth? How else might this loan pay off in goodwill, connections, more profitable loans to the venture later and other possible "sweeteners" such as convertibility or warrants for common stock?

Stakeholder help

Debt can come from many potential stakeholders, including insiders such as partners, and outsiders such as customers and suppliers, as well as firms such as banks, that are in the business of renting money in the form of loans. Leasing is also a form of debt. The most common source of added cash through borrowing is through banks and finance companies. Beyond those sources, each of which will be considered shortly, are some other sources such as community and other organizations, both formal and informal.

Two founders of a photo portrait studio wanted to get a $25,000 bank loan to buy equipment. The bank said that the equipment alone did not represent enough collateral. One founder consequently pledged another $10,000 of collateral personally to get the loan. That founder took 100 percent of the venture's stock with the understanding that he would give half of it to the other founder after the bank loan was paid off. The venture succeeded in paying off the note ahead of schedule, and the stock was shared as agreed.

— • —

The founder of a restaurant tried to get a bank loan for start-up cash but was turned down. He proceeded to apply at a second bank and then six more banks, each of which also turned him down until finally one agreed verbally to grant the loan. Upon further review by the bank, however, this application too was denied based on the applicant's young age, 19 years, and shortage of collateral.

Appealing to friends he managed to persuade one to pledge her house against the loan for which she in turn required 30 percent interest in the business. The loan went through, the restaurant succeeded and the loan was repaid. The guarantor retained her 30 percent of the firm.

— • —

Two young men who had worked for restaurants during college decided to start one of their own upon graduation. They wrote a business plan and took it to several banks, of which they later said "funny thing about banks … they don't want to loan money to a couple of young guys with

no assets … especially going into the restaurant business." The answer for these two, after many rejections from banks and other sources, turned out to be the grandmother of one of them, who loaned them the money for a successful start.

Any of these arrangements could be criticized. The founder in the first example who personally pledged $10,000 in the long run took the risk of losing that if things did not work out. But when they did work out, he ended up with only the same deal as his partner who did not take that additional risk. Thus, for his incremental risk he received no incremental reward. His defense of this action, however, might be that this way he wound up with part of a business he otherwise would not have.

In the second example it could be argued that 30 percent of the business was too much. After all, the guarantor did not actually invest any money and yet reaped a substantial percentage of the business. Her rate of return numerically was infinite. But still, she had a risk. If the bank had experienced difficulty in collecting its loan it would have moved on her house immediately, not waited to learn what it could get on the equipment alone. Arguably, she had more to lose than to gain, so the founder got a good deal. Conveniently, all three of these ventures succeeded. Had they not, and some don't, the stories could have been much sadder.

Supplier credit

As noted by Cooper et al., about 6.3 percent of the time suppliers appear to play an important role in capitalizing start-ups. Like customers, they have a vested interest in what the venture will produce. What they are most likely to extend, however, is credit rather than cash. But most will not do even that for a start-up unless there is evidence of past performance in paying bills. This can become easy to understand by reading through published lists of bankruptcies. The lists are long, and each name on them represents a failed individual or company from whom creditors are unable to recover what they have lent. Consequently, many suppliers require payment on delivery or in advance by start-up entrepreneurs. After the venture gets going and shows reliability, they will likely relent.

Stakeholder help

Supplier credit

Leasing

If the venture needs equipment to get started, it may be able to meet that need through leasing rather than buying. The lessor retains title to the property, and the entrepreneur is thereby freed from having to come up with the money to buy it. Maybe the venture has rights to buy the property at the end of the lease, or maybe not. Either way, it is obligated to make all the lease payments, much the same as if it were bought with a loan. But it does not show as a line item on the balance sheet, and so may cause the venture to appear less heavily leveraged than it really is. For this reason leasing is sometimes referred to as "off balance sheet financing."

Vehicles and all sorts of other equipment, provided it is standard and can be sold or leased to someone else, can be obtained on leases. Computers, laboratory equipment, manufacturing machines, furniture, billboards, and office equipment can be leased, for example. It has been estimated that nearly one third of all business equipment is obtained through leasing.[157]

Advantages of leasing include reducing early cash outlays thanks to no down payment and possibly a long payout time. Leasing may also, depending upon the contract, offer a hedge against obsolescence or maintenance problems. For many years IBM leased rather than sold its computers, keeping them both maintained and updated for users. Leasing typically does not impose loan covenants or require reporting to the funds provider.

Leasing disadvantages can include in effect a higher interest cost than borrowing, and possible reduction in tax advantages, if for instance ownership would allow more rapid depreciation than the lease deductions allow. By leasing, the venture loses the solidity that goes with ownership, and yet it is still stuck with paying for the item, and in fact the leased equipment may become obsolete before the lease runs out.

Thus, there are many possible "it depends" aspects to consider about a lease, and it should therefore be read with care before signing. When will it start and end? Is there a right to buy at the end, and if so on what terms? Who will carry what insurance, and who will be responsible if any of a list of things go wrong with the item being leased? What if obsolescence happens, or if modification of the item being leased is needed? What will it cost, and how will that compare to buying outright or borrowing and buying? What payments are required, and what happens if any are late? Can step-up payments be made that will accelerate the termination date? What are the cancellation penalties? What if the equipment becomes obsolete? Is there a security deposit, and if so what are the conditions for recovering it? Is there insurance that the lessee must pay for? Who must provide what information and when? Does the lessor have the right to inspect anything, and if so, under what conditions and when? What has been the experience of others with the particular leasing company? How complex will the deal be? Will there be reporting requirements? How complex will the overall picture be if there are also other lessors to deal with, and how much will it cost to deal with them?

The verbal technology of leasing, including provisions of the Uniform Commercial Code (UCC) and Tax Code and such terms as side letters, security agreements, disclaimers of warranty, and master leases, can become quite complex. At a more basic level there are (1) operating leases, under which the lessee treats the payments as expenses and the lessor depreciates the asset, and (2) capital leases. Under the latter, the lessee lists and depreciates the item as an asset while recording the payment obligations as a liability against which the payments are applied. Accounting niceties of leases can call for help from a CPA.

2. Bank choices

From both the Cooper et al. and *Inc.* survey results described in the preceding chapter, it appears that banks typically play a strong role in the initial financing of companies, being used by 33 percent and 45 percent, respectively, of entrepreneurs responding to those two studies.

---

[157] Bob Benjamin, "How to Finance Your Venture with Leasing," *Journal of Entrepreneurship, Northwest Venture Group*, Volume 13, No. 4, November 1997, p. 1.

Yet often entrepreneurs say they could get no funding from banks in the early stages of start-up. The cliché is that "a bank will loan you money only if you don't need it." Banks don't have loan departments for start-up ventures. However, banks sometimes do make loans to individuals and to ventures, and they also help ventures with information and other contacts.

As discussed in Chapter 4B, certainly there is reason for banks to be cautious. First, the money they hold is not their own. It belongs to depositors, who expect to be able to withdraw any or all of it whenever they please. For the bank to have it loaned out to ventures that cannot repay immediately, or perhaps at all, cannot be allowed. Secondly, banks are severely limited in what they can charge as interest. Thus, while they can lose all, they can't win much. It does not make sense for them to give risky loans.

So why do banks seem to participate in financing so many ventures, according to the surveys? One explanation probably is that a fairly large fraction of the ventures surveyed were not actually start-ups but rather acquisitions that had assets to pledge. A second is that even among start-ups the banks may have lent money not at inception but only after the start-up was running and showing promise of strong solvency. Moreover, some of the entrepreneurs may have had sufficient personal assets to provide guarantees on the loans.

Despite the risks, there are also positive reasons for banks to make loans to start-ups. Banks are in business to rent money, and doing so is therefore competitive. Every good customer helps, and founders who are aided by banks in the early days of their ventures often stay loyal to those banks after the ventures have grown and become attractive and profitable borrowers. Banks know this and therefore sometimes will loan money unsecured to start-up companies if they have highly credible founders and solid sales prospects.

Loan types

Commercial banks typically make two types of loans: personal loans and commercial loans. Sometimes people can borrow personally and use the money for commercial purposes, as noted in the preceding chapter. And business loans sometimes require personal guarantees by the entrepreneurs who want them for their ventures.

Each commercial loan is an individual decision by the bank, for which somebody in the bank will be held responsible. A given bank may have its own nomenclature for further classifying types of loans, any of which may have its own custom "wrinkles," but generally they fall into some typical categories.

Unsecured loans

Usually small in amount, unsecured loans are given where the bank is confident about the reliability of the individual to repay, thanks to familiarity with the bank, wealth, reputation, or accomplishments. If, for instance the individual owns a home, has lived in the community a long time, is personally respected by the banker or others whom the banker respects, and perhaps has purchase orders from a strong and respected customer, that may be enough to loan what is needed in working capital to deliver on the contract and receive a billing, which in turn will be applied against the loan, possibly through direct payment by the customer to the bank.

Secured loans

If the company or the entrepreneur has assets that can be sold it may be possible to pledge them as collateral to obtain secured loans.

Equipment

It may be possible to lease, rather than buy equipment. But before deciding to lease the entrepreneur should consider the alternative of buying based on a commercial bank loan. Banks, more than leasing companies, try to build relationships by offering an array of services, which leasing companies don't. Bankers themselves may take an interest in the ventures they serve, with objectives of building up a business over time. So the choice between leasing and bank borrowing as alternative forms of debt is worth thinking about with care before signing up. The payments on a lease are periodic expenditures that once undertaken will be hard or impossible to reduce, regardless of what else is happening in a venture. Leases and loans each have different tax consequences, and it may be cheaper to pay interest on the loan than the premium over what the machine can be bought for that a leasing company may charge.

Other assets

Accounts receivable and other commitments to pay the company may occur at its inception, but will more likely enter later, as will company-owned real estate. The assets can be either those of the company or those of individuals willing to help support it financially.

Personal guarantee

If the loan is to a company whose legal form, such as corporation, limited partnership, or limited-liability company (LLC), insulates the owner(s) from liability, the person borrowing on behalf of the company may be required personally to guarantee repayment. At the next level of caution, the bank may loan against the signature of the borrower, if that person has personal assets to back up his or her guarantee, or against the signature of some other person who does. A couple of examples were mentioned earlier where outsiders pledged specific assets to back up the loan. In the next one the individual guaranteeing the note was a strong enough candidate that simply a general guarantee from him was enough.

> A young Seattle woman who wanted to start a food catering service and had no personal wealth to speak of persuaded her father to co-sign a $30,000 note at the bank. He was reasonably well off, solvent, and had done business with the bank for 30 years. She commented, "With that support I didn't even need a business plan. The money was right there." But she prepared a plan, complete with cash budgets anyway, to show him she was in earnest. It also helped, she said, to think through the business on paper first. It was still successful ten years later.

Although the actual loan is to the entrepreneur or the venture, and theoretically the entrepreneur should be the first for the bank to go after in recovering the money in the event of a default, in fact it will usually go after the guarantor, because that is easier. So the guarantor is really the first in line to take the hit if one is to be taken. It makes business sense for the guarantor to require some sort of benefit in return for taking this risk.

> Financier Arthur Lipper often prefers to participate in ventures through personally guaranteeing a bank loan. He personally does not put up any money, but the bank knows it can collect from him if the venture defaults. In return for this guarantee, he will require some sort of participation in the upside potential of the business, possibly a royalty percentage, such as 3 percent to 5 percent on sales, or warrants to buy stock at a favorable price some time in the future.

The guarantee could also come from other parties, such as a supplier, customer, or governmental or other agency that, for its own reasons, wanted to help financially in order to have the venture succeed.

SBA guarantee

The U.S. Small Business Administration (SBA) has a variety of programs to help with financing, mainly through guarantee of bank loans up to some percentage of the loan. The SBA "7(a) Loan Guarantee Program" backs 90 percent of a loan if a bank is willing to risk the other 10 percent. The contact for pursuing this course of action is the bank willing to take that risk. However, even a 10 percent loss is very significant to a bank, so approval is far from automatic.

The business must first attempt to get the money from the bank without the guarantee. Then the SBA will guarantee only if certain requirements are met. First is that the bank will, with a guarantee, make the loan. Second is that all owners of the business personally guarantee the loan as well. Third is that other debt be subordinate to the SBA guarantee. That is, in case of trouble, the SBA gets paid off first. Beyond that, the SBA will want to see that the owners have personally invested capital in the business comparable in amount to the loan that is being guaranteed. Other constraints include that the amount is limited, it can be used only for certain types of cases, and the borrowing cost on these loans tends to be high.

On the plus side, many ventures have obtained capital in this way and the rate of default has not been bad. Less inspiring is the observation of one venture consultant about SBA financing, "We could not find a single use of it in famous start-ups or in the interviews of companies we have dealt with over the years since this research started in 1981."[158] Thus, it appears that perhaps SBA-guaranteed loans are, in effect, more for "the little guys." Even there, however, it may still not work, as illustrated by the following experience.

> Debra Cox wanted to borrow $275,000 to buy equipment plus produce and sell more embroidery, heat transfer, and graphic arts products. "I've been to every bank in St. John's County (Florida), plus the SBA. If you don't have real estate, they won't even talk to you." Failing to find bank money, she also tried advertising on the Web through financehub.com, but again without success.[159]

Something lenders look for in assessing a loan prospect is a healthy debt/equity ratio, which is to say a ratio where the equity capital, cash, put into the company by its owner(s) compares favorably to the amount it wants to borrow. Apparently, that was lacking in this case.

The SBA 7(a) program has special sub-categories for loans depending on size and purpose. Information about them can be found on the agency's Web site, sba.gov.

Going concern bank debt

After a start-up gets going in business and has more assets to borrow against, other types of loans are more likely to be available. Some types of assets, and what percentage a bank might loan on them, are listed in Exhibit 5b-2.

A consequently obvious step for a would-be entrepreneur who is thinking about seeking financing for a venture is to make a list of such assets for an expected point in time that financing would be sought and add the amounts to see how much money might be there. Then, allowing for time needed to seek it out, map a plan for seeking it from such sources as might be available, including banks and others.

Seasonal loans

Most businesses fluctuate seasonally in sales volume. For some the swings are less severe, for example supermarkets, and for others they are much more extreme. Sporting goods are an example of the latter.

> Rusty Surfboards and Apparel, a San Diego company of 40 employees handcrafting surfboards and licensing related clothing, found that the stores it sold to start building their inventories of surfboards in March and April. That meant manufacturing had to be going strong in February to supply them. This cost cash for materials and payroll that would not come back for up to six months later in some cases, since stores typically took 120 to 180 days to pay. Consequently, Rusty drew down a line of credit each year to bridge the cash flow gap.[160]

With a new venture such a loan should not be taken for granted. If the cash flow forecast shows a pattern that might justify some sort of revolving loan whose repayment can be anticipated with high reliability, then the possibility should be discussed with the bank, or better yet more than one bank, in advance to be sure that it will loan against that prospect. After the business has been operating for one or a few years, it should be easy to get such a loan. But for a start-up it can be problematic.

Line of credit

Based upon short term assets, such as inventory and accounts receivable that may fluctuate over time, banks sometimes extend permission to borrow up to some level at will.

Exhibit 5b-2 What banks loan on going-concern assets[161]

Asset	Borrowable percentage range
Contracts and purchase orders	0–100%
Accounts receivable (within 60 days)	70–90
Raw materials inventory	20–50
In-process inventory	0–10
Finished goods inventory	20–50
General purpose equipment	40–70
Special purpose equipment	0–30
Commercial real estate	70–90

---

[158] John L. Nesheim, *Hi Tech Startup* (Saratoga, CA: Electronic Trend Publications, 1992) p. 209.
[159] Jane Easter Bahls, "Cybercash," *Entrepreneur*, March 1999, p. 108.
[160] "Spring Forward," *Business Advisor*, September/October 2000 (Los Angeles: Baumer Financial Publishing) p. 42.
[161] Bruce Blechman and Jay Conrad Levinson, *Guerrilla Financing* (Boston: Houghton Mifflin, 1991) p. 29 (adapted with modifications).

Two founders of a steel fabricating company needed working capital at an early stage for raw materials and labor on contracted jobs. They had been able to get financing for their equipment from a large bank. But now they wanted a line of credit, and the bank they were dealing with just kept giving them "the runaround," they said. Consequently, they checked out some other banks and shifted the remainder of their banking business to a smaller community bank, which readily helped them out. The company was profitable from the start, lost money in only one of its first ten years of business, and by the year 2000 was still prospering with the smaller bank.

Banks are in business to profit by making loans, just as other companies sell their goods and services to earn profits. As with sources of other goods and services, it can make sense to shop around for the best place to deal with, as this example illustrates.

Long term borrowing

If the money is to be used for buying real estate or some other major asset that can be resold, then the bank may be a source of initial capital for that purpose. But commitment to purchase such long-term major assets usually doesn't fit until later in development of the venture. If the business is heavily dependent on the asset, such as real estate for a new marina, shopping center, or ski chalet, then there may be no way around such a loan. But the interest and payments impose a dangerous burden for a fragile new company.

Variety in banks

Most banks would prefer to have monopolies on their customers. As the president of one $991 million institution put it, "I don't want to have my best customers dealing with another bank, and every time they want something, they go to both of us to see who will give them the best deal." But many entrepreneurs use two or more banks at the same time,[162] either for different services, or one for personal accounts and the other(s) for business, just to have connections and be ready to move if one or the other is acquired and changes its personnel or policies.

Some banks are more hospitable to start-ups and small firms, according to the U.S. Small Business Administration's Office of Advocacy. A summary of the results was reported by Griffin and others.[163] The listing gives best banks to try, most of them smaller and not nationally well known, in each state and also the best among the large bank holding companies. Topping the big bank list was Wells Fargo & Company.

Many entrepreneurs report having been turned down by several banks before finding one that would grant them credit. Hence it can make sense to shop around, evaluate at each the individual banker who would handle the account as to rank (banks have lots of vice presidents, some of whom outrank others—higher rank means more power to approve the loan), knowledge and interest in the business, years of experience, particularly with businesses similar to the venture, accessibility, likelihood of permanence, and personal rapport. Comparison should also be made of estimated loan application turnaround times.

Choosing a bank

Rules sometimes suggested for choosing a bank include going with a local bank rather than a branch of a larger one. The arguments are that the local bank will take more personal interest in the company, be able to move faster and more flexibly with decisions, and be staffed with people who are less likely to be moved to another location. Also, the entrepreneur should be able to know and possibly deal directly with top people among the bank's executives.

The following entrepreneur recalled as a mistake the fact that he had not done more shopping around earlier to find a good banking fit.

I made a major error at this point that almost killed the deal. I assumed that my best chance for financing the acquisition was to approach the larger banks in Laurel, the town where the business was located. As a result I didn't go to any local Annapolis banks where friends could get me in the door at the right levels. The banks in and around Laurel wanted nothing to do with me, or my deal.

---

[162] Cynthia E. Griffin, "Spread the Wealth?" *Entrepreneur*, October 1999, p. 32.
[163] Cynthia E. Griffin, "Voted Most Friendly," *Entrepreneur*, July 1999, p. 114.

I was incredulous. I had assumed that putting the financing together would be a matter of a couple of weeks, at the most.

It took six. I was extremely embarrassed to tell people the banks were stringing me along. What was I, some kind of deadbeat?

In desperation, I called several friends for help. They got me in to see Annapolis bankers (I didn't know anyone from the local banks because, although I lived in Annapolis, I had worked in Washington since moving to town). They listened. They checked me out. Then I got a yes. Then another yes. Then another, and another. All but one were from strictly local banks. I wasn't a deadbeat after all. In fact, I was able to get pretty good terms.[164]

Contrary arguments are that a larger bank will have more widespread connections, better information sources, more services to offer, and ultimately greater financial capacity to serve the venture if it grows large or spreads to other geographical areas. The following two entrepreneurs tried to go with large banks but found themselves deflected:

> The founder of a discount buyers' club through which people could buy a variety of goods and services for below-retail prices, chose to work with a major bank because he wanted to be able not only to do online-banking but also be able to process credit card transactions remotely, not just from the office. Smaller banks, he found, could not offer both these services. However, he could not find a large one that would give him a line of credit. His line of business, he was told, was too high risk. Consequently, he ended up working with a medium-sized bank because it would lend to his company and he felt he could get along well with the banker. He found he could buy credit card processing services, which the bank did not offer, through an independent company.

In shopping around, it may be helpful to cast a fairly broad net, including small as well as large banks and some with distant headquarters also, much as it may be comforting to try to work with the top people of a locally headquartered bank. The following entrepreneur's comment is illustrative.

> Don't overlook the out-of-town banks with commercial offices in your home town. They are usually hungrier than the local lenders and often will do deals that the hometown keepers of the cash won't touch. Minneapolis's three biggest banks wouldn't give me the time of day as we went through our whirlwind of growth in the mid eighties, but two out-of-town banks, one from Boston and one from New York, were beating my doors down.[165]

Bankers

Sometimes the question is not so much which bank as it is which banker a founder should choose. Here again, there is conventional wisdom. "Choose a banker who will get to know you and understand your business."

Contrasts between what is called for by the job of a banker versus that of an entrepreneur that may help the entrepreneur understand a banker's point of view include those in Exhibit 5b-3.

Still, every banker is different, as illustrated by the experience of Patrick Kelly who, with two working partners and one investing partner, created the multinational medical supplies wholesaling firm PSS/World Medical.[166]

> The four partners had contributed to the venture $40,000 in equity plus $60,000 of debt, mostly lent by the outside partner, who had in addition personally guaranteed a $100,000 line of credit at the bank and then given a second guarantee for another $100,000. Needing $50,000 to meet payroll, Ryan visited the banker, drew $50,000 against the line of credit and deposited it in the venture's checking account ready to write paychecks.
>
> As he left the bank he suddenly found the banker coming after him with a request that he return to the bank for further conversation. Back at the bank, the banker reached across the desk, lifted the new $50,000 deposit receipt out of Ryan's pocket and informed Ryan that the guarantor had changed his mind, so the loan was cancelled. (Later, it occurred to Ryan that this cancellation by the banker might have been illegal.)
>
> Payroll was met, but only for employees besides the three salesmen. The guarantor subsequently was persuaded to reestablish the guarantee. But Ryan was now convinced that there should be more equity in the company so it would not be

[164] Hendrix F.C. Niemann, "Buying a Business," *Inc.*, February 1990, p. 38.
[165] Jim Schell, *The Brass-tacks Entrepreneur* (New York: Henry Holt and Company, 1993) p. 38.
[166] Patrick Ryan, *Faster Company* (New York: Wiley, 1998) p. 48.

Exhibit 5b-3 Entrepreneur versus bankers imperatives

Entrepreneur	Banker
Goes to the customer	Available for the customer to call
Initiates	Responds
Makes own rules	Must obey institutional rules
Approaches few bankers	Approached by many supplicants
Seizes opportunity	Preserves depositors' money
Dreams about upside	Worries about downside
Seeks to influence people	Must control cash
Is more independent	Is an employee
Is more autonomous	Is more a subordinate
Focuses on vision	Focuses on details
Wears many hats	Occupies one position

so much at the mercy of lenders. He offered to sell preferred stock to all employees with a par ten times its book value. If the company failed, they could collect as much of the book value as was left after lenders were paid. If it succeeded, they would have the option at the end of three years of selling the preferred back for the amount they had paid for it plus 10 percent annual interest or, alternatively, of converting it to common. The employees shortly put up a total of $151,000. PSS/World Medical was on its way to becoming an employee-owned company. It also changed banks, but with efforts not to antagonize the one it left. "In business you never want to burn your bridges," Ryan commented. "You just want to learn from your mistakes."

Appreciation of such differences as these can help in choosing bankers. With it, an entrepreneur will know better what to expect and how to prepare for it in advance to reach a desired agreement. But such understanding does not necessarily come by instinct to the entrepreneur. Cultivating a bank relationship can be a long-term process.

Because they could not get a bank loan when they first started their casual clothing business in 1988, Steve and Andi Rosenstein struck up an acquaintance with the account officer responsible for their checking account. Through him they met a lending officer, and every year for four years they made it a practice to sit down and visit with him. Eventually, this yielded their first line of credit at the bank. By 1999 their business had grown to $28 million in sales and the bank, they said, now gave them "everything we ask for."[167]

An open question, perhaps, is whether it would have been well to cultivate acquaintance with a second banker, just in case.

Tom Novak, a cell phone distributor managed to get a $15,000 line of credit by pledging his home, car, and the $15,000 certificate of deposit owned by a friend. But he could not persuade the banker to come see his business. The banker's attitude, he said, was "I don't care what you're doing. All I want is for you to make your loan payments."

So, networking through his customers, Novak looked for another bank and found one willing to extend a $65,000 line of credit against only inventory and the CD. Again, he tried to develop a relationship. He recalled, "I'd talk to my loan officer every day and keep him informed about everything that was going on in my company." Beyond that, he said, "We've lived up to our loan covenants, and we've made our loan payments on time. And in return, often without our even asking for better rates, our banking costs have decreased. Our credit line—which has now grown to nearly $1 million—is down to prime plus one half a point, from prime plus two points."[168]

Shopping around earlier may lower the risk of having to do it under pressure and when things are not going well. Doing it later may more sharply define the reason for it and the target to aim for. Ideally, the venture's banker should be a commercial loan officer who either knows about, or wants to learn about the business and its industry, who is doing well at the bank, with whom the venture CEO has a good personal rapport and who would like to do business with the venture.

---

[167] Mike Hoffman, "Hot Tips," *Inc.*, October 1999, p. 88.
[168] "Ways to Keep Costs Low," *Inc.*, March 1999, p. 100.

3. Building credit

Working on the loan proposal can proceed in parallel with finding the right banker and learning what he or she will require.

Loan proposal

If a business plan has been written for the venture, it may need adaptation to suit it as a loan proposal and to fit what the particular banker wants. Some tasks in the process of preparing it include the following.

1. **Get business financial data**, including insofar as possible, data on comparable firms. Note pertinent factors such as seasonality and lease commitments.

2. **Include personal financial data**, including last three years' tax filing, and personal financial statements on all partners.

3. As part of the market data, **list who customers will be** and where the information came from.

4. **Describe competitors** by name, what has been happening and can be expected to happen with them. Include a competitor-advantages grid. If location is important, include analysis of it. Cite data sources.

5. **Prepare a forecast**—show where you will plan to use the money and let it be clear where the repayment will come from.

6. **Forecast cash injection sources** and timing. Who else may put money up? Will there likely be future cash injection stages? What are the longer-run financial aims of the company?

Some thoughts that will likely be on the banker's mind in reviewing the proposal include the following.

1. Is everything the venture wants to borrow for **really necessary** for the business?

2. Are the founders willing to **sign personally** on the loan? What other debts do they have?

3. Who, if anyone, might serve as **additional co-signers**?

4. Will any **founders be taking out** more money personally than needed?

5. Will the company be **extending credit**, and if so to whom and how reliable are they?

6. Can some **assets be sold** and replaced with leased items if need be?

Whatever time it takes the banker to explore these questions and others that follow below, is time that might be applied to other opportunities for the bank, serving other customers, seeking new customers, and dealing with the bank's own internal operations. Whether the venture's business really is worth that is something the banker must consider.

Credit evaluation

To become confident that they are choosing loan opportunities prudently, bankers are said to look for the following six C's.

Character Is the person truthful? Will the person keep a promise? Will the person do his or her best to pay back the loan?

Capacity Does the person have a proven capability to earn the amount of money needed to pay back the loan?

Capital How much investor money does the would-be borrower currently have in the business relative to what it will owe after borrowing?

Collateral What assets of the business or the borrower will the bank be able to take over and sell if need be to recover the loan money? How hard will it be to sell them, and how much net cash should result from doing so?

Coverage Is appropriate insurance protection in place to cover assets, including the life of the borrower as protection for the loan money?

Conditions What could go wrong that would jeopardize the borrower's repayment capability, how likely is that to occur, and what can be done about it?

Conditions, the sixth C mentioned above, obviously vary among companies, and beyond the company vary in the economy. To hedge that uncertainty, a banker simply has to anticipate the worst and try to loan only in such a way that the other C's are strong enough to cope with it.

Two other C's that might be added to this list are

Credit history Has the loan applicant borrowed before and repaid the loan on time?

Loan proposal

Credit evaluation

Cushion Is the applicant asking for enough money to do the job plus some extra to be able to respond to possible surprises?

Other elements that can be influential in getting a bank loan include:

- How solid the customers of the venture are and how certain they are to buy. A government or big company contract can make a big difference.
- How fully "loaned-up" versus hungry for loans the bank is.
- How good the bank's recent experience has been with loans like this.
- The extent to which this loan might help relations with other customers, such as perhaps suppliers to the venture.
- How confident the banker is that he or she understands the venture.
- How satisfactory the bank's recent experience has been with businesses of this type.

Credit scoring, long used for consumer loan applications, is a mechanical procedure for rating and applying weighted criteria that produces a numerical score of attractiveness from the bank's perspective based upon its prior lending experience. It is sometimes used also for commercial loan evaluation, particularly for smaller borrowing amounts and particularly by larger banks.

If the loan is to be personally guaranteed, then a further question, which can also involve credit scoring, is what that individual possesses that is not obligated elsewhere and can be used to back up the guarantee. Possible assets include the following.

Residential real estate (about 75 percent of market value).

Life insurance cash value.

Stocks and bonds market value can quickly change.

Collectibles, such as coins, jewelry.

Auto, **airplane**, **boat**, if late model in good condition, fully insured.

Finding an effective combination of such elements can take considerable homework and searching. The entrepreneur may be able to get a jump on this process by both venture planning and becoming acquainted with prospective bankers in advance of seeking a loan.

As usual in business, there are exceptions to the general rules. The approach used by the following entrepreneur to get a loan would not work for everyone in dealing with a bank, but it did for him.

In May 1978, the founder of a fried chicken restaurant had located and, with his wife, brother, and brother-in-law, bought a building for it and engaged an architect to design the remodeling. He approached one bank after another, as his request for a loan to complete the start-up was turned down and he was told to prepare a business plan. To enhance his capability for doing so, he enrolled in banking, business, and health classes at a nearby community college. To earn a living and pay the architect, he also took two jobs, one in health care and the other in entertainment, giving him a workday from 6:30 AM to 2:00 PM.

From the bank he had settled on as most receptive, however, he kept encountering nothing but delays and criticism of his plan, which he kept refining. He suspected, although there was no proof, that the bank's decision might be influenced by his lack of a high school diploma and the fact that he was African American.

Finally, after more than a year, an approval came. He was required to pledge his home in addition to the restaurant and its equipment. In addition, to his outrage, he was told that the bank would not actually give him the money. Instead, he would have to bring any due invoices and let the bank pay them for him directly from the loan.

He refused, and instead began picketing the bank. He also found opportunity to be interviewed on a radio talk show, where again he aired his complaint. The bank backed down and let him have the money.

Review by the bank will introduce delays in the process, accompanied by clues about the bank's position. If the loan is small enough, looks solid enough, and is being reviewed by an officer of high enough rank, he or she may approve the loan directly. Otherwise, the message may be, "I'll have to run this by the bank's loan committee."

If the loan officer says "Come with me, I'd like to have you meet our president," it's a good sign. But if not, it's not necessarily a bad sign. More likely a poor sign is if the hand-off is to a more junior person. If the bank decides it wants an SBA guarantee on the loan, several more weeks may be added to the review process. In short, there will likely be uncertainty and delays in the approval process. So this should be anticipated in planning.

Loan documents

If the loan is approved, documents will be involved, and possibly time and legal costs of having them appropriately reviewed. Those documents will include a promissory note and company authorization. If there is to be a guarantee, that will call for another form, indicating whether it is limited or general. There may be a security agreement if specific assets are pledged against the loan.

The loan agreement will include covenants specifying what the venture agrees to do, or not do. Fairly standard covenants include what level of working capital is to be maintained, what any spending limitations should be observed by the venture, what financial statements should be provided to the bank and when, what insurance should be taken out, how much key executives can be paid, whether the venture can enter into leases, and what rights the venture has to sell collateral.

Things to be negotiated as part of the loan include such covenants as these as well as (1) what the interest rate will be on the loan, (2) what other fees may be part of the deal, (3) whether the venture can pay back ahead of schedule, (4) whether the venture must maintain certain deposit account balances, and (5) who, if anybody, must co-sign.

These negotiations can result in the venture getting lower costs and more freedom, or the opposite, and are therefore important. It may have to accept relatively unfavorable terms at first because of newness. Over time, if the entrepreneur does a good job on the bank relationship and the venture lives up to its promises, terms more favorable to the venture may be developed, particularly if other banks also take an interest in getting the venture's business. Both the banker and the borrower have work to do in maintaining each other's business.

Maintaining the bank relationship

Finally closing the loan deal will be just the beginning of a relationship between banker and entrepreneur that will need much further care and attention. Both parties will hope there are no unpleasant surprises. These could be produced by events or policy changes within the bank that might cause it to stop further extension of credit in either amount or time. Or they could be caused by problems that arise in the venture. In the following example, it was behavior by the entrepreneur that soured the relationship, as was recalled by a young MBA who had recently joined the venture.

The young MBA had met the founder of a small research and product development company through a school project. Subsequently, the founder invited him to join the company as a business manager; his first task would be to help the company find more capital. Through family connections, the graduate introduced the founder to both a venture capitalist, who, after meeting the company and the founder, decided to invest, and to a banker who agreed to loan cash against orders from customers who were known to be powerful and could be relied upon to pay their bills. Among other responsibilities, the graduate was put in charge of the venture's bookkeeper, who wrote and sometimes signed the company's checks.

One Tuesday, the founder asked the graduate to go see the banker to borrow cash for the forthcoming payroll on Friday, explaining that he would do so himself, except that he had to fly out of town to handle the affairs of his mother who had just died.

The graduate saw no problem with this until the founder added more facts. To obtain the loan that the company already had, he had promised the banker that when a certain large customer paid its bill, the money would be used to pay off the existing loan. When the payment arrived, however, the founder asked the bookkeeper to apply it instead to bills owed by the venture to one of its suppliers who was threatening to cut off supplies unless paid. Additionally, as the graduate later learned, the founder instructed the bookkeeper not to tell the graduate about this. Now, it seemed, the deed was done, and the banker had found out about it. It astonished the graduate that the founder, a scientist with a respected record who was always courteous, never swore, lived conservatively, and had always seemed so upright would have acted so duplicitously.

On Thursday at the bank, the graduate asked for the payroll loan and was subjected to a long and furious tongue lashing by the banker for having influenced the bank to do business with someone who had not kept his word. Eventually, the banker granted the payroll loan, lest the company fail and lose money already owed the bank. But he further stipulated that the company would get no more credit beyond that and that it should look for another bank.

The graduate before long left the company which, although it did pay off the bank and then managed to borrow from another one, eventually failed. His memory of how the seemingly upright founder had cheated under financial pressure, and how strongly the banker had reacted to it, survived.

Working rules

Personal operating rules for working successfully with bankers make common sense but are worth thinking about specifically to ward off mistakes such as the pattern illustrated above. Some do's to put on the list include the following.

- Shop banks and learn how to size them up.
- Discuss in person, not just by phone.
- Listen carefully.
- When in doubt about meaning, request explanation.

- Prepare complete homework with appropriate documents and records.
- Ask for enough.
- Be ready to compromise if need be.
- Put promises to be relied upon in writing.
- Negotiate terms and interest.
- Provide requested information fully and truthfully.
- Keep promises.
- Invite visitation.
- Send referrals (as a favor to both them and the bank).

Don'ts such as those below should also be included on the list of personal operating rules for maintaining bank relationships.

- Don't just drop in; phone first.
- Don't push.
- Don't bluff.
- Don't argue.
- Don't quit when rejected.
- Don't be late on payments.
- Don't get the wrong type of loan for the venture's needs.
- Don't surprise; keep the bank informed, especially if there is bad news.

Such rules may serve many other categories of business relationships as well, including dealing with possible sources of debt other than banks.

4. Non-bank debt sources

Inventory

Accounts receivable

Many organizations besides banks engage in lending. Banks are in some ways handicapped by regulations designed to protect borrowers.

Inventory

Auto companies provide loans to customers for buying cars. They also provide "flooring," which is to say inventory that is in effect on consignment to dealers to provide them with a variety of models for the dealers' customers to choose from. Other equipment makers engage in similar deals with customers, both to enhance their sales and, in the case of customer financing, to gain interest on their money. Credit unions and stock brokerages make loans, both personal and business.

Accounts receivable

Banks follow rules on lending against accounts receivable, which causes them to turn such loans down for reasons that are not always well justified, such as the borrower being too new or too small.

Factoring

Another alternative for the venture to obtain money out of its accounts receivable without waiting for customers to pay whenever they feel like it is to sell those receivables to a factoring company. This is a very old form of financing for which there are well-established practices.

Essentially, the factoring company, or factor, reviews the receivables and offers to buy those it likes at a discount off their face value. How much the discount, or, in effect fee, is depends on how risky the receivable is judged to be and on whether the factoring is on a recourse or non-recourse basis. Recourse means that the venture selling the receivable retains some responsibility for collectability of the receivable. If the customer does not pay the factoring company, the venture has to help out with the bad receivable thus created, such as by collecting it from the customer or accepting it back and putting up something else in its place. Also, under a recourse arrangement, the factoring company may require a cash reserve, or an amount in addition to the fee withheld from the face value when the receivable is bought. Because non-recourse factoring is more advantageous in amount raised and risk escaped by the venture, the factoring company will charge a higher fee. Compared to other forms of debt, factoring tends to be very expensive.

Individual buyers of receivables

That, in turn, can make the creation of a factoring enterprise an attractive venture opportunity for some other entrepreneur who either has a lot of resources or is able to recruit them.

Steve Shaughnessy, a Seattle bank loan officer, became frustrated with what seemed to him overly conservative and rigid rules for accepting accounts receivables from small companies as collateral for loans. Consequently, he quit the bank, marshaled his own personal assets and started buying accounts receivable from his former bank customers who had not been able to sell them to the bank. To this writing after several years in this practice, he had never bought a receivable that was not easy to collect. His biggest challenge, he found, was to find more receivables to buy, because he had, by now, become able to borrow plenty of cash against his own resources to buy them.

Bridge loans

Sometimes in the course of obtaining financing the borrower will have to wait for routine procedures and paper work to run their course. In the interim to fill in the cash need, either finance companies or individuals will extend an interim loan for a short period of time from days to weeks. Such loans are called bridge loans and they will carry a fee of a very few percent to the service. Sometimes attorneys or other insiders who are helping with the paperwork of a financing package will happily offer bridge financing that an entrepreneur, who has to cover the time gap somehow, will accept, also happily, perhaps without thinking too hard about the cost.

If the small percentage charge is extrapolated to a yearly amount it will be seen to represent an extremely high interest rate. Individuals also sometimes obtain such advances from paycheck cashing services, which similarly receive extremely high rates. For instance, a charge of 1 percent to get the money one week early amounts to a 52 percent simple interest rate annually.

Quasi-commercial cash sources

Sometimes cash can be obtained from organizations, either governmental or private, that have goals of creating jobs or advancing the wealth of communities.

State and local agencies

The SBA is not the only governmental agency that helps small firms get loans. To help economic development in certain geographical areas, there are both state and local agencies that can help with guarantees, or in some cases direct loans, as well as with tax breaks, hiring subsidies, direct contracts, and other assistance. A good place to start asking about them is with state departments of commerce and local chambers of commerce, as well as with banks. A "guerrilla financing" approach might be to call government employees who run things and ask what help sources might apply.

Community development

Community finance institutions also make bridge loans, usually motivated by desire to help a company retain its capability to serve the local community, or out of social concerns such as helping minorities or other disadvantaged entrepreneurs.

Joe Salinas, founder of a networking software company in Austin, Texas, needed $150,000 to expand his company of 15 employees doing

$750,000 in sales to take on an additional $4 million in expanded orders. His first approach was to try banks, he recalled. "We tried some pretty good sized banks, but they felt we had grown too fast, that we had too much business; they wanted to see how we would manage growth before lending to us."

Instead, he approached the Austin Community Development Corporation. It granted him a bridge loan of $50,000, which carried his venture to a point where banks were willing to loan him the rest.[169]

Affinity groups

There are many types of affinity groups that engage in lending for various reasons. Credit unions, community-lending agencies, even clubs and churches sometimes make loans, usually for policy reasons and goals beyond simply earning interest.

Two Southeast Asian immigrants became impatient with the low-paid employment they were able to obtain and began looking for something better. Through friends they heard of a Vietnamese restaurant for sale. After negotiating a $25,000 purchase price with the owner, they set about recruiting funds. Some came through loans from their families and friends. The rest came from a pool system they said was common within their community. Under this arrangement, members of the pool would contribute over time to a common fund, which then would be lent to one or more of the contributors, who then would repay it on specified terms. Among the terms, because members of their pool were Muslims, was the absence of any interest charges.

Three of the seven founders of Seattle's Speakeasy Café, a restaurant with Internet terminals

for patrons to use, were computer professionals. The others included a playwright, a lawyer, an architect, and the news director of a television station. The lead founder, a CAD professional, put up $10,000 from personal savings, while the others tapped their savings accounts or took out loans to put up another $200,000.

Self searching

There is room for individual imagination in raising money, as illustrated, perhaps, by the following experience of author Bruce Williams, who advertised to find it.

When I went into the nursery school business in 1961, I ran a classified ad in the Wall Street Journal. I found a colonel in the Air Force who had inherited money and was looking to invest it, but that failed to work out … I had a fellow walk into my living room with a briefcase full of bright green cash. 'How much do you want?' he asked me. I couldn't wait to get him out of the house. Obviously, I was being offered underworld money. … I eventually borrowed money through an attorney representing a couple who had inherited a lot of money from a European relative they knew nothing about.[170]

The advertising in this case was done in a formal way. Informal advertising, simply asking contacts about possible sources for money, is also feasible. However, it is important to be clear about whether the venture is simply looking for sources of money or, in contrast, is advertising the sale of securities, whether equity or debt, as will be discussed in a subsequent chapter. Legal implications of this distinction about public offerings are serious.

5. Beyond the loan

One ideal scenario with debt is that it is paid off from retained earnings of the company, and thereafter the company is able to grow without it via plowing earnings back, thus eliminating the expense of interest. In some businesses where the margin is high and sales grow steadily, such as has happened with successful software firms, this is possible. In others, where

margins are lower, capital intensity is higher, or there is major seasonality in sales, it may be best to operate with a line of credit and borrow against it to meet the swings.

It still could be possible to meet the swings with reinvested earnings if they were large enough to build up a buffer, investing them in short-term securities when cash needs were low

[169] Cynthia E. Griffin, "Bridging the Gap," *Entrepreneur*, March 1999, p. 30.
[170] Bruce Williams, *In Business for Yourself* (Lanham MD: Scarborough House, 1991) p. 88.

and pulling them out, instead of borrowing, when seasonal needs rose.

If the company is one of very high growth, however, and also has anything like normal capital intensity, even in a software firm where, despite high margins there was need for large spending to write code or to advertise, something more than seed capital plus borrowing may be needed. How to accomplish that will be the subject of later chapters on venture capital and on public offerings.

Exercises

Text discussion questions

1. How should the appropriate level of debt for a start-up be determined?
2. How should an entrepreneur decide between one source of debt and another depending upon what debt sources have already been tapped?
3. How should lease commitments be handled on a balance sheet or in analyzing the appropriate level of debt for a venture?
4. What are the pros and cons of an entrepreneur leasing a company car for the venture?
5. Under what conditions would you be willing to guarantee a note at the bank for a venture of someone else's?

Case questions

5B-1 Sally Corbin

1. What steps should Sally Corbin take to maximize her chances of getting debt financing for her venture?
2. If Sally approached you as a bank loan officer and your bank was not "loaned up" at the time of the case, how would you respond to her request for a loan?
3. List the terms you would require on a loan for Sally's venture if you were a banker.
4. If you, as a student, decided to take on a four-credit–hour independent study project to help Sally apply for a bank loan, what would be your work plan?

5B-2 Greg Thompson

1. What should be Greg's pitch to the bank's float control officer to obtain a contract for ferrying checks by air to the Federal Reserve Bank for clearance and why?
2. What should Greg's pitch be to a commercial loan officer at the bank for obtaining a loan to buy an airplane for ferrying checks to the Federal Reserve Bank?
3. As CEO of the bank, what would you see as the pros and cons of being Greg's first customer, and what would you do about it?
4. List the sequence of steps Greg should take next at the end of the case.

Portfolio page possibilities

Page 5B-1 Potential non-bank debt sources

List potential non-bank debt sources for your venture, indicating (1) how much might be sought from each, and (2) what can be done to maximize eligibility from each source. Be sure to footnote appropriately any potential debt sources you actually talked with.

Page 5B-2 Debt funding schedule

Prepare a calendar schedule of borrowing for the first year or two of your venture. Include all sources and types of borrowing, including in-kind and possibly borrowing of assets as well as repayment intentions.

Page 5B-3 Loan application high points

In as much detail as one page allows, write out the main points you would make in a bank loan application for your venture.

Term Projects

Venture history

1. What debt financing did the venture pick up to extend its initial equity financing and when along its timeline?
2. What trade credit became available to the venture and at what time points?
3. What different types of debt did the venture choose not to use, and why?
4. How much interaction with bank officers of what rank, did the founders have? Were any personal guarantees involved?

Venture planning guide

If you have not done so already, visit commercial loan officers at two different banks and seek their counsel on how to make use of the bank most effectively.

CHAPTER 5C – Outside Investors

Topics

1. Main outside investors
2. Angels
3. Venture capital organizations
4. Limited offerings
5. Full registration

Checkpoints

a. What is the basis for distinction among the three outside investor types?
b. Who are angel investors and how do they operate?
c. How are angel investors to be found?
d. How are venture capitalists different from angel investors?
e. What different types of venture capital firms are there?
f. Why do venture capital firms have to seek big wins and avoid small deals?
g. What kinds of criteria do venture capital firms use for choosing investments?
h. How are venture capitalists to be found?
i. Why don't all firms go public?
j. What are the different types of public offerings?
k. What is the role of an underwriting firm in a public offering?
l. What is a direct public offering?
m. Explain the procedure for trying to sell stock in a venture over the Internet.
n. Describe the pros and cons of going public.

Entrepreneurs who need more cash than insiders can provide turn to various types of outside investors, such as those that will be described in this chapter. The reasons for these greater needs may be that the venture has to begin big, as did Amazon.com and Federal Express, or that it will have to operate for a long time before sales bring in cash, as in the case of pharmaceutical start-ups, or that it has to grow fast to avoid losing out to competitors who jump in and try to pass it up.

This chapter will describe types of outside investors, what they look for, how they operate, and what rules, particularly legal ones, must be observed.

1. Main outside investors

Three general categories of outside investors in ventures are (1) individuals sufficiently wealthy, (2) venture capital firms, and (3) other members of the public. In more detail:

1. **Wealthy individuals** sometimes invest either as silent partners who put money in and hope the company does well, or as informal participants with founders in helping the company operate and develop. These latter

are sometimes referred to as *angels* or *informal venture capital investors*. Informal venture capital has been estimated to invest a total of tens of billions of dollars per year.[171] Respondents in the Cooper[172] study reported that 7.2 percent of all ventures began with outside individual investors and 5.6 percent said they received 40 percent or more of their funding from outside individuals.

2. **Venture capital firms** (or *formal venture capital*) is funding that comes through people who make a profession of investing in start-up and fast-growing ventures. Most of them work for organized venture capital firms, most of which are independent and some of which are parts of large corporations that, for strategic reasons, invest in outside ventures. The total in 1998 was estimated at $17 billion.[173]

3. **Other members of the public** can be approached for financing under two general categories of securities offerings.

   a. **Limited offerings** apply to the two categories of investors above plus, within limits, other members of the public. A variety of laws and rules must be observed depending on the size and target audience of the offering as well as the amount of money to be raised and which of several legal paths is chosen. Generally, the rules get considerably tighter for offerings to groups characterized as "unaccredited" or "unsophisticated."

   b. **Full-registration public offerings** are aimed at anyone in the public at large. These offerings may occur in a series over time beginning with an initial public offering, or IPO. Many have the purpose of creating a market through which employees can cash in on stock options given to them as incentives by the venture. Others are to raise cash for major development efforts in the venture. They require governmental approval, and the procedures for getting it are demanding and complex. Also required for this process are powerful channels for selling the securities. Altogether, it is an expensive process.

Sometimes these alternatives are applied in the sequence listed above after personal savings plus "friendly" and borrowed money sources have been tapped out. But any could apply at inception of the venture, and in fact various sequences can occur, as will be discussed below.

2. Angels

When a venture requires more capital than a founder can muster from savings plus possibly working partners, family, friends, and commercial borrowing, a natural next step is to reach out through personal contacts to find others who might be interested to invest, both for the possibility of a profit and possibly as a participant with advice, counsel, or other participation. To find them may be easy or may take considerable searching. Here is how *Time* magazine was initially financed.

With the idea that they were going to start their own magazine, Briton Hadden and Henry Luce obtained seven week's leave without pay from their newspaper jobs in Baltimore and on February 8, 1922 left for New York. They showed a dummy issue to others in the publishing business, trading on their contacts among Yale alumni the fact that Hadden had been top man in the class of 1920, Luce had been Phi Beta Kappa, and both had been on the board of the *Yale Daily News*.

To raise a capital target of $100,000 they wrote a prospectus. It included a statement of editorial policies aimed at distinguishing it from its main established competitor, the *Literary Digest*, and stating "no publication has adapted itself to the time which busy men are able to spend on simply keeping informed." They also showed their idea to a list of prominent personalities, including Franklin Roosevelt, Bernard Baruch, the president of Yale, and a number of others, obtaining endorsements of the idea.

Their expectation was to persuade each of 10 rich Yale classmates to put up $10,000. But none did. Looking for smaller amounts among J.P. Morgan partners and others, they managed to raise $35,000 after six months. Then a Rockefeller partner agreed to put up $5,000 and introduced them to his mother, who added $20,000.

[171] R.J. Gaston, Finding Private Venture Capital for Your Firm (New York: John Wiley and Sons, 1989).

[172] Arnold C. Cooper and others, New Business in America (Washington, D.C.: The NFIB Foundation, 1990) p. 16.

[173] 1999 *National Venture Association Yearbook* (National Venture Association, 1999) p. 24.

Through her they also met her daughter, who happened to be married to a classmate, and who put in another $5,000. By October they had raised $86,000 and decided to start, although still $14,000 shy of their capital target. Their advertisement in the *New York Tribune* stated as a goal "to summarize the week's news in the shortest possible space."

The first issue sold 9,000 copies, less than 40 percent of its 25,000 goal. Its 28 pages included only six pages of advertising, sold at cut rates, in contrast to the same week's issue of its established competitor, *Literary Digest*, whose 88 pages included 39 pages of advertising. By the end of 1923, circulation was 20,000 copies per week and losses for the year were $39,454. To the founders it appeared that success was surely on the way, and they raised their salaries to $40 per week each. Time's breakeven occurred in 1927 on double the sales of the preceding year, and four years after its first issue in March 1923. As the stock market dropped toward the bottom of the depression in 1931, *Time's* stock was sky-rocketing from $360 per share in 1929 to over $1,000 where it would be split 20 to 1.[174]

A study by Gaston[175] reported that there were a half-million informal, or angel investors in the United States, but this is hard to verify, as is the estimate that they invest around $30 billion per year in ventures. It can be noted that there are something over two million millionaires in the country. Not all angels are millionaires, although most probably are.

Such a backer may invest only once, or may make multiple investments. The money may be advanced as a loan rather than a permanent investment, possibly with rights for conversion to equity ownership. Someone who invested years earlier, but not recently, may or may not still be considered an angel investor. People may invest their own money, or they may invest for others, and they may invest directly or through another company. The latter have been referred to as *quasi-angels*. Attempts to learn through surveys about these various types and how they operate have been frustrated by low response rates, averaging around 5 percent.[176]

Typically angels seem to invest amounts ranging from $25,000 to $2 million in backing around 50,000 start-ups per year. Based on a tracking of 1,200 such investors between 1989 and 1999, it appears that about 70 percent lost all or part of their investment, notwithstanding their profit objectives. A fraction of the remainder achieve high enough returns to show that spectacular profits are possible as was earlier the case with *Time* and more recently with Intel and many other high-technology firms.[177]

When Robert Noyce and Gordon Moore quit Fairchild Semiconductor to start their own company, Intel, Fairchild hired a new top executive from Motorola, C. Lester Hogan, who soon replaced the remaining Fairchild managers with others he brought with him. The last to go was Fairchild's sales and marketing director, Jerry Sanders.

Given a year's salary in compensation, Sanders rented a Malibu beach house to relax in while he considered his next move. Shortly he heard from four other Fairchild employees saying they wanted to quit and form a new company and asking him to help them raise money. He agreed to do so, providing he could add still others to the team and that the start-up would pursue the same product goals as Intel.

Contacting the Los Angeles investment firm Capital Group Companies, he managed to get a $50,000 personal check from its chairman to provide temporary living expenses for his team. Preparing a 70-page venture plan, he also contacted Arthur Rock, the venture capitalist who had first raised money from Sherman Fairchild to back Noyce and Moore and then 10 years later had raised money for them again to create Intel.

The plan described products aimed at markets that should grow rapidly, specified prices, and included financial forecasts predicting profitability after seven quarters and positive cash flow after ten. It also included resumes showing strong technical qualifications of the founding team and a start-up capital need for $1.75 million.

Rock declined, based on two points. First, he said, there were already too many companies ahead in the race. Second, the only companies he had ever lost money on had, he said, been headed by men who, like Sanders, came from marketing.

[174] W. A. Swanberg, *Luce and His Empire* (New York: Charles Scribner's Sons 1972) p. 85.

[175] Gaston, *Private Venture Capital*.

[176] Barry Singer, "Contours of Development," *Journal of Business Venturing*, 10, no. 4, July 1995, p. 310.

[177] John Cotter, *Secrets of Successful Startups* (La Jolla, CA: University of California Summer School of Entrepreneurship, 2000) p. 17.

Several weeks later, Sanders had still received nothing but rejections from people he approached for money, most of whom declined either because they did not understand the technology enough to appreciate its great potential or because, like Rock, they had a good appreciation for the competition that was already underway and doubted Sanders and his team could catch up. Moreover, his team was growing restive, particularly those who had by now already left Fairchild and felt they were unfairly more at risk than the others who up to this point still were employed there.

Summoning them all to his house, Sanders urged them to commit to joining the new company formally on May 1, 1969. To those still with Fairchild he gave copies of letters they should use in resigning. These commitments, he said, would help reassure prospective investors that the new company was really going to happen. When asked whether financing was available, he promised he would have $1.55 million by June 20.

In the nick of time his promise was finally made good by a check for $25,000 from a Pennsylvania investor that arrived with five minutes to spare on June 20 and pushed the total $5,000 above the $1.55 million. Among the other investors was one with very powerful credibility, Robert Noyce of Intel. He had placed a bet on the new company, AMD, even though he could see it would likely become a competitor of his own firm, which it did.[178]

Who they are

The variety of individuals who invest in ventures was examined by Aram in a study of 55 eastern Great Lakes region angels. They were mostly business owners and managers with a mean age between 40 and 50 who made an average of two risk capital investments every three years. The average investment was just under $50,000. A third of the investments were made within 10 miles of home and three-fourths were within 50 miles. Over 90 percent co-invested with typically four other people. Half of the investments were in start-up firms. Typical target returns on investment were over 35 percent for high technology firms and about 25 percent for others. Those are averages, however, from which individuals might deviate widely. Some entrepreneurs have been lent capital at no interest, for instance, with comments such as, "Somebody helped me when I was starting my business; now I figure it's my turn to put something back." A summary of angel characteristics based upon several other studies by Kelly and Hay included being:[181]

- A middle-aged male (that was then, now is different) with
- Reasonable net income and personal net worth and
- Previous start-up experience who
- Made one investment a year, usually close to home, and
- Preferred to invest in high-technology and manufacturing ventures with
- An expectation of selling out in three to five years.

In addition, these authors found that such investors in a majority of cases backed entrepreneurs who were personally known either to them or to the person who referred the deal to them. They also pointed out that there is much variety within the informal investor population, with many not actually yet having made any investments, while another smaller group known as serial investors has made many and probably accounts for most of the total investment to date. The latter group, moreover, subdivides into some who stick mainly to operating alone and others who mainly invest with syndicates of others, including formal venture capital firms. Studies have given conflicting claims as to which group is more populous.

Foreign investors seem to be a rare source of money for U.S. ventures so far. One three-year-old venture said to have tapped such sources was headed by a former U.S. Assistant Secretary for International Trade. Likely his government work had conferred special know-how, connections, and credentials.[182] Theoretically, foreign

---

[178] Tim Jackson, *Inside Intel* (New York: Penguin, 1997) p. 47-49.

[179] John D. Aram, "Attitudes and Behaviors of Informal Investors toward Early-stage Investments," *Journal of Business Venturing*, 4, no. 5, September 1989, p. 333.

[180] Freddie Laker, *Fly Me, I'm Freddie* (London: Weidenfield and Nicholson, 1980).

[181] Peter Kelly and Michael Hay, "Serial Investors," in *Frontiers of Entrepreneurship Research* 1996, eds. Paul D. Reynolds and others (Wellesley, MA: Babson College, 1996) p. 329.

[182] Ellyn E. Spragins, "Globetrotting for Dollars," *Inc.*, August 1990, p. 116.

sources could also be approached for start-up financing by more "ordinary" entrepreneurs. But geography, even within the U.S., is a barrier. William Wetzel, a scholar at the University of New Hampshire, observed that they preferred to work with lines of business familiar to them and within a day's drive because they wanted to be actively involved with their investees.[183]

How angels operate

Angels include many successful high technology entrepreneurs who, having acquired wealth from their own start-ups, shift to an advisory role by investing in start-ups aimed at high growth. Their motivations include making money, but also being part of the action, enjoying the product or service that the venture creates, working with and mentoring founders, leveraging what they have learned, and sharing bragging rights of another success.

Examples include the following:

Dean Morton, who took up investing in start-ups after retiring as chief operating officer of Hewlett-Packard in 1992, observed, "I like the excitement of a start-up, as do many of the entrepreneurs who are involved as angels. You miss it once you leave the active management of a company you helped grow. Also, you feel like you've learned something along the way. I'm sure there are people who just want to make more money, but the angels I've been involved with are genuinely interested in helping someone else have the experience of success and satisfaction that they've had."

— • —

Jack Carsten had run Intel's microcomputer business, which, he observed, had spawned a number of important innovations, such as modem chips and microcontrollers. In the late 1980s he left to join the venture capital firm U.S. Venture Partners. There he was frustrated by the large number of ventures he had to spread his time across, serving on the boards of 10 companies and responsible for a portfolio of 30. So he decided to leave and invest on his own. "The idea was to put some of my money to work in companies where I could really spend some time …

"Ten years ago if you were doing venture investing you were competing with the venture funds. But today, their minimum investment has

escalated, so that we don't find ourselves competing with them anymore. However, in about one third of the deals it is obvious that we are just the seed round, and that the company will need traditional venture capital if they are successful … I have found that one of the toughest parts of angel investing is 'letting go.' In a venture fund, when a company is in trouble, you go before your partners and put up a fight to save the company, but you usually get shut down. So then you can tell the entrepreneur, 'I did my best, but my partners voted me down.' In an angel deal, you are out there all alone. You have to be willing to look the entrepreneur in the eye and tell him that you are going to pull the plug on their dream. It is hard to do."[184]

— • —

Charlie Gaylord had prospered from stints in two successful software companies, as Chief Executive Officer of Chipsoft and as Executive Vice President of Intuit. During 1999 he invested as an angel in two enterprises out of about 150 whose business plans he read. He commented that in looking at the business plan, *I don't much read the financials, just the model that generated them … Is it a business or just a product? If a business, is there a business/financial model that supports a $50 million plus company?*

If I hear no one is in the market, I worry that there is no market. If I hear some serious players are in the market, I worry that you will be crushed. What I tend to like are 'emerging' markets which are based on a fundamental improvement in something meaningful.

Other criteria Gaylord lists include (1) the prospect of a way to exit with a tenfold return on his investment in three to five years, (2) a team with relevant experience that is scalable (can handle growth), (3) demonstrated commitment, such as having personally invested, and (4) an operating plan that tells how success will be accomplished and that can be summarized clearly in two minutes.

Finding angels

Not wanting to be swamped with solicitations, most angels maintain low profiles and are not on published lists. The best way to find them is by asking around and working through other contacts. Leads include other entrepreneurs, bankers, stockbrokers, real estate brokers, ac-

---

[183] "Angel Hunting Tips," *Inc.*, March 1999, p. 100.
[184] Christina Darwall and Michael J. Roberts, *The Band of Angels* (Boston: Harvard Business School, 1998) p. 7.

countants, and attorneys as well as business and personal acquaintances. Some contacts, such as stockbrokers and real estate agents, expect commissions on deals that come from leads they provide. Others, such as bankers, do not. Looking for ways to return favors of anyone in the search can help the process. Each contact can lead, and so should be asked about, to other contacts so the search becomes one of exploring a web of individuals to find the one who happens to have the sought-for link. Attending showcases, such as the MIT Venture Forum and others like it in many cities (ask the Chamber of Commerce), can also be a way to acquire leads.

Time needed to find the right angel, according to Wetzel, averages six months, followed by another six months while the angel investigates the venture, works out a deal and invests.[185] One entrepreneur, Jim Schell, said angels were like highway patrol, known to be around somewhere, but hard to find. He continued:

> *Finding an angel requires persistence, a black book with a wealth of networking contacts, a clean reputation, and more than a little luck. But somewhere within the framework of our acquaintances is a banker, an accountant, a lawyer, a business broker, a friend, or someone within our industry who knows where to find an angel.*
>
> *I once needed $300,000 to get National Screen-print through another holiday crunch. Thanks to a friendly banker's tip, I found my designated angel hovering between deals. He poked and prodded under my company's hood on his one and only visit. The questions he asked were designed to probe inside me more than into our financial statements.*
>
> *He departed after a one-hour meeting with a noncommittal good-bye, then called the next day and suggested I stop by and pick up a check for $300,000. He charged us 4 percent over prime for four months, by far the easiest deal I ever made. No equity, no meddling, no lawyers[186]*

There are computer-matching systems at the University of New Hampshire and some other universities. But they keep investor names confidential. The SBA (sba.gov) operates a matching service called ACE-net (for Angel Capital Elec-

tronic network, www.acenet.org). An accredited investor, which means one with annual income of $200,000, or net worth of $1 million or more, can register for a fee, set by individual states, and receive a password to enter the database, which lists plans of entrepreneurs who have also registered to be listed. The San Francisco Peninsula (Silicon Valley) area also operates such a network. No statistics have been published, however, about the volume of investments that result or how well they work out.

Silicon Valley has an organization called the Band of Angels, with around 100 investors. Begun in 1994, it developed to include meetings where entrepreneurs were invited to present proposals for funding and became the forerunner of more such groups around the country. One deal arrangement they tried without success to include was a put, which provided that investors could require the company to buy back the angel's stock at three to four times its original value. But subsequent investors balked, so the provision was dropped.[187]

Angels can bring advantages or disadvantages. They may be less demanding, more flexible to work with, willing to go into smaller deals and to accept lower rates of return than are venture capitalists. But they may also lack the breadth of contacts and financial capacity to extend further funding as the venture advances. Giving them ownership can impede later funding, because it makes ownership more complex for other funding sources to deal with. But they also may take close personal interest and be able to help founders get later funding elsewhere on better terms.

Some questions to consider in checking out potential angel investors include:

1. Why might they be interested in your firm in particular?

2. Do they have familiarity and connections in your line of work or market?

3. What else can they add besides money and advice? Bank contacts, recruiting key people, customer introductions?

4. How involved do they want to be and how well would such involvement fit the venture?

---

[185] "Angel Hunting Tips," p. 100.
[186] Jim Schell, *The Brass-tacks Entrepreneur* (New York: Henry Holt and Company, 1993) p. 39.
[187] Christina Darwall and Michael J. Roberts, *The Band of Angels* (Boston: Harvard Business School, 1998) p. 6.

5. What amounts of financial capacity do they possess or have prior working relationships with?

6. What are their financial expectations and desires?

7. How do they feel about risks? Have they been through it before and dealt with setbacks gracefully?

8. How do they feel about dilution of their interest should other investors follow?

9. What is their expectation about other investors being brought in later?

10. When and how do they want to exit?

11. How well do their goals match those of the founders and the venture?

Working things out

Whether individuals should become investors in such ventures is problematic. For them, or for professional venture capitalists, or even for major corporations contemplating new product development projects, the odds are higher by several fold that the enterprise will fall short rather than meet or exceed expectations. In contrast, the odds by investing in stock of listed corporations are that the investment will, on average, grow healthily. Moreover, by investing in listed stocks an investor has a clear path for cashing in, whereas by investing in a venture it is not at all clear that such a path will ever be open.

Occasionally, it is. If a venture is extraordinarily successful, a Microsoft, Yahoo, Google, Cisco Systems, or Starbucks, it may one day go public and make all initial investors colossally rich. The same result can come from the venture selling out or merging, as did Netscape and AOL. Meanwhile, the venture investor may be actively engaged with management in helping the venture develop through contribution of ideas, counsel, and contacts he or she brings to the venture for a spiritual as well as a financial win.

This assumes, of course, that the investor has such additional things to add, that they fit the venture and that he or she wants to spend the time and effort to contribute to them in addition to coping with the financial risk. But even then, the company management may or may not have the time or inclination to provide the investor with desired information, or to draw upon what the investor offers and use it effectively.

Even if these elements are favorable the venture can fail, causing the investment to disappear entirely, as did many early microcomputer makers that showed exciting promise, won for a while, but then sank entirely in a market soaked up by a few big winners, IBM, Hewlett-Packard, Apple, Acer, and Dell.

A venture can sometimes be operated in such ways that managers and employees make money but investors do not. It can stay private indefinitely, so that no investors, particularly if they hold only minority shares, can ever sell out advantageously. Personal relationships can become bitter, as investors see their money used by employees who have little interest in seeing investors gain benefit from it. Managers of the company can become antagonized by resentful communications of the investors. The result can be further adverse to the venture and eventually the only ones to profit may be lawyers paid for the consequent lawsuits.

Arthur Lipper recalled the bitterness of one entrepreneur toward the private investors who had backed his company as follows:

> In an extreme case, a desperate entrepreneur, whom I had helped by arranging for all of the capital initially required, ultimately threatened to slit my throat when his company defaulted on its obligations to the investor group, which had provided the capital in a form that the entrepreneur perceived as being too protective of the angels' capital.[188]

3. Venture capital organizations

In contrast to solo angels, venture capitalists operate as part of formal organizations that invest other people's money along with their own. They generally do bigger deals than angels, and are sometimes thought of as a later stage of investor, either in terms of the size or the time in a venture's development, although some do invest early on.

---

[188] Arthur Lipper III, *The Guide for Venture Investing Angels* (Columbia, MO: Missouri Innovation Center, Inc., 1996) p. 8.

There were approximately 700 such firms in the U.S. in 1992 according to Bygrave and Timmons[189] and 800 in 2000 according to Sherman.[190] The SBA has estimated that they invest approximately $10 billion per year in roughly 2,000 ventures, or an average of about $5 million per venture. Some are independent, while others are linked to government or other organizational funding.

Independent venture capital firms

In the larger and most prominent venture capital firms, full-time professionals manage pools of money put up by individuals or entities such as pension plans. Most venture capital firms are private. A few are publicly held. Deals are often structured as limited partnerships in which the firm is a general partner. These firms are typically the pacesetters of the venture capital industry and are noted for having led the way on such ventures as Apple, Yahoo, Google, Calgene, Amazon, Tandem, and numerous other high-technology success stories.

Government-linked venture capital firms

By agreeing to observe certain federal guidelines restricting investments, Small Business Investment Companies (SBICs) become qualified to borrow federal money at attractive rates and thereby leverage their investment capital. They are typically much smaller than the funds managed by private venture capital firms and not as famous for big wins, although both Intel, the leading chip producer, and Callaway, the largest golf club manufacturer, drew upon SBIC investments early on, as did the office supply chain Staples.[191]

Amateur venture capital groups

Sometimes a small group of individuals will pool savings to invest in ventures as a sideline, hobby, recreation, social activity, or learning experience. Inexperience can mean they will more often than professionals make mistakes such as interfering too much or too little in the venture, arranging deals with counterproductive terms, or giving the venture inappropriate advice. Their funds are also more likely to be limited, so that when the entrepreneur needs further capitalization, they will be unable to help. Worse, they may become fearful and defensive, blame the entrepreneur for creating a predicament, and thereby generate more problems for the venture.

Corporate venture divisions

Some large corporations, such as General Electric, Intel, Cisco, Siemens, Nokia, and Monsanto, have venture organizations of their own. Their goals, in addition to return on capital, sometimes include drawing upon ventures they invest in for technical information to serve R&D. This occurs through interaction between their respective technical employees and sometimes through merging the venture into the corporation later. Each of these possibilities can have major implications for those running the venture.

> Linda Rhode, the CEO of Virtual I.O., was surprised to learn from experience that big corporate investors don't much care about several million dollars poured into a start-up. They care about how the venture can impact their technological and marketing power through new technology and product development. In fact, she said, they typically wrote off the monetary investment on their balance sheets as soon as they put the money in.

Executives of the corporations care first about their jobs and performance of their own companies. One entrepreneur recalled:

> The controller of TCI was on our board, and when TCI got into trouble he kept leaving the board meeting to take phone calls about progress on sale of TCI's three corporate jets, which it was trying to get rid of. At one point all we could get out of some of the Fortune 500 executives on our board was copies of their resumes because they thought they might need new jobs.

Institutional private placements

Other institutions with money that sometimes invest in ventures include insurance companies, pension funds, university endowments, community development funds, family

---

[189] William D. Bygrave and Jeffry A. Timmons, *Venture Capital at the Crossroads* (Boston: Harvard Business School Press, 1992) p. 72.
[190] Andrew J. Sherman, *Raising Capital* (Washington, DC: Kiplinger Books, 2000) p. 159.
[191] www.nasbic.org

trusts, credit unions, foundations, and other variations. Some are profit-oriented, while others have other goals, such as social causes, education, and economic development.

Meeting an investor through an investment banker may cost around 5 percent for the broker, another 1 percent to 2 percent as a commitment fee to the institution making the loan, and anywhere from $20,000 to $100,000 in legal fees, which renders them appropriate only for multimillion-dollar investments.[192]

Combinations

It can be awkward to get a venture started with one set of investors and later want to change to other investors. The first group may have bought in on a set of priorities for the venture that a later investor group does not like. The first group will probably also believe that the later group should pay a higher share price because now, after all, the venture is farther along and the risk consequently lower. Getting more funding from the first group instead of shifting to a second should be more efficient because all the parties have had time working together to increase their capabilities for collaborating.

Where venture capitalists fit

High rates of return on large investments are the aim of venture capital firms. One angel, Jack Carsten, who had previously worked as a venture capitalist (VC), commented that professional venture capitalists gained higher rates of return than angels did.

> *From what I can tell, the data suggest that the track record of returns on angel investing is not as good as for professional venture capital funds. This isn't surprising, since anyone with a checkbook can be an angel, but it takes a good track record as a VC to raise a big fund … But I don't need a 40 percent return. I'm happy with a healthy return and the chance to enjoy the personal satisfaction that comes from being involved in these start-ups.[193]*

The strategy of venture capitalists is to cash in by having the ventures they invest in either be bought by another firm or go public within typically five years or less. This can conflict with goals of an entrepreneur who might rather keep it closely held longer.

A typical VC, according to Nesheim, invests in only six out of a thousand business plans received per year. About 10 percent of the investees prosper greatly and manage to make up for the non-performers to win an average profit about 8 percent above the average of Standard and Poor's.[194] To aim that high, VCs typically seek a patent-protectable new product that can win high demand in a fast-developing new market.

Average returns on 131 venture capital funds, according to a study by Bygrave et al., ranged from 32 percent in 1980 to less than 10 percent in 1985. This varied greatly, however, according to the age and founding date of the fund, some reaching between 40 percent and 50 percent in peak years and others going negative.[195]

VCs quickly screen most proposals out, seeking the tiny fraction capable of yielding enough to (1) pay for the time to find, screen, and work out terms with them, (2) cover losses on those that don't work out, and (3) provide return on capital. While about 10 percent of ventures selected achieve their hopes, another 10 percent are complete losers and those in between are simply disappointing. For example, Sevin Rosen Funds, a venture capital firm with $1.7 billion in successful public offerings of investees, including such companies as Lotus and Compaq, found that 10 out of the 45 start-ups it backed failed.[196]

To back up their investments, VCs typically require one or two seats on the board of directors. Less formally, they provide connections, counseling, coaching, and sometimes replacements for the entrepreneurs in whom they invest. Some ask for interest on the money they put in by extending it as interest-bearing debt or preferred convertible into common stock at their option. Others charge consulting fees and become more actively involved in management

Where venture capitalists fit

---

192 Ellyn E. Spragins, "The New Quiet Money," *Inc.*, June 1989, p. 125.

193 Darwall and Roberts, *Band of Angels*, p. 9.

194 John L. Nesheim, *High Tech Startup* (Saratoga, CA: Electronic Trend Publications, 1992) p. 2.

195 William Bygrave and others, "Rates of Return of Venture Capital Investing," in *Frontiers of Entrepreneurship Research, 1988*, eds. Bruce A. Kirchhoff and others (Wellesley, MA.: Babson Center for Entrepreneurial Studies, 1988) p. 275.

196 "Risky Business," *Inc.* March 1990, p. 31.

of the venture. Still others impose no fees or interest, preferring to minimize expenses of the venture so it can reach profitability quicker.

Most VC firms are less likely to put in early seed money than angels are. A tabulation by VentureOne showing the VC pattern appears in Exhibit 5c-1.

In 1997 Zider reported that out of a total of $10 billion invested by venture capitalists that year, somewhat less than 10 percent went for R&D, and only 6 percent, or $600 million went to start-ups, while 80 percent went for scale-up of later stages such as expenses of expanding manufacturing and marketing and investments such as fixed assets and working capital.[197]

How they work

VCs tend to be less personal than angels, with office staffs and attorneys to back them up. They generally have deeper pockets, more money available for additional rounds or emergencies, than do angels. If they have been in business long they will have experience and a track record. Most specialize in narrow sectors of hot industries, which is to say where they think they will most likely be able to find within a few years a public market or established company interested in buying the venture's shares.

VCs usually expect to see a well-thought-out venture plan, written personally by the founders. If in reading it they get past the executive summary, seriously into the rest, and still have interest in the venture, they will typically send the plan for selective review to one or more consultants who are experts in the venture's proposed line of work. Then they deliberate at a pace of their own choosing. They tend to make decisions committee-style, and hence may be slower than angels to act. Jerry Kaplan, founder of the first pen-operated laptop, commented from his experience in raising money from them.

Venture capitalists are masters of procrastination. Their standard practice is to keep all options open until the last possible moment, often abandoning some hapless entrepreneur at the altar after months of reassurances that there is just one final question to answer before they will invest. The VCs know that time is on their side: the less money a venture has, the more desperate it will be to make a deal. They stand on the sidelines with their hands in their pockets like bystanders afraid to get involved, while small companies slowly bleed away their precious remaining cash. This is why frustrated entrepreneurs sometimes refer to VCs as "vulture capitalists."[198]

Unlike angels, who mostly work solo, VCs often work deals in syndication with other venture capital firms. They are sometimes said to operate like penguins, each hesitating to move until another does, then cascading in one after the other as a deal comes together.

To some extent there is a natural progression from personal capital to borrowing, then angel investors followed by venture capital firms and finally public stock offerings. But the sequence does not have to be in that order. Sometimes VC firms not only put up seed capital for start-up, they even initiate ventures by recruiting a lead entrepreneur and founding team.[199] Other times VCs may have been left out entirely by entrepreneurs who skipped past them from start-up to public offering.

Exhibit 5c-1 Venture capital firm investments, 1996 ($ millions)

Stage	Number of deals	Total amount	Amount per deal
Start-up	109	247	2.3
Development	589	2,947	5
Shipping	859	5,380	6.3
Profitable	142	1,506	10.7
Restart	10	44	4.4
Total	**1,709**	**10,124**	

[197] Bob Zider, "How Venture Capital Works," *Harvard Business Review*, November-December 1998, p. 132.
[198] Jerry Kaplan, *Startup* (Boston: Houghton Mifflin, 1995) p. 59.
[199] Barry Werth, *Billion Dollar Molecule*, (New York: Simon and Schuster, 1994).

Selection criteria

To appeal to VCs a venture must, of course, appear highly promising. Ideally, it should be

- Able to employ enough money to make investigation and investment effort worthwhile. Deals under $500,000 probably aren't worth VCs' consideration, although there can be exceptions. Elango et al. found that investment limits ranged according to the size of the VC funds.[200] At the small end were some whose limits ranged from a minimum of $300,000 to a maximum of $1.4 million, while in the larger funds the limits ranged from $1.1 million up to $10 million per investment.

- Able to earn a high annual rate of return on that capital. In the sample of Elango et al, hurdle rates ranged 33.5 percent to 42.2 percent, with a slight indication that the earlier the stage of investment, the higher the rate imposed.[201]

- Appear likely to be salable, either to another company, or to the public within five years so investors can cash in.

- Compatible with the kinds of investment interest, expertise, and personalities of the venture capitalists.

Criteria may be both broad and narrow, such as those described by John Barry of Prospect Street Ventures[202] as follows:

Management team Proven capability to rebound from major setbacks, turn seemingly unsolvable problems into opportunities, and deal with rapid change in a fast-growth environment.

Market size Large enough so that top entrants can achieve several hundred million dollars in revenues, growing at 20 percent to 30 percent per year.

Market share Dominant position based upon being a first mover with protectable intellectual property such as patents, trademarks, copyrights, and trade secrets.

Margins high, capital intensity low.

Likely to become a candidate for exiting through public offering and also alternatively through selling out, while at the same time being capable of operating on earnings without need for doing either.

Guidelines another venture capitalist, Robert J. Kunze,[203] used for developing a venture capital portfolio that ranked number one by Venture Economics, a company that tracks venture capital firms, generally included investing only if careful investigation indicated that the venture:

- Could break even in three to five years or,
- Could demonstrate the importance of its technology for less than $3 million,
- Would be differentiated from its competition by something unique,
- Would need less than $20 million in total,
- Could reach revenues of $100 million within five to ten years, equity capital to break even, and
- Had original employee founders who were high achievers, experts in their fields and had proven functional skills such as engineering, marketing, or research.

Institutional investors, such as pension funds, that might invest in ventures tend to judge their credit ranking somewhat differently by such things as:

- Industry rankings of market share, growth rate, and profitability compared to competitors.
- Formulas such as those of Standard and Poor's or Moody's.
- Expected profit multiples of interest coverage.
- Debt-to-equity ratios and evidence of repayment capacity.
- Credibility evidence, such as use of distinguished accounting and law firms.

---

[200] B. Elango, V. Fried, R. Hisrich, and A. Polonchek, "How Venture Capital Firms Differ," *Journal of Business Venturing*, 1995, 10 (2): pp. 157-179. [the lateral and vertical formatting is off on this one]
[201] Elango and others, "Venture Capital Firms Differ," p. 165.
[202] John F. Barry, "Prospecting for Ventures," *American Venture*, April-June 1999, p 37.
[203] Robert J. Kunze, *Nothing Ventured* (New York: Harper, 1990) p. 26.

Finding the right VC firm

An important aspect when there are successive funding rounds is that risk tends to decline with each round and with it the entrepreneur's cost for money, whether as interest or share of equity. Hence, there is incentive for the entrepreneur to hold off seeking outside equity cash. But not for too long. Time is needed for finding and meeting the investor and negotiating for needed cash, while at the same time getting the venture itself going. Getting cash too early can make cash infusion cost too much, but so can seeking it too late under time pressure.

Beyond the general criteria shared by many venture capitalists are more specialized criteria that individual VC firms choose based upon particular interests and expertise. For instance, in 1998 Joe Levi chose to specialize in Internet investments because he and the other principals in his firm, AlleyTech Ventures, had long personal experience in computers. Among Internet ventures, his criteria were that they:

- Were beyond the seed stage.
- Had an experienced management team, including "a CEO who can listen and take advice."
- Offered a product or service based on proprietary technology, as opposed to just content.
- Derived revenues by directly selling a product or service, rather than from advertising.[204]

Rejection reasons found to be most common from a survey of nearly 250 venture capital companies, in rank order, were

1. Lack of an experienced and complete management team.
2. Mismatch with industrial or geographical preferred investment criteria.
3. Market too small.
4. Inadequacy of strategy-execution steps.

Other reasons mentioned included inadequate company growth potential, lack of industry entry barriers, inadequately high margin prospects, and overestimation of venture worth by the entrepreneur.[205]

It has become a venture capital cliché that "It is better to invest in a grade A team with a grade B proposal than a grade B team with a grade A proposal." Experience has taught that problems with any idea are bound to arise, and a grade A team is more likely to recognize them early and find effective ways to succeed in spite of them. Also important in the view of many venture capitalists is the extent to which founders of the venture have committed their personal assets to it, which is taken as indication that the entrepreneur strongly believes in the venture and also will be highly motivated to make it succeed.

Finding the right VC firm

Locating VC firms is generally easier than finding informal investors, and the Web is a good source. Locally they are generally known among banks and local stock brokerage firms. SBIC-type venture capital firms in particular can be identified by clicking on a map that appears on the SBA's home page (sba.gov). Pratt's *Guide to Venture Capital Sources*, lists venture capital firms with addresses, phone numbers, and investment preferences.

Criteria for seeking an appropriate VC funding source should include convenient location and match of interests with what the venture will deliver. Questions to consider in checking out potential firms include how well they will understand the venture and its industry, what assistance besides money they typically provide, what their reputation is in the financial and venture communities, how fast they can move, and to what extent they have deep pockets (capability to add cash in later financing rounds).

For approaching such firms, introductions by recognized sources, such as others who have dealt with those firms, or are known to them, can help. References familiar with prior accomplishments of the entrepreneur(s) who seek cash can be especially helpful for the VC's screening process.

Notwithstanding occasions when a brief sketch on a single sheet of paper may have sufficed for a business plan, as happened with Intel, generally it is better to have a well-written plan to show a venture capitalist. A high-quality executive summary and, if possible, a prototype, pictures, or even a sketch of one can, in that order, help. The plan should also make clear how and when investors

---

[204] Joe Levi, "AlleyTech Ventures," *American Venture*, April-June 1999, p 25.
[205] Brian E. Hill, "Why Venture Capitalists Say 'No,'" *American Venture*, April-June, 1999, p. 9.

could cash out. Full rehearsal of oral presentations of varying lengths in front of sympathetic but savvy and candid listeners can be invaluable.

Deal terms

The deal, if they do one, will be formulated by the venture capitalists, not the entrepreneur, probably including such provisions as:

- Debt or preferred stock convertible into equity, probably with a requirement that it be redeemed by the venture before common shareholders receive a return.

- A conversion rate that depends upon performance; better performance by the venture to mean less equity for the investors.

- Interest or consulting fees.

- Purchase of "key person insurance" by the venture on certain founders.

- A nominee from the venture capital firm on the venture's board of directors.

- Controls on spending, or specification of financial ratio limits, violation of which permits investors to take charge and influence potential downside investment loss.

Deal terms

How much ownership and control investors will want is a natural concern of entrepreneurs seeking capital. But the VCs don't want either. What they care about is the return they get on capital, and how fast, not who owns how much of the venture.

4. Limited offerings

The government has, in response to investor discomfort and financial injury over the years, taken responsibility for combating money-raising swindles. Consequent laws and regulations, both federal and state, impose red tape on financing initiatives. In selling any securities, such as stock or debt promises, caution is required to make sure the Federal Securities Act of 1933 and any corresponding state laws are not violated. Such violation exposes the entrepreneur and venture to lawsuits by investors and prosecution by the government. Massive lawyer fees, fines, and jail terms sometimes result.

Hence, entrepreneurs who anticipate offerings of securities for their ventures need to be legally aware. Usually they also need to hire professional help, although it is legally possible to get by without a lawyer and some entrepreneurs have. The basic principle is that there should be full disclosure on financial aspects investors should care about. To accomplish that takes careful work.

Private offerings

Government policymakers want to see legitimate entrepreneurship, including pursuit of needed capital, flourish, and so have made efforts to reduce red tape by allowing some types of end runs on paperwork. Exemption from registration, or the filing of forms for government approval, is allowed for selling securities to financially sophisticated individuals such as angels and VCs. Recruiting directors or working partners who add cash and help run the venture can be done informally without much concern about government oversight because such people can be presumed to know what they are getting into.

Federal Regulation D

Registration on a simplified basis for selling venture securities to less sophisticated investors under certain conditions is allowed. Those conditions generally consist of restricting how much money can be sought and/or how many investors can be solicited. Such offerings of venture securities are generally covered by Regulation D (Reg D) of the Federal Securities Exchange Commission that covers private offerings and, within some limitations, offerings to other individuals and companies. Some official paperwork, such as filing a Form D (notice of sale of securities) can in some cases be tricky, but nowhere near as burdensome as full registration.

Moreover, under Reg D an enterprise can try to sell the securities first and then only file for the exemption from registration later if sales occur, provided it does so within 15 days after the first sale. Filing under Reg D requires use of either Form D, or alternatively Form U-7, which can be simpler but tricky with the Securities and Exchange Commission. Additional

Private offerings

Federal Regulation D

filings are required every six months after that until the offering is sold, and another 30 days after the final sale.

Investor types

Records on qualifications of each person approached for sale of the securities must be kept in a permanent file at the company. The government cares whether a person can be considered an accredited investor, a sophisticated investor, or neither. To be accredited, the person must have an income of $200,000 per year (or $300,000 with spouse), or a net worth of $1 million (with or without spouse), or be an officer, director, or general partner in the company. Some types of companies, such as banks, also qualify as accredited investors.

The definition of a sophisticated investor is less sharp, because it refers to someone who essentially has enough business savvy to evaluate risks of the venture deal realistically, either alone or with the help of a professional who does. Proving that a person was thus qualified if they later decide to sue with a claim that they were fooled on the offering can be problematic.

Alternative private offering types

Each offering memorandum or prospectus describing the venture and offering to investors should be numbered and discussions with each investor must be noted and dated. Local securities laws, sometimes called blue sky laws, vary from state to state and must also be observed. Further provisions of Reg D to escape registration impose the following conditions:

Rule 504 (small offerings) permits the venture to sell up to $1 million in securities without registration, subject to the above requirements. The offering can be advertised, within restrictions such as putting out no mass mailings or press releases, and it can be sold to any number of investors, regardless of their qualifications or level of wealth.

Rule 505 (medium offerings) permits selling by issuers not including investment companies up to $5 million, minus whatever was invested in the company earlier, of securities to any number of accredited investors and up to 35 others in a 12-month period. If there are unaccredited investors, a disclosure statement must be prepared containing the information that would be provided in a full registration statement. Accredited investors include (1) institutions like banks, insurance companies, and pension funds with assets over $5 million; (2) individual investors who put in over $150,000, have over $1 million in assets, or earned over $200,000 in each of the past two years; and (3) directors, officers, and general partners of the venture. Public advertising of the offering is not allowed. Audited statements are required.

Rule 506 (big offerings) permits the sale of any amount to any number of accredited investors and up to 35 others. As with Rule 505, no public advertisement of the offering is allowed, but 506 lifts the 12-month time limitation and the restriction on sales by investment companies. Non-accredited investors must be sophisticated enough to understand the risks and merits of the investment. If there are unaccredited investors, a disclosure statement must be prepared containing the information that would be provided in a full registration statement. Audited statements are required. If, on the other hand, all the investors qualify as accredited, then the disclosure documents can be looser. In what ways they can is something to work out in each individual situation with suitably experienced advisers.

SCOR refers to a still more simplified form of registration under Reg D, the **Small Company Offering Registration** (SCOR). In some states the name is Uniform Limited Offering Registration (ULOR). Under this form a company can raise up to $1 million per year provided it has a stock price of $5 or more per share. The stock can be freely traded, and there are no SEC reporting requirements. The relatively simple form U-7 is used to file for permission. Clearance time, in the State of Washington at least, takes four to six weeks. However, every advertisement for the offering must also be cleared by the state. Rules can vary from one state to another.

Limited public offerings

For selling stock or other securities of a venture to wider constituencies there are additional alternatives. Some require federal registration and others don't.

Intra-state offerings

A venture can qualify for exemption from federal registration to sell its own securities through an **intrastate public offering** under a state's blue sky laws. To qualify, the venture must be incorporated and headquartered in the state, obtain 80 percent or more of its sales within the state, and have the securities it sells stay within the state for at least two years. This type of offering cannot be combined with others that are out of state within that time to broaden the range. Rules for this path vary among states. Some states have passed laws to allow qualification in coordination with Reg D, but most have unique rules about it.

Merger

Another end run around federal registration can be to merge a venture with the "corporate shell" (i.e. a legal corporation that may or may not possess any assets) of a company that has already gone public even though it may be no longer in operation or traded. If shares of the shell have warrants attached for shareholders to buy more shares, these can be used to raise more capital after the merger.[206] If the shell already contains capital, that too helps. Moreover, the shell may do another public offering in addition to the one that made it public earlier. But permission will again be required, and if it is public, the shell will already have reporting requirements to comply with. This approach is legally complicated and not much used by new ventures.

Limited federal registration

To get other dimensions of freedom for selling its securities a venture can register at federal level under two alternative paths, one where the registration process is simpler but more restricted and a second where permission costs more to get but the freedom in selling is greater. The first is limited registration under Regulation A or "Reg A."

Federal Regulation A

Regulation A of the federal securities law permits freely tradable offerings up to $5 million. Reg A offering requires registration with a regional office of the Federal Securities and Exchange Commission (SEC). State permission is also required, but usually follows easily once federal approval is obtained.

Unless the Reg A offering is to be less than $100,000, there must be an offering circular, or prospectus, which is reviewed and approved by the SEC prior to stock sales. Approval typically involves several rounds of submitting drafts of the prospectus, having the SEC reject them because of errors it finds, then fixing and resubmitting them until the draft finally passes inspection.

After that, the company can sell up to $5 million worth of securities within 12 months. Financial statements must be filed for up to the preceding two years, but they need not be audited. Once approved, the offering can be sold to any number of buyers regardless of their qualifications.

A lawyer can be hired to carry out this drafting, submitting, redrafting, and resubmitting, or the entrepreneur can do it personally. Either way, several months may be required. A more experienced lawyer will probably accomplish it faster and cheaper, albeit at a higher cost per hour of the lawyer's time. The entrepreneur can do it personally, rather than hiring a lawyer, by visiting the SEC regional office, looking at the filings of some companies that have done it before and imitating the way they did the paperwork. Lacking experience, the entrepreneur will have to spend a lot more hours to obtain clearance. But some do it successfully.

The main trade-off is between the time a lawyer would take, much less but at a high cost, versus the time the entrepreneur would take to complete the process. But trying to work without a lawyer can be tricky. For instance, it is permissible to discuss, but not perform, sale of a Reg A offering with prospective buyers before seeking approval.

Also important to weigh is the effect that performing a Reg A or other limited offering, even if it is successful, may have on the venture's chances of raising more money later. Shareholders it obtains through its first offering will thereby become a constituency to be reckoned with later. Will that constituency by then be happy or antagonistic? How will they be polled? What say will they want to have in terms of a later offering? Will those to whom the later offering is to be sold have to pay a

---

[206] Ellyn E. Spragins, "Back-Door IPOs," *Inc.*, September 1989, p. 121.

higher price for shares in order to keep the first shareholders happy, and if so, will that make the later offering harder to sell?

Federal SB-2 registration

A less limited form of registration than a Reg A uses the form SB-2 and can be applied to firms that are going public with less than $25 million in revenues. The main difference from full registration, the S-1 offering which will be further discussed shortly, is that the paperwork is considerably less complicated.

For all these types of public offerings, limitations exist with regard to resale of the securities. They vary both with the types of offerings and with individual situations. There are also reporting requirements, and spreading the venture's ownership among many people can make it impossible to raise money from angels or venture capitalists.

5. Full registration

A second form of federal registration, in addition to Reg D, is known as full registration and is often referred to as an S-1 offering because to get permission for it, the company must complete and file an S-1 federal registration form. Doing so is a complex and costly process, requiring paperwork several inches thick, formal offering circulars, audited financial statements, a considerable amount of expensive help from lawyers and accountants specializing in securities regulation, plus months of time. And after the offering, the requirements for disclosure and dealing with large numbers of shareholders continue.

Consequently, it is used less by start-ups and more by companies that have justifiable needs for large amounts of money and records of major accomplishment, such as rising profits over time, sufficient to gain major public interest. Data from a study by Roberts, for instance, indicated that well over 90 percent of high-technology companies that went public did so after they had broken even.[207] Aside from the aberrant example of the dot-com bubble, companies generally go public only after three or more years of solid and growing profitability attested to by fully audited financial statements.

But the appeal in the idea of going public is strong, as noted here by *Inc.*[208]

> Of all the temptations that contributed to the new economy's opulent mirage, few were as enticing as the initial public offering. How things have changed. In the second quarter of 1999, 139 companies filed an S-1 with the Securities and Exchange Commission; for the same quarter of 2001, that number fell to 26. Going public has gone from a cakewalk to a slow crawl over hot coals. HPL Technologies Inc. CEO David Lepejian spent 18-hour days hyping his company's IPO to newly skittish moneyed types who were reluctant to add to their growing portfolios-cum-compost of incorporated carrion. HPL, a software developer for the semiconductor industry, made it through the gantlet of wary investors, however, and by the closing of its July 31 market debut the company's share price was up 21 percent, to $13.35.

> — • —

> Wal-Mart first went public in 1970 at $16.50 per share. By the year 2000 after 11 splits one share had become 2,048 shares worth $116,736.[209]

The upshot of such events is that many companies see full-blown public offerings as a way for existing shareholders and option-holders to cash in that is worth the great expense and effort to pull it off.

Process

For a given company, there are questions of why it should consider going public, whether it is ready to, and whether the market will want to buy its stock. Is the offering only for existing shareholders to cash in, or is it to meet needs of the company for more cash? Will it be selling enough securities to justify the costs of paperwork and the selling needed to persuade shareholders to buy? Is the company in a growing industry with enough romance to attract buyers? What has the company shown it can pro-

---

[207] Edward B. Roberts, *Entrepreneurs in High Technology* (New York: Oxford University Press, 1991).
[208] *Inc.*, October 1, 2001.
[209] Robert D. Hisrich and Michael P. Peters, *Entrepreneurship* (New York: McGraw-Hill, 2002) p. 560.

duce in sales and profit growth, both absolute and relative to competitors? Major national underwriters typically require that a company going public have an offering justifiably worth at least $15 million.

Beginnings

Groundwork for full registration must begin well ahead of the event with management learning what is involved, developing appropriate acquaintances among attorneys, accountants, and underwriting firms, and beginning to prepare needed back-up materials such as financial statements audited by a well-respected and known CPA firm.

An S-1 offering must be a major team effort undertaken cooperatively between the venture going public and an underwriter such as a major stock brokerage firm. Personal contacts will be key to finding and engaging experienced, accomplished, well-reputed, and well-connected professionals for the process. Choice of the brokerage or investment-banking firm, which will have its own lawyers to work in cooperation with those of the venture, should be based on such things as:

- Which investment firms will consider the size of the deal and the performance and romance of the venture sufficiently attractive to sell.
- Industry specializations of the investment firms.
- Reputation and track record of each firm on other IPOs, including aftermarket follow-through and support.
- Research strength of each firm relative to others.
- How good a syndicate of other brokerages the firm can muster for the deal.
- Sales strength of the brokerage firm.
- What priority with which of its people the firm will apply to the effort.
- Personal chemistry between people in the venture and people in the firm.

An implication of these factors, particularly the last one, is that groundwork and getting acquainted with prospective underwriting firms should begin several months before the underwriter selection process comes to a head. More-

over before that the company must have had its performance and statements in order for two or three years.

Paperwork

Once the underwriter and professionals are engaged, there will be a week of meetings to get started on authorizing shares to be issued, scheduling tasks, (such as preparation of a prospectus and registration statement), and starting the preparation of these items and other paperwork, which can easily require one or two months to complete.

Documents such as powers of attorney, amendments to articles of incorporation, directors' resolutions, an underwriting agreement, selling-stockholder agreements, a blue sky memorandum, and correspondence with relevant stock exchanges must be prepared and reviewed.

Drafts of the registration statement and the prospectus, which will be printed first in the form of a red herring (a prospectus on which the stock price has not yet been set and which has some sections printed in red-ink) must be cycled through various readers to make sure they are correct. Again, the job will call for teamwork between the venture, the underwriter and their various specialists.

SEC filing

After two to three months of preparing the paperwork, the applicant should file it with the Securities Exchange Commission and the appropriate state agency. Around the same time, the red herring should go out to other securities firms in the underwriting syndicate and a "tombstone advertisement" should be published in one or more papers to inform the public of the forthcoming offering.

Another month or so later, criticism letters will come from the governmental agencies. Then the registration document and prospectus will have to be revised again. This process, including further negotiation of these with the agencies, should be completed in another week or two.

Road show

During these couple of weeks, the company executives will participate in a road show, where they make presentations about the company and its offerings around the country at brokerage firms who will be participating in the syndicate that sells the offering to the public.

Except for the road show and red herring distribution, the company is restricted from talking about the offering publicly. This is called a quiet period.

Action

Finally, the offering price will be set by the lead underwriting firm based largely on responses from the road show. The underwriting firm may choose to offer the stock as a firm underwriting, which means it guarantees to buy the stock for resale, or a best-efforts basis, which means it will try to sell the stock but not guarantee that it will sell. It can also decide how long it will "make a market" in the stock, which is to say actively buy and sell it between shareholders.

Following the offering there are a host of rules to be followed in auditing, reporting to the government, divulging information to shareholders, and responding to them. Some managements regret having gone public because of these impositions.

> Warren Avis recalled how unpleasant it was "playing nursemaid to thousands of stockholders," going to analysts' meetings and boards of directors' meetings. "Furthermore," he said, "government regulations and requirements proliferated at an alarming rate when we got into the public arena."[210]

In summary, both pros and cons to going public are as follows:

Pros—The offering

- Provides capital with no interest or repayment required.

- Strengthens financial base (DE ratio) for stability and borrowing.
- Legitimizes, enhances image.
- Gives a market-driven valuation.
- Sets up a path to liquidity for shareholders and stock option holders.
- Makes the wealth level of shareholders greater and more apparent.

Cons—The offering also

- Exposes confidential information.
- Reduces entrepreneur's control.
- Dilutes ownership.
- Increases red tape requirements.
- Imposes heavy expenses for the process without guarantee it will succeed.
- Increases pressure for short-term performance.
- Increases legal exposure and expenses.
- Introduces the pain of informing and responding to many shareholders.
- Virtually eliminates possibility for any further private offerings.

Direct public offerings

An alternative for going public with either a limited or full registration is to do a direct public offering (DPO). This has been done since 1976 with both Reg A and Intrastate offerings where entrepreneurs sold the issues themselves rather than working through underwriting firms. More recently, some companies have undertaken to sell their offerings over the Internet. The first was by Spring Street Brewery in 1996, which went on to use that experience for setting up its own online combination of investment bank and brokerage firm. In 2004 Google did a full-registration offering of its own stock on-line.

---

[210] Avis, *Take a Chance to be First*, p. 187.

Exercises

Text discussion questions

1. How should an entrepreneur choose among the different types of outside investors?
2. Explain the differences in investment criteria of angel investors versus venture capitalists.
3. Explain how venture capital firms specialize and why.
4. Discuss the reasons why public offerings are so complicated.
5. Explain the conditions under which public offerings are most versus least advisable for a venture.
6. Explain from an investor's point of view the reasons for investing money as an angel versus putting it into a venture capital partnership versus buying public shares in a venture.

Case questions

5C-1 Arthur Lipper

1. After responding to the first question, list in rank order the additional information you would ask of the entrepreneur for each of the above ventures in order to be more certain about the financing terms that the investor should offer.
2. What specific terms would you suggest for each of the two investment deals Arthur is considering and why? Which should he take?
3. What is your assessment of the philosophical statements about investing that Arthur has made?
4. What should be Arthur Lipper's personal pattern of actions to find more and better venture opportunities like those described in the case?

5C-2 Bill Foster

1. How would you rank what you see as Bill Foster's main financing alternatives?
2. What is your assessment of his actions thus far in seeking capital?
3. What would most concern you about the ownership split he has in mind?
4. What series of action steps should Bill take next?

5C-3 Byron Spain

1. What is the best advice you can offer Byron Spain about how to accomplish a public stock offering based on the information you have?
2. What other information from the company do you think would most help you improve on that advice?
3. What other information from sources outside of the company do you think would most help you improve on that advice?
4. What actions to raise money should Byron take next ?

Portfolio page possibilities

Page 5C-1 Private investor search

1. Describe the sort of private investor beyond friends and relatives you would seek for a venture like this and why that sort of person, if interested, would be preferable to others for this particular venture.
2. Describe some approaches you might apply for seeking such a person, rank order those approaches, and explain the rationale behind that ranking.
3. Explain why the venture should be of interest to such a person and how that kind of appeal could be enhanced for him or her.

Page 5C-2 Venture capital appeal

1. Describe briefly a strategy by which your venture could conceivably appeal for growth financing from a venture capital firm.
2. Outline as fully as space permits on the page the presentation you would make to present that strategy to a venture capital firm partners' meeting.

Page 5C-3 Public offering plan

1. Sketch out a sequence you would follow to check out the practicability of one day making a public offering.
2. List the contacts you think you might use, including specific professionals by name and what their services might cost.

Page 5C-4 Public investor pitch

Write what you think might be an effective pitch for selling stock or other security interest in your venture personally to public investors at some point in the future that you specify. Insofar as page limits permit, also describe as part of the rationale for this pitch what pattern of achievement the venture should seek over time to justify such a securities offering.

Page 5C-5 Road show presentation

Sketch out the highlights of what you might expect to use in a road-show presentation to brokerage firms if your venture were some day to go public.

Term Projects

Venture history

1. How did the entrepreneur(s)' opinions about including outside investors change with experience as the venture proceeded?
2. If outside investors were used, how were terms worked out?
3. What other potential outside investors did the venture's founders think they could have tapped, and why didn't they?
4. What negotiating processes were involved in getting outside capital if the venture got any? Or, if it managed to get by without any, how was that accomplished?

Venture planning guide

1. Meet at least one wealthy private investor whom you have never met before and ask for reactions to your venture as an investment possibility.
2. Repeat, or precede, the above with either a venture capitalist or an investment banker.

Part 6

SETTING UP

Many elements are involved in setting up to do business, and this section concentrates on three of them: (1) protecting intellectual property, such as the name of the business and one or more ideas that make the venture novel, (2) arranging facilities in which to work, and (3) establishing the venture's location, at least initially.

Somewhere along the line in developing the venture, intellectual property will be created. It may be an invention that crops up before the venture is even considered, and it may be the discovery of some person other than any founder. It may be not an invention but only the name of the business or a Web site name. But if the venture occurs and succeeds, that intellectual property will have value that the founder can devise ways to protect. Hence, part of setting up a venture effectively is to design a protection scheme as soon as it appears there will be need for it, and to implement that scheme as soon as it fits in the setup process. Protecting ideas is the topic of Chapter 6A.

The three most concrete protection avenues are through trademarking to protect the name and logo of the company, copyrighting to protect written works of the company and possibly artistic creations it may have, and patenting to protect product designs, software, and formulas it may have created. Registration of a domain name is a recent addition to the types of intellectual property protection and one which every venture arguably should seek.

Somewhat less concrete but nevertheless powerful protection mechanisms are the maintenance of trade secrets and the strategy of out-competing or inventing good new ideas faster than the competition does. Possibly best of all is to combine all these types of protection, some of which can even overlap, to form a circle of defense around the venture's intellectual property advantages.

Chapter 6B on set-up, preparing the venture to commence business, focuses on arranging facilities for whatever its operations will be. Choices here will depend importantly on not only what kind of output the venture must generate but also upon which tasks behind that output will be performed by the venture and which will be farmed out or outsourced to other companies. Each approach has its advantages and disadvantages, but especially for new ventures the advantages of gaining the expertise of ongoing outside suppliers plus the flexibility of being able to scale up or down how much is bought from them and avoiding the need to invest in plant and equipment tend to weight the scale toward outsourcing. Sometimes, however, these benefits are outweighed by needs for closer personal control of processes and for secrecy that insourcing can give.

Every venture needs a location. For some ventures it is a dominantly important choice, while for others it does not much matter. Many entrepreneurs are able to start out with the legendary dining room table or garage location. Some start and remain in remote sites while others have to locate near heavy foot traffic or with ample parking nearby. Still others are confined in location by zoning requirements related to the production processes they use. Cost versus convenience is an important choice in locating for some entrepreneurs, as is whether to buy or lease a site.

CHAPTER 6A – Protecting Ideas

Topics

1. Motivation
2. Identity protection
3. Aesthetic protection
4. Functionality protection
5. Other idea protection methods

Checkpoints

a. What is intellectual property?
b. Explain the pros and cons of attempting to protect different kinds of intellectual property.
c. How is software protected?
d. What are the pros and cons of registering a copyright?
e. What are the main different kinds of patents?
f. How is the purpose and operation of a trademark different from that of a copyright?
g. How long are patents, trademarks, and copyrights good for?
h. Under what circumstances might it be possible to copyright, trademark, and patent the same object?
i. How else, besides patenting, trademarking, and copyrighting, can ideas be protected?

Ideas in general are easy to come by and of little value, but excellent ideas are rare and can be extremely profitable. Most of Microsoft's profits, which in the 1990s made William Gates the richest man in the world, came from the DOS (disk operating system) software package to which Microsoft bought exclusive rights cheaply from Tim Paterson, another entrepreneur who wrote it. Without protection through copyright, patents, or secrecy, anyone could have taken the system for nothing. Thus, protection for an idea can be very important.

1. Motivation

Because the federal government wants to encourage people to develop new ideas, it has provided legal ways for those who do so to enjoy monopolies on them. Copyrights, patents, and trademarks are those legal mechanisms, and each applies to certain categories of ideas. These legal monopolies can be tremendously powerful for creating and sustaining a business in some cases, although in others they are worthless. Hence, an entrepreneur should have some understanding of them. It is also useful to know that they are not the only ways of protecting ideas or gaining monopoly power.

The importance of proprietary rights in entrepreneurship, as well as business in general, would be hard to overstress. The men who developed the first spreadsheet did not end up owning exclusive rights to it and did not become wealthy. The company that exploited it and did protect the rights, Lotus, made its founder very wealthy. The man who created the Web did not obtain or exploit commercial rights to it and did not become wealthy, although eventually he was given recognition through a prize. People who did obtain proprietary rights in countless ventures that exploit the Web have become billionaires. Linus Torvalds deliberately avoided protection for his operating system Linux, and has never been noted for his wealth, though undoubtedly he could command high pay. In contrast is Microsoft, which jealously protected its Windows operating system and made all its founders and thousands of employees multimillionaires.

Ring of protections

The kinds of protections provided by law that can be chosen for protecting ideas include patents, trademarks, and copyrights. Beyond those are secrecy and competitive performance. It can be possible to combine such protections so that together they become more powerful than any of them alone by forming a kind of ring of protections around whatever it is that the company wants to protect. How much to invest in creating this defensive perimeter, because most of these protections cost time, money, or both to adopt and exercise, is a strategic decision for any entrepreneur or venture. Investing too little, investing too much, or applying the investment inappropriately can all lead to poor or even fatal venture performance. So careful design and creating a ring of protections is worth the effort in learning, thought, and action. Trying to think of candidate items to include in that ring for a particular venture, such as possible features to patent, trademark, copyright or keep secret, may make reading this chapter, with its numerous lists, easier and more worthwhile.

Avoiding conflict

In starting a company with intellectual property, the entrepreneur should consider safety tactics as soon as it appears there may be something to protect. Keeping a notebook and having it witnessed in the idea discovery stage was mentioned earlier. Another early line of defense concerns protection from others who might

charge the venture with theft. In leaving a former employer, nobody in the start-up should have brought along any of the employer's property, such as drawings or customer lists. The employer should have debriefed them on what the company considered its intellectual property, such as secrets, and none of those should be divulged or used in the start-up. This concerns gray areas, legally, so there is always potential for dispute. Netscape, even though it had tried to start cleanly, nevertheless got drawn into a dispute that came close to killing it at inception.

Jim Clark and Marc Andreessen decided to have the product of their start-up be a better Web browser than Mosaic, the one Marc and his fellow students had developed at the University of Illinois. Jim began by hiring away the whole team, all of whom were graduating students except for one full-timer, and naming the company Mosaic Netscape and its first product Netscape. The University of Illinois was meanwhile starting to license Mosaic commercially. Thousands of sites had downloaded and were using it free.

Jim insisted that his programmers write completely fresh code for the new browser, without a single line taken from the original Mosaic. He wanted to be legally safe, and he worried about rumors that the University of Illinois might take legal action against the start-up. He recalled, "I had to head this off before any of the private mutterings became public complaints, or even legal threats. Any belief on a potential customer's part that we were selling purloined goods and might face a protracted court fight would stop any deal dead in its tracks."[211]

The University did decide there was possible infringement of its rights, and meetings between lawyers began. Demands were made and rejected for agreement to pay royalties and drop the company name. One of the University lawyers said, "You are intrinsically in violation of our intellectual property because of the information in the heads of those who worked for and thereafter left the University." Netscape prepared to sue first so that the trial would take place before a California, rather than Illinois, jury.

As time and negotiation, with offers and counter offers, dragged on with Netscape consuming cash, Netscape informed the university of its intention to sue, terrified that it might have to follow through, which could easily sink Netscape. But the University decided not to fight and a settlement

---

[211] Jim Clark, *Netscape Time* (New York: St. Martin's Press, 1999) p. 161.

was reached, in which Jim's company removed the word Mosaic from its name, an action resented by some of the employees. The University granted rights to Microsoft, which subsequently went into fierce competition with Netscape and was hit with antitrust litigation by the U.S. Justice department. Netscape eventually sold out to America On Line.

Because litigation is so expensive relative to the financial and management resources of a start-up, efforts to anticipate and avoid it if possible make sense. One thing to avoid is the charge, as above, that the venture has misappropriated others' intellectual property. The other is to have intellectual property of the venture, including its name or its inventions, misappropriated by others. A way to make this other less likely is to take strong precautionary actions, such as trademarking, copyrighting, and patenting early.

2. Identity protection

The importance of company (as opposed to the entrepreneur's) identity ranges from fairly low for such companies as small subcontractors, wholesalers, independent investment counselors, casket producers, customs brokers, or prosthetic makers, to very high for big consumer products companies in toothpaste, fast food, and soda pop. The world's most valuable brand is Coca-Cola. If the company producing Jones Soda has its way, Jones too will take on greatly heightened new value.

Choice of name

Each entrepreneur must make some choice about what name to do business under. One choice can be the person's own name, as in "Smith Roofing." Another can be to give the company a trade name, which is any name used for a business that does not include the personal names of all the owners.

Any business with a trade name is supposed to register it with the state where the business is headquartered. If it is not registered, the owner(s) will not be able to bring any lawsuit on behalf of the business if it is legally wronged by anyone. The state maintains a database of names that have been registered, which of course does not guarantee that the name is not being used by someone else who has simply not yet registered it. From that database anyone can learn who all the owners are of any registered business.

It is necessary that the trade name include exactly the owner's name, although it may also include more than that in some cases. If a corporation, such as Ginger Sweet's, Inc. wants to do business as simply Ginger's, it has to register that name separately. If a proprietor, John J. Smith, wants to do business as John J. Smith Enterprises, no separate registration is required, but to do business as J.J. Smith, it is. Some conversation with the state office responsible for registration may be needed to get it right.

Investigation of what names are already owned and registered may also be needed to get it right.

Choice of name

> When Gordon Moore and his former boss at Fairchild Semiconductor, Robert Noyce, set out to start a microchip company of their own the first name they chose was "NM Electronics." But this met with less than enthusiasm from associates. So they searched for other possible names. After about a dozen additional rejects Moore came up with "Integrated Electronics." Noyce suggested they shorten it to Intel. But shortly after the papers of incorporation were drawn up with that name on July 16, 1968 they learned that there was another company already using the name Intelco. Rather than change it or deal with a possible lawsuit they agreed to pay $15K for permission from Intelco to use the name Intel.[212]

With millions of companies in business and thousands per day being started, it can be a challenge to find an effective logo for a new venture. The choice of name is important because, like picking a location, it can stand in lieu of great expenditures in advertising if done well. Compared to a location choice, it will probably remain with the company longer. Should it indicate what the company does (e.g. Software Arts) or not (e.g. Eveready)? Should it be a word with some intrinsic meaning (e.g. Apple) or not (e.g. Kodak)?

---

[212] Tim Jackson, *Inside Intel* (NY: Penguin, 1997) p. 23.

There is room for disagreement. The November 1972 name change from Standard Oil to Exxon was based upon review of 10,000 computer-generated names which were narrowed to 234, then 16. Finally, eight were selected for linguistic studies to establish that they had no meaning. In addition, 15,000 telephone directories were checked for prior use and 10,000 people were interviewed. After Exxon was chosen, another $100 million was spent to change the names on stations, pumps, trucks, maps, billboards and 224 million shares of stock held by 780,000 people.[213]

Some companies may risk losing identity through name change. Exxon is big enough to impart meaning to any word. Univac was a familiar name, as was Honeywell. But did the money spent on creating the name Unisys to replace them both add to familiarity or image? Who can remember what familiar company names were abandoned to form it? To some extent there is a conflict between what makes a name legally protectable, namely a word that has absolutely no meaning, and one that is memorable and effective in identifying the business to customers. One possible approach is to include both unrelated and business-related terms in the name. Apple Computer, the two words, and Pennzoil, one word, are examples.

If a company becomes large it will ultimately make its name familiar. Ford and Hershey were not particularly evocative words by themselves. On the other hand, some names probably do help. Santa Monica, California in the mid-1950s saw the opening of a new soda fountain somewhat off the main thoroughfare, on 16th Street. The name, Sweet Sixteen, quickly became familiar and is still known to old time and former residents who long since have forgotten other stores' names, although the enterprise itself is no longer there.

However, the name will not make the company. For years, the name Astrodynamics was owned by an electrician on Hollywood Boulevard who did nothing with it except keep the registration current because he thought it had promise. It was not the name of his electrical contracting company. No great company grew out of it. But it could probably have been a good name for the right enterprise.

It is important to choose a name that is not already owned by another firm for the territory where the new venture will operate. Once chosen, the name should be registered with the state department of commerce where the company will be operating and possibly with the U.S. Patent Office to tie up national rights. If international rights may one day have value, then ways of registering in foreign countries as well should be sought.

There are consultants who specialize in company names and there are also references on the subject. There are also attorneys who specialize in determining the registerability of company names. But the best place to start is probably the U.S. Patent Office. For this the Web contact is uspto.gov/web/menu/tm, which provides helpful information about how to fill out the forms, after which application can be made electronically.

Entrepreneurs typically invent the names of the start-ups themselves. Some, like 3M or Safeway, have no apparent relationship between the name and the nature of the business. Others do, as illustrated by the top ten winners in a name contest conducted by *Business 97* magazine,[214] listed in Exhibit 6a-1 below.

Domain name

Most businesses that deal beyond a local area, and many that don't as well, benefit from having a Web site and consequently a Web domain name, or URL (Universal Registration Locator). Several sites offer registration services for such names. One is Network Solutions in Herndon, Virginia, which was the original source authorized by the U.S. Government to provide them. Application for a name can be made at the company's Web site, www.networksolutions.com, or other sources such as Godaddy.com. Beyond registering, it may, to gain advertising advantages, be important to have the name linked to browsers, such as Yahoo. This can be initiated by finding the "add your site" button on the browser and then responding as instructed.

---

[213] Frank H. Foster and Robert L. Shook, *Patents, Copyrights and Trademarks* (New York: Wiley, 1993) p. 183.
[214] Winners!!!!!!! *Business 97*, October-November 1997, p. 45.

Exhibit 6a-1 Name contest winners[214]

Rank	Name	Business	Location
1	Fannie Wrappers Lingerie	Lingerie & novelties	San Luis Obispo, CA
2	Bushwackers Tree Service	Tree pruning	Isle of Palms, SC
3	First Feast	Lactation consultation	Ellicott City, MD
4	The Barking Lot	Pet grooming	San Francisco, CA
5	Den of Antiquity	Antique store	Bluffton, SC
6	In Other Words	Language translations	Los Angeles, CA
7	Nature's Calling	Portable toilets	N. Charleston, SC
8	Jitters & Shakes	Coffee and juice bar	San Francisco, CA
9	Duzitall	Home renovation	Columbia, SC
10	H2-OH!	Retail swimwear	North Augusta, SC

Finding from a registration service that a particular domain name has not been claimed does not necessarily mean that the venture can obtain and use it. Beyond not being a registered domain of anyone else, it also must not have been trademarked by anyone else. This is a good reason, among others, to search for possibly conflicting trademarks and probably to apply for a trademark.

Trademark

Beyond state registration of a company name is the option of registering the name, and possibly a logo, at national or international levels, a process called trademarking (for products, or service marking for services). National registration involves applying for a trademark with the U.S. Patent Office, a process which requires a fee, takes a year or more, and involves a public notice period when anyone can challenge the applicant's right to the exclusive use of a name. Information about trademarks is available on the Patent Office Web site, uspto.gov, which can be used to learn the rules, to search for prior trademarks that have been filed and either abandoned or kept in force (Trademark Electronic Search System or TESS), and to make application on line through the Trademark Electronic Application System (TEAS), which are both available on the uspto.gov Web site. The current fee for filing is $335 per category under which the trademark appears.

The trademark of a product (or, in the case of services, a service mark) applies to either the words of a name, or a visual design or emblem. A key consideration is that to be registered the purpose served by the mark must be to distinguish the product or service of the applicant from those offered by others.

But the trademark must not otherwise be functional for the product. A color may be protectable for the right product. Owens-Corning managed to trademark pink to identify its product, because pink is not a particularly natural color for Fiberglas. But Pepto-Bismol could not register pink because the Patent and Trademark Office construed it to be a soothing color, and therefore functional for the product.[215] Even the sound of a product has been the basis for a trademark application. In 1995 the Patent and Trademark Office announced that Harley-Davidson had filed for a trademark on "the sound of applicant's motorcycles, produced by V-Twin common-crankpin motorcycle engines when the goods are in use."[216]

An ordinary word, like *water*, cannot be trademarked, but a non-word, like Kodak when it was first used, can. If a word becomes ordinary through use, as *Zipper* did, then it cannot have trademark protection. The decision rendered on *Zipper* (is it really an ordinary word?) illustrates how, as usual, a gray area surrounds what qualifies for protection. Some trademarks that have been declared generic include Nylon, Cellophane, Thermos, Aspirin, Linoleum, Shredded Wheat, Yo-Yo, and Monopoly. Generally, if someone else has already been using the name or mark, even without registering it, they can't be stopped from continued use and may even be able to prevent use by others. The government's objective is to let a company prevent others from confusing customers about whether they are buying what it produces or what someone else produces.

Trademark

215 Foster and Shook, *Patents*, p. 165.
216 David Edwards, "Letter to Willie G., No. 2," *Cycle World*, July 1995, p. 10.

Page 223

Goods bearing the trademark must be "sold or transported in commerce" interstate to qualify for federal protection of the mark or, under an important 1989 change in the law, the applicant must be able to show a good-faith intention to so use the goods. An intent-to-use application can be filed, and if application is approved and the product is shipped with the mark, the registration will date back to the filing date. Evidence of such shipment need not be submitted for up to 30 months following the intent application.[217] State governments also register trademarks without this interstate requirement. For trademarks issued after 1989, the life of a trademark is 10 years. It may be renewed each additional 10 years.

Before registration, the letters TM or SM (for *service mark*) may be used after the name, provided the mark has not been ruled invalid. After the trade- or service mark is registered with the Patent and Trademark Office, it may carry the mark ® or the words "Registered Trademark" to so indicate. It is important not to use this indication of registration until the mark has been certified; otherwise, registration may be denied. The name of a company, as opposed to the trademark of a product, or service mark of a service, may be registered at the state, but not the federal, level. (Some tactics for protecting trademark names appear in shaded area below)

Trademarks may be extended from an established product to a new product that conveys the same benefits to a new market (Neutrogena soap to Neutrogena shampoo), or to a new product that conveys new benefits to the same market (Tom's of Maine toothpaste to baking powder).[218]

Because international agreements cover trademarks, in applying for them it is advisable to consider filing applications in other countries as well. Trademarking in the United States does not automatically protect the mark elsewhere. The European Community (EC) of 15 countries allows application for a single Community Trademark (CTM) that gives exclusive use rights in all those countries, even if the company uses those rights in only one of the countries. Prior registration in the United States can sometimes be of help in applying for trademarks in other countries. For instance it allows registration in a other countries which agreed under a Madrid Protocol to allow filing a single application with the international Bureau of the World Property Intellectual Organization through the U.S. Patent and Trademark Office.

Complications can be introduced when making contracts with companies in other countries concerning not only trademarks but also other protected intellectual property. The rules and court decisions there can be different on patents and secrecy agreements, as well as royalty agreements, non-compete agreements, and termination rights. An obvious implication is to check those out before putting intellectual property at risk there.[219]

Tactics for protecting trademark names

- **Seek non-descriptive words.** The purpose of the mark is to distinguish between products, not to describe them. "Celestial Seasonings" is all right, but "Tasty Seasonings" would be hard to protect.
- **Search** for any **other users**, both before applying for registration and after registering. After registration, go after any imitators promptly.
- **Register the mark** at the state level and, when it is clear that it will be used interstate, at the federal level. Renew it six months before it lapses. (Registration is not required to prove ownership of a mark, but it gives better protection.)
- **Use** the mark **as registered**. Do not alter it. If change is needed, register a new one.
- Refer to the **trade name as a brand**. Examples are "Scotch Brand" and "Kleenex Brand."
- **Avoid using** the name as a verb. Xerox is careful not to use the term Xeroxing, which could make the term generic.
- **Be cautious in licensing** anyone else to use the mark. If others fail to maintain the quality the mark represents, it may be deemed to have lost its identity.
- **Flaunt the mark.** Otherwise it may be deemed to have been abandoned. Put it on the product, advertisements, displays, tags, and manuals.

[127] *American Venture*, April 1997, p. 9.
[218] "Will It Travel?" *Inc.*, April 1990, p. 116.
[219] *American Venture*, July 1997, p. 9.

3. Aesthetic protection

Although trademark protection does apply to appearance, its purpose is to prevent confusion as to the source of a product or service, not to prevent copying it. Two other paths of protection are aimed at control of copying, copyrights, and patents. Copyrights aim to protect artistic originality. Information about them, including prior registrations, is available online through copyright.gov.

Copyrights

Written materials and works of art can be protected by copyrights, which are issued by the Library of Congress. Under international agreement the U.S. protection is automatic in more than 80 other countries as well. The procedure for securing a copyright begins with writing on the "work of art" a "c" with a circle around it (©), followed by the name of the idea's creator and the year in which it is created. If the work is produced and distributed with that mark, it is automatically entitled to legal protection.

Taking the further step of contacting the U.S. Copyright Office in the Library of Congress and registering it, there is a way to assure that the creator of the work has laid claim to copyright protection on that date, in case anyone else should attempt to claim the work as theirs. The procedure for copyright registration consists of filing an application and including with it two copies of the work (or a photo if it is art), and a check for $30 with the Copyright Office, Library of Congress, Washington, D.C., 20559. The work can also be submitted on a CD-ROM or online.

- Registering a copyright may be done at any time, but there are advantages to registering sooner rather than later:
- Registration permits the holder to sue any infringers immediately.
- Registration allows collection of damages from the time of registration.
- Registration within five years establishes validity even if the work is published without a copyright notice.

- Registration at least three months before any infringement allows imposition of attorneys' fees and statutory damages in addition to actual damages and profits in successful infringement suits.

It takes about five months for a copyright to be issued following submission, and the life of a copyright equals the life of the author plus 50 years. There is a statute of limitations on infringement. Suit must be brought within three years of infringement. Copyright infringement requires that the infringer have had access to the work infringed upon. If the work is proved to have been created independently, there is no copyright infringement. Prior registration is not necessary and can be applied for any time. Documents can also be registered at www.firstuse.com.

There can, however, be significant advantages in not waiting. Delay in filing precludes recovery of statutory damages, which can exceed $100,000, and attorneys' fees for infringements that occurred prior to registration. The copyright holder can recover only actual damages. Some courts have even barred recovery of statutory damages for infringements that occurred after registration when they judged such infringements to be of the same character as those that occurred prior to registration. Most copyrights apply to written works, but there are other important applications as well, such as the following.

Web site designs

The art and writing work of Web sites can be copyrighted just as written material can, but development and expanded use of the Web is introducing a host of new dangers and legal issues. An early one is the question of who owns copyrights on what the site displays, including text, icons, graphics, and layout. A hired Web site designer is likely to want copyright ownership on what he or she creates for the venture, or alternatively, to want more money for the job. If the designer uses works of others on the site, such as clip art or other materials scanned

Copyrights

in, that may require negotiating and paying fees for permissions. Even creating a site that someone else thinks looks too much like theirs could be the basis for a demand that the venture stop using it, or risk being sued.[220]

Important to consider in such negotiations is who will have what rights to data collected at the site. Should the Internet service provider be free to share information about such things as the number of hits received by the site? What should become of the venture's contact data if the venture shifts to another website? Contacting an attorney who specializes in such issues and, to the extent possible with such a new technology, has experience in dealing with them is probably essential, but after first thinking through such issues insofar as possible.

Is it all right to introduce links to the Webs of others? Some site owners are choosing to do it only after first writing the other sites and saying they hope there is no problem. But sometimes there is. For example with deep linking, the user of one site may be able to bypass the Web page of another site to obtain information from that site without having to pass through the advertising banners of the site to get there, which is disadvantageous for the advertisers and consequently also the site being contacted. Ticketmaster, for instance, sued Microsoft over just this issue.

Another problem concerns copying material that is copyrighted from a site, some thing which the Web, more than any other medium, makes easy.

> Shannon Entin, owner of a site providing information on health and fitness found, in surfing the Web, another site that had duplicated one of her articles completely under someone else's name. She immediately sent the site an E-mail saying they were violating her rights. Conveniently, they pulled the article.[221]

Information about copyrighting on-line work is contained in Package 125, available from the Copyright office at (202) 707-9100. But Web site content can run afoul of the law, not only on copyrights but also on trademarks, patents, rights of publicity and privacy[red], and not only in the U.S. but also in any country. Hence it can be worth anticipating what can go wrong and how to ward off lawsuits before taking what seem like potential chances.

But the rules regarding how much can be copied from another Web page design are as yet far from fully clear. To contact a lawyer for guidance in setting up a Web site, one approach is to call some local law firms and ask for names of lawyers who have experience in such work and are currently involved in it, particularly because that aspect of law is so new and fast developing. A relevant Web site is that of the American Bar Association at www.abanet.org/buslaw/cyber.

Semiconductor chip designs

The Semiconductor Chip Protection Act of 1984 provides that the Copyright Office can issue protection for the design of an integrated circuit chip for a period of 10 years. During that time it is illegal to reproduce, import, or distribute chips that were made using the mask for that chip without permission. The circuit package must bear the mark "mask work" or *M*, or an "M" with a circle around it to signify that it is thus protected. Unlike copyright protection on other works, which may be filed for any time after creation, mask-work protection must be filed for within two years of commercial introduction. Innocent purchasers of pirated mask works are not liable.

Software

Copyrighting can protect software code from literally being copied, and therefore may be worth filing for. But it cannot protect the underlying ideas of the code. Patenting may or may not be able to give that protection, as will be discussed below. In addition to filing for copyright protection, it may be possible to keep at least some aspects of the software secret.

Music protection

Music can be protected by copyright, and the composer is entitled to royalties from anyone who makes money by playing it. The American Society of Composers, Authors and Publishers (ASCAP) is an organization dedicated to enforc-

---

[220] Phaedra Hise, "Who Owns a Web Site?," *Inc.*, February 1996, p. 107.
[221] Deborah L. Jacobs, "Legal Traps on the Web," *Inc.* October 1999, p. 101.

ing this protection. Radio stations are obliged to pay royalties for playing music over the air, and business establishments that play radio music are also obliged to pay. ASCAP employs roving observers to enforce these rules.

As with virtually anything legal, copyrights have their gray areas where disputes are always going on and never fully settled. Currently, computer software copyrighting is a hot legal battleground. In 1992, for instance, a decision was rendered in favor of a company that had been sued for disassembling copyrighted software for purposes of "reverse-engineering."[222] Another decision was rendered in favor of a company that duplicated a copyrighted piece of software in order to understand it.[223] Navigation in such shifting seas calls for attorneys who specialize in that particular gray area.

Nevertheless, copyrighting still begins with the simple imprinting step that does not have to wait for an attorney's help.

Defending such a legal monopoly when someone else infringes on it is where attorneys are most needed and also are most expensive. The copyright itself does not prevent anyone from imitating the original work. Only the action of a court can do that. For the court to act, a lawsuit must be filed, a verdict must be rendered and action must be taken to get it implemented. Such a process takes time, work, and money. Decisions could go either for or against protection on that particular creation. How much legal expense is justified must continually be decided by whoever is paying for it as the litigation moves forward.

4. Functionality protection

The First Congress of the United States began creation of a patent system for protecting inventions with a statute passed on April 5, 1790, that was signed into law on April 10 by President George Washington.

Patents

Over 200,000 patents are issued each year in the U.S. Summaries of new patents are published weekly in the *Patent Gazette* and by the U.S. Patent and Trademark Office, and made available online at uspto.gov. Large firms receive about two thirds of those issued, with individuals and small firms getting the rest. IBM, for example, received 1,742 patents during 1998. About 5 percent of inventions have typically become products. Most recently, Internet-related inventions have accounted for over 80 percent of the applications.

Patents are of three types. **Utility** patents are used to protect ideas for machines, processes, and chemical compounds. **Design** patents pertain to the shape and design of useful objects. **Plant** patents apply to living organisms and other life forms such as DNA. Most patenting efforts are directed at the first of these three.

Only features of products and processes that are new, different, and not an obvious discovery (which can be tricky to define) to someone "skilled in the art" are protectable. To be patentable, a patented item must be able to work and be potentially useful. Expert patent examiners employed by the Patent Office decide which claims in a patent application qualify for that distinction. Patenting requires proof that the conception can physically work, but a physical model may not be needed to do that.

Application for a patent typically involves high attorney costs and time both to work the application through and wait for around two years to learn the verdict. If issued, a patent gives its owner a right to sue anyone who violates its approved claims.

Claims stated in the patent describe specific individual attributes of the invention that the inventor wants to protect. The inventor would like to obtain protection on claims that are as broad as possible and that preclude imitation of any aspect of the invention. But the Patent Office generally requires that they be narrow and specific, and usually when a patent is is-

Patents

---

[222] "Seega Enterprises, Ltd v. Accolade," *Inc.*, 977 F.2nd 1510 (9th Cir. 1992).
[223] "Atari Games Corp v. Nintendo of America," *Inc.*, 975 F.2d 832 (Fed. Cir. 1992).

sued it grants only some of the claims—maybe very few. Possibly the claims granted will be valuable. An infringer on the claims can be required to pay damages for past activity (manufacture, use, sale, or importation of the invention), and the amount can be high. Moreover, the court will issue an injunction prohibiting any further infringement of the patent backed up with such penalties as seizure of equipment and imprisonment.

Investors, particularly venture capitalists, like to see patents as part of a business proposal for two reasons. First, their possession indicates that a search has been performed that found someone else did not own rights to the idea that could prevent the new venture from using it. Second, they give reason to hope that the venture can have a monopoly advantage on the idea that will stop others, at least until they manage to design some way around it.

But if claims granted by the patent pertain only to inconsequential details, the patent containing those claims may offer little protection and be essentially worthless for at least the latter purpose. Hence, it is important, if a patent is to be applied for, that the application process, including claim formulation, be done carefully.

Alternatively, from the viewpoint of a potential attacker, the possession of a patent by an existing company should not be assumed to make it unassailable unless a review of the claims indicates that they truly protect what will be vital to competing. The patent may turn out to be toothless. It will be toothless for either party if it cannot afford the high expenses of legal combat.

The concept of a patent right is simple, but defending it can be costly, complex, and chancy. A suit alleging violation of a patent's claims may prevail. Or it may not, and the court may declare the patent invalid. And even if it is valid, the court may decide that the alleged violator is not violating it. If a judgment is rendered in favor of the patent holder, the damages awarded may justify the time, expense, and trouble of the lawsuit—or they may not.

Applying for patents

Application for a patent can be made personally without a lawyer, as illustrated by the following example of a gun entrepreneur.

Bill Ruger developed as a boy a life-long interest in guns that would lead eventually to his becoming a prominent manufacturer of them. During two years spent in college, he got permission to use a shop in the chemistry building for experimentation, which he used to work on a belt-fed machine-gun design. Through his mother's lawyer he met a patent attorney, who helped him obtain the first of his eventual 70 patents and from whom he learned how to perform a search.

Later, he began doing more of his own application work. At age 23 he wrote home that he had not yet landed a job, but was off to see another patent attorney, whom he had not yet met but had heard good things about. He wrote his mother, "I did prepare the patent application complete, myself, drawings and all. It was the toughest job I ever did, but I did it well, even if it did take a month. At least I tested my own ability, and it may save me a lot on the attorney's fee."[224]

There is a cost to do this personally in terms of time to learn the procedures and how to avoid following them incompetently. Patent lawyers gain experience with years of practice that lets them to the job better.

Steps for getting a patent are different from and more complicated than those for copyrighting. The first step is to start as soon as possible keeping and dating records (including sketches) that describe the idea and how it works. As these are extended over time, the various changes and experiments should also be dated and recorded in a page-numbered notebook. These records should be periodically witnessed, dated, and signed in ink with a phrase like "read in confidence and understood" by a couple of other people who are capable of understanding them. This will help prove that the inventor kept working on the idea to improve and "reduce it to practice."

Instructions for setting up and keeping a notebook to seek patent protection are described in material available from the U.S. Government Printing Office and in commercially published

---

[224] R.L. Wilson, *Ruger & His Guns* (New York: Simon & Schuster, 1996) p. 95.

works.[225] Among the rules are that the notebook not have removable pages, that each page be dated and signed by the inventor, that the book be witnessed and signed by others, and that pursuit of the idea's development be continuous and diligent. The purpose is to demonstrate that nobody else developed the idea sooner.

It is important to realize that once an inventor has either made public or sold an invention, there are only 12 months left in which to file a patent application, or the idea will become unpatentable. If two people apply for a patent on the same concept, it is the one who discovered it first who wins, provided it can be proven. Because the date of conception is so important, the inventor should consider filing a Disclosure Document with the Patent Office as soon as possible. This is not the same as applying for a patent, and application for the patent should still be made when ready. If the patent application is not filed within two years, the Patent Office will discard the disclosure document.

Two reasons for studying earlier patents in connection with an idea are first to make sure that using the idea will not violate a patent someone else holds on it. Second, to apply for a patent requires listing prior related patents. Anyone can search for them at a patent library, but a professional should do it better and faster. Although patent searchers are listed in the Yellow Pages, the best way to pick one is with help from a respected patent attorney. Copies of issued patents are available from the U.S. Patent and Trademark Office. Summary descriptions of new patents appear in the Patent Gazette.

Searching personally in a patent library or online is another option. The sequence for searching out precedents for a new toothbrush design, an example cited by Gary Lynn,[226] is as follows:

1. Look in a document called the *Index to Classification* for "Tooth" and "Teeth." There is a listing for "Brushes" which cites Class 15, Subclass 167A.

2. Seek further subclasses of "Brushes" in a second publication, the *Manual of Classifications*. It shows there are subcategories R and A.

3. Check a third document, *Classification Definitions*, which for Class 15, Subclass 167A says "Implements of the brush or broom type especially adapted for cleaning the teeth or nails."

4. Look in a fourth document, the *U.S. Patent Classification—Subclass Listing*, where it will be seen there are 91 patents listed.

5. Pull out each patent itself and check it for precedents of the new design. Notice also the other patents it lists as precedents.

Utility patents historically were good for 17 years from the date of issuance. Beginning June 8, 1995, however, the law was changed so that on applications filed after that date, the patent rights begin when the patent is granted and continue, if maintenance fees are paid, until 20 years from the day that the inventor filed a utility patent application or 15 years for a design patent, which involves no maintenance fees. On a patent issued on an application filed before June 8, 1995, the patent term will expire after either 20 years from the earliest U.S. filing date or 17 years from the date the patent is issued, whichever is longer. On patents already in force on June 8, 1995, the new patent laws specify that, again, the term will be the greater of either 20 years from the earliest U.S. filing date or 17 years from the patent grant.

This is a contrast to rules in most other countries, where the 20-year countdown begins on the date application was filed. Approval can take five years, which then reduces the life after issuance to only 15 years. Other parts of the world also allow publication of the application before the patent is granted, the objective being to hasten use. In the U.S. the application is kept secret until issuance of the patent, because there is an objective of protecting the inventor's interest and motivation to patent. The extent to which the U.S. should shift to the world standards has been the subject of intense debate.

To facilitate obtaining an early filing date, the law allows filing a provisional application with fewer formalities and lower cost. No patent is issued based upon the provisional application, but once that application is filed, the inventor has 12 months to file a regular patent

---

[225] Gary S. Lynn, *From Concept to Market* (New York: Wiley, 1989).
[226] Lynn, *From Concept to Market*, p. 72.

application and claim the provisional application filing date. Filing a provisional application requires the following:

1. A clearly written **description** of the invention.

2. Any **drawings** needed to understand the invention.

3. A **filing fee** that depends on whether the applicant is an individual inventor or a "larger entity."

4. A **cover sheet** identifying the application as being provisional and including the inventor(s) name(s), residence(s), invention title, name and registration of attorney/agent, correspondence address, and any U.S. Government agency that has a property interest in the application.

Application can either be **provisional**, which is simpler in procedure and cost, but marks the application date and holds for up to 12 months. After that it will lapse unless followed up with a full non-provisional application.

Patents cannot be renewed. After a patent lapses, the patented design or process enters the public domain. Exceptions occur in the case of drug patents, which may be extended if sales have been significantly delayed by the Federal Drug Administration.

To counter lapsing, patent holders often continue to develop refinements to the original design and patent those. This can generate a race in which competitors, who may not have as much experience but may as a result be fresher in their thinking, also seek to patent refinements to the original design. Such a race, coupled with other corruption inside the company, almost killed Gillette's Safety Razor Company according to his biographers.

> Gillette's patented razor consisted of a T-shaped handle with three round pins protruding across the top of the T, over which a thin flat rectangular blade with three holes to match the pins slipped and was clamped with a cover that screwed down over it. His fortune was made, not by selling the razor, but by selling replacement blades. In spite of occasional bouts with counterfeiters, he managed to maintain and further fortify his patent-protected monopoly with distribution channel saturation and brand-building advertising expenditures.

> When the company's basic patent lapsed in 1921, it began encountering more powerful legitimate competition, not only in blades, but also in sharpening machinery in which Gillette had made enormous investments, and was reluctant to scrap in response to others' improved designs. One company in particular, AutoStrop Razor, had also developed what its inventor, Henry Jacques Gaisman, claimed was a better blade, the Probak. It broke less easily by virtue of different metallurgy, and it featured three diamond-shaped mounting holes that would let it fit on a Gillette razor although the round holes of Gillette's blades would not fit on a Probak razor.

> Gillette spurned Gaisman's offers, which began in 1926, to sell out, and instead looked for ways to leapfrog his designs while also contending with other imitators. Finally, a design with diamond holes, but also differently shaped ends that would distinguish it from the Probak, was chosen. At an executive meeting to approve the new design, a Gillette executive, looking over some prototypes of alternatives, noticed one with a short bar on the blade cap that slipped through a slot on the blade and nestled in a groove atop the handle. He proposed that the groove and bar be lengthened to make a blade that would not possibly work on a Probak.

> Later, the Gillette people would claim that there had been Probak spies to blame for the fact that Gaisman beat Gillette to the Patent Office with his design and got it on the market first. Gaisman partisans claimed that Gillette had stolen the idea from Probak's shop. After trumpeting its readiness to do battle in court, Gillette backed down and agreed to merge. Audits performed as a result of Gillette's search for the buy-out money subsequently revealed that the company books had been seriously cooked and Gillette was in real trouble. As a result, following the merger Gaisman wound up in charge of the company, and some of the Gillette directors, although not Gillette himself, were financially, as well as reputationally, ruined.[227]

If the venture becomes strong enough before the patent litigation occurs, it may very well be able to spend enough money to win. Or if it loses it may have enough to survive the penalty.

> George Eastman had been inspired to search out a way to make a dry photographic plate by the damage done to his luggage when he included photographic gear for a vacation trip.

---

[227] Russell B. Adams, Jr., *King C. Gillette* (Boston: Little, Brown and Company, 1978) p. 149.

Through experimentation he came up with a better way, which he patented in 1879 at age 25, first in England and then in the United States. He sold the English patent and used the proceeds to set up a plate-making shop in Rochester, New York.

He chose the name Kodak which, because it had no intrinsic meaning, was easy to protect as a trade name. It was also clear, easy to pronounce regardless of a person's native language, easy to spell, and hard to get wrong.

Through continued research he found a way to replace the cumbersome glass plates with film as his company continued to prosper and grow. However, he ran afoul of patents held by another man, Hannibal Goodwin, on flexible film, and in 1913 was forced to pay Goodwin's family and others $5 million in compensation. Despite this settlement, which at the time was enormous, his company was strong enough to continue. By 1927 it employed over 15,000 people and had become a household name.[228]

Patent application in foreign countries must be made separately. Unlike the U.S., where first-to-invent wins, foreign countries follow a first-to-file rule. In the U.S. an inventor has a one-year grace period after first publication or sale of the invention in which to file. But someone who sees that can run and file on it in a foreign country and win, unless the U.S. inventor has already filed somewhere first. If application is made in the U.S. before any publication or sale of the invention, applications can then be made in other countries in the ensuing 12 months without losing rights by claiming priority based on the U.S. application.[229] Whether to apply in foreign countries depends on the potential markets in those countries. Action against copying in the foreign country cannot be taken until a patent is issued there. But action may be taken to prevent foreign-made copies from being imported or sold in the United States.

Utility patent application costs $690, plus $72 for each claim beyond three, and $20 for each claim over 20. The issuance fee is $1,130. These fees may be halved if the applicant is declared a small entity, which includes independent inventors. Maintenance fees must be paid at years 4, 8, and 12; otherwise the patent will lapse. It is advisable to pay these fees several months in advance to be safe.

A larger expense will be involved in hiring a patent attorney and preparing the application. It is necessary to show that the idea can be made to work. If chemicals are involved, they must be specified and the process for using them must be detailed. If machinery is involved, it must be drawn and verbally described in sufficient detail for someone of ordinary skill to be able to make and operate it without a lot of experimentation. Developing this degree of detail to prove workability may cost considerable time and money in addition to the legal fees.

Once a patent application has been filed, it cannot be amended to make changes or improvements in the invention. Instead, a new application that incorporates those changes must be filed. Until the patent is issued there is no legal protection from copiers, so it may be best to keep the product or process secret. Writing *patent pending* on a product during this time may discourage copiers because they may fear that issuance of the patent will make them abandon their attempt to profit from it. However, there is no legal protection from copiers under the term *patent pending*.

Whether the expense of searching and—assuming the search indicates patenting is likely—filing for a patent is justified is one of the judgments that may be called for in pursuing a venture. Costs can run into thousands of dollars, and the costs of defending the patent against infringers can cost tens of thousands or even millions more. This may seem discouraging, but possession of a strong patent can be powerful in recruiting capital to develop a venture, or in licensing the idea to another company in return for cash and/or a royalty. It can also pay off by protecting the venture's market. Tony Maglica, for example, concluded that it had been worthwhile to spend $16 million in lawyers' fees over six

[228] Peter C. Wensberg, *Land's Polaroid* (Boston: Houghton Mifflin, 1987) p. 24.
[229] *American Venture*, January 1998, p. 7.

years to protect features of a flashlight around which his company was built.[230]

Sometimes the process is cheaper than that.

Michael Walker, a cabinet maker, spent $25,000 to bring a new product to market, but only $5,000 of that was for legal fees to patent it. When he lost a $700 fishing rod in 1991, he conceived the idea for a pocket mount that would attach to the side of an inner tube or a pontoon boat to hold the rod safely. He developed a prototype and began a patent search, which turned up 12 similar holders. After defining the elements he considered unique in his design, he made application to the U.S. Patent Office, which turned up another dozen. Persisting in refinement of his product, he resubmitted his application and eventually received his patent, number 5,697,183, in 1997.

Meanwhile, he sought to license the idea to other companies. When that failed, he learned about plastics fabrication and sought out start-up capital from his family and friends. He created an assembly line where he could make 500 units a day and started attending trade shows where he would demonstrate and sell the product. Sales in 1998 and 1999 amounted to 10,000 "Rod Pockets," which wholesale for $3.95 and retail for $16.95, yielding enough to pay for travel to the shows, but not to live on. "The money is certainly important, but it's more a sign than I've succeeded," he commented.[231]

As with copyrights, patents grant rights only to sue imitators. Sometimes imitators are able to design around the claims of issued patents, and thereby in effect nullify them. Some companies never file for patents, figuring that the technology will be obsolete too soon to benefit from patenting, that courts will not back them up, or that the ideas they protect are not sufficiently valuable. Others obtain dozens of patents on ideas that are not profitable, sometimes just for the sake of having them. They are a form of property, after all, and they do demonstrate genuine invention.

With so-called *submarine patents* some inventors attempt to blanket some area of technology that may have potential by filing vague claims which, in a give and take with the patent office, they refine as the technology advances, so that they have an advance position on the territory when it becomes clear enough for patents to begin issuing. Some inventors have become enormously rich with this strategy, while others have decried the practice as a perversion of what the patent law is supposed to accomplish, namely rewards as incentives for true discoveries.

Occasionally patents prove to be incredibly powerful, as did those that protected Polaroid's camera from competition by Kodak. The experience of Exac, a start-up with a better flow meter, illustrates how patent contention can have an enormous effect on the fortunes of a start-up—and can also sneak up as a surprise.

Exac was founded by an inventor who had developed a flow meter capable of higher accuracy than existing meters. Another company, Micro Motion, developed a meter that utilized a similar principle, and was bought by a large company, Emerson Electric. When Emerson learned, after buying Micro Motion, that Exac was introducing a flow meter that would outperform Micro Motion's, Emerson filed a lawsuit accusing Exac of patent infringement.

Robert J. Kunze, a venture capitalist who had put up the money for Exac, observed, "It's tough to get clear answers from patent attorneys. Exac's patent lawyer assured me we had nothing to worry about, but he was equally quick to point out that it was impossible to predict what might happen in court. He then told me that the Polaroid/Eastman patent suit on instant cameras illustrated that the courts had become very sympathetic to patent holders and very harsh on infringers. For a man who was telling me not to worry, he gave me a lot to worry about."

Seeing that millions of dollars might be needed for defense, because Emerson refused to settle and insisted on going to court, Kunze decided that Exac would have no hope of obtaining further venture capital, observing, "A cardinal rule of venture investing is the money must go for building a company, not to a bunch of lawyers," and decided to seek a buyer. He arranged a deal whereby another large company, Monsanto, agreed to shoulder the patent litigation costs, which eventually reached $5 million, in return for an option to buy Exac.

In court the jury unanimously found in favor of Exac. Monsanto exercised its takeover option. The investors in Exac reaped three times their

---

[230] Paul B. Brown, "Magnificent Obsession," *Inc.*, August 1989, p. 89.
[231] Rebecca Smullin, "Inventors Mine Ideas from Puget Sound Area's Strengths," *The Seattle Times*, January 25, 1998, p. F1.

money, but the litigation had been debilitating to Exac, with the uncertainty, disruption of work by the employees being interviewed, and legal expenses.[232]

Because the life of a utility patent is limited and there is no option of renewal, it is necessary to keep exploiting and improving what it protects with additional patentable features that render the original design obsolete and extend the protection time further. Foreseeing how others might foil or supersede a patent was outstandingly exemplified by John Ryan.

> The co-founder of Macrovision, a Cupertino, California company, Ryan developed and patented an anti-copying system to protect videotapes. Then to foil those who would make devices to circumvent his system, he also developed and patented the technology required for circumvention. With this second patent, his company filed 21 infringement suits against would-be makers and sellers of circumvention "black boxes." Four manufacturers of the boxes settled with his company before the suits, three more settled as a result of them, and all 12 distributors agreed to stop selling the boxes.[233]

A patent holder does not have to commercialize what the patent covers or license it to anyone else. He or she can keep it off the market by the legal monopoly power that it conveys. It is a privilege extended by the government to encourage invention.

But that purpose also leads to a catch. When the patent is issued, the inventor must make public the technology it embodies so that others can learn how it works and become motivated and enabled to build on it with further useful inventions. The Patent Office keeps the application secret unless and until a patent is issued on it.

Patent law requires that the patent application disclose the best ways of practicing the invention. If the applicant reveals only inferior ways and keeps one or more better ways secret, that may invalidate the patent. Hence, publication of the patent gives competitors an opportunity to learn what is protected and what is not. They can then try to get around the

patent. Moreover, if a foreign patent is applied for, the information in that application may, by that country's rules, be made public even if no patent is issued.

Another catch can be the typical wait required to have a patent issued. For some products that change quickly, this may be a longer time than the product itself lasts. If, however, claims in the patent can be obtained that are broad, they may cover not just the first version of the product, but also later versions that follow when the initial version is phased out.

Software patents

Software could be patented as part of a software/machine combination or, if sufficiently novel, by itself, at least until October 31, 2008, at which time a federal court ruled that a process technology had to be tied to "a particular machine or apparatus." Until that ruling, which will likely take some time to play out and be tested, a patent gave broader and stronger protection to software than could copyrighting. Better yet was to apply for both and, insofar as possible, keep some parts of the program secret as well. Patenting could conceivably keep someone else from using important features of the code even though they did not copy it line by line.[234] But what the future holds for either enforcing existing software patents or obtaining new ones became, in late 2008, an open question.

Web tools are a form of software that has become an area of intense patent activity that may also be open to new attacks. Firms that offer site for Web stores, for instance, employ software that they may have developed and patented for such things as displaying the store site, tracking hits, and processing orders, as well as tracking, analyzing, and reporting data. Using the software of an intermediary, such as an Internet service provider or a Web store site in some other E-firm's mall to advertise or route responses and orders for a new venture on the Web runs the risk that the venture will remain tied to that provider. One solution for the venture may be for it to create all its own software. Another is to negotiate with the Internet service provider (ISP) a

[232] Robert J. Kunze, *Nothing Ventured* (New York: Harper, 1990) p. 161.
[233] "Defending Anti-copy Rights," *Venture*, September 1989, p. 72.
[234] *American Venture*, January 1999, p. 39.

price for rights to own the graphical user interface, including permission to take it along in any move to another ISP. A license to use whatever software is required for editing the site may also be needed as part of the package, permanently or at least temporarily.[235]

Business patents

Some enterprises have even been issued broader patents on forms of doing business over the Web that they hope to use for charging royalties to any enterprises that use those general forms. Priceline.com's patent, for instance, covers "bilateral buyer-driven commerce," an example of which is their own application in which a person who wants a airline ticket offers over the Web site a price for the ticket and a credit card number. If the site finds a ticket at the price, the deal is made. This could apply to purchase of anything, not just airline tickets. The Priceline patent is owned by Walker Digital, a company formed in 1994 with $50 million in capital to create and patent new business models like Priceline. By the end of 1998, it had filed over 200 patents; the one on Priceline was the first to be issued.

Another company that received patent protection on a general business model for the Web is CyberGold, which obtained rights on the practice of paying consumers in various ways, such as with flyer miles, money, or other products, to spend time paying attention to Web advertisements. Litigation seemed likely to ensue.[236]

However, the October 30, 2008 federal court mentioned above, declared that to be patentable under U.S. law, a process technology had to (1) be tied to a particular machine or apparatus, or (2) physically transform a particular article into a different state or thing. Early reactions in the blogosphere, remaining at the time to be further tested, were that this meant business process patents would no longer be defensible.

Design patents

Design, as opposed to utility, patents cost $220 to file and $400 for issuance. They are issued for 14 years. Someone may infringe on a design patent without having seen the original; such infringement is illegal, even though it might be inadvertent. This is different from copyrights. Because design patents are based on shapes, not mechanisms, they can often be easy to design around through simple alterations in configuration, and therefore are generally considered less protective than utility patents.

5. Other idea protection methods

Secrets

Patents, trademarks, and copyrights are not the only ways that ideas can be protected.

Secrets

When Robert Noyce and Gordon Moore left Fairchild Semiconductor to start their own company, Intel, they took with them knowledge about chip technology they had developed there and about the frontier goal of making a semiconductor memory to replace the old magnetic core memory technology. The approach they eventually used, although they also explored two others in their new firm, was silicon gate, which had been invented at Fairchild in the laboratory headed by Noyce. A former employee of both companies alleged, in fact, that "Intel was founded to steal the silicon gate process from Fairchild." Intel hired dozens of employees away from Fairchild, eventually including the technician who had been working most closely on the silicon gate process.[237]

Historically, this was a time when practices for protecting proprietary information were becoming much tighter, and Intel was part of the trend. No longer were engineers free to discuss with friends after hours over drinks what they had been doing at work lately. Noyce and Moore when founding their company said of its purpose only that it would focus on product areas no other manufacturers were supplying, that it would avoid government business, and that it would provide components, not end-user products. When asked on a technical panel about results of experiments Intel was rumored to have been making with aluminum nitride, Moore would say only, "We got the results we were pre-

---

[235] Hise, "Web site," p. 107.
[236] Leigh Buchanan, "A Business Model of One's Own," *Inc.*, November 1998, p. 83.
[237] Tim Jackson, *Inside Intel* (NY: Penguin, 1997) p. 1.

dicting." In fact the experiments showed no useful effect from the material.

As time went on, Intel became even more aggressive in protecting its technology. Tim Jackson's biography of the company reported that eventually, "It launched a string of long-running lawsuits against competing chip design teams, former employees, semiconductor manufacturing plants, venture capitalists, and at one stage the computer companies that were its customers. Intel's legal department spent hundreds of millions of dollars. At one point, the general counsel who headed it was told that performance appraisal was a fixed number of new lawsuits to start each quarter. [238]

Instead of filing for patent protection, it may sometimes be better to keep the technology of a product or process secret. Things that can be protected include formulas; mathematical algorithms; production techniques; customer, dealer, or supplier lists; and technical drawings or instructions. To qualify for legal protection, the information of a secret must (1) have economic value as a result of (2) not being generally known or readily ascertainable by others through legal means, and (3) efforts must be applied to maintain secrecy.

The recipe for Coca-Cola is not patented, but rather is kept secret, although author Mark Pendergrast[239] claimed to have come across it in company archives. Many manufacturing processes that perhaps could be patented are kept secret. How colored adhesive plastic tapes used in graphics are sliced to very thin widths has been kept secret for decades. This has both avoided competitor imitation and saved the substantial costs of searching, filing, and defending patents.

Secrets require taking precautions for protection. A starting point is to consider what, if any, information is worth protecting. Phone records, correspondence, recopied computer disks, receipts giving names of suppliers, credit card records, old bank statements or cancelled checks, minutes of meetings, invoice copies telling who the customers are and what they buy for how much,

documentation on products such as design specifications, drawings, bills of material, test results, customer complaints or service records all could turn up in the company's waste bin where the wrong person might get access to them. Making as complete as possible a list of what competitors might find useful is a starting point.

Another is to consider how sensitive items might be divulged. The waste bin was mentioned already. But there are others, such as employee conversations with others, roving eyes of suppliers, customers, or other visitors, messages left on answering machines, and possibly computer break-ins. As Ira Winkler, an expert on corporate espionage observed, "The smoking areas outside major office buildings are great places to pick up information through casual conversations. I've heard of spies taking up smoking specifically to exploit that vulnerability."[240] As many as possible of such potential leak areas should also be listed, along with ways of plugging those deemed to matter. There is even the possibility of deliberately allowing misleading information to leak, if espionage is suspected to be going on.

The legal rules of trade secrecy are far less codified than those for copyrights and patents. In part they derive from common law, which is to say precedent decisions of the courts. Over the years, judges have made reasoned decisions aimed at fairness, and in time, those become general guidelines. In part the rules derive from contract law, wherein there is an agreement between people working together. Finally, tort law forms part of the basis for judging disputes over trade secrets. It concentrates on whether one person is wronged by another, and, if so, what compensation the wronged person deserves from the wrongdoer—in this case, through unfair handling of a secret given in confidence. There are no legal time limits to trade secrets. Most states have adopted a Uniform Trade Secrets Act. (Some tactics for protecting trade secrets appear in the following shaded area.)

[238] Jackson, *Inside Intel*, p. 8.
[239] Mark Pendergrast, *For God, Country, and Coca-Cola* (New York: Charles Scribner's Sons) 1993.
[240] Ira Winkler, "Corporate Espionage," *Inc.* June 1997, p. 95.

Precautions for protecting trade secrets

- Explicitly identifying the categories of information that are secret for the venture.
- Pointing out to all employees the categories and secrecy rules that apply to them and how, issuing reminders of the rules and policies periodically and when any employees leave. Employees should not have to guess what is covered. To be protected, the employer must make clear what is versus what is not secret.
- Setting up policies that restrict people's access to that information on a need-to-know basis.
- Having new hires and, when appropriate, visitors sign secrecy agreements, contracts under which they promise not to tell others what their venture secrets are or to use those secrets themselves to compete with the venture. If existing employees are required to sign such agreements, they must be paid something explicitly for that to make them enforceable.
- Having new hires sign non-compete agreements in which they agree not to solicit former customers when they leave. It is illegal for them to take customer lists, but not for them to remember and reconstruct such lists later.
- Reminding employees who are leaving of what the rules were and what they signed. It may also help to notify their next employer, if known, about their prior access to confidential information that could get them in trouble if that employer makes use of it.
- Arranging physical facilities insofar as practicable, as by labeling documents or containers to indicate confidentiality, posting signs on sensitive areas, having locked cabinets, using guards and alarms to keep information secret, maintaining complete records, such as numbering and logging copies in and out to track access, and disposing of such materials so they can't be retrieved.
- Drafting with care to protect secrets in any licensing agreements that share information or rights with other companies.

Owner versus employee

If secrets are stolen, legal action will be needed in addition to proof that such precautions have been taken in order to collect damages from any secrets that may have been divulged. Court decisions balance different ways of looking at secrecy disputes and therefore tend to be on a case-by-case basis. Key questions concern whether a secret really existed, whether someone breached a contract or duty and what should be done to remedy the situation.

Reverse engineering to discover a secret is legal, but taking customer lists or formulas from an employer and revealing or using them in competition is not. In one case it was judged illegal to fly over a plant under construction and take pictures of it before the roof was on to discover how it would operate. Falsely posing as a customer or negotiating a contract in bad faith just to learn a company's secrets, taking an insider job to learn these secrets, or bribing employees to disclose company secrets is illegal.

At the same time, an employee's general experience in working for a company would not prevent him or her from using that experience in a job elsewhere. Independent discovery of a way of doing something that another company regards as secret does not prohibit the independent discoverer from using that method. Discovery of a secret by reading public literature or visiting public areas of a company is also legal.

Courts have mixed feelings about supporting secrecy rights. They like to encourage development of improvements, and by supporting secrecy rights they give businesses incentive to do so. But at the same time, courts also like to encourage competition and curb monopoly power, which is what secrets give their owners. Courts also lean in favor of an individual's right to earn a living, although at times that may be at the expense of another's right to maintain a secret.

Owner versus employee

The ideas an employer pays somebody to come up with belong to that employer. One implication for an entrepreneur leaving a job to start up is that the entrepreneur's employer may have rightful claims on ideas that are part of the start-up. Hence, an entrepreneur not sure may be well-advised to check this out before leaving.

Another implication is that if the entrepreneur hires someone else to develop technology for his or her venture, that technology will belong to the venture and the employee should know that. Such awareness can help ward off extremely costly and time-wasting disputes and legal fees. Things to consider including in an employment agreement to protect the venture's rights are:

- A confidentiality agreement.
- A non-compete covenant with specified time and geographic limits.
- A clause stating that the employee assign all inventions conceived on or related to the job during the time of employment to the venture.
- An agreement not to solicit the venture's customers to transfer their business to the employee or to encourage other employees to defect.

Some of these protections may exist even without the agreement, but by having a written agreement, they can be made clearer and stronger.

Finally, in hiring an employee who may have developed new technology for another company, it is important to make sure no stolen intellectual property is brought along. If the employee claims he or she has rights to intellectual property where there may be question, there should be written confirmation of that claim either in the patent or from the prior employer to avoid losing a lawsuit that disputes ownership.[241]

Out-competing

Most companies are not able to gain protection of much power from patents, copyrights or secrecy. After watching two lawyers who cost her $200 per hour each argue with four opposing lawyers for hours over such terms as *collateral estoppel* (impermissibility of claiming something that was ruled against by the court when claimed before), Mary Baechler, inventor of the highly successful three-wheeled jogging baby stroller, commented:

> Frankly, I doubt that patents and trademarks do any good, anyway. We know it's going to cost $150,000 for us to take through the court system a case against a competitor who has infringed our patent. Lately, my competition has been countersuing us for unfair trade because we used our patent to sue it. Add another $100,000 to pay for the countersuit.[242]

Eventually, her company went bankrupt.

Aside from patents and copyrights, trademarks are only as good as what people believe them to represent in terms of product or service quality and value. Consequently, the main mode of protection used sometimes has to be simply competitive performance in producing, pricing, selling, and delivering a product or service.

Donald Beaver invented a better way to soak up industrial fluid leaks. Rather than the current practice of spreading kitty litter on the floor, he proposed using sausage-shaped socks full of absorbent matter, which could be laid as more effective barriers and more easily picked up afterward. Calling it a PIG ("Partners In Grime"), he patented the product and in 1986 put it on the market. Within three years he gained over 8,000 customers and annual sales of $10 million.

The sales also attracted over 60 imitators. Rather than suing them for their attempts to design around his patent, Beaver adopted improvement tactics, principally in service, to stay ahead. These included:

- Catalog plus telephone plus computer linkup to four warehouses to allow next-morning shipment and three-day or faster delivery on all orders.
- Twenty-day free trial with invoicing only after a company representative has called and found the customer satisfied. (Result: 95 percent pay up)
- In case of product failure, replacement of the product within hours, no charge on that purchase and 10 percent off on the next one.
- Working with customers to make sure the company's products are used as effectively and efficiently as possible.
- Creation of new products through careful attention to customer problems or requests that existing products don't satisfy.

---

[241] *American Venture*, July 1997, p. 9.
[242] Mary Baechler, "My Life Without Lawyers," *Inc.*, December 1996, p. 37.

– Including in the annual catalog articles on industrial clean-up to help customers learn better ways to accomplish it.

– Calling each customer twice per year to make sure names are updated and correctly spelled.[243]

Out-competing may or may not begin with a better idea. It should aim to include better refinement and execution of the idea. Keeping track of what competitors are up to may also help. Information about them can be obtained legally through a number of means, including talking with suppliers, customers, and former employees of the competitors.

Their products and services can be bought and examined, and they can be investigated on the Web.

Other precaution areas

Paperwork challenges rarely make or break a venture, perhaps because they are fairly easy to handle adequately. But they can impact the bottom line by affecting legal expenses, tax rates, insurance expenditures, and revenues. Choice of name and logo are important enough to some companies that they spend millions in efforts to get them right. Having appropriate insurance coverage can potentially determine whether recovery from a calamity to the venture is possible.

Exercises

Text discussion questions

1. Describe conditions under which intellectual property laws should not be enforced.
2. Explain how you would go about making a decision for a new venture about:
   a. Whether to make application for a patent, trademark, or copyright.
   b. How much to be willing to pay for prosecuting such applications.
   c. Circumstances under which you would sue another party for violating any of them.

Case questions

6A-1 Hoyle Schweitzer

1. Read the Windsurfer case and abstract the main points about intellectual property law that it contains.
2. Be prepared to discuss their potential significance for a competitor.
3. What are Hoyle Schweitzer's other "protection ring" options for protecting his concept besides trying to enforce the patent?
4. What should Hoyle do next?

Portfolio page possibilities

Page 6A-1 Protection ring

1. Describe on one page as specifically as possible the combination or "ring" of intellectual property protections you would invest time and money to build into your venture, and explain your rationale.
2. Insofar as space on the page permits, also describe the fallback plans you think most likely needed if the first line of defenses is breached.

Page 6A-2 Trademark application

1. Find a trademark application instruction (www.uspto.gov) and describe your main entries for it. (To see details of the electronic form TEAS an "x" can be used for making required entries.)
2. Explain the reasoning behind your trademark design and/or choice, including what you did to determine whether it would likely conflict with some other existing trademark.

Page 6A-3 Other paperwork

Describe how you would handle for your venture (1) any government approvals needed, (2) insurance, and (3) location formalities.

---

[243] Rachel Meltzer, "Fending Off the Copycats," *Venture*, February 1989, p. 62.

Term Projects

Venture history

1. What different types of intellectual property did the venture develop or acquire and how?
2. How would the founders now characterize the value of the venture's intellectual property?
3. How much did the founders know, think, or learn about protecting intellectual property before and/or during start-up?
4. How far would the venture go legally to defend the property it owns, and how much do the founders think that might cost?

Venture planning guide

1. Check idea notes to confirm dates and witness signatures.
2. Identify and if possible meet a preferred patent attorney.
3. Describe the full strategy for protecting your venture's intellectual property.
4. Sketch out an application to the Patent Office for either a graphical trademark or a patent on some aspect of your venture idea.
5. Search for patents or trademarks that conflict with your idea and note your findings.
6. Impanel a focus group and search for ways of (1) competing with your planned product or service and (2) improving it to stay ahead of competitors.
7. Meet a patent attorney or two and ask how they can help you.

CHAPTER 6B – Facilities

Topics

1. Start-up time versus tasks
2. Make or buy
3. Shop and equipment
4. Location
5. Lease or buy

Checkpoints

a. How many set-up tasks can you name for an ambitious venture?
b. Describe how dimensions or features of a product or service might impact the set-up of a shop to produce it.
c. What are the important considerations in a start-up's make/buy decision?
d. How do production specifications impact outsourcing for a new venture?
e. What sorts of venture-specific knowledge should be involved in obtaining production equipment?
f. How does choice of location depend on the type of venture being started?
g. What should be investigated in checking out a site for a start-up?
h. How do terms matter in leasing a venture start-up site?

A glimpse of the drama that may be associated with setting up plant and equipment in a new venture was offered by futurist George Gilder in the following description of the chip-making start-up Micron Technology:

Development of its first product to meet performance specifications that could prevail in the marketplace was a key requirement for the start-up of Micron Technology. But there were others as well, not the least of which was to get facilities up and running in Boise that would let it compete with competitors in Silicon Valley and elsewhere around the world.

The founders had to find land, erect a building, assemble equipment, attract, hire and train personnel. And it had to coordinate all these efforts into a crescendo of technical virtuosity and productivity unequaled in the history of industry. Anything short of this climactic triumph would leave Micron as just another listing in the endless annals of entrepreneurial overreach, just another forgotten name in the record-breaking catalogs of bankruptcy in the world wide recession of the early 1980s.[244]

1. Start-up time versus tasks

A 1989 survey by Inc. magazine of its 500 fastest-growing small firms found that 26 percent of the companies had, during start-up, taken only "a matter of weeks" to go from idea to beginning operations. For 37 percent the time lapse was a few months, for 28 percent it was between six months and a year, and for 9 percent it was more than a year.[245] Cooper et al. reported from their sample of 2,994 non-fast-growth start-ups that, "Although the majority went through a relatively lengthy planning period prior to business entry, 87 percent reported that the time between their

---

[244] George Gilder, *The Spirit of Enterprise* (New York: Simon and Schuster, 1984) p. 230.
[245] John Case, "The Origins of Entrepreneurship," *Inc.*, June 1989, p. 54.

first business expenditure of $500 or more and their first cash receipt (sale) was three months or less. Just 3 percent reported the time to be seven months or more."[246]

Setting up shop may require substantial effort. Jim Clark, the founder of Netscape, recalled the office set-up needs for his Internet browser start-up as follows:

> The time had come to sweat the small stuff.... The casual gatherings at my house had hatched an idea, the idea had attracted the talent to make it happen, and now a company was becoming a reality, with the hundreds of needs any company has. Office space had to be found, computers, phones, chairs, desks, conference tables, refrigerators (bring on the Jolt!), and so forth had to be bought and set up. The specialized wiring required for a modern communications company, even a small one, had to be installed. Every new company passes through this underbrush of details, of course; I'd gone through it before myself. It's always a peculiar combination of annoyance and excitement. I've had other entrepreneurs tell me that it's at this stage, when per square foot rent is settled on and cash begins to flow out for equipment that they have their first vague anxieties about the possibility of failure.[247]

Myriad tasks must be performed in setting up even seemingly simple businesses. Which tasks apply naturally depends upon the type of business. Although some can be done quickly, others may take considerable time and effort. Collectively, for a founder who may have to give top priority to finishing development of a product, raising capital, or generating sales, the other things to be done can make the total activity load almost overwhelming.

A laundry list of typical set-up tasks appears in Appendix 6b-1. Description of some governmental requirements that extend the list further appears in Appendix 6b-2. Types of insurance that may be called for are noted in Appendix 6b-3.

The time required for these set-up tasks can vary for many reasons. Some, such as the nature of the company, may already be fixed in the early concept stage. But others may be subject to influence by the founders and those with whom they collaborate in the process. Then the time required may be controllable to some degree. Tradeoffs in terms of dollar costs and risks of error may arise. Balancing these and applying ingenuity to optimize set-up is an early challenge that can set the venture apart favorably from its competitors. Bearing this in mind may help make otherwise prosaic elements of set-up more interesting, challenging, and worthwhile to anticipate.

Anticipating production

Dimensions of the product or service that can have significant implications for how a shop should be set up to produce it, as well as how it will generate sales, satisfy customers, and yield a profit, are listed in the shaded area below.

How these elements are balanced to win and keep customers is central to the venture's competitive strategy and to setting up shop.

Production process

Setting up to produce what the venture will sell, whether it is a product or a service, can be approached by describing the production process in terms of what will be created and how it will be delivered. A list of tasks for accomplishing this can be developed in the form of one or more flow charts or sequence maps that indicate:

1. Steps in the process.
2. Equipment needed to accomplish them.
3. Skills required for doing the process well.
4. Material flows involved.
5. Information needed to make decisions in the process.

Implicit in the map will also be cash and credit flows that are reflected in the operations parts of the financial forecasts of the business plan. Following from this map will also be implications for the equipment, plant, and location most appropriate for the business.

Two further considerations important to decisions about plant and location are what the company should make versus buy and

[246] Arnold C. Cooper and others, *New Business in America* (Washington, D.C.: The NFIB Foundation, 1990) p. 5.

[247] Jim Clark, *Netscape Time* (New York: St. Martin's Press, 1999) p. 70.

Features influencing facilities decisions

- **Functions the product or service performs** Making a drawbridge requires some types of equipment and facilities. Making flow meters or apple pies requires other types. Providing consulting services on taxes requires little in the way of equipment and can be done at home.

- **Quality as perceived by the customer** Colored announcements can be made on copy machines, or computer printers, which may be quite adequate. Alternatively, they can incorporate glossy prints of much higher fidelity, showing truer colors and more detail, but which require entirely different devices and skills to produce.

- **Convenience** Customers may care about how close the venture's plant is to their own location and how much parking is available. Alternatively, it may be important for the venture to be close to a work force of suitable skills, which may be far from customers. Attributes of the surrounding area, such as noise, safety, and beauty may or may not matter to customers. Level of rent and zoning may be crucial to operation.

- **Cost** Starting an airline to fly out of Denver's new airport may provide service that is more convenient for customers. But flying out of Colorado Springs, 70 miles away, may be enough cheaper for some people from Denver to drive the distance and fly from there instead, particularly if several are traveling together.

- **Speed of delivery** This usually requires a larger production or warehouse capacity. If customers are willing to wait, a smaller capacity may satisfy the same needs by producing more steadily (the tortoise competing with the hare) and perhaps more cheaply.

- **Dependability of delivery** More reliable production equipment and/or workers may be needed for dependable timing because shutdowns cannot be tolerated. Flexible delivery timing may allow the use of production facilities rented from others, when available, probably with a savings in investment capital but at higher production cost.

- **Flexibility** Special-purpose equipment and standardized products and services can lead to a streamlining of operations that enhances quality and dependability in the venture's output. Flexible output often requires more general-purpose production equipment that operates slower, while requiring greater set-up efforts and employee learning to accommodate the changes.

- **Follow-up service** If field service is needed, customers can either buy it from someone else, or the venture can provide it. The skilled workers, facilities, tools, and communication equipment needed will depend on the service offered and whether the venture survives to a point where follow-up on its products is necessary.

- **Rate of modification** Some products and services become obsolete fast because they are fads, while others must be updated to keep pace with changes in technology and/or customers' preferences and competitors' actions. This may require flexibility in the venture's production and/or service. It may also require special equipment for engineering design and prototyping to create upgrades.

how choices about that should be expected to change over time. Laying out a PERT chart depicting steps and their timing for setting up operations of the various stages in production can be helpful and probably should also be included as part of the venture's business plan.

2. Make or buy

Whether to make or buy what the company will sell, as discussed earlier in connection with the profit chain, can be a major issue in setting up shop. Important considerations in making this choice will include:

- What the company should try to be best at ("sustainable competitive advantage").

- What quality of output is most likely to result, how adequate the timing of delivery will be.
- How much one versus the other will cost.
- How appropriate the delivery timing will be under either alternative.
- How much money will be required for investment under either alternative.

- How much flexibility there will be to change important elements such as timing, quantity, properties of the output including design, and suppliers.
- How much of the investment will be lost if results are not adequate.
- What the odds of success are.

Other questions include how well quality, output, and costs can be controlled over time, how easy it will be to communicate, how much clout the contact within each supplier will have, and possibly to what extent confidential aspects of the operation must be divulged. Given the large number of potential variables as well as sources, it may be helpful to create a matrix that lists alternative combinations of make versus buy across the top and criteria down the side and then apply weights to evaluate alternative choices. A similar approach may be helpful for selecting individual suppliers, as will be discussed later in the chapter on Operations.

Out-sourcing

Having someone else make the product or service while the venture does designing and selling only may allow lower initial investment, because then entrepreneur(s) will not have to buy as much in the way of equipment, rent as much space, pay the costs of installing machinery, and recruit or train people as much. It may also be faster and reduce the number of tasks that the founders must perform.

But buying from outside also means that the founders will have less control over methods of production and also over readjustments in quality standards. Effort will be required to find the best suppliers and to work out contracts describing exactly how much product should be delivered, by when, and to what specifications.

Production specifications

Every level in the value chain needs production specifications, for how a product or service is advertised, produced, delivered, serviced, and finished off. These specifications in turn must somehow lead to attainment of another set mentioned earlier, the performance specifications of the product or service. When different suppliers are used, the formulation and

enforcement of production specifications are likely to require special vigilance, especially on the part of a fledgling venture that may be short of both power and sophistication for the particular line of work.

When Janet Luhrs and Renee Williams started getting major orders for their "Babypack" (mother's pack for carrying a baby in the front), they found it would be most economical to produce it overseas. Through inquiries they identified a person who could connect them with suppliers in Asia. They sent a sample of their product to a Taiwanese supplier, who agreed to produce it. To receive the shipment, they first had to pay.

When the shipment arrived, they found that the product was fine in many ways, except the supplier had used cheaper materials than the two women had expected. At that point, however, they owned the shipment. On subsequent orders they were careful to specify more completely not only how it should be made, but also exactly what materials should be used.

Important as these specifications at the producing level are, the starting point where the customer makes the decision on whether or not to buy is probably more important, because that can set standards for specifications all the way back up the value chain.

For suppliers of a start-up, some payment is likely to be required in advance, possibly the whole amount of the production order. If the founders discover that changes in the product specifications are needed, these will have to be renegotiated, which will not only take time, but will probably increase costs and delay delivery. Working with the supplier may require the venture to divulge information it would prefer to keep secret. Moreover, the supplier will build into its charges a profit that will thereby be lost to the venture itself. The supplier may even become a competitor, as Warren Avis learned.

Our big mistake was to allow this other company to assemble all our parts and ship the product to our customers. We even spent a half million dollars teaching this company how to produce and distribute the product! As a result, they had access to our total business operation—and they made the most profitable use of it.

The upshot was that this subcontractor set up another company and began to put out a similar prod-

uct. We brought a patent suit against them. But we soon found that we couldn't win because of a technicality. … The whole thing was a disaster.[248]

Seeking suppliers overseas has become a major trend in recent times, with manufacturing in the United States declining markedly in recent years as a result. But for a start-up entrepreneur unfamiliar with how to deal with such suppliers, it can have many pitfalls, as illustrated by the following.

In mid-1985, two Canadians decided to collaborate on a product one had developed, a belt-like device with fabric pouches for carrying audio tape cassettes. How fast to move on it was a question. They wondered whether they should seek sales in the forthcoming Christmas season even though most stores had already done their advance ordering. The pair lacked both the resources and know-how to set up a production line, which they expected would take too much time to accomplish anyway.

Their options seemed to be either to drop the Christmas target or seek out a supplier willing to perform a rush order. Among suppliers, the alternatives were either domestic or foreign. Through personal contacts, one partner found a supplier in Hong Kong not only willing to do the work, but to do so at a fraction of the cost compared to domestic producers. A deal was struck.

Some Christmas sales were made, but not as many as hoped. The company survived, but not very profitably. A main benefit from this fast action, the two said, was learning that:

– Overseas cost savings are eroded by (1) travel costs to arrange the deal, (2) long distance phone costs to keep things moving, (3) air shipping costs to cope with late deliveries, and (4) correction costs of inability to oversee quality.

– Having to spend extra time on production subtracts time from marketing and reduces sales.

– Even with good contacts, effective control of production and quality at producers who are located far away is difficult and sometimes impossible.

– When a distant producer promises delivery immediately it may mean two weeks, and a promise of one month may mean six to seven weeks.

– Plants in Asia take Christmas orders in February and gear up their plants to deliver by August. Persuading them to reschedule for rush orders, even though they are willing to do small ones, costs extra.

The two concluded that this adventure, despite its problems and disappointments, had been worthwhile because now they had a business going, knew more about the market, were working on new ideas for expanding their product line and had improved both contacts and know-how for doing better next time. More advance thinking about possible problems and ways of mitigating them were precautions they would add.

In-sourcing

Producing in house also has its potential pitfalls, as will be further discussed in the chapter on Operations. To be able to produce at a competitive level of excellence usually requires practice and possibly training. Even with those things, there can be problems if the plant and equipment are new and somewhat unfamiliar, as occurred in the following venture.

In March 1973, three people, an experienced potter, an architect, and an investor, founded a company to make stoneware dinner plates. Equity of $42,000 plus loans of $16,000 from the founders was supplemented by an SBA guaranteed loan of $40,000. The founders signed a lease for plant space and ordered production equipment. The needed pug mill to prepare clay, RAM press to form it, and kiln to fire it arrived during July and August. Set-up and debugging of the equipment continued through the summer, and the first firing occurred in October. It produced samples for test marketing in local specialty shops, but not a production run.

Only 10 percent of the output was of adequate quality, and the remainder had flaws, which the company continued to struggle with month after month. Enough "firsts" were produced by December to create a display for the Los Angeles gift show in January, where responses to the line seemed favorable and $15,000 worth of orders were received. However, the company's pug mill seemed to be producing inadequate clay, and flaws were also showing up in the glazing process.

In-sourcing

[248] Warren Avis, *Take a Chance To Be First* (New York: Macmillan, 1986) p. 173.

By March the company was almost finished. It had not been able to deliver on orders, its capital was used up, the bank was demanding payment, and one of the founders wanted out. The many months of struggle with production problems finally began to produce better results, however, and failure was narrowly averted. By late 1975, the company was operating at a profit, though not a large one. Subsequently, however, it lost out to competitors and disappeared from the scene.

This great a delay in accomplishing high-quality production is hard to excuse when the technology is well established. The company's failing seems to have been in not obtaining adequate expertise, which it could certainly have bought with less cash than it took to grope through a self-education experience. While the problems are going on, however, that can be harder to see. Every day there is hope that the solution will soon be found. The last experiment was almost right but didn't work well enough.

3. Shop and equipment

Strategic power

What equipment is needed for setting up a venture obviously varies greatly depending on the type of business. A new dot-com can be started with a laptop computer and an Internet service provider link. A real estate office may need just furniture and phones. Technically, there need not even be an office, just an address in some form for customer money to come to, although that could be by electronic deposit. There will still be some red tape to deal with, such as filing tax forms and obtaining and renewing a business license, but not much more. So the set-up cost for some set-up alternatives can be low.

Examples of low-cost facilities include the fabled dining-room table that countless entrepreneurs have used for their initial working areas. More elaborate and costly facilities may be required for some types of ventures, such as development and production of a new drug or supercomputer. Between these extremes lie innumerable intermediate choices, whose adoption will depend on such factors as what resources are conveniently available, how much capital is required, and, most importantly, what the venture will seek to produce itself, versus outsource, in order to please customers.

A new bank requires lots of cash and paperwork, as well as modest furnishings for dealing with customers. Protection systems will probably require help from specialists to provide proper safe space, locks, and alarms. Security systems are also needed for doing classified government contracts.

A new in-house manufacturing company requires production equipment, tooling, shop space, appropriate wiring for machines, scrap disposal means, safety equipment, and possibly security alarms. Beyond that, equipment needs further depend on what type of manufacturing, whether a cement plant, an electronics shop, or a fish processor, each with its special kinks to be resolved to get ready for a workforce, which in turn will add another new host of details to be worked out. For foundry manufacturing in particular, there can be serious pollution control restrictions and equipment needs. Secret work requires security arrangements, and chip-making calls for clean rooms, all of which can be done well or badly, and may be overpriced for an inexperienced buyer.

Those details may be familiar to someone in the venture by virtue of experience in similar work. Otherwise, they will have to be discovered through engaging people on either a short- or long-term basis who do have such familiarity, or else through trial, error, and point-to-point treasure hunting.

Strategic power

If a manufacturing venture is on a frontier of innovation, the equipment and facilities may be central to strategic success, as illustrated by the agricultural processing business of Jack Simplot.

With profits from raising some "discarded" sheep and then pigs, Jack Simplot bought land, equipment, and animals to do his own farming in Idaho. Profits were hard enough to come by that he worked winters sorting potatoes for a local warehouse for more income. The tedium of this work sensitized him such that when he heard mention that someone in a nearby town was building an electrically operated machine to sort them, he recruited a partner to join him in buying one.

The two men subsequently fell out over the issue of whether to use it only for their own potatoes or to serve other farmers with it, thereby incurring the wrath of some workers whom it displaced and some farmers who were not included among the number it could service. Simplot solved the argument by proposing the decision be made by a coin toss, which he won. With that start he began building more warehouses and sorting equipment. By 1940, 13 years after he heard about the first sorting machine, he was employing 1,000 people at thirty potato and onion warehouses whose sorting machines at three each were processing 10,000 boxcars of produce per year.

His next big facilities investment was for onion-drying equipment. He had been selling cull onions to an exporter in Berkeley, California who had run up an $8,400 bill without paying. To learn what was going on and collect the bill, Simplot drove to the exporter's office. When the middleman showed up, Simplot asked for the money he was owed. The man agreed, but when asked where the dehydrating was done, dodged the question. Simplot left, but also followed one of the man's trucks that happened to be pulling out. When that truck arrived at the processing plant, he entered and asked where the drying equipment was produced. He then drove to the equipment producer and ordered six tunnel dryers for making powder and flakes.

He then spent months looking for a site with suitable transportation connections and where the smell would be allowed. When the new plant finally swung into operation, many things changed. The smell was welcomed by onion growers, who now started making good money on cull onions they formerly discarded. Simplot's profits from the plant quickly rose to $50,000 per month.

He next started working on ways to dehydrate potatoes to reduce both spoilage and shipping weight. A grievous problem, how to remove the peels, was finally solved when he came up with the idea of first boiling the potatoes and then blasting the skin off with high-pressure water spray.

His market for dehydrated products expanded tremendously with the onset of World War II and need by the U.S. armed services for easily transportable food supplies. He worked frantically to expand against obstacles such as obtaining raw material and supplies such as cardboard boxes, setting up new plants, getting rid of waste peelings, and expanding the workforce.

After the war he looked for other processes. One of his chemists suggested they experiment with freezing the potatoes, and despite prior attempts showing that turned them to mush, they found that by first cooking the potatoes and then squeezing out the right amount of water, they could be turned into frozen French fries. There were still problems with grease going rancid, but eventually these were overcome, and finally frozen fries made it to supermarket shelves where sales took off.

Then he urged McDonald's, one of his customers for fresh potatoes, to try the frozen fries. At first there was major resistance, rooted in the belief that the present fries were the chain's most successful appeal. But Simplot managed to sell the idea of experimentation in a few stores, and soon the results made his case. His sales of frozen fries rose from two million pounds in 1951 to a billion pounds in 1980.[249]

In addition to illustrating the crucial role that facilities, processes they permit, and location can play in the development of a venture, the experience of Jack Simplot shows that letting them be seen can sometimes be crucially helpful to a competitor, that being where he got some of his most important tips for success.

In the next example, the role of plant and equipment did not lead to such a major enterprise, but it had the effect on a small one of directing the entrepreneur from one line of work into another completely different.

The Portland, Oregon operator of a photography studio inherited some welding equipment from a relative. Although he had no experience with such equipment, he did have a college degree in fine arts and an interest in artistic creation. He began trying to weld, then to experiment as his skill increased. For his own satisfaction he began welding decorative pieces, then furniture. He placed some of it in his photo studio; a high-backed chair, coffee table, stool. With his photo skills and experience he prepared a sales

---

[249] George Gilder, *The Spirit of Enterprise* (New York: Simon and Schuster, 1984) p. 40.

brochure. Then extending some selling experience he had obtained in the insurance business before going to art school, he called on an interior decorator and got an order for furnishings. Further sales came from more cold calls and mail advertising. Eventually, he closed the photo studio, moved his manufacturing facilities to a small town near the beach and continued his successful furniture manufacturing business.[250]

Creation of a ski-manufacturing company that became the world's leader was similarly guided by manufacturing know-how and equipment.

Bill Kirschner and his father operated a small company selling medical equipment to veterinarians from Vashon Island in the Puget Sound of Washington State. Bill liked to ski, and when his skis wore out, he worried about how to replace them. The business produced a skimpy income and they had searched for ways to build it larger. One attempt had involved a contract with the University of Washington's medical research program to manufacture rat cages with rounded corners that would render them easier to clean. The Kirschners had, after trying various fabrication approaches, settled on use of molded fiberglas for making the cages.

Now, worrying about how to cope with the cost of buying new wooden skis, Kirschner thought he would try using some of the fiberglas materials and skills he had acquired on the hospital contract. The result was a successful pair of skis that led to creation of the K2 ski company, which during the '50s and '60s became the world's leading producer of skis.

Costs

Often the role of plant and equipment is routine, as when a dry cleaner buys washers, a printer buys presses, a travel agent buys only office furniture and computers, or a retail store buys shelving and a cash register. But equipment for the seemingly simple business may still be expensive, as illustrated by the following food business.

Two Seattle men, having become tired of working in the computer industry, decided to go into some sort of food business instead. After considering several possibilities, they settled on the idea of producing bagels. To set up shop, one partner called a friend at Starbucks to learn how food-

manufacturing equipment could be obtained. This yielded a list of food equipment dealers, from whom he began to learn about prices for equipment and maintenance costs. Eventually, he settled on a San Francisco equipment distributor whose 10-page quote included description of an 18-step manufacturing process and a list of equipment totaling $1,171,770, not including installation and set-up to produce bagels.

Cheaper and easier, perhaps, would have been ordinary cooking and serving equipment such as might be used for ice cream scooping or making hamburgers. But there would still be need for proper refrigeration and sanitary equipment to meet health code requirements and inspections.

Ben Cohen and Jerry Greenfield thought they would start a shop that would produce and deliver fresh bagels, lox, and cream cheese each morning and be called UBS, for United Bagel Service. But when they visited a restaurant supply house and saw the cost of equipment for making them, they decided to pursue their second choice, ice cream, instead.

To prepare for that, they took a course in making ice cream. Ben took a couple of jobs, first as a baker's assistant, from which he was fired for ruining a batch of rolls with too much salt and making a mess of separating egg yolks, and then in a diner, where he was fired for complaining about lighting in the kitchen.

They sought out used equipment for the venture by visiting auctions, where in his enthusiasm, Ben sometimes bid against himself. (Along the way on one trip, Ben invested $2,000, half the $4,000 he needed for his half in capitalizing the business but had not yet fully saved up, to buy a sailboat and trailer.)[251]

Setting up for a high technology business, even if not as massive as Micron Technology, can be enormously expensive. Brian Golson recalled setting up facilities for Everdream, a start-up to provide microcomputer system support for small businesses.

There are a lot of up-front fixed costs in a business like this. We spent $400,000 last month to build a server room. Some companies outsource this function, but we felt it was necessary to do this ourselves in order to guarantee that our many systems were integrated effectively. Also, building a call center is very expensive; for example, we spent $800,000 on

---

[250] Personal communication.
[251] Fred "Chico" Lager, *Ben & Jerry's: The Inside Scoop* (New York: Crown Publishing, 1994) p. 13.

the implementation of Siebel CRM (customer relationship management—which might give quick access to all customer information, such as service history and past purchases) software.[252]

It was earlier suggested that to minimize start-up cash needs it might be well to lease, not buy; build, not buy; or buy used, not new, in order to save money on equipment. There is no general choice, but at least such alternatives can be considered before making commitments.

Earl Tupper was able to borrow rather than build the facilities he needed for development of new plastic products, at least during the development stage.

> In 1937 Tupper got a job as a sample maker for DuPont in The Doyle Works, a Leominster, Massachusetts manufacturing company that he had learned about from a contact who had lent him shop space for working on his inventions. Doyle agreed to give Tupper a 10 percent commission on any idea he conceived that made or saved them money and also sent him to local trade fares to keep up on new products.
>
> On his own time after doing the sample-making work for DuPont, Tupper worked on inventions of his own like toothpaste and shaving cream dispensers with self-closing caps that he thought he could patent. Informally, Doyle agreed to do the production work if they could profit by it. Baby rattles, Japanese comb designs, novel belt buckles, eyebrow dye shields, egg peeling clamps, flour sifters, and dish draining rack designs came from his observations and mind. He ordered stationery in 1937 that identified him as "Industrial Inventor/Designer."
>
> He traveled to fairs, sought out new plastic products and reported them to Doyle as well as DuPont, which was trying to build a good name in consumer products, in part to put behind its record of profiteering during World War I (when its profits increased twelvefold). He also window-shopped, talked to retail clerks, and enlisted his wife and other relatives in looking for product ideas and in testing them. In 1939 he formed the Earl S. Tupper Company to market some of his items. By 1940 items included among his line were a combination nail file and comb disguised as a fountain pen for men to wear in a top pocket and a Lucite illuminated tongue depressor manufactured by a competitor. His first polyethylene container was

developed in 1942. Stackable containers followed, and in 1949 came design of the seal for an airtight top lid, along with a catalog of 22 standardized products.[253]

Safety

On installing equipment there may be choices between doing it personally and hiring professionals. The latter cost more but save time and may do the job better. The following experience of a day care center illustrates how problems can cascade if power wiring is not done correctly:

> A short in the wiring started a fire that ruined $54,000 worth of the day care center's equipment, including refrigerators, microwave ovens, television, video recorder, toys, furniture, books, and rugs. Fortunately, nobody was hurt and insurance covered replacement of these items. But business had to stop immediately and customers took their children elsewhere. Until the insurance could be collected, there was no income, and rent payments were draining away the owners' capital.

It turned out in this case that the day care owners were able to persuade the landlord to let them delay, although not discontinue, rent payments. They then implored local community service agencies for donations to help recovery. Customers were asked to return when rebuilding was accomplished, and enough of them did to allow restart of the business.

These examples only touch for illustrative purposes upon a few specks in the galaxy of possible tasks and problems to be dealt with. Each new start-up has to amass and install its own production plant individually. Projective thinking—creating scenarios and imagining what might benefit from advance remedies—can be a helpful thought mode in making facilities and equipment decisions. How will the shop be laid out? Where are bottlenecks most likely to arise? If the company grows, where will the bind first be felt? What chain of calamities could follow from a breakdown? At what points along a growth curve should the next expansion problem be foreseen and from what clues? How far ahead should action be taken to forestall such problems?

---

252 Christine Darwell, *Everdream* (Boston: Harvard Business School Publishing, 2000) p. 3.
253 Alison J. Clarke, *Tupperware* (Washington, DC: Smithsonian Institution, 1999) p. 26.

4. Location

What matters about location depends on the type of business. For one where walk-in customers are important, different things matter than for another that operates entirely over the Web. Some start-ups need space that is high priced. For others low rent should be a goal.

There is generally some evident logic to the location of new ventures. For raw materials like coal, steel, and oil it was proximity to the resource. Oil later shifted from location near sources to location near markets and transportation, as did the beef industry. For movies, the start was in the New York area, where there was high population density and available theaters. It was also near where Edison, building upon precedents in Europe, was advancing moviemaking technology. But the final concentration in Hollywood sprang from a different rationale—scenery.

> Moviemaking technology had spread from Europe to the United States, where in New York vaudeville theaters began using "flickers" to shoo patrons out, also calling the primitive movies "chasers." Then movies started becoming main attractions. Former furriers Marcus Loew and Adolph Zukor, cloth wholesaler William Fox and the Warner brothers, sons of an immigrant cobbler, all pooled their resources to buy a used movie projector and open a theater. Louis B. Mayer, a scrap dealer employee, picked up a lease on a theater and started building a chain of them.[254]
>
> Sam Goldfish, later Goldwyn, a Manhattan glove salesman, noticed how the new theaters were prospering as crowds grew and considered starting one. But, thinking it would take less capital, decided to try producing movies instead of showing them.
>
> He campaigned with several others to join him in a venture that would make better movies, not just the short chasers, but multi-reel features of more substance. The first was his brother-in-law and vaudeville performer, Jesse Lasky, who happened to have lost $100,000 on an unsuccessful play and counter-proposed that they seek to gain control of a concession in New York for tamales, a food new to the area with which

Lasky was familiar from his home in San Jose, California. Goldfish countered with the idea of calling the company the Jesse L. Lasky Feature Play Company, saying "that sounds better than 'Lasky's Hot Tamales,' doesn't it?" Lasky agreed to head the company, though he would continue working in vaudeville.

> For a director Goldfish approached D.W. Griffith, who was starting to make innovative movies but declined, and then Cecil Blount DeMille, a stage-play writer and director with a theatrical family. DeMille wanted a change from Broadway and agreed to join as director. Visiting Thomas Edison he obtained permission to see how movies were made. To DeMille it looked like improving dramatics of the filming process would be simple.
>
> For $4,000, the new company picked up rights to a hit stage play on Broadway, The Squaw Man, a love story western, figuring it could be filmed outdoors to save cash, and even against the stigma actors associated with movies, they recruited successfully by offering shares in the business.
>
> The location at first was to be New Jersey, where the one-reel chasers were shot. But established producers were known to employ goons there for busting up attempts to start up in competition. So the site was changed, a technical advisor and a cameraman were hired, and the producing group boarded a train for Flagstaff, Arizona. Goldwyn and Lasky, the organizers and financers, stayed behind.
>
> Arriving in Flagstaff, with some 20 pages of penciled script ready for typing and rehearsal, the group was disappointed to see no scenery, only dull flatlands. Immediately, they re-boarded the train, on which they stayed until they reached Los Angeles. DeMille sent a telegram to Lasky in New York that read, "Flagstaff no good for our purpose. Have proceeded to California. Want authority to rent barn in place called Hollywood for $75 a month. Regards to Sam."[255]

Alternatives

A natural initial goal for most start-ups is to reach first for low cost if possible, because that way, less is lost if the venture fails. Sometimes that is possible, sometimes not.

---

[254] Neal Gabler, *An Empire of Their Own* (New York: Crown Publishers, 1988).

[255] A. Scott Berg, *Goldwyn* (New York: Ballantine Books, 1989) p. 39.

Home office

The first site for many start-ups is home. Hewlett and Packard's choice of a garage was not too far off the typical mark, although with microcomputers the site is more likely to be inside the home, or as in the case of Sandra Kurtzig's Ask Computer, a spare bedroom in the apartment.

Even in the case of *Inc.* magazine's 1998 fastest-growing firms, 54 percent were begun in the founder's home.[256] Coincidentally, in that year, 36 percent of the total were computer-related and another 21 percent offered business services, both types of work not calling for massive plant facilities, even when in full operation. Home location is, of course, a natural choice for many Web-based businesses. If the company operates virtually, contracting out the delivery of everything it makes and/or sells, it may even be able to be based in a laptop computer, going wherever its owner wants to operate for any length of time.

With growth, however, most ventures need commercial sites; this brings other choices into play. Easiest may be to take the first location found vacant, or to pick one close to home so as to reduce commuting time. The lowest rent or best purchase terms may appeal. But these may be the wrong site-selection criteria for a particular business. Alternative types of sites in general include the following.

Downtown and business districts

Traditional downtowns range widely in size and activity. Office workers provide one type of steady clientele. Other inhabitants of the local area may come to shop or for entertainment. Depending on the town there may be tourists. Not to be forgotten as potential locations are older buildings where space may be cheaper for businesses that don't depend on walk-in traffic. Also easy to overlook may be second floor sites that are easy enough to reach from the sidewalk and possibly even basements. Most likely a problem will be parking, for which there may be some compensation in public transit. After-hours crime may be a problem.

Shopping centers

Successful shopping centers draw large amounts of traffic, beginning with such anchor stores as supermarkets and large drug stores, and hence can greatly help sales in retailing and food ventures. But rent in them is correspondingly high. In addition, there are typically fees for common maintenance, mall advertising, and other purposes.

A few centers are unsuccessful in drawing a critical mass of retailers, in which case space in them may be available at very low cost, including convenient parking, for businesses that don't need high traffic nearby, such as wholesalers, warehousing, antique stores, or appliance repair shops.

Neighborhood centers and strip malls

Building and operating establishments like these can be a lucrative form of small business in itself. Strip malls generally lack large anchor stores and are dependent on having specialized draw for particular businesses, such as exercise equipment, dry cleaners, or vacuum cleaner repair that people will plan a trip to reach. Because traffic is fairly low, parking is usually not a problem.

Countryside

The lowest territory in cost and overhead may be raw or farm land. Wal-Mart's rise began on such property, with Sam Walton scanning the territory from his own airplane. An attractive feature of such locations is that in time they tend to become more urban, with corresponding increase in value of the land in and around them, which can be a reason to buy nearby rather than rent in such a site.

Manufacturing districts

Manufacturing districts usually are well suited to their purpose. Zoning restrictions are likely to be fairly open, though a company that pollutes will be required to clean up what it emits. Truck and possibly rail access is likely to be easy, as is parking. Foot traffic will be close to zero, and the only firms that sell to local customers may be small restaurants catering to workers and truckers. For cheap space in which to develop, test, or make things, an alternative

---

[256] "Overview Almanac," *Inc.* 500, October 20, 1998 p. 18.

Dependence on business type

for a start-up to look for may be unused space in some shop that happens to be working below capacity or have extra space that it has not yet grown to fill. Borrowing or renting shop equipment at low cost during off hours may also be possible.

Industrial parks

In more recent decades some industrial districts have been designed and developed specifically to accommodate desired types of companies, such as those in high technology. Generally, they are more attractive and rationally laid out than old industrial districts. But they also tend to have higher rent.

Incubators

Small industrial areas of buildings that may house auto repair, woodworking, and other small manufacturing and industrial service firms are sometimes referred to as *incubators*.

Incubator sites are also set up by some universities and local governments specifically to cultivate start-ups. Some provide cheap rent for a year or two. Many provide ancillary services such as copying, phone answering, secretarial, and possibly accounting and legal help. If the incubator is affiliated with a university, it may also provide access to use of laboratory facilities and to help from faculty and students. Association with other entrepreneurs using the incubator may provide useful contacts as well as moral support and mutual problem solving.

The number of incubators, according to the National Business Incubation Association, grew from 55 in 1984 to nearly 400 by 1990,[257] more than 100 of which were linked by electronic mail.[258] The largest fraction of incubators (39 percent) are those affiliated with local government agencies and development agencies. Next (17 percent) are those of universities, followed by centers run for profit (14 percent), according to the above association.[259]

As an indication of performance, one incubator in Chicago, begun with a $1.7 million federal grant, was able to report after nine years of operation that it had served 142 companies

with such things as cheap rent, shared services and space, business plan help, group consulting, and eventually low-cost loans. Only 16 percent of the clients had failed. One who had grown to 17 employees commented, "It's a shame not all start-ups have this kind of assistance."[260] At the same time as noted earlier, however, assistance often has a price and its value must be weighed against that.

Mobile facilities

Some garage mechanics will fix cars anywhere, coming to the site in a van, as do plumbers and other home repair service people. Semi-mobile are fairs, which some businesses such as handicraft manufacturers follow from site to site.

Dependence on business type

Law firms retained by major corporations or wealthy clients are typically ensconced in high-priced downtown suites with expensive furnishings, spacious conference rooms, and up-to-date office equipment. Job machine shops may contain high-technology numerically controlled machine tools, but most are located in grimy industrial districts with old and/or cheap furniture in the entry office, giveaway calendars on the wall, and no furnished waiting room. Both types of premises probably fit equally well the firms they serve. More economy in the law firm office arguably would lose it the kind of customers it wants, and more elegance in the job shop would simply increase expenses without expanding sales, and therefore hurt profits.

Appearance can be crucial to some businesses. To a retail store, display windows, types of neighboring firms, lighting, fixtures, wall textures, and cleanliness matter. In food service, it may be important to fit the style of decoration to the menu, whether elegant, thematic, or designed to encourage quick eating and departure. Such choices as furniture, floor covering, and background music (including type and volume) can affect how much money goes into the cash register.

[257] Leslie Brokaw, "New Businesses," *Inc.*, May 1990, p. 25.
[258] Martha E. Mangelsdorf, "Hotline," *Inc.*, July 1990, p. 27.
[259] Leslie Brokaw, "New Businesses," *Inc.*, August 1990, p. 21.
[260] Martha E. Mangelsdorf, "*Inc.*'s Guide to 252 'Smart' Government Money," *Inc.*, August 1990, p. 60.

Remote-serving

The history of ventures that serve customers from remote sites goes back as far as foreign trade, when the customer might ask an emissary to convey an order to be brought back by caravan or ship. In the modern age, mail order began with advertisements for everything from plows to brides offered to settlers on the frontier. Sears & Roebuck built a retail catalog empire by serving farmers. Telephone sales of products advertised in catalogs and other media were boosted as credit cards came into vogue, allowing people to order directly and more conveniently by phone. Ironically, Sears closed out its catalog business just as smaller catalog companies, such as L.L. Bean and The Sharper Image were growing through telephone sales service to narrower, more specialized markets. That closeout concluded just before use of the Internet came to life as a burgeoning competitor to all the catalogs. It may be instructive in hindsight to speculate about how Sears could have won rather than lost to start-ups, in this evolution of the remote-serving industry from mail order to Web order.

Where best to locate a Web-related company is an open question. Amazon.com was attracted from the East Coast to Seattle by several factors. One was the presence of a large software workforce. A second wasabsense of a state income tax. Third the fact although that although residents of the state would have to pay sales tax on purchases from the company, the population of the state was relatively small compared to other states where sales tax would not apply. Good communication infrastructure and attractive living conditions probably also were influential.

Most dot-com companies probably start where their founders happen to be.

Service

As illustrated above by law firms and machine shops, what matters about the location depends heavily on the type of business. Aircraft maintenance companies typically operate near runways. Boat yards, on the other hand, may or may not be on waterfront, because waterfront property is often expensive and most boats are easy to haul around by trailer.

A service company for which location was the key to starting is Avis Rent-A Car:

> Warren Avis was frustrated as a combat pilot in World War II when he arrived at airports and could not get good ground transportation. It was expensive to pay cab fare for a ride to town to rent a car from Hertz. Better, he thought, would be to be able to rent a car at the airport.

> As the first to set up car rental agencies at airports, Avis had to decide at which ones to locate the initial operations. He recalled, "My targets with the car-rental concept were first the Detroit Willow Run airport, and then, Miami. I chose the Detroit airport because I lived there for many years and knew the area like the back of my hand. Miami was also a natural because it was the hottest car-rental community in the world at the time … Our growth exploded like dynamite."

> Avis introduced the first use of credit cards in car rental, brochures that became forerunners of airline magazines, renting only cars that were new and fresh, employing women to staff rental counters, running cooperative magazine advertisements with airlines, and persuading airlines to let their reservation services be used for renting Avis cars as well.

> Meanwhile, Hertz remained on the sidelines, believing Avis would fail. Avis continued, "Then after about three years, when we had proved that the system would work, Hertz made their move. They jumped in and began to copy everything that we had pioneered."[261]

For auto lubrication service in particular Steve Spinelli, the founder of Jiffy Lube, said the main factors to consider in location were

- Zoning.
- Cost.
- Ingress/egress.
- Population density.
- Traffic level and pattern.
- Visibility.[262]

How to measure each and reach judgments about the combinations that exist then becomes a matter of both analysis and experience.

Walk-in retailing

For walk-in retail stores, eating places, and some kinds of services, such as shoe repair, location is a crucial variable. Such factors as foot

---

[261] Avis, *Take a Chance*, pp. 14-16.
[262] Steve Spinelli, "Franchising," in *The Portable MBA in Entrepreneurship*, ed. William D. Bygrave (New York: Wiley, 1997) p. 363.

traffic density, visibility, convenience to walk in, safety, and parking as well as proximity to other non-competing attractions are all potentially important. Observing the traffic and purchases at nearby stores can help with assessment.

To make intelligent guesses about whether sales volume will cover costs and generate a profit, the following must be weighed against the rent level per frontage foot or per internal square foot:

- Target customer profiles.
- Number of potential customer types within a certain radius.
- Availability of parking.
- Level of foot traffic.
- Kinds of other stores in the vicinity.
- Regulations about permissible signs.

Examples of what can go wrong in locating at sites that at first glance might seem quite acceptable have been noted by Luigi Salvaneschi, a former executive with several retail chains, including McDonalds, KFC, and Blockbuster Video.[263]

In **New York City**, people did not like ketchup on their hamburgers, and in Dallas, people wanted fresh lettuce and tomatoes on their sandwiches.

In **Tifton**, **Georgia**, Blockbuster tried to open a store near the headquarters of a local video chain, but was driven out by intense local loyalty.

In **Louisville**, **Kentucky**, the home of KFC, any would-be new competitor is targeted for a devastating marketing counterattack.

In **St. Etienne**, **France**, a location on the main commercial street in front of a major tramway exchange, McDonald's attributed disappointing sales to the fact that the local population was blue-collar, unionized, politically red, and anti-American.

In **Rotterdam**, **Netherlands**, McDonald's found a cluster of high-rise residential buildings that housed a population of 80,000 people, yet there was no local restaurant. Religious convictions of the residents encouraged family meals at home.

Most of these considerations lend themselves to objective analysis; weighing their importance requires subjective judgment. Advice from other people experienced in similar lines of business may be helpful in making such choices, but only if it is heeded.

When Donald Hauck decided to open a small department store in Montevideo, Minnesota, the first site he chose, which was in the middle of the business district, was "too expensive, we thought." He ignored another retailer who said "Don't be afraid of the rent. If you find the right spot, the rent will take care of itself."

Instead, Hauck took the recommendation of a banker who offered enough credit to open the new store in a building Montgomery Ward had vacated. "That alone should have told us something." Hauck recalled. It was located not centrally but rather "about 40 feet too far north" and had no similar stores near it. But the rent was cheap.

A variety of attempts to attract customers with advertising, promotions, sales, changes in decor and even changes in line failed, and Hauck eventually closed the store. But he drew upon this experience in setting up his next store, a bridal shop. This time he chose a site directly across from a major shopping center with a huge lighted sign. "Almost half our customers find us because of that sign," Hauck observed. "I'll never again make the mistake of being 40 feet too far north."[264]

The possibility of such a degree of mislocation, just 40 feet, puts a fine point on what may be called for in an overall location analysis. Aspects of the broader population makeup within striking distance of the store include age levels, gender, income levels, sex, marital status, how many people per household, and ethnic background. U.S. census bureau data provide some of these data by four-digit numbered census tracts. More details can be obtained from other sources such as metropolitan newspaper offices, chambers of commerce, and other studies done by economic development agencies or private firms. A listing of companies and market research magazines, including Web sites, that offer such data has been published by Salvaneschi.[265]

---

[263] Luigi Salvaneschi, *Location, Location, Location* (Grants Pass: Oasis Press, 1996) p. 18.

[264] Donald Hauck, "Location, Location, Location!," *Venture*, April 1987, p. 100.

[265] Salvaneschi, *Location*, Appendices A and B.

Who will come to the store does matter. A check of license plates in local parking areas may reveal that some people have come from long distances. Possibly, they will even be attracted from long distances by the new venture, as has been the case with large new shopping malls and discount stores. The kinds of cars, who gets out of them, and what stores already in the area they visit and buy from can also be useful clues about what type of new venture in the area they might patronize. A look at cash register lines and amounts rung up can add still further clues, and beyond that there is, of course, the possibility of asking the customers and perhaps employees of other local stores some questions.

Sometimes even competition is helpful. Fast-food outlets attract fast food customers, who may patronize different outlets on different days for variety. So locating yet another fast-food establishment nearby to serve such customers may be effective. But there is also danger that enough others may think the same way as to over-saturate the area.

> McDonald's found that one of its stores had the highest sales in the Midwest, not just because the owner had enlarged the parking lot and the store, but because there was no other such store within a 30-mile radius.

> —•—

> A franchisee in Pittsburgh had 18 stores with excellent sales. Closer analysis indicated that the area could support as many as 40. Progressively more were added successfully until there were 56.[266]

There are at least two significant implications of these last examples. One is that excellent sales can come from having the only store of a particular kind in a large territory. The other is that discovery of that fact can bring in more such enterprises until saturation of the market area is reached.

Manufacturing

In a manufacturing business, location requirements would be different from those for a consumer-oriented retail or service establishment. Considerations of importance for manufacturing might include some of the same factors as for auto lubrication, such as zoning, cost, and accessibility. But it could also bring others into play such as safety, access to needed suppliers and ancillary services, availability of appropriately skilled workers, availability of rail connections, insurance costs, local tax and red tape requirements, and room to expand.

What operations are done in-house also matters. If the product is software, code writing can be done any place that programmers with the needed skills can be found. Moreover, the other functions of the business such as management, advertising, duplication, packaging, shipping, and paperwork can all be handled at other sites. There are suppliers who do nothing but replicate copies. Others offer fulfillment, which is to say storing inventory, packing, shipping, and receipt of returns, all for a price. Location of the headquarters then can be wherever the owners want it.

Two graduates of the Wharton Business School in 1999 started a company to produce and sell computer mice one of them had designed in the shape of a golf club driver head. Manufacturing they contracted out while they worked on building sales through such channels as Brookstone stores, country clubs, gift shops, and the Net. For the first year they headquartered the company in their two-bedroom apartment. Then they moved to a converted shed measuring 6 by 30 feet, into which they crammed two desks and three file cabinets. "It's not much," one commented, "but it's relatively inexpensive, has phone and network connections and it's conveniently located two doors down from our former strategic boardroom: Starbucks."[267]

Richard Branson's problem in producing a magazine was to find a place at low cost that would fall within the zoning requirements. After having his company evicted for trying to operate in an apartment against the rules, he recalled finding another site.

> *We scoured the neighborhood looking for somewhere to rent. The best deal, no rent at all, was offered by the Reverend Cuthbert Scott. He*

---

[266] Salvaneschi, *Location*, p. 176.
[267] Timothy Archibald, "Two Guys and a Start-up," *Inc.*, February 2001, p. 77.

liked the work of the Advisory Centre and offered us the use of the crypt at Saint John's Church, just off Bayswater Road, for no rent. I put an old slab of marble across two tombs to make my desk, and everyone found themselves somewhere to sit. We even charmed the local post office engineer to connect our phone without having to wait the normal three months. After a while none of us noticed that we were working in the dim light of the crypt surrounded by marble effigies and tombs.[268]

Here it seems initial location conditions did not matter. But that could change with time and require moving, in which case moving costs should be anticipated. High technology companies sometimes shift location at great expense get closer to a larger technical workforce or to reside in more attractive geographic areas. The workforce of Mosaic moved from Illinois to the San Francisco Bay Area. Sierra Online moved from the Bay Area to Seattle. And Gateway Computer moved from the Midwest to San Diego, for such reasons. Later, in 2004, Gateway acquired E-Machines, another microcomputer company, and moved 77 miles north to Orange County where E-Machines was located and more space was available for expansion.

Wholesaling

In the next example, a wholesaler, it was more the nature of the building than where it was located that became decisive.

When a frozen-food distributor vacated a cold-storage building and moved to a larger one in another part of town, a young man who had been renting a small space in the building to store tree seeds, which he harvested as a part-time job, thought he saw a good opportunity to set up his own cold-storage business. The plant was over 50 years old but in good working order, and the rent seemed to him very low. Without much thought he signed a lease.

He then went looking for clients to fill the space but learned that many wanted not just storage space but also services such as processing and packaging in addition to receiving, storage, and shipping. He found himself short on both experience and equipment for these. There was no "sharp freeze" capability. The layout included four floors, a very slow elevator, and small rooms with many corridors and doors to be navigated, all of which made work slow. The elevator capacity was so limited that each floor needed its own forklift. Low ceilings, small rooms, wooden floors, and limited ventilation made the building unsuited to processing lines. Both the loading dock and the approach alley were inadequate to the traffic.

Negative cash flows resulted and prompted him to seek partners. Eventually, he persuaded one to join him in financing legal action to break the lease, move to another plant, and begin the business over again—this time he'd do it right, but no longer as sole owner.

This entrepreneur knew from experience bought at a high price what to look for the next time. Had he done more investigation into what factors were important for a cold-storage location to work well, he might have fared better the first time.

Site investigation should include not just whether a location is suitable at present, but also whether or not it is likely to remain so. For instance, zoning restrictions could be all right today, but change tomorrow. If they did change, perhaps a business not within those new rules would be given an exemption to continue under some sort of grandfather provision. But if later it needed to expand, the exemption might not apply and the firm might be forced to move. A few further considerations, illustrating how finer distinctions can arise, are listed in Appendix 6b-3.

Investigation

Because location can be so powerful in determining performance for a retail store, investigation that may cost much time and effort, and even after that, abandoning the effort on any given site may be warranted. Personal visits to the area to become familiar with it can be used to become acquainted with the other stores of the area and the type of people who run them as well as those who buy from them. Learning the history of the area can reveal what moves it forward or pulls it back and which way it seems to be headed in the future. How high and consistent rents are and how they have been changing may be a clue.

---

[268] Richard Branson, *Losing My Virginity* (New York: Random House, 1998) p. 52.

Walking around, driving past, and even fly-ing over an area each should reveal different features that matter. Do people move past the site or stop short? Do they stop at nearby sites, or just ones farther away? Is the site relatively visible, or does it tend to be overshadowed by others in the area? Are the parking spots used by different visitors, or mostly tied up by the same cars whose owners just periodically feed the meters? How long does it take to traverse the area, and do people window shop on the way or just rush past? Each site will be differ-ent, and they all should be subjected to a pro-cess of compare, compare, compare.

Local government agencies may have other important information about such things as:

- Zoning laws and building codes and how they may be changing.
- Street changes, new parking areas, stop signs, alternate routes being opened.
- Building permits for structures that may change the area.
- Plans in the works for new parks, low-cost housing, or government buildings.
- Urban renewal projects that may disrupt traf-fic temporarily or permanently.
- Public utility district plans.
- Environmental clean-up disputes or projects coming up.
- Possible condemnation or takeover of private property in the area by the government.

Other private parties who can be helpful include commercial real estate agents, local bankers, and the chamber of commerce, as well as the phone company, cable TV companies, and Internet service providers of the locality. If part of the venture plan depends upon mak-ing changes in rules, whether public or private, pertaining to the site, then inquiry about how such things are accomplished in that particular area is called for.

Finally, hiring one or more professional pri-vate inspectors may be appropriate to check out aspects such as structural adequacy, compliance with building codes, environmental hazards, or possible pests that must be dealt with.

Maps should be developed that show in topographical form (sometimes as amoebic-shapes) the makeup of the surrounding popu-lation, competition, and expected densities of customers in relation to how far they are from the site. Others should show the roadways and traffic flow patterns of the site and surrounding areas. Where are the big attractions, such as su-permarkets that will pull people to the vicinity? What and where are the attractions that may pull people toward, past, or away from the site of interest? Where are there barriers, such as un-crossable streets, canals, or blight zones that can cut off traffic flow? How long does it take to get from one part of the territory to another at relevant times of the day? What parts of the territory may be underserved and so draw at-tractions in the future? Where have interviews been conducted? These can be marked on the maps with coloring or other coding that indi-cates the nature of the findings.

Notwithstanding the many actions that can be taken to get location right, it alone is not necessarily enough.

> When Ben and Jerry finally decided their ven-ture would be an ice cream scoop shop they reasoned that a good type of location would be a college town with no other homemade ice cream parlor. They chose Saratoga Springs, New York, which had Skidmore College, a race track and many summer tourists. There they spent several months saving money, scouting equip-ment, and laying plans. But to their dismay an-other home made ice cream shop opened in town, dashing their plans.
>
> Looking for a new site they settled on South Burlington, Vermont, near the University of Ver-mont with its 12,000 students, plus three other smaller colleges. The town population was only 40,000, but another 60,000 lived within a 10-mile radius. The only competitors were a coffee shop at the bus station and a pinball arcade that sold a commercial brand of ice cream. Vermont was the only state with no Baskin-Robbins store. The only drawback seemed to be a relatively large amount of cold weather. To cope with that, they decided to add crêpes and soups and call the business, after considering alternatives, includ-ing Josephine's Flying Machine, Ben and Jerry's.
>
> They wanted to rent a long-vacant drug store that had a soda fountain with a marble counter top and a row of chrome-based stools, but it was tied up in probate legalities. So they chose a for-

mer gas station one block from the retail center of town that had most recently served as a plant store and farmers market. They picked up equipment from an auction, hired help for plumbing, offering to pay with "free ice cream for life" instead of cash, and did other fix-up work themselves. They had no plans to grow beyond one outlet.

Sales began on May 5, 1978 and averaged $650 per day through the summer, but yielded no profits. Variations were tried, such as different menus and piano music as the two partners performed all chores themselves and supplemented their diets with crêpes and sundaes left behind by customers.

Despite experiments with various promotions, ranging from "Lick It" bumper stickers to fairs and free movies in the street, that produced sales double their projections of $90,000 in the first year, the company failed to earn a profit. A move into wholesaling ice cream to restaurants in response to requests from a few of them in-

creased sales further, but also left the venture still below breakeven. A new production plant was added in a bobbin mill a few blocks from the scoop shop. New equipment included a better freezer and a bigger truck with its own refrigerator. Two seasonal scoop stands were added, but proved failures—the losses continued.

What changed the company fortunes most was hiring a plant manager and then shifting away from the practice of selling large tubs of ice cream to restaurants. Instead, they started selling smaller pint containers to grocery stores along the truck route, priced high with a money-back guarantee to retail customers and to stores on any inventory that did not sell. With that approach, sales tripled in 1980 and the business turned its first profit.[269]

Notwithstanding the popularity of the cliché, "location, location, location," location may not be enough.

5. Lease or buy

Leasing

Renting rather than buying space is the choice made by most start-ups. The commitment is less, the flexibility is greater, and cash can be used for other things through renting. However, sometimes a venture can make more profit on the real estate than it makes on doing business. So the choice is not necessarily a foregone conclusion.

Leasing

An entrepreneur who chooses to economize capital by renting rather than buying premises should also give forethought to the impact that lease terms can have on the venture. This is illustrated by the following experience.

Having obtained a $10,000 line of credit to set up an imported smoked-meat sandwich booth in a mall, an entrepreneur signed a "standard" lease for the site and built a booth himself with the help of his brother and his wife. When it opened, business started slowly, but then gradually grew. As a complementary activity, the owner started wholesaling meat to a local supermarket chain. Attempts to sell to other markets, however, failed.

Noticing the growth in business at the booth, the building owner allowed three other fast

food stores with similar products to start selling, notwithstanding a clause in the lease that the first entrepreneur had understood would forbid such competition. He considered suing but decided that the time and money costs would be too high. Sales growth slowed, but still continued, and net cash flow became strong enough, when coupled with the supermarket wholesaling, to pay an adequate living income plus some accumulation of capital.

Then the building owner closed a deal to put up a new building on the same site and exercised a demolition clause in the lease, which put the sandwich stand out of business. Not seeing a site he considered suitable for another such stand, the sandwich shop owner started looking for partners to raise enough cash to begin a restaurant, even though he realized it would require different practices and skills from those of the sandwich stand.

Customarily a standard lease has a lot of fine print in addition to custom terms of rental amount, timing, and conditions for renewal that will be negotiated and written in. It should all be read and considered with care, possibly with the help of a broker friend or another entrepreneur. Essentially, everything in the lease should be considered negotiable, and before

[269] Lager, *Ben & Jerry's*, p. 14.

signing it should be reviewed by an attorney with strong recent experience in commercial real estate transactions.

Some other terms and conditions to take note of in reviewing a lease before signing include the following:

Charges

Base rent Rent is usually stated as a flat amount, but should also be computed for comparisons as a monthly cost per square foot and possibly per foot of frontage.

Sales percentage Retail stores are sometimes obliged to pay in addition to base rent a percentage of sales or percentage of sales above a given level.

Inflation escalator Some leases build in an escalator amount to increase them on the basis of rises in cost of living.

Service fees In a mall or shopping center, maintenance of common areas to make repairs, keep things clean, and take care of the grounds, as well as buying common advertising, paying taxes for the common areas, and possibly remodeling work, may be part of what the landlord will charge, usually as a percentage of the rent or based on square footage. These fees may also be escalated on the basis of how much space is un-rented in the center, which tends to be a regressive feature, because lower occupancy means less foot traffic and causes higher rent.

Further terms

Renewal Being able to renew a lease may make the difference between survival and failure of a business. Conditions for doing that should be considered with care.

Bailing out Being able to break the lease if sales don't reach a certain level, or if an anchor tenant leaves may be worth negotiating.

Leasehold improvements Modifications may be needed to accommodate the venture to the leased space with such things as fixtures, plumbing, electrical outlets, and decoration. It may be possible to negotiate some sort of construction allowance with the landlord to cover this. Decoration in particular may be a

major task, particularly if it is to be important to the image and trademark of the business. In that event, professional help should probably be hired to get it right, unless someone on the founding team happens to be an interior decorator with experience appropriate to the venture's particular line of business.

Other contingencies Also to be considered are such things as whether or not it is possible to sublease; what the landlord will provide in the way of security or parking; whether or not competing enterprises can obtain leases in the same building; what happens if the nature of surrounding businesses changes or too many of them move out; and how flexible the landlord has been in dealing with the leases of other tenants. Considerable negotiation may be required to work out terms.

> Warren Avis put up $10,000 of his own cash (a lot of money in the '40s) and borrowed another $75,000 to work out rental arrangements with airports. He found that there was little demand for counter space near the baggage areas, which was just what he wanted. Even so, working out the details he found very demanding:
>
> There were endless discussions about exactly where we could place our car rental counters, the kinds of signs we could put up, and where our parking spaces would be located. At that time, at our insistence, they were always in the parking lot opposite the main terminal.[270]

Expansion from site to site

If the venture succeeds and prospers, it will likely need to move to other sites to get more space, and that too should be anticipated in working out terms of the lease and setting up facilities.

> By the spring of 1949, he had moved again to a space five times as large. By mid-1951, this 5,000-square-foot space was too small and he had to move again. This time, he searched out and bought industrially zoned land, hired an architect, and built a 20,000-square-foot facility at a cost of $18,000 for the land and $70,000 for a building that took two years to put up.[271]

Buying

There can also be advantages to buying, rather than leasing, a site. Doing so introduces the need

---

[270] Avis, *Take a Chance*, p. 13.
[271] Max Holland, *When the Machine Stopped* (Boston: Harvard Business School Press) 1989.

to have the site inspected before committing to buy, then working through the transaction, including making arrangements for financing, presumably through a mortgage. If the business does not work out, there will be need either to lease out or resell the property, all of which keeps money tied up and takes time.

Through buying, the entrepreneur will have the added financial strength of property ownership, and may derive some personal satisfaction from it as well. But the decision to buy may not be an option, or even if it is, may not be all that rational.

> The would-be founder of a fried chicken restaurant had found a general metropolitan area he preferred for setting up his venture. He noted a KFC store and Church's fried chicken store in the area, which were separated about a half mile from each other and seemed to have all the business they could handle. Driving around he noticed, separated from the two somewhat like the third point of a triangle, a shut-down burger restaurant. Inquiring, he learned it had been closed for violations by the Health Department.
>
> Calling the Department, he learned the name of the owner, whom he contacted to ask whether he could obtain a lease. The owner said he had no interest in a lease, but would sell on favorable terms. The new venture now had a permanent site.

Advantages of buying include the assurance that a landlord will not refuse to renew the lease or may increase the rent exorbitantly, which in either case will force the business to move and thereby perhaps lose benefit of whatever habits customers have associated with the existing site. There would then also be the time and expense of moving. Whatever leasehold improvements the entrepreneur may have contributed to the leased property will be a complete write-off.

Updating plans

By the time these actions to set up the business are being taken much of the plan writing, if any, may have faded into memory. The start-up process will take on a life of its own, and most decisions will usually follow automatically from obvious choices. It may help occasionally to refer back to plans for assessment of how things are going. It may be necessary to update plans as a way of thinking through major decisions or to apply for further financing. But the main guide to start-up action in entrepreneurship must be action itself.

Exercises

Text discussion questions

1. Which facilities decisions are easiest to make and which are hardest?
2. Which facilities decisions are likely to be most important and which least?
3. What kinds of expert help should be of most value in facilities planning?
4. How are facilities decisions likely to vary in sequence from one line of business to another?

Case questions

6B-1 Dave Powers

1. List pros and cons of the arguments put forth by each of the two camps in this case.
2. List specific facts you would ask of each of the two camps if you wanted to cross-check the reasoning behind their recommendations.
3. Which two prior entrepreneurial experiences presented in the chapter do you think would be of most benefit to someone in Dave Powers' position in this case?
4. Whom all should Dave bring in to the decision process at this point and what should he say to them?

6B-2 Dave Williams and Mike Ruffo

1. Which topics in sections 3, 4, and 5 of this chapter do you think would have most bearing on the decisions Dave and
2. Mike are making about physical set-up of their firm?
3. What will likely be the most critical success factors for Dave and Mike's venture?
4. What is your assessment of the way they have proceeded thus far?
5. What should Dave and Mike each do next?

Portfolio page possibilities

Page 6B-1 Production process flow
Sketch out a process flow diagram for production of what your venture will offer.

Page 6B-2 Facilities and equipment need
1. Describe for your venture as specifically as possible the facilities it would need, what would be the best source(s) for those facilities and what would be the cost and timing for their purchase, delivery, and installation.
2. If pertinent, sketch a diagram on part of the page showing layout of the facilities.

Page 6B-3 Workplace layout
Draw a map of the layout for a shop to perform the business in. Include a guess of the dimensions you would look for, recognizing that the ideal might not be available.

Page 6B-4 Location
1. Find two specific sites you would consider appropriate for your venture to start in and, if there is still room on the page, to expand to in the future.
2. Explain what would be entailed in obtaining those first sites as specifically as possible, including terms of any rental agreement (aside from what a standard lease would include).
3. Which lease or purchase terms would be most important for the venture to seek and/or hardest to get?

Term Projects

Venture history
1. To what extent were all the most important paperwork and action steps in start-up anticipated and handily taken care of?
2. How was the real estate used by the venture obtained and at what point(s) along a time line of the venture's creation and development?
3. What did the founders learn as time went on about the important features of its particular location, lease (or title), and insurance needs?
4. What levels of spending during design and start-up were applied to fixed assets, and how satisfactorily were costs controlled as the founders see it?

Venture planning guide
1. Shape this section of the plan in response to portfolio suggestions above.
2. Describe and explain your supplier arrangements including (1) from whom the venture should buy what, (2) what should be appropriate terms of discount and required date of payment, and (3) sources of back-up for these suppliers.
3. Prepare a budget of the expenses required to set up your venture's facilities.
4. Visit two established firms in lines of work similar to your venture and ask their operators where you should place the most concern among facilities decisions.
5. Estimate the facilities costs of two firms similar to your venture and list how those costs and the risks associated with them can be controlled.

Part 7

TEAMING

To make things happen requires personal capability. It begins with capability of the entrepreneur, who must expand it through recruiting the cooperation and support of others, because business is inevitably a multi-party activity. Information, effort, plus possibly raw material, money, and other resources must come from other people. Decisions about how to obtain that help are therefore crucial to the venture and worthy of study, experimentation, and practice in anticipation of venturing.

Teaming to get help will be explored in the two chapters of this section: first, in Chapter 7A, the inside team beginning with founders and working partners; and second, in Chapter 7B, the outside team of helpers, such as bankers, lawyers, and others. Hiring employees to get help will be taken up as a third category in a later chapter.

Not all entrepreneurs take on partners, and whether more should or not is debatable. It is sometimes a choice and other times a matter of necessity. Advantages of going solo when that is possible include freedom to make decisions without having to consult a partner and being able to retain personally all the wealth that the venture represents rather than splitting it with someone else.

Advantages of having partners can include access to the capital, experience, and contacts that one or more partners can bring. Partners can also provide a backup for the founder in case of emergency and the addition of another perspective and cross-check on judgments by someone who cares as much about the venture as the lead founder. Venture capitalists, those who aim to bet their money on only the biggest winners among ventures, absolutely insist on the presence of a balanced team of founders.

If teaming is chosen, then there are other issues to think through from the outset about who should be responsible for what, who should contribute what and how big a piece of ownership each partner should get. Also important are the working rules by which the partnership should operate. Appendix 7a-1 describes alternative legal forms such as partnerships and corporations.

Chapter 7B in this section is on teaming with outsiders and is presented in two main parts. The first lists and briefly describes sources of help from individuals and institutions, some of which directly cost money and others of which do not. Generally, familiar sources are professionals such as lawyers and bankers. Others are institutions and associations with special links and knowledge that may serve the venture.

Finally, there is a section on getting help from other companies through development of working relationships such as joint ventures, where the venture and another company form and own a third company for some special cooperative purpose in which both share ownership. Strategic partnerships are a second form of collaboration where the venture exchanges help with an established company in such areas as technical development, marketing, and operations. It is generally an easier concept to understand than to implement.

CHAPTER 7A – Inside Team

Topics

1. Building capability
2. Whether or not to partner
3. Recruiting
4. Sharing and legal arrangements
5. Working together

Checkpoints

a. What are the pros and cons of inside teaming versus solo start-up?
b. Describe the different ways that inside team members help?
c. What kinds of things go wrong with teams?
d. Explain what can be done to keep an inside team functioning well.
e. On average, what sources of help are used more and what sources less in start-up?
f. Describe how teaming correlates with odds of success and odds of growth.
g. What should be considered in deciding whom to recruit for a start-up team?
h. What should be considered in dividing ownership among start-up team members?

To create a venture an entrepreneur must either have or develop collective capability. Some will be possessed personally and some must be obtained from others. It may come from many categories of people, including family. A study of small firms by Cooper, Woo, and Dunkelberg found for instance, that two thirds began with teams working together closely.[272] Sometimes team members were related. Although the best known in a venture may be the main founder, there is often a less visible but highly important sibling or spouse. Sam Walton and Walt Disney, for instance, had brothers for partners. In Mary Kay Cosmetics and Mrs. Fields Cookies, there were very active husbands.

Some advantages of starting with a team, either as co-owners or as hired outsiders, rather than solo, include:

- To cover more areas of needed expertise in greater depth.
- To bring more brainpower and balance to bear on major decisions.
- To share the massive workload of start-up.
- To provide backup in case of timeout or departure need.
- To be able to grow further before having to recruit more people.
- To have more personal material resources available.
- To add more contacts.
- To enhance credibility.
- For moral support when conflicts arise.

Pulling together a team, which can include insiders who work in the company on its payroll, outsiders who don't, partners who own varying levels of shares in the company, and others who instead are engaged as needed, should build greater capability for winning. Venture capitalists are convinced it does, universally insisting not only that the companies they back be headed by teams,

---

[272] Arnold Cooper, Carolyn Woo, and William Dunkelberg, "Entrepreneurship and the Initial Size of Firms," *Journal of Business Venturing* 3:97-108.

but also that those teams be balanced among the different facets of business management. Supporting this position are academic studies of start-ups, which generally report a positive correlation between shared ownership and venture growth.

Yet many start-ups are created solo and succeed. So there is reason to consider that approach also. It is one way of avoiding conflicts with partners that frequently arise. Being lucky is another way. More reliable is probably the approach of being aware of problems that can arise in partnerships and through forethought designing ways to mitigate them.

1. Building capability

1. Building capability

Input areas

The process of coalescing capability through teaming may begin either before or after discovery of the venture opportunity or venture idea. Needed capability includes knowledge, talent, skills, connections, and other resources. How the team is composed can determine what directions an idea search takes, what it finds, and how start-up is accomplished.

Input areas

Areas where input from other people may be valuable can broadly be grouped into four categories: (1) information, (2) production, (3) resources, and (4) sales. Helpers who can contribute in these four areas can be grouped into seven categories, most of them outside the company: partners, employees, financers, suppliers, advisers, institutions, and channels. Overlap can occur among these seven. For instance, partners may also be financers, and employees may help as advisers. Each of the seven categories can also be subdivided; there are many types of advisers, including professionals such as accountants and lawyers, plus informal

advisers, such as other entrepreneurs, to whom a founder might turn for ideas.

Each category of helper will tend to contribute mainly to one area of need for the venture and will possibly contribute to others secondarily. Exhibit 7a-1 illustrates what the patterns might be. Advisers contribute mainly information and financers mainly resources, for instance. Using this table, an entrepreneur might rank either categories of help by type of helper who might be most useful (rank the rows in each column), or type of helper by areas of capability to serve (rank the cells for each row). The point of doing so is to clarify mentally just what help is needed by the venture and who might be able to provide it. Getting the wrong person for a particular need can be expensive.

The following ambitious start-up was undertaken by an entrepreneur who lacked important prior experience, and therefore needed considerable help to get it going.

Greg Braendel, described by *Inc.* as "a 44-year old itinerant Hollywood actor," had a cousin working in England for Thrislington, a company

Exhibit 7a-1 Input types and sources

| | What the party can help with | | | |
	Information	Production	Resources	Sales
Inside				
Partners				
Employees				
Outside				
Financers				
Advisers				
Institutions				
Channels				
Alliances				

producing unusually decorative bathroom partitions, who visited and persuaded Braendel to help sell them in the U.S. "My idea," Braendel said, "was to find a manufacturer and then sit back and collect my royalties for 10 years or so. Then I could pursue my acting career."

A U.S. partition maker whom he approached declined the job but suggested a distributor, who liked the product and in turn introduced Braendel to a manufacturer's representative. A representative of the British producer came to help Braendel find a U.S. manufacturer, but without success. Then the Briton suggested Braendel make them himself. Braendel obtained production rights from the British maker in return for a royalty on sales and set about forming a company. *Inc.* summed it up as follows.

"Add it up. He was setting out to build a company—something he had never done successfully—in an industry he knew next to nothing about. He would be making a low-tech product that, while distinctive, could easily be copied. To succeed he'd have to line up reps and distributors all over the country, set up and operate at least one factory and ultimately several more, persuade architects and interior designers to gamble on a new and still-untested manufacturer—and do all this before competitors moved in on his turf. Braendel figured that he could count on his parents back in Pennsylvania for some seed capital, but he had little money of his own and little notion of how to raise more.

"As for the start-up team he assembled, well, an optimist would say that they made up in enthusiasm what they lacked in relevant experience. Braendel's friend, Jack Dunsmoor, 42, gave up a marketing job at Republic Pictures to become Thrislington's vice president. Dunsmoor's half-brother, Tim Haase, only 26, became manager of production, and a young actor named Bo Rostrom, 27, became marketing coordinator. Jo Strate, 63, a friend who was training director for General Nutrition Center, managed the office and kept track of the cash."

Braendel chose well-known professional firms for help. A prestigious Los Angeles law firm, White and Case, helped with trademark and logo protection plus preparation of a private placement memorandum. For a fee of $14,000, Peat Marwick helped with preparation of a business plan and was expected to help further with set-up of a computerized accounting system and possibly executive search. Suppliers also helped. DuPont and Formica both sold materials needed in the partitions and offered to help with cooperative advertising and distribution of literature.

Disappointments also followed. A company engaged to perform assembly let the venture down and Braendel and his partners ended up doing the work themselves. One bank agreed to make a loan, but only against Braendel's personal collateral. Later when his venture was going and sought more working capital, it was turned down at that same bank and elsewhere. A venture review panel at an "Entrepreneurial Forum" sponsored by Stanford alumni criticized Braendel and his group for undertaking a line of work in which they had no experience. One venture capitalist commented that "We took a vote of five or six people after the meeting and it was unanimous. They wouldn't get the money they needed, and they wouldn't succeed if they did." Two years into the business, however, sales had risen to $2.7 million annually and the company was still going, with plans for continued expansion.[273]

Whether this venture succeeds in the long run or not, it shows how entrepreneurs find help. They start with whatever acquaintances they have and work through them, and they make cold calls on professionals such as lawyers, accountants, bankers, and suppliers to find people who can provide the needed help.

Collective muscle for start-up may be recruited through coincidence, intent, or both.

William Boeing was born wealthy in the Midwest but didn't like his stepfather. So he moved to the west coast where he invested in lumbering and bought a boat yard to have a yacht made.

Like many people at the time he took interest in news of the Wright brothers' successful first flight. Later he met another flying enthusiast, Eric Westervelt, a military officer who, like Boeing, had studied engineering. Boeing bought a plane made by Martin, took flying lessons, and persuaded Westervelt to join him and contribute technical expertise for making a plane of their own, using fabrication capabilities of the boat yard. When war broke out in Europe, Westervelt was recalled by the army to the east coast and he left the partnership with Boeing.

Ideas

Teaming can precede occurrence of the venture idea, and searching for ideas with a team is a good way to discover them. Silicon Valley, from its early

---

[273] John Case, "With a Little Help from His Friends," *Inc.*, April 1989, p. 132

days, was known as a place where pairs and small groups of engineers would break from their jobs at lunch and meet in the parking lot to discuss ideas for starting companies of their own.

For founders of the *Inc.* 500 fastest-growing small firms, help on development of business ideas came most often from potential customers, followed by a variety of others as listed in Exhibit 7a-2. Hence getting out and talking to potential customers for their helpful input also makes sense.

Exhibit 7a-2 Sources of help on business ideas for Inc. 500 founders[274]

Source	Percent of firms
Potential customers	52%
Spouse	51
Partners	50
Colleagues in the same industry	44
Suppliers	29
Professionals such as lawyers, consultants, etc.	26
Potential backers	19

Alternatively, a would-be entrepreneur may first discover an idea and then set out to amass capability for executing it, contacting others as needed for refining, designing, financing, setting up shop, getting sales, producing, and delivering.

Expertise and effort

In the following venture, a capability was created by two friends joining forces and then recruiting two others who had complementary experience plus motivation, but only for a while.

Jeff Dennis co-founded a company to syndicate commercial real estate properties. He and his three partners would find a property, make a small deposit to have an option on it for a short period of time, then find investors to put up the money to close the acquisition, on which they would take a cut. Trained as a lawyer, Jeff designed the deal and handled the paperwork. Then he and one of his partners, Grant, provided management services on the property.

The task of the other two partners was to sell the deals to investors. But as the venture started to do well and become highly profitable, these

two backed off on selling to enjoy the winnings. Then the real estate market turned down and arguments broke out among all the partners as to whether they were mainly in real estate or in syndicating deals. The partnership was terminated.

Jeff and his first partner then formed a new partnership and recruited a new potential partner with expertise in tax shelters. They tested him first on a small deal, three million dollars Canadian, then took him in as a partner. Their deals grew larger, to 10, 30, 100, 200, and 300 million dollars in size, until finally they sold out to a buyer who went on to hit 600 million.

This example also illustrates the importance of timing for the capability to be valuable in particular markets. Being ready when the market opportunity opens up, as well as sensing where a given capability can be used, is what can permit an entrepreneur to outperform competitors. Developing in advance a personal contacts portfolio from which a team can be created quickly to meet opportunity can provide strength for capability push.

Although the help needs of no two ventures are exactly alike, it may be useful to review the history of a start-up and identify the entrance of help at certain important points during its development. The following sequence occurred during the early days of cable television.

In 1962 an entrepreneur-to-be began working for his brother helping install TV cable in a major city. The following year, while he was visiting in a suburb of the city that did not yet have cable, he noticed on a friend's set that the reception was poor. Knowing he could help and that money could be made with a cable system, he knocked on the doors of several households in the neighborhood and asked if they might be interested to see whether a cable could improve their reception. The replies encouraged him.

Using his car as collateral, he borrowed $1,000 from a bank, bought some used equipment from a dealer and started a sideline business of setting up a system. Over the next year he installed a cable system for 17 charter subscribers, and brought in enough cash to pay off the bank.

Six months later, in mid-1965, he got a call from city hall in the suburb telling him he needed a city franchise for his cable system. He duly submitted an application and received the franchise without problem. This sequence raised

[274] John Case, "The Origins of Entrepreneurship," *Inc.*, June 1989, p. 54.

concern in his mind, however, that perhaps he should tell the phone company that he was using its poles. In response, the phone company demanded he obtain a $5,000 bond to cover any possible damages as well as a lease fee.

Concerned about the implications of liability that had been raised, the entrepreneur decided he should reform his cable company as a corporation. He was not sure how to do this, but had noticed the nameplate of an accountant in one building where he had worked. Now he approached this man for assistance. The accountant said he would help in return for some stock and a small salary. He introduced the entrepreneur to a friend of his who was an attorney. For a customary fee he helped with incorporation, registration of a company name, obtaining a bond and setting up a contract with the telephone company in late 1966.

While these arrangements were being made, the entrepreneur had heard about another nearby suburban area where some homes had poor reception. Knocking on some doors in the area to verify this, he noticed a nearby hill where a reception antenna to serve the area might work. He applied for a franchise at the end of 1967 and a year later had an approval for it.

During the wait for approval, he began seeking sources of cash to build the next system. By now he had concluded that he had picked the wrong accountant, paid more than he should have for help in setting up the company, and made a mistake in sharing stock. Determined not to share more of it, he tried to borrow for the company expansion from several potential financers whom he approached, but they all wanted stock.

He decided to scale back initial capacity in the new antenna system, seek another bank loan and develop the system incrementally. Pledging his personal assets he borrowed $5,000 and began construction. Costs grew faster than revenues, however, payments to suppliers began to slip, and one supplier brought suit in an effort to take over the company. The entrepreneur hired another lawyer to defend him, who discovered that the supplier had not properly registered his own firm with the state and therefore could not demand payment.

By letting this account payable continue to run and issuing more stock shares with which to pay friends and relatives for help, the entrepreneur completed set-up of the new system in early 1968. Revenues now grew, bills were paid, the number of subscribers expanded, and the

entrepreneur asked a real estate agent to help find permanent quarters for the company. The company also hired its first full-time employee in addition to the entrepreneur.

Decision making

Answers to several questions worth exploring about what an entrepreneur needs in order to implement a business idea successfully can be worth thinking about beginning with this example.

1. Whose cooperation did this entrepreneur draw upon to accomplish his venture?
2. What personal attributes probably helped him get it?
3. What capabilities did he possess that another might not for accomplishing this venture?
4. To what extent does it appear that he knew the right people in advance?
5. What did he not know that others had to guide him on?
6. How could he best find them?
7. Why did they render the help?
8. How could he go wrong in getting the help?
9. What should he have learned from this experience about getting help?
10. What could he have studied in advance of encountering his opportunity that might have made him more effective?
11. Would it have made him more likely to prevail if a competitor discovered the same opportunity at the same time?
12. How might the help that another entrepreneur might need with another venture differ from the experience of this man?

Information in the next few sections should help broaden the picture.

Decision making

Some decisions in a start-up call for expertise that can be hired outside. Others benefit from input by people who are part of the internal team and therefore more closely familiar with daily events of the venture. How much prior experience they should bring in addition to that immediate familiarity depends. Warren Avis, based on experience with many ventures both as an entrepreneur and as an investor, observed that adding gray hair can be either a plus or a minus.

If you think about it for a moment, it just makes good sense: Any new venture is going to be stronger if there are one or more top people who can confront a tough new problem by saying: 'I've been through this before. From my own experience, I can tell you that here's what's likely to work … and here's what's likely to fail.'

But then he commented further about a danger in having "too much gray hair":

… many people with much experience may become battle weary. They tend to think in terms of what can't be done, rather than what the possibilities are with a new business project.[275]

Who is picked for the team can not only influence decisions about ongoing operations but also determine significantly the main direction of the company.

FloScan, a Seattle start-up, was begun with an idea for producing illuminated road curbing. It consisted of a string of small lights encased in a plastic shield to form a structure shaped like a length of road curbing. Laid as a segment of curb, outside a restaurant doorway, for instance, it could be switched on either to help attract attention or to be seen easier for disembarking car passengers. Substantial financial backing was recruited and development began.

When it proved too hard to find customers, Wilfred Baatz, the team member brought in for his engineering experience, came up with another brand new product, a gallons-per-mile meter for cars. When car companies did not buy it and auto parts stores could not sell it, the engineer redesigned it as a gallons-per-hour meter for boats, and on that basis the company went ahead.

On major decisions the venture's board of directors, if there is one, comes into play. Along the way other outside team members such as bankers, lawyers, and accountants do also, as will be discussed in the next chapter.

2. Whether or not to partner

2. Whether or not to partner

Successes both ways

Team members can be either outsiders who mostly work elsewhere, such as the board and professionals just mentioned, or insiders with significant ownership in the company as partners or stockholders.

Many entrepreneurs are fiercely independent, and some truly are predominantly solo. The lone prospector looking for ore; the fisherman who sails out, either alone or personally hiring a crew to bring in the catch, which is offloaded to the plant of a processor; the mechanic with a hired hand or two, or possibly none; the independent pharmacist; artist; housepainter; gardener; inventor; beautician; veterinarian; job machine shop owner; and bush pilot may run their whole shows alone or with only very few subordinate employees. Rarely do their enterprises expand much, but they may do well, although most probably survive marginally. Still, some certainly become rich and famous. Examples include, for instance, Ted Turner, Paul Newman, and many authors ranging from fiction writers to authorities like Jim Collins and Tom Peters.

Others, and even some of those, may seem more solo than they are.

Bill Lear, founder of a series of companies including Learjet, was highly individualistic, had to have his way, and was hard to get along with. He seemed very solo, but he always had either partners, employees, or both.[276]

Successes both ways

Success happens both with co-owning partners and without, as illustrated by the list of some highly successful ventures divided into solo- versus partner-started in Exhibit 7a-3. But it is easier to find high-success examples among partner-started firms than solo-started firms, especially in more recent years.

From a questionnaire administered to 15 highly successful managers, 13 of whom had been a founder or cofounder of their firms, Hills[277] found strong agreement (79 percent) with the statement: "It is critical that the right leadership team be assembled." This supports the notion of teaming, but leaves open the

---

[275] Warren Avis, *Take a Chance To Be First* (New York: Macmillan, 1986) p. 158.

[276] Richard Rashke, *Stormy Genius* (Boston: Houghton Mifflin, 1985).

[277] Gerald E. Hills, "Opportunity Recognition by Successful Entrepreneurs: A Pilot Study," in *Frontiers of Entrepreneurship Research*, eds. William D. Bygrave and others (Wellesley, MA: Babson College, 1995) p. 105.

Exhibit 7a-3 Solo versus partner start-up examples

Solo starts	Partner starts
Ampex	Apple
California Airmotive	Ben & Jerry's
Carnegie	Boeing
Charles Schwab	Control Data
Dell	Costco
Douglas	Digital Equipment
Electronic Data Systems	Disney
FedEx	Genentech
Fluke	Google
Ford	Hewlett-Packard
Getty Oil	Intel
Gillette	Kleiner, Perkins
Head Ski	Liz Claiborne
Holiday Inns	Lucasfilms
LeTourneau	MGM
Marion Laboratories	Microsoft
Mary Kay Cosmetics	Mrs. Fields Cookies
McDonald's	Nike
McDonnell	Polaroid
Simplot	Sony
Standard Oil	Southwest Airlines
Tektronix	Tandy
Tupper	Wal-Mart
U-Haul	Yahoo

question of how to recruit that team, whether with pay or by sharing ownership.

Pros of sharing ownership

A report by Cooper et al.[278] stated that 69 percent of founders began their businesses without partners. Twenty percent started with one partner, 7 percent with two, and the remainder with more. (Apparently some had outside investors whom they do not consider partners, because only 63 percent said they owned 100 percent of the equity.) In subsequent years after founding the fraction of ventures with partners increased, but by only a few percentage points.

Odds of survival

However, the same study also found that those whose ventures were more likely to survive for three years:

- Were more likely than not to have had full-time partners (30 percent in surviving firms vs. 25 percent in non-surviving firms),
- Started with more employees,
- More often got important help from accountants (47 percent vs. 41 percent), bankers (35 percent vs. 32 percent), and lawyers (20 percent vs. 17 percent).

Roberts reported from extensive investigations of high technology start-ups in particular, that 80 percent were still going after five years and that over half of them had been formed with more than one founder. In other studies of technology companies he reported that the fraction with partners ranged up to 80 percent.[279]

Odds of growth

From the 1989 list of *Inc.* 500 firms that quickly grew large, it appeared that owners more often shared ownership rather than retaining it all. The amounts of equity still held by founders and their families by the time their firms reached 500 status was as shown in Exhibit 7a-4.[280]

Exhibit 7a-4 Inc. 500 ownership still held by founders and their families

Fraction of *Inc.* 500 firms	Fraction of equity held by founder families
39%	100%
18	75 to 99
22	50 to 75
21	less than 50
100	

An argument sometimes advanced for sharing ownership is that 50 percent of a $100 pie is worth more than 100 percent of a $25 pie. From this *Inc.* 500 sample, however, it appears that a fair percentage of entrepreneurs, almost 40 percent, managed to retain 100 percent of some very valuable pies.

McMullan, Lischeron, and Cunningham reported that growth followed an apparent J-curve pattern among start-ups, with specific figures as shown in Exhibit 7a-5 below.[281]

---

[278] Arnold C. Cooper and others, *New Business in America* (Washington, D.C.: The NFIB Foundation, 1990), p. 5.
[279] Edward B. Roberts, *Entrepreneurs in High Technology* (New York: Oxford, 1991) p. 64.
[280] Case, "Origins," p. 58.
[281] W. Ed McMullan, J. Lischeron, and B. Cunningham, "Building Entrepreneurial Teams: Some Options, Rewards and Barriers" (Working Paper #88-13, presented TIMS/ORSA, Denver, October 1988).

Exhibit 7a-5 Company growth, 1978–83 vs. ownership distribution

Ownership	Average Sales Growth	Average Employment Growth
Founders and financers only	156.6%	75.8%
All above + managers	64.6	20.4
All above + profnl/technical employees	91.0	125.3
All above + operations/clerical/others	597.0	312.1

At the left tip of the J, with fairly high performance in terms of sales and employment growth, were companies in which all ownership was retained by founders and investors. In the bottom of the J, with lower performance, were companies in which founders and investors shared ownership with key managers and technical people only. At the high right-hand end of the J were companies with shared ownership throughout their employee populations. Not reported were either the stage at which ownership sharing expanded or the extent to which sharing seemed to be a cause versus an effect of growth. Another basic reason for sharing ownership is to provide extraordinary incentive, to people who might alternatively simply be hired as well as to recruit people who could not be hired without an ownership share or options to buy it on favorable terms.

Cons of sharing ownership

Notwithstanding this apparent endorsement for sharing ownership, there is a view among many entrepreneurs that it is better to go without partners and retain 100 percent of ownership if possible, even if it means that the company will not grow as safely or as large. Although no systematic study has reported on the hindsight judgment of entrepreneurs who had partners, as contrasted with those who did not, it appears anecdotally that it is easier to find entrepreneurs who succeeded but had trouble with partners and who would not want to have them again, than it is to find entrepreneurs who succeeded without partners but wish they had had them.

Solo would have been better

The sole owner of a small manufacturing company was approached by a man who said he could help with sales. As proof of his sales ability, the man obtained from a potential customer a letter of intent to buy enough to increase the company's volume fivefold for the year. The two formed a corporation, divided the stock 50/50 and co-signed a note at the bank to obtain working capital. Sales, however, turned out to be far slower than forecast, and with a large inventory, the company began to have trouble paying its bills. Creditors, including the bank, pressed for payment. The original founder became increasingly unhappy with his sales partner who had not met his promises.

When, in addition, the founder learned from the bank that the salesman had sold the company truck to help raise more cash for selling expenses, he was furious. He approached the bank and offered to pay off his half of the bank obligation personally with cash. The banker agreed. Then the founder approached the salesman, condemned what the man had done and offered to pay off all the company's suppliers personally if he could have the inventory. The salesman complied, but said it would be a mistake and that things would pick up soon.

The founder replied that the only mistake had been their becoming partners. He wrote the salesman's lawyer saying his name could no longer be used in connection with the business. Thereafter, the founder operated as a sole proprietor, sold off the inventory, and started expanding the business. His conclusion was that the $15,000 he had lost in this process had been tuition for an educational process about caution in taking on partners.

Sometimes there is no other workable choice but to share ownership. If there is possibility of choice, the argument about whether or not to do it can go either way.

3. Recruiting

When sharing ownership is the chosen way, the next tasks are to clarify desired qualities, find the best available candidates, and work out terms. Not that many entrepreneurs follow those steps. More often partners are chosen out of what comes easiest with present acquaintances. Or, if nobody is obvious at hand, the search goes only as far as the first possibility found. Sometimes that works well. Often it does not. It may be forced by time pressure. Or it may simply be a path of least resistance or apparent effort.

If reaching for better results seems worth the effort, then some questions for directing the quest for a partner(s) include:

1. What tasks must be performed to make this company go? (The answer can be cross-checked by asking founders of similar businesses to review what has been stated about them in the business plan.)

2. What tasks does the founder know how to perform at various levels compared to those with more experience in them? (Both how well the founder can perform them and how long it will take compared to having pros carry them out should be considered.)

3. For what tasks can the founder recruit help, and at what cost? (Some asking around will probably be needed to ferret out answers to this question.)

4. How are answers to these questions going to differ from one point in future time to another as the venture develops?

These questions may best be worked on in parallel, balancing what seems possible against what would be more ideal. Other questions to consider while searching for partners is whether or not the venture is ready for them yet, how long particular skills and experience will be important to it, and how well it is designed to be appealing to them.

Balance is an important quality to consider. All important line and staff areas of business, notwithstanding that the organization may be tiny, need to be covered. Someone on the team must be sufficiently expert in its area of technology and operational tasks to enable it to compete with other companies that have those skills. The newness of the venture's offering may be enough to let it break into the market. But to survive, it will have to perform at a high professional level as soon as competitors come. The venture's appeals, as well as competence it needs, will likely change over time.

Finding candidates

Finding candidates

Friends and work acquaintances are logical places to start, but probably not finish, looking. Frequently, people know others with common interests, and when they align with a venture, it is natural for them to choose each other. William Boeing, as mentioned above, met his partner for the aircraft venture first as a coincidence and then chose him as they both found they shared enthusiasm about airplanes.

Many times the choice comes automatically, without either the possibility or perhaps even the need for further checkout, as illustrated by the experience of Mary Kay Ash.

After 25 years of experience with other companies in so-called multilevel-selling, Mary Kay Ash decided to try going on her own. She would train and supervise other women as "Beauty Consultants" to sell her own brand of beauty products. Using her life's savings, she had assembled a beginning inventory, recruited several other women to sell, and agreed with her husband that he would handle the administrative end of the business.

At breakfast one month before opening day, as he was commenting on projected figures and she was half-listening, he suffered a fatal heart attack.

Soon she had advice. Her lawyer urged her to drop the business idea and sell off whatever she could, commenting, "If you don't, you'll end up penniless." When she suggested to her accountant that she still wanted to start the business, he reviewed her situation and then said, "You can't possibly do it. This commission schedule will never work. It's just a matter of time before the company goes bankrupt—and you along with it."

On the day of her husband's funeral, she met with her children and said she still wanted to continue. Her 20-year old son, who was off to a successful start in selling life insurance, agreed to take a 50 percent pay cut to join her venture. Over the objections of other relatives and friends, he quit his job and moved his home to join her. Her older son, at 27 a married father of two, handed her the passbook showing his life savings of $4,500 and told her to use it.

One month later the business opened with Ash, her younger son, and nine salespeople. "If Mary Kay Cosmetics failed I wasn't going back into easy retirement" she observed. "I'd be broke!" Eight months later she needed help with expanding the warehouse and the older son took a 66 percent pay cut to join in and help with it. Still later, her daughter joined the company. As for the comments of her accountant and her attorney, she observed, "They didn't understand the business as I did."[282]

Sometimes an outside helper becomes an insider, as illustrated by the following event in development of Tom Fatjo's garbage collection company.

Two years into start-up, Fatjo had sought to raise money through a private placement. In that process he met Lou Waters, head of the underwriting department in the firm helping with the process.

The underwriting was successful, but Fatjo's actions to acquire other companies were not. He had been on the road for a year seeking out prospects and trying to work out acquisition deals, but not one was successful. Finally, he turned to Waters for advice and was told, "I see basically three difficulties: one's the lack of proper organization, another's your lack of financial credibility and negotiability for your stock, and third, there's the lack of really large company management experience."

Fatjo would later recall:

I realized then that the ingredients Lou had pointed to were essential to the building of a national company, and I simply didn't have them.

After spending the afternoon with Lou, I saw that, for an undertaking as large as the one I envisioned, we needed to have someone with these financial abilities leading us.

And Lou Waters was the logical choice. But with his experience and stature there was no place for him in our organization except at the very top. It seemed strange to ask someone to come in at that level, and

I had an uneasy feeling about giving up the number-one position in my own company. But I remembered that my goal was to build the largest and best company of its kind in the world. And I knew we really needed Lou's experience to accomplish that.

So, after several months of negotiations, we finally convinced him to be the Chairman of the company.[283]

When the coincidence doesn't happen, a natural approach is to ask around further, exploring industrial circles related to what the venture will do, whom it will buy from, or through whom it may sell. Attending industry shows or calling, as well as visiting related companies can turn up leads. People there will bring more relevant experience, catch on quicker, and have more appropriate further contacts. A parting question to raise with any contact is who else to ask.

Choosing

Recognizing what to look for and what to avoid in partners and other potential helpers can call for hard-headed assessment—what have they done before, what do they know, what reputation do they have among those with whom they worked, what are their ambitions, how much compensation do they want, and in what form? It also calls for subjective appraisal—is this person enjoyable to work with, does he or she seem enthusiastic and reliable, are we getting along well, do motivations match?

The following entrepreneur could have avoided some problems by using as much caution on his first partnership as he did on later ones.

Fresh out of school, Mike Meek started an Internet consulting company, solo at first. A year and a half later, he took on a partner and by doing so, he said, enabled his venture to recruit professional businesspeople, which he said "helped catapult me to a much higher level."

Unfortunately, the partner also spent a lot of money based on his arrangement with Meek. If Meek had checked, he would have learned that the man's own credit was bad and also that he did not have either of the two PhD degrees he claimed. Fortunately, thanks to having a written partnership agreement, Meek pressured him to quit and, agreeing to pay off all the venture's debts

---

[282] Mary Kay Ash, *Mary Kay* (NY: Harper, 1987), pp. 4-6.
[283] Tom J. Fatjo Jr. and Keith Miller, *With No Fear of Failure* (New York: Berkeley Books, 1981) p. 36.

himself, got him to do so. Meek then changed the name of the company and kept it going.

He then took in another partner, but with the proviso in a written agreement that the partner would produce at a specified level or higher. When he failed to do so, Meek used the agreement to force him out. "That was a tough one," Meek recalled, adding that "because there was nothing negative between us. It was simply a performance issue."

Subsequently, Meek went on to form several further partnerships that worked out successfully thanks to lessons he had learned about performing background checks, exploring "what ifs," and signing lawyer-prepared written agreements.[284]

4. Sharing and legal arrangements

Working out terms with a prospective helper or partner has two sides: who should add what, and who should get what? Each side has its objective and subjective aspects. Different people value different things, and what they value can change over time, so some learning about what is important to the other person is an important part of dealing for both parties.

Who should get what can be examined through developing answers in specific terms, quantitatively insofar as possible, although there may be non-quantifiable benefits also desired. The founder needs to consider the relative dollar costs of partnering versus hiring to get the needed help.

The prospective partner needs to consider the opportunity cost of joining the venture. How much money and other benefits could be gained elsewhere? Can the partner get a special tax break, such as being able to deduct expenses of the business from personal income? Might the partner enjoy insulation from some problems of the business by having part of it set up separately in such a way that the partner shares only some particularly appealing aspect, such as a tax break? Or perhaps a separate partnership will be set up for sales or for ownership of certain facilities. These may be unencumbered, while another part of the business copes with past losses or other risks.

Thinking about what can go wrong should be part of setting up a deal, not because things necessarily will go wrong, but because they might, and thinking ahead may mitigate or head off problems.

Contributions

Presumably, the lead entrepreneur has already contributed the venture idea, some planning thoughts, possibly also some capital, and time. Part of giving time, for either partner, may be the important sacrifice of relinquishing a job elsewhere.

What the partner should add can be sorted out in terms of the four categories mentioned earlier: information, production, resources, and sales. These four can be aligned with capabilities of the potential helper to see how good the fit should be. Usually, information is easiest of the four to obtain, while the other three—production, resources, and sales—may be both harder to get and more important because they require more serious commitment.

Performance measures for the expected contributions are also worth considering. The more specific they are, the less room there will probably be for misunderstanding and later argument. In law firms an important measure is amount of business brought in by a partner. Another is the number of billable hours produced by each partner. Both connect directly to income generated for the firm.

The venture can go very wrong if the entrepreneur makes the wrong suppositions about what a prospective partner expects to contribute. The following entrepreneur expected to get experienced management help as well as financing, but only got the latter.

Tina Holden accepted an offer of $30,000 from an experienced entrepreneur for 50 percent interest to start-up an exclusive AT&T wireless dealership. She provided the client base, selling work, management, and all her savings. Think-

Contributions

---

[284] Jana Matthews and Jeff Dennis, *Lessons from the Edge* (New York: Oxford Press, 2003) p. 134.

ing she and her partner were going to work on the venture together and also bring in another person to help her run the company, she gave up further ownership to him. But instead of hiring help, he started withholding her paychecks.

She left the business and started again, applying her savings, borrowing against credit cards, and recruiting credit from suppliers. After the person she hired this time to help her out did not do the job, she pared the business down to the minimum and worked on her own until a large order turned it around. Then again she hired, and this time it worked out.[285]

From the fact that she was able to leave and start over successfully it appears that this entrepreneur did not really need a partner when she took one on. Something she could have done to check his intentions further would have been to propose a trial period of working together. If that had been working successfully, then the partnership agreement could have been drafted to reflect the terms that were implicit in how it was working.

Part of what can be revealed in a trial period is to what extent the prospective partner is under pressure from outside commitments. Another is just how they will get along with the entrepreneur and the venture. A third is whether or not their values are in alignment. How committed are they to working cooperatively on solutions to unanticipated problems or conflicts? Do they agree on values and priorities?

Rewards

The main incentives for becoming a partner are usually three: (1) ownership, which can come in the form of either shares or options for shares; (2) control, which is based on the shares held; and (3) pay, which is mainly in the form of money, although other perks, such as retirement contributions, use of a company car, or travel allowance are possible.

One purpose for allocating rewards is to provide incentive to become a partner. Another is to reward valued resources and service and thereby motivate partners to strive in the venture's best interest. Running through all these rewards is the issue of fairness, which may be perceived in different ways by different partners.

Ownership

The biggest financial gains for venture partners generally come from ownership of shares. These may be divided any way the partners choose, and usually can be bought and sold to others. Theoretically they should be worth in total the discounted expected present value of the venture's future net cash flow. But because that is a matter of speculation, they represent in fact what the owners hope for. Misjudgment or disagreement about that can lead to discontent and dispute.

Jim Clark, founder of Silicon Graphics, remembered the financing deal he got from a venture capital firm, the Mayfield Fund. The venture, he figured, included 10 years of his own personal experience, three years of work by seven students, and three senior executives in place. The fund took 40 percent of the company for $800,000 it invested.

Later, he decided that he had not been adequately compensated. In founding Netscape he valued the work of its seven students at $3 million, put in $3 million of his own cash and in return took 50 percent of the stock.[286]

How others may have viewed the fairness of either of these deals was not reported. Most likely there would have been a range of opinions.

Control

Clark's decision to award 50 percent of the shares to himself, however, carried with it a certain amount of risk that the other shareholders could have joined forces to deadlock with him in attempts to exercise control.

Warren Avis experimented several times with 50/50 ownership and found that "without exceptions major problems arose … my mistake? I should have asked for 51 percent."

In one case a venture started going well and the partner demanded an increased share. When Avis refused, his partner formed a new corporation and sold all the assets of the partnership to it. When Avis sued, the court ruled that the partner's corporation belonged to the original partnership. But now all its officers were appointees of the partner who had formed it. Avis owned half and could appoint half of the board of directors. However, with that he could not overrule

[285] Matthews and Dennis, *Lessons*, p. 141.
[286] Jim Clark, *Netscape Time* (New York: St. Martin s Press, 1999) p. 57.

the partner's appointed people, who "took out the company profits in the form of salaries, profit sharing, bonuses, stock options, country club memberships, company cars, insurance policies, you name it."[287]

Avis sold out to this partner on the cheap.

It is possible to be equal in ownership but unequal in control if some of the shares issued are non-voting or are in preferred stock. Changes in fraction of ownership can come downstream through issues of more shares to raise further capital or reward performance.

Pay

Another way to separate control from ownership is to reward a partner with cash rather than shares. For the recipient cash is much less risky, easier to spend and can be spent immediately, which for some people may be important or even imperative. But it does not carry with it the potential for growth in value if the venture succeeds. Pay can take the form of other benefits than cash, such as those the partner of Warren Avis mentioned above took as perquisites. But they can be cut off at any time. Generally, whoever has controlling ownership gets to determine how much the person working for pay and perquisites receives.

For the founder who wants to attract partners a dilemma arises on issuance of shares versus pay. Because cash is likely to be in short supply early in the venture's life, it is hard to give to partners. But because ownership carries voting power and has the potential to grow in value, it can be painful to share.

A tactic sometimes used by founders is to offer a large number of shares during recruitment as pay in the form of stock, but only after issuing in advance so many shares that the large number offered as pay is a small fraction of the total. The logical response for a recruit who is thus offered shares in lieu of pay in cash is to ask what fraction of the total of shares issued is represented by those being offered.

Commitment to writing

At some point putting the agreement in writing is usually very important. If nothing is written, a partnership will be judged by the courts to be equal in ownership among the partners, which may not be fair for reasons just mentioned. Waiting too long to settle the matter can also raise problems, as in the following example.

> Julie Pearl decided to bring another lawyer to her law practice to gain more time for personal affairs, including birth of a baby. First, she agreed to grant the recruit a 5 percent interest in the firm, though nothing formal was signed. Then when she became pregnant and wanted more time off she let it go to 10 percent. The new attorney then asked that her name be added to the firm's title, which Julie granted, and three months later the newcomer said, "By the way, I want 50 percent and the right to veto anyone else getting profit sharing." Julie refused and the new person left. Fortunately, no formal partnership agreement had been signed. But the new person had mishandled work and run up $20,000 in bills the firm had to pay. It was later discovered that she had spent much of her time sending out resumes and looking for another position. Pearl concluded that she should have looked harder at the strengths and weaknesses of the new person before agreeing in principle to make her a partner.[288]

When the deal is written, it is also usually essential to have it done by a lawyer, although legally that is not required. A lawyer experienced in writing such deals can help raise issues that may otherwise be overlooked and also offer different ways of tuning the deal technically to achieve desired ends. For instance, if stock is to be granted, when should it be vested, that is technically owned by the recipient permanently? The attorney knows how to write a vesting agreement, whereas a person not legally trained probably would not. Sad experience that can result in absence of professional legal help was illustrated by the following example.

> Three partners in a fish farm negotiated with some potential silent partners to obtain capital. The understanding of the three partners was that the investors would pay the company in a lump sum to be used for expenses during start-up, and they attempted to include this provision in the investment agreement, which they

[287] Avis, *Take a Chance*, p. 185.
[288] Matthews and Dennis, *Lessons*, p. 124.

Commitment to writing

wrote themselves. Shares were duly issued to the investors, but the latter chose to mete out the cash slowly, which frustrated the founders. The investors claimed that costs of start-up were becoming higher than promised and therefore they were entitled to more ownership. The founders sought legal counsel, and were disappointed to learn that the agreement they had drafted left loopholes that gave the investors the upper hand.

Legal form

Something to have written by a lawyer are formal papers describing the legal entity that the venture will have. More details on the legal entity alternatives appear in Appendix 7a-1. Broadly, there are four types as follows:

Proprietorship (one person, no partners).

Partnership (regular or limited, partners may be equal or not).

Corporation (main two types are federally designated as "S" or "C".

Limited Liability Company (some advantages of numbers 2 and 3, above).

At the outset which legal form will be best and when may not be clear. There are other things to do—gathering market information, working on prototype design, checking out the competition, locating needed contacts, looking for alternative capital sources, and so forth. If the entrepreneur is working alone, a proprietorship is the natural default for the company's legal form. Later, a decision can be made about whether to incorporate and in what form. In the meantime, if the entrepreneur is operating alone or with a spouse, the form will automatically be a proprietorship. That happens by default without any paperwork.

If the entrepreneur and one or more others are working on the venture together, and particularly if they are spending their own money on it, they automatically have a partnership, even if there is no paperwork. Any of them then can make commitments for the venture and all are liable for actions of the venture. Absent any paperwork to the contrary, moreover,

they all own it equally. If one or more of the partners does not like that arrangement, then papers should be written by an attorney saying what the partners want the arrangement to be. That document may leave the venture as a partnership, perhaps a limited partnership, or may shift it to one of the last two legal forms, corporation or Limited Liability Company.

Hence, if the entrepreneur is not working alone, however, but is developing partnership-like arrangements with one or more other people, a written document should immediately be prepared. David Packard recalled the first written formalities, minutes of a planning meeting for creation of a company with his college friend, William Hewlett:[289]

> During my visit to Palo Alto I got together with Bill Hewlett, and at that time we had our first 'official' business meeting. The minutes of the meeting, dated August 23, 1937, are headed 'tentative organization plans and a tentative work program for a proposed business venture.' The product ideas we discussed included high-frequency receivers and medical equipment, and it was noted that 'we should make every attempt to keep up on (the newly announced technology of) television.' Our proposed name for the new company: The Engineering Service Company.

Packard was still an employee of the General Electric Company in New York at the time, and his main reason for going to Palo Alto was to visit his future wife, not to form a company. He returned to New York and stayed with General Electric until June 1939, almost two years after the business meeting with Hewlett. The shift from partnership to corporate form did not take place until eight years later, as Packard wrote:[290]

> In 1947 we incorporated Hewlett-Packard. This allowed for some tax advantages and also provided more continuity to the business than a partnership could. By that time we had also put in place a good part of the top-management team that was to guide the company over the next thirty years.

Fred Burg started a machine tool company based on first one and then a second significant invention to improve shop performance.

[289] David Packard, *The HP Way* (New York: Harper Business, 1995) p. 32.
[290] Packard, *The HP Way*, p. 64.

To cope with demand, he took his son and his son-in-law in as minority partners. Five years after inception the company was booming and needed more capital. A consultant explained to them that by incorporating the company it would be able to retain more of its earnings with which to grow. It became Burg Tool Manufacturing Company, Inc. in mid-1951, apparently without incident.[291]

These examples illustrate that the legal form of the business need not be elaborate at the start and can shift to other forms later. But each has its advantages and disadvantages, and one may be better than another from the outset.

5. Working together

Not all problems can be anticipated in committing a partnership agreement to writing, but some of the possibilities can, including provision for dissolution. Careful thinking and discussion of what-ifs with each partner, other advisers, and an attorney can help anticipate problems and mitigate them. These explorations should consider the problems from each party's point of view for best understanding and resolution.

Anticipating problems

It is to be expected that business circumstances, personal pressures, and individual ambitions of partners will change over time. One partner will be more ambitious for the firm than another. One will want more time off and an easier pace than another. Quite possibly, each will feel that he or she is giving up more, doing more, and working harder than the others will appreciate. Sometimes these pressures can lead to ethical compromises not foreseen.

> Two men formed a machining company. At year-end the wife of one of them took a look at the books to prepare taxes and found that the partner had been making unauthorized withdrawals from the company bank account and attempting to disguise them as supply purchases. The partnership was dissolved.
>
> — • —
>
> Louette Glabb, a sales representative for a company that replicated CD-ROMs, thought the work could be done better, hence quit and invited another sales representative to become a partner in starting a new replicating enterprise in 1992. Five years later she found he was writing checks for personal items on the company's account. She also found he was

mistreating and alienating customers by such actions as accusing them of being past due on paying what they owed when they were not. When she threatened to have the company books audited, he agreed to sell his interest in the firm for $50,000 and leave. Aided by a pickup in the market, performance dramatically improved and, after reviewing the books, she concluded that despite money he had taken, other money he had wasted, and damage he had done, the company was still worth $1.5 million.[292]

Both of these examples underscore the importance of being alert, maintaining partner access to good records, and checking up on them.

Solving problems over time

Another point the above example brings out is the need for someone to exercise leadership and deal with unforeseen problems as soon as they come to light.

> Two doctors formed a clinic. One started feeling progressively more overloaded and wanted to hire a third doctor to get some relief. His partner, however, resisted because he knew doing so would cut into profits. After considerable debate, the two agreed that the new doctor would be hired, but the doctor interested in maintaining profits would take no cut in his draw. The other did take a cut in draw. But it turned out to be brief because, to the surprise of both, with the new doctor available, business and profits soon increased enough to replace the cut.

In a larger partnership the problems and remedies can become more complex. In the 1950s the architectural firm of Daniel, Mann, Johnson and Mendenhall, which had

Anticipating problems

Solving problems over time

---

[291] Max Holland, *When the Machine Stopped* (Boston: Harvard Business School Press, 1989) p. 21.
[292] Matthews and Dennis, *Lessons*, p. 233.

300 employees, was troubled by the following partner problems:[293]

- Lack of consensus on votes.
- Suspicion and quarrels between partners.
- Imbalance of workload among partners.
- Partners pulling rank and upsetting subordinates.
- Confusion over partners' duties.
- Partners operating outside the company strategy.
- Lack of coordination in such activities as hiring.
- Confusion about what was going on ("Don't ask me").

After trying numerous remedies, including psychological tests, hiring a consultant (which worked until he became a partner), dividing into autonomous divisions, overloading everybody with work or with information, rotating roles among partners, and hiring professional managers, they distilled through trial and error over time a list of 12 policies that seemed to work best.

1. Equal salaries for all partners with half of the firm's profits reinvested.
2. Partners have separate social lives.
3. At least one partner on every job.
4. Each partner sees through at least one job per year.
5. All partners pass on all major designs.
6. All partner decisions must reach unanimous consensus.
7. One partner is general manager, clearly in charge.
8. Each partner is an owner on policy matters, and employee otherwise.
9. Annual meetings are held at which:
   - Each partner's performance is reviewed;
   - Long-range plans are hammered out; and
   - General managers report on each partner's happiness, output, and job fit.
10. Update meetings are held monthly.
11. Any partner can call a complaint meeting.
12. A code of ethics applies in which each partner:
    - Takes responsibility for bringing in a pro rata share of business;

- Agrees not to make disparaging remarks about other partners; and
- Agrees not to take arbitrary positions.

This pattern might not fit any other firm, and in time probably had to be changed anyway. In a typical start-up where people were added over time, it is extremely unlikely that all would receive equal ownership or pay. Moreover, most companies are not composites of individual customer projects as they were in this firm. Instead, the company will have one main thrust and the whole enterprise will be one team to pursue that. Individual co-owners will not likely be responsible for pro rata selling. Rather, there will be one group concentrated on sales. Thus many things will be different. But working out and writing out how owners are supposed to work together, as this firm did, will likely still be well worth the effort.

Divorce

Notwithstanding good effort at developing a partnership it may one day need to be broken up, and that possibility should be anticipated from the beginning. The break-up may or may not be hostile, and the company may or may not survive it. The first of two break-ups below was hostile and yet two companies survived out of it. The second example was friendly, and also resulted in two separate firms.

> Bob Ohlson, one of four partners in a computer cable company, saw the other partners as both lacking in vision as to what their company could become and not pulling their weight. He tried persuading first one partner and later a different one to join with him to take over from the other two. Eventually, however, the other three all aligned against him and offered to buy him out.
>
> Ohlson rejected the deal, claiming that both the price and the condition that he sign a promise not to compete were unacceptable. Instead he quietly set about organizing a new company in the same line of business. He recruited key employees to come with him, offering shares of ownership in his new company as part of the inducement. Suddenly one day, his partners were surprised to find that he and 18 of their 80 employees had left, including three-fourths of the salespeople. They struggled to recover, however, and by a year and a half later the company had

[293] Karl H. Vesper, *New Venture Mechanics* (New York: Prentice Hall, 1993) p. 132.

grown to 95 employees. The partner in charge, John Berst, felt he had nevertheless lost something. "With Bob Ohlson I bared my soul," he said. "Now, I'm reluctant to totally confide in anyone."

Ohlson's new company had also managed to survive and was now up to 36 employees. Reflecting on his departure from the partnership, he commented, "If I had had enough money, I probably could have cleaned the whole organization out. This was a super move on our part. Obviously, I'm more cynical about personal relationships. At one time I would have considered John Berst my best friend in the whole world. And then he went and stuck a knife in my back." [294]

— • —

Greg Ferguson, experienced in real estate development, met and teamed up with a developer who had resources but needed help. As he saw it, Greg brought logical thinking and his partner brought out-of-the-box thinking. Together they generated what Greg described as "some terrific office systems, a terrific network with investors and banks and we built ourselves up to a significant sized company."

Two other partners joined, but then the first partner started getting the company into projects that Greg judged to be too distant and flawed on which the company started losing money, something Greg felt he could not abide. He commented: "So, we're dividing up the business and I'm setting up a new company in separate office space. It's going to be an amicable separation. We know that we are on different wavelengths." [295]

To cope with the possibility that the cause of break-up may be death of a partner, the venture should consider taking out a Key Person insurance policy, which indemnifies for the loss.

There should also be a Buy-Sell agreement, which describes how a partner may leave or be forced out. That agreement may provide for holding an auction among the partners to set the price at which one or more of them will leave. Or there may be a shoot-out clause, which states that either partner can buy out the other on the terms he or she offers provided the other has the right first to buy on the same terms and declines to exercise it. In this circumstance, each party has a different advantage. The person who proposes the deal presumably does it

when he or she thinks the timing is right for themselves, as opposed to for the other party. The other party has the advantage of being able to choose whichever option seems preferable.

To use another analogy, whichever party cuts the sandwich is bound to be off by at least a little bit from getting the pieces equal, and consequently has to let the other party choose the larger piece.

Summary guidelines

At the risk of leaving out a rule that may be important to a particular venture or adding one or more that don't apply, here are some guidelines to consider in forming an internal team for the venture.

1. Perform a background check on any new partner. Look at their resume. Ask for references. Ask about negative references. Perform a credit check.

2. Look for skill set fit and its overlap versus full coverage of important areas. Consider how it will change over time.

3. Explore how well values, goals, priorities, work ethic, enthusiasms, and time availabilities fit.

4. Clarify what each partner is expected to contribute in terms of work, finances, and otherwise and consider how that fits with their corresponding capacities.

5. Discuss openly the what-ifs. Brainstorm what could go wrong, including potential health problems and failure of the business.

6. Consider exits possible under contrasting circumstances.

7. Learn what the legal rules and the responsibilities of different participants are for whatever form the business will take.

8. Consider the personal risks relative to ambitions of each partner and risks that the partnership will break up.

9. Plan for full, timely, audited, and accessible financial disclosure of all partners.

10. Plan for periodic review of individual performance and for revision of roles and responsibilities.

11. Get it in writing.

12. Have a lawyer finalize it.

---

[294] Edward O. Welles, "Blowup," *Inc.*, May 1989, p. 63.
[295] Jana Matthews and Jeff Dennis, *Lessons from the Edge* (New York: Oxford Press, 2003) p. 137.

Exercises

Text discussion questions

1. Why do some people strongly believe in having partners and others strongly believe in not having them? What might change the mind of either?
2. What set of procedures would be best for working out terms between partners in a prospective start-up?
3. What sequence over what time period would make sense for working out partner terms in a start-up?
4. How would you rank order the likely partner disputes to be expected over time, and what rules would you suggest for coping when they occur?

Case questions

7A-1 Bruce Milne (A)

1. Assess the implicit criteria Bruce used versus ideally should have used in recruiting partners, if any.
2. Sketch a list of responsibilities for the venture and who should cover which.
3. Develop a grid showing percentages of initial ownership each founder should receive in this venture, and be prepared to explain your rationale.
4. What should Bruce say to each of his partners about ownership?

7A-2 Ampersand (B)

1. What other types of individuals, if any, should the Ampersand team plan to recruit, either for money and/or effort?
2. Whose company should Ampersand be/become, and on what specific terms?
3. What should the Ewings ask for and be willing to give?
4. What should the team propose to the Ewings about ownership terms and how?

Portfolio page possibilities

Page 7A-1 Founding team

List on one page the most important questions, in rank order, in picking for your venture: (1) Working partners, (2) Silent partners whose main contribution is to put up money, (3) Banker, (4) Lawyer, (5) Accountant, (6) Consultant, (7) Potential corporate strategic partner.

Page 7A-2 Partner terms

List on one page the terms you would want to have if you were going to have a working partner. Rank them in importance and to the extent that space permits indicate what your negotiating flexibility might be on the trickiest terms.

Page 7A-3 Team member negotiations

Describe the sequence you expect to go through in selecting team members from among possible candidates and working out with them what their responsibilities will be. Include a time schedule.

Page 7A-4 Team member assignments

Forecast a timetable of tasks you would expect, although through negotiations they may change, to have different team members complete and by when. Explain how you will present it to them.

Term Projects

Venture history

1. How was ownership and control of the venture divided over time and what problems, if any, arose regarding it?
2. What legal form was chosen for the business, what was the rationale for that, and who did the paperwork on it?
3. How have the lead founder's views about sharing ownership changed over time and due to what experiences?
4. What rules for getting along with partners would the founder(s) recommend to others? What experiences prompted them?

↓

↓

Venture planning guide

1. Assess your strengths and task-relevant experience for carrying through your venture. Note areas where complementary talent capabilities from others should be most helpful.
2. Ask someone else to review and comment on the above assessment. Write a summary of what that person said.
3. Formulate composition of the team you can recruit, discuss it with them and describe it, along with copies (possibly "anonymized") of their resumes.

CHAPTER 7B – Outside Team

Topics

1. Directly paid specialists
2. Indirectly paid professionals
2. Other individuals
4. Institutions
5. Corporations, strategic alliances

Checkpoints

a. Explain how to choose a lawyer, banker, and accountant.
b. Describe the different ways outside team members are compensated for what they contribute to ventures.
c. What is an entrepreneur's invisible organization and why does it matter?
d. What is the role of a board of directors and how should directors be chosen?
e. How is a board of advisers different from a board of directors and why?
f. How are joint ventures and strategic alliances different from each other?
g. What different types of strategic alliances are there?
h. Explain the roles of closers, enforcers, and advocates in strategic alliances.
i. Describe what sorts of things go wrong in strategic alliances and what can be done about them.

Every business, including a start-up, needs help from outsiders, people who can provide information and guidance but are not employed in the company. An entrepreneur can benefit by becoming acquainted with a number of outside-help sources and their costs. Government agencies and libraries provide information without fees. Some types of professionals, lawyers for instance, charge directly for their services. Others, such as bankers and insurance agents, provide counsel without charge and get paid for the other services they offer. Still others offer free counsel on a volunteer basis; for instance, retired executives who work with the SBA, students at business schools, and other business people who serve pro bono as advisers to small firms.

Whether free or recompensed in some way other than in dollars, all of these help sources cost time to use, and an entrepreneur must weigh the benefits of outside help against both the time and money costs of obtaining them. Most specialists cost money but save time because they know what they are doing and don't have to stop and learn as a newcomer does.

More important than the cost in either money or time is the quality of outside help that the venture receives. People who have the strongest proof that they can deliver high-quality performance often tend to charge the highest prices. Is the venture really worth enough to justify such investment? High-priced help may easily be justified if its benefits can be spread across a large operation. But how can a small one justify such costs? And if it can't, what is an entrepreneur to do? Juggling these dilemmas is not impossible. Entrepreneurs do it all the time. It calls for imaginative and energetic management.

1. Directly paid specialists

Time-Paid

Many different types of specialists are available to help ventures. Some provide information, others production, resources, or sales help. Many also provide introductions to other useful business contacts. Generally the more successful the professional, the better the contacts he or she can provide. Direct payment for their work is generally based either on the time they apply or else on the task that they perform, but not both.

Time-Paid

Professionals who are typically paid by the hour include lawyers, accountants, consultants, artists, and craftspeople.

Lawyers

Conventional wisdom advises entrepreneurs always to put important agreements in writing, read and understand the fine print, and hire the most competent lawyers they can afford to help with these tasks and keep them out of legal trouble. The law never requires that lawyers be hired, and many entrepreneurs have successfully accomplished their own legal work ranging from filing for incorporation to drawing up contracts, conducting their own trials, handling their own public offering applications, and writing their own wills. But the advice to hire good legal help persists, with the support of virtually all who have done so. A lawyer costs more money than handling legal work personally, but there is usually a more-than-offsetting saving in time expenditure and mistake reduction.

What an entrepreneur needs to know about the law is (1) where it generally comes into play, (2) how to go about becoming better-informed in those areas where it is likely to become especially important for the particular business, (3) how to find an appropriate lawyer, and (4) how to use legal services effectively and efficiently. The variety of legal specialties is very large as can quickly be seen from listings on the Web. For some specialties it can be hard to imagine much connection with entrepreneurship: maritime law, insurance law, constitutional law, personal injury law, medical malpractice, and labor law, for instance.

For others, such as the following, potential connections with entrepreneurship come to mind quickly. Lawyers help with:

- **Entity formation** (Should the venture be incorporated, and if so, with what provisions?)
- **Relationships** between owners, employees, and others (Will the venture need non-disclosure agreements, union contracts, or non-compete agreements? Should it have pension or profit-sharing plans?)
- **Protection** of intellectual property (Should the entrepreneur file for a trademark or patent? Should the venture sue for theft of trade secrets?)
- **Contracts** (What should be the wording with suppliers, customers, landlords?)
- **Lawsuits** (Where are the litigation risks greatest and how can they be mitigated?)
- **Taxes** (What are the allowable deductions, what must be paid when, and what must be reported when?)
- **Government permissions** and requirements (What records must be kept? What applications and reports must be filed and in what form?)
- **Issuing securities** (What advance preparation is advisable? What can and cannot legally be done, and how are approvals obtained?)
- **Personal property** issues (What estate planning should the founders do? Should they be leasing assets to the company?)

An entrepreneur should attain some knowledge of the meaning of each of these categories and the kinds of issues that might arise within them. Some issues are suggested above in the parentheses, but each issue is complex, and the list is by no means exhaustive. Moreover, the ways of dealing with these issues depend on the individual circumstances. Incorporating as a sole owner can be simple, but with partners it tends to become complicated. Government permission for selling stationery is simple. Opening a foundry is complex in some situations and virtually impossible in others. Some start-ups won't ever sell shares publicly and need not worry about rules governing that. Others eventually will and should therefore explore whether they need to get started right away with certified accounting audits in order to qualify later, and so forth.

Information about each of these topics is available in libraries, particularly law libraries, which are operated both by law schools and by governmental agencies. The standard reference on law firms is Martindale-Hubbell.[296] On the Web, Findlaw.com lists specialties, individual firms by geographical area, and articles on a host of legal topics.

Talking with other entrepreneurs in related lines of work or who have faced similar situations, and reading up are two free ways to become prepared to answer such questions as:

1. Is something legalistic called for?
2. Should a lawyer be engaged to help with it?
3. Should the lawyer be a generalist or specialist?
4. Should a large or small firm be engaged?
5. Which firm should be hired?
6. What should be bought from it?
7. How should the budget for its future services be handled?

Answers will vary with the source of the opinion as well as the kind of business situation the entrepreneur faces. For instance, many if not most lawyers will advise engaging them early to help with the decision of how and when they should be used. A lawyer from a large firm will point out that large firms have the advantage of employing many specialists to provide most efficient, informed, and up-to-date information on whatever legal assistance the entrepreneur needs.

A lawyer from a smaller firm will counter that the large firm will typically assign top partners to the major accounts and use the small firm as a training ground for younger and less-experienced members of the firm. In contrast, the small firm may assign a top (or maybe the only) partner, and where specialists are needed, it will refer the entrepreneur to whomever is the best specialist in the business rather than

simply to one whom the firm already employs and therefore must use.

The big firm may respond that it has more numerous and powerful contacts (but why should it draw upon them for a small venture?) and a better-known name to enhance the venture's image. But it will likely charge more. Some big firms, such as the one described following, have subunits that specialize in start-ups, particularly those involving high technology and ambitions.

> Gray Cary, a large multi-office California law firm, set up a "Venture Pipeline" unit in 2001 specifically to help start-ups. It reviewed over 1,000 business plans in its first 14 months of operation, 200 of which were judged to warrant "a closer look," 40 of which were judged "strong enough to shop" and seven of which were able to raise money. All supplicants are offered advice and, said a member of the firm, nobody was brushed off with simply, Thanks, but no thanks. Those that are accepted as clients are charged an initial $15,000 to take on the legal start-up work, though payments on this may be deferred, plus 1 percent of the venture's equity.[297]

According to a study by the Technology Executives Roundtable, 45 percent of high technology entrepreneurs found their lawyers through business acquaintances, and another 15 percent found them through accountants and bankers. Large law firms were the choice of 41 percent and sole practitioners of only 11 percent.[298]

Will the premium price of a large firm be better spent on that or on advertising, quality improvement, employee training, or research and development? Investigation and application of judgment by the entrepreneur are required. Some feeling for a law firm can be obtained by briefly discussing with it such matters as these before deciding whether to hire it. It is always appropriate for the customer to ask whether or not the firm thinks it should be hired, how much it will charge, and when the meter will start running.

There should be no charge for getting acquainted, only for giving information about

---

[296] *Martindale-Hubbell Law Digest* (New Providence, N.J.: Martindale-Hubbell). Also findlaw.com.
[297] *San Diego Business Journal*, September 30, 2002, p. 121.
[298] "Hands On," *Inc.*, July 1989, p. 99.

the law, or for giving requested advice. Other questions to which free answers should be sought include: How much experience has which partner in the law firm on the particular legal issues faced by the venture? Which lawyer in the firm will be the venture's main contact after it is engaged? Junior partners in the firm have to learn on somebody, presumably with back-up by a more experienced partner. Will it be on the venture? It is appropriate to shop around before choosing a law firm and also to use different firms for different specialties.

It often works well to have one main law contact, whether in a small or large firm, and to pay that firm an advance retainer for future services over time. The firm on retainer to the venture should, for its part, give priority response when the venture calls, and should refer the venture to other law firms in situations where their specialties fit a particular legal problem better. And, of course, it should give prompt billings against the retainer, reporting down to a few minutes the time for which the venture is being charged.

Although very little research has been done on how entrepreneurs should use lawyers, there does seem to be common wisdom that is not often disputed about ways not to try saving money. One is by hiring a cheaper lawyer rather than the best one obtainable if the case is important. A second is to let the lawyer of the other party in a contract write the contract and not personally hire a different lawyer to review it. A lawyer's job is to take the side of the party paying for the legal work, not to be unbiased.

Accountants

Accountants, like lawyers, also generally work on an hourly basis. Also like lawyers they are available as sole practitioners, partners of small firms, and members of large firms, which charge higher prices but embellish the financial statements with their brand names. Those names, in turn add more respectability and

prestige to the statements, notwithstanding the fact that famous accounting firms sometimes commit colossal blunders, as symbolized by the failure of one of the biggest, Arthur Andersen. Tasks they perform include:

- Setting up financial reporting and control systems.
- Auditing and certifying financial statements.
- Tax computation and reporting.
- Evaluating financial performance.
- Anticipating financial needs.

As regards this last task, however, Bodsky[299] suggests a caution about accountants, which is that the perspective demanded of them in auditing and preparing financial statements is backward in time towards the past ("followment, as opposed to management"). So as forecasters they may be severely handicapped, and even as counselors they may be overly inclined to extrapolate earlier experience, rather than concentrate on impacts of future events.

Cooper et al. found in their survey of National Federation of Independent Business firms that initially bookkeepers were most often considered important sources of counsel (46 percent), followed by bankers (32 percent), other business owners (28 percent), and suppliers (28 percent). Later in the venture's development, the accountants were still regarded as high in importance, while bankers were regarded as less so.[300] Bankers are chosen, according to a survey by the Technical Entrepreneurs Roundtable, much the same way as lawyers, at least by technology entrepreneurs. Most frequently business acquaintances are the source of referral (44 percent), while bankers and lawyers are the source only 18 percent of the time.[301]

Some accounting firms also offer more general business consulting services on other subjects such as pension and profit-sharing plans, and corporate strategy.

Consultants

The list of specialties for which consultants, who also generally charge by the hour, can

---

[299] Norm Brodsky, "No Accounting for Success," *Inc.*, June 1996, p. 25.
[300] Arnold C. Cooper and others, *New Business in America* (Washington, D.C.: The NFIB Foundation, 1990) p. 7.
[301] "Hands On," p. 114.

be hired is virtually endless. A few examples include, in addition to those just mentioned for accountants:

- Choosing appropriate software for special situations.
- Computer system selection, installation, familiarization, debugging, expansion.
- Cost reduction.
- Expert witnesses for lawsuits.
- Industrial design.
- Labor negotiations.
- Location analysis.
- Market research.
- Pay setting.
- Plant layout.
- Plant safety.
- Product failure analysis.
- Recruiting.
- Setting up or fixing computer systems.
- Training programs of all sorts.

Some of these categories break down into other specialties. For instance, computer-system help can include repairs, network installation, selecting system software, setting up a Web site, training employees in operation of it, and so forth. Even for a restaurant, more than one of these could apply, and special consultants could be hired for menu design, furniture selection, kitchen set-up, interior design, and more.

For finding consultants with the right specialty, the method is to ask around. For picking the right one, the method is to ask how many other similar jobs the consultant had done and also for references from enterprises in the same line of business that had the same kind of work done.

Consultants can be found on virtually any topic. Unfortunately, some will claim expertise on almost any issue, even though they may not have that expertise. Making inquiries with other business people who have bought a particular consulting service is probably the best way to check it out. Some specialize in helping prepare business plans, but those who read the plans usually prefer that they be written by the entrepreneurs who will carry them out.

Task paid

Some help sources are paid in cash on other bases than hourly, such as a bid for the job, usually described in a proposal they submit to get the job. Advertising agencies often charge a percentage of the cost of the advertising program they develop for a company.

Financial advisers

Sometimes companies use financial advisers or finders in seeking capital. This has been an area of sad experience for many who hired advisers, paid them advance fees for their work, and then never received results. A lesson from that experience is to check the references and track record of such a person carefully and consider the advice of other people before engaging one. Terms of the relationship should be written out, including:

- What transactions the help is to apply to and how broad ranging that application is.
- Whether the person has any type of exclusive rights.
- Amounts of money the person is to receive, including fees, expense reimbursements, timing, and any other parts of the deal.
- How long the relationship is to last.

Advertising professionals

Advertising agencies help with:

- Invention of effective themes, slogans.
- Design of brochures, displays, packages, advertisements.
- Placement of advertisements.
- Placement of public relations messages.

The *Standard Directory of Advertising Agencies* lists all but the smallest. For a start-up company with drastically limited cash, however, the smallest may be preferable, and that must be found locally by asking around.

Designers

Industrial designers help with:

- Graphics, plus styling of products and packages.
- Human factors such as ease of use, "foolproofness," comfort, safety, and so forth in design of products.

Designing packages, brochures, and general product configuration is something anyone can do and something the would-be entrepreneur who is dreaming up a business will likely do automatically as part of the thinking process, probably making sketches along the way.

But unless that person is trained, skilled, experienced, and with the times in taste, the result is virtually certain to be amateurish and likely to be out of tune with the times. Hence hiring a professional to help is advisable.

Sophia Collier considered package design to be so important to her SoHo soda pop start-up, that after reading extensively at the library about printing and packaging. she sought professional help. After choosing a general style, "art deco-ish," she looked for designers specializing in that style. One of them, Doug Johnson, expressed interest in the project until she told him she had no money. Then he told her to forget it.

But she persisted, and eventually persuaded him to accept a royalty for his help. "The fact that I kept coming back suggested that I would be as tenacious with other things," she said. "It gave him more faith in me."[302]

Other elements of Sophia's advice in addition to persistence included taking the time to learn about printing, the effects it can produce, and how to get them most economically, then making the designer a working partner by selecting one who is personally compatible, providing information as completely and early as possible, staying in close touch as the job progresses, and paying on time.

2. Indirectly paid professionals

Bankers

Suppliers

Anyone can walk into a bank and get information without charge. Banks profit by renting money, so they are interested in meeting prospective borrowers and they have reason to learn how to help borrowers succeed. In the case of commercial banks, those that service businesses as borrowers, they develop some expertise concerning how businesses can survive and prosper. They also become acquainted with appropriate information sources and many contacts. The way they get paid is through interest on successful loans.

Bankers

Specifically, bankers help with:

- Raising money.
- Obtaining credit reports on other companies.
- Anticipating financial binds.
- Providing introductions to helpful contacts.

Banks themselves, of course, offer numerous other services such as payroll processing, foreign exchange, and trust management as well as account functions familiar to individual customers.

Critical elements in a banking relationship, aside from whether or not the banker has expressed willingness to lend money to the venture and on what terms, are which bank officer will handle the venture's account, how much interest that person takes in the venture, how comfortable the entrepreneur is with that particular person, and how much weight that person carries within the bank. When a banker responds to a loan request with "I'll have to take that up with the loan committee," it is usually not a favorable sign. When the banker who is dealing with the entrepreneur moves to some other activity in the bank and is replaced by someone else as the venture's contact, it is sometimes very bad sign.

Suppliers

Suppliers have a vested interest in seeing a new venture that might be a future customer, succeed. Consequently, they are predisposed to help if they can and if it will not cost them too much. Large corporations with well-known names may have both talents and connections of value to the venture. They may be able, for instance, to use the venture in their advertisements to capture favorable interest for themselves, while the venture itself gets free advertising. Useful advice in product development, contacts for other help, provision

---

[302] J. Donald Weinrauch and Nancy Croft Baker, *The Frugal Marketer* (New York: AMACOM, 1989).

of samples, and extension of credit all may come from suppliers.

Against potential gains from giving help to the venture, suppliers must weigh three possibilities: first, that the venture either will not succeed and therefore not be able to pay the suppliers back at all; second, that it will survive but remain very small and therefore not return the investment made to help it; and third, that after it gets going, the venture will shift to other suppliers. It is natural for suppliers to favor their most important customers and to avoid those who lack a proven track record of paying bills. Even with such precautions, suppliers continually absorb bad debts. Bankruptcy filings typically report liabilities in excess of assets, which is an indication of bills that suppliers are unable to collect.

The way to find suppliers is by asking around from one referral to the next until the needed suppliers are found. Some places to start in this search process in addition to the Web include:

- Yellow Pages of the phone book.
- A manufacturers' directory for the city or state.
- Thomas Register in the library.
- Firms that might use the same type of supplier.

Once a suitable supplier is located, a selling job by the customer (entrepreneur) begins. Quality, delivery time, price, and credit terms, if any, must be arranged, and usually the start-up founder is at a disadvantage. Some suppliers are sympathetic to entrepreneurs, but most are not so generous that they will jeopardize either money or other customers to help out. They may require payment on delivery or even in advance. They may put other orders ahead and deliver later than promised. They may compromise any prior arrangements, and for that reason the entrepreneur must stay in close touch. This may be difficult with all the other demands to be met during start-up, but it may be necessary to get the needed help.

3. Other individuals

Unlike company executives, entrepreneurs don't have staffs of specialists to help them out on either general advice or specialized areas of expertise. Sometimes, as will be discussed later, they fill this need by hiring outside experts. But there is often much help available free that can be tapped first. Hence, networking is a valuable skill to develop, and building a network is a worthwhile activity that can begin at any time, preferably long before the venture so it will be in place when needed. According to a study by Butler and Hansen, breadth in social networks appeared to expand the set of options open to entrepreneurs for start-ups.[303]

Networks

The crucial value of an entrepreneur's invisible organization and of close versus loose ties was discussed in Chapter 1. It's not possible to know during design and start-up of the venture exactly which types of contacts will be needed; having a bigger network to draw upon is better than having a small one. But having one that understands, trusts, and is willing to help the entrepreneur can also be important. So both close and loose network contacts can be valuable.

Since drawing upon contacts in the network may not cost money, but it will cost time, there is reason to think about managing the network, starting with being willing to meet people, seek people out, and initiate acquaintances. At some point it will be helpful to build a computerized address book and possibly acquire a digital business card reader to make part of the process easier. A Web site devoted to networking, where subscribers can tell about their talents and what they can offer as well as what they want, (ryze.com) was set up by an early investor in Napster. As of 2004, it claimed to have 140,000 members and be profitable. Other networking sites include Ecademy.com, Tribe.com, and Lindekin.com, intended for corporate officers who want to communicate with

Networks

---

[303] John E. Butler and Gary S. Hansen, "Managing Social Network Evolution and Entrepreneurial Benefits," in *Frontiers of Entrepreneurship Research*, 1988, eds. Bruce H. Kirchhoff and others (Wellesley, MA: Babson Center for Entrepreneurial Studies, 1988) p. 430.

each other. Scott Allen, founder of OnlineBusinessNetworks.com, commented on the efficiency of such sites:

> You might spend five hours, counting drive time, going to an industry event and come back with two or three good contacts, if you're lucky. Spend the same five hours online, and you can post meaningful messages on a dozen sites, each of which has hundreds or thousands of the kind of people you need. I guarantee you'll make more quality contacts.[304]

Entrepreneurs

Many entrepreneurs have a philanthropic streak sometimes expressed in a phrase like, "When I was getting started some other people helped me. Now I figure it's my turn." So long as the start-up is not a competitive threat, and sometimes even if it might be, they take pleasure in sharing their experiences, expertise, and sometimes financial assistance.

Some entrepreneurs find that demand for their expertise becomes so high that they can't afford the time cost and consequently start charging for it, possibly thereby entering a new line of business, consulting.[305] Michael Dell commented that he tried to surround himself with smart advisers.

> In 1985 a venture capitalist, Lee Walker, was recruited as CEO for Dell Computer and promptly helped the company further by calling a banker he knew and arranging for a line of credit. Later, he also helped the company recruit some distinguished and highly successful people for its board of directors.[306]

All these types of advisers may be able to help in finding other useful contacts. The way to evaluate such advisers is to learn about what they have done before and to talk with other people who have worked with them. This leads naturally to further contacts. As a general rule, smaller companies do better working with smaller professional firms and agencies. That way they represent a relatively larger share of the professionals' business and are more likely to get the attention of top members in the professional firms rather than being relegated to apprentices.

Board of directors

If the venture is incorporated, as it likely will be when outside investors are involved, it must have directors, which provides yet another basis for recruiting advisers in that capacity. Technically, the role of directors is to represent shareholders and see to it that the corporation is run in their best interests.

In fact, the situation is a bit more complicated than that. An important question concerns which shareholders are in fact represented. If one shareholder holds controlling interest, then that shareholder can appoint the majority of directors, who may in effect become a "rubber stamp board" for the wishes of that shareholder. If the directors are shareholders themselves, they may be biased to have the corporation conform to their own personal interests, rather than the interests of all shareholders. Directors, in addition to serving on the board, also do business with the corporation as customers, consultants, or other suppliers, and they may be biased to comply with what the company wants in order not to lose the business they personally have with the corporation. Even the fees they receive for being directors or the prestige they may feel from being on the board may bias them not to think and speak independently or on behalf of the shareholders as they are supposed to. According to Jack Savidge, whose experience has included serving on over two dozen boards of directors in companies large, small, old, and young over the years, a directors' meeting subject to such biases might go as follows.

> The directors get there about 11 a.m., all shake hands and chat a bit and then ask, 'What's for lunch?' Then during lunch the CEO will say something like, 'Well, let me tell you how the company is. It's all OK and going OK.' The directors say, 'Terrific. What's for dessert?' and that's the end of the board meeting. This sort of situation, where the CEO is strong and the board is weak, then sometimes leads to problems that show up later as scandals in the newspapers where things were done improperly and illegally in the company, resulting in trouble for everybody and possibly legal prosecution for some.

---

[304] Chris Tucker, "Joined at the Chip," *Southwest Airlines Spirit*, June 2004, p. 48.
[305] Tucker, "Joined," p. 48.
[306] Michael Dell, *Direct from Dell* (NY: Harper, 1999) p. 21.

The right type of board is, in Savidge's view, one that is "actively decisive." This type of board comes to directors' meetings prepared to ask management tough questions. Moreover, they will be able, as the tough questions begin to expose problems, say things like, "All right, I should be able to make a couple of quick calls that can help fix that, because we faced that same problem in another company I worked with," and offer constructive suggestions based on their experience.

Providing help as a director usually requires effort, and effort usually calls for compensation. There may be some people who will provide effort gratis to a start-up. Here and there an entrepreneur who has prospered and wants "to give something back," or a retired executive who is more concerned with being active than with compensation may be willing to contribute to the venture without compensation. Most others will require it, either in the form of pay, ownership, or possibly expenses to meet at a vacation spot. How to provide enough compensation with meager resources can be a major problem for a start-up wanting help from directors. There may be the alternative of an exchange of free help in return from the entrepreneur, but the entrepreneur may not be able to afford the time.

The board formally should have a compensation committee that annually reviews both what top management is paid and what the directors themselves are paid. Beyond the board are shareholders who elect it, and if shareholders disagree with the decisions the board makes about pay, they have the right to vote on replacement of board members.

There will also be an audit committee, whose responsibility is to make sure that arrangements are in place and people with the appropriate skills and motivation are engaged to keep the books and reporting straight. In addition, there may be a nominating committee charged with appointing and renewing the appointments of officers and of directors.

As the new venture gets started and grows, it will likely need changes in the board from directors whose experience is with start-ups to directors more familiar with problems that arise downstream and eventually perhaps to directors who have experience dealing with management in large companies. It is unlikely that the directors will be sufficiently immersed all the way along to develop changes in their expertise from one level of company to another. At early stages, for instance, directors have responsibilities to shareholders and to society for obeying the law and having the corporation do so; these responsibilities open them to the potential of lawsuits and prosecution. Insurance can be bought to protect against lawsuits in performance of their work. But it is usually expensive, reflecting the fact that the risks are significant. These in turn impose a disincentive for people to become directors.

Advisory board

A partial solution for some companies it to appoint, in addition to its board of directors, a board of advisers who can ask helpful questions and provide guidance and expertise, but not have formal responsibility for how the company is run.

If a company has great ambitions of growing and perhaps one day going public and it can back those ambitions up with a convincing plan, it may be able both to attract prominent directors and use them to bolster its image. However, that rarely seems to happen. Even among the *Inc.* 500 companies, which were selected for their high growth rates, 43 percent were found to have no outside directors.[307] At start-up and among more "ordinary" small firms this percentage would likely be as great or greater.[308] It appears that those companies that add such directors most often seem to do it out of needs that arise downstream from start-up when they and directors can both offer more to each other.[309]

Investors

Those who put money into the venture thereby become allies, at least in helping it move

[307] "Hands On," *Inc.*, October 1990, p. 151.
[308] Flynn Bucy and Sam Seaman, "Relationship Between Role, Composition and Perceived Benefits of Boards of Directors for Privately Owned Firms," in *Frontiers of Entrepreneurship Research*, 1988, eds. Bruce H. Kirchhoff and others (Wellesley, MA: Babson Center for Entrepreneurial Studies, 1988) p. 499.
[309] Elizabeth Conlin, "Unlimited Partners," *Inc.*, April 1990, p. 71.

forward when they invest, and ideally beyond that. It is in the entrepreneur's best interest to make them glad of the investment and, as the venture prospers, in their best interest to continue helping it, perhaps by investing further and possibly in other ways as well.

Silent partners

Those who put money into a company but do not participate in its management are sometimes characterized as silent partners.

Being silent, however, does not mean that they don't have rights, don't ask questions, don't make their views known, or don't exert influence. At the time of their investment, they may impose requirements as part of the deal, and these may be written into the partnership agreement giving them rights, such as access to certain information or to step in if the venture is managed adversely or gets into trouble.

4. Institutions

Associations

Government

Institutions

Recognition that new ventures create jobs and add useful new products and services has inspired institutions of various types to help them.

Associations

Trade associations can be very helpful providers of information on specific industries. Sources of information about them include The Encyclopedia of Associations and the Directory of the National Trade and Professional Associations of the United States. The associations themselves gather and share information, providing contacts, newsletters, and meetings where members can exchange helpful suggestions and moral support.

Government

Federal government agencies attempt to favor small firms in making purchases and issuing R&D contracts. The SBA in particular helps by guaranteeing bank loans to start-ups and small firms. It also offers free consultation services, seminars, and literature on many aspects of starting and running small businesses. A telephone call to the nearest SBA office can provide an inventory of services available from the agency. Three government programs under the SBA that provide direct assistance to smaller firms are the Small Business Institute Program, in which participating universities assign student consulting teams to work with the company, the Service Corps of Retired Executives (SCORE), in which retired executives donate their services, and the Active Corps of Executives (ACE), in which currently active ex-

ecutives do so. None of these programs costs money to the company.

State governments usually seek to help start-up and small firms through publication of booklets on requirements for setting up a business in the state, and sometimes other services. City governments also try to help in various ways. Both the local chamber of commerce and the state department of commerce are places to call for finding out what help is available. The pros and cons of drawing upon government programs vary from case to case. Some impose strings, while others do not. Some cost money and others are free. The effectiveness of a given program depends upon the particular government people running it, what their prior experience is, how heavily they are scheduled at the moment, and so forth. So it can pay to investigate, provided not too much time is spent on that task.

Institutions

Universities provide extension courses on starting and running businesses. Participating in such a seminar can be a way to meet other entrepreneurs who can help. Some universities also operate Small Business Institute programs in which students provide consulting services to entrepreneurs, as mentioned above, for course credit. Some universities also operate Small Business Development Centers in which professionals are employed to provide free consulting services to small firms.

Places to contact at the university are its office of extension programs and its business school. If the entrepreneur has a particular type of help in mind, such as market research or setting up an accounting system, then contact with the chairperson of the department teaching that subject may also be a good place to start.

Incubators

Facilities designed to house start-ups and small businesses take many forms, from conventional industrial parks to university centers that provide access to faculty. Some charge low rent thanks to subsidies. Others are conventional industrial real estate. All have the advantage of proximity to other entrepreneurs with whom to share problems, solutions, comfort, and experiences.[310]

Whether a particular incubator is right for the venture or not will likely warrant some investigation. Some small industrial parks are simply collections of buildings operated by landlords primarily for earning as much rent as they can in areas zoned for business activities. Others are operated by communities or non-profit organizations for alternative primary objectives such as developing jobs in the community, even if rents are not maximized.

Still others attempt to provide services for start-ups to increase the odds of their succeeding. Universities with incubators sometimes trade on the availability of faculty and students to provide special expertise or low-cost help. But, as Esser points out, this help will probably have a price that may be worth considering before signing up. About the Cambridge Incubator at MIT she said:

> To ensure that the companies that move into the incubator will be able to obtain the resources they need as soon as they need them, the incubator fixes the company up with a few members of its special "leadership team."
>
> I wonder how much control an entrepreneur would have over the business that he was trying to build when the people who control his purse strings are

sitting right on the other side of the office. And then I wonder how a new entrepreneur—a person who has quit his job and assumed the significant financial risk of starting his own company—would feel about sharing the control of his company with 'experts?'[311]

To this she adds echoes from three other entrepreneurs:

– You're going to get some advice; you're going to get some facilities assistance. And how much do you want to pay for that in the equity side of your business?

– We never considered using an incubator. It was too expensive. If you're a resourceful person, you'll find a way to get things done.

– The best advice is from your customers.

Information sources

Web sites for entrepreneurs are innumerable and include:

entrepreneur.com *Entrepreneur* magazine
inc.com *Inc.* magazine
sba.gov The U.S. Small Business Administration
kauffman.org The Kauffman Foundation

In addition to the two magazines mentioned among these Web sites, all the major business magazines and papers such as *The Wall Street Journal* carry entrepreneurship stories and information. Business sections of local newspapers also frequently carry news of recent entrepreneurial exploits in their business sections. Most major U.S. cities also have weekly local business newspapers, such as the *Puget Sound Business Journal, Los Angeles Business Journal, Orange County Business Journal, San Diego Business Journal,* and *Crain's Chicago Business,* each of which tells about the adventures of recent start-ups in its metropolitan area. Occasionally, individual entrepreneurs write histories of their experiences in detail.

5. Corporations, strategic alliances

One or more outside corporations may be the most powerful help source a start-up can have, but only if the relationship works right. The corporation may have virtually everything

the start-up lacks: abundant resources, credibility, connections, expertise, quite possibly a market, and staying power. A study of electronics companies with sales under $100 million

---

[310] Raymond W. Smilor and Michel D. Gill, Jr., *The New Business Incubator* (Lexington, MA: Lexington Books, 1986)
[311] Teresa Esser, *The Venture Café* (New York: Warner Books, 2002) p. 50.

Joint ventures

reported in the June 1990 issue of *Inc.* found that 71 percent had some sort of strategic alliance, most often for market channels.[312]

Large manufacturers, such as automobile, aircraft, and electronics makers typically have hundreds of small suppliers. In part their relationships may be adversarial, as when the large company purchases from the suppliers on competitive bidding that pits the suppliers against each other. Large retail chains also sometimes operate that way. In recent years, however, many large corporations have decided it is more to their benefit to develop longer-lasting relationships that include loyalty and reliability.

Motivations for established corporations to help new ventures include: (1) gaining windows into new technologies and embryonic markets while they are still niches, (2) gaining help on research and innovation from founders and employees of start-ups and small firms, (3) getting new ideas with a flexible organizational unit that can move quickly to try them out, (4) gaining a customer, (5) opening additional sources of supply, (6) retaining productive efforts and access to talents of employees who prefer to operate on their own, (7) getting to know potential recruits with new ideas, and (8) putting cash to work through investment in start-ups whose markets and technologies they understand and with whom they may gain other benefits through mutual cooperation. Corporations may be able to get these things from start-ups with cash, or they may do so through collaborating with them either informally or formally.

Even competitors form strategic alliances. Microsoft writes software for Apple's operating system, which competes with Microsoft. General Motors collaborates with Toyota. Aerospace companies like Boeing and Lockheed and Martin, each bringing with it a host of smaller subcontractors, form coalitions to bid on government contracts. They work together on the proposal or a series of proposals, then prototypes, and finally in the case of the winning consortium, they jointly carry out the production contract for a new weapon system.

What is to be gained from the venture's point of view can include: (1) financial support, (2) market connections, (3) credibility by association with a powerful name, with suppliers, customers and prospective employees, (4) employee expertise, (5) use of equipment or space, (6) cross-licensing of complementary technology, (7) servicing help, and (8) cooperative advertising.

But these mutual benefits do not necessarily come easily or even at all. They may come early and then go away as circumstances, leadership, or motivations of either party change. Even with the best initial intentions, strategic alliances between companies, including those between start-ups and corporations, can end up as negative experiences. Therefore it makes sense to approach them with investigation, understanding, and care.

Joint ventures

One mode of strategic alliance is joint venturing. A joint venture is a distinct enterprise, or multi-organizational agreement, created as an alliance between two or more parent organizations that design, own, and oversee it. Joint ventures may involve the parent companies' sharing equity, or they may be contractual, where the payoff is other than ownership. There may also be passive investors or silent partners in the deal.

Alliances are often used for global collaboration where an established company in one country that wants to enter business in another country does so by partnering with another company in that other country to form a jointly owned subsidiary for doing business there with both parents sharing the benefits.

In other cases, a company with a new technology may join forces with another that possesses complementary technology to share in the benefits of combining both. Joint venturing is common among biotechnology start-ups, where massive amounts of cash are required over a long period of time with no revenues coming in while development efforts aimed at earning FDA approval play out. Particularly in current times when technologies are changing fast this approach is useful, but its practice goes far back.

The Radio Corporation of America (RCA) was formed in 1910 as a joint subsidiary between

---

312 "Hotline," *Inc.*, June 1990, p. 33.

General Electric and Westinghouse to capitalize on their common interests in the new technology. It produced the first radio sets for popular consumption, and the first broadcast network. In 1932 after 22 years of operating jointly, it was forced to become independent by U.S. government antitrust action. Later, it went on to introduce the first TV sets for popular consumption and the first color TV.[313]

According to findings of Woodside and Pitts, a joint venture is more likely to succeed if its purpose is to exploit a product-market opportunity for both firms, than if the opportunity is just for one of the firms or if it is in response to a crisis in one of the firms. Typically, joint ventures take six months to three years to implement. Failures to get off the ground arise from poor fit in working out details to implement the shared vision. Rates of failure in joint ventures are high—7 out of 14 terminated.[314]

Joint ventures, the same authors point out, tend to be inherently unstable because circumstances constantly change and are more likely to introduce divergence than co-linearity of goals. Two main causes of failure are perception of unequal benefits and decline in resource availability at one or both of the partners.

More successful joint ventures were found to:

- Focus more on aggressive market growth as opposed to market defense.
- Put less emphasis on short-term profits.
- Aim at both financial and market objectives simultaneously.
- Emphasize product superiority as a distinctive competence.
- List a greater number of distinctive competencies.
- Put more responsibility at the operating level.
- Put more emphasis on teamwork and group responsibility.
- Put less emphasis on hierarchy.
- Make less use of variable and ad hoc job specifications.

Important third parties often involved included banks, suppliers, distributors, and possibly customers.[315]

Other types of strategic alliances

In contrast to ventures which are set up and jointly owned between corporations are strategic alliances between corporations and ventures that are operated by independent entrepreneurs and other investors. Advantages are similar to those mentioned above, although the venture ownership by independent entrepreneurs can impart stronger motivation and dedication, which may work for or against harmony with the corporation.

Harrison and Mason reported that 77 percent of Massachusetts software companies formed alliances.[316] For example, introduction of the first microcomputer was accomplished by an alliance between a small hardware corporation (MITS) and a start-up software company (Microsoft). But getting such alliances to work can be tricky, as that particular one illustrated by falling apart when Bill Gates and Paul Allen wanted to go their separate ways.

Katila found from a study of 103 new biotechnology companies that technological collaboration had contradictory effects: while a number of partners and their average industry tenure were positively related with start-up growth and total innovative output, collaboration sometimes became "a liability for radical innovation."[317]

For technological enterprises strategic alliance mechanisms include exchange of technological information, investment, and cross-licensing. Hewlett-Packard, Epson, and Canon, for instance, have cross-licensing agreements that allow each to use printer technology patented by the other. Monsanto, Intel, and other large corporations have invested in start-ups to gain the windows on new technology that the start-ups are working on. Microsoft works closely with independent software developers to help them develop products that work with windows.

---

[313] "RCA's New Vista, the Bottom Line," *Business Week*, July 4, 1977, pp. 38-44.

[314] Arch G. Woodside and Robert E. Pitts, *Creating and Managing International Joint Ventures* (Westport, CT: Quorum, 1956).

[315] Woodside and Pitts, Creating, p. 134.

[316] Richard T. Harrison and Colin M. Mason, "Entrepreneurial Growth Strategies and Venture Performance in the Software Industry," in *Frontiers of Entrepreneurship Research*, 1997, eds. Paul D. Reynolds and others (Wellesley, MA: Babson Center for Entrepreneurial Studies, 1997) p. 449.

[317] Riitta Katila, "Technology Strategies for Growth and Innovation," in, *Frontiers of Entrepreneurship Research*, 1997 eds. Paul D. Reynolds and others (Wellesley, MA: Babson Center for Entrepreneurial Studies, 1997) p. 405.

Purposes of such collaborations, according to Hitt, et al. include (1) reducing the time from development to market entry, (2) maintaining market leadership, (3) establishing industry standards that competitors then will have to follow, (4) reducing the risks of research and development, and (5) reducing the uncertainty of technology and market. Alliances can either be vertical in the profit chain or horizontal.

Collaboration can also take the form of less formal cooperation. Trade associations make this possible in a structured way, where companies within an industry meet, share contacts, and cooperate on developing contracts and exchanging tricks of the trade. Less formal networks within industries also make successful use of such exchanges. Human and Provan[318] reported that such exchanges, even among competitors, were effective.

Alliance setup work

A host of factors can influence how well alliances work. Most powerful for small manufacturing firms, for instance, seems to be the closeness of collaboration linkages between a firm, its customers, and its suppliers in what Naumes and others[319] characterized as a "vertical supplier and customer network" where producer companies collaborate with marketing companies. There they found product and process innovation, facilitated by such linkages, were more important in competing than was price.

The tasks involved in setting up a strategic alliance are similar in some respects to those for developing a personal partnership in a venture. A summary list of steps appears in Exhibit 7b–1. They begin with recognition that partnering could have some advantages such as those mentioned above for both parties. The large firm or the entrepreneur may either happen upon or seek out a partner. Searching systematically to find a better partner than the first one that turns up may be worth the effort.

Exhibit 7b-1 Sequence for strategic alliance

1. Identify purpose of alliance.
2. Weigh alliance against other ways of achieving the purpose.
3. Seek and assess candidate corporations.
4. Get introduction or learn name and position of contact in corporation.
5. Identify alliance objectives of both organizations.
6. Identify potential sources of conflict, present and future.
7. Meet key participants in the corporation (recognizing they may change).
8. Work out plan for cooperation and solving future problems.
9. Develop contract and have it reviewed by start-up's counsel.
10. Work to make the most of the alliance.

For the venture seeking alliance with a corporation, getting a meeting with the right people in the corporation tends to be more complicated than seeking one with an individual. Whom to seek out in the corporation and how to get into contact with the right person may be hard to work out, unless the entrepreneur has special help from a connection who can make appropriate introductions. Three roles to be aware of in the corporation are (1) the closer, (2) the enforcer, and (3) the advocate.

The closer is the person who persuades or reinforces upon the entrepreneur that joining in alliance is a good idea.

The enforcer role is more legalistic. If negotiation begins with a person in the corporation high up, the details of working out the deal will likely be delegated downward to someone who feels pressure to work out terms that are at least as advantageous to the corporation as the higher-up proposed, or preferably more advantageous, which is to say worse for the entrepreneur. After that, the enforcer's job will be to make sure that the corporation does not fail to take advantage of terms it has in the deal.

---

[318] Sherrie E. Human and Keith G. Provan, "External Resource Exchange and Perceptions of Competitiveness Within Organizational Networks," in *Frontiers of Entrepreneurship Research*, 1996, eds. Paul D. Reynolds and others (Wellesley, MA: Babson Center for Entrepreneurial Studies, 1996) p. 240.

[319] William Naumes and others, "Competitive Advantage of Small Firms," in *Frontiers of Entrepreneurship Research*, 1992, eds. Neil C. Churchill and others (Wellesley, MA: Babson Center for Entrepreneurial Studies, 1992) p. 326.

The advocate's job is to try to make the deal work for both parties. How well he or she will be able to do that will be a function of how high the person is in the corporation, whom they report to, what their boss wants, how much they care, and how competent they are. If these factors are poor, the venture may be in for a rough time of it, while the entrepreneur attempts to deal with or go around the person.

The advocate or liaison person will be the corporate person responsible for making the links between corporation and venture work over time. Generally, the higher the position of the advocate, the more that person can do to help or hurt the venture. But also the higher the advocate's position, the lower the priority that person can give to working with the venture, as opposed to taking care of other responsibilities in the corporation.

These roles may be played by the same person or by different people in the corporation. Part of the entrepreneur's job is to figure out who they are and what pressures are acting on them, as well as how they operate. Those pressures may come from the nature of the corporation and how it works inside. They may also come from events outside the corporation, as it attempts to make the most of its own strategic position relative to both its industry and the opportunity that it and the venture are linking up to exploit.

Ways an alliance can go wrong unless they are anticipated include misunderstanding these roles and their expectations, changes over time in motivations, miscalculation of what was possible, feelings that things are working out unfairly, personal hard feelings between the responsible representatives of the companies, failure to gain the advantages that were sought, and of course changes in the venture's circumstance introduced by other events unrelated to the alliance in particular.

Things that sometimes go wrong include:

- Setup costs exceed expectations.
- Coordination costs are too high.
- Erosion of competitive position.
- Emergence of adverse bargaining position.
- Dependency weakening both parties.

- Outcomes become less certain.
- Disagreement over authority and decision-making power arise.
- Management time demands are too great.
- Key people leave or get transferred.
- Imbalance in benefits develops.
- Imbalance occurs in commitment and motivation.
- Communication delays and misunderstandings cause mistakes.
- Response to new problems or opportunities slows.
- Negotiation time is excessive.
- Disentanglement or divorce raises expenses and leaves resentments.

Cautionary questions

From a list of things that can go awry, such as the above, should follow thoughts about how to avoid them, possibly by looking further for a partner or by tabling the quest for an alliance. Some questions that may help with this decision are as follows:

1. Is the partner being chosen as best, or just as convenient?
2. How well are interests really aligned and likely to stay aligned?
3. Is the timing right for both venture and prospective ally? For how long?
4. What are the prospective benefits and costs over time for both partners?
5. Who will have to carry how much "maintenance load" at the venture end?
6. How clear and likely to be stable are the motivations of the prospective partner?
7. What might change and obsolete the prospective arrangement?
8. Do the odds of its working out warrant the time to investigate and negotiate?
9. Which person at what level will be the continuing contact in the other company?
10. How may the venture's freedom to deal elsewhere be affected by this deal?

Contractual provisions

Considerations to include in working out a formal agreement between the companies are numerous and include nature and scope, mutuality of interest, structure, ownership, copyright, trademark, patent and secrecy rights, voting rights, liquidation rights, valuation of assets, contributions (cash or other?), allocation of costs, divestment procedures, board of directors, management contract, payments, royalties, fees, salaries, operating expenses, resolution of disputes, assistance, training, quality control, handbooks, manuals, sale of assets, purchase of assets of various sizes, transfer of know-how, any performance guarantees, right to observe or obtain information, duties to report, exclusivity (e.g., using the technology beyond the contract), secrecy and confidentiality, reporting requirements, technology sharing requirements, sharing or divergent use of facilities, uses of IP, settlement of disputes, timing requirements, handling of tax disputes, and penalties for violations.[320]

Help on complexities

As the massiveness of these lists and considerations suggests, working out a strategic alliance can be a very challenging job. It is also one where specialists can help. Clearly, there will be need for legal help in working out contracts. Consultants may also be able to help as finders for potential partners and in subsequent stages of the process which, with experience, can to some degree be routinized. The entrepreneur below built a business based on buildup of experience in alliance formation.

> As a sophomore night student at Brigham Young University in 1986, Sarah Gerdes took a full-time job at a 350-employee software company, WordPerfect, where her assignment in the marketing department included reviewing business plans of companies wanting alliances with her employer. She recalled, "It was amazing to me that CEO's would tell me that 25 to 30 percent of their time was spent 'creating alliances,' but so few knew how to structure, create, and execute them." Big companies had trouble finding the right small ones and small companies had trouble finding whom to talk to in big companies and how.[321]

> She started working as a consultant to different software companies, developing progressively more contacts as she gained expertise in how to help companies find the right partners and work out alliances more effectively and efficiently. She said, "I went with the market demand and developed my key contacts from there. The value of my past experience was primarily in identifying an opportunity, correctly targeting the decision maker, pitching the idea, and then delivering the goods." She created a Microsoft contact, for instance, by calling an employee there whose name she noticed in a press release. "Elapsed time: 10 minutes."

> From software she branched into helping potential partners in other industrial areas gain alliances, taking payment partly in fees and partly in stock. By late 1999, she had achieved sales of $4.7 million per year and built up a client stock portfolio worth $4.8 million. She published a book in 2003 describing the lessons learned and systems developed through her experience as a strategic alliance consultant.[322]

Indication of the power of practice can be seen in the reduction of time taken to form partnerships and the increase in return in investment on them in clients of Gerdes' firm. At the start, the average alliance took from 18 to 24 months to develop and yielded $35,000 per year. Later, after her firm gained experience in helping form some 400 alliances, average development time had dropped to five months and average return was $3 million per year, presumably on bigger and more complex deals.

The entrepreneur in need of outside help, whether on legal, marketing, strategic alliance formation, or some other facet of the venture, will often have to decide whether to spend cash to get greater speed and higher performance from a professional, or to do the work personally at greater cost in personal time and possibly with higher odds of something going wrong.

---

[320] M.B. Rao, *Joint Ventures* (New Delhi: Vikas Publishing, 1999).
[321] Christopher Caggiano, "Hotlinks," *Inc.*, October 1999, p. 74.
[322] Sarah Gerdes, *Navigating the Partnership Maze* (New York: McGraw-Hill, 2003).

Exercises

Text discussion questions

1. Why are some professionals directly paid and others indirectly paid, and how might exceptions occur?
2. What tradeoffs might point to choosing a lower versus higher paid professional for help?
3. What might explain the finding of Woodside and Pitts about when a joint veture is most likely to succeed?
4. If you were working in a start-up and were asked to explore the prospects of adding competitive strength through forming an alliance, how would you go about it?

Case questions

7B-1 Andrew Hammoude

1. Develop a list of outside team members Andrew Hammoude should seriously consider trying to recruit for his company.
2. Rank order the above list two ways, (1) in importance, and (2) in sequence for being approached for recruiting. As part of this, estimate how he should recruit them.
3. Which remarks from the audience seem to be most valuable and why?
4. If Andrew wants to implement what you suggest in answer to the above questions, what actions should he take to do it?

7B-2 Jerry Kaplan

1. Which outside participants has GO (a) fared best with, versus (b) worst with so far and why?
2. What rules, in rank order of importance, should GO follow in dealing with partners from this point forward?
3. Could there be other ways to create a company for producing a product like this than through strategic partnering with other companies?
4. What, as best you can tell from events up to the time of his appointment as CEO at the end of the case, should Bill Campbell have done next?

Portfolio page possibilities

Page 7B-1 Outside team recruitment

1. List on one page the most important questions you would use, in rank order, for recruiting outside team members for your venture.
2. Indicate both the type of individuals and their most important functions.
3. Where possible, also list names, contact information, and expected charges.

Page 7B-2 Outside team budget

Prepare a budget of both time and money you would expect your outside team members to cost during the first two years of start-up.

Term Projects

Venture history

1. What outside specialists were used during start-up, how were they picked, and how did their costs range?
2. How did the benefits gained from outsiders compare to the above costs, both in time and in money, of using them?
3. How would the founders feel about giving assistance to other entrepreneurs who were starting up, and why?
4. What experiences with firm strategic alliances during start-up, whether formal or informal, did the founders have and what did they learn from them?

Venture planning guide

1. List the names and qualifications of the most critically important suppliers of goods and advice, and briefly describe what they will be needed for, what they will cost and on what payment terms.
2. Explain the rationale behind your choice of lawyer(s), accounting firm, and commercial bank that the venture will use.
3. Explain whom you expect to have for directors, if your firm incorporates, what the cost of appropriate liability insurance for them will be, and what you will do about it.

Part 8

STARTING UP

Two chapters comprise this section. The first deals with generating sales and the second with developing productive operations to deliver on those sales. That order of topics may fit the sequence with which the venture actually starts. Or the order may be reversed, with operations beginning first to create the output to be sold.

Compared to established companies, start-ups have special advantages and disadvantages in selling. Shortage of company reputation and established relationships are some of the disadvantages, while novelty, freshness, and enthusiasm are typically among the advantages. A variety of routes exists for gaining sales, each of which fits one venture or another at one time or another, and all of which can therefore be worth considering in preparing to venture.

Most likely, a combination of tactics for gaining sales will be used. Selling involves choices of price, channels, communication, and timing as well as just what product and/or service combination is to be offered. Each of these can set precedents that linger. Low prices can be hard to raise later, but high prices may attract competitors sooner. Channels take push to start, and push to change, particularly for a new company with no reputation. Investing in education of the wrong market wastes resources. Failing to educate the right one produces no sales. Rolling out a sales campaign either too early (product not really ready yet?) or too late (competitors have already entered the market?) can be fatal, as can simply (because of inexperience?) doing it incompetently.

An important initial advantage most ventures have in selling is that the CEO of the venture personally does it. It counts with customers that the top executive of their supplier is their contact in the transaction. The entrepreneur at the same time benefits by being in direct contact with customers to understand their desires and reactions as a basis for directing the company to satisfy them, and understand their future needs and preferences better than competitors do.

Operations, the topic of the second chapter in this section, must fit with selling to complete that satisfaction of customers. In this area too, starting anew will afford the venture special advantages and disadvantages to be planned for and dealt with. Suppliers will likely be slow to extend credit and, because the venture's first purchases will probably be small, suppliers also may not be motivated to go full out in providing attractive prices and top service. The need to develop new working relationships may also put an extra load on the venture.

Recruiting employees may pose challenges because of the lack of resources and initially precarious existence. Job security and fringe benefits may not match those of established companies with which the venture competes in recruiting employees. And, of course, everyone in the venture is importantly learning new working patterns, which take time to smooth out.

But newness gives the venture a chance to build the culture that best fits it, whereas established companies are essentially stuck with cultures they have and can't change. Culture largely determines how well the company works, how efficient and innovative it is, and how its employees cooperate. Crucial in setting the direction of culture are such things as how jobs are defined, who is hired, what rules and instruction they are given, and what example(s) the founder(s) set. With a start-up these are all open territory.

CHAPTER 8A – Selling

Topics

1. Start-up selling as special
2. Alternative paths to sales
3. Responding to customer requests
4. Personal dealing
5. Site selling
6. Reaching out

Checkpoints

a. How are the 4 P's of marketing different for new ventures?
b. What special hurdles do start-ups face in selling?
c. Explain the advantages entrepreneurs have in generating sales.
d. What kinds of customers invite entrepreneurs to sell to them?
e. Who typically makes the first sale for a start-up and why?
f. Describe three types of sites start-ups can set up to seek sales.
g. What combinations of sales approaches might a start-up use?
h. Describe four patterns of selling through other people in a start-up.

Selling is a continual job for many entrepreneurs, and not just in the marketing end of the business. Other parties who must be sold include money providers, network contacts, prospective cofounders and employees, suppliers and advisers whose help is needed, and customers from whom orders to buy and payment of subsequent receivables are needed. However, it is upon selling to customers that this chapter will focus.

The importance of selling can be seen in a study by Terpstra and Olson.[323] Based upon responses from 120 of the *Inc.* 500 high-growth firms in 1987, they found that by far the most frequently encountered problems during start-up were in sales and marketing, as displayed in Exhibit 8a-1 below.

This emphasis puts selling to customers at the center of the venture founder's concerns.

A profile of first sales in *Inc.* 500 from 1994 indicates that 45 percent started with a marketing plan, and the average firm spent an average 8.5 months studying the market before launch. Fifty-eight percent did their own selling, and the remainder used independent representatives. The average time to make a sale was 3.8 months, the same as it had been in 1990.[324]

Exhibit 8a-1 Frequency of problems during start-up

Problem areas during the first year	Frequency percent
Sales and marketing	38%
Obtaining external financing	17
Internal financial management	16
General management	11
Product development	5
Human-resource management	5
Production and operations management	4
Economic environment	3
Regulatory environment	1
Total	100

[323] David E. Terpstra and Philip D. Olson, "Entrepreneurial Start-up and Growth: A Classification of Problems," *Entrepreneurship Theory and Practice*, 17, no. 3, Spring 1993, p. 5.
[324] Stephanie L. Gruner, "Benchmarks," *Inc.* January 1996.

1. Start-up selling as special

1. Start-up selling as special

Seven start-up selling hurdles

Based on their experience with some 200 ventures, a group of 14 Chicago venture capitalists interviewed by Hills[325] indicated that on a scale of one to seven, marketing management by entrepreneurs should be rated 6.7, more important than any other business function. They also saw new ventures as facing different marketing challenges than established firms, in particular to cope with inability to spread advertising costs, difficulty in linking to good distributors, and inability to gain access to retail shelf space, among other handicaps.

How new ventures differ in sales problems, both from established firms and from each other, varies. In terms of the 4 P's of marketing lore, some differences for start-ups include the following:

Product   The new venture is completely centered around a new offering, as opposed to already having one and possibly adding variations of it.

Pricing   The new venture lacks a precedent of its own on price, probably has to experiment, has limited resources for making mistakes, but has the advantage of low overhead.

Place   Channels must be chosen and entered for the first time against unfamiliarity, but without being bound by prior commitments.

Promotion   Brand image must be established fresh and probably with limited resources, but also without baggage of prior expectations or embarrassments.

Each of these four categories could be explored further for implications about choices in generating sales effectively for a new venture. But to avoid falling back into ruts of thinking that were developed mainly for established enterprises, a different classification scheme may be worth considering.

Seven start-up selling hurdles

Selling for a new venture typically poses some special hurdles, but there can be ways to get around them, and in addition start-ups possess some natural marketing advantages that may be worth making the most of. This discussion will consider first seven hurdles, then seven advantages, as background for exploring what marketing channel or combination thereof should serve a particular venture best.

Hurdle 1. Credibility

New firms typically lack reputation in the marketplace by which customers can judge them and what they offer. Will the product or service be done well? Will the start-up be around for back-up parts or service?

Founders often bring credibility, sometimes even customers, from prior work. In some fields, such as biotechnology and other sciences, adding distinguished scientists to a board of advisers is essential for credibility in addition to having some on staff. For other lines of business, such as sports products, endorsements from celebrated performers help. In still others, a major contract from a big company or the government may suffice.

Hurdle 2. Habits

Prior customers, as well as suppliers and employees all develop habits that can sustain an established company but are missing in a start-up. Because habits are hard to create and can be even harder to undo, they can represent a great sustaining asset for a going business and a tough barrier to overcome for a new one.

Ways to buy the favor of patronage from someone else's traditional customer can sometimes be found. Free samples, a prize or premium, extra service, or attention may help. New banks usually offer extra personal attention to take depositors from established banks. New restaurants may give out coupons offering discounts. New industrial customers may be offered free freight for deliveries or other extra services on orders as get acquainted deals. Occasionally, existing firms will help out by overpricing or going slack on quality and service.

Hurdle 3. Salespeople

Start-ups lack staff, including those in sales, and also the personal contacts those sales and staff people would have.

---

[325] Gerald E. Hills, "Marketing and Entrepreneurship Research Issues," in *Research at the Marketing/Entrepreneurship Interface*, eds. Gerald E. Hills and others (Chicago: University of Illinois 1987) p. 6.

It is not legal to take customer or prospect lists from other companies, including former employers. But it is all right to remember names and go looking for old acquaintances who may be willing to help. Trade show meetings can add new help, as can disciplined cold calling. Start-ups call upon employees to be flexible in order to cover many different tasks with few individuals. Serving as salespeople can be one of those tasks.

Hurdle 4. Data

Over time, established companies accumulate data on their customers and competitors, some of it in files and other of it in employees' memories, but most of that remains inaccessible to a start-up. This can limit the start-up's feel and basis for judgments about selling decisions, including how to price, advertise, and focus efforts.

To some extent, the same things that help compensate for missing sales staff can help with this as well. Beyond that, a start-up can take advantage of its greater freedom to experiment and thereby learn faster, while established companies remain more bound by both their habits and old expectations that have been developed in their markets.

Hurdle 5. Scale

Lacking volume in sales and operations probably limits breadth of the product line that the venture can offer and of the market it can reach with advertising other than a Web page and possibly a few advertisements. This will likely also handicap it in establishing a brand.

If the venture's niche is small enough not to attract competitors, it may be able to seek out an attractive margin there. To work with larger markets, it may be able to form marketing alliances with larger firms if they can see it as a profitable complement, possibly one they will eventually buy out. Buell Motorcycles was simply a small shop hopping up Harley-Davidsons. But when the performance of its souped-up machines did well enough, Harley bought it out.

Hurdle 6. Resources

Limited financial capacity is a handicap linked to limited scale. The venture can't spend enough to roll out major marketing campaigns.

Entrepreneurs seek out all sorts of ways to market on the cheap. They use press releases and, if technically qualified, write articles to gain attention in periodicals. They engage sales representatives on straight commission and operate out of cheap quarters. They buy piggyback space in the booths of other trade show presenters. And, of course, there is much that can be done on the Web at low cost for most start-ups to stimulate sales.

Hurdle 7. Pressure

With resources stretched to the limit and many things to do, the entrepreneur may find that selling can get lost in the bustle. Costly mistakes can't be afforded, and experimenting on a small scale to avoid them may result in progress that is too slow.

Planning ahead to minimize backtracking and selectively head off problems where that can most help, recruiting assistance in advance, debugging before selling, and working fast and hard may increase odds of landing and delivering on enough sales to make it through the knothole.

Seven start-up selling advantages

Advantage 1. Something better

From the market's point of view, justification for the venture's existence should be that it offers something better. Selling may still be required to put across what that something is, but the free economy is designed to allow that, and it is working all the time.

Thinking and experimenting to understand and improve the something better, lengthening its list of advantages continuously will probably help.

Advantage 2. The CEO sells

The chief executive officer will almost certainly make the venture's first sale. This will distinguish the venture favorably from most companies, because customers care about that kind of attention and most companies can't afford their CEOs to provide it. Later, if it grows, the venture will not be able to either. So working to make the most of this advantage early and then move beyond it judiciously should be a disciplined goal.

Advantage 3. Sympathizers

Except for those companies that see the venture as a direct competitor, sympathy will be a natural reaction to the start-up effort by established companies and particularly by other entrepreneurs, who will consequently help it gain customers so long as it does not cost them much. Therefore, identifying those sympathizers who can help most and soliciting their aid, even before starting up, can give the start-up unique selling advantages.

Advantage 4. Flexibility

Unconfined by past deals and policies, a start-up can tailor fresh sales propositions and tune them more tightly to individual customers. Part of the selling job should be to look for rigidities of competitors' deals and shape propositions that fit better, and then tout them, but without forgetting that this will set new patterns for the future. Today's custom delivery may become tomorrow's customer expectation.

Advantage 5. Speed

With no hierarchy that decisions have to flow through, the venture should be able to give customers fast answers and delivery, which in turn can save them time and money as a reward for dealing with the venture.

Advantage 6. Low overhead costs

The uncomplicated and focused nature of the start-up should let it set prices low or alternatively let it add to features without pricing high.

Advantage 7. Motivation

Excitement should be especially high during start-up, and channeling it to focus on gaining sales and delivering high quality should come naturally, because they are crucial to survival. How best to progress into a longer-range pattern that will capitalize most effectively on inception should be worth rethinking as the venture advances, to build new advantages as those of inception fall behind.

2. Alternative paths to sales

One way of subdividing the general array of tasks for selling to customers appears in the list of activities of Exhibit 8a-2, which further suggests how one small group of 20 entrepreneurs rated the items in an investigation reported by Ram and Forbes.[326]

Because the sample is small, and the companies are at different stages of development and in different lines of work, the percentages in Exhibit 8-2 are subject to uncertainty. But the list of tasks illustrates variety in the issues of new venture sales.

Six topics under which venture selling paths will be considered here are

1. Responding to customer requests.
2. Personal selling—hitting the road.
3. Opening a storefront.
4. Setting up a Web site.
5. Advertising for orders.
6. Building synergy and reaching further.

Although the main selling path choice may come naturally to a venture, most will use at least two, advertising on the Web plus one or more others, possibly changing combinations over time.

Exhibit 8a-2 Difficulty of marketing activities

Entrepreneur percent characterizing as difficult	
Developing distribution outlets	80 %
Right packaging	73
Right product/service	67
Creating product/service awareness	58
Conducting market research	53
Building customer loyalty	53
On-time delivery	50
Allocating advertising budget	50
Developing an advertising campaign	47
The right pricing	47
Developing a prototype	40
Getting shelf space	40
Choosing a brand name	28
Physical distribution	22
Identifying target market	15

[326] S. Ram and Sandra J. Forbes, "Marketing Variables that Affect Entrepreneurial Success," in *Research at the Marketing/Entrepreneurship Interface*, eds. Gerald E. Hills and others (Chicago: University of Illinois 1990) p. 101.

3. Responding to customer requests

An especially encouraging basis for starting a venture arises when the founder has been asked by a customer to provide something that the founder is well-qualified to deliver. In that event, three requisites for a sale are automatically present, namely the presence of a desire, the ability to pay, and the willingness to buy what the entrepreneur can deliver to satisfy the desire.

> Steve Jobs and Steve Wozniak were both employed at other companies, and pursued microcomputer development as a hobby as members of the Homebrew Club on the San Francisco peninsula. When friends asked for copies of the computer they had developed for fun, the two decided to look into it. Steve Jobs proposed it to his employer, Atari, and Steve Wozniak proposed it to his, Hewlett-Packard. Rejection by both companies channeled them into producing it themselves for the ready customers.

> — • —

> After Cornelius Otis had created for his employer a safe elevator that would not drop if its rope broke, he decided to go prospecting for gold in California. Requests from other companies for copies of the elevator interfered with his departure and caused him to start the Otis Elevator Company. He already had customer orders.

An especially nice feature of these customer requests as paths to first sales is not so much that they came, but also that it appears they came without competition. Whether they did or not, there was some reason why the particular entrepreneur was solicited, most likely having to do with what that person had previously demonstrated in the way of capability.

Requests for proposal

More often customer requests are not to deliver, but to bid for a contract. Those are very common among homeowners who approach contractors, and among commercial companies that advertise for suppliers. They are also common among various levels of government that are required by law to solicit competitive bids. When they don't, as when Halliburton Corporation was issued non-competitive contracts for Iraq war work, there is sometimes public protest.

The *Commerce Business Daily* (www.cbd.savvy.com), for instance, prints notices of things the U.S. government would like to buy. It awards contracts totaling $200 billion per year, of which about $40 billion goes to small firms. State and local governments spend even more, an estimated $1.02 trillion in 1999, for instance, rising to an estimated $1.31 trillion over the ensuing five years.[327]

Federal agencies are encouraged by policy to buy from small firms when they can. The SBA helps police these rules and is a good contact to make for information. Other helpful documents are *The U. S. Government Purchasing and Sales Directory*, and *Doing Business with The Government*. State governments also post notices of things they would like to buy, and provide information for those interested in bidding on them. Federal agencies can buy up to $2,500 by credit card. Larger purchases generally require bidding. A contact point for registering to become a contractor for the U.S. government is http://pro-net.sba.gov.

Catches in serving as a government contractor include the possibility that some other contractors may have established relationships with agencies that give them advantages in competitive proposals (for "solicited unsolicited" contracts). Governmental agencies generally prefer making award decisions based on past performance, something new ventures, by definition, lack. Other drawbacks include drawn-out approvals, slow payment, programs coming and going capriciously at the whim of Congress, and red tape. The following company apparently encountered grief from a combination of governmental factors.

> Comcraft, an independent young phone installation company, noticed a "request for quote" (RFQ) in the *Commerce Business Daily* in 1987 for installation of a phone system in an Army Corps of Engineers office. Terms of the government

---

[327] "Selling to the Government," *Entrepreneur*, October 1999, p. 168A.

request were that the system could be either a key system or a more complex PBX system. For the latter system, however, approval of the General Services Administration would be needed because a PBX would duplicate to some degree a system already used by the GSA, which owned the building used by the Army.

The company's founder, Dominick Macaluso, Jr., discovered that the Army would save over 75 percent of the charges it was paying for use of GSA lines if he installed a PBX system. He said, "We were told that the Army would get anything it wanted, that it would march four-star generals down if it had to." Concluding that he could give the Army a bargain, a PBX system capability for a key system price, he proposed a PBX. Two Army technical evaluators visited the company, examined its equipment, and were "enthralled." Comcraft received official notice that it was the most technically qualified, lowest-cost vendor.

Before it could celebrate, however, the company received another notice, this time from the GSA, that it had disapproved the proposal. Comcraft began a series of appeals. But the end of the government's fiscal year was approaching, motivating government agencies to spend up their budgets. Hence before the appeal process was complete, another company had been given the contract. Instead of the Army getting its savings, the GSA kept its rental income. The GSA telecommunications chief said, "We had already paid for those lines." Comcraft had no contract and was out approximately $25,000 spent on pursuing it.[328]

Help in navigating the maze for obtaining federal contracts is available from the SBA, which has an Office of Government Contracting (www.sba.gov/gc). It also has people assigned to provide help, including representatives stationed at federal agencies that buy a lot of goods from the private sector. Literature and workshops are also provided to help small enterprises find their way. State governments, to varying degrees, also offer such help.

Large companies typically use many subcontractors and also put out word of things they would like to obtain. Over time they develop qualified bidder lists of companies that they contact when they want particular products and services. Becoming part of the in group is usually a matter of becoming known to buyers in the supply chain, and developing credibility with them.

Practical devices to facilitate responding to customers who may want to contact the venture for what they may need from it are a Web site, a toll-free telephone number, and possibly an answering service. Costs include installation plus any directory listing costs, and a rate per call depending on where it comes from. A Boston company selling live lobsters, for instance, found it cost them $200 for installation, $1,500 per year for directory listing, and roughly $2,000 per month for calls, as compared to twice that amount previously spent on responding to collect calls. Web communication would presumably be cheaper if customers can be persuaded to use it. Developing a Web site can be done personally with available software tools or with the aid of a professional designer.

4. Personal dealing

Hitting the road, calling on customers, and selling personally is a second approach to create sales in a new venture. The first sale by the new venture, if made by a person, not just from a Web site, will almost certainly be done by the lead entrepreneur. Even if made remotely through a medium such as mail or Web order, its processing will likely have been handled by the CEO. As noted earlier, this can be a major advantage for getting that sale. Customers generally like the idea of dealing with a CEO.

In 1982 Julia Duren arrived as an immigrant from Germany with two young children and $2,000, which she immediately spent on rent deposit and an old car, which shortly failed. She pawned her jewelry for another $600, which she spent on a sewing machine and some leather, determined to develop her own business. "I had specialized in leather," she said, "and was doing some innovative stuff. It was very difficult then to be an entrepreneur in Germany because there were strict regulations as to what kind of degrees you had to have to train other people. I knew I couldn't train other workers if I needed them."

[328] Ellen Forman, "Deal Carefully with Uncle Sam," *Venture*, September 1989, p. 14.

After arranging day care for her children, she started producing handmade leather jackets and selling them personally to retailers. "I went from store to store, pretended I was a rep, and got some orders," she continued. "Then I'd hop on the bus, pick up my kids from the public day care, and make the things. There was a long period when I slept three and a half hours a night."

Ultimately, she branched into handbags as well, and cultivated bigger accounts. In 1989 she bagged Nordstrom, which five years later listed her firm as its "vendor of the year." By 1999 her firm employed 25 people and was generating annual sales of $1.8 million.[329]

For those other sales beyond the first one, moreover, selling will probably remain the top priority interest of the lead entrepreneur. But trying to raise money also requires personal selling, as does recruiting, negotiating for facilities, dealing with federal agencies, and working out deals with suppliers and potential strategic partners, possibly even dealing with competitors.

An important place to start is with understanding the person to whom the sale is to be made. Who is the person who makes the buying decision, what would that person want enough to buy, and why? What makes the venture different from other sources of that or of its substitutes?

In personal selling, a particularly important quality is credibility as perceived by the potential buyer. What will convince the potential buyer that he or she can't lose? Would a guarantee, references, samples, or a free trial period help? Some way must be found to let satisfaction seem adequately certain, as illustrated by the following example.

In 1974 a young man from the Pacific Northwest with an interest in photography learned of the success that a cousin in Southern California was having in producing and selling wall-sized photographic murals. He decided to set up a firm like his cousin's and installed the necessary photographic equipment in a darkroom to do it. Then he began calling on potential customers, telling them what he could do and asking whether they had favorite photos they would like to have made into decorative murals. Unfortunately, his verbal descriptions were not adequate to obtain orders.

Consequently, he prevailed upon his cousin to lend him page-sized photographs illustrating different applications the cousin had made in California. When accompanied by these examples, his sales pitch was successful, orders began to come, and before long he was able to replace his cousin's examples with those of his own.

Persistence, working the numbers, may also be essential. It has been estimated that on average about five noes will be encountered before getting a yes, with an average cost of $800 per sales call in person. But that only illustrates a principle, namely the value of effort and experimentation to learn what works and apply it. The number of hits per miss may start much lower than one in five, but should increase with practice and refinement of the pitch.

Because time is such a scarce resource for a founder, it is vital to define with care whom to go after, what to seek from them, how much effort to apply in each attempt, and how to assess the results in planning each next action. Contact building constantly calls for judgment. Insufficient persistence can render efforts futile. However, too much of it applied on the wrong tack can be even more wasteful.

A set of steps entrepreneur Clint McCowen found through experience to work in selling to chain store purchasing agents products that ranged from wireless microphones to flashing earrings are described in the shaded area on the next page:[330]

McCowen recalled how effectively his system had worked on one product versus another:

> Negotiating global distribution for my wireless microphones took about six months using these techniques. But my success with Lobe Strobes was almost immediate. I obtained an appointment with the senior buyer at Spencer Gifts in New Jersey, and presented my products based on the principles I've discussed. At the end of my presentation I immediately received a purchase order to supply Lobe Strobes nationwide through 500 stores.

Major chains, like K-Mart, Sears, and Wal-Mart have their own rules for vendors, and the place to begin is typically by visiting one of their stores, figuring out where on the shelf a new product should be placed, and why that will

[329] Geoff Williams, "Tough as Leather," *Entrepreneur*, April 1999, p. 102.
[330] Clint McCowen, "How To Get the First Big Order," *American Venture*, January-March 1998, p. 24.

Selling to chain stores

1. **Create** a list of alternative stores by searching the Web with key words like *retailers, wholesalers, or distributors.*
2. **Narrow** the list by eliminating independent stores, chains not carrying products similar to the venture's, and those without a central buying office.
3. **Phone** the buying office and learn who is the senior person authorized to sign a purchase order for the product. Don't accept someone else. Keep trying. "Normally you'll get the runaround for the first few calls or even several months. Patience is required."
4. **Prepare a demonstration** with the real thing, a video, or professionally done poster boards showing favorable use of the product.
5. **Have answers ready** for the buyer on such things as competitive comparisons, delivery, capacity, warranty, quality, costs, legality, safety, insurance, return policy, displays, volume or quantity discounts, shipping costs, minimum order quantities, exclusivity, and advertising help.
6. **Price** the order to assure **profits for the buyer**.
7. Go prepared with **high, low, and most-likely** projections of both sales and gross profits for the store based on whatever information can be obtained about the store and its number of outlets.

Paying others to sell

present a better deal for customers than what is on the shelf at present. Next is to learn how the chain's buying system, which has 21,000 suppliers, works. An example can be seen on the Web site walmartstores.com.

If there is a technology side to what the venture will offer, then one way to offer that technology to prospective customers may be to invite them to seminars where it will be explained.

> William Delphos became expert in low-cost government resources for smaller firms to develop overseas sales when he worked for four years as a White House appointee in foreign investment. To find customers as a consultant on the subject, he spent $1,000 putting together a humorous cartoon slide show, then persuaded an electronics trade association to include it among the programs available to their 21 councils across the country, which continually offer various programs to their members. This exposure, he said, gave him both credibility and opportunity to display his expertise to prospective customers for his consulting services. He found it best not to attempt any selling at his seminar but to follow up afterwards with a letter to each participant.[331]

Other ways of personal selling that particularly lend themselves to sharp focus on selected audiences include writing and calling.

- **Personal letters** to acquaintances from individuals in the venture.

- **Phoning.** Although it is sharply focused with respect to the market, this approach is expensive in time compared to letters or email. Advantages, however, are that it allows progressive interrogation of the people called, and can yield much better information. The best way to find what works will probably be to write out a script, follow it, and modify it with each call until it peaks out in effectiveness. The final version is almost certain to be greatly changed in both content and performance.

Paying others to sell

Some enterprises, especially smaller ones, believe everyone in the company should sell, partly because opportunity to do so can arise in almost any aspect of doing business, and partly because adoption of a selling goal throughout the company can help guide the efforts of all employees better to please customers.

Other alternatives include (1) hiring salespeople, (2) engaging independent representatives, or (3) selling to middlemen such as brokers, wholesalers, catalog houses, retailers, or dealers. Each of these costs time to recruit and money to employ, making the cost of an average sales call around $1,000. Costs differ depending not only on what is being sold, but also the type of representative used, what the representative does and, of course, how well the selling effort is managed.

---

[331] J. Donald Weinrauch and Nancy Croft Baker, *The Frugal Marketer* (New York: AMACOM, 1989).

There are also costs of training, which average in the range of $5,000 to $10,000.

Although Earl Tupper's injection-molded polyethylene bowls and lids were good products, they did not sell nearly as well as he had hoped. Placed in retail stores, the products sold better with demonstrations than without them. But the demonstrations cost money. Mail order selling was cheaper but didn't work well. Some institutions, such as hospitals bought the products, but Tupper wanted to see them in homes. He also wanted his to be a household name. A major advertising in magazines, and displays in collaboration with major department stores where patrons were invited to "yank it, bang it, jump on it," and endorsements of important personalities helped sales but cost too much in relation to the interest they generated. Company correspondence also took note of "home demonstration companies," but initially concluded that they were too peripheral and inconsequential.

Orders from the field, however, told a different story about sales through "hostess parties." This form of selling, in which women would demonstrate home products to each other, had been introduced by Wearever Aluminum in the 1920s to sell pots and pans. An offshoot of this company in 1932 was Stanley Home Products, which sold a variety of goods through home sales. Mary Kay Ash, who would later open her own direct-selling company, Mary Kay Cosmetics, learned the business as a Stanley representative. Some Stanley representatives also started adding Tupper's products to their lines, and one who produced particularly outstanding results was Brownie Wise, a Detroit secretary and divorced mother who wanted the extra income and had built an effective collection of saleswomen to help her generate what she called "Poly-T Parties" where, at the home of a housewife who was given incentives to be hostess and invite friends, the products would be demonstrated and sold. Her cheerleading of dealers included a weekly bulletin, the Go Getter, which Wise wrote and circulated. Impressed with her performance, despite her lack of formal management experience, Tupper recruited Wise to develop a national organization for his company. After that, sales soared, making Tupperware the household name Tupper wanted it to be. [332]

Ironically, Wise did not prosper. She had no ownership in the business, and Tupper eventually fired her. She tried to start up independently by recruiting salespeople who had formerly worked for her, but failed.

With each mode of selling there are tradeoffs to consider. For example, independent representatives typically work on 30-day cancelable contracts and are paid only if they accomplish sales, which eliminates the risk of paying for no performance. Commissions, which are paid as a percentage of sales, range considerably as shown in figures of Exhibit 8a-3 below from *Sales and Marketing Management* magazine's annual "Survey of Selling Costs."

In addition to the commission, however, there are costs of samples, literature, communications, and training that the venture must pay. Moreover, independent agents typically concentrate on only those sales that are largest or come easiest, which is likely to leave out the product of a new company. And the company must still run the risk that customers may be bad credit risks. Credit checks can be bought online (hoovers.com).

Selling through brokers and wholesalers lowers the risk of collection problems, but they must be convinced that retailers will buy from them, or they will not stock the line. Similarly,

Exhibit 8a-3 Sales commissions in different lines of business

Line of Business	Percent of commission paid		
	High	Average	Low
Advertising	24.2%	16.2%	8.1%
Toys, novelties	12.8	9.3	5.9
Robotics	12.4	10.3	8.2
Building supplies	10.7	7.7	4.6
Electronics	10.4	8.5	6.5
Consumer electrical	6.7	5.6	4.6
Lumber	6.4	5.1	3.7

[332] Alison J. Clarke, *Tupperware* (Washington, DC: Smithsonian Institution, 1999) p. 96.

retailers must be convinced that consumers will buy, which may require the venture to spend money on advertising and promotions which, if not successful, can break the venture. Failure can also occur if the venture is successful in persuading consumers to buy, but wholesalers and retailers do not stock up fast enough to serve them all.

Susan Sargent started her home furnishings venture in a Vermont barn intending to run it "very differently from traditional furnishings companies" using "the very best of creative talent." All sales she intended to outsource to 120 independent representatives across the country linked through e-mail and phone, with access to her real-time inventory and working under guidance from her sales manager in San Francisco.

To her dismay, the representatives rarely used her system, did not sell her newest products, and sometimes took orders for products not in stock. Some sales were lost, others were made to stores ill-equipped to showcase her products. From stores came the message that "You never have what I want," she recalled.

Her remedy was to drop 118 of the 120 reps in favor of six local phone representatives at headquarters, and replace the San Francisco sales manager with one in Vermont. Deals were arranged with 35 stores to carry her products in floor locations. Sales rose to $3 million.

Disillusioned with the virtual-company concept, she observed, "When you're evolving madly every day I can't see a substitute for having everyone in one place."[333]

Lest this seem like a formula for all companies, it should be remembered that the continued existence of countless independent sales representatives demonstrates that for some companies they are the preferred selling alternative.

Start-up allows setting policies unencumbered by precedents. But their absence also provides less to go on in forecasting. Should compensation of salespeople be salary, commission, or some combination with bonuses, and at what levels? How big should territories be, and under what conditions should accounts be house accounts, which is to say that the company gets all credit on them instead of a salesperson getting sales credit on them? Should selling in some territories be handled by company employees and in others by independent representatives, or some combination of those two? If the company manufactures products, should it ship them direct to customers, or to wholesalers who stock inventory and ship from there?

Cannondale, a Connecticut bicycle manufacturer tried something it had not done before by starting up "Cannondale Europe" in 1998. Contracts were negotiated with European distributors, and sales in the first year quickly rose to $1.5 million. But margins dropped because the distributors who brought in the biggest orders did so by discounting prices, which in turn reduced the prices other distributors were willing to pay, and a downward spiral ensued.

To counter the trend, Cannondale decided it had to buy out the distributors' contracts, at 5 percent of annual commissions, hire its own sales force, rent its own office and warehousing space in Europe, and sell direct. This was successful, and by five years later sales were approaching $32 million in Europe. But in hindsight, management saw the first sales strategy as an expensive mistake.[334]

If the founders haven't gained experience in selling through others, they should consider recruiting others who do have such experience.

5. Site selling

Easiest to see physically are ventures that begin their sales through opening a physical storefront. Important variations on this approach are to set up a display at shows, fairs, malls, flea markets, and auctions. Shows break down further into consumer shows (autos, boats, motorcycles, home improvement, for instance), which are open to the public, and industrial shows (computers, machine tools, gifts, film festivals), which are usually restricted to members of the industry. The newest variation of storefronts,

[333] Susan Greco, "There s No Place Like In-House," *Inc.*, February 1999, p. 38.
[334] Susan Greco, "From Easy Orders to Disorder," *Inc.* April 1995, p. 107.

Storefront

Shows

those that appear on the Web, will be taken up separately.

Storefront

Choice of location, selection of inventory, pricing, credit policies, methods of display, advertising, selection and management of salespeople, and practices of dealing with customers are variables that influence results in retail storefronts. For some name-brand chains, there are elements of science in controlling these variables. But the science is never perfect, and for new ventures there is inevitably considerable suspense in first opening the store. For some new retail stores the customers show up soon, as the founder of Wendy's, Dave Thomas, recalled.

> The first day we opened our doors for business, customers were lined up down the street, and the business caught on right from the start. … The opening of Wendy's wasn't backed up with fancy market research, but I had a nose for trends in the restaurant business. (Research isn't everything. Not long after we started, Burger King paid a lot of money for a research study that explained why Wendy's wouldn't work.)[335]

For others it takes time to build up a clientele. The fact that many storefronts change tenants from lease to lease demonstrates that for many stores the clientele never becomes adequate to continue the business.

Because the process of simply buying, displaying, and reselling can be done so simply, competition is high, margins are thin, and failure rates are high. Occasionally, newcomers have broken in with large success using exceptional strategies. Placing large warehouse stores in low-rent areas and selling at discount to move large volumes to gain low prices from suppliers was an innovation that has worked for entrepreneurs for a long time. Sam Walton began in the late '40s, following behind the wave of entrepreneurs like Sears, Penney, Kresge, and others in the '30s. More recently have come still others such as Costco, Home Depot, Builders' Emporium, and Eagle Hardware. Costco and Eagle started with financing in the millions. Wal-Mart began with considerably less.

Sam Walton learned selling as a J.C. Penney clerk just graduated in economics at the University of Missouri. He later recalled the company founder showing him how to wrap a package adequately with less string and paper, a lead-in perhaps to Walton's own penchant for frugality in overhead expenses.[336] He also remembered loving to sell but making a mess of records. "I couldn't stand to keep a new customer waiting, and I'll have to admit, it did cause some confusion."[337]

Several years later, after army service in World War II, he opened his own first storefront. After much moving around with the army, his wife preferred to settle down in a small town. He found a "Ben Franklin five and ten cent store" for sale in Newport, Arkansas, population 5,000. Borrowing $20,000 from his father-in-law, he bought the furniture, fixtures, and franchise and took over the lease.

Throwing himself into the job, hiring people who worked well, becoming active in the local community, and running the store effectively paid off. He experimented with a popcorn stand outside on the street, then an ice cream machine as well. In purchasing he sought out cheaper sources of supply than the franchiser, who still could require that 80 percent of the merchandise was bought from it. Sales rose from $75,000 per year, lowest in the region to $250,000 per year, highest in the region.

Aspects to consider with a storefront include not only location and cost, as discussed earlier, but also innovative merchandising as in the example above, appropriate decor, use of signs and point-of-purchase displays, optimal amount of inventory, best methods for display, and effective store layout. Storefronts can be either stationary or mobile, permanent or temporary and, most recently, virtual.

Shows

Another form of storefront is display at a show, of which there are several types, some for retailing and others for gaining sales through other channels. They include those mentioned on the following page in the shaded area.

---

[335] R. David Thomas, *Dave's Way* (New York: Putnam's, 1991) p. 93.
[336] Vance H. Trimble, *Sam Walton* (New York: Signet Books, 1991) p. 42.
[337] Sam Walton, with John Huey, *Sam Walton, Made in America* (New York: Doubleday, 1992) p. 18.

Alternative shows for selling

Fairs These usually provide sites for retail display and make money by charging visitors for admission and merchants for display space.

Consumer shows Examples include auto, boat, motorcycle, motor home, and home improvement shows. They aim at retail customers and make money both on general admission and on booth space, as well as advertisements in the programs.

Franchise shows Aimed at people who want to go into business, these shows make money for their backers on booths, admissions, and seminars. A frequently repeated message among the displays at franchise shows is how easy it is to make money with the particular system.

Trade shows These sell booth space to producers and distributors. They attract competitors, wholesalers, agents looking for lines to represent, and industrial customers. Examples are gift, fashion, and toy shows; computer conventions; military weapons demonstrations; and industrial machinery shows. They make money on booth space rental plus sale of admission tickets to the booth-holders, who in turn give them free to attendees on a selective basis.

Web

At trade shows, companies in similar lines of work can make their existence known, test customer responses to what they offer, study what competitors offer, and recruit sales agents. The venture can open its own booth or, to save money, may be able to rent part of the space in someone else's booth. Where the booth is physically located is an important variable, and charges for the space vary accordingly.

A guide to trade show costs is published annually by the International Exhibitors Association of Annandale, Virginia. These costs include those of the exhibit itself, plus the entry fee, travel, transportation, set-up, samples, and literature expenses. Other helpful information about shows and their costs is published in Trade Show Week (2,000 shows) and Exhibit Schedule (10,000 shows).

Things to be mapped out clearly in advance include who will be coming to the show(s) selected; what information will be sent in advance, given out at the show, or sent later as follow-up to show attendees; what information will the venture seek to obtain from attendees; what sales results will the venture seek to accomplish through the show; who will help out (sometimes suppliers and/or local governments will); and how the activity itself will be managed. Innumerable tips on making the most of trade shows are available in books and magazines that can be located through such sources as those above or the National Association of Exposition Managers. Another way to learn is simply to attend local shows. The state department of commerce, chamber of commerce, or local convention bureau can provide information about shows coming up.

Designing a layout and display, whether for a store or a show, is an art form that can be helpful to sales, if done well. Someone with visual talent and originality may have inspiring ideas for how to do it. Those less gifted in that way can either study the displays of others and copy what works, or ask for help from those with the talent.

Web

The Web can be viewed as a combination of the other pathways, as suggested in the tabulation following. Its power is evident by the many multimillionaires and billionaires it has produced almost instantly, examples being the founders of Netscape, Yahoo, Hotmail, eBay, and Google. Each of the traditional selling pathways has its new equivalent on the Web. Broad alternatives for selling via the Web are listed in the shaded area on the following page.

The Web has become a multi-faceted sales realm in itself, expanding and evolving at a rate that no book can keep up with. It is an educational source for customers and also for the company selling over it, because the company can post educational material and the customer can interrogate the site or the company itself to

Web selling alternatives

Response Customers search the Web to find suppliers. Among other things, this lets a small and highly specialized venture, such as one selling exotic tropical fish, become easily discoverable by the whole population of Web users worldwide.

Storefront The venture can set up its own Web site and storefront, or can rent one on the site of others, such as Yahoo for a fee and a cut ranging around 1 percent of sales.

Advertising Banners, pop-ups, links, and other displays can be placed by the company on others' sites. Press releases can be distributed online.

Personal selling Sending messages personally via the Web is an obvious, low-cost, and widely used option. But its intrusion can sometimes alienate people and getting it past spam filters can be a challenge.

---

learn more. As a market research mechanism, the Web can be used not only as an information search site, say to look up databases on demographics, but it also can collect customer information from cookies, such as what sites they visit, what information they seek, how many times and for how long they do it, what they buy, when, and to some extent why.

Particularly appealing features of the Web for starting a business are that (1) it is very low in cost, (2) the site physically can be geographically anywhere, (3) relatively little equipment and facilities investment is required, and (4) the steps for performing set-up, particularly as the march of technology toward greater user friendliness advances, can be learned fairly easily and quickly by a person without any technical background, or alternatively hired out. An example is the experience of the following car dealer who faced failure.

> Pete Ellis, as an owner of 16 car dealerships, including the largest Jeep Eagle, Chrysler outlet in the U.S., saw it all head into a fatal dive when the economy turned downward in 1990. One by one he closed or sold outlets to cover debts until he had only the big one left. Then it too, had to be sacrificed, leaving him with less than nothing. He recalled, "I owed $5.6 million on a piece of property that was worth $3.6 million. I decided to kill myself."
> Instead, he retreated to a bedroom and started exploring on a computer to see what could be done in the way of selling cars through the Internet. For help, he decided to approach the executives of Prodigy, the on-line service. He prepared a presentation, made an appointment, and flew to New York. Five minutes into his prepared one-hour presentation they interrupted him to say, "Let's try it."
> When the program was set for launch, Ellis was hoping it could generate 500 purchase requests per week. Instead, it generated 1,348 on the fourth day alone.[338]

Although Pete Ellis used help from Prodigy to begin his site, an individual can now do it alone with very little help, using a book or a service such as Godaddy.com.

For as much as analysis may be involved in the process, refinement of Web sites is an art form. Problems to be dealt with include both attracting customers and retaining them. Reasons found from one poll that customers, once attracted to a site don't complete transactions on it include those listed in Exhibit 8a-4.

Some aspects of tuning, an entrepreneur without experience may be able to do personally. Others may become easier as technology escalates user friendliness. Still others may require consulting help.

Exhibit 8a-4 Reasons for non-response to Web sites[339]

Site was too slow	41%
Site looked unprofessional	20
Site would not accept credit cards	16
Couldn't find the checkout areas	14
Couldn't find return policy	12

---

[338] Edward O. Welles, "Burning Down the House," *Inc.*, August 1997, p. 67.

[339] Melissa Campanelli, "Are You Losing E Customers?" *Entrepreneur*, November 1999, p. 56.

6. Reaching out

6. Reaching out

Advertising

Advertising

A fourth way to get sales is to advertise. The most obvious starting point for retail and service firms is to buy an advertisement in the Yellow Pages. Thumbing through a phone book makes it quickly apparent that the advertisements vary in size and content. Each advertiser has made independent decisions about which design will be most effective for what purposes. Choices must be made about which directories to use, in which geographical areas, what sizes of advertisements, how many to list, under what names, and with what contents and graphics. The phone company may be of some help, and beyond that an advertising agency may have good advice. Visiting and asking some advertisers what their advertising experiments have taught them can also be informative.

Paid advertisements in newspapers, magazines, radio, and television are other avenues of advertising. Yet another is to write articles that papers and magazines will print free as information. Posting notices, passing around flyers, sending sales letters, literature, newsletters, staging free lectures, public relations events, or stunts, and sending samples through the mail are ways of putting out news of what the venture has to offer. Either starting a catalog or seeking space in another company's catalog is also an option.

- In the heyday of hi-fi, many companies started by advertising do-it-yourself kits for building amplifiers, tuners, and such in magazines.
- In the early days of the microcomputer, companies such as MITS, IMSAI, and Osborne rapidly generated large sales through advertisements in magazines (although once high performers, none of those companies survived long term).
- Flyers stuck under auto windshield wipers and home doormats are familiar to most.
- Coupon books can be handed out free to students and to homeowners.

Each of these techniques can be simple or complicated, prosaic or imaginative. The technique of brainstorming originated in the advertising industry and has great power there, as illustrated by the following example involving coupons. It arose in the next venture of Dave Pitassi and Wally Klemp, who lost their diaper-manufacturing start-up when the investment banker who helped raise capital for it used the terms of their limited partnership agreement to expel them from the enterprise.

Determined to start over, the two men set up an office consisting of folding tables, a phone, and metal chairs in the unfinished basement of Wally's house. After 15 months of seeking start-up capital, including turning down some potential investors based on more careful investigation than they had done before, the two managed to raise $2.5 million to begin again producing and selling diapers with their own brand, Drypers.

This time Procter & Gamble, which had lost sales to the earlier start-up, preempted them by contacting stores in advance and pointing out that the new entrant would, by offering equivalent but cheaper diapers, undercut the stores' sales of their private diaper brands, not just those of Procter & Gamble's. P&G followed this preemptive attack as soon as the new venture started selling its diapers, with a campaign of 20 different coupons in newspapers, magazines, and other places offering $1 off.

Applying sculpture thinking (looking at the business from different perspectives) combined with brainstorming, the entrepreneurs spent 15 hours searching for remedies. They would put numbers 1 through 10 on a blackboard, put a potential solution by each one, then add 10 more for each of those 10 until late at night. Then someone noticed on the box of pizza they had ordered for dinner that there was a statement that the pizza store would accept the coupons of its competitors.

The entrepreneurs decided to offer customers multiple advantages on competitive coupons. To avoid hurting the stores' private-label diaper sales, the new venture specified that its offer would apply only to big-company brands, Pampers, Huggies, and Luvs. "They send us three $1 Pampers coupons, we send them a sheet of ten $1 Drypers coupons," Dave recalled. "It might sound like a lot of liability, but we knew people don't keep or redeem all of their coupons."

Then the entrepreneurs added another twist, which was to put a coupon converter on each of their Dryper packages so a customer could apply a competitor's coupon to the purchase of Drypers directly at the store, which would accordingly give the customer a discount. The store was then to collect the coupons and return them to Drypers for reimbursement. But some stores in error sent them back to P&G instead. "This Judo strategy," Dave said, "took the momentum of the giant and turned it on himself. It caused P&G such a fit that they actually stopped couponing diapers."

Drypers became the fastest-growing company of the *Inc.* 500 in 1993 with sales of $175 million. By 1997, sales had reached $300 million and David Pitassi had formed his own venture capital company.[340]

Another variation on advertising is the use of public relations techniques to get word out about the venture's product or service without paying for advertising space. Approaches for doing this include the four listed in the shaded area below.

Saving cash

How much to spend on advertising and publicity is a special problem for a new venture. For advertising expenditures in established companies, there are often rules of thumb, such as 1 to 5 percent of gross sales. But that is after a company already has a sales record and cash to buy adver-

tisements. Moreover, a new company is usually unknown and therefore may have especially great need for advertising. With small resources, it must seek the most advertising for the least money. Beyond seeking free publicity, possibilities include:

- **Business cards** and flyers are inexpensive.
- **Homemade newsletters** can be more effective than slick advertisements for some markets.
- **Many small, inexpensive ads** can add up to major impact over time.
- **Classified ads** are much cheaper than display ads.
- **Piggybacking** on ads of others can allow cost sharing.
- **Suppliers** often **share** advertising costs.
- **Off-hours** on radio, back corners in trade shows, poor locations for signs, and last minute fill-ins are often available at low rates and sometimes work.
- **Advertising departments** of papers, magazines, and radio stations will provide free help in ad design.
- **Advance payment** may yield discounts.
- **Bartering** may substitute for cash.
- Strategic **marketing alliance** with another company or cooperative advertising to split costs can help.
- **Frequent checking** to see whom the ads are affecting and how can help cut costs.

Public relations advertising

Writing technical articles for magazines or journals where the publicity can help, or where the publication can be held up to substantiate the technical validity of what the venture sells. Testing the articles by asking other authorities in the field for critiques can help shape them into forms more likely to be accepted.

Sending press releases to newspapers, magazines, or other media announcing what is new about what the venture is up to. These have to contain elements that would be considered news. Testing and comparing ideas for their content against other published news items can be a way of assessing their likely publication. Brainstorming with sympathizers can help generate ideas for making the releases more catchy or newsworthy.

Seeking interviews with radio or TV to demonstrate what the venture will offer. Practicing on audio or videotape and possibly sending copies of the final tapes to stations may help with invitations. These too should be catchy, with visual displays, specimens, props, demonstrations, and possibly participation by the interviewer or audience in order to retain interest.

Becoming involved in causes, public events and/or stunts to draw attention to the company. Corporate contributions to Public Broadcasting System and National Public Radio programs, local arts and music programs, student contest prizes, and charities are one form. The founders of Fratelli's Ice Cream, for instance, chose to co-sponsor Fourth-of-July fireworks for local visibility in Seattle.

[340] Dave Pitassi, "My Startup, Lock-out, Buy-out Journey to Success," *American Venture*, January-March 1998, p. 5.

Information about advertising costs can be found in publications of the Standard Rate and Data Service, available in many libraries as well as online (srds.com) from the service itself, whose address is 1700 Higgins Road, Des Plaines, IL 60018-5606, (847) 375 5000. Service Center 800 861 7737. It lists, for instance, thousands of cooperative advertising programs available from manufacturers throughout the country. The bad news about advertising is that the average American is hit with an estimated 500 or more advertising messages per day, but remembers only about a dozen of them. How to be remembered on an extremely small advertising budget calls for careful thought and very sharp focus of the message.

Specialty advertising involves imprinting a company name on any of innumerable gift items such as calendars, mugs, clocks, rulers, pencils, pens, knives, paperweights, jewelry, bumper stickers, decals, combs, and so forth. Although expensive on a per-person basis, such advertising is usually sharply focused so that the total cost is not so great and the impact is high. One company that gave empty flower pots and followed up with flowers to put in them estimated that its campaign was more effective and cost around $5,000 in contrast to an estimated cost of $20,000 for print advertising, or $200,000 for a magazine campaign. An important question to consider, aside from cost, is whether the gift will be more effective as a door opener, a reminder, or a memento of thanks after a sale.

Combinations

It is not unusual to sell through a combination of the above approaches. For instance, advertising in the Yellow Pages at minimum and by other means as well, is widely used in combination with a storefront for retailing. Also common is to start with one means of selling and shift to others over time. Some examples include:

An electronics company sold its first few products personally, then rented a booth at a trade show where it distributed advertising brochures and recruited manufacturers' representatives. Technical articles were written for magazines to get word of the products out further. Ultimately, sales grew to a point where the company began adding its own sales employees in place of the manufacturers' representatives.

— • —

An olive oil company began packaging and shipping in a garage and selling to wholesalers. Due to zoning restrictions, the founders moved their operations to an empty storefront. Passersby started asking to buy directly, whereupon the founders changed the storefront to a retail operation and moved packaging and shipping to another rented plant.

— • —

A bakery producing muffins started by selling retail out the front door but found it could make more by selling wholesale out the back door to restaurants.

— • —

An ice cream company set out to introduce another brand of premium ice cream, only to conclude that it was too late. Other companies had grown too dominant in that market. Consequently, the company dropped its own brand and shifted its sales efforts to persuade stores to buy its premium product under their brands instead.[345]

— • —

A food packaging company, rather than develop its own brand, leased the brands of other well-known companies for royalties ranging from 3 percent to 5 percent of its gross sales and did the selling itself.[346]

Another variation worth considering, particularly after the venture has developed some marketing muscle of its own, is to exchange that capability through joint distribution with another company that is strong in a different marketing territory. Each can be a commissioned agent of the other, sales leads can be exchanged, costs can be shared on advertising, trade shows, and incoming phone calls. Each can help the other with information about competitors and ideas for sales campaigns. However, as with any partnership, the load and benefits can get out of balance and lead to breakup, so attention must be given to fairness to keep such a relationship working.

Companies that provide good results to their first customers tend to find other customers coming to buy because they have learned through word of mouth that the companies are

---

[341] Paul B. Brown, "When Quality Isn't Everything," *Inc.*, June 1989, p. 119.
[342] Tom Richman, "A New Lease on Growth," *Inc.*, July 1990, p. 107.

good suppliers. A common factor among ventures that succeed in building sales and having them expand through word-of-mouth seems to be effective concentration on maintaining what customers perceive as a high and consistent level of quality.

Going global

Starting sales on a global basis is common in countries with smaller domestic markets, such as Canada and Scandinavia. U.S. ventures have been slower to follow that path because the domestic market has, for most of them, been large enough to support a profitable volume. With the advance of e-commerce—which makes international communications so much easier and cheaper—this will likely change, giving U.S. entrepreneurs more reason to start globally and also threatening them with more foreign competition.

A key element for many companies in quest of overseas sales has been to link with a partner already in business there. These links seem mainly to develop from contacts that a firm already has.[347] The extent to which that will continue to be requisite with expansion of e-commerce remains to be seen.

Experimentation

Selling is inevitably an experimental process, especially for a new venture. Even if one or more of the founders is experienced in a similar line of business, the reactions of customers to a start-up will be shaped by special aspects, such as the lack of a track record for the company, the widespread perception that new ventures are risky and therefore not as much to be trusted for quality and reliability. Will the entrepreneur be there to follow up if something goes wrong, or will it just go out of business? Buying may be more of an experiment for the customer than selling is for the entrepreneur. The purpose of experimentation, for both parties, is to find a way to a workable arrangement so sales can be closed.

Randy Weiss decided to use some of the money he had earned by developing a software company and selling it out to Lotus for starting another new venture, this time one that would sell contact lenses for chickens. Tinted red, the lenses caused chickens that wore them to be less likely to peck at other chickens they were cooped up with, a behavior pattern that destroyed as many as 20 percent of farmers' flocks. He had calculated that a 30 cent pair of lenses could save a farmer 68 cents on average.

The initial sales strategy called for (1) advertising in poultry publications, (2) sending free trial kits with order forms to larger ranchers, and (3) offering volume discounts. It didn't work.

In response, the venture's strategy was changed to sell experiments to ranchers instead of products. This, they found, obtained easier access to ranchers and, when the ranchers bought, yielded better information about how the product worked, which in turn led to improvement of the product through redesign, and to sale of more experiments and gathering of more data. Lenses were made available in different configurations, for instance, when it was found that different chicken breeds had different eye structures.

With this new approach sales significantly improved.[344]

This example is a reminder that it is important not just to sell, but to learn from the process so selling can be done better. Not just making the sale, but also gathering information systematically can begin to build a body of data for the venture that can be used for organizing the sales process, making decisions about which paths work best and how, and training new people in what works best to get sales.

What the body of data should contain is something each venture must figure out from among the endless array of possibilities on the basis of its own individual makeup. Two examples, for instance are the following:

A consulting firm for banks keeps a running historical dialog describing the history of selling activities with each customer; appointments, letters, proposals, and activities of the salespeople in contacting 3,000 customers and leads per year.

[343] Nicole Coviello and Hugh Monroe, "International Market Development and Growth of Entrepreneurial Firms," in *Research at the Marketing Interface*, eds, Gerald E. Hills and Sumaria T. Mohan-Neil (Chicago: University of Illinois, 1994) p. 217.
[344] Neil C. Churchill and Daniel F. Muzyka, "Animalens, Inc.: The Pioneering of a New Product and Process," in *Research at the Marketing/Entrepreneurship Interface*, eds. Gerald E. Hills and others (Chicago: University of Illinois, 1991) p. 239.

—•—

The operator of a consumer show records objections of sales prospects as well as personal information helpful in figuring out what appeals best for some 6,500 customers and leads per year.[345]

An assortment of customer relations management (CRM) software programs available for recording contact data conveniently includes GoldMine, Maximizer, and Sharkware, for examples. The question then becomes what data to obtain and how to analyze it to screen prospects effectively. Books on how to sell effectively are myriad and constantly coming out with fresh ideas.[346] Magazines and seminars produce a torrent of tricks, tactics, tools, and novelties about how to sell faster, better, easier, more, bigger, and cheaper. But the entrepreneur must distill what works for not just any company, but his or her company, one that is distinguished by, among other things, freshness.

Exercises

Text discussion questions

1. What are the causes of differences in selling by start-ups versus ongoing firms?
2. How could someone who does not like selling nevertheless become a successful entrepreneur?
3. What are the reasons why some organizations deliberately seek to have start-ups sell to them, and how can start-ups best exploit those reasons?
4. How should a start-up go about determining the optimum pattern of paths to sales that it should (a) begin with, and (b) reshape over time?
5. Describe steps an entrepreneur could take to develop an everybody-sells culture from the beginning of a start-up.

Case questions

8A-1 Jim Russell

1. What actions, if any, should Jim Russell take to check out the strength of the Extractor patent?
2. Which path of sales, direct or indirect, should Jim recommend and why?
3. What terms should he propose in response to the engineers' requests concerning selling agreements?
4. What action should Jim personally take next to help with sales?

8A-2 Kevin Scheevel

1. What is your assessment of Kevin's strategy?
2. What marketing decisions must he make, and how should he make them?
3. Which start-up advantages and disadvantages apply to a venture like this?

8A-3 Bruce Milne (B)

1. How does Kevin's sales strategy align with the special advantages and disadvantages of new ventures, as listed in the chapter, for getting sales?
2. What novel tactics for reaching out can you think of for him?
3. What novel approaches to selling can you think of for a situation like Bruce's?
4. What sequence of steps should Bruce take next?

Portfolio page possibilities

Page 8A-1 Pricing rationale

Describe and explain the rationale behind the pricing and terms for your venture's product or service.

Page 8A-2 First sale scenario

Describe a scenario for your venture's market rollout and first two or three sales. Include characterizations of the customers and the sales pitch.

↓

[345] Susan Greco, "Good Cheap Data," *Inc.* August 1997, p. 94.
[346] Susan Greco, "The Rating Game," *Inc.* January 1998, p. 93.

Page 8A-3 Advertisement rationale
Prepare an advertisement and display it along with explanation of the rationale behind it and indication of any reactions you got on it from others you specify.

Page 8A-4 Advertisement professionalization
1. Depict an advertisement for your product or service.
2. Insofar as space permits, also describe who could help you professionalize it.
3. Include estimates of the costs of both professionalizing and displaying it.

Page 8A-5 Personal sales pitch
1. Write out in one paragraph an oral sales pitch script for your product or service, noting what audience it was designed for.
2. Describe in a second paragraph the price and rationale for your product or service.

Page 8A-6 Promotion program
1. Brainstorm a promotion program for your venture and cost it out.
2. Design the venture's Web site.

Term Projects

Venture history
1. Who landed the first three sales by the company how?
2. What selling channels came into play over time as the company took hold, and how well did their patterns of development align with expectations?
3. How were prices set for whatever the venture sells, and in hindsight how appropriate were they?
4. Did the venture experience any returns, and if so, how?

Venture planning guide
1. Prepare a detailed selling expenses budget in both dollars and founder hours monthly for the first year of your venture.
2. Explain the rationale by which prices were arrived at for your venture.
3. Describe the venture's system for tracking competition and forecasting its moves.
4. Describe policies, staffing plans and procedures, and budgets for keeping the venture's product or service up to date.

CHAPTER 8B – Operations

Topics

1. Satisfying customers
2. Arranging output capacity
3. Starting to hire
4. Building a workforce
5. Aligning disciplines

Checkpoints

a. Distinguish between the challenges of starting operations in a new firm versus
b. managing operations in an established firm.
c. Describe qualifications that are important in discussing quality.
d. Explain cautions a start-up should consider in choosing suppliers.
e. What is meant by *virtual capacity* and what is its importance for a start-up?
f. Explain steps involved in building a workforce from scratch.
g. Where does culture begin in a new company?
h. What precautions should an entrepreneur take to avoid running out of cash?

New, as opposed to established, enterprises face somewhat different challenges in producing, profiting, and staying solvent. Established firms have advantages in terms of experience, coordinated relationships, credit with suppliers, procedures that have been "shaken out" to work effectively and, perhaps most importantly, a workforce of people with habits of collaborating to deliver the product or service to customers effectively and economically. Going concerns also have advantages in finding and hiring the talent they need.

A new venture, in contrast, may face an uphill battle to build these capabilities before cash runs out. A start-up's disadvantages include diseconomies of small scale, lack of bargaining power with suppliers, inevitable fumbling and groping to find the best connections, lack of specialists to assure that each area of activity can be done with high competence, being spread too thin because of short resources, and the need to break new employees free from now-ill-fitting ways of working that they may have acquired in prior employment.

A start-up must be designed to do things better than established competitors. Among those is to focus more tightly on satisfying customers, and to be fast and flexible in accommodating their preferences. To its advantage, the new venture should be less encumbered by dysfunctional routines that may have grown obsolete in an established firm. Venture employees, if well chosen, should be enthusiastic about in the opportunity to start fresh. This all has implications for how production should be planned, started, controlled, and progressively refined for the longer term.

1. Satisfying customers

The central aim in venture operations should be to deliver the right amount of whatever it sells on time with appropriate quality at a cost at or below target.

Seeking quality

An example of falling short on quality with disastrous consequence was described by Jim Schell, the founder of National Screenprint,

Seeking quality

a company that nevertheless grew to 200 employees and sales in 1990 of $25 million.

> *I lost $18 million one day in 1972.*
>
> *That was National Screenprint's first day of business. I was there as the first shirt rolled down our dryer belt. I didn't know it at the time, but during the course of that day the workmanship of one out of every twenty shirts we would print would be something less than our customer would consider acceptable …*
>
> *I set the quality standards for our company that day. Not by what I did but by what I didn't do. I didn't reject a single shirt … Our customers and our employees would know our product forever by my actions that day, and we would live with the consequences for eighteen long and expensive years.*
>
> *Perhaps I wanted to save the two bucks that each mediocre shirt represented. Or maybe I didn't want to hurt a printer's feelings, or spoil the euphoria of that opening day.*
>
> *How was I to know (I rationalize now) that hundreds of thousands of National Screenprint products over the years would be produced and go unrejected, thanks to the example I set that day? How was I to know that my acceptance of mediocrity would cost us countless hours of rework time, and invoicing credits, and spoilage write-offs, and (the most telling hit) an untold number of customers who would take their business elsewhere.[347]*

As noted earlier, studies by the Boston Consulting Group and others have shown that typically higher profitability is associated with higher share of a served market. The Strategic Planning Institute has found similar results and also that market share tends to be driven by higher quality.[348] Moreover, higher quality allows both higher prices and higher margins. Thus, aiming for high quality is often a logical way to seek high profits.

High quality can also be a requirement for doing any business at all if the venture aspires to manufacture and sell products to other companies, particularly large ones, many of which have adopted the Six Sigma (introduced by Motorola) or ISO 9000 (International Organization for Standardization in Switzerland) international quality standards. These impose such quality measurement goals as allowing no more than 3.4 defects per million units. The system,

which covers not only output, but also processes and records, must be continually reviewed to check for compliance. The standards number over 14,000. Published by the ISO with collaboration of 148 countries around the world and managed by some 3,000 technical committees, subcommittees, and work groups, they cover most of the products made in the world. The process for meeting them and being certified for compliance usually requires hiring a consultant who knows them, takes typically 3 to 18 months to become compliant, and costs from a few thousand to over one hundred thousand dollars for such things as equipment, documentation of procedures, and computerization to track and monitor production flow, as well as training of employees to follow the rules.

In a start-up firm, there are two more reasons for emphasis on top quality. First, as an unknown the firm may have a hard time attaining credibility. Demonstrating exceptional quality may help with that problem. Second, by selecting a segment of the market that desires exceptional quality, the venture may narrow the front on which it must compete. The smaller the segment, or niche, the less it may be of interest to larger competitors and the more the venture can concentrate its limited selling resources.

Defining quality

Just how quality should be defined deserves careful attention. Sometimes a quality problem—that is, a gap between the actual and the appropriate quality—is obvious, as may be seen in this experience described by the venture capitalist Robert J. Kunze:[349]

> *One meter failed our quality control pressure test by exploding. Since our meters were hooked up 'in line' by customers, an exploding meter could cause a flood of potentially dangerous materials. We had to shut down production, find the cause of the failure, and fix the problem.*
>
> *After a week of nail biting, we discovered the welding on the flange of the meter was defective because of contamination. This was a break for us because we could inspect all weldings by X-ray to determine which ones were bad. We screened out*

---

[347] Jim Schell, *The Brass-tacks Entrepreneur* (New York: Henry Holt and Company, 1993) p. 94.
[348] Robert D. Buzzell and Bradley T. Gale, *The PIMS Principles* (New York: Free Press, 1987).
[349] Robert J. Kunze, *Nothing Ventured* (New York: Harper, 1990) p. 162.

a few dozen bad flanges, repaired the defect, and were shipping safe meters within two weeks. That episode cost Exac about $300,000 in lost sales and unabsorbed overhead. A bigger problem would have destroyed the company.

The most important definition of quality is not necessarily what the entrepreneur thinks is high-quality, how the ISO defines it, or even what the customer says it is. Rather is implicit in the customer's buying decision, Ferreting out this real definition can begin with careful thought and armchair analysis, but may also require customer observation and interviews, analysis of past customer buying decisions, focus group comparisons against competitors' offerings, systematic quantitative analysis of product, or service features and, importantly, experimentation.

Production specifications

Defining quality inside the company is the task of production specifications. In manufacturing, these may take the form of drawings that indicate dimensions and how much those dimensions can vary, or chemical formulas with quantitative indication of how precisely the weights, measures, timing temperatures, and so forth are to be controlled. In a service business, production specifications may include, for instance, steps to be followed, the way they are to be performed, timing to aim for, and how results should be checked for quality.

Continuing innovation

Satisfaction of customers is not enough if it takes place only in the present. The venture must aim at satisfying them in the future, and it must do so relative to what competitors will be offering both presently and in the future. That will almost certainly require innovation that is beyond the innovation the venture is starting with. To avoid being leapfrogged by competitors, there must be at least thought, and probably also expenditure of effort, on anticipating what the path of further innovation will be.

A conflict that can arise then becomes how big a step in the innovation process to take on the first introduction of the product or service versus the timing and magnitude of future steps. A phrase sometimes used in manufacturing innovation is that it is time to "shoot the engineer," which is to say it is time to stop adding improvements, or allowing "feature creep," and get the present version out and on the market, lest that step be put off until too late. However, putting a product on the market too early, before testing is adequate and production processes are working well, can also be disastrous. Avoiding these perils will probably require more cash than originally planned. Hence there is also need continually to monitor and forecast cash flow.

2. Arranging output capacity

The sequence that leads to orderly operation may be relatively smooth if the company develops slowly, building on the competence of a founder with a talent for managing and leading as well as producing. However, in start-ups involving the development of new technology, the pressure to beat competitors to market can be, at best, harrowing or, at worst, fatal. Robert J. Kunze observed that initially things may work fairly well while the team is small, everyone knows each other, communication lines are short, goals are clear and shared, and everyone pitches in whenever something needs to be done. But then, he says, comes the hard part:

Within months of the start-up anguish usually sets in. Though everyone has worked hard, no important goals have been met, at least not those that would reduce the fragility of the business. During this time new people have been hired and no one has had time to integrate them into the company's work plan. The boss has continually set unrealistic and unachievable goals, and everyone has bought into them. The employees have done their best, but after a while they start to grumble. Prototypes don't work and need to be re-engineered quickly. If anything, there seems to be more, not less, risk, more questions, fewer answers. The 60- to 80-hour workweek takes a physical and mental toll. Life outside work takes a real licking. Some companies never escape this hellhole. After six years of banging away, they run out of money and go south.[350]

Anticipating problems

The folklore of new projects, including entrepreneurial ventures, has absorbed an awareness that accomplishments tend to take longer than expected and cost more than predicted, there tend to be more ways that things can go wrong than right and no matter how many things are done right, only one thing done wrong can undo the whole effort. A whimsical codification of such observations has taken a form referred to as Murphy's Laws, listed in Exhibit 8b-1.

Exhibit 8b-1 Murphy's Laws

1. Anything that can go wrong will.
2. Of the things that can't go wrong, some can.
3. The thing that will go wrong is the one that will do the most damage.
4. If it can be done wrong, it will.
5. Nature always finds the weak spots.
6. Bread, when dropped, always lands butter-side down.
7. Things always go from bad to worse.
8. If everything seems to be going well, look again.
9. If the prototype works perfectly, the production units will fail.
10. It is impossible to make things foolproof—fools are too ingenious.
11. No matter what goes wrong someone will have known it would but not have said so.

However, many ventures do ward off fatal problems, survive, and prosper by building in at least some anticipation and remedies. Problems that management should be able to head off include:

- Too little inventory or output.
- Inadequate or inappropriate workforce.
- Insufficient or incorrect instructions to employees.
- Equipment failure due to improper maintenance.
- Lateness due to lack of planning.
- Flaws due to slack quality control.

Other problems that management may not be able to head off but may still anticipate mitigate impacts of include:

- Natural disasters, such as fires, floods, and earthquakes. Insurance, as discussed earlier, can help.
- Man-made problems such as robbery, arson, and riots. Defensive measures can reduce the likelihood of these, and insurance can help compensate for their occurrence.
- Customers changing their minds about what they want without warning. Contingency plans may help the venture respond to these.

Kunze described the instance of a biomedical start-up by a researcher whose plans neglected consideration of how to mass-produce the new vaccines it created. Eventually, the founder was fired by the investors as the company struggled to solve technical problems, missed its forecasts, and overspent. Kunze told how, under new management, operations were straightened out as follows:[351]

Gradually, piece-by-piece, we began to solve the manufacturing problems, cost problems, and quality problems. The entire staff attacked the problems in parallel. The financial people developed, revised, and finally installed a cost accounting system that worked. This required immediate price increases in products we had thought profitable but that turned out to be big losers. We didn't lose a single customer.

Research and development people worked in the factory, teaching the new production workers how to work consistently, to control all the variables such as temperature and ingredients, and to measure precisely the passage of time. This research and development exposure to the factory had an additional benefit. Our scientists learned firsthand about production problems and were able to go back to their laboratories and improve the processes.

The biggest help in operating the business came from stabilizing or fixing the sales-forecasting technique. Because the manufacturing cycle took two months from start to finish, the vaccine-in-process could not be increased, decreased, or changed without discarding the entire batch. The salespeople, trying to expand their territories and

---

[350] Kunze, *Nothing Ventured*, p. 212.
[351] Kunze, *Nothing Ventured*, p. 128.

eager to please, had influenced the manufacturing people to change direction every week. The management stopped what should have been an obviously misguided operating mode, developed a two-month forecast system, and stuck to it.

Aiming output levels

With either a new product or a new service, another challenge will be to set output levels appropriately. If initial output is too high, it may create too much inventory to carry, or worse yet, the second generation may have to be introduced before the first one is sold out. Too low an output will likely mean higher unit costs due to setup expense and may mean risk of running short on supply, thereby leaving an opening for competitors. In an established company, guidance for setting output levels can come from trends that are apparent in hindsight, and from familiarity with customers and their needs. In a new company, the guessing will lack historical information as a basis.

A model rockets hobbyist decided to start producing them for others. The rocket would be 14 inches long, consisting of an aluminum tube capped by a Styrofoam nose cone. For sales the founders planned to advertise in hobby magazines and sell direct by mail for $10.95. This was about 10 percent to 20 percent more than products of competitors. But whereas competitors' rockets used flammable fuel, this one would be powered by Freon from cans usually sold to power horns.

Costs of the product were estimated to be $3 each, and the founders figured that if they built an inventory of 300 and spent $200 on the first advertisement, it would leave just enough of the capital to cover operating expenses. The question of what volume to produce was thereby automatically limited. They chose to manufacture in batches of 100 to simplify scheduling, accounting, and analysis. Actual order volume turned out, conveniently, to average about 300 rockets per month.

Recruiting suppliers

Suppliers, as noted earlier, can be regarded as part of the venture's external team and are often very helpful beyond simply selling what the venture wants to buy from them. But they can also make problems for a start-up. The relationship is new and the venture's purchase levels may be small compared to those of established buyers. Moreover, it may be unclear to suppliers whether the start-up will be around long. As a consequently less-appealing customer to suppliers, they may penalize the start-up with slow delivery, high prices, poor quality, and demand for payment in advance.

If the entrepreneur instead begins the relationship by offering to pay in cash and by working at personal communication, supplier service should be better. But doing that can require liquidity, time, and effort that, in a start-up, are usually hard to come by. Easier to gain may be leverage for choice by seeking out alternative sources of supply, even though that takes more work and the suppliers themselves may not like it.

Actions an entrepreneur can take to bolster supply access consequently include:

- Searching out alternative suppliers and requesting bids to stimulate competition among suppliers.
- Using alternative suppliers at least occasionally, if not regularly.
- Strengthening the venture's image, by obtaining introductions or putting up a good front.
- Deducing which elements of performance on the supplier's part are most important and requesting written guarantees on those by trading off other elements of less importance, or by offering a premium price or payment in advance for a guarantee of a particular quality, quantity, and/or delivery time.

In the following example, more drastic action seemed called for and was taken.

In 1985 Hollis Savin started the Yuppie Gourmet, Inc. to produce upscale snacks. In October 1986, the candy company she had contracted with to manufacture her product suddenly confronted her with a demand for cash payment and as an alternative offered to buy her out for a low price. "He had us backed against a wall," she recalled. "He had our inventory locked up in his warehouse. I was resigned to selling it. I was going to hand over $400,000 in unfulfilled orders.

"But my mother convinced me not to give up." Instead, Savin rented a lock cutter plus three trucks and talked her way past the security guards. "We got the boxes packed up when no one was paying attention and were off to southern Illinois, where my husband had found another candy company with the facilities we needed. They produced thousands of pounds of product and shipped it out. We met all our Christmas orders." By early 1989 the company had sales of $1.7 million.[352]

As the start-up begins to survive and grow, it should be able to pick and choose among suppliers, based in part upon which of them have given it the best service initially. Feelings of gratitude may appropriately play a part in building good supplier relationships for the longer run. But developing a rationalized rating system for choosing suppliers on more than just the terms of a current deal can also help. Eight criteria suggested by two small-business scholars based upon a survey of 449 firms in six industries include those shown in Exhibit 8b-2 below.[353]

The authors suggest that such criteria be weighted, and that each supplier be given a numerical score such as from one to five on each criterion, which is then multiplied by the weighting of that criterion, after which the weighted scores are added to give an overall score to each supplier. This information can provide a rational basis for choosing suppliers and can also give feedback to suppliers. Diplomatically handled, this can help suppliers improve and earn their gratitude, to the advantage of the start-up.

Ordering supplies may call for careful estimating and decision-making. Larger purchase orders usually yield price breaks from suppliers as well as possibly better service and delivery from them. However, trade credit needed to obtain supplies, which often is at best hard to get on small orders, will probably be even harder to get on larger ones. Hence bigger orders require more start-up capital. They also raise the risk of loss if what is ordered turns out not exactly to fit the venture's need. If the initial inventory is too small and the lead-time for ordering is long, however, there may not be time to restock before what is on hand runs out. Thus forecasting in this area can be an important part of setup decision-making.

Building virtual capacity

Some enterprises are referred to as virtual companies, because with minimal facilities, they manage to operate as if they were bigger, either by collaborating with other independent firms whose activities are complementary or by outsourcing selected functions. Some advantages of using virtual organizations versus advantages of performing the work in-house are listed in the shaded area on the following page.

Other firms attain partial virtual operations by keeping a hired workforce near zero through using temporary help only on occasions when it is absolutely necessary. Rather than paying workers directly, the venture can engage them through temp firms that recruit them, pay

Exhibit 8b-2 Supplier selection criteria

		Weight	Points	Score (= Weight x Points)
a.	Consistent quality	___	___	___
b.	Dependable delivery	___	___	___
c.	Net price	___	___	___
d.	Attitude of supplier	___	___	___
e.	Reputation of supplier	___	___	___
f.	Production capacity	___	___	___
g.	Technical assistance	___	___	___
h.	Financial stability	___	___	___

[352] Jeannie Ralston, "Specialty Food with All the Trimmings," *Venture*, February 1981, p. 43.
[353] C. David Wieters and Lonnie L. Ostrom, "Maintaining Effective Suppliers: A Small Business Approach," *Journal of Small Business Management*, 1, no. 2, Spring 1986, p. 149.

Advantage of virtual versus in-house organizations

Advantages of adopting virtual organization approaches can include:

- **Flexibility** The company can hire only the skills it needs for only as long as it needs them.
- **Simplicity** The work of employee recruiting, records, training, red tape, payroll processing, and laying off is minimized.
- **Speed** Time lag is reduced on processing job applications, training, sick leave layoff, or discharge.
- **Cash flow** Whereas employee payroll absolutely must be met on time, it may be possible with a contractor to negotiate trade credit, thereby delaying payments.

There are, however, also advantages to hiring an in-house workforce for the venture, which include:

- **Lower hourly cost** By not using an outside labor source the venture can avoid having to pay for the overhead and profit that the outside employer must earn for providing labor assistance.
- **More refined skill** Whereas an outside worker may have high skill within an area, a company employee should be able, through more consistent practice, to develop still higher skill pinpointed at the special needs of the individual venture.
- **Greater innovation** To the extent that employees can be motivated to "live the job," their creative capabilities that work independently of hours and of conscious thought may be influenced to generate better ideas for the venture.
- **Higher dedication** Commitment by the venture to continuing employment of its workers can motivate workers to do more for the company.

them, and take care of their payroll deductions, insurance, and governmental paperwork. Then the venture must pay only their employer, thereby avoiding payroll busywork.

A second way to escape those complications is to hire individuals as independent contractors rather than employees, letting them take care of their own payroll deductions and insurance. Individual consultants, for example, are employed in this way. Caution is required, however, to follow the law. If the government gets the idea that these contractors are really employees of the venture just masquerading as independent, it will move in to stop the practice and impose fines. Tests it will apply include whether the individuals keep their own hours,

have their own work facilities, direct their own efforts, report self-employment income, and work occasionally or steadily for the venture.

Hiring employees only part time, defined by the federal government as less than 1,000 hours per year, is a third way to gain flexibility and some simplification. Further information about hiring rules can be seen on the legal Web site Findlaw.com.

When the technology is new and sophisticated, the convenient solution of hiring expertise outside may not be available, and the entrepreneur may have no choice except amateur experimentation, which should be considered in planning and budgeting.

3. Starting to hire

In setting up the venture initially there may be just a founding team of a few owners. There may also be occasional engagement of professional advisers; beyond that perhaps contracts with outside suppliers, with the venture operating largely as a virtual organization with no regular payroll.

By handling many or all of the operations tasks personally, an entrepreneur may avoid having to share ownership, spend money to hire help, or take much time to coordinate with helpers. But also then the founder will have to operate outside his or her zone of greatest competence as a jack of all trades and carry a personal time overload, which can both slow down progress and reduce performance quality. Venture capitalist Robert J. Kunze described problems with this approach in a venture he considered financing:[354]

> *Dr. Black was an accomplished researcher on paper, but he had only managed a few laboratory technicians and a secretary. He had been a product manager and twice successfully transformed technical theories into successful commercial products. All his work had been done with RCA's checkbook and infrastructure, however. The availability of a corporate infrastructure meant that if Black needed special equipment, someone researched the problem and bought it for him; if a fixture needed to be machined, the head of the machine shop took care of it; if he needed a micrograph, the analytical laboratory made one; if his telephone broke, someone fixed it.*
>
> *TM (the new venture) would have no infrastructure. Dr. Black would have to take care of almost everything himself, from getting the permits to work in the building to locking up at night.*

These were limitations that Black apparently initially learned to live with. Hiring only a secretary, a maintenance man, and an engineering graduate, he set about designing, building, and delivering machines. However, sales were minimal and some customers were sending their machines back. For operations to progress beyond the barest inception point, more qualified people were needed, but Black was not getting them. Kunze continued:

> *When I asked him about his people and dealing with the tasks at hand, and plans to sell milling machines while rapidly developing the deposition machine, Black dismissed my concerns with a wave of his hand. He had done this type of work before, he said. He had created an electron milling machine that worked, and left alone, he would build a deposition machine in six months. No, thank you, he didn't need to hire any hotshot engineers (or marketing people). He needed people who would do what he wanted when he wanted it, nothing more, nothing less.*

Kunze declined to invest in this venture and Black raised money from others, who demoted him to director of engineering. Some time later

the company went bankrupt, after which Black was convicted of selling technology secrets to the Russians.

Hiring acquaintances

The first hiring of regular employees by a new venture is often done among existing acquaintances without formal search. Usually, it begins with personal and working acquaintances of the founder(s) rather than systematic analysis and campaigning. Advantages of this approach are that it is fast and the people hired have already been evaluated through personal experience with them. Possible disadvantages are that the experience may not have been indicative of what the new tasks of start-up will call for, and even if they are, there may be better candidates not yet known to the founders who could be discovered through searching more widely.

Avoiding errors

To the extent that employees are to be hired for steady work, regardless of the organization size, the tasks of (1) choosing them well and providing (2) effective training, (3) motivation, and (4) leadership for them are extremely important. These four tasks will determine how well they do their jobs, which will become how well the company does its job and, in the long run, how successful a company it will most likely become.

Some examples of difficulties encountered by entrepreneurs in producing with their own employees include the following:

> The founder and 65 percent shareholder of a security systems company was out of town inspecting work on a new job when the operations manager, controller, and marketing manager, concerned about loose management of the company, approached the company's bank and suggested that it tell the founder either to resign or have his loan called. Upon learning of this, the founder contacted his lawyer and the two visited the banker, whom they informed firmly that all relations between the bank and founder were to be kept confidential. They vowed to file suit against the bank for conspiracy if any damage to the company resulted from the bank's meetings with the company's employees. The employees

---

[354] Kunze, *Nothing Ventured*, p. 105.

were given the choice of resigning or being fired, and chose the former.

— • —

The factory of a jacket enterprise burned down. Arson appeared to be the cause, but when the owner appealed to the insurance company for compensation, both it and the local fire department indicated they believed management had been behind the fire to gain insurance money. The owner hired a former FBI agent to investigate. This man found in the fire department records, notes from a interview with a woman who had been eating in a restaurant near the plant when the fire broke out and had reported seeing a young man enter the restaurant muttering somewhat incoherently about the blaze. An amateur artist, she had also submitted a sketch of him to the fire department. The FBI man showed this sketch to the owner of the jacket enterprise and learned it depicted a former employee. Investigation of the employee's background turned up earlier troubles with the law. Eventually, the employee confessed to setting the fire, the insurance firm paid up, and the jacket enterprise continued.

— • —

The founder of a restaurant said employee stealing was a never-ending problem. Tablecloths, silverware, pots and pans, food, and other supplies continually disappeared. He recalled firing one cook who had stolen large quantities of food, including whole beef roasts, by putting it in plastic bags, placing them in the garbage and retrieving them from the dumpster after hours. The only solution the owner could think of was to be eternally vigilant and accept the fact that some things were bound to go wrong.

These examples illustrate only a small fraction of problems that arise with employees. A new venture at least offers opportunity to start out right with careful employee selection coupled with care-ful management, including clear formulation and enforcement of rules. Starting a pattern of careful attention to employee needs and problems can set a positive trend from the beginning, and head off later need to fix dysfunctional habits.

Meeting government requirements

Caution is also needed regarding governmental rules on employment. As employees are added, progressively more governmental restrictions and requirements apply. A list of federal employment laws and regulations showing the company size at which they kick in appears in Exhibit 8b-3.

Such consequences of growth are why some entrepreneurs permanently keep their enterprises small.

In addition there are workers' compensation laws varying from state to state requiring the company to pay for job-related injuries. There are also EEOC (Equal Employment Opportunity Commission) guidelines for what any employer can ask a job applicant. For instance, questions about age (unless the applicant may be too young), religion, number of children or pregnancy, arrests (unless there was conviction), health condition (unless work-related), race, or ethnicity, even where the person learned English, are not appropriate.

Employees can still sue if they think they have cause and might be able to collect from the venture. Discharge policies, Internet policies, sexual harassment policies, disclosure of information about dangerous people, and spreading damaging information about present or former employees, if another company should ask, can all lead to lawsuits.

Exhibit 8b-3 Federal laws and regulations on employment

Rules	Application threshold (Number of employees)
National Labor Relations (unionizing) Act	1
Taft-Hartley (unionizing) Act	1
Immigration Act	1
Occupational Safety and Health Act (OSHA)	1
Civil Rights Act	15
Equal Pay (for equal work) Act	15
Americans with Disabilities Act	15
Age Discrimination in Employment Act	20
Family and Medical (rights to) Leave Act	20
Vocational Rehabilitation Act	50

4. Building a workforce

Definitions

Recruiting

Beyond the first few informal hires, the processes for recruiting and managing should become systematized more like those of established firms.

Definitions

Earlier, in connection with designing and setting up facilities, the tasks to be performed in using them were discussed. Another step is to write out job descriptions, both for the venture to be clear about its needs and to clarify for each applicant just what the company expects. Each job description should tell (1) what the name of the job is, (2) what its holder is expected to do, (3) whom the person should report to, (4) what qualifications the job holder should have, and (5) indication that the company reserves flexibility to assign other duties as it sees fit.

Targets for hiring

Underlying the sales and output projections of the business plan are implications about how many recruits will be needed, and for how long. Ventures vary in this regard. Rock concerts hire people for a night. Construction companies may hire them for days or weeks. Manufacturing and selling companies often hope employees will stay for years, continually improving their know-how and skills. Restaurants and other service firms usually fall in between. High-technology companies need at least some people with esoteric know-how and high ability to innovate on some technical frontier. Each venture must define its needs and preferences in terms of both quantity and characteristics of employees to be sought.

Search criteria

Careful thought, discussion with co-founders, if any, and with advisers should be applied to determine the make-up of people to be recruited. It can be terribly expensive in both money and lost time, as well as to others in the organization to hire people who turn out to be wrong for the organization, as illustrated in examples described earlier. Criteria for the people to be hired should be written down and

reviewed by advisers. Doing so can help also in preparing written job descriptions.

Technical qualifications and work experience are some qualities of interest, but possibly not the most important. Qualifications in the way of personality, style, and ambitions also matter. Will the person be egotistical and resentful, or a supportive, possibly leading, team player?

Recruiting

There are always many people looking for jobs. But hiring from among them those who fit the venture's criteria best can require major effort.

Finding candidates

If the venture is in the same line of business where the entrepreneur has had work experience, the logical first place to search is among contacts in that line of work, including people presently working for or helping the venture plus, of course, their own networks. Beyond those are the options of running advertisements in newspaper classified sections and on Web sites such as Monster.com, MSN Jobhunt (careers.com), and Guru.com. Some tactics for seeking candidates appear in the shaded area at the top of the following page.

Thoughtful effort on preparation of job descriptions and listing criteria should help to sharpen the focus of search so as not to be swamped with candidates most or all of whom don't fit. If a job is important enough to justify hiring a search firm (head hunter), then it too can help sharpen the focus. If the job is technical, other options include university placement offices, job fairs, and technical society meetings.

Competitors may also be suitable sources, although if alerting them to the venture's need may reveal otherwise unknown vulnerabilities, doing so is unwise. Also, competitors may regard the venture as a place to get rid of employees they don't want. For instance, in telling about an engineer who produced poor results, resisted having his work reviewed, and was late but finally left the company, G. Gordon Bell, head of research at Digital Equipment Corporation for 23 years observed that "Outplacing negatively

Tactics for seeking job candidates

- Design the venture to be an attractive employer.
- Build in ways to have employees achieve their career aims.
- Start collecting recruiting connections before they are needed.
- Ask among present and past acquaintances, suppliers, customers.
- Ask all present members of the venture to help in the search.
- Advertise in journals, at trade shows, and association meetings.
- Visit college placement offices.
- Attend networking meetings, such as entrepreneurship groups.
- Stay in touch with former applicants and employees.
- Contact individuals profiled in newspaper business sections and magazines.
- Seek people offshore through immigrants here.
- Let needs be known in media interviews and news releases.
- Hire a recruiting firm.
- Collect resumes, keep a list of possibilities, and build on it over time.

productive people with a potential competitor can do wonders for a firm's competitive lead."[355]

Checking out candidates

Individuals experienced in hiring find their own tricks for screening candidates, sometimes through uncomfortable experiments and other times successful ones.

A big company physicist who, on the side, started a high-fidelity speaker company, thought it most important to hire unusually bright people. The people he hired agreed with him. For screening they gave candidates an IQ test, then picked those with the highest scores. He paid them largely with stock, eventually lost controlling interest through dilution of his shares, and finally was fired by his employees. The company failed.

— • —

Elmer Ward, founder of a high-performance electric motor company, Task Corporation of Anaheim, California, believed it was important to test people's task-relevant performance. To engineering applicants he gave a dimensioning problem to lay out the measurement tolerances on the shaft of a motor. The company produced innovative and well-engineered products. But in other areas it did not fare so well, lost money, and was sold off by its main shareholders.

Screening to find the most promising recruits from among candidates not already known through personal acquaintance or contacts can be a lot of work that scales up with the number of candidates. But hiring an unsatisfactory candidate or missing out on hiring an exceptionally good one can be much more expensive. Hence successful companies tend to apply substantial effort and resources to get it right.

Take time as needed. Managers who fill openings too quickly often regret it sooner or later. The cost of a bad hiring decision can be very high. List desired qualities and specific skills needed for the job in advance. Then allocate time to seek them. Figure on using resumes, interviews, possibly testing, plus reference-checking as part of the process.

Resumes are a starting point, but almost certainly biased. If factually correct, they give good information about education, jobs held, and references. But then they must be checked for truthfulness and omissions. Why does the person want a different job from what he or she had, and how well do their qualifications fit future needs?

For interviews ask colleagues or advisers to help frame questions that will reveal whether the candidate has what it takes, and later to help evaluate the answers. Consider all the skills needed in the person's skill set to do the job well. Prepare and follow an interview script. Figure that an interview may take as

---

[355] G. Gordon Bell, *High-Tech Ventures* (Reading, MA: Addison Wesley, 1991) p. 133.

much as two to three hours if a candidate does not bomb out sooner.

In the interviews, try to put candidates at ease because they will then feel better about the venture and also probably reveal more. Listen to them without talking and ask that they hold their questions for afterward. Taking notes can reduce bias, help with refining the process, and add protection against any claims of improper questioning or discrimination. Keep the hiring goals in mind when evaluating answers. Important to notice is the level of interest that the candidate has in the job; the higher the better.

Use open-ended questions that yield more information rather than asking yes or no questions. Ask for examples, descriptions, explanations, and interpretations of specific experiences and the results they produced. Seek to learn how candidates thought and acted about different situations at work. Consider how relevant those experiences are to the tasks that the venture will need done.

Ask about proud accomplishments, and the reasoning and actions that brought them about. But also ask about limitations, maybe worst as well as best experiences, and what the candidate thinks future learning should be aimed at. Look for clues on all the needed skills, not just those that show up best. Seek counsel from others again in assessing the results.

A good technique to use when possible is the situational interview. For that, the interviewer and advisers make up descriptions of situations the candidate might face and also formulate and rank in quality the range of most likely responses. Then the interviewee is asked what he or she would do in a particular situation. Following the interview, the answers given by each interviewee are graded according to which of the pre-formulated and ranked responses they gave.

Checking references is also important. But it can be complicated by the reluctance of respondents to say unfavorable things that might bring down upon them either resentment or possibly lawsuits for doing so. One tactic can be to ask in person, rather than in writing, for comments. Another is to call references when they are likely to be out of the office, such as during lunch, and asking that they call back as a reference about the person in question. If they call back it will likely be because they have good things to report.

Persuading preferred recruits to join

In attempting to recruit job candidates, start-up firms have some handicaps and advantages as listed in the shaded area at the bottom of the page.

Larger firms can capitalize on economies of scale in hiring. They can spread over many re-

---

Start-up handicaps versus advantages in recruiting employees

Handicaps include:

- Relative financial insecurity.
- Relatively low pay.
- Limited, if any, fringe benefits.
- Lack of opportunity to move around within the company.
- Little or no formal training opportunities.
- No association with a name brand.

To be weighed against these are such advantages as:

- A more personal environment.
- Capability of the company to grow and change faster.
- More responsibility and breadth of coverage in work.
- Opportunity to make a visible difference personally in the fortunes of the company.
- Opportunity to rise faster as the company expands.
- Part ownership can be given as compensation, which could become very valuable.

cruits the costs of widespread advertising, formal testing, fees for recruiting firms, formal job study costs, and travel expenses for interviewing. Start-ups and small firms may have to accept applicants that established firms either overlook or don't want.

At the same time, large firms simply don't appeal to some people because of their standardized and bureaucratic treatment of the recruiting process plus a regimented, hierarchical "no fun" work environment. With more rigid and formalized decision making, large firms may less be able to accommodate individual exceptions, including favorable as well as unfavorable ones.

It is up to venture founders to pitch these potential advantages effectively, and often their own enthusiasm and excitement during start-up help them do that. Consequently, start-ups, in spite of their handicaps, sometimes manage to recruit excellent employees. By being small and flexible, they can accommodate unusual people who do not fit well in established firms, or simply don't like the regimentation such firms impose in pursuit of efficiency. Homemakers, part-timers, members of the family, military people in off-hours, school teachers during summers, people with disabilities, and retired people can be more readily accommodated by start-ups than by companies whose routines have grown more firmly fixed.

> Advanced Financial Solutions, number 491 on the *Inc.* 500 list of fastest-growing small firms in 2001, needed to recruit technical professionals to work in Oklahoma City, far from most hi-tech communities. The solution adopted was to invite selected applicants to go there for a week to become familiar with the company and its town, after which the company would decide whether to extend an offer and the candidate would decide whether to accept. This gained the company the people it needed for an average cost of $7,500 each, not including recruitment firm fees. The amount was well justified because of the problems it forestalled in the view of the CEO, Gary Nelson, who commented, "You can't put a price tag on aggravation and grief." Turnover in the firm as it grew from 60 to 190 employees in three years was 1 percent.[356]

Offering to share ownership is often a most powerful hiring incentive that start-ups are in a good position to use. The company can offer shares directly or on the basis of stock options that the recruit can exercise after a certain period of time if the employment works out. Professional legal help is likely to be needed for doing this right, because there are tax consequences according to how it is handled. Also important to remember is that by thus sharing ownership the venture may end up having paid dearly to recruit the person. At the same time, that is why it can appeal strongly to them.

Beginning culture

Actions in hiring will set the basis for building the culture of the company, and culture determines what the priorities of the company are in the minds of its employees. How hard they work, how much they cooperate and support each other and the company, what ethical rules they follow, how loyal they are, and how much they care about customers, quality, and service are both causes and effects of corporate culture. Some companies have found that by sharing financial statements with employees and educating them about connections between employee performance and financial results, particularly if those results directly impact employees' pocketbooks through sharing ownership and profits, employee attitudes toward their work and their coworkers' work changes. They find ways to make products better, render improved service, and reduce costs so that company performance markedly improves.

Treatment of financial information, however, is by no means the only, or even most powerful, shaping force on company culture. What kinds of people are hired is powerful, because people tend to continue being the way they are, and the way they are has much to do with their attitudes about customers, coworkers, company expectations, and quality of performance.

What rules the founders lay down will strongly influence what kind of company to work for the venture turns out to be. Being autocratic, like the military, may initially save time and

---

[356] Jane Saladof MacNeil, "Hey, Look Us Over," *Inc.*, November 2001.

reduce the chances of misunderstanding and error. But will it turn on or turn off the kinds of employees the company wants to recruit and retain? It will probably not help employees develop their own decision-making strengths as much and consequently leave more load on management later, which can bog it down with details it is also not good at handling.

Examples management sets by its own behavior will also strongly influence how the venture's culture will develop. Will the founders be on site or absent a lot? Will they put in long hours or short? Will they have special parking places or fly different class than subordinates? Will they be open with information or cagey? Will they be interested in personal problems of subordinates, or focused sharply on business?

How much will the founders care and seek to learn about the aspirations of employees? How strong will priorities of the venture be on seeking ways to help employees achieve them? Will employees be encouraged to experiment with ways of doing things to learn, or will they be required to follow company procedures believed to be most efficient?

How will the company handle the trade-off between higher pay and lower fringe benefits such as health care, educational support, or retirement benefits versus the opposite for a given amount of labor cost? If orders slacken, will the company lay some employees off or reduce the pay and workweek for all employees? How much exceptional treatment will it give to employees with personal emergencies or problems?

A company particularly noted for a congenial and effective culture has been Hewlett-Packard, and many of its values seemed to be expressed in "Bill and Dave" anecdotes, such as the following.

> The company's headquarters in Palo Alto was a plant where many employees came and went to some degree on their own schedules. A woman recently hired from another company where employees tended to exit at 5 p.m. was just starting to rush from her desk to reach the exit at that time. Bill Hewlett happened upon her as he was passing through the office, saw what she, in contrast to the other employees, was doing, gave her a big smile and said "I'll race you to the door!"

> —•—

> A Hewlett-Packard engineer took an extended vacation, flew with his family to the East Coast, bought a sailboat and sailed it to San Francisco Bay. Along the way he learned navigation and sailing, endured rain pouring through cracks in the cabin roof, sweltering days getting through the Panama Canal, and even losing a child overboard, whom he and his wife managed to pull back aboard with a lifeline. By the time the boat was moored in Redwood City, he was deeply tanned, had calloused hands and feet, and felt quite uncomfortable trying to re-enter the discipline of work at his engineering desk.

> Hearing about this, Hewlett called him in and said "Tony, why don't you have our travel office get you some tickets to fly out, visit oceanographic institutions on both coasts, and look for ways we might be able to develop instruments for marine science and industries?"

Coincidentally, Hewlett-Packard had an easy time hiring when other technical companies found it hard, even though its pay was relatively low (though it had high fringe benefits), and few of its employees left (even though it offered to help them become independent suppliers to it if they chose to). Both its growth and profits were exceptionally high for its industry at that time and for long after.

That is not to say that culture or congenial management is necessarily a formula for certain success, as the following may illustrate.

> Seattle had two family-owned steel fabrication companies that were struck by their union. Jorgensen Forge's management took a hard line, fought the union, and wouldn't budge. Isaacson Iron Work's management was conciliatory, made concessions to the union, and went back in production. Eventually, Jorgensen too, was back in production, notwithstanding the union's hard feelings, and before long Isaacson failed financially, went out of business, and saw its production equipment shipped to China.

Congenial culture by itself is not enough. Hewlett-Packard coupled it with strong spending on innovation and high standards of product quality, even though they coupled with high prices. Southwest Airlines, noted for a culture strong in fun on the job, built its outstanding long record of growing sales and high profits, even when its industry was declining, by coupling that culture with cost-saving work rules, shrewd choices of routes, and many other strategically advantageous policies.

5. Aligning disciplines

Among the important dimensions of performance in the venture will be how well it maintains quality, innovation, delivery, and service work, as well as how fast its sales grow, topics treated in the preceding chapter and the first part of this chapter. Measures of effort must be developed implicitly for sales and production as well as measures of performance. Important to measure in the area of finance are those of sales, expenses, and cash flow. Seeking to achieve good performance on these measures then becomes the responsibility of both management and the other employees, guided by strategic choices and the company culture.

Keeping important records

Companies need all sorts of records for taxes and other reasons. A catch in setting up records for a start-up is that need for some of them may not appear until the company has been in business a while and something goes wrong. Examples include the following.

A company was prosecuted by state tax collectors for not collecting state sales tax from customers who might have used personally some products they bought for resale from the company.

— • —

An attorney who had not kept adequate time records for billing clients found himself losing money because he was undercharging in an attempt to avoid overcharging.

— • —

An office machine repair company found itself running out of some types of parts, which delayed work, while having excess inventory of other parts. Also, some employees' time on jobs was not fully accounted for in billings.

— • —

An architecture firm found itself having to substantiate for a lawsuit hours of work it had done on a building where the contractor had stopped working because the customer contested some of the work and refused to pay.

In each of these cases the best time to set up good records was at the start of business; the easiest thing to do, and in the short run the cheapest as well, was not to.

Anticipating cash shortages

Operating under the pressure of a cash squeeze is a common necessity in start-up ventures, and for many it leads to shutdown. Three means of dealing with this squeeze are to minimize expenditures, maximize collections, and recruit more capital infusions as the venture continues—in other words keep cash outflows down and inflows up. The former includes both controlling costs and controlling disbursements related to both costs and accruals. The latter includes collecting from customers, pursuing trade credit, and possibly borrowing cash or selling securities.

Three elements that determine the need for cash in a company are its margin, its growth rate, and its capital intensity. If the margin is too slim, the venture can lose money and cash. If its growth rate is high, there will be need to support more receivables, inventory, and possibly plant and equipment. A high enough margin may be able to cover these with retained earnings, but not if capital intensity is high. Consequently it is easy for a venture to need more cash. Without it the founders will at best have to cut back on expenditures, give up more equity, or possibly see the venture fail.

In 1974 a Seattle man undertook to start an indoor tennis club. He sold 150 memberships, obtained a bank loan, built a facility that could accommodate 600 members, and opened the doors in September. He found that to break even he would need at least 250 members. Month after month the club lost money while he sought to recruit more members. This depleted his cash and soon creditors were pressing for payment. As the deficit grew he was compelled to shift his efforts to recruiting investors rather than members. Eventually he was able to put together a consortium of Canadian and American investors to take over the business and its $50,000 loss.

Keeping important records

Anticipating cash shortages

He was left with no business and no job, but relieved that he had not let down the members whom he had initially recruited.

In hindsight this entrepreneur might have seen that there were at least three things he could have done better. The first would have been to forecast cash flows with more care, which would have revealed sooner the crunch that was inevitable. The second would have been to line up more adequate financing in advance, rather than having to seek it when things were desperate. Third, he could have controlled operating costs more carefully and thereby reduced cash drain.

The discipline of managing cash with maximal efficiency is one many entrepreneurs learn out of necessity and one which can give their ventures an advantage over older competitors long beyond start-up. The importance of watching cash closely was emphasized by Harvey Quadracci, the founder of a printing company whose sales by 1990 were $375 million.

> Nobody understands what cash flow is unless they've lived by it. The experience changes you permanently. I have a telephone in planes, trains, cars, and bedrooms because I have a phobia. I break out into a cold sweat if I'm away from a phone. It goes back to those days when I was always calling to ask, "Did the check come in the morning? OK, release those other checks."[357]

If cash is short it means either too little came in, too much went out, or both. The result if it continues is certain failure of the venture. Ways cash shortfall comes about include:

- Failing to foresee needs adequately.
- Lacking good financial controls.
- Waiting too long to seek capital.
- Underestimating effort required to raise capital.
- Pursuing capital sources that don't fit the venture.
- Selling stock to an investor who has inadequate capability to help further.
- Taking on too much debt.
- Agreeing to a misunderstood deal.
- Losing credibility by failing to meet commitments.

- Paying too much for capital.
- Misapplying the capital.
- Asking for money without adequate preparation.

The first line of prevention against cash shortfall is to forecast carefully what cash will be needed for and where it should come from.

Rochelle Zabarkas did it right in many respects, designing a specialty food store for Manhattan, choosing a busy site, thinking through, and writing out a business plan, and lining up enough personal financing to qualify for $245,000 in bank loans to cover her start-up costs. Sales of her mix of gourmet foods and spices took off in 1992, as magazines wrote enthusiastically about her venture, and by 1993 were up another 40 percent to over $1,100 per day.

But the initial seed capital was not enough to support the growth, and she ran short of cash. She defaulted on a $145,000 bank loan and also the mortgage on her condominium. Suppliers went unpaid, and in desperation she even misapplied a $5,000 New York State check. Her mistake, as she saw it in hindsight, was to estimate that she needed $285,000 to start the business, when in fact she needed $350,000. A friend of hers, also in retail, put the estimated need at more like $450,000 to start. A consultant familiar with such situations said she forgot to consider, "What do I need in operating capital to keep me going for at least two years."[358]

Curbing cash needs

Seeking to minimize cash needs is worthy of continued attention and effort as the venture begins to take hold. There may be natural inclinations to add expensive but non-essential things: new facilities and equipment, bigger inventory, refurnished offices, and maybe company cars. As the venture becomes visible, it will also become a target for others who have things to sell, such as computer systems, accounting services, advertising ideas, security systems, and charitable causes. These may play on a founder's ambition to build a bigger and more

---

[357] "Going for Broke," *Inc.*, September 1990, p. 35.
[358] Brent Bowers, "This Store Is a Hit but Somehow Cash Flow Is Missing," *Wall Street Journal*, April 13, 1993, p. B-2.

successful company by implying that such accomplishment can be bought and erected like a stage prop or a window display.

Desire to increase sales and please customers can allow accounts receivable to string out. Why antagonize people by pressing for payment if it might cause them not to buy as much? Sales are needed to break even and earn profits. There is plenty else to do without worrying about how fast customers are paying. It's easy to be comforted by the fact that receivables are a symbol of successful sales, the more the better. Besides, the receivables can always be used for borrowing at the bank if more cash is needed. It's also easy to forget that the bank will loan at most only a percentage of the receivables, not the face value, and maybe nothing at all. Moreover, the borrowed money will cost interest and probably other charges that constitute further cash drain.

> Donald Weck and Harvey Levine started Love At First Bite in 1981 to make pâtés and quiches. In the second year they started borrowing money to add staff and equipment. Weck recalled, "We spent way too much money on things we had no business spending money on. We took out a $15,000 loan for a computer that we didn't need. We hired a controller for $30,000 when we were only grossing $400,000 a year." By 1985 the company, $200,000 in debt, was advised to declare bankruptcy. Instead Weck fired the controller and the bookkeeper, reorganized the production staff, persuaded the bank to restructure its loan, and managed to restore profitability. By 1988 the company was debt-free with sales of $1.2 million per year.[359]

Constant vigilance is needed to minimize cash drain, and staying constantly informed of any cash commitments is something a founder must do. Signing all the checks is one action that may help. Others are to keep a running file on receivables aging, and to discuss any major financial commitments with a banker or someone likely to hold conservative views on spending. Maintaining a cash flow forecast and paying careful attention to it particularly before making any commitments for expansion should be another rule.

Monitoring expenses

Although incurring expenses and having cash outflow don't necessarily coincide, minimizing expenses is a natural companion to minimizing non-cash assets to conserve cash. The value of vigilance appears in the following case.

> A machine shop owner noticed that his total materials costs were running far in excess of the amount he was estimating on jobs. Seeking the reason, he also noticed that scrap from the shop seemed somewhat too abundant. Figuring that excessive material waste might be occurring because workers had free access to the shop's materials inventory, he decided to hire a stock clerk who would check both incoming freight and shipments against invoices, have workers sign for materials checked out against jobs, and maintain a running inventory of not only raw materials but also work in process and finished goods. Materials costs shortly came into line with expectations.

A logical approach to controlling costs might seem to be going line by line through the income statement and looking for ways to cut. But that is not the way CEOs of high-performing small companies do it, according to the editors of *Inc.* who interviewed them. Instead, they reported, "The motivation to cut costs becomes a departure point for something much more far-reaching. It forces a CEO to reexamine the entire company, to rethink its structure, what it does, even his or her role in it."[360] Examples the article cited to illustrate this point included the following.

> A construction company operator knew there was waste, but not where. The first task, rather than seeking cost cuts, was to make financial information on jobs uniform so they could be compared. This revealed that big jobs were more profitable than small ones and gave better ideas about what types of business to seek.
> — • —

> A quick oil-change operator who emphasized having a qualified staff and providing exceptional service, found his margins slipping. Looking for places to cut costs, he decided the only option was to reduce advertising. However, upon further analyzing ways to increase profits rather than cut costs, he decided it would be better to leave advertising alone and expand capacity.
> — • —

[359] Ralston, "Specialty Food," *Venture*, February 1981, p. 43.
[360] Bruce G. Posner, "Squeeze Play," *Inc.*, July 1990, p. 68.

The CEO of a company selling computer printing equipment, supplies, and services analyzed how the people in his company spent their time and concluded that too much of it went to less profitable activities. Rather than cutting costs, he changed the composition of his workforce, adding some people with new expertise and laying off others whose specialties were less profitable.

— • —

The owners of a security systems company found that installation costs were exceeding estimates they used in bidding. A new incentive system that paid installers by satisfactory job completion rather than hours brought costs down.

Cost control can begin much earlier than these examples display. Dan Bricklin, one of the founders of Software Arts, which introduced the first microcomputer spreadsheet program, Visicalc, but subsequently failed to distinguish itself successfully, recalled missteps reaching back to company conception.

We had no models for a software company, so we operated on the book-publishing model, which turned out to be wrong. We thought we could just develop neat products and sell them—without realizing that different organizations were needed for different types of products. We didn't appreciate that the overhead appropriate for one product might be totally inappropriate for another. So there was a lot of waste. I could see it in my company, and I saw it even more when I did consulting for Lotus. It wasn't purposeful. People just didn't understand what was necessary and what wasn't.[361]

Figuring out which costs are necessary is something the initial business planning process can help with. But it is likely to require some trial and analysis, as well. Venturing is largely a process of experimentation. Although the entrepreneur may have a clear vision of what the venture is to be and perhaps even plans that have been carefully thought out, reviewed by other knowledgeable people, and refined based on feedback from them, there will still be continual adjustment of important dimensions and possibly major changes in the venture's strategy as it moves forward.

Warren Avis observed that in setting up his airport car-rental agencies, he had not been careful enough in checking up on revenues the company was owed by licensees.

It was only after having sold Avis Rent-A-Car that I learned about one of my biggest blunders with the licensees. I was quite trusting and rather naïve. It didn't dawn on me that some of them might try to cheat by reporting lower revenues than they were actually taking in. Also, I felt I couldn't afford to run auditors all over the country checking up on them. Besides, I didn't want to!

That attitude turned out to be wrong. The people who took over the company from me did send out auditors. As a result, they recovered many times more than they had to pay the auditors to investigate.[362]

Preventing cash leaks

Businesses have to operate largely on trust, and most of the time that works well. But the possibility that it will not should also be clear in mind from the beginning of a venture to forestall unnecessary unpleasant financial betrayals.

Avoiding bad receivables

Eagerness to get sales can blind a company to the fact that not all potential customers can pay for what they buy.

Future Pages, an advertising agency specializing in college newspapers, was surprised by collapse of a large dot-com client who owed $250,000 and expected to raise money with a public stock offering but went bankrupt instead. To cope in the short run with this uncollectable bill, the agency negotiated with its suppliers to delay its payments to them and at the same time sold what good accounts receivable it had at a discount to a factoring company. In the longer run it was more cautious to make sure its customers would be able to pay, and sought to avoid depending too much on any one of them.[363]

In retail stores and services where customers pay with cash, there is no need to worry about bad debts. But where the company is asked to extend credit to firms whose solvency is not obvious from their size and prosperity, it pays to be cautious, run credit checks, and in some instances require guarantees from solid backers.

[361] "My Company, My Self," *Inc.*, July 1989, p. 35.
[362] Warren Avis, *Take a Chance to be First* (New York: Macmillan, 1986) p. 14.
[363] Jana Matthews and Jeff Dennis, *Lessons from the Edge* (New York: Oxford University Press, 2003) p. 175.

Avoiding embezzlement

From 1996 to 2001 the number of arrests for embezzlement in the United States rose from 15,700 to 20,157, indicating that it is both a common and an increasing crime.[364] New and small firms can be especially vulnerable to this because they tend to be less formal, they have not had time to work out fail safe systems, and they may not be able to be as picky in recruiting employees.

The founder of a company that sold computer products was contacted by an employment agency to ask if he needed an assistant. He replied that he did not, but that he did need an accountant to replace the one who had just quit. The agency recommended one, who impressed the entrepreneur favorably and was hired. The entrepreneur, who wanted to concentrate his own attention on sales, accepted the agency's strongly positive recommendation, and hired the accountant without further background checking. The accountant, he said, "quickly made friends with everybody. Before long, everyone thought he was a great guy. He took people out to lunch all the time, and he was a very sociable guy."

But the founder was not getting financial reports. According to the accountant, a software problem was delaying them. The founder soon concluded that the accountant was incompetent, and within three months fired him.

After that the founder started going through the records and found that the accountant had forged a signature card enabling him to sign company checks, which he then used to buy the "free" lunches and other gifts for various people as well as providing himself with cash, all of which added up to $200,000 embezzled from the company. For that he was apprehended, convicted, and jailed for two years.[365]

The founder in this case was surprised to learn that whereas the average blue-collar thief took an average of $3,000 and went to jail for five years, the average white-collar criminal took $60,000 and got only six months in jail, depending on the amount stolen.

Precautions to consider include checking references for clues to past behavior, and instituting systems to catch malfeasance. Having two people sign all checks, one being the CEO or other officer, using a check-writing machine that makes forgery difficult, reviewing cancelled checks to see if there may have been alterations after they were signed can help, and looking over bank statements to see where the money went. If employees are permitted to charge items on company accounts or use company credit cards, then those statements too should be cross-checked for any unusual patterns, such as charges at vendors that the company would not likely buy from. Taking out a fidelity insurance policy is another alternative. The insurance company will probably be glad to help suggest precautions, because they can help reduce risk.

To the extent that employees feel their best interests are better served by helping protect the company from wrongdoers, the odds of their helping combat theft should also increase. But they too can be fooled. Embezzlers succeed by not looking like the sort who would steal, and they can kill a company. Consequently, vigilance is part of the discipline that should be built into the venture from the beginning.

Exercises

Text discussion questions

1. Distinguish between the challenges of starting operations in a new firm versus starting new operations in an established firm.
2. How might venture-specific knowledge about operations differ from general information such as this chapter mainly presents?

---

[364] John Grossmann, *Inc.*, May 2003.
[365] Matthews and Dennis, *Lessons from the Edge*, p. 188.

Case questions

8B-1 Matt Fleck

1. What is your assessment, as best you can tell from the limited information about it, of the process through which Matt Fleck's restaurant was designed?
2. Try sketching what you think a PERT diagram might look like for opening the restaurant.
3. Is there anything Matt Fleck should have done earlier to reduce the level of anxiety he seems to feel now about staffing the new enterprise?
4. What actions would you recommend Matt take for coping with the start-up operations challenge?

8B-2 Ampersand (C)

1. What, if anything, should the Ampersand team have done differently so far?
2. How many person hours should each team member allocate among what tasks?
3. How might conflicts about team members' assignments arise and how should they be settled?

8B-3 Ampersand (D)

1. What other course of action could the team reasonably have followed over term break, and how would that compare to what they did?
2. What lessons about production has the team encountered to date?
3. What new policies regarding development of production capability should be considered at this point, and why?

Portfolio page possibilities

Page 8B-1 Gantt chart

Prepare a Gantt chart of the actions needed to start up production.

Page 8B-2 Troubleshooting

List things that could go wrong during your start-up and rank them according to (1) likelihood, (2) cost, and (3) difficulty of prevention.

Page 8B-3 Follow-up

Tell how after-sale follow-up will be done to earn customer loyalty.

Page 8B-4 Sequenced organization charts

Create organization charts for two different time points over the growth cycle of your venture and explain the changes.

Page 8B-5 Workforce building

Tell how your employees should be found, selected, recruited, and trained.

Term Projects

Venture history

1. Develop, in hindsight, a PERT diagram with dates for producing.
2. How were the production skills and procedures needed by the venture acquired?
3. What employees and suppliers were recruited for start-up and how?
4. How was early cash flow and accounting managed by whom and with what, if any, difficulties?

Venture planning guide

1. List things that could go wrong during start-up and rank them three ways, according to (1) likelihood, (2) cost, and (3) difficulty of prevention.
2. Describe the systems to be used for managing inventory levels as sales increase.
3. List main areas for development of employee policies, indicating which are trickiest and how they will be dealt with.
4. Describe critical operations policies, including incentive systems, for (1) directing activities, (2) quality control, and (3) cost control. Include indication of what figures will be used for tracking performance and how.
5. Prepare a PERT chart of the actions needed to start up production.

Part 9

ACQUIRING

A shortcut for becoming the owner-manager of a business without having to create it is to buy an existing enterprise. Advantages are that historical data on performance will already be available and start-up time will be avoided. If the business has a profitable track record over time, odds are that profits will continue, absent the emergence of some new fatal flaw that can probably be checked for in advance. New management may be able to improve performance, at least marginally. Businesses tend to have momentum that can be hard to change, either way. They operate largely as collections of human habits, of customers, employees, and suppliers. Human habits tend not to change quickly, either for worse or better.

A problem with acquisition is that many people realize it is an effective entry mode, so they try it. This makes it competitive, which can raise both the costs of prospecting and the price of buying. Every seller would like a buyer who will offer a higher price and whose ability to pay it is assured. Also preferred is a buyer who has demonstrated by past performance that he or she can manage the business successfully, both to pay for it on time and to preserve it as a specimen of the seller's accomplishment.

Effective management of searching to find a good buying opportunity, assessing the business, developing appropriate price and terms, designing a deal and conducting takeover, are thus called for. Development of appropriate acquisition criteria and a thought-out acquisition strategy, as well as doing the search, evaluation, and negotiation work, and implementation of the strategy will be time-consuming and possibly expensive. Along the way there will likely be discouragements. So dedication and persistence will likely be needed.

The first chapter in this section will focus on developing a personal search strategy and applying it to find promising acquisition candidates. The chapter after that will treat working out a deal and taking over. The third chapter will then explore a somewhat different alternative, which is to buy a franchise for copying a proven venture, rather than originating one.

The last section of the book, consisting of two final chapters, will explore management and eventual disposition of the venture after getting into it, whether through start-up or acquisition.

CHAPTER 9A – Prospecting

Topics

1. Rationale
2. Strategy
3. Discovery
4. Credibility
5. Screening

Checkpoints

a. What is the nature and significance of personal strategy in pursuing a buyout?
b. Why is it possible to buy a going concern?
c. How important is having experience in its line of work to buying a business?
d. Describe the pros and cons of buying versus starting a venture.
e. What are the best sources of leads to buyable companies?
f. Explain the significance of personal credibility in seeking to buy a business.
g. What are things to look for and to beware of in seeking a business to buy?

1. Rationale

Many firms outlast the desire of their owners to manage them. Hence there are opportunities for others to take them over, including through purchase. It has variously been estimated that around 15 percen t to 20 percent of all businesses and that on average an owner keeps a business for about seven years. That there are around 15 million businesses in the U.S. would suggest over two million businesses come on the market for new owners each year. Moreover, the rise in entrepreneurship and new firm formation in recent decades has made this an increasingly prevalent possibility.

The owner of a carpet installation company sold out, he said, simply because of burnout, recalling that,

I just got tired of employees not showing up for work, or quitting without notice, leaving me in a panic to fulfill commitments to customers. Then my partner neglected to pay state sales taxes until they were three months behind on about $350,000 in sales per month. That meant we had to file late and pay penalties of about $100,000. Because I had more personal net worth than my partner, it was clear that the state would be coming after me first for the money. So one day everything seemed to be fine, and the next day I was on the line for that much money.

Then another time I got a call from the bookkeeper asking why there had been no Visa transactions out of the store. I said we had them every day, and she said there had been no bank deposits from them. It turned out the transaction confirmations were on my partner's desk. He had neglected to report $15,000 worth of them. Moreover, because most were over 72 hours old we now had to call up every customer and get them to sign another receipt. Of course, when we went out to do that, they would often want us to make some other changes in the job that they had managed to think of since we completed it.

Things like that, doing 50 houses a month with 40 employees and all the problems of dealing with them just wore me down to where I wanted out at any price. I sold out for about three cents on the dollar.

Some acquirers are other corporations wanting to invest spare resources or expand their empires. Some are private investors who see potentially higher returns in majority ownership of smaller companies. Recent years have seen many venture capital firms follow this invest-ment path.[366] Some acquirers are entrepreneurs with both work and investment aims.

What they acquire are sometimes whole on-going companies and sometimes selected assets that permit them to take over the sales and op-erations, perhaps excluding accounts payable, real estate, or some equipment that is not really essential to continuing the business.

Prefabricated packages of assets in the form of franchises are also always available. The fran-chisers who offer them include in the packages alternative combinations of such elements as an established brand, procedures, and equipment that have been developed, tested, and proven, plus training in how to perform functions of the business, guidance in selecting a location and running the business, and possibly help in financing it. By this approach, the entrepreneur can acquire a business that is only semi-inde-pendent, because the franchiser also has some interest and imposes some rules on it.

How to find and check out an independent venture for potential acquisition will be the focus of this chapter. How to evaluate it, work out a deal, and take over will be the focus of the next chapter. Franchise acquisition as a mode of acquiring selective parts of a business will then be examined in the third chapter of this section.

Acquiring versus starting

In some ways, starting a new firm and taking over an existing firm are similar. Entering any business usually requires physical resources, in-cluding such things as a shop, equipment, and inventory. These can be obtained either new or used to start up fresh. Or they may be obtain-able through buying either a whole ongoing business, or only selected parts of one, such as the business name, customer lists, procedures, contracts, accounts receivable, trademarks, se-crets, and perhaps consulting help from the former owner.

About one in three entrepreneurs enters self-employment via acquisition, while two-thirds start businesses from scratch.[367] Advantages of buying a going concern rather than starting one from scratch to enter independent busi-ness include:

Time savings from eliminating set-up and start-up activities, which usually require much more than expected.

Risk reduction from existence of a track record upon which to evaluate the busi-ness. Cooper et al. found for instance, that firms acquired by entrepreneurs were more likely to be still operating after three years (69 percent) than those started fresh (63 percent).[368]

Reduced personal resource require-ments if the seller will advance credit and the buyer can borrow additionally from other lenders against company assets.

Pre-established systems and habits of employees, suppliers, and customers, which can be costly to set up, but are already in place with an acquisition.

A systematic approach can work to either seek an idea for a start-up or to locate an acquisition, but it is much easier to find examples of individ-uals who succeeded in finding companies that they acquired through systematic searching than who found good start-up ideas that way.

Whereas successful start-ups, particularly in higher-profit enterprises, tend to be accom-plished by people with relatively high expertise in their start-up's line of work, it is not at all unusual to find people who acquired going concerns in lines of work where they had lit-tle or no expertise other than general business savvy and nevertheless succeeded. Finally, the number of conceivable acquisitions could be viewed as close to the number of businesses in existence, and most of them are easy to find. The catch is that most are not up for sale and the number of potential buyers is much greater

---

[366] Natalie T. Taylor and Frederick A. Hooper, Jr., "Entrepreneurial Buyouts Developments and Trends 1978-1988," in *Frontiers of Entrepreneurship Research*, 1989, eds. Robert H. Brockhaus, Sr. and others (Wellesley, MA: Babson Center for Entrepreneurial Studies, 1989) p. 575.

[367] Arnold C. Cooper and others, *New Business in America* (Washington, D.C.: The NFIB Foundation, 1990) p. 5.

[368] Arnold C. Cooper, William C. Dunkelberg, and Carolyn Y. Woo, "Survival and Failure: A Longitudinal Study," in *Frontiers of Entrepre-neurship Research*, 1988, eds. Bruce H. Kirchhoff, and others (Wellesley, MA: Babson Center for Entrepreneurial Studies, 1988) p. 234.

than the number of sellers. Finding owners who really want to sell is hard; competing with other buyers to acquire one that is for sale on a price and terms that make business sense can be much harder yet.

This should not rule out pursuit of an acquisition approach. But it does argue for facing in advance the challenges it presents and adopting a personal strategy designed to cope with them effectively. Logical preliminaries can include reading about acquisition as an approach and talking with others who have had experience with it, such as business owners, business brokers who put buyers and sellers together for a price, and bankers who have helped arrange financing for acquisitions. In talking with any particular business owner, a question to consider is, "Would I want either to run this business or to own it, whether I ran it or not?"

Reflecting on these questions should help clarify the entrepreneur's purpose for seeking an acquisition and guide development of criteria for the kind of acquisition to be sought. Is the goal simply to get a better job, and if so, what dimensions of better are important? Is the goal to gain higher income, to have more freedom, to be a manager rather than a subordinate, or to own an income-generating asset run by someone else? Or is the goal to buy and then resell the business to achieve a capital gain profit? Or is it to develop a collection of businesses, possibly to reap efficiencies by consolidating them?

Is there a preference for operating as a lone buyer, or inclination to join with one or more partners in developing one acquisition, a portfolio, or a sequential chain of them? In exploratory discussions with others, all of these questions may be helpful to keep in mind.

2. Strategy

Thinking about not only personal goals but also strategy is a good starting point for considering acquisition entry, just as it is for pursuing start-up as a path to business ownership. Start-up usually makes more sense when the entrepreneur has a better idea for some new product or service. Acquisition often makes more sense when the person does not have that and is not inclined to go hunting for such a better idea. Both approaches take time for exploratory searching, and both are made more feasible by prior accumulation of personal capital and respectable business accomplishments. Either can be taken up or dropped as an opportunity search activity at any time, and either can be done either solo or teamed with one or more other people. But both can also benefit from sustained rather than sporadic effort, if for no other reason than that is more likely to recruit help from other people.

Process

The company acquisition process can be divided into six general stages: (1) mapping out a strategy for acquisition, (2) finding a suitable company to acquire, (3) becoming accepted by the seller as the person he or she wants to sell it to, (4) evaluating the business, (5) negotiating the acquisition, (6) taking over the acquisition after the deal, which presumably includes managing it, for either a short or long time, and then (7) ultimately selling it again or possibly closing it down. The two hardest parts above are most likely to be number two, finding the right acquisition, and number three, establishing personal credibility with its owner(s). Fortunately, both of these challenges can be deliberately worked on to raise the odds of becoming a successful acquirer.

Recruiting allies

Other people not only can help in the acquisition process, but some will be essential to it. A list of candidates from whom to seek help is something that can be developed and used as the search for potential acquisitions begins and moves forward. Certainly there will be need for a lawyer in drafting a contract to buy the acquisition, and certainly the business, hence the entrepreneur, will need a bank connection. Probably there will be need for a CPA to help with reviewing the books and de-

Process

Recruiting allies

termining tax implications of the acquisition. The business will likely need a review of insurance alternatives, which an insurance broker or consultant experienced with business insurance in particular can provide. Possibly, one or more appraisers as well as real estate and business brokers will be involved. Beyond these there may be need for expert help from other owners of businesses that are somehow similar, and from suppliers and customers of companies similar to the one being considered for purchase.

When to acquire such allies will in part come naturally and can in part be worth calculated planning. Recruiting any will take time that will be at least partly controllable. Some, like lawyers, will cost money. Others, like brokers, may want a contract. Most will value their own time, and therefore be concerned with how much of it to spend on the searcher, which will cause them to want information attesting to that searcher's capital, credibility, character, capabilities, and history.

Each ally the entrepreneur is able to recruit for the team should, in turn, be able to help establish the entrepreneur's credibility for recruiting yet other helpers, as well as, eventually, for approaching potential sellers. So can the entrepreneur's growing accumulation of acquisition know-how and relevant data at any given point in the search process. Sharing intelligence can help recruit allies.

Search criteria

Weak criteria to reach beyond in seeking potential acquisitions are "anything might be OK," and "I'll know the right firm when I see it." Such statements both make it hard for anyone else to help and, which is worse, tend to undermine the searcher's credibility. Some fumbling early on using such search phrases may serve for an experimental warm-up—maybe only in the entrepreneur's mind—to help develop appreciation for what may lie ahead. But they should probably not be expressed in asking others to help. Better will be to define criteria first, then ask for search help. Here, for example, are two contrasting sets of criteria.

Jerry Eisen, a Seattle company acquisition consultant, helps acquirers learn what is involved, prepare for a search, conduct the search, negotiate and close the acquisition deal, and move in to take over. In his view there are no best types of acquisitions in general. Winners can be found in loser industries and vice versa. But there are certainly firms not worth buying, either because the price will be too high, or they aren't worth the effort and resources required to operate them. Example criteria he suggested he suggested include:

- Location is desirable to the buyer.
- Owner has strong reason(s) to sell.
- Company can afford a 25 percent starting salary increase for the buyer.
- Return on buyer's cash investment is attractive.
- Business has operated for at least five to seven years.
- Profit history has been positive and consistent for at least two years.
- Growth rate can be financed from earnings without outside capital infusion.
- Lease extends long enough for the business to be paid off and resold.
- Franchising (competitor saturation) is not prevalent or becoming so in the industry.

— • —

Dave Ederer, a Seattle entrepreneur, built an extremely successful career out of acquiring over time literally dozens of companies, beginning first with smaller local ones, then moving to others both larger and in more distant geographical areas. The criteria he used were:

- Seller is aging owner who wants to cash out and retire (not someone who wants to shuck a failing company).
- Company has insistent record of profitability as verified by tax filings.
- Only industrial, not consumer, markets are served by candidate firms (preference is to sell things people must have, not just want to have).
- Only capital-intensive firms are eligible, such as machine shops with machinery or industrial supply firms with inventory (so as to be able to borrow against the assets for down payment).
- Price must allow present cash flow rate from the company to cover the payments and interest. ("A good way to make a million dollars is to buy a business for a million dollars that can pay itself off in three or four years.")

None of the businesses Ederer bought was very glamorous or fast growing. But he kept adding to a portfolio of them until collectively they represented great wealth. Over time his success qualified him to move into larger acquisitions. This was desirable because, he found, they were no more work to obtain than smaller ones. Also, the more he succeeded with, the more deals tended to come to him, so that eventually he no longer had to search for them. To capitalize on this emergent deal stream, he set up his own business brokerage firm as another venture of his own, though not his main interest.

The fact that any particular criteria worked well for someone else does not mean that they would for all. Those best may vary from one buyer to another. Some successful acquirers will deal only in consumer product companies, and others want only companies in high technology. Still others prefer services, because their slim assets tend not to support a high price. Having clear criteria still does not preclude consideration of opportunities that may pop up outside of them. It also does not preclude changing them as experience grows.

Sashimi approach

With criteria defined, a logical next step is to play the numbers. Try many sources. Seek many leads, including but not limited to impersonal ones such as bizquest.com, using a *sashimi approach* (with the sources being tapped successively over time and overlappingly like tunafish sliced and overlaid on a plate Japanese-style like a fanned deck of cards) Build up a list of prospects, bring two or three under careful examination, and add others as the least attractive ones under analysis are eliminated. Keep several ranked candidates in the analysis pipeline. Terminate unacceptable candidates with minimal delay to avoid wasting time on them, and keep hunting for new ones. Be prepared to stay at it over time.

To stretch hunting possibilities, classify and group candidates in categories by size, industry, type of owner, location, proprietary versus commodity, high versus low technology, degree of vertical integration, type of customer or customer relationship, geographical scope of market, capital intensity, and other such search criteria, which can also be refined over time. With the variety of company types that should be apparent in this list, coupled with the variety of potential sources for trying that will be expanded below, it should not be hard to form and maintain a respectable queue of prospects.

Likely to be deleted earlier are less attractive acquisitions, such as small businesses with profit records that are marginal or worse, that require long, tedious hours of work for low pay, that are prone to failure, and that are easy to find through business opportunities sections of newspapers. Leads from commercial real estate brokers may be even less attractive, both because the brokers will be shopping them around to get competing buyers and because the brokers will be entitled to a commission on any deal. However, to justify eliminating such leads, better ones must be discovered, and many of the acquisitions that work out do come through business brokers.

More promising might seem to be businesses that have a significant proprietary advantage in a brand, product, expensive tooling, or skilled workforce. But such businesses are also more likely to be sought after by many buyers. Small manufacturing companies with such advantages are frequently approached by established firms on the prowl for acquisitions. Owners of such sought-for companies, however, often enjoy owning them and are not anxious to sell. When they do reach a point of wanting to sell, they can fairly easily find interested buyers and typically prefer to sell to those buyers with the greatest resources and/or demonstrated business success record indicating they can carry on the acquired company successfully. For would-be buyers who lack such advantages, finding an attractive firm whose owner can be persuaded to sell to them can be a challenge. That can be a reason to work all the harder at searching.

*Chance
encounter*

Acquisition opportunities can be found through (1) chance encounters without searching, (2) searching out revealed candidates, companies that have exposed an interest in being acquired, and (3) searching out hidden-candidate companies whose owners have not revealed an interest in being acquired or possibly not yet even have thought about it.

Chance encounter

There is always the possibility that an acquisition possibility will arise without being sought.

Employee buyouts

Some acquisition opportunities arise through employment. An aging owner may want to change lifestyle and therefore sell the company to a younger employee. Or in a larger company, top management may decide to sell off a department or division to interested employees for one or more of the following reasons.

- The division no longer fits well with the corporation's main thrust or goals.
- The division is losing money and distracting management attention from higher priorities.
- The corporation is short on cash and can increase liquidity by selling something off.
- The employees have seen a way to make the division worth more and are consequently offering a price higher than the corporation feels the division is worth as part of the corporation.

An example of employee buyout as a way of entering business is Leslie Otten.

> In his mid-20s, Otten was working for a ski resort in Vermont when his employer dispatched him to manage another smaller resort it had recently acquired in Maine. "He was stuck in the back of nowhere," Leslie's wife Chris observed, "and people paid little attention to him….Every spring he'd say, 'We're outta here,' and we'd write up a new resume. But then he'd stay around to paint the chair lift."
>
> It troubled Otten that the owners showed no inclination to invest and build the small enterprise up further, and around 1976, four years af-

ter he had joined the company, he began talking about what he would do "if this were my place."

> By 1980 the resort was losing $240,000 per year on revenues of $541,000, and the owners had become open to selling it. "I turned 31 years old," Otten said, "and I was ready for something. You could have put me almost anywhere, into almost any venture." He arranged with the owners to take ownership of the business in exchange for an $840,000 note.
>
> He began by cutting costs, then adopted a strategy that contrasted with other ski resorts by emphasizing the quality of the skiing rather than amenities of the lodge. Financial performance turned around. By 1986 the company's profits were over $1.6 million per year and by 1988 they were over $6 million.[369]

Management-led buyouts

John Case, an *Inc.* editor, noted that Michael C. Jensen had seen that "managers buying a division had built-in advantages over the previous owners. Their financial rewards depended solely on the performance of the business they were running. They had no incentive to 'milk' the company or to build up little empires or bureaucrats; indeed, because of their high debt load, they had to run the business as efficiently as possible." Moreover, company productivity, according to a study of census data by Frank R. Lichtenberg of Columbia University and Donald S. Siegel of the National Bureau of Economic Research, increased by about 20 percent after buyout.[370]

Seller search

Presumably, company owners should lay careful plans for passing their companies on to family members, employees, or other companies. But many don't. Some wait until necessity drives them to go looking for buyers. They may approach brokers, or more likely they will begin by informing people they already know and trust, such as relatives, their banker, lawyer, accountant, or other professionals whose services they buy.

---

[369] Bill McGowan, "The Turnaround Entrepreneur," *Inc.*, January 1990, p. 53.
[370] John Case, *From the Ground Up* (New York: Simon and Schuster, 1992) p. 69.

The owner of a small manufacturing company that produced kitchen equipment fell terminally ill and, given only two or three months to live in a physically weakened condition, set about seeking a buyer. He called business acquaintances and relatives. Several potential buyers emerged, but most were hesitant, wanting to spend more time than the owner felt he could endure for careful check-out and negotiations. One of his distributors offered him in cash three times his earnings as reported to the Internal Revenue Service minus all accounts payable. A relative offered approximately four times earnings less accounts payable, with one third down and the rest to be paid over ten years. Wanting to gain as much as he could for his widow's retirement, the owner took the relative's offer. Under the relative's management, the business failed, and the four times earnings part of the price turned out to be two times instead. A consultant later estimated that with better planning the business could have sold for at least twice as much.

This buyer got a bargain both because he was a relative with easier access to information about the opportunity, and because the seller had not laid plans earlier for selling and consequently found himself under pressure to get out fast. No systematic study has been made of how often such a combination occurs or of what searching methods work best when it does not occur. But it does appear logical that some approaches, such as calculated and systematic searching to find a good acquisition, are likely to work better than others and particularly than simply hoping to run into luck like this.

Exposed candidates

There is an exposed market where sellers make known through advertising, posting on the Web, and/or listing with business brokers their desire to sell. Sources of exposed market leads include:

Web sites Among Web sites that advertise companies for sale are bizquest.com, bizbuysell.com, and businessbroker.net. Google lists others, usually specialized in some way such as geographical region.

Seller-placed advertisements Classified ads in the business opportunities sections of both local and national newspapers list businesses for sale among other things. In local papers small service firms will predominate, along with "hustles" for making money without knowing much, doing much, or investing much, so they will say. Classified advertisements for more substantial types of businesses such as manufacturing companies are more likely to be found in national papers such as *The Wall Street Journal*. Also, *Inc.* magazine typically runs a series of descriptions of businesses for sale, including information about assets, historical earnings, and asking prices, along with commentary about the attractiveness by the magazine. These postings represent national exposure that would cost far beyond anything the sellers could afford, and so may in a sense demonstrate advertising's maximum selling power for small businesses. Results of the exposure, as shown in Exhibit 9a-1, seem to indicate that some businesses are extremely hard to sell. The average of about one year for a deal to close (range was two months to two years), given the exposure, probably seemed long to sellers. This may reinforce the judgment that advertised businesses are simply not very attractive.

Business brokers Usually, these are real estate brokers whose licenses permit them to claim brokerage fees on sales of businesses as well as properties. Some business listings will be small or virtually non-existent sidelines. (If a business for sale were highly attractive, why would the broker not buy instead of sell it?)

Auctioneers or auction advertisements in local newspapers may pertain to many different types of goods, but also businesses that are liquidating. In such a case there is always the possibility that a deal could be struck to buy all the assets pertaining to a closed business and thereby get as close as possible to everything needed to restart it.

Hendrix Niemann, who, after losing his job ("If 'resigned' suggests that it was entirely my doing, that's not a fair characterization.") went searching in the exposed market for an acquisition, included the following comments on ex-

Exposed candidates

Exhibit 9a-1 Sales of businesses for sale displayed in Inc.[372]

Business	Real Estate?	Asked $ thous.	Got $ thous.	Got % of asked	Actual Price/Earnings	Actual Price/Sales
Fitness center	no	185	92	49.7	85.9	1.90
Old movie theater	yes	135	100	74.1	5.4	1.33
Model boat kits	no	365	331	90.7	4.5	1.17
Bowling alley	yes	3,600	1,300	36.1	2.7	1.01
Winery	yes	5,900	4,000	67.8	2.0	0.93
Casino	yes	2,300	1,500	65.2	4.2	0.82
Chocolate shop	no	40	40	100.0	2.7	0.75
Diving magazine	no	500	220	44.0	4.4	0.68
Crafts cataloger	no	150	127	84.7	1.6	0.44
Motorcycle dealer	no	1,100	900	81.8	3.0	0.34
Billiard hall	no	190	60	31.6	1.1	0.23
Comedy club	no	350	110	31.4	1.1	0.15
Record store chain	no	1,500	500	33.3	1.3	0.14
Travel agency	no	150	105	70.0	0.8	0.06

perience with both advertisements and brokers in a diary he kept.[371]

> I started by wading through the ads slowly, one by one…ANSWERING/BEEPER SERVICE…ANTIQUE RESTORATION…AUTO BODY/PAINT….I had absolutely no idea what I was looking for—but I'll know it when I see it. Certain names and/or phone numbers kept popping up. These must be the brokers or agents for the owners.

> I had started my first business, a regional magazine, along with my college roommate when I was 24. We ended up being taken over five years later. I started a magazine for someone else…and I had been the CEO of an independent TV news company in Washington.

> This time I wanted to do it all myself; no partners, no investors, just me…. I'd contact all the lawyers, accountants, and bankers in Annapolis. Surely they would have a client or friend who wanted to retire. I pictured a friendly man of around 65, getting tired, nobody to turn the company over to, wanting to take care of his longtime employees. Not greedy, doesn't want a lot of money down, a nice long-term payout. I'm his salvation, and the company's. A nice little business doing a couple million. Doesn't really matter what it is. No retail, of course, but maybe light manufacturing or some kind of distributorship, or a niche service business… How tough can it be to find something like this? I'll probably have several to pick from.

> Nothing. A dry hole. Dead ends….The time had come to take on the business brokers….I started

with the one offering the hospital transcription service. Like many business brokers, he was a realtor who had kind of backed into selling businesses. He had no formal business or accounting background. He came to our appointment armed with a confidentiality agreement and four typed pages about the transcription company. The first three showed revenues and expenses for 1986, '87, and '88. The fourth sheet was a projection for 1989. There was no balance sheet, no customer list, no promotional literature, no written history of the business. He said none of that existed, that he had spent days just pulling together what I held in my hand….

> On to the next….He said, 'I need some venture capital. I happen to be a small investor in a company that's going to make a computer screen that will revolutionize the industry.' He told me all about it, for an hour and a half. I asked him if he had any companies for sale that I might be interested in. 'Not right now. I'll call you.' And so it went.

The difficult task of search continued, and eventually Niemann located a lead, which worked out for him, through answering a blind classified advertisement in *The Wall Street Journal*, "after 17 business brokers, dozens of blind ads and four months." The advertisement had been placed by a business broker.

Commenting on this exposed market, Jerry Eisen, the Seattle consultant (not a broker) mentioned above who specialized for a fixed fee in helping would-be buyers find and com-

371 Hendrix F.C. Niemann, "Buying a Business," *Inc.*, February 1990, p. 28.
372 "Where Are They Now?," *Inc.*, June 1996, p 58.

plete acquisitions, observed, "Very few winners are ever advertised for sale in the newspaper. Some brokers are very selective, but most are not. Only about 14 percent of the businesses that sell go through brokers or the newspaper. So if you are using only those sources you will never see the other 85 percent."

Hidden candidates

By this statement he was referring to a second type of market which is, in effect, hidden, and includes both sellers who are searching for buyers and other potential sellers who may be on the verge of wanting to sell. Sources of leads for searching this hidden market include those listed in Exhibit 9a-2 below.

A positive aspect of seeking to buy a hidden-market business is that the task of finding one lends itself much more to systematic searching than does the opportunity for starting a new one. That is not to say the finding is easy. But the num-

Exhibit 9a-2 Some sources of hidden sellout candidate leads

1. **Cold calls** on companies that look interesting. The fact that a business is not looking for a buyer does not mean its owner would not sell it if the price and terms were right. The owner may be comfortable and not willing to consider anything but an unjustifiably high price. Or possibly the owner will have become unenthused about the business and just not yet reached a point of seeking a buyer. Entrepreneurs have found firms like the latter simply by walking in office doors and asking at one company after another until hitting pay dirt.

2. **Running an advertisement** describing the type of company wanted. Not just owners possibly interested in selling, but also friends, families, and acquaintances who know about them, as well as brokers and other professionals may respond with leads.

3. **Direct solicitations** of firms likely to fit the buyer's criteria, possibly found in the Yellow Pages, a manufacturers' directory or online searching. Jerry Eisen said he typically contacted 1,000 businesses per month for a given client, receives responses from about 30, and winnows that to one or two for closer checkout.

4. **Other contacts.** People who might know about firms potentially for sale but not yet revealed include:
   a. *Bank trust officers* responsible for custody of inherited companies.
   b. *Attorneys or insurance agents* whose clients want to rearrange their estates.
   c. *Commercial loan officers* who may have loans out to firms in need of new management and funding.
   d. *Companies that are recruiting* for a new CEO or general manager.
   e. *Accountants or consultants* with clients who need management help or want to get out of their firms.
   f. *Suppliers, customers, competitors, or landlords* in the industry of interest. *Discontented owners* sometimes share their woes with such people.
   g. *Employees of the types of businesses of interest* have reason to be aware of how other companies such as the one they work for are faring and may know of one whose owner could have reason to sell.
   h. *Other entrepreneurs who know of colleagues* who should want to sell out.

5. **Media articles** about owners who are aging or who are faced with attractive alternatives to retaining their businesses.

6. **Customers, competitors, suppliers, and employees** of the type of company being sought.

7. **Trade associations and chambers of commerce**, Rotary and other business clubs.

8. **Personal acquaintances** who may know, possibly because of awareness of personal or health problems, of prospective sellers.

9. **Advertisements by companies** seeking new management.

10. **Articles about firms** whose founder/operators have become old or recently died.

11. **Courthouse records** of divorce or bankruptcy filings.

12. **Auctioneers** who liquidate stock and equipment of failed enterprises.

ber of possibilities, although large, is at least finite, and they can readily be located, categorized, and checked out on a discretionary schedule.

Method

A daunting aspect of searching is that the number of possible directions for looking is bewilderingly large. Moreover, the odds are that it will take 15 to 40 hours to screen a business. An unpublished survey of business brokers in Northern California found that a seller can be expected to be contacted by about 54 buyers while listed. Moreover, only about 3 percent of the deals that went into escrow actually closed. So a buyer should expect that a business for sale will very likely be in contact with several buyers who may take it off the market at any time, and any deal pursued can fall through as late as escrow. It therefore makes sense for the buyer to hedge the search by always looking at several potential deals in parallel until one of them clicks.

An arguable conclusion from considering the number of potential sources of leads to the hidden market, plus the number of businesses for sale per year, the number of buyers likely to be hitting each prospective seller, and the odds of a particular buyer succeeding, is that it makes sense for the searching buyer to work out a rational search strategy in advance, not simply start anywhere looking for leads, as Hendrix Niemann, mentioned above, apparently did.

Instead, the searcher should begin by first formulating a list of criteria for the business to buy, as suggested earlier.

One systematic activity that can help is to make a list of the possible search avenues and contact sources such as those listed above, then make a numerical count of the number to be acted on in parallel. Then a record can be kept of the number and quality of leads produced by each type of source as a basis for deciding which type should be emphasized more and which type less.

A record can also be kept of the script followed in conversation with sources. Experimentation will likely change it from the initial lines to a modified script that may be less logical but much more effective for producing the desired information quicker from each person contacted.

Quick search

A preliminary way to get started is to perform a quick search of possibilities by first reading about how acquisition works and then tapping some of the above sources quickly before settling down to develop clear criteria and mapping out a systematic search sequence. The scan should include (1) visiting some companies listed for sale, (2) trying cold calls on a few, (3) talking with some sources of free information such as bankers, and (4) meeting one or two business brokers to ask how they work.

4. Credibility

To succeed, an acquirer must convey personal credibility. The seller is likely to care greatly about four things. The first is that nothing important be lost by exposing either personal or company information to scrutiny by the prospective buyer. Second is that the time wasted in dealing with prospective buyers who don't work out be minimized. Third is that if a deal is struck, then full payment for the business be received. Fourth is that the business continue in satisfactory condition, maintaining jobs for its employees and carrying on the entity that the seller grew accustomed to regarding as an original proprietary creation, personal property, or

both. To feel assured that these will happen, the seller will want the company sold to someone of integrity who is capable and dedicated to accomplishing them.

Victor Kiam had gained experience in selling, managing other salespeople, plus managing divisions as an executive with such larger companies as Playtex and Lever Brothers. He had negotiated and managed takeovers for Playtex, sometimes successfully (Sarong) and sometimes not (Jantzen). Since childhood, when he bought cold soda pop for resale to people coming home from work on hot days, he had also developed other smaller side ventures of his own, mostly centered in jewelry imports and in partnership with his wife.

An advertising executive acquaintance who knew of this background and happened to handle the Remington account, told Kiam in 1976 that Remington's owner, Sperry Corporation, wanted to sell it. Preoccupied with making other acquisitions for Benrus watch at the time, Kiam passed up the Remington opportunity, although two years later he would come back to it and become the man on Remington television commercials who would say, "I liked the razor so much I bought the company."[373]

While Kiam was the kind of buyer sellers want to find, there are other purported buyers whom they want to stay away from, and this can raise barriers against all who are seeking acquisitions, as illustrated by the following.

A buyer who was having difficulty obtaining business information from an owner who wanted to sell became not only frustrated, but also suspicious as to reasons why. Had the owner cheated, possibly as part of some other deal, a customer, a supplier, the Internal Revenue Service? Pressing persistently for an answer, he finally got an answer. The owner, who was at the time engaged in a bitter divorce with his wife, had been contacted earlier by someone presenting himself as a buyer. Negotiations progressed through sharing of confidential information up to a point where they suddenly stopped. Then the buyer could not be found. Even his phone had been disconnected.

Later, the seller learned that the prospective buyer had in fact been a private detective who had been hired by his wife to investigate whether he might be hiding assets by keeping two sets of books as part of their divorce litigation. In fact, he had.

A record of integrity can be vital to the negotiation process for both parties in an acquisition. Some safety for the buyer can be to require that the seller formally attest to claims about the business, so that if there is deception, the buyer can take legal action to recover damages from assets backed up by the business. But then the seller is more vulnerable. The potential buyer could let damaging information slip to competitors, suppliers, or employees. Proving that had been done and collecting any damages could both be impossible.

Moreover, the seller's vulnerability may increase further after the sale, because the buyer will still owe money on the business. After takeover the buyer will be in a position both to loot the business and to let purchase payments lapse. A tight contract may be able to mitigate damage from such acts to some degree, but cannot prevent them entirely. If a buyer with integrity cannot be found, the seller would likely be better off either to keep the business or to liquidate it.

Personal qualifications

Before letting the buyer peek behind the curtain of privacy in the business, the seller should want to see a resume of the prospective buyer that includes (1) description of work experience and accomplishments and (2) references, both personal and business. Additional items that may be required later if buyout discussions seem to be progressing seriously are (3) personal financial statements of the buyer and any others who may be putting up or guaranteeing money for the deal, (4) a list of people on the buyer's team, and (5) a written promise to maintain confidentiality.

Resume

For the buyer it can be helpful to prepare a resume that is written with buyers' likely concerns in mind. Having it critically reviewed as part of the preparation process by either professional intermediaries or business acquaintances with experience that equips them to understand a seller's perspective may also help highlight aspects sellers are most likely to care about, which will vary to some degree among sellers.

Even though successful acquisitions are frequently made by people without the advantage of having worked in the same industry as a company they buy, such related experience can be helpful. It can help the buyer know what to look for about the business, size it up more quickly, and better see what to do with it and why. At the same time, the seller should more easily be able to explain advantages of the business and to evaluate the buyer, both directly and through industry contacts in the same line of work.

---

[373] Victor Kiam, *Going for It* (New York: Morrow, 1986).

More relevant in some ways, however, will be prior management, as opposed to simply working experience, in either the same or other lines of business, because it might better demonstrate the buyer's capability to run the business after buying it. Also, aspects of experience that demonstrate industriousness, reliability, follow-through, and concern for factors most likely to produce profitability may count more than schools attended, hobbies, community service, or honorific awards.

A natural seller question about the buyer will be, "What has this person done before that demonstrates he or she can tackle a difficult problem and see it through to a solution despite major obstacles?" Another is, "What challenges has this person failed to tackle, or tackled and failed to meet?" Asking for personal references and asking the references for other references are logical ways for a seller to seek answers, though not all sellers will. Family status may also be considered important by the seller as an indicator of personal commitment and reliability.

However, that is not to say the buyer must be strong on all these counts. Most buyers aren't. But generally, the more strength, the better the buyer's bargaining position.

Financial strength

A buyer with savings may be able to make a substantial cash down payment to solidify the deal. Being willing to pledge other personal assets, such as home equity, may also help. Of still further help may be co-signature by another individual with substantial assets.

To go with the resume, a personal balance sheet, also designed with potential sellers in mind, can enhance credibility. Simply the skill displayed in its preparation can constitute evidence of financial savvy that can enhance the buyer's image as a good financial bet.

The seller may specifically want to see (1) tabulated values of what the buyer owns, (2) a list of all debts, mortgages, and notes on which the buyer owes money, and (3) a listing of the buyer's income broken into such categories as the Internal Revenue Service requires. A copy of the buyer's 1040 tax form should suffice for the last of these. The stronger the buyer's financial backing, the higher the buyer's credibility to the seller.

But demonstrating too great a financial capacity can also be dangerous, because it may cause the seller to reach for a higher price and the pledging of greater guarantees. Hence, it may make sense for the buyer to include on the statement only those assets that fit the purchase situation and, importantly, that the buyer is willing to risk on it. The others may be regarded as not-riskable and hence be left off. An argument against providing the 1040 information may be to point out that after acquisition, the buyer's income from other sources will change, and hence be less than fully relevant during negotiations.

Confidentiality agreement

Maintenance of confidentiality can matter in varying degrees to both seller and buyer. Employees, customers, competitors, and suppliers can all be affected by knowledge that potential sale of a company is in progress. Both prospective buyer and seller may want as much secrecy as possible for as long as possible. Even if potential sale is not secret, there may still be sensitive information about financial, legal, or personal aspects of either party's situation. Both parties may want the protection of a confidentiality agreement. Examples of such agreements can easily be found online. But tailoring to the individual case and making sure the agreement fits can best be assured by getting help from an appropriately experienced attorney.

Buying team

Several types of specialists can help the acquisition process, and the prospective buyer should consider in advance who would be of most value. These can be regarded as the buyer's team, and letting the prospective seller know who they are can also enhance the seller's image of the buyer. A one-person-show is not nearly as likely to seem a good bet to the seller as one complemented by qualified professionals and possibly also by experienced and accomplished teammates.

The attorney, banker, accountant, consultant, and partners, if any, of the entrepreneur can all have impact. Some may be helpful as buffers to handle tricky aspects in negotiating that the entrepreneur is unfamiliar with or uneasy about. One of these may be last-minute demands by the seller, perhaps by a statement, just when it seems everything is wrapped up except for final signatures, such as, "You'll have to throw this in too, or the deal is off." Or, it could be that the buyer will want to make such a statement.

Doing that through an intermediary may make it easier or more effective and may enhance credibility in general. The team should be also helpful as a sounding board against which the buyer can test ideas, both to avoid getting caught up in emotion and doing something ill-advised on impulse. Some friends and relatives may help as an audience against which the buyer can rehearse or role-play to improve negotiation performance.

Selling is inescapably an emotional experience, and sellers prefer to pass their companies along to people they like. Diplomatic handling of the checkout and negotiations by the buyer, in addition to careful study and forecasting for the firm's future, should help compensate for other weaknesses the buyer may have.

Seller's urgency

Lack of other buyers who are qualified and prepared to act fast enough to suit the seller obviously will be an advantage to the buyer. Sometimes, sellers postpone selling too long, and then get in a hurry to close a deal.

> Doug Talbot heard in 1969 that a company with hot dog street carts, Lucky Dogs, was for sale at a price of $200,000 set by the owner and founder of the company, Stephen Loyacano. With total annual sales of only $40,000 at the time

Talbot thought the price seemed too high and said so to Loyacano, who immediately dropped it to $65,000. "He just wanted to get out," Talbot observed, but he still declined the deal because there were "so many negatives," including such health code discrepancies as no refrigeration, washing facilities, or sneeze guards. But Loyacano would not give up, pleading with Talbot to "just give me an offer." Finally, Talbot, "just to get him off of my back," offered $15,000. Loyacano accepted, Talbot bought, and still owned the business 30 years later.[374]

The seller also should be prepared to demonstrate important elements of credibility. How good does the product or service itself seem to be? What do others think, and what does the buyer think?

> Two years after first declining to pursue the possibility of buying the Remington Razor Division of Sperry Corporation, Victor Kiam wanted to make an offer with two partners to buy another company, Maui Divers, which harvested coral for jewelry. But the partners fell out, and coincidentally Kiam read in a Saturday news article that the CEO of Sperry Corporation said he would rather sell one computer than a hundred thousand razors, which were made by the company's Remington division. Two days later, Kiam called the CEO to express renewed interest in acquiring it. He was referred to Sperry's CFO, who offered to make the division's books available. Kiam said he would be by to pick them up in an hour.
>
> Soon he had them spread out on his dining room table, and when his wife came home, he asked if they could remain there while they ate dinner in the kitchen. When he explained that he was investigating the potential acquisition of an electric shaver company she asked, "How can you even think of considering that company? You've never shaved electrically in your life."
>
> The next evening, he recalled, she gave him a Remington shaver and he tried it. He recalled, "How good was the shave? Well, as I've said a few times, I liked it so much I bought the company."[375]

5. Screening

Once the seller has accepted a buyer as a satisfactory candidate to negotiate with, the prospective buyer's next task is to check it out both for possible surprises and for fit. This process must continue to work from viewpoints of both owner and buyer. From the owner's perspective, why might this be the best buyer available? Will this buyer be willing to pay the price of a reason-

Seller's urgency

[374] Leigh Buchanan, "The Taming of the Crew," *Inc.*, August 1999, p. 35.
[375] Kiam, *Going for It*, p. 184.

able deal, or simply fold somewhere along the line, quite possibly at the last moment? Unless the buyer is going to pay cash, what is the assurance that he or she will be effective enough after takeover to assure that the business will survive and make its payments on time?

From the buyer's side a different set of questions applies, first to determine what the company's performance has been, second to assess what shape it is in now, and third to forecast what its future can be under a new owner.

First look

Businesses typically have momentum that causes them to change slowly with time. This momentum factor exists because companies are, in one sense, basically a collection of habits possessed by the various participants, employees, customers, and suppliers. Consequently, early checkout questions should include how long the firm has been operating, what its current performance is, and what its trends of performance have been over time.

How good is the company's product or service? A company with a well-accepted product or service can be hard to kill, while one lacking that may be hopeless, regardless of how dedicated and intelligent the new management may be. If the present owner has been supported by the business for ten years or more, it is probably a sign that the product or service is fine. Otherwise, the owner would have cleared out earlier. Maybe the reason for selling now is that the owner has simply become tired of running the firm, which is not unusual. Age too can be a reason.

Obviously, other reasons include any number of things that may be wrong with the company. What are the stated reasons that the seller wants out? Can any unstated reasons be discerned? Who might know? Can they be asked?

A brief look at what the company is physically and what is currently going on there is a natural early step. Does this look like the company is delivering something the market wants, and does the activity seem to be accomplishing that objective? It is not necessary that things look great. If the company is a bit run down and not performing at high speed but still is operating at a profit, that may be all right. Profits can probably

be improved. But if losses, instead of profits, are being generated the prospect is probably much dimmer and maybe hopeless. The momentum factor can apply to losses as well as profits.

Close behind meeting the owner and a first view of the physical operation should come a look at documents, beginning with financial statements, to verify any claims about the profit history of the company and what assets it has. These should be examined with progressively more attention to detail until the buyer is satisfied with what they can tell. Historical profits may be verifiable by checking the owner's and/or company's tax filing. These and some other documents to ask about are listed in Exhibit 9a-3.

Tax filings tend to be reliable because their truthfulness is required by law with penalties for distortion. They also tend to state profits conservatively in order to minimize taxes by not overstating sales and by expensing as many things against them as legally possible. However, if cost of goods sold is computed based upon inventory valuations that were already marked down in prior years, then current cost of sales may be an understated cost and stated profits may be misleadingly high. Another understated cost may be depreciation if equipment was already written off in prior years. Therefore not only the most recent tax filing should be exam-

Exhibit 9a-3 Company documents of potential interest

- Financial statements, both balance sheet and income statement.
- Lease.
- Important contracts with customers.
- Facilities and equipment owned by the company or leased, and on what terms.
- Patents, trademarks, copyrights, possessed or pending.
- Licenses.
- List of main accounts receivable by age.
- List of main accounts payable by age.
- Contracts with individual employees.
- Any formal appraisal.
- Lawsuits in process or pending.
- List of key employees, their pay rates, and anything owed to them.
- Shareholders and what they have coming.
- Any information about audits.

ined, but also those that preceded it over the past few years. Possibly, the company will have a separate set of income statements designed to reflect current operating performance aside from making allowable tax deductions that may alter the appearance of that performance. If so, the two should be reconciled and any contrasts should be understood.

Questions to keep in mind and perhaps make notes on in this review process include: What might a new owner be able to improve? How might sales be raised? Do all the expenses seem to be there, including for instance appropriate owner salar(y)(ies)? Which expenses might be reduced without injuring performance?

Going through the balance sheet and making sure it can be reconciled with the income statement will let the prospective buyer see what the company claims to have in the way of assets and what it claims to owe. Later, if negotiations seem likely to be headed for completion of the acquisition, it will be important to understand in more detail and verify financial statement items, and perhaps other assertions of the owner.

> The prior general manager of an auto dealer decided that he would like to own his own dealership instead of working for someone else's. Through a broker he found a dealership that was for sale. The present owner showed financial statements indicating a book value of $800,000 and said book value was the price he wanted. When the prospective buyer wanted to discuss and explore it, the dealer refused, saying he was not willing to negotiate. He had set the basis of his price, take it or leave it.
>
> The manager took it. Then he learned more about the financial statement items. There was an item of $300,000 for prepaid expenses. These, the former owner explained, were to reflect the fact that the local utility district had done some construction work that had interrupted business for the dealer. When the dealer protested, the district had apologized and indicated willingness to compensate for the disruption. However, there was no signed contract to do so, which left the buyer stymied.
>
> Another item was prepayment for advertising in the amount of $200,000. However, the new owner could not see how to take advantage of it, and no refund was possible. By the time he and

his accountant had worked through the books he found that a closer figure for the company's true book value was half of the former owner's claim, or $400,000.

The reason for looking at company history is to explore the more important, but also more slippery, question of what the company's performance can be under a new owner, and this inevitably calls for projection of what can be expected as future cash flows of the business.

Can the company, if acquired, achieve cash inflows needed to meet its needs, plus personal income needs of the new owner, plus whatever payments are required to carry out the purchase terms? Exploring this question will call for closer examination of all facets of the company.

Delving deeper

Obviously, cash flow projections must be made, and to do that, the prior financial records must be examined and understood in more detail. What are the biggest items that checks were written for, and on what time cycle? How quickly did receipts follow sales, and can that pattern be expected to continue if the firm gets a new owner? The prospective buyer should formulate and check off each item on a list of documents to be reviewed as part of the check out, and should develop a cash flow projection plus pro forma financial statement forecasts. Creating these forecasts should be much simpler than creating them for a start-up because here there is historical precedent to work from. It should be relatively simple to go through a recent historical statement line by line and write in a best guess about how each number is likely to change after takeover.

A fuller summary of questions to consider, working from the company's past financial statements and other documents—coupled with physical observations, intermiews, and projections by the prospective buyer—includes those in the shaded area on the following page.

Discretion may be appropriate in moving ahead to check out such questions. Doing so will take time, and if the deal does not work out, it will be wasted. So a balance should be designed between offer, response, and investigation. A buyer can start by accepting to a

Some financial statement items to consider

Assets

1. Which assets will be bought as part of the deal and which will not? Is the location important and will the building stay with the owner? If so, what will be the terms of the lease? If those terms had applied in the past, how would the company's income statements have looked? If there is already a lease, is it transferable, how long will it run, and are there rights to renew, reassign, or sublet? Will the landlord have the right to raise rent as a result of changing the tenant? Will the lease constrain the business from carrying out new plans, perhaps involving increased sales? Are there any present or expected zoning constraints, and is the company within compliance?

2. Are there any contracts with suppliers, customers, employees, unions, or others in addition to the landlord that are important to the company, and will they transfer to the new owner? Do any of the company's customers consider it important to do business with the old owner personally? If so, then perhaps there should be a contract keeping the old owner on to help the business as needed for a specified period of time.

3. Facilities. What other facilities, installed equipment, or tools come with the establishment? Are there liens against any of them? Are their types and condition suitable for the future? How much could they be sold for separately? How much would it cost to replace or upgrade them?

4. Company name, patents, trademarks, licenses, logos, style, or formats for advertisements and correspondence, customer lists, mailing lists, and credit records should be checked out. Is there important know-how for performing the work or an ongoing pattern of employee and customer activities to be maintained? How hard would it be to replicate them? Will the seller or competitors have incentive to undercut them or be able to do so? What is the company's reputation? According to whom?

Liabilities

5. Accounts payable. What will they consist of at the time of sale?

6. Hidden liabilities. Are there any non-apparent liabilities, such as impending lawsuits, customer claims, outstanding warranties, or other obligations of the company?

7. Credit. Does the company have any problems with suppliers that may surface later? Will suppliers give the new owner the same credit as the seller had?

Cash flow

8. How much working capital has the company needed in the past, and how will this change under new ownership? How will the timing of payments to suppliers and collections from customers shift after the sale?

Non-financial factors

large degree within reason, the seller's claims about the company. Preliminary negotiations can be based on those assumptions, and if a handshake deal can be struck from those, then more detailed checking of the assumptions can be done.

Non-financial factors

Perhaps more important than any of the above checkout questions is whether any other issues of importance have not been considered. What do competitors and customers say about the business? Has it ever been subjected to formal appraisal? Every business is a special case with unique issues. Might there be new legis-

lative, competitive, demographic, or technical changes in the works that deserve special consideration? Possibly, the entrepreneur will think of new questions through development of a plan to make the most of the business.

Other people, besides the new owner, who hold the keys to future success include customers, employees, and suppliers. They will be needed, as will perhaps the landlord, neighbors, and local government which controls permits and zoning. Although discretion and time limitations are to be considered, interviews with these parties, to the extent possible, can help with assessment of future prospects and may reveal information of great consequence for the business.

Experience by the buyer in the line of business or in a similar one may help in not only establishing credibility with the seller but also in checkout of the firm. However, it is clearly not a prerequisite for success with an acquisition. Many entrepreneurs who took over firms in lines of work where they had no experience have succeeded magnificently. Interestingly, it is not so easy to say the same for companies that acquire other companies.

Conclusion

This chapter has dealt with a subject that, although basically straightforward, also raises topics that can become complicated. A bifocal view will be needed both to develop appreciation of details and how they can become important, and at the same time view them with broader perspective for managing and moving ahead on goals of acquiring, taking over and managing a company. What to analyze closely and what to gloss over in order to move ahead are matters of judgment that make up an important part of the acquisition process to be examined in the next chapter.

Exercises

Text discussion questions

1. What sequence of actions would you take if asked by a relative who became seriously ill to help sell his or her small custom manufacturing business?
2. Why might a buyer be concerned about confidentiality?
3. How might a person go about setting up an enterprise to specialize in the sale of local small firms?
4. Why do entrepreneurs seem to fare better with acquired companies than corporations do?
5. How might a given individual likely change strategy for seeking an acquisition at different stages in life?
6. How might acquisition-seeking change an individual's start-up process?
7. How might start-up designing help a person be better in seeking an acquisition?
8. How should an individual decide whether start-up or acquisition is the better mode for seeking to enter independent business ownership?

Case questions

9A-1 Brumveld and Johnstad

1. What is your assessment, against the points and examples presented in this chapter, of Paul and John's acquisition strategy?
2. What is your assessment of the way they have implemented that strategy so far?
3. How would you rank the candidates they have found?
4. What should they do next?

Portfolio page possibilities

Page 9A-1 Personal strategy
Describe in as much detail as you can on one page a personal strategy you would use if you decided to seek out and acquire an ongoing firm.

Page 9A-2 Discovery contacts
1. Name five contacts you would approach in search of a business you could buy.
2. Try the first three sources on your list and describe the responses you got.

Page 9A-3 Available businesses
1. List in rank order of promise the businesses for sale that you can find in the current edition of a metropolitan newspaper.
2. Explain the rationale behind your ranking.
3. Attempt to make contact with three of them and describe what happened.

Page 9A-4 Confidential information

1. List in rank order a dozen or so documents or other possessions of the company that you would consider most important to examine personally.
2. Describe the steps and their timing that you would follow in asking for the above.
3. Write out a draft non-disclosure document you think might serve for the above.

Page 9A-5 Acquisition partner

1. Describe the sort of person you would seek out if you wanted to join with a partner to buy an ongoing firm.
2. Describe an approach you might make to that person and the rationale behind it.

Term Projects

Venture history

1. How was the decision to seek an acquisition made and how did the strategy for doing it develop?
2. What qualifications did the buyer and helpers have for establishing credibility with company owners/sellers?
3. What strategy and set of screening criteria (explicit or implicit) were adopted for seeking buyout candidates and how?
4. What checkout procedures were used to verify what might be bought?
5. What array of candidates did the buyer find and how did they rank?

Venture planning guide

1. Describe your personal strategy for seeking a company to acquire.
2. Describe the results you gained from your search for an acquisition.
3. Prepare profiles of the three most promising acquisitions you found, telling how you would rank them and why.

CHAPTER 9B – Dealing

Topics

1. Seller's price
2. Buyer's assessment
3. Deal terms
4. Due diligence
5. Takeover and beyond

Checkpoints

a. Briefly describe alternative methods to value a business for sale.
b. What are the main variables of concern in an acquisition deal?
c. Contrast the viewpoints and motivations of buyer versus seller in acquisition.
d. Explain the role that negotiation should play in acquiring a business.
e. Define the term *due diligence* as applied to entrepreneurial acquisition.
f. What are the pros and cons of making a consulting contract part of buyout?
g. What are the pitfalls of taking over management of a going concern?

Further analysis of acquisition candidates that pass the early screening, as described in the preceding chapter, can begin with the scrutiny of documents acquired under a non-binding letter of intent. If the firm is one whose location is important, then the lease or real estate acquisition arrangements are crucial. Contracts and obligations may come next. Even more important may be retention of key people in the company, especially if the acquiring entrepreneur is not familiar with the firm's line of work. This in particular can be a sticky item if the seller does not want to inform employees that selling the firm is under serious consideration. On the other hand, employees may know more about it than management thinks. The need for selling may be obvious to them in any number of ways, and there can be many other clues to the negotiation process that tip them off. Secrecy may or may not be the best policy.

1. Seller's price

If the seller proposes a price for the business, the buyer can choose whether to haggle or accept that price and perhaps negotiate on other terms instead. Sperry Rand proposed a price for the Remington Razor Division it wanted to sell. Even two years after Victor Kiam had learned of its interest in selling, Sperry still clung to that original price and responded to the suggestion of a lower one by Kiam as follows:

> This is all very well, but the price is twenty-five million dollars, and we're not going to lower it. We can make certain concessions on interest rates and time frames. But we're not going to sell this company for less than book value.[376]

For Kiam this was intended to convey "take it or leave it." But that did not necessarily mean he had to. A variety of alternative approaches could be proposed, some of which would likely carry more weight with the seller, while others would be favored more by the buyer.

Just what part(s) of the business is being sold of course matters. Corporate stock is one thing; parts of a business, whether it is a corporation or not, are others. Will the buyer take

[376] Victor Kiam, *Going for It* (New York: Morrow: 1986) p. 189.

the whole business, including assets and liabilities, or only assets? If assets are to be sold, then will it be all or only some, such as inventory, receivables, equipment, building, and/or land? Fractionation will require valuing assets one at a time. The discussion here will, unless otherwise noted, take the simpler case of buying the whole business.

Some sellers propose a price for their business based on sentiment. "I want a million dollars" (because it sounds so good), or "My neighbor sold his business for half a million, and that's what I want for mine," or "I bought it for $300,000 ten years ago and I figure it should be twice that by now," and so forth. Seller's offered price may also be influenced substantially by the seller's desire to get out.

More likely to be put forth by the seller as a rationale for price are four approaches that include: (1) market value, (2) replacement cost, (3) book value, and (4) appraised value, which are more fully described in the shaded area following. To some degree they are bound to generate different values, and the seller will probably prefer the highest.

Accuracy of appraisals

Several formalistic alternative approaches have been advocated for appraisers, and they are all likely to produce different results as can be seen from Exhibit 9b-1. Based on information from sales of 258 closely held firms in the southwestern and western United States, Harper and Rose found that combination methods of valuation appeared to be the most accurate. They compared the valuation figure obtained by various individual and combination valuation methods with the prices at which the companies were actually sold and found that the average difference or error was 6.7 percent. All the individual methods, such as book value, discounted cash flow, and so on, yielded sub-

Buyout pricing approaches sellers tend to favor

1. **Market value** indicated by offers from other buyers. If some other person or company has made an offer for the company, then that should identify a level where that other party thinks the company is a good deal. It may also establish a hurdle that the next would-be buyer must meet or surpass. It is also possible, however, that the other party has overestimated value, is bluffing, is motivated by different factors, has different conditions that mitigate price, or simply won't be able to raise the money to make good on the offer. Sellers and brokers sometimes like to intimate to a prospective buyer as a motivation to move quickly that there is someone else who may get the deal if they don't move fast and generously.

2. **Replacement cost** The seller may find advantage in adding up the cost of replacing assets and estimating what it would cost to buy them and start the business for fresh. Likely this method of valuation will generate a high price for the seller. But for the buyer it could also produce a more fresh and up-to-date version of the seller's company.

3. **Book value** The value listed on the company's books as the difference between its assets and its debt obligations can be favorable to the seller by inclusion of intangible assets such as start-up costs, intellectual property, contracts, and possibly goodwill as a going concern. However, it may also yield a value on the low side if these intangibles are not listed and if the owner has written down some assets such as inventory and equipment to reduce income taxes.

4. **Appraised value** Hiring a professional appraiser is straightforward. Companies use such help not only for sale pricing, but also for establishing a company value for inheritance tax purposes. When an owner dies, for instance, the value of all that person's assets must be determined in order to compute inheritance taxes. What an asset might be worth in an estate, however, could be different from what it might be worth as part of an acquisition. In an estate or even a lawsuit, the asset might more likely be left to languish and lose value longer than if an acquiring entrepreneur takes it over to keep a company going. So fresh appraisal may be appropriate for pursuing acquisition. Appraisals are also sometimes needed for ESOPs (Employee Stock Ownership Plans), divorce settlements, and disputes among shareholders.

Exhibit 9b-1 Accuracy of alternative valuation methods[377]

	Valuation method	Avg. # firms	Absolute error %	Error %
1.	Adj. bk. & capitalized earnings	61	6.0	9.0
2.	Cap. earnings & comp. sales	10	-6.3	8.3
3.	Past transactions	7	-7.4	9.8
4.	Adjusted book value	9	8.2	12.9
5.	Cap. earnings or P/E	31	-9.7	11.4
6.	Adj. bk. & comparable sales	9	10.5	11.6
7.	Comparable sales	16	14.8	18.1
8.	Capitalized dividends	5	-19.8	24.1
9.	Discounted cash flow	6	19.9	23.9
10.	Replacement cost	5	24.4	24.4
11.	Capitalized revenues	7	36.8	36.9
12.	Unadjusted book value	7	-35.5	35.5
13.	Other combinations	81	8.9	11.5
14.	Other single methods	4	-26.7	26.7
	Total	258		
	Overall Average		6.7	13.9

stantially higher errors than this, while the two most effective methods, on average, were the combinations of (1) adjusted book value and capitalized earnings, or (2) capitalized earnings and comparable sales. (Absolute error ignored which way an individual erred.)

Appraisal results varied not only with method used, but also among appraisers, as can be seen from the comparative results displayed in Exhibit 9b-2. Interestingly, venture capitalists appear to have been the most off actual price and consultants closest to it.

Exhibit 9b-2 Accuracy of different appraisers[378]

Appraiser background	# firms	Error %	Error %
Industry consultant	9	6.0	9.9
General consultant	26	-8.0	10.4
Academic faculty member	34	8.5	8.9
Industry employee	8	13.0	13.0
Buyer's business broker	37	-14.1	15.8
Seller's business broker	27	16.7	17.0
Venture capitalist	38	24.7	25.7
Other, or no response	79	9.2	10.9
Total	258		
Overall Average		6.7	14.8

2. Buyer's assessment

The buyer too should look at the above pricing approaches but can draw different conclusions from them. Market or existing offers are significant, for instance, to the extent that other buyers will be able to follow through on them. Might other would-be buyers have temporary options from the seller for specified prices while they seek financing which they may or may not be able to get for paying those prices? Are the alleged offers contingent upon review and satisfaction by other presumed buyers?

---

[377] Charles P. Harper and Lawrence C. Rose, "Accuracy of Appraisers and Appraisal Methods of Closely Held Companies," *ET&P*, 17, no. 3, Spring 1993, p. 21.
[378] Harper and Rose, "Appraisers," p. 21.

Seller and buyer valuations may differ for not only market value but also for replacement cost and book value, depending upon assumptions and levels of optimism about the business. Even appraised values of seller and buyer can differ significantly if each hires a different appraiser, as can be seen in Exhibit 9b-3.

Beyond the valuation approaches often taken by sellers as noted earlier are five others a buyer should consider, which are further described in the shaded area on the page below, including: (1) payback time, (2) liquidation value, (3) price of comparables, (4) ratio comparisons, and (5) rules of thumb.

As a rule-of-thumb example *Inc.* magazine described a window cleaning business for sale in 1999 with previous-year sales of $556,000 and recast earnings (i.e. before interest, taxes, depreciation, and owners' draw) of $204,544. The seller's offer was $439,000, or 79 percent of sales. Noting that companies in janitorial and related services typically sold for 55 percent of annual sales, the magazine judged this asking price as too high.[279]

Dimensions used in this example and often applied in valuing smaller firms that are not necessarily reflected in P/E ratios of listed company stocks are recast earnings and adjusted cash flow. These two terms generally mean the same thing and are intended to

Buyout pricing approaches buyers should not overlook

1. **Payback** This is the price by which the company can, with appropriate salary to the buyer, pay for itself including any down payment, installments, and interest, within a reasonable length of time, such as perhaps one or two years for service firms and three or four years for asset-heavier manufacturing firms.

2. **Liquidation value** How much money will the company yield if it is broken up and its individual assets are sold? Some companies, like furniture retail firms, are typically worth only what they can be liquidated for. Two scenarios can be considered: planned liquidation and forced liquidation. Planned liquidation should yield a higher value for each category of assets in the company: receivables of different ages, inventory at various stages of use, equipment, and so forth. Professional appraisers can help with estimation about how much may be realized.

Comparables

Companies, like houses, can be valued by comparing them with what similar companies have sold for. Appraisers do this, just as do stock analysts. Many alternative dimensions can be used for comparisons. The main three are:

3. **Price of similar companies sold** If a company like the one being considered has recently sold, then a similar price may fit. Probably, there will be some adjusting to do for different sales levels, locations, or other relevant features. Also, it may be hard or impossible to learn just what the other compan(y)(ies) sold for or, perhaps more importantly, on what terms, which can sometimes influence price greatly.

4. **Ratio comparisons** For companies whose stocks are listed on an exchange (public companies) the market value is indicated as price per share, which can be seen daily in newspaper financial sections as well as online. If multiplied by the number of shares outstanding it produces the capitalization ("cap") value, which is the total market value of the company. A ratio commonly used to indicate value versus risk is the price/earnings ratio (P/E ratio), which is often listed alongside the price per share. A qualification to be borne in mind with that valuation approach is that the earnings are of the preceding year (or so), whereas the real question is what they will be in the future, particularly with entirely new ownership. Price/book value or price/sales ratios of comparable companies may also be instructive.

5. **Industry rules of thumb** For some industries there are rules of thumb for company valuations, as illustrated for various types of companies in Exhibit 9b-3 below. Adjusted cash flow (ACF) in these rules is computed by taking company taxable net income and adding back interest, plus the owner's draw, taxes, and benefits, plus non-cash expenses such as depreciation, amortization, and nonrecurring extraordinary expenses, then subtracting any one-time nonrecurring revenues.

[279] "Business for Sale: Rocky Mountain Window Cleaners," *Inc.* August 1999, p. 124.

Exhibit 9b-3 Some rules of thumb for small firm valuations[380]

Type of business	Times adjusted cash flow	Or	Or
Auto repair	1 to 2.5	2.5 x monthly revenues plus inventory inventory	1.5 x fixed expenses plus owner salary 35% of annual sales
Small eateries	1 to 2	1.5 x annual net cash flow (acf) plus fixed assets & inventory	
Computer repair	1 to 2		
Printing & publishing		0.5–3 x acf plus fixed assets & inventory	
Retail stores		1–2 x acf plus fixed assets & inventory	25% to 50% of annual gross sales

make comparables more comparable by washing out factors that may arbitrarily discriminate between them. The approach they refer to will be illustrated shortly.

Among small manufacturing businesses a much wider range of valuations can be justified. A firm with effective patents, well-protected secrets, a solid repeat-customer list, and/or strong brand can be worth much more than one that is easier to copy. At the low end, such a firm may be worth around three times the sum of owner's draw plus before-tax profits. At the high end, competitive advantages to be gained by the buyer can be worth up to hundreds of millions of dollars.

As suggested by the ranges in these figures, many factors can come into play that must be considered for any individual case. How long are the sales and earnings records? What are important non-tangible assets such as valuable leases, reputation, proximity to home, and prospects for the industry, and what are the competition threats? Will departure of the old owner immediately cause some customers with whom that person had a close relationship to fall away under new management? Generating a list of such questions is worth considering.

Value disagreement

Seller and buyer can argue for very different values on a given company, as the following example which uses recast earnings illustrates. Assume annual sales are $1.5 million, profits are $75,000, and the asking price of the business is $600,000. Further assume the interest rate is 8 percent and principal is to be paid off in equal installments.

How the seller may argue that this is a good deal, perhaps preceding that assertion with a general statement to the effect that, after all, cash is king and net cash flow is the true test of value, is illustrated in Exhibit 9b-4. The bottom line here may look fairly lucrative, even though the seller may admit that income taxes have been left off because neither knows the other's personal situation on taxes.

How a prospective buyer might judiciously look at the same deal differently is shown in Exhibit 9b-5, which indicates that the same company will not generate near enough cash to cover payments owed to the seller.

Exhibit 9b-4 Sellers' description of an attractive cash flow

Recent level of profit	$75,000
Increment added by the new owner improving performance	15,000
Adding back of "discretionary" costs that could be cut	130,000
Prospective cash flow potential from the business	220,000
Minus annual principal payment on debt	(80,000)
Business "discretionary cash flow"	$140,000

[380] Scott Gabehart, *The Upstart Guide to Buying, Valuing and Selling Your Business* (Chicago: Upstart Publishing, 1998) pp. 221-231. Also Lawrence W. Tuller, *The Small Business Valuation Book* (Holbrook, MA: Adams Media, 1994). Both books list other helpful references.

Exhibit 9b-5 Buyer's different view of the same cash flow

Recent level of profit	$75,000
Less income tax	25,000
Equals real business "discretionary cash flow"	50,000
Less real cash outflows:	
Owner's draw for working in the business	40,000
Payroll tax on owner's draw	6,500
Owner's health insurance premium	2,500
Owner's auto and travel expenses	5,000
Repair and replacement of depreciating assets	20,000
Interest on principal owed	4,000
Minus annual principal payment on debt	80,000
Cash shortfall after principal payment	($158,000)

Conveniently overlooked earlier by the seller, in addition to taxes, were cash items that the buyer might have been told are "up to you. Of course, you could add something to cover debt interest if you want, but it winds down over time, and anyway, it is not a large item. Put it in for the first year, if you like. It doesn't make a huge difference." And so forth.

Pro forma financials

Both seller and buyer care about future performance of the business as long as they expect to have an ownership interest it, but the buyer presumably expects to have it longer. To the buyer the price must be justified for the future by how much the company will pay off, both in annual cash flow after taxes and in eventual cash-out value, which will likely be a function of profits achieved.

Preparation of pro forma financial statements, suggested in the preceding chapter as part of delving deeper in the screening process, is essential to pursue further here. Full forecasts of an income statement, balance sheet, and cash flow statement should be prepared. The buyer should work from historical statements of the past that have been corrected for expectations about how individual numbers in them can be expected to change in the future. The first three to six months should be especially detailed, perhaps even weekly, because they will include non-routine costs and investments needed to take over and keep the company running. Beyond these, monthly statements for the rest of the first year

and probably second year may be appropriate, followed by annual projections for a year or two beyond that. As with a start-up, especially crucial will be to have alternative scenarios for not running out of cash. Working out the forecast statements line by line, with footnotes listing how the largest numbers in them were determined, is the best way to prepare these.

Pro forma statements will also provide a basis for calculating a present value of discounted future cash flow, the theoretically right way for pricing the business. But it can become complicated. Should cash flow include owner's draw, and how does that depend on how much the owner was working in the business? More importantly, what discount factor should be used for the computation of present value? Just how was the future cash-flow stream determined and how reliable does that process seem likely to be? Should a premium be added for being the person who will have control, albeit with more responsibilities?[381]

Finally, preparation of the pro forma statements should include estimates of how financing the acquisition will be accomplished. Will the company be able to borrow so that loans become part of the balance sheet while adding cash for working capital? Which assets can be sold or pledged? Can help be obtained from customers by their paying off accounts receivable faster? Can suppliers help by allowing extension of accounts payable longer? Or will the opposite happen as a result of the buyer being new to the business?

---

381 Ellyn E. Spragins, "Locking Up Good Value," *Inc.*, November 1989, p. 157.

It is important for company valuation to consider what salary and other fringe benefits accrue to the buyer, such as retirement and health plans, and possibly key-person insurance, as well as taxes or bills due and, especially, interest due on either debt of the company or on principal due in the acquisition process.

One-time fees of consultants, brokers, attorneys, or accountants who help with the deal may also be significant. These may, particularly in smaller firms, be much greater than the profits. Whether they or other customary company expenditures have changed recently and thereby affected the apparent profit level can also be important. Other financial items easy to overlook are the need for working capital and the need to repair or replace equipment that wears out or becomes obsolete.

One way of viewing a prospective venture that may help in valuation is to consider acquisition versus start-up of the same firm, which could avoid many of these inherited problems. Could the prospective entrepreneur accomplish such a start-up? How much would it cost and how much time would be required? Answering these questions should help bracket the high end of what could justifiably be paid for the company.

3. Deal terms

Whether any deal is good or bad is inevitably a matter of opinion. Calculations should certainly figure into it, but probably seller and buyer will see even those differently. As preparation for negotiating, it should be helpful to formulate alternative valuating and financing scenarios, then weigh them, including nonfinancial as well as financial elements, from the viewpoint of both buyer and seller.

Three main parts to a deal are (1) what is being bought, (2) for what price, and (3) on what terms. A simple deal is summarized in Exhibit 9b-6.

In this deal the buyer must come up with not only a down payment and balance over time, but also money for working capital beyond inventory and for any paid help in raising cash, doing the paperwork, moving in, and taking over.

Leveraged buyout

If the down payment in the above example could be borrowed at a bank or some other place so that the buyer managed to get the business without personally putting any money down, the deal would be a completely leveraged buyout. The buyer might still have to use personal savings to live on until the company generated enough cash to meet payroll, plus debt payments and salary for the buyer. Savings might also be needed as a reserve for coping with unwanted surprise, such as a machine breaking down, a theft, or some supplier wanting advance payment. But just for obtaining ownership of the company and needed assets to run it, the buyer would not be putting up any cash.

Hendrix Niemann described how he got such a deal. His business broker, Lauren Finberg, sent a package of information that included proposed terms.

> *Of greatest importance to me was a two-pager showing how I could purchase the company with 100 percent financing, get the owner his purchase price, service the debt, and still take out 75 percent of what I had been earning before.*
>
> *Subsequently, however, an item-by-item physical valuation of the assets, coupled with new figures showing decline in earnings, low-*

Leveraged buyout

Exhibit 9b-6 Example of price and terms

Price: *$600,000 for going concern, name, tooling, equipment, customer list, and records, plus inventory valued at $200,000, to be verified by mutual physical count at time of deal; price to be adjusted according to any discrepancy. Seller will keep company bank account and receivables. Seller also agrees to pay all payables outstanding at time of purchase. Buyer assumes the existing lease.*

Down Payment: *One third of price at time of closing, $200,000.*

Other terms: *Balance of $400,000 to be paid to seller over five years with interest at 2 percent over prime on unpaid balance.*

ered the company's estimated worth and cash-generating ability.

When the inventory was complete, it came in at 60 percent of its stated value on the balance sheet and $16,000 less than my accountant's worst-case scenario. We talked about what the company was worth and agreed that with the combination of the ongoing losses for the year, the old receivables, and the inventory reductions, it was worth about half the previous year's book value. And that was to be our offer, no more, no less, take it or leave it. Book value. Period. The purchase price had come down a full 50 percent from the amount we had agreed to that July day in the hot, unlit Italian restaurant. The offer was accepted within 24 hours.[382]

The shop itself, if the company owns it, may be included in the deal, or the seller may sell all the assets except real estate, and lease the shop to the buyer. From the buyer's perspective, leasing can lower the purchase price as well as initial cash required. From the seller's viewpoint there will be an income stream from rent, and the comfort of still owning the property that the buyer needs for operating. In thinking through such a case, of course, the buyer needs to add to rental expenses that did not appear in historical statements of the company as a charge that would have taken a bite out of its profits but that will do so in the future.

As another tactic to lower the price and down payment, the seller may keep some furniture or some general-purpose equipment of the company not immediately needed for production, and perhaps lease it to the buyer if needed for operating the business.

Points of view and remedies

A natural point for contention between buyer and seller will always be what the company's prospects are. The buyer may fear that it will be impossible to continue an uptrend, if the company has one, or to counteract stagnation or downtrend if that happens to be impending.

The seller, however, will likely assert that the company is attractive, express optimism about profit potential, and even suggest that with the buyer coming in with fresh energy, ambition, ideas, and willingness to get out and sell harder, the company's fortunes are bound to improve. The buyer can use this to support the idea that a leveraged buyout should be safe for the seller who is thereby assured of being paid off.

For the seller it will be natural to fear that the buyer, unfamiliar with the business and how to run it, will make mistakes that are ruinous to the business and will undermine both the buyer's ability to pay for it and the firm's value to anyone. To head off this line of argument, the buyer may suggest that the seller stay on with the company as a consultant for pay that will also represent part of the purchase price. The advantage to the seller will be a chance to improve the odds of success and also opportunity to monitor the business and pursue actions to ward off deterioration if it starts to appear.

Advantages to the buyer will not only be that the consulting contract may gain help from the seller without raising the cost of purchase, but also the consulting payments will make the consulting part of the purchase price tax deductible to the business. The seller will have to pay income tax on the consulting payments, but having left behind any salary or dividends from the business, that tax will be on a reduced personal income and possibly therefore at a lower tax rate than before.

Possibly to make the deal still more secure to the seller, the buyer may offer not to take any cash out of the company personally, living on income provided by a spouse perhaps, until a certain percentage of the outstanding debt is repaid. Or possibly the buyer's promise to pay can be backed up by a co-signer, who guarantees to pay off any unpaid balance of the purchase debt if the buyer fails to do so. Obviously, it will be important that the co-signer be a person with enough resources to make good on that promise. Moreover, that person may have to be one who thinks he or she can take over the company and succeed with it if the buyer fails to make payments.

Incentives for the co-signer to take such a risk may be personal, as when a relative with resources chooses to back the buyer, or financial. Payment to the co-signer can take the form of a

---

[382] Hendrix F.C. Niemann, "Buying a Business," *Inc.*, February 1990, p. 38.

job with pay in the business, ownership of some share of the business, dividends, or a royalty on sales. Less risky for the company would perhaps be to give the co-signer some amount of preferred stock that would have to be redeemed at some specified price by the company before the company could pay any salary above some specified amount to the buyer.

Royalties

If the seller asserts that the company has higher earning potential than the buyer believes, then the buyer can suggest that part of the price be in the form of a royalty on sales, conveniently tax-deductible to the business, for a specified period of time based upon the seller's claim.

A nice feature of being offered royalties from a seller's point of view is that they come off the top of the income statement and are therefore not vulnerable to anyone's potentially adverse accounting interpretation or manipulations. A correspondingly adverse feature of royalty payments from the buyer's point of view is that they have to be paid whether the company generates profits or not.

The buyer might raise the possibility that a royalty will kick in only above some specified level of sales that the seller claims should be possible but the buyer has reason to doubt. A risk for the buyer is that such an arrangement may reduce incentive to work as hard or risk other investments for the sake of increasing sales. Which way this argument goes may depend upon how great a percentage the royalty will be as well as at what sales level it will take effect.

Taxes

A major impact on the amount of cash the buyer must relinquish to the seller can be produced by tax consequences of decisions made

in the deal. For instance, if assets are bought in the deal, then the seller will immediately pay capital gain tax on any value allocated to goodwill, but the buyer will have to amortize it over time. The tax on any inventory value gain will be at the ordinary income rate for the seller. On recapture of any fixed-asset depreciation, the seller will be taxed at the ordinary income rate, and so forth.

Financing

Four general sources of financing come into play in company acquisitions by entrepreneurs as listed in Exhibit 9b-7.

By approaching potential financing sources early in the acquisition process, two advantages may be gained. First, the sources may be able, through their knowledge and that of their contacts, to help with the search. Second, it can give time and working knowledge that strengthen credibility that may help with both search and the negotiations, as well as in obtaining the financing smoothly when it finally becomes needed.

> When Victor Kiam set out to buy the Remington Razor Division of Sperry Corporation, he expected it would be hard to obtain financing, because the division had been such a historically money-losing enterprise. He solicited advice from friends and associates about how to do it, and also set about hiring a bank to help him seek financing.
>
> He expected that cost of such help would be a conventional finder's fee of around $50,000 non-refundable cash up front plus an additional $50,000 if and when the financing was obtained. Instead, to heighten the incentive, he offered $5,000 up front plus another $200,000 upon receipt of the funding. He also learned, in making his proposal, that other banks had been recruited to seek financing for other people aspiring to buy the Remington Razor Division.

Exhibit 9b-7 Four buyout financing sources

1. The **entrepreneur's personal savings** and borrowings, possibly from friends and family, and possibly collateralized by personal non-cash assets.
2. The business being bought and/or its **owner who agrees to sell on time** probably with a down payment from the buyer, including a negotiated rate of interest on the unpaid balance.
3. A lending institution, probably a bank or finance company, that agrees to extend **credit, probably secured by assets** of the acquisition, and probably also by a personal guarantee by the buyer.
4. Other **outside individuals** as lenders or investors.

Finally, when he had most, but not all of his financing pieces in place, he agreed to give Sperry a letter of intent to buy the division together with a non-refundable check for $250,000, and a promise to give another $250,000 check thirty days before finalizing the deal that would be refundable if the deal did not go through.

This agreement triggered an article in *The Wall Street Journal* about the deal, which in turn prompted a phone call to Kiam from a consultant who had been arranging financing for another prospective buyer. The consultant offered, for a $50,000 fee, to finalize that other buyer's deal for Kiam to use, instead of what Kiam was still trying to set up. Kiam accepted and consequently received full ownership of the company for the $25 million price Sperry wanted while personally putting up only $750,000 cash of his own and signing a note for the rest. In other words, the cash he put up to buy the business was less than 4 percent of the full purchase price, while the fee he paid for help in getting the deal was $50,000 instead of the $250,000 he had expected.[383]

Obviously, an unforeseeable coincidence can sometimes have major effects.

Non-compete agreement

As part of the deal, it may be appropriate for the seller to sign a non-compete agreement, thereby promising not to enter into competition with the purchased firm. This document must specify the time period and geographical scope to which it applies. These, moreover, must be limited reasonably so that a court will not later throw them out as unduly in conflict with the basic notion that a person should have a right to pursue gainful employment in what they know how to do.

Negotiation

If the seller believes the buyer is highly credible, negotiating the purchase can be short and simple. Daryl Mitton was a division officer in a privately held aerospace corporation when its CEO decided the company should rid itself of the division.

No sooner did he announce that my division was to be sold, than he suggested that I buy it. We came to an agreement on terms of the sale in very short order. I would buy the 'hard' as-

sets at book value. His firm would loan the total amount for the purchase of these assets, with the loan secured by the assets and repayable over five years. I would purchase the existing inventories for cash, payable in 90 days. His firm would supply headquarters support services for up to 90 days at cost.[384]

Mitton knew the division, and present management knew Mitton, giving the company good reason to believe it would be paid for as agreed to, so they unilaterally made him an offer.

In contrast, Hendrix Niemann had no experience working in the company he wanted to acquire and his path to a purchase agreement was correspondingly bumpier.

He repeatedly ran into problems on such things as down-valuing of assets, finding hidden liabilities, learning that key employees were set to leave, being rejected by banks when trying to obtain financing and, at the last minute, resistance from the seller's attorney. The deal was on the attorney's desk two weeks before closing. But it received no attention, drew no suggestions for changes, and provoked no objections until Niemann went to the bank, got a down payment check on which interest immediately began accruing, and arrived at his attorney's office, where Lauren Finberg, the broker, was already waiting with the seller, Peter Klosky and Peter's lawyer to close the deal. As Niemann described it:

Peter and his attorney were late. When they did arrive, they wanted to rewrite the whole deal. Better for Peter's taxes this way. We're not changing any amounts, just the way it's paid out. And, by the way, we're not satisfied with the collateral you're using to secure the note to Mr. Klosky. Did we neglect to mention that before? Well, it doesn't really matter if we settle today, does it?[385]

Niemann and his attorney refused to yield, gambling that the seller would give in which, as it turned out, he did, and the deal went through. Had it not, there would likely have been further protracted negotiations, more legal expenses, and in the end, perhaps no deal at all, just need for Niemann to find another job and pay off his legal expenses.

[383] Kiam, *Going for It*, p. 192.
[384] Daryl C. Mitton, "The Anatomy of a High Leverage Buyout," in *Frontiers of Entrepreneurship Research*, 1984, eds. John A. Hornaday and others (Wellesley, MA: Babson Center for Entrepreneurial Studies, 1984) p. 414.
[385] Niemann, "Buying a Business," p. 38.

Preparation can help. Something Niemann arguably did right was to include his attorney in the closing process. Whether or not they talked through the possible points of discussion (an expensive activity if the attorney's meter is running) was not reported. But pre-thinking or at least pausing to think out responses on important issues carefully, rather than shooting from the hip as discussions progress, can reduce mistakes.

Warren Avis recalled an instance where negotiation failed to give him what he needed.

Some young businessmen approached me with what looked like a surefire deal to buy a company in Canada. We agreed that I would put up 75 percent of the money and they would put up 25 percent. Also, they would personally guarantee any bank loans that were taken out.

The young businessmen had assured him they already had the bank loan. But, he found, they did not, the deal was more complicated than it appeared, and this caused them to drag their feet. Bank financing would be needed for the deal, but Canadian exchange laws required that the bank be Canadian, and that would in turn require approval from the Canadian government. The sellers also wanted assurance of Canadian government approval so they would not be stuck with the plant. So, Avis recalled,

The Canadian government wouldn't give its approval without our owning the company; yet the bank wouldn't grant us a loan without government approval.

Avis sought other financing and lined up some possibilities. But he could not move because his partners, although they had become frightened by the deal, would not agree to step aside. Avis said,

Finally we did manage to put together a rather creative financing arrangement which would undoubtedly have worked. But then in the eleventh hour, the company was sold out from under us to a competing Canadian corporation. And the company was now making a million dollars a month!

Furious at this outcome, Avis concluded that,

The wise thing would have been to include a clause in the basic contract that would have allowed us to move in under certain conditions of failure. So I took the lesson to heart: I resolved that in future deals I would insist upon the right to take over within a certain time period if the partner failed to meet within reasonable time limits certain projections or goals.[386]

There are countless books, courses, lectures, videotapes, stories, and lore about negotiating. The number of variables that may come into play, given the diversity of personalities who may be involved, is limitless. There are guidelines, rules, aphorisms, maxims, and exhortations about how to do it right. To mention a few:

- It may be helpful to have a professional intermediary present the buyer's offer, so the buyer can then remain a good guy in the negotiating process.
- Written documents of the deal should be drafted by a professional having strong and successful experience in similar deals.
- The deal has to seem like a win to the seller as well as the buyer. Preferably, this perception should continue after the deal is done.
- The seller may be able to help with the company in many ways after the deal is done.
- It will work to the buyer's advantage to have the reputation of being a good person to deal with.

4. Due diligence

As final terms come together, the buyer should have suitable documents drawn up. These should be presented to the seller with the expectation that the seller will have his or her attorney go over them, after which there may be further haggling before they reach final form for signing.

Letter of intent

If the potential acquisition continues to appear attractive after screening and price check-out, the seller can prepare, presumably with help from an attorney or broker, a **letter of intent** setting forth a proposal about price and terms. It should briefly describe what would be bought, how much down payment would be made, and what the payout and interest schedules would be. It should also state that the offer will be contingent upon further checkout of the company or due diligence by the buyer be-

Letter of intent

---

[386] Warren Avis, *Take a Chance to be First* (New York: Macmillan, 1986) p. 190.

fore it becomes fully formal. This, then, should set the stage for negotiating about further deals of the specific price and terms.

Even so, however, negotiations can be tripped up or dragged out by any number of events beyond the buyer's control, as illustrated by the following example.

> A venture capitalist decided to apply what he had learned about valuing firms and structuring and negotiating deals by doing a buyout of his own. Young and not yet wealthy, he recruited 12 investors to back him during the search and help finance the deal. He formulated criteria and sent a brochure listing them, along with the names of his advisers, to nearly 1,000 intermediaries. He reviewed over 275 companies, made offers on six, and finally entered closing negotiations with the 80-year-old founder of a proprietary manufacturing firm who concluded that he didn't want to sell out because he had a son performing much of the management.
>
> But six months later the son died, and the owner called back to say he had decided to sell after all. Negotiations began with a fairly wide spread in price, then began to move toward closure. But before a deal could be struck the wife of the son who had died stepped in to block the deal. After nine months of wrangling negotiations ceased. Then they started again, but after a month the founder was felled by a stroke and the bookkeeper left.
>
> Then the founder's second son stepped forward and negotiations started all over again from the beginning. Again, there was a spread in views about appropriate price. By the time the deal finally closed, two years had elapsed and a fourth of the original investors had dropped out. The buyer's conclusion was that it would have worked better at the end if the letter of intent written earlier had included fuller explanation of reasoning behind the price and terms developed in the early stages of negotiation with the founder.[387]

Disappointment in the true value of assets, as opposed to what the seller claims they are worth, is a frequent occurrence among buyers. Another entrepreneur who bought a company that included general-purpose machines recalled a setback even after he had taken the precaution of having a used-equipment dealer give him an appraisal on them.

> I had bought equipment before based on appraisals. Normally, there would be a statement at the bottom of the dealer's appraisal sheet to the effect that "as of this day we will agree to pay X dollars for this equipment." That lets you know that it is really worth the figure they give. But this time I did not notice that the statement was different, and instead it said something to the effect that "this is our best judgment as to what this equipment is worth." As it turned out, the equipment was actually worth only about 60 percent of the estimate, and I got stuck.

This company buyer also found other problems with the business. Financial statements prepared by his own accountant turned out to contain substantial errors which lowered the value of what he thought he had bought. The company's job costing system was woefully inadequate and had to be revamped. Finally, the head man in the shop, who knew the most about how to run it and had been considered invaluable to the buyer, turned out to have a serious drinking problem and had to be let go. The buyer ultimately was able to keep operating at a profit, but one substantially lower than he had projected.

Of crucial importance is the question of whether the new owner will be able to make the company perform adequately. The odds are that it will continue along the performance trajectory, which is fine if the company was doing well. But if it was not performing well, the buyer should explore carefully why, before assuming that he or she will be able to turn the company around after takeover. Victor Kiam concluded from prior investigation of Remington that he could.

> After verifying the numbers on Remington, Kiam next searched to learn what Sperry had done wrong with it. The division had done well when first taken over by Sperry. The original owner continued to run it successfully under Sperry, but when he retired a couple of decades later, Sperry, mainly a high-technology company, replaced him with an engineer who greatly escalated emphasis on technical innovation. A series of model changes in the razor followed, which frustrated retailers as the models on their shelves

---

[387] Russell Robb, *Buying Your Own Business* (Holbrook, MA: Adams Media 1995) p. 266.

repeatedly became obsolete. Consequently, they cut back on orders and sales declined.

Remington had also added a variety of other product lines besides shavers after the management change. As part of selling the division, these had been eliminated, but some of the personnel associated with them, such as their different product managers, were still on the payroll, pulling profits down. These things Kiam had discerned through his due diligence analysis before buying the company. But still more were to come after takeover.[388]

The list of possible angles, consequences, and restrictions needed to protect both seller and buyer can be long. Can the buyer pay off any loan faster if, for instance, interest rates fall below what the buyout agreement requires? Can the buyer sell off selected assets? Does the seller have rights to check on the company's condition while it is still being paid off? What freedom of action does the seller have to try to save the company if it seems to be failing under the buyer's management? What steps can the seller take if the buyer defaults on payments due, and can those steps be put into effect fast enough to prevent fatal deterioration of the company before they are completed? Exactly when will the transfer take place? How will keys be transferred and when will the locks be changed?

Whether the seller may have partners should be investigated, and there should be assurance that the seller actually has full rights to sell. If there are partners involved on either side, they too must be informed and agree to the transaction.

If any licenses are required, the procedure for obtaining them should be checked out. If there is an operations manual, is it up to date? It may now be time to reveal more about what is going to happen to people who were not informed about the sale earlier. Which people in the company know how the operations are to be done? Who is best informed about the software and any network operating procedures? Who is qualified to get needed upgrades, debugging, or repairs done? How will they feel about staying on? Should the possibility of employment contracts be further explored with any key employees?

The assets to be transferred should already be listed, and the list should perhaps again be checked against what is present. Liabilities not to be assumed by the buyer should also be rechecked, and so should a statement of assurance that there are no others. Who should pay which legal and other fees involved in the transfer should all be clear. Some of the many other details to be considered as part of due diligence are listed in Exhibit 9b-8 below.

Although there may have been agreement during negotiations on the terms of a deal acceptable to both parties, the deal is not final until documents are signed confirming closure. Assumptions made during the earlier screening process and the negotiations should be verified before

Exhibit 9b-8 Illustrative due-diligence details

1. What assets of the business guarantee any note the seller may be accepting? Must other loans to the company be subordinated?
2. How will the current assets be valued at the time of closing?
3. Is every single asset to be transferred listed in the agreement?
4. Should the seller sign a non-competition agreement, and if so, for what activities, time, and geographical area?
5. Who will get any shares of any stock, articles of incorporation, and minutes of shareholders' meetings that happen to exist?
6. Is there certification that shareholders have duly authorized the sale?
7. What does the seller guarantee about outstanding liabilities, claims, or lawsuits against the company, either present or impending?
8. Does the seller have partners, and if so, are they signing too?
9. Exactly when does the buyer take over what?
10. What if something is missing at takeover?
11. Are there any protections for the seller to cover things the buyer might do after sale?
12. What are the buyer's longer-term aims for the firm?
13. Are there any constraints on how the buyer can dispose of assets or the business?

---

388 Kiam, *Going for It.*

signing the deal by final cross-checking. Are customers really as happy as claimed? How important to the business are which employees, what are their aspirations, what do they know about the sale, how do they feel about it, and what do they think should be changed, or not? Does the firm have any liabilities or litigation threats not known of earlier? Is the equipment really as up to date and in condition as good as it seemed to be? Is the inventory as fresh as assumed? Checking into such factors, once an informal agreement has been reached, may give grounds for further negotiation of the final terms.

The following example illustrates two important points about following through on a deal, the importance of (1) making sure that values received by the buyer don't deteriorate before takeover, and (2) employing professional help, not just any, but help with the right experience, to avoid pitfalls:

> A CPA became intrigued with the beautiful work produced by a cabinet shop and, when he found out the owner wanted to sell, negotiated to buy it. Two items of value considered particularly important to the buyer were (1) inventory and equipment in the shop which he, as an experienced accountant, valued at $200,000 and (2) a backlog of firm orders with financially sound customers amounting to another $200,000. He agreed to pay $500,000 for the business and put up $150,000 to clinch the deal.
>
> But the next day when he went to take over the shop he found things had changed. The selling owner had engaged three shifts and worked overnight. The inventory and equipment had now been reduced to $50,000, and the backlog was also down to $50,000 thanks to an early morning shipment. Now the company was short on working capital, and the accountant saw no other choice but to inject another $150,000 to keep it afloat. Eventually, after four years of operation, he sold the business for half the price he had paid for it.

Had the purchase agreement been written to link price to conditions as of the time of takeover, these problems could have been reduced or eliminated. An attorney or consultant experienced in business sales and employed by the CPA, not by the seller, should have been used. That is not to say that all problems can be

avoided, but they can be diminished. Further off-balance-sheet items to check appear in Exhibit 9b-9 below.

As numerous and long as such lists may seem, there is always room for other wrinkles to crop up and always reason to be cautious in either accepting what is presented by the seller at face value or figuring that legal action will be an appropriate remedy in case of seller fraud.

> Victor Kiam was stung on purchase of the Benrus watch company from its Swiss owners by an inventory of unusable watch cases. They had been made to house a watch movement that became obsolete and was discontinued. After taking ownership of them as part of the acquisition, he looked for another movement that could be put in them, but found none. He also investigated having another new movement produced to fit them, but found it would be enormously uneconomic. Consequently, he concluded, "Half the book value was an illusion." Because the watch cases had been represented by the seller as good inventory, he could have sued them for fraud. But his legal advisers said doing that would take years and much money to do so, more than the chance of an uncertain recovery was worth. "The experience taught me," he said, "never to buy a company without examining every bit of it."[389]

Paperwork and forms

Paperwork required for conclusion of the sale will vary depending on whether the buyer is purchasing assets or, if the company is a corporation, stock. If the seller is to be paid over time, there will have to be a promissory note specifying the amounts, interest, timing, and what happens in case of default. If some specific assets are pledged to guarantee the note, then a chattel mortgage form will be in order. That, in turn will raise questions about who is responsible for maintaining the assets in what ways, what rights of inspection the seller has, whether insurance must be carried on the asset, under what conditions the asset can be sold, and what happens in case of default.

An important law pertaining to sale of assets in a business is the Uniform Commercial Code adopted by all states. It provides, among other things, that the bulk transfer of inventory

Exhibit 9b-9 Some off-balance-sheet commitments to be checked

1. **Payments maybe due in near term**
   a. *Deferred compensation or bonus obligations.*
   b. *Past service obligations, such as pension payments.*
   c. *Profit sharing plan obligations.*
   d. *Health plan premiums or reserves.*
   e. *Cost of new services needed by acquisition.*
   f. *Debt payment obligations.*
   g. *Equipment lease expenses.*
   h. *Royalties due either to or from acquisition.*
   i. *Capital expenditure required for upgrading.*
   j. *Costs of refurbishment.*
2. **Other foreseeable near-term expenses**
   a. *Deferred-tax plans.*
   b. *Outstanding purchase commitments.*
   c. *Service contracts, such as with ISPs.*
   d. *Unbilled services due to prior customers.*
   e. *Vacations or other awards due to employees.*
3. **Other items of possible financial consequence**
   a. *Uncovered insurance needs.*
   b. *Order backlog, whether asset or liability.*
   c. *Special purchase terms extended by suppliers personally to the seller.*
   d. *Surplus assets to be sold.*
   e. *Any licenses with companies or government agencies needed to continue operations.*
   f. *Warranties held by prior customers.*
   g. *Union contracts.*
   h. *Assets or guarantees pledged.*
   i. *Stock options outstanding.*
   j. *Repurchase agreements.*
   k. *Rights to the names and logos of the company and its products.*

requires that suppliers from whom the seller bought the inventory first be paid. But exceptions to the law are also possible and may be worth exploring. One possibility may be that the buyer can explicitly assume such liabilities as part of the sales agreement.

Representations and warranties statement

The buyer is entitled to receive assurance that the seller has not hidden deficiencies in the company. This can be guaranteed by the buyer through explicit statement of representations and warranties such as those listed in Exhibit 9b-10. Actual wording of such documentation should be reviewed by the buyer's attorney, whether prepared by the buyer or the seller. Examples can be found in the literature.[390]

Signing an acceptable (hopefully good) deal will complete the third of four big tests involved in business entry via acquisition. Takeover and operation come next.

Exhibit 9b-10 Some representations and warranties statement items

- *All debts owed are included in the purchase agreement.*
- *Seller has full rights to sell the company assets.*
- *Seller is not defaulting on any legal commitment of the company.*
- *All required tax returns have been filed.*
- *Buyer has been informed of any impending lawsuits, liens, attachments, and guarantees.*
- *Financial statements and other records of the company have been disclosed and are truthful.*
- *Permits and licenses required for operation are valid.*

---

[389] Kiam, *Going for It*, p. 194.
[390] Gabehart, *Buying, Valuing and Selling Your Business.*

Formalizing

If the deal is good enough for the buyer to accept, the next step is for the buyer to put up earnest money in anticipation of finalizing it. Once the earnest money is accepted by the seller, the seller is essentially locked in. The buyer can still back out of the deal, but only by leaving the earnest money behind with the seller as what legally is considered part of liquidated damages. Legally the seller will then be said to have been damaged by having to hold the company in limbo, possibly passing up alternative deals that would have been even better while the buyer was failing to follow through.

In practice, unlike theory, the buyer can probably word the earnest money agreement in such a way that backing out is possible. Phrases such as "subject to inspection" or "subject to inspection of the facilities by a professional inspector to the buyer's satisfaction" may provide a back door of escape for the buyer.

Even so, actually having to put up a significant amount of cash imposes a certain amount of discipline on the buyer not to be frivolous about the deal. The seller may regard the magnitude of the earnest money as an indicator of the buyer's seriousness and capability to follow through on the deal, and as a result may be willing to give the buyer a better price or terms if the buyer puts up more earnest money.

To carry through this part of the transaction, both parties may agree upon one escrow attorney or firm to make arrangements for handling the earnest money and following through on paperwork that completes the transaction.

5. Takeover and beyond *and beyo*

Although systematic statistics are limited, entrepreneurs appear to fare better with their acquisitions than do corporations.[391] They know they are dependent on existing employees; consequently they treat them with care and respect for their views and interests. Because they are typically risking everything they own and will earn for the foreseeable future, entrepreneurs simply must find ways to make their acquisitions work out, and usually they do.

Nevertheless the events that will follow a decision to pursue business entry through acquisition can still be hard to predict, according to one business broker. Noting that virtually all the acquisition customers he encountered came to him as a result of some particular company he had advertised for sale, less than 3 percent of those who bought acquired the company they came in for. He offered two examples as follows:

A restaurant executive with long-time experience in managing restaurants successfully, and especially in turning around failing units to make them profitable, came to inquire on behalf of his wife about a travel agency for sale. The agency was losing money, and to the broker reasons seemed obvious. The owner had not been controlling expenses. For example, he had installed 27 telephone trunk lines costing $1,000 per month each when he had only 10 employees using them. By cutting unnecessary expenditures such as this, the broker, who had combed through the company's financials, computed that it should be possible to transform the company's $36,000 annual loss into a profit of $85,000.

The owner's asking price was $600,000, based on a rule of thumb that travel agencies typically sold at about 10 percent of annual bookings, which in this case were $6 million. Considering the losses, however, the buyer was able to negotiate a price of only $270,000, and the deal was done. The broker expected to see great success.

He was surprised about six months later when the new owner drove up in an extremely high-priced car and said his wife wanted to sell the business and move to the southwest. When asked for recent records, the new owner brought in a box of papers and apologized that there was not much in the way of operating statements. The broker found bank statements in the box, however, and these indicated that the company's bank account had been overdrawn in each of the past three months by $100,000. Instead of cutting expenses, the buyer had extravagantly increased them. Consequently, the outcome

[391] Robert B. Brown, John E. Butler, and Karl H. Vesper, "Performance after Acquisition: The Role of Entrepreneurs," in *Frontiers of Entrepreneurship Research*, 1989, eds. Robert H. Brockhaus, Sr. and others (Wellesley, MA: Babson Center for Entrepreneurial Studies, 1989) p. 575.

was not resale of the business, but bankruptcy. The broker concluded, "Apparently he could manage other people's money, but he couldn't manage his own."

— • —

Two men came to the broker's office saying they wanted to buy either a manufacturer, a distributor, or a wholesaler. They seemed open-minded and the broker thought it would suit them to take over a highly specialized employment agency because it might have potential for expansion, which seemed to him their real goal. Net cash flow the previous year had been $135,000, but six months later it was running at $165,000 per year. The sellers were asking $230,000. Total fixed assets of the business could be bought new for less than $10,000 and installed in a 10 by 10 foot room. Disparity between the asking price and value of the tangible assets had, the broker said, scared off all potential buyers for six months.

But the new partners thought they saw ways to connect the business to their desire for making an enterprise grow. It had, after all, been growing, and its low capital intensity could make further growth possible without heavy financing. By three years later the enterprise had expanded to three additional states, and sales were running at $6.5 million with a very healthy profit.

As discussed earlier, the first task of an acquirer is to find an acceptable company to buy, and although it strongly makes sense to define clear criteria and focus the search among the huge array of possibilities, flexibility can also be appropriate. Second is to demonstrate credibility to the seller. Third is to work out the deal, and fourth is the transition to new management.

After takeover

Some acquisitions at this fourth stage, particularly when the acquirer is a larger corporation, falter and ultimately fail. Corporation managements tend to perform heavy-handed acts, such as changing the name of the acquisition, imposing new internal systems and new managers, showing disregard for methods that have traditionally worked well for the acquired company, and disrespect for its employees. Such measures add confusion and drive out key employees who have other options. Then the acquired company, even though it may be able to draw on greater financial strength from its new parent, becomes weaker and possibly gets sold again or closed down.

Most acquisitions by independent entrepreneurs, unless the businesses are fatally flawed, succeed and improve, perhaps because the entrepreneurs feel themselves faced with no other tolerable choice. Always they find problems, but also solutions.

Dave Ederer, a CPA who bought the heat-treating company owned by one of his clients, knew nothing about its technology. Shortly after he took over the business, the two lead men who best understood it and upon whom he depended to run it left, one as a result of arrest for something unrelated to the company and the other because of divorce. Dave concluded he had to bring in qualified replacements for them before work went wrong and before competitors found out. How would he accomplish that? He chose three steps.

First, he ran advertisements in the newspaper classified section for experienced heat-treaters. Many responded, but whom should he choose? Second, he privately interviewed each to get a feel for the person's style, values, and aspirations. But how could he know whether they were really qualified without tipping off competitors? Third, he sent those who passed this test back to talk with his employees, telling them to choose carefully, saying, "If you pick the wrong people, I will lose the company and you will lose your jobs." The choices succeeded, as did that company and other companies Dave went on to acquire, notwithstanding he understood none of their technologies in depth.

— • —

Upon taking over Remington Razor from Sperry Corporation, Victor Kiam stopped the product design changes and dismissed unnecessary personnel. But the employees remaining knew that the money drain from losses had formerly been covered by cash from Sperry, which Kiam was not in a position to replace from his now-empty pockets. Consequently, some of those most needed by the company began to leave.

To cope with this, Kiam held meetings with employees where he presented the upside potential he saw for the company, introduced new incentive compensation systems whose cash payouts would be in the future, and cut other costs through eliminating things such as the executive dining room and first-class air tickets, which saved cash immediately. Soon other savings were achieved by eliminating frills on the shaver and its case and by consolidating manufacturing operations in one place.

Dropping price on the simplified product and introducing a sales campaign emphasizing how the company's new policies would be better for stores succeeded in lifting sales. Advertising campaigns stressing superior performance in the razors boosted sales further.

Other problems arose, such as disputes in other countries where Kiam closed operations to centralize manufacturing (workers in the company's French plant even sabotaged a production run) and a lawsuit by the company's main competitor, Norelco, charging trademark infringement on a new product name. The suit was unsuccessful. Company profits soared.

Success was strong enough for the company to pay off its bank loans in one year, which was nine years ahead of schedule. Kiam observed that actions had brought this about, but also that "this turnaround began with the basic product. I could have been blessed with the powers of Merlin, but if the shaver hadn't been any good, the company wouldn't have survived."[392]

Beyond the two business-entry modes considered thus far, start-up and acquisition, one more will be described in the next chapter, which is to buy a franchise for copying an existing firm.

Exercises

Text discussion questions

1. Is there a fundamental reason why there is a variety of alternative ways of valuing a business that is for sale? Explain why or why not.
2. What is basically the best way for a seller versus a buyer to value a business for sale?
3. Which are the most important, in rank order, pros and cons of attempting a leveraged buyout for the purchase of a business?
4. When would it be better to buy just the assets of a corporation, as opposed to the stock, and vice versa, in a buyout?
5. What are the most important, in rank order, pros and cons of incorporating royalties in a company buyout from the viewpoint of buyer versus seller?
6. Discuss possible reasons why buyouts by entrepreneurs seem to work out better than buyouts by corporations. What would you do first the day you got title and the key to a business?

Case questions

9B-1 Cliff Dow and Steve Shaper

1. Describe two alternative deal strategies with terms Cliff and Steve should consider best bets for seeking to acquire and develop this business.
2. Describe two alternative deal strategies with terms from the seller's point of view.
3. Draft a brief script for presenting an offer from either side to the other.
4. List the first action steps Cliff and Steve should take upon closing the deal.

Portfolio page possibilities

Page 9B-1 Negotiate a sale
Pick whatever small business you either know or can learn the most about, both operationally and financially. Pair up with a classmate who has done the same, imagine that person as a buyer, you as owner, and negotiate a sale.

Page 9B-2 Negotiate a second sale
Repeat the above for the firm investigated by your classmate.

Page 9B-3 Investigate a sale
Interview some small business owners until you find at least one who bought the business. Learn what you can about the sequence of events, and describe, as best you can, how the price and terms came about.

↓

---

[392] Kiam, *Going for It*, p 206.

Page 9B-4 Investigate a second sale
Perform a second interview as above and describe how the two were different versus identical.

Page 9B-5 Letter of intent
Draft what you think might be a suitable letter of intent for buying a particular local business, assuming it were for sale.

Page 9B-6 Plan after takeover
Sketch on one page the highlights of a plan for takeover of a particular local business, assuming you had bought it.

Term Projects

Venture history

1. How did the buyer, versus the seller, develop and rationalize a purchase price?
2. Who all participated in creating the deal terms and through what processes?
3. To what extent was the negotiation involved and how did it operate?
4. What surprises, if any, occurred during the takeover process after buying?
5. How did company performance change after takeover?

Venture planning guide

Prepare an assessment of a company to buy, including:

1. A checklist of items gone over,
2. Pro-forma financial estimates,
3. Deal terms,
4. A letter of intent, and
5. A loan proposal for a bank to provide the down payment.

CHAPTER 9C – Franchising

Topics

1. Franchise variety
2. Performance
3. Choice
4. Checkout
5. Moves

Checkpoints

a. Describe the range of variety in franchises.
b. Contrast and explain the performance of franchises versus independents.
c. How may a UFOC be helpful to an entrepreneur who is considering franchising?
d. Contrast the roles of franchiser versus franchisee and their attractiveness.
e. What franchisees become wealthier than others and how?
f. Explain the pros and cons of becoming a franchisee for the learning experience.

The franchise alternative for business ownership combines some elements of taking a job, starting a new company, and taking over one already going, but these advantages come with significant costs.

1. Franchise variety

The underlying concept of a franchise is that a company that has developed a successful product or service brand allows someone else to use its name to sell the same service or product in return for money either as single payment or installments over time. The cost to the franchisee is often structured as an up-front franchise fee plus a royalty percentage on sales. The percentage of sales may be fairly small, such as 5 percent or less, but as a percentage of profits, it will of course be substantially larger.

There are two types of franchises, trade name and format. **Trade-name franchises** typically refer to dealerships, such as those of carmakers, oil companies, and soft drink producers. A trade-name franchisee commits to display a particular supplier's logo and sell its goods among any others, but is an independent business in other respects. The key value is the trademark, which is preferably widely advertised and well known.

In the second type, a **format franchise**, some company (the franchiser) with a proven operating formula, such as 7-Eleven, sells the right to use its brand and formula, along with some degree of support, to someone (the franchisee) who wants to use them for a business of their own. A format franchiser also provides the franchisee with help on a variety of facets of the business for delivering the branded product or service, including how to operate it, how to advertise, and possibly what would be a suitable location. Typically, the franchiser will require that the franchisee follow a set of written rules for operating the business. Exhibit 9c-1 below illustrates variety among format franchises by category in column 1, by brand in column 2. It also lists the number

Exhibit 9c-1 Examples of format franchises[393]

Category	Franchiser	Franchises	Branches
Training	Kumon Math & Reading	19,667	14
Hamburgers	McDonald's	16,319	4,908
Convenience stores	7-Eleven	14,549	2,535
Sandwiches	Subway	13,395	1
Commercial cleaning	Jani-King	7,038	35
Chicken	KFC	6,635	2,975
Frozen desserts	Dairy Queen	5,800	50
Bakery products	Dunkin' Donuts	4,813	0
Fitness centers	Jazzercise	4,909	2
Hardware	Snap-on Tools	4,157	237
Mexican food	Taco Bell	2,927	2,221
Rental	Budget Rent A Car	2,490	640
Electronic	Radio Shack	1,963	4,992
Motels	Super 8	1,575	0
Video	Blockbuster	1,010	5,223
Computer training	Futurekids	996	10
Oil change	Jiffy Lube	963	598
Mufflers	Meineke	878	3
Transmissions	Aamco	713	2
Auto painting	Maaco	535	0

of franchisee-operated outlets in column 3 and franchiser-operated outlets in column 4.

The idea with a format franchise is that a would-be entrepreneur who wants to create his or her own business may end run the need to (1) invent a new product or service, (2) develop a plan, (3) figure out location criteria, and (4) design financing by instead imitating what someone else has already developed and tested, in return for an up-front payment plus a percentage of sales to a franchiser. A table listing other ways an entrepreneur could seek those same benefits as an independent start-up appears in Exhibit 9c-2 below.

Both approaches to business formation are very widely used in the economy. Among the 2,994 responding small firms, Cooper et al. found that one quarter (26 percent) began operations with some type of franchise, though only 12 percent reported that three-quarters or more of their sales came from franchised goods or services. The latter 12 percent corresponds to the number who operated under a franchise name (11 percent). No relationship existed between survival and the possession of a franchise or operation under a franchise name. However, a negative relationship existed between growth and the percent of franchised sales.[394]

Exhibit 9c-2 Benefit comparisons of franchises versus independents

Franchiser-offered benefit	Other ways for seeking the same benefit
1. Proven idea	1. Most ideas can be copied
2. Operational expertise	2. Look for an appropriately experienced partner or hire a consultant
3. Training	3. Take a job in something similar, maybe working for free, and/or take classes from other sources, public and/or private
4. Price breaks from volume buying	4. Trade associations can get them too
5. Name brand identity	5. Build one up locally with clever ads, good quality, possibly price promotions financed by the franchise fee, and royalties avoided by starting independently

[393] "Franchise 500," *Entrepreneur*, January 1999, p. 212.
[394] Arnold C. Cooper and others, *New Business in America* (Washington, D.C.: The NFIB Foundation, 1990) p. 5.

Motivation

The typical format franchise begins with an entrepreneur who has created a small business that wins. That business became successful, possibly quickly as an instant good idea, or possibly over time as the entrepreneur experiments to refine it. As it becomes successful, the original entrepreneur considers ways of capitalizing on that success. If it is the type of business that sells locally and the local area becomes saturated, then growth will require expanding to other locations.

One growth option is to add new branches in other locations. But those branches will have to be financed and also well managed to extend the first outlet's success. If the company is wealthy or can raise the cash, then it may be able to afford to finance the expansion, including recruitment and training of competent managers for the branches. In addition to the work and money it must invest, it will also have to carry the risk of those branches working out.

Or, it can choose to sell the use of its format or success formula to others, who thereby become franchisees, take on the role of managers, and put up the financing for additional outlets, which, instead of branches of the original company, are the franchisees' own enterprises. Each of those outlets now benefits from implementation of the proven good idea that the franchiser created, with rights to use it under conditions of the franchise agreement. The franchisee typically gets exclusive rights for some specified geographical territory, free of competition. Ideally, the format will work as well in the franchisee's territory as it did for the entrepreneur who invented it. But that is a risk.

As can be seen in Exhibit 9c-1 above, some franchise companies also operate branch outlets that are owned and operated by the company while others do not. The branch outlets are often used as learning and test sites. Starbucks stores are all company-owned rather than franchised, except in China where for political reasons they are locally owned. With company stores the company's management believes it can exercise more effective control of quality, costs and culture.

When a franchiser's good idea is employed at franchised outlets, which are paying up-front fees and royalties, the franchiser can invest in further refinement of the idea, better training programs, and advertising to benefit progressively more outlets. Expansion can mean opportunities to buy equipment and supplies in greater quantities in order to gain volume discounts, and it increases the total experience being acquired by both the franchiser and franchisees to make the business work more effectively and economically. Thus the second factor, economy of scale, can work for all the outlets.

Extent

Franchising took off in the American economy during the '60s, and it was estimated by 1989 that there were over 3,000 franchise chains in the U.S. operating around 500,000 outlets.[395] Restaurants were estimated in 1990 to account for 102,000 outlets, gas stations for 112,000, and business aids and services for 67,000, with the latter having grown 21 percent since 1988.[396] By 1995 the number of outlets was up to 663,000 and still rising, with sales of $1 trillion or 40 percent of all U.S. retail sales.[397] In all, according to the U.S. Department of Commerce in 1998, franchising accounted for one third of all U.S. retail dollars. Growth continued in the '90s so that by 1996 according to the U.S. Department of Commerce it accounted for 45 percent of all U.S. retail sales, and employed a million people. Its significance by 1998 can be seen in its share of sales for 18 industries appearing in Exhibit 9c-3 below.

Annually *Entrepreneur* magazine publishes a list of top ten franchisers based on such numerical measures as age, size, and growth of the franchiser, litigation, percentage of franchises terminated, growth, financial strength and stability, and whether or not they provide financing. How these measures are weighted is not stated, nor

---

[395] Carol Steinberg, "The Right Deal," *Venture*, June/July 1989, p. 53.
[396] Leslie Brokaw, "New Businesses," *Inc.*, May 1990, p. 25.
[397] International Franchise Association and Horwath International, *Franchising in the Economy 1990* (Evans City, PA: IFA Publications, 1991) p. 1.

Exhibit 9c-3 Franchising share of sales in 18 U.S. industries[398]

Industry	Aggregate sales ($ millions)	Franchise share (%)	Franchise sales ($ millions)
Restaurant	139,281	46.2	64,280
Nonfood retailing	88,485	26.4	23,344
Construction, cleaning	53,291	9.9	5,296
Hotels, motels, camps	51,146	38.6	19,749
Real estate	38,145	15.5	5,923
Convenience stores	36,100	38.5	13,896
Auto products, services	32,343	35.1	11,363
Accounting, collection	28,607	0.6	165
Employment services	19,924	23.4	4,661
Specialty food retailing	18,500	55.1	10,184
Miscellaneous business	18,136	16.3	2,951
Auto, truck rental	16,441	40.3	6,617
Entertainment, travel	14,062	25.2	3,543
Educational services	12,860	2.1	272
Equipment rental	9,884	6.9	678
Laundry, dry cleaning	6,103	27.9	1,700
Printing, copying	1,978	71.4	1,413
Tax preparation	905	67.2	608
Total, average	586,191	30.4	176,643

is there any information about franchisee satisfaction. As can be seen from lists of the top ten franchisers for the years 2006, 2007 and 2008 appearing in Exhibit 9c-4, there is both repetition and change from year to year, albeit unexplained. A table in the magazine lists 500 franchisers, including these, with more data, importantly including start-up cost and royalty charges, which are typically a percentage of sales, but sometimes a flat fee per month. Important to remember is that these charges come off the top line, whether the company makes a profit or not.

By 1999 *Entrepreneur*, which ranks the top 500 franchises in 137 categories, based upon a combination of objective factors such as financial strength and stability, size, and growth rate, but not including franchisee satisfaction or profitability, put Yogen Fruz at the top, followed by McDonald's, Subway, Wendy's, and Jackson Hewitt Tax Service, in that order.[399] A few years later, some of the same pattern was still in place, as shown in Exhibit 9c-4. Many franchises also are sold abroad. 7-Eleven had nearly five times as many stores abroad as in the U.S. (25,062 versus

5,580), according to the January 2008 *Entrepreneur* magazine tabulation.

Numerous advertisements for format franchises can be found in newspapers and magazines, often suggesting the promise of pleasant work, attractive returns, and financial independence. Many carry photographs illustrating what work people do in the franchise, usually with broad smiles, or sometimes with looks of confident concentration on some task of the business. A prolific source of current information about available franchises is *Entrepreneur* magazine which includes a section on that subject at the rear of each monthly issue. It may be noted, however, that this section contains mainly advertisements, which are paid for by the franchisers and are an important source of revenue for the magazine. Hence, it tends to contain mainly upbeat and enthusiastic articles about the various franchises and franchisees who have bought them. Not much described are situations of unhappy franchisees, of whom there have also been many over the years. Although there are in fact many happy franchisees, there are also

---

[398] Steven C. Michael, "To Franchise or Not To Franchise," *Journal of Business Venturing*, Volume 11, Number 1, 1996, p. 63.
[399] *Entrepreneur*, January 1999, p. 209.

Exhibit 9c-4 Top ten franchisers by recent year

2006	2007	2008
Subway	Subway	7-Eleven
Quiznos Sub	Dunkin' Donuts	Subway
Curves	Jackson Hewitt Tax	Dunkin' Donuts
UPS Store	7-Eleven	Pizza Hut
Jackson Hewitt Tax	UPS/Mail Boxes Etc.	McDonald's
Dunkin' Donuts	Domino's Pizza	Sonic Drive In
Jani-King	Jiffy Lube	KFC Corp.
RE/MAX Int'l	Sonic Drive-In	Intercontinental Hotels
7-Eleven	McDonald's	Domino's Pizza
Liberty Tax Service	Papa John's	RE/MAX Int'l

always unhappy ones, many of whom have lawsuits in process against franchisers. It is not hard to imagine in reading the list of ten touted advantages below how disappointment and disillusionment in franchise relationships could sometimes arise.

The argument for becoming a franchisee, rather than doing an independent start-up, rests on the franchiser offering help in come combination of elements from among those listed in the shaded area on the following page.

2. Performance

Central overhead in the franchiser's home office can be seen as adding burden to all the outlets. Part of this is the time cost to the franchisee of dealing with the franchiser. Another part lies in expenses for the central office, which does not produce goods and services, but just oversees. It includes costs of communicating with the franchisees, running training programs, complying with franchiser reporting requirements, and dealing with problems and complaints of franchisees, as well as those of customers at large. Executives in the central office will likely draw large salaries and expense accounts, all of which will be drawn off what the franchisees put in. If one or more franchisees for any reason becomes disaffected and sues the company, all the other franchisees will likely in effect carry the costs. Clearly, how these central costs weigh against the economy of scale benefits will importantly affect competitiveness of the outlets in the long run.

Profitability

Of more significant interest to the prospective franchisee should be the level of profitability. Cooper et al. found that franchise-based start-ups grew faster than independents. However, profitability assessment must take into account (1) the amount invested in shop, equipment, and inventory, (2) the cost of the franchise fee, and (3) the impact on profits of any royalty fees. After subtracting those, discounting for a suitable return on the investment in the business, and taking into account the hours worked, the income to the franchisee may not be very attractive. It will probably cost more to start a franchise than to buy or start a comparable business, and the profits, after royalties, may well be less with a franchise. Certainly, the freedom to manage will be less.

A for-instance look at prospective franchisee profitability can be seen in the projected income statement for a new pizza franchise reported in 1990 by Inc.[400] and shown in Exhibit 9c-5 below. Of the $325,000 investment required, it was projected that $75,000 would be for equipment, $13,000 for a point-of-sale system, and $135,000 for the modular building to house the store. Experts in similar industries polled by the magazine were divided about whether the concept, fast window-pickup pizza, would succeed. Most said no.

Profitability

[400] Joshua Hyatt, "The Next Big Thing," *Inc.*, July 1990, p. 44.

Ten advantages offered by franchisers

1. Brand

Familiarity can be a powerful draw. A family with children will recognize the golden arches and know exactly what a meal there will be like. Someone with a Ford will know that factory parts will be installed at a dealer with that name on its sign. Someone looking for a mail drop may choose Mail Boxes Etc. out of familiarity, even though the drop is owned by an independent operator, who has bought the right to use that name, and the parent company gives no guarantee that service there will be more reliable than any other mail drop store. People tend to assume there is reliability behind a name brand, whether there is or not, and that helps draw customers. Coldwell Banker, a familiar name identified with high-quality service in the United States, does not necessarily take any responsibility for actions of real estate enterprises that operate under its logo in Mexico.

2. Formula

Franchisers put great stress in selling their franchise contracts on the idea that the contract gives an entrepreneur the right to start with a "proven" formula. Whether Colonel Sander's secret recipe, or McDonald's special sauce, some combination of features in the product or service offered claims to have a unique appeal to customers. These may seem simple, but they are harder to copy than it might seem. Independents who try find that out, and rarely manage to break into competition with established franchises.

Wendy's broke into the hamburger market against Burger King and McDonald's, but by operating differently, not just imitating. Wendy's offered fresh cooked, while the other two offered pre-cooked and warmed-over meat. That sometimes left Wendy's with fresh cooked meat that is not bought quickly enough to make a fresh burger. But they have used this as an opportunity. Chili is an alternative application for the cooked meat.

3. Procedures

Part of the franchise formula includes procedures for operating the business in the best way found by the franchiser. The franchisee will probably have no choice but to follow them, and the contract will say so. Food franchisees, for instance, don't have the option of trying out new recipes of their own unless given specific permission by the franchiser to do so.

4. Training

The franchiser will likely have its own training program to teach its franchisees the correct way to run the business. Typically, they will travel to the company headquarters for a few days to get this instruction.

5. Location help

Location matters for most franchisees, though not all. For instance, it is probably not critical that a Snap-on tool office be located to attract walk-in traffic. For fast food franchises, on the other hand, location is very important. Sometimes fast food outlets benefit by locating near their competitors, because together they can attract more customers overall than separately. The franchiser should gain location experience from each new franchisee, which can then be applied to others that follow.

6. Advertising help

Part of the contract may cover how the franchiser, who can spread advertising costs over multiple outlets, will help with advertising. For individual franchisees, it will cooperate in providing material and may also help with expenses. Or it may require that the franchisee contribute money for advertising, or both.

7. Purchasing volume price breaks

A selling point the franchiser will likely use will be the claim that it can gain volume discounts on very large bulk purchases of equipment and supplies that it then passes along to franchisees. As with several of the claimed benefits offered by franchisers, comparable advantages can often be gained by an independent through joining a trade association for the particular type of business.

8. Troubleshooting

If a franchisee has trouble with equipment, procedures, or unanticipated developments, the franchiser ideally should be available to help out. For franchisees who want to sell out, the franchiser may help with finding prospective buyers.

Ten advantages offered by franchisers (continued)

9. Research

The franchiser should be looking constantly for ways to improve performance of the formula to meet changing conditions or cope with moves of competitors. New equipment, recipes, ways of working, locating, advertising, and managing can help the franchiser by helping the franchisees. Company-owned, rather than franchisee, sites are typically used for this work.

10. Kindred spirits

Purchasing a franchise can be like joining a club whose members are owners of the same franchise in other locations with whom experiences can be profitably shared. For educating and updating franchisees, the franchiser will likely organize some meetings, typically at resort sites where franchisees can meet and learn from each other, get updates from the franchisee, relax, and enjoy themselves on a tax-deductible basis. Again, it should be noted, however, that trade associations offer many of these same benefits to enterprises in similar lines of business.

The first of these, a well-recognized brand, may be hardest to replace. McDonald's is highly vigilant in seeking out businesses that attach Mc to just about anything, except human beings whose names happen to start with those letters, and bring suit to stop such use. Franchisees who appreciate that importance pay much more for the right to use a strong brand than one less well known.

Some independents go to great lengths to attract attention as a substitute. A Seattle car dealer in the 1970s, for instance, advertised on TV by slamming a five-pound sledge hammer down on the hoods of some new cars. Amazingly, some customers came in specifically asking to buy those particular cars that had been hit.

End runs to franchising as a way of obtaining others of these ten advantages touted for franchising have been noted at some other points on the list, and the reader's imagination can probably generate further such ideas.

How economically attractive franchising is on average for an individual depends on the individual and how much he or she could make in other ways. Individuals who decide to take up franchising, according to one study in the U.K. by Stanworth and Kirby,[401] seem to be similar in background to those who become independent small business operators. Whether these two categories of entrepreneurs reap the same economic benefits, however, is an issue of stark disagreement, at least in the U.S.

A comparison between U.S. independent entrepreneurs and franchisees across 26 industrial categories reported in 1999 that an entrepreneur who self-selects into franchising could expect to earn $18,075 per year, whereas one who had no other alternative but to establish an independent business could expect to earn $3,957. The study also reported that an independent owner could expect to earn $19,704 as an independent owner, but as a franchisee that same person could expect to earn $90,882. Thus, the economic argument in favor of franchising seems to be quite strong.[402] The extent to which these higher profits for a franchisee should be discounted to take account of a higher required investment for the franchise fee was not noted.

Exhibit 9c-5 Proposed new pizza franchise sales and expense projections

Sales		520,000
Expenses		
Food purchases	140,400	
Other costs of goods	36,400	
Labor and benefits	145,600	
Royalty	20,800	
Advertising	26,000	
Land rent	25,000	
Utilities	15,000	
Delivery expenses	6,500	
Miscellaneous	28,900	
Depreciation	43,642	
Total expenses	488,242	
Net profit before tax		31,758

---

[401] John Stanworth and David A. Kirby, "Franchising and Franchising Entrepreneurship: Socio-Economic Considerations in Development," in *Research and the Marketing/Entrepreneurship Interface*, eds. Gerald E. Hills and others (Chicago: University of Illinois, 1993) p. 331.
[402] Darrell L. Williams, "Why Do Entrepreneurs Become Franchisees?" *Journal of Business Venturing*, Volume 14, Number 1, January 1999, p. 120.

Other authors have found a less attractive return for U.S. franchisees. Based on a sample of 71 franchisees in varied lines of business Michael and Moore found that the average return on investment in the business was 4.5 percent, which they characterize as "low given the risk of failure and the return compared to alternative financial instruments." They further note that franchisee profits averaged about 4 percent of sales, roughly the same as the franchisers' royalties. An implication seems to be that franchisers take away in royalties what they add in other ways to the franchisee's bottom line.[403]

How franchisers take away profitability was suggested in a study by Phan and Butler. These authors studied 160 entrepreneur-franchisees in the truck retailing industry and found that whereas franchisees were motivated to maximize profits, possibly by spending less to get additional sales, franchisers were motivated to maximize sales, even though that might run counter to franchisees' interests. Franchisers could not directly tell franchisees what to do, but they could influence them through such things as site visits, daily telephone calls, periodic network-wide conferences, and training programs.[404]

An even more negative picture of franchising was reported by Bates, who found that among small businesses started nationwide in 1986 and 1987, franchises generated average first-year pretax profits of negative $4,501, while independents averaged positive $15,511. This was despite the fact that annual sales by year-old franchisees in 1987 were $440,193, or more than five times the average of $86,489 for independents, and it was despite the fact that the franchised firms had more substantial investment as well, averaging $94,886 versus $29,329. He concludes that a main cause of dismal average results may be that many franchise buyers are simply naive.[405]

Although the average individual franchisee may or may not fare poorly, particularly considering the long hours of hard work, the top layer of most successful franchisees are still alleged to fare well, and likely some do. The secrets of such performance probably lie in straightforward application of good management disciplines, careful attention to many fine details and, above all, finding ways to motivate employees to provide exceptional service to customers.[406] It follows that someone who considers becoming a franchisee should analyze carefully the prospect of franchising and of any franchise chosen before signing up.

Survival claims

Claimed advantages of starting with a franchise are that the entrepreneur need not look further to find a business idea, need not invest time in puzzling out a plan for the business and learning how to pick a location, and may not have to search for financing, which the franchiser company may conveniently provide. There are also claims that odds of failing are lower, because the formula has already been proven to work at other locations. Doubt about the latter claim, at least, has appeared in the study of 2,994 firms by Cooper et al., which found no relationship between possession of a franchise or operation under a franchise name and survival three years after start-up.[407] No doubt survival of some franchises is higher than others.

Buy second-hand?

It might seem that a safer approach would be to buy a franchise already in operation, because then it will have a performance history for assessment. Franchises can be acquired second-hand as going concerns, just as can independent businesses. But unfortunately even the fact that the franchise may be well known and that the unit for sale may have records of its performance does not assure that the buyer is getting full value for the purchase price.

A 41-year-old Seattle man had worked independently in home remodeling and operating

---

[403] Steven C. Michael and Hollie J. Moore, "Returns to Franchising," in *Frontiers of Entrepreneurship Research*, 1994, eds. William D. Bygrave and others (Wellesley, MA: Babson Center for Entrepreneurial Studies, 1994) p. 601.

[404] Philip H. Phan and John E. Butler, "Entrepreneur-Franchisees: The Impact of Non-contractual Interactions" in *Frontiers of Entrepreneurship Research*, eds. William D. Bygrave and others (Wellesley, MA: Babson Center for Entrepreneurial Studies, 1994) p. 605.

[405] "Look Before You Leap," *Inc.*, July 1995, p. 24.

[406] Curtis Hartman, "The Best-Managed Franchises in America," *Inc.*, October 1989, p. 68.

[407] Cooper and others, *New Business in America*, p. 5.

his own auto generator repair shop. Through an acquaintance he learned of a transmission repair shop for sale operating under a well-known franchise. Records indicated that the present owner had been able to draw an income from the business that the prospective buyer found attractive.

Several days after taking over he was told by the employees that they had been promised raises and would quit if they did not receive them. Not knowing how he would replace them, the buyer agreed, and found his labor costs were now 70 percent of revenues instead of 60 percent. Shortly after that he found that many people who needed transmissions repaired were poorly prepared to pay cash for the work, and as a result his cash flow squeezed ever more tightly.

Total sales were also disappointingly below what they had been under the previous owner. Discussing this with workers in the shop, the buyer was told that prior management had seen to it that virtually every car brought into the shop for inspection was found to need expensive repairs urgently, regardless of its condition. Such a procedure had not occurred to the buyer, who prided himself on honest business practices.

Finally, order processing in the shop, he found, was sloppy. Estimates were lost, there was no way to trace labor costs on jobs, transmission parts could not be found, and it was impossible to reconcile the company checkbook. To correct these problems, the buyer started a job-numbering system to trace labor and parts costs, hired a part-time bookkeeper to reconcile accounts, negotiated with a finance company to provide cash with which customers could pay for work, and raised prices to cover his increased labor costs.

Sales, however, continued to lag, and the buyer consequently resold the business at a loss, took a job elsewhere, and struggled to collect from the new buyer, who soon had trouble making payments due on the shop.

Thus this entrepreneur shifted from one strategy to a second. The first was to operate as a franchisee. The second was to buy and resell a franchise already in operation. There is reason for a newcomer to beware this approach, not just because it did not work for this particular situation, but because both the franchiser and others with existing franchises will know about it first, be in better positions to assess it, and be

more likely to pick it off, if it is truly promising, leaving for newcomers only the rejects.

The other two most likely ways to make substantial profits on franchises are either to find a successful business formula and sell it by becoming a franchiser or to acquire multiples of franchises, if possible in the early days of a to-be-successful franchise, before the price of it has gone up.[408]

Drive of independence

Personal aspects can play an important role in performance. One advantage, perhaps the most important one of all, possessed by the independent non-franchise entrepreneur is the intense motivation that comes with independence, carrying all the risks, and reaping all the gains that come with independence. The manager of a company outlet has to be motivated by the attractions offered employees, pay, possibly bonuses, and the comfort that may come with letting someone else do most of the worrying about success or failure of the business. These motivations, although they may be sufficient to draw excellent work from some people, are likely less intense than those of independent venturing.

The franchiser hopes to capture as much as possible of those independent venture motivations. The franchisee, like the independent entrepreneur, risks the financing, has more independence than the paid manager and a tighter connection to the bottom line of the outlet. But the risk may not be as great, and certainly the independence will not be as great as that of the independent entrepreneur. So motivation may be compromised for the franchisee, and that may be a handicap on the franchise outlet as compared to one that is independent.

From franchisee to independent

Franchising is not for everyone, as illustrated by the following example.

I had a Burger Chef franchise when I was 21. It was terrible. I was thrown into two weeks of training at a hamburger school, and I didn't understand anything. I worked seven days a week, 12 to 15 hours a day. I took off one afternoon for my wife's uncle's funeral. I didn't know what was going on. I

---

[408] Jeannie Ralston, "Franchisees Who Think Big," *Venture*, March 1989, p. 55.

couldn't tell day from night—for seven months. I must have been one of the worst managers Burger Chef ever had. But I had so many things go wrong. We were in a shopping center that was under construction, and there was a big economic crisis. Interest rates shot through the roof. So they stopped building the shopping center and shut down the road in front of us. The whole thing was a disaster. My father-in-law helped finance the deal, and we lost everything he put into it—$70,000.[409]

This same entrepreneur later became highly successful in building an independent venture, American Photo Group, which he sold to Eastman Kodak for an estimated $45 million.

The pattern here of an entrepreneur failing at a franchise in spite of the competitive advantages it should give but succeeding as an independent may seem unlikely. But, according to Bates, it is more widespread than generally realized. He cites another example, this time of a person older than the one just described above.

Leo Weissman, 51 years old with an advanced degree in mathematics, left a career at IBM and used his retirement savings to buy a fast-food franchise. After spending $120,000 unsuccessfully trying to make a profit, and with the franchiser demanding that he invest another $60,000, he gave it up. A year later he had set up an independent ice cream shop of his own, was bringing in higher revenues than he had with the franchise, had lower costs, likely thanks in no small measure to the absence of an annual royalty, and was optimistic about the future.[410]

Bates goes on to present statistics that clash with those of the International Franchise Association, which claims that 97 percent of franchises opened nationwide were still in operation five years later. His own survey found that whereas 62 percent of independents were still running their start-ups five years later the rest having either sold the business (6 percent) or shut down (32 percent), only 54 percent of franchisees were doing so, the rest having either sold out (8 percent) or shut down the business (38 percent).

3. Choice

3. Choice

Starting points

An obvious question is which particular lines of business might be acceptable, not just to invest in, own, or even to manage, but also to enter and work in at the ground level. Taking on a franchise business is not an absentee activity. The daily work activities—selling and serving customers personally, hiring, demonstrating what employees should do and how, keeping track of details, and following them up, all of which can involve long hours of hard work for a specific business—must be acceptable.

Ideas for franchises categories to consider can quickly be found through searching online, from advertisements that appear in publications such as *The Wall Street Journal* and *Entrepreneur* magazine, or by attending franchise trade shows that appear periodically in major cities. Some franchisers and some franchisees will provide historical profit information on a personal basis. Others won't.

Starting points

Following up any such leads will yield further information about any particular franchise, but is also likely to produce requests for personal information about the person who wants it. Providing details should then yield further information in return as both parties weigh the value to be gained by spending more information exchange effort. The starting points for five people interviewed by Tomzack who successfully resolved the matter of personal fit were as follows:[411]

Corporate subsidiary president laid off. Preferences: No overhead, no salaried employees, operate from home, customer continuity so not always selling, residual income buildup, new franchise with prime areas still available. Source: Franchise show. Choice: Unishippers, a shipping service for smaller users.

— • —

[409] "Thriving on Order," *Inc.*, December 1989, p. 47.
[410] "Look Before You Leap," p. 23.
[411] Mary E. Tomzack, *Tips and Traps When Buying a Franchise* (New York: McGraw-Hill, 1994) p. 33.

Auto agency manager, highly paid, but over-worked. Preferences: Recession-proof, repetitive, low-capital intensity, low overhead, minimal franchiser oversight. Choice: Wedding Pages, a wedding information publication selling advertising.

— • —

Fortune 500 glass ceiling. Preferences: No high-tech, no food, professional service, high ethics, well managed, a whole region available. Choice: Ledger Plus, a young accounting service for small firms.

— • —

Computer software and hardware sales. Choice: Fastsigns, a sign company. Appeal: Fast, clean, computer-oriented, and industry-driven. Others Rejected: Retail card shop, frozen yogurt shop. Why Rejected: Performance too dominated by location.

— • —

Employee opposed to company relocation. Preferences: Customers come without cold calls, niche without high-powered competition, repeat business, no major capital requirement. Choice: Check Express, a check cashing service.

While these venturers formulated preferences and then searched for franchises that fit those preferences, still others in the sample followed a different searching approach. They simply scanned available franchises and responded to those that appealed most.

Tomzack also reported sad stories among her sample of franchisees, but those were not described. Mistakes were made, she indicated, when prospective franchisees did not apply enough effort to investigating their alternatives. Failure to appreciate the kind of work involved, time requirements, personal interests, and capacities can lead to poor choice, both of whether to buy a franchise and, if so, which particular franchise.

Costs to the franchisee

In return for franchise privileges, the franchisee pays either an up-front franchise fee and/or a royalty on sales. An informal survey of 50 widely varied franchisees in 1994 found that franchise fees ranged upward from under $5,000 for only 2 percent of the sample to over $30,000 for 14 percent of the sample. Annual royalties as a percent of sales in the sample ranged from zero for 8 percent of the sample to over 10 percent for a comparable fraction of the sample, with most (48 percent) clustering in the range of 5 to 6 percent.[412] Some indication of how those figures had changed by 2008 can be seen in the examples of Exhibit 9c-6.[413]

Of as much or more interest, perhaps, was how franchisees felt about their enterprise. Over half said they were completely satisfied, while only 2 percent said they were totally unsatisfied. How bad a figure the latter is depends, of course, on how many franchisees did not report their dissatisfaction because they had already left the business.

Satisfaction level

Franchisee satisfaction level was investigated by Spinelli and Birley. From results of a questionnaire with 81 variables answered by 51 franchisees they reported that just over half (59 percent) were satisfied, while 19 percent were ambivalent, and 14 percent were angry.[414] Unfortunately, the study did not delve into what seemed to make the differences. So whether, for instance, it is better for would-be franchisees to seek out larger, better-established franchisers or newer and smaller ones, remains an open question. More powerful ones are probably safer, but probably cost more money,

Exhibit 9c-6 *Franchise cost comparisons*

Name	Offering	Began	Franchised	Royalty	Fee($)	Startup costs($)
Subway	Sandwiches	1965	1974	8%	15K	76.1K–227.8K
Zero's Subs	Sandwiches	1967	1996	5%	20.0K	138K–242K
Buffalo	Chicken wings	1982	1991	5%	42.5K	842.2K–2.9M
Wings Over	Chicken wings	2000	2002	4%	20.0K	156.2K–338K
Curves	Women fitness	1992	1995	5–6%	44.9K	31.4K–53.5K
Gold's Gym	Men fitness	1965	1980	3%	25.0K	961.5K–3.6M

[412] Tomzack, *Tips and Traps*, p. 33.
[413] "Meet the Winners, Top 10 Franchises for 2008," *Entrepreneur*, January 2008.
[414] Stephen Spinelli, Jr. and Sue Birley, "A Multivariate Assessment of Franchisee Satisfaction," in *Frontiers of Entrepreneurship Research* 1994, eds. William D. Bygrave and others (Wellesley, MA: Babson Center for Entrepreneurial Studies, 1994) p. 607.

impose tighter restrictions, and yield smaller returns on investment.

Self assessment

Important aside from financial considerations is the extent to which the entrepreneur will find the work of franchisee satisfying. A franchise contract typically places very significant restrictions on flexibility in managing. What products or services to offer, how to make them, how much to charge, how to advertise, what decor to have in the store, and how to run operations may all be tightly controlled by the franchiser, leaving the franchisee feeling more like a middle manager or shop worker than an entrepreneur. Perceptions vary among franchisees, however, and some see their work as more entrepreneurial than others.[415]

Consequently, self assessment becomes important. Which fits better, a regular job, an independent start-up, or the somewhat in-between option, becoming a franchisee? This question applies at two stages in the search process. First, is a franchise the thing to look for based upon the general properties of that approach relative to the others? Second, if it does, then after one or more candidate franchise opportunities has been identified, again how good is the fit? The nice thing about franchises is that it is easy to find many legitimate ones to pick from, and if one does not fit, there are plenty of others in view.

At the more general level, some questions to consider are

1. Does it seem likely that a good independent venture idea can be found or is already in view, or does seeking a franchise, with its limitations, seem better?

2. Is working within the confines of a franchise contract going to be more comfortable than taking a job or starting independently?

3. Are personal savings adequate to cover the franchise fee and the negative cash flow associated with initiating options?

4. Would it be better to buy the business of an existing franchisee who wants to leave it and move on?

5. Are the long hours of work and possible monotony of operating a franchise acceptable, or alternatively, could someone else be hired to do it without intolerably reducing profit and return on investment?

4. Checkout

Effort to seek out satisfactory franchise propositions can logically begin with adopting skepticism about representativeness of the advertisements with smiling or earnestly contented faces, and about the red carpet treatment that may be rolled out when the franchisee visits the franchiser's sales office. Prudence argues for careful data-gathering and analysis, and for visiting other franchisees of the firm to learn about their experience with that franchise. A list of current franchisees may be found in the franchiser's Uniform Franchise Offering Circular, which will be described shortly. If not, and if the franchiser is not willing to provide them, it is probably a signal that merits heed.

Because of some franchiser abuses in the past, laws have been developed to curb and control them, and these vary from state to state. Consequently, it is advisable to engage a lawyer who specializes in franchises and has extensive experience in the state where the entrepreneur's business is to be located. Checking not only with other franchisees who have bought from the same franchiser, but also with some of their employees is another obvious precaution to take before buying. The Chamber of Commerce, the Better Business Bureau, and banking connections may also be able to add helpful information to that which will be provided by the franchiser.

It seems natural, both from a neoclassical economic perspective, as noted by Spinelli and Birley,[416] and also from observation for there to be both an alliance and a tension with poten-

---

[415] Cecilia M. Falbe, Ajith Kumar, and Thomas C. Dandridge, "Industry and Firm Influences on Entrepreneurial Behavior Among Franchisees," in *Frontiers of Entrepreneurship Research*, 1989, eds. Robert H. Brockhaus, Sr. and others (Wellesley, MA: Babson Center for Entrepreneurial Studies, 1989) p. 559.

[416] Steve Spinelli and Sue Birley, "Toward a Theory of Conflict in the Franchise System," *Journal of Business Venturing*, Volume 11, Number 5, September 1996, p. 339.

tial of creating dissatisfaction between the franchiser and franchisee. Both want the franchisee to succeed, because that way they both make money. But the franchisee will favor the idea of more help from the franchiser in such things as advertising and possibly training, whereas the franchiser sees these as benefits for which the franchisee should pay. Moreover, the franchiser wants to protect such interests as the trade name and reputation, while the franchisee will likely feel urges toward more independence and freedom of action. The franchiser in some ways has the upper hand, and in others does not. Laws provide important safeguards for franchisees. Ways that a franchiser may run up against them appear in Exhibit 9c-7 below.

How problems can arise between franchisers and franchisees as regards control of supply sources is illustrated by the following example.

Chicken Delight, a franchiser, required all franchisees to buy from it such things as packaging items (paper plates, spoons, napkins), food (batter preparation and barbecue sauce), and equipment (fryers made by Chicken Delight) at higher prices than franchisees would be able to buy them elsewhere. Unhappy franchisees banded together and filed a class action suit, claiming that this was a "tying arrangement" and therefore a violation of the Sherman Antitrust Act.

A tying arrangement means that a seller offers two separate items for sale but will not sell the first item unless the buyer agrees to buy the second item. Whether that is illegal or not depends on how dominant the seller is on the first item, whether substantial interstate commerce is involved, and how logically justifiable the tying is. In this case, the first item would be the franchise and the second would be the supplies and equipment.

The judge ruled that this situation did represent a tie, that the company's trademark gave it market dominance, and that there was a "not insubstantial" amount of interstate commerce involved, but left open the question of logical justification on the basis that perhaps there was need for the franchiser to control quality and to protect the company trademark. This last issue was decided by a jury in favor of the franchisees.

Moreover, beyond that, the court held that damage was done to the franchisees by overcharging them for the tied products. Chicken Delight tried to argue that the overcharge was simply an added fee for the use of the trademark to compensate for the fact that no separate charge for such use was imposed. But the court replied that careful reading of the franchise agreement indicated that no such additional charge was to be imposed.[418]

Exhibit 9c-7 Control by franchisers and some legal boundaries[417]

Control desired	Justification	Legal risk
Site selection	Expertise, desire to space outlets	Liability if selection is incompetent
Premises Appearance	Uphold company reputation, defend trade dress (similar to trademark)	Liability for injury to customers or for violation of environmental or disability laws
Hours open	Consistent service to public	Franchisee may legally become an employee
Things sold	Defend quality reputation	Possible antitrust violation
Supply sources	Protect secret formulas, maintain quality	Antitrust violation
Resale prices	Protect competitive position, keep franchisee solvent	Sherman antitrust violation
Bookkeeping procedures	Assure orderly and consistent records, regardless of franchisee skill and understanding	Possible price-fixing scheme or tie-in violation of antitrust laws
Advertising and promotion	Protect company image, marks, and logos	May run afoul of price-fixing laws
Customers	Prevent sales to discounter	May be antitrust violation

[417] Glickman, *Franchising* (New York: Matthew Bender, 1996) p. 93.

Illustrated by the Chicken Delight example is how complex the legal issues can become that result from a seemingly simple dispute over whether the franchiser can rightfully specify what items must be used as part of doing business under its name by the franchisee. Even if it cannot specify whom the items must be bought from, it can still write specifications for their makeup.

What, moreover, constitutes market dominance was not clean cut either, but rather was debated in terms of quantity sold or degree of competition, each of which leaves open the question of "how much is too much?" The fact that the franchisees won in this case, and remember they ganged up to do it, does not mean that another franchisee would necessarily win, even in a somewhat similar case. Thus, buying a franchise can open the door to risk of having to litigate if the franchiser does something unfair, and the litigation can be a costly affair with a chancy outcome, particularly for a thinly financed franchisee up against a wealthy franchiser.

To ward off disappointment and potential litigation later, a major informative document for any prospective franchisee to read with care is the franchiser's obligatory Uniform Franchise Offering Circular (UFOC). Government guidelines require that it cover the following, here oversimplified, 23 topics as shown in Exhibit 9c-8, and it may be several hundred pages long. A copy must be filed with the state government, where it becomes public information.

In spite of a carefully written contract and UFOC, legal problems can still arise leading to expensive court battles. Relevant lagal princi-

Exhibit 9c-8 Summary of UFOC contents

1. Concise description of the franchiser, what it offers, its history, predecessors, trade names, and address.
2. Five-year business experience description of the franchiser's executives.
3. History of litigation against the company or its key people over the preceding 10 years.
4. Indication of any bankruptcy filings by the franchiser or its directors during the past 15 years.
5. Initial franchise fee, terms of payment, how the money will be used, whether they have been changing over time, and whether refund is an option.
6. Other fees including royalties, advertising, insurance, training, accounting, audit, consulting, or other charges in connection with the franchise deal.
7. Estimate of initial investment the franchisee must make for such things as fixed assets and working capital, as well as who gets the money and whether refunds are possible.
8. Restrictions or requirements as to sources of supply the franchisee must or must not use, and whether the franchiser receives payments from any required suppliers.
9. Requirements of the franchisee to buy according to stated specifications.
10. Any financing programs for the franchisee offered by the franchiser.
11. Service and support, such as training, site selection, market research, and advertising to be provided by the franchiser.
12. Any exclusive territorial rights given by the franchiser to the franchisee.
13. A list of any trade names, trademarks, service marks, logos registered, and a list of the states where they have been used.
14. Patents and copyrights held by the franchiser.
15. Any obligations of the franchisee to participate actively in the business.
16. Any limits on commercialization of goods or services by the franchiser.
17. Rules about renewal, termination, repurchase, modification, or assignment of the franchise agreement.
18. Any arrangement for endorsements of the franchise by public figures.
19. Optionally, any actual or projected financial performance figures. There is no requirement to provide them, but the franchiser can if it wishes to.
20. Information on number of franchises sold, in operation, terminated (including reasons), and signed but not in operation, as well as the number of company-owned branches.
21. Financial statements of the franchiser.
22. Copy of the franchise agreement that is to be signed.
23. Acknowledge of receipt by the franchisee.

---

[418] "Siegel versus Chicken Delight, *Inc.*," *Georgia Law Review*, Vol. 5, Number 1, Fall 1970, p. 151.

ples for the franchiser to keep in mind include that (1) having proof is essential to win against a franchiser, (2) if the franchiser sold the deal in bad faith and it can be proven, the franchiser can lose, (3) contracts are presumed by the legal system to have an implied covenant to deal fairly and not deny to a party something the contract was supposed to let them have, and (4) a signed contract carries a tremendous amount of weight in case of dispute.

Pitfalls

Pitfalls that others have run into in dealing with franchisers in the past, notwithstanding governmental rules, have included those shown in Exhibit 9c-9. Many of the problems that might arise, however, are difficult to anticipate either with or without a list.

Although location is not highly important for some businesses, such as plumbing shops, tax services, and to some degree travel agencies and real estate offices, it can be crucial for other businesses such as hotels and restaurants. That, after all, is why commercial real estate rents for such higher prices in some areas than in others.

Encroachment can be a major source of grief for a franchisee, and so is something to be worried out in signing a franchise agreement. It happens when a franchiser in effect undercuts the market of a franchisee by (1) allowing other outlets with its brand to open up sufficiently nearby as to take away customers, (2) making its products or services available through a different channel that takes away sale from the franchisee, or (3) letting its trademark be used in other ways so that pulling power in sales is lost for the franchisee.

From a franchisee's point of view, one of the worst things that can happen is for a franchiser, after having sold the contract to the franchisee, collected the fee, and possibly some years of operating royalties, to set up a company outlet or allow another franchisee to open up sufficiently close by as to take away business from the first franchisee in the area. From the franchiser's point of view, this is a natural way to collect more fees and royalties. From the franchisee's standpoint, it is destructive competition. So specification of territorial rights is a highly important provision in franchise agreements.

Following are three examples illustrating disputes that went to court:

> Adrian Eichman, a franchisee of Fotomat, sued it as franchiser on a list of complaints and lost right down the line. He claimed that Fotomat:
>
> 1. Breached its contract with him by putting company branches near his store that took away business from him. But the court said his contract did not explicitly give him exclusive territory.
>
> 2. Wrongly would not permit him to relocate his store. But the court said the contract said Fotomat had discretion regarding location.
>
> 3. Overcharged him for supplies. But the court noted that he did buy from other suppliers with no objection from Fotomat, even though the contract said he should ask Fotomat for permission.
>
> 4. Failed to live up to its agreement to maintain his store. The court noted that Fotomat did repair some chairs and that although some plants or shrubs died from lack of water, Eichman did not prove that he lost money by that.
>
> 5. Failed to notify him of promotions. The court noted that the contract did not require it to.[419]

Exhibit 9c-9 Pitfalls some have encountered with franchisers

- Formats that may sound good but don't really work
- Promises of training that are not fulfilled
- Fees and charges by franchisers that eliminate franchisee profits
- Franchisees becoming stuck with unsalable inventory from the franchiser
- Promises of advertising that are not fulfilled
- High-pressure selling that does not allow the prospective franchisee to evaluate sensibly
- Failure to reveal negative aspects of the franchise firm's past performance
- Failure by the franchisee to appreciate just what it will be like to work for the franchiser
- Failure by the franchisee to obtain input from other franchisees and a qualified franchise lawyer before signing the franchiser's contract

[419] "Eichman v. Fotomat," *Federal Reporter*, Second Series, Volume 880, p. 149.

Vylene, a restaurateur who went bankrupt, blamed it on a franchiser, Naugles, under whom she operated successfully for a while. But then things went bad and she went bankrupt. She sued, saying failure occurred because the franchiser opened a company store nearby that reduced her sales by 35 percent. The franchiser argued that there was nothing in the franchise agreement giving her exclusive territorial rights, just as in the Fotomat case above. But this time the franchiser lost because he had violated an "implied covenant of good faith and fair dealing," and she was entitled to expect that the franchiser would "not act to destroy the right of the franchisee to enjoy the fruits of the contract." He had, the court said, acted in bad faith when he had:

- Kept and hid vendor rebates she was supposed to get.
- Tried to physically take over her operations, firing many of her employees.
- Resisted her attempt to open an unrelated restaurant, causing her to lose her home and ownership in other businesses.

- Given out coupons in her area for promotions she could not be offering.
- Raided her employees to work in a company-owned store.[420]

— . —

Steven Scheck sued Burger King claiming it damaged his business by letting Marriott open another Burger King two miles away. His contract did not give him any exclusive territorial rights. It was not disputed that a Burger King vice president had told him and several franchisees together at a company meeting that he could not believe that the company would allow Marriott to do what it subsequently was allowed to do. The court said it was the written contract that ruled. Scheck lost.

An obvious lesson from such experience is to check out the franchise contract with care before signing. If it does not specify an exclusive territory, there isn't one. A host of other lessons have been learned by franchisees over time, some from happier and others from unhappier experiences. Examples include those listed in Exhibit 9c-10.

Exhibit 9c-10 Some lessons franchisees have learned

- *The contract is negotiable until signed, and then is not. So do the checking first.*
- *Beware and compute the high impact of top line royalty upon bottom line income. A 5-percent royalty takes away half of a 10-percent bottom line.*
- *Selling is the central activity in most franchises, so relish that activity or don't become a franchisee.*
- *Working in a franchise or firm similar to the one of interest for a while can be a good way to size it up.*
- *Before buying a franchise, browse some trade journals in its field and talk to some independents in that field to learn how attractive they think buying a franchise in it would be, as well as how else they would recommend entering that field.*
- *Expect vanishingly small personal income for the first year or two at least in opening a franchise.*
- *Concepts that can be franchised spawn more franchisers until saturation occurs and some fail, leaving the rest, and their franchisees, with thin margins. What rules and policies apply regarding saturation of local markets?*
- *If profits do manage to rise over the years and the business is put up for sale, how many years will the franchise contract still have to run (about 10 years total is typical), and what effect might that have on a prospective buyer?*

5. Moves

The more seriously interested the entrepreneur becomes in a particular franchise, the more digging will likely be called for in checking out both that franchise and the idea of buying a franchise at all, perhaps versus going to work for a similar business in any capacity and then starting a new one in the preferred field of interest. If by good work and luck such a start-up became successful, the entrepreneur then might consider creating a franchise around it. Thereby the entrepreneur might capitalize on having studied earlier the alternative of buying a franchise in the first place.

---

[420] "Vylene v. Naugles," *Federal Reporter*, Third Series, Volume 90, p. 1472.

Making visits

Many things to consider investigating have already been described. An obvious early choice is to check out periodical and Web sources for written information. Beyond that should come visits to a variety of places, including franchise outlets and their operators, franchise trade shows, and eventually franchisers themselves. Different questions to explore will fit with the different sources. How they might vary is illustrated in the list in Exhibit 9c-11.

Early conversations with franchisers can take place at shows. If one or more offerings becomes of serious interest, those conversations will become more intense, and if pursued still further, will likely lead to visiting a franchiser's home office.

Preparing to visit the home office

Corporate headquarters is the franchiser's home turf, and the franchiser will likely have given serious thought, extended by experience with having prospective franchisees visit, to how the signing of a contract and collection of money from them can be brought about. Quite possibly red carpets, nice lunches, gracious offices, glossy brochures, and cordial, maybe even deferential, behavior may be part of the show.

Assess how ready management is to share and discuss its UFOC. If they say they can't legally

Exhibit 9c-11 Different questions for different sources

1. **Checking the contract**
   a. What conditions and time periods apply for upgrades of the shop?
   b. What would be required for reselling the franchise?
   c. How can fees change or the contract expire?
   d. Are there requirements to participate in anything or to permit inspections?
   e. What equipment or supplies must the franchisee buy and from whom?
   f. Are specific working hours and days of operation required?
   g. What rules about territory saturation with other outlets may apply?

2. **Checking with industry sources, including meeting competitors at a franchising expo**
   a. How does the franchiser's display and presentation compare to others?
   b. How many franchisees has this franchiser had for how long?
   c. What is the financial condition and performance record of the franchiser?
   d. How have performance claims compared to historical performance?
   e. What has been the franchiser's legal history and litigation?
   f. What is the franchiser's reputation generally?

3. **Visiting other franchisees (maybe try working for one or for a similar business)**
   a. Based on observation, how consistent are standards among outlets?
   b. What are other franchisees' backgrounds and how into the work are they?
   c. Did the franchiser provide adequate training and help as promised?
   d. How well has the franchiser responded to calls and problems?
   e. How reasonable has been the price relative to the return?
   f. Will you get the same deal they got?
   g. Have there been hidden charges and requirements, like equipment tie-ins?
   h. Would they advise buying a used franchise from someone who wants to get out?

4. **Asking the franchiser (remembering information from other sources)**
   a. What has been the rate of sales versus loss of new units?
   b. How fast did what percent of outlets become how profitable?
   c. What litigation is in progress or anticipated?
   d. Have there been fee and rule changes over the years?
   e. What has been the rate of product changes and their profitability?
   f. How stable have relationships with suppliers been?
   g. What changes in franchiser management or ownership have occurred or are expected?

Entering negotiations

Aiming farther

discuss typical financial figures of their units, be suspicious. It isn't true.

Learn about the franchiser's advertising policies and how much they will help the particular outlet under consideration, as opposed to their outlets in general or, worst of all, simply the recruitment of other franchisees. And assess carefully the completeness, usability, and likely helpfulness of the operating manuals and training program that go with the franchise.

Entering negotiations

It may take conscious effort to retain skepticism when visiting the franchiser's headquarters. When the franchiser says it cares more strongly about other characteristics of a prospective franchisee than the financial resources of the franchisee ("What we care about is you"), beware.

Consider relative bargaining strengths. Better-known franchises get customers much faster at the start, so are probably worth more. Similar franchises in an area may indicate that it draws the traffic desired. Competition sometimes kills off and other times helps all competitors. Keep thinking.

New franchises are riskier and should be correspondingly cheaper. With less well-known franchisers, it should be possible to drive a harder bargain. Often things that should be negotiable aren't and other things claimed to be non-negotiable actually are negotiable. How much harder it would be to create the same business independent of a franchiser?

Aiming farther

Four ways to use franchising as a path to greater prosperity are to (1) buy and sell franchises, rather than simply operating one, (2) acquire a second nearby franchise, then others to achieve economies of scale, (3) acquire a master franchise that can perhaps give not only more existing outlets but also the option of actually starting still more within an area, and (4) become a franchiser rather than remaining simply a franchisee. In the following example three founders were stymied in seeking to pursue the third of these options, a master franchise, and followed instead the fourth, becoming franchisers.

> The father of Aaron, Michael, and Simon Serruya had been a bagel shop franchisee, and was willing to lend them $100,000 in 1985 to buy master franchise rights in Canada, their home, from a major U.S. frozen yogurt franchiser. Aaron recalled, "I was 19 at the time, and Mike was 20. We didn't get much respect when we went to see those franchisers."
>
> In response, they hired help with the money to design their own store. Michael engaged a design firm on the concept for a new company, Yogen Fruz, while Aaron worked with a food technician to develop the menu. The first store opened in 1986 and was so profitable that they were able to repay their father six months later. From there they franchised the concept and expanded to 3,600 stores in 81 countries by 1997 with total sales of $360 million.[421]

This chapter concludes examination of ways to enter business, whether by creating a new one, buying from somebody else a company that is already ongoing, or copying with guidance the business developed by a franchiser. The next two chapters look beyond entry to what follows that. How the business grows or not, what problems may arise if it does, how can they be handled, and finally, what path the entrepreneur may choose beyond the creation process, and possibly beyond ownership of the business will be topics of the two concluding chapters of the book.

---

[421] Charlotte Mulhern, "The Big Chill," *Entrepreneur*, January 1998, p. 190.

Exercises

Text discussion questions

1. Why do both franchises and independents exist in competition, rather than one winning out and eliminating the other?
2. How might the personal nature of a happy franchisee, a happy franchiser, and a happy independent in the same line of work compare and contrast?
3. What determines what lines of industrial activity are best suited to franchising versus independent businesses?
4. Why has government regulation come to apply to franchising?
5. What might explain the fact that some franchise firms operate company-owned branch outlets while others do not?

Case questions

9C-1 Raheed Sahemi

1. What cautions for Raheed are raised by topics in this chapter?
2. In what ways is the Temploy franchise attractive versus unattractive?
3. What further information about Raheed might help you decide what he should do?
4. What plan of action would you recommend for Raheed based on the case information?

Portfolio page possibilities

Page 9C-1 Pick a franchise

From a recent *Entrepreneur* magazine's "500 issue," pick and compare two franchises you find most interesting. Tell which you would find more attractive to own yourself, and explain your reasoning plus what further you would seek to learn about it to be sure, and how.

Page 9C-2 Franchise versus independent

Observe a local company and describe as best you can imagine the pros and cons of attempting to start and operate it as an independent entrepreneur versus as a franchisee.

Page 9C-3 History of entry strategies

Interview local business owners until you find one who is a franchisee and one in a similar business who is not. Compare their approaches for entering and operating their businesses.

Page 9C-4 Critique a UFOC

Browse some UFOCs (either by visiting a state office or obtaining one either from a local franchisee or a franchiser's magazine or newspaper advertisement) for franchisees licensed in your state, then compare and critique two.

Page 9C-5 UFOC versus a business

Interview local business owners until you find one who is a franchisee. Obtain a copy of the UFOC for that franchise and critique it in view of whatever you can observe about the actual business in operation.

Term Projects

Venture history

1. How did the entrepreneur decide to become a franchisee, rather than start a company independently or buy an ongoing company?
2. How were candidate franchises identified and prioritized?
3. What was done to check the franchise out?
4. What tactics did the franchiser use to sell the franchise?
5. How fully did the franchiser's promises come true?
6. How, in hindsight, did buying a franchise compare to start-up or buyout?

Venture planning guide

Write out a full work plan for carrying out a franchise of your choice.

Part 10

DOWNSTREAM

This book is focused on becoming a business owner successfully. Most entrepreneurs undertake that through creation of a new firm. Others, less numerous, attempt it through takeover of going concerns. Important either way is to have the business prosper and pay off adequately longer term. Anticipating that longer-term goal should be part of designing entry into business via either path.

The next two chapters are intended to tie into that design process. The first explores growth. The second and last considers paths by which the entrepreneur may move on first from management and eventually from ownership in the venture.

Growth of the business, both in terms of speed and extent, which combine to form a trajectory of the venture's size over time, will be considered first. An important question is how much influence the entrepreneur can have over that and through what choices. Some ventures grow while most do not, and there can be a tendency in hindsight to give credit to whomever was in charge if the growth was high. Probably it is safe to say at least that management did not prevent whatever growth occurred, although it probably could have, and it seems reasonable to recognize that. But it is also reasonable to consider elements of luck involved.

If growth doesn't occur, then there may be inclination to think that perhaps management actually did not want it, and some managements don't. Or if management wanted but did not achieve it, then an obvious explanation to consider is if elements beyond its control have caused shortfall. Even if a competitor succeeded while the venture did not, there may be identifiable differences between the two firms other than management that explain their contrasting performances. Or maybe, in fact, management did make the difference.

When growth does occur it often introduces new problems that to some extent are similar among ventures. Their patterns and ways of mitigating their undesirable effects will be covered, although not in depth. How to influence growth and how to respond to such problems as it may cause are obviously topics too broad and complex to explore in only a chapter or even two. But considering them can provide leads for further learning.

The same can be said for examining the longer-run careers of entrepreneurs beyond business entry. How might they depend upon personal capabilities and preferences, how the venture goes, and what personal options present themselves to the entrepreneur downstream from venture entry? Certainly, it will matter to the entrepreneur and likely it will consequently matter to the venture. Hence, this topic, which was introduced in the first chapter of the book, will be raised again in concluding.

CHAPTER 10A – Trajectories

Topics

1. Staying small
2. Growing from within
3. Success drivers longer term
4. Coping with growth
5. Growing through acquisition

Checkpoints

a. Why do some firms grow more than others?
b. What limits a firm's growth?
c. At what points is growth trajectory determined and how?
d. How much choice does an entrepreneur have at start-up about growth?
e. What are the main theories of success causes?
f. How should an entrepreneur decide how much growth to aim for?
g. Illustrate the roles of design versus luck in achieving growth.

Three broad alternatives for longer-term development of the new venture will be considered in this chapter: having the venture remain small, growing the venture from within, and growing it through acquisition of other firms. Sometimes there may be little or no freedom to choose among these. Still, it may be possible to foresee and plan for coping with some challenges likely to arise.

1. Staying small

As discussed in the first chapter, there are different types of ventures and roles that a would-be entrepreneur can hope for, possibly aim for, or maybe even choose. The variety of possible venture trajectories in terms of growth in sales, employment, and profits is virtually limitless. Some enterprises end before making a single sale. Others go on to unimagined success. In between, most new ventures never grow large. The overwhelming majority peak out with fewer than five full-time employees.

Enterprises that defy expansion to large size include top-quality restaurants, although a few manage to achieve multiple outlets, and lines of work where personal attention or individual art is important, such as portrait photography, dance, martial arts, and acting studios. A master artist may supervise a ring of subordinates, assistants, and apprentices, but the firm's perimeter is still limited by the central personage unless the work can be reduced to a formula. Franchising or chaining as a growth strategy works only for enterprises reducible to routines.

Tool and die shops that make special tooling to order, and similarly job machine shops that make single items or small production batches, usually stay small. They can't be developed as chains or franchises because they specialize in the exceptional rather than the repetitive. They typically do not advertise and may not even have marketing departments, but instead let orders come to them based on their reputations for special expertise. If more orders come than they can handle, they may add a few employees temporarily, then shrink again, or more likely, they will simply quote slower delivery dates and perhaps thereby deflect additional business elsewhere. Sometimes then some of the more skilled employees may accommodate delayed customers by taking work home, which in turn leads to them forming their own new, and small, shops.

In contrast, some start-ups in other industries grow large fast on trajectories that go steeply upward from inception by capitalizing on a few products or services that can be standardized for sale to expanding numbers of customers. In an earlier age, development of the Otis elevator was an example of a strong take-off trajectory with fast growth continuing from the outset as ever taller buildings were constructed. Auto companies did the same later, then electronics companies. More recently, of course, microcomputer, software and Internet companies have followed fast-growth patterns, as may companies in genetics technology and green energy.

Between the extreme trajectories of stable smallness and fast take-off are intermediate firms that may start less spectacularly, rise a bit, flatten off at a fairly low level, then later take off steeply upward. Some with this pattern have included Ball Brothers (canning jars), Bissell Carpet Sweepers, Xerox, McDonald's, and Starbucks. Ben and Jerry's started as an ice cream scoop shop very slowly, mainly concerned simply about surviving ("Our slow-growth strategy wasn't one"[422]), then stumbled upon better combinations, such as delivering to grocery stores and emphasizing liberal social values, and through experimentation, progressed from small to an ever steeper curve of growth.

Struggling with choice

The importance of contemplating during start-up what the later evolution and ultimate disposition of a venture will be varies among participants. An entrepreneur may believe there is plenty to think about in working through the many immediate tasks of start-up without worrying further ahead. But others may feel differently. Outsiders who put money

into the enterprise will likely want to know just how and when they will get it back. Employees may be interested in longer-term career implications. Customers may want assurance that the venture will endure to back up what it sells them. Suppliers will care about being paid, and beyond that, whether the venture will afford them opportunity for more and better orders. Growth not only is likely to make the company stronger, it may be crucial to survival, lest competitors with greater clout enter and squeeze it out. Thus founders may inevitably have to consider the possibility of expansion as a goal.

A Southern California entrepreneur founded a company making high-performance electrical rotating equipment such as motors, fans, and pumps. He loved designing and working on his products, and the company succeeded in gaining a series of contracts, first from the defense department and then from commercial aircraft makers. This built sales rapidly, but because the work did not carry especially high margins and was fairly capital-intensive, the company needed external capital for expansion. Through private placement it raised investment money, but the founder had to give up voting control to outside shareholders. They wanted profit growth and he liked technical challenges. If a motor failed in some distant city, he would typically catch a flight to go see what was wrong, fix it, and devise improvements in the design.

But when he did, other aspects of the company, such as contract completion, cost control, personnel recruitment, and training, as well as bidding on new contracts, would tend to slacken or drift off target, and before long profits would diminish, sometimes into the red. When this happened some investors would become upset and start badgering the founder about sticking to his job as CEO rather than design engineer. In response, he would "get back to business," and profits would come back into line. But only for a while, because then he would relax, delve back into technology, and the loss cycle would return.

Outside investors, after several years of discomfort with this pattern and, not finding anyone whom they felt could replace the founder, reached an agreement with him to sell the company to a larger corporation where he would continue division head of his company under higher management. He soon left to start another new firm, which he kept small to retain com-

---

[422] Fred "Chico" Lager, *Ben & Jerry's* (New York: Crown 1994) p. 154.

plete control. Eventually, his new firm acquired his old one from the big company, under whose ownership it had done poorly, to the disappointment of many.

To this entrepreneur the desire for independence and being able to follow technical enthusiasms were more important than building a large company or maximizing wealth. Other entrepreneurs may have other goals as well as other constraints on their freedom to choose. Many may have to take what they can get. Some may, as this one did the next time around, be able better to shape the venture to their preferences by envisioning in advance alternative scenarios downstream.

Managing benefits

Growth tends to impose demands and constraints on management: the need to raise more money and hence answer to those who provide it, the need to hire more people and then train, direct, and respond to them, and probably a need to duck the supplications and criticisms that can arise from jealousy toward a leader perceived to have new power and wealth. In addition, with growth of the workforce come more governmental labor requirements, and if the company becomes publicly held there are more governmental and shareholder reporting requirements.

Choosing not to grow will likely mean less opportunity to become rich, powerful, and famous, but it can be a way to avoid the above penalties and in addition it can have some advantages that are hard or impossible for larger firms to enjoy. Top management can hand pick and know personally every member of a workforce that is smaller, and members of the workforce themselves can all know each other better. Relationships with customers, suppliers, and the community where the company is located can be more personal and warm. There can be a greater sense of common purpose, passion, and mutual support, both within the firm and between the firm and its outside contacts.

Small giants is a term used by author Bo Burlingham[423] to characterize companies that choose to trade off such power as they have to grow or to maximize profits against alternative goals instead such as producing higher quality output, enjoying work activities and other people more, having more sense of common purpose with customers, suppliers and the local community, and enjoying greater occupational freedom coupled with less regulation, strain, and grief. As one of his dozen-plus examples he tells about Norm Brodsky, a frequent contributor to *Inc.* magazine.

In the no-entry-barriers, and therefore highly competitive and low margin business of providing bicycle-courier service in Manhattan, Norm Brodsky managed through the early 1980s to build an exceptionally large and profitable business by responding to an advertising agency operator who said she would employ any messenger service that could provide invoices showing which of her clients should be charged back for each delivery. At the time microcomputers were new and unfamiliar, which left this job hard for other firms who typed invoices by hand. Brodsky, in contrast, developed software to make it simple and thereby passed up his competitors to grow with ease. His goal became "to have a $100-million company, and I was willing to do almost anything to get it," he recalled.

He bought, then merged with, one of his competitors that was publicly held, bringing his combined sales to the $45-million level. Then he bought another with $75 million in sales, and finally surpassed his growth goal.

But then came problems. The second company kept needing cash infusions. Then, a stock market crash in 1987 toppled many of that company's customers. On top of that, fax machines became more popular, reducing the need for messengers and shrinking his company's business by 40 percent within a few months. In 1988 he filed for Chapter 11 bankruptcy protection from creditors. When his firm finally emerged from this process in 1991, sales had fallen to below $2.5 million and the number of employees from 3,000 down to 50. His conclusion, according to Burlingham, was that "he had single-handedly destroyed a solid, profitable business by putting it in harm's way."

As to motivation, Brodsky himself observed,

I had to admit that I'd done it because of something in my nature. I enjoy risk. I like to go to the edge of the cliff and look down. We had to have armed guards in our offices. We had guys coming

---

[423] Bo Burlingham, *Small Giants* (London: Penguin 2005).

up who were extremely angry, and I couldn't blame them. They hadn't had any warning because I couldn't announce our Chapter 11 in advance. So one day they had a job, and the next day they didn't—through absolutely no fault of their own. I can't tell you how hard that was. Today I never ever make a decision that will jeopardize anybody's job, but that's something I had to learn the hard way.[424]

Another entrepreneur who also had the opportunity to grow his business greatly, but decided through a different line of reasoning not to was Robert Catlin.

> Having developed a system that let his 16-person mortgage company outperform much larger rivals, he explained how he passed up the option of expanding it farther beyond its Canton, Ohio headquarters.

> *People tell me all the time, 'You're crazy, pal. You're missing a golden opportunity.' I say, 'Hey, I'm doing just fine. I have control. I have freedom. I have family time and travel time. What more can I ask for?'*[425]

Although Burlingham's selected sample of companies that are highly successful but deliberately kept small was very limited, the variety within it was great. All were privately held by owners who worked in them. But some firms had founders who shared ownership with employees and some others were programmed to become completely employee-owned through ESOPs (Employee Stock Option Plans). Most were service firms, but a couple were manufacturers, a pattern that is reflected also in the *Inc.* 500 fastest-growing companies population. Employee participation in management decisions appears to vary widely among the small firms. One reached to employ relatives of employees, while another flatly banned doing so.

There were also commonalities that seemed to go with determination to remain small. Each firm, according to Burlingham, tended to have such close relations with its local community that to imagine it being anywhere he said was virtually impossible. Also, the need for eventual replacement of top management appeared to be very problematic among these successful companies. Most had not yet done it (which may or may not mean his sample wasn't big enough). Of those that tried some had to give up and sell out. But morale and satisfaction in the firms seemed to be high in all of them, and turnover correspondingly low.

A permanent unknown seems to be what fraction of small firms have the capability to choose between being ordinary, becoming small giants, or succeeding at the more popular ambition of growing greatly.

2. Growing from within

Two broad approaches for seeking growth are to do it externally through acquisitions or to do it from within via managerial policies and actions. Both approaches are used, both can work or not, and management can choose both whether to attempt them and how.

High growth can emerge from within when not expected. One poll of the *Inc.* 500 fastest-growing small firms in America revealed that 50 percent began as "regular but small" businesses and 48 percent began as informal operations in a garage or home. Only 2 percent began with all systems in place for fast growth.[426] However, none of those written up in the magazine's articles seem to have grown against their wishes. Although some firms do deliberately choose smallness, it appears that most entrepreneurs whose firms grow are glad of it, and the business plans of most seem to indicate that they aspire to make growth happen.

Reaching beyond start-up for growth of a firm from within may be possible through several types of initiatives, including those listed in the shaded area on the following page.

Pursuing any growth initiatives will raise impediments from both inside and outside for management to deal with. Inside there are the usual problems of personalities, frustrations,

---

[424] Burlingham, *Small Giants*, p. 15.
[425] Burlingham, *Small Giants*, p. 41.
[426] John Case, "The Origins of Entrepreneurship," *Inc.*, June 1989, p. 54.

Management initiatives for growing from within

Quality improvement Individuals and organizations tend to find ways over time to improve their performance. Management can encourage this by giving it priority. Stressing to employees its importance, organizing "quality circles" where they are urged to propose, discuss, and experiment with improvement ideas, providing incentives for them to do so in terms of recognition and rewards, instituting training that improves skills and carrying out experiments can all help.

Economy Lowering price may or may not help, depending upon how customers feel about it. If quality improvement is great enough, they may even buy more at higher prices.

Innovation Introducing new products and services has proven extremely powerful, not only for starting new companies, but also for expanding existing ones, both large and small. Some industries where companies can be seen constantly fighting back and forth on innovation are chip-making, where AMD, Intel, Texas Instruments, and Motorola battle, television where networks fight for ratings with new programs every year, and toys, where companies of all sizes compete with countless fresh products, especially at Christmas.

Selling Increasing advertising, promotion, and discounts, and strengthening personal sales through hiring and training are straightforward ways to push for more sales.

Channel expansion Adding sales outlets, either in the same territory or expanding into new territories, including abroad, is also straightforward, though not necessarily easy. There may be a choice between adding outlets by opening company stores versus selling franchises for others to open them. Both of these approaches offer advantages and disadvantages that are easy to imagine in such areas as motivation, training, control, and financing.

Collaborating Strategic alliances, both informal and formal, as well as joint ventures with other companies, are ways of extending reach and gaining help, though they also can introduce pitfalls, particularly in the form of partner disagreements.

Spending A catch with all these activities is that they use both money and time. Hence, a crucial question is how much to spend on them, as opposed to concentrating entirely on such regular day-to-day affairs of the company as productivity, cost control, and quality, while letting growth happen or not as it will.

---

mistakes, jealousies, and calamities, any combinations of which can cumulate into deterioration, slack performance, creeping malaise, and bureaucracy. Outside there will arise competition for the new sales needed for growth.

Big idea, big break, or other

A 1989 study by the author of 122 companies that had grown to become household names found that about one-fourth had taken off on a high-growth trajectory from the start.[427] The other three-fourths came into a growth spurt farther downstream from start-up through an opportunity not pursued at start-up. About two thirds of the take-offs appeared to be propelled by a "big idea," such as introduction of a new product, as can be seen from Exhibit 10a-1 below. Another 9 percent seemed to have benefited from a "big break," such as a war that boosted demand for what the company was well positioned to deliver, as hap-

pened with Clark candy bars, which suddenly encountered high demand as U.S. Army rations when World War I struck. The remainder of companies, fewer than one-fourth, seemed to have accomplished major growth simply from something else, which presumably included skillful evolutionary management.

One striking feature of this array is that most take-offs occur downstream from start-up. A "side-street effect" seems to be at work, which is to say that as consequence of entering business the company in operating becomes exposed to more information, as in traveling down a boulevard from the point of start-up, thereby catching glimpses down side streets from time to time where opportunities that were not apparent until travel down the boulevard revealed them. These glimpses might later be recalled in such forms as, "One of our customers asked us," "At a trade show we noticed," "When we took on a bigger customer we had to change

Big idea, big break, or other

---

[427] Karl H. Vesper, "When's the Big Idea?" in *Frontiers of Entrepreneurship Research*, eds. Robert H. Brockhaus, Sr. and others (Wellesley, MA: Babson College, 1989) p. 334.

Exhibit 10a-1 Antecedents to fast company growth (n=122)[428]

Big idea	Number	Percent
At company inception	30	24.6%
Downstream from start-up	50	41.0
Not sure when	4	3.3
Big break rather than big idea	11	9.0
Not sure what drove rise	27	22.1
Total	122	100.0%

how we did things, and when we applied those changes to working with our small customers we got many more," or "We had to think of a way of coping with new competitors, and it made us much stronger."

A linkage of growth trajectories with influential antecedents was described by Chandler and Baucus in 1996, based upon plotting the sales trajectories of five mainly high-technology companies from 1970 to 1995.[429] Most grew without major discontinuities, except for one company that rose rapidly for six years then tapered off. The main performance enhancers were said to be (1) a stable and balanced management team, (2) acquisition of key personnel for new product introduction, (3) close customer linkages, (4) impact on markets by government action, and (5) not hiring external managers.

However, while these five firms were riding out relatively smooth hills and valleys of growth between half a million and five million dollars in sales for roughly a quarter century, others such as mainframe computer companies, fast food chains, discount retailers, and oil companies were rising fast, with much of the difference apparently attributable to industry big events.

Propitious industry circumstances and adequate execution obviously matter in connection with a big idea or any other basic success driver. This can be seen from the record of *Inc.* magazine's annual list of fastest-growing companies and how it changes over time. Aging of the population coupled with advances in medical technology create new opportunities for health care companies. Government response to the need creates new programs, agencies, and

red tape, which in turn opens opportunities for creation and growth of consulting companies to help private firms and individuals cope with the red tape, and amid the consulting companies that grow some surpass others. Invasion of another country creates demand for all sorts of military equipment and new technology, such as better bullet-resistant jackets, drone aircraft, and contractors.

This hot industry effect can be seen in the *Inc.* 500 list for 2007. The largest number of companies (55) was in information technology services and the smallest was in insurance. If other things electronic are combined with information technology (computers, 12; telecommunications, 24; and software, 37), they account together for 25 percent of the total 500 companies.

But high technology clearly cuts across other industrial categories as well, including manufacturing, consumer products, energy, health, and security. Most of the 48 advertising companies on the 2007 *Inc.* 500 list were centered on utilization of the Internet, which is also a relatively new technology.

Financial prosperity of the companies is hard to assess, because no profit or investment figures are given. However, it can be seen that the highest revenue per company and per employee occurred in the health and the real estate sectors. It seems likely that the first of these will continue to prosper as the population ages and the second, real estate, will likely drop next time around, since the 2007 list came out just as the industry was undergoing substantial collapse from the sub-prime bubble. At a general and simplistic level, such tabulations suggest that growth

428 Vesper, "When's the Big Idea?" p. 341.
429 Gaylen N. Chandler and David A. Baucus, "Gauging Performance in Emerging Businesses," in *Frontiers of Entrepreneurship Research*, 1996, eds. Paul D. Reynolds and others (Wellesley, MA: Babson College 1996) p. 491.

among generally young and start-up companies is particularly to be expected on the backs of larger waves in the society and economy.

Closer looks at individual ventures within categories of *Inc.*'s 500 population of fast growers illustrate further how growth also results from leaders as companies tune their strategies to innumerable smaller features of the main waves. This can be seen by contrasts in the lines of business of the following three companies that were highest ranked by growth in the general field of health care.

1. The top company in the list, Member Health, has only 157 employees and was started in 1998, generates revenues of $1.2 billion by helping people manage their Part D coverage of the federal government's Medicare program. Its founder, Charles Halberg, earlier had worked as a mergers and acquisitions lawyer for a drugstore chain. Then he started a company to help people get discounts from drug companies. After selling that company he started Member Health in 1998, whose big event for growing came in 2002 through winning a major contract from the state of Ohio. "Part of what set us apart," he recalled, "was that people in our plan needed only one card," while other companies required a different card to obtain benefits for each drug company.

2. The second health company listed, which began in 2002, owns and operates acute care hospitals in which the doctors are co-investors.

3. The third manufactures sports supplements with names like "Endorush" that are sold by retailers and gyms. The company began in 2001 by recruiting name athletes as customers, then using their names to gain credibility with others.

From this tiny sample of fastest-growing small ventures in the 2007 *Inc.* 500 (which is itself a small sample, albeit somewhat spectacular, of the overall U.S. economy), can be seen how much contrast in product or service exists within a general category such as health care. The angles that have led to growth are similarly varied in other industrial categories as well. Left to the imagination are questions of which competitors of each firm could have beaten that firm to its special angles for succeeding.

A common theme seems to be that the starter ("founder," "entrepreneur") comes into the venture's line of work already possessing experience in it, which leads to glimpses of opportunity not only for starting the venture, but also for expanding it. But also sometimes the builder may be a different person from the starter.

MediConnect was started in 1996 as a company to retrieve, digitize, and organize medical records for insurance carriers, but it needed more cash. At the behest of a venture capitalist who was considering investing in it, Amy Rees Lewis was asked to evaluate the company. With experience both as a reseller of software out of her home for doctors' offices and later 10 years in managing information technology firms, she concluded that MediConnect was unpromising as an investment, although she liked its technology.

She recalled that after telling the venture capitalist not to invest, she received a call from the venture's CEO who said, "You seem to get what's broken here. Can you come in and turn us around?" Both he and the venture capitalist wanted her to take over his job and run the company. "So I came in," she said, "and I told them, you can either increase sales or cut your costs; let's try to do both."

Several changes resulted, the biggest of which was to shift the mix of documents processed from mostly medical records to mostly legal records by adding the latter. This put the firm, with $26.9 million in sales and 1,200 employees, among the top three in the country in that line of work.[430]

Product versus market moves

To expand sales the company can choose along two dimensions, the customers served and the products/services offered. In the first example above, Member Health, it appears that Charles Halberg had a somewhat different clientele to whom his company offered similar, but not identical, services. So there was some of each. In MediConnect it appears that a considerably different clientele, lawyers instead of doctors, was where the sales came from for the similar service of records processing. So the main change was in customers. The possibility of such strategic departures from the prior orientation of an enterprise can be visualized along two axes as depicted in Exhibit 10a-2 on the following page.

[430] Amy Rees Lewis, "How I Did It," *Inc.*, September 2007, p. 100.

Exhibit 10a-2 Product/Market growth possibilities

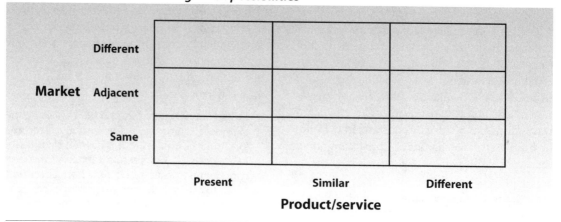

Least likely, perhaps, is the prospect that management will introduce a fork in its strategy that pursues two very different markets with very different products. But there may be some value in stretching imagination to consider many possibilities, including that combination. One entrepreneur who branched widely from one product and market to an entirely different one, for instance, was Charles Kaman:

> After graduating in aeronautical engineering from Catholic University in 1940, Charles Kaman worked for a helicopter pioneer, Igor Sikorsky. Five years later, with ideas of his own for better designs, plus a $2,000 investment, and equipment from two friends, he set up his own helicopter-manufacturing company. In 1947, the first Kaman Corporation helicopter began flight tests, equipped with a new patented servo-controlled rotor. Two years after that, Kaman introduced the first helicopter powered by a gas turbine. The first twin-turbine helicopter came in 1952, followed in yet another three years by the first remote-controlled helicopter. The company's H-43 model flew more rescue missions in the Korean and Vietnam wars than all other helicopters combined, and was the only military helicopter never to experience a loss of life or accident attributable to design weakness.
>
> In parallel with these developments, Kaman also applied some of his knowledge about vibrations learned from helicopter design to create a guitar made from aerospace composites rather than wood, that nevertheless had a natural sound. This new branch of Kaman Corporation

eventually became the world's largest independent distributor of musical instruments. Kaman and his wife also developed a breed of German Shepherd better adapted to serving needs of the blind.[431]

Although not common, there are nevertheless many other examples of departures in both market and product by innovative companies: (1) Seiko from mechanical watches to microcomputer printers (Epson); (2) Kyocera from spark plugs to artificial emeralds and then, when gem dealers would not accept the product, to opening its own retail jewelry store in Beverly Hills, California; (3) Tandy Corporation from hi-fi and electronics to digital computers; (4) Signode Corporation from loading-dock strapping to TV dinner trays; (5) Apple from microcomputers to music downloads and cell phones; and (6) Task Corporation from wind-tunnel instrumentation to high-performance pumps, fans, and electric motors, including one of 250 horsepower weighing only 187 pounds to power a remote-controlled helicopter to serve as an observation extension for submarines.

Essential to such departures in product and/or market are nevertheless important linkages to capabilities of the companies and their leaders that can be seen as the key ingredients mentioned in the first chapter for new ventures in general: (1) technical know-how, (2) a better idea, (3) physical resources, (4) personal contacts, and (5) customer orders in one sequence

---

[430] National Inventors Hall of Fame Web site: invent.org.

or another. Thus creation of one successful venture can be seen as sometimes providing key ingredients for other new ventures as well.

Richard Branson started publishing a magazine called *Student* when he was 15, started selling records by mail at 20, opened a chain of record stores called Virgin Records (since renamed Virgin Megastores) at age 21, began a recording studio at age 22, and at 23 released a record that sold over 5 million copies. Eventually adding the works of artists including Janet Jackson and the Rolling Stones, his studio became one of the six largest in the world, and was sold for $1billion in 1992 when Branson was 42 years old.

Branson's holding company, The Virgin Group, included Virgin Airlines, which he created in 1984 and expanded with funding from the record business and its sale, plus other ventures in the Internet, mobile phones, another recording company, railroad, hotel, and other leisure industries, including a venture in space travel. Along the way he attempted less successful forays into running lotteries and acquisition of TV franchises. Still, by 2007 his holding company included some 200 different enterprises around the world employing over 50,000 people, and he had been knighted by the Queen of England.

Although the venture diversity generated by these entrepreneurs can be seen as including radical departures in both markets and products/services, they can also be seen as building upon established capabilities possessed by their founders, the least specialized of which were financial resources they had acquired and could therefore experiment with.

3. Success drivers longer term

What will determine whether a start-up will one day become great? Success theories include the company's (A) strategic position, (B) big idea, (C) right cast of characters, (D) strong property, (E) exceptionally effective systems, and/or (F) powerful culture.

A. Strategic position

A rising economic tide, sudden demand, or change of technology in any industry can spawn new companies and make others grow almost regardless of their management's actions, at least until competitors catch up. When the oil crisis hit in 1974, filling stations were bound to lose and oil drilling companies were bound to win. Wars win for steel, airplane and spacecraft, gun, boat, combat electronics, and truck companies, among others. Technological breakthroughs in computers, telecommunications, and microchips spawn cascades of new growth that some companies exploit. Pundits introduce terminology like hyper-competition, first mover, early adopter, and s-curves to flag emergence of these forces with trendy articles and books. A new wave rises, some paddle to catch it, those who happened to be in the best position, or to notice it first, or to paddle most effectively, get the best rides on it. Some are thus likely to win, or in an opposing tide, to lose, although a few may succeed in bucking the tide.

A systematic search to find correlations between management moves and profitability over time was conducted by the Strategic Planning Institute, a Cambridge, Massachusetts consulting firm. Researchers there entered numerical data on close to 40 variables. Independent variables ranged from industry economics, management budgetary decisions, capital investment, and spending on such things as R&D, marketing, and quality improvement. Dependent variables they chose included such company performance figures as sales level and growth, market share, price-to-book, price-to-earnings, sales-to-book ratios, and return on investment, this last being what they decided was of most merit.

Then the researchers fed data on some 3,000 businesses and business units into a digital computer and had it seek out correlations between the independent and the dependent variables to learn what patterns of management decisions on independent variables seemed to have produced wins on the dependent variables of interest. The computer's finding was that if a company had the follow-

A. Strategic Position

ing four elements in its strategic positioning, it was certain to be winning:

1. Operating in a market growing faster than the country's gross national product.
2. Having a large market share relative to its two next largest competitors.
3. Offering differentiated rather than commodity products.
4. Producing with low capital intensity.

These findings are fairly unsurprising and easy to rationalize, with the possible exception of capital intensity. (Higher intensity evidently reduces company flexibility.) But lack of any of these four advantages does not mean a company is not winning, just that it may not be. Interestingly, it did not matter what the industry was, such as high or low technology. Also, companies could be winners without matching this list. The nagging question, however, is how should a company go about attaining such winning characteristics? For that there are other success theories below.

B. Big idea

It is easy to think of companies that won by virtue of home-run product ideas. Ford, Apple, and Google are familiar examples. It is also easy to find companies, such as Hiller Helicopter and Montgomery Ward, that were felled by inferior ideas, while still others, like 3M and HP, despite starting with mediocre ideas, triumphed by moving on to better ones.

Edwin Land, a brilliant and charismatic self-taught physicist, set out to produce polarized headlight lenses and eyeglasses that would relieve motorists from the glare of oncoming car lights at night. That product idea failed, but the effort to make it produced polarized sunglasses, which were a great success. But Land's subsequent idea for the patent-protected instant camera, which he was able to develop thanks to the sunglasses win, is what did most to make his Polaroid Corporation great. Along the way, this company Land had started won a monumental lawsuit when Kodak introduced a similar instant camera. The court forced Kodak to withdraw its instant camera from the market in 1986, return the money of all who had bought it, and pay Polaroid damages. Then Land had an encore idea for an instant movie, as op-

posed to the successful still camera. This big idea was too late for a market that was moving from film to magnetic recording, first on analog tape and then on digital disks. The result was that the once-great Polaroid Corporation failed and filed for bankruptcy in 2001.

The big idea can also take the form of an insight. In the stock market Roger Babson got the idea that stock market statistical analysis could have more power than the intuitive hunches of investors, and it made him rich. Later, Emerson W. Axe used detailed analysis to make investment decisions and also, whether by brains or luck, most probably both, managed to predict accurately the timing of the 1929 crash, which earned him enough fame to attract wealthy clients to his investment counsel firm and make it a success. Along the way, by hook and crook, Joseph P. Kennedy, scion of the political clan, also had big ideas about how to capitalize on both the timing and possible manipulations of the market, to build a fortune for his family.

Big ideas can come later in company development and rest upon not only imagination but also careful calculation. Boeing's gambles on the KC-135 and the 707 set its course for airliner leadership, as had Douglas's earlier bet on the DC-3 before the engine it required had been developed.

But such calculations do not always work correctly. DeHavilland actually introduced the first jet airliner. But in a couple of years it failed because of design weaknesses that caused it to disintegrate in mid-air, as later happened with a prop-jet, the Lockheed Electra. Sony had a better technological idea for the Betamax camcorder system, but its strategy idea, which was to introduce that product as a monopoly rather than shared system, lost its market to VHS, which other companies shared.

Apple's idea was to monopolize the microcomputer market with its better operating system. But Microsoft took away the lion's share of the market by letting any microcomputer companies use its DOS operating system, later to be called Windows. Apple tried licensing its operating system to other computer makers, but found the results unsatisfactory. So it returned to selling its system for use on its machines only. Eventually its market share rose as it began to offer both operating systems on its, and only its, computers.

Which big ideas are good and which are not may sometimes be discernable only in hindsight. But their power can be enormous.

C. Right cast

Sometimes the big ideas come from clearly identifiable individuals, as can be seen in examples above. Other times, it's not so clear. Whose idea was the airplane or the bicycle? Creative individuals over time build on ideas of other creative people and at some point one or another of them may turn out to be an entrepreneur.

Vivid individuals also star in other ways. Professional athletic teams and movies display this obviously, not only in the names of individuals that become familiar, but also in the far-out-of-line free-market salaries and/or high positions they command. But not always rightly, because they sometimes lose and eventually are ousted. Ray Kroc was an individual who made McDonald's great, but single-handedly Sewell Avery almost destroyed Montgomery Ward. Phrases characterizing this phenomenon include, "Every great company is the shadow of a man" [sic], and the venture capitalist adage, "When the light at the top goes out, it gets dark all the way to the bottom."

Different kinds of talent may star also entrepreneurially. W. Clement Stone was a super salesman who built an insurance company, and Lee Iacocca, another super salesman, turned around Chrysler. Andy Grove starred as a tough, hard-driving smart production manager who drove Intel up the curve of success, although he was not part of the original team of other star technologists led by Gordon Moore and Robert Noyce, who initiated the company.

"Our most valuable asset is our people" is a cliché. Venture capitalists repeatedly stress getting the right people, and they frequently replace the founding entrepreneurs whose companies they invest in to put the right people in charge.

And when acquired companies yield disappointing results under the imposed regimes of those who took them over, it is frequently seen in hindsight to be because after takeover, the best people left.

D. Strong property

Property in a variety of forms has been crucial to the development of many companies. Only if a company has very high margin and very low capital intensity can it expand without cash infusions, as have many software and Internet companies. Microsoft had no need for outside capital to grow because replicating its main product, the leading PC operating system, involved low capital intensity and high margin.

But most high-growth start-ups do need substantial investment cash. Howard Hughes, Fred Smith, and the McCaw brothers did wonderful things, but had they not inherited major assets, they probably would not have had such impact. It was thanks to his inheritance that William Boeing was able to build a lumber business and then create his airplane company, which then benefited from U.S. government money for air mail service and warplane development. Seymour Cray was able to obtain millions for starting his supercomputer company because of the reputation he possessed based on technical accomplishments of his prior career at IBM. The American railroads were built largely with the necessary benefit of property provided by the U.S. government.

Other forms of property also play powerful roles. Without its trademark, which is a form of property, McDonald's would be vastly less well off, and consequently the company protects it vigorously by suing whenever any new Mc-something appears on the commercial scene. Valuation of intellectual property is high for many other things, including all sorts of prepared foods, and especially soda pop. Coca-Cola has had the most highly valued trademark for decades. Harley-Davidson's trademark transfers to other products so well that it operates clothing stores that don't even sell motorcycles. Starbucks puts its logo on not only ever more stores, but also on more products.

Mining companies own rights to minerals at specified locations, without which they would

C. Right cast

D. Strong property

E. Effective
systems

F. Powerful
culture

be nothing. Oil companies benefit from both land rights and trademarks of great value. Small companies sometimes have reason to cherish most the locations they own or hold lease rights on, which are also forms of property often critical to success.

E. Effective systems

A major finding reported in best-selling business books by Jim Collins is that differences between companies that are good versus those that are even better are determined not by extra charismatic leaders, home-run product ideas, or property, but rather in large part by operational systems that are highly refined and applied over time by diligent employee effort.

Effective systems can yield reliable high-quality performance and strong control of costs. Big companies use them to outperform competitors. When small companies are able to develop and codify good systems, they sometimes thereby enable expansion through chaining and/or franchising, as described in the preceding chapter. Winning through effective systems can apply in all types of companies, including agriculture, consulting, education, financing, health care, manufacturing, mining, and shipping.

The first development needed to harness this success driver is to invent, polish, and codify rules that work exceptionally well for operating the business successfully at some size. The second is to develop ways of transmitting the rules to managers and suppliers so that they in turn can spread application of the system to lower cost employees who perform needed functions throughout the company for eventually delivering good results to customers. Quality control and cost control are important end objectives to be attained through effective managerial application of the systems. Ultimately, however, their effective application depends on the people employed and managed to bring them about and how they are managed.

F. Powerful culture

It has been said that any system will work if the people want it to, and no system by itself can work in a company if the employees don't want it to. Organizations are collections of human habits and behaviors, and these are largely governed by common understandings of "the way we do things," which is all part of the organization's culture. From the culture come interactions with customers that either bring them back for more or don't, ideas for how to do things better or not, attention to details that may be covered by formal systems of the company, or may not.

Some long-time favorite companies among those who study corporate culture are Hewlett-Packard and 3M, both firms with long-time strong financial performance, many innovations, and low rates of turnover, notwithstanding lack of reputation for particularly high pay.

None has starred so much for the strength of its culture in recent years, however, as Southwest Airlines, which continued to profit and grow as other airlines suffered losses and some failed entirely. Interestingly, Southwest did not win from a single big idea, although it introduced many novelties in its operation over the years. Contrary to the four winning economic determinants identified by the Strategic Planning Institute, Southwest operates in a commodity industry and one that has high capital intensity, both features that other airlines typically suffer from greatly. As a somewhat late starter, Southwest has never been known for having property, such as cash, privileged landing rights, or contracts to give it advantage over other lines.

That leaves only three of the six noted success determinants on which it depends for advantage. First is its cast of characters, beginning with its lead founder, Herb Kelleher, who set and maintained from the outset the management style and basic "think fresh with common sense" policies, particularly as regards efficiency and low cost. Second is the work ethic, style, and focus on customer service that followed in the workforce culture from this management style. The third success determinant is composed of the innovative and effective systems for operating noted in the preceding section.

4. Coping with growth

Behind the glamour of fast-growing companies can be all sorts of problems that may only appear in the headlines if the companies happen to fail because of them.

Top management at Federal Express decided the company had to grow fast or die. To offer package delivery competitively, it had to cover the entire country before competitors did. This required first capital for expansion, which was hard to get because the company had to incur losses to build its system and attract freight volume. It also had to bring about new government rules to let the company use larger planes and thereby keep up with increasing volume in an efficient manner. Opposing this were established freight airlines such as Emery, Airborne Freight, and Flying Tiger, plus passenger airlines that used leftover baggage space to carry freight as well.

Company growth brought union attempts at organizing plus need to redesign the organization and management structure. It also fueled ambitions for "next breakthroughs," and some of these proved very expensive. An idea for installing seats quickly to serve passengers when planes were idle during the day was quickly scrapped, as was the idea of carrying freight supersonically in the Concorde, carrying it slower using blimps, and even using rocket boosters to put a new satellite communication system in space. An attempt at greater decentralization was introduced then abandoned.

In 1986 another big idea tried was an even faster form of communication than overnight, namely, use of fax machines in FedEx offices that could send letters instantly once they were brought in. FedEx messengers could then deliver them quickly to their destinations. After three years the project, called "ZapMail," was written off at $357 million. Widespread use of personal fax machines wiped it out.

This was followed in 1989 by acquisition of a controlling interest in Flying Tiger, an air carrier of large freight with around $2 billion in sales compared to FedEx at $4.5 billion. In trying to develop sales outside the U.S., FedEx had experienced difficulties and losses. Flying Tiger already had worldwide routes and seemed to Fred Smith, who negotiated the acquisition personally, like a natural complement for expansion.

But then came other problems. Some of the planes acquired were in poor condition, Flying Tiger's 970 pilots were unionized, and its 5,500 ground workers seemed to have a different culture from that of FedEx. Flying Tiger worked through freight forwarders for entry and exit of its large shipments at airports in contrast to FedEx, which handled its small packages with company personnel directly. Trying to arrange compatibility caused trouble with employees in both organizations, while competitors took advantage of the consequent dip in performance. For the first time since going public in 1978, FedEx lost money in 1991. Operations were slashed in Europe with layoff of 6,600 employees. One analyst said, "A smart person has one brilliant idea in their entire life. It is unlikely that the same person is going to have two or more brilliant ideas."[432]

In short, chasing after new big ideas to keep growth high can also produce costly problems.

Problem variety

Based on information from 120 of the 1987 *Inc.* 500 fastest growing firms, Terpstra and Olson[433] reported that problems encountered after start-up were most frequently in sales and marketing, as can be seen in the rank order of problems by frequency in Exhibit 10a-3 below. As mentioned in Subchapter 8A on selling, the high rank of sales problems was even higher during start-up (38 percent top ranked at start-up versus 22 percent later). But in other categories, ranking changed. External financing problems dropped to last later from second during start-up, while human resource management and organization design problems rose to much higher significance later than where they had been earlier.

The nature of growth bottlenecks varies with line of business, location, and time. For example in wartime, all industrial manpower may be in short supply. Similarly, with the fast growth of software and Internet companies, programmers are hard to hire. In contrast, for liberal arts teaching jobs, the supply

---

[432] Vance Trimble, *Overnight Success* (New York: Crown Publishers, 1993) p. 325.
[433] David E. Terpstra and Philip D. Olson, "Entrepreneurial Start-up and Growth: A Classification of Problems," *ET&P*, 17, no. 3, Spring 1993, p.5.

Exhibit 10a-3 Fast-growth problem areas beyond first year (Terpstra and Olson)

Problem areas mentioned	Frequency %
Sales and marketing	22%
Internal financial management	21
Human resource management	17
General management	14
Production and operations management	8
Regulatory environment	7
Organization structure/design	6
Product development	2
Economic environment	2
Obtaining external financing	1
Total	100%

of interested candidates tends to be high, and consequently, wages in relation to educational investment are low.

Outside the company competitors, new as well as old, add efforts to make inroads. Countless prospering small companies were displaced as retailing demand rose by large chains like Sears in an earlier age and Wal-Mart more recently. Areas of product technology, such as platter phonograph records, bamboo phonograph needles, slide-rules, mechanical adding machines, typewriters, and dial telephones have phased out as technology advanced. Unfavorable economic events, such as inflation and credit restrictions sometimes depress performance, as does crime. Shifts to foreign suppliers sometimes cause industrial capabilities, from telephone help lines to various types of manufacturing, to phase out domestically in favor of imports.

Another list of organizational problems encountered by most companies as they mature, according to Eric Flamholtz based upon both his studies as a scholar and his experience as a consultant, appears in Exhibit 10a-4 below.[434]

Remedies for such problems, says Flamholtz, include four steps. First, audit the current effectiveness of the organization. Second, formulate plans to remedy problems. Third, implement the plans. Fourth, monitor and assess results. Participation of employees in these review and remedial activities is crucial and it may also be important to spread the activities over many months, possibly years, to have them work well. External events, he notes, can also complicate the challenges of such reform.

Exhibit 10a-4 Flamholtz' fast-growth problem areas beyond year one

1. Employees of the company
   a. Find there are not enough hours in the day.
   b. Spend too much time putting out fires.
   c. Are inadequately aware of what fellow employees are doing.
   d. Lack understanding of company goals.
   e. Believe the only way to get things done right is to do them personally.
   f. Consider company meetings a waste of time.
   g. Find plans inadequate and not followed up.
   h. Feel insecure about their circumstances in the company.
2. Sales people find that inventory they took orders for had already been sold.
3. Some vendors are paid several times for the same goods; others aren't paid.
4. Quality drops and the reasons are not apparent.
5. People quit when the company needs them more than ever.
6. Confusion arises when important files and records can't be located.

---

[434] Eric G. Flamholtz, *How To Make the Transition from Entrepreneurship to a Professionally Managed Firm* (San Francisco: Jossey-Bass, 1986).

Sequences over time

Many authors have observed that growth problems seem to occur in predictable stages. Several have described typical sequences, beginning with Buchele's "Key Crises."[435] To this have been added Steinmetz' "Critical Stages,"[436] Thain's "Corporate Stages,"[437] Greiner's "Evolution/Revolution Stages,"[438] Churchill and Lewis' "Five Stages,"[439] four more from Seligman,[440] and most recently, description from the experience of Tatum[441] in building a financial services firm and then consulting with others on problems of their firms as they grow. A synthesis of different authors' stages, problems, and remedial actions includes the following, grouped for conceptual convenience, but not because they fit regularly, into three broad phases: (1) inception, (2) development, and (3) arrival.

Inception phase

a. Imbalance crisis The founder's strengths, if not complemented by a well-rounded team, can produce a start-up strong in some areas, such as technology or marketing, but weak in others such as production or finance where things therefore go wrong. The most likely remedy is to recruit complements or subcontract help where weak. The start-up study by Cooper et al., found that at the earliest venture stages a typical owner personally participates in production of the venture's product or service. This can give rise, according to author Michael Gerber, to an entrepreneur erroneously assuming that "If you understand the technical work of a business, you understand the business that does that technical work."[442] A logical solution is to seek partners or hire help that complements technical know-how with other business experience.

b. Personal cash crunch crisis Typically founders finance initially with personal savings, with hope they will carry the enterprise farther than they do. A logical, but often neglected, precaution is to forecast cash flows and develop potential sources of infusions ahead of needs,

then maintain and monitor effective records to tap them in time. But start-ups typically need more cash than anticipated, even with careful planning. Product development or initial sales, for instance, may come slower than expected. Consequently, rent and utility expenses may get ahead of expected cash inflows. Maybe the amount budgeted for a lawyer was too small for actual start-up needs because a contract became complicated or more trademark advice is desirable. Or an important supplier, uneasy about the start-up's lack of demonstrated stability, asks for cash in advance. Having to arrange for more cash from the bank or from family and friends requires time that can put the venture even farther behind. Consequently, some start-up veterans give advice to "estimate your needs as well as you can, then double that number and arrange in advance for enough to cover it."

c. Delegation crisis The venture starts to move beyond the founder's ability to personally "be the business," in close touch with every customer and job. Some customers start to feel demoted or palmed off by the CEO. Mistakes occur because the CEO is trying to make all the important decisions and can't keep up as they proliferate. Alternatives are to hire more help, take on partners or, insofar as time allows, train others to manage. Systematization of operations to make the company itself good at what only the founder(s) were good at initially becomes crucial to maintaining relationships with customers. Important for accomplishing this will be to reflect upon and clarify just what it is that customers, suppliers, and employees value and want from the company. Goal and reward systems that include feedback and updating increase in importance. As the CEO of Teradyne, a high-growth test equipment company, Alex d'Arbeloff, recalled:

Suddenly, you find yourself facing the need to change everything about the way you run the business except the basic values. You have a fundamental dilemma. The company has become complex, and you've got to hire specialists and create divisions to keep it together. But the very process

[435] Robert B. Buchele, *Business Policy in Small and Growing Firms* (Scranton, PA: Chandler Publishing, 1967).
[436] Lawrence L. Steinmetz, "Critical Stages of Small Business Growth," *Business Horizons*, February 1969, p. 29.
[437] Donald H. Thain, "Stages of Corporate Development," *The Business Quarterly*, Winter 1969, p. 33.
[438] Larry E. Greiner, "Evolution and Revolution as Organizations Grow," *Harvard Business Review*, July-August 1972, p. 37.
[439] N.C. Churchill and V.L. Lewis, "The Five Stages of Small Business Growth," *Harvard Business Review*, May-June 1983, pp. 30-50.
[440] Lawrence Seligman, "The Creative Use of Tension," in *Managing Take-off in Fast-Growing Companies*, eds. Raymond W. Smilor and Robert Lawrence Kuhn (New York: Praeger, 1986) p. 59.
[441] Doug Tatum, *No Man's Land* (New York: Penguin Group, 2007).
[442] Michael E. Gerber, *The E Myth* (New York: Harper, 1986) p. 10.

of imposing formality on an organization tends to create bureaucracy and parochialism. These forces in turn can cause people to lose their business judgment and to focus on the more particular needs and agendas of their own division, department, or function. At that very time you, yourself are no longer as close to the details of the business as you once were. I used to run customer seminars and I used to be out there selling, so I knew firsthand what was going on. I can't do as much of these things anymore. And you have to adapt, or else the vitality of the business—the innovativeness, the responsiveness to changing external events—will fall between the cracks. The CEO simply can't have his finger any longer on the day-to-day pulse of the organization to the extent he used to—there are just too many pulses. The job becomes one of somehow helping each employee think like and behave like a founding owner-entrepreneur. But there's one thing you can't delegate, and that's the job of maintaining the critical balance between innovation and control.[443]

Development phase

d. Leadership crisis Start-up top management is likely to be autocratic and/or ad hoc. Even with delegation from the founder, mistakes arise with further growth if those to whom responsibilities have been given cannot further delegate and develop the leadership capabilities of their subordinates. More formal communication channels become needed so leaders will not be besieged by every decision. More formal organization structure, control systems, training programs, budgeting, and work standards also become needed. The aim must be to build systems that let the company continue doing what it does best even though the tasks of doing it are now delegated and possibly fractionated among employees who did not invent and may not have a good feel for them. A larger workforce will require leadership by managers who are experienced in larger organizations. Particularly tricky will be not only to find and recruit them, but also to give them appropriate titles. Beware hasty decisions. Titles such as "vice president of sales" or "head of manufacturing" may need to be rescinded from early employees or partners who easily gained them when the company was small but can't merit them in a larger organization. Retracting titles can be painful for all.

e. Beyond-personal cash crisis To recruit managers for growth and to build the organization will again, unless the company has customer advances or a high ratio of margin to capital intensity, require more cash from outsiders. More money may also be needed for equipment, space, training and, almost certainly, working capital. An easy catch to overlook is that cash hunting can become a very different game when needs move beyond personal borrowing from either friends or a bank. Now the personal financial resources of the founder(s), though they may be solid, are no longer large enough to back up loans to the company, and lenders have to start betting on the financial strength and prospects of the nascent company itself for carrying larger debt. Time and energy to seek more cash may rob too much attention from running the company. Ownership may have to be shared outside. Then privacy must be sacrificed to get money for the company to grow further. Possible solutions will include seeking help from outside professionals such as bankers, consultants, and lawyers, as well as a stronger board of directors carefully chosen as individuals with relevant experience. Anticipation of such needs can be crucial.

f. Prosperity crisis The company may have to walk a tightrope toward growth without falling into complacency on one side or chaos on the other. This calls for self-criticism, complemented by bottom-up reviews and participation at all organizational levels, help from knowledgeable outsiders, careful monitoring of performance, forecasting, planning and evaluation, and correction. The company must adapt ahead of increasing competition that will be attracted by the market that allows growth. Some companies benefit by intentionally having one person who steps on the gas and another who works the brake, one who disrupts the routine and another who smooths it out, an idea person versus a critic, an optimist versus a pessimist. The company's culture will inevitably be taking shape, with emergence of rules, many unwritten, some more subtle, and others more obvious, that comprise the company's internal code of conduct and social order, and that let people know "what kind of people we are" and "how we work together here." This culture will be crucial to the trust needed for people to work together effectively. Management must attend to its development.

---

[443] Donald Clifford and Richard Cavanagh, *The Winning Performance: How America's High-Growth Midsize Companies Succeed* (New York: Bantam Books, 1985) p. 13.

Arrival phase

g. Bureaucracy crisis Systems set up to cope with chaos can increasingly impede flexibility, innovation, and eventually, productivity. Central management may encounter problems with diversity among different segments of the business. A logical response is to divisionalize into different strategic business units, which are then granted autonomy so that they can regain greater flexibility. Profit centers will be a logical way to monitor divisions almost as separate companies. But complications arise as central overhead is allocated and common systems are applied to all units even though they fit some less well than others. Central management must struggle to balance freedom against control.

h. Sprawl crisis The autonomy can lead to less coordination among units. Line incompatibilities and resource allocation disagreements will occur between divisions. Product lines may match less well, and direction may become unclear under the decentralized approach. Imposed attempts at solutions may include some merging of units, more formal planning, review procedures, policy statements from headquarters, and coordination sessions between division heads who may or may not view themselves as allies, particularly in competition for resources.

i. Stagnation crisis The policies, reporting, and meetings imposed to control sprawl drain off energy and stifle initiative needed to maintain clear thrust. Bureaucracy can rise again. Poor financial performance may lead to contention with shareholders as well, while organizational infighting dampens morale and wastes resources.

j. Vacillation The cycle of tightening central authority versus decentralizing can go back and forth. Products mature and profits may rise, at least for a while, leading to diversification efforts, and perhaps corporate venturing. Those can consume capital while the mature products become obsolete, leading to losses, cutting off innovation efforts, retrenching, restructuring, more centralizing, and the cycle begins again.

These stages and solutions are oversimplified characterizations of complex processes. They may or may not all fit any particular company. No studies have demonstrated that in fact the whole series has applied regularly to any given company. How far the venture grows can sometimes be seen as controllable, which offers reason to consider, even if only briefly, these possibilities for problems and remedies as lying ahead.

Arrival phase

5. Growing through acquisition

Growth, instead of being built from within, can also be pursued through acquiring one or more other companies. Buying out a competitor can expand sales to the company's present market or others, and possibly extend a product/service line as well. It happens in many lines of business. Washington Mutual Savings became large mainly through acquiring other savings and loan associations, which worked well for a while, though eventually it collapsed. Microcomputer software companies like Microsoft, component companies like Intel, and hardware companies like Hewlett-Packard have acquired innumerable companies over the years and continue to do so, often as a way of adding complementary products, expertise, or market connections.

Diversification into different products and markets is occasionally stated as purpose for corporate acquisitions, the theory being that occasional declines in some of their industries may be averaged out by acquisitions in other industries faring better to provide a more stable overall pattern. That was an argument once used by Ling-Temco-Vaught for developing a conglomerate in businesses ranging from steel production to fighter planes. But as it turned out, a stock market illusion was also part of the act.

James Ling, originally an electrical contractor, found he could buy a company using shares of his own company, combine the two, and then use shares of the combined company to buy yet another. Thus, his first company "grew," and because of its growth, the value of its shares of stock relative to earnings also grew. This stock with a boosted P/E ratio could then be used to buy yet another company with lower P/E ratio, and when that company was folded into the conglomerate, its P/E ratio also rose from a halo effect. Thus a pyramid began and was imitated by a wave of takeovers by other companies doing the same. Eventually, of course, there was a collapse in this conglomerate industry, because no truly new value had been created, and many who got into the game lost when the market woke up to it.

Sometimes the acquisition motive seems to be growth for its own sake, either on the faith that bigger is stronger and therefore better, or for the challenge of building a bigger empire, rationalizing through bigness such perks as higher executive pay and bigger corporate jets, not to mention more power, and perhaps induction into higher social strata. Executives who embark on such growth binges may believe they are building greatness, and sometimes that may be right, but often it's not.

It has long been known that corporate acquisitions of other companies on the average do not work out well, whether in the case of AT&T acquiring NCR and then having to dump it, Daimler and Chrysler merging then breaking apart in worse condition, or Time-Warner buying AOL and producing another industrial debacle. A *Business Week* analysis of corporate mergers between 1998 and 2000 found that 61 percent of them had destroyed shareholder wealth for the acquirers and that a year later the losses got worse. Four reasons were given for the disappointing results:

1. The buying corporations paid too much.
2. Synergies and cost savings did not meet expectations.
3. Integration frustrated employees and customers.
4. Emphasis on cost-cutting and short-term profits weakened selling.[444]

An acquisition may be already failing when taken over and then simply not be cured. But more often the takeover company makes trouble by managing, notwithstanding earlier promises not to interfere, but if it is currently successful, rather to leave the acquisition alone after takeover. But the promises get broken, perhaps beginning with the corporate accounting department, which after all has responsibilities for monitoring financial developments. So it points out that standardizing accounting methods of the venture to mesh better with those of the parent corporation would be more efficient.

Then the human resources department says the same about insurance, other fringe benefits, and personnel policies. Marketing in the acquiring corporation may advocate imposing the name of the acquiring company on the new acquisition, or will leave its name and append something like "a division of ..." So identity becomes diluted for employees of the formerly independent company and morale in the acquisition suffers.

But it is when the parent company sends in its own managers, possibly as promotions for them, to occupy key positions in the newly acquired enterprise that the most severe damage happens. This damage takes the form of the most valuable employees of the acquisition leaving amid complaints that the acquiring company:

- Dropped their managers on us without explanation.
- Tried to squeeze fast profits out of us to make themselves look good.
- Imposed goals on us without regard to our resources.
- Assumed we'd follow new rules without telling us what those rules were.
- Made no attempt to appreciate our talents or capitalize on them.
- Took away our opportunities for advancement.

Amid those who don't leave may be new fears, defensiveness, distrust, resistance, disloyalty, lack of dedication at best, and possibly deliberate sabotage at worst. Precautionary remedies to avoid this include identifying and including key people in the transition process early, talking through things that may go wrong and working out solutions for them in advance, and moving carefully to avoid errors.

There may also be an option of being slow to interfere with the acquisition's culture and how the acquisition operates by leaving it autonomous as simply an investment. Some companies are formed simply for the purpose of making acquisitions to build a kind of holding company. The idea is that the central office will, through acquisition, enable owners of a firm to sell out and realize thereby cash or salable stock for their companies, while the holding company will add the value of the acquired company to its balance

---

444 David Henry, "Mergers, Why Most Big Deals Don't Pay Off," *Business Week*, October 14, 2002, p. 62.

sheet, enabling it either to borrow money or sell stock to make more acquisitions.

The overall firm may enjoy some economies of scale, perhaps on central office functions and financing as well as some stabilization through diversity. K2 Skis sold out to Cummins Engine because the latter could provide seasonal cash injections needed by K2 to make and ship ski inventory to shops in advance of the snow season, thereby enabling the shops to sell their inventory first and then pay for it. General Electric prospered through being in a wide variety of "first to sell and then to pay for it" industries such as appliances, nuclear plants, plastics, aircraft engines, steam turbines, and financing. It also applied great effort to development and application of systems for managing its diversity effectively.

Some other corporate acquisition strategies that worked well seem to be those of Berkshire Hathaway and Teledyne. Warren Buffet has practiced acquiring mainly as an investor who buys whole companies in whose managements and prospects his analysis sees promise. Teledyne prospered from the outset by acquiring companies whose technologies, principally in microelectronics and control systems, were interrelated. Both emphasized selecting companies that they believed had solid management and then worked to retain and support that management.[445]

Roll-ups

If the acquisitions are in a similar line of business and the holdings, usually small firms, are integrated to gain economies of scale or scope, the activity is referred to as a *roll-up*, the idea being that a bundle of similar small companies may in effect become a single bigger and more profitable non-diversified company. The following small firm grew through focused acquisition.

Two young Seattle entrepreneurs, largely through borrowing, managed to buy a restaurant. Then, borrowing against that restaurant's assets, they bought a second, and folded both into a single corporation. They arranged for a small public offering through which employees and outsiders could buy into the business, and also used stock from the corporation to buy another restaurant, fold it in, and then buy another. Most of the restaurants they bought were unprofitable, which was why they were able to buy them with stock. When they had done this with a half dozen restaurants, they picked the theme of the one most profitable, changed the themes of all the others to match it, closed those that did not become profitable, and thereby attained both overall profitability and growth, which enabled them to grow still further, and through economies of scale advertise, to become the well-known chain Sea Galley restaurants in Seattle.

Open issues

Considering the amount of acquisition and merging that has taken place and continues to do so, it is interesting that so far there has been relatively little academic study of the subject. How the challenges of managing acquisitions might best mesh with those of coping with growth from within is, for instance, an open question.

The other side of the bargain in acquisition, which has not been examined in this chapter, is that of the seller. It will be examined in the next chapter as one of several ways through which the relationship between the entrepreneur and the venture can conclude.

Exercises

Text discussion questions

1. How might it happen that a venture would miss the boat on growth opportunities?
2. Why do problems arise if a venture grows?
3. How could a company fail by growing?
4. Discuss the proposition that challenges of bringing about growth call for different managerial skills from those of coping with growth problems.
5. Can any company grow large if the management is smart enough? Explain.

---

[445] George A. Roberts, *Distant Force* (No publisher given, apparently self published, 2007, ISBN 978-0-9796363-0-6)

Case questions

10A-1 Meximeals

1. What success drivers does, versus could, Meximeals have going for it?
2. What are the pros and cons of growing Meximeals larger for two different growth strategies?
3. Which strategy should they adopt and why?
4. List some specific actions that should be taken within the company to pursue the strategy you recommend.

10A-2 Ampersand (E)

1. What are the pros and cons of accepting further investor capital to carry on the venture?
2. What should the team propose as positive covenants to be a good model for other companies if they go for the capital injection?
3. What, if anything, should worry them about proposing that?

10A-3 Ampersand (F)

1. What lessons about how to grow sales has the Ampersand team been exposed to up to this point?
2. How has the experience of Ampersand thus far determined what should be its long-run growth strategy?
3. What should now be the top three goals on Ampersand's list?
4. What assignments should be given to which Ampersand team members at this point?

Portfolio page possibilities

Each page, bearing the date and your name, should be one single-sided sheet, based upon this chapter, stating from your present impressions and information (quite possibly to change later) the following:

Page 10A-1 Growth trajectory possibilities

Describe two contrasting scenarios of growth trajectories your venture could follow, including developments both within the company and within its industry.

Page 10A-2 Most natural trajectory

Estimate the growth trajectory that would be best for your venture to aim at considering its product or service, market and intrinsic capabilities, and explain your reasoning.

Page 10A-3 Future growth markets

Portray potential growth markets for which your venture's strengths should be well constituted relative to existing and potential future competitors.

Page 10A-4 Most ambitious departure

Explain the most ambitious departures from the trajectory you described above that you might hope to succeed with and how you could attempt that.

Page 10A-5 Anticipating growth problems

Project a scenario of possible most-severe problems your company might encounter on an optimistically high growth trajectory and how they might be forestalled or coped with.

Term Projects

Venture history

1. What growth trajectory did the venture aim at versus achieve?
2. What growth mechanisms and success drivers seem to be working for the venture versus competitors, as displayed on a grid?
3. In what ways does growth seem to be something the company can choose at will?
4. What growth problems has the company experienced and how were they dealt with?

Venture planning guide

1. Prepare a plan for developing your venture beyond start-up.
2. Prepare a plan B for the best way of growing your venture if it starts to fall short, and at what point that plan should kick in.

CHAPTER 10B – Eventualities

Topics

1. Relinquishing leadership
2. Parting with ownership
3. Termination
4. Recovery
5. Careering

Checkpoints

a. What are the reasons entrepreneurs withdraw from top management?
b. Which of the six divestment methods do entrepreneurs expect to use most?
c. Which method of terminating a business is preferable and why?
d. What is the purpose of bankruptcy and what does it involve?
e. How is turnaround possible?
f. What is serial entrepreneurship, who does it, and who does not?

Regardless of any venture's trajectory, its original leaders must change roles eventually. Sometimes different talents are needed, and at other times more attractive opportunities may arise. Alternative exit paths may be shaped by events or choice. Economic downturn, emergence of superior competition, need for outside funding faster than it can be obtained, decline caused by management mistakes, withdrawal because of health or family problems, or simply the desire to do something else, for any number of reasons, including weariness of the routine, may prompt the entrepreneur's personal move, either out of management, out of business ownership, or both.

1. Relinquishing leadership

In some ventures management phases out quickly around inception and in others much later. Ideally, a founder's withdrawal should receive careful consideration and planning well before it happens, so others of consequence to the company, managers and non-managers alike, can adapt constructively. But events can thwart that. Founders can be peremptorily ousted by investors, and owner-managers can withdraw for any number of reasons. Those who sell their companies without adequate preparation may do so at too low a price or on poor terms. Or if they stay too long they may bungle, reducing the venture's value and consequently their returns from it. So all shareholders have reason to care about handling departure well.

It has long been common for entrepreneurs who raise money from venture capital firms to find themselves pushed aside after the capital comes in and the company gets going. *Venture* magazine estimated that this happens in at least one out of three venture capital financed start-ups, observing that:

> Most venture capitalists will try to ease out an inept entrepreneur as painlessly as possible. "You try to prepare the entrepreneur to come to the conclusion (that he should step aside)," Fred Warren of Brentwood Associates, Los Angeles, says. "And after the board of directors has come to the conclusion, they will designate one or two in their ranks to convince the individual that additional management horsepower is needed to

protect his investment." Some investors even make the entrepreneur's eventual dethronement an a priori condition of investing in his company. "We discuss the issue even before our investment is made," says Brent Rider, president of Los Angeles-based Union Venture Corp.

"We raise the subject from time to time early on," he continues, "making sure the entrepreneur is ready to accept it. If you handle the issue in advance, both sides are better equipped to handle it, and the reins are amicably turned over." [446]

To this observation Art Wilkes, founder of a firm where he was pushed aside after takeover by a big company, after which he founded a second firm where he was again pushed aside, this time by a venture capital firm that had invested in it, concluded:

> *Having absolute power is a hard thing to give up gracefully. But when you can say 'it won't upset me,' you have gone a long way toward insuring the success of your stock holdings. And just because they set you aside doesn't mean you're a bad guy. The venture capitalist recalled that the move was necessary to make room for a marketing person, while Wilkes returned to the laboratory to run the company's advanced development group.*

Even a founder who becomes highly successful as CEO can come under scrutiny for possible replacement. In mid 1999 *Business Week* observed of Southwest Airlines[447] that it was time to look for a successor to its founder, Herb Kelleher.

For most of Southwest's 28 years, the Wild Turkey-gulping, chain-smoking, Elvis-impersonating Kelleher has made precious few missteps in building one of the most profitable and admired airlines, now a model for low-fare carriers around the globe. But for all of his success, Kelleher's toughest challenge may lie ahead: hand over the controls in the right way at the right time to the right person.[448]

The article goes on to point out that Kelleher was holding the top three jobs personally, Chairman, CEO, and President, while also managing to dominate the board, serve as lead energetic role model, and be chief spokesman for the company both on Wall Street and in Washington D.C. The company's performance, profits, and stock price were all soaring. But who, observers wondered, would keep things that way when Kelleher left? By 2007 the question was still open. He was still chairman until July of that year and remained on the board until 2008.

Presumably, founder replacement can be planned for so it will transition at its best. But with other tasks of running the business and no thoughts of retirement in the near term, preparation for succession may not seem necessary right away. However, all that can be upset by surprise impulse or necessity arising from any number of causes, including illness, death, or rise of an alternative that is personally more attractive to the founder than staying on.

2. Parting with ownership

Reasons for shedding ownership include not only to cash in or to pass a company on to heirs, but sometimes also to free up time and resources for exploiting even better opportunities.

How the various owners of 359 firms, over three-fourths of which had sales of less than $14 million, expected to cash out of their enterprises was reported in 1990 by the American Institute of Certified Public Accountants[449] as can be seen in Exhibit 10b-1 below, which indicates rough equality between the fraction who anticipated selling out to another com-

pany, to outside private investors or to family members. A small minority expected to go public or liquidate.

At least these seem to have been their hopes. Not reported was how these owners actually did eventually part with their enterprises. But each method doubtless gets used by some, can to some extent be planned for, and is therefore worth considering. Missing from the list is a failure category, unless the last two categories, liquidation and unknown, are presumed to account for that.

---

446 John J. Fried, "When Entrepreneurs Lose Their Companies," *Venture*, December 1979, p. 59.
447 Kevin Freiberg and Jackie Freiberg, *Nuts!* (Austin, TX: Bard Press, 1996).
448 Wendy Zellner, "Earth to Herb: Pick a Co-Pilot," *Business Week*, August 16, 1999, p. 70.
449 *1990 Small Business Report* (New York: American Institute of Certified Public Accountants, 1990). See also *Inc.*, October 1990, p. 152.

Exhibit 10b-1 Expected ownership transfer methods

Method	Percent
Sell to another company	26
Sell to outside investors	25
Pass along to family	22
Sell to insiders	16
Go public	3
Liquidate	2
Don't know or Other	6
Total	100

A study by Cardozo,[450] which defined failure as termination of a business unable to pay all its bills, versus closure as termination without loss to creditors, summarized various other studies that estimated the ratio of closures to failures as ranging from three to twenty-four. From his own investigation of some 38,000 company registrations in Minnesota, he concluded that failures through bankruptcy accounted for 5.3 percent of firms that had disappeared, while failure with losses to creditors but not involving bankruptcy accounted for another 2.2 percent, and mergers appeared to account for around another 20 percent. There was no comment concerning the extent to which the remaining 72.5 percent of firms might have changed names, possibly after being sold in whole or part to other owners, or simply closed without losses to creditors. Still, it appears that the expectations of owners shown in Table 10b-1 underestimate the likelihood of involuntary liquidation as an eventual outcome, presumably one to avoid.

A. Passing along to family

A logical first exit thought for many founders is that some family member(s) may take over and carry on the business. But that can pose special issues. Heirs may or may not have good knowledge of the firm or the kinds of special capabilities required to run it profitably. Employees on the way up in the company may see their advancement opportunities reduced or eliminated by nepotism. Customers, lenders, and suppliers may or may not have faith that the heirs can manage a transition effectively.

But also it can work. Malcolm Forbes, Jr., Howard Hughes, and Ted Turner carried on quite successfully the firms they inherited. Johnson and Johnson, the bandage company, carried on profitably under family heirs, and so did Johnson Wax.

Three major decision areas in connection with bequeathing a venture to heirs are those of taxes, ownership, and management. Each can cause major problems that can even lead to failure of the business.

The main tax problem arises from the fact that there is a limit on how much wealth can be passed along to heirs upon death of an individual before the federal government begins taking 55 percent of every dollar. In 2008, that tax-free limit was $2,000,000. In 2010 the maximum inheritance tax rate dropped to zero, and was scheduled to return to 55 percent in 2011 unless changed by Congressional action. In addition, any individual can in any tax year make a gift of $12,000 tax-free to any number of other individuals, and that can include gifting shares of ownership in the business.

However, then the heirs become co-owners, so now the founder(s) have additional partners, who in turn may right away start pushing views about how the business should be run. Granting ownership to more than one heir can raise other issues. Should it be equal to minimize potential jealousy? Should an older child receive a larger share, to recognize that he or she had waited longer to receive it and that there is a time value to money? Or should one person receive a larger share to recognize greater dedication, past or future, to the business? How much power should which heir receive when?

The founder of a successful wholesale hardware business had a son and daughter. The son went to work for the firm, and his sister married an accountant. Then, when the son also married, expanded the firm, and diversified it into construction work, the accountant became uneasy about limitations he could see for his own separate career. Meanwhile the daughter became

---

450 Richard Cardozo and Patricia S. Borchert, "The Disappearance of Businesses," in *Frontiers of Entrepreneurship Research*, 2003, eds. William D. Bygrave and others (Wellesley, MA: Babson College, 2003) p. 19.

uneasy about the difference in living standards between herself and her sister-in-law.

She appealed to her father, the founder, who thereupon agreed to take her husband, the accountant, into the firm to train for management. Soon, he had taken charge of the office and begun to influence policies. When he started cracking down on slow-paying customers, his brother-in-law, the son of the founder, began to argue with him that the good will of those customers was important. When the founder then backed up his son, the daughter appealed that it was not fair for the father and son to gang up on her husband. Her father relented, urged his son to do the same, and the accountant forged ahead, assuming more authority, at the urging of the daughter, in reorganizing the business.

The son's wife now became uneasy about the accountant's growing power in the company and asked for a job in the company herself. Under pressure from the father, the accountant looked for things for her to do, but she was not satisfied that they were important enough. More infighting followed until the father, frustrated at his inability to combine peace in the family with running the business, decided to retire, leaving his son in charge. Unable to dispatch the accountant, however, partly because he loved his sister to whom the accountant was married and partly because she was bequeathed half ownership of the business, the son began avoiding the business in favor of expensive recreation. Then the accountant did too.

The owner, seeing his business deteriorating, returned from retirement to rescue it with the aid of three new managers hired through an executive recruiting firm. Daunted by the rebuilding job needed to avoid bankruptcy, however, he decided to sell out for something less than sixty cents on the dollar.[451]

Oddly missing amid management books and research articles, in light of the great importance to business that it often plays, is the role of jealousy, a force that can take on particularly great power in family-owned firms.

B. Selling to insiders

Employees sometimes buy the company they work for. It does not always work well, as the experience of United Airlines attests, but other times, as in the case of SAIC, a large company that is somewhat anonymous outside its clientele, principally the federal government, it greatly succeeds.

Sharing ownership with employees can both motivate them in the company's best interests and help them learn and appreciate more about the company so they can help it perform better. This can come about either by giving them shares of ownership, which will of course have tax consequences for them, or by selling them shares, either personally or through issuance by the company.

Sell-off to employees can also be done through an Employee Stock Ownership Plan (ESOP), which is set up as a separate trust that borrows from a bank or other financial institution the money to buy stock in the venture from the entrepreneur and any other investors. The bank loan is guaranteed by the venture. A federal tax break given to encourage this process includes elimination of capital gains tax for the former shareholders if they buy other U.S. stocks or bonds, provided that the ESOP has at least a 30 percent ownership of the venture. Another tax break is that the lender need pay tax on only half of the debt interest if the ESOP owns at least 50 percent of the venture.

Potential drawbacks under an ESOP are that it can cut off opportunity to sell or merge the business elsewhere, and that it entitles employees to information about financial matters of the company such as salaries, which management might prefer not to disclose.

Jack Stack, at age 30 in January 1979, had just been appointed plant manager at Springfield Remanufacturing, a subsidiary of International Harvester that had been set up five years earlier to rebuild diesel engines and parts for industrial and farm applications. In the previous year it had lost $2 million, and in March the employees, so far non-union, would vote on whether to join the United Auto Workers or the Teamsters. Jack was given six months to decide whether the plant should be shut down.

He called a meeting of all 140 plant employees, whom he recalls greeted his introductory remarks with totally immobile faces. When he finished, their only question was, "How old are you?"

As it happened, he had four years earlier been put in charge of another of the company's manufacturing operations, one whose four foremen

451 Howard J. Klein, *Stop! You're Killing the Business* (New York: Mason and Lipscomb 1974) p. 2.

reporting to him were all over 50 and whose 400 employees had just managed to rank last in productivity out of seven shops in the plant. Within his first three months, that rank changed to first. His cure began with giving each foreman a copy of the division's daily productivity figures broken down by foreman and compared in total with each of the other six divisions. The first time his new group beat its previous high score he gave his foremen coffee. The second time it was coffee and doughnuts, and the third was celebrated with pizza, poker, and beer at his house.

At Springfield he learned that the reason employees had called for a union vote was their hope that it might enable them to get more parts and tools they needed. He went after those and also began to introduce new incentive pay systems he had developed earlier. Morale quickly improved, along with productivity, customer servicing, safety record, and profits, which reached $250,000 after nine months. The union proposal lost by a 75 percent margin, and over the next year later profits rose to $1.1 million.

But then problems arose with the parent company. Though happy with Springfield's performance, International Harvester, due to a national economic recession in 1981, took a major downturn in sales. Top management announced that company capital constraints would require severely restricting Stack's division's growth or possibly even closing it.

Stack conferred with his group then proposed to upper management that he and the other Springfield employees buy the Springfield plant for $6 million. He was encouraged to seek potential outside investors. Things got worse for Harvester, which fell $4 billion into debt. Seeking ways to sell off assets, management gave Stack a one-month deadline to present a firm deal.

He did so, and with $100,000 from 12 managers, a $6 million loan from Bank of America, plus $1 million extended by Harvester, a deal was signed. Stack and all his workers were fired by Harvester, and a new business was formed under an ESOP in which they all shared ownership. Stack installed a control system that made all company finances transparent to employees, and began classes instructing them how financial performance worked, particularly on the income statement. Armed with this understanding, the employees figured out ways to operate with rapidly increasing efficiency, and

consequent profitability that soon put their new enterprise in the black.[452]

C. Selling to another company

An entrepreneur may profit by selling a venture to another firm, small or large, in return for shares in the other company and/or cash. Because larger acquiring companies, especially, often pay high prices for companies they buy, this can be a lucrative way to cash in on venture ownership. Selling can, depending upon terms of the deal, permit anyone who holds either stock or options in the venture, such as perhaps employees or earlier investors in the venture, to harvest their stake. Hence, it may strongly appeal.

Cardozo found only two studies comparing mergers with closures, one indicating that about 50 percent of some 250 high technology companies that disappeared had merged with other firms, while another found that 88 percent of California savings and loans that disappeared in the 1970s and 1980s did so through merger.[453]

Many corporations are constantly on the prowl for acquisitions to enhance growth, as noted in the preceding chapter. Consequently some entrepreneurs who own promising companies, especially if they possess valuable proprietary elements such as intellectual property or brand loyalty, find themselves frequently approached by scouts of larger firms. In addition to growth per se, as discussed in the preceding chapter, what companies seeking acquisitions may hope to gain is summarized in the shaded area on the following page.

Any of these seemingly good reasons for corporate acquisition may be undermined by other factors, such as poor choice, bad management, or wrong pricing that strip away advantages, as was noted in the preceding chapter. A case in point is the story of Burg Tool Company.

> Fred Burg, a European-trained machinist who had immigrated to the U.S., invented and patented a better production machine tool, founded a company in Los Angeles to produce it and, with the help of his sons, built it to prosperity. Success brought it attention from big corpora-

---

[452] Lucien Rhodes, with Patricia Amend, "The Turnaround," *Inc.*, August 1986, p. 42.
[453] Cardozo, "The Disappearance of Businesses."

Strategic advantages sometimes sought through acquisition

- A place to invest profits rather than paying them out as dividends to shareholders.
- Expansion of operating capacity faster or cheaper than can be done anew to gain economies of scale.
- Frontier technological know-how possessed by the acquired company, including R&D capabilities of key employees.
- Additional market connections, political clout, locations, and brand presence.
- Integration forward and/or backward in the profit chain.
- More stability through diversifications such as complementary seasonality, government versus commercial, or consumer versus industrial markets.
- More balance in capital structure, as where a corporation that is cash rich takes over a smaller firm that needs money for attractive opportunities or to balance seasonal swings. Cummins Diesel, long on cash at one point, acquired K2 Skis, which needed money to operate amid seasonal cash swings in the ski industry.
- Tax advantages where a corporation with good profits takes over a firm with R&D losses to reduce income taxes through integration.

tions seeking acquisitions, but the family for years rejected their overtures.

Eventually, however, as innovation from competitors was intensifying, sales were growing, and Burg Tool Company's capacity was becoming strained, Fred, now approaching seventy, reconsidered. He did not relish the challenges of expansion, and turning the business over to his sons also did not seem a satisfactory way to cope.

So when a large suitor, Houdaille Industries, made inquiry in mid-1965, he agreed to discuss selling out. Houdaille too had been built by a driving entrepreneur, a Frenchman who had contributed innovations in shock absorbers for cannons during World War I that would later be used in autos and other machines. By the mid-1960s, however, he had retired and been replaced by an executive good at numbers and trained as a lawyer who specialized in finance. His goal was to increase shareholder value, particularly through acquisitions. Buying Burg Tool was a logical move under this strategy with Fred Burg nominally still in charge.

But after takeover many changes were imposed on Burg. There were soon different managers, different rules, different reactions by employees, and different marketing and product development priorities. There was a new plant and more money, but also more paperwork, reporting, and constraints from top management.

Major ups and downs in the industry coupled with efforts by competitors to beat Burg's new moves added challenges. Efficiency, productivity, and innovation were talked about as goals for

Burg, but didn't happen. Before long the old man and his sons were out. The company went through a leveraged buyout by a Wall Street firm, KKR, but then ran out of cash and was liquidated.[454]

Did Fred Burg say yes to the wrong acquirer? Did he accept the wrong terms for a deal? Could he have influenced the direction of the company more effectively after takeover? Or was the unhappy outcome inevitable? Answers can be proposed, but not known.

Certainly, some entrepreneurs reach happier business outcomes through corporate takeover, as seen in another Southern California company, Ryan Aircraft.

Claude Ryan, 1898–1982, began his work life driving a wagon for his family's laundry in Parsons, Kansas, later delivering newspapers. When his parents bought a citrus grove and moved to Orange, California, young Ryan, fascinated by the new romance of flying, persuaded his father to sponsor lessons for him at a private flight school. But the school went broke before he could finish, and he went off to study mechanical engineering, the closest subject he could find to aeronautics at Oregon State University. After graduation and another stint in the family orchard, he managed to get accepted for flight training by the army, after which he flew patrol for the U.S. Forest Service.

Tiring of that, he tried a couple of other lines of work, auto parts selling and a laundry, before getting the idea of imitating other pilots who did stunt flying for a living. In San Diego he

---

[454] Max Holland, *When the Machine Stopped* (Boston: Harvard Business School Press, 1989)

found he could buy a war-surplus biplane for $400. Adding the sale of his Ford for $300 to his $150 in savings left him with the plane plus $25 to hire a mechanic to help him ready it for flight and another $25 for working capital. The San Diego harbormaster let him defer a $50–per-month fee to use a waterfront field, where in 1922 he initiated the Ryan Flying Company, offering flight training, aerial taxi service, and excursions. Eventually, he began also buying and selling used planes, then modifying some of them with bigger engines and widened bodies for more carrying capacity.

A wealthy 23-year-old acquaintance, B. Franklin Mahoney, proposed that Ryan join him in starting a regularly scheduled year-round airline, the nation's first, flying between Los Angeles and San Diego. It began in March 1925, with Mahoney providing the money, Ryan doing the rest, and the two splitting the profits. That same year Congress passed legislation allowing commercial companies to fly U.S. mail.

Already modifying existing planes to carry passengers, Ryan decided to design a plane specifically for mail freight. The result was the M-1, which proved to be a precursor to a plane designed to fly non-stop across the Atlantic, Charles Lindbergh's Spirit of St. Louis. More aircraft manufacturing followed for the military over ensuing decades. Aeronautics was an industry on the build, supported largely by war spending.

By 1959, Ryan Aircraft had shifted from making planes to building parts of them for other companies such as Boeing, and had also moved into making experimental missiles. Then in 1969, it was sold to a conglomerate, Teledyne Corporation.[455] Now wealthy and famous, Ryan retired to work on other airplane ideas with his son.[456]

The outcome differences of Burg versus Ryan might trace to many things: different industries, histories, acquirers and vicissitudes of the marketplace. Burg's technology was lower, his company was smaller, its marketplace was private industry, and competition was closing in. Ryan went into takeover as mainly a government products subcontractor. Houdaille Corporation, which took over Burg, was a manufacturer of commercial products, while Teledyne, which bought Ryan, was more of a conglomerate in advanced technology and had extensive experience in acquiring other companies and keeping them in operation.

Entrepreneur buy-backs

Sometimes when buyout degrades an acquisition the original entrepreneur may be able to buy back and repair it.

In 1980, John G. Robinson and David McKelvey sold their software company, Information Associates, to Westinghouse for $7.5 million. Three years later in August 1983 when it was losing money under corporate management, they bought it back for $2.5 million and returned it to profitability within a year. Explaining the turnaround, Robinson commented, "At Westinghouse the focus was on internal management, not the customer."

— • —

In 1971, Joe Hrudka sold his company, Mr. Gasket, to W.R. Grace and company for $17 million and signed an agreement not to compete. Ten years later the non-compete agreement lapsed, and when he threatened to compete with his old venture, Grace let him buy back five of its marginally profitable product lines for $4.3 million. He promptly cut overhead by one-third through termination of 85 managers and consolidation of channels. He also added new lines and within two years managed to raise profits to $5.1 million, at which point he took his reclaimed company public and profited again.[457]

D. Selling to outside private investors

Just as for a would-be buyer it makes sense to look through a variety of potential sources to find potential sellers, it similarly makes sense for a would-be seller to consider a variety of sources for potential buyers. It is easy to find business brokers willing to help, particularly if they can have exclusive rights as sales agent for some fixed period of time. But that is probably better a last, rather than first place to start. Instead, personal connections with bankers, accountants, attorneys, and other such professionals are more likely for openers.

Ben and Jerry decided to sell their company and signed an agreement with a broker to help them. The broker found a buyer. But then they

---

[455] George A. Roberts, *Distant Force* (No publisher given, apparently self published, 2007, ISBN 978-0-9796363-0-6) pp. 85-88.

[456] Ev Cassagneres, *The Spirit of Ryan* (Blue Ridge Summit, PA: Tab Books, *Inc.*, 1982).

[457] Daniel Cohen, "Buying Back Your Company," *Venture Magazine*, January 1984, p. 46.

decided not to sell. The broker demanded a commission, as called for in the contract. Ben and Jerry refused to pay. They also pulled all the cash out of their bank account and deposited it in a personal account at a different bank in another state. The broker sued, Ben and Jerry lost and were forced to pay.[458]

How public to be about the company's availability depends on impact such information might have on customers, employees, and suppliers as well as how much it might help in finding potential buyers. It may or may not be desirable to inform personal acquaintances and business associates through whom the information might leak to competitors. But because the process of finding potential buyers, letting them check the company out, and then negotiating with them, may take months, secrecy may not be practical.

Buyers will want to see the plant and meet employees, as well as examine records. Employees may wonder who these people are and begin speculating. Because there are many possibilities for leaks, it may be better to explain the process so employees can participate in it and see that their interests are being taken into consideration. Employees then may help it go better, whereas if they know about selling but are not supposed to, they might make it go worse.

Because sale to an individual or small group will probably include some down payment plus a balance over time, it is important that the buyer(s) be able to keep the company profitable during the payout. Hence, a check of prior job performance and personal record of keeping commitments, credit and otherwise, is desirable. Employees can probably help in sizing up the prospective buyer, because they understand what it takes to make the business go, have their desires about the kind of person they will want

to work for, and should realize that their jobs will still be on the line after takeover.

E. Going public

Public stock offerings were discussed in Chapter 5C as a way of raising capital for expansion and providing a market for employees to cash in on shares or options they may hold. Obviously, public offerings can also be a way for existing owners to sell out entirely. Alternatively, publicly offering part of the business can be combined with sale of another part to another company, as the following example from the United Kingdom illustrates.

> A private multi-division company in pharmaceuticals, Gordon, enjoyed profits of over 1 million pounds in 1993. Its management realized it was a potential float candidate but was unclear about the implications of a float. Flotation involves selling a fraction of shares to outside companies or the public to get the company listed on an exchange.
>
> Advisors conducted an in-depth review of the business, analyzing its marketplace, organizational structure, financial anatomy, and reputation within its industry and among other interested parties. Potential underwriters for a float were introduced to the company and reviewed it. Valuations, organizational structure, market strategy, and growth potential were all discussed.
>
> The report triggered a complete review of the business plan process and possible decentralization into separate units. One division was to be groomed for development using external finance and geographical expansion. Another was to be floated free in three to five years with specific action plans.
>
> Over the forthcoming six years one non-core division, a retail pharmacy chain, was sold to a competitor at a favorable price. The main business was taken public on the London Stock Exchange at a market capitalization of 772 million pounds.[458]

3. Termination

Entrepreneurship requires optimism. More than 30 percent of founders estimate their

chances of success at 80 percent or higher, according to the data of Cooper et al,[460] even

---

[458] Fred "Chico" Lager, *Ben & Jerry's* (New York: Crown, 1994) p. 63.

[459] Ian Smith, *Growing a Private Company* (London: Kogan, 2001).

[460] Arnold C. Cooper and others, *New Business in America* (Washington D.C.: the NFIB Foundation, 1990) p. 4.

though in fact many more start-ups fail. When failure happens, many people may be let down: founders, suppliers, investors, customers, and lenders. The less they are let down, the better, and it therefore makes sense, regrettably, to consider in advance such questions as:

1. How, in order of likelihood, could things go wrong and cause failure?

2. What might give warning of one or more such events?

3. What advance actions could minimize the chances of failure?

4. What advance actions could minimize costs of failure?

But it is also fair to consider how answering such questions might have prevented the following disappointing outcomes.

It looked like a natural combination to win. Joe Burnieika had been a partner in a large advertising agency, sold his share, then opened his own public relations firm, and operated it successfully for six years. In 1994 he joined Robin Emerson and Larry Bearfield, who had successfully operated an advertising and marketing firm of their own for 10 years that had done $5 million in business the preceding year. The trio formed a new joint enterprise with projected sales of $5.5 million for 1995.

They spent heavily on new equipment and expanded the workforce to 18 employees, some of them highly priced, in anticipation of growth. But actual business yielded only $2 million that year.

Searching for more work to cover expenses, they started bidding low on advertising projects. Margins fell by over half and some customers started stretching out payments. In October 1996, the firm was shut down and the partners separated, with Joe Burnieika working to collect the remaining receivables to pay debts. His hindsight conclusion was that the firm should have cut staff faster and hired freelancers to reduce costs before the cash ran out.[461]

— • —

In 1990, Sue Mackarness and her husband, Christopher Notley created Transworld Teachers, a school in San Francisco for teaching English to foreign students. The school used a novel easygoing, participative approach developed by Mackarness. Enrollment grew, 390 students graduating the first year with 80 percent getting jobs. In 1994, sales reached $550,000.

But by then the company, which the partners had regarded, according to Notley, as "just our little mom-and-pop store" was in serious financial trouble, little to no attention having ever been paid to formal planning, definition of responsibilities, or financial controls. Unable to obtain bank loans, the couple borrowed cash and sold stock to friends and acquaintances however they could. One lender, for example, was granted a 300 percent return on a $5,000 loan. The partners had deemed love of the work more important than profitability. But problems of covering payroll and other expenses finally convinced them they needed managerial help.

A consultant, Neville Fridge, whom they contacted at the suggestion of one of their investors, offered, to the owners' grateful relief, to join the company, take stock in lieu of salary and invest $7,000 himself for 29.6 percent ownership. Then he took over the office and fired the bookkeeper, whom later he accused of embezzlement based upon an audit. He subsequently bought out another shareholder who owned 26.2 percent, adopted the title of president, called an emergency shareholders meeting, appointed new directors, and fired Mackarness. Legal warfare followed for 14 weeks.

In response to being fired, Mackarness froze the company bank account, whereupon Fridge obtained a restraining order barring Mackarness and Notley from entering the school. The court relented when it learned Mackarness' credentials were essential for operations. Many employees felt Fridge, who had been meeting payroll with checks that could, for a change, be cashed right away, was more competent at running the business.

Eventually, Mackarness and Notley bought Fridge's shares back for $40,000. But they had spent $43,000 on legal fees and divorced. They tried to recreate the business, this time in Prague. But that failed, and they filed for Chapter 7 bankruptcy.

Meanwhile, Fridge formed a new school in San Francisco, which he named New World Teachers, hiring some of the prior staff and introducing a curriculum which one observer described as a photocopy of the old one. By 2008, New World Teachers appeared to be advertising as a Web-based source of contacts in San Francisco for teaching English programs around the world.[462]

---

[461] Phaedra Hise, "Boston Ad Agency Finds Cost of Doing Business Doesn't Add Up," *Inc.* February 1997, p. 25.
[462] Stephanie Gruner, "Takeover," *Inc.* April 1997, p. 72.

How to tell when a venture is not working is not always simple. It depends on both how the venture is supposed to work and where it is along the path of development. If there is a written business plan, then one early danger sign may be failure to meet forecast. But progress can sometimes seem on schedule when it is not. If, for instance, the company has produced its goods, sold them, and collected from customers, the financial statements may look all right. But customers may be having trouble with the goods that will lead to large returns and/or collapse of the market. Possibly deliveries have laid a basis for lawsuits. Or the venture may be on track, customers may be happy, and just ahead are as yet unannounced moves of competitors that will eclipse the venture. Many new microcomputer firms, for instance, were doing fine until IBM and Microsoft introduced the DOS standard, which became dominant in the marketplace, rendering obsolete ventures using any other systems.

Some signs that a venture isn't working may be obvious, as when it can't raise needed capital, recruit key people, obtain supplies, or get customers either to buy or to pay for what they bought. Other signs such as impending technical obsolescence may be harder to discern. Even the tightening of credit in the economy can sink a business as the bank decides not to renew a loan, other banks in turn decline to extend one, and the company has to shed its assets to pay bills. That can force the company into bankruptcy, even though it may have been otherwise healthy. How best to detect potential danger signs should be thought through as part of the planning process, so that if the venture is liable to sink, at least the founders can act early to minimize their downside losses, even if it requires shutting down the business and moving on.

Recalling some of his many ventures that did not work out as well as many others that did, Warren Avis said:

> The first loss is always the cheapest. So don't allow yourself to get frustrated or discouraged if something unexpected and inexplicable happens in one of your early entrepreneurial outings. Things get off track for everybody at one time or another. When that happens, usually it's best to sell a losing or disappointing business for what you can get for it; stop worrying about any loss; and then move on to the next profitable opportunity. (If only I always followed my own advice!)[463]

Staying alert for other potential side-street opportunities may be possible despite the heavy demands of starting up. They may even strengthen the entrepreneur's hand by providing useful information to give to others who may at some time be able, in turn, to help the entrepreneur.

Shutdown

Procedures for closing down a company depend on whether it is a proprietorship, partnership, or corporation and whether it is solvent. Cases of insolvency will be discussed later in connection with bankruptcy.

Simplest to close as well as to set up is a proprietorship. Paying all the bills and notifying the state and city to stop the renewal of business licenses are the only legal requirements. There may also be employees to pay, assets to sell, leases to terminate, signs and telephone listings to remove, customers to notify, and warranties to honor. If the company has set up retirement plans for employees, these may need attention. Presumably, the reason for closing down will be that not much has been going on with the company. Otherwise, there should be something to pass along for someone else—possibly employees or an outside buyer—to run.

Partnerships are more complicated. A partnership may automatically be terminated by the death of a partner, depending on how the arrangement is legally structured. State laws govern partnerships, and three things are generally required under those laws to terminate them. The first is dissolution, which means that the partnership agreement is ended by the withdrawal or death of a partner, or by other action. The second is winding up, which essentially means stopping operations, fulfilling obligations, paying creditors, collecting receivables, and selling off assets. The third is distri-

---

[463] Warren Avis, *Take a Chance to be First* (New York: Macmillan, 1986) p. 195.

bution of assets according to provisions of the partnership agreement.

In addition to state laws governing the existence of a partnership are federal laws recognizing it for tax purposes. Federal rules as to what constitutes the termination of a partnership are different from state rules. For instance, either the buyout by one partner of another partner's interest or the cessation of operations constitutes federal termination. The rules may change at either state or federal level at any time, thus it is generally advisable to hire a lawyer who specializes appropriately and is up to date on these rules for help with the process.

Corporate termination is also complex and governed by state law as well as federal tax rules. Death of an owner does not affect the life of a corporation as it does a partnership. A corporation has its own life. State laws specify what is required to terminate it; as with partnerships, legal help is advisable.

Liquidation

An important part of shutdown will be to dispose of company assets. The going concern or goodwill value of the business in shutdown is zero. Equipment, whether sold at auction or to someone else, such as a used equipment dealer, will probably be worth only pennies on the dollar. Tooling will be worth a fraction of its scrap value. If there is inventory, it may have perhaps some value if it is new, and most likely zero value if it is in-process.

There are companies liquidating all the time, as the announcements of auctions will attest. And if the real objective is to scrap the business, whether to retire or to get a fresh start, auctioning off assets will do it. To see how auctioning works at no risk anyone can find one that involves company liquidation to watch. Metropolitan newspapers advertise them.

At a liquidation auction will be the equipment and any inventory of a failed company, the auctioneer, potential bidders, and possibly a few other spectators. Likely, one observer will be the business owner, perhaps partly out of nostalgia and curiosity, and probably to verify that nothing gets "lost" in the auction process.

At the auction of a manufacturing company in Seattle the shop floor was covered with equipment, furniture, and supplies. A crowd of about 80 people wandered around, most carrying a large card with a number that identified them as a bidder, looking over the merchandise, and occasionally making notes of things that interested them. A member of the family that had owned and operated the failed business, a trailer manufacturing company, was there. Proceeds would go to the SBA, which had foreclosed on the business for defaulting on a loan.

The auctioneer walked over to a numbered item or pile, said into his microphone a few words of praise for the goods, followed by something like, "We'll start the bidding at…" some specific dollar amount. He would then invite higher bids, recognize each bid by repeating it, then invite a still higher one, sometimes suggesting a higher number himself. His incentive was that he would receive a percentage of the receipts.

Occasionally he would cheat, indicating that higher bid had been offered, even though it had not, and asking for a still higher number, then sometimes indicating someone had, through some presumed nod or wave of their numbered card, offered the amount. If nobody responded to this he would back down to a number less, but still far above the last valid bid, and ask for offers from there.

After all the items had been bid, he announced that he was accepting an offer of someone who had bid a price for the entire lot. So all the other offers were then moot. The person who bought the lot was a stranger from another city who wanted to start a similar company there. Several weeks after the auction, the buyer confided to an acquaintance that he had "persuaded" the auctioneer to accept his terms for the lot by informing the auctioneer that he had heard the auctioneer, before the auction began, tell an assistant to load a stack of electrical cable from among the inventory into the trunk of his car. Essentially, the stranger threatened to inform on the auctioneer about this theft if his offer for the lot was not accepted. He got it.

Failing in business can be traumatically unpleasant in many respects. In the case of the above company, the family who had owned the business lost everything, because they had been required to guarantee with all their personal assets the loan that the business could not repay. So had an outside investor, a fairly well-known

256 "Overview Almanac," *Inc.* 500, October 20, 1998 p. 18.

local personality. Employees of the company lost their jobs and the wages they had coming when the company closed.

Bankruptcy

Sometimes a business does so badly that it and/or the owner ends up with debts so large that no way can be seen to repay them in full. To deal with that possibility there are bankruptcy laws, the purpose of which is to provide a way to make such repayment as is possible with assets remaining, do it in a way that tries to be fair with creditors, and at the same time leave the debtor with enough to survive and possibly make a fresh start. It was estimated in 1998 that at least 30 percent of all bankruptcies stemmed from unsuccessful company start-ups.[463]

At the simplest mechanical level, bankruptcy amounts to filling out standard forms and filing them along with a fee of a few hundred dollars, depending upon the type of bankruptcy, in a bankruptcy court. This filing is an agreement to give the court control of all the venture's assets or, in the case of personal bankruptcy, the owner's assets, except for certain assets specified as exempt to allow the fresh start. These might include personal effects and perhaps interest in a residence or a car.

Reasons for learning about bankruptcy in advance are to know what rights to such assets may exist, what steps to take for preserving such rights, and whether there may be better ways to deal with hopeless indebtedness than going through bankruptcy. For instance, bankruptcy stops any collection from lawsuits against the company. Those suing must stand in line with other creditors, and that may help. On the other hand, going through bankruptcy

can permanently hurt a reputation and ruin credit. Bankruptcy stays on a person's credit history for ten years and can impede borrowing or obtaining credit cards, although it may not make them impossible to get.

Undesirable consequences can sometimes be mitigated by proper planning. For instance, a bankruptcy court can force the sale of assets to pay creditors and can cut or eliminate the owner's salary. If, however, the owner earlier had entered into a written employment contract with the company and formally pledged selected assets of the business as collateral for the contract through public filing of notice, then the owner would have become a secured creditor of the business with first rights to ownership of the pledged assets ahead of other creditors.[464]

Help from an attorney in thinking through whether, when, how, and which form of bankruptcy to pursue if things get bad may be necessary. But probably money can be saved and some mistakes can be avoided by reading about the subject first in books, such as *Surviving Bankruptcy*.[465] Filing for bankruptcy can be done without a lawyer by filling out some fairly simple forms and paying the fee in cash. Doing this immediately freezes any lawsuits pending against the business, and creditors of the company lose all power to collect. Hence, there is a point of timing to consider. Maybe the company can work its way around bankruptcy by letting creditors know it is a possibility and negotiating a settlement with them. Or maybe bankruptcy should be declared just before they can crack down and take assets that could be helpful for attempting recovery. More about bankruptcy appears in Appendix 10b-1.

4. Recovery

What happens after failure? Systematic data on this subject are limited. Most people suffer personal setbacks, even those who become great successes eventually. Winston Churchill

failed at most things he tried in politics until World War II, but his brilliance with words made him a great success. Life goes on.

---

[463] Rodney Ho, "Banking on Plastic," *The Wall Street Journal*, March 9, 1998, p. 1.
[464] Wilson Harrell, *For Entrepreneurs Only* (Hawthorn: N.J., Career Press, 1994) p. 124.
[465] Dan Goss Anderson and M.J. Wardell, *Surviving Bankruptcy* (Englewood Cliffs: Prentice Hall, 1992).

Restart after failure

Countless entrepreneurs fail in business, sometimes repeatedly, but start again, and eventually succeed. Well-known examples include Henry Ford, Milton Hershey, Forrest Mars, and Karl Eller.[466] Others are less famous, like Isodoros Garifalakis, who was forced into Chapter 7 bankruptcy by his bank, then restarted his welding business with help from former customers, or Sam Casternovia, who was creating a real estate empire by building malls but went broke during the crash of 1986, then acquired a billboard company and built another fortune.

Bill Ruger's interest in guns since a boy had led him to designing them during World War II for Auto-Ordnance, a submachine-gun producer. After the war he quit, and with a partner, whom he later bought out, set up the Ruger Corporation to develop a hardware tool line and a .22 Automatic Pistol. He profited as a parts supplier to his former employer, but lost money on a government contract and on developing a line of small hand-held drills, which proved too expensive for consumers. He recalled, "The harder we worked, the poorer we got, until finally the company went bankrupt and into receivership and that was the end of it."

The pistol he had designed gained admiration from a prospective investor, Alexander Sturm, who agreed to put up $50,000 and let Ruger restart with equipment bought out of the old company in receivership. The leaders of other pistol companies, High Standard and Colt, predicted failure. But a highly favorable article about the weapon in *The American Rifleman* precipitated a large number of mail orders with checks enclosed. As Ruger recalled, "Alex Sturm came around for lunch one day in late 1949 as I was writing out the check to cover our payroll. I said to him, 'Alex, this is the last of that $50,000.' But fortunately that day we had a hundred pistols ready to ship, and Alex took a hundred $37.50 money orders to the bank. Now we were really in business."[467]

How many failed entrepreneurs take another job, retire, go back to school, or restart is not recorded, but readily available anecdotes clearly indicate that many do.

Variety in recoveries

Many examples of less widely known entrepreneurs restarting after failure have been described in business periodicals such as *Success* (which, ironically, failed in 2000) including the following:[468]

Chellie Campbell bought out her partners in a bookkeeping service in 1988 and built it to sales of $36,000 per month. But when her head bookkeeper left, taking along key clients, sales dropped by 75 percent, which led to bankruptcy in 1994. Chellie restarted by offering "Financial Stress Reduction Workshops," a sideline she had developed a knack for several years earlier. This tripled her personal income the first year and by 1998, raised it to $140,000 per year.

Brett Kingstone published a how-to entrepreneurship book for college students in 1981.[469] Later, he started a fiber-optic custom-lighting company, which did well until it was sued by a rival firm for alleged theft of trade secrets. His firm lost in 1989, and he was ousted. He grew a beard and sailed the Bahamas for six months. By the time he returned, his former firm had failed and was being liquidated. He bought some of its equipment, and in 1990 started another company in the same line of work. By 1998, it was reporting sales close to $1 million per month.

Mark Kvamme founded a software distribution company in 1983 that was forced out of business in 1986 when two of its major customers went bankrupt. He took jobs in marketing for technology companies over the next three years, then co-invested in a buddy's 1989 advertising venture. A third partner also joined, and over the next ten years the firm grew, going public in 1995, to employ 600 people and report 1997 sales of $133.6 million.

Scott Schuster experienced a theft in 1993 of virtually everything in his recording studio (including the toilet paper!) that put him out of business. Consequently penniless at age 29, he and his family were evicted from their apartment, following which his third child was born with medical problems. He filed for bankruptcy.

---

[466] Karl Eller, *Integrity Is All You've Got* (New York: McGraw Hill, 2005)

[467] R.L. Wilson, *Ruger & His Guns* (New York: Simon & Schuster, 1996) p. 23.

[468] Elaine Pofeldt, "They Rose from the Ashes" *Success*, July 1998 p. 40.

[469] Brett Kingstone, *The Student Entrepreneur's Guide* (Berkeley, CA: Ten Speed Press, 1981).

Moving himself and his family in with a friend temporarily, he drew upon his experience in computer programming to start his own consulting firm in 1996, whose sales by 1998 were approaching $14 million per year.

Not reported in the article, regrettably perhaps, was how these entrepreneurs saw their alternatives or whether they considered any.

5. Careering

Based on acquaintance with thousands of business owners during a long consulting career, Leon Danco observed that:

> *Old entrepreneurs and their money are easily parted by the simple act of telling them, 'Of course you can do it again.' I've seen too many successful business founders, free of the responsibility of management because they 'sold out,' who take their money and say to themselves, "I did it once. I know the secret. I can do it again." Mostly they fail—taking with them much (sometimes all) of the money they accumulated the first time, plus the cash, credit and reputation of those who believed in them. It's sad to watch, but you can't tell them.*
>
> *What this indicates to me is that success is a combination of timing, relevance, luck, and opportunity, coming together at just the right time, with just the right amount of energy, guts, and resources. This means, any given successful founder's activities just may not be duplicable—all the more reason why their creations must not be allowed to disappear.*[470]

Whose responsibility it might be to follow through on Danco's injunction he does not say. But first the responsibility for sustaining entrepreneurs' creations will fall upon the entrepreneurs themselves.

Howard Schultz withdrew after many years as CEO of Starbucks in 2007. The company declined, he returned and was working, amid some layoffs, to restore it in 2008.

— • —

Bill Gates withdrew from management of Microsoft in favor of Steve Ballmer, but continued active involvement in both the company and the microcomputer industry as a strategist and spokesman while shifting the majority of his efforts to giving away his fortune through creation and leadership of the Bill & Melinda Gates Foundation, a nonprofit organization devoted to humanitarian causes. In 2008, he withdrew as active spokesman for the company to concentrate on his foundation.

Serial entrepreneurship

Entrepreneurs sometimes choose between staying with one venture and continuing to build it over time, or moving on to start one venture after another in series, not just a second one, but sometimes whole strings of them, which has inspired the appellation *serial entrepreneur*.

Steve Jobs stayed with Apple, was displaced from Apple, returned to Apple leading it to vastly higher success, and in between tried Next, another computer company that did not last, and Pixar, a movie company that did last and which he has also stayed with.

— • —

Richard Branson started out in the music business and went on to create new businesses in a variety of industries including both air and space travel. By 2008, he operated over 50 businesses with over 200,000 employees around the world, all from beginning with his first office in a burial crypt, the only space whose rent his first venture could initially afford.

Somewhat more mixed was the final outcome of William Lear, whose ventures were characterized not only by their number but also by their variety in both type and level of success.

By age 24 Bill Lear had started a radio store with a partner, sold out, started a store of his own, and gone bankrupt. He had built a kit biplane in his backyard that did not fly, and on contract a radio station that did work. In Chicago, then the nation's largest radio manufacturing center, he became a technical troubleshooter in that industry, which was expanding explosively, the number of home sets having jumped from 30,000 in 1922 to 1.5 million five years later. At the first radio show in 1927, there were some 8,700 people and companies registered. Using his family's apartment as a lab, Bill and an employee who had worked with him previously in the radio store undertook to develop fixes for

---

[470] Leon Danco, *Inside the Family Business* (Cleveland, OH: Center for Family Business, 1980) p. 28.

technical bugs that produced squeaks, buzzes, hums, and squawks among the fast-changing new radio models.

Soon he was producing his own radios, violating, as were numerous other radio-makers, the patents of RCA, which now held some 2,400 of them, over half the total number issued up to that time. As a small producer among the 250-odd radio companies, he was overlooked and got away with it.

Soon, he introduced a better coil design of his own. A larger producer, Galvin Radio, started buying coils from him, then hired him as chief engineer, but still let him freelance on designing radios for other companies. He developed the first fully practical automobile radio, which became the start of Motorola.

He also became interested in developing instruments for airplanes that would help pilots navigate and started a new company to make and sell homing radios for aircraft. Most pilots weren't interested, so for a while he lived on car radio patent royalties.

At age 32 he moved from Chicago to New York to be at a busier airport, but within three months had fallen so deeply into debt that the future seemed hopeless. In his head were new product ideas, including a direction finder design. But engineering competition was greater in New York, and he had essentially no capital. Recalling how he fell behind on alimony payments to his first wife and payroll to his employees, he later jokingly claimed, "I bought a bottle of Scotch and spent my last dollar on a room in the tallest hotel I could find. I planned to jump. But when I got to the room I remembered that I am afraid of heights. So I drank the Scotch and went to bed." It was not the last time he contemplated suicide.

More practically, he deliberately filled his mind with all the radio problems he could think of and, on the advice of some book he read, commanded his subconscious to find solutions. Looking at an electronic signal generator owned by a friend, he got an idea for a better multi-band radio, and through the friend he met a Navy engineer who helped him obtain a Navy development contract for it. Another friend whom he told about it gave him the idea of proposing it to RCA. He asked the company for $500 and a box of components, and with that in two weeks developed a prototype that he demonstrated to RCA's president. RCA, it turned out, had a patent

on the technology Lear had used, but they paid him for the idea anyway, $50,000 down for rights plus $40,000 per year for four years.

Lear now concentrated his efforts completely on aviation radios and instruments, occasionally borrowing so much to pay for development and sales efforts that did not pay off that he neared bankruptcy. At one point when his wife Moya became anxious about it he told her, "Honey, you don't have to worry because they can't bankrupt my mind. There's an infinite supply of ideas in there, and all I have to do is dip into it."[471]

World War II and its need for aircraft instruments took Lear's avionics company to prosperity, but following it the military market slumped and one employee recalled that "there were pay periods when people took a few shares of Lear stock in lieu of cash ... The (office) would complete paperwork against the military contracts, fly to the Air Force to get it signed, then fly to the bank in Detroit for a loan against the contract to meet the payroll."[472] But shortly, Lear produced another new instrument that won the company a contract worth nearly a billion dollars over the ensuing twelve years.

Next, he went into conversion of military transports to executive airliners, and from there he began exploring designs for an executive plane of his own, first a pusher-propeller design and then a jet based on a Swiss-designed fighter. By now his avionics company Lear Incorporated was publicly traded, and Lear had a reputation for mercurial performance. Airplane production did not appeal to shareholders, and in 1962, Lear was squeezed out of the avionics company, which was merged with another to form Lear-Siegler, leaving him rich.

With that money he concentrated on creation of what would become the Lear Jet. By mid-1965, a prototype had been made and flown, and there were firm orders for over 100 Lear Jets. One of them set three world speed records on a Los Angeles-New York round trip. Again though, Lear skirted insolvency. When the FAA was slow (as he perceived it) in certifying the plane, he stretched his credit to the limit and threatened to close the plant. Approval did come, however, and stock sold to the public in mid-1964 at $10 per share traded a year later at $83.

But still there arose operating bugs and crashes, including a fatal one in 1965, that had to be dealt with, and they were. December 1965 be-

---

[471] Richard Rashke, *Stormy Genius* (Boston: Houghton-Mifflin, 1985) p. 140.
[472] Rashke, *Stormy Genius*, p. 151.

came a record month for sales. But then in 1966, economic recession hit, the IRS rescinded a tax credit amounting to $50,000 per plane, and sales slumped. Unsold new aircraft began piling up outside the factory. Lear had been expanding the plant, and also developing a next generation model, which used up capital, and he had embarked on another new venture, eight-track tape decks for autos. Aircraft sales fell and losses started piling up. To get more cash, Lear began bypassing his dealers and selling directly. Insolvency loomed.

Under pressure, Lear sold out to Gates Rubber Company, and the days of the Gates Lear Jet began. Lear himself was again cash rich but out of a job. Friends and family became worried about his mental state. His wife Moya on a hunch cut short an errand and came home to find him leaving the house with a small suitcase. Coaxing him inside, she found a note announcing that he was going to fly a plane out over the Pacific until the fuel was used up. He later joked that there was really no danger because, "The only plane available was a Lear Jet, and I wasn't about to waste one."[473] (Also, perhaps, who packs for a suicide?)

He next explored a series of possible ventures ranging from real estate development to mining, and somehow he became intrigued with steam engines as a solution to problems of energy conservation and pollution. He spent $17 million developing prototype steam engines and testing them in cars and buses. He also appealed for help to the chairman of General Motors, Senator Barry Goldwater of Arizona, and even President Gerald Ford, but all without success, and in 1975, he gave up on steam power.

That same year, however, he also proposed a new aircraft design on which he collaborated with an aircraft engineer. Rights to the design were bought by Canadair, Limited, of Montreal the next year for $375,000 plus advances, if it exercised certain options on the design that would amount to $7 million. But about a year later this working arrangement collapsed in disputes about the design, and a new deal was struck that would advance Lear $50,000 per year against royalties. Soon, however, that deal dried up too. Canadair lost interest.

Next, Lear started working on another new aircraft design of his own. It would have a turbine-powered pusher propeller mounted at the back and be called the Lear Fan. This would be a novel arrangement intended for quiet operation and high fuel efficiency. Also new would be the engines it would use and construction materials consisting of composites.

Design work and construction of a mockup began and in late 1977 Lear made presentations in Denver to pilots, in Dallas to LTV aircraft manufacturing executives, in Washington to congressmen, and in New York on the Today Show where he talked about advantages of the new craft. He also recast his personal will to direct that proceeds of his estate be devoted to following through on the plane if he should die. As it turned out he did die a few months later, and his remaining estate was largely spent on finishing the plane, although heirs contested his will.

Moya Lear devoted herself to carrying out Bill's desire that the Lear Fan be carried on. On New Year's Day 1981, after expenses of $6 million, it flew flawlessly. Plans were made to certify it in Reno and manufacture it in Belfast, Northern Ireland. The project moved on through a series of different backers, eventually consuming $260 million from all sources without ever becoming certified. Fan Holdings, Inc., the third company to take ownership of it, filed for bankruptcy in May 1985.

Whether Lear's final venture, the Lear Fan, produced a success or a failure could be argued. The plane flew well, but as a commercial product it did not survive. Lear himself experienced both success and failure with many projects and products. Certainly, his technical contributions were prodigious, valuable, and acknowledged. Along the way, he also apparently had many times of triumph and pleasure. He died wealthy, though not greatly so because of the great costs of his unsuccessful efforts in steam power and the investment he had made on his Lear Fan. Had he been able to devote more years to the plane perhaps he would have succeeded with it, even though others did not.

For everyone, life as we know it ends. Some organizations created by entrepreneurs last only briefly and others for many lifetimes. Some of the better products and ways of doing things they introduce may go on forever. Quite possibly innovations that were developed in the Lear Fan's design are still flying.

---

[473] Rashke, *Stormy Genius*, p. 300.

Exercises

Text discussion questions

1. What are the pros and cons of thinking about withdrawal from management when writing a business plan?
2. To what extent should parting with ownership be discussed with potential founding team members when working on a venture plan, and how?
3. What are the pros and cons of the best three ways of parting with ownership of a venture?
4. What issues in relation to termination of a venture should be considered when preparing to start one, and why?
5. What factors should determine whether a person becomes a serial entrepreneur, and how should they be acted upon at different points in venture formation?

Case questions

10B-1 Pradeep Singh

1. How would you answer the question Pradeep Singh offers at the end of the case?
2. What main strategic option(s) should Pradeep's company pursue?
3. How should the company maximize the value of its employees' stock options?
4. What should Pradeep Singh's personal strategy be, looking forward from this point, whom should he communicate it to, and how?

10B-2 Ampersand (G)

1. What should the venture's strategy be from this point on?
2. Upon what sorts of conditions, if any, should which members of the team be moving on to jobs away from the company?
3. If the team participating in the venture is reduced in number, how should their ownership participation in the venture be determined?
4. What should team members do about possible job opportunities in other directions that may have been offered to them with grace periods?

Portfolio page possibilities

Each page, bearing the date and your name, should be one single-sided sheet, based upon this chapter, stating from your present impressions and information (quite possibly to change later) the following:

Page 10B-1 Evolution of management

Describe two contrasting sequences through which managers of the company with significant ownership shares could, over a specified time, withdraw from management, including how specific successful performance of the company can be sustained.

Page 10B-2 Departure of owners

Describe two contrasting scenarios through which owners of the company could cash out, including potential impact on performance of the company.

Page 10B-3 Beyond the first venture

Project a future career path for one or more founders of the company leading up to and beyond personal departure from the venture.

Term Projects

Venture history

1. How close has the company ever come to failing and how was it handled?
2. What are the founders' aims for eventual disposition of the business?
3. What are the founders' aims for their own careers both within and beyond the venture?
4. How much money and unpaid effort did the founder(s) put into the business, and what is your quantitative estimate of the eventual time-discounted return on the founder(s)' investment?
5. How does the above payoff probably compare to what employment in others' organizations would have given the founders?

↓

Venture planning guide

1. Write a job description for your replacement, noting the stage and circumstances of the venture when you think that would most likely fit.
2. Write a personal plan for parting with ownership of your venture, noting when and why.
3. Explain how much your venture is worth right now and how much you think you could make it worth within two years.
4. Tell how you would hope to prepare for parting with ownership of your venture, and by when.
5. Prepare a written assessment of the pros and cons of serial entrepreneurship for yourself.

APPENDICES

Table of Contents

Appendix 4A-1 Morris Unified Business Model[1]

Component one: **How do we create value?** (select from each set) *(factors related to the offering)* 1. offering: primarily products/primarily services/heavy mix 2. offering: standardized/some customization/high customization 3. offering: broad line/medium breadth/narrow line 4. offering: deep lines/medium depth/shallow lines 5. offering: access to product/product itself/product bundled with other firm's product/service 6. offering: internal manufacturing or service delivery/outsourcing/licensing/reselling/value added reselling 7. offering: direct distribution/indirect distribution (if indirect: single or multi-channel)
Component two: **Whom do we create value for?** (select from each set) *(market factors)* 1. type of organization: b-to-b/b-to-c/both/other 2. local/regional/national/international 3. where customer is in value chain: upstream supplier/downstream supplier/government/institutional/wholesaler/retailer/service provider/final consumer 4. broad or general market/multiple segment/niche market 5. transactional/relational
Component three: **What is our source of competence?** (select one or more) *(internal capability factors)* 1. production/operating systems 2. selling/marketing 3. information management/mining/packaging 4. technology/R&D/creative or innovative capability/intellectual 5. financial transactions/arbitrage 6. supply chain management 7. networking/resource leveraging
Component four: **How do we competitively position ourselves?** (select one or more) *(competitive strategy factors)* 1. image of operational excellence/consistency/dependability/speed 2. product or service quality/selection/features/availability 3. innovation leadership 4. low cost/efficiency 5. intimate customer relationship/experience
Component five: **How do we make money?** (select from each set) *(economic factors)* 1. pricing & revenue sources: fixed/mixed/flexible 2. operating leverage: high/med/low 3. volumes: high/med/low 4. margins: high/med/low
Component six: **What are our time, scope and size ambitions?** (select one) *(personal/investor factors)* 1. subsistence model 2. income model 3. growth model 4. speculative model

[1] Michael Morris, Minet Schindehutte and James Richardson, *The Entrepreneur's Business Model,* working paper, Syracuse University, 2003, included with permission.

Venture Plan Rating Form

University Of Texas, Austin

International Moot Corp®

This appendix presents forms used by judges for evaluating the submissions in an invitational collegiate venture plan competition conducted annually by the School of Business at the University of Texas, Austin. They are registered and are reproduced here by permission.

MOOT CORP® COMPANY EVALUATION

Company: _____

Please evaluate the <u>business plan</u> on the following aspects:

(Using this rating system: 1=very poor, 2=poor, 3=fair, 4=adequate, 5=good, 6=very good, 7=excellent)

I. Elements of the Plan (20%)

    1. Executive Summary
       (clear, exciting, and effective as
       a stand-alone overview of the plan)   1   2   3   4   5   6   7

       Comments/Questions: _____
       _____
       _____
       _____

    2. Company Overview
       (business purpose, history and
       current status, overall strategy
       and objectives)   1   2   3   4   5   6   7

       Comments/Questions: _____
       _____
       _____
       _____

    3. Products or Services
       (description, features and benefits, pricing,
       current stage of development,
       proprietary position)   1   2   3   4   5   6   7

       Comments/Questions: _____
       _____
       _____
       _____

    4. Market and Marketing Strategy
       (description of market, competitive
       analysis, needs identification, market
       acceptance, unique capabilities,
       sales promotion)   1   2   3   4   5   6   7

       Comments/Questions: _____
       _____
       _____
       _____

    5. Management
       (backgrounds of key individuals,
       ability to execute strategy,
       history of team, personnel needs,
       organizational structure)   1   2   3   4   5   6   7

       Comments/Questions: _____
       _____
       _____
       _____

In rating each of the above, please consider the following questions:
- Is this area covered in adequate detail?
- Does the plan show a clear understanding of the elements that should be addressed?
- Are the assumptions realistic and reasonable?

Please evaluate the <u>financials</u> of the plan:

These should be presented in summary form in the text of the business plan and follow generally accepted accounting principles.

(Using this rating system: 1=very poor, 2=poor, 3=fair, 4=adequate, 5=good, 6=very good, 7=excellent)

II. Summary Financials (20%)

1. Cash Flow Statement

   (effective as record of
   available cash and as planning
   tool: Detailed for first two years,
   quarterly/annually for years 3-5)

       1   2   3   4   5   6   7

   Comments/Questions: _____
   _____
   _____
   _____

2. Income Statement

   (consistent with plan and effective
   in capturing profit performance;
   Quarterly for first two years
   Quarterly/annually for years 3-5)

       1   2   3   4   5   6   7

   Comments/Questions: _____
   _____
   _____
   _____

3. Balance Sheet

   (Effective in presenting assets,
   liabilities and owners' equity)

       1   2   3   4   5   6   7

   Comments/Questions: _____
   _____
   _____
   _____

4. Funds Required/Uses

   (Clear and concise presentation
   of amount, timing, type, and use
   of funds required for venture)

       1   2   3   4   5   6   7

   Comments/Questions: _____
   _____
   _____
   _____

5. Offering

   (Proposal/terms to investors—indicate
   how much you want, the ROI, and
   the structure of the deal;
   possible exit strategies)

       1   2   3   4   5   6   7

   Comments/Questions: _____
   _____
   _____
   _____

Please evaluate the <u>presentation</u> on the following aspects:

(Using this rating system: 1=very poor, 2=poor, 3=fair, 4=adequate, 5=good, 6=very good, 7=excellent)

III. Presentation Skills (20%)

1. Overall organization

(Materials presented in clear,
logical and/or sequential form.)   1   2   3   4   5   6   7

2. Ability to relate need for the company

(Meaningful examples, practical applications,
etc.)   1   2   3   4   5   6   7

3. Ability to maintain judge's interest   1   2   3   4   5   6   7

4. Responsiveness to judges

(Answered questions, adapted to judge's
level, needs, etc.)   1   2   3   4   5   6   7

5. Quality of visual aids

(Slides, outlines, handouts, etc.)   1   2   3   4   5   6   7

In rating each of the above, please consider the following:
- Do the presenters demonstrate competence in their presentation skills?
- Are they poised, confident and knowledgeable?
- Do they think effectively on their feet?

Strengths of Presentation

Weaknesses of Presentation

Additional Comments

Please evaluate the <u>viability</u> on the following aspects:

(To be completed after reading the plan and viewing the presentations)
(1 indicates definitely no, while 7 indicates definitely yes.)

IV. Viability of Company (40%)

	Definitely No						Definitely Yes
1. Market Opportunity							
(There is a clear market need presented as well as a way to take advantage of that need.)	1	2	3	4	5	6	7
2. Distinctive Competence							
(The company provides something novel/unique/special that gives it a competitive advantage in its market.)	1	2	3	4	5	6	7
3. Management Capability							
(This team can effectively develop this company and handle the risks associated with the venture.)	1	2	3	4	5	6	7
4. Financial understanding							
(The team has a solid understanding of the financial requirements of the business.)	1	2	3	4	5	6	7
5. Investment Potential							
(The business represents a real investment opportunity in which you would consider investing.)	1	2	3	4	5	6	7

Company Strengths

Company Weaknesses

Additional Comments

Venture Plan Rating Form

San Diego State University

This appendix presents the forms given to judges for evaluating the venture plans of an international venture plan competition conducted annually by the School of Business at San Diego State University. They were adapted by San Diego State from forms prepared and copyrighted by Dr. Alan J. Grant for use in a venture plan contest held annually at Babson College for Babson students and are reproduced here with permission.

SAN DIEGO STATE UNIVERSITY
Entrepreneurial Management Center

NORTH AMERICAN INVITATIONAL BUSINESS PLAN COMPETITION

Spring 1993

EVALUATION CRITERIA

Feasibility of the Business Plan. The winner(s) will be the individual or team whose plan conveys the most promising combination of significant capital gains potential, attractive investment possibilities, and actual implementation; i.e., the more likely the plan is to become a going venture, the better.

Product/Service Description. The business plan should provide a clear description of the proposed product or service offering.

Marketability of the Product or Service. The business plan should be able to demonstrate that there is a viable market for the product or service. It would be helpful to use the results of market surveys and demographic studies to support your argument. Specifically, the plan should focus on size of the market, growth potential of the market, and strategies to enter the market.

Strength of the Management Team. The business plan should profile the key members of the firm's management team. You must demonstrate to the reviewers that the management team possesses the necessary skills, drive, and desire to carry out the plan in an effective and efficient manner.

Description of Operations. The business plan should present a logical approach to resource procurement, product development and distribution. Plans for layout and design of facilities should also be included in this section.

Assessment of Risk. The business plan should recognize the types and nature of risks associated with starting the new venture.

Sales Analysis and Forecasts. The business plan should include sales forecasts for at least the first three years of operation. Heavy emphasis will be placed upon your ability to present a logical argument in support of the projections.

Capital Requirements. The financial projections contained in the business plan should demonstrate that the firm will have sufficient capital to implement the idea.

Return on Investment. The financial projections should be able to demonstrate that equity investors will be receiving a satisfactory return on investment over a three- to five-year period.

Organization of the Business Plan. The final business plan should be put together in a professional and logical fashion. Writing style and overall appearance are important. Each business plan should contain a two-page executive summary that highlights the critical elements of the overall plan.

BUSINESS PLAN OUTLINE

The format of the following guide is intended to help the Business Plan author include responses to the evaluation questions most asked by investors/venture capitalists and others who might be interested in taking a debt or equity position in an enterprise.

The general guidelines provide rules for the organization and cosmetics of the Plan. The balance of the guide suggests that the details of the Plan be best organized into the underlined ten section titles. This is not intended to be a firm rule of Business Plan composition but is so stated for the sake of completeness.

Except for the Executive Summary appearing as the first section, the presentation of the Plan can be made with whatever emphasis the author believes will be of most interest to the prospective investor.

Plans should include, on the cover page, a proprietary caution and a request that the Plan not be reproduced and be returned if there is no interest. Most investors will verbally indicate that they will be careful not to disclose the contents of the Plan to others, but few will sign any confidentiality agreement.

Firms, such as venture capitalists, see many plans that contain overlapping technical and/or marketing strategies. For the most part, they are extremely ethical and, although they will not sign such an agreement, will comply with the author's requests.

GENERAL GUIDELINES

IS there a cover page on which the company is identified by name, address, and telephone number? IS the date and Copy number included?

IS there a concise Table of Contents <u>with</u> page numbers?

IS it less than 40 pages, including Exhibits?

IS it neatly assembled and covered?

ARE <u>all</u> Figures and Exhibits discussed and referenced in the Text?

TYPICAL SECTIONS

<u>EXECUTIVE SUMMARY</u>

CAN it be read in 5 minutes, i.e. IS it no more than 4 pages long?

DOES it share the entrepreneur's dreams?

ARE the objectives stated and qualified?

WHAT are the highlights of the plan?

HOW many $$s will be needed WHEN, and for WHAT use?

WHAT ROI can the investor expect at the time of the exit scenario?

PRODUCT/SERVICE DESCRIPTION

WHAT is it?

WHY would it be desired? by WHOM?

HOW will it benefit customers?

WHAT will it replace?

CAN it be legally protected or defended?

MANAGEMENT & ORGANIZATION

WHO'S running the show? WHAT'S his/her or their background?

WHO will provide professional business guidance to the enterprise, e.g., the Board of Directors, Outside Accountants and Legal Counsel?

WHO will handle the functional specialties of financial communications and controls, marketing, engineering, manufacturing, administration, etc.?

WHAT is the corporate pace, i.e., objectives, milestones, Gantt chart, organization progression?

OPERATIONS (for a product)

HOW is it made? WHERE is it made? WHAT are the key components?

WHAT will be the make/buy components strategy?

HOW much will it cost?

OPERATIONS (for a service)

WHAT value or benefit will be provided?

WHY would the user choose this company?

HOW are the services differentiated from other providers?

IS the cost/benefit economics evident to potential customers?

MARKETING STRATEGIES

WHAT is the size and growth potential of the market sectors _available_ or to be _created_ for the product?

WHO are the potential customers? Have any of them shown initial interest?

WHO are the competitors?

WHAT are their strong and weak suits?

WHAT are the barriers for others to enter?

MARKETING TACTICS

HOW is the product to be differentiated?

HOW is margin to be obtained? Quality / Promotion / Price / Service?

HOW is the product made available to the end user?

FINANCIAL ASSESSMENTS

WHAT are the key financial parameters that describe the company over the five-year period, e.g. sales, income, break-even, positive cash flow?

WHAT are the premises upon which they are based? ARE they optimistic, most probable, pessimistic? Describe each case!

FINANCING

WHO owns the company? to WHAT extent?

HOW many $$s are needed and

HOW will they be used?

WHAT portion of the company can be shared?

On WHAT terms?

WHAT return can the investor expect? WHAT are the exit scenarios?

RISK EVALUATIONS

WHAT are the economic, competitive, human, and financial resources risks?

WHAT changes might they have on the plan's financial parameters?

HOW many more $$ might be needed if the plan's goals are missed?

HOW will delays in development and manufacturing be made up?

TYPICAL EXHIBITS

Five-year pro forma statements

These must be prepared using GAAP and contain the standard schedules, i.e. Income Statement, Balance Sheet, and Changes in Financial Position. A Cash Balances schedule is mandatory.

Organization Progression

A chart or charts showing first and last year's structure with names, positions, and titles.

Milestones

Gantt- or Pert-type charts depicting the probable start and completion dates for key objectives.

Product Descriptions

Sales literature or clearly legible drawings showing relative size and other designated characteristics.

<u>Resumes</u>

Applicable background data on all officers and directors prefaced by a brief title and position statement.

<u>Market Statistics</u>

Published industry data showing date and source of material.

Market research backup materials.

Appendix 6B-1 Laundry List of Start-up Tasks

Marketing
1. Pick a name.
2. Set up an Email address.
3. Get help on graphics, logos, and advertising.
4. Buy business cards,
5. Set up a Web site.
6. Get listed in the Yellow Pages, if appropriate.
7. Formulate pricing and discount schedules.
8. Codify returns policies and warranties.
9. Print brochures and price lists.
10. Contact distribution channels.
11. Design, negotiate, and roll out advertising and sales campaign.

Operations
1. Formulate employment policies.
2. Seek out and interview potential helpers.
3. Check references.
4. Design, prepare, and sign confidentiality and non-compete agreements.
5. Set up employee and casualty insurance.
6. Identify and evaluate suppliers.
7. Work out supplier agreements.
8. Buy inventory.
9. Set up servicing arrangements.
10. Refine written plan.

Site
1. Find space, check zoning, and apply for permits.
2. Work out lease terms and sign.
3. Make rental deposits.
4. Copy and distribute keys.
5. Have phone and communication lines installed.
6. Arrange for an Internet service provider.
7. Obtain office furniture and equipment.
8. Put up a sign.

Accounting and finance
1. Create payroll system.
2. Set up an expandable accounting software system.
3. Set up cash-tracking system.
4. Open a company bank account. (require two signatures on checks?)
5. Seek needed cash sources.

Paperwork

1. Register a domain name.
2. Pick a law firm and work with attorneys on idea protection.
3. Set up correspondence software with letterheads and forms.
4. Obtain a city business license.
5. Obtain a federal employer identification number.
6. Obtain a state business license and tax ID number.
7. Arrange and set up tracking systems.
8. Buy envelopes, and rubber stamps.

Appendix 6B-2 Government Approvals

A simple one-person business may be able to get away without registering with any government agencies, although it will have to report income to federal and possibly state agencies. The federal form is a Schedule C, which becomes part of the owner's personal income tax filing. Technically, a city business license may be required, but it is simple and inexpensive to obtain, and failure to get it may not be noticed if the business stays small, as in the case of a couple of college students cutting lawns or painting houses on the side.

If the business becomes more visible, however, it will have to observe more registration and reporting requirements at the local, state, and federal levels of government. Requirements may vary with geographical locale. In Washington State, for example, they can include the following:

Local

- City Business License. Easily obtained at City Hall for a nominal fee. Forms will automatically come to the venture for paying a Business and Occupations tax based upon sales.
- County Licenses. For businesses that deal with tobacco, juke boxes, shuffleboard games, and so forth, additional licenses must be obtained from the county clerk. Forms will then come in the mail for county property and inventory taxes.
- Certificate of Firm Name. Filed with the county clerk.

State

- Certificate of Registration. Filed with the State Department of Revenue. Tax forms will be sent automatically.
- State Licenses. Must be obtained for many specialized activities such as contracting, barbering, practicing law or medicine, operating beauty shops, or running employment agencies. The State Department of Commerce or Department of Licensing can be contacted for a list.
- Corporate Name Reservations. Obtained and annually renewable from the Secretary of State.
- Employer's Requirements. Needed if the firm is going to employ people other than the owner. These requirements include:
  - Registration and Industrial Rating Number from the State Department of Labor.
  - Employer's Identification Number for Employment Security from the State Employment Security Department.

Federal

For particular lines of work other forms of regulation may apply. Mail order is regulated by the Federal Trade Commission, franchising by state agencies, airlines by the Department of Transportation, trucking by the Interstate Commerce Commission, radio and TV broadcasting by the Federal Communications Commission, importing and exporting by the Federal Trade Commission, and so forth. Some agencies, such as the Occupational Health and Safety Administration, and the Environmental Protection Agency cut across many lines of work.

Regulations can change any time, and so must always be checked on a current basis. One source of information to begin with is the SBA, which can suggest other points of contact. Another is the State Department of Commerce. Best, however, may be to contact other businesses in similar lines of work and ask what government agencies they must deal with. Cross-checking with more than one source is also advisable.

Need for regulatory approval can sometimes completely stymie a company even though it may have a product that would ultimately be approved. How this could happen is illustrated by the reaction of a solid waste manager, John Conaway, to a new foam product developed by a start-up company, Rusmar, for reducing the costs and extending the life of a landfill.

"Rusmar looks to have a good product, but here in California the permit process will be a big pitfall. I'd be using Rusmar's foam right now if it weren't for the regulatory nightmare. We have a severe capacity crunch. But any time you file for a major operational change here—and foam would fit into that category—you need new permits from three separate agencies.

"It would cost us more than $1 million just to apply for them, given all the monitoring and documentation they require. I can easily see being required to do a very complicated and expensive series of ground water tests and surface/air emission tests. Some of these are fly-emergence tests, where you have to get people to come out and actually count the number of flies that emerge prior to using the foam, and then after using it. And even then there's no guarantee we'd get approval."[2]

Still, notwithstanding such barriers, new companies do get started by introducing products that successfully hurdle them. But often they must bring to bear more effort and ingenuity, spend more money, and take more time to accomplish start-up than they expected. A case in point was the start-up of Southwest Airlines.

Herb Kelleher, a lawyer, filed an application with the Texas Aeronautics Commission (TAC) in November 1967 for his proposed airline to fly between Dallas, Houston, and San Antonio. It was approved three months later on February 20, 1968. The next day, a competing line, Continental, managed to have a restraining order issued against the approval. The case went to trial that summer. Three established lines, Braniff, Continental, and Texas International, argued that there was no room for another carrier, and the court agreed. Seven months later the case went to appeal in state court and the decision against Southwest was upheld two to one. So far, it had cost the start-up $543,000 in legal expenses.

At this point several directors of the company proposed to give up. But Herb Kelleher proposed otherwise, commenting: "Gentlemen, let's go another round with them. I will continue to represent the company in court, and I'll postpone any legal fees and pay every cent of court costs out of my own pocket." After debating his proposal, the directors agreed. An appeal to the Texas Supreme Court prevailed; Southwest received its certificate to fly, but only in Texas.

The legal battle to get that permission, however, was not yet over. Continental appealed the case again, this time to the U.S. Supreme Court. In 1970, the Court refused to hear the case, and start-up work again continued. In January, 1971 a CEO, Lamar Muse, was hired to commence operations of the company, which by now had only $142 in the bank against $80,000 in overdue bills. His first task was to raise money, not only to buy airplanes and get them flying, but also to obtain permission from the Civil Aeronautics Board (CAB) to fly beyond Texas. Complaints to the CAB by Braniff and Texas International alleging that Southwest was going to fly outside Texas without permission were still keeping the new line grounded.

Braniff also put pressure on the firm that was going to help Southwest raise capital. But Southwest found another underwriter, and in June of 1971, got the money. One week later news came that the CAB had rejected the Braniff and Texas International complaint. But those two lines had managed to get another restraining order.

---

[2] Jay Finegan, "Down in the Dump," *Inc.*, September 1990, p. 98.

Herb Kelleher went personally to see the Texas Supreme Court judge who had earlier written in favor of Southwest, and the judge agreed to call the other justices together the following morning to hear his appeal on an informal basis, saying "Herb, you've got to figure out what you're going to do." After digging in the law library and working in the State Attorney General's office all night, Kelleher found a precedent and worked up his argument.

Without an appeal that is formal, it is unusual for an appellate court to order a trial court to dissolve an injunction, but Kelleher's presentation the next morning persuaded the Justices to do so. Kelleher called Muse, who said that notwithstanding the court's order, he was still worried that the sheriff might show up to enforce the injunction if planes started taking off. Kelleher recalled saying "Lamar, you roll right over the son of a bitch and leave our tire tracks on his uniform if you have to." The next day, June 18, 1971, Southwest had planes in the air.[3]

---

[3] Kevin Freiberg and Jackie Freiberg, *Nuts!* (Austin: Bard Press, 1996) p. 16.

Appendix 6B-3 Insurance Types

Anticipating what can go wrong should inevitably be combined with thinking about not only how to prevent problems but also how to insure for those that occur anyway. For instance, if a visitor to the business bumps into a stack of boxes in the plant, causing one to fall and hurt his foot, he may sue the business. If it is a proprietorship or partnership, the owners may be liable. Even if it is a corporation, he may sue the people in it who should be responsible for maintaining safety. To deal with this the company should be protected by appropriate insurance, liability insurance in this case.

Some types of coverage to be considered include:

- Liability: product, directors', property
- Fire
- Theft
- Vehicles: company's and/or employees'
- Business interruption
- Workers' compensation
- Key employee's life
- Health
- Disability
- Accounts receivable

There are ways to save money. Carefully list and review the things that could go wrong, produce accidents, and attract lawsuits. Then apply imagination to the task of reducing the risks of each of those things happening. Design of the product, production, warning labels, layout of the plant, instructions to employees, types of equipment used, application of safety guards and warnings, maintenance of the equipment and plant, storage and handling of hazardous materials, alarm systems, fire extinguishing and escape systems, education of salespeople and customers, and plant security are all areas where precautions can be considered.

There are ways to get help on the task. Employees can help reduce accident possibilities. They can also be motivated to take more care of their own health by being required to share costs of health care. Government literature and inspectors can provide useful suggestions. Insurance consultants and company representatives have experience they can share about how to lower risks and costs of coverage. The state workers' compensation bureau can provide information about how to qualify for discounts based on favorable safety experience ratings.

Some ways to reduce costs of the insurance directly are to (1) consider higher deductibles on policies, (2) consider introducing hold-harmless agreements to get around needs for some kinds of liability coverage, and (3) obtain premium quotations from several competing insurance carriers. A way to check on the financial soundness of the carriers themselves is to look at their ratings in *Best's Insurance Reports* at the library.

Appendix 6B-4 Other Location Details that May Apply

Other local features that can trip up a site where many factors seem to be favorable include:

1. Type of traffic in the area. Are people working, shopping or just passing through? How interested might each type be in what the venture will offer?
2. Type of business. Breakfast sells better on the side of the street where people head toward work.
3. Where does the street lead, and will travelers want to stop where the venture is?
4. The shady side of the street can be preferable in some climates, while the sunny side is preferable in others.
5. Generally, the far corner (right hand side across the intersection) with a level site is preferable, not on a near corner, a one-way road or the inside edge of a curve. In a strip mall, however, being in the middle rather than on a corner is sometimes better.
6. Fast-food stores tend to do better where other fast food stores are situated.
7. Night shopping is more adversely affected in high-crime areas than is day shopping.
8. The nature of the store next door sometimes matters. Meat market next to a pet store or mortuary?
9. Changes in zoning or local construction projects can hurt, or even wipe out some businesses and help others.
10. Gentrification of a neighborhood attracts richer people and raises rents, while a neighborhood in decline loses residents and may suffer from more crime.
11. Change in an adjacent or more distant part of the city may draw clientele away from or add more clientele to the business location being considered.

Appendix 7A-1 Business Legal Entity

Either by initiative or default, some legal form must be chosen for the business. Four choices include proprietorship, partnership, limited liability company, and corporation. Within each of these, particularly the latter two, are other choices to be made. Reasons for choosing one business form over another are easy to identify.

Federal taxes to be paid include the following:

- Corporate income tax, if there is a corporation.
- Personal income tax withholding on all employees.
- Social security tax on all employees.
- Medicare tax on all employees.

Proprietorship

A proprietorship is what the business will be if no action is taken to make it something else. It is part of the owner. If the business is sued, the owner is sued. If the owner dies, the assets of the business individually are part of the owner's estate and debts of the business are owed by the owner's estate.

If the proprietorship operates under some name other than the owner's it may be referred to as a DBA (doing business as) enterprise. Most states require that such an enterprise be registered with the county government with some sort of certificate of doing business under an assumed name.

A proprietorship pays no corporate income tax, but the proprietor must still pay personal income tax, including quarterly prepayments of the estimated tax. At the end of the year the income and expenses of the proprietorship are reported on a Schedule C form as part of the proprietor's 1040 personal filing. Social security and Medicare taxes then are computed as part of a self-employment tax, which is also a regular part of the 1040 filing. Schedule C's have been the most common source of audits by the Internal Revenue Service. Factors favoring this form of organization are

- It's easy, happens automatically. Like any business, it will require a license, which really just amounts to letting state and local authorities know that it should be on the tax rolls. But no written description must be filed.
- It's cheap. There is no need for a lawyer.
- It's clear. The proprietor owns everything, gets all the profits, need not obtain anyone else's approvals on decisions.

Partnership

A partnership is what the business becomes if more than one person owns it, but no action is taken to separate it legally from its owners. There need not be any paperwork to have a partnership, just ownership by more than one person. Such an arrangement can be created by, for instance, more than one person contributing assets, doing the work of the business, or withdrawing profits from it. Actions like these may even create a partnership inadvertently.

Unless there is paperwork to the contrary, the state will assume ownership is equal among the partners. That can produce discomfort if personal goals or work habits of the partners diverge. For instance, if one partner works harder than the other, the profits of the business will nevertheless be divided equally, unless the partners reach some other agreement between themselves or, better yet, not only do that but put it into writing in a formal partnership agreement.

Also, any partner can commit the business to obligations or be sued for debts of the business unless there is some agreement to the contrary. Or, the mistake of one partner who overspends or who causes the business to injure someone can automatically obligate the other partner(s) to assume responsibility for the mistake, and have to pay for it as well. These can be reasons for arranging the legal form and ownership of the business in a formal manner using legal help. To formalize a partnership, some sort of certificate of partnership may have to be filed with the county clerk.

A partnership can come into being by default as co-founders begin working together and representing themselves as being in business together. To guard against the unlimited liability that can arise for a partner through the action of any other partner, White has suggested a form, such as the following, which should be signed by each partner, and also be signed and dated by two or more witnesses:[4]

> I, _____ as a co-founder and co-owner of _____ (venture name), realize that we must operate as a partnership in the public's eyes until we are ready to incorporate. I realize that my co-founders and co-owners are placed in jeopardy by my actions and by my commitments on behalf of the venture. Therefore, I agree not to spend over $ _____ in cash purchases or to commit my company to over $ _____ in any agreement without the prior approval of the other partners.

Other statements to consider formalizing at this time include a non-disclosure agreement to be signed by any participant to whom secrets of the venture are revealed and in which the participant promises not to divulge confidential information about the venture to anyone outside without permission, plus a non-compete agreement in which a co-founder promises not to enter competition with the venture. The non-compete agreement must specify precisely what lines of business would constitute competition, in what geographic areas, and for what period of time. It is important to remember that courts are generally loath to prevent people from working for a living, even if it involves competing with former employers or partners, and the terms therefore should not be too broad.

Formulating these documents, although they are generally quite simple, may point up the desirability of getting help from a lawyer. However, many people manage without such help at this stage. Those who do get legal help sometimes run into expensive lawsuits later if the cooperative spirit between partners breaks down. Harmony is probably more important to seek than legal shielding, but seeking both is probably better yet.

If a partner dies, a partnership automatically terminates, unless there is specific provision to the contrary in the partnership agreement. Hence part of the legal task of creating a partnership is to consider what disposition of the business should be made in such event.

Partnership agreements can specify that partners are not equal and can spell out such things as duration, conditions for partner withdrawal, division of responsibilities, assets, income, and so forth. These agreements should be written, signed, notarized and filed with a county or state agency to maximize their enforceability.

Limited partnership

A limited partnership (Ltd, or LP) is a variation in which liability for obligations of the company are limited for some partners. There must still be a general partner whose liability

---

[4] Richard M. White, Jr., *The Entrepreneur's Manual* (Radnor, PA: Chilton Publishing, 1971) p. 79.

is not limited. The partnership agreement can specify any arrangements about relationships between partners as above. Venture capitalists sometimes set up investment pools as limited partnerships. The capitalists run the partnerships, and get paid, while the limited partners put up most of the money and have certain rights to participate in winnings of the investments but no say in operations. After a time specified in the paperwork, the partnership is liquidated and investors receive their specified share. They are owed whatever the partnership says they are.

As with a proprietorship, income taxes of the partnership arise as part of each partner's personal income picture. In 1998, only 4 percent of the *Inc.* 500 fastest-growing firms used the proprietorship or partnership legal forms. The other 96 percent were corporations.[5]

Partnerships, whether limited or not, can be tricky. Each is custom designed and therefore is in a sense an experimental model. The partners, presumably with the help of a lawyer, essentially make up their own rules about not only who owns how much, but how it will be run, who will be in charge, how partners can join and leave, how assets will be divided, how long it will last, what can end it, and so forth. A lawyer with little experience will likely be little help and together with the partners will create a partnership agreement that inadequately anticipates the what-ifs, which will likely lead to trouble sooner or later.

A lawyer with a great deal of experience is better to bet on for drafting the agreement, but it is crucial on whose behalf that lawyer works. The following example illustrates how an unhappy outcome can result.

> Dave Pitassi joined the diaper division of Procter & Gamble after college, impressed by the fact that it accounted for 25 percent of the profits of a company with $30 billion in sales. When he learned that retailers typically offered the product at loss-leader prices to recruit young customers, it occurred to him that offering retailers a better price might enable a new diaper producer to enter the market. He and a former college friend, Wally Klemp who now worked for a big accounting firm, Coopers and Lybrand, quit their jobs, wrote a business plan, and went in search of $2 million to set up a company and lease a multi-million dollar diaper-making machine that could put out 400 diapers a minute.
>
> They managed to raise only $465,000 with the aid of an investment banker who structured the deal as a limited partnership. Proceeding anyway they started production, but encountered disappointment in sales. They then cut back production to conserve cash and sent a memo to the brokers who handled their product saying, "We have a limited supply, therefore we are going on allocation."
>
> To their surprise the brokers passed along to grocers a different message, namely that the product was selling so fast that the new venture could not keep up with demand. Grocers immediately responded by placing much larger orders so as not to miss out, and sales suddenly took off, leaping five years ahead of projections in the venture's business plan to $20 million. Dave and Wally immediately bought new houses and matching white Cadillacs.
>
> They also got a call from their investment banker, who personally had put no money in the company, informing them that with the support of the investors he was taking control of the company. Visiting an attorney, they were told that under the partnership agreement they had signed there was no recourse. When Wally returned to the venture to retrieve his coat and go home he found that his key no longer worked at the office. The locks had already been changed.
>
> In hindsight he saw the partnership agreement as an important cause of his loss. "I didn't know a lot about them or the other structures available: LLC's, S-Corporations, C-Corporations. Limited partnerships are not designed to keep money in a growing company. However, entrepreneurs want to build something that lasts for a long time, and in that process you need to put

---

[5] *Inc.*, October 1998, p. 25.

capital in, not take it out. Our LP structure allowed capital to be taken out of the business, which was absolutely the wrong thing to do."[6]

Limited liability company

The limited liability company (LLC) is a newer legal form that includes some advantages of a partnership and others of a corporation. Liability, as the name indicates, can be limited, as in a limited partnership, but with an LLC there is no need for a general partner who does accept liability. Like a partnership, it allows owners to deduct losses from their personal income, and they pay taxes on any income only once and at their personal tax rate. These advantages are similar to those of a Sub S corporation, to be discussed below, but in addition the LLC has more flexible rules that a Sub S concerning ownership.[7]

Because it is a relatively new form, however, neither the law nor the boilerplate (routine formats that law firms typically develop as part of their own working files) is well developed. Therefore the law firm is likely to charge several times as much to work one up, it will take more time to put in place, and the expenses of working with it, particularly if bugs show up in the way it is cast, will also be higher.

It is possible to convert an existing partnership into an LLC, the most likely way being to first form the LLC, then merge the partnership into it. Some states, including Delaware, have set up conversion statutes to make the conversion process easier by reducing the need for third-party consents. There can be tax complications, depending on how the conversion is handled, so it should be done with help from a lawyer who learned the process by practicing on other people's cases first. The same general process and qualifications would also apply to conversion of an LLC into a corporation.[8]

Incorporation

Corporate form is the path chosen by most companies that grow beyond the one- or two-owner stage. Setting up the business as a corporation theoretically separates it from the owners in terms of liabilities and taxation. Technically, owners are no longer liable for debts of the business, although lenders may refuse credit unless the owners agree to waive this feature. If the corporation is really set up as a way of getting around the law, the government can easily prosecute the owners. If, for instance, it is set up with insufficient capitalization for debt it takes on, or if the owners use its accounts for their personal affairs, the corporate shell will not protect them.

If owners commingle their own assets with the corporation, again the protection may be lost. Spending significant amounts of corporate money on personal expenses could do this. So could making substantial use of company assets for personal purposes. If owners made frequent use of a company plane for personal purposes and one of them through negligent operation of it injured somebody, that person might be able to pierce the corporate veil in suing for damages.

Some other favorable features of a corporation in addition to its usual protections from liability are

- If owners die or give up their shares in a corporation, it continues. If any partner withdraws ownership from a partnership, the partnership does not automatically continue but rather must be reformulated.

---

[6] Dave Pitassi, "My Startup, Lock-out, Buy-out Journey to Success," (*American Venture*, January-March 1998) p. 5.
[7] *The Essential Limited Liability Company Handbook* (Grants Pass, OR: Oasis Press, 1995).
[8] *American Venture,* October 1998, p. 16.

- It is easier to issue, sell, and exchange corporate shares than partnership shares. For these conveniences and the liability protection, owners often set up businesses as corporations, despite such disadvantages as requirements for meetings and more paperwork.
- In the eyes of some people corporate form is more impressive. Formation establishes a date of inception that in later years may give the impression of solidity, tradition, and reliability. A corporation must have officers who have formal titles like president, treasurer, and secretary, and to some these convey prestige, which may in fact be real.
- If the corporation is very simple, an owner can set it up personally by purchasing the forms and filing them with the appropriate state agency. Usually, however, there are enough complications to warrant engaging a lawyer who is experienced in the task for help in making sure it is done properly. The cost, depending on how many special what-ifs it is supposed to deal with, should be around $600 to $1,200. Hiring a lawyer is also advisable in terminating a corporation.

On the negative side, a corporation is usually more costly to set up, certainly more than a proprietorship. Even though not required, hiring an attorney for help is usually advisable. Fees must also be paid to the state for filing.

Corporations are more complicated to maintain. Separate bank accounts must be set up, separate special tax filings must be prepared, officers must be elected, regular meetings must be held at least once per year, and at them minutes must be kept. Records must also be kept of transactions and relationships with other parties. Finally, winding down a corporation can be complicated, with requirements for settling out with all concerned parties.

S versus C corporations

There are two types of corporations, S and C. A principal difference between them is how they are taxed. Each type has its own tax forms, separate from those of its owners. An S corporation is taxed essentially the same as a proprietorship or partnership, namely only once and at the personal tax rate of each owner, which tops out at 42 percent as of this writing. If the S corporation has losses, those can be deducted from the personal income of the owners to reduce their taxes.

A C corporation pays taxes separately from the owners at the corporate rate of 34 percent maximum for profits up to $10 million. If it loses money, the owners cannot take that as a deduction on their personal income in computing their taxes. However, the corporation can carry forward those losses, and if it has prior profitable years, it can also carry them back.

If the owners withdraw salary from the C corporation, they pay personal income tax on that salary. That reduces the profits of the corporation. If enough salary is deducted to reduce profits to zero, then there is only one round of tax, namely at the personal rate just as in an S corporation. If the profits are not zero, then the corporation pays tax on its income, at which point there is just one round of tax again. If at a future point in time, however, the corporation pays out those profits to the owners, say as dividends, those dividends, which were already taxed once as corporate profits, will be taxed again as dividends at the shareholders' personal income rates, making a second round of taxation.

Sometimes it is possible to pay enough salary to reduce the corporate rate to a low level, and yet not pay enough salary to put the owner in a high bracket, so that the whole tax is minimized, at least for the time being. This practice, called income splitting, still leaves the retained profits of the corporation to be dealt with at a later time possibly as dividends. But also possibly the owner will by then be in a low income bracket because of retirement or will alternatively sell off the business with the profits still in it, paying only a tax on whatever capital gain is realized through the sale.

The subchapter S form is usually preferable if the corporation is paying out its earnings; that way they are taxed only once. In contrast, in a regular C corporation, earnings are taxed at the corporate level and then a second time at the personal level. Moreover, S corporation losses can be deducted against personal income of the owners, thereby giving them a tax break if the venture loses money, which often occurs in early stages. However, an S corporation also imposes qualifying requirements:

- It can have no more than 35 shareholders, and none can be nonresident aliens;
- It can have only one class of stock, although there can be differences in voting rights;
- It cannot have active subsidiaries;
- It must derive at least 20 percent of its revenues from U.S. sources;
- It must derive at least 75 percent of its revenues from active sources (i.e., not dividends, rents, or royalties).

If the firm is a Sub S corporation it might seem that the owner(s) could escape the social security and Medicare taxes by simply taking out no salary and hence having a zero base on which to compute those taxes. In fact, however, the entrepreneur(s) must be paid a reasonable salary on which those taxes are computed, reported, and paid as deductions from pay. Amounts above that salary, however, can be taken as a distribution of profits to the entrepreneurs without such deductions. Some fringe benefits, such as health plans, company car, group-term life insurance, and disability insurance are deductible expenses for an S corporation, only if they are considered part of compensation for owners, in which case those individuals must pay personal taxes on them. But a C corporation can deduct them without the individual having to report them. Retirement program expenditures are treated the same in terms of deductions under both types of corporations only if the programs are designated as qualified under the IRS rules.[9]

A C corporation may be converted to an S corporation and vice versa, but there are restrictions and also advantages not widely known. For instance, set-up or conversion of the venture into a C corporation, if done early enough will, under certain conditions, permit founders to exclude half of a gain on the shares held for at least five years, say by going public or selling out, up to $10 million or 10 times the basis paid in for it. Technical details of these requirements can be complicated, but well worth working out where they apply. Legal help in assessing them is advisable.

Sometimes it makes sense to incorporate different parts of a business in different ways. A part that loses money might have more appeal to an investor in a high income bracket, for instance, because that person can deduct the losses against a high tax rate. So it may make sense for high-income founders to buy real estate or other assets the company needs, rent them to the company at a relatively low rate to help profits of the rest of the company, and take a depreciation deduction against that rent that reduces the high-income founder's taxes.[10]

In return, that founder may get more shares or other privileges in the other part of the venture that rents the assets from him or her. This part that makes more profit will carry less tax impact against an owner in a lower tax bracket. Ultimately, the high-income owner will,

---

[9] *Inc.*, December 1995, p. 126.
[10] *American Venture*, October 1998, p. 16.

of course, want to recoup the losses to come out ahead in the long run. That recovery might perhaps be done advantageously at a later time when the person is no longer in such a high bracket, possibly after they have retired or maybe have gone on to another start-up that is showing early losses against which they can credit the recouped income.

For example, John DeLorean, when organizing a new company to start producing stainless steel-bodied sports cars in Ireland for sale in the U.S., first set up the DeLorean Manufacturing Company (DMC), followed by the DeLorean Motor Company and then a series of other related companies. He explained:

> "Suppose I established a corporation whose business was to design cars, build cars, sell cars, make tires, and invent products for use in automobiles. Now suppose that the research section was extremely successful in creating new products, which were worth $1 million this year and, predictably, $100 million in five years. But then the portion of the corporation that was building cars discovered that no one wanted their products. All the dealers refused them, and they had a loss of $7 million. In addition the tire division made a mistake in the rubber formula and the first 400,000 tires they built fell apart after being driven only 1,000 miles despite a money-back guarantee paying for each tire if it did not last 40,000 miles. Again there would be a loss of millions of dollars.
>
> "With a single corporation handling many different projects, all losses are combined, weighed against the profits of whatever division is successful, and the bottom line proves the fate of the business. In the example I just provided, the losses would be so great that the entire company would be bankrupt, despite the fact that the research division was showing such spectacular potential. Thus, a company might fail simply because it was trying to serve too many different purposes.
>
> "By comparison, many businesses form what are known as umbrella corporations. They start with one corporation that is essentially an empty holding company, usually consisting of just two or three people. This is the "umbrella" for other corporations created to handle individual functions.
>
> "I wanted a corporation involved in research and development so that any products with broader applications than just my car could be sold wherever such a sale would be appropriate. If the car failed I might still have a separate, though related corporation that could make money for the investors. At the same time, if the research and development company was not successful, it couldn't hinder the sales in the car activity."

Unfortunately in this case, none of the companies worked out. DeLorean did manage to struggle through the thicket of governmental red tape, raising money, and coping with skeptical unions to set up his plant and produce 8,758 cars, many of which are still running as collectors' items. The company broke even and made a profit in its first year. But it ran short of cash, and along the way John DeLorean was accused by the FBI of conspiring with the mob to do a drug deal to provide more cash for the company. His story was that he was trying to "take" the mob for financing, and did not deal in drugs but was framed, presumably by the mob, to whom he was going to sell a European DMC corporation for $10 million that was mostly an empty shell. After a high-profile trial he was acquitted of any wrongdoing on the jury's first ballot.[11]

More normal reasons for forming more than one corporation include not only the advantage of protecting the profits of one from the losses of another, as DeLorean noted, but also the greater ease of taking one company public if it has separate financial records. Further, there are limits on how much an owner can take as salary from a C corporation. Because the salary

---

[11] John Z. DeLorean, *DeLorean* (Grand Rapids: Zondervan Books, 1985) p. 105.

is a tax deduction for the corporation, the IRS seeks to limit its amount to what it considers reasonable. Separation of a business into more than one corporation may allow justification of separate salaries whose reasonable limits added together are greater than what would be accepted from one combined corporation.

Arguments against separate corporations, rather than one, mainly concern cost. Administration, paperwork, accounting, legal expenses, and insurance costs will likely be higher from losing economies of scale. Some states, moreover, impose a minimum tax on each corporation. Merging a less profitable corporation with a more profitable one in such a case may eliminate such a tax on the former. The entrepreneur in the following example weighed these and still other reasons in deciding to go set up separate corporations.

> Fran Greene's two firms in Orlando, Cakes Across America and Sun State Electronics, were in entirely different lines of business. "Each of my businesses runs on a different mentality," she commented. "With Sun State, we take advantage of opportunities open to us as a woman-owned business. With Cakes, we're focused on reaching the individual consumer. As a manager, it doesn't make sense to try to pretend that these businesses are really just two parts of one whole."
>
> She further noted that it would be necessary to have separate accounting and financial reporting systems regardless of the corporate formalities, so there was no loss from having separate entities. Longer term, she figured that separate companies would give her greater flexibility for having any of her six children take them over, or alternatively for taking either company public.[12]

A consideration sometimes important in forming a corporation is that its stock be issued under provisions of **Section 1244** of the Internal Revenue Code. Essentially, these permit initial investors to charge any loss up to $50,000 from disposition of their stock as a loss against their ordinary income, rather than only against capital gains that they may or may not have. Among the requirements for this declaration are that the stock has been issued to individuals; that it has been issued in return for cash, not other securities; and that the company be a domestic corporation with less than $1 million in capitalization.

The procedure for creating a corporation involves filing articles of incorporation with the appropriate state agency, and depositing at least the minimum paid-in capital amount required by the state. The state issues a certificate of incorporation, which means that the corporation now exists. Beyond that are tasks of issuing shares, appointing directors, electing officers, setting up bylaws, and commencing business.

The main items of paperwork in this process are the articles of incorporation and the corporate bylaws. What the articles must contain is specified by the state. In Washington State, for instance, the following must be specified:

- The company name and address.
- How long the company is to last (e.g. "in perpetuity").
- What its purpose is (e.g. "any legal business").
- What kinds of shares and how many are to be issued.
- How many directors it will have.
- Names and addresses of the incorporators.

Answers to these questions may be simple or complex. For instance, stock issued may be common. Or it may be preferred, voting, or non-voting, carry all sorts of different rights, and

---

[12] "Incorporation Issues," *Inc.*, April 1996, p. 115.

so forth. Simple answers an entrepreneur may be able to provide without help. More complex questions probably require assistance from a suitably specialized lawyer.

Generally, it is desirable to keep the articles of incorporation as simple and open-ended as possible, to maximize flexibility that the corporation can exercise without changing them. Further structure can be added, to the extent desired, in the corporate bylaws, which need not be filed with any government agency. They remain private and can be changed as the directors wish. Bylaws are enacted by the directors at their first meeting. Typically, bylaws include the following:

- Where and when directors meetings will be held
- What constitutes a quorum
- Who can vote
- How proxies work
- What powers directors will have
- Directors' tenure terms and replacement
- What officers' jobs there will be
- Who the officers will be
- How corporate records will be handled
- Who can sign checks and contracts
- Issuance and replacement of stock certificates
- How bylaws can be amended
- Shareholder rights, such as inspection of records and receipt of financial reports
- Any restrictions on transfer of shares

Standard forms for bylaws, as with articles of incorporation, partnership agreements, and business licenses, can be obtained from legal supplies stores and possibly from other entrepreneurs. The entrepreneurs, however, may have to do some hunting for them because once issued, they are rarely looked at again during operation of the company.

Tax aspects

All businesses pay several layers of taxes. All pay the same federal taxes, and in addition, state and local taxes that depend upon location and lines of business.

Federal taxes

All companies must pay the following types of taxes to the federal government.

1. Income taxes that depend on legal form of business as discussed earlier.
2. Payroll taxes for any employees, including income withholding, social security (FICA) (called self-employment tax in a proprietorship or partnership), and Medicare must be withheld. The easiest way to handle payroll taxes correctly is to let a bank or a payroll service take care of the records, check issuance, and deposit of the tax money in a special account. Some owners get into serious trouble by handling these accounts themselves and using money from them for their purposes other than taxes. A first step is to apply with the IRS with a form SS-4 (www.irs.gov) and a copy of the *Employer's Tax Guide* giving further instructions.
3. Unemployment taxes that depend upon payroll and must be reported each year.

Federal tax forms and instructions can be downloaded from the IRS Web site, www.irs. gov. A free IRS document called *Business Tax Kit* includes a section on Starting a Business and Keeping Records. The Internal Revenue Service offers training under a Small Business Tax Education program.

Fringe benefit programs, such as retirement, profit sharing, and pension plans, have additional special rules and requirements for reporting, both to the federal government and to the employees. Complying with the Employee Retirement Income Security Act (ERISA) of 1974 can become complicated and warrant considerable study, and/or help from a professional who works with those rules all the time.

State taxes

States, counties, and cities impose taxes of their own that vary from one to another. The following state taxes are imposed, for instance, in Washington State.

1. Excise and/or business and occupation tax based upon total revenues (not on net income in this state, where there are no personal or business state income taxes).
2. Sales taxes on goods sold within the state. These have both a standard state percentage as well as a county and city percentage that varies depending on location.
3. State unemployment tax, in addition to federal noted above.

In addition, state laws require companies to get workers' compensation insurance for their employees, so that they can pay for care in the event of injury or sickness on the job. The cost of this insurance, which is bought from a state fund, varies with the riskiness of the work the employees do. This insurance is also required even if workers work at home, which can be tricky, given the possibility that an injury sustained at home might be construed by one person as work-related and by another as not.

Prepayment plus a quarterly report are required, as are the posting of notices to inform policies that the insurance exists. Complete records of all injuries must be kept, but only those requiring medical attention need be reported. There are special taxes for some activities, such as selling fuel or real estate.

The following are city taxes imposed in Seattle, Washington.

1. Excise and/or business and occupations tax as a percentage of total revenues.
2. A component of the sales tax, as noted above.

Although the Internal Revenue Service may be the most feared tax agency, state and local agencies should not be dismissed as weak.

In March 1988, a software developer opened a microcomputer hardware company, Microworkz.com, as a sole proprietorship operating out of a Seattle storefront, and soon made the startling announcement that it was going to start selling PCs for just $299. A city inspector walked into the store in the fall of 1998 and found that the company lacked a city business license. The owner later obtained the license, but did not pay Seattle city taxes. He incorporated the company in November 1998, and in early 1999 moved to an adjacent city, Lynnwood. Later, in June 1999, he was charged by Seattle with failing to pay city taxes and threatened with up to 90 days in jail and a $1,000 fine. A warrant for his arrest was issued in August 1999 but quashed in September when he posted $500 bail. He claimed that Seattle had sent notices to the wrong address for six months, a claim which Seattle denied. In August 1999, he publicly conceded that *his company needed "more seasoned management" and stepped aside as CEO. His attorney said, "We are having ongoing discussions with the city to resolve this tax issue quickly and amicably." The city director of revenue said, "We'll work with the taxpayer as long as we see progress." Meanwhile, Microworkz had announced a $300 million deal with AT&T over three years to provide low-cost or free Internet access.*[13]

---

[13] Peter Lewis, "Microworkz Faces City Charge," *The Seattle Times*, September 30, 1999, p. C1.

Appendix 10B-1 Bankruptcy Alternatives

To give either individuals or companies a way to escape debts so large they can't repay them, federal law provides several types of bankruptcy.

Chapter 7

By far the most common type is Chapter 7, or straight bankruptcy. It is used mainly by individuals, but also by partnerships and corporations, who face debts they don't think they can handle. It requires liquidation, selling off assets, and closing out the books. It can be voluntary if declared by the owner, or involuntary if it results from a lawsuit brought by creditors who have not been paid. It requires $295 in filing fees. There were 450,332 Chapter 7 filings in the twelve months ending June 30, 2007, down 61 percent from 2006.[14]

Some lawyers specialize in bankruptcy cases, and hiring one to help if filing a petition for bankruptcy with the bankruptcy court is usually advisable. Within a couple of weeks after filing, the court will send notice announcing the date that a meeting of creditors will be held. After that meeting, creditors, who may or may not appear personally, have 60 days to file with the bankruptcy court any objections to the bankruptcy they may have. Another 60 days later, absent any continuing contest, the bankruptcy will become final. A trustee, either elected by creditors or appointed by a court, will then take charge of the business's assets so that creditors may be paid off from what remains of them. However, often virtually nothing is left of those assets after legal and accounting fees are paid. A waiting period of six years is required with this form of bankruptcy before it can be filed again.

Chapter 13

Second most common are Chapter 13 work out bankruptcies, of which there were 294,693 in 2007.[15] This type is essentially intended for wage earners, and applies to individuals and proprietorships only, not corporations. It costs $274 to file and must be entered into voluntarily. Provided that unsecured debts are less than $250,000 and secured debts less than $750,000, the individual submits to the court a plan for paying off debts on extended terms for the following, in order of priority:

1. Secured creditors (those who have specific claims on certain assets that were pledged against debts)
2. Administrative expenses
3. Operating expenses of the business
4. Wage claims up to $2,000 per person
5. Employee benefit plan contributions
6. Claims of consumer creditors
7. Taxes
8. Other creditors

If the court agrees to the proposed plan, the entrepreneur is allowed to retain all personal assets, and may continue operating the business to follow the bankruptcy plan under

---

[14] "June 2007 Filings Drop Compared to 2006," *U.S. Courts: The Federal Judiciary Newsletter* (Washington, DC: Administrative Office of the U.S. Courts, 2007).
[15] "June 2007 Filings," *U.S. Courts*.

supervision of the court. Creditors must go along with it whether they want to or not, and the process is under supervision of the court. There is no waiting period on filing again after Chapter 13 bankruptcy.

Chapter 11

Most often reported in business news stories, although the least common type of bankruptcy, is filing for protection from creditors under Chapter 11 reorganization. Costs start at $15,000, including $1,039 to file; it is used by corporations to keep operating in an attempt to recover from the fact that they cannot pay all their bills. There were 5,586 such filings in 2007, down from a high of 24,740 in 1986.[16]

Under Chapter 11 a plan for dealing with creditors must be submitted to the U.S. Bankruptcy Court proposing specifically how claims will be handled. The plan may propose to pay only a portion of what the corporation owes, or to stretch payments over a longer period of time, or to offer stock to creditors in place of repayment. If the plan is approved, the company, which gets to retain its assets as a debtor in possession, must follow it and attempt to fulfill it. Less than a fourth of such firms manage to do so, usually because they waited too long before filing for protection. A waiting period of six years is required with this form before it can be filed again.

The rationale for this alternative is belief that the company is worth more to creditors if it is intact than if it would be if immediately liquidated. Because different obligations of the company are handled in different ways in the bankruptcy process, it can be worthwhile to consider their nature and treatment in advance. Debt secured by collateral, for instance, will likely result in confiscation of that collateral. If it can be sold on better terms by the business before bankruptcy, then it may be possible to take care of those debts better ahead of time by selling the collateral and giving what's collected to the creditor.

But before doing that it may be helpful to investigate what types of property are going to be exempt from confiscation. Many dependencies can be involved, including the type of bankruptcy and also which state the business is located in. For instance, in some states private pension plans are exempt and in others they are not. But sometimes federal courts disagree with the states and can overrule them.

Hence, making an inventory of assets and asking an experienced bankruptcy lawyer for help in classifying assets as to which are exempt may be worthwhile, depending on the value of the assets. It may be possible to sell assets that are non-exempt (i.e. that can be confiscated), and put the money into assets that are exempt and hence can be kept for a restart. It is important to sell them for the highest possible price, however. Trying to give a deal to some friend or relative can be interpreted as intent to defraud creditors, which is illegal.

Finally, if it is in the best interest of creditors to help avoid bankruptcy, then it may make sense to work with them toward that end. In that case, it is also important not to leave any of them out. If that is not possible, then it is probably time to see a bankruptcy lawyer.

---

[16] "June 2007 Filings," *U.S. Courts.*

CASES

The cases and their sub-chapters in this section appear in the same order as the case assignments that appear at the ends of the chapters. Please refer to the table of contents for listings both by assignments and by cases alphabetically.

Cases in order of chapter assignment

Eric Chang

School, venture, both, or ... ?

In mid-September 1998, Eric Chang had to decide whether to proceed at full speed with a new venture he had formed with three companions, set the venture aside to pursue an MBA program to which he had been accepted and that was about to begin, or strike some sort of compromise between the two.

Eric had become acquainted with computers through working in a computer store after graduating with a degree in Chinese Literature and training in art in 1994. He had also worked as a consultant on computer graphics, Web site design, and animation for two years. He had become friends with three others similar in age, one his roommate, who together with him began in 1996 developing a screen-saver featuring an aerial view of downtown Seattle. Two were programmers, one of whom had done projects featuring 3D programs for viewing geographic areas and the other had worked extensively in computer graphics. The third partner was an architect with six years of industrial experience.

The partners pooled their savings and spent their spare time developing the screen-saver product before and after work hours of their full-time jobs. Eric recalled that particularly in the first few months he would get up at 5 a.m. and wake the others so they could all make headway on developing their product before going off to their day jobs. Then after work they would get back on the project again until late into the night or early morning. It was, he said, very demanding, but they enjoyed it.

The first run of their screen-saver consisted of 1,000 units at a cost of about $6 each, which they sold to stores for $14 each and the stores resold for $25 to $30. Notwithstanding its cost to the end user being over double that of many other screen-savers, the run sold out quickly in 1997. "Putting demo units in the stores that customers could play with was what overcame the competition," Eric said. "What we did was buy obsolete computers cheap and put them up free. That alone probably doubled our sales."

A second run of 5,000 units sold out by fall 1998, and another 5,000 had been ordered and would arrive shortly. Eric handled most of the marketing and selling effort, which essentially involved calling on retail stores and persuading over 30 of them to carry the product. The unit cost of this longer production run, Eric noted, was less than that of the first run. Each CD copy this time cost about $1, and the box cost another $1. Printing and packaging cost about 50 cents, bringing the direct cost per copy to $2.50. Eric estimated that if the run size were increased to 100,000 units, this cost would drop to about $1.

Eric pointed out that a difference between his product and other screen-savers was that his was interactive and included sound. A viewer could maneuver over the city for different aerial views and also click on different sites for other information. Cars moved on the streets and honked their horns, Volkswagens tooted with a sound like real Bugs, tourists hailed taxis, and meter readers held up traffic. An advantage for stores carrying the product seemed to be that the product itself, when running in the store, would hold the attention of customers and keep them in the store longer.

The team thought of many ideas and benefited from others' input about how the product, which so far seemed to be the only one of its kind, could lead in other directions of opportunity. Similar savers for other cities would be one possibility, perhaps through collaboration with programmers in those cities who might like to work up the code and maybe even help with selling in their areas for a share of the profits. Eric noted that the registration cards that had come back so far indicated that customers would like to have a screen saver that concentrated on their particular city and neighborhood.

Another possibility might be to develop further the game features included in the display. One novelty they thought might be amusing would be to make it possible for users to select the Kingdome stadium and blow it up (which was, in fact, the method used two years later for planned demolition). Or an application of the program to a Web site could be developed for selling advertising space and other companies' products.

Pursuing any of these would cost much more time and money, both of which were limited for all members of the team. They had received invitations to work on lucrative consulting projects that could greatly enhance their incomes; they also knew they could obtain progressively higher salaries by moving among jobs. The market for the kinds of technical skills they possessed was booming, particularly in the greater Seattle area, which currently boasted over 2,000 software companies.

"We have friends who have gone to work for companies like Amazon.com and received stock options whose value has far surpassed what we have earned by doing this company," he noted. To seek out and undertake more lucrative employment of that sort, however, would take time and likely lengthen their work weeks, so that having more money would in effect have to be bought at the expense of less time to work on their screen-saver venture.

Eric in particular was facing another potential major time demand because he had applied to and been accepted by the MBA program at the University of Washington. If he were to pursue that, he would have to cut back not only on his job at the bookstore, which provided needed income, but also the screen-saver venture, which had been set up formally as a limited liability company with the name "4i Software." Eric took seriously the admonition of his mother, who pointed out that an MBA would likely lead to better employment and enhancement of his income, plus also make him more effective as a businessperson. It seemed to him that such training could make him more effective for building 4i, if and when it would be destined for real growth.

Important lessons about business, Eric believed, could also be seen in experiences that his father had gone through with inventions. One was a shut-off valve for lawn sprinklers if they happened to get broken off, for instance, by being run over by a lawn mower. Mr. Chang had successfully sold rights to a large company, which gave him an initial payment and agreed to a royalty on future units sold. However, Eric said, the company had bungled development of a production model of the valve and thereby rendered it unsalable, so that the royalties never materialized.

A second invention was a water-saving toilet valve that used line pressure, rather than the gravity pressure of water in the tank, for flushing with a smaller amount of water. There were other such products, but Mr. Chang's valve included features that enabled it to be much more cheaply made, and it also operated more quietly. Plumbing manufacturers were approached whose engineers expressed admiration and enthusiasm for the product. However, their sales people were put off by a delay of a few seconds required in its flush cycle that they feared would deter customers. So no way seemed to exist for making money with this invention, which like the sprinkler valve, had taken Mr. Chang years of time and personal funds to develop.

It was clear to Eric that a new product could have better features that appealed to many people and still not be commercially viable. He expected that to mount a campaign for expanding geographically with their screen-saver, and to add other products such as maps of other cities and even the overall United States, would cost much more money than he and his partners presently had. It also seemed apparent that the software and Internet industries were experiencing very rapid change and many new business entries, so that slowing or delaying a project could easily spell the venture's doom.

Should Eric and some or all of his partners shift to better-paying work, such as consulting, and drop or slow down their proprietary software development? Or should they shift their time to seeking financing by sharing the business in order to concentrate on it more and either accelerate development of geographic interactive screen-savers or diversify into a broader line? "I talked with the team about responsibilities, and it looks like the largest share of the job if we go ahead will fall on me."

Eric noted that because of the time cycle on which he had applied, he would not be able to put off his MBA acceptance as a way of concentrating a bit longer on the business. Classes were about to begin.

Kerry Tye

Whether to join a venture

In mid-April 1998, Kerry Tye was considering how she should respond to an invitation by a founder of iTango, an embryonic software company, to quit her present job with Group Health, a health maintenance organization (HMO), and join the new venture. The position offered was that of product manager for development of software pertaining to health care. What the product was supposed to consist of and do, however, was not yet clear to her. Accepting the job would require that she accept a $15,000-per-year pay cut, although she would receive in return payment in stock from the new venture.

After graduating from the University of Washington in 1991 with a bachelor's degree in business administration, Kerry had studied French in Belgium for a year and then taught language at a mission in Zaire. In 1992 she had moved back to Washington State to work for Group Health as a facility and operations manager, first in the Spokane branch and then in Seattle. Next she became director of a for-profit branch of the hospital devoted to treating hearing disorders. She developed budgets, managed expenses, helped develop strategy, consulted for other units of the organization, coordinated remodeling, helped install computer networks, and administered vendor contracts. Her responsibilities included supervision of 24 employees, including hiring, training, evaluating, and firing.

She became acquainted socially with the two founders of iTango. She and her husband, a real estate manager, helped them find facilities and work out lease arrangements for the new venture. One of the founders had attended Harvard Business School with a friend who had since become a venture capitalist. From that personal acquaintance, the founders obtained a commitment for $1.8 million in venture capital without even developing a business plan. The first two employees were a software developer and a graphics specialist, both of whom came from another software venture that had failed. Now they wanted someone to help with management of product development, and so had called upon Kerry.

Kerry's familiarity with the business was limited except for the work she did voluntarily to help it obtain real estate. She knew that the two founders had worked for Microsoft earlier and then for other enterprises with which she was not familiar. They had conceived some sort of software architecture for drawing information centrally out of a variety of distributed databases, organizing and redistributing it as desired. Kerry's understanding was that they had assumed there would be commercial applications for such a program and decided to try forming a company to exploit it.

The partners asked a few people for advice about where to apply their program; they suggested that the health care industry was the best place to look for applications. The idea was that a package could be developed that would enable health care clients both to obtain and to communicate information about themselves with health insurance companies more time-efficiently. The entrepreneurs had learned that Kaiser Permanente, a large health care company, had said that reduction of the average customer-support call by 10 seconds would save it between $10 million and $15 million annually.

They also heard that there were 223 million individuals with health insurance in the U.S being served by approximately 90,000 insurance brokers or agents in dealing with some 1,845 health insurers.

No one in the company had figured out, however just how to sell a time-saving software package to some part of this market, and they wanted Kerry to help them. However, she understood that the two founders had changed market direction in their thinking three times during the preceding two months, from higher education to telecommunications, and now to health care. So she was not sure this one would or should retain its top priority.

She had a high respect for the founders, both technically and personally, and felt pleased that they had invited her to join them. In her present job she was experiencing frustration with the fact that her responsibilities and pressures seemed to be increasing but nobody in her area had received any raises for three years. She had thought of seeking work at other established companies, but expected that such a change would require that she start again at a lower level and work her way up as she had done at Group Health.

At the same time, she knew from the media and acquaintances that working in a start-up company could be exciting. It could let her see all aspects of the business, be able to make a significant impact on the firm herself, and be able to identify clearly the differences that she personally made to the organization as it developed. The $15,000 pay cut she would have to take was to be made up through payment in stock at a valuation of half of what the venture capital firm was expected to pay for it. She foresaw the possibility of making a great deal of money if the venture prospered. But she expected her work hours would be longer if she joined the venture, and her benefits would also be reduced from those she currently received.

She knew there was no assurance that the venture stock would ever be worth anything. The venture capital firm had not yet actually put in its money. Instead, one of the founders had been paying all the venture's expenses out of his savings, which would also be the initial source of her pay. In addition there would be the income from her husband's job, but they had just finished building a new house, and there was a mortgage to pay.

Byron Osing[1]

From school to venture

In 1999, three years after finishing his Ph.D. at age 33 in Marketing with an Entrepreneurship minor, Byron Osing had created two companies, one of which he sold for $200,000,000 US. Here he recalls the path he followed.

I grew up in a little southern Alberta farm town named Milk River, the only son of a farmer. Like most farm kids I started driving around in a truck as soon as I could see over the dashboard. I also found better ways to make money than working in a grocery store. At around 13 or 14 I decided to become a gardening contractor and spent the summer around town roto-tilling peoples' gardens with a tractor that my parents let me have. They probably spent more money on it than I made through the summer, but then again they probably thought it was good experience. During high school I always had a summer business. It was window washing one summer and contract painting the next.

My dad said that he would rather work fifty hours a week for himself and make less money than work forty hours a week for somebody else. His dad, my grandfather, was the biggest contractor around. With a big crew he built half the town. My dad saved nickels from working for his dad, and eventually bought a truck to make his first million dollars hauling coal. In those days they didn't have hoists, so he'd back up to the mine, load the truck eight to ten feet in the air with a big shovel, drive someplace, and unload it, all day, every day, until his back went out.

I showed enough aptitude for hockey to play Junior A by the time I was 14 which, back then, was basically unheard of. But it wasn't just love of the game that made me want to go pro in the sport. One of my pro hockey goals was to make and save enough money in a short period of time to finance business ventures. Hockey careers can be short. By age 17 I was already sick of the incredible bus travel, the politics, and the coaches. So I quit playing Junior A and went off to the University of Lethbridge.

Undergraduate years

I played university hockey but got a good liberal arts education in the process. I studied psychology more because I found it interesting and because it offered insight into human behavior, which is very important in business. I stayed an extra year for a management undergraduate diploma that included the ten core courses of the management program.

Next I worked in the Solicitor General's Office counseling kids in jail. That was a really sad experience. I don't know if I am not just a warm 'give them a hug' kind of person, but I ended up really disliking these kids as opposed to wanting to nurture them. It seemed to me that they didn't want to be helped, or that they knew the system and how to work it. They felt more comfortable there than out on the street. It was a nasty experience that convinced me I needed a drastic career change.

In that fifth year I also spent some time with the Flames hockey farm system in Salt Lake City. I was getting scouted heavily and had a contract in Germany, but then I blew out two discs on my back in my final year, which stopped the hockey thing then and there. (I am quite happy that I can walk and play golf at this point.) But that left the question of what to do for a living. In Lethbridge you either live to farm or you retire to die. It is not a great place to develop a business career.

---

[1] Prepared by W. Ed McMullan of the University of Calgary in 1999 and used with permission.

While playing hockey and going to university in Lethbridge I also had a rose and flower business. I'd take in an order of 500 roses every Thursday, then cut and put water tips on them. Girls would come by pick them up, go to bars and sell them at night. It was good particularly because it took about $300 in capital and everything was a variable cost. Net cash out was about $5000 per month for just hanging out in the bars a couple of hours a night on weekends to see what was going on. I got the idea from a really bad Tom Cruise movie called "Cocktail." He was a bartender but always had a stack of books on "how to be an entrepreneur" or "500 businesses that you can start on a shoestring."

I wanted to be an entrepreneur so badly that I read every one of those cheesy books. Surprisingly, you can get some good ideas out of them, like the rose and flower thing. It was years before they ever did that in Calgary. It was going on in the US so I thought, "Hey, let's do this in Lethbridge," which I did. Lethbridge is right in the heart of the Bible belt, and articles appeared in its newspaper on how this business must be a front for prostitution or something. It was unbelievable. But I had a good time, learned a lot, and earned enough money to pay my way through school.

It always seemed to me that a key to success was opportunity identification. I remember looking through all these off-the-shelf ideas on businesses that you can start. I also read about using the Yellow Pages. Once you tweaked onto an idea it was always useful to get the Yellow Pages from four or five metropolitan cities to see if anyone had actually satisfied the need that you had identified. If you didn't see anybody in that business it meant you had stumbled upon something unique. Whenever I came up with an idea, I would go research it. This was unlike most people who would come up with an idea, then make a few phone calls, and if their friends liked it, they would try and start a business. I always recognized that researching an idea would make it fall flat on its face or heighten it.

I also realized from growing up on a farm that I wouldn't make a good employee. As a poor farm kid with no rich relatives or friends and no access to capital, the only way that I was ever going to be able to raise the money to start a business was to somehow add some credibility to my resume. Credibility wasn't going to come from the jobs that I had in the past; it was going to come from putting some academic degrees behind my name. That, in fact, did help a lot.

MBA years

To get a career change I decided to go back to school for an MBA. One reason I chose the University of Calgary was its emphasis on entrepreneurship and new enterprise development. I had good enough marks as an undergrad to go anywhere, but I liked the school. Their courses included a lot of interactive work with businesses and I could actually take an emphasis on entrepreneurship.

I started the program at 26, fresh from undergraduate school, with long hair. In class there were a lot of older people who had been working for ten to fifteen years, carrying brief cases and wearing suits, Type A, bankers and accountants. I felt quite intimidated without such business background.

The MBA culture, though, was more like high school than undergraduate school. It seemed "cliquier" with people moving off into their social groups. Accountants hung out together. Engineers hung out together. Bankers hung out together, leaving the rest of us out in the cold as sort of a mish-mash. But I was a pretty serious body builder, so I could come in and just intimidate the hell out of everybody physically. I also played a little hockey on the MBA team. I earned their respect, you might say.

After the first semester I felt comfortable and fit in, but up until that time it was a painful integration process. There were only two or three people I really got to know well in the early period. There were some tough times emotionally in that there were a lot of pseudo-intellectual things happening. People who had direct business experience really wanted to strut their stuff and show the class who they were. I was weak at finance and accounting and had to work hard to catch up. People with all the financial wizardry and accounting background lorded it over the rest of us. Then again they couldn't market their way out of a paper bag. It all kind of evens out in the end. I acquired some good friendships and business acquaintances that come into play at the current time. During the program I spent a lot of time on the nightlife since I found the big city exciting. My GPA in my first year was not sparkling, just 3.3 or something like that.

When the Alberta government decided to privatize its wine stores a friend of mine from class and I jumped all over it in an entrepreneurship class. We did a whole business plan—did the research and started raising money—before we took a really hard look at the industry and concluded that this wasn't a good thing. We took it a long way but then, based on the research and our own feelings, we said, "No, this is not a good opportunity."

Ph.D. years

In the second year of the program I met a professor of international marketing who was recognized as a guru in Europe. I took some international marketing classes from him and got to know him well. I really admire this man. He has about 15 books and 85 or so publications. He speaks six languages. In Europe they treat him like a god but over here it is like "who are you?" He convinced me early in my second year that I should probably stick around and do a Ph.D. I was able to pull out a 3.7 in my second year, barely enough to squeak into the Ph.D. program.

I really had to lobby to get into the Ph.D. program because the professors who knew me felt that I didn't fit the mold of a pure academic—far from it. When you get into a Ph.D. program, it is the antithesis of an MBA program that is pragmatic, real-world oriented, and working with business. The Ph.D. is academic, esoteric, and theoretical. They kept asking me what I was doing and why I wanted to be part of this—so I had to lobby hard. The first two years of a Ph.D. are very difficult. If you think the workload is heavy in an MBA, and it is, then double or triple it for a Ph.D. We were in one class where we had ten textbooks to read for the first class. In 18 months I took sixteen Ph.D. classes over and above the MBA. You find that there is a high dropout and burnout rate in the Ph.D. program, because the workload is brutal. You have to get your dissertation idea put together, defend that idea, and do comprehensive exams, both written and oral, all at the same time. I finished the coursework in April at about the twenty-month point. I had the summer to study for all of these exams and did them in August. It's a grueling, grueling process.

Then once you have done that you can start the work on your dissertation. Mine was a monolithic 540-pager. Some of the comments that came back from the reviewers were that this dissertation has the potential to make an impact on the entrepreneurship and marketing world. I still owe it to my supervisor to get some articles out of it.

Fifty percent of people who start a dissertation never finish. These are all bright, hard-working people. What you have to do with a dissertation is develop a piece of knowledge that is unique and adds to the body of knowledge in your field. That becomes a daunting task in that people get really jammed up because they go, "Oh man, look at all the research literature in this realm that I am working in. How can I possibly do something different here that is meaningful?" So a safe way is just to split something off somebody else's work and add to it. So what if it is not meaningful, it will slide by.

I took the opposite approach where I did the armchair theory approach. I sat back and went, "Okay, what do I think is happening out there in the world?" I did a lot of reading in the entrepreneurship and marketing areas. I saw strains converging in two areas, one called market orientation and the other called entrepreneurial orientation. One thing that always interested me was firm performance. In the business world if you are not adding to the bottom line and firm performance, then it may be esoteric and pretty, but it is valueless. In the real world I thought that market orientation and entrepreneurial orientation were fairly highly correlated or similar. Market orientation is about how well a company executes marketing strategy. How much market research do they do? How much competitive research do they do? How differentiated are their products? How well do they deliver value added to customers? All those good things make you a better marketing company. There are a lot of great marketing companies out there, but surprisingly, the research in the area demonstrated a pretty weak correlation between marketing orientation and bottom line performance. Nor was entrepreneurial orientation related to the bottom line either. Entrepreneurial orientation is somewhat different but correlated. You have to be market-oriented to be a good entrepreneur. You are looking for opportunity, for trends. You are hostile to your competitors. You are aggressive. You are innovative, so you do a lot of market research and competitive research. That is where the overlap comes in.

My big "aha" idea was that the high performance firms would demonstrate both an entrepreneurial and a market orientation. In my way of thinking it was the interaction effect that was the critical element that really generated firm performance. That is what I set out to test. When I examined the scales that the researchers had created to measure market and entrepreneurial orientation, I concluded that they had done a poor job for the size of firms that I wanted to research. Their instruments were aimed at measuring "Fortune 500" companies, but I was interested in a broad range of companies anywhere from 10 employees to 20,000 employees. So I redid the scales. I reoperationalized them, as it is called, preparing new, more appropriate questions. What resulted was a pretty thick measurement instrument. I tossed these things into a statistical analysis that threw out all of the interaction between the scales, or multicollinarity as it is called. So off I went and sent off nearly two thousand questionnaires and got a response rate of over 20 percent.

The neat thing at the time was that few theses were generating statistically significant support for their research hypotheses in the social sciences (or in business, which in the university is really a social science). When the results came back, about seven of my twelve hypotheses had statistical support greater than 0.05 and several that had 0.01 probability. So I had taken an idea from armchair theory and ended up thankfully with some strong support. I absolutely shocked a lot of professors by producing one of the best theses that had been generated at the Faculty. (This was the reviewers' opinion of my work not just my own ego.) It turned out to be a rewarding experience.

Opportunity identification and evaluation

All of those stupid entrepreneurship books that I read as a kid had one thing in common. If you read between the lines they said that you don't create opportunities, you recognize them when they come to you. The whole art of the game is being open and seeing the opportunity when it does pop up in front of you. At various times in my life I have worked very hard to create an opportunity or to think of one. I have to start a business—what is it going to be? You do all this hard work. It is like the old exercise of here is a toaster and here is a hammer. Create a new product out of the two of them. You can always come up with some goofy thing. But is it going to add value and will people pay money for it? I think that the trick to recognizing opportunity is seeing it when it is in front of you.

It doesn't have to be an aha that will change the world. It doesn't have to be a cure for cancer. It just has to be some deviation of something that somebody else is doing but in a better way that adds value to some group of consumers who will pay money for it. Much of the business world has become mature and commoditized. When you are selling a car, there are ten other people selling that car at about the same price. The real question is how do you add value to that product and to that sale so that people will buy that car from you, and in such a way that you have a better profit margin built in. The whole key to business opportunities is recognizing the differentiated value added of that opportunity. People walk by opportunities every day and don't even realize that they missed them. You first have to see them. Then you have to see them in the clear light of how this adds value to the consuming world in a way that nobody else is doing it. It doesn't have to be that significant; it just has to be something that people will pay money for.

Through the years ideas were always coming to me—constantly. I would say that once a month I would pick a pretty good one out that you could run with. For every ten things that popped up, one would be a real gem. Once a year I would find something I wanted to go with. It got to the point that I was almost looking too much. I was driving myself crazy, almost desperate to find the next one that looks good. I concluded as I got older that it was better to sit back and be acute enough to recognize them when they come up. Then you do your research and either act or don't act. A lot of people tend to take what they like to do as a hobby and turn it into a business, or perhaps they are working in a business and they find a way to take it over. I took a little different approach in that I was always starting businesses from scratch. My perspective on business was that I am here to make money. If I want to enjoy myself I will have a hobby. If I happened to really enjoy the industry or business I was in, then that was a bonus. Whenever an idea came up the first thing that I would do was look for competitors and do walk-rounds. Walk through their stores. Walk through their operations. It was clandestine and not open. I would act like a customer. By posing as a customer you can find out a heck of a lot about a business operation. The sales reps are really eager to sell you something so they will open right up. That hands-on competitive research was something I always did a lot of.

I always play the role of devil's advocate on any idea I come up with and shoot as many holes in it as I can. If it can survive my attempts to take it apart, then it is a pretty good opportunity. Once I get my head around it and I can't make it go away, I start getting more enthusiastic about it. Then I start looking for the upside. I'm not looking to support something. I am looking to take the risk out of something. I want to know what the chances of success are here. My goal is to never have a business failure. Basically I am risk-averse. I have felt that for a long time I couldn't afford a failure. When I recognize that something is a valid opportunity and in my mind a low-risk opportunity, then it is easy to be passionate about it. When you take it to people looking for financing or looking for various resources and you have done your homework, then you can answer their questions, especially the negative ones. That carries it a long ways towards the launch process. It's a matter of believing in what you are doing. I believe the passion should come from a lot of hard work so you can really believe what you are saying; it isn't just promotion.

To start a window-washing business as a university student, you just go and talk to twenty or thirty people in various parts of the city and ask, "For x amount would you let me wash your windows once a week or once a month?" You can find out very quickly whether there is a business opportunity there or not. Same with the rose and flowers kind of stuff; you just go talk to the nightclub owners. It's easy to run the numbers on that kind of business. Here is what it costs. Here is what it will sell for. You just have to find out whether the club owners will let you in or not. Each business type has a different research requirement.

Starting executive centers

While the Ph.D. is esoteric, and not necessarily a business-fundamentals kind of program, I did do a lot of work on the entrepreneurship side of things, which certainly didn't hurt my knowledge base. I looked at the Ph.D. as partly a work-study program, in that I started three businesses while I was there. I was learning hands-on while also practicing the academic side, plus consulting with companies and learning from their mistakes and their strengths.

Then in September on the two-year anniversary of starting, I began work on my dissertation. I thought that it would be okay and I could coast a little. Then I got the idea to start a business. My wife had been working in something called an executive center. This is where you take a whole floor and lease the space then sub-lease the space to independent businesses in single offices or clusters. You supply them with telephone answering, business machinery to use, and service. I began examining the business and decided that the guy running the center was a moron. He was not a very nice individual and treated his employees horribly.

I said to my wife, "Betty, if you want to start a business we can do this. We have learned from this. Here is the opportunity. Business conditions are depressed out there right now, but that gives us opportunity to lease up some space inexpensively on a long-term basis. The center's customers love you, and if you leave they will come with you." So we went to all of the customers beforehand and polled them quietly. We asked if she left would they be willing to come, and said, "Here are some incentives for coming to our new center." This was our risk-reduction strategy.

We had no money but scraped together a few thousand dollars. Thankfully at that time the Treasury Branch had government-backed guaranteed loans you could get for small business. I got one of them.

So we did it, and most of the customers bailed out of that center and came along behind her. We started our own executive center in Kensington called Kensington Business Center. Within about two months of opening we were at two-thirds capacity, just operating on a shoestring. Within six months we were full to capacity and never had more than one or two offices open in six years.

About a year into the first executive center when we could actually relax a little, we bought another one. There was one down the street that we had beaten into the ground and the owner offered it to us at a good price. My wife recently sold out because now she is spring-boarding into retirement at age 30 thanks to the software venture that followed, and is becoming acquainted with the couch and the TV.

While I was working on my dissertation I would get up at 6 AM, I would work all day long getting the businesses up and running them with my wife, I would also consult (typically marketing feasibility analyses and financial feasibility), because we needed the money, till 6 PM. Then I would come home, have a quick supper, then sit in my big easy chair with my laptop, and write on my dissertation until one or two in the morning. It took about 18 to 20 months of typically 18-hour work days.

Software business opportunity

While working on my dissertation with executive centers were up and running, I also had the bright idea to start a software company. Again, I wasn't stressed out enough or tired enough—I had to add something else to the mix.

Life has this funny way of taking you in the directions that it feels like it is going to take you in. I could barely turn on a computer. I was one of the most computer illiterate people. In my MBA time I had to take an MIS class and thought that it was painful as hell. What is this stuff? And lo and behold I end up running a software company.

In one executive center we had a client who was a VAR, which is a value added reseller, of storage technology—typically hard drives, DLT tape arrays, RAID arrays, and things like that. We got to know each other and got talking. I asked him where the future was going in the storage management business of the high tech industry. It was early 1994 when we started talking about it.

Laptops and mobile computers were starting to become a big thing—not omnipresent as they are now, with everybody and everywhere, but nevertheless a big thing. As we started talking about it we realized that the people using these things were executives or sales representatives. These people had really valuable information on their computers and they were never getting backed up. If you drop it or lose it, you have lost a big piece of your life. So we said that there has got to be a way to protect this.

Lo and behold he had a partner in Vancouver in an office who, in selling hard drives, had stumbled across an ex-University of British Columbia management science professor who had set up his own little software company to develop remote backup software. He wanted to back up computers over the phone line or an Internet connection or a wireless modem, back to a centralized host system that had the server and storage capacity. When we recognized the connection we said, "Wow!" After that we just kept talking about it over a few months. One day when the partner went in to sell the professor some product, he found out the guy had closed his business and was in the process of shelving his work.

We quickly struck a partnership, two VAR guys and me. These two had a business and said that they would provide the money. As they put it: "We have a hundred thousand up front and another hundred thousand to follow. We will be equal partners, and you take the business and you run with it. You go and acquire this product then off we go." I thought that was a pretty darn good deal.

The Internet was my main research methodology for analyzing this business. It allowed me to find a heck of a lot of information on businesses in my niche around the world. I found some historical data on companies that had tried and failed. I learned why they failed by phoning some of their old customers and asking where they fell down. (I also advocate that when you do find competitors, phone their customers and find out why they are using them. Find out what value is being added and what someone else is doing.)

After we struck the partnership deal, it was my job to acquire the technology. I just phoned the professor out of the blue and said: "Listen, I understand you are not pursuing this any more. It is on the shelf and you ran out of money. We would be interested in licensing the technology from you and running with the business opportunity." He was amenable to talking. He didn't like the fact that we had no money. But if you are passionate about something you can sell people on your ideas and where you are going to take it. We struck a 10 percent royalty deal. There would be no cash up front, but he would get ten cents out of every dollar of software we sold.

Honing vision

In addition to the Internet I found the Management Library at the University of Calgary to be phenomenal—particularly their online database (all the Statistics Canada material).

Building a business plan around secondary data is difficult. They teach you to do that a lot in business schools, but all you are really doing is tracking some macro trends. You are not really getting down to the bread and butter of what makes a business run or not. Here is the whole market and it is growing at such and such a rate but that is a really 40,000-foot level analysis. It isn't the stuff, however, that will tell you whether an opportunity will fly or not.

On Telebackup I must have put in two-and-a-half to three months of solid work before we decided to run with it. It was a high-risk, high-reward kind of thing. I had to know what it was going to take and what were the failure points. There have been five or six similar companies that tried this and failed dramatically. It takes a lot of footwork and phone calls to find out why these other companies failed.

I also talked to different analysts and other people in the industry to frame out a business plan that felt right. It convinced me that there was a future market for this. But I didn't know what our positioning should be. I didn't come from the industry so I didn't have background knowledge. It was completely new to me. It was also a sophisticated opportunity, so it took a lot of investigation.

Every single business I ever did I had a business plan for. The one for Telebackup Systems had a one-page executive summary, followed by a ten-page version of the business, followed by appendices. The whole thing was, maybe, a 50- to 60-page document with appendices in fine print. But what I took to the bank for bank financing was something different, 15 to 20 pages.

We recognized that there were major players out there with great backup software but they concentrated upon network PCs bound to servers and mainframes. We could have created a product with a lot of sophistication and competed head-on with them. What I recognized was that we had a value-added opportunity. We could build a technology that added value to their technologies, something that they didn't have. We wouldn't even brand it. We could be OEM specialists. That's what we did.

We didn't even try to sell our products, because we knew how tough it was to get into distribution. We knew how expensive and time-consuming it was to build a direct sales force. Instead we could claim that we built this wonderful OEM technology. This is what you guys have. This clicks right on top of it and we can brand it and make it look exactly like your product. You can walk into your existing accounts using your technology and do a value-added sale to them. Keep more money for you. Keep control of your account. Keep your competitors out. This is because it adds value to that part of the organization that they don't cover, which is the remote and PC unit.

That was the perfect strategy. It was a non-competitive strategy, a non-threatening strategy with value added. That is what I recognized right up front. This was a value added to anything else already being done in the backup world. In the technology game it is not the best technology that wins. It is usually second-rate technologies that win. It is smarter companies that win: companies that know how to market, that know how to position, that know how to control distribution and customers. You have to know how to play the game and it is always in a value-added capacity.

Partners

A really good lesson in life is to really know who your partners are before you go into business with them. Every bit of pain that I have had in business has been due to having partners who are not who they seem on the surface. So we strike this partnership, and I go and acquire this software technology, in very rudimentary form. It was old DOS format technology. It stumbled along and worked but we ended rewriting 98 percent of it. It did, however, have several key algorithms in it that no one else in the world had. This professor really had some aha ideas. But he didn't know how to build a commercial product, or take it to the market, or raise money. Another guy who should have stayed in academia instead of trying to start a business, but a very bright individual.

We acquired this thing and set up in one office with one programmer on one little PC and that was the start of our business. At the end of the day after four years when we sold the company in June 1999, we had about 50 employees, the business did about $6,000,000 in yearly sales, and it was recognized as the best remote backup technology of its kind in the world. So it came a long ways.

The early days were tough and the $200,000 that these guys promised me turned into $22,000. That was all of the money that they could actually scrape up. So we started on $22,000 with one employee, and I worked like a dog for 18 months with no salary, my wife and I supporting ourselves with our other businesses and my consulting until such time as we could pay me a little bit of salary. I earned my position through sweat equity. These guys just gave me $11,000 each and coasted, and each came out with about $30,000,000 four years later. If you want to talk about falling onto the golden goose's nest, it does happen sometimes.

A couple of years into the business we recognized that to succeed we'd have to be a takeover target, and you can't have that 10 percent royalty overhang there. It would really kill any deal. So I ended up renegotiating the royalty deal with the ex-professor. He ended up getting $50,000 a quarter as a minimum payment but with a takeout clause where we could buy him out at any time for $2 million. As part of the deal he also got 200,000 shares of the company, and by now he might be able to sell his shares for about $7.2 million Canadian. It wasn't always a trusting relationship. I had to really beat on the guy to do the deal. I literally had to threaten to sue him to walk away from the original deal based on the fact that the technology we thought we were getting didn't turn out to be good technology. We thought that it was much better than it was. The Alberta Research Counsel who reviewed the technology really screwed up on their analysis.

He didn't like any of these takeout deals. He got greedy and wanted to be paid millions a year forever. I just said that is not the way it is going to work. The big companies will not do that. We just pressed him until he agreed. At the end of the day it wasn't a trusting relationship, it was a pure business relationship. If he flinched then I nailed him or visa versa. He never even phoned me to thank me for the $7-plus million. That is fine. That is reality. He was kind of hard to deal with because he was more a pure academic than a businessperson.

Raising money

We found out very quickly that in Western Canada you couldn't raise money for early-stage software companies at that time. We ended up going to friends, relatives, and business associates. I raised $150,000 at 25 cents a share on the first round. We did another $300,000 round at a dollar. That was $450,000 we raised in love money. We also matched the love money with $500,000 in loans from the Royal Bank. This for me was shocking because I knew banks to be asset-based lenders. When you are talking about software companies, there are no assets of the type banks want. It is all intellectual property. Lucky for us Royal Bank had started a program called "knowledge-based industries" to try and show the world they were different and progressive, and that they were trying to support the high-tech world. They badly needed some success stories they could point to, so they ended up lending us money with no guarantees and no assets to back it. Nothing, just here is $500,000.

The deal with the bank was at prime plus 2 percent. Repayments on principal were not required for two years. It was an extremely attractive deal. The government underwrote only 10 percent. The deal was really dependent on a banker who bought into our deal. When the banker got a promotion and left for Toronto they ferried in another banker. He came from the retail side and the first thing he did was ask us where our cash flow was, then tell us we were six months behind plan, yap, yap, yap. "We have to consider taking some actions here." I nailed him at a public-speaking forum about high-tech financing. I said basically that we were open for business and "renegotiating our bank loan." He happened to be in the audience. A week later we had things where we needed them plus another $150,000 line of credit. That money basically carried us until we went public.

Three years ago August I took the company public and learned that it is like uncorking a wine. You go too early and it is a really sour experience. We did it because there were no alternatives. There was no good venture capital money available in Canada. The only individuals interested in us wanted to burn us—70 percent of the company for a few dollars. It was horrid.

So we went public. A little firm called Jennings Capital here in town took a gamble on us and undertook to raise us $2,000,000. Everything that could have gone wrong did. Sprott Securities, a co-financier in the offering, dropped out because the guy who was our champion at Sprott quit and the people in Toronto didn't like high tech stuff—just oil and gas. So Jennings was stuck by itself. But Jennings had no retail sales force, so they had to piece it out to all the other institutions. I am not going to name the bottom-feeding institutions, but there are some here who do all the Junior Capital Pools and have only junior representatives. We ended up having to have those firms place two thirds of the deal. This was really painful later on when we had to get rid of them. They are like parasites.

We filed all of our documents with the securities commission, but it only had two analysts at the time. Instead of being a six-week process it turned into three months for our prospectus to clear. But the lawyers had forgotten to file something with the exchange called a preliminary listings approval. So back we went for a four-week approval process. Then we had to go back to the commission. That took another two weeks.

All told, it was about four months before we could try to raise the money. The trouble was that you have to sell a public offering on momentum. You have to get people excited. You have to be over-subscribed. People have to feel that they have to get a piece of it. The brokers did a good job of that. They had this thing oversold two to one, but it took three months before we could actually sell it.

Everyone had expected approval to take six weeks, not 4 months, so that by the time we got it, we were about half way to the two million dollars. The day we were cleared by the commission was the start of the Calgary Stampede. Who does business during the Stampede, right? How do you raise money in Calgary during the Stampede? For ten days we sat. So Stampede is over and we are all geared up and ready to go. Guess what happens. The NASDAQ crashes by 24 percent. One of the worst crashes in years. So the word is out to stay away from technology stocks.

We started to claw away and get on the phone. Everyone was working hard to get this thing done. We got up to a minimum. The minimum on the offering was $1.6 million and the maximum was $2 million. We were all celebrating because it took so long to get through this thing and we were broke. We were so close to being under that we couldn't make the next payroll without the new funds.

"Gauntlet of thieves"

Then the bottom-feeders phoned us and said: "Listen, if you guys can't get this thing subscribed to the maximum (so that it looks good) we are dropping out. We are not going to see a $1.25 share go onto the market and then drop to fifty cents. You guys sell $400,000 or we are out." I got on the phone and in three days I sold $400,000 worth of stock. It was to friends, neighbors, and business associates. It was really touching how many people who had no money came out of the woodwork having somehow found $5,000 or $10,000. They are all thanking me now when the shares are at $25 or $27. A lot of these people made a half a million dollars. Now it is a rewarding experience. For a year I had sleepless nights. Losing my own money is one thing. Losing money from those close to me is something else. It is something that I couldn't have dealt with. So it was very stressful that way.

A week before we closed one member of our executive team got anxious for the same reason—some of his family was in this thing. He went and did a deal with some guy in the UK to sell the company out from under us for a couple hundred thousand bucks. He called me up in the middle of the night from Toronto saying that he had just struck this deal. I am flying home on the "red eye" for tomorrow's board meeting and I want you to support this. I asked him if he was nuts. The money was raised, we were in the closing process and were days away from getting it. Then we will have $2,000,000 in the bank and we are off. He called me maybe four times in the middle of the night trying to coerce me into supporting this. I just said, "Give me a break." So he shows up at the board meeting the next day and stands up and tries to have me fired for some reason he made up—I can't remember. It was just completely crazy. The board just looked at him and told him to sit down—this was stupid.

In the meantime I had this really nasty board member on there. I don't know how he ended up on the board. To this day I don't know. He saw the opportunity to seize the company for himself. I didn't know that he had been in cahoots with my CFO at the time. They had actually set up the board meeting (knowing that things were shaky) to seize control of the company. They took the opportunity to say that the partners are fighting like idiots. "This is irresponsible. Yak, yak, yak. We are going to take control of the company," he said.

He tried to lever us into it by threatening to quit. He was a big name on the board and a big, fat ex-retailer. The nastiest human being you ever have met. He said, "If you don't give me this company, I will quit the board and phone the commission. My quitting is a material issue and that means you will have to re-file your prospectus. That will kill your IPO and the company." He said that he wanted x million shares including a million shares for his good friend, the CFO. He wanted this and he wanted that.

We went through a three-day period of gut-wrenching issues. He brought his lawyers in, and we had our lawyers there. It was nasty. All the other board members just tucked their tails between their legs and hid from this guy. They were trying to protect their own liability. The only thing that saved me at the end of the day was that I went into the board meeting where there were about a dozen lawyers with a little tape recorder in my pocket. I played on this guy's ego and really pissed him off. He said in front of all these lawyers, "If you don't give me this company I am going to kill this IPO (by doing this and this and this)."

When you boil that down it amounts to extortion. "If you don't give me your money (the company) I am going to do the following." But as a director of a company you are duty-bound to do the right things for the shareholders and the company itself. You are not supposed to be looking out just for yourself. I turned off the tape recorder and asked everyone to leave the room but the guy. Then I said: "Listen you fat bastard. You have two choices. I'll either call the police and everyone else, and charge you with extortion, and I will make sure that you never sit on the board of another public company, or you can sit there and shut up, then resign quietly after the IPO. That is your choice." He brought his lawyer in and they conferred. I could see his lawyer telling him he was dead in the water. So that saved the company. I don't know how many times we were saved at the bell. We finally got public.

Professionalizing

As a start-up entrepreneur you begin as a one-employee company. As you keep adding employees, your definition of who you are and what you do changes. Once your company is really up and growing, you move from being an entrepreneur to being a manager, which didn't sit well with me. So what I always did was to position good people around myself to be the management. This let me continue doing entrepreneurial tasks: looking for new moves and directions to take the company, raising money, and promoting the organization to the financial community.

I always had a clear definition of what I was good at and what I wasn't. You have to know what your weaknesses are so you surround yourself with people to buffer that. Your strengths should be key to your businesses survival and progress. In my case it certainly was. Unless I had a clear self-definition of who I was and what I did well, I don't think that the business would have succeeded. If I hadn't let the management team run with what they were supposed to do, it would have just got in the way and slowed everything down.

I also cleaned up the board. At an early stage you may take any board members with big names that you can get. Mine turned out to be completely useless. After the fiasco where I threw the one guy off the board, I told the others that they would have to resign. "Enough of this crap; you could have done the right thing and stood up for me and you didn't, so you're out of here." So they all left. We replaced them with good people who made a real impact on the company. When you start off in a company you start with one thing and then professionalize along the way.

Things went a little better after that. We still had tough times and we still ran low on money. The next financing that we did out of Toronto was a $5,000,000 round with a firm called Thompson Curnahan. They actually did a good job and there were no big hiccups except that we were almost out of money and we had to bridge-finance the company through the directors.

I went into this never having worked in a high-tech company, let alone run one. From what I know now, I would do things differently, including not going public at such an early stage. In retrospect it all worked out but it was painful.

The single most important trait of an entrepreneur is the humility to recognize your weaknesses and that you can't do it all. The smartest thing you can do is surround yourself with the best people that you can find. I literally dragged executives out of retirement. My executive team had an average of 25 years' experience. The whole reason that we could recruit them was that the company had upside potential. It had a story. They could tell that I was committed to it. I lived, ate, and breathed this thing. We optioned the heck out of them and they all came out multi-millionaires. It was that management team that made all of the difference.

A lot of people can build a brilliant technology for the high-tech market but they have no idea how to execute on marketing strategy, operations management, or getting into distribution channels. That is where management experience pays dividends and really separates the bright star that just dies from the one that evolves, matures, grows up, and becomes a success. That was the critical success factor—the people.

This is particularly true in a high-tech company where the only thing that you really have is your intellectual capital. It is 500,000 lines of code on a CD-ROM and that is worth $200 million-plus dollars. The value is in the people who generated that code and managed the generation of that code and managed the distribution of that code. There are some entrepreneurial awards coming up in the near future that I know that I have won, and that will be an opportunity for me to get up there and give the credit to the right people, finally.

Selling the company

The company that bought us was called Veritas Software in Mountain View, California, right in Silicon Valley. They are a big company. They are going to do $600 million this year. Next year they will do a billion. They are the fastest-growing company in the business. I think that they will be the next Oracle or Microsoft in five years, because we got bought by a real winner.

When we struck this deal initially it was worth a $120 million. By the time we closed it was worth $200 million. Now it is worth $275 million or $280 million depending on what Veritas stock is currently trading at. The next biggest software deal that was ever done out of Western Canada was Hyprotech at $93 million. So we have really eclipsed that and set a new record for the value of an acquired software company.

Veritas is a great company and I am working for them right now as a mergers and acquisitions person. I am one member of a four-person team in a 2,500-person company. I can fly everywhere, see all these neat companies, cut these deals, and rub elbows with all of these big merchant bankers around the world. They pay me $250,000 base salary with enormous stock options. If I stayed for four years until all my options vest, I would be pulling down $2,000,000 a year as a salary. The truth of the matter is, however, that I am throwing this opportunity away. I am already in the process of resigning. There are some personal reasons to do with family. But also once you are already loaded up with money, the salary doesn't really matter. It is kind of a different perspective. It changes your life in some ways and you realize what is important: your family and your friends and people who are close to you. More than that, I love starting companies and running companies and doing my own thing and starting from scratch and building something.

Some entrepreneurs who have had success will want to take all the credit. Some will recognize that it wasn't them but the team they built around them. In general, it is the latter group that will keep moving to the next echelons and build big companies. Their people tend to follow them everywhere. So they take their successful people from one opportunity to another and just keep replicating their successes. That is what I am doing.

Starting again

I have now formed a new company. There are five of us, all high-tech people who have had some big successes. I am the junior guy in this bunch. These guys have all built and sold two or three high-tech companies. We have formed a company called Launchworks. Just this month we are going to start pulling the covers back.

The high-tech industry, more than any other industry in the world, is incestuous. Everybody who has been in it for a while and has been reasonably successful knows each other in one way, shape, or form. You have bumped into each other in this event or the other. You have done business. Five of us have got together and have become pretty good friends. We have all been through the grinder.

In Canada we have tremendous resources. We are desperately trying to transition from being hewers of wood and drawers of water and trying to produce high-value-added products, including technology. Canada is trying to push a technology thrust. We have a tremendous talent pool for architecting and building technology. We have very bright people. Our immigration policies are such that some of the best and brightest people in the world are coming from Asia and Eastern Europe.

We have very little capability in financing to grow software companies. We have little capability of getting into distribution channels in the US. That is why probably eight out of ten of these early stage ventures fall on their face. Typically the people starting these companies are technology people. Techies shouldn't run technology companies. People who can build technology are not typically people who can run a technology company. Yes, there are some who rise to the top. But typically technology people have very big left brains and very small right brains. To run a company and to know how to position your technology and market it and to take it to the next steps and to have the charisma to be able to sell your story with passion and get the world excited about it—people who write software code are not typically those types of people. They are not CEO material.

How do you get a company that has a very intelligent technology founder and great technology from point A to point B? That is what we set up Launchworks to do.

We realized access to capital was limited so we are going to change that. We just raised our first capital pool. There are some very serious people who put money into this capital pool. It is small. It is $5.5 million. We are going to do $20 million to $30 million on the next shot. What we designed Launchworks to be was a true incubator. Not a physical incubator but a money- and people-provider incubator. We are only looking at software companies typically in the e-commerce, business-to-business software applications, or Internet space because that is where a lot of the growth is right now. We provide money. We provide people.

We have this entire stable of people who have been with us and are willing to go anywhere with us and do anything, so we plug these people into the companies to provide that senior management on short-term contracts of six or twelve months. These people, in turn, get optioned up, and if the company is really successful they make half a million or a million bucks, every time. They love these opportunities.

Moreover we provide all the strategic planning. We sit with these companies and we develop their strategies and their execution plans for them. We make introductions for them into the distribution channel and to the big players we know. Like any other industry, you can kick on a door for a year and no one will answer it if they don't know who it is. We can make one call and have this company working on a deal within one week. That is the shortcut to success: changing a five-year cycle to an 18- to 24-month success cycle. So we provide all those things and we call that launch capital.

If you look there is seed and love money down here. There is venture capital and early stage IPO and mezzanine capital up here. In between the love capital and the traditional VC capital (which is never less than $3 million to $5 million) is what we call launch capital. That launch capital is typically $250,000 to $1.5 million. But with that money come the people and the expertise and the contacts.

With the five of us working hard at it, and with some of the very significant people who invested in it at an early stage, we think we can make an impact not just in Western Canada, but also across Canada and the Pacific Northwest. We were down in Seattle today looking at a deal there. Capital is even scarce there. We hope to make a real impact and change the way that software companies get financed, incubated and cuddled, and how they grow up to become successful. Make no mistake, we are not just doing this out of the goodness of our hearts. We intend to make a lot more money at this, but we also intend to add social value. People who meet our criteria, who have done a good job of building those early stages, and do business with us will have a high probability of success compared to their counterparts who are still out there slugging away on their own.

So that is my next gig. Hopefully, I will be out of Veritas within the month and joining Launchworks as CEO again. One of the other gentlemen will be president, and we will run the company cooperatively. I think there will soon be news articles on this thing.

Reflections on education and success

In terms of life style, ten years ago I started an MBA program with nothing. I was basically a poor farm kid. Now I guess by any standards I am really wealthy. We live on a great acreage, raise our dogs, and do some very nice things.

I see some people who have had a little bit of success and made a couple of million, or started a cash-flow business like a nightclub, and they do pretty well. A lot of them get really high on themselves and forget about the people who were there for them when they had nothing and were on their way up. I find that those people tend to typically crash and burn, and never see any huge success.

The people I have gotten to know more recently are extremely wealthy and have turned out to be extremely nice. The people who were with them at day one are still with them today. They all have gotten wealthy along with them because they have taken other people along for the ride.

Yes there is always a wall there. You will find that when you meet people who have become very successful. You have to have walls. I get dozens of calls a day now from people wanting money. You can't make everybody happy. So you have to put up a wall that is tough to get through.

But once you get through that wall, I find that these very successful people are very nice. Typically they don't show a lot of flash in their lifestyles. They are not living the lifestyles of the rich and famous in a huge mansion being chauffeured around. Yea, a guy came up from Chicago in his own Lear jet this weekend and we took him fishing. He is still a nice guy. If you didn't see his Lear jet you wouldn't know he's rich. The guy walks around in Bahama shirts, shorts, and sandals. He has this big ponytail and beard, and looks like a beach bum. Yet he is one of the real players in the technology industry.

When I think about how my education contributed to my success the most important component was very clearly the MBA program, without a doubt. I honestly don't think I would be where I am now without the MBA. It was a turning point in my life. As a result of the MBA, I was more receptive to the high-tech field which providence brought to me. Cash flow businesses are really nice. But you can work all your life and only cash out for half a million dollars. I could cash out my position for $30 million now, and I am just getting started. The probability is much higher that without the MBA, I would be doing a cash flow business because they are much simpler to run. They require a lot less expertise and a lot less sophistication. The people running a lot of them may be completely incompetent, and somehow they still manage to survive. When you get into the high-tech field it is a damn sophisticated business and it moves at the speed of light.

The people in high tech are extremely smart and well educated, people on the business side. To be able to understand technology it takes more education than in a lot of other industries. The people who are running the bulk of the successful technology firms are older, savvy people who have worked in the industry twenty or thirty years. The thirty-year-old wonders you hear about are exceptions.

It is a completely different game, and unless you have a tool chest that makes you capable of playing at that game, you are not going to get anywhere. What I sniff out is that many of these people who make it early have wealthy families behind them to support the business. Without the MBA program and some of the Ph.D. experience, I wouldn't be there. In any knowledge-intensive industry, the people respect education.

Yes, I had had various small businesses. And I even put together full-blown business plans for gyms and fitness clubs I wanted to pursue. But I realized through the planning process that they weren't good businesses. These were things I loved to do and wanted to make a business out of. At the end of the day, I realized that this was crazy. You couldn't make money at it. I did that all in undergraduate, during my management diploma days. I came to realize that I still lacked skill sets required to operate a big business. I didn't want a little two- or three-person lifestyle company. I wanted to be a real businessman.

I see that a lot of the entrepreneurs these days are older. They have been taught management skills by going to school. Then they have learned hands-on in a business for ten or twenty years. Then they come out with a little money or they inherit some money and off they go to start a business. I didn't have that ability. I had always worked for myself in little businesses but those were simplistic things relative to what I wanted to do. I recognized that I needed the experience that an MBA program could bring, especially the hands-on aspect of it: working on case studies and working in other organizations to see how they operated, and getting feedback from people who ran those businesses.

In hindsight there were things that I should have spent more time on and I didn't. There were things that I loved and spent a lot of time on but I was good at any ways. Being in a business, I realize how critical finance and accounting are—particularly the finance side. I didn't like that when I was taking it in school, but I did well enough at it, and worked hard enough at it that it did arm me to go out and raise money. The new venture finance class I took was a very good one and it helped a lot.

Now I find myself in a business that finances other businesses, so I'm on the other side of the table. Still the things that I learned in that class ring true from both sides. I do have a true appreciation of everything that I learned there. The strategy classes and the clinics where you worked hands-on with entrepreneurial organizations were extremely useful. I loved all my marketing classes because that is what I was good at, as well as the entrepreneurship stuff, because that is what I liked. Anything to do with the new venture classes was typically good because you got that hands-on learning experience with established entrepreneurs who always had a lot of their own insights. A lot of times they would say, "The stuff you are learning in the book is crap. Let me tell you what it is really like." So you got both sides of it. I learned the finance on my own afterwards but it would have been handier if I had learned it while I was there.

What most prepared me, though, was taking entrepreneurial courses. That made a tremendous difference. I worked with seven or eight different entrepreneurs through the MBA program. Some of them became good friends as a result. I typically was working with the CEO or the founder. The amount of time I spent with them varied a lot. Sometimes I met with them five or six times over a semester for a few hours. Other times I was with them pretty well nonstop for five or more hours a week for weeks on end because they viewed me as free labor. One of those guys became the closest thing to a mentor that I have had. A big part of his business was expansion through acquisition, so he taught me a lot about finance from a street level that I didn't know and didn't get anywhere else.

All my university programs helped. First, although people say that the Ph.D. is esoteric, something important that program really reinforced in me was the work ethic. With the businesses and consulting included I put in 18-hour days for two years.

Second, it teaches how to think both analytically and creatively (especially to come up with ideas for your dissertation). It also teaches you time management. Your mind is just functioning at a higher level than it typically would be. My armchair theorizing during the Ph.D. program was valuable because I was drawing on my personal entrepreneurial experience and my MBA, consolidating my thoughts about what makes a successful company. I got a chance to see if I could support my ideas in the literature. My findings further convinced me that my vision was sound. When I was building Telebackup I kept in mind all those things which are required both to build a strong entrepreneurial and a strong market orientation. I told people on my management team, "This is my research, and you can laugh at it if you want because it is academic, but this is what really makes companies tick and I want to do these things." Even in the company that bought us, I was checking them out against my model. They had all the right things that make them a great company. Again I am using my model in setting up my new firm. Everything that we have done is in line with my Ph.D. findings. When I look at my competitors, they are not doing these things.

Third, the undergraduate diploma in management was good because all that I had up to then was the off-the-shelf, how-to-be-an-entrepreneur stuff. And the psychology degree was a definite fourth.

Credibility to acquire capital was certainly a prime reason for my getting the degrees. Without the MBA degree to back me, I don't think I would have got bank financing for Telebackup. People would recognize that you were intelligent enough to be accepted into a Ph.D. program and that you had the work ethic to see it through. That didn't hurt either. The Ph.D. can be interpreted as being a negative thing in some industries, but not the high-tech industry that I was in. In the technology industry a Ph.D. is widely regarded as a feather in your cap since the industry is built on smart people and intellectual capital.

John Morse

Systematic search for business ideas

Midway through a two-year MBA program at the University of Washington, John Morse had begun a venture search with the objective of achieving self-employment upon graduation. Now graduation was just two weeks away and, although he had generated many possible venture ideas, John had not yet found one he was sure he wanted to pursue. He felt it was time to review the steps taken in his search to date and decide whether to continue it or to adopt a different approach.

Background

As the ninth of 12 children, John spent the first 18 years of his life (1952-1970) growing up in a suburb north of Chicago, going right from high school to college. He spent one year at Boston College, his sophomore year abroad in Rome, and finished up the last two years at Northwestern University in 1974 with a B.S. in Sociology. During the next four years, until starting his MBA program in 1978, he held the following jobs: waiter, bartender, phlebotomist, law clerk, factory worker in a sausage plant, hospital purchasing agent, and purchasing agent for a printing plant. John said his experiences working with other individuals as his supervisors and "carrot danglers" were not very rewarding or fulfilling.

> *I seem to be intimidated and uninspired in that environment. I suspect it would be a frustrating life for me as an employee, and it would probably be riddled with continual disappointment. My nature is especially attracted to the independence associated with being one's own boss. I am far more secure with the uncertainties this entails. Three or four years ago, in 1976, I realized what I wanted out of a career in business was to run one, ideally my own. My plan was to get a master's degree in Business Administration, spend three to five years as an employee gaining experience and capital, and then launch a business.*

For part of his MBA program, John spent a year as an exchange student in England. While there, he took a course in entrepreneurship which triggered the thought that it might be possible for him to start a business of his own following graduation, if he could line up a suitable venture idea. Upon returning to Seattle in June 1979, he approached one of his professors at the University of Washington about doing a feasibility study of a new venture idea as an MBA research project. Since John did not have a specific venture idea in mind, the professor suggested that he come back before fall quarter (three months hence) with a study proposal.

During the next three months, once or twice a week John would go into a vacant classroom for a couple of hours at a time with a notebook. He would try to force himself to think of business innovations. He relied largely on his imagination and inspiration. He would try to picture in his mind where business trends were headed. Some ideas that came out of those sessions were:

1. Develop a product for a fast growing market segment—senior citizens.
2. Start a service to capitalize on the increase in foreigners visiting Seattle (for example, day care or tour bus guide service).
3. Develop a marketing device (for example, a nondefaceable billboard to put up on stall walls) to take advantage of the captive market in public toilets.
4. Set up camps for adults.

5. Begin a service to alleviate some of the difficulties facing the growing number of women executives traveling alone to Seattle on business.
6. Organize an information network with subscribers hooked up via computer terminals.

About three weeks before he was scheduled to get back to his professor with his proposal for a topic, John came across an article in Newsweek on "Snob Ice Creams" that he said "came the closest to eureka" since he began searching for a business idea. He now wanted to investigate the feasibility of manufacturing locally a top-quality ice cream to compete with brands currently imported from the Midwest. During the next week-and-a-half he tried to get a feel for what he was considering. He went to the library and pulled some books on ice cream manufacturing. He called all the local ice cream manufacturers to find out what they manufactured in the way of high-quality ice cream. He contacted, either by phone or in person, a number of retail ice cream stores to find out whose ice cream they were distributing and what sort of demand it was generating.

This informal research left John less than convinced that his ice cream manufacturing idea was bound to be a sure-fire success. His professor also expressed doubts, noting that the gourmet brand uppermost in John's mind was imported not only to Seattle but also to Los Angeles from the Midwest. If the Los Angeles area with its many millions of people did not represent a large enough market to justify setting up a local manufacturing plant, the professor asked, how could the Seattle area, which was only a fraction that size and even closer to the Midwest, justify doing so? Instead of plunging ahead with the "hot flash" idea of manufacturing gourmet ice cream, he suggested that John might undertake, under his sponsorship, a methodical search for a business venture as a research project. The professor pointed to three donated boxes of IEA (International Entrepreneur Association) manuals as a possible source of ideas but left the door open to any other sources John might want to mine.

John took a sample of an IEA manual home and discovered it to be a report on a business venture that might appeal to an aspiring entrepreneur. It outlined, step-by-step, what an individual might do to pursue the profiled venture. Some of the items covered were market research, a suggested list of readings, sources for equipment and supplies, and typical cost figures. At the end of each manual was a section devoted to business, legal and governmental considerations in establishing a new venture. A list of manuals available to him in the school library appears in Exhibit 1.

Unsure how he was going to approach the search, but with the desire to do it, John arranged with his professor to begin the MBA research project in fall quarter, two weeks away.

Anticipating a market

Weeks 1 and 2

In discussion with his professor, John decided to attempt a systematic search for a business venture by reviewing the various manuals in the light of his desires and Seattle's business makeup. But he began the search far from convinced that this method would lead to anything tangible or practical. He chose to combine his search through manuals with a review of the Puget Sound area. It seemed to him that it should be possible to view the marketplace as a "case study," and analyze the Puget Sound area for its demographics, economic factors, market profile and any apparent trends. From some such combination of information, he figured, it would be only a matter of deduction to recognize where opportunities existed for a successful start-up.

Week 3

John began his search with a visit to the Seattle office of the Washington State Department of Commerce. He asked for any information that they had on local and state demographics, market studies, consumer profiles, trade figures, growth projections, economic forecasts and anything else they thought relevant.

> *What stumped both them and me was the question: relevant to what? Since I wasn't really sure what information I was seeking, I couldn't be specific. They gave me all the publications they had that might have any connection, even remotely, to the somewhat broad boundaries of my request.*

They included a 1978 Pocket Data Book of the State of Washington (a reference volume of population, economic, government, education, and human resource statistics and trends), a "Community Level Target Industry Identification Program" report, the "Washington State Economy Review of 1978, Outlook for 1979," "Washington State Exporter's Guide," and the "International Trade Directory." He also spent an hour speaking with the Small Business counselor in that office about general trends in the state, as he perceived them, and what he felt were the areas for opportunity. Energy and transportation were cited as the industries providing the greatest opportunities.

Later that same day John visited the Seattle Chamber of Commerce with the same request for information. They too indicated that his request was very broad and gave him a number of publications, including a 1978 Economic Review of the Seattle-Everett area, a booklet entitled "Corporate Headquarters: Central Puget Sound Region," a sample of "Business Profiles," a "Business Migration Study: An Analysis of Out-Migration Patterns in Seattle Firms," and a listing of other publications available through the Chamber of Commerce. Both the state and city Commerce Departments recommended a visit to the Seattle City Library's business department.

Week 4

Skeptical about where his search was going, John next visited the city library with the same request used at the Commerce Departments. The librarian in the business section presented him with a large volume of statistics profiling metropolitan Seattle consumers. "It could conceivably have been a great marketing aid, but since I didn't know yet what I was trying to market, I had a hard time extracting any value out of that book," he recalled.

The librarian also pointed out a file cabinet of resource documents which contained a drawer devoted to the Small Business Administration. John perused that file and while finding it of general interest, came away with no concrete information.

> *At this point I had accumulated a small library of information and the more I looked through it, the more confused I became as to what I was trying to learn. From all this data I discovered that trying to absorb all the information available on the Puget Sound area and then translate it into some business opportunity(s) was far too broad, difficult and abstract for my purposes and abilities. I also discovered that the approach I was taking could offer no more direction than that which I was already bringing to it. The flip side of that, however, was the realization that there is a wealth of information and assistance available to the individual who knows exactly what information he is seeking.*

Four weeks into the project John was still devoting most of his mental energy searching for a business idea that would anticipate a market, either a new product or service that would capitalize on a currently unmet need or else a business that would take advantage of a growing market demand. He began to think that perhaps the best way to enter a market would be to let an innovative or quality product or service lead him into the market rather than entering a market first and then searching for an idea.

Week 5

> *I remember once reading an article which stated that even when you are not looking for a job, it is prudent to keep an eye on the "Help Wanted" classified ads so that you can get a feel for which employers are having a hard time finding and/or keeping employees, which professions are (not) in great demand, pay scales for various positions, and so forth. Using that same line of thinking I started to read the `Business Opportunities' section in the classifieds to learn what I could about the business climate as evidenced by what types of businesses were up for sale, where, and at what price.*

So far, John was still avoiding analysis of the IEA manuals, feeling they were "somebody else's song," which he did not want to imitate. He was trying to be highly methodical, keeping and analyzing a log of his time and the degree of output different approaches were producing for him. The log was something he had agreed with his professor to do as part of the research paper he was supposed to produce for course credit. However, he found the chronicling difficult and was acutely aware that the sixth week of the search was at hand and, so far, no satisfactory venture idea had turned up. He intensified his efforts at becoming more systematic.

Establishing a list of possible ventures

Week 6

John observed:

> *My single most difficult step in undertaking a methodical and rational search for a business (and it really didn't begin until this point) was overcoming the gut feeling that it is inspiration and innovation that lead the entrepreneur to the marketplace, not scientific inquiry. The prospect of starting or buying a business before having an outstanding idea or product seemed like the proverbial cart before the horse. At the same time, there was fear that by forcing entry into one market, I could be preempting the discovery or recognition of a successful enterprise in another field. Fortunately, I came to see that line of thought as counterproductive. The way I was able to bridge the gap between my desire to be creative and methodically arriving at a list of possible ventures was the belief that the latter does not have to preclude the former.*

Next he began to write down what it was he was looking for versus what he was trying to avoid in various types of businesses, as shown in Exhibit 2. As he did this, he also noticed that the venture search project was becoming the main focus of his school interest, notwithstanding three other courses he was taking.

Weeks 7 through 12

A help, John found, was Kenneth Albert's How to Pick the Right Small Business Opportunity. One of its features was a capability assessment guide, which he used to take an inventory of his strengths and weaknesses. He continued:

> *The Alberts book revealed to me that it was easy when looking at existing entrepreneurs and executives to be impressed with what I don't know without counterbalancing it with how much I do know, which is also important.*
>
> *A hard part of trying to be systematic was figuring out what step to take next. As with any exercise, if you know where you're going to end up, the direction of your steps is fairly obvious. But otherwise, it's confusing.*
>
> *One thing I discovered, though, in thinking of potential business ideas, was that step-by-step progression had to take place in their development, and that I should avoid sitting back and viewing the 'go-no-go' decision as a quantum leap.*

Other outside reading John did at this stage was Sandman and Goldenson's, How to Succeed in Business Before Graduating,* plus the record of another student's venture search and an article in the Harvard Business Review on the origin of venture ideas.** The Sandman book seemed to him limited to ventures of only short-term viability. The other student's study did not seem to have found much pay dirt. The article suggested that most venture ideas come from jobs and hobbies rather than from any systematic study such as John was pursuing.

Also in the seventh week of the project, John xeroxed a 13-page index of major groups in the Standard Industrial Classification. His intent was to go through this index and circle any industry or product that he could conceivably get involved with in some capacity. In weeks eight and nine, he went through this list two more times on different days to check and recheck his choices. He applied the same procedure to a Seattle Yellow Pages index. By the end of the fourteenth week, he had consolidated the products and services list as shown in Exhibit 3. A couple of hours scanning the Thomas Register and the National Directory of Associations revealed to him no additional ideas or categories that weren't already covered in the consolidated list.

Week 13

During spring break John began reading through some of the IEA manuals in an attempt to identify positive and negative features of each of the profiled ventures (Exhibit 4). He commented:

> Some of the available manuals (e.g., Christmas tree lot) I didn't even glance at, either because they were too small-time or they didn't even have a minimal attraction. The ideas most worth serious consideration in the manuals I read seemed to be a cookie shop, a secretarial service and a mobile restaurant. The mobile restaurant (vending truck) seemed potentially viable as a business to take downtown during the lunch hour rush. After thinking about it, however, I decided that I didn't want to get involved with retail food service. That clouded the cookie shop idea as well.
>
> The secretarial service had the appeal of low capital required and seemed like maybe it could be a good interim step and experience-builder in case I didn't get something else going. But those advantages still left me feeling unmotivated, so I decided not to follow through with it.

It began to seem to John that the more effort he spent defining what he was looking for, the less time he would have to spend searching for it, but with the trade-off for defining versus searching not being one-for-one. This impression persisted. John sketched what he meant on a time-line as follows:

The first of these two patterns, he believed, was more difficult but more efficient. It also occurred to John at this time that his search process might be helpful in clarifying what he was seeking in a job, even if it did not yield a business.

Week 14

By the fourteenth week of the project, John felt ready to narrow his search further. He began by listing 11 criteria he considered important in the evaluation of a business. Then he took a list of product and service areas he had consolidated earlier and went through each business category, rating it against his criteria (see Exhibit 5). He assigned plusses and minuses subjectively based on how he felt about it. He also assigned priorities to the criteria (indicated by the number next to each criterion in Exhibit 5). "I asked myself how I would assign 30 points or allocate $30 among the criteria to indicate its importance to me," he recalled. Then, although his knowledge of what these businesses entailed in terms of financial, technical and personal resources was sketchy, he computed two scores for each line of business: one by counting the number of plusses and the other by multiplying the number of plusses by their respective criteria priority weightings and adding up those totals.

With these numerical values computed for each of the business categories, he selected eight products and five services that were both high-rated numerically and comfortable to his "gut feeling." They were:

PRODUCTS	SERVICES
Frozen Desserts	Circulation Library
Ice Cream	Day Care
Sporting Goods, Wholesale	Freight Forwarding
Cookies and Crackers	Lodging, hotel, motel, hostel
Cider, Fruit and Vegetable Juices	Delivery Service
Woolen Goods	
Salad Dressings	

Next, he began pruning this list, beginning with day care. He commented:

A friend who is a good friend of a woman who runs a day care business told me about all the headaches she encounters trying to run a business that deals with people's most precious concern, their children. That conversation and subsequent reflection made day care an easy deletion. Owning a lodge struck me as beyond my immediate skills, experience, finances and interests so I dropped it from the list. The circulating library is really a take-off on the information services that I was trying to structure in my thoughts before I began this project. I realized that unless I had something concrete, this business idea would have to wait. Since six of the remaining eight products were food-related, I decided to concentrate my interviews with the food industry and the remaining two services on my pared-down list, freight forwarding and a delivery service.

Interviews

Weeks 15 and 16

Now began what John regarded as the most enjoyable and rewarding phase of the project, interviews with business owners and executives. The interview process, visiting firms, talking with people about getting into businesses like theirs, and getting around to see and hear what was happening, gave John what he described as the most tangible feelings of accomplishment and progress.

Throughout this project I felt my status as a student was a real asset and could probably make information and individuals far more accessible than they may be otherwise. It seemed a natural and logical move then to contact business owners and executives and see if I could draw on their experiences and knowledge to aid in my search.

He prepared a questionnaire (Exhibit 6) to guide his interviews, then visited nine people, all of whom were in the food business, either manufacturing or wholesaling. Which questions on his list were appropriate varied among interviews. Sometimes items would come up in the interview that led to new questions.

To find interviewees John used two references, the King County Manufacturer's Directory and Contacts Influential. He chose these sources for three main reasons: (1) they listed companies by their S.I.C. (Standard Industrial Classification) numbers, which made it easy to locate prospects; (2) they gave valuable information about these companies such as when they were established, their sales volume, number of employees and whether the office is a branch or headquarters, and (3) they listed names of company presidents or owners.

He was hesitant to let interviewees know that his reason for pursuing this project was to consider entering their lines of work as a potential competitor. He suspected they would be reluctant to answer the questions. John's professor argued to the contrary and, as it turned out, John's fears were unjustified. In fact, he found all whom he interviewed were helpful and encouraging. Two of them spoke with him over lunch, and one invited him to sit in on his annual marketing meeting.

In reviewing the notes taken during the interviews, John said the following points appeared to represent a consensus of the interviewees' remarks:

> An individual must have money and related experience to get started in the food business. Also mentioned on more than one occasion as necessary were traits of courage, desire, ambitiousness, and determination.

> The most instrumental factors in determining a company's success seemed to be good business management (awareness of costs and cost efficiencies, working capital management, and common sense), good product, and integrity in that order of frequency among the interviewees.

> Respondents were about evenly divided on the relative advantages and disadvantages of a small business in the food industry. On the plus side for small firms were quick response time, simplicity and close supervision, while heavy investments, distribution channels, and governmental requirements favored large companies.

> The trend in the food industry is toward more convenience foods and prepared high quality frozen foods.

> Good business sense, obviously, is important. Also frequently mentioned were the ability to get along with and motivate people and the ability to be a jack-of-all-trades.

> In order, the three biggest problems facing the businesses seemed to be (1) government (local and federal) interference; (2) finding and keeping good employees; and (3) financial management, maintaining good cash flow and finding money to expand the business.

To date, John had not looked for possible acquisitions, and none had presented themselves. But he recognized that buying a business was another possibility worth considering.

> A product-oriented business, especially manufacturing, seemed to call for buy-out rather than starting from scratch. Product development could take too much time; equipment and setting up would cost too much capital. In contrast, an established business, if its owner were willing to sell it for a small down payment borrowed at the bank, and take payments over time, could be a way around those problems.

Services seemed less difficult capital-wise, but they presented other problems. Among delivery service firms, for instance, John called five individuals before one agreed to speak with him. The owner described a heavy role of government licensing and regulating in his business, as well as in freight forwarding. John decided that line of work was not for him.

Week 17

By the seventeenth week of the project and halfway through his planned interviewing, John said he was disappointed with his progress and frustrated by the shortage of time left before he would be done with school and have to move on.

> Up to this point, I hadn't really considered what I would do if the right opportunity didn't turn up. But a glance at the calendar and a pinch of foresight was telling me that, ready or not, school

was almost over. Thinking it would help me clarify my thoughts, I took out a piece of paper, titled it "Going For It" as immediate entrepreneurship, and then listed the pros and cons of pursuing a venture tenaciously right away (Exhibit 7). Even though I didn't really make a conscious decision, judging from the subsequent six weeks, I chose to continue trying to arrange something.

Having already established a set of business criteria and attached relative weightings to them (Exhibit 5), John slowly began to conclude during the interviewing process that a good share of the criteria would be met only if the business he attempted were successful.

Selecting a business

Week 18

In the eighteenth week of the project, and with graduation only a few weeks away, John saw two major concerns in deciding on a business venture. First, he was approaching this decision as though he had a gun with only one bullet, so the aim had to be excellent. Second, it seemed to him that undertaking risk was directly related to conviction. Starting and/or running a business seemed likely to require heavy investments in time, energy and probably money, at least relative to his meager resources. Without a solid commitment and the necessary determination, that investment could be wasted.

As he reflected on his situation, several options were on his mind. One was to continue searching. In that line, he felt he should consider not only the degree of effectiveness his procedure had demonstrated so far, but also how it could be done better. He had collected a log of activities and time spent, as shown in Exhibit 8, which he thought might be useful in refining his process. There was also the question of whether one or more of the ideas generated so far should be carried further.

Overall, there seemed to be four broad choices: (1) continue searching for more ideas, (2) investigate several present ideas further, (3) select one idea and put all efforts into going ahead, and (4) look for employment in someone else's organization.

EXHIBIT 1 International Entrepreneur Association (IEA) manuals

1. Dive-For-A-Pearl-Shop	20. Swap Meet Promoting
2. Plant Shop	21. Art Show Promoting
3. Balloon Vending	22. Bicycle Shop
4. Tennis & Racquetball Club	23. Rental List Publishing
5. Athletic Shoe Store	24. Liquor Store
6. Pizzeria	25. Popcorn Vending
7. Pet Shop	26. "Who's Who" Publishing
8. Handwriting Analysis by Computer	27. Antique Photo Shop
9. Tune-Up Shop	28. Tool & Equipment Rental Service
10. Flower Vending	29. Ghost Dog Making
11. Furniture Store	30. Contest Promotions
12. Window-Washing Service	31. Parking Lot Striping
13. Instant Print Shop	32. Maintenance Service
14. Adult Bookstore	33. Antique Store
15. Mail Order	34. Pet Hotel & Grooming Service
16. Hamburger Stand	35. Janitorial Service
17. Quit-Smoking Clinic	36. Do-It-Yourself Auto Repair Shop
18. Consignment Used Car Lot	37. Old-Fashioned Ice Cream Bar Stand
19. Cheese & Gourmet Food Shop	38. Dry-Cleaning Shop

EXHIBIT 1 *(continued)*

39. Copy Shop
40. Stuffed Toy Animal Vending
41. Adults-Only Motel
42. Robot Lawn Mower
43. Mini-Warehouse
44. T-Shirt Shop
45. Muffler Shop
46. Worm-Farming (expose)
47. Psychic-Training Seminars
48. Trade School
49. Auto-Parking Service
50. Rent-A-Plant
51. Auto-Painting Shop
52. Employment Agency
53. Furniture-Stripping Service
54. Carpet-Cleaning Service
55. Ten-Minute Oil Change Shop
56. Fried Chicken Takeout-Restaurant
57. Mobile Restaurant
58. Bonsai Collecting
59. Day-Care Center
60. Coffee Shop
61. Earring Shop
62. Stained Glass Window Manufacturing
63. Low-Cal Bakery
64. Lie Detection by Voice Analysis
65. Bust-Developing Product
66. Sunglass Shop
67. Custom Rug Making
68. Newsletter Publishing
69. Self-Service Gas Station
70. Flea Market-Finding Products
71. Homemade Candy Stand
72. Seminar Promoting
73. Mattress Shop
74. Hot Dog Stand
75. Hot Tub Manufacturing
76. Car Wash
77. Vinyl-Repairing Service
78. Yogurt Bar
79. Weight Control Clinic
80. Skateboard Park
81. Cookie Shop
82. Computer Store
83. SBA Financing-New Businesses
84. SBA Financing-Existing Businesses
85. Hidden Franchise Laws
86. Roller Skate Rental Shop
87. Free University
88. Roller Skating Rink
89. Burglar Alarm Manufacturing
90. Import & Export
91. Burlwood Tables Manufacturing and Retail Store
92. Homemade Cake Shop
93. Digital Watch Repairing Service
94. Sculptures by Computer
95. Video Cassette Recorder
96. Liquidated Goods Broker
97. Selling Your Business
98. Pinball Arcade
99. Kitchen-Remodeling Service
100. Gift Shop
101. Women's Apparel Shop
102. Used Car Rental Agency
103. Windsurfing School
104. Free Classified Newspaper Publishing
105. Promotional Gimmicks
106. Candid Key Chain Photos
107. Used Bookstore
108. Handicrafts Co-Op
109. Salad Bar Restaurant
110. Sculptured Candle Making
111. Coin-Op TV
112. Plastics-Recycling Center
113. No-Alcohol Bar
114. Health Food Store
115. Donut Shop
116. Shrimp Peddling
117. Soup Kitchen
118. Pipe Shop
119. Roommate-Finding Service
120. Backpacking Shop
121. Hobby Shop
122. Discount Fabric Shop
123. Paint & Wall Covering Store
124. Do-It-Yourself Cosmetic Shop
125. Secretarial Service
126. Furniture Rental Store
127. Pet Cemetery
128. Seasonal Christmas Tree And Ornament Business
129. Tropical Fish Store
130. Gourmet Cookware Shop
131. Flower Shop
132. Do-It-Yourself Framing Shop

EXHIBIT 1 *(continued)*

133. Insulation Contracting
134. Automobile Detailing
135. Private Post Office
136. Telephone Answering Service
137. Sailboat Leasing
138. Exterior Surface Cleaning
139. Consulting Service
140. Intimate Apparel Shop
141. Flat-Fee Real Estate Agency
142. Travel Agency
143. Chimney Sweep Service
144. Sandwich Shop
145. Cross-Country Trucking
146. Specialty Bread Shop
147. Security Patrol Service
148. Maid Service
149. Children's Apparel Shop
150. Coin Laundry
151. Shell Shop
152. Churro Snack Shop
153. Jojoba Plantation
154. Video Store
155. Financial Broker
156. Vitamin Store
157. Raising Money
158. Hottest New Businesses and Future Trends
159. How to Get Free Publicity & Promote Your Business
160. Manufacturing & Distributing Products

161. Legal Ins & Outs of Small Business
162. How to Intelligently Buy a Business
163. Getting Into Import & Export
164. Women Getting Into Business
165. Businesses You Can Start for Under $1,000
166. Mail-Order Business
167. How To Franchise Your Business
168. Franchise Pros & Cons
169. Selling Ideas
170. How to Develop a Successful Plan
171. Businesses You Can Run and Keep Your Present Job
172. How to Make Quick Profits in Real Estate
173. Tax-Saving Angles for Small Businesses
174. Advertising Techniques for Small Businesses
175. Recession-Proof Businesses
176. Preventing Bad Checks, Pilfering & Embezzlement
177. Four Millionaires Tell How They Did It
178. Negotiating Techniques
179. How to Protect Your Ideas
180. How to Test Market Your Products & Ideas
181. Millionaire's Secrets to Success

EXHIBIT 2 Thoughts about preferences

LOOKING FOR

Something that I can be proud of; a product or service that is a contribution; allows for quality input/differential.

A business that I can sell.

Stability - a business that I can sink my feet into without concern that its market/usefulness will quickly vanish.
A business that I am interested in, will make it easy to spend the extra hours to make it fly.

A business that will utilize my talents, staple, no gimmicks.

Challenge - competitive.

Ideally a product rather than a service

A business that can be flexible in its location, allow for the best of two worlds.

Opportunity for eventual absentee ownership.

Very profitable business, both financially and spiritually. One that will give me and the company the power (freedom) to enact some positive contributions.

Flexible work hours; both in days and hours.

Slow, healthy growth in a growth industry.

Independence.

A business of ideas, innovation in substance, not style.

A business centered around communications, communication skills important.

Success criteria that match my abilities.

A market that I can relate to, get excited about and enjoy dealing with. Not necessarily high labor intensive; will allow for small, sole beginning.

AVOIDING

Franchise; a business that appears to be a commodity.

Faddish business, more a fashion.

High technology/capital requirements.

Being a middleman, a conduit.

Fast buck business.

Fabricated need, product oriented.

Business/industry in tail-end of product life cycle.

High capital requirement.

Art, cultural, design business.

EXHIBIT 3 Products and services from S.I.C. list and Yellow Pages

Products	Services
Bakery	Amusement Park
Cocoa and Chocolate Products	Bridge Teacher
Coffee	Camps
Dairy Products	Chauffeur Service
Fruits and Vegetables, Wholesale	Circulating Library
Frozen Desserts	Cold Storage Lockers
Frozen Fruits	Day Care
Games	Messenger Service
General Merchandise Store	Food Lockers
Wholesale Groceries	Freight Forwarding
Retail groceries	Gymnasium
Hardware; Wholesale and Retail	Motel, Hotel, Hostel
Ice Cream	Laundry
Knit Mills	Linen Supply Delivery Service
Wood Products Dealer	Picnic Grounds
Musical Instruments	Resort
Records and Tapes	Trucking, Local Cartage
Slippers	Air Port Terminal Services
Sporting Goods; Wholesale & Retail	Accounting & Bookkeeping Services
Book Store	News Dealers
Hobby, Toy and Game Store; Whole- sale and Retail	Floor Laying
Wooden Goods	Library and Information Center
Vaults and Safes	Rental Business
Children's Vehicles	Taxicabs
Wines; Wholesale and Retail	Local - Suburban Transit
Cookies and Crackers	Transportation, Chartered, on Land, Rivers, Air, Etc.
Salad Dressings	Transportation Broker
Stereo, Video Cassette Equipment, Retail	Food Broker
Pies	
Bicycle Rentals	
Camping Equipment	
Carpet and Rug Dealer	
Cider	
Vending Machines	
School Supplies	
Dehydrated Foods	
Fruits and Vegetables	
Nuts	
Soda Fountain	
Swings	
Vending Trucks	

EXHIBIT 4 Survey of IEA businesses

**FREE CLASSIFIED
NEWSPAPER PUBLISHING**

+ high return
+ could lead to many more opportunities
    in related fields
+ little know-how necessary
- mechanical
- not very exciting, largely a money
    machine

GIFT SHOP

- retail
- high risk
- out of my league

DONUT SHOP

+ food
- restaurant business, retail headaches

BACKPACKING SHOP

+ product line
+ growth industry in good area of
    country
+ personality of market
- high investment, risk
- barriers to entry
- retail

PIPE SHOP

+ clientele
+ specialty
+ stable
- boring
- retail

GOURMET COOKWARE SHOP

+ specialty shop
- cannot relate to the market
- retail
- risk

TROPICAL FISH STORE

+ product
- small time
- risk

HEALTH FOOD BAR

+ could be an idea whose time has come
- a tavern, or a restaurant; either one
    is unacceptable

SCULPTURED CANDLE MAKING

+ product
+ has low investment, easy startup
- small time
- art and art shows, flea markets

PAINT AND WALL COVERING STORE

+ stable
+ reasonable profit
- not a comfortable industry
- heavy investment

SECRETARIAL SERVICE

+ good employee relations
+ reasonable investment
+ tap marketing skills
+ reasonably stable
+ easy growth/management
- lack of familiarity
- competition, mature market

EXHIBIT 4 *(continued)*

HOMEMADE CANDY SHOP

+ easy start up
+ quality output
+ business atmosphere (customers)
+ growth and expansion potential
+ stable
- product
- roadside scenario

SEMINAR PROMOTING

+ an idea that has its financial merits
+ down the road it certainly offers a
    source of revenue
- not exactly what I am looking for

STAINED GLASS WINDOWS

although it is a product, it does
not offer anything other than a
short term attraction

CAR WASH

- doesn't grab me
- high risks
- high investment
- out of my ball park

FURNITURE RENTAL STORE

+ stable, over established
+ profitable, easy absenteeism
- doesn't excite me
- high investment
- little outlet for quality, creativity

INSULATION CONTRACTING BUSINESS

+ timing
+ seasonal
- not my style
- this is where the pack is
- heavy investment in money & time to
    get going

FURNITURE STRIPPING

+ appears to involve minimum startup
+ craft
- reasonably stable
- tough to break away from "Mom & Pop"
- small ROI

SCULPTURE BY COMPUTER

- not me

MOBILE RESTAURANT

+ dealing with food
+ relatively low start up
+ opportunity for creative application
+ reasonably simple
- difficult quality input
- questionable future in terms of growth
    and potential

EXHIBIT 4 (continued)

SUN GLASS SHOP

+ stable market
+ low investment
+ easy absentee
- too narrow
- not exciting enough

NEWSLETTER PUBLISHING

- lack of interest/expertise

YOGURT BAR

+ product, different
- market seems saturated
- somewhat faddish

KITCHEN REMODELING

- do not have the skills to do the job
- high investment in time and money

DIGITAL WATCH REPAIRING

+ low start up
+ work and location flexibility
+ good growth potential
- an area I do not feel comfortable with
- seems high risk

DAY CARE CENTER

+ good future
+ good product-opportunity for
    contribution
+ good customer base
+ room for quality differential
+ could be fun
+ survives on its own momentum
- dependent on high volume
    high start up costs
- governmental influence
- competition can be fierce, money

EXHIBIT 5 Comparisons

BUSINESS PRODUCTS	Favorable Content	Business Flexibility	Product	People Contact	Independence	Quality Differential	Artistic Contribution	Fun	Stability	Status	Income	Total "+"s	Total Points
Weights	2	3	3	2	3	3	1	2	5	3	3		
Cookies and Crackers	+	+	+	–	+	+	–	+	+	+	+	9	27
Bicycle Rentals	+	–	–	+	–	–	+	+	–	–	–	4	7
Camping Equipment	+	+	+	–	+	+	+	+	+	+	+	9	27
Carpet and Rug Dealer	+	–	–	+	–	+	–	–	+	–	+	5	15
Cider	+	+	+	–	+	+	–	+	+	+	+	9	27
Vending Machines	+	–	–	–	–	–	+	–	+	–	+	4	11
School Supplies	+	–	–	+	–	–	+	+	+	–	–	4	11
Foods (Dehydrated)	+	+	+	–	+	+	+	+	–	+	+	9	23
Fruit and Vegetable Juice	+	+	+	–	+	+	–	+	+	+	+	9	27
Nuts	+	+	–	–	+	–	–	+	+	+	+	7	21
Soda Fountain	+	–	–	+	–	–	–	+	+	+	–	5	14
Swings	+	+	+	–	+	+	+	+	+	–	+	9	27
Vending Trucks	+	–	–	+	–	–	+	+	–	–	–	4	7
Woolen goods	+	+	+	–	+	+	–	+	+	+	+	9	27
SERVICES													
Amusement Park	+	–	–	+	+	+	+	+	–	+	+	8	19
Bridge Instructor	+	–	–	+	+	–	–	+	–	+	–	5	12
Camps	+	+	–	+	+	+	+	+	–	+	+	9	22
Chauffeur Service	–	–	–	+	–	+	–	–	+	–	–	3	10
Circulating Library	+	–	–	+	+	+	+	–	+	+	+	9	24
Cold & Food Storage Lockers	+	–	–	–	+	–	–	–	+	–	+	4	13
Day Care	+	–	–	+	+	+	+	+	+	+	–	8	21
Messenger Service	+	–	–	+	–	+	+	+	+	–	–	6	15
Freight Forwarding	+	–	–	+	–	+	+	+	+	+	+	7	20
Gymnasium	+	–	–	+	–	+	+	+	–	+	–	6	13

EXHIBIT 6 Interview questions

COMPANY_____INTERVIEWEE_____

1. What does an individual need to get started in your business?
2. What factors are most instrumental in a company's success in your business? (e.g., service, location, contacts, product).
3. How much is product and how much of it is service?
4. Do you feel that a small company is at a distinct disadvantage in your business?
5. How important are economies of scale?
6. What trends do you see developing in your industry? Why?
7. Do you see a market that is currently not being satisfactorily served?
8. Do you see any opportunities in the _____ industry? Why do you think this is?
9. Would you characterize your industry as extremely competitive?
10. What are the competitive pressures?
11. What skills or attributes do you consider most essential in successfully running a _____?
12. How are they different from running, say, a cardboard box plant?
13. How much people-contact do you have? What type?
14. What do you consider to be the biggest problems you are faced with in running your business?
15. How large a market is there for top-of-the-line _____?
16. Are you currently trying to serve it? Why? Why not?
17. What sort of work week does your _____ have (# of days, shifts)?
18. What sort of work week do you have?
19. Could you, if you wanted, have a non-conventional work week?
20. Could you locate anywhere in the greater Seattle metropolitan area without serious consequences?
21. Can you think of anything particular to your industry that would influence a decision to buy a going concern vs. starting from scratch?
22. What background did you bring to your business?
23. What experience do you consider most helpful in running your business?
24. What attracted you to the _____ business?
25. Were your expectations and hopes realistic?
26. If you knew then what you know now, what would you do differently?
27. Would you start up your business today? Why(not)?
28. If you were to start your business from scratch today, what do you think would be the biggest difficulty?
29. If you were to start your business today, how much technical and product know-how would you need?
30. Dealing with such a stable and established product, do you sometimes find this too staid, too conventional?
31. Are there opportunities for creativity?
32. What do you feel are the greatest rewards from your position?
33. What do you find exciting about your work?
34. What do you consider to be the biggest challenges in running a _____?

EXHIBIT 7 Going for it

PROS	CONS
Little to lose, in a position to take a risk, short-term needs are mounting.	Precarious financial situation; short.
The earlier I dedicate the time, the easier it should be.	Lack of experience/exposure.
Personal financial needs are slight.	Am I prepared to handle the setbacks?
It's what I want to do.	Will I choose a business only for the sake of choosing?
It would be exciting.	Want vs. need (is the timing right)?
I owe it to myself/personal tranquillity.	Is the opportunity really there? Am I forcing it?
Pass?	
If not now, when?	Do I need the pressure this search is causing?
Overcome a fear.	
Start up something and sell it in a few years if it's not what I'm looking for.	
I'll be disappointed.	
Quit delaying; sink or swim.	

EXHIBIT 8 Time log

CALENDAR	ACTIVITY	TIME EXPENDED
Weeks 1&2	Trying to figure out what I was going to do and how I was going to do it.	?????
Week 3	Visited State Dept. of Commerce (and spoke with Maurice Alexander)	two hours
Week 4	Went to downtown branch of the city library (business section)	four hours
	Read booklets and pamphlets gathered thus far.	six hours
Week 5	Started reading "Business Opportunities" section in Times and P-I classifieds	one hour
Week 6	Started log; started writing down what I'm looking for and avoiding in a business.	three & 1/2 hours
Week 7	Xeroxed S.I.C. index; started circling interesting categories	two hours
	Read "Business Opportunities"	one hour
Week 8	Read Sandman's book " Albert's book " Business Opportunities"	two hours one & 1/2 hours one hour
	Screened S.I.C. index twice	three hours
Week 9	Skimmed *Thomas Register*, *National Directory of Assoc.*	one hour one hour
	Read "Business Opportunities"	one hour
Week 10	Drew up "Capability Assessment Guide" Began screening index to Yellow Pages	two hours five hours
	Read "Business Opportunities"	one hour
Week 11	Continued screening Yellow Pages index	four hours
	Read "Business Opportunities" Read Alberts book	one hour one hour
Week 12	Read "Business Opportunities"	one hour
Week 13	Read or skimmed twenty IEA manuals	eight hours
	Read Albert's book Read "Business Opportunities"	one hour one hour

EXHIBIT 8 *(continued)*

CALENDAR	ACTIVITY	TIME EXPENDED
Week 14	Read or skimmed twenty IEA manuals	eight hours
	Consolidated the Yellow Page and S.I.C. indices and narrowed the list via the criteria checklist.	six hours
	Read "Business Opportunities"	one hour
Week 15	Devised a questionnaire for interviews	two hours
	Used Manufacturers' Directory and Contacts Influential to locate prospects for interviews	three hours
	Read "Business Opportunities"	one hour
Week 16	Called to arrange interviews	1/2 hour
	Interviews with: Bill Mynar	one & 1/2 hours
	Howard Stanford	one hour
	Eugene Holland	one & 1/4 hours
	Bob Lindsay	two hours
	Used Contacts Influential to locate prospects in freight forwarding and delivery service	one hour
	Read "Business Opportunities"	one hour
Week 17	Called to arrange interviews	1/2 hour
	Wrote down pros and cons of "Going For It"	one hour
	Interviews with:	
	Jim Reynolds	one hour
	Henry Gai	one & 1/2 hours
	Paul Baertch	one & 1/2 hours
	Cecil Neilsen	one & 1/2 hours
	Dave McDonald (including sitting in on marketing meeting)	six and 1/2 hours
	Read "Business Opportunities"	one hour

Note: The time expenditures listed above are rough estimates. They represent time spent only on listed activity and do not include travel time, waiting time, time spent locating information, etc.

Michael Shane

The first time you try to start a business is the easiest. Everyone expects you to fail. It's the second or third time around that can shake your confidence. People expect you to do better than the time before; and if you don't, they think that something is wrong. Not only that—you're going into another unknown area, just when you've gotten comfortable with what you've been working on so hard before.

Michael Shane, was reflecting on his "third time around" for starting a business. His latest idea for a venture was to get involved with the growing computer industry—perhaps as a distributor for retail computer stores. Two months earlier, in December of 1979, he had assembled a core of five people to find out if a "super distributor" was needed. In addition to himself, Michael's brother, Tom Shane, and sister, Sandy Fromm, were helping in planning and learning about the industry through calls to computer stores and going through trade magazines. His administrative assistant, Elaine Cresto, had worked for Michael in his previous business for the past five years and agreed to help with this possible venture. To survey stores, Michael had just hired Dick Sanders, the only one of the five who would admit to knowing "a little bit about computers."

Now, in February of 1980, the five were working out of Michael's recently purchased condominium in suburban Boston. Each had a telephone line for making calls to stores and manufacturers throughout the United States to learn about trends and needs in the industry. Michael explained that if there was need for a "super distributor," their next step would be to develop a strategy for the venture. If not, perhaps they might be able to discover through market inquiry another niche relating to computers that would afford them a business opportunity. The trick, Michael emphasized, would be to interpret the information they got correctly. Otherwise, the past months of preparation and nearly $20,000 already invested in the unnamed venture could turn out to be a complete loss.

Wig Flair

Michael Shane was 17 years old in 1967 when he started his first business. Using $235 in savings he began selling wigs, which he bought from New York wholesalers for $35 and sold for $35 out of the trunk of his car. His mother had owned several beauty salons and most of the wigs she carried cost from $38 up. He reasoned that by starting at a low price and building volume he would be able to buy in larger quantities at lower costs to net a profit. Emphasis on service and fast delivery paid off. Soon his cost dropped to $30 per wig, then dropped further as his sales rose to $100,000 per month by the end of the first year.

He rented 2,500 square feet of warehouse space in Canton, Massachusetts, and quit Babson College as a sophomore to become a wig distributor. He chose the name "Wig Flair" for the business and began selling to retail stores. With profits he began to buy larger volumes and varieties of wigs and go to more exclusive boutiques and retail chains. Timing decisions, he said, came from an intuitive sense, based on casual observation of fashion trends, that the market was ripe for wider distribution of wigs. Enlisting his younger brother, Tom, to help in the stock room after school, Michael developed contacts for buying wigs directly from a Hong Kong-based manufacturer instead of going through New York suppliers.

To support further growth he took in as 50-percent partner a customer who ran a wig salon at night and worked as a meat salesman during the day. By 1969, their joint company had developed a nationwide network of sales representatives who called on beauty supply houses. It also employed a telephone sales force, which sold to wig wholesalers. All Wig Flair sales were C.O.D. Volume continued growing, and in 1970 Wig Flair bought its own Hong Kong manufacturing plant.

Later that year, with sales at $12 million, the two sold out for 150,000 shares of U.S. Industries, then traded on the NYSE at $12 per share. They also received employment contracts of $60,000 per year each, plus dividends of $100,000 per year each. In addition, they received incentive options, which could earn them up to another $5.5 million over the next five years, if performance met projections. The projections were, in fact not met, as the market for wigs declined in profitability. But Michael was able to sell his U.S. Industries shares at $27.

His partner stayed on, but Michael left Wig Flair a year after selling out. He explained.

> *It wasn't like we were building toward anything, and I hated it. I realized that my partner was only interested in the money. I was interested in money, but also in creating something. Just sitting there and drawing money on my five-year employment contract and not making waves was of no interest to me. When I left the company, I didn't know what I was going to do. I was 21 years old and I had good instincts and some money. I wanted to be independent. I figured I'd dabble in some things for a while.*

Michael started investing, mostly in real estate. One deal his accountant introduced him to was a retail blue jeans business needing capital. He invested $25,000 in what became a five-store operation. He also arranged with the Wig Flair plant in Hong Kong to make jeans with its spare sewing capacity. The first $300,000 order, however, was patterned on Hong Kong styles unacceptable to Americans. Michael wrote off his investment and gave his interest to a store manager.

Faded Glory

Subsequently, however, the manager had a dispute with his partner that threatened to break up the jeans business. The Hong Kong plant manager called Michael in a panic to say that he was going to lose the jeans business. Michael had been thinking that there was still opportunity in jeans. His brother, Tom, commented on Michael's vision:

> *He told me in 1973 that he thought the next thing in fashion would be blue jeans that went beyond the traditional concept of dungarees. He turned out to be right.*

Michael purchased $10,000 in denim, and set up the factory to begin production of private label fashion jeans. His own vision of the situation was as follows:

> *In those days, there was no fashion denim like we know fashion denim today. Hard blue denim, like Levi's, that's all there was. They weren't even washing them out. But you had to be stupid not to see everybody bleeding their blue jeans out in the bathtub. So we took them, washed them out, and put studs on them or dragons or pansies, or whatever, and that was fashion. We were fashion, and the first year we had $12 million in sales.*

This new business, Faded Glory, was a family affair. Michael allowed some of his brothers and sisters to obtain ownership on favorable terms, but retained voting control himself. His brother, Jim, managed internal administration, while Michael took care of marketing and other "outside" functions. Tom continued to work in the back room, filling orders and taking inventory in his spare time from undergraduate work at Boston University. Sandy joined the two in early 1974 to set up a sales force and telephone system to keep in touch with retail customers. She recalled:

My job was to build a sales group that would rely on telephones as the main way to get orders and service accounts. I started by myself, sitting with one phone in a big empty room. Five years later, there were over 40 people working the phones and a field sales force of 100, calling on thousands of stores we had as customers.

Although Faded Glory had a head start in fashion jeans, competitors quickly appeared, not only with other designs but also aggressive prices and service. Telephone salespeople called individual stores periodically to inform retailers of lines and promotions available. The calls also obtained information about retailer problems, such as late delivery, with suppliers' services.

In addition, a field sales force called on stores to get orders. Eventually, phone salespeople collaborated to coordinate for better service. For very large accounts, a VIP "hot line" was set up to provide still better service. Mass mailings were also used to provide stores with posters, product announcements and promotional literature.

Tom Shane continued his description of how Faded Glory developed and grew:

Initially, we were selling to specialty retail stores—boutiques—which were relatively small. I was responsible for seeing that the orders were filled, and Jim made sure that the volume of the jeans we needed came from overseas at the right times. In the early days, you would get the requisition from the salesperson, grab a basket, and walk around the back room filling the order. We added data processing capabilities as our sales increased, and we finally had to move out of our original warehouse to larger facilities.

Faded Glory's distribution system provided retail stores with much better service than they had previously received. We had a competitive edge because we could make large volume purchases, promise shipments to be ready at the start of the five or six fashion seasons each year, and maintain service credibility with individual stores.

Refining distribution capabilities

While Wig Flair relied on relatively few accounts, keying on large retail department stores for sales, Tom recalled that Faded Glory had developed a more extensive distribution system:

In the case of Faded Glory, we were selling to specialty retail stores, which were relatively small. I was responsible for seeing that the orders were filled and the volumes of the jeans we needed came at the right times. At first, it was pretty simple. You would get the requisition from the salesperson, grab a basket, and walk around the back room filling the order. As our sales increased, we added data processing capabilities and finally had to move from the Canton warehouse to larger facilities.

In the company phone bank, Sandy had directed employees who called stores periodically to inform retailers of the different lines of jeans currently carried and any special promotions being conducted, and to learn of any problems stores might have in terms of delivery or other parts of the relationship. A field sales force also called on stores to obtain initial orders and solicit reorders. Sandy recalled that over time they merged the two functions so that the person on the phone handled both sales and service of a particular account:

We divided the workload by geographic region so a person might be handling all the stores in North and South Carolina, for instance. The field sales force still recruited new accounts and helped with promotion and displays. As for any national chains, they typically bought from one central area, such as New York, so the person who had New York would handle that particular chain.

Sandy added that much of a typical phone salesperson's time was spent on responding to incoming calls and taking orders for a particular design of jean. A "VIP hot line" was set up to provide quick service to the company's largest customers. Mass mailings provided stores with posters, product announcements on accessory outerwear, and other promotional literature. These efforts, according to Tom, provided retail stores much better distributor service than they had previously received. Making large-volume purchases, having shipments ready at the start of each of the five or six fashion seasons per year, and maintaining service contact with individual stores was a competitive edge he cited as central to the firm's success. He commented:

> A lot of things we did were strictly by seat of the pants. But it didn't take long to find out which jeans were the dogs and which ones were the stars. You simply tried to order less dogs and more stars and make sure that the retail outlet got the kind of attention that you knew you would like to have if you were in their shoes.

Faded Glory's sales grew to $40 million in its second year, as it focused on the high-end fashion business. Pretax profit was about $6 million. Gross margin reached 45 percent and Michael guessed it might reach 60 percent. Instead, however, it started dropping, down to 32 percent as sales reached $50 million. The company booked $175 million in orders its third year, but delivered only $55 million because the Hong Kong supplier refused to expand capacity.

Michael went looking for suppliers elsewhere and soon took over a Nicaraguan plant that had been foreclosed by its bank. Progress there, however, was shortly terminated by a revolution. One of the plant managers was shot. The factory was closed and a $700,000 write-off was taken by Faded Glory.

The search for yet another supplier in Guatemala was interrupted by a disagreement between Michael and Jim over how Jim managed. The company now had 600 employees, including eight of Michael's relatives. In 1978, Michael asked to be bought out. He recalled:

> I wasn't interested in keeping the company at the $50 million level. Also, I was getting up every morning and saying, "There's got to be more to life than the garment business and making money." I wanted to do other things. I was a little interested in politics among other things, so in early 1979, I sold out to my partner and my brother.

His brother, Jim, and sister remained with Faded Glory, as did his administrative assistant, Elaine. Tom had graduated from Boston University in 1977 and was now entering his second year of law school at Suffolk University.

Considering a computer venture

Michael spent the end of 1978 and first half of 1979 working with one of the major political parties in its Washington, D.C. office. He developed a friendship with the director of an East Coast educational institute and recalled that whenever he visited or traveled with this friend, the man would be carrying around a portable computer. He showed Michael how the machine worked and the capabilities microcomputers have for problem solving. Michael said his friend's fascination with computers further piqued his own interest in the machines. A subsequent trade show he attended inspired him to serious discussions with his brother about the prospect of entering the computer industry. He observed:

> I was attending a blue jeans trade show at the Coliseum in New York. Half of the floor was being used for jeans while the other half had a trade show for personal computers going on. I wandered over and started talking with some of the sales manufacturers representatives and manufacturers and found out that they regarded themselves as the kingpins of the future. I realized that computers could be a good bet if I started another business.

I met with several guys who owned retail stores. I was willing to match the capital they had in the business for a 50 percent interest, but I was perfectly happy to let them run it. I'd have been delighted to have been a passive investor, just talking to them once a week or so, and offering them my expertise where it was needed. What I was looking for was someone I saw eye-to-eye with in business philosophy and who had the ability to run a big company. But I never found the situation I was looking for.

Elaine Cresto had joined Faded Glory in 1974 as a result of seeking part-time work through an employment agency, which in turn, referred her as a two-week replacement for a secretary on vacation. She recalled fearing that if she insisted upon a permanent part-time referral, the employment agency might never call her back. But now, six years later, she was still working for Michael. Her duties gradually increased, as she kept telling Michael, "I don't have enough work to do." One aspect of her work, she remembered, was occasionally clipping an article on computers from a magazine at Michael's request, and filing it for future reference. She said the articles ranged from impacts computers were expected to have on society to information about major manufacturers and their product lines. When Michael asked her to help think about a new venture that would be involved with the computer industry, Elaine said it came as no surprise to her.

By autumn of 1979, Michael, Tom and Sandy were contemplating ways to begin dealing in small computers and peripheral equipment. Their consensus was to explore whatever gaps might exist in distribution channels between manufacturers and retailers. Michael stated that start-up capital would be provided from his personal savings and that the apartment complex where he lived could serve as an office initially. It had recently been converted to condominiums and he decided to make a down payment on both his unit and the one immediately above it.

Michael requested another three phone lines for the condo, in addition to the two already present, and ordered subscriptions to magazines carrying computer advertisements and information. Sandy and Elaine scanned the magazines to find names of computer stores and products that they most often sold, as well as information about their typical customers. Tom spent much of his time talking with the stores by telephone, calling manufacturers to inquire about their products, and discussing overall strategy with Michael.

The common advice to get a good lawyer and accountant to start a business was true, Michael said. "But first and foremost," he emphasized, "you need a good market researcher." He placed an advertisement in the Boston Globe in late November for someone to conduct studies for the prospective venture. Elaine screened the respondents by phone, commenting that she was looking for persons who had experience in the computer industry and who seemed to come across well over the phone. One person whom she advised Michael to interview was Dick Sanders, who recalled his reaction when he first read the ad and later met Michael:

I told myself this must be a waste of time; it was a real small ad. On the other hand, I was out of work because the company I was with had just gone bankrupt. My job prospects were pretty dim except for a major local mainframe manufacturer, and I had the feeling that I would just get lost in their type of environment. So I went in to interview and was immediately impressed to find out that Michael had an entrepreneurial spirit. I quit interviewing elsewhere and was hired in three days. Most managers look for the big, glossy position announcements and tend to value a job by the size of ad in the classified section. I'm glad that this time I didn't.

Dick had spent most of his professional career with a Boston-based market research firm which specialized in the computer industry. In his words: "I've been doing market surveys all my life." He said his task now was to design a survey to send computer stores that would determine:

1. Whether need for a distributor existed.
2. How such a venture should be set up.
3. What type of services should be provided to both manufacturers and retailers.
4. How to position the business to take advantage of growth trends and set it apart from other competitors.

He explained that the "hunch" they were all basing the venture on presumed that computer retailers were not getting good service, nor low enough prices to encourage wider sales of microcomputers and related peripheral equipment. At the other end, he said, manufacturers were burdened with selling small lot quantities to individual stores. This required maintaining nationwide sales forces and inventory systems, which drained manufact- urer's resources away from their primary strengths in product development.

By December, the five had each "mapped out" their own work responsibilities to learn more about the computer industry and plan the venture. Dick was focused on putting together his mail survey. Michael was calling on manufacturers to learn about products and discuss terms that could be established for a distributor relationship. Elaine was still compiling information on manufacturers and distributors by going through magazines and reading about them. She also reviewed advertisements sent in by a hired clipping service. The service had been instructed to send any ads by computer stores that appeared in major newspapers around the country. Dick said they soon found that the information was of little value to them:

> You get charged 50 cents an article and they started pulling every Radio Shack ad in the country. Needless to say, we didn't rely on them too much after that. We've ended up doing most of the clipping ourselves.

Sandy and Tom were responsible for planning operations of the potential venture. Tom said he expected inventory control and shipping to require methods similar to those used in the jeans business. Sandy added that they would likely use a phone bank as a sales and service link with retail stores:

> I've found out that when you set up a telephone system like we used with Faded Glory, you don't need a telephone for every person. If you have nine outgoing lines for every 12 or 15 people, that should be enough. Part of their time is spent recording information on each store in a loose leaf notebook, which all of the sales people use. They also might be reviewing literature on a particular product that we're trying to sell. The question of whether you can get by with nine lines or 12 is based to a large degree on how many incoming phone calls you expect to receive.

She explained that the Faded Glory sales force had attempted to call each retail store at least once every two weeks. This allowed each retailer to keep abreast of any promotional activities and also stay in touch with the distributor. It was, she said, a means of showing that service was being stressed.

Besides dealing with likely operational issues, both Tom and Sandy were also contacting computer stores by phone and through personal visits to outlets in the New England area. Tom estimated that everyone was averaging at least 50 hours per week on the potential venture, and Sandy guessed she was putting in up to 80 hours a week if her week-end visits to computer stores were included. Having a telephone for each person was a logical step in Tom's view:

I probably spend 40 percent of my time on the phone. Michael's probably on the phone 70 percent of the time. Sandy's on the phone about 30 percent and Elaine 20 percent—the phones are not going unused.

Often, Dick said, the owners appeared to be people who were simply opportunistic and/or interested in computers but had little, if any, business knowledge or financing capacity. The flow of newcomers into this industry was pointed up, he noted, by a recent Datamation article, which predicted that, by 1983, there would be over 2,000 computer stores in the United States.

Working on a market survey

Dick said he usually followed a number of rules when putting together a market survey. First, the mailing list should include precisely those people or firms whom the survey was trying to reach. Second, the questions should be written out. Then they should be reviewed by several people to make sure that they wouldn't be misinterpreted by respondents. "Finally, and probably most important," Dick added, "is to ask yourself, just what is it that you want to find out."

He said that reviewing the questions for clarity wasn't much of a problem, since he had been doing surveys for so long. He recalled that a questionnaire typically took him about two hours to write and proof. Dick related his methods in composing a survey:

You want to stay away from essay-type answers; have questions they can check answers to. You want to keep the appearance light. Otherwise, they'll look at it and say, "I'm not going to take the time to finish this." Make sure that they receive a copy of the results and assure them that the survey won't be published without their permission. And finally, offer a little reward up front—it doubles the response rate. On our last survey we estimated that by offering a drawing for a camera we roughly doubled our response rate.

The four prepared their own lists of retail computer stores from names out of magazines. The only other alternative, Dick said, was to purchase a list from one of the subscription houses or magazine publishers.

Current distribution patterns of the microcomputer industry

While considered an "infant" when compared to established industries such as autos, steel and chemicals, data processing equipment was widely hailed in media articles as "the greatest growth and glamour industry since World War II." Technological advances had made it possible for computing power to be packaged in ever smaller equipment that was easier to use in a variety of applications and by people with little, if any, technical background in electronics or computer science.

Current terminology divided computer products into three major classifications: mainframes, minicomputers, and microcomputers. Each was designed to address a particular customer application and evolved as advances were made in data storage.

Mainframes came from the industry giants such as IBM, Control Data, Honeywell, and Cray Research. The machines were designed for very complex and exacting scientific and analytical needs and could cost well over a million dollars, including software and peripheral equipment. Distribution in this segment was by one of two routes: the manufacturer sold directly to the end user, thus using a strategy called OEM (original equipment manufacturer), or sold to an intermediary systems house. The systems house would then add peripheral equipment made by other manufacturers and custom design software for more specific applications. The final product was then sold as a "turn-key" package, where the buyer would simply have to turn on switches and the system would be operational.

Page 529

Minicomputers were generally less expensive units with substantial computing power, memory and speed, although less than that of mainframes. Recent products called "super minis" had somewhat blurred the distinction between minis and mainframes. Distribution channels for minis were similar to mainframes, with salespersons typically making four or five calls to a prospect before a purchase was made. Principal manufacturers included Hewlett-Packard, Digital Equipment, Data General, Prime computer and Tandem. Customers were considered to be medium and large businesses or government agencies, with lengthy lease or purchase periods and service agreements with the manufacturer or the systems house.

Microcomputers represented a radical departure from other computer products in several respects. Microprocessor chips as a form of central processing unit or "brain" for the computer instead of massive cabinets full of electronic circuits and magnetic tape drives had been in existence only since the mid-1970s. These chips made microcomputers unique in size. For the first time, computers could be small enough to be placed on top of a desk. Previously, computers had to be housed in special rooms with temperature and humidity controls. Now, not only did they not need such rooms, but they also cost tens of thousands of dollars less, under $10,000 for the first time. Programming also became vastly simpler and for the first time software was becoming standardized, as well as much cheaper, easier to use and widely available.

Users for the first time included small businesses, home hobbyists who would use the machines for recreation or developing applications for personal use, schools, and larger businesses. An increasing number of companies had started manufacturing peripheral equipment specifically for microcomputers, including printers, memory storage units, special-purpose plug-in circuit boards and plotters. The largest manufacturers were Apple Computer, Tandy's Radio Shack division and Commodore. An assortment of companies followed, from IBM to small ventures, some of which had already failed, including two of the earliest, MITS and IMSAI. It was widely expected that there would be many more entries and many more failures among the makers of microcomputers before the industry stabilized.

Since the value added per unit with microcomputers was much less than that for minis and mainframes, the use of direct sales people calling on individual accounts didn't make economic sense. Apple, for example, had used mail order as a strategy to build sales and gain a leadership position in the industry but was currently selling mainly through regional distributors to retail computer stores. Distributors were mostly regional, serving at most two or three states.

Radio Shack added its TRS-80 microcomputer to its existing line of stereo equipment and sold the machine in the retail outlets it had developed throughout the United States and overseas. Other manufacturers used a combination of mail order and retail sales through locations such as the estimated 700-1,000 computer stores in the U.S. For mini and mainframe builders, as well as peripheral equipment manufacturers, the addition of a microcomputer to their product line could be touted to existing customer accounts as an added product from their sales forces.

The fact was, Michael pointed out, that no clear distribution pattern yet existed for microcomputers. He said the trend toward selling microcomputers in retail computer stores appeared to be the most likely avenue to persist. Whether the stores would remain largely independent, be comprised of chains such as Radio Shack or Computerland, or be a retail outlet of a computer manufacturer, such as Digital Equipment's computer stores, he hoped he could divine from the market survey.

Sandy commented that the inquiries they had made to date had already provided some clues as to what they could expect from Dick's more formal survey:

We've found that the retail outlets are used to waiting five or six weeks for delivery on an order and when it comes, the manufacturer often requires them to pay C.O.D. In part, the payment terms are due to the fact that most of the retail stores are fairly new. Another factor is that these store owners come from a technical background, and they have no concept of what retailing is all about. So they often fail. If you look at a list more than six months old, many of the store numbers have been disconnected, and people have gone out of business. About one out of every six stores we tried to contact had gone out of business in the last six months. But for every one that closed, two more are opening up. At that rate, we figure there will be about 1,500 independents by the end of 1982.

She added that the people running the retail stores were much more willing than the jeans store operators to talk on the phone about their products. They gave their thoughts on where the industry was headed, even though she gave them only her name and simply said she was interested in learning more about computers. In many ways she thought retail personal computer stores were similar to stereo outlets in the 1960s, when hobbyists were the major "promoters." The general public was just becoming aware of the products offered and what the terminology meant in terms of performance or application.

Michael continued his commentary concerning difficulties that computer retail stores seemed to be up against:

Retailers aren't getting the newest products as fast as they want, nor can they reorder quickly. The underlying issue here is that entrepreneurs in any new business always have limited capital. To compete in the long run with the big manufacturer's stores like Radio Shack and Xerox, the independent computer retailer needs fast delivery of the best products available. This way he ties up and risks less capital. There is need for someone who will do the market research and take the risk of stocking new products, so stores can concentrate on what they do best, which is making sales. What is needed is, in a sense, a buying service.

A printer possibility

Michael had sent requests for product information to every manufacturer in the microcomputer business he could locate. The response of one company, LRC, was to send a salesman to call on him. Michael recalled:

The LRC salesman said his company is coming out with this new 40-column printer and they want us to carry it. He had no sales figures because there are no 40-column printers on the market, as yet. Everyone is selling 80-column printers, but the salesman said it is logical that hobbyists using a small computer will want a small printer. His argument makes sense to me.

When we asked about terms, he said if we take 55 printers COD, LRC would give us a $5,000 credit limit. We figure the gross margin would be about 14 percent. We don't like the terms, but I know we're not in a good negotiating position. Here he is calling on us in our condominium where we have nothing at all to show him.

Other start-up issues

As Dick faced the task of designing a survey, the other four were concerned about other issues. Education about the products and the industry was a must, according to Michael, since none of them had a technical background in computers or electronics. Dick was acquainted with computers from the perspective of following the industry and market trends, although he admitted that he still had trouble trying to figure out how to simply turn on a machine:

We'll have manufacturers come in to talk about their product and they'll start in on some heavy technical presentation. They don't realize that Michael and I are thinking about goats when they're talking about ROMS and RAMS. So, we've got some catching up to do in learning about the jargon and products.

If the venture were attempted, Michael thought they should try to develop a sales force dedicated to maintaining close contact with the stores and keeping up with product developments. Sandy pointed out that this might be hard, since experienced technical sales people were in short supply and were prone to switching companies for higher salaries or improved benefits. "Company loyalty doesn't seem to extend very far down the ladder in the computer industry," she lamented.

Dick remarked that people they had talked to with computer experience "want the moon for a salary." The five were hoping to start people at $12,000 per year and increase the amount as they developed experience. With Faded Glory, the sales staff had worked on a straight salary basis. Whether any commission incentive should be included in this venture idea wasn't yet known. Dick added that they would probably settle for people who simply had general sales experience, figuring that someone who had sold Tupperware was better than someone with no sales experience at all.

Another concern was finding a more suitable office and warehouse facility to work from. The Canton Massachusetts warehouse, which had been used in previous businesses, was currently under lease. The tenant indicated he might vacate it when the lease expired in April, but Tom and Sandy continued to spend part of their time searching for other space in the Boston area.

Another question was what their initial product line should include. Michael suggested distributing first some relatively non-technical product with potential for high volume to offset the low margins he expected they would be able to command. He wanted 20- or 30-percent-margin product lines but believed that realistically, they would have to settle for 10 to 15 percent to attract manufacturers to an unknown business like theirs.

One possible initial product to distribute would be floppy disks and diskettes. A manufacturer they had investigated seemed to have a good reputation for such products, yet held a mere 3 percent market share in sales. Michael and Dick reasoned that if they told the manufacturer they could boost market share to over 10 percent, they might be able to get advantageous distribution rights. Their strategy would then be to build on that success by adding micro-computer peripherals to their line. Another emphasis, they stated, would be to concentrate on products compatible with the leading computers such as those of Apple, Radio Shack, and Commodore—which together currently comprised 60 percent of the total installed base of personal computers.

Industry standards for negotiating margins followed the assumptions that retail stores required 30 percent off list price for every item sold. Michael and Dick estimated they would need between 20 and 30 percent to act as a full service distributor, even though some distributors in the industry were taking as little as 6 percent on products. Dick pointed out that these companies simply purchased products from manufacturers and resold them to retailers with no attempt to provide service or assistance beyond product delivery.

The two figured they could attempt to purchase from manufacturers at 50 percent off the suggested retail price. They would keep 40 percent of the discount and pass the remaining 60 percent along to the retailers. To be successful, manufacturers would have to agree to forego 10 to 20 percent of the list price which they were now keeping for themselves.

Another element of strategy Michael believed would be extremely important was advertising. He commented that since the venture would be starting from scratch, a disproportionate amount would be needed for promotion. He said that they would probably spend 10 percent of annual sales on advertising for the first year or two until the venture became recognized as a leading distributor of computer products.

Dick said conversations with retailers and manufacturers indicated that a gap did exist in terms of distribution. Most of the retail emphasis was being put on carrying only the leading printer, CRT, or other peripherals for each particular product line. One result was that periodic price cutting, rather than product variety, was the major competitive tactic being used, and lesser known manufacturers were having difficulty selling their products. Another result was that retailers became dependent on a small number of suppliers. At the mercy of those suppliers, the retailers found that fast delivery was the exception. Maintenance and repairs often required shipping machines back to a manufacturers and could take weeks to accomplish. Shortages of user-oriented software impeded selling new microcomputer systems to the general public.

Possible implications of a formal market survey

As March 1980 approached, Dick considered it important to find out what a formal survey could tell him about market potential for the prospective venture. He, Michael and Tom believed that, if they decided to move ahead, conclusions from the survey should form the basis for structuring the venture. If the type of service, markets, pricing and related issues were handled appropriately, the business could succeed. If not, Michael's third attempt in starting a business might result in failure.

Dick reviewed a number of questions that he hoped the survey results would help answer:

We want to find out what the stores think of the manufacturers and their products. Which one are the best? Worst? Where are the retailers getting their sales people? How are they hiring them? Who are the stores selling products to? What needs could a distributor fulfill?

We want to know what kind of money it takes to start a store. Who are the store's competitors? What about problems with software and maintenance? How much do they spend on advertising? Should they put out a catalog featuring the store's product line? Does the store use mail order?

What does the future hold for retail computer stores? Where would they invest capital if they had more of it to spend: inventory or another store? What are their sales revenues? What about in three years?

The answers to these questions will tell us if there is a place for us as a distributor. And it will tell us how to structure our business, in terms of what products to go after and what services to offer. Also, we'll be able to develop some expectations about growth and competition down the road.

At the same time, we can't forget the importance of getting our name out to people in the business. That's very important. Right now, we have manufacturers come to the condominium with their product, they look at the five of us, look around the room in disbelief, and say, "Hey! What's going on here? You call yourself a business?"

Laurence Osborne

Laurence Osborne was frustrated in February 1981 by his lack of success in attempts to refinance his new enterprise, First Watersign Corporation of Cambridge, Massachusetts. Its product was a small appliance that could, among other things, enhance the potency of a drug which, although illegal, was beginning to show some promise as a medicine and, he believed, might some day be legalized. He noted that the drug, marijuana, was widely used socially, and he thought this fact, coupled with the high cost of law enforcement, which was having only limited success anyway, might eventually lead to legalization under government control, as had happened with alcohol and the elimination of prohibition.

Mr. Osborne's product, called the "Maximizer"™, was a redesigned electric hotpot converted into a double boiler. It is depicted in Exhibit 1. As the water boiled, steam surrounded an inner container, bringing the contents to exactly 100 degrees centigrade. The water itself served as a timer. The moment that the unit boiled dry a thermostat turned it off to complete a calculated heating cycle. Data from U.S. government research on marijuana showed relationships between the heating cycle and potency in activating the drug, THC (tetrahydrocannabinol). Depending on the sample, narcotic potency could be increased by as much as 50 percent through regulation of this heating process.

Osborne said that although marijuana remained illegal, its acceptance for treatment of cancer chemotherapy patients seemed to be growing in the medical community. He had filed for a patent covering his cooking process, which could be used to regulate potency for either medical or commercial purposes. He commented:

> The upshot is that when we get that patent, we'll have virtual control over any form of legal marijuana processing for 17 years. Between now and then, I'm betting that we'll have legal medical marijuana, and we'll be the only ones with the technology. Somebody is going to pay well for this mini-autoclave we made out of kitchen appliance parts. And besides, it's a dandy rice cooker as well.

At present, however, Mr. Osborne was out of cash. Developing the product, including injection molds, jigs, and four-color mail-order advertisements in *High Times* had used up his initial investment capital, which had come mainly from old friends and by borrowing on his life insurance. His first manufacturing run was also partly financed by pre-selling much of it to retailers highlighted in the first advertisements. The first 5,000 Maximizers, whose assembly and shipment he directed and participated in himself, sold as fast as they could be put together.

Following this first run, Osborne located a manufacturer to whom he could subcontract the entire assembly and packing operation. After work had begun on the second run, however, the U.S. Drug Enforcement Administration unveiled a new set of statutes designed to criminalize makers, distributors, and users of "drug paraphernalia." Included in this newly illegal category were small pipes, rolling papers, and virtually anything else that was sold to be used with marijuana. Despite a letter to Osborne from the National Institute on Drug Abuse which affirmed, in response to a query from him, that a double boiler was not such paraphernalia, he saw the marketplace for his product falling apart. Stores known as "head shops" because they sold the newly condemned paraphernalia went out of business throughout the country, eliminating Maximizer sales through that channel. With sales of *High Times* magazine, in which his advertisements ran, also under adverse pressure, the mail order component of his sales dropped by 75 percent in three months. His firm barely survived the summer of 1980. He could foresee that without Christmas advertisements, sales would continue to drop, leaving him with an apartment full of unsalable cookers.

In order to pay his creditors, refinance the company, and move his operation forward, Mr. Osborne prepared a written business plan as a prospectus for recruiting more capital. Excerpts from this document appear in Exhibit 2 of this case. As he began using it in search of backing, he encountered repeated rejections and soon became concerned that his creditors might seize the inventory on hand, or even attach his company's bank account.

Laurence Osborne

Starting businesses was something Larry Osborne had done from an early age. As a young boy, tired of his lemonade stand, he located a clam bed during summer camp and "cornered the market." He traded clams as fish bait for comic books and traded comics for candy bars. Later, as a Harvard freshman in 1962, he led a rock band and promoted it vigorously. Taking it to Los Angeles the summer of 1963, he returned with a surfboard and started a chain of surf shops called "Surf City" on Cape Cod, as well as in New Hampshire and Maine. He plowed all his earnings back into this seasonal business, which he finally sold in 1968.

Following graduation from Harvard in 1966, Larry taught writing at the University of North Carolina. His attempt to join the Army ended when he told recruiters that his skills would be useful in the Saigon black market. Classified 4-F, he entered the Harvard Business School instead in 1967, graduating in 1969. During the summer between his first and second years of MBA study, he was funded by a Kansas City industrialist to design a media workshop for young African Americans. Then in the second year of MBA studies, he completed two final projects: a truck rental plan for Ryder systems and a study of marijuana as a free-trade phenomenon within a regulated economy.

After he received his MBA, *Time* magazine asked Osborne to contribute to one of the first school-oriented drug abuse efforts. Deciding he could do it better himself, he gathered a group of experts who specialized in the field, and soon, he recalled, became a minor celebrity when William F. Buckley. Jr. publicly praised his small educational publishing firm, The Creative Learning Group. It was during this time that Osborne developed the professional friendships with those in the field of drug research that led ultimately to the marijuana process on which he later applied for a patent.

His publishing firm began growing. Within two years it was selling drug education curricula to schools nationwide, as well as to the U.S. Army, the U.S. Navy and the Smithsonian Institution. In 1973, however, President Nixon eliminated federal funding for school drug education, forcing The Creative Learning Group into receivership.

From what he had learned about marijuana from reports of U.S. federal experimentation with it, he undertook in 1973 to obtain a patent on the process for creating from it the narcotic, tetrahydrocanabinol. He recruited a chemist to help him, with the understanding that the two would share ownership in the patent. They were also going to share in the costs of applying for the patent but, to Osborne's disappointment, the chemist neglected to do so.

When The Creative Learning Group terminated, Osborne undertook to continue in the publishing business by dropping drug education and instead following a new direction. He used his limited remaining resources to develop the first Russian language computer typesetting system. His aim was to reproduce current Russian articles for use in Russian language classes. These were needed, he explained, because the only other Russian language writings widely available in the U.S. were very old classical works of less current interest. The lack of current works was apparently due to the high cost of setting Cyrillic type, over $100 per page, which pushed up printing costs to levels schools could not afford. He found that with a computer he could do it much cheaper, recalling: "Even *Pravda* could not do it as cheaply as we could."

Just as he began to enter the market with this innovation, however, the U.S. Congress passed the "Jackson Amendment" that denied favorable trade status to the U.S.S.R. because of its emigration policies. BORIS (Binary Operated Russian Interface System) was liquidated after only six months. With the office space and publishing facilities he had available, he struck up an alliance in 1974 with two men who had just left their jobs with a magazine to form one of their own, *New Age*. Eventually, their magazine grew beyond the space Osborne had available, and they moved out.

Meanwhile, after learning through personal friends that Harvard University had a trove of antique glassware that it wanted to sell, Osborne formed a company called University Antiquaries to purchase, clean, catalog and pack nearly 20,000 of naturalist Louis Agassiz's original hand-blown specimen jars. These he sold at a gallery in Boston and through mail order advertisements.

In 1976, Osborne received news from the U.S. Patent Office that the patent he had applied for had been granted. Having earlier been disappointed that his chemist partner had not paid the share of filing expenses that Osborne thought he should, Osborne now contacted the man and again asked him to pay up. Osborne recalled:

> I told him that if he wasn't going to pay up, I was not going to pay the required $100 issuing fee and our application would lapse. He said, "fine, let it lapse." So I didn't pay the fee, and a month or so later, it lapsed.
>
> My hope was that he would not apply for the issuance himself. He could have, but didn't. I also didn't, because I wanted to wait until marijuana was closer to legalization before I started the expiration clock that would begin ticking when the patent was issued with its 17-year life span.

By 1977, the jar venture inventory was exhausted. Osborne, also exhausted, took a break by attending Harvard Divinity School. In the spring, financial pressures led him to perform freelance air courier deliveries. Tiring of that, he dropped by the Harvard Business School and read on the bulletin board about a harpsichord company that wanted consulting help. He recalled:

> The founder had died and his widow was concerned that the company was losing money. It turned out they were trying to operate with only a 15-percent markup. I fixed that, developed a mailing list and started a newsletter for them to help promote their products. That turned it around and I found myself with some success in the management consulting business. That fall I joined another consulting firm, Management Directions, where I worked on jobs like developing product sales manuals and multimedia for sales meetings in companies like BMW, Volkswagen and American Optical.

The cooker design

One day the attorney who had helped Osborne with his marijuana process patent called to say that *Playboy* had talked to him about an article they were developing on the question of who would get rich if marijuana were legalized. He suggested Osborne give the reporter a call, which he did. During the conversation, the reporter asked Osborne why he did not make a machine to carry out the optimal cooking cycle Osborne had developed. When Osborne replied that it would take expertise, the reporter said, "Well, you're a consultant. Why don't you hire one?"

Taking up the challenge, Osborne began calling cooking appliance companies and asking them where he could find a good consultant on how to design one. Following up the names he was given, he called one consultant in Connecticut, who said he would give the job some thought. Osborne described what happened next.

> One week later, the consultant called and said, "I think we have your problem solved. The fee will be $1,200. Do we have an agreement?" I asked if the cooker could be designed to sell for around $29.95. When he said he thought so, I said then we had a deal, and asked what the secret was.
>
> Then he proceeded to tell me that he would control the temperature with a fluid that vaporized at exactly 100 degrees centigrade. The time would be controlled by having a circuit close when just the right amount of this fluid boiled away.
>
> I asked what sort of fancy fluid we would have to get for that mechanism. He said, "Now just think a minute. What readily available fluid vaporizes at exactly one hundred degrees centigrade?"
>
> I said, "My gosh! You just charged me $1,200 for telling me about a double boiler!"

In the spring of 1979, the cooker project moved ahead. Using a quickly-written prospectus offering 20-percent interest-bearing bonds, Osborne was able to raise enough money to pay for the designer, the model makers, the injection molds, and advertising layouts to roll out the product in November.

He also decided to try reactivating the process patent he had applied for earlier, since now he would be using that process in his new cooking appliance.

Initial operations

Since he expected the Maximizer would be used by those wishing to improve marijuana potency, Osborne decided to place his first advertisements for it in the *New England Journal of Medicine*, directed to the attention of medical researchers. Other small advertisements, which he placed in *New Age* magazine, described the Maximizer as a small steam cooker without reference to any other use. If his product were going to end up in *High Times*, Osborne reasoned, let it first be marketed as a "medical instrument or a simple appliance." A researcher at the Mayo Clinic ordered one, as did a number of *New Age* readers who said they used it as a versatile steam cooker and praised its efficiency.

By August 1979 Osborne had raised only $30,000. Although he regarded this as "a drastic under-capitalization," he went forward with a production run of 5,000 units to coincide with a November double-page advertisement he had scheduled with *High Times*. The ad offered to mention the names of any shops buying more than two dozen Maximizers. This brought in enough orders to yield what Larry characterized as his "last increment of investment" from his own customers, the shops. By the day the first order was shipped the venture's bank account had been reduced to less than $250. But the product sold readily, and within six weeks the entire run had been shipped.

With the cash that was coming in from these first sales, Osborne started his second production run. He also worked on a prospectus for raising more capital, which he believed was desperately needed. He calculated that he had enough either to keep advertising or to finish the second run, but not both.

A process patent

Osborne regarded his Maximizer product as the financial engine that was keeping First Watersign Corporation afloat. He expected, however, that the process patent embodied in the Maximizer, rather than the product itself, would be by far the most valuable asset of his corporation. So far, he had learned that no patent identical to the one he was applying for had been issued in the interval since the earlier application had lapsed. So he thought the chances of getting it again were good.

With the help of his patent attorney, he had identified three areas that he believed could be protected:

1. The method of treating the plant material to maximize and/or stabilize the THC content.
2. The device which provided the environment to effect the process.
3. The means of storing the processed plant material.

If the first two claims were granted, Osborne expected that his company would control not only the device, but the process itself, in the same manner that DuPont had benefited by its patent on the process for making nylon. A process patent, he said, could be more lucrative than a product patent because it generally reserved to the owner the sole rights to both the process and the product as well.

The search for more capital

The result of his quest for capital Osborne summarized as follows:

> My search for funding for the MAXIMIZER was a long story that I can make short. Nobody wanted to touch it.

Possible investors Osborne had approached during his initial fundraising included several venture capital firms that specialized in startups. He recalled:

> They loved the prospectus. Some said it was the best written business plan they'd ever seen. But they felt the area was taboo. The fact was that the burgeoning paraphernalia industry was generating considerable profits, but few people had any solid numbers and the major players were, to say the least, considered marginal operators and novelty distributors.

It seemed to Osborne that the first production run had demonstrated that manufacturing costs could be contained and that the market was nearly unlimited. Hence, he reasoned, it should be easier to attract investors for the second run. In fact, however, it seemed harder to raise money for the second run than it had for the first one nearly a year earlier. He observed:

> Here I am with a 400 percent R.O.I. after the first run and still nobody is putting in the money we need. I stopped pursuing institutional investors a long time ago, and now it's just rich eccentrics. Recently, I almost got $15,000 from a family friend, but then, just as he was about to sign the check, his son was committed to a drug abuse clinic.
>
> So here I am, in debt, with 750 Maximizers from the second run ready to sell and not even $45 to pay for a mailing, which would sell at least $1,500 worth. I need to pay my parts suppliers or they'll never go along with a third run. I have to pay for the Christmas ads, and I'd love to send something to my investors as well. I'm pretty certain we'll get that patent, and I'm not sure that those paraphernalia laws are constitutional in the long run.

The bottom line is that I would be making more money doing just about anything if I dropped this venture. But if I hold on, I might end up with the entire technology for medical, or even legal, marijuana.

Sometimes I think this is pioneering; sometimes I think that someone must have put some pot in my corn flakes to get me to even try the idea. You tell me. What would you do? Hang in there, or just let it go?

EXHIBIT 1 The Maximizer

EXHIBIT 2 First Watersign Corporation prospectus

(This document has been abridged to reduce case length.)

CONTENTS PAGE

FIGURES (Several omitted to reduce length)

EXHIBIT 2 *(continued)*

IN BRIEF

Purpose

The First Watersign Corporation, a small privately held research and manufacturing firm in Cambridge, Massachusetts, is raising $200,000 for expansion of their business operations. A first year test-marketing through limited channels sold nearly 9,000 of the company's unique and proprietary product. The enthusiastic response of customers, wholesalers, and retailers has demonstrated both feasibility and profitability of the product, and indicates a likelihood of rapid growth once the total market is aware that the product simply exists. For the purpose of raising expansion capital, 25 percent of the common stock of the company is being offered. The offering price is $53.35 per share, and purchasers will receive with each share a warrant good for purchase of one further share at the same price during a two-year period.

Product

The company's product, the MAXIMIZER™, is a unique time-cycle multi-purpose appliance. Although it is marketed chiefly as an all around cooker, it incorporates proprietary techniques which allow it to increase the potency of marijuana by as much as 200 percent through the non-destructive decarboxylation of precursor plant cannabinoids. Units have been supplied to every research project in the country where legal marijuana is used by medical volunteers participating in the national testing of THC and smoked marijuana as a therapeutic medicine. The sale of the appliance through food channels has already prompted a special letter from the National Institute on Drug Abuse affirming the legality of the MAXIMIZER™ for production and sale to all markets.

Return

The entire offering will be returned in profits the first year if 0.1 percent of the estimated market responds. Should marijuana become legal for medical or recreational use, the company will probably control the processing patents and all machinery for the potency control/increase used in the entire industry.

Taking into account all production and marketing costs, the total potential profitability, before taxes, is nearly $34,000,000. At a ratio of one unit sold at wholesale ($4.00 net at $16.00) to one unit sold through mail order ($16.00 net at $29.95) the figures add up as follows:

$$1,700,000 \text{ units wholesale x } \$4.00 = \$6,800,000$$
$$1,700,000 \text{ units retail x } \$16.00 = \underline{27,200,000}$$
$$\$34,000,000$$

The $29.95 price came from a standard marketing formulation which suggests a price of "five times cost of goods" as a retail price which will permit enough flexibility for wholesaling and marketing. Since the manufacturing cost at normal levels reduces at $6.00 from the current $8.00, the $29.95 price was not only still within "impulse purchase" range, but conformed to standard pricing formulas.

EXHIBIT 2 (continued)

It was also noted that the original "Isomerizer," which sold at $129.00, did not lose sales volume when the "KIK" appeared at $69.00. In fact, both items were able to sell at the same volumes (approximately 8,000 units per year) simultaneously. It appeared that as the price dropped, this market grew proportionately. It was felt that the $29.95 price would absolutely insure a market test of nearly 10,000 units in that particular market. Despite the unexpected effects of the paraphernalia ordinances, which drove the two other manufacturers out of business, the company was able to enter this market, and sell nearly 8,000 units during the first year.

The MAXIMIZER™ was designed to be manufactured from parts which are readily available and which are, for the most part, either stocked or easily manufactured by a number of domestic suppliers.

A primary consideration was that the manufacturing process not be defined by the test market, and that the early seed capital not be expended for permanent dies or molds. Accordingly, the major part of the product is assembled from an already available appliance which is taken from its manufacturing process at an intermediate stage and sold to the company in lots of 5,000. The only part of the product which is produced in company molds is the polypropylene top.

Since entering the market at the 1979 Christmas season was considered important, design and early manufacturing were done almost simultaneously. When the company contracted for final assembly suddenly was unable to handle the job, untrained workers were used to produce the first 4,200 units. Although unit cost was high, due to multiple revisions of design, parts, and manufacturing operations, it was indicative of the simplicity of the product that the job was completed in less than six weeks.

Enthusiastic acceptance of the product in the marketplace resulted in stock-out by the first week in February. Due to long lead times on some components, assembly of the second run was not started until the last week in April 1980. At this time, the company had located an appliance firm with private-label manufacturing as a specialty. Current manufacturing procedure is to ship all parts to this company, which then prepares the sub-assemblies, assembles and tests the product, and packs it in 12-pack cases.

Since there is no part of the appliance which cannot be made or obtained in large volume, and the assembly firm is geared towards much larger runs for other customers, production could be increased to well over 200,000 units per year without the necessity of seeking any other suppliers or assemblers. The new assembly procedure has provided an almost defect-free run while cutting the labor cost in half. (Exhibit 19).

Personnel

Since the founding of the company, it has been solely managed by Laurence O. Osborne. Osborne, who previously managed a small-business consulting firm, has a long history of managing start-up situations. Familiarity with the drug field came through his management of a major drug-abuse publishing company in the early seventies, a position which also provided extensive training in the area of printing, publishing and communications. Management of a direct-mail marketing firm (1974-77) provided experience in that area. His biographical information sheets are included as Exhibit 20.

EXHIBIT 2 *(continued)*

Throughout the first year, Osborne has been aided by a number of professionals functioning either as consultants, part-time employees, or suppliers. Judith Preston, who holds an MBA from Boston University, is active as the corporate treasurer and comptroller. Office management and shipping functions have been assumed by several individuals as the office became more systematic, and manufacturing is handled entirely by the Appliance Development Company of Boston.

One of the major reasons for the placement is to obtain the funds necessary to provide trained management to help manage the expansion of the corporation into its new and growing markets.

<u>Financing</u>

At this time, 30 percent of the stock in the company is held by Laurence Osborne, 10 percent by Donald A. Jenkins, Esquire, the patent attorney, and approximately 5 percent by outside stockholders and holders of convertible debentures. The remainder is authorized, but unissued, treasury stock.

The original bondholders invested in the project at the ratio of $100,000/15 percent of the corporation. The value of the corporation was arrived at by a formula of five times estimated profits at 20,000 units-per-year sales. So as not to dilute initial investors, the original ratio has been maintained for the purposes of the offering. To further facilitate the placement, investors are offered warrants which may be exercised at any time during the next two years and which allow purchase of an equal number of shares at the same price.

The offering represents an enlargement of the original offering, which was for convertible debentures, rather than for common stock. As $35,000 was raised during that offering, the current offering will raise approximately $165,000, returning $125,000 to the corporation after payment of commissions. Since the corporation currently has 12,500 shares of common stock authorized, the price per share is $53.35. The objective is to sell 25 percent of the common stock. When this is accomplished, Osborne will still own 30 percent, Jenkins 10 percent, outside shareholders will own 30 percent and will be able through the use of their warrants to increase their holdings to 60 percent of the corporation during the next two years, if company performance indicates a highly profitable investment.

Investors should regard the company as a speculative investment which provides its payouts either in the form of regular dividends or in the appreciation of the value of the stock in the case of a possible buy-out by a larger firm in the appliance or biomedical field. At sales levels of more than 30,000 units annually, the one product alone would return in its profits more than the total amount of this offering. Should growth proceed as expected, the company could be sold for several million dollars within its first three years of operations.

EXHIBIT 2 *(continued)*

<u>MAXIMIZER MANUFACTURING COST BREAKDOWN</u>

PART	COST
Drawn aluminum body	1.30
Tubular heater	.55
Phenolic base	.48
Top, with valve	.50
Inner container (screen bottom)	.58
Inner container (solid bottom)	.38
Screen	.04
Cord set with strain relief	.28
Thermostat	.65
Pilot light	.13
Label for bottom	.05
Box	.24
Boxwrap	.04
Label for box	.05
Two instruction booklets	.08
Guarantee-Registration card	.05
Plastic lens	.05
Order entry form	.05
Shipping, all parts	<u>.20</u>
PARTS TOTAL	$5.70
Slot base	.10
Finish on body	.25
Coating on body	.10
Logo on body	.05
All assembly and packing	<u>1.75</u>
TOTAL MANUFACTURING COST	$7.95

EXHIBIT 2 (continued)

Figure 16 FIRST WATERSIGN CORPORATION CASH FLOW PROJECTION FOR THE 12 MONTHS ENDING JULY 31, 1981

	AUG	SEP	OCT	NOV	DEC	JAN	FEB	MAR	APR	MAY	JUN	JUL	TOTAL
Cash Balance	2,500	2,167	7,317	3,692	16,527	26,452	23,422	16,924	3,439	2,864	15,674	16,88	3,200
Cash Receipts													
Wholesale	4,960	6,160	8,400	11,600	10,800	6,800	6,000	7,600	8,800	9,200	10,000	10,800	101,120
Mail Order	3,744	9,360	15,600	18,720	20,280	6,240	7,800	6,240	6,240	7,800	8,580	9,360	119,964
College Reps	—	5,000	7,000	12,000	9,000	4,000	2,000	4,000	7,000	10,000	4,000	2,000	66,000
Magazine Features	—	—	—	9,360	15,600	6,240	3,120	1,560	780	780	312	—	37,752
Direct Mail	—	—	3,120	7,800	6,240	2,340	1,560	1,560	780	780	312	312	24,804
TOTAL SALES	8,704	20,520	34,120	59,480	61,920	25,620	20,480	20,960	23,600	28,560	23,204	22,472	349,640
Cash Available	11,204	22,687	41,437	63,172	78,447	52,072	43,844	37,884	27,039	31,424	38,878	39,355	352,840
Cash Disbursements													
Manufacturing	1,747	10,020	23,845	20,695	23,845	10,675	10,020	21,045	10,675	—	—	—	132,567
Shipping	440	1,000	1,550	2,600	2,300	1,025	1,050	1,050	1,150	1,400	1,145	1,110	15,820
Marketing	1,500	6,000	7,000	15,000	10,000	4,000	7,500	4,000	4,000	4,000	7,500	7,500	78,000
Salaries	3,350	3,350	3,350	3,350	3,350	3,350	3,350	3,350	3,350	3,350	3,350	3,350	40,200
Office	2,000	2,000	2,000	2,000	2,000	2,000	2,000	2,000	2,000	2,000	2,000	2,000	24,000
TOTAL DISBURSEMENT	9,037	22,370	37,745	43,645	41,495	21,050	23,920	31,445	21,175	10,750	13,995	13,960	290,587
Minimum Cash Desired	3,000	3,000	3,000	3,000	3,000	3,000	3,000	3,000	3,000	3,000	3,000	3,000	3,000
Total Cash Needed	12,037	25,370	40,745	46,645	44,495	24,050	26,920	34,445	24,175	13,750	16,995	16,960	293,587
Excess (or deficiency)	(833)	(2,683)	692	16,527	33,952	28,022	16,924	3,349	2,864	20,674	21,883	25,395	59,253
Financing													
Borrowing	—	10,000	—	—	—	—	—	—	—	—	—	—	+10,000
Repayment	—	—	—	—	2,500	—	—	—	—	5,000	5,000	2,500	15,000
Interest (@ 20%)	—	—	—	—	—	4,600	—	—	—	—	—	4,600	9,200
Total Effects of Financing	—	—	—	—	—	—	—	—	—	—	—	—	—
Cash Balance, ending	2,167	7,317	3,692	16,527	26,452	23,422	16,924	3,439	2,864	15,674	16,883	18,295	45,053

EXHIBIT 2 *(continued)*

Figure 16 (continued) CASH FLOW PROJECTION (60% OF ORIGINAL ESTIMATES) FOR THE 12 MONTHS ENDING JULY 31, 1981

	AUG	SEP	OCT	NOV	DEC	JAN	FEB	MAR	APR	MAY	JUN	JUL	TOTAL
Cash Balance, Beginning	2,500	2,167	5,133	7,897	16,200	35,942	31,629	23,747	8,088	533	6,719	9,344	1,700
Cash Receipts													
Wholesale	4,960	4,321	5,760	8,160	4,800	3,360	3,840	5,280	5,280	5,760	6,240	6,720	64,480
Mail Order	3,744	5,616	9,360	11,232	12,168	3,744	4,680	3,744	3,744	4,680	5,148	5,616	73,476
College Reps	—	3,000	4,200	7,200	5,400	2,400	1,200	2,400	4,200	6,000	2,400	1,200	39,600
Magazine Features	—	—	—	5,616	9,360	3,744	1,872	936	468	468	187	187	22,651
Direct Mail	—	—	1,872	4,680	3,744	1,404	936	936	468	468	187	187	14,882
Total Sales	8,704	12,937	21,192	36,888	35,472	14,652	12,528	13,296	14,160	17,376	14,162	15,423	215,099
Cash Disbursements													
Manufacturing	1,747	10,020	23,845	10,675	—	—	10,020	18,475	10,675	—	—	—	85,457
Shipping	440	600	233	1,560	1,380	615	540	630	690	840	687	666	8,881
Marketing	1,500	4,000	6,000	8,000	6,000	3,000	1,500	1,500	2,000	2,000	2,500	2,500	40,500
Salaries	3,350	3,350	3,350	3,350	3,350	3,350	3,350	3,350	3,350	3,350	3,350	3,350	40,200
Office	2,000	2,000	2,000	2,000	2,000	2,000	2,000	2,000	2,000	2,000	2,000	2,000	24,000
Total Disbursements	9,037	19,970	35,428	25,585	12,730	8,965	17,410	25,955	18,715	8,190	8,537	8,516	199,038
Minimum Cash Desired	3,000	3,000	3,000	3,000	3,000	3,000	3,000	3,000	3,000	3,000	3,000	3,000	3,000
Total Cash Needed	12,037	22,970	38,428	28,585	15,730	11,965	20,410	28,955	21,715	11,190	11,537	11,516	202,038
Excess (or deficiency)	(833)	(4,867)	(12,103)	16,200	35,942	38,629	34,747	8,088	533	6,719	9,344	13,251	14,751
Financing													
Borrowing	—	10,000	20,000	—	—	—	—	—	—	—	—	—	+30,000
Repayment	—	—	—	—	—	—	—	—	—	—	—	—	—
Interest (20%/annum)	—	—	—	—	—	7,000	—	—	—	—	—	7,000	14,000
Total Effects of Financing	—	—	—	—	—	—	—	—	—	—	—	—	—
Cash Balance, Ending	2,167	5,133	7,897	16,200	35,942	31,629	23,747	8,088	533	6,719	9,344	13,251	14,751

EXHIBIT 2 (continued)

Figure 17 FIRST WATERSIGN CORPORATION UNIT SALES AND INCOME PROJECTION FOR THE 12 MONTHS ENDING JULY 31, 1981

	AUG	SEP	OCT	NOV	DEC	JAN	FEB	MAR	APR	MAY	JUN	JUL	TOTAL
Retail Outlets	125	140	160	180	200	205	210	230	240	250	270	280	280
Inventory of Units	2,203	1,763	763	213	113	313	1,788	2,388	1,338	188	1,288	2,143	2,203
Units Produced	—	—	1,000	2,500	2,500	2,500	1,500	—	—	2,500	2,000	500	15,000
Unit Sales													
Wholesale	320	450	600	850	500	350	400	550	550	600	650	700	6,520
Mail Order	120	300	500	600	650	200	250	200	200	250	275	300	3,845
College Reps	—	250	350	600	450	200	100	200	350	500	200	100	3,300
Magazine Features	—	—	—	300	500	200	100	50	25	25	10	—	1,210
Direct Mail	—	—	100	250	200	75	50	50	25	25	10	10	795
TOTAL UNITS SOLD	440	1,000	1,550	2,600	2,300	1,025	900	1,050	1,150	1,400	1,145	1,110	15,670
End Inventory/Units	1,763	763	213	113	313	1,788	2,388	1,338	188	1,288	2,143	1,533	1,533
Gross Income/Sales	8,864	21,560	35,320	61,480	59,120	24,420	20,880	22,160	23,600	28,960	23,604	22,872	352,840
Less Manufacturing	3,520	8,000	12,400	20,800	18,400	8,200	7,200	8,400	9,200	11,200	9,160	8,880	125,360
Shipping	440	1,000	1,550	2,600	2,300	1,025	1,050	1,050	1,150	1,400	1,145	1,110	15,820
GROSS PROFIT	4,904	12,560	21,370	38,080	38,420	15,195	12,630	12,710	13,250	16,360	13,299	12,882	211,660
Less Marketing	1,500	6,000	7,000	15,000	10,000	4,000	7,400	4,000	4,000	4,000	7,500	7,500	78,000
Salaries	3,350	3,350	3,350	3,350	3,350	3,350	3,350	3,350	3,350	3,350	3,350	3,350	40,200
Office	2,000	2,000	2,000	2,000	2,000	2,000	2,000	2,000	2,000	2,000	2,000	2,000	24,000
Interest	1,850	1,850	2,050	2,050	2,050	2,050	2,050	2,050	2,050	2,050	2,050	2,050	24,200
Depreciation	180	180	180	180	180	180	180	180	180	180	180	180	180
Net Profit	(3,976)	(820)	6,790	15,500	20,840	3,615	(2,450)	1,130	1,670	4,780	(1,781)	(2,198)	45,080

EXHIBIT 2 *(continued)*

Figure 17 *(continued)*
UNIT SALES AND INCOME PROJECTION (60% OF ORIGINAL ESTIMATES) FOR THE 12 MONTHS ENDING JULY 31, 1981

	AUG	SEP	OCT	NOV	DEC	JAN	FEB	MAR	APR	MAY	JUN	JUL	TOTAL
Retail Units	125	135	140	145	150	150	150	150	150	150	150	150	150
Beginning Inventory/Units	2,203	1,763	1,163	233	173	1,293	1,678	1,138	508	1,318	2,978	3,291	2,203
Units Produced	—	—	—	1,500	2,500	1,000	—	—	1,500	2,500	1,000	—	10,000
Unit Sales													
Wholesale	320	270	360	510	300	210	240	330	330	360	390	420	3,912
Mail Order	120	180	300	360	390	120	150	120	120	150	165	180	2,307
College Reps	—	150	210	360	270	120	60	120	210	300	120	60	1,980
Magazine Features	—	—	—	180	300	120	60	30	15	15	6	—	726
Total Units Sold	440	600	930	1,560	1,380	615	540	630	690	840	687	666	9,402
Ending Inventory of Units	1,763	1,163	233	173	1,293	1,678	1,138	508	1,318	2,978	3,291	2,625	2,801
Gross Income/Sales	8,864	12,936	21,192	36,888	35,472	14,652	12,528	13,296	14,160	17,376	14,162	15,423	216,789
Less Manufacturing	3,520	4,800	7,440	12,480	11,040	4,920	4,320	5,040	5,520	6,720	5,496	5,328	75,216
Shipping	440	600	233	1,560	1,380	615	540	630	690	840	687	666	8,881
Gross Profit	4,904	7,536	13,519	22,848	23,052	9,117	7,668	7,626	7,950	9,816	7,979	9,429	132,692
Less Marketing	1,500	4,000	6,000	8,000	6,000	3,000	1,500	1,500	2,000	2,000	2,500	2,500	40,500
Salaries	3,350	3,350	3,350	3,350	3,350	3,350	3,350	3,350	3,350	3,350	3,350	3,350	40,200
Office	2,000	2,000	2,000	2,000	2,000	2,000	2,000	2,000	2,000	2,000	2,000	2,000	24,000
Interest	600	800	1,100	1,100	1,100	1,100	1,100	1,100	1,100	1,100	1,100	1,100	12,400
Depreciation	180	180	180	180	180	180	180	180	180	180	180	180	2,160
Net Profit (loss)	(2,726)	(2,794)	889	8,218	10,422	(513)	(462)	(504)	(680)	1,186	(1,151)	299	13,432

EXHIBIT 2 (continued)

Figure 18a BALANCE SHEET AS OF JULY 31, 1980 (Financial statements prepared by CPA without audit)

ASSETS

Current Assets
Cash	2,502.00	
Accounts Receivable	5,538.00	
Prepaid Advertising	1,188.00	
Inventory	24,244.00	
Total Current Assets		$33,472.00

Fixed Assets
Proprietary Molds	$5,200.00	
Mold Inserts and Mandrils	1,155.00	
Factory Tools and Machinery	1,162.00	
Office Equipment	4,850.00	
Total Fixed Assets	$12,367.00	
Less: Accumulated Depreciation	1,582.00	
Net Fixed Assets	10,785.00	

TOTAL ASSETS $44,257.00

LIABILITIES AND STOCKHOLDER'S EQUITY

Current Liabilities
Accounts payable	$5,748.00	
Accrued expenses	478.00	
Accrued Interest (Note 2)	5,175.00	
Total Current Liabilities	$11,401.00	

Long-Term Liabilities
Bonds Payable (Note 2)	$36,000.00	
Loan Payable – L. Osborne (Note 3)	3,337.00	
Loan Payable – B. Osborne	5,000.00	
Total Long-Term Liabilities		44,337.00
Total Liabilities		$55,738.00

Stockholder's Equity
Common Stock	0.00	
Retained Earnings (Deficit)	$11,481.00	
Total Stockholder's Equity		(11,481.00)

TOTAL LIABILITIES & STOCKHOLDER'S EQUITY $44,257.00

"See Accountant's Compilation Report"

EXHIBIT 2 *(continued)*

Figure 18b   STATEMENT OF INCOME & RETAINED EARNINGS FOR THE YEAR
ENDING JULY 31, 1980

Sales		$120,217.00
Cost of Goods Sold:		
Parts	$73,339.00	
Labor	12,026.00	
Total	$85,365.00	
Less: Ending Inventory	24,244.00	
Total Cost of Goods Sold		61,121.00
Gross Profit		$59,096.00
Operating Expenses:		
Advertising	$18,403.00	
Professional Fees	8,408.00	
Telephone	7,185.00	
Commissions	7,087.00	
Office Expenses	6,990.00	
Refunds and Bad Checks	6,200.00	
Shipping and Mailing Expense	5,690.00	
Interest Expense	5,175.00	
Rent	2,250.00	
Depreciation	1,583.00	
Marketing	444.00	
Bank Charges	383.00	
Accounting	250.00	
Mass. Corp. Excise Tax	228.00	
Travel	228.00	
Insurance	46.00	
Total Operating Expenses		70,550.00
Net Loss		$(11,481.00)
Retained Earnings - July 31, 1979		
Retained Earnings (Deficit) July 31, 1980		$(11,481.00)

"See Accountant's Compilation Report"

EXHIBIT 2 (continued)

Figure 18c STATEMENT OF CHANGES IN FINANCIAL POSITION FOR THE YEAR ENDING JULY 31, 1980

SOURCE OF WORKING CAPITAL

Operations:		
Charges not requiring use of working capital		$1,583.00
Issuance of 5-year bonds		36,000.00
Receipt of loans payable		12,000.00
Total Sources of Working Capital		$49,583.00

USE OF WORKING CAPITAL

Operations:		
Net loss for the year	$11,481.00	
Purchase of Fixed Assets	12,367.00	
Decrease in loans payable	3,664.00	
Total Uses of Working Capital		27,512.00

TOTAL INCREASE IN WORKING CAPITAL $22,071.00

COMPOSITION OF WORKING CAPITAL

	End of initial year	Beginning of initial year	Increase or (decrease) in working capital
Current Assets			
Cash	$2,502.00	— 0 —	$2,502.00
Accounts Receivable	5,538.00	— 0 —	5,538.00
Prepaid Advertising	1,188.00	— 0 —	1,188.00
Inventory	24,244.00	— 0 —	24,244.00
Total Current Assets	$33,472.00	— 0 —	
Current Liabilities			
Accounts Payable	$5,748.00	— 0 —	5,748.00
Accrued Expenses	478.00	— 0 —	478.00
Accrued Interest	5,175.00	— 0 —	5,175.00
Total Current Liabilities	$11,401.00	— 0 —	
Working Capital	$22,071.00	— 0 —	
TOTAL INCREASE IN WORKING CAPITAL			$22,071.00

EXHIBIT 2 *(continued)*

Figure 18d NOTES TO THE FINANCIAL STATEMENTS FOR THE YEAR ENDED JULY 31, 1980

Note 1   SUMMARY OF SIGNIFICANT ACCOUNTING POLICIES:
Inventory is stated at standard cost, which approximate actual cost on a first-in, first-out basis and does not exceed market.

Depreciation of equipment is computed using the straight line method over the estimated useful lives of the assets.

The tax year ends on December 31 and as of this date the initial State and Federal Tax Returns for December 31, 1979 have not been prepared.

The Corporation was incorporated on July 31, 1979. This financial statement of July 31, 1980 presents the activity during the 12 months since incorporating. Some start-up costs were paid for in June and July of 1979 and all have been expensed during this fiscal year ending July 31, 1980.

Note 2   BONDS PAYABLE:
The 5-year bonds consist of the following:

20% Notes due August 1984	$11,000.00
20% Notes due October 1984	11,500.00
20% Notes due November 1984	2,500.00
20% Notes due January 1985	11,000.00
	$36,000.00

These Notes are secured by all assets. Interest of 20 percent per year is payable semi-annually on the date of purchase. As of July 31, 1980, $3,600 of interest has become due but unpaid. The bonds are convertible into a percent of common stock, calculated at 15 percent ownership for every $100,00 of bonds.

Note 3   LOAN PAYABLE L. OSBORNE:
The original amount of the loan to Laurence Osborne was $7,000. The balance has been reduced by taking repayments against the loan in lieu of salary.

Note 4   ERRORS
There are two errors in this statement. The amount for "bad checks and returns" is high by $3,400. The accountant noted this debit memo in the bank return, and it was not reconciled with a later deposit of the same amount. A large check had been mis-endorsed, and had to be redeposited. The gross sales would likewise be over-stated by the same amount.

EXHIBIT 2 *(continued)*

Figure 18d (concluded)

The accounts payable are closer to $15,000. Two pages of the older payables were somehow not included. They do exist, although there has been about $3,000 of payments made on them since the end of July.

Finally - the first run was a production debacle. A firm hired to do the assembly went suddenly bankrupt, and we had to become an appliance manufacturing firm on the spot. Only a small portion of the workers were trained, and the entire assembly line was makeshift. We managed to get 4,400 out in about a month of continuous effort, but the labor cost per item was close to $4.00 when the smoke finally cleared. Added to this much higher cost, 1,100 of the first run were sold at an average of $9.50 to distributors to obtain the cash to complete the run.

This combination of high cost and a low average sale price on the first run is combined with the much more efficient second run, the costs of which are accurately represented in the $7.95 cost of goods sold total in the exhibit. One banker insisted that our unit cost was close to $10.00. If we hadn't learned how to make them after the first run, that could well have been true - but since May, the second run, we've got that cost contained.

Janet Luhrs and Renee Williams

In October 1988 Janet Luhrs and Renee Williams were moving forward with a product idea Renee had developed called "Babypak," a fabric sling for a parent to use in carrying a baby. Traditionally, American mothers had carried babies in front and Japanese mothers in back by means of such slings. After trying both methods, Renee had preferred the Japanese arrangement and had consequently developed a Japanese-style sling with what she regarded as improvements in configuration and strength over the Japanese product.

After considerable work on improvement of the product, unsuccessful attempts to sell through mail order, design and development of a box-type package and exploration for suitable manufacturers in the Orient, the two had visited the headquarters of Toys 'R Us and received an order for 15,000 units, to begin with a first shipment of 5,000. This put them, Janet observed, "in the process of trying to figure out the best way to set up our business so it will be a successful one."

Renee Williams

Renee Williams had attended art school and beautician school following graduation from high school, and then gone to work as a beautician. She commented:

> One of my classmates who had dropped out before graduating from high school had also become a beautician, and by the time I was ready to go to work she already had her own beauty salon. So I went to work for her.

After working a while in other shops, Renee decided in 1977 to open her own. She recalled her reasoning at the time.

> I figured, that if my friend could set up her own business without even graduating from high school, then I ought to be able to do it, too. Besides, the shop I was working for at the time didn't seem to me to be treating people very well. I wanted to leave, and it turned out some of the other beauticians did too. So when I opened my own salon several of them came to work for me.

A problem, she said, was that running a salon and managing other people was very demanding work, which provided meager returns. Beauticians who worked for her, she found, often made more money than she did after she paid for wages, rent, health insurance and other costs of doing business. The salon was always profitable, but revenues in the best year were only $150,000, leaving income after expenses for her and her husband, who worked as receptionist, of around $30,000. When the difficulty of operating it was compounded by arrival of her first baby in 1982, she sold the salon and opened a small solo salon in her home, to which some of her clients followed her.

Occasionally she came up with other product ideas.

> I've always been inventive. Even back in school I used to think I would like to invent something and patent it. The trouble was that at the time I couldn't think of any products worth patenting.

While operating the salon she had tried commercializing some ideas with a friend she had met in art school, Janet Luhrs, about whom she said:

> Janet is also inventive, and we had fun working together even though our ideas didn't pan out.

They had tried making some products they called "Terrific Toilets," which were toilet covers, and packaged "Schmores" for microwaves. A combination of peanut butter, cookies, chocolate and sugar in plastic bags, the schmores were supposed to be a product that could be quickly heated to a sweet, gooey consistency in microwave ovens. Renee recalled the result:

> The trouble was that the sugar crystallized into a hard substance that made the schmores hard to eat.

Renee and Janet had also tried working up a video program for high school students. After paying a small fee the students would progress through a series of videotaped lessons presented by well-known personalities. After watching these, the students would prepare and present their own fashion show. Renee recalled:

> We showed it to schools and they liked it. The problem was they didn't have any money to pay for it, so they just took the lesson plans we had developed and used them on their own without the tapes and without paying us anything.

Baby Pak

Then had come the Baby Pak idea. When Renee's first baby arrived in 1982, a Japanese lady had given her a sling from Japan, which Renee had used with pleasure and then passed along to another mother when her baby outgrew it. Arrival of Renee's second baby in late 1986 had prompted Renee to wish for another such sling and consequently to design a copy for herself which a friend who was skilled as a seamstress helped her make. Working through a series of a half dozen prototypes, Renee added improvements to the design which fitted it better to the baby and made it stronger. A flyer depicting applications of the Baby Pak appears in Exhibit 1.

Having created what she considered to be a superior product, she decided to try selling it. She had noticed advertisements for baby products offered by other individuals in a diaper service newspaper and decided to telephone some of them to learn how selling through the paper worked. Running the advertisements cost, she found, around $60 per month. After enlisting her mother-in-law's help as a seamstress to make the products, she ran advertisements in that paper and in *Mothering* magazine, but found that the volume of sales did not cover the costs of advertising.

She concluded that she needed to find a source of greater sales volume and it occurred to her that a store like K-Mart or Toys R Us might afford such an opportunity. For help in writing letters to them, she decided to ask her friend, Janet Luhrs. "If there's one thing I can't do it's write anything," Renee observed, "and Janet is a good writer."

Janet Luhrs

Janet picked up the conversation from there.

> Writing and art are two strong points with me, so when Renee asked me in April to help her out with these letters, I was glad to.

Following high school Janet had gone to art school, where she met Renee. Janet recalled her own career.

> In high school I had been the best in art. But in art school everyone else had been the best, too. It was really competitive, and I just didn't feel like buckling down on it at that point. So I needed to move on to something else and went on to the University of Washington where I got a bachelor's degree in journalism.

After journalism school I worked for a while in the newspaper business and then did my own freelance writing. Then I went to law school. I had met my husband, and he had gone to law school. A woman I had worked with in the writing business had also gone to law school. So why hadn't I gone to law school? One morning I woke up and said 'I think I'll go to law school.' I had been getting tired of the writing anyway, and thought maybe going to law school would lend another dimension to my writing and my research.

Law really wasn't for me, although I enjoyed parts of it, like working for the public defender up in Alaska and conducting trials. A lot of it is just too dry. I'm good at writing and artistic work. But in law you just gobble up what some judge said and spit it back out in a nice way.

Then when I had a baby I found I couldn't flip my brain on and off to do law. That work is intense and I found I could not do it all day and then go home and say goo goo. And besides I just didn't want to work full-time any more. It was just too much.

Also, I had continued to do freelance writing all through law school, and in fact, I have one account, a newsletter, that I still do work for. Then I got pregnant again, and when I'm that way, I'm just a wreck and can't do anything.

But about three months after I had the second baby, I started to get "antsy" again and think about what else to do. I thought maybe I'd start writing again, and then Renee approached me with this baby pack design and asked if I wanted to go into business with her. It was perfect, so I said sure.

First steps

The two women asked advice of anyone whom they thought could help. Renee told her hairdressing clients what she and her partner were trying to do and through one of them met a successful inventor in Bellingham, Washington who gave them suggestions and leads on packaging the product. Janet asked her husband, a maritime lawyer, for leads and through them located a man who specialized in making arrangements for manufacturing in the Far East. Through inquiries with manufacturers' representatives they learned about sales markups and "hidden" costs. For instance, there might be a requirement that 98 percent of the products be perfect or else the buyer could cancel the deal. And to obtain a UPC bar code for the box they found they would have to pay $300 to a company which monopolized the standard code.

A manufacturer's representative told them that the best way to follow up on the encouraging mail response they had received from Toys R Us would be to make a personal appointment and both fly to New Jersey to meet with the buyer. Renee recalled:

It was hard for me to accept the idea of such a big expense. But we did it, and everything worked out perfectly.

Janet added:

Others told us either we wouldn't get in to see the buyer at all, or if we did, he'd only give us five minutes. But he was very friendly, we had no trouble getting in, and he spent two hours looking over the product and giving us helpful advice.

One of the things a sales representative told us was that we had to ask for an order to get one. If he had not told us that, I would have just waited for the buyer to tell us he would place an order. And he probably never would have. But in the interview we did ask for the order, and we got one for 15,000 units, the first delivery to be for 5,000. He didn't even try to beat us down on price, but took what we offered, $15 a unit.

Renee concluded:

I couldn't believe we would be able to get an order without a successful test marketing program first. But we did.

The partners had also explored possible manufacturing arrangements. Currently, it appeared that a local firm would be able to have them made in the Orient and deliver them to the partners for $7 per unit, including customs. It also appeared that there would be no problem with import restrictions that applied to clothing.

The supplier wanted guarantee of payment on delivery, however. This would require more cash than either partner could provide and consequently they had started to prepare a business plan, excerpts of which are attached in Exhibits 2 and 3, and approached banks for possible loans. Rainier bank had said it could probably provide a letter of credit guaranteeing payment if the two women could produce enough cash to back up the letter. Renee figured she could raise part of the money from her house but not enough.

Next concerns

A question on the mind of both women was how to turn these beginnings into a longer term business with high profitability. A schedule of activities Janet saw as necessary to start the company appears as Exhibit 2. She had also prepared a financial forecast which appears as Exhibit 3. Both had young children and wanted to be able to stay home with them. Neither had much capital. Janet observed that she hated borrowing money and did not want to be in debt personally. Renee said she had thought of selling stock, but did not want more partners and was not anxious to have the profits diluted by other owners.

> *I read in a magazine about two women who were making a lot of money selling designer bottles, and we heard about a couple of women back east with another product. The first pair seem to be making a lot of money and the other two are just squeaking by. We want to know what will determine which we will be like and figure out a way to be like the ones who are really successful.*

EXHIBIT 1 Baby Pak advertising flyer

Baby Pak
The Best Baby Carrier!

P.O. Box 25332
Seattle, Wa.
98125
(206)633-4514

1 - Although Baby Pak is best used as a back pak:

2 - You can also use Baby Pak as a front pak for smaller babies.

3 - Or as an emergency high chair. (Directions: Sit baby in contoured seat of Pak. Insert legs through leg holes. Criss-cross shoulder straps across baby's chest, and around chair back, criss-cross and thru D-rings and tie straps.)

4 - Or a safety seat for shopping carts. (Use directions from #3 above.)

5 - Or a safety seat for high chairs. (Use directions from #3 above.)

If baby falls asleep while on your back, use receiving blanket folded into a triangle to hold baby's head close to your body. Tuck corners of blanket under shoulder straps, or simply use a shawl around baby and yourself.

EXHIBIT 2 List of activities (copied from handwritten notes)

Sept '88
        Letter of credit - #1 for $53,000
        Manufacturing Order - # 1 Thaw, 5,300 paks
        Miscellaneous - Incorporate
Oct. '88
        Loan on A/R, Bank Pays - #1 Box co. $3,500 for 5,000, R. Mann $1,000
        Box Orders - #1, 5,300 boxes
        Miscellaneous - Work with R. Mann on box design
Nov. '88
        Make Sales - 2,400 pks to Kids R Us, Target
        Miscellaneous - Source RSVP better price on pak mfg.
Dec. '88
        Box Orders - Receive Box #1
        Payments to others - Box co $1,590 #1
Jan. '89
        Letter of credit - LOC for run #2
        Loan on A/R, Bank Pays - Loan on A/R - Pays Thaw $53,000
        Manufacturing Order - Order Thaw 5,000 pks #2
        Deliver to Stores - 5,000 pks to Toys R Us #1, 100 pks to REI, run #1
Feb. '89
        Receive payment from stores - REI $1,500, apply to box co #2
        Box Orders - Order box #2
        Payments to others - Box co, $1,500 #2
Apr. '89
        Letter of credit - LOC for run #3
        Payment to Bank - $60,000 #1
        Receive payment from stores - Toys R Us $75,000 less 3,000 hold back
        Manufacturing Order - 5,000 paks #3 Thaw
        Box Orders - Receive boxes #2
        Payments to others - Box co $1,500 #2
May '89
        Loan on A/R, Bank Pays - Loan on A/R #2
        Box Orders - Order boxes #3
        Deliver to Stores - 2,600 pks Toys R Us, 560 Kids R Us, 100 REI, 1,755 Target, run #2
        Payments to others - Box co $1,500 #3
Jun '89
        Make Sales - Large sales push for run #5 K Mart
Jul '89
        Letter of credit - LOC's for run #4
        Manufacturing Order - Thaw for 5,000 pks #4
        Box Orders - Receive box #3
        Make Sales - Dallas trade show
        Payments to others - Box co $15,00 #3
        Miscellaneous -
Aug. '89
        Loan on A/R, Bank - Loan on A/R #3
        Payment to Bank - Pay $50,150 on loan #2
        Receive payment from stores - $75,000
        Deliver to Stores - 2,600 pks to Toys R Us, 560 Kids R Us, 100 REI, 1,755 Target, run #3
        Payments to others - Box co $1500   #4

EXHIBIT 2 *(continued)*

Oct. '89

      Letter of credit - For run #5

      Manufacturing Order - Thaw run #5, 13265 pks

      Box Orders - Receive boxes #4

      Payments to others - Box co $1,500 $4

Nov. '89

      Loan on A/R, Bank - Loan on A/R #4

      Payment to Bank - $50,150 From Thaw #3

      Box Orders - Order box #5, 0.47/box, 13,265 pks

      Deliver to Stores - 2,600 toys R Us, 560 Kids R Us, 100 REI, 1,755 Target, run #4

Jan. '90

      Letter of credit - LOC #6

      Manufacturing Order - 13,265 pks, Thaw, #6

      Box Orders - Receive box #5 for 13265 pks, $3,117, 0.47/box

      Payments to others - Box co $3,117

Feb. '90

      Loan on A/R, Bank - $132,650 on #5

      Payment to Bank - pay on #4

      Receive payment from stores - Receive #4, $75,000

      Box Orders - #6 for 13,265 pks, $3,117

      Deliver to Stores - #6, 5,015 Service PX, 8,250 K-Mart

      Payments to others - Box c $3,117

Apr. '90

      Letter of credit - #7

      Manufacturing Order - 13,265 pks, Thaw #7

      Box Orders - Receive #6 for 13,265 pks, $3,117

      Payments to others - Box co, $3,117

May '90

      Loan on A/R, Bank pays Thaw - $132,650 on A/R #6

      Payment to Bank - #5

      Receive payment from stores - Receive #5 for $198,975

      Box Orders - Order box #7 for 13,265 pks, $3,117

      Deliver to Stores - #6 to first yr accts 5,015 and to K-Mart 8,250

      Payments to others - Box co, $3,117

Jul. '90

      Letter of credit - #8

      Manufacturing Order - Thaw #8 for 13,265 pks

      Box Orders - #7 for 13,265 pks, $3,117

      Make Sales - Dallas show

      Payments to others - Box co. $3,117

Aug. '90

      Loan on A/R, Bank Pays Thaw - $132,650 on #7

      Payment to Bank - Pay #6

      Receive payment from stores - #6 for $195,975

      Box Orders - #8 for 13,265 pks $3,117

      Deliver to Stores - ## to first yr accts 5,015, to K-Mart 8,250

      Payments to others - Box co, $3,117

EXHIBIT 2 *(continued)*

Oct. '90

    Letter of credit - #9
    Manufacturing Order - Thaw #9
    Box Orders - Receive #8 for 13,265 pks $3,117
    Deliver to Stores - #8 to first yr accts 5,015, to K-Mart 8,250
    Payments to others - Box co $3,117

Nov. '90

    Loan on A/R, Bank Pays Thaw - $132,650 on A/R #8
    Payment to Bank - Pay #7
    Receive payment from stores - #7 for $198,975

Feb. '91

    Payment to Bank - #8
    Receive payment from stores - #8 for $198,975
    Deliver to Stores - #9

EXHIBIT 3a Financial forecast Sept. '88 – Aug. '89 (copied from handwritten notes)

	Sep'88	Oct'88	Nov'88	Dec'88	Jan'89	Feb'89	Mar'89	Apr'89	May'89	Jun'89	Jul'89	Aug'89	Totals
Revenue													
Toys R Us								72,000			37,440		109,440
4% Hold Back													
REI						1,500					1,500		3,000
40 Sm. Specialty											3,000		3,000
Kids R Us											3,375		3,375
Toys R Us Canada											1,125		1,125
Toys R Us Intnl											900		900
Target											26,325		26,325
K-Mart													
Total Revenue						1,500		72,000			73,665		147,165
Cost of Sales													
Thaw		5,300			53,000				50,150			50,150	153,300
Eagle Box				1,590		1,500		1,500	1,500		1,500		12,890
Richard Marin		1,000											1,000
Total Cost of Sales		6,300	—	1,590	53,000	1,500	—	1,500	51,650	—	1,500	50,150	167,190
Gross Profit		(6,300)		(1,590)	(53,000)	—	—	70,500	(51,650)	—	72,165	(50,150)	(20,025)
Expenses													
Salaries $1K Each								2,000	2,000	2,000	2,000	2,000	10,000
Payroll													
Outside Services													
Supplies													
Repairs and Maint													
Advertising													
Deliv and Travel			1,500							1,500	1,500		4,500
Acctg and Legal		50	50	50	50	50	50	50	50	50	50	50	550
Rent													
Telephone		20	24	24	24	24	24	24	24	24	24	24	260
Utilities													
Insurance			200	98	98	98	98	98	98	98	98	98	1,082
Other Expenses													
Total Expenses		70	1,774	172	172	172	172	2,172	2,172	3,672	3,672	2,172	16,392
Net													(36,417)

EXHIBIT 3b Financial forecast, Sept. '89-Aug. '90 (copied from handwritten notes)

	Sep'89	Oct'89	Nov'89	Dec'89	Jan'90	Feb'90	Mar'90	Apr'90	May'90	Jun'90	Jul'90	Aug'90	Totals
Revenue													
Toys R Us			37,440			37,440			37,440			37,440	149,760
4% Hold Back		3,000				1,560			1,560			1,560	7,680
REI			1,500			1,500			1,500			1,500	6,000
40 Sm. Specialty			3,000			3,000			3,000			3,000	12,000
Kids R Us			3,375			3,375			3,375			3,375	13,500
Toys R Us Canada			1,125			1,125			1,125			1,125	4,500
Toys R Us Intnl			900			900			900			900	3,600
Target			26,325			26,325			26,325			26,325	105,300
K-Mart									123,750			123,750	247,500
Total Revenue		3,000	73,665			75,225			198,975			198,975	549,840
Cost of Sales													
Thaw			50,150			132,650			132,650			132,650	448,100
Eagle Box		1,500	3,117		3,117	3,117		3,117	3,117		3,117	3,117	23,319
Total		1,500	53,267		3,117	135,767		3,117	135,767		3,117	135,767	471,419
Gross Profit													
Expenses													
Payroll													
Salaries $1K ea.	2,000	2,000	2,000	2,000	2,000	2,000	2,000	2,000	2,000	2,000	2,000	2,000	24,000
Outside Services													
Supplies													
Repairs and Maint													
Advertising													
Deliv and Travel											1,500		1,500
Acctg and Legal	50	50	50	50	50	50	50	50	50	50	50	50	600
Rent													
Telephone	24	24	24	24	24	24	24	24	24	24	24	24	288
Utilities													
Insurance	98	200	98	98	98	98	98	98	98	98	98	98	1,278
Other Expenses													
Total Expenses	2,172	2,274	2,172	2,172	2,172	2,172	2,172	2,172	2,172	2,172	3,672	2,172	27,666
Net													325,134

EXHIBIT 3c Financial forecast, Sept. '90- Aug. '91 (copied from handwritten notes)

	Sep'90	Oct'90	Nov'90	Dec'90	Jan'91	Feb'91	Mar'91	Apr'91	May'91	Jun'91	Jul'91	Aug'91	Totals
Revenue													
Toys R Us			37,440			37,440		1,560		1,560		1,560	
4% Hold Back			1,560			1,560							
REI			1,500			1,500							
40 Sm. Specialty			3,000			3,000							
Kids R Us			3,375			3,375							
Toys R Us Canada			1,125			1,125							
Toys R Us Intnl			900			900							
Target			26,325			26,325							
K-Mart			123,750			123,750							
Total Revenue			198,975			198,975		0		0		0	
Cost of Sales													
Thaw			132,650										
Eagle Box		3,117											
Total		3,117	132,650			198,975		1,560		1,560		1,560	
Gross Profit		(3,117)	17,425			198,975							266,863
Expenses													
Salaries $1K ea	2,000	2,000	2,000	2,000									
Payroll													
Outside Services													
Supplies													
Repairs and Maint													
Advertising													
Deliv. and Travel													
Acctg and Legal	50	50	50	50									
Rent													
Telephone	24	24	24	24									
Utilities													
Insurance	200	98	98	98									
Other Expenses													
Total Expenses	2,274	2,172	2,172	2,172									
Net	2,172	2,172	2,172	2,172									

Knight Brothers

In November 1980 Richard Knight and his brother, James, were reviewing the business plan they had prepared for setting up a retail store to sell microcomputer time by the half-hour. They had chosen a location in Harvard Square, a very busy intersection in the Boston area, and had lined up computers they would lease and set up for operation in the store. What remained, as they saw it, was to obtain venture capital, set up the store and open for business. To do this, they felt their plan needed to be in good order, and they needed an idea of just how much capital they should seek from what sort of people, and on what terms. A copy of the plan, such as they had prepared it to date, appears in Exhibit 1.

Born in Providence, R.I. in 1944, Richard Knight had attended boarding school and earned a B.A. degree from Colorado College. After a tour of duty in the U.S. Army, he took a job with the First National Bank of Boston. In 1970 he decided to leave the world of corporate finance, remarking, "I hate suits and I hate, absolutely despise, organizational politics." Subsequently, he and his wife traveled to many parts of the world, until she injured her leg, and they decided to return for extended medical care in Boston. He recalled:

> At that time I had nothing to do. I was interested in finance, the stock market, data manipulation, forecasting, and so on—just things I had picked up since leaving college. But I wanted to learn more about business and to try fooling around with forecasting and computers, so it seemed like business school would be a good thing to get involved in.

He enrolled in the MBA program at Boston University and found a professor who would allow him to store data on his computer account. As a part-time student, his course of study took several years, during which he made extensive use of his computer access to develop forecasting programs.

> The tuition at B.U. was fairly high, but I figured I was getting around $30,000 worth of computer time that more than made up for it.

When his access to the terminal ceased upon graduation in 1979, he turned to microcomputers to carry on his work, operating in conjunction with a Boston stock brokerage firm.

James Knight, Richard's brother, who was 10 years younger, had earned an undergraduate degree in banking at Boston University and more recently had applied for admission to the MBA program at Dartmouth. Soon after graduation, with his wife expecting their first child, he looked around Providence for a company to buy and develop. Failing to find one, he moved to New York, where he became involved in Dynamotion, a company which manufactured a jingle-bell box for point-of-purchase sales. James commented:

> It was such an odd concept that I thought we should get orders first and then manufacture the product only after we were sure there was a market. But the financial backers disagreed, made me president and told me to go ahead anyway. A month later I left to join an investment firm. Three months later Dynamotion went broke.

At the investment firm James worked first in institutional sales for five years and then in mergers and acquisitions.

The Knight brothers had also tried a venture together as crude oil brokers in the late 1970s. Their father had suggested the opportunity as one that might yield commissions as high as $250,000 or more per day if they could close a big deal. Over a six-month period the brothers ran up a phone bill of over $4,500 attempting to set up oil purchases between suppliers and sellers, with themselves as middlemen, but they could not close a deal. Richard remarked:

> *Everyone was too greedy. Sales kept falling through because different people involved all wanted bigger and bigger cuts, first $1 million, then $2 million and so forth. There was so much money involved. It was hard for us to believe that a multimillion dollar deal would be entirely aborted because it wasn't more "multi."*

During that time, Richard negotiated to take over a bankrupt oil refinery in Puerto Rico, but that deal also fell through, just before papers were signed. "Too much graft, corruption and payoffs involved," Jim observed. Nonetheless, both men looked back on the oil endeavor as "an incredible adventure." By contrast, Jim said his work in mergers and acquisitions at the New York investment bank made him "bored to tears." Richard said he felt the most important lesson from the oil venture was understanding the reason they failed.

> *The scheme was entirely feasible, but we had no credibility and no credit. We had not proven to anybody that we could conceive and capitalize a venture, so they refused to believe in us or back us.*

Some other venture attempts by Richard that never progressed beyond the pencil and paper stage included selling thermostats, a Mazda dealership and a pasta pushcart to provide homemade pasta with several alternative sauces from a small wagon in Harvard Square to people rushing out of the subway stations headed home without groceries.

The decision to pursue the idea of a computer time rental store was made in the fall of 1980 when James came from New York to Boston on personal business. He and Richard met for lunch at the Parker House and discussed the concept. Richard had suggested the idea 18 months earlier, but James had flatly said it would not work.

> *Richard wanted to set up a store full of APPLES with $15,000, but I figured it would cost 10 or more times that much.*

Since that time, however, James had noticed the spreading popularity of microcomputers. The idea of renting them on an hourly basis in a retail store to hobbyists, small business managers and larger firms with temporary word-processing overloads seemed like it might succeed. Rental cost in Harvard Square, he and Richard knew, would be high, in the range of $2,000 per month for a suitably sized storefront on ground level. But the traffic in the area was high, consisting largely of college students, but also shoppers and business people going between the local subway station and downtown Boston. It also included many who were fairly affluent. The two men knew of no other computer time rental store in the country. The only related firms they knew of in the area were an arcade with pinball machines and computer games approximately one-third mile east of Harvard Square, and a small microcomputer retail sales store approximately one-third mile north of the Square.

Harvard, which was right on the Square, was among the most expensive universities in the nation to attend, and included many bright students who were both "well-heeled" and fascinated with computers. Recently it had made computer programming literacy one of the requirements for liberal arts graduation. In addition, many of its graduate students had use for the machines in their studies and research. The two brothers started preparing a prospectus and soon produced the document appearing in Exhibit 1, replete with computer generated alternative financial forecasts.

Beyond the initial store, they contemplated additional enterprises. They figured they would expand from the first store to 20 others at different locations within a year-and-a-half. After that, they surmised that their concept might become obsolete as larger companies moved into retailing on a larger scale and more people installed microcomputers at home. Second, however, they wanted to explore the concept of a laser printing service. Xerox was just introducing a machine which would allow quick and very high-quality printing with any defined typeface, and the two could see that it would permit them to provide a high-quality and very flexible printing service to any customer in the country by telephone. The machine would cost on the order of $150,000 to install, however.

Third, they wanted to market a new point-of-purchase marketing aid consisting of a "light box" about a foot long with 50 spaces for L.E.D. letters and numbers, which could be individually programmed by a retailer to flash advertisements on a running loop basis like a stock exchange ticker tape display or the Times Square News. This too would take substantial capital.

Their immediate objective, however, was to raise capital for the first store. Once they were able to do that, they felt they would have established credibility in the financial community, which would let them move on to additional and larger enterprises in the future.

EXHIBIT 1 Think Tanks business plan

I. INTRODUCTION

It is our intention to form a partnership to purchase microcomputers (hardware) and the peripheral equipment necessary to adapt the microcomputers to many different uses along with the programming (software) that will facilitate adaptation of the microcomputers to the greatest number of prospective clients.

In connection with this we intend, once established, to offer our clients the opportunity to lease or purchase the computers, peripheral equipment and the programming from us, should their need for access to a computer make it more sensible for them to have it at their place of business or residence instead of coming to us.

We intend to lease store space in the Harvard Square area of Cambridge. Renovations will be made to the store to make it modern and suitable to our needs. We will advertise primarily on the radio in the Boston/Cambridge area to make people aware of the services we are offering.

The general partners will keep the limited partners apprised on a timely basis of the completion of the various stages of development.

II. CONCEPTUAL PLAN

Over the next 10 years, usage of microcomputers by the average American household will undergo a major expansion. It has been established that the demand will exist in the next decade for the home computer to handle such matters as the family bank account, grocery shopping, and budgeting of family energy consumption among many other uses. Given this need, the American public will have to become far more familiar than currently with the computer and its uses. As this is primarily an educational process, the benefits to the organization that can establish a foothold in the confidence of the American household will be sizable. Establishing our store, which we plan to call Think Tanks, at this time will allow us to take full advantage of the opportunities outlined above.

A perceived roadblock to the widespread use of the computer in the home or small business is the cost of acquiring a computer. From marketing studies we know that the consumption of high-ticket home usage items can be readily achieved. As evidence of this, the BETAMAX system and the VHS system have become extremely popular. A BETAMAX, or comparable machine, costs slightly under $1,000.00 per unit. The cost of the microcomputers currently available appears to present a certain argument for elasticity of the demand for high-ticket items for the home.

Even though we cannot control the cost of the hardware to the consumer, we can offer a far less expensive way for the typical consumer to explore the product and have use of it. An individual will be able to walk into our store and will be met by one of our employees. The employee will be familiar with the operation of microcomputers and will attempt to ascertain the exact interests of customers while helping them learn and experiment with the various systems. We feel that the ability to offer many different microcomputer products and allow customers to investigate the advantages and disadvantages of each system will bring us people who are not only curious but also interested in purchasing.

EXHIBIT 1 *(continued)*

In addition to the regular computer services the client might wish to perform, a separate area of the store will be devoted entirely to computer assisted games. For example the person interested in playing backgammon with one of the acknowledged experts could sit down in front of a television type screen and attempt his skill. The customer interested in this type of service will have access to the games on the computers in return for the payment for the time the computer is used. The inherent market for this type of service in the proximity to a college should be large.

The success of the game SPACE INVADERS is well-documented. We will be able to offer many games of this type on a comparable cost basis.

The use of the CRT, or Cathode Ray Tube, is an important part of the concept. The idea of sitting in front of a simple keyboard and typing is not appealing, but the ability to look at what you are typing or look at the game you are playing is quite intriguing.

Computers now being tested as a learning tool with children in school systems have been quite successful and the reception to them has been quite good.

III.   DEFINITION OF MARKET

We project that the average age of our initial customers will be on the low side. Somewhere in the mid-twenties to start is the best estimation that we are able to make. We would hope that the age will rise, as people in the area become more familiar with our store.

The application to so many areas is exciting. We believe that the possibilities for the near future from the neighborhood concept are of a most exciting nature. Once the store becomes a member of the community, the sales potential for servicing local business accounts in, for example, accounts receivable or inventory control is tremendous. A local doctor might send a secretary down to our store at the end of every week to input data on patients the doctor has seen during the week, what types of problems they sought help on, what the diagnoses were, how much time the doctor spent with each patient, and billing information. This would computerize the doctor's records, giving cross-reference ability on ailments and telling where the doctor stands from a personal financial point of view so he or she can plan accordingly.

If initial demand meets our expectations, we want to be prepared to expand into other sectors of the greater Boston-area market. This area is one of the largest population centers in the United States, and it has an extraordinarily high percentage of students because it contains many colleges and universities. In the Harvard Square area there are five: Harvard University, Massachusetts Institute of Technology, Boston University, Northeastern University, and Boston College. Their combined student population exceeds 100,000.

Cambridge is regarded by industry as a high-technology center and was the forerunner of what is currently described as the Route 128 technology belt.

We foresee the prime customers for our concept to include: small businesses, professionals, students, leisure-time users, elementary schools, high schools, learning systems users and data-base users. Let us consider each of these perceived potential markets.

Small Business

There exist well in excess of 2000 small businesses in the immediate area of the proposed store location. The potential for this market is substantial. Traditionally, small business has not been able to take advantage of many factors which for the larger businesses bring about economies of scale. One area in which the small business has been at a severe disadvantage has been information systems.

Typically, the small business has not had any form of sophisticated inventory control. The application potential of the microcomputer to this area is extensive, from information aspects to reporting and keeping accounting control. How many small businesses can monitor their cost of goods sold in an efficient manner? The time required in taking inventory could be eliminated with a computer providing all this information. The business owner could tell at any time what type of a mark-down should be used while still remaining profitable.

EXHIBIT 1 *(continued)*

Keeping track of accounts receivable is a problem, and their aging can cost the small business a lot of money. Using a microcomputer the small business could analyze the profitability of various products in inventory. In planning, this would be most useful information. Many accounting costs which the small business now sustains could be reduced by adding a microcomputer. Many other applications are possible with the use of a microcomputer, but the above gives a feel for the potential of this segment of the market.

Even though the microcomputers address themselves to the small-business market, there is still a gap. We believe that the problem is twofold, the first being the educational or confidence gap. No one likes to be regarded as unsophisticated or unintelligent. The owner of a small business who lacks expertise to operate a small computer may consequently hold back from buying one. If to this inhibition we than add the factor of cost, we would expect to find that a large sector of the potential market has not purchased. We propose to solve these two roadblocks by offering computer time on a low cost basis so users can learn without any type of capital contribution.

Then, should a customer decide that the benefits of the microcomputer are as extensive as we think, and that acquisition of a computer is desirable, we will offer to sell or lease one. This makes sense because of the reluctance of the small business to commit to a capital expense. We would offer attractive terms to induce business owners to enter into the lease and get the hardware installed.

To summarize, for the small business the microcomputer's advantages are extensive, incorporating such positives as inventory control and the ability to compete effectively from an informational decision-making point of view with large businesses of the same industry. Our approach to this segment of our market is to show customers the obvious advantages of adding the expertise of the microcomputer to their business. This can then be accomplished in three ways; leasing time on our microcomputers, leasing the customers their own microcomputers, or selling them microcomputers.

Professionals

Programs at our store will offer multiple uses for the professional sector of the economy including some of the same advantages provided to the small business sector. The professional is typically in a service-oriented business involving significant personal interaction with each client. One factor that places a ceiling on effectiveness of practitioners is their ability to handle the flow of information and statistics on each new client. The strain placed on a professional's time is significant, and there is an optimization point after which the value of additional clientele can become negative. Although this optimization point can be raised by adding more staff, there is a cost trade-off which makes this impractical beyond a certain level. More importantly, the time of the professional becomes occupied with managing the increased staff, rather than drawing an enlarged clientele and thereby increasing the revenue base. Insofar as we help increase the time that professionals can spend on increasing their income, we provide a valuable service.

There are the additional benefits allowing the professional with a small office to compete effectively with larger offices. This becomes especially important as we examine the move to more advertising and competition on the part of professionals, from doctors to accountants to lawyers. The professional who does not have all the cost effectiveness of the large firm will be forced to innovate in order to survive. We offer innovativeness to the professional with a smaller office.

The uses take several forms. Word processing and accounting are only two of many useful capabilities for professionals. For lawyers, time records could be stored on the microcomputer which, in turn, would easily handle the billing of the clients. The information which the lawyer keeps on his clients could be stored and cross referenced.

For doctors the uses include standard office accounting work, as well as keeping track of lab reports. An MD could cross reference all of his or her cases, which would provide the ability to analyze types of services being provided to the community on an on-going basis. The ability to call up a patient's prior records in legible hard copy just before the patient arrives for an appointment should be a definite plus.

EXHIBIT 1 *(continued)*

Other professionals have many needs for services we are discussing. There are many one-person accounting offices that do both individual and business work. Addition of a microcomputer would allow the accountant to prepare the quarterly statements for an organization in a fraction of the time currently needed. It would also allow opportunity to compare the results of the client company over comparable periods of time. This would be a most useful tool as it could reveal discrepancies quickly and help the accountant home in on important changes in financial position.

To other professionals the aid of a microcomputer will be invaluable. Stockbrokers in smaller firms now lack access to the type of computer capability which larger firms afford their employees. To be competitive with counterparts in larger firms, stockbrokers in smaller firms need computerized help in such areas as cross-referencing of clients' holdings by position. Most larger firms already have such a service in place. In addition, it would be of significant benefit to have the computer maintain a call sheet that the broker could use to track conversations with present and prospective clients regarding their holdings and suggestions they were given.

It is readily apparent that the uses for professionals are manifold in nature and exciting in scope. The capability of a professional to provide more and better services on a more timely basis will be greatly enhanced by use of a microcomputer. Further, the option of not having to increase overhead by making a substantial purchase should make time-renting or leasing alternatives attractive to professionals.

Students

One of the most fascinating of all the markets for the services we are proposing is the student population. Advantages of the Harvard Square area in this connection are readily apparent. The student population of the area, which exceeds 100,000, makes the location ideal for marketing the services of the store to students.

As you will recall, in conceptually analyzing the project we came to the conclusion that one of the major roadblocks for some market sectors was an educational gap. That is not true of the student market. There, that educational factor should work very much to our benefit. The younger the customer on average, the greater the prior exposure to computers. Students in college today are products of the computer age, where it is natural to rely on the machine for part of the work. The more quantitative the field of study in which the student is engaged, the greater the interaction with data processing equipment.

We do not envision students as likely candidates for purchase of computers. However, the interest they should have in using our facilities we feel will be significant. Uses to which students can put our microcomputers appear to be never ending. Let us analyze a few of them.

Presently, students have access to computers only through their schools, and the schools set very definite restrictions upon who can use computers and for how long. The emphasis in time-sharing at those institutions goes to the statistically oriented courses. In addition, it is quite unlikely that there is a computer for the eye to see. Many students are simply allowed access to terminals which operate remotely via telephone connections with large computers from which the university leases time. The advantages of students actually seeing computers in front of them we feel are significant. This will encourage them to be more participants than just programmers of homework into keyboards.

For students taking courses in quantitative areas, the benefits of working with numbers and formulas is apparent. Moreover, the word processing-related functions are helpful with writing and on-line editing of manuscripts. The writing and reorganization of term papers becomes far more facile. Development of quality resumes is one of the prime concerns of students in their last year. We could assist in development of resumes.

Access of students to data bases in conjunction with empirical research can aid some required schoolwork. A student will be able to tie from our computer directly into many large data bases, such as Dow Jones, with a telephone hook-up, which we will provide. Cross-referencing ability will be beneficial to students outside of the normal work which would be called for by their colleges.

EXHIBIT 1 *(continued)*

Our store will provide many other services which we believe will interest students. The largest of these falls into the leisure time sector of our services. We will offer many games with various degrees of sophistication on the microcomputers. Among sophisticated games a student can choose to play backgammon against some of the best players in the world to improve skill. This holds true for many other games, including gin rummy, poker, blackjack, chess, checkers, cribbage and others too numerous to mention. The microcomputers will be programmed to play at different skill levels, which will accommodate anyone from beginner to the most advanced of players.

Less sophisticated games we envision installing include some now available through such manufactures as Atari. These will be available in the store in an area slightly separated from the computers in a physical sense. In this way those who are playing the games will not disturb the more serious students who might be working on formulas. The range of games will be more than enough to satisfy even the most enthusiastic devotee. We envision a different pricing structure for games which are less complicated. These pricing policies will be discussed later when we will take up the entire pricing structure of the store.

We believe that student demand will be a function of intelligence and curiosity level. Students are today far more accustomed to computers in their day-to-day life than older people. Most students have been using computers on a regular basis since high school and have been made aware over a period of time that there are many other functions which computers can perform in addition to homework assignments. The interest of students in the sophisticated games the microcomputers will offer has been documented in our research in the university systems. There is today a definite demand in this area made up of the students who wish to spend time playing chess on the computer, for example. In summary, we feel that the student sector offers us a large untapped market for the store's services.

Graduate Students With Degrees

The application for the services in this store should run somewhat congruently with those of the student population, but with an important difference. Undergraduate students have access to computers of the university to aid them with their studies. But many graduate students must do research on their own under limited budgets. We will be able to offer this sector the most cost-effective manner in which to use computers.

Word processing capabilities of the microcomputers can be important to the graduate student who is attempting to get published. The store will offer a full complement of computer on-line word processing type functions which would be helpful with a doctoral dissertation. The more quantitative the work that the individual is engaged in, the better we will be able to service him or her.

Leisure Time

The leisure-time sector of our perceived market is large indeed. Even though not all sectors of our market may be as versed in computers as the student population, we expect that the surrounding community in general is sophisticated. This statement is backed by voluminous amounts of empirical data on the socioeconomic composition of the Harvard Square area. We believe that leisure-time activities in this community are such that it would be perfectly normal for individuals to stop in to our store after hearing about us and experiment with various products we offer.

We anticipate demand from this sector of our market for the following services: sophisticated games which can be played on the microcomputer; less sophisticated games, that a parent might bring children in to play on a Saturday afternoon; the learning about microcomputers to ascertain practical fit with a household; and the pursuit of other outside hobbies or interests. Cooking could be an example. A person would be able to access a vast number of recipes. A dieter could select recipes screened to exclude cholesterol.

This market segment is exciting in offering so many different possibilities. There are, of course, many more than have been discussed here, and new combinations of services are being developed every day.

EXHIBIT 1 (continued)

<u>Elementary and High Schools</u>

Many schools already use computers in one way or another as a learning aid. However, the budgetary crisis that confronts most school systems aids us in that we offer a less costly service through our leasing option, and as a result of the low cost of the microcomputer. We could provide programming to schools that would enable students to learn how to use computers all by themselves. The additional advantage of the microcomputer that comes into play here is that it is in front of the student who is working on it. It is not some abstract "thing" that the student never truly understands. We will explore the feasibility of offering part or all of these services on a limited basis as a good-will gesture to build up our community identity and bring us additional business from other market sectors, such as, for example, the parent who hears from a child or the person who reads about the concept in a newspaper.

The amount of programming available in this area and the instructive games which can be demonstrated are exciting.

<u>Instructional Systems</u>

Instructional systems will become more microcomputer-oriented in the future. The market here is large and the ability of our store to exploit it is great. A tremendous amount of learning takes place outside the formal classroom structure that can be economically accomplished on the microcomputer. This can be seen by looking at self-teaching aspects of microcomputer programming. Certainly if the microcomputer can teach the individual who is operating it how to do so without any outside help, then it will be able to teach accounting, cooking, English grammar or applied statistics. What could be more exciting than being able to expand into new areas of learning on your own time and in accordance with your schedule? Courses for the microcomputer to provide will be developed by leading authorities in their fields.

For businesses interested in teaching salespeople a new marketing approach, we could develop a system to their specifications. For a brokerage firm wanting to provide institutional clients with explanation of a new product in the financial futures area, our store could prepare computerized teaching materials and other services. The possibilities are expansive for servicing this market sector.

<u>Data Base Access</u>

The final perceived market is in data base access. Throughout the country there are large data bases on everything from the number of golden retrievers who had litters last year to the movements of multi-national corporations into new markets overseas. These data bases are being added to every day by all of us. All we must do is write a check and the bank upon which we wrote the check is increasing its data base. The possibilities for data base access are far too numerous to mention so we shall only discuss a few here.

The electronic mail concept widely discussed for the last few years in connection with the office of the future is currently available to larger corporations. They can send mail on an overnight, or if they wish immediate, basis through expensive equipment. But if an individual or small- to medium-sized business should wish to accomplish this, the cost is prohibitive.

The application of microcomputers we will offer in this area is exciting. An individual will be able to walk into our store and access a data base or send a letter to Texas for delivery the next day. We will be able to offer these services to the person who has no other access to them. A local business interested in expanding sales but handicapped by limited capital and lacking an extensive sales organization will be able through our store to reach buyers based upon extensive information about each of them.

Among more whimsical uses of the data bases, we could generate the record of every major league football team against another team and screen for factors such as the defensive nature of the team in the past to form conclusions as to advisable coaching directions and the amount of passing they should utilize. In connection with this, we could provide information on how all the various people who predict these outcomes are thinking.

This mentions just three of the endless possibilities.

EXHIBIT 1 (continued)

Summary of Market Sectors

We must conclude that the uses of the microcomputers that we will install to meet the demands of the markets are limitless and bounded only by the imagination and the software available. However, our store will not enter all of the above-mentioned markets on the first day of operation. We believe that a gradual rollout of services is better in keeping with sound financial practices and the common good of the partnership. It is our intention to provide those services through the store that are in greatest demand. That will maximize cost effectiveness for the partnership and contribute to optimization of return to the limited partners.

Experience of the General Partners

Richard D. Knight is 36 years old and has lived in the Harvard Square area for the past nine years. He holds a Bachelor of Arts degree from the Colorado College in Colorado Springs, Colorado, and a Master's in Business Administration from Boston University with a major in the application of microcomputers. For the past five years he has been an independent computer consultant specializing in the microcomputer area. Most recently his work has included the development of volume momentum models for stock, commodity and option trading for Burgess and Leith, an investment banking and brokerage firm in Boston, Massachusetts.

James A. Knight is 26 years old and a resident of New York City. He holds a degree in finance from Boston University. He lived in the greater Boston area for four years while associated with the investment banking firm of Shearson, Loeb, Rhoades, most recently as a vice-president. He has extensive experience in all facets of the financial markets and the capital raising process.

IV.   PRODUCT SCOPE

Products offered by our store will vary from the low end of Atari games to the high end of a Hewlett-Packard computer with disc drives and a color plotter. Equipment will cost from $600 per game to the Hewlett-Packard at $25,000. In between will be small microcomputers from Apple and Radio Shack with the add-on equipment necessary to expand functional performance of the units. In addition, because we believe that a significant portion of our revenues will initially come from our word processing capability, we have projected the purchase of two Digital Equipment (DEC) word processors that are, in our judgment, among the very finest available in cost-effectiveness. In the high-quality area, we intend to purchase a color graphics printer, which will give us the finest possible hard copy output for the demanding segments of our perceived market.

We will also have a large selection of software to meet user requirements. The cost of the software is low in relation to the time utilization.

The scope of the product must also include certain cards, chassis, monitors, plugs, connectors, modems, etc. One of the more interesting peripheral components will be two Apple graphic tablets, which will work in conjunction with the Apple computers and enable users to perform a far broader range of functions.

In summary, we intend to cover the microcomputer market thoroughly. Installation of the various units must be timed from a cost effective roll-out point of view. The microcomputer field is expanding so rapidly that new product substitutions might occur within the next few months if they offer better scope or less cost.

V.   LOCATION

Why Harvard Square? Well, it has long been one of the leading high technology areas of the country. The Greater Boston Area presents excellent demographics for this type of product introduction. Especially important to us, as we analyze the location, is the combination of high percentage student population with high-income level in the rest of the population. A study done for the Cambridge Seven group was filed with the city of Cambridge and the Commonwealth of Massachusetts, in connection with the proposed building of residential housing in place of the old

EXHIBIT 1 (continued)

subway yards in Harvard Square. Extensive demographic analysis done in connection with that study identified as target groups for the housing project families with $45,000 in annual income and young (under 35) professionals. It concluded that there were more than enough in these groups to justify the building of a major multi-million dollar housing project.

These results indicate first, that the area is conducive to new investment on a large scale; second, that the income level of the local community is such that it can justify an expensive housing unit expansion; third, that type of clientele we would like to attract exists in the area and; fourth, that the overall outlook for the Cambridge/Harvard Square area is excellent.

We conclude that Harvard Square offers us the best overall mix on high income level, proximity to the universities, large professional population, technological interest and cost effectiveness.

VI. COST ANALYSIS

In estimating costs for setting up the store and beginning operations we have made some assumptions, which follow:

1. The cost of equipment will range in the $150,000 area.
2. The space in Harvard Square area will be available immediately.
3. The renovations can be completed within 30 days.
4. The cost of the microcomputer hardware, software and add-on equipment will not materially vary before the end of the year 1980.
5. We will be able to hire adequate staffing.
6. The store will be in operation in 1980.
7. The amount allocated to rent includes heat and electricity.

In line with this, we intend to purchase the following equipment:

<u>Hardware</u>

Six APPLE 48K	$6600.00
Twelve disc drives (APPLES) four with monitor	5640.00
Four APPLE soft cards	50.00
Three Zenith 19" color monitors	2250.00
Three PAPER TIGER with graphics	3000.00
Three APPLE graphics tablets	2100.00
Two Centronics 636 Printers	1700.00
Four SANYO black and white monitors	600.00
Two Centronics printer interface cards	380.00
Five APPLE serial intersect cards	1000.00
One APPLE clock/calendar card	250.00
Two Silenttype printers	1000.00
Two APPLE expansion chassis	1100.00
Two Corvus 10 megabyte Hard Disc	8800.00
One Diablo Daisywheel letter quality printer	3000.00
One Hewlett-Packard HP-85 with disc drive	5000.00
Five DC HAMET micromodem II	2000.00
One PRINACOLOR IS 8001 (color graphics printer)	6000.00
Two Digital Equipment word processors	40,000.00
One Hewlett-Packard 32K with disc drives and color plotter	25,000.00
Four Radio Shack 264002,64K with one drive	14,000.00

TOTAL HARDWARE.............$130,170.00

Page 575

EXHIBIT 1 *(continued)*

All hardware is subject to replacement by comparable equipment.

<u>Games</u>

Five Texas Instruments $3000.00
Five Atari .... <u>3000.00</u>

TOTAL GAMES .... <u>$6000.00</u>

<u>Software, Etc.</u>

Software, Cables, plugs, connectors, parts,
library inventory, disc inventory, data base
subscription, paper inventory .... <u>$16,600.00</u>

<u>Working Capital Costs</u>

Rent $90,000.00
Telephone 5,000.00
Salaries 43,200.00
Advertising 20,000.00
Renovations 20,000.00
Office misc .... <u>2,500.00</u>

TOTAL .... <u>$180,700.00</u>

<u>Sales Analysis and Pricing</u>

The pricing formula we have determined to be best is based on the sophistication of the machine. The more sophisticated and costly the machine, the higher price it will rent for. At the low end of the spectrum is the game segment, which will be priced at $1.25 per quarter hour. The APPLE segment will be priced at $12.00 per hour. The Digital Equipment word processors will be priced at $19.00 per hour. The top end of the equipment represented by the Hewlett-Packard equipment with the graphic plotter will go for $21.50 per hour. We expect to do the bulk of business in the lower sectors of our pricing structure.

VII.   STAFFING AND INVENTORY

Under the projections we have run for the store, there is essentially no cost to carry the inventory because there is virtually no inventory, except for discs and programs, which are not material.

Staffing of the store will be accomplished primarily with graduate students of the area in need of extra money. Richard Knight has agreed that during the start-up phase, he will devote his efforts on a daily basis to operation of the store. He, plus one full-time staffer, should be adequate for administration and handling customer inquiries. We do not anticipate any dramatic increase in staff, even if the utilization rates should hit the higher end of our prediction.

VIII.   PROJECTIONS

In the equations we ran to estimate revenues at various levels of equipment utilization, we assumed that the store would be open six days a week for 52 weeks per year. We assumed alternative machine utilization rates in the computations shown below for different activities to examine their impacts. For example, Assumption One shows everything at a 30 percent rate of use and in Assumption Two we increase the use on the games up to a 50 percent rate. In Assumption Three we project that the games are used 70 percent of the time. Costs remain constant throughout, because we have budgeted our fixed expenses to meet the different levels of demand. It is interesting to note that the optimization of revenues and therefore of profits comes from the APPLE system.

EXHIBIT 1 *(continued)*

In the projection below all equipment will be assumed to have a utilization rate of 30 percent except for the games which will have the following utilization rates: Assumption One, 30 percent; Assumption Two, 50 percent; Assumption Three, 70 percent.

NAME(GAMEW) = GAMEW

UNDER THE 30-PERCENT ASSUMPTION 11/16/80

PROJECTIONS FOR MICROCOMPUTER UTILIZATION
UNDER 3 ASSUMPTIONS

	Assumption One	Assumption Two	Assumption Three
Revenue	272,160.00	324,000.00	375,840.00
Expenditures	160,700.00	160,700.00	160,700.00
Profits	111,460.00	163,300.00	215,140.00

The effect of other assumptions on profits can be seen in the table following.

IX.   CONCLUSION

It is our belief that the demand for the product we intend to market will be significant in nature and require us to expand our operations in the near future. The potential of expanding the number of stores in the greater Boston Area and then expanding into other markets in other cities is high.

We believe this concept is the tip of the future and will enable our investors to participate in what we consider to be the coming boom in the microcomputer market. The evidence of this exists partially in the offering of Apple on Wall Street and the enthusiastic reception that company is receiving.

As a final note, this offering memo and the projections which it contains were prepared by a microcomputer of the type we intend to utilize.

EXHIBIT 1 (continued)

OTHER UTILIZATION RATES ASSUMED (%)				PROFIT CALCULATIONS ($)		
GAMES	APPLES	DIGITAL	HEWLETT	REVENUES	EXPENSES	PROFITS
30	30	30	30	272,160	160,700	111,460
50	30	30	30	324,000	160,700	163,300
70	30	30	30	375,840	160,700	215,140
30	50	30	30	361,029	160,700	200,329
30	70	30	30	449,897	160,700	289,197
30	30	50	30	286,231	160,700	125,531
30	30	70	30	300,302	160,700	139,602
30	30	30	50	298,821	160,700	138,121
30	30	30	70	325,481	160,700	164,781
30	50	50	50	401,760	160,700	241,060
50	50	50	50	453,600	160,700	292,900
70	50	50	50	505,440	160,700	344,740
50	30	50	50	364,731	160,700	204,031
50	70	50	50	542,469	160,700	381,769
50	50	30	50	439,529	160,700	278,829
50	50	70	50	467,671	160,700	306,971
50	50	50	30	426,939	160,700	266,239
50	50	50	70	480,261	160,700	319,560
30	70	70	70	531,360	160,700	370,660
50	70	70	70	583,200	160,700	422,500
70	70	70	70	635,040	160,700	474,340
70	30	70	70	457,303	160,700	296,602
70	50	70	70	546,171	160,700	385,471
70	70	30	70	606,898	160,700	446,198
70	70	50	70	620,969	160,700	460,269
70	70	70	30	581,719	160,700	421,019
70	70	70	50	608,379	160,700	447,679

Mark Juarez[1]

What business to make of a new product

In March 1991, Mark Juarez, an American living in Berlin, Germany, worked under contract as a masseur. He had invented a product that he found helpful in his work and was considering what to do with it. The product consisted of five wooden balls, four small ones approximately one inch in diameter that were connected to a larger one, about two inches in diameter, with wooden dowels that angled out about one inch each from the bottom of the large ball, as depicted in the Exhibit following.

In use, the product was gripped by a masseur as an aid in transmitting pressure to the client, reducing the strain on the masseur's hand while applying the pressure more firmly at the same time. It had been well received by a few of Mark's colleagues, to whom he had given copies, and by their customers.

How, he wondered, should he apply his time and very limited personal financial resources to capitalize on it? Should he pursue licensing, manufacturing, patenting, or investigating whether there were already other such products on the market? What sequence of specific actions should he follow? Should he simply stick to his massage work and let this simple product find its own way into whatever market might or might not exist? What would be involved in creating a company to produce and sell it, and how might such things best be done, if that were the chosen path?

Background

Mark had held a number of different jobs prior to his present occupation. In the mid-1970s he studied marketing at Chabot Community College in California while working nine months for a wine company, followed by seven months with ARA Services, a national company providing laundry services for institutions and restaurants.

In early 1977, he began working in sales for a company that marketed energy-efficient air conditioning systems for the home. Although successful, Mark felt by 1978 that his life was unrewarding and his lifestyle was incompatible with his ideals. He took an unexpected leave for two weeks, and just drove up and down the West Coast. He then decided to quit his job and fly to Europe to travel and explore. Ten of the next 15 years, he spent in Europe working odd jobs in his travels. Whenever he ran out of money, he would go back to the U.S. and work to save enough to go back to Europe. During these return visits to the United States, he started a landscaping company, worked in sales for a company that made environmentally-correct living/work spaces, and participated in other small ventures.

In 1987 Mark was in Berlin and became interested in massage. At first, he thought it would be difficult to learn locally, since he did not speak German and did not have much money to pay for massage classes. But a massage teacher who encouraged him to learn more about massage explained that massage could be learned regardless of the language barrier, because massage was about touch and the body, both universal subjects. To further encourage Mark, the massage teacher offered him a job at the massage school. By year end Mark was a certified massage therapist. Eventually, he too, became a massage teacher. He also learned

[1] Karl H. Vesper, 1998, based upon a case written by Susan Devan and Michael Pisenti under the supervision of Dr. William B. Gartner at San Francisco State University College of Business, with the support of the Corporate Design Foundation, as a basis for class discussion rather than to illustrate either effective or ineffective handling of a business situation.

that traditional techniques of massage were very tiring to the hands. Many massage therapists developed carpal tunnel syndrome, a painful disorder of the nerves in the hands and forearms.

One February morning in 1991, through a vision in a dream, Mark conceived of a device that might help with his work. He envisaged a wooden ball with four wooden legs protruding from it, each leg having a smaller wooden ball at its outer end, as depicted in Exhibit 1. He also envisioned having a smiley face on the big wooden ball.

He told a friend about his idea. She encouraged him to go to a wood doweler, someone who carves wood on a lathe and who could make the parts for his design. With this help, Mark made some prototypes and tried them on his students. The students said they loved the device, went off with the prototypes, and the following week requested copies of it for their friends. Mark provided them and demand for the new massage tool rapidly increased.

Concern about copycats

Because of this student enthusiasm for his apparently novel product, Mark began to think about how to protect his design idea from imitation, perhaps by patenting it. He visited an American patent attorney in Berlin, who told him the cost would be $4,000 for researching prior patents to see if someone already laid legal claim to it. This task was not to be confused with actually filing to receive a patent on the new device. Either a researching attorney or a patent research service would simply look through the records of U.S. patents to ascertain whether or not the same product features had already been patented. If there were none, then Mark could try to obtain a patent, which would cost much more in legal fees.

Different types of patents existed. Life forms, computer programs, plants, and chemical processes could, if conditions and features were right, be patented. Most familiar were "utility patents" which had to do with the functions of an object and how its mechanism worked. To qualify, features of the mechanism had to be both novel, which was to say not used or patented before, and unobvious. The idea of making a concrete blob to pound nails would not qualify for a utility patent.

Inventors fortunate enough to be granted U.S. "utility" patents based upon adequately ingenious inventions involving new mechanisms found that the approval process typically took about two years and cost them from tens to hundreds of thousands of dollars for legal and other assistance.

Another form of patent simpler to obtain than a utility patent was a "design patent," which had to do with appearance of an object rather than any operating mechanism of it. Although quicker and easier to get, a design patent was also harder to defend, because to get around it, a copycat had only to change the configuration a bit, such as by adding a bump, or some other change in shape so that it looked a little different, although it might still operate in the same way. A concrete blob with indentations for fingers to grip it to be used for pounding nails might qualify for a design patent if there seemed to be something significantly novel about it. But also possibly another person could get around the patent with a blob with some variation, such as different shaping of the indentations.

If he were to spend the needed time and money to prepare and submit a patent application, wait and possibly work through any revisions that might be required in the application process, and after that be fortunate enough to get a patent, Mark would then have the right to sue anyone who imitated whatever features the patent covered in the country where the patent was issued, and claim that they were violating his patent. If the patent court then decided in his favor, he could try to prevent further such imitation and perhaps collect money in damages.

If it did not decide in his favor he would be out the cost of application and suing, and have to let anyone similarly copy his product.

Seeking a low cost patenting route, Mark found a book, *Patent It Yourself*, by John Pressman and published by Nolo Press. To pursue that path he returned to the United States in April 1991. At the New York Public Library he undertook his own patent search to see if someone already owned a legal rights on his product idea.

Not finding one, he moved on by bus to the United States Patent Office in Washington, D.C. and asked for help in filing for a patent. When the clerk responded that he should get a patent attorney for that, he replied that he had little money. When in response to his persistence the clerk asked what his product was, he pulled out his product, and demonstrated it, first on that clerk and then on others in the office. In response, the clerk called a patent examiner, who agreed to spare "a minute" if Mark could get to her office within ten minutes. He ran all the way, about a block.

After seeing his product, the examiner invited to him to return the next day, when she gave him a list of tasks for patent application, starting with a search of prior patents, and then visiting the art department for suggestions on his drawings. The next afternoon he filed application for a design patent. Three days later, a much shorter time lapse than the six weeks normally required, he received notice that his application had been accepted. The design patent itself, "Des. 328,328," was issued three months later, on July 28, 1992. Now he could legally imprint on his massage tool that it was patented.

From product to business?

Whether the product idea could be defended with such a patent was another question, and at this point Mark, with little money, had no business to produce and sell it. Should he look for a shop that could turn out his product at larger volumes, or try to set one up? But either way, where should he look, how should he decide how many units to make, and to what standards? If he could get permission to use a couple of spare rooms in his mother's house and/or maybe her garage for storage, should that determine the quantity? Or should he look for a warehouse?

There was a whole host of still more questions about how to go about trying to design a business to exploit his product. How should he get sales for it? Go door to door, and if so, where? Hire someone else to do it? If so, pay them on what basis? Might mail order work, and if so, how? Should he rent a trade show booth, and if so, which show, and how should it depend on cost? Should he try to advertise? If so, what message should he transmit, and through what media?

How fast should it all happen to anticipate possible competition? At what point would there be need to hire help for what aspects of the business, and on what terms? How should he go about deciding the appropriate people to seek?

Mark had, in his travels and job experiences, developed some views about how a company should operate. Visiting the Scottish town of Findhorn, for instance, he had noted that despite its reputation for being good at operating with idealistic views of how humanity and community should work together, the place nevertheless seemed to have typical problems. Taking this up with residents, he was told that was quite all right because, "All of us share the vision. We want to reach this goal, and our journey is getting there."

Could a philosophical idea like that apply to designing, starting and managing a massage tool venture, and if so, how? Could a company be created that would "Let work be love made visible," a phrase that had captured Mark's imagination? Could it put the integrity of products, employees and customers before profits and survive? Could it incorporate recycling in every production phase and still operate efficiently enough to cover costs? Could it aim to make massage affordable and accessible to everyone, provide U.S. jobs rather than just produce cheaply overseas, encourage employees to contribute to the community, offer customers a life-time product warranty and still stay in business?

For any action path, there was the question of how much money to spend and where to get it. But how much choice he would have about that would probably depend upon how plausible the design of his business was and the extent to which he could support the claim that it should work.

EXHIBIT 1 Massage tool

Charles and Barbara Ewing

Turning an invention into a business

In mid 1992 Charles and Barbara Ewing were contemplating whether they could create a profitable and substantial business around a product Charles had developed and named "Clayboard." Its purpose was similar to that of a canvas used by artists, but instead of being cloth stretched across a frame it was a thin rigid board covered with a hard, smooth, absorbent coating of white clay on one side for drawing and painting.

He had recently sold a few Clayboard panels of various sizes to individual artists. In 1991 a local Colorado art supply distributor had encouraged Charles and Barbara to put the art panel into distribution for the art supply retail trade. Their first major move towards a relationship with this distributor began with a commitment the Ewings had made to introduce the panel in a major art supply trade show. The two were producing it in the garage of their home in southern Colorado, but they were having problems with both the quality and quantity of production. As they prepared for the show, Barbara asked:

> But if a lot of people decide to buy the panel, how can we make enough to meet demand? We can't keep up with the orders we already have.

Charles, covered with dust in the summer heat from sanding clay surfaces replied:

> And we aren't really making much on it either, at least if you put any value on our time.

The product

Clayboard consisted of a mineral coating that was applied to a hard, rigid sheet of one-eighth-inch thick Masonite to produce a superior painting panel. Charles Ewing, an artist living in Colorado, had developed it for his personal use. When he showed it to other artists and local art classes, he found that they liked it too. He sent out samples to other artists. Written responses had included a number of complimentary comments. A few art stores in Colorado had bought the product from him. Barbara had designed packaging for the product, which read "Clayboard, real neat stuff."

Charles had been exploring the possibility of obtaining patents on the composition and process, but had not actually filed. Essentially, the coating involved a complex mixing and ingredient process. The coating, which cost under $0.50 per square foot, was applied to Masonite, which came in 4x8 foot sheets costing around $15 each that were cut into standard-size rectangles ranging from 8"x10" to 18"x24". After applying the coating and allowing it to dry, the surface had to be sanded smooth, something Charles accomplished with a hand-held electric orbital sander bought from a local hardware store for around $100. The process was slow and tedious, limiting the number he could produce to less than 300 Clayboards per week.

Clayboard was better than paper for drawing and painting on for several reasons. One was that it could be used directly without the need for some other backing such as a drawing board. Unlike artist papers, it did not bend or warp under repeated applications of water. The mineral surface of the panel allowed multiple erasures without affecting the surface texture. Erasure was accomplished by rubbing with steel wool to remove applied colors. However, when sealed with a clear acrylic fixative coat an artwork on Clayboard could be framed to last without need for glass covering.

Painting on panels went back at least as far as the Renaissance. Many artists, including Michelangelo, painted on wooden panels that had been coated with chalk gessoes.[1] While Charles Ewing's product was not an entirely new concept, he had developed a coated panel with a level of smoothness he explained was not easily attainable by modern-day artists. Many artists would spend days preparing wooden panels for painting. The coating Charles had developed also allowed an artist to manipulate the surface extensively. His art panel accepted all types of paints, including ink, pencil, watercolors, oils and acrylics. It would not age or yellow, and could be erased. Pictures on Clayboard could be framed easily without other backing.

The other art surface on the market with a coating similar to Clayboard was "scratchboard." This paper-based panel was clay coated with a top layer of ink that could be scratched away to develop etching-type drawings, commonly known as "scratchboard" art work. Other competition consisted of papers and canvas panels for painting. Estimated typical prices at retail for these alternative surfaces compared approximately as shown in Figure 1 below.

Figure 1   Costs of alternative art surfaces

Material	Typical Size	Cost[2]
Quality Watercolor Paper Gessoed (Primered)	22"x30"	$14.65
Masonite	18"x24"	8.13
Scratchboard	19"x24"	15.55
Pre-Stretched Canvas	18"x24"	10.00

Background

Charles Ewing had studied wood technology at Colorado State university. In the early 1970s he had taken a Peace Corps assignment at a University in Chile. His father had been a commercial illustrator who did fine art as a hobby. He did not encourage Charles to take up art; but when he died, Charles inherited his art tools and took them with him to Chile. There he began taking art lessons at night on the side, using his father's tools.

When Chile was swept by the turmoil of a new political regime, Charles lost his position at the university there and transferred to another Peace Corps group that was preparing a book on Chilean mammals. With his newly-learned art skills, he became their illustrator. Eventually, that project ended, and after some other travels, he returned to the southwestern U.S. and opened an art gallery in Cimarron, New Mexico. It burned down. Broke, he returned to a cabin owned by his family in the thinly-populated southern area of Colorado.

To earn a living, he began producing art and selling it through galleries. The typical arrangement, he said, was for the artist to set the price, then display it on consignment in the gallery. If and when it sold, the gallery would keep 25 to 60 percent, depending upon the prominence of the gallery.

During summers Charles worked for a local outfitter leading hunting parties. When the outfitter decided to retire, Charles recruited a partner and the two took over the business. He recalled:

> I was still painting. That went on for about five years, and then I got out of the outfitting business. I could get by on painting alone, and the outfitting took too much time away from it. Being a painter is something like being a musician. Unless you keep practicing, your skill drops off.

---

[1] Webster defines gesso as "plaster of Paris prepared for use in sculpture or bas-reliefs, or as a surface for painting."
[2] Charles explained that prices ranged fairly widely with quality. Art paper and canvas, for instance, might sell well below the cost of Clayboard or well above it, depending upon grade.

Like most artists, I tried different things, watercolors, oils, sculpting, pen and ink. Typically an artist will find that one particular thing sells better than others, and for me that turned out to be drawing on scratchboard. I enjoyed the technique, but not its lack of permanency. It had to be mounted on a backing board with glue and framed under glass, which was tedious. But what was worse was that sometimes it bubbled up in the middle where the glue came loose. I had some work come back to me with that problem from unhappy customers.

So I went to the hardware store and bought some Masonite and glue. Then I went to a pottery store and bought some white clay. I mixed it with the glue, painted it on the board with a brush, let it dry and then sanded it smooth, so I could paint on it. That seemed to work fine, so I began doing my artwork on it from then on.

This, as best he could recall, took place in the late 1970s, and Charles kept using his product. He was essentially the only one who did anything like it for the next fifteen years. He would make just two or three sheets at a time, a process that was very laborious but produced a surface he liked to use and that did not give him problems later due to lack of durability.

Occasionally, someone else would use his board. For instance, he sometimes taught local art classes. When students saw him use the Clayboard, some took an interest in it and wanted some. He would then sell some, but the volume of sales was minuscule from invention of the board through the 1980s.

Producing for the art supplies market

In early 1991, Charles was told by the owner of an art supply store in Alamosa, Colorado that there was an art supplies distributor who might be interested in selling Charles' Clayboard product. The distributor had been having a hard time finding good sources for scratchboard, most of which was imported from England. The store owner had told him about Clayboard. He told Charles: "If you can make it, he can sell it."

Taking down the distributor's phone number in Denver, Charles gave him a call. The man expressed interest and, after seeing samples, offered to buy it for resale. The two worked out an arrangement. Charles gave a retail price of $9 per square foot, with 25 percent to 50 percent off for the distributor.

As a result, the distributor began buying Charles' product, starting with all the inventory Charles had available. He resold it to stores. He also let Charles share his booth to demonstrate Clayboard at the NAMTA (National Art Materials Trade Association) show in Denver during July of 1991. This too produced orders, and some letters came from other artists complimenting Charles on his product. Charles and Barbara started thinking in terms of creating a business around it. She quit her job as a health care professional to help. He began experimenting with more efficient production methods.

Charles' formula for making the boards was in part secret. A reason for his hesitation to file for a patent was that he understood issuance of a patent would make public the details of his process. Also, he had been told that legal fees in the application process would probably be in the range of $3,000 to $10,000.

Increasing the volume of production produced problems. Setting the boards out to dry took much more room than he had needed before. Sanding the boards was very laborious, even with electrically-powered, hand-held sanders. The process produced a great amount of dust which made working conditions difficult. And the time needed for all this work kept him busy about 60 hours per week, even though Barbara helped about 40 hours per week, and in addition they hired a laborer at $4 per hour who put in another 40 hours per week. Having to hire someone, Charles said, added annoying paperwork:

I never had any idea how much red tape and expense would be involved in hiring someone— unemployment insurance, workmen's compensation insurance, tax deductions—not to mention all the taxes and forms I have to file on account of buying materials and selling the boards.

The most they could produce, Charles and Barbara found, was around 1,000 square feet of finished board per month in sizes typically around two to three square feet each. Even the packaging, he found, was much more work than he had anticipated. Each board was wrapped in a sheet of spongy plastic to protect the surface, then taped and labeled. This wasn't really hard work, just time consuming and monotonous. It was taking Charles' time away from painting, and he didn't like that.

Seeking sales

Getting sales also took more work for less results than expected. There was demand and complimentary letters from users, but no great flood of orders as they had hoped. Charles found he had to demonstrate the product and found himself traveling to other cities to do so. Even then, many artists would pass it up. He commented:

Some artists are just very conservative and stick to traditional materials like oil on canvas. Some pick up a particular medium because that is what their mentor used, and they stay with that. Others may experiment, but mostly when they are just getting started. Then when they find something that works for them they hang onto it.

Every material requires practice for becoming proficient with it. It is obvious to me that you can do many things with my board, pen and ink, watercolors, oils, all sorts of things work with it. But for someone who hasn't seen it before, it can take time to figure these things out. If I demonstrate it for them they catch on faster, but even then a lot of them just watch, say it looks nice, and go back to what they were using before.

The cost should not be a big deal for them. The board only costs around $10 for a painting they might sell for $200. They buy other materials that cost that much. With mine, they can sand down the surface and start over if they don't like the way a picture is turning out. They can't do that with the other materials, although they may be able to paint over with more layers if they are using oils. But the fact that cost should not be a problem doesn't mean it isn't. The best people for me to sell to might be students, since they are less likely to be set in their ways. Unfortunately, they tend to care about cost of materials because they don't have much money, and they rarely get good prices for their work at that stage.

The dream we have is that if we can just get established in the market, then people will stick with our product, and we can have a good business. I'd like to have some people do the selling, someone else be the foreman and get out the product, and get myself back to producing art before I get rusty at that.

But right now I find myself doing all these other things. On top of that, I have been struggling with how to get little bubbles out of the clay that always seem to form. They have never been a problem for me personally, but my impression is that stores like to sell a product that looks perfect. Otherwise people take off the wrapper, decide there is something wrong with the product and the store has to give their money back. Then what should the store do with the board, send it back to me? And what should I do with it?

Prize-Winning Venture Plan

The business plan following was prepared by a student team at the University of Texas at Austin both as a basis for starting a business and for entry into a series of competitions. In the first competition, which took place in professor Gary Cadenhead's entrepreneurship course in December 1992, the team won first place with this plan and received a $500 prize plus free office space in the Austin Business Incubator.

The second contest anticipated by the team would be the International Business Plan Competition at San Diego State University on April 30, 1993 where first prize would carry a $5,000 cash award. Third would be the International Moot Corp® competition at the University of Texas on May 5, 1993 which did not offer a cash prize. The plan is reproduced here with the team's permission as a basis for class discussion.

For prior information about the source of the project and the product, please refer to the case entitled Charles and Barbara Ewing.

AMPERSAND
ART SUPPLY

Graduate School of Business
The University of Texas at Austin

Management Team

CEO	Elaine Salazar
VP of Marketing	Katherine Henderson
CFO	
VP of Operations	
Faculty Advisor	Dr. Gary Cadenhead

Copy ___ of ___

Confidentiality Agreement

This business plan is the property of Ampersand Art Supply. It is to be used by the official judges of the International Moot Corp. Competition at the University of Texas at Austin May 6, 1993 for evaluation purposes only. The information contained within this plan is not to be divulged to a third party without the express written consent of the owners of Ampersand Art Supply.

© Copyright 1992

TABLE OF CONTENTS

EXECUTIVE SUMMARY

1.1 The Opportunity

Ampersand Art Supply will establish itself as a provider of high quality art products with its initial product, Claybord TM. This exciting new art surface has the potential of $4.6 million in annual sales by year five. This business opportunity exists because:

- Claybord addresses a fundamental need shared by artists for a surface product that will enhance their creativity.

- A $2.4 million target market in a $2.8 billion industry demonstrates the vast potential for Claybord.

- Ampersand's aggressive marketing and manufacturing strategy, and trademark and patent protection will sustain long-term profitability.

- Ampersand's management team has the breadth of experience and skills needed to capitalize on this lucrative opportunity.

1.2 Products and Benefits

An artist's surface is his/her fundamental tool. Its versatility determines the degree of freedom and range of expression an artist will have when approaching his/her work. Claybord's rigid clay-coated surface provides artists with a level of control and flexibility unmatched by any other surface on the market. For example, without ruining the integrity of the surface an artist using Claybord can completely erase and rework his/her design multiple times until the desired effect is achieved. This flexibility is impossible with any other surface product. Additional product features provided by Claybord and demanded by professional artists include durability, freedom from smudging, pH-neutrality, consistent quality, and a wide range of sizes. Finally, Claybord's acceptance of all types of media including acrylic, oils, pen and ink, pencil, and watercolors makes it a desirable surface for all artists.

1.3 The Market

Claybord's primary market is the 2.4 million professional artists in the United States who are characterized by their need and willingness to pay for high quality surfaces. Within this market, Ampersand has targeted 1.2 million pen and ink artists as its primary segment and 1.1 million artists working in oil and acrylics as a secondary segment. In extensive test marketing, these artists found Claybord to be an exciting addition to the surfaces they currently use. By targeting both market segments Ampersand will achieve an 8.5% penetration of the professional artist market by year five, representing 1,200,000 board sales to 200,000 customers.

1.4 Competitive Strategy

Ampersand will create effective barriers to entry and achieve a sustainable competitive advantage through its marketing and manufacturing strategies and its trademark and patent protection. An aggressive marketing and distribution strategy will be employed to quickly establish the Claybord brand, create product awareness, generate customer demand, and build volume sales. Outsourcing manufacturing in strategic market locations will enable Ampersand to produce and transport Claybord to its customers at lower costs than any potential competitors.

1.5 Management

Ampersand's management team collectively has over 20 years of real world experience in the areas of entrepreneurship, corporate and small business finance, marketing and design. Elaine Salazar and Kathy Henderson have extensive backgrounds in marketing and distribution, including experience starting their own companies and working as consultants to small businesses. Kathy Henderson also has an extensive art background and an intimate knowledge of the needs of Ampersand's customer base. Ampersand also has an advisory board of talented individuals, including Charles Ewing, the inventor of Claybord, who will contribute their vast experience as business professionals, artists, and entrepreneurs.

1.6 Financial Summary and Offering

As a result of Ampersand's aggressive marketing strategy, the company will break even in fiscal year two. Revenues are projected to reach $4,500,000 by fiscal year five. The company's average gross margin is approximately 60% across the five-year projected horizon. Average operating cash flows and net margins are estimated at 20% and 25%, respectively. Ampersand is seeking $200,000 in equity capital. This will be used to fund working capital requirements during the first year of operations. In return, the investor will receive at least 25% of the pro-rata outstanding common shares of Ampersand with a projected compounded annual rate of return of 70%.

COMPANY OVERVIEW

2.1 Company Background

Claybord was invented by artist Charles Ewing to meet his own requirement for a high quality surface for his fine art. As illustrators and fine artists became familiar with Mr. Ewing's work on Claybord, many sought the product for their own use. In July Mr. Ewing approached Ampersand's CEO Elaine Salazar with the proposition of developing a partnership to manufacture and market Claybord.

2.2 Current Status

Mr. Ewing, in exchange for equity, has agreed to give Ampersand the exclusive right to manufacture Claybord. The patent application and trademark registration for the Claybord name will be completed under the direction of Winstead, Sechrest and Minick, Esq. This Texas law firm has completed the initial review of our patent search and has determined that patentability exists.

Ampersand has identified World Research Company (W.R.C.) in Tyler, TX as the first of the company's outsourcing facilities. W.R.C. will provide the flexibility and capacity needed in the initial years of operation. Since consistent quality is critical to Claybord's success, Ampersand has recruited a team of UT students involved in a Total Quality Management class to develop a quality program for Claybord.

Distribution options have been analyzed and channel members have been contacted. Claybord is currently being evaluated by selected retailers, mail order catalogs, and major distributors. Pearl Paint, one of the largest art retailers in the US, contacted Ampersand within one day of receiving a sample of Claybord. They expressed a serious interest in Claybord and are currently testing additional samples of the product.

Finally, Ampersand has occupied office space in the Austin Technology Incubator. In the next six months Ampersand's management team will continue to build the infrastructure for the company and establish contracts and financing in order to launch the business upon completion of their MBA's in 1993.

Timeline

| 1/93 | Start 8/93 | Intro of Product 1 2/94 | Intro of Product 2 11/94 | End of Fifth Year 9/98 |

MARKET ANALYSIS

3.1 Market Research Conclusions

To determine the viability of Claybord in the art materials market Ampersand conducted a number of test marketing initiatives.

A random sample of 40 professional illustrators was selected from a national mailing list of science and medical illustrators. These illustrators were asked to test the product and complete a short telephone survey. Ampersand selected this group of artists as the basis for its test marketing because of the segment's familiarity with scratchboard and illustration board - products that most resemble Claybord. Following are highlights of the survey results. (Exhibits M-1 and M-2 contain a complete summary of survey results and selected comments from these artists.)

The results of the survey illustrate that (1) Claybord offers unique advantages for pen & ink applications and (2) Claybord is a superior and preferred product when compared to even the highest quality scratchboard and illustration board.

Ampersand also tested Claybord in three drawing classes at the University of Texas Department of Arts. The reactions in the classroom mirrored those of the professional artists. Students working in pen and ink found the surface exceptional. Students working in other media found the board's versatility and manipulation attractive for experimenting and developing unique styles.

Purchase Likelihood	Percentage
Definitely	81%
Probably	7%
Occasionally	6%
Seldom	0%
Never	6%

Favorite Characteristics	
Ability to Take all Media	76%
Erasability	73%
Pen & Ink Application	58%
Easy to Work With	55%
No Surface Glare	22%
Durability	22%
Feel of Surface	22%
pH-Neutral	11%
Size	11%
No Puddling Effect	11%

Average Number of Boards Purchased per Year

5-15	30%
15-30	38%
30-50	26%
50+	6%

In order to assess the potential for Claybord's use in commercial art programs, Ampersand asked the Austin Community College to evaluate the product. Four professors who teach illustration and design evaluated Claybord for classroom use and concluded that they would prefer to use Claybord when teaching scratchboard technique. As a result, Austin Community College has committed to order Claybord for its second semester classes beginning in January.

Management also asked other professional artists working in oils, watercolor and acrylics to test Claybord. These artists all indicated that the surface's acceptance of these media rendered the Claybord an excellent medium for their work.

To test artists' response to direct mail promotions designed to encourage product sampling, 200 artists were selected from the mailing list of *Science and Medical Illustrators*. Within the first 3 weeks after mailing, 20 requests for samples were received. This appears to indicate a high level of interest given that typical responses to direct mail promotions average a 1.5% response rate.

Finally, Ampersand acquired three major studies that provided critical data for its analysis of the market and industry. The 1991 National Artists Survey, sponsored by *Artists Magazine,* provided a broad base of statistically valid data on artists, art activity, and art product purchasing. The 4th Annual Art Supply Store Survey gave Ampersand extensive information on retail channel characteristics and the *Yearbook of Who's Who in Art Materials* provided us with data on manufacturers in the industry. Both these studies were obtained from the National Art Materials Trade Association (NAMTA).

3.2 Customer Profile

According to the 1991 National Artists Survey (NAS) there are 13.2 million artists in the US. Seventy eight percent or 10.3 million of these artists do their primary art activity in pencil, acrylics, oils, pen and ink, and pastels. Approximately 24% or 2.4 million of these artists are professionals who rely partially or entirely on their art for their income. It is this segment of the art market that Ampersand Art Supply will target with our introductory product, Claybord.

This professional art segment is less price sensitive when purchasing art supplies and is more prone to experiment with a new product. A fine artist who commands $300 to $10,000 for his/her work will not hesitate to pay for a high quality surface. Moreover, professional artists by their very nature are constantly experimenting with new products and looking for ways to differentiate themselves and create their own unique style. Claybord offers these artists the opportunity to explore and expand their techniques, thereby creating a unique approach to their work.

Ampersand Art Supply has segmented the targeted 2.4 million professional artists in line with its two-phase strategy for entering the market. Ampersand's primary segment is pen and ink artists and its secondary segment is artists who work primarily in oil and acrylics. Additionally, Ampersand will target schools and programs of science and medical illustration and commercial art.

Exhibit M-3 outlines the number of boards that will be sold yearly in each of Ampersand's target segments. The volume estimates are extremely conservative given that Ampersand's test market results showed that artists use anywhere from 5 to 50 sheets of scratchboard or illustration board per year. Ampersand's volume estimates for the first three years of sales are based on 5 Claybords per professional artist per year and 2 claybords per student.

Target Segments

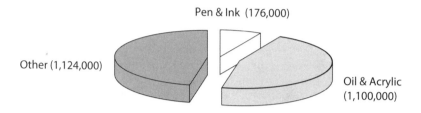

Pen & Ink (176,000)

Other (1,124,000)

Oil & Acrylic (1,100,000)

3.3 Primary Target

Of the 2.4 million professional artists, 176,000 work in pen and ink as a primary activity. There are approximately another one million professional artists who work in pen and ink as a secondary activity. By targeting these pen and ink artists Ampersand expects a 1.0% penetration rate by year two. This penetration will be followed by a 2.2% and 3.7% penetration in years three and four, respectively. This penetration represents sales of 700,000 boards by year five. This number is conservative when one considers that the total number of artists who work in pen & ink, both as a primary and secondary activity totals 4.96 million.

3.4 Secondary Target

Ampersand has found through its test marketing that artists who work primarily in oil and acrylics find the surface exceptional. According to NAS there are approximately 1.1 million professional artists who work primarily in acrylic and oils. In targeting the acrylic and oil segments Ampersand is keenly aware that its competition is no longer pen and ink surfaces, but quality pre-stretched canvas and gessoed masonite. In year two, Ampersand will target these artists with a version of our Claybord product at a price comparable to that of the surfaces these artists currently use. Approximately 116,000 boards will be sold in the first year of introduction and grow to 532,000 boards in year five.

3.5 Schools

Ampersand also will target schools of science and medical illustration and commercial art programs. In discussions with these schools across the country, Ampersand found that scratchboard is taught as a technique and students are required to purchase products similar to Claybord. Many of the professors, however, expressed that students are often frustrated with the technique due to the inferior quality of the scratchboard currently available. The ease of working with Claybord makes it an ideal product for these schools.

There are 130 commercial art programs in the country and 52 schools of illustration and design, including medical and science illustration. In these programs, we have estimated, an average of 60 students per year will be required to purchase products similar to Claybord. Ampersand will contact these schools in the first year through direct mail and telemarketing. Targeting this market is key for future sales growth. The NAS showed that 36% of artists are influenced by their teachers' and peers' choice of art product brands. A 25% penetration of this segment is projected in years one and two and growing by approximately 10% yearly. Ampersand's focused marketing efforts justifies these penetration estimates.

3.6 Customer Benefits

The surface an artist chooses to use is one of the most critical decisions he or she will make when creating a work. Surfaces are often fraught with problems that artists must find ways around. Claybord solves many of these current surface problems.

Current Problems	**Claybord Solutions**
Limited surface size	Many available sizes
Surface glare	Soft, nonglare surface
Fragile	Durable
Limited erasures	Up to 30 cut-ins & erasures
Yellowing	pH-neutral
Limited media application	Accepts all forms of media
Smudging	No smudge surface
Inconsistent quality	Top quality manufacturing
Poor availability	Strong distribution strategy

THE INDUSTRY

4.1 Industry Overview

The $2.8 billion art supply industry is dominated by six major companies who control approximately 80% of US retail sales volume. The remaining 20% is shared among approximately 300 other manufacturers. Similar to Ampersand's strategy, the majority (81%) of the industry's manufacturers produce either a single line or limited family of products and grow by introducing line extensions. Very few surface manufacturers produce a diversified product line. A breakdown of the manufacturers in each product area is shown below:

Art Supply Manufacturing Breakdown

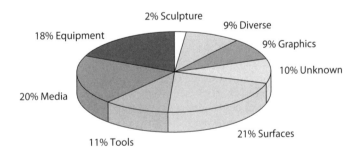

4.2 Distribution

Retail stores are important players in the art materials industry. According to NAMTA, the majority or 60% of all retail stores had gross revenues of under $250,000 while 23.5% reported revenues in excess of $1 million. 17.6% of the large resellers reported revenues in excess of $10 million. Many of these resellers operate warehouses and sell out of multiple retail locations and some act as distributors for other retailers. The retail channel is powerful in the industry, commanding 65% margins from manufacturers. These margins clearly indicate that a successful manufacturer must maintain low manufacturing costs in order to achieve meaningful profits.

4.3 Competition

Claybord's attributes make this product most similar to "scratchboard" products. There are approximately six companies currently who manufacture scratchboard. Four of these companies produce low-priced, low-quality products targeted at elementary education and craft markets. Claybord's price point and product positioning places it in competition against only two existing scratchboard products—Essdee Scraperboard and Paris Scratchboard, representing the higher quality scratchboard on the market. These products are both produced in Europe and imported into the US.

Our test marketing has shown that Clayboard appeals to a wider spectrum of users and therefore will be competing with other surfaces as well. The three most popular surface types are paper, canvas and film products (e.g. vellum, acetate, etc.). In the US market there are approximately 62 manufacturers who sell art surface products. These manufacturers are primarily specialists and can be aggregated by product type.

Three manufacturers, Canson Talons, Windsor Newton and Strathmore are large volume producers of art surface products, mostly paper. These manufacturers focus on volume and target the price sensitive 75% of the art supply industry. They rarely manufacture specialty products. From our discussions with these large manufacturers we found that because the manufacturing process of Claybord differs significantly from their core competency, these players do not pose a serious threat to Ampersand's market. In fact, these industry leaders often form partnerships with successful small manufacturers of specialty products.

The smaller manufacturers are Ampersand's greatest threat, since they are often able to produce and distribute specialty products at low costs. The emergence of national mail order catalogs has provided a low-cost distribution channel for these small manufacturers, making the barriers to entry low in the industry. It is clear that Ampersand must create strong barriers against these manufacturers to maintain its profitability.

4.4 Competitive Strategy

Ampersand has strategically positioned itself to be successful in light of these industry challenges. Ampersand will (1) provide a unique and high-quality product that will differentiate Ampersand from other manufacturers, (2) incorporate a strong marketing strategy to create demand which in turn will exert pull on the powerful distribution channel, (3) target the 25% of the market consisting of professional artists who are less price sensitive and currently not the primary target for industry leaders, (4) erect trademark and patent protection barriers to other manufacturers from copying our product, and (5) achieve a low cost structure with low fixed costs in order to deliver the necessary margins to the retail channel while maintaining a high profit margin for the company.

MARKETING STRATEGY

5.1 Overview

In order to achieve our projected sales volume of 1.2 million boards by year five, Ampersand will launch an aggressive marketing campaign to quickly establish our product and generate customer demand. According to NAMTA over 90% of all retailers, regardless of size, indicated that customer demand was the primary influencer in stocking new products. The $130,000 in marketing expenditures forecast for Year 1 will be used for direct mail promotions, print advertising, product demonstrations, trade show participation, and retail sales support. Our product introduction efforts will precede and overlap retail product release. This will ensure an active customer base for sales partners. This strategy will allow Ampersand to quickly establish the Claybord brand and trademarked name, thereby creating a marketing barrier against potential competitors.

5.2 Direct Mail

In terms of Claybord, our market research has shown product acceptance and purchase intention are enhanced when the artist has an opportunity to sample the product. To facilitate sampling, a direct mail promotion to 100,000 artists in the primary target group is planned. Mailing lists will be obtained from state-wide artist guilds and professional organizations. The mailing will consist of an informational brochure that includes a coupon enabling artists to request a sample. A small "shipping and handling fee" will be required to qualify respondents. Finally, a mailing list of samplers will be compiled and forwarded to our retailers as sales leads.

5.3 Advertising and Promotion

To support product introduction Ampersand will place 1/2 page advertisements in industry publications for three consecutive months. This campaign is to create top-of-mind awareness of the product in our target market and the retail channel.

Brochures, press releases, reproductions of articles, and product samples will be mailed to all state artists guilds. Typically these organizations produce monthly newsletters and hold monthly meetings. To increase product awareness and to facilitate product demonstrations we are developing an instructional video to be used as an integral part of the Claybord demonstration and sales support program. The video will highlight the advantages and applications of Claybord. Accompanying the video will be product samples and brochures. Product media material will include information on how guilds can request the loan of the video and free samples. Additionally, Ampersand will target national meetings of artists in our primary target market and provide live demonstrations to these groups.

Finally, we will contract with well-known illustrators/authors for articles on the features and benefits of Claybord. These articles will be published in trade journals and used in our promotional efforts. Well-known science illustrator Trudi Nicholson recently published an article about Claybord in the national newsletter of the National Science Illustrators Guild. The response to this article has been immediate and very encouraging. Ruth Lozner, illustrator for the *Washington Post* and author of *Scratchboard for Illustration* also has offered to write articles for publication.

5.4 Trade Shows

According to the Art Supply Store survey, over 95% of all retailers attend trade shows to identify new products. The most influential trade shows for retailers are sponsored by the National Art Materials Trade Association (NAMTA) and are held three times a year in various geographic locations. According to sources at NAMTA, new products are showcased at these trade shows. A team of influential retailers present awards, and a video highlighting promising new products is produced and then distributed to NAMTA's retail members. In addition to the NAMTA shows we will attend and demonstrate Claybord at national meetings of artist guilds.

5.5 Product Distribution

A majority of artists interviewed stated that they purchase the bulk of their art materials from art supply retailers and mail order catalogs. They indicated product selection and price as the primary factors. According to NAMTA over 65% of large resellers operated warehouses and sold products out of multiple retail locations. 46.5% acted as distributors for other retailers. Also, large resellers carried on average twice the number of product lines in each general category as small retailers and had lower annual inventory turns. 98.9% of large retailers carried a variety of art surfaces and 64.5% cited surfaces as one of their most "successful" product categories.

Initially we have targeted twenty large retail outlets and national mail order catalogs as our primary distribution channels. This will allow us to focus our resources on building product awareness and demand by utilizing the most supportive and easily penetrated channel members. Once product acceptance has been achieved and a sales history established, we will expand our distribution to include small and medium sized retailers by working through national and regional distributors.

5.6 Channel Strategy

Initial contacts with the targeted retailers indicated a high level of interest in the product. Product samples are currently being evaluated by channel members who are providing sales estimates to support our sales projections. We will provide standard industry discounts and incentives for volume purchases and prompt payment. All retailers contacted reported monthly to bimonthly ordering. Stock balancing and product returns are not significant factors in this industry with the exception of damaged merchandise which is typically returned to the manufacturer for credit. To protect against damage and to enhance product visibility Claybord will be individually packaged.

To support our sales partners' efforts we will provide dealers with sales leads and sales kits to include product samples, brochures and training videos. A training video will be used to introduce sales staff to the features and benefits of Claybord and can be used as a basis for in-store workshops. Live in-store demonstrations are planned to enhance visibility, to educate sales staff, and to obtain feedback from channel members and customers.

Mail order catalogs will offer the standard Claybord product line as well as an "Introduction to Claybord" product. This product grouping will include three 8" x 10" boards, instructional brochures, and training video. It will be used to encourage product trial. According to buyers in the mail order industry this type of SKU, called a "put-up," is a popular and successful way to establish a new product. It will allow our customers to learn about and experiment with Claybord with a minimum of risk. Historically, once customers are successful with the put-up they continue to experiment with the product and will purchase "open stock."

With the introduction of our second product in Year 2 we will expand our distribution into second-tier retailers and college bookstores by working through national and regional distributors. We will follow the same pattern of product introduction, retail sales support, and discounting.

5.7 Products and Pricing

Within the first two years of operation we will introduce two different Claybord product families. The initial product, Claybord Premium, will be priced in competition with Essdee Scraperboard and Paris Scratchboard. Claybord Premium is a superior product and addresses many of the weaknesses found in competing products. Sixty two percent of Ampersand's survey respondents said that our proposed prices for Clayboard Premium were in line with what they would expect to pay for this type of quality art surface. We will offer nine different sizes of Claybord in a smooth surface.

A second product, Claybord for Oil & Acrylic, will be offered in fewer sizes and with a textured surface. It will also have a thinner coating of clay and a different hardboard backing. This product will be targeted at oil and acrylic painters and will be priced to compete with high-end surfaces currently favored by these artists. These surfaces include pre-stretched canvas and gessoed masonite board. Cannibalization of Claybord Premium with the introduction of the oil and acrylic line is not expected to be significant. Each product has unique attributes that are targeted to meet the needs of two distinct customer segments.

Ampersand Product Pricing

Size	Variable cost/unit	SRP (1)	Wholesale (2)	Gross Margin
Claybord Premium				
8" x 10"	$0.37	$2.00	$0.75	50.7%
9" x 12"	$0.50	$3.60	$1.35	63.0%
11"x14"	$0.71	$5.50	$2.06	65.5%
19"x12"	$1.06	$10.00	$3.75	71.7%
14"x18"	$1.17	$9.10	$3.41	65.7%
16"x20"	$1.48	$12.00	$4.50	67.1%
18"x24"	$2.00	$14.00	$5.25	61.9%
20"x24"	$2.22	$16.00	$6.00	63.0%
24"x30"	$3.33	$23.70	$8.89	62.5%
Claybord Oil & Acrylic				
9" x 12"	$0.37	$3.00	$1.13	67.3%
14"x18"	$0.85	$6.25	$2.34	63.7%
18"x24"	$1.46	$9.00	$3.38	56.8%

Notes: (1) Suggested retail price (2) Price received by Ampersand

Price Comparisons

Type	Size	SRP	Wholesale
Claybord Premium	18"x24"	$14.00	$5.25
Essdee Scraperboard	19"x24"	$15.55	$5.83
Paris Scratchbord	19.5"x25.5"	$13.20	$4.95
Claybord Oil & Acrylic	18"x24"	$9.00	$3.38
Gessoed Masonite	18"x24"	$8.13	$3.05
Pre-stretch canvas	18"x24"	$10.00	$3.75

MANUFACTURING

6.1 Overview

To ensure a successful and sustainable entry into the market, Ampersand must have low fixed costs to achieve high profit margins. Ampersand will therefore outsource its manufacturing to World Research Company (W.R.C.) in Tyler, TX. W.R.C. has been in operation for four years providing flexible manufacturing to the custom hardboard industry and has the facilities and capacity to meet Ampersand's current needs.

6.2 Process and Quality Partnership

Claybord is currently being manufactured by hand by the inventor in small quantities. With the precision and accuracy required in the type of artwork for which Claybord was designed, quality is a critical factor. In mass production the primary determinant will be the capabilities of the surface application process. Because the current process can achieve appropriate quality levels with hand application, we are confident that the decrease in variability resulting from automation can produce the product within the same levels and with less post-production patchwork.

Ampersand also plans to integrate a quality program to ensure the consistent integrity of the Claybord surface, and has engaged a project team from the UT MBA program to explore the issue. Ampersand's partnership with W.R.C. in building this quality initiative will ensure long-term customer satisfaction.

An additional advantage to Ampersand's partnership with W.R.C. is flexibility. As a smaller but automated manufacturer of custom hardboard products, W.R.C. not only has the ability to customize their process to meet our requirements but can also offer us one to two week lead time on production. This flexibility is critical as Ampersand begins its operation and builds its volume sales.

6.3 Packaging

Appropriate packaging will be developed in-house during the initial months of preparation. Although similar products simply "stack" on shelves in retail outlets, some form of surface protection is necessary. Innovative packaging also will promote the image of a brand new type of product.

6.4 Manufacturing Barriers to Entry

Ampersand's manufacturing strategy is designed to sustain profitability by maintaining a low cost structure. After we have finalized the process with W.R.C. and generated sufficient demand for the product, we will spread our manufacturing to similar facilities in locations closer to our distributors. By doing this we will generate cost savings both in production and in transportation. Through volume-based contractual agreements with these manufacturers and the decrease in shipping costs, we will erect a significant cost barrier in later years.

Initially, however, our barriers will be of a different nature. Not only will Ampersand have trademark protection and the protection of the patent pending label, but we will also have equity in the Claybord name generated from our expansive marketing strategy and first mover advantage.

RESEARCH AND DEVELOPMENT

7.1 Overview

Beginning in Year 3 our product development efforts will be focused on expanding our surface product line, creating Claybord accessories, and developing completely new products. The research and development costs on the financial statements are intended directly for this purpose.

7.2 Inventor Involvement

As a part owner of Ampersand, Charles Ewing will play a significant role in research and development. An inventor by nature with an intimate understanding of the needs of professional artists, Mr. Ewing already has a number of products under development, including surface product line extensions and prototypes of several erasing tools.

7.3 Surface Product Line Extensions

By altering the composition of the surface, products similar to Claybord Premium but designed to meet the specific needs of artists working in various media can be produced. Prototypes of boards designed specifically for artists working in oil and acrylics, watercolor, and pastels have already been developed and are currently being field tested. Eventually, a full line of high-quality surface products will be manufactured and marketed under Ampersand's direction.

7.4 Claybord Accessories

Because Claybord is a unique surface with unusual properties, the opportunity for adjunct products is considerable. The majority of these will involve manipulation of the surface, especially in erasing or removing pigment from the board. At this moment the recommended tool for erasing is different grades of steel wool. However, greater precision and ease of use could be obtained with an object designed specifically for that purpose. This is one area we would like to explore. Other areas for development could include: surface cutting tools, texture creators, display products, color manipulators, board cutting tools, etc.

7.5 New Products

One of the major needs that Claybord fills is something that afflicts most artists—the need for new opportunities in which to express themselves creatively. Ampersand will continue to explore new media, surfaces and applicators. Through the vigorous identification and definition of the specific needs of specific groups in the art community, Ampersand will be able to introduce products which satisfy a niche yet provide opportunity for the masses.

MANAGEMENT

8.1 Management Team

The management of Ampersand Art Supply is one of the company's greatest strengths. The members collectively have more than 20 years of real world experience in the areas of entrepreneurship, corporate and small business finance, marketing, operations management and design. The individual members of the management team and their positions are listed below.

Elaine Salazar, Chief Executive Officer - Ms. Salazar has a background in marketing and small business operation. In addition to serving as a small business consultant for the past five years, Ms. Salazar has founded and operated an FM radio station located in Southwest Colorado. She also founded the public radio industry's first national broadcast training program in her capacity as the Director of Training for National Public Radio (NPR).

Kathy Henderson, Vice President of Marketing and Distribution - Ms. Henderson has more than 10 years experience in marketing and entrepreneurship. In addition to developing the marketing and distribution strategy for two existing companies, Ms. Henderson currently serves as founder and co-owner of her own successful software publishing company. Ms. Henderson is an artist in her own right, with several years of formal art training.

8.2 Role of the Inventor

Charles Ewing, the inventor of Claybord, is a well-known southwestern artist. His work can be seen in galleries throughout the country. He is often commissioned to render major works of art for large corporations and art connoisseurs. Charles Ewing is excited about the opportunity Ampersand Art Supply and its management present to turn his invention into a lucrative endeavor.

This partnership meets the artist/inventor's goals and needs. Mr. Ewing's first and foremost priority is to focus his attention on his art work, and not the manufacture of Claybord. Building this partnership with Ampersand Art Supply enables him to accomplish this goal while creating long term value from his invention. Mr. Ewing will be a critical member on Ampersand's board of advisors and will support the company's initial marketing efforts by conducting many of the live demonstrations planned.

8.3 Board of Advisors

The Company has selected a number of individuals to serve as its Board of Advisors. A number of these advisors will assume positions on the Company's Board of Directors on the date of formal incorporation. The selected advisors were chosen because of their valuable experience in the art and small business industries.

Mr. Charles Ewing - The inventor of Claybord is a well-known southwestern artist. His work can be seen in galleries throughout the country. He is often commissioned to render major works of art for large corporations and art connoisseurs. Mr. Ewing is often asked to teach workshops on illustration and drawing techniques for professional and student artists. As an equity partner, Mr. Ewing will play a key role in the development and operation of Ampersand Art Supply.

Mr. Alex Howard - Partner, Howard Frazier Barker Elliott, Inc. - Since 1972, Mr. Howard has prepared or supervised numerous studies encompassing diverse industries for both private and public companies ranging in size from revenues of less than $1 million, to over $1 billion. These studies were performed for purposes including corporate and estate planning; estate, gift, and income tax requirements; going-private situations; mergers and acquisitions, and others.

Mr. Robert Santangelo - Mr. Santangelo is a patent attorney and operates his own private law firm in Fort Collins, CO. Mr. Santangelo has been involved in the patent search process for Claybord. He also has served as an advisor to dozens of small businesses in the Rocky Mountain area.

Ms. Ruth Lozner - Ms. Lozner is a renowned illustrator for the *Washington Post* and a fine artist. She is the author of *Scratchboard for Illustration* and is a professor of illustration at the University of Maryland.

FINANCIAL PLAN

9.1 Deal Structure

Ampersand is seeking $200,000 in equity capital. Management will contribute the remaining $100,000 required. In return, the investor will receive 25% of the outstanding common shares of Ampersand and the right to select a pro-rata share on the board of directors. The remaining 75% of the outstanding shares will be divided among Charles Ewing and management. Upon completion of the transaction Mr. Ewing will own approximately 37% of the company, with management retaining equal shares of the remaining 38%. We would note that these ownership percentages are negotiable. Therefore the transaction, as represented herein, represents one of many possible avenues available to the investor. The following table illustrates varying rates of return given different ownership levels.

% Ownership	ROI
25%	69.6%
30%	75.9%
35%	81.4%
40%	86.3%

9.2 Use of Funds

Given that Ampersand intends to fully outsource all manufacturing of the product, the primary use of funds generated from the private placement will be financing of working capital requirements. The largest component of these requirements will be advertising and marketing expenses (approximately 50% of operating expenses in fiscal year 1). As mentioned previously, management believes that an aggressive marketing and advertising campaign, coupled with sufficient patent protection, will serve to erect formidable barriers to entry.

9.3 Financial Review

The five year pro-forma summary financials for Ampersand Art Supply are included below.

	Fiscal Year 1	Fiscal Year 2	Fiscal Year 3	Fiscal Year 4	Fiscal Year 5
Revenues	$271,925	$840,378	$1,925,060	$3,009,805	$4,585,495
Cost of Product Sold	65,076	353,995	813,797	1,251,342	1,883,365
Gross Profit	206,849	486,383	1,111,263	1,758,463	2,702,130
Operating Expenses	280,864	293,812	506,975	637,736	833,219
Operating Income	-74,015	192,571	604,288	1,120,727	1,868,911
Taxes (@34%)		65,474	205,458	381,047	635,430
Net Income	-74,015	127,097	398,830	739,680	1,233,481
Total Assets	194,646	396,575	1,015,913	2,136,224	3,981,141
Book Value	194,646	387,217	991,504	2,112,231	3,981,141
Cash Flow From Operations	-173,096	115,400	346,743	1,144,584	1,423,282

The illustrated financials represent the "Most Likely" case analysis. In addition to this scenario, two other scenarios were created (Best and Worst cases) which differ primarily with respect to market penetration and terminal operating cash flow (EBDIT) multiples. Exhibit F-1 illustrates the assumptions made for each case. We feel that these areas represent the most significant areas of risk to the investor. In the above illustrated case, Ampersand expects revenues from its Claybord product to grow at an annually compounded rate of approximately 103% over the analyzed five year horizon. While this growth rate may initially seem somewhat ambitious, management would note that these projections are based on extremely conservative assumptions as discussed previously. Full five year financials are included in Exhibit F-5.

9.4 Investor Return

Exhibit F-3 illustrates the calculation of the investors' return on investment (ROI) given the Most Likely Case scenario. Two possible exit strategies exist for the investor at the end of the five year projection horizon. The first option is an equity offering in which the investor could offer his/her shares to the public. The second option will involve the sale of the Company. The Most Likely Scenario yields an ROI of approximately 70%. This ROI is largely dependent upon the selection of the exit multiple. Management has determined, in consultation with venture capitalists and valuation experts, that an EBDIT multiple of approximately six times is appropriate for a firm with growth and earnings characteristics similar to those of Ampersand. The resulting return is in line with the relatively high risk level associated with the venture (i.e. start-up firm, no interim returns, etc.). Once again, we would note that these exit strategies represent platforms for negotiation. Staged exits (as well as entries) are possible given our current projection framework. Note, however, that such staging strategies (especially exit strategies) will result in lower aggregate returns.

9.5 Sensitivity Analysis

Exhibit F-8 illustrates sensitivity analyses for revenue, earnings and cash flow given management's three case scenarios (Best, Most Likely, Worst), as well as a graph illustrating the sensitivity of return on investment (ROI) to these scenarios. The primary areas of risk in the deal are associated with over-all market projections and terminal valuation parameters. As the graph illustrates, returns at all levels of possible market conditions are quite favorable to the investor in terms of ROI, given the inherent riskiness of the deal.

EXHIBIT CONTENTS

EXHIBIT M-1

Survey - Overview of Artists' Responses

Survey Respondents	# of Artists
Illustrator Only	17
Illustrator/Fine Artist	26
Fine Artist Only	12

Do you work primarily with one medium or many types?

Response	# of Artists
Mixed Media	41
Primarily One Medium	13

What is the primary surface you use?

Response	# of Artists
Scratchboard	21
Illustration board	14
Gessoed masonite	4
Canvas	4
Quality paper	4
Other	8

How many boards do you purchase yearly?

Response	# of Artists
5-15	17
15-30	21
30-50	14
50+	3

Where do you find out about new art materials?

Response	# of Artists
Journals	25
Word of mouth	35
Newsletters	42
Conferences	27
Catalogs	11
Trade shows	0

How did Claybord compare to your current surfaces?

	Inferior	Same	Superior
Erasability	1	8	46
Manipulation	1	11	43
Line Control	1	17	37
Detail	0	17	38
Versatility	1	4	50
pH neutral	0	7	48
Durability	0	0	55
Surface (smooth)	1	24	30

Will you purchase Claybord?

Response	# of Artists
Definitely	45
Probably	4
Occasionally	3
Seldom	0
Never	3

Where do you currently buy your art materials?

Response	# of Artists
Local retail stores	35
Mail order catalog	28
Direct from manufacturer	5
Other	8

What did you like best about Claybord?

Response	# of Artists
Pen & Ink Application	32
No Surface Glare	12
Size	6
Ability to Take all Media	42
Manipulation of Surface	40
Durability	12
pH Neutral	7
Easy to Work With	30
No Puddling Effect	6
Feel of Surface	12

Note: These results are based on a survey of 55 artists. Forty of these artists were selected using a random sampling of science & medical illustrators. Another 15 artists who work in other media were asked to test Claybord.

EXHIBIT M-2

Selected Comments from Artists*

Margy O'Brien, Albuquerque, NM, Fine Artist

Surface quality is critical for me. I need to have a surface that is absolutely smooth to do my silver point drawing. Besides being smooth I have to make sure that the surface will accept silver point. I loved the Claybord! It was so smooth and tactile. The soft feel of the surface made it so inviting to work on.

Craig Gosling, Indianapolis, IN, Medical Illustrator

I run a medical illustration department of four people. I had each of my illustrators try the board and they all loved the way it accepted pen and ink. It didn't smudge and the ability to erase the ink was remarkable. I personally see the Claybord as a replacement for scratchboard because it is far superior. I also think it's perfect for rendering beautiful originals. I'm planning to do my next set of wildlife illustrations on Claybord.

Jan Bishop, Denver, CO, Fine Artist/Illustrator

I happened upon Claybord when I mentioned to a colleague of mine that I was having a hard time finding a surface that would take egg tempera well. He told me that I might want to try Claybord so I called Charles and asked him to send me a few boards. I was amazed the way the surface took the tempera-- it was perfect! I also tried my pen and ink techniques that I use on scratchboard and again, found Claybord to be superior. The surface was so smooth and did not create the puddling that you sometimes get with scratchboard and illustration boards. I love the way the surface sucks the paint in.

Ed Heck, New York, NY, Illustrator for the American Museum of National History

I liked the idea of a more stable surface and really liked the tone of the board. Claybord was much easier to work with than any other board I've used. I do a lot of wildlife illustration so creating fine detail is important. On the Claybord I could achieve the detail I wanted much easier than with Essdee scratchboard, for example. Also, the medium was so forgiving -- this was great! I'm really excited to try water media on the board to see how it takes it.

Lynette Cook, San Francisco, CA, Fine Artist/Science Illustrator

Claybord is certainly a superior substitute for scratchboard but I think it's so much more. The fact that I can now apply guaches, inks, watercolors and oils to one single medium is amazing. This is going to give me as an artist an entire new set of tools for expression.

Lloyd Logan, Osawatomie, KS, Fine Artist/Science Illustrator

This is by far the most durable surface available. I was able to have so much more control of the pigment I was laying down and I was able to experiment with the entire range value on a color so easily.

June Mullins, Blacksburg VA, Science Illustrator

Claybord is so much better than scratchboard. You can build up an image so much easier and you can achieve different levels of color gradation so easily it really is amazing. The board (Claybord) allows for so much more correction.

* From telephone conversations with the artists.

EXHIBIT M-3

Boards Sold in Each Target Segment

	Year 1	Year 2	Year 3	Year 4	Year 5
Claybord Premium (Prof. Artists)					
Penetration	0.48%	0.98%	2.20%	3.67%	3.67%
Number	11,400	23,626	53,039	88,479	88,479
Boards/Artist	5	5	5	5	8
Boards Sold	57,000	118,130	265,195	442,395	707,828
Claybord Oil & Acrylic (Prof. Artists)	2,400,000	2,400,000	2,400,000	2,400,000	2,400,000
Penetration	0.00%	0.93%	2.33%	3.26%	4.66%
Number	0	23,157	58,017	81,174	116,034
Boards/Artist	0	5	5	5	5
Boards Sold	0	115,785	290,085	405,870	580,170
Total Prof. Penetration	0.5%	1.9%	4.6%	7.1%	8.5%
Claybord Premium Schools (182)	10,860	10,860	10,860	10,860	10,860
Penetration	15.50%	25.00%	35.00%	50.00%	60.00%
Number	1,687	2,715	3,801	5,430	6,516
Boards/Artist	2	2	2	2	2
Boards Sold	3,374	5,430	7,602	10,860	13,032
Watermedia Board					
Claybord Oil & Acrylic Schools (1,500)	90,000	90,000	90,000	90,000	90,000
Penetration	0.00%	10.00%	15.00%	20.00%	20.00%
Number	0	9,000	13,500	18,000	18,000
Boards/Artist	2	2	2	2	2
Boards Sold	0	18,000	27,000	36,000	36,000

EXHIBIT F-1

Overall Assumptions

Revenue Assumptions

Most Likely Case	50% of original Projections
Best Case	Most Likely Case x 1.5
Worst Case	Most Likely Case x 0.75

Expense Assumptions

Administrative Expense	Increases at rate of inflation between years 2-5
Payroll Expense	
Salaries	24,000 per officer, Increasing by 10% per year
Payroll Taxes	13% of salaries
Warehouse Rental	5,000 square feet x $0.32/sq. ft./year, Increases by inflation in years 2-5
Research and Development	10% of revenues beginning in year 3
Advertising	See Exhibit F-2
Inflation	5%
Tax rate	34%
Accounts Receivable Terms	
Sales received in month of sale	10%
Sales received one month after sale	30%
Sales received two months after sale	60%
Accounts payable terms - raw materials	Cash terms first year, Net 30 thereafter*
Accounts payable terms - production	Cash terms

*Note: All inventories that appear on the balance sheet are raw materials <u>only</u>. We plan to utilize a just-in-time inventory control system with respect to our finished goods inventory. This is possible because our customers allow a 4-6 week lead time while our manufacturer has a 1-2 week lead time. Thus, calculated inventory turns of 20-26x are overstated because CGS includes production costs which are paid in cash.

EXHIBIT F-2

Marketing Expenditures - Year 1

Conversion Fees $3,000
    Costs involved in contact with retail channel. Includes product sampling,
    postage, telephone, etc.

Print Promotions $600
    Press release creation and mailing.

Print Advertising $20,000
    Ad production and media fees for three consecutive half-page ads in
    Artist magazine and *American Artist*. Combined circulation 410,000.
    Average C/M $20.51.

Direct Mail $55,000
    Targeted mailing 100,000. Includes design, production, printing,
    mailing list, postage, mail house fee and product sampling costs.
    Print quantity 150,000

Trade Shows $12,250
     Includes trade show booth design, registration fees and transportation
    costs. Seven scheduled shows including three sponsored by NAMTA.

Retail support $13,700
    Production and packaging of video training systems and "how to" brochure.

Telemarketing $4,176
    Follow up on direct mail to educational institutions.

Live Demonstrations $11,667
    Site visits to retailer locations. Includes transportation and materials.

Dealer Sales Kits $10,000
    To include video training and sales support materials. Estimate 100 training kits.

EXHIBIT F-3

Ampersand Art Supply
Return on Investment Calculation

(a) Invested Value	$200,000
(b) Percent of corporation	25.0%
(c) Exit Value Multiple (EDBIT) (Note 1)	6.0
(d) EDBIT at Year 5 (See Exhibit F-4)	$1,868,910
(e) Terminal Value at Year 5 - (d) x (c)	$11,213,462
(f) Share of terminal value at Year 5 - (e) x(b)	$2,803,365

Cash Flows

Year 1	-$200,000
Year 2	
Year 3	
Year 4	
Year 5	$2,803,365
ROI (Note 2)	69.6%

Notes:

(1) This figure is representative of transaction multiples for firms with earnings and growth characteristics similar to that of Ampersand's. (According to valuation experts at Howard, Frazier, Barker, Elliot, Inc.)

(2) Compounded annual rate of return.

EXHIBIT F-4

Ampersand Art Supply
Pro-Forma Summary Financials
Most Likely Case

	Fiscal* Year 1	% of Total	Fiscal Year 2	% of Total	Fiscal Year 3	% of Total	Fiscal Year 4	% of Total	Fiscal Year 5	% of Total
Revenues	$271,925	100%	$840,378	100%	$1,925,060	100%	$3,009,805	100%	$4,585,495	100%
Cost of product Sold	65,076	23.9%	353,995	42.1%	813,797	42.3%	1,251,342	41.6%	1,883,365	41.1%
Gross profit	206,849	76.1%	486,383	57.9%	1,111,263	57.7%	1,758,463	58.4%	2,702,129	58.9%
Operating expenses	280,864	103.3%	293,812	35.0%	506,975	26.3%	637.736	21.2%	833,219	18.2%
Operating income	-74,015	-27.2%	192,571	22.9%	604,288	31.4%	1,120,727	37.2%	1,868,910	40.8%
Taxes (@34%)			65,474	7.8%	205,458	10.7%	381,047	12.7%	635,430	13.9%
Net income	$-74,015	-27.2%	$127,097	15.1%	$398,830	20.7%	$739,680	24.6%	$1,233,481	26.9%
Total assets	194,646		397,092		1,014,704		2,137,556		3,981,141	
Book value	194,646		387,217		991,504		2,112,231		3,981,141	
Cash flow from operations	-173,008		113,902		365,519		1,102,943		1,376,143	

EXHIBIT F-5.1

INCOME STATEMENT Year 1

	Sept	Oct	Nov	Dec	Jan	Feb	Mar	Apr	May	June	July	Aug	Total	%
Revenue						$37,696	$38,073	$38,454	$38,839	$39,227	$39,619	$40,016	$271,925	100.0
Cost of Goods sold						13,505	13,640	13,776	13,914	14,053	14,193	14,335	65,076	23.9
Gross Margin						24,192	24,434	24,678	24,925	25,174	25,426	25,680	206,849	76.1
Operating Expenses														
Administrative														
Office rent	500	500	500	500	500	500	500	500	500	500	500	500	6,000	2.2
Office supplies	100	100	100	100	100	100	100	100	100	100	100	100	1,200	0.4
Telephone	300	300	300	300	300	300	300	300	300	300	300	300	3,600	1.3
Postage	1,000	1,000	1,000	1,000	1,000	1,000	1,000	1,000	1,000	1,000	1,000	1,000	12,000	4.4
Total Admin. Expense	1,900	1,900	1,900	1,900	1,900	1,900	1,900	1,900	1,900	1,900	1,900	1,900	22,800	8.4
Payroll Expense														
Salary	8,000	8,000	8,000	8,000	8,000	8,000	8,000	8,000	8,000	8,000	8,000	8,000	96,000	35.3
Payroll Taxes	1,040	1,040	1,040	1,040	1,040	1,040	1,040	1,040	1,040	1,040	1,040	1,040	12,480	4.6
Total Payroll Expense	9,040	9,040	9,040	9,040	9,040	9,040	9,040	9,040	9,040	9,040	9,040	9,040	108,480	39.9
Equipment														
Warehouse rent	1,600	1,600	1,600	1,600	1,600	1,600	1,600	1,600	1,600	1,600	1,600	1,600	19,200	7.1
Total Equipt. Expense	1,600	1,600	1,600	1,600	1,600	1,600	1,600	1,600	1,600	1,600	1,600	1,600	19,200	7.1
R & D														
Advertising														
Distributors	500	500	500	500	500	500							3,000	1.1
Print promotion/PR			300	300									600	0.2
Print advertising		6,667	6,667	6,667									20,001	7.4
Direct mail campaign		10,000	45,000										55,000	20.2
Trade shows	2,042		2,042		2,042		2,042		2,042		2,042		12,250	4.5
Retail support			13,700										13,700	5.0
Telemarketing					833	833	833	833	833				4,167	1.5
Live demos						1,667	1,667	1,667	1,667	1,667	1,667	1,667	11,667	4.3
Dealer sales kit				10,000									10,000	3.7
Total advertising	2,542	17,167	68,209	17,467	3,375	3,000	4,542	2,500	4,542	1,667	3,708	1,667	130,384	47.9
Total Operating Exp.	15,082	29,707	80,749	30,007	15,915	15,540	17,082	15,040	17,082	14,207	16,248	14,207	280,864	103.3
Operating Income	-15,082	-29,707	-80,749	-30,007	-15,915	8,652	7,352	9,638	7,843	10,968	9,178	11,474	-74,015	-27.2
Income before tax	-15,082	-29,707	-80,749	-30,007	-15,915	8,652	7,352	9,638	7,843	10,968	9,178	11,474	-106,354	-39.1
Income taxes														
Net Income	-15,082	-29,707	-80,749	-30,007	-15,915	8,652	7,352	9,638	7,843	10,968	9,178	11,474	-106,354	-39.1

EXHIBIT F-5.2

INCOME STATEMENT ($)

	Year 2					Year 3					Year 4		Year 5	
	Q1	Q2	Q3	FY 2	%	Q1	Q2	Q3	FY 3	%	FY 4	%	FY 5	%
Revenue	146,831	209,403	230,347	840,378	100.0	310,534	403,577	525,483	1,925,060	100.0	3,009,805	100.0	4,585,495	100.0
Cost of Goods sold	57,163	88,847	98,530	353,995	42.1	133,372	171,815	221,777	813,797	42.3	1,251,342	41.6	1,883,365	41.1
Gross Margin	89,668	120,555	131,816	486,383	57.9	177,162	231,763	303,706	1,111,263	57.7	1,758,463	58.4	2,702,129	58.9
Operating Expenses														
Administrative														
Office rent	1,575	1,575	1,575	6,300	0.7	1,654	1,654	1,654	6,615	0.3	6,946	0.2	7,293	0.2
Office supplies	315	315	315	1,260	0.1	331	331	331	1,323	0.1	1,389	0.0	1,459	0.0
Telephone	945	945	945	3,780	0.4	992	992	992	3,969	0.2	4,167	0.1	4,376	0.1
Postage	3,150	3,150	3,150	12,600	1.5	3,308	3,308	3,308	13,230	0.7	13,892	0.5	14,586	0.3
Total Admin. Expense	5,985	5,985	5,985	23,940	2.8	6,284	6,284	6,284	25,137	1.3	26,394	0.9	41,570	0.9
Payroll Expense														
Salary	26,400	26,400	26,400	105,600	12.6	29,040	29,040	29,040	116,160	6.0	127,776	4.2	140,554	3.1
Payroll Taxes	3,432	3,432	3,432	13,728	1.6	3,775	3,775	3,775	15,101	0.8	16,611	0.6	18,272	0.4
Total Payroll Expense	29,832	29,832	29,832	119,328	14.2	32,815	32,815	32,815	131,261	6.8	144,387	4.8	158,826	3.5
Equipment														
Warehouse rent	5,040	5,040	5,040	20,160	2.4	5,292	5,292	5,292	21,168	1.1	22,226	0.7	23,338	0.5
Total Equipt. Expense	5,040	5,040	5,040	20,160	2.4	5,292	5,292	5,292	21,168	1.1	22,226	0.7	23,338	0.5
R & D						31,053	40,358	52,548	192,506	10.0	300,981	10.0	458,549	10.0
Advertising														
Distributors	1,500	1,500		3,000	0.4	788	788	788	3,150	0.2	3,308	0.1	3,473	0.1
Print promotion/PR	300	300		600	0.1	158	158	158	630	0.0	662	0.0	695	0.0
Print advertising	13,334	6,667		20,001	2.4	5,250	5,250	5,250	21,001	1.1	22,051	0.7	23,153	0.5
Direct mail campaign	55,000			55,000	6.5	14,438	14,438	14,438	57,750	3.0	60,638	2.0	63,669	1.4
Trade shows	4,083	2,042	4,083	12,250	1.5	3,216	3,216	3,216	12,863	0.7	13,506	0.4	14,181	0.3
Retail support	13,700			13,700	1.6	3,596	3,596	3,596	14,385	0.7	15,104	0.5	15,859	0.3
Telemarketing		1,667	2,500	4,167	0.5	1,094	1,094	1,094	4,375	0.2	4,594	0.2	4,823	0.1
Live demos		1,667	5,000	11,667	1.4	3,063	3,063	3,063	12,250	0.6	12,863	0.4	13,506	0.3
Dealer sales kit		10,000		10,000	1.2	2,625	2,625	2,625	10,500	0.5	11,025	0.4	11,576	0.3
Total advertising	87,917	23,842	11,583	130,384	15.5	34,226	34,226	34,226	136,903	7.1	143,748	4.8	150,936	3.3
Total Operating Exp.	128,774	64,699	52,440	293,812	35.0	109,671	118,975	131,166	506,975	26.3	637,736	21.2	833,219	18.2
Operating Income	-39,106	55,586	79,376	192,571	22.9	67,491	112,788	172,540	604,288	31.4	1,120,727	37.2	1,868,910	40.8
Income before tax	-39,106	55,586	79,376	192,571	22.9	67,491	112,788	172,540	604,288	31.4	1,120,727	37.2	1,868,910	40.8
Income taxes				65,474	7.8				205,458	10.7	381,047	12.7	635,430	13.9
Net Income	-39,106	55,586	79,376	127,097	15.1	67,491	112,788	172,540	398,830	20.7	739,680	24.6	1,233,481	26.9

EXHIBIT F-5.3

BALANCE SHEET

	Sept	Oct	Nov	Dec	Jan	Feb	Mar	Apr	May	June	July	Aug	Total	%
ASSETS														
Current assets														
Cash	285,918	256,212	175,463	142,449	123,497	98,161	82,495	91,503	98,710	109,034	117,195	127,992	127,992	65.8
Accounts Receivable														
Due in 30 days						11,309	34,040	34,380	34,724	35,071	35,422	35,776	35,776	18.4
Due in 60 days						22,618	22,844	23,073	23,303	23,536	23,772	24,009	24,009	12.3
Total Receivables						33,927	56,884	57,453	58,027	58,608	59,194	59,786	59,786	30.7
Inventory				3,007	6,044	6,105	6,166	6,227	6,290	6,353	6,783	6,868	6,868	3.5
Other current assets														
Total Current Assets	285,918	256,212	175,463	145,456	129,541	138,193	145,545	155,183	163,027	173,994	183,172	194,646	194,646	100.0
Total Assets	285,918	256,212	175,463	145,456	129,541	138,193	145,545	155,183	163,027	173,994	183,172	194,646	194,646	100.0
LIABILITIES														
Current liabilities														
Total payables														
Short term debt														
Other current liabilities														
Total current liabilities														
Shareholders' Equity														
Paid in capital	300,000	300,000	300,000	300,000	300,000	300,000	300,000	300,000	300,000	300,000	300,000	300,000	300,000	154.1
Common Stock	1,000	1,000	1,000	1,000	1,000	1,000	1,000	1,000	1,000	1,000	1,000	1,000	1,000	0.5
Retained Retained earnings	-15,082	-44,788	-125,537	-155,544	-171,459	-162,807	-155,455	-145,817	-137,973	-127,006	-117,828	-106,354	-106,354	-54.6
Total shareholders' equity	285,918	256,212	175,463	145,456	129,541	138,193	145,545	155,183	163,027	173,994	183,172	194,646	194,646	100.0
Total liabilities & equity	285,918	256,212	175,463	145,456	129,541	138,193	145,545	155,183	163,027	173,994	183,172	194,646	194,646	100.0

EXHIBIT F-5.4

BALANCE SHEET ($)	Year 2 Q1	Q2	Q3	FY 2	%	Year 3 Q1	Q2	Q3	FY 3	%	Year 4 FY 4	%	Year 5 FY 5	%
ASSETS														
Current assets														
Cash	58,671	90,791	158,682	241,894	60.9	279,694	340,082	443,978	607,413	59.9	1,710,356	80.0	3,086,499	77.5
Accounts receivable														
Due in 30 days	44,308	63,468	69,828	76,951	19.4	95,739	124,448	162,068	211,447	20.8	226,832	10.6	463,569	11.6
Due in 60 days	39,322	43,208	47,554	52,424	13.2	67,586	87,888	114,503	149,447	14.7	151,328	7.1	323,074	8.1
Total receivables	83,630	106,676	117,382	129,375	32.6	163,325	213,336	276,571	360,895	35.6	378,160	17.7	786,643	19.8
Inventory	19,830	21,239	22,828	25,824	6.5	24,410	31,498	40,723	46,396	4.6	49,040	2.3	108,000	2.7
Other current assets														
Total current assets	162,131	218,706	298,893	397,092	100.0	467,429	583,916	761,272	1,014,704	100.0	2,137,556	100.0	3,981,141	100.0
Total assets	162,131	218,706	298,893	397,092	100.0	467,429	583,916	761,272	1,014,704	100.0	2,137,556	100.0	3,981,141	100.0
LIABILITIES														
Current Liabilities														
Accounts payable	6,592	7,310	8,120	9,875	2.5	12,721	16,420	21,236	23,199	2.3	25,325	1.2		
Short term debt														
Other current liabilities														
Total current	6,592	7,310	8,120	9,875	2.5	12,721	16,420	21,236	23,199	2.3	25,325	1.2		
Stockholders' Equity														
Paid in capital	300,000	300,000	300,000	300,000	75.5	300,000	300,000	300,000	300,000	29.6	300,000	14.0	300,000	7.5
Common stock	1,000	1,000	1,000	1,000	0.3	1,000	1,000	1,000	1,000	0.1	1,000	0.0	1,000	0.0
Retained Earnings	-145,460	-89,604	-10,228	86,217	21.7	153,708	266,496	439,036	690,504	68.0	1,811,231	84.7	3,680,141	92.4
Total equity	155,540	211,396	290,772	387,217	97.5	454,708	567,496	740,036	991,504	97.7	2,112,231	98.8	3,981,141	100.0
Total liabilities and equity	162,131	218,706	298,893	397,092	100.0	467,429	583,916	761,272	1,014,704	100.0	2,137,556	100.0	3,981,141	100.0

EXHIBIT F-5.5

CASH FLOW STATEMENT

	Sept	Oct	Nov	Dec	Jan	Feb	Mar	Apr	May	June	July	Aug	FY 1
Net Income	-15,082	-29,707	-80,749	-30,007	-15,915	8,652	7,352	9,638	7,843	10,968	9,178	11,474	-106,354
Operating Activity Adjust.													
Asset & liab. changes													
Accounts receivable				-3,007	-3,007	-33,927	-22,957	-569	-575	-580	-586	-592	-59,786
Inventories					-30	-60	-61	-62	-62	-63	-431	-85	-6,868
Total changes				-3,007	-3,037	-33,987	-23,018	-630	-637	-643	-1,017	-677	-66,654
Cash from operations	-15,082	-29,707	-80,749	-33,014	-18,952	-25,335	-15,666	9,008	7,207	10,324	8,161	10,797	-173,008
Cash flows from investing													
Plant additions													
Other													
Cash flows from financing													
Short term debt													
Long term debt													
Long term repayments													
Sale of equity	1,000												
Capital contributions	300,000												300,000
Total	301,000												300,000
Net cash incr. (decr.)	285,918	-29,707	-80,749	-33,014	-18,952	-25,335	-15,666	9,008	7,207	10,324	8,161	10,797	126,992
Beginning cash balance		285,918	256,212	175,463	142,449	123,497	98,161	82,495	91,503	98,710	109,034	117,195	
Ending cash balance	285,918	256,212	175,463	142,449	123,497	98,161	82,495	91,503	98,710	109,034	117,195	127,992	127,992

EXHIBIT F-5.6

CASH FLOW ($)	Year 2 Q1	Q2	Q3	FY 2	%	Year 3 Q1	Q2	Q3	FY 3	%	Year 4 FY 4	%	Year 5 FY 5	%
Net Income	-39,106	55,856	79,376	192,571		67,491	112,788	172,540	604,288		1,120,727		1,868,910	
Adjust. for Operations														
Changes in op assets & liabs														
Accounts receivable	-23,844	-23,046	-10,706	-69,589		-33,950	-49,011	-64,235	-231,520		-17,265		-408,483	
Inventories	-12,962	-1,408	-1,589	-18,955		1,413	-7,087	-9,225	-20,572		-2,645		-58,960	
Other current assets														
Accounts payable	6,592	718	810	9,875		2,846	3,699	4,816	13,324		2,126		-25,325	
Other current liabilities														
Total changes	-30,215	-23,736	-11,485	-78,669		-29,691	-52,400	-68,644	-237,768		-17,784		-492,767	
Cash flow from operations	-69,321	32,120	67,891	113,902		37,801	60,388	103,896	365,519		1,102,943		1,376,943	
Cash flows from investing														
Short term borrowings														
Long term debt														
Debt repayment														
Sale of Equity														
Capital contribution														
Net Cash Increase	-69,321	32,120	67,891	113,902		37,801	60,388	103,896	365,519		1,102,943		1,376,143	
Beginning cash	127,992	58,671	90,791			241,894	279,694	340,082						
Ending cash	58,671	90,791	158,682	241,894		279,694	340,082	443,978	607,413		1,710,356		3,086,499	

EXHIBIT F-5.7
REVENUE DETERMINATION Year 1

Product #1

Quantity of Item	Share %	Sept	Oct	Nov	Dec	Jan	Feb	Mar	Apr	May	June	July	Aug	FY 1
8" x 10"	4						335	338	342	345	348	352	355	2,415
9" x 12"	4						335	338	342	345	348	352	355	2,415
11"x14"	4						335	338	342	345	348	352	355	2,415
19"x12"	4						335	338	342	345	348	352	355	2,415
14"x18"	20						1,674	1,691	1,708	1,725	1,742	1,759	1,777	12,075
16"x20"	20						1,674	1,691	1,708	1,725	1,742	1,759	1,777	12,075
18"x24"	20						1,674	1,691	1,708	1,725	1,742	1,759	1,777	12,075
20"x24"	20						1,674	1,691	1,708	1,725	1,742	1,759	1,777	12,075
24"x30"	4						335	338	342	345	348	352	355	2,415
							8,370	8,453	8,538	8,623	8,709	8,796	8,884	60,375

Revenue per Item	Price $	Sept	Oct	Nov	Dec	Jan	Feb	Mar	Apr	May	June	July	Aug	FY 1
8" x 10"	0.75						251	254	256	259	261	264	267	1,811
9" x 12"	1.35						452	456	461	466	470	475	480	3,260
11"x14"	2.06						690	697	704	711	718	725	732	4,975
19"x12"	3.75						1,255	1,268	1,281	1,293	1,306	1,319	1,333	9,056
14"x18"	3.41						5,708	5,765	5,823	5,881	5,940	5,999	6,059	41,175
16"x20"	4.50						7,533	7,608	7,684	7,761	7,838	7,917	7,996	54,337
18"x24"	5.25						8,788	8,876	8,965	9,054	9,145	9,236	9,329	63,393
20"x24"	6.00						10,043	10,144	10,245	10,348	10,451	10,556	10,661	72,449
24"x30"	8.89						2,976	3,006	3,036	3,066	3,097	3,128	3,159	21,469
							37,696	38,073	38,454	38,839	39,227	39,619	40,016	271,925

Product #2

Quantity of Item	Share %
9" x12"	33
14"x18"	33
18"x24"	33

Revenue per Item	Price $
9" x12"	1.13
14"x18"	2.34
18"x24"	3.38

Market Projections	Size $	Market Penetration	Number Purchasers	Board/ Artist	Boards Sold	Growth Rate	Factor
Product #1	2,410,860	0.52%	12,617	4.79	60,374	1%	7.21
Product #2	2,490,000				60,374		
Case Adj. Factor							

EXHIBIT F-5.8

COST & INVENTORY Year 1

Total Costs	Sept	Oct	Nov	Dec	Jan	Feb	Mar	Apr	May	June	July	Aug	FY 1
Raw Mat'l 1						557	562	568	574	579	585	591	4,017
Raw Mat'l 2						425	429	434	438	443	447	451	3,068
Board						2,025	2,045	2,066	2,086	2,107	2,128	2,150	14,607
Raw Materials (Inventory)						3,007	3,037	3,068	3,098	3,129	3,160	3,192	21,692
Production						10,497	10,602	10,708	10,816	10,924	11,033	11,143	43,384
Cost of Finished Goods Sold						13,505	13,640	13,776	13,914	14,053	14,193	14,335	65,076

Raw Mat. Order Schedule

Raw mat'l lead time, mos (1 or 2) 1
Finished goods lead time, mos 1

	Sept	Oct	Nov	Dec	Jan	Feb	Mar	Apr	May	June	July	Aug
Raw Mat'l 1 purchased at end of mo				557	562	568	574	579	585	591	665	607
Raw Mat'l 2 purchased at end of mo				425	429	434	438	443	447	451	508	463
Board purchased at end of month				2,025	2,045	2,066	2,086	2,107	2,128	2,150	2,418	2,207

Item Costs	Sq. In.	Raw Matl 1	Raw Matl 2	Board	Raw	Prod	Total	Margin $	Margin %
8" x 10"	80	0.02	0.01	0.06	0.08	0.29	0.37	0.38	50.60
9" x 12"	108	0.02	0.02	0.08	0.11	0.39	0.50	0.85	62.95
11"x14"	154	0.03	0.02	0.11	0.16	0.55	0.71	1.35	65.38
19"x12"	228	0.04	0.03	0.16	0.24	0.82	1.06	2.69	71.84
14"x18"	252	0.05	0.04	0.18	0.26	0.91	1.17	2.24	65.77
16"x20"	320	0.06	0.05	0.22	0.33	1.15	1.48	3.02	67.07
18"x24"	432	0.08	0.06	0.30	0.45	1.56	2.00	3.25	61.89
20"x24"	480	0.09	0.07	0.33	0.50	1.73	2.22	3.78	62.95
24"x30"	720	0.14	0.11	0.50	0.74	2.59	3.33	5.56	62.49

Raw Mat'l 1 cost/sq. in. 0.0002
Raw Mat'l 2 cost/sq. in. 0.0001
Board cost/sq. in. 0.0007
Production cost/sq. in. 0.0036

EXHIBIT F-6

Pro Forma Summary Financials - Best Case ($)

	Fiscal Year 1	% of Total	Fiscal Year 2	% of Total	Fiscal Year 3	% of Total	Fiscal Year 4	% of Total	Fiscal Year 5	% of Total
Revenues	407,887	100.0%	1,260,567	100.0%	2,887,590	100.0%	4,514,708	100.0%	6,878,242	100.0%
Cost of goods sold	97,614	23.9%	530,992	42.1%	1,220,696	42.3%	1,877,013	41.6%	2,825,048	41.1%
Gross profit	310,274	76.1%	729,575	57.9%	1,666,894	57.7%	2,637,694	58.4%	4,053,194	58.9%
Operating expenses	280,864	68.9%	293,812	23.3%	603,228	20.9%	788,226	17.5%	1,062,494	15.4%
Operating income	29,410	7.2%	435,763	34.6%	1,063,666	36.8%	1,849,468	41.0%	2,990,700	43.5%
Taxes (@34%)			148,159	11.8%	361,646	12.5%	628,819	13.9%	1,016,838	14.8%
Net Income	29,410	7.2%	287,603	22.8%	702,020	24.3%	1,220,649	27.0%	1,973,862	28.7%
Total assets	281,900		731,700		1,817,942		3,666,786		6,718,427	
Book value	281,900		717,663		1,781,329		3,630,797		6,621,497	
Cash flow from operations	-119,213		320,006		677,349		1,885,254		2,246,516	

Pro Forma Summary Financials - Worst Case

	Fiscal Year 1	% of Total	Fiscal Year 2	% of Total	Fiscal Year 3	% of Total	Fiscal Year 4	% of Total	Fiscal Year 5	% of Total
Revenues	203,944	50.0%	630,283	50.0%	1,443,795	50.0%	2,257,354	50.0%	3,439,121	50.0%
Cost of goods sold	48,807	12.0%	265,496	21.1%	610,348	21.1%	938,507	20.8%	1,412,524	20.5%
Gross profit	155,136	38.0%	364,787	28.9%	833,447	28.9%	1,318,847	29.2%	2,026,597	29.5%
Operating Expenses	280,864	68.9%	293,812	23.3%	458,849	15.9%	562,491	12.5%	718,581	10.4%
Operating Income	-125,728	-30.8%	70,975	5.6%	374,598	13.0%	756,356	16.8%	1,308,015	19.0%
Taxes (@34%)			24,132	3.8%	127,363	8.8%	257,161	11.4%	444,725	12.9%
Net Income	-125,728	-61.6%	46,844	7.4%	247,235	17.1%	499,195	22.1%	863,290	25.1%
Total assets	151,018		229,012		614,898		1,370,943		2,720,247	
Book value	151,018		221,993		596,592		1,352,948		2,660,964	
Cash flow from operations	-200,038		13,097		181,440		774,249		941,961	

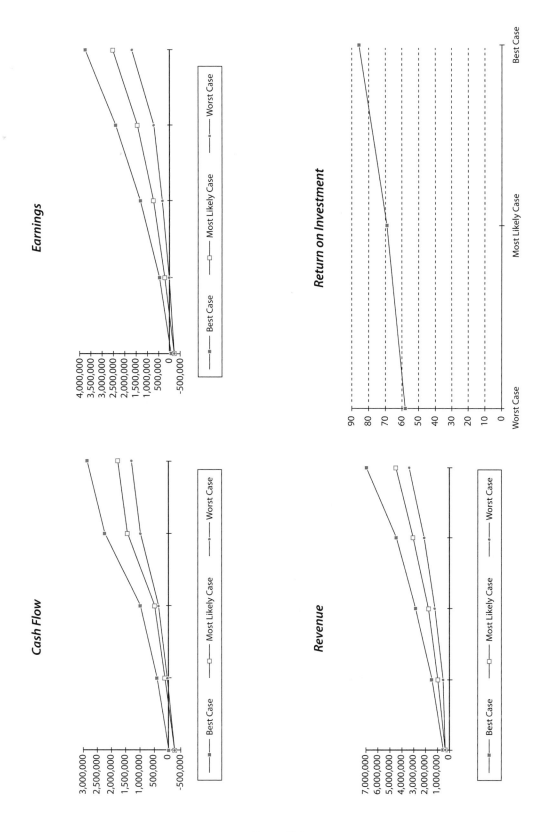

EXHIBIT 0-1.1

Elaine Salazar

3209 IH-35 South #2051
Austin, TX 78741
(512) 444-9706

Education	The University of Texas at Austin, Austin, TX	August 1993
	Master of Business Administration Marketing/Operations	
	The Colorado College, Colorado Springs, CO	June 1982
	BA History	

Experience

Summer 1992   **SLV Economic Development Council**, Alamosa, CO
Marketing Associate (Summer Intern)
- Consulted eight companies in marketing, operations, and financial areas.
- Designed and executed four major marketing initiatives to bring new products into the market.
- Conducted major research project to identify potential for increasing market share in the institutional market for selected food products.

11/86-8/91   **National Public Radio**, Washington, D.C.
Director of Training
- Created NPR's Department of Training. Planned and managed all staff and financial resources for the department.
- Designed the first comprehensive national broadcast training program for 400 public radio stations.
- Designed and implemented curriculum for management training programs and launched the first interactive satellite training program in the industry.

6/83-11/85   **KRZA-FM**, Alamosa, CO
General Manager
- Built and managed a public radio station to serve southern Colorado and northern New Mexico.
- Initiated and secured financing for construction, equipment, and operations.

Honors
- Consortium for Graduate Study in Management Fellowship Recipient
- The Thomas J. Watson Fellowship Recipient, 1982
- Josephine McLaughlin Fleet Award for Scholastic Achievement & Community Service, Colorado College, 1981
- Alpha Lambda Delta Honor Society, Colorado College

Activities
- National Association for Hispanic MBA's
- Mexican American Women's National Association, Vice President for Communications on national board of directors, 1989-1991
- Hispanic Graduate Business Association, UT Austin
- Graduate Business Women's Network, UT Austin
- Academic Affairs Committee, UT Austin

Personal
- Fluent in Spanish

EXHIBIT 0-1.2

Katherine M. Henderson

2502 Cedarview Drive • Austin, TX 78704 • (512) 326-3009

Education	**The University of Texas at Austin**	August 1993
	Master of Business Administration: Marketing / Management	

Southern Illinois University - Carbondale May 1981
Bachelor of Science: Journalism / Advertising
University Scholar, Awarded certificate of achievement for academic merit

Experience
Summer 1992

Apple Computer, Inc., *Marketing Analyst* Cupertino, CA
- Researched alternate distribution channels for development tools and training software
- Made recommendations based on projected reach, cost effectiveness, and profitability
- Delivered white paper and presentation to key management

1990

Blue Poppy Productions, *Co-Founder* San Diego, CA
- Identified a business opportunity and founded a software company that required zero start-up capital
- Developed a distribution system targeted at mail-order and direct mail channels
- Created a computer-based instructional enhancement program for secondary teachers and coordinated product development using royalty programmers
- Number 2 unit sales producer in catalog of 260 items

1985 to
1991

Chariot Software Group, *Director of Marketing* San Diego, CA
- Established in-house marketing department for an Educational Software Publisher which resulted in an increase in sales to end users from 0% to 65% of total revenue
- Analyzed alternative means of product distribution and successfully recommended establishment of a mail order catalog which was profitable its first year; current circulation 80,000+, annual sales over $1,000,000
- Planned for company growth through product and market diversification

1983 to
1985

Over-Lowe Co., *Sales Promotion and Advertising Manager* Englewood, CO
- Created promotional and sales support materials; designed and coordinated press releases, direct and co-op advertising for a construction equipment manufacturer
- Managed the administration of trade shows, sales meetings and training programs
- Provided in-house sales, support, and demonstration equipment allocation

1981 to
1983

BHCD Engineers, Inc., *Marketing Coordinator* Denver, CO
- Initiated and designed promotional programs including corporate identity program and project marketing materials for a large Mechanical Engineering firm

Activities

Graduate Women's Business Network, Board of Directors Liaison
Membership in various professional organizations, 1981-1991: Macintosh Software Publisher's Association, Direct Marketing Club of San Diego, Society for Marketing Professional Services, Student Advertising Association/AAF

Art Background

Nineteen hours college level art training plus numerous courses under private instruction since age 5. Exposure to all types of media. Current interests include watercolor, charcoal & pastels, and ceramics. Experience: Free-lance desktop publishing, paste-up, layout, design and process camera work.

Ampersand (A)

Coalescing venture elements

In January 1993 as the resumption of school approached following New Year's vacation, Elaine Salazar and Kathy Henderson, students at the University of Texas, Austin, were considering how to allocate their energies and resources on a project they had begun the preceding term. With two other teammates, who had since withdrawn, they had developed a venture plan, which appeared earlier in this book as the Prize-Winning Plan case. They had also taken a number of steps toward actually starting the business.

Before them were two goals they had set for themselves. One was to continue starting the venture. The other was to win another venture plan contest to be held in a few weeks at San Diego State University. First prize in the contest consisted of $5,000, an amount that they believed would help them greatly in their start-up. How best to work toward both goals at the same time was a question they considered important.

Aiming for a venture

When, over a year earlier in September 1991, they had begun their first year in the MBA program at the University of Texas, Austin, Elaine and Kathy both dreamed of some day starting their own business. Elaine recalled:

> *My plan in enrolling in an MBA program was to learn more about business, get a job where I could learn about some line of business, and then use that knowledge to start one of my own. Kathy's thinking was similar.*

Vitas presenting the prior education and experience of both women can be found in the Prize-Winning Plan case.

Toward the end of the first year of their MBA program, both had signed up for Professor Gary Cadenhead's entrepreneurship course, which would start in the fall term of the next school year, beginning September 1992.

The course would require preparing a plan for a new business. At the end of the term in December the class would include a competition in which the plans were submitted both in writing and orally to a judging panel comprised of both faculty and business practitioners, including venture capitalists. The oral presentations would be advertised publicly and held in an auditorium where anyone could attend.

In the summer of 1992, prior to Professor Cadenhead's class, Elaine worked with Charles and Barbara Ewing as part of a summer internship on a project sponsored by the Colorado Economic Development Council in Alamosa, Colorado. The Ewings, who had known Elaine's brother for many years, had signed up to gain help from the Economic Development Council's "Leading Edge" consulting program to seek ways of expanding their business. Elaine continued:

> *As part of my summer work in the 'Leading Edge' program, I identified some more art schools and told them about the program at the University of Texas where I might be able to recruit some students to work on developing a fuller plan for creating a business. So I asked them if they would let me bring Clayboard to U.T. and use their product as the subject for developing a business plan for the International Moot Corp℠ project. I needed an idea to work on and they needed someone to help them conduct market research and put together a business plan. It was a win-win situation.*

The Ewings had encountered some demand for Charles' painting panel invention which he referred to as "CEC," or "Charles Ewing Clayboard." Description of the product, its background and what the Ewings had done with it so far can be seen in the case entitled "Charles and Barbara Ewing."

Elaine found that the Ewings had prepared the beginnings of a business plan. Their sales so far had consisted of a small volume of Clayboard sold directly to a few artists and to a couple of art stores in the Denver area. An art distributor had met them, liked the product, and said he could sell more of the product if the Ewings could make it. He said he wanted to take some Clayboard to the National Art Materials Association trade show that summer and put it on display.

Barbara Ewing had expressed concern about how to meet demand if more orders came. Elaine recalled:

> The Ewings were trying to put Clayboard on the market, but they finally decided that it was too much for them. They wanted to scale back. They had decided not to show Clayboard at the National Art Materials Trade Association Show in Las Vegas the summer of 1992, fearing that they would not be able to meet demand if the trade show went well.

Recruiting a student team

The day entrepreneurship course began in the fall of 1992 Elaine showed Kathy the Clayboard and asked if she might be interested in working with her on the business plan. Not only was Kathy interested in the venture idea, but she also had an art background. Elaine continued:

> I approached Robert Tavarez, but at that time he said he wanted to work on something a little more high-tech.
> Two other students, Drew Tingleaf and David Shackleton were also approached. David was an industrial designer and Drew had a finance background. They agreed to join the team.

The name, Ampersand, was suggested by David who stressed the importance of choosing a name that was unique and yet could easily become familiar so it would stick in customers' minds when they saw the company's product. Ampersand is the name of the "&" sign.

Now the team had 12 weeks to crystallize their business idea and develop a plan to carry it out. Their goal, however, was not just to satisfy requirements of the course, but to help Barbara and Charles create a real business plan.

Early explorations

Elaine and Kathy drove to visit the Ewings, learn more about the product and see their shop. Kathy recalled:

> I wanted to get more background on the product and how it was positioned, since I was going to look at the marketability of it. Because Elaine and I were more driven by doing the business than getting a grade we started this project with skepticism. Even though Charles Ewing had received personal endorsements from several happy customers, we wanted to know whether there was really a profitable market for Clayboard.
> We picked up some samples and then started by calling a few retailers. They sounded interested.

Elaine continued:

> We mapped out information we needed to know. Kathy explored and researched the retail channel and I worked on discovering artists' reaction to the product. We sent out samples and

followed up with calls to over 100 artists and others in the industry. We paid for the mail and phone bills out of our own pockets. During our research we explained to those we spoke with that we were a team of students doing a research project on the art industry for one of our classes. People were more willing to give business information to students than to other businesspeople who might be prospective competitors.

One person they talked to was a professor in the University of Texas Art Department. He suggested that they contact the country's largest art supply store, Pearl Paint in New York City, which sold both direct from its premises and through its own mail order catalog. Kathy called Pearl's purchasing department and described Clayboard, which the team had now given the new name "Claybord," after their attorney had advised them to seek a name less generic as a stronger basis for trademarking. Pearl responded to the phone call with a suggestion that the team send a sample. When asked to whom in particular, they said simply the purchasing department.

In November 1992 via second day express, Kathy sent a Claybord sample to Pearl Paint requesting feedback. Four days later they received a phone call from Pearl saying the store was very interested and would like to explore the possibility of carrying Claybord.

Kathy had looked in the library for appropriate trade associations and through one of them had obtained a list of companies that sold art materials, including wholesalers as well as individual stores. There were many questions regarding how to set up the distribution strategy. Should the venture sell to individual stores like Pearl Paint which was a chain of 10 stores or should it sell through wholesalers? What sales support materials should it provide? Should there be any kind of sales training program for anyone?

To establish a price for the boards, the team felt they should consider what Charles Ewing had been selling them for, what competitive materials such as art panels and scratchboard sold for, how attractive artists were likely to consider the product, and what they would be willing to pay, as well as the industry discount structure.

Through their contacts with the stores and manufacturers' representatives, the team learned about discounts in the art supply channels. The typical arrangement was to give wholesalers a discount off retail price of 50 percent plus another 25 percent on the remaining 50 percent. The wholesalers then gave 50 percent off retail price to the stores. Manufacturers' representatives typically operated on a commission from 5 percent–10 percent on whatever they sold.

A win at the end of the term

Meanwhile, the term was rapidly coming to a close. The team had to make assumptions and wrap up their plan for oral presentation and written submission. Nine other teams in the course would compete with them. Two rounds of presentations would be held before panels of judges that included not only instructors but also venture capitalists, entrepreneurs, bankers, advertising agents and other professionals.

First prize would include a stipend of $500 plus free rent and an office space at the University of Texas business incubator, a facility provided to help startup companies by offering low-cost office space complemented by ancillary services such as phone answering, fax and copy services and the companionship of other entrepreneurs. The first round of competition would eliminate half of the teams and the second would pick the overall winner. Kathy commented:

We were not too surprised when we made it through the first round. We felt we had a promising product and a good plan, even though there were still a lot of questions to be answered.
But we thought the odds would be against us on the second round. All the other teams had high tech products or ideas, and we just had a very simple-looking low-technology product. Most

of the entrepreneurs and venture capitalists on the judging panel seemed to be oriented toward high technology, so we thought that would give the other teams an important advantage.

When we took first prize in the second round, it just amazed us. As it turned out, our low technology may have worked in our favor, because the judges could touch and feel the product. We had market affirmation and a solid plan. I don't know if that is what worked for us, but anyway, we won!

Comments from the judges included questions about how reasonable the inventory figures were in the team's balance sheet projections and whether the team might have trouble controlling quality, since none of the team members had much experience in manufacturing. One judge expressed the view that this venture should indeed go forward. He said he would personally consider investing, probably lending the money and taking some equity in the business.

Elaine's trip to New York

During the term break in early 1993 after the team won first place, Elaine flew to New York and visited Pearl Paint. She recalled:

It happened that the buyer who had initially reviewed our product was no longer there. It had been turned over to a man named Victor. We met. I showed him samples and what the product could do. I explained that we were not ready to go nationwide with it, but we would like to run a test market to obtain more market information and before we launched a national sales campaign. Victor said, "Why don't you put together a proposal for a test market program and send it to us, and maybe we will try it."

That seemed encouraging, but I wasn't sure how to take it. The store was like nothing I'd ever seen. Five floors of art supplies. Each floor was dedicated to some particular category of supplies, but it seemed so disorganized with very little merchandising. There were 10-foot high shelves with everything imaginable on them. No point-of-purchase displays, just paper brochures hanging off the shelves. I called Kathy and said, "This store is very different from what I expected. I don't know if they'll be able to move our product or really help us identify the right national campaign."

Kathy recalled:

When Elaine called and said that Pearl, the biggest art store in the country, was interested in placing an order, it just about blew me away. It sounded as though Pearl might order as many as 2,000 Claybords as part of a test market experiment.

Elaine passed along the good news to Charles and Barbara Ewing and suggested that perhaps together they could find a way to expand production in southwestern Colorado to fill the Pearl order. They realized, however, that this would require a substantial expansion of capacity from the 300 boards per week that Charles was currently able to produce only if he sacrificed his art work.

Looking ahead

As the March 15, 1993 beginning of spring break approached, the founding team of Ampersand was optimistic, based upon conversations with Pearl Paint in New York, that they would soon be receiving a $5,300 order for 2,000 Claybords. Kathy commented:

When Elaine came home from New York, we drafted up a one-and-one-half-page letter proposing a test market order for 2,000 boards. We figured the customer, Pearl Paint, would buy on some sort of consignment where they could return the product if it didn't sell, and then if that happened, we could find out why and use the information to shape our marketing strategy. We offered to be at the store for a week and demonstrate the product for their sales staff and customers. Now it sounds from phone conversations as though they will be giving us an order for 2,000 Claybords without any contingencies except that we will have to deliver them by the end of May.

The team again called Charles Ewing, and asked how fast he could make Claybords. He replied that he could produce at most 300 per week, and that much not for long because it interfered too much with his work in art. About the same time, the team was selected as one of the five teams to compete in San Diego State's North American Venture Plan Competition in April. Since they were also taking classes full time, they figured there would be much to work on over the one-week spring break.

Anticipating production

In anticipation of sales, they had regarded arranging for production as an important task. With David Shackleton's help the team had searched for ways to accomplish production on a larger scale. Paint shops, they found, were not equipped either to handle their thick mineral coating or to dry these panels once they came off their coating lines. The closest shop interested and willing to coat the panels was nearly 200 miles away in Tyler, Texas. Elaine Salazar and Charles Ewing had visited the shop, persuaded the owner to sign a non-disclosure agreement, and discussed with him the process of putting the mineral coating on the Masonite. The owner had said the team could come and experiment with coating a small batch.

After being coated the 4x8 foot Masonite sheets would need to be cut into standard sizes of 8x10, 11x14, 16x20 and 20x24 inches. The edges of these smaller panels then had to be routed to round their corners and sanded to make the coated surface smooth. This was the most labor-consuming part of the task, which Charles Ewing had accomplished with a hand-held orbital sander. He had expended considerable time and effort learning what grade of sandpaper to use on the sander and how to get the surface smooth.

But he could not do it speedily. The materials for Claybord were relatively cheap. Masonite sheets cost about $15 each and could be cut into several smaller boards. The coating consisted of limited amounts of relatively inexpensive materials. Labor in cutting, routing to round the edges and sanding, on the other hand, could take as much as five minutes per board. By performing this work himself and selling direct to end users, Charles had saved the labor cost and had also been able to escape the high discounts to retail stores. But it consumed more of his time than he wanted to spend.

Changes in the team

When David and Drew decided not to continue with the venture during the second term beginning January 1993 Elaine and Kathy had recruited two new team members. One was Robert Tavarez, who had graduated from San Jose State University in 1988, then worked for Silicon Graphics and for Lockheed Missiles and Space Systems as a Business Systems Analyst, then for Hewlett Packard as a Software Applicatons Specialist before enrolling in the Texas MBA program. He had declined to join the Ampersand team earlier, and commented:

I wondered, why did my venture lose and theirs win. I realized that they had a great team and had spent 90 percent of their time on market research. My team had spent 10 percent on that.

At the beginning of the next term I was passing down the hall, and Elaine said, "We need a CFO, because Drew dropped out. How would you like to do that?" I said, "Well, it sounds like a commitment; let me talk to my wife."

The other new member, Scott Bryant, had graduated from Texas A&M with a bachelor's degree in mechanical engineering, and then worked for Anderson Consulting for four years in operations management where he became a senior analyst before enrolling at Texas. Scott recalled:

> My training had been in mechanical engineering and I had some experience with manufacturing through work with a consulting firm. I had not come to business school with a goal of having my own business, but rather just to learn more about business. At the end of the first term I went to see the venture plan presentations because I had heard that there were great professors in the entrepreneurial area and the program was interesting.
>
> The presentation by Elaine's team really impressed me because the venture they were planning looked so straightforward and feasible. Other ones that had to do with robots and high tech didn't look like the students could really pull them off. But this team's product just seemed to be mud on a board that should be easy to make, and the team had really checked it out with artists. They had strong evidence that the market was really there. I told Elaine, "Hey, if any of the other people don't stay on, be sure to contact me."
>
> In the middle of January, I was signing up for job interviews in the career center where I bumped into David, who had been on the team. It surprised me because I thought he was going to do the venture. I asked him what he was doing there and he told me he had dropped out of the venture. I went right to Elaine. I repeated to her that I would like to join the team, and she asked me to meet with her and Kathy.
>
> One thing she specifically asked about was whether I was capable of fixing machinery. She had lived on a farm. Machinery on farms frequently breaks down, and farmers get good at fixing it. I had studied mechanical engineering, so I knew the theory and something about the reality of machines. But I had never run a production line.

Robert and Scott both committed to joining the team at least for the rest of the term and possibly for longer.

Anticipating needs

In January 1993 the venture had received office space in the incubator rent free plus $500 prize money from winning the Texas class competition. If they could win the San Diego State University venture plan contest in April too that would give them another $5,000.

Was there anything else they should do to their venture plan to increase the odds of that happening, they wondered? Criteria to be used by judges in the San Diego contest appear in Appendix 4b-1 of this book. Those to be used by the judges in the International Moot Corp competiton, which would be held in May, appear in Appendix 4b-2. A copy of the team's plan, as noted earlier, appears in the Prize-Winning Plan case.

Following through on the Pearl order was clearly going to require capital. The four guessed that they might need around $10,000. Members of the team would be able to come up with some. There was debate about how much money would be absolutely necessary to tide the venture over at least until it could win the $5,000 prize in San Diego.

The team began to talk about each member perhaps contributing $1,250 for starters to carry the project forward. But how should it be handled? Was this an investment in a business or simply expenses for carrying through a class project? It seemed desirable to aim for as much equality as possible in order to have all team members feel fairly treated and motivate them on the venture.

Also, what sort of formal arrangement, if any, should be established with the Ewings. They too had not only created the product, but had been working for about two years on trying to make a business out of it. And they had invested an estimated $40,000 to bring that about, including legal expenses for a patent application which was still being worked on.

In addition, each of the team members had other classes, since all were full-time students aiming to graduate at the end of May. At the end of the first term Elaine had asked all team members to consider seriously whether they wanted to continue on the project as a real venture, since it would likely call for increasing investments of not only time but also money.

The team members expected to interview for potential jobs at the campus career center, which would demand an appreciable amount of their time. One open time that would be available to produce Claybord for Pearl's test market, if the hoped-for order came, was a one-week spring break from school in early March. There seemed to be a variety of issues calling for resolution and then a considerable amount of action required. Meanwhile, there was the substantial demand of school work.

The new team of four decided to meet at Scholz's, a local bar, and map out member assignments for the coming term.

Knight Brothers (B)

In conjunction with their business plan, which appears as the Knight Brothers (A) case, the two brothers had also drafted an investment proposition, as follows below:

November 16, 1980

The following is a business proposal for the formation and operation of a limited partnership. This memorandum is to provide a limited number of investors information pertaining to the private placement of Units of Limited Partnership Interest in THINK TANKS, a New York limited partnership organized to purchase microcomputers and operate them in a retail store.

SUMMARY

INVESTMENT OFFERED Limited partnership interests are offered in the aggregate amount of $300,000.

MINIMUM PURCHASE The minimum purchase is $25,000.

PAYMENT SCHEDULE The first payment of $12,500 upon subscription. The final payment of $12,500 on March 15, 1980.

OFFERING PERIOD The offering will terminate at 5 p.m. on December 15, 1980 (unless extended by the partnership to not later than December 30, 1980 or the commencement date, if earlier).

CONDITIONS TO CLOSING THE OFFERING All subscriptions will be returned to investors unless received prior to December 15, 1980 (or December 30, 1980 in the event that the partnership has extended the offering), the partnership has accepted subscriptions for interests totaling $300,000.

BUSINESS OF THE PARTNERSHIP The partnership will purchase microcomputers and will sell time on them through a retail store in the Harvard Square area of the Cambridge, Massachusetts. In addition, the partnership intends to purchase microcomputers for lease or sale to individuals and/or businesses.

MICROCOMPUTERS The partnership intends to spend approximately $150,000 in the acquisition of microcomputers and related high-technology equipment.

MANAGEMENT The managing partner will be responsible for the managing of the partnership's business. Mr. Richard D. Knight and Mr. James A. Knight, individual general partners, have an aggregate in excess of 10 years' experience in the computer and financing businesses.

FINANCING The general partners do not anticipate the need for debt financing of any kind in connection with the purchase of the microcomputers or the operation of the business.

PAYMENTS TO THE GENERAL PARTNERS The partnership will pay the general partners a management fee of $30,000 per annum plus an amount equal to 3 1/2 percent of the net profit (payable monthly).

ALLOCATION OF THE PROFITS AND LOSSES Profits and losses of the partnership will be allocated 95 percent to the limited partners and 5 percent to the general partners until the sum of the cash distributions to the limited partners equals the amount contributed to the partnership by the limited partners. Thereafter profits and losses will be allocated 80 percent to the limited partners and 20 percent to the general partners until the sum of the cash distributions is equal to TWICE the amount contributed to the partnership by the limited partners. Thereafter profits and losses will be allocated 60 percent to the limited partners and 40 percent to the general partners.

PARTNERSHIP DISTRIBUTIONS The general partners will distribute quarterly, in their discretion, the amount of cash in excess of that required to conduct the business.

SUMMARY OF PROJECTED
RETURN PER $25,000 INTEREST

YEAR	Cash Investment	Tax Loss	Investment Tax Credit	Cash Flow
1980	$12,500	$2000	-$0-	-$0-
1981	12,500	10,250	412.50	2,000
1982		2775	-0-	18,000
1983		1450	-0-	22,000
1984		-0-	-0-	30,000
1985				30,000
1986				30,000
1987				30,000
1988				30,000

The assumptions which are made in the summary table with regard to the projected tax losses and the investment tax credit are in line with the business plan of the partnership and generally accepted accounting principles.

The projections as to the cash flow are based upon the business judgment of the general partners in connection with the utilization studies which have been performed projecting the store's sales.

Sally Corbin

Looking for a loan

In March 1998, Sally Corbin was preparing to apply for a bank loan to expand her hobby of candle-making into a for-profit business. She had written a brief description of what she planned to do (Exhibit 1), a summary of sales and materials expenditures so far (Exhibit 2), and a cash-flow forecast (Exhibits 3 and 4). Her objective was to obtain a bank loan to develop the business.

Sally's new venture, Phantastick Candles, custom designed, manufactured, and sold candles, mostly wholesale but also retail, from a low-rent facility in Seagull, Georgia. The market ranged from Miami to Boston and west to Portland, Oregon. Most sales were to stores in Boston and Miami. The typical buyer at wholesale, which accounted for about 95 percent of current sales, was a retail gift shop. Sales were obtained by mailing out postcards and catalogs with a price list, though most new customers to date had been recruited through a salesman and the founder, Sally, making direct cold calls. The company also had sales agreements with representatives on a straight 15-percent-commission basis in Boston and Miami, who sometimes displayed the company's candles at gift shows. Approximately 65 percent of sales by her customers' stores occurred during September and October in preparation for Christmas.

Competitors included numerous other small companies with which Phantastick contended on the basis of its product quality, designs, and sales efforts, as well as much larger companies, against which Phantastick competed by accepting smaller orders and more varied combinations within orders.

Typical order sizes for Phantastick were close to its $100 minimum, whereas larger companies typically had a minimum of $300. Most smaller companies, according to Sally, made very low profits, and consequently came and went. Larger companies, she believed, were the only ones making high profits. Versatility and flexibility, she said, were what allowed the small companies to survive. Phantastick would supply smaller orders than most of its competitors and would create special orders of almost any design. Typical types of candles included pillar, votive, sand, and molded candles in a wide variety of colors, scents, and containers. The company also offered a line made from recycled wax at a price discount for customers who saved and brought in their own wax. Sally commented:

> *Other candle makers have been impressed by our candles because they can't see the seams. We take a lot of care and pride in how they look.*

Although the company was somewhat hard to find because the telephone company misspelled its listing as "Fantastick," sales from the date of founding in February 1997 through the end of that year were $30,010, and left Sally with a gross profit of $18,005, as shown in Exhibit 2. This also left the company with a debt on Sally's credit card, which was the sole source of financing, of over $12,000, which she hoped to pay off by obtaining a bank loan.

Sally said entrepreneurship had long been an activity in her family. Her father had operated his own trucking business, her grandfather had owned a ranch in Arizona, then later a restaurant, and Sally had previously owned and operated, with a partner, a dried-flower store in Cave Town, Georgia from 1980 to 1985. They closed the store in 1985 when the partner was offered "too good a job to pass up" elsewhere. That store was, in Sally's view, too much for her to manage alone. Besides, she had a young daughter to whom she wanted to give attention, and her mother was getting up in years. Sally decided to move to Seagull, near the Florida border, where her mother lived. She recalled:

> The dried flower store was a good experience. It gave us a living for five years. If we had known more about management when we were running it we might have been more profitable.

The two partners closed the store, cleared out and disposed of the furniture and equipment, and moved on. Sally became a waitress in Seagull, and continued to pursue, her hobby of painting.

The business idea

After 11 years Sally grew tired of working as a waitress and started thinking about other things she could do. The dried-flower store had worked out for her and her partner before, but she was not particularly interested in starting another one of those. She now had no partner, and the dried-flower business had been a lot of work. She commented:

> I wonder if anyone makes much money running a gift shop. Especially in a small town, I doubt they ever do. So I looked for other ideas.

She considered selling her paintings, but said she rejected that idea because she tended to become attached to them. This, she said, made it hard for her to accept criticism or rejection of the paintings by possible customers, and also hard to part with them if people did want to buy them. Ceramics and candles were alternatives. Candles seemed simpler, so she bought a book on candle making and, in April of 1996, an electric wax melter. She continued:

> I didn't know people who made candles, and hadn't made them before myself. But I was interested in aromatherapy, and candles seemed like something I could make where I wouldn't have trouble not wanting to part with them or being sensitive to criticism. A candle's just a candle.
>
> But making them was harder than I expected. I tend to be a perfectionist, and I had trouble getting them to come out right at first. After a while, though, I became able to make them well and began thinking about opening some sort of gift store where I would make candles in the back and sell them out front.

She tried selling candles at retail by opening a booth at a Wal-Mart store, something the store permitted local artisans to do experimentally. There she got her first sales of candles, but from the small resultant income concluded that "unless the volume is going to be a lot bigger than this, retailing won't work."

This changed the direction of her plan toward manufacturing and wholesaling, rather than retailing. That not only promised higher volume, but also gave her more flexibility with her time to concentrate on craftsmanship, which she enjoyed more than tending store. Moreover, it reduced her rental expense, since now she wouldn't need a high-traffic location. Seagull, she said, was not a very good town for retailing anyway.

Sally obtained her first major load of wax, three boxes at $30 each, from a local woman who had been left ten boxes from her former husband. With the wax she also got some molds that she later found defective and threw away. After that, she obtained her supplies from commercial sources.

She found them and other sources of helpful information by starting with "wax" in the Yellow Pages and then phoning from one referral to another. That way she also found a trade association for candle-makers, which she joined. Through it she received a monthly newsletter with problem-solving information and tips on how to improve operations, and was able to obtain addresses of retailers to whom she might sell.

At first she worked in her home, but then as the candle-making began to require more space for equipment and inventory, she looked for bigger space. A prominent local business man, who owned a used car lot (where she had bought a car) plus other real estate and had been one of the founders of a local bank, offered her space in one bay of a building he owned on a back street. Rent he set at $75 per month, with $25 of that deferred, and no charge for utilities, including electric power from an already-installed 220-volt outlet that she used heavily for melting wax. She transferred her candle-making supplies and equipment in February 1997. Buying furniture and equipment for the new shop, she said, was fun.

Sales began at a Wal-Mart booth and then developed through some craft fairs where Sally displayed her products. Her first wholesale order came from the gift shop of a Best Western motel where she had worked as a waitress. In January 1977 she hired, as a salesman on 15 percent commission, a former waiter she knew, who began calling on other stores and brought in her first order from out of town. She observed:

> People here in Seagull think my candles are expensive. But in Boston they seem to be regarded as cheap.

In April 1977 Sally went by auto on a sales excursion to Arizona and New Mexico to try selling a candle line decorated with Indians and cactus. The trip proved to be eventful, not so much for sales it generated as for what went wrong. She fell ill in Gunnison, Colorado and needed an operation plus a week and a half in the local hospital that left her with a $12,000 bill to pay upon her return home. She recalled:

> I pay off a little here and a little there, as I'm able to. Some people told me I was lucky because if I had fallen ill in Miami it would have cost a lot more.

Sally began advertising by mail to other stores, which brought in some orders. Her phone number, which she had printed on a label at the bottom of each candle, started bringing in repeat orders. By June of 1997 sales were small but slowly growing, and by early fall they began to pick up substantially, then rose further as the Christmas season got underway.

She continued to experiment with different designs. The work, she said, was somewhat similar to making and selling artificial flowers, but a bit more creative. Molds for different shapes cost between $75 and $100. One she found amusing produced a candle shaped like a skull, and she found she could make combinations with red wax on the inside and white on the outer surface. Scratching through the white could produce a gory appearance.

The production process, she said, was generally straightforward. Although her daughter helped, Sally found it tiring work, the hardest part of which was handling the heating properly. The $55,000 bank loan she sought would let her buy larger quantities of wax, install equipment to make candles faster, hire another salesperson to replace the present one, who wanted to quit, and hire another person to help with production. She said she might go on the road personally to seek sales by visiting stores, and perhaps also participate in some fairs, although that was an activity she did not find attractive. "It's very tiring and not much fun."

EXHIBIT 1 Summary description

Phantastick Candle Creators (PCC) started as a home business in August 1996. Because of the enthusiastic customer response at craft shows, it quickly outgrew kitchen space and is currently located at 222 King Street in Seagull, Georgia. Initially, PCC supplied hand-crafted candles to small gift and specialty shops along the coast and has now grown to supply over 80 stores from Miami to Boston. During 1997 PCC showed an 11 percent average growth in sales per month.

The mission of PCC is to produce hand-crafted high-quality candles, soaps, and aromatherapy aids with zero defects at a lower price than its competition. PCC is committed to a high level of customer service, maintaining personal contact between its clients and the principals of the company by collaborating to produce candles to suit customers' specific needs. Because of this PCC is gaining a reputation for flexibility, creativity, and dependability.

Sally Corbin and Al Brown are the principals of the business. They design and manufacture hand-crafted candles of many styles with zero defects achieved through outstanding quality-control standards. PCC is a sole proprietorship owned by Ms. Corbin, who is also financial manager. Mr. Brown is responsible for sales and marketing.

Currently PCC produces candles on a per-order basis. The time from order placement to delivery is three to four weeks. Ms. Corbin and Mr. Brown can produce $4,000–$5,000, at wholesale, of candles per month as the sole producers. Within this framework PCC has reached its production capacity and has been able to service only its established accounts since October of 1997. The company was not able to take on new accounts for the 1997 holiday season because demand exceeded PCC's capacity to produce. According to the National Candle Association, seasonal (Christmas holidays) business accounts for approximately 35 percent of the yearly U.S. market of the candle industry.

Historical data from 1997 prove that PCC has developed an excellent product to market. To supply the demand for PCC products, the company needs capital in order to expand facilities and satisfy demand for present and future business. PCC is asking for $71,074. (For further details see the financial forecast that follows this section.)

1) Hire a sales representative by April of 1998.
2) Produce a catalog of PCC products by May of 1998.
3) Increase PCC inventory in order to improve order time and service mail-order potential.
4) Create a Web page for advertising on the World Wide Web by May 1998.
5) Promote and market PCC products through local candle parties starting October 1998.
6) Open a retail shop by fall of 1998.
7) Design new products starting in June of 1998.

PCC anticipates rigid control of expenses and improved gross margins throughout 1998, 1999, and 2000. Based on PCC marketing assumptions for these three years, the company projects a 205 percent increase in sales for 1998, followed by a 15 percent growth in sales for both the years 1999 and 2000 to permit settling in and stabilization of the business. Currently, PCC spends 40 percent of its gross sales for goods and supplies. This percentage will decrease to 29 percent with the advantage of buying these goods with volume discounts. This will create 11 percent savings in the cost of goods. These savings will be applied toward offering a commission for a sales representative, which should increase sales 40 percent. The company's projected net profit before taxes for 1998 is $36,612; for 1999 it is $29,143 (this is after hiring an additional employee, as well as an anticipated change in the company's rental agreement that will increase PCC fixed expenses), and for 2000 it is $35,712.

EXHIBIT 2 Sales and materials costs for 1997

Month	Sales	Materials	Gross profit
Jan	0	0	0
Feb	375	150	225
Mar	1,530	612	918
Apr	2,057	823	1,234
May	2,219	888	1,331
Jun	2,667	1,067	1,600
Jul	2,688	1,075	1,613
Aug	3,633	1,453	2,180
Sep	3,494	1,398	2,096
Oct	3,913	1,565	2,348
Nov	4,024	1,610	2,414
Dec	3,410	1,364	2,046
Totals	30,010	12,005	18,005

EXHIBIT 3 Cash flow for 1998

Months	Jan	Feb	Mar	Apr	May	Jun	Jul	Aug	Sep	Oct	Nov	Dec	Total
Beginning cash	245	471	632	1002	19120	5159	4480	7125	5662	8445	13907	19868	23651
Total sales	3560	3810	4191	5867	8214	10678	10892	11110	11665	12248	13105	8900	104,240
Cash receipts													
Cash sales	3026	3239	3563	4987	6982	9077	9259	9444	9916	10411	11140	7565	88,609
Credit sales	512	534	571	628	880	1232	1601	1633	1666	1749	1837	1965	14,808
Payment													
Loans				55000									55,000
Total cash	3538	3773	4134	60615	7862	10309	10860	11077	11582	12160	12977	9530	158,417
Receipts													
Begin cash+recp	3783	4244	4766	61617	26982	15468	15340	18202	17244	20605	26884	29398	158,417
Cash disbursements													
New material	1054	1128	1241	19344									22,767
Equipment					4052	375	1563	2806	1250				10,046
Supplies	50	50	50	1083	0	2117	0	2426	500	100	100	100	6,576
Transportation	200	200	200	200	200	200	200	200	200	200	200	200	2,400
Phone & elect.	100	100	100	100	200	200	200	200	200	200	200	200	2,000
Professional services					71	71	71	71	71	71	71	71	568
Advertising	50	50	50	50	1350	100	100	100	100	100	100	100	2,250
Insurance	25	25	25	100	147	147	147	147	147	147	147	147	1,351
Rent	75	75	75	75	75	75	75	75	75	75	75	75	900
Loan payment	188	188	188	13175	760	760	760	760	760	760	760	760	19,819
Capital purchase				3500	8500								12,000
Tax, payroll				100	100	100	100	100	100	100	100	100	900
Labor	370	396	435	1972	2569	3195	3249	3305	3446	3595	3813	2744	29,089
Owner draw	1000	1200	1200	1200	1200	1200	1200	1200	1200	1200	1200	1200	14,200
Other expenses	200	200	200										600
Maint, repair				1598	1599	1648	50	50	50	50	50	50	5,145
Training & pdt dev					1000	800	500	1100	700	100	200		4,400
Total expenses	3312	3612	3764	42497	21823	10988	8215	12540	8799	6698	7016	5747	135,011
Ending cash	471	632	1002	19120	5159	4480	7125	5662	8445	13907	19868	23651	23,651

EXHIBIT 4 Footnotes to cash flow 1998

1. Sales growth is based on historical sales enhanced by hiring a salesperson.
2. Local newspaper advertising will increase from biweekly to weekly.
3. PCC-related credit card debt will be eliminated by consolidation.
4. Insurance increases will be due to putting a second auto under coverage, adding life insurance for the founder, and adding liability insurance for future employees.
5. A repair budget is added because there wasn't one and because the company's rental agreement is being changed to make it responsible for repairs.
6. Advertising increases will be due to expanded direct mail, plus addition of a sales representative and a Web page.
7. Accounting firm is to be hired.
8. One full-time employee will be added through the South Coast Employment Corporation.
9. Taxes added for employees.
10. Increase due to change in PCC's rental agreement to include utilities.
11. This expense eliminated with hiring of sales representative.
12. Loan payment.
13. Nominal increases for balance of year for stabilization of the business.
14. This figure represents the first two weeks of December only. The principals focused on production during this period and went on vacation during the last week of December.

Greg Thompson

Proposing to a bank

In late September, three years after receiving his MBA degree from the University of Washington, Greg Thompson was thinking about preparing two proposals. One would be for presentation to a bank executive to solicit a contract for flying canceled checks from bank branches in southern Washington to a central office in Seattle. The second would be to a bank loan officer for financing the purchase of an airplane with which to carry the checks. Questions facing him included what information to include in the proposals, how to obtain it, and how to present it.

Personal history

Flying had been a favorite hobby of Greg's for over 10 years. He was a licensed pilot and had served on the board of directors of a local flying club, "where I learned the many difficulties of doing things by committee," he recalled. In studying for his MBA, he had led a team of students in preparing a prospectus for a commuter airline as part of an entrepreneurship course. That project was not carried further than the class, however. Greg recalled:

> We abandoned the commuter airline idea because it simply required too much financing. So after graduating we took different jobs. Two members of the team started a small restaurant after hours to serve Mexican food, and the third one set up a manufacturer's rep operation in Denver.
>
> I vacationed around for a while after getting my degree and then innocently sat back waiting for the phone to ring with job offers. By the time summer ended, it was clear that would not happen, so I began to hustle. Through the placement office, I interviewed with a small contracting firm that really looked interesting, but they didn't offer me a job. I sent some applications to Boeing and had two or three interviews with them. At the time I really didn't know what I wanted to do, but it began to become clearer to me what I didn't want to do. These were big government contracts where I would be some sort of coordinator or administrator. I had never been comfortable with the prospect of being a tiny cog in a huge machine, and that was what this was. The jobs were ambiguous, with no clear idea what was expected of you. Somehow you were responsible for something, but with no clear authority over anyone or anything—just shuffling papers.
>
> The life insurance routine also left me cold. At first I thought, "Why not sell life insurance?" My major had been in marketing. But when I went for an interview to one of the companies, they kept me waiting for half an hour. During that time I wandered around the office and came across a chart on the wall that showed what volumes of business the different salesmen were doing. A very few were doing big volumes, but more were far below that. Then when they got around to interviewing me, they told me about commissions, sales volumes, and what I could expect. They made claims about what other salesmen typically did, which were way out of line with what I had seen on the wall. That convinced me I didn't want to work for them.
>
> But by now my savings and student loan money was running out, and I needed to get a job somehow. So I got hold of a Boeing company telephone book and started looking through the different sections that made up the company. The hydrofoil program caught my eye. I had been in the navy for three years before returning to graduate school, and I liked the sea. So I called up the marketing manager of the hydrofoil program from his number in the book, and told him I had majored in marketing and transportation, and that I wanted to go to work for him. That got me an interview, and the interview got me a job as a market analyst.

Greg was still in this position when the idea for air-freighting bank checks came up, and although he now worked for a very large company, he liked his job.

> *The part of Boeing I work in is actually a small one. In it I can see the whole picture of what I'm doing and how it fits in. In our small group a salesman and a market analyst work together on each project. We learn about the prospective customer, work up a demand analysis and cash flow, and build the basis for a sales and financing proposal. I like being able to see the whole thing and follow it all the way through to a sale.*

Check flying service idea

In July Greg read in the newspaper about the crash of a helicopter near Seattle. He was surprised to notice in the article that the craft had been used just to fly canceled checks between bank offices. This, he thought, was certainly an expensive way to move checks around, since air transport in general is fairly high-priced; helicopters are especially costly to operate, generating expenses per mile and per payload pound that are two or three times as much as those of airplanes. He figured it must be worth a lot to banks to get fast delivery service on canceled checks. It occurred to him that with a plan he might be able to out-perform other modes of transport for some routes. But he did nothing further with the thought at the time.

Then in early September he attended a cocktail party where, by chance, he met a man who happened to be on the planning staff of a major Seattle bank, one of the three banks that had been experimenting with the helicopter service for transporting checks from nearby cities around the Puget Sound. The air transport subject came up, and Greg let it be known that he might like to try ferrying checks by airplane—perhaps from more distant areas where advantages over the helicopter would be greater. The planning officer said he knew the bank's float control manager, who was responsible for arranging transport of the checks. Greg recalled:

> *He gave me his card, told me to call the man, and said he would contact the man himself to announce that I would be calling. I probably would not have called the man, but this setup really didn't leave me much choice. I felt literally pushed into it.*
>
> *The phone call lasted nearly two hours. The float control manager and I just seemed to hit it off right from the start. It turned out the bank was dissatisfied with the combination of air and ground service they were using for various routes and was open to new possibilities. They can save a great deal of money by getting checks in just a few hours or even minutes earlier to beat deadlines on interest at the Federal Reserve Bank. So it doesn't help when their contract delivery service sends the bank an announcement that its schedule is going to be changed. The delivery service does this because it is a big outfit with many customers, and it finds a way to reduce its costs by striking a new compromise in delivery timing among them, rather than accommodating each individual customer on an individual basis. At the bank such changes can disrupt handling and processing schedules, making things harder and possibly adding delays that cost the bank more money.*
>
> *It also doesn't help when check shipments get mixed up or lost, which had happened to the bank at times on commercial airlines where their freight may be stacked with everyone else's. The checks are not negotiable, but it is enormously inconvenient and expensive for the bank.*

At the close of their meeting, the float control manager suggested that Greg come back in a few days with a proposal for ferrying checks from Vancouver in southern Washington to Seattle, roughly 140 miles north. He gave no indication of present costs on the route or of the expected price for Greg's service, but did describe the present method of transport, which was by truck and typically took two hours and 25 minutes per trip.

Another option Greg quickly noted was to bring the checks by commercial airline, perhaps with a special attendant to make sure nothing happened to them. From flight schedules at the airport he laid out three sequences for using commercial service out of Portland airport. A copy of his tabulation can be seen in the Exhibit. From the bank's description of its needs, he estimated that roughly 25 percent of the checks would be ready for departure by 3:15 p.m., another 50 percent by 4:15 p.m., and the remaining 25 percent by 5:15 p.m.

If he had a plane, Greg expected he could fly the routes himself. He could use the international airports in Portland and Seattle, for instance. Or he could use smaller local airports, since his plane would be small. To reach Portland, Oregon, he could fly in and out of a local airport just across the state line in Vancouver, Washington. That would cut the driving time from airport to Portland down to roughly 5 to 10 minutes, or about half the time it would take from Portland International, where the commercial flights went. Loading and taxiing the aircraft would take perhaps another 10 to 15 minutes, and flying to Seattle between 70 and 90 minutes. Then taxiing and unloading at Seattle might require roughly 10 to 15 minutes. To reach Seattle, he could use Boeing field, which was about 10 minutes from downtown, rather than Seattle-Tacoma airport, which was approximately twice that time away from the city. The purchase price of a small plane suitable for these routes and capable of carrying the load he expected would be roughly $45,000 to $54,000. From personal savings he expected he could raise about $45,000 for down payment to buy it, but still need a bank loan for any difference in purchase price plus other start-up expenditures.

At present he enjoyed his market analyst job at the Boeing Company, and he was not particularly anxious to leave. His work involved several international trips per year, often to exotic places like the South Pacific, where there was interest in hydrofoils for tourist excursions. His salary was not particularly high, around $39,000 a year, but it was enough to live on and do some recreational flying on weekends. He observed:

> *Making more money or being my own boss are not things that particularly motivate me. But I certainly would like the idea of being able to own an airplane and do more flying. I wonder how feasible it would be to try combining a check transporting service with personal flying. Would I have to quit my job at Boeing? How big a dip would it put in my income, and for how long? What kind of help should I be able to get from the bank? What should I present to them to persuade them to grant that help, and what steps should I take to prepare that presentation?*
>
> *Should I be concerned about whether they might just take all the work I might put into a plan and use it to give the job to someone else instead of me? Should I propose a trial period with them? If so, how long, and what would be the best way to keep going with them beyond that? I imagine there might be quite a few people out there who now pay to fly, like I do, and would gladly offer low-cost service to get a subsidy for their flight time by taking over the work. Should the pricing I put into my proposal be based on this or on how much it's now costing the bank to fly checks by helicopter? How should the pricing basis, whatever it is, change with time? Or should it? What are all the most important issues, like this, that should be considered in my proposal to the bank? What should be the most effective way to organize and to present them?*

EXHIBIT Airline delivery time using flight schedules

Check pick-up time	3:15 p.m.	4:15 p.m.	5:15 p.m.
Arrival Portland International	3:50	4:50	5:50
Ready for departure (90 min. check loading to plane)	5:20	6:20	7:20
Next available commercial flight	5:45 (flt 792)	7:55 (flt L09)	7:55 (flt 10)
Arrival Sea-Tac	6:30	8:30	8:30
Ready for pick-up (1 hr. unloading to truck)	7:30	9:30	9:30
Arrival computer center (35 min. driving time)	8:05	10:05	10:05

Arthur Lipper

Alternatives for attracting capital

Arthur Lipper, an experienced investor in young companies, was reflecting in the summer of 2000 on some investment opportunities he currently faced. He had experienced a long career with investments, most of it working with Wall Street. Among other companies, he had owned his own institutional investment brokerage and banking firm with a seat on the New York Stock Exchange and offices in New York, Washington, London, Geneva, Tokyo, Singapore, and Buenos Aires. He had also created various Lipper mutual funds performance-ranking services, which became Lipper Analytical Services, a well-known investment information firm. For several years he had also owned *Venture*, a magazine concentrating on entrepreneurs, and he had written five books on investing in privately owned firms. He had moved from New York to Del Mar, California, where he worked mainly as a consultant and investment banker specializing in financing deals. As he reflected on three current potential investments, he expressed the following views:

> The challenge facing an investor in private companies is to realistically structure the investment so as to gain as much appreciation as possible while assuming as little real risk as is practical.
>
> The entrepreneur will likely accept, especially after a series of predictable rejections by other funding sources, almost any proposal that is expected to be accompanied by a check. Therefore the full responsibility of designing the initial capital structure of the company will fall to the first non-family, or friend investor.
>
> Typically, an entrepreneur will seek to present in person and by business plan the case for investing in the venture, and may also propose that the investor purchase a specified amount of common stock for a price sufficient to produce the amount of money thought to be necessary.
>
> The investor may view several things as wrong with this procedure. First of all, probably the amount of money sought will be too little to accomplish the stated objective, and the time required will have been underestimated. Others with more experience than the entrepreneur estimate the time required better.
>
> Questions of concern to the investor may include what determines the most appropriate objective(s) to be accomplished by the initial funding. Is it achievement of revenues, or just to get the business started? Is it proof of concept for a device or product? Is it to gain certain relationships?
>
> Why should the investor, having a large number of alternative opportunities to invest in, ever accept common stock in a private company? Who should bear the most in a private company? Should it not be 1) those making the predictions and 2) those having the most to gain relative to their cash investment or exposure? If so, then shouldn't they carry the most junior of securities?
>
> Other issues to be addressed by the structure of the initial funding include whether the present management should be continued or changed, whether a corporation is the form of commercial organization which best suits the needs of the investor(s), and, if so, who should have control of the venture's board of directors. There may be issues of corporate domicile and location of the operations, as well as of form and amount of executive compensation. Why should not these be determined through application of the Golden Rule of Private Company Investing, "He who has the gold shall make the rules."

Arthur believed he should apply these investment principles in considering the following two potential investment opportunities. The question was how they should be applied.

Opportunity #1, Sigmacom

Sigmacom, a small company of about 12 people, was in the business of creating computer software and installing computer and communication equipment. The company had a vision of creating video conferencing capabilities for large multi-location companies. Its managers said they believed that sales would take off if they had funds for additional marketing efforts. In Arthur Lipper's view the skill sets of the company included understanding of programming, communications, and equipment installation. Three executives owned most of the company stock and functioned much as if they were partners. They had personally invested in the company and also guaranteed loans to provide its initial cash but now said they needed an additional $600,000 from outside. They projected a high level of profit on revenues once a relatively low breakeven point was reached.

Opportunity #2, DKS Technologies

DKS had invented a "Fuel Stabilizer System" that consisted of a device to pre-heat fuel before combustion in diesel engines of large diesel trucks and buses. The device consistently reduced fuel consumption by 8 percent to 12 percent and substantially reduced noxious gas emissions. Users of the device provided glowing endorsements of satisfaction and tended to buy additional units. The Bill of Materials (BOM) for the device was less than $200 and the suggested installed selling price was $1,200. The fuel savings for a fleet of trucks or buses were said to be sufficient to pay for installation of the DKS equipment in less than 12 months.

DKS was operated by a Canadian immigrant who had been characterized by the person who told Arthur Lipper about him as "a mature and dedicated person who employed and was assisted by his son and wife plus one other person to deliver a product with limited intellectual property protection." The Company requested funds for the development of marketing material estimated by management to cost $100,000.

Bill Foster (B)

By the end of January 1980 Bill Foster was shifting his attention from working out the details of his venture plan to seeking a commitment for start-up capital. He knew that striking a deal with a venture capital group for financing would involve continued negotiations until both sides were willing to accept the terms presented. There were no assurances that the process would be completed within a week, a month or even later. Only one of his four partners had been associated with a start-up; none had been involved with venture capital financing.

Needs, he expected, would be for $6.2 million to cover a three-year development and market introduction effort. He would need about $2 million the first year to develop a working prototype and establish credibility of the team and concept. The founders themselves would personally be able to put in about $75,000 cash at most.

Possible capital sources

While recruiting his founding team and working out details of a business plan, Bill had also been gathering information about alternative potential financing sources.

> My philosophy has always been "It doesn't hurt to talk to anybody. You might learn something." So I followed up every lead I got, whether it had to do with raising money, finding people or anything. You may run up a phone bill, but people are generally very helpful. I got leads from headhunters and investors, lawyers and friends. I talked to other people who had started companies. They were probably the most helpful of all—those who had recently experienced what I was going through. They would reminisce about those exciting times. Of course, if they were successful and got their operations off the ground, they always liked to talk about it.
>
> I got many of the new company leads by reading magazines. Some of them have articles about companies that have just started up. I'd just call some of the presidents of the companies that had been interviewed out of the blue, tell them what I was doing, and ask their advice. I met several of the people out in California through those articles.

Bill had found three major options venture capital firms, private individuals, and other operating corporations. There appeared to be significant differences in the way each of these groups made investments and in the types of deals that might be struck.

Venture capital firms

The venture capital firms were the most obvious possibilities. There were a large number of venture firms actively seeking investments. In addition to the best known and perhaps most prestigious firms, there were a wide range of other, less well-known, firms he considered worth contacting. Most were smaller, more recently started, or simply chose to keep low profiles. Contacts with two of these latter firms who expressed interest in Alta had come through one of Bill's partners, Gardner Hendrie. When Gardner was considering joining the team, he had called an old friend, Charles Meyers, for advice. Charles had worked with Gardner 15 years earlier in an engineering company, then gone to California to become involved in venture capital, and through it became very successful. When Gardner explained why he was interested in learning the climate for venture capital, Charles said his company, Pacific Ventures, might be interested. Bill recalled:

> Before I know it, Charles hops an airplane to come and talk with us. Right away he's very interested, partly on the strength of the business plan and partly because of his personal association with Gardner. But he felt we should have an East Coast firm in the lead. He'd be very happy

with the New York firms we knew, but also suggested we contact Davidson-Mills, a lesser known Boston company they'd done some business with before. (It seemed that the best known Boston firms generally preferred second-round financings.) I had heard of Davidson-Mills, but had never bothered to call them. I didn't think they did start-ups, and I didn't think they were big enough. But Charles said they'd be good, and they'd feel good about our idea. One of the their partners had prior experience in the timesharing business and knew something about computers himself.

During his early discussions with the venture firms and in talking to the other recently started companies, Bill discovered some apparent ground rules in the venture capital community:

One rule is that you're not going to raise $7 million on day one. No one has put in that much money. The going first round for my kind of deal is around a million and a half. Maybe you can get close to $2 million, but probably not more than $2 million for a team of untried people. That much would get us just past a working prototype.

Number two is that they are going to have control—at least 51 percent. They're going to do it—there's no way you can get around it. At the same time, they won't commit to anything on round two. They'll talk about what they'll do if you do a good job, but if they don't like what you've done, you may not get that second-round money.

None of it is cast in concrete. You can talk and you can go through scenarios. They'd sit me down and tell me what other companies did. "In 1974 Tandem gave up 74 percent of their company for $1 million. The investor got 72 percent of Prime Computer for $600,000 in 1972." The new start-ups did a little better—the going rate seemed to be giving up about 60 percent.

I also found that many of the venture capital firms without technical backgrounds used outside consultants to help them evaluate high-technology ventures. The people they relied on were heavily booked and might take weeks to schedule.

Private individuals

Another possible source of financing was from wealthy individuals. Certain tax provisions could make investments in firms such as Alta appealing; most of Alta's early expenses would be for research and development. If the funds for the R&D were provided by a limited partnership most of the expenditures could be deducted by the individuals against other sources of ordinary income. This would effectively lessen the actual after-tax amount at risk for those individuals. If the research proved successful, the investors would typically receive a royalty (normally 7 to 10 percent) on resulting sales. Such royalties would be taxed at long-term capital-gain rates.

Bill had been put in contact with a young individual who had taken an idea from an MBA thesis and built it into a very successful company, which he had recently sold for about $6 million. Now, to invest some of the proceeds he offered to lead a private placement with about 10 individuals each putting up $300,000 to $400,000. Because of potential tax benefits of such a placement and because some of the individuals in it did not get to see as many deals as venture capital firms did, Bill hoped his team would not have to give up so much ownership, maybe only 40-45 percent, if money could be raised this way. However, he expected this route would be more complicated and might require preparation of a private placement memorandum nearly as complex as a full-blown prospectus under SEC Rule 242. This might also require review by the state "Blue Sky" commission. "The SEC might not consider that even a wealthy lawyer is necessarily a 'sophisticated investor' when it comes to a computer start-up," he said.

Other non-venture corporations

Once again, Bill found that people recommended to him as advisers for dealing with venture capital became capital sources themselves, as he began discussions with another company that soon expressed interest in financing the entire Alta start-up. Bill's contact, Gary Jameson, had formerly worked for a venture capital firm. Now he was vice president of administration in a company offering a product that depended on reliable computer systems. This company bought computers from major suppliers, then incorporated them in systems it sold to telecommunications firms. These systems required continuous absolutely reliable operation. Bill commented:

> Gary's employer said they were very interested, and even though they were not in the venture capital business, they might fund us to the tune of $7 million. Again, this would be set up as partnership so that this company could get the more immediate tax benefits of expensing the R & D.
>
> Gary said it might be impossible for me to raise money through venture capital sources— and I could be wasting my time talking to venture capital firms. Even though I had run R & D teams, I had never been the chief executive officer of a company, had never run the whole show. He said that venture capitalists were really conservative investors, and it was unlikely that any venture group would invest millions of dollars in a company in which the chief executive officer didn't have a proven track record.

This was the only non-venture capital company Bill had contacted for financing. After seeing the interest it expressed, however, he thought perhaps some other non-capital companies might have similar interests. He had heard that some major industrial corporations, such as General Electric, had in-house venture groups, but he wasn't sure how their investment strategies might differ from those of traditional venture capital companies.

Other considerations

Striking a deal with any of the financing sources would, Bill expected, require detailed negotiations of unpredictable length with no assurance that a deal would ever be reached. The risks seemed heightened by the fact that the Alta team was untried in launching a company. One factor in their favor was that there had been a number of recent success stories of computer firms starting up and becoming industry leaders. Those deals also served as a growing data base to determine the increased values of the company for each round of financing.

Recent increases in the availability of venture capital also worked to Alta's advantage. Bill pointed out that more money now chased roughly the same number of high-quality investments, so his founding group should have good leverage in negotiating a deal. This could enhance terms for Alta on a whole range of issues, including relative percentages of ownership between investors and venture, relative privileges shareholders might seek through different types of common stock, preferred stock, or debt instruments with convertible provisions or warrants. The extent of voting privileges and membership on the board of directors would likely also be areas for negotiation.

Valuation of the company had to be considered somewhere in the process. With on-going companies, investors could look at the asset-bases and price/earnings ratios. With a start-up, the investor had to consider the concept, the projections, and the team, then decide on the venture's likely future value. Bill expected that more than one round of financing would probably be needed. How the first round of capital was priced and structured would, he supposed, influence the terms of later investment rounds.

Bill commented that an investor's main concern would be the likelihood of the venture's achieving a specified level of profitability in a given period of time. The track records with new products of his founding team could, he said, be a big plus. It had been in the start-up by Gene Amdahl whose record in the computer industry from his prior accomplishments at IBM had allowed him to marshall $17 million in start-up capital. Also in Alta's favor, Bill believed, was the fact that there had been a number of recent success stories of computer firms starting up and becoming industry leaders. Such venture precedents helped determine how stock prices and splits were negotiated between investors and founders at each round of funding.

Working out terms

All Bill's team members said they would agree to take smaller salaries than they had earned before. His own would, he expected, be less than half of this former salary and the others would be about 80 percent. The four founding members of the company would split whatever equity they could retain by dividing the number of shares by 4.2. Each of them would receive a 1/4.2 part except Bill. He would receive 1.2/4.2 or a "120 percent" share for putting the team together. Employee stock ownership and shares for other key employees also had to be considered.

Cash equity available among the team totaled between $50,000 and $75,000. Thus, to raise the necessary funds, a differential for stock paid by the venture capitalists and the founders would by required. No formula existed for setting a ratio differential. In some cases, the venture group might pay 10 times the rate of the founders; other times the ratio might go as high as 30 or 40. The figure was partly a function of initial funding required, available equity, willingness by the founders to give up a substantial or even controlling interest in the firm, and expectations on the time frame for future funding or start of shipments to generate revenues. Bill commented:

> Let's say there are 3,000,000 shares in the company and that if the stock was being publicly traded, the current selling price was $10 a share. That would indicate that the value of the firm is $30,000,000. But what would it have to earn to produce that result? If current earnings are $1,000,000 for example, then the price/earnings ratio would have to be 30. Investors would have to be willing to pay 30 times present earnings for access to future earning streams in the company.
>
> For a start-up like ours, you can look at what our profits are projected to be in the future, adjust that by some perception of risk, and see what similar companies on the stock exchange are selling for in terms of their price-earnings ratios. Or, you could look at the historical pricing of other private placements in start-ups.

Another factor Bill thought important to consider was that more than one round of financing would most likely be needed. If progress as measured against the plan went as scheduled, he expected a better stock price and/or differential could be negotiated in the second round. On the other hand, if delays occurred, he and the three partners would be in a weaker bargaining position and, at worst, might find themselves unable to raise any additional capital at all.

Byron Spain

Early public offering

In the spring of 1997, Byron Spain, a retired Boeing engineer, was puzzling about how best to raise between $4 million and $20 million to move his company, Rodi Power Systems, toward profitability. Together with six associates and his wife, he had been working on development of a better diesel engine for large trucks for ten years, concentrating on it full-time for the past two. So far the company had not sold any engines, but it had developed three working prototypes, one of which was currently powering a Freightliner truck. With $4 million the company would aim to produce 10 more engines for testing. With $20 million there would be another 25 engines produced, which would provide more extensive testing. The company's comparative balance sheets for the past two years appear in the Exhibit.

Financing

So far the company had been financed through private loans and stock sales. To get larger amounts Byron believed a public stock offering would be needed. The problem, he said, was how to present information that would persuade prospective investors that the company was a good bet and still be within the laws enforced by the Securities and Exchange Commission. In a memo Byron made the following observations about obstacles to the stock offering he believed the company had to find ways of overcoming:

> There are federally approved processes to raise first round capital funding through the sale of equity using a broker. When seeking first-round capital funding by using a federally approved equity sale, the most difficult issue is defining how to commercialize the product. Demonstrating how to make money for the investor is the critical issue that must be comprehensively developed in order to generate interest.
>
> A serious limitation to aggressively addressing this issue is the very negative tone dictated by the SEC and state securities offices in the preparation of a prospectus.
>
> Factors most affected by this problem are
> 1. Asking price of the stock.
> 2. Acquiring reputable legal counsel, audit firm, and broker.
> 3. The requirement for a minimum subscription balance.
> 4. The broker making a "Best Efforts" sales agreement rather than underwriting.
>
> The correct structuring of the manufacturing and marketing plans plus believable (read: very conservative) Pro-Forma financial projections are a major challenge since no participating party wants to accept any liability. Since start-up companies are always broke, dissatisfied investors historically sue the legal counsel, audit firm, and broker if the Company does not perform as promised. Hence a terribly negative business plan is required for the prospectus.
>
> How should we solve this problem?

Background

The idea Byron had started working on originally in 1985 was that of a "rotary" diesel engine, one using rotary vanes rather than conventional pistons to cycle the fuel/air mixture and produce power. But by 1985, he had shifted to a two-cycle piston design using "reverse flow scavenging." The concept was not new, but it was not used in truck engines. This was despite some advantages it offered, and the reason for it, Byron said, was that "the truck-makers have coerced all of the big three diesel makers (Caterpillar, Cummins, and General Motors) to make their engines clones of each other."

He further pointed out that the diesel sales of these companies totaled approximately $11 billion per year. Over 200,000 U.S. trucks were produced in 1995 that used the class 8 engines with which Rodi would compete. In addition, there could be sales as replacement engines in some of the 2.3 million trucks already on U.S. roads with this class, and beyond that there could be international sales.

The main advantages of his design, he said, included (1) lighter weight and smaller size for the same power than the four-stroke clones, (2) higher efficiency than other two-strokes because of the way scavenging worked, plus the capability of turning off some cylinders during light load, (3) a 40 percent lower manufacturing cost because two-strokes are simpler, and (4) lower cost rebuilding because it could be accomplished with only partial disassembly. One particularly advantageous application was expected to be in short-haul vehicles such as dump trucks and cement trucks, because they typically went out full and came back empty, which meant they could return with one bank of cylinders turned off to save fuel.

Byron and his partners had written a description of development plans of the first engine design, the HT1-450 as follows:

> Further development of the HT1-450 will be required before this product can be commercialized. Tests are planned to enhance performance and increase maximum power output of the HT1-450 by greatly increasing air flow through the engine by optimizing air cycle components such as intake valves, exhaust port geometry, supercharger volume ratio, and turbocharger matching. Variables to be tested include various exhaust system geometry changes; the use of four intake valves per cylinder and using several types and combinations of supercharger and turbocharger. Optimizing the air cycle of a two-stroke engine is a complex trade-off of many characteristics that are interrelated. Recently completed cylinder liner and piston design changes are expected to resolve past problems associated with oil cooling and will be verified by testing during the first phase of the pre-production engine development program. However, until these design changes are tested, there are no assurances that they will be successful.

The final sentence in this statement, Byron pointed out, was the sort of thing that apparently had to be emphasized in obtaining clearance to sell stock in the company. After they had the clearance, he added, they would have to compete for investors against stock issues in glamorous industries like software, biotech, and the emerging Internet phenomenon.

Some claims Rodi would be able to make were that the company had taken precautions to maintain secrecy and that it had filed for trademarks and also applied for one patent. It could not, however, comment on what the secrets were or what exactly they hoped the patent would be granted on, at least not until the patent was issued, which could be two or more years away.

It could also state that they planned to seek another round of financing in another year beyond the first one, and that there were a number of further technical thrusts that they were working on. These included designing a V-8 in addition to the HT1-450, which was a V-4, and a 4-stroke engine that would use some features of the two-strokes plus run on natural gas for specific application in running electric power generators and water pumps. Byron had achieved a record of innovation during his 23 years at Boeing, where he was named "Inventor of the Year" three times, and he expected to continue applying that capability at Rodi.

Expert opinions on prospects for the new motor included both pessimism and optimism. Bruce Wadman, the editorial chairman for *Diesel Progress Magazine*, said:

I would have to say it's a risky venture. Byron Spain is trying to make Rodi a revolutionary product for an evolutionary business. The question is, does he have enough unique design advances that will bring him into a position of prominence?

However, David Marks, an independent consulting engineer who had worked at Cummins Engine for 17 years, including as director of research, and before that as an engineer for Packard Motor, Chrysler, and Fairbanks-Morse, commented:

It's a pretty salable program. They've got a pretty unique approach to a two-cycle engine, which I think could be very competitive.

It might be possible to state all these things in an offering circular to attract investors through a public offering. But would that be enough, and if not, what would?

EXHIBIT Comparative balance sheets

	4/30/96	4/30/97
ASSETS		
Current		
Cash	225,206	20,377
Receivable loans & other	0	40,070
Prepaid	5,257	32,757
Total current	230,463	93,204
Fixed		
Property and equipment at cost		
Machinery and equipment	178,359	175,843
Computer equipment	99,161	99,161
Leasehold improvements	49,672	49,672
Total	327,192	324,676
Less depreciation	(133,311)	(187,081)
Other	3,950	4,102
Total assets	428,294	234,901
LIABILITIES AND EQUITY		
Current		
Payables	42,035	46,669
Accrued	36,391	32,913
Total current	78,426	79,582
Long-term debt		
Payable to officers	262,895	352,895
Equity	86,973	(197,576)
Total liabilities & equity	428,294	234,901

Hoyle Schweitzer

The start-up

Hoyle Schweitzer's inspiration to start a company to manufacture sailboards came from a 1965 conversation with an acquaintance, Jim Drake. The two were comparing two sports they enjoyed, surfboarding and sailing when it occurred to them that it might be possible to combine the two by mounting a sail on a surfboard to propel it.[1]

They began constructing prototypes in quest of a design that could be steered without a rudder, as a surfboard was, but with power coming from the sail rather than a wave. When they achieved a design that worked they applied for a patent for a "wind-propelled apparatus in which a mast is universally mounted on a craft and supports a boom or sail." Twenty two months later, in January 1970, the patent was issued as number 3,487,800. An excerpt from the *Patent Gazette* containing the announcement of this patent appears as Exhibit 1.

Schweitzer, his wife and Drake formed a company, Windsurfing International, to make and sell their invention. The novelty of it attracted attention and even practical jokes: When they displayed it at a boat show, someone modified the sailboard by adding a large helm and portable toilet. But it began to catch on. The Schweitzers bought out Drake in 1973.

Success of the product, however, inspired imitators, and to protect it Schweitzer filed suit for infringement of his patent. In the legal combat that followed, it was discovered that another man, S. Newman Darby, had created a similar device which looked like a door with an upside-down kite stuck into the socket in the center. The rider stood in front of the kite and leaned back against it as the wind blew it forward and propelled the flat door-like board across the water. Darby made no attempt to patent his invention, but a description and photograph showing it in operation appeared in a 1965 issue of *Popular Science*. Thus Schweitzer's patent became threatened.

Schweitzer claimed that his design represented a significant innovation beyond Darby's "prior art," as required to keep his patent valid, because of differences in design of his windsurfer's triangular sail and boom in contrast to Darby's kite-like arrangement. This novelty, Schweitzer asserted, gave much more control to the operator.

Would-be competitors disputed Schweitzer's claim of advance beyond prior art and sold imitations as the sport caught on and the market for sailboards rapidly grew. Schweitzer sued one imitator after another, resulting in a series of court decisions. By 1981 he had spent over a half million dollars on lawsuits and won 40 of them. But there were by then over 100 imitators still doing business. The U.S. Patent Board of Appeals decreed in favor of Schweitzer that his "hand-held wishbone rigging combined with the vehicle swivel mast attachment produces, in our opinion, a unique sailing apparatus which functions with the user in a manner that is completely unrecognized in any art before us." But subsequently the Patent Office rejected that decision, which in turn led to another appeal.

The litigation continued, leading to still further decisions. One from the U.S. Court of Appeals which was rendered in early 1986 appears in Exhibit 2.

---

[1] Mamis, Robert A., "Hoyle Schweitzer's Decade of Discontent," <u>Inc</u>, February, 1982, p. 54.

EXHIBIT 1 Excerpt from Patent Gazette, January 6, 1970

3,487,798
SEWING MACHINE FOR PRODUCING BELT
LOOPS AND THE LIKE
Nerino Marforio, Milan, Italy, assignor to S.p.A. Virginio
Rimoldi & C., Milan, Italy
Filed Aug. 28, 1968, Ser. No. 755,932
Claims priority, application Italy, Sept. 7, 1967,
20,221/67
Int. Cl. D05b *23/00, 37/04*
U.S. Cl. 112—121.27   11 Claims

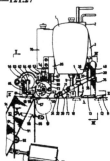

A sewing machine for producing belt loops and the like
from off-cuts of random length which are sewn end-to-
end to form a continuous lengthwise strip, including
means for preventing the cutting knife from cutting said
strip along any portion thereof which is of a thickness
other than the uniform thickness required for the loops,
and also including means for automatically sorting reject
loops from satisfactory ones, as well as a counter means
adapted to count only the satisfactory loops.

3,487,799
ROOF SEAMING MACHINE
Sven Olof Grönlund, Marumsgatan 16, Skara, Sweden
Filed Apr. 12, 1968, Ser. No. 721,024
Int. Cl. B21d *39/02, 19/04*
U.S. Cl. 113—55   2 Claims

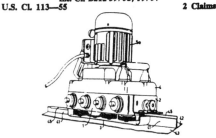

The present invention relates to roof seaming machines
for forming standing seams to interconnect adjacent roofing sheets and is of the kind comprising a carriage with
pair-wise arranged rolls which successively perform the
seaming operation when the carriage is moved along the
upstanding sheet flanges. One of the rolls of each pair,
hereinbelow termed the folding roll, is adapted to be displaced outward relative to the other roll, herein termed
the counter roll, and is acted upon by a compression
spring such as to be biased toward the counter roll and
to assist in folding the upstanding sheet flange or sheet
flanges for producing a single or double seam. Accordingly, one of the rolls must be movable towards and away
from the other roll in order to enable the spring to act

on the folding roll and to enable the folding roll and the
counter rock to adjust themselves to various thicknesses
of the seam.

3,487,800
WIND-PROPELLED APPARATUS
Hoyle Schweitzer, 317 Beirut, Pacific Palisades, Calif.
90272, and James Drake, 385 Mesa, Santa Monica,
Calif. 90402
Filed Mar. 27, 1968, Ser. No. 716,547
Int. Cl. B63b *15/02*; B63h *9/10*
U.S. Cl. 114—39   14 Claims

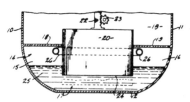

Wind-propelled apparatus in which a mast is universally
mounted on a craft and supports a boom and sail. Specifically a pair of curved booms are arcuately connected
athwart the mast and secure the sail therebetween, the
position of the mast and sail being controllable by the
user but being substantially free from pivotal restraint
in the absence of such control.

ERRATUM

For Class 114—77 see:
Patent No. 3,487,807

3,487,801
METHOD AND APPARATUS FOR STABILIZA-
TION OF VESSELS
Mario C. Calvi, Santa Susana, Calif., assignor to The
Ralph M. Parsons Company, Los Angeles, Calif.,
corporation of Nevada
Filed Oct. 31, 1966, Ser. No. 590,728
Int. Cl. B63b *43/06*
U.S. Cl. 114—125   16 Claims

A ship stabilization system having passive tanks
opposite sides of the ship with an interconnecting pa
sage for the flow of liquid between the tanks. The effec
tive cross-sectional area of the interconnecting passage
varied to maintain the natural period of flow of the liqu
in excess of the period of roll of the vessel. The cro
sectional area is varied in one embodiment by shifti
transversely one of the walls defining the passage, and

EXHIBIT 2 U.S. Court of Appeals decision, January 28, 1986[2]

Background

(1) Proceedings in District Court

Windsurfing International (WSI) sued AMF, BIC and Downwind, alleging infringement of its '167 patent. AMF then sought a declaratory judgment that the patent is invalid for obviousness, unenforceable because of patent misuse, and not infringed. Also, AMF sought the cancellation of WSI's registrations of "WINDSURFER" and related trademarks[3] on grounds that the marks had become generic. BIC sued WSI, seeking a declaration that the '167 patent is invalid for obviousness, unenforceable, and not infringed.

Consolidating the three actions, the district court held a non-jury trial on 13 dates between November 19 and December 11, 1984, filed an opinion July 15, 1985 and entered judgments on September 11, 1985. AMF, BIC, and Downwind appeal from the judgments holding the '167 patent valid and infringed. AMF and BIC appeal from the grant of injunctions.[4] WSI cross-appeals from the judgments holding it misused its patent and refusing to enjoin Downwind.

(2) The '167 Patent

The patent in suit relates to the sport of "sailboarding,"[5] in which participants ride boards propelled by wind striking sails attached to the boards.

A preferred embodiment of the claimed invention is shown in Figure 1 of the '167 patent:

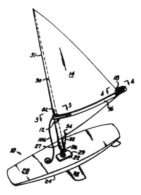

A participant stands on the top surface of surfboard 10 behind universal joint 36, grasps boom 16 or boom 18 (depending on wind direction), and controls the speed and direction of the board by maneuvering the boom to which sail 14 is attached. If a participant begins to lose control in a sudden wind surge, he or she merely releases the boom and the universal joint allows the sail to fall freely into the water.

---

[2] 282 F 2nd 995 (Fed. Cir. 1986)
[3] U.S. Trademark Registration No. 962,616, 997,974, 1,180,024, and 1,195,641. The district court held that WSI's trademarks have become generic. The district court has not yet entered judgment to that effect and the trademark issue of genericness is not part of this appeal.
[4] The district court permanently enjoined AMF, but "preliminarily" enjoined BIC pending termination of a related action by Intervener James R. Drake claiming an ownership interest in the '167 patent.
[5] We refer to the patented structure as a "sailboard" and not as a "windsurfer" because whether the latter term has become generic is not yet final.

EXHIBIT 2 *(continued)*

Claim 15 from the patent is representative:

Wind-propelled apparatus comprising body means adapted to support a user and wind-propulsion means pivotally associated with said body means and adapted to receive wind for motive power for said apparatus, said propulsion means comprising a mast, a joint for mounting said mast on said body means, a sail and means for extending said sail laterally from said mast *comprising two opposed booms secured to said mast for guiding said sail therebetween and adapted to provide a hand-hold for said user on either side of said sail while sailing*, the position of said propulsion means being controllable by said user, said propulsion means being substantially free from pivotal restraint in the absence of said user, said joint having a plurality of axes of rotation whereby said sail free falls along any of a plurality of vertical planes upon release by said user.

The understood limitation sets forth the boom and was added when WSI's U.S. Patent No. 3,487,800 was reissued as the '167 patent.

Issues

Did the district court err in: (1) holding the claimed invention nonobvious[6] (2) finding infringement; (3) holding patent misuse; (4) enjoining AMF and BIC; and (5) refusing to enjoin Downwind.

<u>Opinion</u>

(1) Non-obviousness

On appeal, AMF[7] argues that the district court erred in upholding the '167 patent because it: (a) improperly deferred to decisions by the U.S. Patent and Trademark Office Board of Appeals (Board); (b) compared preferred and commercial embodiments with the prior art; and (c) considered commercial success having no nexus with the claimed invention.

(a) Deference

[1] In deferring to the Board's decisions concerning the allowance of the claims in the reissued patent, the district court was recognizing the statutory mandate that all patents are presumed valid. The district court carefully considered whether the evidence not presented in the "fiercely contested adversarial proceeding" before the Board would ease AMF's burden of proving facts compelling a conclusion of invalidity.[8] Concluding that the evidence at trial

---

[6] 35 U.S.C. § 103 provides:
A patent may not be obtained…if the differences between the subject matter sought to be patented and the prior art are such that the subject matter as a whole would have been obvious at the time the invention was made to a person having ordinary skills in the art to which said subject matter pertains.
[7] Because BIC raises many of the same arguments, and Downwind relies principally on the arguments raised by BIC and AMF, this opinion hereinafter refers to the three parties collectively as AMF, unless otherwise indicated.
[8] The "proceeding" referred to comprised the initial application for reissue, a protest, an appeal to the Board, a remand to the examiner, a second appeal to the Board, and an appeal to the Court of Customs and Patent Appeals. The district court described these events in its opinion. 613 F. Supp. at 942-44, 227 USPQ at 934-35.

EXHIBIT 2 *(continued)*

was merely cumulative of that before the Board, the court correctly held that evidence did not enable AMF to carry the burden.

AMF contends that, because the Board did not mention the obviousness of replacing the rig, shown in a publication referred to as the "Darby reference," with the boom disclosed in the '167 patent, no deference is due the Board decisions. The district court carefully reviewed the administrative record and stated that such argument "oversimplifies the depth of the Board's review and assumes the Board ignored other issues raised in the parties' extensive briefs." We agree. Merely because a decision does not mention a particular point "forms no basis for an assumption that it did not consider those elements." Moreover, the district court correctly noted that "the Board...reaffirmed its original holding that combination of the hand-held wishbone rigging [boom] with the vehicle swivel mast attachment produces...a unique sailing apparatus....'" We are satisfied that the district court did not err in this case in giving "deference that is due to a qualified government agency presumed to have properly done its job."

(b) Comparison

[2] The district court conducted a thorough *Graham*[9] analysis before concluding that the claimed invention at the time it was made would not have been obvious to one of ordinary skill in the art. AMF attacks the district court's findings as clearly erroneous, asserting it compared to the prior art not the claimed invention but commercial and preferred embodiments as representative of the claimed invention (claims, not embodiments, are focus of obviousness inquiry). Those embodiments include a "scoop" on a slimmer hull-shaped board, a skeg (or fin on the bottom at the back), and footstraps. Thus, they argue that the advantages found by the court are attributable to a combination of those design improvements and not to the claimed invention.

The district court did determine that it would have been obvious to replace a kite sail with a force and aft sail, and to add a second opposed boom.[10] Properly looking to the claimed invention at the time it was made as a whole, the district court correctly concluded that "the combination of the hand-held wishbone rigging with the universal joint produced a vehicle that performs in a manner previously undisclosed by any of the prior art references before us and, indeed, a vehicle with a performance potential that is even now not yet fully realized."

WSI's expert, Dr. Bradfield, conceded that certain advantages were due to particular added improvements, but he consistently maintained that the overall performance capabilities of the claimed invention were mainly due to the combination of the universal joint and the wishbone rigging. The district court found that testimony credible and AMF has shown no basis on which this court could engage in the normally inappropriate process of substituting a contrary credibility determination for that of the district court.

---

[9] Graham v. John Deere, 383 U.S. 1, 17-18, 86 S.Ct. 684, 693-94, 15 L.Ed. 2d 545, 148 USPQ 459, 467 (1966).
[10] Contrary to BIC and Downwind's contentions, a conclusion that it would have been obvious to replace the sails and add a boom does not require a conclusion that the claimed invention considered as a whole would have been obvious. The claims include more, e.g., a universal joint and its relationship to board, mast, boom and sail.

EXHIBIT 2 *(continued)*

(c) Nexus

Before concluding that the combination of the universal joint with the wishbone rigging would not have been obvious, the district court reviewed the objective evidence, and correctly sought a nexus between WSI's commercial success and the merits of the claimed invention.

In essence, AMF says that the commercial success found by the district court was due in large part to "other economic and commercial factors unrelated to the technical quality of the patented subject matter." Particularly, AMF argues that the great commercial success found by the district court was due to (1) sales of accessories amounting to 10-15 percent of the gross receipts; (2) an extensive advertising campaign and European promotional effort; and (3) more efficient manufacturing and design changes. They argue that WSI's commercial success is of little probative value because it occurred so many years after the date of invention and was not the result of providing any solution to some existing problem or long-felt want.

[3] Having carefully reviewed the record before use, we conclude that the district court did not impermissibly credit the evidence of commercial success. It specifically found that SWI's commercial success should not be "significantly diminished" by testimony that 10-15 percent of gross receipts are from paraphernalia. The court accorded some weight to motivational factors leading to German licenses, but concluded that "widespread recognition and use of the invention" indicated that it would not have been obvious. The commercial success of the invention was found to have been "well beyond the effect" of WSI's promotional efforts.

Absent some intervening event to which success must be attributed, the delay in achieving the great commercial success of the claimed invention in this case does not detract from the probative value of the evidence of that success. Similarly, AMF's suggestion that objective evidence of non-obviousness can be considered only when the invention solves a long-existing problem is unwarranted. Providing a solution to a long existing problem is but one type of objective evidence useful in making obviousness/non-obviousness determinations. Further, the district court correctly noted that copying the claimed invention, rather than one within the public domain, is indicative of non-obviousness.

[4] Having carefully considered AMF's arguments and the evidence relied upon by the district court, we conclude that AMF has not discharged its burden on appeal, i.e., of persuading us that the district court committed reversible legal error in its determination that the invention would not have been obvious, or that the court's probative findings underlying that determination were clearly erroneous. Accordingly, the presumptive validity of the '167 patent remains unscathed and the judgment upholding claims 15-21 of the '167 patent is affirmed.

(2) Infringement

Downwind alone appeals from the judgment of infringement, urging that its structure does not have a "joint having a plurality of axes of rotation." Downwind employs a flexible rubber tube or rod connecting the mast and the board.

[5] Claim interpretation is a question of law, but we have been shown no basis for upsetting the district court's interpretation of the claims as covering a structure that permits the mast to pivot with respect to and about a number of axes. Downwind's contention that a flexible rubber tube is not "mechanical," and does not rotate, and thus is not a "joint" within the

EXHIBIT 2 *(continued)*

meaning of the claims, is without merit. The word "mechanical" does not appear in the claims, the twisting of the flexible tube is about an axis of rotation, and the tube forms a joint between the mast and board.

[6, 7] Whether Downwind's accused device infringes the claims as interpreted is a fact question, and a finding on that question will not be upset unless clearly erroneous. None of the accused infringers has attempted to rebut the testimony on which the district court relied in finding infringement. Downwind has not shown that the claims must be given its own unduly narrow interpretation or that the district court's finding of infringement was clearly erroneous. Accordingly, the judgment of infringement is affirmed.

(3) Patent Misuse

AMF's allegation of patent misuse is based on this paragraph included in license agreements between WSI and 11 licensees:

Trademarks

LICENSEE hereby acknowledges that the terms "WINDSURFER," "WINDSURFING," and "WINDSURF" and the company logo are all valid trademarks. LICENSEE hereby agrees not to use any of the trademarks identified in this paragraph 10 in any form or fashion in its company name or any of its literature or advertising or promotional material or on any products whatsoever.

The district court said that whether that provision gives rise to a patent misuse defense depends on whether the registered trademarks are generic. Having found the marks generic, the court concluded "that Paragraph 10 has an intrinsically inhibiting effect on competition beyond the scope of the patent...."

The court went on to determine that the "level of misuse" did not warrant rendering the patent entirely unenforceable because the court found the "record insufficient to determine fairly the extent to which WSI sought to enforce the provision and the extent of any monetary gain to it" and also found the record insufficient to support a finding that "WSI necessarily would or should have known that its mark had become a common descriptive name for the product."

The court set the damages issue for determination at a later time, deferred until that time "the resolution as to what relief, if any, WSI's misuse of its patent privilege warrants," and decided to enforce the '167 patent.

In its cross-appeals, WSI contends that a mere inclusion in a patent license agreement of a promise not to infringe a licensor's trademark does not constitute patent misuse. Acts constituting misuse, says WSI, must be "coercive" toward an improper advantage. WSI argues that it was merely asserting rights it possessed under the trademark laws and, thus, the patent misuse defense should fall.

[8] The doctrine of patent misuse is an affirmative defense to a suit for patent infringement, and requires that the alleged infringer show that the patentee has impermissibly broadened the "physical or temporal scope" of the patent grant with anticompetitive effect. We have seen cited to no authority, and are aware of none, for the proposition that patent misuse may

EXHIBIT 2 *(continued)*

be found on the basis of a patent license agreement provision recognizing and forbidding use of the licensor's validly registered trademarks.

[9, 10] To sustain a misuse defense involving a licensing arrangement not held to have been per se anticompetitive by the Supreme Court,[11] a factual determination must reveal that the overall effect of the license tends to restrain competition unlawfully in an appropriately defined relevant market. A provision in a patent license agreement requiring the licensee to acknowledge the validity of registered trademarks, and to avoid their use, cannot possibly restrain competition unlawfully in an appropriately defined relevant market. The license agreement provision merely asserted and recognized WSI's rights derived from the trademark laws. The assertion of trademark rights can have procompetitive effects, and thus under only the most rare of circumstances could such assertion, separately or as a provision in a patent license agreement, form in itself the basis for a holding of inequitable conduct such as that labeled "patent misuse." It is not an uncommon precaution when licensing a product sold by the licensor under a trademark to prohibit the licensee from using the licensor's trademark on the licensee's product. That is but a matter of business prudence and in no manner misuses the patent right.

That the marks were found generic after trial and long after execution of the license cannot of itself prevent a full enforcement of the '167 patent. Trademark registrations enjoy a statutory presumption of validity. As the district court found, AMF failed to show that WSI granted the licenses or enforced its rights in the marks with knowledge that they were or had become a common descriptive name, and AMF failed to show that WSI should have had that knowledge. On the present record, the district court was improperly persuaded to rest its holding of misuse entirely on an after-the-fact determination that the marks are generic. Because that was error, the holding that the facts of record established a misuse of the patent right must be reversed.[12]

(4) Injunctions

[11] The law empowers district courts to "grant injunctions in accordance with the principles of equity to prevent the violation of any right secured by patent, on such terms as the court deems reasonable." The statute makes clear that the district court's grant or denial of an injunction is within its discretion depending on the facts of each case. Hence, the district court's grant or denial of an injunction is reviewed under an abuse of discretion standard.

The holding of misuse having been reversed, we need not address AMF's contention that the district court should not have enjoined further infringement of the '167 patent in light of that holding.

AMF argues that the district court improperly ignored its intervening rights, a defense it contends was raised in the pleadings and at the injunction hearing, citing *Seattle Box Co. v. Industrial Carting & Packing, Inc.,* made no mention of its intervening rights defense at the trial.

[12] Nothing in *Seattle Box* addresses the point at which the intervening rights defense must be raised to preserve it. Intervening rights, however, is "an affirmative defense . . . that

---

[11] Recent economic analysis questions the rationale behind holding any licensing practice per se anticompetitive.
[12] We need not, in view of our determination, discuss the parties' contentions respecting the purging of misuse.

EXHIBIT 2 *(continued)*

must be raised at trial." That it failed to make any attempt to prove the defense at trial is in this case fatal. AMF cannot be held to have resuscitated the defense by the mere submission of affidavits at a post-trial hearing. To so hold would run counter to the finality attaching to trials. District courts are under no obligation to consider a defense abandoned at trial. Accordingly, no abuse of discretion having been shown, we affirm the district court's grant of injunctive relief against AMF and BIC.

On its cross-appeal, WSI urges that the district court abused its discretion in refusing to enjoin Downwind. In denying injunction relief against Downwind, the district court stated from the bench:

I am prepared to say at the present time that I do not believe that an injunction against Downwind is appropriate. As bad as Windsurfing's problems I am prepared to believe may be, I do not believe that enjoining Downwind, which is such a small operation, would solve their problems, not that I think an injunction's purpose is simply to solve its problems; and so I mention that because I don't think you need to argue further on that.

The relative size of multiple infringers should not alone serve as a basis for enjoining continued infringement by some and not by others.[13] The district court articulated no other basis for denying injunction relief against Downwind. On the present record, therefore, we must conclude that the district court abused its discretion in refusing to enjoin Downwind. Accordingly, we remand the case to the district court to reconsider WSI's request for an appropriate injunction against Downwind.

CONCLUSION

The judgment of the district court upholding the validity of claims 15-21 of the '167 patent and finding them infringed, and the grant of injunctions against AMF and BIC are affirmed. The judgment that WSI is guilty of patent misuse is reversed. The case is remanded with instructions to vacate the order denying an injunction against Downwind and to reconsider WSI's request for that injunction.

The appeal is affirmed in part, reversed in part, vacated in part, and remanded.

---

[13] Downwind said its infringing sales were between 1,000 and 2,000 sailboards a year since it began operations in 1981. AMF was selling about 1, 800 sailboards a year during the same four-year period. That sailboards are Downwind's primary product, and that an injunction might therefore put Downwind out of business, cannot justify denial of that injunction. One who elects to build a business on a product found to infringe cannot be heard to complain if an injunction against continuing infringement destroys the business so elected. The district court, recognizing the absence of bad faith on the part of all parties, weighed the effect of its orders on each. In so doing it indicated that WSI's entire business was built on sailboards and accessories, and thus that Downwind and WSI were in the same boat. Under those circumstances, no warrant appears on this record or denying the requested injunction against continued infringement by Downwind.

Dave Powers

Production facility dilemma

One calamity after another had beset Power Battery Corporation over several years as its owners struggled to achieve profitable start-up. Its product was a flashlight-type battery whose end could be flipped out to extend prongs that enabled it to plug into a conventional electric outlet for direct recharging. Its inventor, David Person, had initiated its development out of frustration with the cost of batteries consumed by his children's toys.

There were essentially three parts to the battery: (1) the rechargeable cell, which was purchased from large suppliers who provided it to many other users, such as makers of electric razors and other appliances; (2) the metal prongs that would plug into a wall socket and were held by a circular plastic disk fitted to the battery; and (3) a miniature charging circuit that transformed the alternating current from the wall socket to lower-voltage direct current to charge the cell.

David Person had exhausted his personal savings developing the unit and trying to sell it with what turned out to be an inferior nickel-cadmium cell. To sustain the venture he had sold rights to another company that persuaded him to use a lead-acid cell instead. But that turned out to perform even worse than the nickel-cadmium cell, and the partnership fell apart.

At that point another entrepreneur, David Powers, acquired rights to the product, formed a new corporation, and recruited investors. After two years of further work and expenditure of another $2 million, the Power Battery Company, had reached what he regarded as a critical decision.

Refinement of the design and development, prototype testing, Underwriters Laboratory approval, Federal Communications Commission approval, and pilot production of samples to check performance and quality had been accomplished. The "Power Flip-Top Size D" battery was, as David Powers saw it, ready for production. The engineers on the development team had released the design and delivered to the venture documentation confirming readiness of the product for mass production and the marketplace. Powers saw his task as that of transforming the venture from what he called a Development House to a Production House.

He had just closed a third round of financing and there was now approximately $1 million on hand from a group of investors eager to see the Company deliver goods to the market and finally start reaping profits. The current monthly cash burn rate was $50,000, all of which was going to general, administrative, and selling expenses. There were orders on hand for 50,000 Flip Tops. Estimated production costs, at $12, were still higher than the $10 sales price to stores but expected to come down with volume production.

Clash of opinions

But now two opposing camps emerged within the Company about how that production should be accomplished.

First camp: Slowly but surely

Power Battery's chief development engineer had spent most of his career in medical products design and manufacture. He was adamant that the first production run should be done locally and in very small volume (1,000 to 5,000 units) in order to expose the development team to debugging needs of the product and to facilitate refinement of quality assurance processes as volume was ramped up. He insisted that a three-month shakedown process must be followed through despite the certainty that it would be very expensive. Only when that had been successfully accomplished would he consent to volume production outside the country where costs could be dramatically lowered.

Second camp: Go for scale economies

Power Battery's vice president of operations was a seasoned battery industry manager with a strong appreciation of the competitive strength of other battery producers. As he saw it, Power Battery had a window of opportunity to be the "first mover" with a new product and backorders that no other company in the market could duplicate in the near term. He was adamant that a production run of over 10,000 units per month should be initiated immediately in a contract factory that had been located and evaluated in Tijuana, Mexico. Lower assembly cost, he insisted, could provide economies of scale almost immediately, and a majority of the orders on hand could be filled within the three-month period that the chief development engineer wanted instead to confine to a relatively tiny pilot production run.

Arguments gained in fury over a three-day period as others connected with the venture began to take sides, some of them almost coming to blows. To Dave Powers it seemed time to step in and implement a decision.

Dave Williams and Mike Ruffo

Site seeking

In the summer of 1998, Mike Ruffo, who with his friend Dave Williams, had been working to implement their business plan for a new store to provide do-it-yourself pet grooming, made the following entry in his diary:

> *It has been a summer of learning. I learned that you are always selling something. Whether it is your idea to a landlord or an espresso cart to some stranger, everything is selling. I also learned that you cannot plan for every obstacle. You can only try your best to overcome it. There have been frustrations this summer, but we will overcome them. We refuse to settle for anything less than success, and a good location is our first step.*

Dave and Mike, MBA students at the University of Washington in Seattle, had prepared a business plan for their venture during school, and entered it in a business plan contest at the University of Oregon, where they won second prize. In October 1997, encouraged by this and by their market research, both primary and secondary, they incorporated For Pet's Sake to implement their idea. Their aim was to become known as "The Nordstrom of pet care by providing upscale products, services, and amenities to pets and their owners."

Their intention was to establish and maintain "an immaculately clean, comfortable, and upscale atmosphere" where pet owners could buy pet supplies and either bathe and groom their pets themselves or have it done by professionals. A modern café facility would be designed into each store to enhance the upscale image. Each café would become a place where pet owners could relax, sip a latte, soft drink, or beer, as well as watch a satellite TV system if they chose to wait for care of their pet.

In May 1998 the two presented their business plan to several banks for start-up funding. Loan approval eventually came in July. Having successfully navigated the labyrinth of scrutinizing and skeptical financiers, they next needed a site for their first location in order to close the loan. This was proving much more difficult than they had expected.

Criteria set up by the two for seeking a site included that it be (1) a semi-rural or urban community that contained the targeted demographic groups, (2) within two miles of at least two major grocery stores, (3) near major fast-food chains and convenience stores, (4) near at least two major banks, and (5) if possible, within three miles of public parks frequented by dog owners. The targeted groups, based upon both literature search and systematic interviews by the founders, included pet-owning households with incomes between $30,000 and $99,000. From interviews they decided that the person responsible for pet grooming was typically a female in the age range of 31–40, but that nearly one-third (28 percent) is between ages 41 and 60. Those who used professional groomers typically visited them twice per month, but many used them monthly. About three-fourths bought their pet food at grocery stores, but the remainder bought it at specialty stores devoted to pets. Based on their study, Williams and Ruffo stated in their business plan that:

> *Pet owners indicated a desire for many full-service pet care options. However, most heavily requested were bathing, quick drying, flea dipping or shampoos, coat clipping and conditioning, or de-matting. A surprising number of respondents (57 percent) indicated a preference for environmentally friendly grooming products. Most pet food buyers purchase both canned and dry*

food for their pets. Twenty-nine percent demand premium or all-natural brands. High-margin specialty items are heavily demanded.

The income statement projected in the business plan for the venture indicated that it could break even by the second month and earn approximately $50,000 before taxes on sales of around $200,000 in the first 12 months, excluding any pay to themselves. They were allowing around $19,000 for advertising and promotions, $9,000 for rent, based on an estimate of $9 per square foot per year, half that for phone and utilities, and $6,000 for legal, accounting, and consulting help.

Now all that was needed was to find a site, set it up, hire help, and open for business. Mike's diary continued:

> *We expected to secure a lease, close the loan, and begin operations by late July or early August. We had already written the business plan. All we needed to do now was execute the plan. We had done our market research and even had the ideal location picked out. The only deadline was the close date on our loan, which we had extended until August 1. Plenty of time. Unfortunately, the rest of the world does not always agree to the plan.*
>
> *We chose Lakewood (in Tacoma about 30 miles south of Seattle) because we are familiar with the area and feel it fits the type of market we will appeal to. We found quite a few potential sites in this area and began submitting proposals to several different locations. This way we would have our pick.*
>
> *At the same time we were scouting locations, we were preparing for the opening. We ordered a phone and placed a Yellow Pages ad. We did not have an address yet, but that could be added at the last minute. We also began to look for an espresso bar which we would operate in front of our store. We expected to open by mid-July at the latest, and to jump right in and open as soon as possible when the lease was signed.*
>
> *The first place we tried was perfect, 2,000 square feet right outside of the Lakewood Mall. The building was brand new and we would share it with two clinics. It was just outside of a large community and had very high visibility. We met the owner and he seemed to be behind our idea. We were very excited and were ready to move in.*
>
> *Unfortunately, just as we were about to fax the proposal, we received a call from the owner. He told us he had run the idea by the doctors next door and they had some concerns. They were worried about dogs creating a bathroom outside of their offices. This is an understandable concern, and I told the owner we would propose a solution. We spent all night figuring one out that included a sign and scoop dispenser that would be mounted to a post implanted in the grass. He wasn't interested.*

Undaunted, the two moved on to another prospect, 1,800 square feet right next to their bank in a center with a McDonald's and a vacant grocery store. The latter, they thought, might enable them to bargain more strongly, since it too lacked a tenant. This time they decided to go through an agent, to whom they faxed a proposal. But they were blocked by the owner of a Mexican restaurant who considered barking dogs next door undesirable.

A chain of further disappointments over sites unfolded, recorded by Mike as follows:

- Pet store moving out. Asking $1,000 per month rent, but on major road with many small stores—inconvenient for walking pets and not the sort of place one would send the kids alone. Maybe acceptable as a fallback if all other options fail.
- Site with competitor near by. Won't allow outside espresso bar (and food inspector will not allow one inside).
- Site will not allow outside espresso bar.
- Site near another where a large pet supply store is already negotiating for a lease.

- Strip mall site—established groomer nearby, owner's son installing an espresso bar.
- Site is long and narrow—may be hard to use—rent is $12 per square foot per year, bakery nearby might be a problem.
- Nice-looking building on the outside, but space is overly large and would require many improvements. Put together a proposal for two-year lease starting at an annual rate of $5 per square foot for the first four months, $6 for next four, and $7 for next four plus year two with option to extend five more years at $8. However, owners wanted annual rent to start at $15 and rise to $17 per square foot. Also, site has very limited parking.

Mike and Dave next made a proposal of $10 per foot on a site in Seattle, but shortly were informed that it had been rejected. They raised their offer on it to $11 for the first six months, $12 on the next six, and then $13 on year two with an option to extend for another five years. This offer too was rejected.

The two believed they had exhausted all existing possibilities in Lakewood. It seemed to them that their failures were rooted in several causes as follows: (1) pre-conceived images and concerns about noise, image, and sanitary conditions as perceived by landlords and neighboring businesses; (2) lack of experience in the industry with nothing but a business plan to convey their intentions; (3) lack of experience in dealing with leasing agents and agencies; (4) start-up failure rates vs. those of established businesses; and (5) lack of financial depth.

One option seemed to be recycling the first alternatives with increased efforts. Another would be to seek more sites in other directions. Dave Williams summarized these possibilities as follows:

1. **Puyallup** is a suburban city near Tacoma and Lakewood and is home to the Puyallup fair. It is located approximately one and one-half hours from Seattle. It contains all the criteria we listed as desirable with the exception of criterion number 5, proximity to public parks. There are many strip malls located in Puyallup, and one located near a popular Gold's Gym and several shopping centers. Puyallup's most favorable aspect is extremely reasonable commercial rental rates in relation to other sites under consideration. Its most undesirable weakness seems to be its remoteness from larger cities.

2. **Kirkland**, east across Lake Washington from Seattle on the Microsoft side, is a very modern city that has undergone considerable growth and development over the past ten years. It is a waterfront community containing middle- to high-level income residents who possess considerable disposable income. Many employees of Microsoft reside here. The location under consideration seems to meet our selection criteria. Commercial and residential rents are higher than other locations under consideration. The specific strip mall is located on Lake Washington Boulevard, Kirkland's most popular waterfront avenue. The lease term is shorter than some other sites under consideration (3 years vs. 5 years) because of a potential future condominium development. This shorter lease could be viewed as a strength if the concept proves unprofitable; i.e., the owners would not be held responsible for an extended lease agreement. However, this short lease could also prove to be a considerable weakness if the venture proves profitable and the business is forced to relocate.

3. **Bellevue**, also east of the lake, has become a capital of the information technology world because of its proximity to Microsoft. Income levels throughout Bellevue are the highest in the Pacific Northwest with a correspondingly high level of disposable income. Both commercial and residential real estate rents are extremely high in relation to other areas; even higher than those of Kirkland. The location under consideration is a strip mall located in North Bellevue, across the street from the big volume store of Eagle Hardware. It is highly visible from a major freeway intersecting the heart of Bellevue. The proposed location seems

to meet the selection criteria for an initial store. A key strength to this location is its proximity to Marymoor Park, a "leash-less" dog-walking park located less than three miles away. Its main weakness is its high rent and potential overhead.

4. **Ballard** is a community to the northwest of downtown Seattle with a somewhat ethnic European (Norwegian) and elderly population of mid- to high-level income. It seems to meet the criteria listed as desirable except for number 5. It is conveniently located within minutes of all the metropolitan areas of Seattle and can be conveniently accessed from (1) downtown via Western Avenue, a major artery, (2) Interstate 5, the most traveled north-south highway on the West Coast, and (3) SR-100, the second most popular highway in Seattle. This highly visible potential location is on the main street of Ballard across the street from Starbucks, SBC Coffee, and several other desirable walk-in business entities. Ballard's main strength is its accessibility; its main weakness is its "average" customer demographic profile.

5. **Capitol Hill**, which sits right above downtown Seattle and looking westward over it, has been referred to as the San Francisco of the Pacific Northwest. The area is known for its open-minded, early-adapter consumer attitudes. It meets all the selection criteria we outlined as desirable to an initial location. Income categories range from lower-middle class (student types) to extremely wealthy, upper-income families. Commercial and residential rental rates vary from reasonable to extremely high, depending on exact location. The location under consideration is located on Pine Street, a main thoroughfare that passes eastward from downtown Seattle through Capital Hill to Madison Park, a very upscale residential area. Capitol Hill's main strength seems to be its proximity to Volunteer Park, a public park that has an off-leash dog walking area. Its main weakness is lack of parking.

Bruce Milne (A)

As 1979 ended, Bruce Milne, the sales manager of a minicomputer sales company office in Seattle, was considering how to structure ownership in a new company he planned to start with two of his co-employees. The company they worked for sold DEC minicomputers to accountants for the combined functions of accounting and word processing. Bruce had watched with increasing interest as microcomputers had expanded in capabilities and he expected that it was only a matter of time before they too would find application in both accounting and word processing. Because they were much cheaper than minicomputers he expected that once they entered the market for those functions they would spread rapidly. His idea for the new company was to capitalize on that opportunity. To get started he wanted Brian Duthie and Lauri Chandler to join him as partners.

Antecedents of the idea

Bruce Milne had been engaged in ventures of one kind or another since childhood. He recalled:

> When I was 8, I was already trudging around selling Christmas cards. I liked to buy the stock, go around presenting it to people, make the sales and collect the money. To me it was fun.

Later, as a business major at the University of Washington, he "always had two or three businesses going at once," he recalled. "It was to prevent starvation, because nobody was paying my way."

For instance while working as a lifeguard, he met parents who wanted swimming lessons for their children. Consequently, he rented time at a local pool and set up a swimming school which employed up to four instructors. He continued:

> I'd been a swim instructor and a coach. Then I became a lifeguard for the city. Parents were always asking if there were someplace they could send their kids for lessons. I saw that there were a lot of private pools, and a lot of people in one housing complex wanted lessons. I went to a private pool there, and they let me use the pool until two o'clock on my own. For instructors I hired some fraternity members at the University. I had all the paper boys in the north end put flyers out, and I had a little pyramid scheme where for every customer you bring in, you get a dollar off on your own child. We had a babysitting service where if you bring them for a half-hour they could have a babysitter for two or three hours, so you could go shopping at the Northgate shopping center. We were deluged because we had the cheapest babysitting service in town, plus swim lessons.

He also bought, repaired and sold used Volkswagens, ran a barber service, sold cookware, imported and sold Swiss watches and renovated houses.

After graduation in 1970, Bruce spent the remainder of his savings on a trip to Europe, after which he returned to Seattle and looked for a job. He made application to the University of Washington Business School. He was accepted, but decided not to go. He worked for a company called Canadian American Security Holders (CASH), which was a collection agency. "I thought you'd make money quick at that," he said. "But it was a fly-by-night operation." He soon looked for another job.

In the newspaper classified section, he noticed two jobs of possible interest, one selling office copiers and the other selling computers. "My dad always told me to go to work for a big company," he recalled. After interviewing both he chose the latter and in 1971 went to work

for Burroughs Corporation, "It was lucky I made that choice," he said, "because the other job would have been a dead end."

He went through Burroughs' training program and became a sales representative. "The job started at only about $600 to $700 a month," he said. "It took me about five years working full time to get up to the level of income I'd had working part time for myself." He once again went to the University, where he took a couple of night courses toward an MBA, but then dropped out.

In 1973 he encountered a new opportunity in the company.

> I had gone to school in Mexico during my sophomore year and always thought it would be interesting to get into international business in some way. There was a guy from Burroughs who was flying through on his way to Japan. My boss said, "I'll see if he can interview you between planes." So I went and said I wanted a job internationally. I was cocky at 24. I said, "I can outsell anybody you have." He said "OK." So I went sight unseen to Puerto Rico. I took a pay cut. I guess a lot of people didn't like that job. It was funny. My three worst subjects in school were Spanish, accounting and computer programming. And so now I was selling computers for accounting applications in Puerto Rico.

By age 24 he became the youngest sales zone manager in the company. He also got married to a co-worker from Burroughs in Seattle with whom he had stayed in touch.

> She had been in real estate sales, and got her job as a Burroughs sales representative after she sold the local sales manager his house—a big 12,000 square foot place in West Seattle that had been a girls' school.

Beginnings of a business idea

Software for computer accounting systems at the time was almost entirely a custom activity in the mid-1970s, he recalled.

> At one point my wife and I set up another business on the side called Systems Analyst Programmers, because Burroughs would not let us hire any programmers, and we needed them to sell and service the systems for Puerto Rican customers. At Burroughs you had to do your own programming, so we did this other business on the side to try to save some of the installations we had. At one point we had guys from about 10 different companies working for us.
>
> I also picked up software on trips to the United States. Wherever I went around the country, to Chicago or Los Angeles, I'd head straight for the software backroom, rip off a copy of everything they had and take it on the plane with me back to Puerto Rico. So I built a library, even though I wasn't a technical guy, because the software they had in South America was garbage.

Then in 1974, Bruce again decided to apply to business school.

> Everything seemed to go in two-year cycles. After about 18 months in one spot I'd start to get the feeling it was time to move on. I applied to Harvard, IMEDE and Wharton. Then to my pleasant surprise on three successive Saturdays I got acceptances from each one. I felt great. My grades had been passable, but not so good as to give me confidence I'd be accepted.

He started at the Harvard Business School in 1975, majored in finance and spent the following summer working as an intern at nearby Digital Equipment Corporation (DEC).

> The question I worked on was basically how do we train the original equipment makers (OEM's) who resold and installed DEC's computers, something DEC itself didn't do. That gave me a great exposure to their OEM channels who developed and sold systems and helped develop the custom software that always had to be part of the package.

During my second year I developed a thesis on "The role of the distributor in a computer environment." It was one of these two-credit courses you could devote your life to. My wife and I sold the report to a number of big companies, including IBM, and made several thousand dollars on it that helped pay tuition. It was the most comprehensive report on that topic available at the time.

It looked at the time like software was going to be a marketing bottleneck. Prices of computers were coming down. People were projecting that computer prices were going to come down by 75 percent, while costs of marketing would triple. Companies like IBM, Burroughs and NCR only sold direct. DEC did almost all its selling through the OEM systems houses. The question was how would you extend the channels around them? How would you manage those channels? How would you recruit? What should be the credit policies, and so forth? Stores selling software were unheard of.

Following graduation in 1977, Bruce and his wife sought a way to return to the West Coast. Bruce took a job with a Portland, Oregon DEC distributor, Alpine Corporation, to help develop a sales office in Seattle. There his belief that better ways of standardizing and distributing minicomputer software were bound to come continued to grow. He recalled:

I said to Alpine management, "you guys already have a lot of software. Why don't you get a guy in Boston, a guy in Philadelphia, and one in Baltimore and make them dealers to resell your stuff so people won't always be reinventing the wheel. You can get leverage and build a big company." There were no big companies selling minicomputers at that time. The biggest we had at DEC was about $3 million a year, and every year the biggest would go out of business, because they would grow, and they would have all this custom software, they'd overextend themselves . . . and we'd be eating their receivables. They were always trying to supply the stuff with lots of custom applications. DEC would help put them out of business because it would take four months to make shipment, and meanwhile the distributors would run out of cash.

His interest in microcomputers also continued to grow as their capabilities increased. In his travels Bruce became acquainted with John Torode, who studied computer science at the University of Washington, then went to Berkeley to teach, while on the side developing a company to make microcomputers. He was the first, according to Bruce, to develop a machine with two floppy disk drives. It seemed to Bruce that it was only a matter of time before machines like that began to benefit from development of standardized software and find application in offices such as those of the accountants to whom he was selling minicomputers.

Teaming

One of the people he began discussing these ideas with was a co-worker, Brian Duthie. Brian had studied industrial engineering and business at Berkeley, then joined Western Electric in 1969, where he worked in product testing. After hours he studied computers at a nearby technical school. Jobs with other companies followed, selling minicomputers for a sales firm, developing software for an insurance company, then working for a computer consulting firm, mainly installing a purchase order system for Boeing. Seeing insufficient growth in that job, he joined Alpine, where he found himself working for Bruce. Together, the two were responsible for over 40 percent of sales in the 40-person company.

When Bruce, frustrated by Alpine's rejection of his business development ideas, first began talking with Brian about creating a new company, the idea was that they might begin developing microcomputer systems on the side. Bruce developed a connection with Altos Computer in California and suggested that Brian might develop software to go with Altos hardware to make a complete system they could sell to accountants.

But attendance at a night course gave Bruce a different perspective. One of the speakers who had developed several successful companies stressed the idea that he had never been able to do it part time. It was necessary, he said, to take the full plunge if the company were going to be ambitiously growth-oriented. Brian, however, was cautious. Neither he nor Bruce had much savings, and Brian's wife was expecting their first child.

Hoping to persuade Brian, Bruce suggested they visit John Torode in California to see his dual floppy microcomputer. On the trip they could also visit the only company Bruce knew of that offered a standard general ledger software package for minicomputers. Bruce commented:

> Brian, like a true techie, was glad for the chance to get inside a computer "factory" and meet the machine's designer. Then we went over to the software company, told them we might be interested in distributing their product, and asked for a demonstration. We had a yellow pad with us that we took notes on. The demonstration was supposed to last 45 minutes. But after 20 minutes we said we had seen enough. The notes we took on the yellow pad were deficiencies and we already had four pages of them. Like any good programmer, Brian always knew he could make something better. And if this was the leader of the industry, they were in for real trouble.

Now Brian was ready to go with the new venture. The idea would be to sell DEC minicomputer systems with existing software for the short term to derive income, which would support development of better software by Brian for the longer term. The software would be for microcomputers, and when it was ready, the new company would sell systems combining it with Altos computers to accountants.

Bruce had also persuaded his secretary, Lauri Chandler, to join the team. Lauri had become skilled at word processing on the minicomputer systems Alpine sold.

Designing the ownership structure

As Bruce saw it, each of the three would bring different ingredients to the new venture. Brian would be crucial as the "resident genius" software developer. He would also be important in helping sell and install minicomputer systems for income while the company was getting started.

Lauri would help with two functions. One would be to run the office of the new venture itself. The other would be to serve as a consultant on the word processing aspects of the minicomputer installations sold during the company's first phase of existence.

Bruce would take primary responsibility for selling minicomputer systems during the first stage. He expected one major problem would be to obtain the computers to sell, since the company, because of its smallness, would not initially qualify as an OEM for DEC. "It's ironic," he observed. "One of the very systems I helped set up at DEC would now prevent us from becoming an OEM for them."

However, Bruce had become well-acquainted with DEC's channels and believed he would be able to buy through contacts he had in a consortium headquartered in North Dakota. This would reduce the discount they would receive on equipment from 30 percent down to perhaps 25 percent, but he expected it would enhance speed of delivery, since the buying consortium always had more units on order than a typical systems house handling DEC products, and therefore could provide faster and more dependable delivery.

Bruce would also be responsible for raising capital. Each of the three, it appeared, would be able to muster $10,000. To do so, the three would have to commit all their personal savings and, in some cases, borrow from relatives. Bruce would be able to go without salary in the near term, thanks to his wife's income, but the other two would need to be paid. So it seemed clear to all three that more capital would have to be raised. Bruce knew of three individuals he might be able to raise another $10,000 each from within a couple of months if they could get the company set up and operating. One was an entrepreneur with a cheesecake manufacturing company to whom Bruce had sold a minicomputer. The second was a lawyer whom Bruce had tried to sell without success, but had nevertheless become a good friend. The third was a former competitor who had recently made large profits from shares he held when his employer went public.

If the new firm were able to raise another $30,000 from these individuals, Bruce expected that it might last only a few months, after which, if Brian were successful in developing the microcomputer software, they would need another infusion two or three times that large to move ahead with its distribution. How he would accomplish that, he was not sure. He supposed it would necessitate recruiting more shareholders from somewhere.

Bruce also knew some sales prospects to whom he thought the new company would be able to sell minicomputer systems in the near term. But as in the case of the potential sources of capital, that possibility remained to be tested.

His immediate problem was how to structure ownership between himself and his two initial colleagues, both to get the company started and to establish a base for further development in the future.

Ampersand (B)

February 1993—Incorporation decisions

In late February 1993, the founders of Ampersand were reviewing provisions to be included in the legal formation of their company. For prior history of the venture, please refer to the Ampersand (A) case. Up to this point they had done essentially nothing about company legal structure.

The company was going to need a commercial bank account. So far, the founders had been paying company expenses out of their personal checking accounts while keeping careful records of the expenditures, which Robert Tavarez was recording with the help of a $100 accounting software package. Expenditures to date had been quickly consuming the original $1,250 each that the founders had agreed to contribute.

To fill the order from Pearl Paint there would have to be substantially greater expenditures which would be awkward to handle from separate personal accounts. Substantial additional cash, whether obtained from winning at San Diego, as the team planned, or from other sources, would have to be deposited somewhere.

To set up a commercial checking account for the venture they would have to obtain business licenses from the state and the city. They would also need a state sales tax license. Robert observed:

> It's a strange situation. You need the licenses to get a checking account, but you have to write checks to get the licenses.

The business had to have some legal form, and it seemed to the team that a corporation was likely the best to adopt. A partnership would probably require more custom legal work and be harder to use for raising money. Elaine called a lawyer she knew back home in Colorado who offered to work on it at no cost. He, in turn, could pass it along to another lawyer whom he knew in Texas to make sure the requirements of that state were met if the team wanted it to be a Texas corporation.

The Colorado attorney raised a number of points that should be considered. It would be simplest, he said, if the shares were all issued to one person, such as Elaine. Later, shares could be issued to others, if need be, through changes in the corporate bylaws. Another decision called for was whether to provide in the articles of incorporation for preemptive rights for existing shareholders. That would mean that if further shares were sold to outside shareholders the existing shareholders, would have the right to buy more shares at the same price per share on a prorata basis. If, Robert observed, there were many shareholders, this could become a complicated procedure.

How many shares to authorize and issue initially was another question the founders would have to decide. These shares would be declared at some par value that would represent the company's initial shareholder's equity, which the team assumed would consist of the $5,000 they had put in so far. How should this be handled if one or more members decided to withdraw from the team?

Another question was whether to choose an S corporation form or a C corporation form. With an S corporation, Robert explained, any losses up to the company's equity basis, $5,000 at this point, and any profits would pass through to shareholders at the personal income tax rate and would not be subject to any separate corporate income tax. A C corporation form, however, would require the company to pay income taxes at the corporate rate, and then if any profits were passed along to shareholders in the form of dividends, those would be taxed again at the personal income tax rate. At the same time, however, a C corporation would allow carry forward of any losses in the corporation without limit.

Moreover, with a C corporation the company could issue other types of stock such as preferred stock or non-voting shares, and stock shares could be held by either individuals or corporations, none of which could be done with shares of an S corporation. Still, an S corporation could be converted over to a C corporation if the shareholders wanted to do so. The reverse was not allowed for five years after conversion. To make this conversion would entail more paperwork and presumably legal fees.

There was also the question of what property the corporation should have at this point. There was as yet no formal written agreement with Charles Ewing concerning his relationship with the venture. He and his wife had been making some sales of Claybord, but they were small and the team had not been following them. He had also spent about $5,000 so far to make application for a patent. But it was still pending and there would likely be more expenses to come, perhaps as much as had been spent so far, before it would be issued. The name Claybord had not yet been registered as a trademark.

As the team member who had been handling most of Ampersand's accounting and paperwork functions, Robert Tavarez felt he should take initiative to make sure its legal choices were handled appropriately.

Andrew Hammoude (B)

The M.I.T. Forum

Dr. Andrew Hammoude and his partners had applied to the Seattle chapter of the M.I.T. Forum to have their business plan reviewed and to receive expert advice for their venture. (Please see the Andrew Hammoude case for further background.) The M.I.T. Forum was an activity organized by the Alumni Office of the Massachusetts Institute of Technology. Entrepreneurs could submit their plans to a local chapter of the Forum, which would then select one for review by a volunteer expert panel. The panelists would be chosen based on relevance of their expertise to the particular venture. They would review the plan, meet with the entrepreneur, examine the product or service and develop appropriate advice.

This advice would be presented at a public, two-hour meeting in the evening. The meeting would begin with dinner. By the time dessert was being served, the presentation would begin. The entrepreneur and his or her colleagues would stand before the assembly and describe their enterprise. Then each member of the expert panel would present his or her observations and advice. After that, members of the audience would be invited to ask questions and make comments, which would conclude the evening.

IMAGEsystems was the subject of an M.I.T. Forum meeting in Seattle on November 14, 1988. The panelists included two founders of profitable and rapidly growing small firms in microcomputer applications, a sales executive from a major microcomputer manufacturer, and an analyst from a venture capital firm. The following is a digest of their comments and those of others in the audience after the entrepreneurs' presentation.

Panelists' comments

Entrepreneur #1

I came out of a very technical background myself and went through much the same thing as you. When we first started our company and were talking to the banks, looking for cash flow commitments to fund our operations and our receivables. The banks were not ready to put more at risk than we were. So you should quit your jobs when you are ready to become a company. Until that, you have not made a commitment that you are a company.

Divide responsibility now. Write it down. Have succinct job descriptions of what each of you is going to do. There is an instinct for all of you to want to be involved in all aspects of the company. The result is that you will all be juggling parallel work, which will lower your efficiency tremendously. Communication is an n-factorial process. When there are four of you, that's not much of an overhead. But when you grow to eight, 16 or 32 people n factorial becomes a very large number. You need to establish clearly defined channels of communication and responsibility. With the latter must go ownership. You must own responsibility. If you have that early on, then you won't be in each other's way, and you will be effective. Decide what it is now and get it done.

You have spent 30 years obtaining technical skills that will give you an unfair advantage in the marketplace. It is important that you obtain similar levels of business skills. You must draw on those to be successful. You must find assistance for those: financial, legal, sales and marketing.

The model we followed was a good one. You don't need a CPA, but you do need a part-time bookkeeper. You need to get off on the right foot. Get in touch with one of the significant accounting firms, have somebody help you set up the books correctly and get you going. Have them recommend someone who can help you on a part-time basis. But get your books set up correctly first. The accounting firm also will know the banking community and can help by making introductions for you there, which can go a long way in helping you get your line of credit.

You don't need a lawyer in house, but you need one to get set up correctly. There are certain issues that we struggled with early on that paid dividends later. Think about your current team. You're all best of friends now. So were the five of us when we started our company. But as our organization matured, our personal goals changed and some of us parted ways. You need to think now, while you're all still good friends, what will you do, how will you divide the stock, what are the rights of people that leave the company with their stock? Should there be buy-back options? Will the company self-destruct if one of you decides to change life-style?

The company will live or die based on its ability to sell products in the marketplace. This is not the time to give somebody in the company on-the-job training in sales. You need to find somebody who has been there before and who has taken a company through the stages you are struggling with. You should consider a staged approach. Somebody who has taken a company to thirty or forty million in sales is not what you need at first. Such a person would be very expensive. But you do need somebody who has taken a company out a few years to around three to five million in revenues. You want that person to have ownership in the company, to own stock, to lust after making it succeed and seeing that stock mature into something of value.

Can you bootstrap the company and grow internally, or do you need outside capital to grow and fund the company? We cannot answer that for you. It is a question you have to answer your-self. But here are some questions to consider.

You are looking at what is claimed to be a fast-growing market with a limited window of opportunity for introducing this product and achieving market penetration. So there are certain boundary conditions that will control whether you can grow from inside or need outside capital.

What is a significant window of opportunity? If you are going after less than 30 percent of the market, you ought to get out right now. How long can you afford not to be a significant player and still be able to capture 30 percent of the market? What do you expect the life of your sales cycle to be? Does it take two weeks or six months from first contact to closing a sale? Each has different implications for recovering return on investment.

How long a production run can you afford? How long will it take to do a run? What are the cash requirements to initiate that production run? When must you pay for all the costs? Basically, the question is what volume of inventory can you support today to support the sales and cash flow? Answers to these questions will reveal whether you can bootstrap your company or will need outside capital to enter the market through the window of opportunity you have.

Be extremely conservative with your costs and sales estimates. A company that fails in this area will not be a candidate for additional venture financing. It's far better to start with more cash than to run out and find you need more and are at the mercy of the venture capitalists.

Judging from your plan, you are positioning your product as basically the "high-priced spread," versus something cheap and ubiquitous. That may be appropriate, but I'm concerned that the company may be driven by academic rather than market goals. What is the real market opportunity for entry? Almost every other word you speak should be "customer." You must be customer driven, market driven. Maybe the high-priced spread is the right approach, but you really need to understand who the clients are and how you can meet their needs.

So in summary, you have a tremendous challenge and exciting time ahead of you. I wouldn't exchange running a company for anything. Yours is an exciting business, and it is admirable that you are asking the questions you are. I wish we had done that at your stage of growth.

Entrepreneur #2

From my experience since starting our company just two years ago, I'd say you have to hock everything you have, take out a personal loan, open a garage someplace and get started. You *need that level of commitment before anyone will be willing to buy your products. They won't buy if they think you are hedging.*

If you want to become known as the lead company in the industry, with 30 percent of the market or more, you will have to buy market share out of profits. You must set a goal of reminding yourself every morning to become a customer-driven company. To do that you must get early sales revenues from somewhere. For a venture capitalist to be interested, you must ask who is the end-user and why will he buy? Are the unfair advantages I have worthy of the price?

I would go out in brute force; buy a list of all the system integrators in the United States. Get on the phone and start calling, working down from the top. You need to wrap something more around the technology that you have for a specific purpose and niche. Look for a niche in which somebody is selling hundred-thousand-dollar-plus workstations, because there you can sell for a higher price. That will let you show some profit, which is the only way you will motivate investors.

The big players are coming into this industry. There are no entry barriers. You have an opportunity to enter with low investment, seed capital and guerrilla tactics, personal loans, licensing of the technology, selling one-offs here and there to individual R&D groups. This can give you a toe-hold. But in about two years these opportunities will not exist. The market you're addressing seems to be a large number of vertical segments—people building products for specific end-user, vertical applications in fairly narrow markets number from 25 to maybe several hundred, if you are lucky.

In a couple of years it's not going to be much of a hardware game anymore. The big computer makers will be bringing in products and pulling the distribution channels together for more effective distribution. That will bring down margins and raise barriers to entry.

Microcomputer company sales executive

You have to be the best in some area and get some wins soon. We are looking hard at the possibilities of this market. We use market consulting firms quite often. Second and third opinions can really help. You have to consider what segments you want to work, how big they are and how fast they are growing.

There are three major areas of distribution we consider: (1) direct sales with your own sales force—loyal but costly, and it has to be large for mass market, (2) distributors—they are order-takers; you must advertise and generate sales for them. (Plusses are that they will hold inventory), (3) value added resellers—people providing solutions to a problem, who take pieces of hardware and software and provide a total solution to their customers; they really know their market. They are people you could really get on the bandwagon with, but only after you decide on what market you are really going after.

Venture capital analyst

What are your goals? To develop a nice little company and maybe sell it off or continue running it? Or to go public? Some entrepreneurs prefer the former, but we are only interested in the latter.

You must understand and properly project your cash requirements. Venture capitalists don't like to be surprised by urgent calls for more cash. How much you aim to raise should be tied to a set of milestones or goals closely aligned with product development and with some sort of customer satisfaction or adoption rate.

If you write a plan and decide you will need $5 million to become self-sustaining, don't try to raise it all at once—that would sell you short. If you can take a smaller amount first and use it to reach a greater valuation for your company, then you can charge a higher price for ownership.

Banks are an unlikely source for you. I am on the board of two companies with sales of around $30 million. Neither of them got bank money until they had three quarters of profitability. Venture capital is next least likely, because it wants hotter deals than yours is at this point.

Our deal structure depends on the business, its plan, prospects, etc. But the typical deal is 60 percent going to the investors and 40 to management, with half of that set aside to cut in other key people the company will need to recruit in the future. There are pros and cons to that, and some other venture capital firms do it differently, but that's the way we typically work.

Individual investors would be a better bet for you. Accountants, consultants and lawyers can lead you to them. Your most likely source, though, is suppliers and customers. See if you can't figure a way to get a customer sold to the point of putting up $200,000 to get you started.

You should go out and hire a big-six accountant. A lot of companies have developed accounting software packages. Each accounting firm has its favorite. Get the right package the first time, because correcting it later can be a disaster. One company I knew had its MRP supplier go into Chapter 11. The company was shipping about $8 million in hardware revenues. The hardware price was over $55,000, there were a lot of parts in it, and we had no idea where they were. We couldn't get the source code, because the company was in Chapter 11.

Part-time bookkeepers can be very helpful in accounting and even beyond that. Having the proper controls set up within the company, so one partner can't take money without the other one knowing it, is very important.

A company we were involved in down in Dallas had two very good people running it. The president was 65. The other was a very bright 35-year-old marketing woman with an MBA from Northwestern, who was one of the sharpest marketing people I ever met. I got a call from her on a Thursday asking me to please come down.

She had done some snooping and found out that the president's wife had terminal cancer. His company had been in trouble since it started, so we had been putting money in every three weeks. That president had been embezzling to pay medical bills, because he wasn't taking any salary, and he had no insurance coverage on his wife. He never told anyone in the company or any of the directors. So you have to set up controls in the company to make sure money doesn't disappear.

Comments from members of the audience

(Each paragraph denotes the start of a different person's comment.)

An engineer is always in the final stages of development. Don't make that mistake.

Could you sell your product to GE or Phillips rather than the user? Their expertise is not image processing but rather in manipulation of the signals coming back. Your opportunity is to sell the OEM a better tool set.

Those big companies are looking for strategic partners because they know they cannot do things fast internally.

To enter the radiologist market you might try selling to medical schools.

There is a company called Strider Technology that does imaging for radiological applications. (Dr. Hammoude) We will have to look into that.

You and your partners should use a Saturday to develop matching lists of goals.

(Response from Dr. Hammoude) We do have different temperaments. I am glad my partners heard you say this. I think we should have more bull sessions, but have encountered resistance from some of my partners. It's hard to justify a bull session when we have got to get software out.

How many people in this room have seen a market research projection from Dataquest, or from Frost and Sullivan or anyone else that was right for three years ahead? You will learn far more from just meeting with several of your clients.

(Computer Sales Executive) The first thing you need to do is identify what market you are really after. We use focus groups of a dozen or so behind a videotaping mirror. It is frustrating the way our message does not get across.

You should visit computer hardware companies in Seattle and Portland to describe your product and get ideas.

If you can get a strategic partner you may be able to use market research they have done.

Four sources of market information are (1) customers, (2) competitors, (3) potential competitors, and (4) market research firms. To get information from that fourth one free, call another company that has bought it and borrow the report from them.

Be careful not to waste your time on people who don't know the market. Identify several thought leaders around the country and go see them.

You could pick one industry, like real estate, and lash together a demonstration of your product, something zippy, then rent a small booth in a show and take orders.

That suggestion is dangerous. If you can't deliver, it can ruin your company.

(Entrepreneur #1) We find that general market data are not very helpful. But specific questions such as "What are the advantages of this competitor" can be very powerful. You can task somebody to go learn that.

(Venture Capital Analyst) Investors may find the "top down" market information of interest because it gives clues about total potential for growth.

It is very hard to get market data from a company like Dataquest about a market that has not developed yet.

(Venture Capital Analyst) You will need some of those reported market numbers to use as references in developing your business plan. You can't pull them out of thin air for that purpose. But since you have not identified a need for what you are developing, I don't see how you could possibly generate any numbers and I can't imagine any source you could go to for numbers. Don't quit your jobs until you know what the need is for your product. Who needs it?

You should get the market reports simply to verify the numbers you have come up with and possibly to identify surprises that you have not thought about.

I used to be a venture analyst, and I remember looking at marvelous numbers in business plans. They never came true.

Don't keep working for perfection. Pick a niche and get started. You can move to other niches later.

I'm not sure you need a niche. Can you make it cheap enough to go after larger markets?

You have no market, no user, no sales experience, no manufacturing experience. You have a product that is difficult to sell because you have to educate. You have no money, consensus or plan. Why don't you sell your technology as soon as possible for whatever you can get for it and do something else.

(Entrepreneur #1) I think there is a lot of merit to that comment. But I think our country would lose a lot of its special value if all the founders of small companies understood the odds that they are up against. They would not do startups. I think it is important that sometimes there is a little naiveté, there is bravery and things are born. I think you are asking the right questions. I think you're going in the right direction. The odds are overwhelmingly against you. But a lot of people have made it.

(Moderator) I think from the M.I.T. Forum's standpoint, we'll close on that comment rather than the previous one. Thank you.

Jerry Kaplan

Collaboration in start-up[1]

In late 1990, as Jerry Kaplan, the founder of GO Corporation was being replaced as CEO to become chairman of the company, there was opportunity to reflect on how the company had progressed and where it should head next amid a web of connections with other firms and individual investors. Kaplan, a computer scientist, had conceived the idea of a pen-driven computer in 1987, and formed GO to develop and produce it. Since inception, the venture had struggled through a series of strategic alliances with mixed success as other companies took varying degrees of interest in collaborating.

Creation of an effective operating system had been a major challenge, but was also where Kaplan expected profit potential would be highest. There were indications that Apple might be working on a competitive product based upon their earlier experience with the unsuccessful "Newton" hand-held computer. Also, Microsoft, when it looked at early development efforts by GO but did not follow up on their visit to the venture, might have chosen to work independently and adapt its own Windows system for use with a pen in place of a keyboard. But GO's engineers thought that would be prohibitively hard, because the modifications needed to adapt Windows to a pen were highly complicated and likely to result in a system that required too much memory, which would, in turn, add too much cost and weight to the laptop.

GO aimed to avoid that cost and weight by designing a system specifically for pen operation. Beyond the operating system there would be need for application programs. Those would mainly come from independent software vendors (ISVs), but GO would have to work with and help them. GO would have not only to recruit ISPs, but also to generate sales or licensing deals on the operating system from producers of the tablet's hardware. To continue, GO always seemed to require more cash infusions, either from existing investors or from new ones with whom they would be compatible. Its burn rate rose to over $1 million a month and kept rising.

1988, Inception financing—Kleiner Perkins

The idea for a pen-driven tablet had occurred to Kaplan in February of 1987, during a plane ride with Mitch Kapor, the founder of Lotus Development. Kapor was having trouble sorting out notes he had made on various scraps of paper. Had they been penned on a laptop tablet instead, he thought, the sorting and reorganizing into a schedule would be much easier.

Kaplan's background included a Ph.D. in computer science from the University of Pennsylvania, research work at Stanford in artificial intelligence, and founding a venture in software for artificial intelligence that he had sold for a good profit. Currently, he was consulting for Kapor to develop what turned out to be Lotus Agenda, a software program for organizing a personal calendar.

The upshot of his pen suggestion was that through Kapor he met a prominent Silicon Valley venture capital firm, Kleiner Perkins (KP), which provided seed money and introductions to investors who also became financial backers. Kaplan hired, from among his prior acquaintances, a hardware designer and a software programmer as the first two employees in the start-up of GO, which he incorporated in August 1987. A few more employees were added

---

[1] Karl H. Vesper based upon Jerry Kaplan's book, *Startup* (New York: Penguin Group, 1994); Harvard Business School Case # 2-297-021 by Abu Zayad and Paul C. Yang under the direction of Josh Lerner and Thomas J. Kosnik; and conversation with Jerry Kaplan.

in each of the two technical areas to pursue a goal of creating a working prototype by June 1988.

There would be three important parts of the proposed computer: (1) the physical machine with its microprocessor chip, plus the pen and screen on which the pen could be dragged to write with "electronic ink" or tapped for actuating command icons; (2) the software operating system that would link the pen, screen, and central processing chip signals to operate with appropriate logic; and (3) software that provided applications such as word processing, arithmetic, and other tasks that a user might want to instruct the computer, through its linkage to operating system's Application Programming Interface (API), to carry out.

Kaplan's experience as a programmer and in study of artificial intelligence indicated that the most valuable thing to own would be the API. User software had to be designed to link with it, which made creators of such applications as word processing, spreadsheet, and graphics programs, for instance, captive to working with whoever controlled that interface.

Two types of specialists, hardware and software engineers, would have to work together closely to make the new machine, which would rest on both technologies. They would also have to collaborate with outsiders, including other computer companies, both large and small. The complexity of designing, refining, producing, and upgrading the countless electronic components and software lines of code was far too great for any start-up to tackle solo. Kaplan told his team:

> So here's the strategy. We should do just enough in each of these areas to interest competent partners. If they're willing to step in, we should let them, and we'll back off. We have to provide compelling economic opportunities for everyone.

As it turned out, the demo prototype scheduled for June of 1988, was in fact shown to GO's board of directors in July. It was as yet only a deskbound version, not a laptop, with its screen sitting on a podium and other working parts underneath the table. It could demonstrate only some principles of the product's intended operation, not nearly all.

Following the demonstration, discussion turned to capitalization. Kaplan estimated that the cash in GO's account would last six more months, maximum. The first $1.5 million was raised for 33 percent of the company at 40 cents a share. This had been followed by another $500,000 at 60 cents a share. Counting the shares issued to employees, that gave GO a theoretical capitalization value of $6 million. Now, given the prototype demonstration, Kapor argued that the value should go to $12 million on the next round. John Doerr, one of the KP venture capital partners who had taken an especially strong interest in GO, argued for $16 million. But from whom should it come?

Kapor proposed approaching independent software vendors who were currently cash rich and would benefit from GO's machine's becoming another platform for which they could create and sell application programs. The big three microcomputer software vendors were Ashton-Tate, Lotus Development, and Microsoft. Doerr worried that Microsoft, with its own operating system, Windows, would "just start a project right away to compete with us."

Kaplan countered that if Bill Gates of Microsoft were sought as an investor he might agree to sign a nondisclosure agreement (NDA) in order to get early access to GO's new operating system and thereby become enabled to develop Microsoft programs for it. Microsoft did, after all, produce software for Apple's operating system. Doerr seemed to like that, rubbing his hands together and suggesting a capitalized valuation for GO of $20 million. Another director cautioned that overpricing could be risky.

The next day Kaplan phoned the CEOs of all three companies and arranged to visit Ashton-Tate and Lotus. At Microsoft, Gates said he would come to see GO. Kaplan cleared an NDA with Gates' attorneys under which Gates agreed that whatever he was told by GO could only be used for considering a business relationship with the venture.

Gates commented during his visit, "You know, Kay Nishi and I talked about a machine like this some time ago. But the technology wasn't ready. Maybe its time is now. I think you've got the right approach here." Subsequently, all three software companies declined to invest, but Microsoft promised to send an applications developer to follow up on possible product collaboration.

By fall 1988, as GO's cash was about to run out, a venture capitalist was finally found who would agree to lead the next financing round by investing $2 million. The trick for getting his pledge appeared to be GO's offer to drop its valuation figure, before the money went in ("pre-money"), from $12 million down to $8 million. Other venture capital firms then soon bought in on the same terms.

1989, Seeking a customer alliance—State Farm

Around the same time through introduction by John Doerr of KP, Kaplan received a sales lead. Doerr's introduction was for an audience on December 1 with Naomi Seligman, who coordinated an informal organization of information technology top decision-makers in 40 large firms. These executives comprised a group called the Research Board, which met periodically to review the latest technical thrusts in computer systems and discuss their implications. Seligman, after hearing Kaplan tell what GO was developing, scheduled him to present to the group in March 1989.

The Research Board, it appeared to Kaplan, was where the major computer makers, such as IBM, got their big sales. The combined budgets of the board members, he estimated, could be on the order of $5 billion per year.

His presentation, to his delight, quickly turned into a discussion in which one board member after another proposed ideas about how a pen-operated computer such as GO's could find applications in his company. At the end of the meeting Kaplan wondered which participant would most likely show further interest.

Doerr cautioned him that such giants were not going to buy from a mere start-up. They would want the kind of delivery assurance that only a major computer maker could provide. GO would therefore need one as an ally. The inducement for it to help GO would have to be access to an important customer through GO.

State Farm soon called. Its data-processing vice president, Norm Vincent, had attended the Research Board meeting and been impressed with GO's product. With 30 million auto policies and 15 million home policies in place, plus all the claims-processing work associated with them, State Farm needed massive computing power. In the preceding year alone it had upgraded over 50 of its IBM mainframes. Prospectively, it might benefit by using a pen-operated tablet like GO's to replace the clipboards and forms on which claims adjusters currently took notes about auto damage.

By invitation Kaplan visited State Farm's headquarters in June 1989 and presented the potential of a GO pen-tablet computer for facilitating this work to a dozen mid-level State Farm managers. Following that he was taken to lunch by Vincent in the executive dining room where they were joined by two more senior people. After the lunch meeting, Vincent drove him to the airport for the return trip home, and said that State Farm was favorably impressed and would be sending out a request for proposal (RFP) on the auto-claims–estimating task.

Four potential suppliers would be asked to propose solutions: IBM, Hewlett-Packard, Wang, and GO. Although somewhat shocked by the sudden injection of several massive competitors to the process, Kaplan agreed to submit a proposal.

GO now had about 30 people on the payroll solving technical problems and was spending cash at a burn rate of about $500,000 per month. Work on the State Farm RFP proceeded in parallel with development work on the computer. Competitive presentations of the RFP invitees were scheduled for a "shootout" at State Farm in late June 1989 to win State Farm as a customer.

Preparing for the presentation—Spring 1989

Technical problems seriously plagued the rush to produce a real working prototype for the competitive presentation at State Farm. For instance, difficulties arose in dealing with some Japanese suppliers. Apparently, without telling GO, Yamaha had changed the specifications on one of its chips needed to manage the display of screen information. Also, the Tokyo supplier of the pen and sensor was not responding with expected deliveries and had become vague about its specifications.

Cultural differences were found to be part of these problems. Although a GO engineer had been making repeated visits to Japan to deal with them, he was apparently handicapped by his "lowly" organizational position. The engineer urged Kaplan to visit the suppliers as CEO, asserting, "In Japan, hierarchy is everything." Kaplan went, and responses improved. At one supplier they found that the Japanese engineers knew about a flaw in GO's design that they had been too embarrassed to tell GO about by fax or phone for fear of offending GO.

Microsoft exchange visits—May 1989

During this time GO was having its first exchange visits with Microsoft. An agreement had finally been worked out with Microsoft under which the latter would study GO's product and application interfaces to figure out what applications Microsoft might want to develop. GO was to provide technicians to help. The agreement specified that neither company would gain any rights to the other's "proprietary, confidential, or trade secret information." Microsoft, which naturally had incentive to develop its own operating system for a machine like that of GO, was to maintain a "Great Wall" between its internal applications operating systems divisions so that they would not collaborate with each other against GO.

There followed visits of Microsoft people to GO, which GO people found time-costly. One Microsoft engineer in particular, Lloyd Frink, "took hours of our time, debating our approach at every turn. He was enamored by Windows, and couldn't imagine why it wasn't suitable for our application," Kaplan recalled.

Those from GO who visited Microsoft under the agreement were frustrated by what they perceived as insinuations that if they did not adopt Windows, Microsoft might compete with them. To GO it seemed clear that Windows was simply too alien to the needs of a machine like GO's to be adapted effectively. The APIs (Application Program Interfaces) that were part of the operating system were the most valuable part to own. GO engineers worried that the Great Wall was not holding when engineers from both applications and operating systems parts of Microsoft showed up for some joint meetings. No more were held.

First working unit—June 1989

Prototype failures persisted as the date of the State Farm competitive shootout approached. Finally, GO engineers were able to get a central processing unit (CPU) to boot, raising spirits.

But then later it wouldn't boot. And even when it did, the prototype's screen did not work, apparently due to some flaw in a chip from Japan. Yamaha didn't seem to understand that GO's machine was not to be a PC clone, and to cope with that, the chip had to meet certain of its own specifications that a PC did not require. GO engineers shifted to working on Tokyo time and staying in constant touch with Yamaha engineers to get a correction. Office arrangements were changed at GO to allow sleeping at work during the day and working on Japanese daytime.

Finally, a GO engineer decided to try a very small change in the circuit. Others watching expected it not to work. But then the screen lit up, inspiring a cheer. Kaplan commented, "It's a small miracle that computers work at all; they function only as the result of endless trial and error, folklore, and superstition."

But then there was a smell of smoke. The working unit quit as flames shot out of its connector slots. Was the flaw in the parts, assembly, or design? Parts for building only one more unit were left. Almost in despair the GO engineers assembled them and turned it on. To the joy of all, it worked. Kaplan wrote on it "6/20/89—first working unit." It contained more computing power in a four-pound machine than had any previous machine that light in weight.

Shootout—June 1989

At the State Farm demonstration program GO preceded IBM. It also had the advantage of a working prototype unit, albeit the software it contained was still primitive and very limited in functionality. The audience was surprised to see the unit, which GO had not promised and they had not expected. When its display lit up and GO's presenter said they were the first audience ever to see such a laptop pen-computer work, they broke into applause. GO continued by demonstrating how it could improve a claims adjuster's speed and accuracy.

Wrapping up his presentation Kaplan predicted what IBM, which was to present the following day, would offer. It would fly attendees to New York on a private jet, feed them sumptuously, and show exciting demonstrations. But it would work from its existing technology that could not do what GO had done. It would only predict, not demonstrate, that its present technology could be adapted to pen operation, and that would be the flaw to look for. Kaplan used for analogy the idea of trying to modify a dog to replace a cat for catching mice. His audience laughed. Later he learned that on the following day when they listened to IBM's presentation they occasionally snickered. GO seemed clearly, at this point, to be well ahead of its competitors.

A week later Vincent called to ask how GO would feel about teaming up on a bid with one of State Farm's regular suppliers. Kaplan asked if that meant with such companies as IBM or Hewlett-Packard. Vincent said yes, and to expect two phone calls.

Alliance with IBM—last half of 1989

This response from State Farm thrilled Kaplan. Not only would it help GO get the business of State Farm, but a major strategic partner like IBM or HP could help it in other areas such as funding, getting introduced to more customers, and persuading independent software vendors to develop more applications for it. Moreover, State Farm had left it up to GO to choose either giant partner. Both telephoned soon after and arranged to visit GO. Kaplan described the meetings with these two companies as sharply contrasted.

First came Al Johnson, the senior IBM salesperson for the State Farm account, accompanied by nearly a dozen people from IBM offices in different parts of the country. They asked seemingly endless questions, tended to fight among themselves, and apparently had trouble believing that State Farm intended to use GO's technology rather than theirs.

The visit by HP was different. There were fewer people. But they asked relevant questions, were easier to deal with, appeared to understand well the advantages of having no projects competitive with GO's, and seemed eager to work with GO.

Jerry Kaplan went over these observations with Robert Carr, who headed up GO's software development:

> We have one potential partner who's skeptical of our technology, divided on whether they should work with us, and resentful of our success with State Farm. The other is cooperative, has no competitive projects to speak of, is headquartered down the road from us, and is anxious to work with us.

The choice, they decided ironically, was to go with IBM because, Kaplan said, "of how much weight they could throw behind our bid to establish our operating system as a standard. In this respect there was no contest."

It surprised Kaplan to learn after choosing IBM and expecting to work with its same senior salesperson for the Start Farm account, that in fact the only IBM person who would return his phone calls was an IBM lawyer, John Kalb. Moreover, the person chosen to head the project inside IBM was Sue King, a relatively critical member of its visiting team. Kalb hired a top New York law firm to help in drafting a complex working agreement. Among other things, IBM would loan GO $5 million on terms providing, among other things, that if GO did not repay it on schedule, all of GO's software, product designs, and patents would immediately belong to IBM.

Beyond that loan, and only after IBM had reviewed GO's technology and plans, GO would get another $5 million by signing an agreement allowing IBM access to GO's advanced technology and rights to relabel and sell GO's products. IBM would have the right, if it wished, to engage in projects competitive with GO, to abandon use of GO's operating system, and to pursue GO's customers.

Sue King reviewed and criticized GO's plans but, according to Kaplan, "at least went to bat for GO with higher management." Other IBM visitors predicted that GO's operating system would be replaced with IBM's, named OS/2, which was trying, without success so far, to compete with Microsoft's operating system.

Then Kalb imposed further terms. The first loan would be divided into four installments to be paid out upon specified deliveries by GO to King's satisfaction. Upon hearing GO's disappointment he said, "We can make you the Microsoft of pen computing, with IBM as your banker."

Provisions imposed by IBM on GO for protection of intellectual property were hundreds of pages long, like nothing Kaplan had ever seen in the industry. GO had to put copies of every technology development and description document in an escrow account, and every quarter send a list of names and home addresses of all GO people who worked on the projects, along with their signatures attesting that they had done the work themselves. IBM security forces visited GO to set up other required precautions, including a chicken-wire barrier under the ceiling tiles to block possible intruders. No secret IBM documents that these measures were implemented to protect ever arrived.

Toward the end of 1989 Kaplan attended the annual Comdex computer industry trade show in Las Vegas, where he had been invited to meet Jim Cannavino, head of IBM's PC division. He asked what Kaplan thought of the technical approach IBM people were taking on the pen computer idea. When Kaplan said he thought that their attempting to add pen adaptations to their OS/2 was a mistake, Cannavino seemed gratified and predicted that the IBM people might drag GO down until it failed. He proposed that Kaplan with GO join IBM and work for him instead.

Passing the venture to IBM could turn a quick profit for GO investors. But to Kaplan it seemed he might thereby be selling his soul. John Doerr, the venture capital partner at KP with whom he most closely worked, seemed to share his aspiration for more than money, and said to tell Cannavino that GO was not for sale.

1990, Seeking more cash—IBM and Intel

In mid-January 1990 Kaplan received a call from an IBM corporate vice president, Mike Quinlan, who invited him to visit IBM in Boca Raton, Florida. Quinlan also sent more information about the agreement for the second $5 million, except that IBM had now reduced it to $2 million. Further it provided that IBM would get half of all royalties GO received from other companies, and royalties from IBM for GO's products would be capped and eventually stop.

Coincidentally, IBM was in trouble itself and about to lay people off for the first time in its history. Kaplan called KP for advice. One partner said, "Come home." Another, John Doerr, said to persist on working out something more acceptable.

The next day Kaplan proposed to Quinlan an agreement giving IBM the option to use current GO technology any way it liked in return for royalties to GO on a sliding scale that would eventually go to zero. In return, IBM should agree to convert the first $5 million loan and the additional $2 million into advances against the royalties that GO was to get from other companies, then pass half of it through to IBM. Also, IBM would agree to continue supporting GO's APIs, which GO would control as part of its operating system.

Quinlan agreed, except for limiting the royalty advances conversion to $4 million, not $7 million. This disappointed Kaplan, because it meant that the worrisome loan repayment guarantee provisions would still apply. But he accepted. Then for the next two months he found himself struggling on details with Quinlan's negotiating team as he tried to collect the additional $2 million loan from IBM before GO's cash ran out.

IBM chose July 18 to announce publicly the new alliance. Quinlan assured GO that Cannavino would make it. But IBM's public relations department representative resisted and became "unavailable" that date, though he would "take calls from the press." A young publicist was assigned to write the IBM press release but got it wrong. Kaplan persuaded Quinlan to write his own, which the publicist then tried to put his own paragraphs back into.

The IBM announcement was finally made. But then Quinlan was transferred to other duties and replaced by someone more subordinate, Kathy Vieth, who coincidentally had not in the past, according to Jerry Kaplan, gotten along very well with IBM's Sue King.

Help from Intel

Meanwhile, to raise still more cash Kaplan approached State Farm, which had a $60 billion investment portfolio. He told State Farm that other investors were willing to pay $2.50 per share, based on the fact that those other investors were linked to KP, which in turn had told Kaplan they would invest once there was a lead investor who would set a price for them to follow. It worked, bringing GO's implicit capitalization value now to $75 million.

The quest for cash also led, through KP's John Doerr, to Andy Grove, the CEO of Intel. During the introduction Grove asked what chip GO was using, then expressed displeasure when told GO's machine would be using Intel's older chip, the 286 rather than the new 386.

This happened because Intel salespeople had not let GO know about the 386 until late, and then had convinced GO to stay with the 286. Grove gave his decision:

> We'll bet five million but with the understanding that you'll upgrade to the 386 as soon as possible and agree that new versions of your software won't be released on competitors' CPU's until Intel's (386).

Kaplan bridled at this special concession that would mean GO might have to hold off on letting its upgrades of its system be released for use on any other company's chip until first it had finished an upgrade for Intel's chip, saying no concession like that was being given to anyone else. Grove replied that GO's being able to announce to the world that it had Intel's backing would add more credibility than would announcements of backing from other investors. Grove delegated further negotiations to a subordinate staff member.

Subsequently Kaplan met with the subordinate who, as the two worked through several meetings on details of the terms and conditions of the financing, again reminded Kaplan about how valuable it would be for GO's credibility to be able to say publicly that it had support from Intel.

Then, just before signing, the staff member said Intel had changed its mind about some things. It would put up only $3 million, not $5 million. And there was to be no public announcement of Intel's participation. GO could tell only its other strategic partners and a few investors, who must first sign nondisclosure agreements. Doerr, when asked for advice about these changes, said to sign and get the money.

Competitive pressures

Elsewhere, while GO had been moving forward, so had other developments of the industry. Steve Sakoman, an Apple engineer who had been part of the earliest discussions with Kaplan and Kapor about the pen idea before the formation of GO, had subsequently initiated at Apple a project that eventually created the Newton, a pen-operated hand-held computer that Apple's CEO, Sculley proclaimed as the first "Personal Digital Assistant" (PDA). Sakoman had also worked with AT&T's Bell Labs to develop a special microprocessor for it called the "Hobbit," which eventually GO would use after Apple switched away from Hobbit to a different chip.

There was also news that Microsoft had been developing pen extensions for its own operating system, Windows.

And the press had been asking where the GO product that had been announced with IBM could be seen. Was it simply "vaporware?" GO responded by initiating arrangements for a presentation at the start of the coming year, January 1991. A name was chosen for the new GO operating system, "Penpoint," with a tag line, "The Pen is the Point."

News of the planned presentation apparently precipitated a call from John Kalb, the IBM lawyer, who now asserted that a revenue-sharing agreement between GO and IBM still needed to be finished. John Cannavino, he said, wanted 25 percent of GO's revenues as an offset against revenues owed by IBM to GO. Moreover, if that 25 percent ever exceeded what IBM owed, then IBM was to be paid the difference by GO in cash. This seemed to Kaplan impossible to accept.

GO had one piece of leverage left: its right, which IBM also had, to walk away from the arrangement between them for working together further or delivering future versions of the operating system. IBM now needed GO's system for working with State Farm and others. Kaplan said he would agree to cancel the "mutual walk-away" right if the new contract would provide only a credit against IBM royalties, not cash to GO, and only after GO had income of at least $50 million. Kalb seemed surprised when reminded about the walk-away option. Now GO had incentive to reduce IBM's market share in favor of other GO licensees, since the licensees would pay royalties in cash, while IBM would just take them as credits against what GO owed it on the loan.

Meanwhile, Kaplan, burdened with expanding demands on his time to deal with both internal and external technical and non-technical problems of the company, asked for help. His directors agreed to move him up to chairman and bring in a new CEO of whom he and others thought highly, Bill Campbell, a marketing executive from Apple.

Epilog

GO eventually failed and, beginning with Kleiner Perkins, lost for its financiers $75 million. But that was not the whole cost that this pen-based pioneering effort generated, because it also stimulated other companies to pursue development of such products. "When you add it all up," Jerry Kaplan observed, "I figure that somewhere around a billion dollars was flushed down the john on pen computing."

However, then he went on to other ventures, including Onsale.com, which he created in 1994, and was intended to be, a somewhat male-oriented garage sale Web site. Again he was given financial support by Kleiner Perkins, the venture capital firm that had lost the most on GO, and whose lead partner John Doerr observed, "If I am given a choice between a guy who has failed a couple of times and a guy who is starting his first company, I will fund the guy who has failed." Two years later the stock market valued this company at around $500 million and Kaplan's share at around $100 million.[2]

Meanwhile, a somewhat similar venture was started as AuctionWeb in 1995 by another entrepreneur, Pierre Omidyar, who changed its name to Ebay.com in 1997.[3]

---

[2] Michael Lewis, "Losers," *Slate.com,* January 22, 1998, at 3:30 AM ET.
[3] D. Bunnell and R. Luecke, *The Ebay Phenomenon* (New York: John Wiley & Sons, 2000).

Jim Russell

Seeking first sales

Two mechanical consulting engineers asked Jim Russell in the fall of 1998 to help them market a new product. They had acquired rights from an inventor to produce and sell what they saw as a better way to lift and open manhole covers, which was currently done by prying with a long crowbar or a pickaxe. It was a task generally relegated to people with very strong backs, which excluded much of the general population. With the new invention, which had been named "The Extractor," almost anyone could do it, and with less chance of injury. An advertising brochure depicting the device appears in the Exhibit.

Jim Russell, a graduate of West Point (1969) and Stanford Business School (1979), had worked in customer support with several companies, including Hewlett-Packard and two smaller firms. He had held executive positions in marketing with U.S. West and several other small firms, and most recently had served as president and director of marketing for a company that manufactured prototypes. Based on this experience, one of the engineers, who had met Jim several years earlier at one of the small firms, asked Jim to consult for the venture on an hourly pay basis. Jim commented:

> They had always worked as engineers, where jobs came to them through word of mouth based on other technical consulting work they had done on such things as aircraft parts, an automatic bicycle transmission, and exercise equipment. They had never tried to go out and sell a product before, or manufacture one either, for that matter. They are accustomed to operating with just a phone line, a bank account, and contracts. Things like compensation programs, company cars, expense accounts, hiring, and financial performance targets are not what they have worked with in the past.
>
> But now they have bought exclusive rights from the inventor who owns a patent on this product. Their idea is to go into manufacturing and build a stable company. As consultants, they are always working their way out of jobs. That can make a proprietary product look fairly appealing. With a stable product you can hope that sales will come as a matter of routine while your factory generates the product and the customers order it.

The engineers personally had sold about a dozen Extractors to date by knocking on doors of utility companies and municipalities, and had managed to get another three dozen units out under test. So it seemed to them a logical way to sell more would be to hire salespeople to sell directly, as they had. A problem with that, however, was that their personal capital had already been used up in designing the product for manufacture, locating suppliers for the parts, putting together the first few units, and making such sales calls as they could fit in. Their time, as well, was short, since they needed to perform engineering work to generate income to live on as well as for their own product and venture development.

They had met one local man who was interested in the possibility of selling Extractors on a full-time basis. Consequently, they had asked Jim to propose terms for a contract with the man and tell them how to manage it. Jim noted that the man would need income to live on, plus money for expenses he might incur in pursuing sales.

Another alternative for selling Extractors had come to the engineers in the form of an offer from an Oregon company whose business was producing and selling chemicals that got rid of tree roots that were blocking underground sewer pipes. This company already sold to municipalities and sewer districts, and thought it would be desirable to add the Extractor as one more product they could offer their existing customers. The chemical company insisted on obtaining exclusive sales rights nationwide, however, and the engineers noted that it presently employed about 20 sales people, half of them telemarketing, and the other half scattered geographically, mainly in the Pacific Northwest.

The engineers asked Jim to tell them what provisions they should consider incorporating in a sales agreement with other companies who, like that one, might carry and sell their product. Jim had at one point developed a marketing program for a company that sold candle lanterns—small aluminum telescoping containers that campers could carry—both through camping goods wholesalers and directly to larger camping retailers. The lantern cost $4 to manufacture; typically, he said, distributors bought the lantern for $8 and sold it to small retailers, who priced it at $20. Large stores paid $8.50 and sold at $17. He further observed:

> To use dealers, you have to offer support and attractive margins, or else they will just list the product and wait for customers to come to them, not caring much whether they do or not. All of them will want exclusives, and territories will have to be negotiated. And none of them will be ideally suited to penetrate all the market segments where the Extractor product might be used. Companies that assemble electric utility trucks don't make fire trucks, and neither of them would have stores or sales forces selling small products like this separately, for instance. Also, you have the companies that have already bought trucks that you might sell to directly, such as electric power companies, phone companies, gas companies, sewer districts, and municipal water works.

They had priced the Extractor at $300 and said that people in municipalities seemed to like the product right away; the price seemed not to be a very sensitive issue. Typically the tool might be carried on a large truck that was loaded with much more expensive equipment for maintaining underground pipe and tunnel systems. Also, Jim noted, if it enabled them to be more flexible in hiring and assigning jobs, not having to select for high physical strength of individuals, and if it reduced the likelihood of back injury to their employees, then the matter of a couple hundred dollars on a tool that could last for many years was a relatively small issue. Moreover, some utilities were subject to regulation of their profits, which might be set as a matter of return on investment, so that if they were able to increase their investment, they could increase profits accordingly.

At the same time, however, selling could be difficult. The person who could make the decision to buy had to be found and persuaded to consider the product. Both of these tasks could be complicated through the nature of the bureaucracy doing the buying and the fact that the individual to be contacted might have many other things to do. If some sort of a committee were involved at the customer end, that too could hinder the selling process. Finally, the nature of budgeting and spending in utilities and municipalities could retard the completion of a purchase. Buying a product in February might require that it be written into a budget the preceding September, after all the approvals had been completed.

No trade-show demonstrations or mailings had been done by the engineers as yet. Jim pointed out that displaying at a trade show could cost upwards of $10,000, and putting out a mailing or running advertisements in trade magazines before the company was positioned to follow up with sales aggressively might increase the likelihood that competitors would spring up.

He noted that the materials and labor required to fabricate the Extractor were said by the engineers to be only $70 per unit, so that potential profits could be attractive to imitators. Although there was a patent on the Extractor, he wasn't sure how vulnerable the protection it offered might be, particularly considering that the engineers lacked money with which to sue infringers. That could cost upwards of $100,000 and take years to play out, after which the company might or might not win the lawsuit and, if it did win, Jim figured the firm might or might not be able to collect whatever damages were awarded.

As soon as this product really starts to show up, somebody in Asia will copy and sell it for less. When that happens, I think the best defense will be company presence and reputation, not legal action, although both would be best.

EXHIBIT Extractor brochure

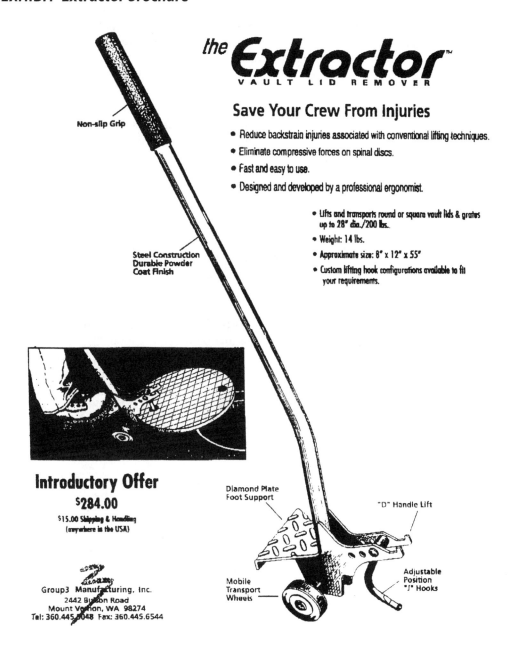

the **Extractor**™
VAULT LID REMOVER

Save Your Crew From Injuries

- Reduce backstrain injuries associated with conventional lifting techniques.
- Eliminate compressive forces on spinal discs.
- Fast and easy to use.
- Designed and developed by a professional ergonomist.

- Lifts and transports round or square vault lids & grates up to 28" dia./200 lbs.
- Weight: 14 lbs.
- Approximate size: 8" x 12" x 55"
- Custom lifting hook configurations available to fit your requirements.

Non-slip Grip

Steel Construction
Durable Powder
Coat Finish

Introductory Offer
$284.00
$15.00 Shipping & Handling
(anywhere in the USA)

Group3 Manufacturing, Inc.
2442 Button Road
Mount Vernon, WA 98274
Tel: 360.445.6048 Fax: 360.445.6544

Diamond Plate
Foot Support

"D" Handle Lift

Mobile
Transport
Wheels

Adjustable
Position
"J" Hooks

Kevin Scheevel

Seeking sales for a new Web page

In February 1999 Kevin Scheevel was pondering how best to profit through a homepage he had initiated under the name of Freight Guy (www.freightguy.com). He had designed it as an aid for shippers who wanted to obtain the status of their shipments in progress. He had also added links to sites for other information that shippers might find of interest.

This, it seemed to him, was a service shippers would find helpful. Those who sold products and services to shippers, he thought, should also find it in their interest to use his site for advertising to shippers. So the site, it seemed to him, should become a profitable business enterprise. What he wondered was how to take possession of that profit potential and protect it. What this called for, he expected, was to acquire users and customers so fast that nobody could catch up with him. The top question on his mind was how to do that.

Kevin had worked as a freight forwarder for 20 years. He characterized himself as a nomad in that profession because he had worked for many different companies. His work consisted of helping companies such as manufacturers that wanted to get their products moved from one site to another as safely and economically as possible given the required timing. He would learn about the shipment requirements, then search out the appropriate trucking, rail, air, and warehousing companies that could accomplish the movement, buy that service from them, follow through to see that all the needed transfers were accomplished, and then bill the manufacturer.

One of his specialties had been booking airline space for freight, space that might otherwise be unoccupied on the flights. The surplus nature of that space would mean that the shipper could obtain it cheaply, and at the same time the airline would receive some payment for the space that it otherwise would not. Kevin's job as a forwarder was to seek out such matches and broker them to both parties. Neither he nor the forwarding companies he had worked for owned trucks or warehouses for handling the freight. They just sought out the information about companies that did, and then used that information to serve shippers.

In earlier years he had done this work mainly by telephone. But it had since become available via computer as the various companies in the chain of logistics went online with data about their capacities and costs. By 1999 Kevin was doing his work from a terminal at his home in the small rural town of Gig Harbor, Washington.

It was during a lull in this work that he got the idea of creating a home page where shipping could be accessed conveniently as a single source, rather than having to pull up needed data from the sites of many different companies in the logistics chains. As a subscriber to AOL he happened to notice a "build your own home page" proposition that triggered the idea. At first, he said, it was essentially a labor of love. He would like to have such a source himself, which was part of the motivation. At the same time, he got satisfaction from thinking what a nice thing it would be, so that the project appealed to him as simply an act of creation.

Sometime during the process he imagined that other freight forwarders like himself might find his offering attractive, and then he starting thinking about making it available to them as well. Possibly it would be a service that they would pay for through some sort of periodic subscription. He sketched out a scheme for how it might work, then contacted freight forwarders in the Northwest to see what interest they might have in it. "Essentially," he recalled, "they all liked it. There were no naysayers at all." He talked to vice presidents of some air freight companies, and found they also responded favorably. They already made their information available on-line. But Kevin's page would add another source for customers to learn about their services.

Eventually Kevin estimated that he wound up contacting around 60 people, visiting them in person to display the idea, talk about its use, and explore how to improve it. He also changed ideas about how to derive money from it. Instead of charging for subscriptions, he would make the information available free to the forwarders. He would generate revenue by charging vendors who served the forwarders to advertise by running banners that would appear on the top of each page as users scrolled through to use the system.

To Kevin it seemed that his professional life might be taking a strikingly new direction. He might still be working on a computer out of his home, but he would have an enterprise with an identity, brand, and property of its own—not just a computer, but also a data base that could bring him revenues directly through sale of advertising space. However, he did foresee a possible downside:

> The problem is, the information that I'll be gathering for my site is available free to anyone, so there is no way I can prevent somebody else from shadowing me and copying exactly what I'm doing. My best hope of winning, it seems to me, is to get sales so fast that I can be bigger and stronger, and therefore not worth trying to overtake. That gives me something to do that I've never done before. How should I do it?

Bruce Milne (B)

In January 1980 Bruce Milne and Lauri Chandler gave notice to their employer, Alpine Data Systems, that they were resigning. Working initially from the den in Bruce's house, they incorporated their venture as Dataword, Inc. on February 22. A third partner, Brian Duthie, joined in the formation, but still remained on the job at Alpine, reluctant to leave because of concern about risks in the new enterprise coupled with the prospect that his family responsibilities would shortly increase with arrival of a new child.

The business plan was not formally reduced to writing at this point, but Bruce was working on it in anticipation that they would need to raise cash beyond the initial $27,000 they could muster from savings and family members. They reasoned that to generate short-term sustaining income the three would continue selling minicomputers with third-party software while working on the side to develop a new software product, which they would bundle with Altos microcomputers to sell as accounting systems for accountants. Bruce would work on lining up suppliers and customers. Brian would develop the new software, and Lauri would run the office. All three would also work on selling the existing minicomputer systems and on consulting, Bruce in accounting systems, Lauri in word processing and Brian on programming.

Because they aimed eventually to provide systems for both accounting and word processing, they chose the name Dataword for their company. In fact, however, they knew they would have to choose initially between the two software packages, accounting versus word processing, for development. Lauri favored word processing because that was her field of familiarity. The other two partners favored accounting, because they had seen what they believed were weaknesses in the market leader of that field, which would give them particularly strong competitive advantages. Accounting was chosen for the initial thrust.

The income-generating strategy did not work as well as they had hoped. They did manage to sell some minicomputer systems as planned, deriving momentum from some leads that came their way as they left Alpine and from their ability to point out that they had proven track records with these established systems. However, a problem all along had been that such major systems invariably required extensive installation and service follow-up work as customers learned to operate them. This took a great deal of the founders' time, and although Brian finally was persuaded in March 1980 to leave Alpine and join the venture full-time, it was still difficult to work on the new software, perform enough consulting and selling to pay the bills and try to line up suppliers and customers for the new microcomputer system all at the same time.

Bruce was able to operate with no salary because of his wife's job, but the other two could not, and there were other expenses of operating the office. It was necessary to add other employees, a part-time secretary and a part-time programmer. Two offices were rented, one in which Brian could concentrate on programming and the other for Bruce's and Lauri's selling and consulting work.

To cope with these expenses as their initial capital dwindled, Bruce undertook to raise more seed capital. From three individuals he raised $10,000 each. One was the proprietor of a cheesecake manufacturing company, a former customer of Bruce's at Alpine who had become a personal friend. The second was an attorney whom Bruce had long tried without success to sell Alpine products, who had also become a friend. The third was a former competitor who had reaped substantial financial gains when his employer, in which he held a share of ownership, had gone public. He too had become a personal friend of Bruce's. The contributions of these investors brought the total capitalization of Dataword to $57,000.

With expenses exceeding revenues by about $10,000 per month Bruce could foresee that something would have to be done soon as fall approached. Although it was not clear that the new software would be ready, he began making arrangements to hold a seminar for accounting firms at which the new system would be displayed and sales orders to buy it would be solicited. This, Bruce observed, would be the first time, so far as he knew, that seminar selling had been applied to microcomputer systems.

The new software was, in fact, not fully complete as the day of the seminar arrived. But there would be enough to display what its capabilities would be. Bruce decided to keep the seminar on schedule. There would, he figured, be a month or two of leeway after taking orders, during which the Altos computers would have to be obtained and delivered to customers, and during that time Brian could put on the finishing touches.

At least, that is what the Dataword founders hoped. Bruce knew they would have reached the limits of their solvency by the time of the seminar. There would still be about $27,000 cash in the bank, but the company would have unpaid bills of approximately the same amount. Brian and Lauri were aware of the cash balance, but not the accounts payable amount. Bruce did not think it would help to have them worrying about financial problems in addition to their other job responsibilities.

But it seemed clear to Bruce that they absolutely had to get orders at that seminar. He had been working on terms of a limited partnership offering which he believed might bring in another $50,000 if they could get orders on books to substantiate that the company had a future. If they could not get the orders, however, it looked to him like they would not be able to raise more capital. In that case he expected they would have to use their cash to pay existing bills and Dataword would be finished.

The seminar was held as scheduled, presenting the new microcomputer accounting system with Brian's developing software package, "Datawrite," and went off as planned. Several accounting companies showed up, asked questions and seemed satisfied that the new system offered a much more economical system, around $25,000 compared to over three times that for other systems, to meet their needs.

The only problem seemed to be that they would not be willing to place orders unless Bruce could answer one more question for them. "We have bought new systems before only to end up with a mess of new problems in getting them to work," they said. "How do we know we will be able to rely on the performance of this new system you want us to order from you?"

Matt Fleck

Need to open fast and well

The Coho Café was to be a new restaurant in Redmond, Washington. It had been in the planning, design and construction phases of development for two years, and its grand opening was scheduled to take place in four weeks. The plan for that called for adding 107 employees who would perform cooking and serving operations, plus acquisition of inventory, getting equipment working, launching a publicity campaign to attract customers, and opening the doors. The person responsible for making this happen on time and successfully was Matt Fleck, one of the three founders. His main concern at this point was how to recruit, train, and initiate management of a workforce that did not yet exist to carry out start-up of operations.

Conception of the Coho Café could be traced back almost five years when the two owners of Arnies, a 20-year-old downtown restaurant, began thinking that their existing business might go out of date. From time to time they would discuss concepts for a new one, perhaps something like a lodge that would have more appeal to a new generation. They would drop the subject for a while, then come back to it. As the Redmond area grew in prosperity, sparked particularly by the success of Microsoft and other software companies, it began to appear a likely spot for trying something new: a suburban restaurant aimed at younger diners than Arnies' and priced lower, around $45 as opposed to $75, for a dinner for two, and "a fun place to eat."

Matt Fleck had been around the operating end of food and drink establishments all his life. His father had owned taverns, and during high school Matt had worked as a waiter. After graduating from business school he had joined Restaurants Unlimited, the Puget Sound-based holding company of several prominent restaurants. He started as a bartender and rose to top management, learning all phases of restaurant operations as he worked through every crew and lower management position. After 18 years he found himself in charge of eight restaurants along the west coast from California to Alaska, plus Hawaii.

Tiring of the long hours and travel that took him away from his family, he began looking for something smaller where ownership and growth possibilities were greater. He recalled:

> I met these two restaurateurs by cold calling. One of them I had worked with about 20 years earlier, so I looked him up and learned that he and his partner now had three stores. I told him what I was looking for, and got no news for two days. Then he called me back and we started talking about possibilities for expanding their existing stores. I joined them, wound up in charge of all three stores, put in new programs, and trained the woman who eventually replaced me.
>
> As this was taking place, the goal of expanding the present stores became replaced by the idea of starting a completely new venture and having it become the path for growth. The founders were both in their late forties and, after 20 years working the same restaurant theme, lacked the right experience in either themselves or their staff to make it contemporary. It had to be a fresh start with new people.
>
> The key we worked from was what is going on in society today: younger people who want to escape from the routine for a meal but can't spend much time doing it. We decided to create a mid-priced suburban, casual, energetic restaurant for them.

At this point the three began a concentrated search for ideas to meet this aim. They met frequently to discuss possibilities, commenting on themes and food they had seen elsewhere, bringing in clippings, and brainstorming. As the ideas began coming together, they settled on seafood, and then started to hire professional help from outside. Matt continued:

> We hired an expert in restaurant space design to sketch out concepts for the overall theme and ways to implement it. That cost about $50,000, and the architect who designed the building cost another $70,000. Besides that there were engineers—mechanical, structural, and electrical—just to get the physical setting designs worked out. I also hired a menu designer whom I had worked with for years to develop graphics and wording appropriate for our theme. We hired a brand company and a graphics company to work out a name and ways of presenting everything. We spent a week with them behind closed doors brainstorming, trying to get something that suggested affordable, approachable, energetic, stylish, and so forth.

> We followed that up by hiring focus groups to give us responses to the ideas, working in special rooms with one-way mirrors, and filming of the whole process. We showed them our ideas with great expectations and then went through big disappointment when they told us that the presentations we thought connoted all the things we wanted impressed them as being like a cartoon. They said it made us look like some cheap fast food places it brought to mind. So that sent us back to rework it all.

> Then we needed a food consultant, who charged $800 a day. After we gave him the general concept and price objectives it was his job to come up with recipes. We chose somebody who had traveled extensively and done this a lot. He came up with ideas that ranged from conventional ovens to woks to smokers. Each week he would propose 10 new recipes. He would come in the morning, cook them up, and have any of us who were around try them out, evaluating for appearance and flavor. All told we've paid him over $21,000 so far. At first he seemed expensive, but when we thought about how important his role was and how his cost compared to other things, he seemed like a real bargain.

> We designed the exterior and the menu, then the interior. We had meeting after meeting. One partner took responsibility for the building, while the other one worked on getting the $100,000 worth of permits we needed, meeting with lawyers, city officials, and citizen review groups who all had to pass on it. My job was to do operations, which involved adding another $200,000 worth of owner-provided items and managing the budget of another $200,000 worth of other pre-opening costs.

> Communication among all these people soon became a problem in itself. So we worked out a decision matrix showing lines of responsibility and authority. It told for different tasks who had straight authority and where consultation was required for decisions to be made.

> We also had to cost everything out, get bids on the work, and work out the timetables for getting it done. We solicited and analyzed bids from seven different construction companies before picking one. The building shell, which is still being worked on, is costing $800,000, and the FF&E (furniture, fixtures, and exterior), which is also not yet finished, is costing another $400,000 over a six-month period.

With four weeks to go before opening, the venture was in its staffing phase. There weren't yet any actual menus, just mockups, plus recipes. Four weeks earlier a general manager had been hired who had served in that capacity with another local chain. Two weeks earlier a chef had been hired. According to plans it was time to hire two assistant managers, and then next week two assistant chefs. Matt continued:

> My big problem now is how to arrange for another hundred people to be hired, trained, and ready to do their jobs right on opening day. Unemployment is low in this area right now, which makes hiring hard. I will need a kitchen crew of about 40, plus waiters, cashiers, and janitors. We expect to pay kitchen wages that are competitive in the industry. But it is very strenuous work, and the average American worker I expect, based on my previous experience, won't be interested.

So we will no doubt get a lot of immigrant applicants. We will have to screen them based in part on their ability to read and speak English. Written and verbal communication to perform work properly will both be critical to our operations. Restaurant margins are thin. Just the food costs 32 percent of sales. That leaves almost no room for error.

My previous hiring experience tells me that we will only be able to hire about 15 percent of the people that our advertising brings in. But first we have to interview them, and at present we have no place to do that for large numbers. The building is still full of construction and installation activities, and my office is small. I have tried to rent space, but so far haven't found anybody willing to agree to a one-month lease.

I also have to get the people we hire trained so that they will present the image that we are trying to live up to with the public. They start out knowing absolutely nothing about us, because as an establishment we don't exist yet. The training will take at least a week once people are into it, and before that the ones we do recruit will have to give the two-weeks' notice to their present employers, if they have jobs, that we would expect them to give us so that we could find replacements if they leave us.

So here we are with $1,800,000 invested in the restaurant so far, the goal of having it succeed as the pilot for a seven-store chain with $20,000,000 in sales by five years from now, and I have to figure out how to generate a nearly instant competent and fast-charging workforce.

Ampersand (C)

March 1993—Starting the first production run

Spring break, which ran from March 15, 1993 to March 20, 1993, had been eventful for the Ampersand team. To meet a scheduled delivery of 2,000 Claybords by the end of May for the order they had received from Pearl Paint in New York, they had managed to get Masonite sheets covered with their mineral coating. But they had not yet sanded them smooth as required. The shop in Tyler, Texas where the coating was applied, however, had essentially told the team not to come back because of difficulties with the coating process.

Then at the next stage in the process, a cabinet shop in Austin had cut the boards and routed the edges as it promised, but then refused to follow through with sanding required to make the boards smooth. After trying one or two, the shop owner had concluded that he would lose money on the sanding work. He also indicated that he was not anxious to have any more of the cutting and edging work either.

So now the coated, cut and routed but unsanded boards rested in the cabinet shop, with the permission of its owner, as the spring school term resumed and the team was obliged to return to class. All members of the team were carrying full course loads, and the problem of sanding the boards awaited resolution. Other present commitments included competition in two more venture plan contests. The first was a contest at San Diego State University on the last day of April. If the team won first place there it would receive $5,000 in prize money that could support the completion of the Pearl Paint test market effort in June. Then on May 5 there would be another competition, the International Moot Corp^{SM}, at the University of Texas. Finally, there was the end of May delivery date for finished boards.

Searching for production alternatives

When the four team members of Ampersand met to divide up tasks, Scott Bryant drew that of vice president of operations responsible for production. Although he had not previously worked in production, his background was in mechanical engineering. He had been attracted to the Ampersand venture in large part because the product had seemed like a simple one that students without extensive experience in the art materials industry could produce. This was a contrast to other student-proposed ventures which were to make high-technology products where students would be up against tough competition from industry experts. Moreover, the Ampersand team was planning to outsource manufacturing to subcontractors initially, so all that should be needed would be to select competent suppliers, seek out favorable bids, apply adequate pressure to meet the delivery time schedule and check quality.

This, he and his teammates found, was easier imagined than done. One early clue was the fact that David, a member of the team during the preceding school term who had taken responsibility for finding suppliers, had experienced difficulty in doing so. He had, however, found one shop, in Tyler, Texas 150 miles from Austin, that might be able to do the job. Much of its customary work was in painting panels and pegboard for store displays. It had a conveyor line that included coating equipment and saws. But the painting it did was mainly layers of lacquer much thinner than the mineral surface Ampersand needed.

A pilot run

Scott arranged to follow through on the small experimental coating run that the Tyler plant's owner had previously agreed to. He ordered some materials and had them sent to the plant. From Charles Ewing, he obtained the new and improved recipe for what he called the "secret sauce" Charles had developed for coating. Then, traveling to Tyler, he mixed up a batch and applied it. After watching the process, the plant's owner indicated that he was not strongly interested in performing the work. It required a much thicker coating than the painting work he was familiar with and required air drying, which he was not equipped to perform. It appeared to him likely to be unprofitable work.

Other searching by the team through calling around had located a cabinet shop in Austin that might be able to cut and sand the boards. The owner had seemed impressed by the potential quantity of the order, 2,000 units and quoted a price of $500 to process the order. However, he could not perform any of the coating work.

Efforts to find one shop equipped to perform all the manufacturing tasks had so far been completely fruitless. Scott explained:

> The way we found people to help us has been to start with the phone and then follow up with a personal visit. I'd call one shop and they would tell me that they can't do the job. So I asked if they had any idea who else might be able to do it. That usually led to more names, which in turn led to others, and so forth. How many calls to keep making, how many of them to follow-up with visits, how far away geographically to reach were all choices that carved up the time.
>
> Some shops might have been steering away from the work because they were already busy with profitable work and this new job presented uncertainty that they'd rather not deal with. Maybe with personal visits we could turn that around. I'm not sure how much that was the case. But to find out would take more time and travel expenditures.

Weekend coating at Tyler

During the week of spring break from March 15 to March 20 Charles Ewing traveled from Colorado to Austin to go over plans with the team and plan for the coating run that Scott had arranged with the shop in Tyler to be carried out over the coming weekend. Renting a truck at a cost of approximately $200, they picked up 100 sheets of Masonite and hauled them 200 miles east to Tyler.

They arranged with the owner of the Tyler painting shop to rent his facility over the ensuing weekend for $500 and began arranging racks to set out the Claybord sheets for air drying after they had been coated. Initially, they had planned to buy fence posts to build the racks, but the shop owner happened to have a stack of two by fours that he let them use for that purpose instead.

As the team completed the coating that evening around 6 p.m., tired and worn, they set up fans throughout the 8,000-square-foot facility to try to get the coated 4x8 foot Masonite sheets to dry by morning. It was questionable whether the thick coating would be dry in time for them to load up early to head back to Austin. They had spent 12 hours coating with five people (Charles, Scott, Elaine, Robert, Kathy). But they were elated by the belief that they now had product to send to Pearl. At this point they had no idea of problems they would encounter shortly at the cabinet shop with the sanding process.

An issue they had become concerned about, however, was that the coating shop owner had basically just told the team that he could not and would not do any more board production for them in the future. He, in fact, encouraged the team to set up their own operation. He gave them names of publications where they could look for used equipment and told them that a minimal investment of $15,000 might be sufficient to buy the equipment. He even offered to help the team set up the shop. The team wondered how they would take their next step as they thought about the next time they would have to produce to fill an order when and if Pearl ran out or when the product was launched nationally. None of this had been anticipated.

After a day on the drying racks, the boards were re-loaded on the truck and driven 225 miles southwest back to Austin where arrangements had been made to have them cut to standard sizes, routed to give them smooth round edges and then sanded on top to make them uniformly smooth by grinding away the "orange peel" or slightly rippled finish that resulted from the coating process. The shop owner had quoted a price of $500 for preparing the 2,000 Claybords in this fashion.

The shop owner became uneasy during the first of these tasks, sawing the boards to size, because it took longer than he had expected. After routing the edges and attempting to sand a few boards it became clear to him that he was going to lose a substantial amount of money if he continued. Consequently, he refused to do so and also said he was not much interested in doing the cutting and routing either because he lost money on that too. He told the team they would have to find another way to accomplish the sanding. He would not do it, but he would let them store the boards in his shop without charge for a few weeks while they sought a solution to the sanding problem.

The procedure used by Charles Ewing seemed safest to the team members because they knew it produced satisfactory Claybords. It consisted of going over each board with an electrically-powered hand-held orbital sander bought at the hardware store. This took approximately two to four minutes to accomplish, depending on the size of the Claybord.

It was now March 21, the first day of classes following spring break. The San Diego competition would begin on April 30. The team would be gone for three days. Then the International Moot Corp^{SM} contest would follow on May 6. Graduation day would be May 22. The 2,000 Claybords had to be shipped May 21 to arrive in New York by the first week in June, ready with appropriate packaging and display materials.

San Diego might net the team the $5,000 prize they had already factored into the financial statements of their venture plan. But why, one team member asked, should the team spend time on the Moot Corp^{SM} contest which carried no such cash award? Didn't the team need every minute it could get to finish and ship that first order, rather than participating in academic sport?

From other members of the team came some agreement and some reasons for competing. Competing had spurred them on and caused them to aim for high performance. They also felt some sense of obligation to follow through, since they had made application to compete and had been accepted. The school had, after all, given them opportunity as well as much encouragement and support. Moreover, their first win, in addition to the $500 and office space, had given them favorable visibility, press write-ups they could show business contacts to indicate that their venture had strong merit. It had also led them to at least one potential investor, the competition judge who had approached the team earlier about financing.

Meanwhile, the team had, because of the experience at Tyler, begun thinking more seriously about the possibility of setting up their own manufacturing operation. They decided to estimate what production costs might be on that basis and came up with the figures shown below in Figure 1.

These estimates, they expected, would bear refining. How validly did they reflect the experience at Tyler? To what extent would that be indicative of having a plant of their own? If so, what sequence of steps, and with what timing, should they plan to follow, first for checking out that idea, and second, for carrying it out? What else might they learn by sanding and packaging the rest of the current production batch? Should they even be thinking about that at this point, or were there more important issues? As these questions awaited answers, the team had to return to full-time classwork.

Figure 1—Estimated manufacturing costs per square foot of Claybord

Direct material	$0.31	32%
Direct labor		
Mixing	0.02	2
Coating	0.04	4
Cut/finishing	0.29	30
Packaging	0.10	10
Mfg. overhead	0.22	22
Total	$0.98	100%

Ampersand (D)

May 1993—Finishing the first production run

> *You know, this just isn't going to work the way we're doing it. We're behind schedule and we're losing money.*

Scott Bryant, vice president for operations of the Ampersand venture, was talking to his team members in the Austin, Texas garage of Kathy Henderson, vice president of marketing. Around them were piles of Claybords, some finished, others being sanded and still others awaiting sanding. The premises were dusty and noisy with four hand-sanders being operated by a workforce of students and street people hired as temporary workers to complete the company's first production run for shipment to Pearl Paint, a retail art supply store in New York.

Robert nodded in agreement with Scott's gloomy pronouncement. The venture would lose money by completing the order, but it would also lose more money if it did not and presumably if they did not complete the order, the work they had done to date would be wasted and the possibility of turning the venture into a success would also be gone. In addition to the cost of the shipment, however, would also be that of sending team members to New York so they could spend a week demonstrating the product for sales employees and customers at Pearl. Was this further investment justified, or might it mean throwing good money and time after bad?

Finishing the first order for shipment

At least Ampersand had more money available for completing the order in May 1993 as the last term of their MBA program drew to a close. The preceding month they had traveled to San Diego and won first prize, $5,000, in the North American Invitational Business Plan Competition at San Diego State University. When asked how their checks should be made out, other teams that had won cash prizes said to divide the money equally among their members. The Ampersand team asked simply that the check be made out to their corporation. They had also followed through with the International Moot Corp[SM] competition at the University of Texas, in which they had won fourth place.

As final examinations were completed, the team returned to the task of completing the 2,000 Claybords that rested in the cabinet shop in Austin where they had been sawed and routed but not sanded. The team had searched for alternative ways of completing the boards, wrapping them, adding appropriate instructions and labels and shipping them. They had considered the possibility of trying to get the boards sanded by some sort of automatic machine, but that seemed risky. If it did not work and the boards were ruined they would be stuck with no boards to finish, and the Tyler shop where the boards had been coated had already told them not to come back for more. The team concluded that they would have to do the sanding themselves using the technique developed by Charles Ewing for hand-held sanders.

With the permission of Kathy Henderson's landlord, Scott and Elaine made numerous trips hauling the load of boards in their small compact cars from the cabinet shop to the landlord's garage. The team then bought four orbital sanders from a local hardware store for around $100 each, rented a shrink-wrap machine for $100 a week from a packaging company and set up tables for processing Claybords on the landlord's back porch, yard and garage.

For labor, the team recruited friends from school and hired workers from among the day labor pool that showed up downtown each morning looking for jobs. Then the noisy, dusty job of sanding began. With the four team members plus two other hired people working from 7 a.m. until 9 p.m. each day for 10 days, they finally finished the boards. In the course of this effort, neighbors had complained of the dust and noise, and the Austin Police Department had come out to see what was going on.

An added complication was discovery that approximately half the boards had to be discarded due to debris found embedded in the clay as a result of dirt that had been in the air during the coating process in Tyler. Fortunately, there was enough extra coated board to overcome this scrap rate, but to use it the team had to return to the cabinet shop and ask the owner to please saw and route an additional 200 Claybords. Recalling his grief on the first load, the owner at first tried to avoid the job, then accepted it at double the rate of the first job and then said he was still losing money on the work.

This final 200 boards at least gave the team enough to complete the order for 2,000 boards. On graduation day, May 22, 1993, they at last sent the shipment off to Pearl Paint. Scott's question to Robert about whether the venture was really worth continuing, however, was still open. Clearly, they had lost money so far, and no certain way to turn it around was yet in sight.

Whether to shift from outsourcing to manufacturing

Since the most serious problems so far had come from dealing with subcontractors, it seemed that possibly a better approach would be for Ampersand to set up its own manufacturing facility. Scott observed:

> Looking for suppliers has been a continuous process for me. I'd call one and when it turned out not to fit, I'd ask them for suggestions about others, and that way I'd find lots of possibilities. But all the subcontractors we had used so far told us to please go away and not come back. When I tried to find new ones, I'd throw out numbers of possible volumes of work and they would get interested. Then they would ask about the process and I would describe it. They would tell me, that it sounded interesting, that they would like to think about it, and they would call us back. But then in fact they wouldn't call; and if I called them, they would tell me that they were too backlogged with other jobs to consider our work.

Prices for machinery, if Ampersand wanted to set up its own plant, ranged into six figures. An automated sander, for instance, they found could cost upwards of $60,000. A paint line might cost an additional $30,000 to $150,000, while a forklift might cost another $5,000—all in used condition. Leasehold improvements, such as shelves, lighting, venting and fans, they estimated, might add $10,000 to the cost of a plant. There would be need for licenses, permits and inspections from various governmental agencies. In all, it appeared that the cost of setting up a shop might range upwards of $150,000, and if things did not work right and had to be modified or replaced, the number would go higher still.

The initial capital had at this point been almost entirely used up. Some founders were at the end of their personal resources. They believed they could finance the product demonstration commitment they had made to Pearl Paint, but not much beyond that. Moreover, the only sale they had definitely lined up so far was that of the demonstration order. Did the company really merit continued effort and substantial further investment?

Against this prospect, team members had received job offers of as much as $60,000 with major successful companies. All had continued interviewing for jobs. Did it make sense for them to continue for little or no pay in trying to start a venture that so far had not collected from a sale and would only have a loss to show when they did collect on the delivery they had made?

Paul Brumveld and John Johnstad

Applying an acquisition strategy

In the spring of 1997, Paul Brumveld and John Johnstad, two students completing graduate degrees in business at Midwestern State University in Illinois, were deciding how to proceed with a project they had been pursuing under independent study. Beyond the course credits, their objective had been to formulate a strategy for building a high-growth business through a systematic acquisition strategy. They had formulated the strategy and undertaken to find acquisition candidates, several of which they now wanted to make decisions about as part of the action plan they would pursue beyond graduation. Both had acquired several years' work experience, Paul as an analytical chemist and John in accounting.

Strategy

Their aim was to locate distressed businesses, buy them with leverage based on assets of the firms, then rehabilitate and resell them for a profit. Paul said this approach had tax advantages. Profit from sales of the firms would be taxed at capital gains rates, which were lower than on regular income (15 percent versus up to 36 percent) and, because it would be regarded by the IRS as "unearned," there would be no Social Security tax involved, which alone could amount to 15.2 percent of income. Thus, this way of earning a living would escape a substantial penalty that applied in conventional employment.

Although they realized that in defining criteria they might pre-exclude some purchase candidates that they might later regret passing over, it seemed to them that they had to adopt some systematic mechanism for selecting among what might be hundreds of candidates, far more than they could evaluate in any depth. Criteria they consequently formulated were as follows:

1. Size—Total selling price of $150,000 or less. Between them the two figured they could muster cash of about half of this amount.
2. Location—The Chicago metropolitan area was one they felt they could navigate without excessive time cost.
3. Industries to avoid due to lack of expertise:
   - High technology, such as electronics, software, and biotech
   - Specialized trades, such as plumbing, law, electrical work, and construction
   - Heavy or complex manufacturing
4. Situations to seek:
   - Companies with distress due to inability to service debt from cash flow, symptoms of which might be total debt approaching market value, cutbacks in expenditures for maintenance or marketing, heavy use of credit cards, or arrears in tax, rent, or debt payments
   - Creditors amenable to working things out
   - No pending litigation
   - Analogous to a "fixer-upper" house, neglected perhaps, but with basically good fundamentals, and restorable to strong condition
   - Preferably, but not essentially, where it was also possible to identify one or more people who might be able to buy the business in two or three years

Newspaper search

Paul and John began their search in the "Business Opportunity" sections of several news-papers. Once or twice a week they would meet to compare notes. They found many listings for marketing and get-rich-quick-and-easy schemes, which they avoided. They also found typi-cally around a half dozen espresso carts and comparable numbers of vending machine adver-tisements, which they also avoided.

Also numerous were advertisements for filling stations. But Paul had some experience in the environmental industry, from which he learned that leaking underground tanks could be a major problem with these. So the two decided to skip them.

Even more numerous were advertisements for restaurants, sometimes as many as 15 in a single paper. Curious about these, they contacted a restaurant consultant with 25 years of experience in that work with whom John was personally acquainted. He pointed out that restaurants tended to be deceptively complex. Few people without extensive experience man-aging kitchens and menus, he said, were successful taking over restaurants. Moreover, those in distress usually had problems related to concept, menu design, or location. Feeling unprepared to deal with those, Paul and John added restaurants to their list of businesses to avoid. Taverns, the consultant said, were simpler, and therefore might be worth a look. So the two left that possibility open.

After several weeks of searching, the two had gone through dozens of leads. Having speci-fications had been effective in weeding out most of them, but not so effective in turning up businesses that actually fit. The only two they had found through newspaper advertisements and not summarily scratched were the following:

1. **Grass-up** This enterprise used a pump truck to spray a mixture of grass seed and mulch as a way of creating a lawn without all the trouble of the traditional method of tilling, seeding, and daily watering. The owner had operated the business for six years using seeding machinery he'd made himself. During that time, however, he had become preoccupied with other business activities, and so decided to sell his equip-ment and the advertising materials he used to obtain customers. Currently he was not actively operating the business.

    Posing as editors of a landscaping trade journal, Paul and John phoned some of the company's competitors. They were told that competition had increased in the seeding industry, causing prices to fall. At the same time, there had been changes in the spray-on raw materials that raised the question about whether the equipment of this business might have become obsolete. This left Paul and John unsure about whether or not to attempt a financial analysis of the business.

2. **Enviro-Serve** This company was advertised in the business opportunities section of a business periodical, with indication that as the result of financial pressures, the owners were strongly motivated to sell at a price of $72,000. Paul and John wrote to express interest in learning more and received a brief description that included the following information:

    a. Firm provides environmental remediation and geotechnical engineering services to major oil companies
    b. Founded in 1993; sellers very motivated
    c. Consistent gross revenues over $1 million per year
    d. Pretax profits of $125,000, $1,000, and $1,500 in 1994, 1995, and 1996, respectively

e.   Shareholder equity $125,000 and short-term assets of $160,000

The reply letter also said that to receive any further information about the business, the "buyer must provide a written offer for purchase of the company at a firm price of $72,000 cash at closing, contingent upon verification of information."

Paul and John had not as yet pursued this lead further, as they continued looking for other sources of leads.

Bankruptcy filings

Bankruptcy filings seemed like a logical place to look for distressed firms, and although these listings did not indicate firms as being for sale, Paul and John expected that if they found one of interest they could always make an offer to its owner(s). Announcements of bankruptcy, however, typically listed only the case number, business name, assets, liabilities—and nothing more. Following up on the list, the two learned that most of the bankruptcies were personal, rather than business, and at present those for businesses were in categories they had ruled out. The best they had found through this source so far seemed to be the following:

3.   **Asbestout** This firm removed hazardous building materials. Brief phone calls to construction firms who might be customers indicated it was reputable. Public records of the Bankruptcy Court provided financial information indicating that the firm had assets of $283,600 and debts of $700,000. There seemed to be misclassification of some of the assets which Paul and John took as possible indication that the filing had not been made by an attorney, or at least not one who was competent in bankruptcy.

According to the owner, who operated from a home office, her firm was forced into bankruptcy when two large contracting firms who had engaged her as a subcontractor contested the quality of her firm's work and refused to pay. Her firm had performed work in response to change orders from the contractors that were not specified in their contracts. She attempted to negotiate a settlement but failed. Meanwhile, work she had done on the job had run up bills that accounted for her large debts.

One complication was that she had enjoyed certain bidding advantages as a MBE/WBE (a minority- or women-owned business enterprise) that Paul and John would not have. A second appeared to be that although she had operated the business as a proprietorship when performing the work, she had subsequently formed a corporation and filed the bankruptcy for that entity. This cast doubt on whether or not the bankruptcy petition (Chapter 11 request to continue operating the business under protection of the court from creditors) would be approved.

Business brokers

As a result of pursuing newspaper advertisements, Paul and John came into contact with business brokers. They also found that these were listed in the Yellow Pages, were sometimes locally owned and sometimes franchised, and charged commissions of 10 to 12 percent based upon the total sales price. To list a business with one, the buyer would be required to sign a contract giving the broker exclusive rights to sell, so it would not be possible to do an end-run around the commission.

Brokers they spoke with stressed the importance of pre-screening buyers, ostensibly to avoid spending time with buyers who did not have adequate capabilities or financing. Paul and John got the impression that the brokers' only real concern, however, was the buyer's cash on hand for a down payment to ensure them receipt of the commission. Showing a strong cash position, they thought, might adversely affect their ability to bargain for a lower down-payment and/or price.

Paul and John gave their list of specifications and financial information to three brokers. Each broker then showed them a portfolio of businesses he represented. Typically for each there would be a brief description of the business, list of assets, owner description, income statement, and photograph or two. Sales prices seemed typically to be three times revenues minus cash expenses except interest, and excluding owner's draw. Many of the leads did not meet their specified criteria. Most, for instance, were not financially distressed situations. All three brokers expressed great concern that all their listing information be kept confidential. The only lead that seemed close to Paul and John's specifications was the following:

4. **Handiclothes** This company manufactured clothing for handicapped people. Founded by a family with a handicapped member, its main objectives were to provide clothing at lower cost for people who had limited financial means, and to pay higher wages than those offered by handicapped workshops to people who found it difficult to hold industrial jobs. The clothing it produced was essentially conventional, but the combination of low prices and relatively high wages had created a steady stream of losses for the founders, who had now run out of money. The price of $20,000 reflected, they said, the value of their customer lists, sewing machines, and office equipment. Readjusting the prices and wages, they predicted, should make the business profitable.

Friends and acquaintances

As Paul and John progressed with their search, leads also began to come from friends whom they had told what they were doing. The three they considered most promising so far from these sources were as follows:

5. **Mybarn Grill** The acquaintance who told Paul and John about this firm worked there as manager and was interested in buying it himself if he could raise the money. Or, he said, he would be willing to partner on a buyout. This bar and grill was situated in a neighborhood that was changing from blue to white collar. That change had earlier put it in distress and led to its purchase by the present owner who was attempting to convert it to a sports bar theme appealing to the new local population. Although that seemed to be progressing, there was still much to be done. The walls, ceilings, and bathrooms were in rundown condition, requiring an estimated $20,000 minimum to renovate, and little had been done to advertise.

The owners meanwhile had encountered another opportunity they preferred and consequently signed with a broker to sell the bar and grill. They wanted $30,000 down and 15 percent interest on the unpaid balance on a $120,000 price, which they said was non-negotiable. The firm's reported receipts and disbursements for its most recent year were approximately as in Exhibit 1.

The manager favorably impressed Paul and John as someone with good education both academically and in the business, a person whom they felt they could work with. He could confirm the expense figures, but indicated there was some question about revenue figures, which were used for tax reporting. Paul and John asked two business brokers who were not involved in the deal about pricing, and were told it was common practice for such firms to under-report revenues. One broker advised pricing the firm at half its reported annual revenues of $170,000. The other recommended six to seven times' reported free cash flow. Each of the brokers had a dozen or more taverns for sale, and some had come on the market in the same vicinity as Mybarn Grill.

6. **Analabs** A former coworker of Paul's in analytic chemistry told him about this firm, which, because of financial stress, had been slow in paying her for consulting services. Analabs performed chemical testing on various materials pertaining to agriculture in a rural area. It appeared to Paul, who was familiar with such testing, that the lab was fully adequate to the tasks and had a good reputation. Moreover, it was the only such facility conveniently accessible to customers in the area and, as long as it did not try to exploit this advantage with excessive prices, would likely remain without local competitors.

The company had, however, fallen in arrears in paying suppliers. Paul could not imagine a valid business reason for cash flow problems in such a firm. Upon visiting the firm and chatting with employees and others in the area who used the service, he gathered that the owner had been traveling extensively to sites such as Las Vegas and Atlantic City on vacations, and had also been purchasing expensive equipment beyond what the company needed, including a company luxury car.

When Paul asked to see financial statements and work records of the company, the owner agreed. But several days passed and the records remained unavailable. The owner explained that this information was highly proprietary and he was therefore having his attorney draft a suitable confidentiality agreement.

Several weeks later the agreement arrived. Having signed several confidentiality agreements earlier in dealing with the business brokers, Paul and John were surprised to see that the length of this one, instead of being two or three paragraphs, was two full pages. Near the end was a clause they had never seen before. It specified that whoever signed it thereby agreed to pay "$30,000 in liquidated damages, collectible at the sole discretion" of the lab's owner if he was in any way damaged by actions of either Paul or John.

The owner's attorney explained that the reason for this clause was to protect the owner against disclosure of confidential information about his business to third parties. Paul and John worried that it might be a device by the owner to enable him through litigation to make Paul and John pay part of his debts. They proposed that a more standard disclosure be used instead, but were rebuffed by both the owner and his attorney.

7. **ShowTowne Theatre** A friend of John's who worked in the film industry informed the two about a movie theater, ShowTowne, whose owner was having trouble paying his creditors. The theater was one he had bought and was upgrading in step with gentrification of a formerly blue-collar part of town. It had lost money since reopening six months earlier, but not every month. John's contact thought a marketing campaign could boost revenues and make it profitable, and said he would welcome an opportunity to participate in taking it over. The company had not kept conventional financial statements. But from records of ticket sales and checks written, Paul and John created the estimated financial history appearing in Exhibit 2.

Working from these figures and with the help of John's contact, Paul and John projected what could happen with increased advertising to arrive at the estimated income statement appearing in Exhibit 3.

Although the projection showed a profit, there remained the fact that it was only an estimate and that the company was deeply in debt. When the present owner had taken over the theater, city inspectors had reneged on some promises, including permission to use a

HVAC film projection system that he already owned, and on permission to install only limited fire equipment. Notwithstanding written assurances of these promises, the city unilaterally reneged, costing the owner over $100,000 in additional setup costs and bringing his total debt to $400,000, of which $63,000 was on his credit cards.

The owner said he did not expect the buyers to pay that much. He would continue to be responsible personally for debt not covered by the purchase price. Paul was concerned about a line he saw in a law book that read, "The fact that the seller is in a precarious financial condition can lead to the acquisition being set aside as a fraudulent conveyance."

He and John were about to graduate and could both look forward to well-paying jobs if they wanted them. They had just invested a lot in schooling and had also spent a considerable amount of time on their search for an acquisition. What, they wondered, had they learned from all this, and what should they do about it next?

EXHIBIT 1 Mybarn Grill approximate receipts and expenditures

Receipts	$170,000
Food & beer cost	75,000
Lease	24,000
Labor	33,000
Maintenance	12,000
Insurance	3,000
Misc.	12,300
Net cash before tax	10,700

EXHIBIT 2 ShowTowne Theatre record of receipts and expenses

	March	April	May	June	July	August
Revenue						
Ticket sales	10,643	6,940	9,676	4,629	9,270	13,470
Concessions	1,417	1,000	1,201	729	1,336	2,131
Expenses						
Film rental	3,725	2,429	3,387	1,620	3,245	4,715
Concessions cost	479	338	406	246	451	720
Rent	1,950	1,950	1,950	1,950	1,950	1,950
Labor	2,600	2,600	3,250	2,600	3,250	3,250
Advertising	240	240	300	240	300	300
Insurance	160	160	200	160	200	200
Utilities	400	400	500	400	500	500
Equipment lease	1,343	1,343	1,343	1,343	1,343	1,343
Other	200	200	250	200	250	250
Net	963	(1,720)	(709)	(3,401)	(883)	2,373

EXHIBIT 3 ShowTowne projected revenues and expenses, 12 months

Revenue	
Ticket sales	$186,613
Concessions	29,858
Expenses	
Film rental	65,733
Concessions cost	10,451
Rent	25,350
Labor	42,900
Advertising	14,400
Insurance	2,600
Utilities	6,500
Equipment lease	15,840
Other	4,550
Net	28,147

Cliff Dow and Steve Shaper

In June 1990, four months after receiving his MBA degree from New Hampshire University, Cliff Dow was contemplating with his wife and with another couple whether to drop his job hunting plans and instead buy a store selling classical guitars in Portland, Maine. He knew he was on the "short list" of a major national consulting firm which had said it would notify him within the next month whether it would hire him. He expected the consulting work would be able to pay him more than working in the store, but the job was not certain to materialize. The store, however, had just been put up for sale by its owner, and both Cliff and his prospective partner, Steve Shaper, expected it might sell soon, as the owner said there were already several buyers who said they were seeking financing and expected to make offers within the next week or two.

The company

Classicraft Guitars was a 15-year-old store in the old section of Portland, which in recent years had been transformed into a chic shopping and tourist area. The first owners of the store had been practicing musicians who had developed it as a sideline and, according to Cliff, given it a good reputation as a source of high-quality instruments with a non-commercial atmosphere. In the back of the store, they had installed several soundproof rooms where they and others gave lessons in classical guitar playing.

Over time, however, the owners found there were conflicts between their occupation as musicians and the work of tending the store, and three years earlier they had sold it to a second owner. The buyer was a guitar maker, who rearranged part of the store into a work area where he both built and repaired instruments. He too, Cliff said, maintained a reputation for handling high-quality instruments and the store was known to have the largest selection of exclusively classic guitars in New England north of Boston. However, this owner had found himself in conflict between his instrument building work and that of tending store, and after three years decided to sell the store and confine his activities solely to manufacturing.

The store at this time utilized about 1,100 square feet on the ground floor of a four story building. It included an entry area approximately 15 feet wide, which opened off a side street near the main thoroughfare in Old Portland. Guitars were displayed in front windows about four feet wide on either side of the front door. Inside, there were guitars hanging along the wall on one side, and on the other side, a display of sheet music, records and instrument cases. At the back was a mahogany office desk with a computer terminal on top and a doorway leading farther back to a hallway with more guitars on the walls, a locked display case with the most expensive instruments costing up to $3,000 and two soundproofed practice rooms where two experienced teachers, one of whom was an initial founder of the store, gave guitar lessons.

Steve Shaper

Steve and Cliff had been friends since working together as retail clerks for a sporting goods store. Steve spent some time in the service following high school, then went on to the University of Maine, where he received both his undergraduate degree and a Ph.D. in English. He then took a faculty position and became a professor of English. He had also been a serious student of classical guitar, taking lessons for many years and playing mainly for personal satisfaction. This avocation he shared with Cliff. The two also shared enthusiasm for long-distance running.

Steve's wife, Sharon, had studied business administration at Portland State and then gone on to become a C.P.A. with the Bangor office of a major national accounting firm. The couple did not have any children, but expected they would in the future.

Cliff Dow

Cliff had gone to the University of New Hampshire following high school. Initially he majored in engineering, but after his sophomore year, he transferred to business administration because it appeared to him that engineering offered "too much dull grind and not enough life. My Dad was an engineer," he said, "and frankly, it didn't look like all that much fun as a career."

Following graduation in 1979, Cliff took a series of jobs in retailing. The same year, he married his wife, Chris, whom he had met at the university through a common interest in running. In retailing he also gravitated toward athletics and worked mainly in sporting goods stores. Chris too went into retailing, starting as a clerk in a women's clothing store. By the time Cliff decided to go back to business school for an MBA degree, Chris had risen to upper management in a chain with 200 stores, over which she had responsibility.

Cliff, however, said he had grown tired of retailing and did not see attractive opportunity for further advancement. He decided to major in finance and international business. On the side he had become interested in Japanese. As part of his degree program, he had completed a summer internship with a firm in Japan. He commented:

> As fate would have it, the Japanese company happened to be in retailing. So there I was again, back where I didn't want to be. But it was a good experience anyway.

Cliff also developed an interest in entrepreneurship, and even went so far as to extend his graduation by one quarter in order to take the university's entrepreneurship course. As a project for the course he developed a plan for a venture. He recalled:

> It was—you guessed it—a retail store. My concept was to start a store in sporting goods, which was something I had lots of experience in. It would differ from most sporting goods stores by offering a wider variety of products, lessons, tours and other sports-related services. It would aim to be the sporting goods superstore of them all. But when I tried to analyze it objectively I could not find a competitive advantage that really seemed likely to work against competitors who could readily imitate anything I came up with, and who would have the resources, skills and established position to do it as well or better.
>
> I learned a lot in the course about how businesses get started. I had developed confidence in some aspects of venturing, but not in my ability to spot a truly workable venture idea or to finance one even if I did find it. At the end I felt frustrated that I had not actually been able to extract from it a truly viable competitive entry wedge. I had wanted the instructor to give me one. But what I found was that by the end of the course, I had developed a plan for a business idea that was not really workable and that I could not finance even if it was.
>
> Worst of all, it seemed that the task of finding an effective entry wedge was still all up to me. It seemed as though all I could do was keep looking and try to be receptive to opportunity if and when it arose without being able to make it happen. So I really didn't see much likelihood of becoming involved with a venture in the foreseeable future, and I put aside the idea of becoming an entrepreneur.

Following graduation Cliff interviewed for jobs in several areas, particularly product management and management consulting. A major national accounting firm had shown serious interest in him as a potential recruit for its consulting activities. Several interviews followed, and the firm had told him that he was likely to receive an offer, but not for a month or two while the firm firmed up its overall staffing plans.

Shop for sale

It was during this interlude that he noticed in a classical guitar magazine the advertisement for sale of Classicraft. He had started learning to play the guitar since before elementary school, and his interest in playing had continued ever since. Classicraft was a familiar place to him for buying instruments and music, and he shared the opinion of other classical guitarists that the store was tops in its geographical area for high-quality classical instruments.

He mentioned the advertisement to Steve Shaper and asked whether Steve might have any interest in pursuing it. As they talked, the idea seemed unlikely to work out. They estimated that the cost of a store like Classicraft would probably be in the range of $100,000 or so. That would be substantially beyond what they could pay without borrowing, and both doubted they would be able to get a loan to buy a business anyway. Cliff said:

> We decided it couldn't hurt to approach the store owner and ask how much he wanted. We were surprised when he gave us a figure right off the bat. Then, when the figure turned out to be $30,000 we were even more surprised, and I had to work hard at suppressing delight. That is the kind of figure we can finance personally from savings.

Records of the store were minimal, consisting of a check ledger for expenses and a general ledger for keeping track of sales. The owner had also made available his tax filings for the preceding two years, copies of which appear in Exhibits 1 and 2. He was proposing to sell all the inventory, fixtures and furniture but retain his guitar building tools. The inventory consisted of finished guitars, sheet music and small items such as strings, picks, stands and cases, which he estimated were worth $19,000. The furniture and fixtures he said were worth approximately $5,000. As a total price, he told Cliff and Steve he wanted $30,000.

Two teachers each paid $150 per month for use of the practice rooms. Lesson charges were typically $25 per hour, of which the store received $2. Steve noted that one had been an initial founder of the store, and was very well known and respected in the local music community. He also taught in the music department of the university as well as at a local school of the arts.

Cliff and Steve had examined the store and made an asset list of their own. Based upon estimated purchase costs of inventory and estimated depreciated value of furniture and fixtures they reached an estimated total for the list of $18,592, as shown in Exhibit 3. Cliff noted that based upon his prior retailing experience, it seemed to him that the inventory turnover rate of some items was low and characteristic, at the values they had given it, of "dead stock." Based on historical figures he had projected turnover rates by category as shown in Exhibit 4. He concluded:

> There should be a turnover rate of at least 2.5 on any category, and on some it looks like the store is doing half that.

Cliff further commented that, although the present owner was a knowledgeable and pleasant person, he did not seem to be operating all that effectively.

> He is very low key and doesn't seem to use suggestion selling at all. At the same time, the store could seem intimidating to visitors. The guitars are not labeled, and they are tied down in a way that makes it hard to take them off the wall so they can be played. The owner doesn't really encourage people to play them, maybe because he's afraid they might get scratched, or because he is preoccupied with making and fixing instruments. Or maybe he just doesn't think people want to play them or would be more likely to buy them if it were easier to do so.
>
> The way he has sheet music and records stacked in milk crates isn't very orderly, and the workshop area creates dust that leaves the overall level of cleanliness lower than you could wish

for. The store seems to me to be entirely out of some items that sell best, probably because the owner has had to make hard choices between taking income and investing in inventory. There aren't any CD's at all in the stock or any electronic instruments or equipment like amplifiers.

Need for a decision

The question is whether we should do it and if so what terms and conditions we should propose to the owner. For me, it would mean dropping the possible job opportunity, which I expect might pay somewhere between $40,000 and $60,000 per year. There is no way Steve is going to quit his teaching job and move himself and his wife to Portland to run the store.

He said he and his wife are willing to put up half the money if Chris and I put up the other half. But then, who takes responsibility for the store? Chris and I can get by on her income, but we definitely plan on expanding our family in the near future, and that will both require money and deflect her activities away from earning it. If I take on the store, that will plunk me right back into—there it goes again—retailing, though I must admit I really like the store, the guitars and other people who are interested in them.

Steve and I figure we have enough interest in this possibility that we should figure out what steps would best be involved in going ahead with it before we decide whether to do that or to drop it. He tells me that, after all, I'm the one who studied business and should be able to spell out all the considerations, contingencies, best plan, pros and cons of going ahead. If we don't move on this thing fast and in the right way, it seems to us very likely that someone else will. So there I am. What should I say?

EXHIBIT 1 Classicraft tax filing for 1988

SCHEDULE C (Form 1040)	Profit or Loss From Business	OMB No. 1545-0074
Department of the Treasury Internal Revenue Service (3)	(Sole Proprietorship) Partnerships, Joint Ventures, Etc., Must File Form 1065. ▶ Attach to Form 1040, Form 1041, or Form 1041S. ▶ See Instructions for Schedule C (Form 1040).	**1988** Attachment Sequence No. 09

Name of proprietor

Randolph Price
Business: Retail Sales - Classical Guitars and Accesories
Principal Business Code: 4333
Business Name and Address: Classicraft Guitars,
    41 Lundy Lane, Portland, ME 04102

E Method(s) used to value closing inventory:
  (1) ☒ Cost   (2) ☐ Lower of cost or market   (3) ☐ Other (attach explanation)

		Yes	No
F	Accounting method: (1) ☐ Cash (2) ☒ Accrual (3) ☐ Other (specify) ▶		
G	Was there any change in determining quantities, costs, or valuations between opening and closing inventory? (If "Yes," attach explanation.)		X
H	Are you deducting expenses for business use of your home? (If "Yes," see Instructions for limitations.)		Y
I	Did you "materially participate" in the operation of this business during 1988? (If "No," see Instructions for limitations on losses.)	X	

J If this schedule includes a loss, credit, deduction, income, or other tax benefit relating to a tax shelter required to be registered, check here. ▶ ☐
If you check this box, you MUST attach Form 8271.

Part I Income

1a	Gross receipts or sales	**1a**	90,462 5:
b	Less: Returns and allowances	**1b**	1,800 00
c	Subtract line 1b from line 1a. Enter the result here	**1c**	88,662 5:
2	Cost of goods sold and/or operations (from Part III, line 8)	**2**	48,186 54
3	Subtract line 2 from line 1c and enter the gross profit here	**3**	40,475 99
4	Other income (including windfall profit tax credit or refund received in 1988)	**4**	
5	Add lines 3 and 4. This is the gross income . . . . ▶	**5**	40,475 99

Part II Deductions

6	Advertising	**6**	650 74	23	Repairs	**23**	51 22
7	Bad debts from sales or services (see Instructions)	**7**		24	Supplies (not included in Part III) .	**24**	305 50
8	Bank service charges	**8**	591 74	25	Taxes	**25**	1,398 11
9	Car and truck expenses . . .	**9**		26	Travel, meals, and entertainment:		
10	Commissions	**10**		a	Travel . . .	**26a**	
11	Depletion	**11**		b	Meals and entertainment .		88 00
12	Depreciation and section 179 deduction from Form 4562 (not included in Part III)	**12**	2,694 91	c	Enter 20% of line 26b subject to limitations (see Instructions) .		
13	Dues and publications . . .	**13**	133 90	d	Subtract line 26c from 26b . .	**26d**	88 00
14	Employee benefit programs .	**14**		27	Utilities and telephone . . .	**27**	3029 95
15	Freight (not included in Part III)	**15**	522 23	28a	Wages . . .		
16	Insurance	**16**	647 27	b	Jobs credit .		
17	Interest:			c	Subtract line 28b from 28a . .	**28c**	
a	Mortgage (paid to banks, etc.) .	**17a**		29	Other expenses (list type and amount):		
b	Other	**17b**	3,878 27		Contributions.....10.00		
18	Laundry and cleaning . . .	**18**			License/Permits 105.00		
19	Legal and professional services .	**19**	295 00		Security System 462.00		
20	Office expense	**20**	271 11		Training/Education 945.00		
21	Pension and profit-sharing plans .	**21**			....		
22	Rent on business property .	**22**	10,625 00			**29**	1522 00

30	Add amounts in columns for lines 6 through 29. These are the total deductions . . . . ▶	**30**	26,704 9:
31	Net profit or (loss). Subtract line 30 from line 5. If a profit, enter here and on Form 1040, line 12, and on Schedule SE, line 2. If a loss, you MUST go on to line 32. (Fiduciaries, see instructions.)	**31**	13,771 0:

32 If you have a loss, you MUST check the box that describes your investment in this activity (see Instructions) . . . .
  32a ☐ All investment is at risk.
  32b ☐ Some investment is not at risk.

If you checked 32a, enter the loss on Form 1040, line 12, and Schedule SE, line 2. If you checked 32b, you MUST attach Form 6198.

EXHIBIT 2 Classicraft tax filing for 1989

DULE C n 1040) *epartment of the Treasury* Internal Revenue Service (3)	**Profit or Loss From Business** (Sole Proprietorship) Partnerships, Joint Ventures, Etc., Must File Form 1065. ▶ Attach to Form 1040 or Form 1041. ▶ See Instructions for Schedule C (Form 1040).	OMB No. 1545-0074 **1989** Attachment Sequence No. **09**

Name of proprietor

Randolph Price
Business: Retail Sales - Classical Guitars and Accesories
Principal Business Code: 4333
Business Name and Address: Classicraft Guitars,
41 Lundy Lane, Portland, ME 04102

					Yes	No
E	Method(s) used to value closing inventory.	(1) ☑ Cost (2) ☐ Lower of cost or market (3) ☐ Other (attach explanation) (4) ☐ Does not apply (if checked, skip line G)				
F	Accounting method:	(1) ☐ Cash (2) ☑ Accrual (3) ☐ Other (specify) ▶				
G	Was there any change in determining quantities, costs, or valuations between opening and closing inventory? (If "Yes," attach explanation.)					✗
H	Are you deducting expenses for business use of your home? (If "Yes," see Instructions for limitations.)					✗
I	Did you "materially participate" in the operation of this business during 1989? (If "No," see Instructions for limitations on losses.)				✗	
J	If this schedule includes a loss, credit, deduction, income, or other tax benefit relating to a tax shelter required to be registered, check here . ▶ ☐ If you checked this box, you MUST attach Form 8271					

Part I Income

1	Gross receipts or sales	**1**	92,046	71
2	Returns and allowances	**2**	250	00
3	Subtract line 2 from line 1. Enter the result here	**3**	91,796	71
4	Cost of goods sold and/or operations (from line 39 on page 2) .	**4**	52,686	64
5	Subtract line 4 from line 3 and enter the **gross profit** here . .	**5**	39,110	07
6	Other income, including Federal and state gasoline or fuel tax credit or refund (see Instructions)	**6**	42	13
7	Add lines 5 and 6. This is your **gross income** . . . . . . ▶	**7**	39,152	20

Part II Expenses

8	Advertising	**8**	2872	16	22	Repairs	**22**	18	92
9	Bad debts from sales or services (see Instructions)	**9**			23	Supplies (not included in Part III) .	**23**	202	13
10	Car and truck expenses . . .	**10**			24	Taxes	**24**	737	69
11	Commissions	**11**			25	Travel, meals, and entertainment:			
12	Depletion	**12**			a	Travel	**25a**		
13	Depreciation and section 179 deduction from Form 4562 (not included in Part III)	**13**	2824	63	b	Meals and entertainment . . 120 50			
					c	Enter 20% of line 25b subject to limitations (see Instructions) . . . 24 10			
14	Employee benefit programs (other than on line 20)	**14**			d	Subtract line 25c from line 25b	**25d**	96	40
15	Freight (not included in Part III)	**15**	353	09	26	Utilities (see Instructions) . . .	**26**	1547	04
16	Insurance (other than health) .	**16**	622	44	27	Wages (less jobs credit) . . .	**27**		
17	Interest:				28	Other expenses (list type and amount):			
a	Mortgage (paid to banks, etc.) .	**17a**				*Security System* 462.00			
b	Other	**17b**	4033	76		*Training/Education* 500			
18	Legal and professional services	**18**	1295	00		....			
19	Office expense	**19**	1211	56		....			
20	Pension and profit-sharing plans .	**20**				....			
21	Rent or lease:								
a	Machinery and equipment . .	**21a**							
b	Other business property . . .	**21b**	10,975	00			**28**		

29	Add amounts in columns for lines 8 through 28. These are your **total expenses** . . . . . . ▶	**29**	27,256	82
30	**Net profit or (loss).** Subtract line 29 from line 7. If a profit, enter here and on Form 1040, line 12, and on Schedule SE, line 2. If a loss, you MUST go on to line 31. (Fiduciaries, see Instructions.)	**30**	11,895	38
31	If you have a loss, you MUST check the box that describes your investment in this activity (see Instructions). . . . . If you checked 31a, enter the loss on Form 1040, line 12, and Schedule SE, line 2. If you checked 31b, you MUST attach Form 6198	31a ☐ All investment is at risk. 31b ☐ Some investment is not at risk.		

For Paperwork Reduction Act Notice, see Form 1040 Instructions.   Schedule C (Form 1040) 1989

EXHIBIT 3 Tally of Classicraft assets by Cliff & Steve as of October 11, 1990 (dollars)

Inventory	Value	Furnishings	Value	Fixtures	Value	Depreciables	Value
		Velvet wall	128	Carpet	234	Fixtures	3,232
Guitars		Posters	81	Floor tile	204	Furnishings	3,051
Carlos 080	400	Flwrs & vase	51	Slide window	51	Total	6,283
Granini 1/4	70	Seashell	8	Slide door	127	(Acc depn)	-2,255
Granini 3/4	73	3 humidifiers	170	Track lights	595	Book Value	4,028
Castilla 3/4	40	Desk chair	68	Adj light fixt	18		
4 F Saez 4A	572	Teak desk	213	Wood doors	20		
P Saez 6A	153	Large fan	25	Wood beam	34	**Assets**	
P Saez 8A	168	Small fan	17	Paneling	82	Inventory	14,596
Artensano 20	137	2 metal chairs	34	Plaster board	51	Book F&F	4,028
Tak C1325	255	2 wood chairs	26	Access. shelf	26	New items	328
Dauphin 535	467	Wood stool	21	Record shelf	10	Total	18,952
Hirade 7	620	Bulletin board	13	Bath shelf	13		
Hirade 8	660	Oak displ case	510	Mirror	4		
Hirade 10	1,050	Small oak case	34	Guitar cabinet	213		
Osterby 17	1,800	Oak shelf	191	Alarm system	359		
Total	6,465	Coffee table	17	Storage cab	213		
		Lamp	51	Book display	127		
Cases		Orientl rugs 2	213	Door alarm	17		
7 GC 318	105	Carpet pieces	4	Hanging sign	510		
GC 316	14	Clock radios 2	26	Wall sign	128		
Used	25	Trunk	42	Door handles	106		
SLM	58	Kitch appli.	42	Front window	90		
AT	65	Humidity gage	13	Total	3,232		
2 ATB Blk	138	File boxes	60				
2 ATB Brn	146	Plastic crates	37				
Total	551	Waste baskets	14	**New items (Expensed)**			
Lights & dec.	51	Floor light	15				
Other (est)		Extension cords	13	Large fan	31		
Accessories	830	Display guitar	38	Small fan	16		
Records	450	Interior signs	64	Folding chairs 4	35		
Music, Books	5,400	Sndwch sgns 2	723	Couch	130		
Strings	900	Fire exting.	34	Phone	56		
Total	7,580	Cash box	4	Calculator	45		
Card table	15	Total	3051	Total	328		

EXHIBIT 4 Classicraft turnover computed by Cliff

	Guitars	Strings	Access.	Books	Records
1990 Proj. Sales	59,235	5,185	3,886	8,286	474
CGS %	56	41	56	68	58
1990 CGS	33,172	2,126	2,176	5,634	275
Inventory @ Book	7,016	900	830	5,400	450
Inv. Turnover	4.73	2.36	2.62	1.04	0.61

Raheed Sahemi

Whether to buy a franchise

In late November 1998 time pressure seemed to be building on Raheed Sahemi. It had been two and a half months since he quit his job with the U.S. Army Corps of Engineers to find a business that he and his wife could own and run. With house payments to make and two young children to provide for, he was keenly aware of each new day without income. He knew also that once he did find a business, there would be additional expenses for moving ahead on it, and likely a further wait before its revenue would exceed its expenditures.

Raheed had emigrated from Iran in 1977 to study soil mechanics and environmental chemistry, and earned his Ph.D. at Washington State University. While there he had met and married another student, who had immigrated from Asia in 1979 to earn her Ph.D. in molecular biology. Preferring life in a larger city, the two subsequently moved to Seattle, where he worked for the Corps of Engineers and she as a researcher for the University of Washington. Although he drew satisfaction from setting up new environmental safety programs, he wanted to advance faster financially than was proving possible for him in the Corps. So he quit to seek a venture with greater upside potential in both money and satisfaction for both him and his wife. They estimated that their present savings could allow a maximum personal investment of around $200,000.

The venture prospect on which his attention was most tightly focused was to acquire a franchise from Temploy Staffing Services of Dallas, Texas. By paying a one-time initial fee of $15,000 for the franchise and agreeing to its terms, he would be able to set up an office under their logo to sell the services of temporary workers to local companies. Temploy specialized in providing workers for truck driving, forklift operation, and warehouse work. And because Raheed had a background in environmental engineering, they said they would permit him to include environmental and laboratory technicians as well.

The basis on which Temploy operated was as follows:

- The franchisee would advertise and also employ one or more salespeople to call upon employers who might need the types of workers agreed to in the franchise contract.
- The franchisee would also place want ads for workers, whom it would then screen with an oral interview protocol, a 100-question form, and a drug test that were provided by Temploy. There were also physical tests, such as lifting, that were to be given to the applicant, depending upon the nature of the job position.
- When a match was found between worker and employer, the franchisee would hire the worker, who would be sent to the job site, and bill the employer for the worker's services, typically at about twice what the worker was paid.
- The employer would send the payment to Temploy, which would deduct its "cut" and send the balance to the franchisee. This cut would be a percentage of gross, which was defined as the monthly difference between the amount billed and what the employee received. The amount was to be 40 percent on the first $50,000, 38 percent on the next $100,000, 36 percent on the next $100,000, 34 percent on the next $150,000, and 32 percent on everything over that.

■ Any worker expenses, such as workers' compensation insurance, beyond salary were to be paid by the franchisee, as were operating expenses of the enterprise such as rent, sales salaries, utilities, secretarial pay, and advertising costs.

Raheed explained that Temploy emphasized the effectiveness of its employment screening methods and also the support it provided to franchisees from its central headquarters in Dallas, Texas. Their questionnaire for prospective employees, they said, had been tested extensively as a tool for weeding out recruits who might be incompetent for the type of work, lazy, or dishonest. The drug testing kit they provided was easy for the franchisee to use. They would also provide assistance on decisions, such as choice of site and facilities, design of advertisements, and marketing efforts, including the structuring of major presentations to prospective employers.

Temploy's organization chart indicated that it included separate divisions specializing in such human resource functions as workers' compensation claims, risk management, productivity, and finance. Raheed observed:

> They have told me that they help aggressively on all these things. They fight every worker's compensation claim, scrutinize every unemployment claim, and will even send a vice president from headquarters if, for instance, I must talk about creativity with a particular employer, and that person will make a polished computerized presentation on the subject.

Raheed had seen much of Temploy's corporate headquarters operations first hand, had interviewed either in person or by phone 12 of their existing 23 franchisees, most of whom were either in Texas or Florida, and was favorably impressed with much of what he heard. He observed:

> This is the future of the workforce. Companies are downsizing and shifting more to temporary workers to make their labor costs more flexible. At the same time, not only industrial companies, but also federal agencies like the Army Corps of Engineers where I worked are getting rid of their HR (human resources) offices. But that HR function still has to be performed somewhere, so companies like Temploy spring up to cover that necessity. With a situation like that and the low unemployment rate, that makes it so hard for employers to recruit people they need, there is no way that a company like Temploy is going to fail, it seems to me.

Temploy had come to Raheed's attention through an advertisement in the Business Opportunities section of the *Seattle Times*, where he had been searching for several weeks. He had followed up advertisements for a couple of gas stations which, he said, grossed a lot and seemed to have high profit potential, but were not attractive to him in terms of the kind of work they would entail. He made inquiries about coffee shops, but found that most of those that were attractive were company-owned. There was a Piccolo's coffee and pastry shop franchise available, but he said that was too small and involved more manual work than he was seeking. He looked at a 7/11 franchise store for sale, and concluded that he could earn more by investing the purchase price in a savings account. He observed that McDonald's was a profitable business, but their stores cost "millions."

He had learned that each state had its own franchising laws and he made contact with the Securities Division of the Department of Licensing where the Washington State franchising registrations were handled. Temploy, it turned out, had not registered until after he had contacted them. He compared the materials that the company sent him with those on file with the state and found that the Temploy materials were more extensive, which seemed to him a good sign about them. Another good sign, he said, was that the company seemed to have grown rapidly in recent years and was aggressively eager to expand further. Before actually closing any deal with them, however, he expected to engage a lawyer specializing in franchise law from the perspective of the franchisee.

An income statement on file for Temploy showed the following recent consolidated income statement for the parent company: (in $ thousands)

	1997	**1996**
Revenue	$43,778	$33,188
Payroll and direct expenses	36,057	26,802
General and administrative expenses	6,566	5,802
Operating income	1,155	584
Other expenses	136	169
Income before income taxes	1,019	415
Income taxes	26	52
Profit after taxes	993	363

Another business possibility Raheed had found and spent some time checking out was a local Denny's restaurant for sale that was owned by the parent company, which was now advertising it as a prospective franchise opportunity. The price was $200,000, and he understood the net profit was $103,000 per year after paying for a $40,000-per-year manager and two assistant managers. The manager, he figured, he could replace with himself, to gain an attractive return. But before he could proceed with a purchase effort, the restaurant, which had been experiencing some litigation based on civil rights laws, was pulled off the market.

Disappointed by that event, Raheed concentrated on delving further into the Temploy possibility. He called the company headquarters in Dallas and was told he should first fill out a form telling about himself for their evaluation. It asked, he said, for financial information about assets and income similar to that required in a bank loan application, plus information about his personal interests, capabilities, and job history. They also sent him newspaper clippings about their firm and its success, plus a copy of their UFOC (Uniform Franchise Offering Circular), a 90-page document describing their company and giving its financial statements as required by law of franchisers.

After they had received his completed form, they called him and offered to travel to Seattle to tell him more about their operation and discuss further the possibility of his becoming a Temploy franchisee. He recalled:

> They seemed very enthused about expanding to the Pacific Northwest, which would be new for them. They had expanded successfully in Florida after growing in Texas from their beginning in 1980. They knew Puget Sound was a booming area where finding employees was hard. Their idea was that if our meeting went well, then I should fly down to their offices, where we could close the deal. I would have to pay my own fare, but they would provide hotel and meals in Dallas.
>
> Instead, I decided to visit them first. In Dallas they gave me eight hours of interviews with their various divisions, and showed me presentations on what they do. It took a day and a half. None of it was rocket science, but they did a competent job of the presentations.
>
> They emphasized the importance of exclusive territories, and asked me what I wanted. When I asked for the three most populous counties in my state, they seemed to balk, telling me that they would not normally permit exclusive rights on a territory that large. I told them my aim would be to have an office in each of the counties within five years. But that was as far as it went.

It seemed to me that I could do well with three offices. They have other offices doing around $2,000,000 per year in total billings. To figure the gross on that, I gather that they pay only $5.50 per hour, which is allowable in Texas. I think that is less than in Washington, maybe because unions are stronger in Washington, although I would not expect to be hiring union people.

They charge employers $9.80 per hour for those workers, so the gross would be something like 45 percent of $2,000,000 or $900,000. If I were getting that and they were taking a cut of around 35 percent, it would leave me about two-thirds of the $900,000, which would be $600,000. Out of that I would pay for my expenses and take my profit. The other expenses I would pay would, of course, vary from state to state. In the figures they used there was a figure of $1.30 per hour to cover workers' compensation, unemployment insurance, and employer taxes.

They mentioned that normally franchisees are also required to pay 4 percent of gross to headquarters for corporate advertising, which is intended to help both company offices and franchisees. But since they have no offices in Washington State, they indicated that they might waive that charge and let me use the advertising money as I saw fit.

My impression was that they do very well on that kind of volume. They now have 18 corporate offices in Texas and another 23 franchisees in other states, particularly the Midwest and Florida. They showed me consolidated financial statements on the company, which I don't fully understand, but their profits looked strong. I gather that they have a line of credit of $500,000,000 of which they are only using $2,000,000.

They could not show me financial statements of the franchisees, of course, since they don't get any from them. The company offices may have separate statements. I'm not sure. But they would probably not be comparable to mine anyway, since the location is so different, they have been in business so long, and to some extent I would be employing different people, such as lab technicians, not just less-skilled labor such as their offices handle.

One thing I wonder is whether I should feel guilty about charging employers twice as much as I would be paying the employees I recruited. Maybe it is appropriate as a customary practice. Also maybe it's right. After all, when I was working with the Corps of Engineers I understood that they were billing other government agencies at nearly 30 times as much for our time as we were getting paid, and that didn't bother me at the time.

Meximeals

Whether or how best to grow

Whether to push for more growth, and if so, how best to do it was on the mind of Don Wilson, the Chief Executive Officer of Meximeal, a Portland, Oregon restaurant firm, in early 1995. The firm, only two years old, had opened four stores and all were currently net cash-positive. Aggregate operating profits of the most recent year were $34,900 on sales of $484,000.

Background

The restaurant had been started by brothers Charles and Calvin Jones. Charles had gone off to college in southern California where he had worked part time in restaurants during school and then joined the software firm of an uncle. He grew tired of the crowded atmosphere in that area, however, and began discussing with his brother how he might find work back in the Pacific Northwest.

Calvin had been working as floor manager in an upscale Portland restaurant, and the discussions about what Charles might do in Portland eventually came around to the possibility of the two men opening an eating establishment. Charles returned to Portland and they developed a business plan for a new deli restaurant.

Next, they began looking for a space to locate it. Because they had little money, they considered it important to find a space with minimal rent. They found this hard, partly because there were few such spaces to be found in areas where people might likely patronize a deli, and partly because without a record of successful self-employment in the restaurant business, landlords were not willing to give them a lease.

Finally, they found one who would. He owned a small food court with several other eating establishments. Located in a tourist section of Portland, however, it was open only from late spring to early fall each year. Moreover, the landlord wanted them to hire his carpenters to set up the facilities, and because there was already a sandwich shop in the court, he didn't want a deli. Mexican food, he suggested, would be more acceptable to him.

Charles recalled the fish tacos he had enjoyed when he lived in San Diego. The recipe had apparently been imported from a Baja California village on the coast of Mexico by some California surfers, but had not yet found its way north of San Diego. A friend of Charles' in San Diego who had collected recipes as a hobby, said he could provide one for the fish tacos. With that, the Jones brothers revised their business plan, borrowed $22,000 from family friends, and started work on their new restaurant, Meximeals.

Don Wilson

The day they opened it in June of 1992, they met Don Nelson, the newly hired manager of the property in which the food court was located. Don had just moved from San Francisco to Portland and taken this job after working as general manager of food services in a large San Francisco office complex that housed several food establishments of various types. After graduating with a degree in history, he had pursued a career as a chef, starting at the bottom peeling shrimp in a restaurant, and working his way up to manager over the next 15 years.

Don felt that he had peaked out in that career and wanted to find something else. So after considering several possible places to live, he had come to Portland. Among other things, he liked the prospect of living where there was more open country nearby for hiking, camping, and other outdoor activities.

He enjoyed meeting the Jones brothers and was intrigued with their new restaurant. Its Mexican theme reminded him of a place in San Francisco where he liked to eat that served large burritos stuffed with meat, rice, and greens. He preferred the burritos to the fish tacos served at Meximeals, but also noticed that Meximeals seemed to be starting off successfully. "They were selling food, paying their bills, and keeping their cash flow positive while they learned as they went," he recalled.

Calvin retained his job at the upscale restaurant and helped on weekends, while Charles worked on the store full time, taking just enough pay to get by. At the end of the tourist season, they closed the store. Charles took construction jobs to get through the winter until it was time to open again.

When the next season came around, Don Wilson began to talk with the brothers about trying the burrito he had liked in San Francisco. Charles was eager to try new ways of expanding. He wanted, Don said, to try building a big business out of the small beginnings and was willing to experiment with ways of accomplishing that. Don flew the brothers to San Francisco, where they too found they liked the burritos.

Adding locations

The three of them formed an equal partnership, with Don Wilson contributing $20,000 from his personal savings. They rented space in an industrial district for their company office and began working on their second store by looking for another site in town that would offer low rent but draw traffic that was less seasonal. During the late summer of 1993, they found one and this time put burritos on the menu, along with some of the taco recipes. When the summer season closed the first store, they opened the second one.

This time sales grew much quicker, and the three looked for a third store. Now they knew still better what they wanted in a site: high foot traffic, many singles living nearby, and cheap rent. Soon they found a woman who owned such a site, but she needed to be convinced that the three could succeed before she would grant them a lease. They gave her a tour of their second restaurant. She said it was favorably impressive, but she did not want the smell of cooking food to disturb her adjacent tenants.

The three told her they would not cook on the premises. Instead, they would do all the cooking at the other stores, chill the cooked food, and only reheat it in microwave ovens at the new location. She agreed, and the third store was opened in March 1994. Sales of this store grew even faster than those of the second store, and soon the three partners were looking for yet another site. They found one with still-higher foot traffic, more singles nearby, and comparably low rent. Opened in June of 1994, this fourth store had sales that were soon double those of the third store.

But now the partners began to struggle with the question of how best to handle the cooking. At some stores they could do it, and at one they could not. It appeared preferable to centralize all the cooking at one site, but none of the stores was big enough for that. So they rented a space in the industrial district near their office to set up a commissary where food could be stored in bulk and cooked for all their stores.

Unfortunately, the only space they could find was much too big for those functions. It included 4,000 square feet of space, about three times what they needed for cooking, and rented at $2,700 per month. So they pursued the idea of opening a fifth store in part of it and renting out part of it for storage by other companies in the area. Don Wilson recalled:

That really put us in a cash bind. Our savings were tapped out. We found a manufacturer who rented some space to store parts, but that was not enough. It took cash to open another store there, and I really worried about whether it would work, since there were no singles living nearby and almost no foot traffic whatever. I told the Joneses to find anything they could to bring us in some more revenue. It was a desperate situation trying to meet payroll.

To his pleasant surprise, Don found that the fifth store became cash-positive quickly. Although the foot traffic and singles nearby that had been vital to success elsewhere were missing, there was another advantage to the new location, namely a scarcity of local competition. People who worked in local industrial plants were glad to have a nearby restaurant and quickly give it good patronage.

Further growth possibilities

Most enthused about the expansions was Calvin Jones, who was eager to keep adding more stores, seeing it as a way to fulfill his dreams of building a large company, while at the same time gaining wealth and providing opportunities for employees to advance. Least enthused was Don Wilson, who was anxious about the cash shortage that building the business created each time they expanded. He commented:

Each time you take a step toward bigger size, it sets you back in cash. Work of all sorts is required to reach agreement with the new landlord, set up the site, hire people, train them, and get things moving. Then you have to hope the customers will come and buy, while you sit there losing money until they do. You have more to lose, because you just made another investment, and unless the new store works right, it can collapse and pull down the rest of the business with it.

Also, the bigger you grow, the farther you get away from the entrepreneurial stage where it is really fun. Things have to be better organized, which means more regimented and more impersonal. Instead of being able to refine what you have to make it more efficient and profitable, you can just be adding more rigidity and more chaos at the same time.

He said it was crucial that the company be run right step by step, lest it slip up and get a smudge on its reputation. He pointed out that the recipes for what they did were "falling-down simple" for someone else to copy. The company, he figured, should do everything it could to make it hard to match the quality of their performance in carrying out this simplicity. Furthermore, he saw appeal in stabilizing the business and looking for ways to reduce the workload of the three partners. They could take turns running the stores and take longer vacations for enjoying the outdoors and other pastimes.

Charles was relatively neutral in the matter, siding a bit more with his brother, though not strongly. Both Calvin and Don thought he could be persuaded, but in opposite directions. Calvin pointed out that the company was profitable even though it had not been going long. Don countered that the profits were not all that large. Calvin replied that each new store took some time to break even, and the most recent additions had not yet come into full play.

Moreover, there had been other expenses of setting up, such as trademarking the company name at a cost of $750, legal fees for incorporating, leasehold improvement and expenses in the offices, plus investment in cash registers and other accounting systems that were largely one-time impacts on initial profits. The company, he said, was doing better financially than its statements yet reflected. The commissary, in particular, he continued was probably imposing a drag on profits because it was not being used at full capacity.

Proposal to franchise

Outwardly, the company was doing well enough that it attracted two people who asked whether they might become franchisees. One was Don Wilson's cousin, who in a nearby suburb was operating a flower shop that, although profitable, she had become tired of.

The second was a man who had successfully owned, operated, and sold out of another restaurant franchise. He said he liked operating as a franchisee because it gave him a proven formula and let him concentrate on operating it efficiently, leaving it to the franchiser to worry about advertising, research and development, lining up good sources of supply, and developing new systems.

He proposed that something like a fee of $5,000 to $10,000 plus a royalty of 3 percent to 4 percent on sales would be reasonable in return for rights to use the company logo, adopt its recipes, buy from its commissary, and learn from the experiences of its other stores. He suggested that a ten-year contract might be suitable, and he was eager to start now.

In thinking through this proposition, the Joneses remembered a relative of theirs who served in a Chicago law firm that included franchise work among its specialties. They contacted the law firm, but they were told that Meximeals was not qualified to become a franchiser. It would need to set up a separate corporation from the one owning the present stores, generate audited financial statements, and post a financial reserve of $50,000 in cash to establish financial solidity. Moreover, the legal expenses of setting up the franchise paperwork would cost around $25,000.

Checking with their Portland lawyer, the brothers heard different advice. He said they might be able to form a simple license contract that would let the new store applicants use the company name for a single up-front fee, and provided they did not include a royalty provision, they would not be in trouble with the law.

The Chicago firm advised against it, pointing out that they would be flirting with the edges of franchise law, and should a dispute break out with any of those with whom they signed the license agreement, they would be sure to lose, because of this infraction.

Calvin favored the idea of franchising anyway, pointing out that it was a way to grow without the heavy investment needed to open a company store, something on the order of $60,000 to $80,000 for leasehold improvements, inventory, working cash, expenses of hiring and setting up, and covering losses while sales were building. In distant areas, he noted, the right franchisee could garner instant goodwill for a new store from their established reputation in the community and provide local knowledge of that area that the company would have a hard time getting any other way.

Don didn't like the franchising idea, partly because of the legal dangers, and partly because he saw it as adding a further enormous complication to the business, a strategy they had no acquaintance with whatsoever at a time when they needed to concentrate on learning how to do their existing stores better.

Furthermore, he pointed out that even if they were determined to expand, franchising would not be the best way to do it. He explained:

> Franchising can be instant riches for a franchisee. They may invest something like $100,000 to get the franchise and open the store. If they pick a good location, that store can become profitable quickly, and suddenly it is worth $200,000. It's an instant way to get rich when it works right.
>
> But that is for the franchisee, not the franchiser. The franchiser just gets its fee and the royalty, both of which are small relative to all the things it has to do to get them. The same store might generate 25 percent of sales in profit if the company owned it instead of just 4 percent if a franchisee does.

For example, there is a company listed on the NASDAQ, Quiznos Subs, which operates 35 stores through franchising. It has a total market capitalization of $15 million if you multiply the per-share price by the shares outstanding. That's a value of only $42,000 per store, which is really small. If those were company stores instead, the market cap might be ten times as large, or $150 million.

So if you are going to expand, which for us is questionable, the best way to do it is through company stores, the method that has worked for us so far.

Ampersand (E)

June 1993—Seeking more cash

In early June of 1993 the Ampersand founders had decided to pursue financing through their mentor, the judge from the first competition who had taken a continuing interest in their adventures, as well as helping them with counsel and contacts. They had each put up $1,250 in January of that year, with the understanding that the company would pay that money back if and when it could. In April they had won the $5,000 first prize in the San Diego State national venture plan contest.

This prize money had carried them through final production and shipment of their first order to the Pearl Paint art supply store in New York City. The test market initiative had been extremely successful. Elaine, Kathy, Charles and Barbara sold well over 600 pieces of Claybord during their one-week demonstration at Pearl Paint in New York City. The store was excited and committed to continue purchasing the product. According to the main buyer, never had a new product been launched so successfully.

Now they felt they were ready to mount a campaign to wholesalers of art supplies across the country and begin full scale production by setting up their own factory. To do that would take much more money, they estimated on the order of $300,000. Their mentor, the December 1992 competition judge, was now firmly offering to lend the company $290,000 in return for 10 percent interest on the unpaid balance plus a 30 percent ownership in the company. He suggested that the team "shop the deal" to see if they could find better terms.

Further conditions he desired were that the company would set up manufacturing in Austin, not Colorado, and that it would serve as a model for the Community Investment Corporation, a local enterprise set up to help new ventures and aid economic development of the area. For instance, its legal papers should be brief, clear and usable as "boilerplate." In effect, this would combine the resources of more than one venture and thereby allow ventures to help each other.

He explained that his goal in creating the Community Investment Corporation (CIC) was to cultivate a diverse group of companies with goals focused on the community. Companies funded through CIC should be committed to reinvesting a portion of their profits in the community, specifically in east Austin, an underdeveloped area. He believed that a new model for corporations should be forged.

As a contrary case, he cited a highly successful company that had begun in Austin and been fully supported by the community in its early years. Now that the venture had grown large it was pressuring the community to give it tax breaks with the threat of moving out if it did not get them.

He, a successful entrepreneur himself, had weathered the ups and downs, run companies himself, taken them public and achieved success. Moreover, he had by now served as a mentor for the team, spent considerable time with it and given guidance the team considered very helpful. Consequently, the team said, his views on corporate philosophy deserved careful consideration.

The team had considered similar philosophies in planning their own company. Some had looked into other forms of enterprise where business and community were considered in combination. One program both the investor and the team had been impressed by was an initiative in Bangladesh where the community provided seed capital, guidance and assistance to local entrepreneurs. These entrepreneurs, when they became successful, then reinvested part of their profits back into the community to continue extending help to others.

Jointly, the investor and team agreed that Ampersand should formulate a list of positive covenants under which it would operate to apply this sort of philosophy in Austin.

Ampersand (F)

July 1993—Sales up then down

By July 1, 1993 the Pearl Paint order of 2,000 Claybords had been shipped and billed at $5,300. Thus a major first sale was on the books. Now the team began contacting major art supply distributors in order to reach hundreds of other stores across the country. In addition, the company's advertising campaign was underway as projected in its business plan.

Ampersand had now received a capital infusion of $100,000 as the first installment of $290,000. Scott Bryant and Robert Tavarez were moving ahead with plans to set up production facilities. They were searching the country for needed machinery and locating plant space.

But then Kathy Henderson called from San Francisco with a disturbing message. The art distributor they had been counting on to serve as a sales channel there had declined to give an order for Claybord, because it did not believe that art supply stores it served would buy enough Claybord to justify wholesaling it. By itself, this news would not have been alarming. But coupled with similar responses that had already come from other distributors, it seemed more ominous. Should Ampersand really be mounting a costly marketing campaign as planned? If not, how should the plan be changed?

Further information about the team's intentions can be seen in the Prize-winning Plan case.

Demonstration at Pearl Paint

The team's idea for the test market at Pearl Paint was to simulate in smaller scale a national rollout of the product, including all display items and advertising copy. This would allow each of the advertising and promotional vehicles, such as the direct-mail initiative and in-store demonstration materials, to be tested prior to a national launch. While attending classes, Kathy found a local art student to help her design the direct-mail brochure. She researched mailing lists to identify professional artists nationwide who would be targeted for mailing. To test the list, she purchased names for the New York City area. Working with a local mail house in Austin, Kathy sent a mailing to 2,000 artists in New York City. Over 200 artists replied, requesting samples of Claybord, a response rate that the team considered outstandingly strong.

In early June, Elaine Salazar and Kathy Henderson together with Charles and Barbara Ewing, went to New York for a week to demonstrate Claybord at Pearl Paint. During that week, the team worked together every day from 10 a.m. to 5 p.m. demonstrating Claybord to the artists shopping through Pearl. They set up a display at a different location in the store each day. Charles Ewing would demonstrate use of the board by painting and illustrating different media techniques. Meanwhile, the others talked to artists and sold Claybord. At the same time, they sought to use the experience for learning, as Elaine recalled:

> *Our week in the store we used to gather lots of information about other products and to talk to the Pearl sales staff on the floor. We learned about merchandising ideas, how the staff perceived the product, and the importance of training floor sales staff on the product. We also had a chance to talk to a multitude of different artists, especially artists working in a variety of different media. We were able to see their reactions to the Claybord and to determine how to position and sell the Claybord in the future.*

Probably one of the most important finds during the Pearl demonstrations is that we began to realize that Claybord was appealing to artists working in all types of media—from inks to oils. Originally, we had positioned the product as a surface for pen and ink artists only.

The team's demonstration drew many favorable comments from artists, and helped the store sell more than 600 units. At the end of the week the store's buyer expressed amazement that sales had been so high. This encouraged the team to move ahead on a program aimed at selling to 10 top distributors nationwide plus 20 of the largest retail stores. These large stores, they estimated, might sell to around 100 customers per day. They were not sure how many bought from Pearl, which was visited by an estimated 10,000 shoppers per week. The team expected to offer Pearl and the other large stores the same discount of 62.5 percent that it gave to wholesale distributors. Small and medium-sized stores would receive 50 percent off retail from distributors, while distributors kept 12.5 percent of the retail price.

National product rollout

Marketing plans called for sending out a direct-mail brochure offering free samples to 50,000 artists, and buying full-page color advertisements in the August issues of two magazines, *Artist* and *American Artist* at $7,000 per placement.

In the Ampersand offices at the Austin Incubator, Kathy and Elaine sat down with a large map of the United States and divided up the country into sales territories and planned sales trips into the ones they assigned themselves. Their goal was to complete their first level of sales calls in all their territories by November. On a limited budget, they planned their trips so that each would be able to take advantage of their acquaintances for free board and room.

They began by telephoning the stores and distributors they planned to visit. A typical response, Elaine recalled, was for the contact to say something like, "We're not interested in ordering at this point, but send us a sample and we'll take a look at it." Ampersand sent the samples, but rather than waiting for further response from the customer, Elaine and Kathy began traveling to make personal sales calls.

Distributors' responses began to fall into a pattern of rejection. Typical comments they made were:

- Leave us a sample and we'll show it to our reps.
- An interesting product, but I'm not sure we'll want to handle it.
- Let us think about it.
- We'll have to see if we get orders from the stores.
- Go out and create a market for it. Then we'll talk.
- We haven't had any requests for it from the stores.

At the large stores contacted, responses seemed to be more favorable, though not nearly as spectacular as the reception Ampersand had received at Pearl Paint. By the end of July, after four weeks of their calling on distributors and stores, no distributors had placed an order. But 1,000 Claybords were ordered in total by 10 stores for delivery by October 1. Typically, a store would order only the $270 introductory package, which included 92 boards of various sizes and a display rack. Each rack displayed the Claybord concept in two slogans. One said to "draw, scratch, wash, ink, erase and paint your heart out." The other said, "Claybord, a better finish to start with."

These slogans had been developed by an advertising agency Ampersand had hired. In addition to the magazine advertisement placement fees, which were paid to the agency to pass along to the magazines, around $15,000 had been paid to the agency for concept development, layout and design.

An estimated 20 stores and five distributors had been contacted thus far, while Elaine and Kathy had spent approximately 15 days on the road and $1,500 on travel expenses. However, the anticipated sales results were not occurring, and they believed that something would have to change.

But what? Should the advertising plan be cut back, postponed, or should it be carried out and let further sales trips come after that, when Ampersand could show distributors that more stores were buying the product? Should the team somehow change what they were offering, or start selling directly to small stores as well as large ones, and if so, at what discount structure? Should they try selling direct to artists? How could the company tell whether its market concepts were appropriate?

Meanwhile, Robert and Scott were also on the road looking for machinery with which to set up a manufacturing plant. To ship product by September 15, they would have to move into an empty shop by August 1, set up production equipment and get it into operation by the end of that month. Prior to that they would have to find empty shop space at a cost that would allow them to make a profit, and also find and order appropriate manufacturing equipment to be delivered at an appropriate time for setting it up. They had heard that real estate costs in Austin were high. But how much could they afford?

As these questions that seemed to call for immediate answers arose, another question also suggested itself. Should they try to delay everything until better information was available? If so, by what steps should they arrange the delay? For how long? What information in particular should they obtain, and how?

Pradeep Singh

Shaping long-term identity

In less than five years Aditi Corporation, led by its founder Pradeep Singh, had grown from his one-man Bangalore, India office to 325 full-time employees and aggregate revenues of $1.35 million per month. He could see possibilities for part of the company that delivered programming services to go public in the near future on the Bombay exchange at a capitalization value of around $200 million. Alternatively, by combining and segregating some parts of the company devoted to e-commerce, it might be able to go public on the NASDAQ at a capitalization that might well exceed $1 billion. Trying to do both might also be possible but could be complex. Moreover, under yet another combination, the company might be able to raise venture capital and exploit a product it was developing that could conceivably lead to a still-higher capitalization figure. But any form of restructuring, it seemed, would require compromises, costs, and risks.

A question Pradeep considered important was how to strike the right balance for both cashing in and continuing to build the company. The company could be viewed as being in several different lines of business that for some purposes were complementary and for others, confusing or even contradictory. To become truly great, it seemed to Pradeep, the company would have to develop in the marketplace an image to customers that was clear and consistent. "In a nutshell," he asked, "what is the picture someone should immediately grasp when they look at our Web page?"

Inception

Motivation to start the company had begun with a personal setback. After awakening in intensive care as a result of a bicycle accident on his way to work in Redmond, Washington, where he was a software developer at Microsoft, Pradeep had reflected on his life and decided he would like to do something that would give back to his native land in gratitude for the engineering education he had received at government expense. He asked for and received permission from his superior to design a Microsoft development center in India that would provide opportunity for Indian software programmers.

When this idea began to shape up as too difficult to implement, he changed to the idea of setting up only a help facility, rather than a development center, which would respond to requests from Microsoft customers who were using its compiler software to develop their own software. A novel aspect of his proposal, beyond the fact that it would be located in India rather than the U.S., was that communication with customers would be via the Internet, rather than voice over telephone, as was the company's current practice. (Netscape had not yet come on the scene. There was only Mosaic.) The present choices available to customers were either to pay for help from Microsoft, after receiving two free help calls, or to feed questions into Compuserve where other developers also fed in questions and tried to help each other with answers. Microsoft and Compuserve collaborated in making this possible. Pradeep's proposed facility would add to these two choices a third at no cost to users.

Microsoft declined to set up such a facility itself, but instead agreed to sign an 18-month contract to cover up to a specified number of calls per month at a fixed price per call. Pradeep, whose stock options as a nine-year Microsoft veteran would let him capitalize the venture, would set up a company in India to carry out the contract. Servicing these calls, he figured, could put Indian programmers in touch with the world market, where they would learn about user needs, which in turn would enable them to identify opportunities to develop proprietary software, which could then make the start-up company great.

Pradeep spent several months developing a business plan to implement his idea, and in March 1995 he wrote the following mission statement for the new Aditi Corporation:

> *Aditi is an intense, creative, people-driven, ethical, socially conscious Indian software company that will build a globally recognized brand by the year 2000 with $100 million in revenues and a $300 million market cap.*

He assumed it would be easy to hire programmers in India, where wages were a small fraction of those in the U.S. and there was an English-fluent population of nearly 200 million. Many of them were well-educated, including a sizable number in computer science.

Arriving in Bangalore for the first time in his life, however, he found the newspapers already carried hundreds of advertisements to recruit programmers. Many were by large corporations, others by "body shops" who either employed programmers as temps to be hired out to companies developing software or, in a headhunting capacity, found jobs for the programmers for a fee. He recalled:

> *I had come to India with the idea that this was going to be easy. I would just arrive with American money in my pocket, run an ad, and take my pick of the best programmers from a pool of smart, well-educated Indians. It was a surprise to learn I was not the first to think of this idea.*
>
> *In fact here I was with my one-man company that nobody had ever heard of—prohibited by contract from using the Microsoft name—up against other names like HP, Motorola, Lotus, and Citibank who had already packed the newspapers with 60 pages of recruitment ads, some of them three pages long! How, I wondered, is anybody going to read my ad with no brand name at all?*
>
> *My solution was a programmers-wanted ad that said, "Before you send me your resume, let me send you mine." Then I went on to mention my education in electrical engineering from Delhi, my Harvard MBA, work with McKinsey and Texas Instruments, plus nine years of job titles at Microsoft.*
>
> *My story line was that if you as a programmer are a mentor to your peer group, then why are you serving a small pond? Come mentor the planet. You will come to understand user needs in other parts of the world, and we will go on to build products for the global community. There is already a large low-level services business in India. But with products you encapsulate services into something that is proprietary that you can make more money with. That leads to brand identity, role models, no more low-level second-class citizenship, which is to say missionary goals.*
>
> *It worked, and our sales took off. We got 32 very smart engineers and hit the ground running. We were profitable from the start, and within two months Microsoft was saying we were doing great! Sales started at $50 thousand a month, rising fast, with a 50 percent margin of profit, and the future looked great. Microsoft called to say that Windows 95 was coming out and they wanted us to ramp up faster. We expanded our recruiting campaign, which was also working well.*
>
> *Of course, there were some problems. I had entered the business knowing essentially nothing about managing help service. I had talked to the people at Microsoft about it before leaving. But my experience was in programming, not help lines, and I had never managed such work. Also, the people I hired were programmers, people good at working on technical problems of their own, not people whose gifts and aspirations were in helping other people solve technical problems, which is a different kind of work. To deliver help you should mostly work from the existing knowledge base, which already has answers for 70 to 80 percent of the problems that come*

up. But programmers are best at adding to the knowledge base, not searching it to answer other people's questions.

I foresaw another problem, which was that this arrangement was not going to last forever. The incentives were not really strong enough for Compuserve. And for Microsoft the arrangement was awkward. They were paying us to give away for free a service that they were offering by phone for a fee. We had incentives to provide help, but only as time-efficiently as possible, and only up to a certain number of inquiries. So we had incentive to short cut on long-answer problems and avoid answering calls that came in beyond our quota. That left some customers less than happy, which was not good for anybody. I said to a friend that the work would not likely last more than three years.

My prediction turned out to be correct except for the time interval. The contract was terminated after one year when in addition to these awkward factors with customers, Compuserve found itself potentially threatened by a new MSN and its relationship with Microsoft broke up. The remaining six months of our contract was bought off for $600,000 and immediately terminated. So here I was with 110 programmers who had nothing to do. If I laid them off after all my recruiting promises I knew I would never be able to fish in that pool again.

So I paid the losses of keeping them on the payroll out of my savings until I could figure out something for them to do. This had to be fast because they were smart, energetic, ambitious people. The only other line of work I could come up with was to compromise my principles and become a "body shop providing temp services." This was already being done by others, and I regarded it as low-grade work. It did not build great companies that gave back to India by establishing Indian brands and making Indian programmers wealthy through stock options.

I had been determined not to do this. I frantically went out making sales calls in the U.S. to replace the service work. Some sales came from other companies, like RealNetworks, but not nearly fast enough, and I was running out of cash. A friend at Microsoft persuaded me to compromise and provide temps by pointing out to me that although it would violate my goals and the programmers would not get rich, they still dearly wanted to work at Microsoft any way they could. So I set up a U.S. company and office to provide in the U.S. programmers on contract as other companies had done.

Expanding into more enterprises

This put the venture back into the black, and all Aditi employees held stock options in the U.S. company, which in turn owned the Indian company. Moreover, the fact that it had begun as an early user itself of the Internet for delivering service had given Aditi experience with that technology, which was now increasing explosively in popularity.

At the same time, Pradeep found that his programmers developed appetites for new challenges as practice made their skills stronger. He began accepting contracts under which his enterprise would not only rent out temps, but would also develop software to specifications for other companies, such as the giant German firm, Siemens. He also initiated an in-house project to create software that would be owned by Aditi for managing e-mail communications, first its own, and eventually those of others. This software would keep track of who called, when, what about, what responses were given, how much time it took, what form-letters should be used for repeat inquiries, what further follow-up should be anticipated, and so forth, no matter whom at the company had been contacted. This would enable a department of people to handle large numbers of calls efficiently, shift calls appropriately among them, and give good service.

By mid-1998 Aditi Corporation was ranked 13th on the *Puget Sound Business Journal*'s list of 100 fastest-growing companies in the region, showing the following statistics:

Year	Employees	Sales ($ millions)
1995	125	0.71
1996	169	2.20
1997	232	3.14

By mid-1999 the company workforce included nearly 300 Indians, most of them doing temp work in the U.S., the remainder doing contract development work in India for clients and for proprietary Aditi product development. The company also employed around 25 U.S.-born programmers, and expected to hire another 75 in the coming year. Pradeep worried about how to recruit, motivate, and retain U.S. nationals if they came to see Aditi as basically an Indian company. The prospect of wealth could help, he expected. But how could they become dedicated enough to apply the 100-hour work weeks and concentration required to keep up with other top software firms?

Lines of business at Aditi now included the following:

1. **Help for programmers via Internet** This activity, which had begun and then been terminated under Microsoft contract, was now coming back, thanks to panicked efforts by Pradeep to find new customers for it when the contract ended. Sales were $3.5 million for the company's fiscal year of April 1, 1998 to March 31, 1999. Pradeep projected sales would be $6 million in the next fiscal year. Net profit margins on this work were approximately 40 percent of sales, tax-free in India.

2. **Temporary workers for product development** Through its Indian subsidiary, Aditi recruited programmers in India who were given programming assignments in the U.S. requested by Aditi customers, such as Microsoft. Sales in the most recent year were $6 million on-site at customer companies and $0.5 million off-site, projected to rise to between $10 and $11 million total during the current fiscal year.

3. **Contract development** Aditi accepted contracts to develop software to customer specifications using its own programmers. Sales for the most recent year had been $2.6 million. Profits from temporary help and contract development combined generated approximately $1.8 million sales in the preceding year. Taxes in the U.S. were approximately 40 percent of sales, but these could be offset through buying products or services from India, where there were no company taxes on profits.

4. **Proprietary product development** With its own funds, Aditi assigned its programmers, principally in India, to develop software for managing e-mail. Products under development included both industrial and consumer versions under the brand name Talisma. Sales were $50,000 in 1998-99 and projected at $4 million in the next year. Product development work cost the company about $3 million in the prior year. In addition to continued programming work, the company was planning to hire six salespeople for the coming year.

    Pradeep knew that at least four other companies had raised capital and were ardently pursuing the same market. This, he said, was a war in which there might be one big winner, and all the others might lose.

IPO possibilities

A significant part of the incentive system in recruiting, motivating, and retaining valuable employees at Aditi was the issuance of stock options. To let these be cashed in for profit, the company would at some point need to go public, and Pradeep saw the following avenues for doing so:

1. **Bombay stock exchange** The Indian stock market was well aware of the economic advantage possessed by companies that employed low-cost Indian programmers for performing high-value work. Consequently, Pradeep said, it was willing to pay high price-earnings ratios for service companies that capitalized on this advantage. He estimated that after such a company had passed $10 million in annual sales it could go public on the Bombay exchange at a price-earnings ratio on the order of 40 to 70. The Bombay exchange, he said, was much less enamored by products because they had never seen Indian companies prosper with those as they had with services.

2. **NASDAQ stock exchange** Here companies with products, such as Microsoft, had good reputations and had proven to command high price-earnings multiples. Service firms, on the other hand, with a few exceptions such as those in e-commerce, were typically less successful in selling their stock, PE multiples of 10 being more common, as opposed to Bombay multiples for service firms. Pradeep observed, however, of particularly high popularity on the NASDAQ had been e-commerce companies. He thought that although the temp and custom code-writing parts of Aditi would not fare well on a NASDAQ offering, the e-service and product parts of it might. He commented:

   The Web used to be just advertisements. Then it became a place to sell products. But now it is becoming a contact point between customers and companies, and guess who understands that better than anybody? We do! So if we isolate our e-commerce lines of work and take those public there, maybe we can get several times what we could get for our broader array of services on the Bombay exchange, although we might have to wait a few years longer, and there would remain some parts of the business we wouldn't know what to do with, namely the temp and custom code writing work.

3. **Downstream venture capital firms** The company's proprietary software products would have high interest, Pradeep believed, with one of the later-stage venture capital firms. By investing, they could fund acceleration of the company's progress either to a stock market or to acquisition by another company. He expected they would want to invest mainly in the products, but they would want all the services activities of the business tied in as a form of security that, because of their earning power, could lessen the blow if the products fell victim to competitors that were driving hard with similar products.

4. **Early-stage venture capital firms** These, Pradeep expected, would be interested solely in the proprietary products. They would want him to concentrate totally on those, cutting away the rest of the company so that the products would have maximum chance to succeed and the company would be able to go public with them or sell out in three or four years at a value in the range of hundreds of millions to a billion dollars.

Pradeep pointed out that success in taking the company public could in itself heavily influence the company's power in the marketplace. If it were a publicly traded stock and performed well, magazine articles would be written on it that would provide, in effect, tremendous advertising, more people would know about it, the brand would be strengthened, and the company could much more powerfully sell whatever products or services it offered. This would in turn increase the value of its stock, which would further strengthen employee loyalty and motivation, while the whole image of success and strength would better improve its recruitment capability.

But he wondered in what line of business all these constituencies should consider the company to be. In an earlier time, the company could have represented itself in different localities as engaging in different things. It could advertise through some channels to companies wanting temps, other channels to those wanting code-writing help, and through still other channels to companies or individuals that might be interested in its proprietary software.

However, the Web had changed all that. Someone writing a story in the U.S. would likely search the Web and find out what image the company was projecting in India. Another writing about products could run across temp services associated with the company name. Anyone could simply look at the company's Web page and see what the company claimed it was involved in. If this presented a mixed message, Pradeep believed it would stand in the way of building credibility and achieving global familiarity and confidence. He commented:

> We can let time and events modify our company strategy. Indeed, we've done that already, and with success. Many companies are changing fast in this new age. But the human memory is not. If we want to build a strong positive impression in it, we need to be clear and consistent. The question, given the activities we have gotten started with, their future potentials, and our basic goals, is how to achieve that clarity.

Ampersand (G)

December 1993—Commitment decisions

Following the successful sales demonstration week at Pearl Paint in June, the Ampersand team had moved ahead on setting up their own production plant. Plant space at a bargain rate had been located through assistance from contacts of the Austin Technology Incubator. Scott and Robert had flown all over the country locating machinery that would be needed for painting, drying and cutting.

They expected to need sharply increased Claybord production the coming months to provide samples and to meet demand as it expanded at Pearl Paint and developed at other stores. The first production run had almost all been shipped, and the team wanted to get more inventory as quickly as possible. But the plant space that had been lined up would not be available until August, and installing machinery seemed likely to take well into September. How could the team get more inventory before that?

The team decided to try repeating the steps they had followed on the first production run. They contacted the shop in Tyler and asked the owner if he would relent on his policy of not taking any more of their work. His answer was a firm, "no." But there was no other choice, they said. They had to have his help for coating the boards. Just this one more time, and then they should be able to do the work in their own plant. Finally, the shop owner agreed, but just this one more time and that was it!

But then there would be another round of all that tedious hand sanding. Scott looked for other alternatives. Based on many phone calls and visits around Texas there did not seem to be any. Finally, Scott located a company near Dallas with an automated sander and the owner there agreed to let the team use it for $1,300 to process the coated boards. Scott commented:

> It sanded the 2,000 Claybords in just six hours. The only trouble, aside from what seemed like an exorbitant charge for that amount of time, was that the sander didn't get the boards smooth enough. It put on scratches that we had to grind away with our same old hand-held sander process anyway.

Maybe, the team thought, a change in the coating process would help. They decided to try a different primer on the Masonite prior to application of the clay layer. Experimentally, they tried different materials, baking a clay layer on them using the oven in Kathy's kitchen. Finally, they found one that seemed to help. This added some cost for the extra layer. But at the same time, it seemed to reduce the sanding needed, although more experimenting would be needed to ascertain how much.

Checking into the cost of obtaining Masonite coated with this primer, they learned that they could buy a single load of 2,000 4x8 foot Masonite sheets with primer already on them for $19,000. Until now they had been paying $15 each for plain panels. How much might this help the bottom line, they wondered, and should they go for the volume purchase? Sales efforts had already consumed much of the money they had raised through borrowing from the competition judge. Estimated financial statements for the period ending December 31, 1993 appear in Exhibits 1 and 2.

One reason to be cautious about the volume purchase, the team could see, was that sales had been considerably below expectation. The team had at first thought they could sell through distributors who would buy in large quantities, around $3,000 on average per order.

The distributors would use these quantities to feed smaller amounts to the hundreds of retail art supply stores around the country. In fact, however, no distributors at all had bought the product as of December 1993, mainly because the stores had not asked them for it.

Kathy and Elaine had consequently retargeted their personal selling efforts at the retail stores themselves. They had mounted an advertising campaign through art magazines and developed an introductory package consisting of a display rack and several sizes of Claybord to be put in it. This package was priced to the store at $270. The team's expectation was that smaller stores would buy just this package and that larger stores would order the package plus additional Claybord in quantities similar to the first order for $5,300 that the company had received from Pearl Paint.

All efforts to recruit distributors had been discontinued in July 1993 as Kathy and Elaine began contacting stores. Typically, they would first telephone, inform the store that a new product was available, briefly mention the advantages of Claybord and ask if they could send a sample. After about one week they would telephone again. They would inform the store that it would receive the same discount structure that normally went only to distributors. Such a discount, the team had learned through its early inquiries in the market, was rarely received by these stores. And they would ask if the store would be willing to place an order.

The typical answer by the store would be to say that they had not really had a chance to try out the product yet and it might be better to call again at some later time. At that point, Kathy or Elaine would inform the store of dates when they were planning to be in the store's area and ask for an appointment or permission to drop by and demonstrate Claybord.

Usually, the store would agree to such a visit. Kathy or Elaine would drop by the store and demonstrate the Claybord. A typical demonstration consisted of marking the board with ink or a marker pen and then rubbing it off. They might also mark on it with colored pencil and suggest to the store owner, "here, you try it." They would point out that the Claybord could be used with all types of media, including inks, oils and watercolors, and show a couple of actual pieces of art on Claybord painted with different media.

They would show the store a picture of the rack that came with all four sizes of Claybord for display and would reiterate the low price to the store that would result from its being given the distributor's discount. With this sales approach, Kathy and Elaine found they were able to obtain orders from about 70 percent of the stores they visited. By December 1993, they had placed Claybord in around 90 stores total.

To their disappointment both the small stores and the large stores were only buying the minimum $270 introductory package. Some chain stores were taking only the minimum order and dividing it among the stores in the chain.

Thus it appeared to the team that they were facing several decisions. Should they seek lower production costs by taking advantage of the volume purchasing opportunity? What should they do about the gap between expected sales they had depicted in their business plan and the actual sales they were getting? They were also aware that their bank balance had been declining.

EXHIBIT 1 Ampersand balance sheet for the period ending December 31, 1993

Balance Sheet

Assets

Cash and Equivalents	$4,655
Accounts Receivable	17,051
Inventory	20,644
Prepaid Expenses	1,872
Total Current Assets	44,222
Plant and Equipment	56,362
Furniture and Fixtures	5,409
Accumulated Dep'n., Plant & Equipt.	(6,693)
Accumulated Dep'n., Furn. & Fixtures	(693)
Other Noncurrent Assets	9,287
Total Other Assets	63,673
Total Assets	107,895

Liabilities

Accounts Payable	$13,766
Accrued Expenses Payable	874
Accrued Taxes Payable	3,328
Current Debt Due	13,568
Long Term Debt	291,107
Other Long Term Note	5,000
Total Liabilities	327,643

Equity

Capital Stock	1,000
Paid In Capital	4,555
Retained Earnings	(225,303)
Total Equity	(219,748)
Total Liabilities and Equity	107,895

EXHIBIT 2 Ampersand income statement for 1993

Income Statement

Revenue

Claybord Sales	$35,465
Artist Tool Sales	0
Other Art Boards	0
Royalties/Other Income	0
Total Revenue	35,465

Cost of Goods Sold

Direct Costs	34,962
Mfg. Overhead	23,198
Depreciation	6,786
Other COGS	1,800
Total Cost of Goods Sold	66,746
Gross Profit	(31,281)

Expenses

Administrative	22,733
Marketing	108,697
Salary	48,697
R&D Expenditures	3,242
Other Expenses	6,297
Total Expenses	189,666
Operating Profit	(220,947)
Other Income	6,064
Other Expenses	10,420
Net Profit/(Loss)	(225,303)

Index